Justice Oliver Wendell Holmes

~

ALSO BY G. EDWARD WHITE

The Eastern Establishment and the Western Experience (1968)

The American Judicial Tradition (1976) (Expanded, 1988)

Patterns of American Legal Thought (1978)

Tort Law in America: An Intellectual History (1980)

Earl Warren: A Public Life (1982)

The Marshall Court and Cultural Change (1988)

Intervention and Detachment: Essays in Legal History and Jurisprudence (1993)

Justice Oliver Wendell Holmes

Law and the Inner Self

~

G. EDWARD WHITE

New York Oxford

OXFORD UNIVERSITY PRESS

1993

Oxford University Press

Oxford   New York   Toronto
Dehli   Bombay   Calcutta   Madras   Karachi
Kuala Lumpur   Singapore   Hong Kong   Tokyo
Nairobi   Dar es Salaam   Cape Town
Melbourne   Auckland   Madrid

and associated companies in
Berlin   Ibadan

Library of Congress Cataloging-in-Publication Data
White, G. Edward.
Justice Oliver Wendell Holmes : law and the inner self / G. Edward White.
p. cm.   Includes bibliographical references and index.
ISBN 0-19-508182-X
1. Holmes, Oliver Wendell, 1841-1935. 2. Judges—United States—Biography. I. Title.
KF8745.H6W47 1993
347.73'2634—dc20
[B]
[347.3073534]
[B]   92-43974

9 8 7 6 5 4 3 2 1

Printed in the United States of America
on acid-free paper

For Susan Davis White

Preface

~

I FIRST wrote about Holmes in 1971, and he has continued to fascinate me over the years. As my scholarship turned to other subjects he remained in the back of my mind, and I expected to do a book on him at some point. But each time I considered my next book, one on Holmes did not seem to be the appropriate choice.

My reluctance was partly due to the subject. Holmes had a very long and accomplished life: there was a good deal to wade through. I had heard stories about previous biographers: one was disconcerted by the prospect of plowing through twenty years of Holmes' decisions on the Supreme Judicial Court of Massachusetts; another alienated by an intensive exposure to Holmes' sometimes cold and distant personality. There were a great many pieces of scholarship and judicial opinions to be considered, and there were his voluminous papers, no longer restricted.

Perversely, the very fact that a book on Holmes seemed more of a formidable undertaking the closer one approached provided a reason for me to undertake one. One could not predict how long such a book might take, or how many more productive years one would be granted—few people live as long as Holmes. The relatively recent availability of the Holmes Papers and the continuing interest in Holmes among scholars and others ensured that other Holmes biographies would appear. When I started the project, no full-scale one-volume life of Holmes had appeared since 1943; since then two such treatments have been published and more may be on the way. I did not want to have begun a project on Holmes knowing that someone else had just completed a particularly distinguished portrait of him. If such portraits were taking shape, I felt, I was better off doing my work ignorant of them.

I also felt that despite the activity that was undoubtedly taking place with respect to studies of Holmes' life, I could bring to the project some interests and experience that others might not share. I had written a fair amount on Holmes and had written another life of a judge, as well as a volume of biographical and analytical essays on judges. I did not expect to find Holmes' scholarship or judicial opinions unintelligible or daunting, although I was well aware of the challenge of saying something fresh and interesting about a body of work that has been extensively studied. I felt that being a lawyer would help me in some places in the project, being a historian would help in other places, and being a (long transplanted) New Englander would help in still others.

Above all I felt I had a perspective on Holmes' life and career that I had not previously seen played out in Holmesian literature. I had an intuition that the two spheres into which Holmes commonly divided his life, his "work" and a sphere "outside" his work, were, despite that attempted division, all of a piece. I believed that there was no essential difference between Holmes the Civil War soldier and Holmes the visitor to English society and Holmes the aspiring scholar and Holmes the "ladies man" and Holmes the Massachusetts judge and Holmes the Supreme Court justice and Holmes the "great jurist." I believed that understanding Holmes' "life" was crucial to understanding his "work," and vice versa. I believed that Holmes' life centered around the relationship between law, his chosen profession, and his inner self. This study has proceeded from those initial assumptions.

The book has taken a long time to complete and has progressed in several stages and drafts. As a consequence I have had a perhaps greater than usual opportunity to enlist the help of others at a time when they may have felt they could save me from one or another embarrassments. Whatever their motivation, those others have certainly improved the end product with their contributions. David H. Burton, Mary Anne Case, Mark Copithorne, Robert W. Gordon, Michael Hoffheimer, Patrick Kelley, Michael Klarman, Alfred S. Konefsky, William La Piana, Helen McInnis, John Monagan, Richard Posner, John Henry Schlegel, and Kimberly Willoughby have read the entire manuscript, in one draft or another. Gerald Gunther, Sanford Levinson, H. L. Pohlman, David Rabban, and Blaise Scinto have read portions of the manuscript. Each has given me the benefit of detailed commentary. Kim Willoughby, William Rolleston-Daines, and Geoffrey Berman also helped with the editorial process of preparing the manuscript for publication.

I would also like to thank Judith Mellins of the Special Collections Department of the Harvard Law School Library for facilitating my access to manuscript collections in the Harvard holdings, checking the form of my citations to those collections, and generally being an invaluable guide to Harvard Law School's voluminous materials on Holmes. Thanks also to Steven R. Smith of the Harvard Law School Art Collection for his help in securing, and his permission to reproduce, the photographs in this book.

Finally, I would like to acknowledge the unique contributions of Hiller B. Zobel, who combines an intimate and detailed knowledge of Holmes with the tireless pursuit of clarity, economy, and sparkle in sentence structure. In the course of providing me with helpful conceptual and substantive comments on each chapter—nearly each line—of the manuscript, Justice Zobel carried on an implicit dialogue with me on the craft of literary expression. I have foregone from adopting some of his stylistic suggestions, but I have adopted many, and have enjoyed and profited from all. As Holmes said, "a word is the skin of a living thought," and one needs to be reminded not to stretch the skin out of shape.

Quotations from material in the Oliver Wendell Holmes Papers, the Zechariah Chafee, Jr., Papers, the Arthur Eugene Sutherland Papers, and the James Bradley Thayer Papers, all at the Harvard Law School Library, are reprinted with the permission of David de Lorenzo, Curator of Manuscripts and Archives. Quotations from material in the Mark De Wolfe Howe Papers are reprinted with the permission of Mr. de Lorenzo and Mrs. Mary Manning Adams. Quotations from material in the Learned Hand Papers are reprinted with the permission of Mr. de Lorenzo, Jonathan

Hand Churchill, Esq., and Professor Gerald Gunther. My thanks to Mary Manning Adams for supplementing my research on Holmes and Lady Castletown, and to George and Robert Boyle for making the Castletown Papers in their family's possession available to me. A special thanks to fellow Holmes biographer John Monagan for his generosity and support. I also want to acknowledge the generosity of the donors of the Sullivan and Cromwell Research Professorship at the University of Virginia School of Law. Holding that professorship for the years of 1990 and 1991 facilitated the progress of this book.

Readers of the preface to my last book, *The Marshall Court and Cultural Change,* might be interested in an update on the status of animals in the author's household. In the last report two Siamese cats were accused of trashing valuable pages of draft manuscripts and two small dogs singled out for less than impeccable control of their bodily functions. Time produces change, and the number of cats in the household has increased, while the dog population, although remaining constant in numbers, is represented by different individuals. Computers are more resistant to paper trashing than yellow legal pads, but ingenious cats can commit sabotage by walking on the wrong function keys, especially when the computer user is marginally literate. Large dogs are more "reliable" than small ones, but a large Dalmatian puppy on the loose is a truly destructive phenomenon. The result is that Annabelle, Grizabella, Hillary, Madeleine, and McCafferty played as small a part as possible in the evolution of this book, and Vronsky and Wendell were ruthlessly barred from exposure to any manuscript drafts. Wendell's nomenclature, however, was a direct consequence of the book. Oliver Wendell Holmes, Jr., never had any offspring, and the White household felt sympathy for him in that respect. Thus Oliver Wendell Holmes III is now in existence. I leave it to more anthropomorphic denizens of the planet than I to assert that the Holmes line has deteriorated.

Time also produces losses, and it is sad for me to think that for the first time George L. White was not able to follow a book of mine through to its completion. With that in mind, it is nice to be able formally to recognize in the dedication page Susan Davis White's great importance in my life, and to underscore the significance of love and continuity in the face of change.

Charlottesville   G.E.W.
January 1993

Contents

~

Justice Oliver Wendell Holmes

~

Introduction

~

THIS BOOK is by no means the first portrait of the life and career of Justice Oliver Wendell Holmes and it will assuredly not be the last. The abiding interest of Americans in Holmes has been a phenomenon in itself. Several reasons suggest themselves as explanations for why Holmes, uniquely among American judges, has been a figure that generation after generation of scholars and laypersons has found intriguing. There is first the simple fact of his distinctively long and accomplished life, spanning a space of time (1841–1935) that made it possible for his grandmother to have remembered the Revolutionary War and for him to have been intimately acquainted with individuals, such as Alger Hiss, who are still alive at this writing. Not only was Holmes' life long, it was conspicuously successful, at least by the ordinary indices of professional success in America. He wrote arguably the most original work of legal scholarship by an American, *The Common Law*; he served with distinction as a judge on the Supreme Judicial Court of Massachusetts and the Supreme Court of the United States for nearly fifty years; in his scholarship and his opinions he wrote phrases that have become staples of legal literature.

Holmes was also an enticing personality. He was exceptionally attractive, especially as he aged and his countenance, with its piercing eyes, shock of white hair, and prominent moustache, seemed to reflect the roles of soldier and jurist that had been so important in his life. He was by all accounts a memorable companion and conversationalist, and his letters, in contradistinction to those of most of his judicial colleagues, rival those of the most celebrated correspondents in their stylistic facility and substantive interest. He was the son of a famous father, Oliver Wendell Holmes, Sr., the physician, poet, and man of letters; a thrice-wounded survivor of the Civil War; a representative of "Brahmin" Boston, with Longfellow, Lowell, and Emerson as his household acquaintances and the intersecting worlds of Harvard and upper-class Boston society as his familiar territory. He was one of the few Americans of his generation to have an intimate acquaintance with English society at the height of the British Empire. He was the darling of young intellectuals in the 1920s and 1930s; he spoke to the nation on radio on his ninetieth birthday.

Finally, Holmes has been an exceptionally resonant and accessible intellect. The details of his scholarship are rarely examined or even remembered, but the arresting generalizations of which he was so fond—"the life of the law has not been logic, but experience"; "to look at the law you must look at it as a bad man"—continue to be quoted. The analytical underpinnings of his decisions may remain obscure, but the epigrams remain: "three generations of imbeciles are enough"; "a word is the skin of a living thought"; "great cases like hard cases make bad law." His epigrammatic style, his penchant for generalization, and his tendency to prefer vivid

[3]

overstatement have meant that his jurisprudence contains snippets of philosophy that have a wide and diverse appeal: he can be quoted as embracing positivism, consequentialism, a commitment to civil liberties, judicial "activism," or judicial "self-restraint." Many an enthusiast for Holmes began his or her interest by reading one of his memorable aphorisms, without, perhaps, realizing that an aphorism pointing in the opposite direction lay within the Holmes oeuvre.

The last comment points, paradoxically, to another source of Holmes' attractiveness. The capacity of his thought to contain diverse and self-opposing points of view, the elusiveness of his ideas, the hints in his personal life that his temperament was layered and complicated, have tempted students of his life to try to penetrate to the intellectual or personal core of their subject. But the ubiquity of Holmes' language and his capacity to take on multiple symbolic roles—as the "great liberal" for one generation of commentators, the "scientist" for another, the "relativist" who was soft on totalitarianism for yet another—appear to ensure that his "core" is unlikely to come to rest, as successive waves of observers reconfigure his image in accordance with their own presuppositions.

Given the long trail of Holmes literature, and the prospect of a comparably long road ahead, this work has had rather particularistic goals. I have adopted the biographical format because it seemed the most appropriate vehicle for implementing my central purpose, to explore the relationship between Holmes' personal and intellectual life. For reasons having to do with the state of source materials on Holmes and my own training, the time seemed ripe for such an exploration. Holmes' private papers have now been made generally available to scholars, so the materials exist for filling in the details of his life past the point—1881—where Mark DeWolfe Howe left off in his authorized biography. Others, whose primary interest has been in the personal details of Holmes' life, have taken advantage of the availability of his papers, and as a result we know a good deal more about the latter years of his life than we did at the time of Howe's death.

Commentators have continued to analyze Holmes' work as a scholar and a judge, in increasing detail and sophistication. Reprinted collections of his earliest writing and his early legal scholarship are now available, as well as detailed treatments of most phases of his intellectual life and career.[1] Few of these commentators, however, have been interested in the parallels between Holmes' private and public lives, the spheres of "work" and "play" into which he divided his life. I concluded that the materials existed to explore these parallels, and that, being trained in history and in law, as well as having some experience in writing biography, I might not be deterred from venturing into both spheres at the same time.

My effort, then, has been to describe Holmes' personal and intellectual life so as to emphasize the presence of certain central personal characteristics, to identify and to explicate certain distinctive ideas that he held, and to examine the relationship between personality and thought. Some readers will doubtless be more interested in one sphere than the other, so the narrative of this work attempts to alternate, where possible, chapters on Holmes' personal life with chapters on his legal contributions. My interest throughout, however, is in the interaction of the personal and professional spheres.

The variety of Holmes' interests, the complexity of his thought, and the singular—one is tempted to say intrinsic—ambivalence of his temperament has meant that the narrative structure of my analysis emphasizes several personal themes in tension. Examples are the themes of what Holmes called "passion," and what he called "action"; the themes of powerlessness and recognition; those of isolation and intimacy; and those of competitiveness and detachment. In addition, I consider other themes that have been more commonly associated with Holmes' thought, such as resignation, skepticism, what he called "jobbism," and the idea, not easily reduced to a label, that life was inherently interesting, enjoyable, and there to be seized. My emphasis, throughout, is on what I take to be the central organizing principle of Holmes' life history—his attempt to integrate, but at the same time keep separate and distinct, the professional and private spheres of his life. This is a study, as its subtitle suggests, of the relationship between Holmes' professional endeavors and Holmes' inner self.

CHAPTER ONE

Heritage

~

O N JULY 2, 1861, Oliver Wendell Holmes, Jr., twenty years old and a senior at Harvard College, composed an autobiographical sketch for his college album. Holmes, at the time, was attempting to secure a commission in a Massachusetts volunteer regiment in order to fight in the Civil War, which had begun that April when Confederate forces fired on Fort Sumter in South Carolina. Since the fall of Fort Sumter Holmes had spent very little time with college affairs, enlisting as a private in the Fourth Battalion of Massachusetts Volunteer Infantry in late April and drilling for the remainder of the spring at Fort Independence in Boston Harbor. In June, on hearing the disappointing news that the Fourth Battalion was being treated as a militia guard, and would not be leaving Massachusetts to fight, he had returned to Cambridge and taken and passed his final examinations. He would officially graduate from Harvard in two weeks.[1] Eventually, sometime in late July,[2] he would receive a commission in the Twentieth Regiment of Massachusetts Volunteers, and in September would be dispatched to Washington, D.C., to see action.

Thus when he wrote the autobiographical sketch Holmes was preoccupied with his future as a Civil War volunteer. Although he intended to leave the Fourth Battalion, he had not yet secured his commission in the Twentieth Regiment. He indicated that the sketch had been written "in haste" and that he was "too busy" to make a very detailed statement of his life to that point. What he produced read as follows:

> I, Oliver Wendell Holmes Jr., was born March 8, 1841, in Boston. My father was born in Cambridge, graduated at Harvard, studied medicine in Paris and returning to Boston practiced as a physician there a number of years. Giving this up, however, he has since supported himself by acting as a professor of the Medical School of Harvard College, by lecturing, and by writing a number of books.[3] In 1840 he married Amelia Lee Jackson, daughter of Judge Jackson of Boston, where he has since resided. All my three names designate families from which I am descended. A long pedigree of Olivers and Wendells may be found in the book called "Memorials of the Dead in Boston.—King's Chapel Burying Ground," pp. 144 and 234-5-6-7-8. Of my grandfather Abiel Holmes, an account may be found in the biographical dictionaries. (He was the author of the *Annals of America*, etc.) as also of my other grandfather Charles Jackson. (See, for instance, *Appleton's New American Cyclopedia* where the account of Judge Jackson was written by my

father.) I think it better thus to give a few satisfactory references than to write an account which is half so. Some of my ancestors have fought in the Revolution; among the great grandmothers of the family were Dorothy Quincy and Anne Bradstreet ("the tenth Muse"); and so on; but these things can be picked up from other sources I have indicated. My grandfather A. Holmes was graduated from Yale in 1783 and in 1792 was "gradu honorario donatur," at Harvard. Various Wendells and Olivers will be found in the triennial, as also various Jacksons; including my grandfather. Our family has been in the habit of receiving a college education, and I came of course in my turn, as my grandfathers, fathers, and uncles had been before me. I've always lived in Boston and went first to a woman's school there, then to Rev. T. R. Sullivan's, then to E. S. Dixwell's (Private Latin School) and thence to College. I never had any business but that of a student before coming to College; which I did with the majority of our class in July, entering without conditions. I was while in College, a member and editor of the Institute (had somewhat to do with our two private clubs), of the Hasty Pudding, the Porcellian, the [Phi Beta Kappa] and the "Christian Union;" not that I considered my life justified belonging to the latter, but because I wished to bear testimony in favor of a Religious society founded on liberal principles in distinction to the more "orthodox" and sectarian platform of the "Xtian Brethren." I was editor in the Senior year of the Harvard Magazine (the chief piece I wrote in it being on "Albert Durer.") I was author of an article on Plato which took the prize as the best article by an undergraduate (for the first year of its existence) in the "University Quarterly." The only College prize I have tried for was the Greek which was divided between one of the Juniors and me. When the war broke out I joined the "4th Battalion of Infantry" and went down to Fort Independence expecting when drilled to go south (as a private). While at the Fort and after we were ordered up I had to patch up a Class Poem as quickly and well as I could under the circumstances, since I had been elected to that office before going (2nd term Senior). We stayed about a month at the Fort and then I came to Boston and on Classday (a week and a half ago) I delivered my poem side by side with my friend Hallowell who was orator and who had also been at the Fort. The tendencies of the family and of myself have a strong natural bent to literature, etc., at present I am trying for a commission in one of the Massachusetts Regiments, however, and hope to go south before very long. If I survive the war I expect to study law as my profession or at least for a starting point.

(in haste)

O. W. Holmes, Jr.

July 2nd, 1861

(N.B. I may say I don't believe in gushing much in these College Biog's and think a dry statement much fitter. Also I am too busy to say more if I would.)[4]

~

It is not without significance that, after listing the date of his birth in the sketch, Holmes chose to discuss his father in the next sentences. Dr. Oliver Wendell Holmes, Sr., was clearly the most important figure in his son's early life, both as a role model and a point of recoil, both as an inspiring and an irritating force. The relationship between Holmes Jr. and Holmes Sr. was sufficiently complex, and central, to merit a brief overview. Holmes' relationship with his father reveals that, whatever the tensions between the two, Holmes Jr. took from his father a "plan"[5] for his own life: a "plan" that explicitly sought to integrate his public work with his private life. In the organization of his own life, Holmes Sr. implicitly presented his son with an effective blueprint for becoming famous and for preserving that fame while simultaneously securing a sheltered and self-absorbed existence.

By coincidence, during the very years that Holmes Jr. was discovering, through his extracurricular college essays, that he had a "strong natural bent to literature," Holmes Sr. was becoming a nationally recognized man of letters for his *Autocrat* essays, which first appeared in the *Atlantic Monthly*, a magazine he had helped found and named, in 1857. When Holmes Jr. began college in 1857 his father was known to a relatively limited number of people as a professor at Harvard Medical School and a lecturer on the Lyceum Circuit. With the appearance of the *Autocrat* essays he became a household word.

It is difficult to reconstruct the great appeal of the *Autocrat* essays in an age in which "table talk" has become a lost art. In the mythical rooming house in which the essays are set the "Autocrat" narrator holds forth on a variety of topics, indulges in witticisms, and plays himself off against a series of stock figures who populate the rooming house's breakfast table. The topics of conversation include religion, the art of conversation, vulgarisms in speech, pseudo-science in medicine, and literary societies. Perhaps the best explanations for the *Autocrat*'s remarkable success are those that link its appearance to the self-consciousness and provincialism of the American literary market at the time. The narrator of *The Autocrat* talked in an educated manner, making classical and literary allusions, but at the same time spoke on provincial subjects, ranging from rowing on the Charles River to walking on the "long path" across the Boston Common. It was as if American readers took pride in the fact that one of their fellow citizens could describe homely, familiar topics with learning and wit.[6]

The author of the *Autocrat* essays was a complex figure. As a youth, growing up in the household of a Calvinist minister, he rejected that calling and became attracted to poetry and literature. Then, when discouraged from regarding writing as a full-time profession, Holmes Sr. experimented with law, which he quickly abandoned, and finally settled on medicine. His junior year in college he had written a close friend that "I am totally undecided what to study; it will be law or physick, for I cannot say that I think the trade of authorship quite adapted to this meridian."[7] A year later he wrote that he had started Harvard Law School, which was "flourishing," and was engaged with "Blackstone and boots, law and lathe, Rawle and rasps, all intermingled in exquisite confusion."[8] But by January 1830 he was writing that "I am sick at heart of this place and almost everything connected with it. I know not what the temple of the law may be to those who have entered it, but to me it seems very cold and cheerless at the threshold.'"[9] And a year later he disclosed that

> I have been a medical student for more than six months, and am sitting with Wistar's Anatomy beneath my quiescent arm, with a stethoscope on my desk, and the blood-stained implements of my ungracious profession around me. . . . I know I might have made an indifferent lawyer—I think I may make a tolerable physician. I did not like the one, and I do like the other.[10]

After two years of medical school Holmes Sr. resolved to continue his studies in France, departing in the summer of 1833 and attaching himself to the pathologist Charles Louis. After a month of following Louis on his rounds he wrote to his parents that "I have more fully learned at least three principles since I have been in Paris: not to take authority when I have no facts; not to guess when I can know; not to think a man must take physic because he is sick."[11] He returned to America in 1835, passed his final examinations at Harvard in February of the next year, and became a member of the Massachusetts Medical Society in May, 1836.[12]

Despite his preference for medicine over law, Holmes was not fully wedded to the life of a medical practitioner. He continued to write poetry in the early years of his practice, and in 1849, after becoming appointed to a professorship at Harvard Medical School, gave up practice altogether. That same year his career as a public lecturer, which he had begun as early as 1838, began to flourish, and by 1851 he earned a yearly income of $1200 for three set lectures, on "The History of Medicine," "Love of Nature," and "Lectures and Lecturing."[13] This formalized a pattern of multiple activities that Dr. Holmes was to engage in for most of the rest of his life. "Until he was seventy-five," one of his biographers has noted, "Holmes . . . taught medicine, wrote for the *Atlantic Monthly*, and entertained his fellow-citizens at dinner-tables and public functions."[14]

The versatility of Dr. Holmes, his son came to believe, had its costs. In a 1914 letter Holmes Jr. wrote his old friend Clara Stevens that

> I think my father's strong point was a fertile and suggestive intellect. I do not care as much as he would have liked me to for his novels and poetry—but I think he had the most penetrating mind of all that lot. After his early medical work, which really was big (the puerperal fever business) I think he contented himself too much with sporadic apercus—the time for which, as I used to say when I wanted to be disagreeable, had gone by. If he had had the patience to concentrate all his energy in a single subject, which perhaps is saying if he had been a different man, he would have been less popular, but he might have produced a great work.[15]

The "puerperal fever business" was a reference to Dr. Holmes' 1843 essay, "The Contagiousness of Puerperal Fever," in which he identified, for the first time, that the sources of a bacterial infection regularly contracted by mothers of infants were doctors and midwives who delivered babies without proper sterilization.[16] The essay, first received almost without comment, eventually became regarded as authoritative after being reprinted in 1855.[17] One could list other "big," and diverse, accomplishments of Dr. Holmes: the poems "Old Ironsides," "The Deacon's Masterpiece," and "The Chambered Nautilus," the last included in one of his *Autocrat* essays; his coining of the terms anesthesia, "Brahmin" (for an upper-class New England intellectual), and the "Hub of the Universe" (for the Boston State House, later generally adopted by Boston itself); the *Autocrat* essays themselves, collected in several volumes. Dr. Holmes was a respected and popular figure in a relatively narrow, but highly influential, late nineteenth-century subculture. But his son's assessment about the "greatness" of his legacy was accurate. The values of "Brahmin" Boston, which emphasized versatility and gentlemanly amateurishness at the expense of single-minded professionalism, steered Dr. Holmes in a direction that resulted in his contributions enduring far less well than those of his son.[18]

The sister of the novelist Henry James, a friend and contemporary of Holmes Jr., kept a journal in which she reported a conversation between Dr. Holmes and James' father in which Dr. Holmes asked the elder James whether he did not find that his sons despised him.[19] From this evidence and other remarks of contemporaries, such as the comment by William James, after having dinner in the Holmes household, that "no love is lost between W. *pere* and W. *fils*,"[20] some commentators have concluded that Dr. Holmes' presence was a source of continual irritation for his son, and that the latter's choice to enter the legal profession, and to devote himself singlemindedly to it, was a conscious rejection of his father's example.[21]

In reality the relationship between Holmes Sr. and Jr. was far more complicated.[22] There is ample evidence that Holmes Sr. was self-absorbed and held a high opinion of himself. His authorized biographer said that he "certainly was an egotist," and that "egotism and vanity found in Dr. Holmes' nature a soil sufficiently congenial to nourish them."[23] Dr. Holmes also seems to have had a tendency, as Holmes Jr. put it later in his life, "to drool . . . over the physical shortcomings of . . . his son and [make] other sardonic criticisms," which "made it difficult for his son to be conceited."[24] In addition to being self-absorbed and inclined to be critical of others, Dr. Holmes apparently enjoyed intellectual competition. There is evidence that conversation at meals in the Holmes household was not unlike conversation at the Autocrat's breakfast table, with participants scrambling for attention: Holmes Jr. wrote in 1928 that his younger brother Edward "used to say that at table I ended every sentence with a 'but' to keep hold of the table."[25] His eldest son duplicated many of his father's characteristics, which doubtless produced a certain amount of strain.

There is other evidence, however, that the same characteristics in Dr. Holmes had some positive effects on Holmes Jr., and that the relationship between father and eldest son was not always strained. In the same letter that Holmes complained of his father's tendency to criticize him he added that Dr. Holmes had "certainly taught me a great deal and did me a great deal of good."[26] Then there is the letter Holmes wrote to his old friend Nina (Mrs. John Chipman) Gray in 1905 that he was "kicked into the law by my father,"[27] and the conversation Holmes had with Felix Frankfurter in 1932 in which he repeated that comment, and then elaborated by saying that after he returned to Boston from serving in the Civil War "my head was full of thoughts about philosophy and in a vague way I thought about the medical school. But my Governor would not hear of that, and put on the screws to have me go to the Law School—I mean he exercised the coercion of the authority of his judgment."[28] Surely Holmes would not have been inclined to follow his father's urging (and one should bear in mind that the elder Holmes had hated law school and had enjoyed medical school) if the two had been estranged.

Just as Dr. Holmes' authoritarian tendencies were not invariably resented, his sardonic criticism was not always meant or taken seriously. A letter Dr. Holmes wrote to Holmes in 1875 provides an example. After receiving a "singular note" from his son, Dr. Holmes responded by suggesting that a treatment of goose-grease rubbed over the hollows of the skull ("the nearest approach to and best substitute for the natural secretion"), asses's milk ("this food will require little or no labor of assimilation"), and the avoidance of pudding ("it goes to the head, and [you have] more than was good for [you] already") would "bring order out of the mental chaos" illustrated by Holmes Jr.'s note.[29] It is hard to imagine that a father who was alienated from his son would have been inclined to tease him in such a fashion. On the other hand, the letter was not calculated to convey unqualified love: it could have been taken by the son as an effort by his father to indulge his literary wit at the son's expense.[30]

Additional insight into the nature of Holmes' relationship with his father can be found in a letter he wrote to a friend in 1908. Dr. Holmes had died in 1894, and subsequently Holmes Jr. organized "a large retrospective of my father in the form of his original writings." He wrote his friend Leslie Scott that in preparing his father's papers "I have an agreeable sense of having sold my governor, as he never realized that I would take any trouble to do him honor, I not spending my time in adoring him when he was alive." His father, Holmes told Scott, had even suggested that he should make "a little worm of a nephew his literary executor," but Holmes Jr. had "told him Not Much, and intimated that perhaps after all I might not be trusted to belittle his reputation."[31] The letter suggests that during his father's lifetime Holmes was disinclined to communicate affection or admiration openly to the Doctor, but also suggests that he did take pride in his father's achievements and felt a proprietary interest in them.

The absence of open praise for father by son, and for son by father, testifies to the mutual competitiveness in the relationship. But that competitiveness bred affection as well as tension. In some of the essays Dr. Holmes collected in 1872, under the title *The Poet at the Breakfast Table*, a character "the Young Astronomer" figures prominently. The character is described as "lonely, dwelling far apart from the thoughts and cares of the planet on which he lives . . . looking at life as a solemn show where he is only a spectator."[32] More than one commentator has seen in the character a representation of Holmes Jr. (known as Wendell) at the time, preoccupied with his own scholarly efforts and professional ambitions, loath to take time out to acknowledge his father, let alone "adore" him. There is doubtless some truth in this impression. But in the same year that the *Poet* was published there was a massive fire in downtown Boston. Holmes Jr. recalled late in his life that he and his father went to witness the fire, which threatened the offices of the brokerage firm Lee, Higginson and Co.[33] Holmes Jr. had left many of his completed notes for the new edition of James Kent's *Commentaries on American Law* that he was preparing with Lee, Higginson for safekeeping, and Dr. Holmes had left some important papers there as well. As both observed the fire, Holmes Jr. remembered, he "was worried about the loss of his father's property, and his father was worried about his [son's]

Kent notes." The fire was eventually extinguished, sparing Lee, Higginson's offices, and Holmes Jr. noted that he had been "pleased the way each thought of the other."[34]

To his son, the senior Holmes' life may well have seemed worthy of emulation. After briefly becoming a youthful celebrity with the publication of the poem, "Old Ironsides,"[35] Holmes Sr. entered a profession, engaged in original, and ultimately renowned, professional scholarship, and accepted a professorship at Harvard University.[36] The primary source of his public fame, however, was his literary accomplishments. With his fame secured, Holmes Sr. continued his association with Harvard, but devoted more and more time to his novels, essays, and literary enterprises. His private life was structured with his public role as a famous literary personage in mind. His household was organized around himself, with his wife, Amelia Jackson, and his children, who consisted of, in addition to Wendell, a daughter, Amelia, born in 1843, and a second son, Edward, born in 1846, assuming supportive roles.[37] After Amelia Jackson Holmes' death in 1888, her role was adopted by her daughter Amelia, and subsequently by Holmes Jr.'s wife, Fanny Dixwell.[38] From Holmes Sr.'s first moment of unquestioned fame in 1857, when the *Autocrat* essays appeared, to his death in 1894, he lived and worked in a household with a woman relative devoted wholly to him. Moreover, the members of the household, as well as his professional pursuits, provided material for his literary offerings.[39]

Thus from at least his sixteenth year on, Holmes Jr. was exposed to a famous father with a quite discernible way of conducting his personal and professional life. And Holmes Jr., after becoming a different sort of youthful celebrity as a thrice-wounded Civil War survivor, would likewise enter a profession, undertake original, and ultimately renowned, professional scholarship, and accept a professorship at Harvard University. Moreover, Holmes Jr.'s public "fame," in the sense of the far wider engagement of the public with his life and career than with most other eminent members of the legal profession, cannot be linked to any of those accomplishments, but instead to what might be called "literature": the memorable language of his judicial opinions and extrajudicial writings. Finally, Holmes Jr.'s private life was also organized around himself and his work. After his marriage to Fanny Dixwell in 1872, his professional pursuits were also the focus of her life. The domestic arrangements of his life were made by others, and his leisure time was spent on activities that he chose.

Yet if the form of Holmes Jr.'s life mirrored that of his father's, its content reflected a more complex legacy. In a history of the two men's relationship, themes of opposition can be emphasized as fully as those of similarity. Holmes Sr. was of short stature and unprepossessing appearance; his son was tall and striking. Holmes Sr., we have seen, did not like legal study and abandoned it; Holmes Jr. wrote William James that he had come to like the law above all other pursuits.[40] Holmes Sr. was at first a skeptic[41] and later a strong enthusiast[42] of the abolitionist cause in the Civil War; Holmes Jr. was at first a strong enthusiast and then a skeptic of the Union War effort. In the flowering of his professional success, Holmes Sr. was the very model of the versatile, educated Bostonian, equally comfortable in medicine, literature, lyceum lecturing, and current events; Holmes Jr. directed his professional energies toward narrowing and refining his field of study, abandoning writing on literature and philosophy along the way. Contemporaries of Holmes Sr. remarked on his vivaciousness, loquacity, and sociability;[43] contemporaries of Holmes Jr., especially during his late twenties and thirties, remarked on his self-preoccupation and singlemindedness.

In sum, it appears necessary, in assessing the significance of Holmes' relationship to his father, to emphasize both the overriding similarities in their professional goals and personal aspirations and the marked differences in their temperaments. Indeed one might surmise, at this early stage in an exploration of Holmes' life and work, that the departures from his father's example that Holmes Jr. made in his own career were conscious, or unconscious, adaptations of the framework within which his father had structured a famous life to accommodate his own search for fame. One might surmise that Holmes Jr.'s "life plan" was a product of the discernible similarity between his father's and his life goals and the discernible difference in their personalities.

~

In his autobiographical sketch Holmes next turned to his mother, Amelia Jackson Holmes. His entire reference to her consisted of two comments. He noted that his father had married Amelia Lee Jackson in 1840, and that Amelia Lee Jackson was "the daughter of Judge Jackson of Boston." The slightness of the reference, with its identification of Amelia as one man's wife and another man's daughter, speaks volumes about the status of women in Boston society at the opening of the Civil War. It is also consistent with, and perhaps forms a partial explanation for, the slight amount of information that has survived about Holmes' mother.

Among that information is contemporary commentary on Amelia precipitated by her marriage to Dr. Holmes in June 1840. One acquaintance found her "singularly energetic and effective," but "too devoted as a wife," although feeling at the same time that her marriage to Dr. Holmes had "vastly improved her intellect, so that she makes a much better appearance in society than I ever expected."[44] Another found that her obvious happiness in her marriage had not made her unmindful of her social obligations: on one occasion she had expressed concern about her husband's tendency to "talk . . . about the different quackeries of his profession."[45] A third assessment, rendered by a contemporary whom Holmes' authorized biographer interviewed much later in her life, described Amelia as "dull and stupid," though "very affectionate."[46] The initial portion of this last characterization requires further investigation, but Amelia's affection is abundantly clear from the limited correspondence of hers that has survived. In a letter to her eldest son in July 1866, when Holmes was traveling in Europe, for example, she wrote that "I assure you that I give more thoughts to [my children] than to anything else in the world. . . . I suppose I bother you sometimes—but I love you very much."[47] Holmes, for his part, seemed to have had no difficulty expressing affection for his mother: during the Civil War he wrote her letters ending "God bless you my darling I love you"[48] and "Goodnight my loveliest and sweetest."[49]

We also know that Amelia felt strongly about Wendell's participation in the Civil War. She wrote a friend, almost two years later, that "I only hope and pray that the war may go on till every slave is free, and that my child will always be ready to defend and struggle for humanity." She added that "it is very hard to have our sons

... go off, but we would not keep them at home if we could," and that while she "hate[d] bloodshed," she "hate[d] slavery more."[50] In the early years of the war Amelia was persuaded to engage in the one public service activity of her life, the presidency of the Boston branch of the U.S. Sanitary Commission, an institution established to raise money and provide supplies for soldiers in the Union army.[51] Nearly thirty years after that service had concluded, she was remembered as having "impressed us all ... as being strong, steady, clear and firm" in her approach to the office.[52]

The retrospective assessment of Amelia Holmes' role as President of the Boston branch of the U.S. Sanitary Commission went on to say that

> [T]he strange thing about her was that she really had the executive ability and the clear mind, as well as the gentle and amiable spirit. . . . When first asked in regard to the proper action in any matter she would be apt to say, "Oh Miss _____ [naming one of us] knows much better than I." But afterward in her quiet way the advice we wanted would come out, and it would rarely fail to be the advice adopted. . . .
>
> She was wont to make many clear-headed and just observations on men and women, betraying the intimate knowledge of human nature. . . . [But] [i]n giving opinions to the public she was exceedingly diffident and tremulous. . . . The humility and sweetness of her nature were its chief charms and its chief distinction.[53]

The impression generated by this reminiscence, and the previously quoted comments, is that of a woman whose "clear-headed" tendencies were suppressed, at least in public, in an affect of extreme diffidence and amiability. "Affectionate," "humble," "sweet," "gentle," "tremulous" in public are the adjectives primarily applied to her by commentators, with "energetic," "effective," "just" being added to complicate matters. Explanations for Amelia Holmes' personal diffidence and humility can be found in the culture of her time. As one commentator has put it, "[h]ers was a typical complaint of the pre-Victorian woman" from an upper-class background, for whom opportunities for "achievement outside the home were rare."[54] She herself, at the age of twenty, observed, to a male cousin, that "I think a girl's life at my age isn't the most pleasant by any means; she is in the most unsettled state: a young man can occupy himself with his business, and look forward to his life and prospects, but all we have to do is pass our time agreeably to ourselves. Not that we do not have enough to occupy ourselves in carrying on our education, but I think everyone likes to feel the *necessity* of doing something, and I confess that I have sometimes wished I could be poor to have the pleasure of exerting myself."[55]

When opportunities arose for achievement within the carefully bounded sphere of domesticity, as interpreted by her contemporaries, Amelia by all accounts readily and passionately grasped them. From the early observation of a female contemporary that she was "too devoted as a wife" to the conclusion by John Morse, the authorized biographer of Holmes Sr., that she was "an ideal wife," Amelia Holmes' peers were unanimous in their assessment that her energies, after her marriage at the age of twenty-two, were directed almost exclusively toward the comfort of her husband and children. As Morse put it,

> The kindest, gentlest, and tenderest of women, she had the chance given her, when her eldest son was three times wounded in the Civil War, to show of what mettle she was; and she did show it, as all who knew her would have foretold of her. For Dr. Holmes she was an ideal wife,—a comrade the most delightful, a helpmate the most useful, whose abilities seemed to have been arranged by happy foresight for the express purpose of supplying his wants. She smoothed his way for him, removed annoyances from his path, did for him with her easy executive capacity a thousand things, which otherwise he would have missed or have done with difficulty for himself; she hedged him carefully about and protected him from distractions and bores and interruptions,—in a word she took care of him. . . .
>
> If in thus ordering all things alike within and without the daily routine with such careful reference to the occupations and the comfort of her husband, she often gave herself in sacrifice,—as no doubt she did—she always did so with such amiable tact that the fact might easily escape notice, and the fruit of her devotion was enjoyed with no disquieting sense of what it had cost her. She eschewed the idea of having wit or literacy and critical capacity; yet in fact she had rare humor and a sensitive good taste.[56]

This assessment, written from the perspective of one who knew the Holmes household well (Amelia Jackson was Morse's aunt), and who found Amelia's subordination of her life in her husband and her family "ideal," presents some additional evidence of Amelia's character and temperament. Again one notes the initial impression of Amelia's "amiability": "the kindest, gentlest, and tenderest of women." Again one sees examples of this trait in her playing self-subordinating roles, such as "smooth[ing] her husband's "way," "supplying his wants," "giv[ing] herself in sacrifice" with "amiable tact" and "no disquieting sense of what [the behavior] had cost her." And again one observes the "mettle," the "easy executive capacity," the ability to "order" the affairs of her husband and her household, the "humor," "good taste," and "critical capacity" she possessed even while disclaiming those attributes.

Despite Amelia's aura of sweetness, generosity, and amiability, it is not surprising to find Holmes commenting, late in his life, that he had "got a sceptical temperament . . . from my mother"[57] and that he had also inherited from her a "perverse" tendency to feel melancholy and unfulfilled in the midst of apparent success.[58] It is also not surprising to find his singling her out to be the first to know that he was leaving military service.[59] At the same time, it is abundantly clear that the managerial tendencies lying beneath the layer of self-deprecation that Amelia erected around herself did not serve to qualify Amelia's love for her eldest son. Here is an excerpt from an 1866 letter she wrote to him while he was traveling in England and on the Continent.

> We have just received your second letter from Europe, and you can hardly realize our happiness at seeing your handwriting again, and reading all that

you have been seeing and doing—I do not find fault with you—I know that
you are very busy, only remember among all the great people, and great sights,
that you have a little mother at home, who is living as quietly as it is possible
for anyone to live, that it is always a delight to her to hear from her beloved
child—You will let me give one word of caution—I am sure that you are
trying to do too much . . . don't feel as you did at home that you must
accomplish just so much each 24 hours. . .

   You touched my heart by saying that you had not had any coffee as good
as ours—You remember my fear that nothing will be good enough for you
when you get home—. . . I think of you every day & many times in the day.
Write when you can—without trouble—remember that the stupidity of my
letters is not owing to any want of affection for you my dearly beloved child.[60]

While Amelia could not resist including a "word of caution" about her son's
"trying to do too much" as he "did at home," the bulk of the excerpt reinforces
the constraints of personality she communicated to intimates as well as to others:
her sense of herself as a "little" person who presented a poor contrast to the "great
people" of the world, who lived "as quietly as possible," whose letters were characterized by "stupidity," and for whom the persistence and force of her love for her
husband and family were givens.

~

From the reference to his mother in his autobiographical sketch Holmes passed to
several sentences about his ancestors.[61] Prominent among them were the symbolic
figures Judge Charles Jackson and the Reverend Abiel Holmes, his grandfathers.
The former represented the mercantile side of Holmes' ancestry, for whom, in the
view of one of Holmes' biographers, "religion and scholarship were, at most, periph-
eral," and worldly affairs, especially business and politics, were central. The other
embodied the "somber ministry and austere scholarship" of an intellectual Calvinist
tradition in which religion was a learned profession as well as a calling.[62] Other
ancestors had been persons of weight: the "long pedigree of Olivers and Wendells"
buried in King's Chapel Burying Ground; the poets Dorothy Quincy and Anne Bradstreet; family members who had fought in the Revolutionary War. But Charles Jackson and Abiel Holmes were the two polestars of Holmes' heritage.

   Charles Jackson served as a justice on the Supreme Judicial Court of Massachusetts from 1814 to 1825. Before that he had been a prominent member of Boston's
mercantile community. He was affluent enough to present his daughter and son-in-
law with a house on Montgomery Place in downtown Boston in commemoration of
their marriage in 1840,[63] and dedicated enough to the law to produce a treatise on
the pleadings in real property cases after his early retirement from the Supreme
Judicial Court in 1825 for reasons of health.[64] He was not, however, identified with
the orthodox Calvinist traditions of Massachusetts. Not only was he a Unitarian, he
had been a member of the Court majority that had reached the heretical conclusion,
from the perspective of Calvinist orthodoxy, that the property of a church belonged
to the parishioners, even though a majority of them no longer professed the trinitarian
doctrines of the church's founders.[65]

The case in which Judge Jackson cast his vote for the church parishioners had a direct bearing on a controversy, nine years later, in which the minister of the First Congregational Church in Cambridge, having found that any embrace of Unitarianism was heretical, was forced from his pulpit after declining to exchange sermons with Unitarian ministers in the area. The minister in question was Abiel Holmes. While there is no evidence that Reverend Holmes and Judge Jackson were even acquainted at the time of the earlier decision, which occurred twenty years before Dr. Holmes married Judge Jackson's daughter, the controversy can be seen as a manifestation of the clash in early nineteenth-century Boston culture between orthodox and reformist attitudes toward religion. Unitarians, including Judge Jackson, his daughter Amelia, and his son-in-law Oliver Wendell Holmes, Sr., believed in a version of religion that embraced the practical dimensions of human affairs; Abiel Holmes' Calvinism was at once less tolerant and more other-worldly. That Abiel Holmes declined to allow Unitarian ministers to exchange sermons with him testified to his severe and scholastic character. He represented the clergyman as intellectual, just as Judge Jackson represented the jurist as man of affairs.

Abiel Holmes, who was born in Woodstock, Connecticut, in 1763, had trained for the ministry, graduating from Yale when, under President Ezra Stiles, its orientation was theological. After traveling to Georgia and settling in a parish for seven years, he had come to Cambridge, Massachusetts, in 1791 and assumed the ministry of the First Congregational Church. In addition to his parish duties, he maintained an interest in writing, publishing a biography of Stiles, whose daughter Mary he married in 1790, a history of Cambridge, and a book of poems.[66]

In 1800 Abiel Holmes began a project that was to be his most important intellectual contribution, a history of American civilization in the form of a record of events he thought significant, ultimately called *The Annals of America*.[67] For each calendar year Abiel would include a list of "noteworthy" events, covering a variety of subjects and ranging from matters of national to purely local importance. As a historical document, *The Annals* serves as a compendium of information about early nineteenth-century America; as a memoir, it provides implicit testimony about the frame of reference from which Abiel Holmes observed the world around him. Some of Abiel's examples of events worth recording continue to be emphasized in contemporary history texts; others appear to have been of special interest to him and his immediate contemporaries. In 1806, for example, Abiel recorded that "[t]he President sent captains Lewis and Clarke to explore the river Missouri, and the best communication from that river to the Pacific Ocean."[68] He also noted that "[t]he Lehigh coal, obtained at the Mauch-Chunk mountain in Pennsylvania, which had for some time been only used by the blacksmiths and people in the immediate vicinity, was brought into [more general] notice," and that one entrepreneur "had an ark constructed . . . which brought down . . . 200 or 300 bushels to Philadelphia."[69] In 1819 he noted that "[t]he case of Dartmouth College was decided in the Supreme Court of the United States," a decision he considered "of great importance to the literary and charitable institutions of our country."[70] In the same year he recorded that "[t]he first steamship sailed for Europe in May."[71]

Abiel Holmes found no conflict between his historical and theological interests, as evidenced by a quotation from George Washington he included in the second edition of his *Annals*. He quoted Washington, with approval, as saying that "[e]very step, by which . . . the people of the United States . . . have advanced to the character of an independent nation, seems to have been distinguished by some token of providential agency."[72] When his son Oliver Wendell Holmes later came to memorialize Abiel's contributions, however, he suggested that Abiel's "highest literary pleasure" in writing the volumes was "[t]o verify a doubtful legend" or "to disprove a questionable tradition," in short, "to get at the absolute fact" of history. That comment suggested that one of the legacies Abiel Holmes passed on to his eldest son, and through him to his grandson, had been that of intellectual curiosity. While Holmes Sr. once told Wendell that he was conscious of getting "the iron of Calvinism" out of his temperament only with difficulty,[73] he had not raised his son in any orthodox fashion. Still, there were echoes of Abiel Holmes in his grandson's early life: Dr. Holmes' refusal to engage in certain activities until sundown on Sunday;[74] Holmes Jr.'s memory, which he later described of "those Sunday morning church bells— and hymn tunes—and the sound of citizens' feet on the pavement—not heard on other days."[75] "The Boston of my youth," Holmes said in a speech in 1902, "was the still half-Puritan Boston."[76]

Ancestral weight for Holmes, then, came not only in the form of the prior accomplishments of Olivers, Wendells, Jacksons, and Holmeses, but also in the form of strongly established religious and scholastic traditions. Abiel Holmes' instructions to Holmes Sr., written during the latter's first year at boarding school, should be placed alongside the Doctor's instructions to his son on the latter's first trip to Europe forty-one years later. In the earlier letter, written in 1825, Reverend Holmes had told his son to "[b]e diligent in your studies; punctual in your attendance at the Academy[77]; and strictly observant of its rules. Avoid bad company, and choose the virtuous only as your companions."[78] In 1866 Dr. Holmes told his son to "see as much of Europe as you can, regard being had to health, safety from detention by quarantines, etc. Try to get strong in Switzerland after the company going of London and the sight seeing of Paris. To do this it is important not to *overdo* walking and climbing as some Englishmen do."[79]

It is not clear how Dr. Holmes responded to his father's suggestions, but there is some suggestion of how he expected his son to respond to his. In a sentence in the 1866 letter Holmes Sr. reminded his son that "there is one comfort—if I should advise about . . . anything except general plans, my counsel would be sure to come a week too late." Among the male members of the Holmes family advice was freely rendered but not, apparently, invariably expected to be followed. Indeed Holmes Jr. recorded in his diary for July 11, 1866, probably soon after he received his father's letter with its warning about excessive walking and climbing, that he and his English companion Leslie Stephen, on a hike through the Alps, "didn't leave the snow till 5 1/2 p.m.—14 hours—and to Eggischorn at 8, burned, stiff, exhausted."[80] Included in the cumulative weight of Holmesian ancestral traditions, then, was that of continual paternal advice that a son noted, if he did not necessarily follow. In 1908, after arranging some of his father's papers, Holmes wrote a friend that "I . . . chuckled to come on a letter or two from *his* father to him at school inculcating virtue in the same dull terms that he passed it on to me."[81]

~

Another dimension of Holmes' heritage can be found in the sentences in his auto-biographical sketch immediately following his discussion of his ancestors. The first sentence read "Our family has been in the habit of receiving a college education and I came of course in my turn." This was followed by "I've always lived in Boston, and went first to a woman's school" in that city, "then to Rev. T. R. Sullivan's, then to E. S. Dixwell's (Private Latin School) and then to College."

Fifteen years and a good deal of life was contained in those two sentences. Taking them in reverse order, the second identified Holmes as having "always lived in Boston." By "Boston" he meant a particular version of that city, Brahmin Boston in the 1840s and 1850s. Brahmin subculture had a distinctive atmosphere. It was one simultaneously liberated by intellectual ferment and curiosity and constrained by orthodox religion and traditionalist patterns of education, one simultaneously imbued with a sense of growing regional and national self-confidence yet deeply provincial and insular. The Boston in which Holmes and his contemporaries grew up was still overwhelmingly a small town, with a closely linked network of mer-cantile and professional families at the apex of its social hierarchy; still dominated by its Puritan religious heritage; still committed to a "classical" education, in which techniques of rote learning predominated for males and no formal schooling was the rule for females; still grouped around the downtown wharves that led up to Park Street, Beacon Street, and the Common. But at the same time it was poised to become the "Hub of the Universe."

Two autobiographical descriptions of the Boston in which Holmes grew up have been provided by rough contemporaries of his. The first is that of Henry Cabot Lodge, born nine years later than Holmes, who was subsequently to promote Holmes' candidacy for a nomination to the Supreme Court of the United States. Lodge wrote that

All that quarter of the town [where his family and the Holmeses lived] was pervaded by the same atmosphere. Hard by was Summer Street, lined with superb horse-chestnut trees, beneath whose heavy shade the sober well-built houses took on in spring and summer an air of cool remoteness. Farther to the east, where Summer and Bedford Streets came together, stood the New South Church, with a broad green in front and trees clustering about it. . . The fact was that the year 1850 stood on the edge of a new time, but the old time was visible from it, still indeed prevailed about it. . . The men and women of the elder time with the old feelings and habits were, of course, very numerous, and for the most part were quite unconscious that their world was slipping away from them. Hence the atmosphere of our old stone house, indeed of Boston itself, was still an eighteenth-century atmosphere. . . The tidewaters of the Back Bay still rose and fell to the west of the peninsula, and that large region now filled in and covered with handsome houses had no existence. The best houses of that day were in Summer Street and its neighborhood, then just beginning to yield to the advance of trade, or elsewhere clustered on the slopes of Beacon Hill. . .

Boston itself was then small enough to be satisfying to a boy's desires. It was possible to grasp one's little world and to know and to be known by everybody in one's own fragment of society.[82]

A more famous description of the Boston in which Holmes grew up has been provided by Henry Adams, who was born three years earlier than Holmes:

> Resistance to something was the law of New England nature; the boy looked out on the world with the interest of resistance; for numberless generations his predecessors had viewed the world chiefly as a thing to be reformed, filled with evil forces to be abolished, and they saw no reason to suppose that they had wholly succeeded in the abolition; the duty was unchanged. That duty implied not only resistance to evil, but hatred of it. Boys naturally look on all force as an enemy, and generally find it so, but the New Englander, whether boy or man, in his long struggle with a stingy or hostile universe, had learned also to love the pleasure of hating; his joys were few . . .
>
> The chief charm of New England was harshness of contrasts and extremes of sensibility—a cold that froze the blood, and a heat that boiled it—so that the pleasure of hating—one's self if no better victim offered—was not its rarest amusement; but the charm was a true and natural child of the soil . . . The violence of the contrast was real and made the strongest motive for education. The double exterior of nature gave life its relative values. Winter and summer, cold and heat, town and country, force and freedom, marked two modes of life and thought, balanced the lobes of the brain. Town was winter, confinement, school, rule, discipline; strange, gloomy streets, piled with six feet of snow in the middle; frost that made the snow sing under wheels or runners; thaws when the streets became dangerous to cross; society of uncles, aunts, and cousins who expected children to behave themselves, and who were not always gratified; above all else, winter represented the desire to escape and go free. Town was restraint, law, unity. Country . . . was liberty, diversity, outlawry, the endless delight of mere sense impressions given by nature for nothing, and breathed by boys without knowing it.[83]

Holmes, who was not fond of Henry Adams' *Education*, once said that Adams had "talk[ed] about Boston and our boyhood with almost genius."[84] The excerpt associates an environment of "extremes" with a consciousness that tended to divide the world into stark spheres of good and evil, so that "duty," "hating," "winter," and "discipline," were juxtaposed against "pleasure," "delight," "summer," and "outlawry." In this division some of the contrast that Lodge had made between an "old time" and a "new time" resurfaces: one feels that in the world of Holmes', Adams', and Lodge's youth, a generation of elders sought to respond to the mixed messages of "summer" and "winter," "new and old" by suppressing or trivializing the "newer," more liberating messages. The "education" of Holmes and Adams was defined by this generation as an indoctrination in the precepts of duty, piety, scholasticism, and discipline. At the same time, however, Holmes', Adams', and Lodge's contemporaries were receiving implicit cultural signals that, as Lodge put it, the world of "[t]he men and women of the elder time with the old feelings and habits" was "slipping away."

One can see evidence, in Holmes' early education, of the elemental themes of Brahmin Boston in the 1840s and 1850s. At the age of seven, having attended a private "dame's school," where one of his report cards contained the notation "talks too much,"[85] Oliver Wendell Holmes, Jr., was enrolled in the Reverend T. Russell Sullivan's School on Beacon Hill, and was presented with a composition notebook. Part of his schooling involved copying passages into that notebook, which were then corrected for errors in spelling, punctuation, and other features of penmanship. Each passage ended with a biblical quotation. The following was the entry for December 8, 1848:

THE GOLD COUNTRY

Gold has been lately discovered in great quantities in California, and a party of people are just going from Boston to California to seek gold. Some of it is found in clefts or rocks, some in the stream; and some washed out in bowls, some with a machine like a cradle. The precepts of the Lord are true and righteous altogether; more to be desired are they than gold, yea, than much fine gold. Ps. 19:9.

"7 corrections" were noted as having been made to this entry.[86] By October 13, 1850, the following entry was copied without any corrections being necessary:

PLYMOUTH SETTLERS

The reason the settlers went from England was because they could not have their own way as to religious worship. First they went to Holland, and thinking that their children's morals would be corrupted, some of them went to America. Here they landed at Cape Cod having before they left the ship chosen John Carver for governor. They found it so cold that they were obliged to make log huts. In these miserable abodes they passed the winter. The whole number was 101, that died 45.

The Lord will make his wilderness the Eden, and his desert like the garden of the Lord Jesus.[87]

In these entries one can observe the presence of the cultural juxtapositions commented on by Lodge and Adams; one can also appreciate why the early education of Holmes and his contemporaries may have seemed to bear only the remotest relationship to the external world they were witnessing. The enthusiastic prospects of the 1848 California gold rush, whose participants, Holmes' entry noted, included "a party of people" from Boston, were first rendered in the concrete details of how one prospected for gold. Just as a seven-year-old boy's imagination began to dwell on those details, however, came a message of quite a different sort: the "precepts of the Lord were "more to be desired . . . than much fine gold." The schoolboy dutifully copied down both messages and submitted his penmanship to scrutiny.

Likewise in the second entry the details of the Plymouth settlement, intriguing for a schoolboy in their references to log huts, numbing cold, and death, were presented in a context in which the religious motives of the Plymouth settlers were emphasized. The settlers had left England because of their interest in having "their own way as to religious worship"; they had left Holland because they feared having their children's morals corrupted. The privations of the settlers that first winter were seen in that same context: their "wilderness" was "the Eden," their "desert" Jesus' "garden." "I was brought up in Boston," Holmes wrote Harold Laski in 1918, "and though I didn't get Hell talk from my parents it was in the air."[88]

Commentators have regularly noted the ambivalence of Holmes toward religion, which Edmund Wilson once characterized as the attitude of one who had "put the old New England God behind him" but was nonetheless, "in his temperament and his type of mind . . . much closer to the Puritan breed than his father."[89] By that statement Wilson meant to suggest that while Holmes, from his undergraduate years on, rejected any orthodox religious faith and denied the existence of some organizing spiritual power in the universe, he internalized some of the secular manifestations of Calvinism, such as the idea of subordinating the pleasures of the self to the obligations of class or profession or social convention. One thinks here of Holmes' omnivorous reading, and his oft-repeated comment that books, however tedious or unenlightening, should be completed once started. His dogged pursuit of books appears as an effort to conform to an ideal of an "educated gentleman," who was expected to have accumulated a fund of knowledge in his lifetime. Holmes would regularly express this sense of obligation in an imagined conversation with some examiner at the gates of Heaven who would quiz him on a list of books "that a gentleman should have read before he dies."[90]

The heritage of Calvinist religion thus primarily manifested itself for Holmes in the Puritan concept of a "calling," which by Holmes' time had evolved from its initial theological context to the secularized world of educated elite professionals. Among Holmes' beliefs throughout his adult life were the need for moderation and self-control, the obligation of continued and persistent education, and a consciousness of the qualities and duties of the "elect," which for him meant not a class of predestined souls but his Brahmin contemporaries. The last set of "class" values included a distaste for "vulgarity," whether in conspicuous consumption or elsewhere, and contributed to Holmes' belief in what he called "jobbism," the idea that someone with Holmes' heritage did his best in his profession not only for self-gratification but also out of an obligation to hold up the standards of the elect.

A year after he penned the entry on the Plymouth settlement Holmes left the Reverend Sullivan's school to enroll in that of Epes Sargent Dixwell, who had previously taught classics at the Boston Latin School and had opened his own school on Boyleston Place in Boston. The Reverend Sullivan, who had written a verse about Holmes in which he spoke of "versatile power in all paths to excel," basing this prediction on Holmes' "inherited talent,"[91] presented Dixwell with a letter of introduction:

> O. W. Holmes, Jr., the bearer, whom, (like his cousin J. T. Morse,) I take delight in calling my young friend, has been for four years under my charge as a pupil. He had been uniformly docile, thoughtful, admirable and affectionate. Young as he is, his habits of application are confirmed, while his proficiency in all the English branches, and his love of study are remarkable for his age.[92]

E. S. Dixwell was a classical scholar, whose curriculum included Latin, Greek, ancient history, mathematics, French, and German. Charles Frances Adams referred to Dixwell's school as a "classical grindmill" with poor teaching materials,[93] but Henry Cabot Lodge, who had also gone from the Reverend Sullivan's to Dixwell's school, gave a more favorable account:

> Mr. Dixwell. . .was highly and deservedly successful. . .[He] was a good deal of a martinet and given to severe sarcasm at the expense of stupid or disorderly boys. . ., [b]ut what I never doubted was that Mr. Dixwell was a thorough gentleman, albeit a rigorous one, and that he was also a scholar and an accomplished man. I can see him now, a slight, active figure, walking briskly into the school in the morning, always most carefully although quietly dressed, and then mounting the platform and calling the school of order in a clear, dry voice. I looked upon him with hostility owning to our official relations, but that hostility was tempered, as I have said, with respect and also with a little fear. He exercised, I am sure, a good influence on me, for he had no patience with slovenliness of mind; he also taught well, as I found when I reached the top of the school and came under him. He was an equally good critic and instructor in declamation. . .[94]

Lodge also gave a description of the curricular emphasis at Dixwell's school:

> The old system was in force. We spent a great deal of time on the Latin and Greek grammars and mastered them thoroughly. We learned to read and write Latin and to read Greek with reasonable ease, going as far as Virgil, Horace, and Cicero in the one and in the other concluding with Felton's Greek Reader, which contains selections from nearly all the principal poets and prose-writers of Greece. . . In addition to the classics we were drilled in algebra and plane geometry, and were given a smattering of French as well as courses in Greek and Roman history. That we should learn anything of modern history or of the history or our own country was thought quite needless.[95]

Lodge agreed with Henry Adams' judgment that "most school experience was bad" as a form of education, and that boys "learned most" from reading Sir Walter Scott's novels and "raiding the garden at intervals for peaches and pears" in the summers.[96] Lodge's "real education," he felt, was "largely physical": learning "to swim and ride, to box and fence and handle a boat" were far more valuable than "[a]ll those dreary hours spent over the Latin and Greek grammars."[97] But while the emphasis in Dixwell's school was firmly directed away from the contemporary lives of Dixwell's students, it had the advantage of fitting admirably with criteria to secure admission to Harvard College. In an autobiographical sketch Dixwell said that the curriculum in his school was deliberately fashioned with the Harvard entrance requirements in mind:[98] Latin, Greek, ancient history, and mathematics, the very subjects Dixwell stressed, were valued at Harvard as well. If Dixwell's subsequent account is to be believed, Holmes was not entirely bored with his schooling. Dixwell wrote Holmes in 1882 that as a schoolboy Holmes had enjoyed walking with his schoolmaster and "talk[ing] of all topics."[99] The episode seems to confirm Sullivan's early perception that young Wendell Holmes had a "love of study," and there is ample evidence that at an early age Holmes had developed the habit of absorbing himself in books, a habit that was to endure for the rest of his life.[100]

~

In 1857, after six years at Dixwell's school, Holmes entered Harvard College. Harvard was another part of Holmes' heritage, his matriculation being a matter "of course," as "my grandfathers, fathers and uncles . . . before me." Harvard must also have been, for a young man of Holmes' generation, a singularly trying experience. One of Holmes' contemporaries gave an eyewitness description of Harvard, in the late 1850s, as

> being rather a primary school, on a grand scale, than the first University in the country. . . . The system of marks is too absurd to require anything but contempt; the standard of scholarship required to obtain a degree, so low that any fool can have the distinction of graduating with full honors from the University. . . . Almost all instruction has become dry and mechanical, tutors and professors rather striving to maintain a wooden old-maidish dignity than to inspire any generous sympathy.[101]

Another said of the faculty that

> [T]he competent and learned instructors did not give us of their best, but having listened to our stumbling recitations and inscribed an estimate of our blunders, would then withdraw to the congenial companionship of erudite religions, contented if collegiate discipline had been reasonably secured.[102]

"Harvard College," Henry Adams said, "taught little, and that little ill. . . . The entire book of the four years could have been easily put into the work of any four months in after life."[103] His brother Charles Francis Adams was equally critical, regarding the teaching methods he encountered as an undergraduate as "simply beneath contempt," and the faculty as "drudg[ing] along in a dreary humdrum sort of way."[104]

An inkling of the educational atmosphere of the Harvard College that Holmes entered in 1857 can be gleaned from the criteria by which students were ranked. Points were assigned for student achievements and reduced for disciplinary violations, so that intellectual performances and what the faculty saw as moral performances were regarded as equivalents. A student could gain 8 points for a perfect oral recitation and 24 points for a perfect written exercise; at the same time he could lose 2 points for missing daily prayers, 8 for missing a class recitation, and 32 for missing public church services. If he were "privately admonished" for a breach of decorum he lost 32 points; if he were "publicly admonished" he lost 64. At the end of a term points were added up and subtracted, and the result was the student's class rank.[105] Between 1857 and 1861 the meetings of the College faculty were principally devoted to the selection of punishments for various student transgressions.[106] One particularly striking decision, seeming to capture the consciousness animating the ranking system, was "that Bradlee and Willard, Seniors, be privately admonished for throwing reflections of sunshine about the College Yard."[107]

Holmes himself was to run afoul of Harvard's disciplinary emphasis. As early as his freshman year, he and a companion were fined a dollar each for "writing on the posts in Tutor Jennison's room."[108] On three occasions he lost points for "playing," "whispering," or being regularly unprepared in class.[109] After his last examinations had concluded in his sophomore year he was "privately admonished" for "creating a disturbance in the College Yard,"[110] and during his senior year he was "publicly admonished" twice, the first for "repeated and gross indecorum in the recitation of Professor [Francis] Bowen," the second for "breaking the windows of a member of the Freshman class." The last two offenses prompted Harvard President Cornelius Felton to write Dr. Holmes about his son, whom Felton characterized as "an excellent young man" but noted that "of late . . . his conduct has been frequently the subject of complaint." Felton added in the letter that breaking windows was normally punished "by dismission from college," but the fact that Holmes had "frankly and honestly confessed" and "made suitable apologies" to the student whose windows had been broken had allowed "the faculty to treat [the offense] as of a less serious character than usual."[111]

Fulton's characterization of Holmes not only demonstrates the extent to which conformity to myriad disciplinary rules played a significant part in the Harvard College Faculty's assessment of its students, it suggests that on the whole Holmes was not perceived by faculty members as unduly rebellious during his years as an undergraduate. Nonetheless there is little evidence that Holmes was any more stimulated by the academic offerings of Harvard than his contemporaries who later publicly expressed their contempt for the college as an educational institution. His courses included Latin, Greek, mathematics, grammar, "Orthoepy" (pronunciation), rhetoric, botany, chemistry, physics, history, political economy, German, and religious instruction. All of these were required except German, which Holmes elected in his junior year, and a fourth year of Greek, which he elected in his senior year. In all of them, with the exception of Holmes' Greek class, of which he still spoke favorably in 1925,[112] the ranking system apparently overshadowed any substantive excitement Holmes gleaned from the offerings. Some, such as Francis Bowen's course in political economy, he positively deplored, and responded to by exhibiting contempt for the instruction.[113]

By the time Holmes graduated from Harvard in 1861, he had accumulated 18,681 merit points, which resulted in his standing 52nd in a class of 96. His standing was deceptive, however, since he had stood 13th in his junior year, and had received a significant number of minus points for missing most of the last two months of his final term because of his enlistment in the Fourth Battalion of Massachusetts Volunteers in the Union Army.[114] The very fact that he chose to leave Harvard to join the Fourth Battalion, and in so doing assumed that he would not be receiving a degree with the rest of his classmates in July 1861, conveys his sense of the comparative value of a Harvard degree. Indeed in late May 1861, when Holmes' battalion returned from a tour of guard duty and training at Fort Independence in Boston Harbor, Holmes, who now had no pressing military responsibilities,[115] did not resume his classes at Harvard, and only took his final examinations after the faculty voted to award him a degree, notwithstanding his long absence, in the event he passed his final examinations.[116]

Harvard College was not, however, a uniformly negative experience for Holmes. On the contrary, it was a time in which he avidly pursued three interests that would engage his attention for the remainder of his lifetime. The first of these was social companionship, a pursuit that was to take a singularly structured form in Holmes' maturity, but whose youthful version appears to have been more informal. The second was reading, particularly works not emphasized in his college curriculum. The third was writing essays on subjects that interested him, whether or not they bore any relationship to his course work.

~

An illustration of the features of Harvard that Holmes found attractive can be seen in a letter he wrote to one of the first women for whom he exhibited some romantic feelings, Lucy Hale, late in his freshman year. In that letter he said that

> College is [a] perfect delight, nothing to hold you down hardly, you can settle for yourself exactly what sort of a life you'll lead. And it's delightful—one night up till one at a fellow's room, the next cozy in your own. In the day, boating, etc. And not too hard (as a general thing) lessons.
>
> Today I've been out to row twice, this after sacrificing History to the fowls [and] afterward reading my letter over in the class clandestinely.[117]

The letter went on to particularize what Holmes found delightful about the experience. First and foremost was being able to "settle for yourself exactly what sort of life you'll lead," having few restrictions "to hold you down." That comment suggests that by "hold[ing] down" Holmes primarily meant being restricted socially. Like many others experiencing college after the combination of attending a structured preparatory school and living at home, he welcomed the relative indifference a college environment exhibited toward how students spent their days or nights.

In short, college was a "perfect delight" for Holmes because it provided opportunities for him to seek education outside the classroom. In his autobiographical sketch Holmes chose to single out some of those opportunities. First were his clubs: "the Institute, . . . the Hasty Pudding, the Porcellian," and Alpha Delta Phi. His father had belonged to the Hasty Pudding and Porcellian, which were primarily social clubs, although the former put on farcical theatrical performances, in three of which Holmes performed during his junior and the fall of his senior years.[118] Two of the clubs seemed to have had literary interests as well: Holmes described himself in the autobiographical sketch as an "editor" of the Institute, and many years later remembered that in meetings of Alpha Delta Phi "the Club used to listen to essays by its members" before turning to "the business of the bottle."[119] In contrast, Holmes' membership in Porcellian, to which he was elected late in his career at Harvard, was an implicit confirmation on his social standing at the college. Several of his immediate friends and family members belonged to Porcellian, including his father, his teacher and father-in-law, E. S. Dixwell, his cousin Henry Cabot Lodge, and Penrose Hallowell, his closest companion at Harvard. In addition, people with whom Holmes was to have significant friendships and associations later in his life, such as John Chipman Gray, Theodore Roosevelt, and Owen Wister, shared a membership in Porcellian with him.

Holmes also mentioned belonging to Phi Beta Kappa, which was then primarily a literary society,[120] and to the "Christian Union." The latter membership he felt inclined to explain further. He did not believe, he said in the sketch, that "my life justified belonging to the [Christian Union]"; he had joined that organization "because I wished to bear testimony in favor of a Religious society founded on liberal principles in distinction to the more "orthodox" and sectarian platform of the 'Xtian Brethren.'" The Christian Brethren, on its formation, had declared that "no person shall be admitted as a member to this society who does not heartily assert to the fundamental truths of the Christian religion," specifying in particular "the doctrines of depravity and regeneration, the existence of one God in three persons . . . [and] the atonement and mediation of Christ." In contrast, the Christian Union defined itself as an "unsectarian and liberal" organization which was prepared to admit to membership "students of good moral character, whatever distinction or sect."[121] Since prospective members of the Christian Union were asked to "claim . . . to believe in the truths of Christianity" before being considered for membership, Holmes may have wanted to signal that in his case that claim was not fully "justified." Indeed there is evidence that his joining the Christian Union was entirely a gesture of protest against the sectarianism of the Christian Brethren, since he apparently never attended meetings of the Union.[122]

Holmes' membership in social clubs, then, served not only as an outlet for companionship, but as a way of "settling" for oneself "exactly what sort of life you'll lead," a form of self-definition. In February of Holmes' senior year one of his Porcellian clubmates, Francis Lowell Gardner, was killed on a shooting trip to Cape Cod, and Holmes, who apparently had accompanied Gardner on the trip,[123] wrote an obituary for the Porcellian Club records. He described Gardner as follows:

> Endowed with virtues which made him the delight of his domestic circle, he also possessed those manly qualities and livelier graces which compelled respect while they won the love of his companions. . .
>
> [I]t needed not intimacy to feel the courage and courtesy which never deserted him, even when most tried, but which always walked hand in hand; his high breeding restraining all needless display of his bravery, and that, in turn, giving to his manners dignity and weight. . . .
>
> In the social circle, and in the walks of friendship we shall feel the void which he has left unfilled, yet we shall recall his memory rather with pleasure than with pain, as one who did honor to his College, his Class, his Club, as a truly chivalrous gentleman.[124]

In the language of this obituary one observes qualities Holmes valued in his social companions at Harvard and implicitly aspired for in himself. "Manly qualities" and "livelier graces," in Holmes' judgment, "compelled respect" and "won . . . love." "Courage and courtesy" were attributes to be celebrated. "High breeding" was to be valued in itself, but also because it "restrain[ed] . . . needless display," thereby giving "dignity and weight" to one's bearing and "manners." In Holmes' view one could bestow no higher praise on a Harvard contemporary than to say he was "a truly chivalrous gentleman" who "did honor" to his college, class, and club.

The sensibility revealed in Holmes' obituary of Gardner seems one preoccupied with associating "high breeding" with manliness, courage, suppression of "needless display," courtesy, dignity of manner, and even chivalry. Such a preoccupation was not unusual for Holmes' Harvard contemporaries. The overwhelming number of his classmates were from upper- or upper-middle-class, Protestant backgrounds, graduates of preparatory schools, residents of Massachusetts, and aspirants to the professions.[125] In so homogeneous a social universe, membership in clubs such as Porcellian, the Institute, or Alpha Delta Phi was an effort to further distinguish oneself socially. The role of the "chivalrous gentleman," in whom the virtues of high freedom, courtesy, modesty, manliness, and appreciation of the "livelier graces" were combined, was a goal of those seeking social distinction. Even if one makes allowances for the formal tone demanded by obituaries, Holmes' tribute to Gardner reveals how fully and unselfconsciously he had adopted the "chivalrous gentleman" model as his own social desideratum.

Holmes' club memberships, and his social contacts, were thus significant features of his Harvard experience. So too was his effort to seek intimate companionship, both with men and women. In those efforts he demonstrated an early manifestation of the strikingly ambivalent attitude toward intimacy, and intimate relationships, that he was to hold for the remainder of his life.

In two of the last public statements of his life Holmes was to employ the word "intimate," which he had regularly used in private letters, to describe states of being that held great significance for him. In the nationwide radio address that formed part of a ceremony to commemorate his ninetieth birthday, Holmes said that "in this symposium my part is only to sit in silence," because "[t]o express one's feelings as the end draws near is too intimate a task."[126] And in a letter to the Justices of the Supreme Court of the United States, responding to a farewell note they had sent him on his retirement from the Court in January 1932, two months before his ninety-first birthday, he referred to "[t]he long and intimate association with men who so command my respect and admiration," noting that such an association "could not but fix my affection as well."[127]

A comparison of Holmes' use of "intimate" in the two statements reveals that while he was associating the word with experiences that were abundantly meaningful to him, the word itself could incorporate quite different emotional responses to those experiences. In the first statement he used "intimate" to describe the "task" of expressing how one felt about approaching the end of one's life. Such a task invited one to summon up feelings about an experience that was sufficiently momentous and personal to defy expression. Intimacy was associated with that most private of expressive states, silence.

"Intimate" in the second statement, however, was associated with closeness to others. It did not describe an overwhelmingly personal and private task, but a "long . . . association" with the kind of men who commanded the writer's "respect and admiration," an association that "could not but fix" the writer's "affection." Instead of intimacy being treated as a state of being that deterred the expression of one's feelings to others, it was treated as a state of being that engendered feelings for others. The writer grounded his feelings of "respect," "admiration," and "affection" for his correspondents on the fact that his "association" with them was not only "long" but "intimate."

Intimacy for Holmes was thus an experience simultaneously associated with closeness to others and with a retreat from communication into the silence of one's private thoughts. It was a state of being that could generate deep emotions but at the same time serve as a justification for not disclosing those emotions to the world at large. It was a double-edged concept, one that could be invoked as a barrier between the self and the world and one through which the self could achieve particularly meaningful relationships with others. It was one of the experiences Holmes most coveted in his life.

Two conspicuous examples of Holmes' ambivalence toward intimacy can be found in a relationship he developed with Lucy Hale during his freshman year at Harvard and in his close friendship with Norwood Penrose ("Pen") Hallowell, also a member of the Harvard class of 1861.

Holmes seems to have met Lucy Hale the summer before he matriculated at Harvard; during his freshman year she was attending a young women's boarding school in Hanover, Massachusetts.[128] In the spring of that year he wrote her two letters that provide some evidence of the nature of their relationship, and also of his general attitude toward intimacy in relationships with young women. In the first of those, a portion of which has been previously quoted, Holmes described himself as "[b]eing of a slightly jealous disposition" and noted that the regulations "about riding with young gentlemen" that existed at Lucy Hale's school afforded him "huge satisfaction," since they restricted the access to Miss Hale of an "artist (going to be) friend" and a "young gentleman who drives *fast horses*," two competitors whose presences, Holmes added, "stick in my memory." In this letter Holmes appears as a conventional courtier, communicating his ardor through confessions of jealousy and competitiveness with other aspirants.

The second letter, written a month later, is more intriguing. Holmes wrote, in part,

> Now almost all my best friends are ladies and I admire and love ladies' society and like to be on intimate terms with as many as I can get. . .[I]f I write in other terms than those of a silly flirtation I know that you at least could have a good influence on me—When you honestly speak to yourself don't you feel these flatterers are not those that you would ever speak to about what you really deeply felt?. . .In the little time I have seen you I tell you frankly that you seemed to me to have a good deal of capability as yet unaroused.[129]

Of particular interest in this letter is Holmes' simultaneous profession that he wishes to get beyond "silly flirtation[s]" and "flatterers" and know Lucy in a deeper fashion, and also that he likes "to be on intimate terms with as many [young women] as I can get." The sentence about intimacy reveals a certain craving for that state of being in Holmes, but it also suggests that Holmes conceived of being "on intimate terms" with young women in an abstract, detached sense, as if he could collect intimate relationships the way he collected, in his later life, the photographs of his female friends and the scarf pins they sent him. Then there is the sentence about "capability as yet unaroused," which comes after one referring to Lucy's "deep feelings." The juxtaposition of the term "capable" with a sexually evocative term such as "arouse" at first seems odd, but is clarified when the earlier sentence reveals that Holmes is talking about a capacity for deep feelings and attachments, lying dormant in the face of so much superficial flattery and flirtations. It is as if Holmes sees himself as the man who will "arouse" his female contemporaries to partake of relationships at a deeper, more intimate level, but at the same time as one who is interested in accumulating a number of intimate relationships.

The second letter thus signifies a complex attitude toward women in Holmes, an attitude in which sexual attraction is associated with a desire for intimacy, but intimacy itself is treated as something of a game. The appearance of this attitude in Holmes two months after his seventeenth birthday is particularly noteworthy, since it was an attitude toward women that he retained for most of his adult life. Holmes' "flirtations" with women were legion, and regularly remarked upon by those in his social circles, but they were not conventional flirtations, either in the sense of being superficial efforts at "flattery" or of being the sexually oriented dalliances of a rake. They can be seen as efforts at intimacy, but of a paradoxically cavalier sort. Just as Holmes, in his adult correspondence, wrote a great many different people with obvious relish, but said similar things to most of them, he "flirted" with a great many women, but treated flirtation as both a treasured opportunity for self-revelation and a parlor exercise. Much later in his life Holmes was to say, as reported by his former law clerk Francis Biddle, that

> The fun of talking to women. . .was that they carried you away, so that you could express your innards with all the appropriate rapture, floating on the exquisite breath of your own egotism; reaching so far that suddenly you might look at her and say: "By the way, my dear, what is your name?"[130]

The letters to Hale thus propel us from Holmes' youth into the themes of his mature life. Likewise his friendship with Pen Hallowell, as he put it, "gave the first adult impulse to my youth."[131] Hallowell was not one of the numerous classmates of Holmes who came from the Boston area: his family were Quakers from Philadelphia. He first became acquainted with Holmes during their freshman year, and subsequently both became members of the Hasty Pudding Club. Hallowell regularly visited Holmes at his family's Charles Street home, and Holmes stayed with Hallowell's parents in Philadelphia during one college vacation.[132] As Holmes noted in his autobiographical sketch, Hallowell was elected Class Orator of the Harvard Class of 1861, and Holmes Class Poet. Hallowell is the only one of his contemporaries mentioned by Holmes in the autobiographical sketch, in which Holmes noted that "I delivered my poem side by side with my friend Hallowell" at the Class Day ceremonies in May 1861.

While Hallowell and Holmes were close friends and clubmates for much of their time at Harvard, their principal tie was their joint decision to volunteer for service in the Civil War. Hallowell had been a fervid abolitionist from his earliest time in college, and it appears that his commitment to abolitionism had a substantial effect on Holmes. In a 1928 letter Holmes spoke of being "deeply moved by the Abolition cause,"[133] and in a 1926 one as being "a pretty convinced abolitionist."[134] On Hallowell's death Holmes described him as a "savage abolitionist, a fighting Quaker who blushed at his own militancy, intolerant of criticism or opposition." He also testified to the impact Hallowell made on him:

> [He was] the most generously gallant spirit and I don't know but the greatest soul I ever knew. . . .We were classmates, officers in the same regiment, lay on the field wounded side by side.[135]

The repetition of the phrase "side by side," forty-three years after Holmes had used it in connection with Hallowell in his autobiographical sketch, suggests the feelings of closeness he associated with Hallowell. In the same letter he referred to Hallowell as his "oldest friend," when his cousin and schoolboy companion, John B. Morse, whom Holmes had known since the age of seven, was still alive and in periodic correspondence with Holmes. By "oldest" Holmes meant "most intimate."

The sort of intimacy Holmes experienced in his relationship with Pen Hallowell was of a different variety from that he described in his letter to Lucy Hale. It more resembled the conception of intimacy illustrated in Holmes' retirement letter to the Justices of the Supreme Court: a set of feelings engendered by regular contact with a member of the same sex for which one had "admiration," "respect," and, as a consequence of those reactions and the length and closeness of the contact, "affection." Holmes' characterization of Hallowell on the latter's death gives an indication of the qualities in Hallowell that made Holmes inclined to seek and to value closeness with him.

Holmes' first descriptions of Hallowell in his tribute associated him with his Quaker faith and his militant abolitionism. It is not unlikely that Holmes' own commitment to abolitionism was influenced by Hallowell's example. It is also possible that his perception of Hallowell as "the most generously gallant spirit [and] . . . the greatest soul I ever knew" stemmed in significant part from his being exposed to Hallowell's distinctive brand of Quaker abolitionism. Hallowell was prepared to fight in a war, an act that ran directly counter to his faith, because of his overriding belief in the justice of the abolitionist cause. Having made that decision, he would brook no "criticism or opposition" on the subject of abolitionism. Holmes took this behavior to be evidence of a "gallant spirit."

Intimacy with Hallowell was thus linked to the admiration Holmes felt for Hallowell's participation in antislavery activities, a participation that led both Hallowell and Holmes to abandon their association with Harvard in order to enlist in a volunteer regiment of the Union Army. The growing involvement of both Holmes and Hallowell with the antislavery movement can be observed in their participation as bodyguards for Wendell Phillips, Ralph Waldo Emerson, and other speakers who sought to address a meeting of the Massachusetts Anti-Slavery Society on January 24, 1861.[136] Prior to the meeting Holmes had received a letter from Richard P. Hallowell, Penrose's elder brother, a Boston merchant who had been influential in organizing protection for antislavery speakers during the winter months of 1860 and 1861.[137] Antislavery speakers commonly had their meetings and addresses interrupted by heckling crowds in the late months of 1860, and the Boston police had shown no evidence of being inclined to protect the speakers from crowd violence. Hallowell's letter instructed Holmes to "call at our store [to] obtain the William [a "billy club"] our young man promised you," adding that "[I] trust you will not use a weapon except as a last resort."[138] No violence ensued at the meeting, but hecklers in the crowd repeatedly sought to drown out the speakers' comments with noise of their own, and eventually the mayor of Boston closed Tremont Temple, the public building where the Antislavery Society's rally was taking place.[139] By April 1861, Hallowell and Holmes had left Harvard and enlisted in the Fourth Battalion of Massachusetts volunteers.

~

The remaining portions of Holmes' autobiographical sketch, with one significant exception, dealt with his involvement in the Civil War. He indicated that "[w]hen the war broke out" he had joined the Fourth Battalion, trained at Fort Independence for a month, expecting to go south "as a private," and was, in light of the Fourth Battalion's being dissolved, "trying for a commission in one of the Massachusetts Regiments. . .and "hop[ing] to go south before very long." He even qualified the statement of his future plans ("I expect to study law as my profession or at least for a starting point") with the words "[i]f I survive the war."

The exception to Holmes' preoccupation with his current military plans in the latter portion of his sketch was his brief mention of some of his intellectual activities at Harvard. After discussing his club memberships, he wrote:

> I was editor in the Senior year of the Harvard Magazine (the chief piece I
> wrote in it being on "Albert Durer"). I was author of an article on Plato
> which took the prize as the best article by an undergraduate (for the first year
> of its existence) in the "University Quarterly." . . .The tendencies of the
> family and of myself have a strong natural bent to literature.

"Literature," which for Holmes encompassed both reading and writing, was the principal intellectual pursuit of his college years, and it was primarily an extracurricular pursuit. While he was motivated by his enjoyment of his Greek class to submit a Greek composition that was jointly awarded the prize for excellence in Greek prose his senior year,[140] his "literary" interests during college were not centered in the classroom. Nonetheless they provide evidence of the first set of important intellectual influences in Holmes, as well as his early intellectual tendencies, and are thus worthy of extended attention.

Early in his childhood Holmes identified himself as someone who took considerable pleasure in reading, and by his last year at Epes' Sargent Dixwell's school, from which he graduated at the age of sixteen, his reading tastes had come to encompass academic subjects.[141] The earliest of those subjects seems to have been the history of art. Holmes had collected prints as a boy, beginning with some his father had bought while studying medicine in Paris in the 1830s,[142] and around the time of his sixteenth birthday was given John Ruskin's *Modern Painters* by his parents.[143] This gift seems to have precipitated a spirit of enthusiasm for Ruskin in particular,[144] and for art history in general,[145] which extended through his college years.

In 1916 Holmes told his young friend Lewis Einstein that his exposure to the art of other cultures and eras "gave me the first breath of a different atmosphere from that of the Boston of my youth."[146] Five years earlier he had written one of his close Washington acquaintances, Charlotte Moncheur, that a re-reading of the novels of Walter Scott had exposed him again to "the old order in which the sword and gentleman were beliefs," which Scott portrayed "in costume, with people who could not have heard of evolution, belated but in its last and therefore articulate moment."[147] In both comments one gets a glimpse of the youthful Holmes' motivation in collecting art or reading adventures and romance: the attraction for him of "a different atmosphere" from that in which he was growing up; of "an old order" filled with people "who could not have heard of evolution."

John Ruskin was one of "the men," Holmes wrote in 1919 to Morris Cohen, "who set me on fire" during his college years.[148] Ruskin's perspective on art history was congenial with Holmes' intuitive attraction to art that generated a "different atmosphere." Ruskin's principal motivation, as an art critic, was to emphasize the degree to which his contemporaries could have an enhanced appreciation of art from the past by emphasizing its historical roots and by observing more closely details of technique so as to better judge the extent to which art was a faithful representation of nature.[149]

As stated, Ruskin's perspective may appear to be confused or naive. If artistic renderings from the past were to be better understood by locating them in a historical context, one would expect that that context might also serve to shape the artist's perspective, affecting artistic representations of experience. It may be hard to understand how Ruskin could thus hope to evaluate art based on a criterion of how faithfully an artistic effort rendered nature, when perceptions of nature themselves would be affected by the historical context in which the artist worked.

Suffice it to say, however, that this apparent contradiction was not given serious attention by Ruskin, Holmes, or their contemporaries. They were among the early generations of nineteenth-century writers and critics to have developed a historicist sensibility, that is, a perspective that defined the course of societal change as continuous and inevitable, so that the "past" was necessarily different from the "present." Only a few generations earlier the relationship between past, present, and future had been characterized in universalistic terms, either as part of predetermined cycles of birth, decay, death, and rebirth, or as the continuous demonstration of universal truths, such as the primacy of religious values and principles.[150] Ruskin and Holmes, intuitively at this stage of his life, had abandoned this "pre-historicist" epistemology for one that emphasized contrasts between the past and the future and saw the course of a civilization as progressive, not cyclical or predetermined by the will of God. At the same time, however, neither Ruskin nor Holmes, in his youth, had taken the further step of equating the progressive and historicist character of human development with a relativistic interpretation of belief and experience. On the contrary, they were both attracted to the possibility that understanding the differences between past and present, and the contextual explanations for those differences, could help observers discern which beliefs and experiences were universally "true." They saw no conflict, in short, between observations of art, or other products of a civilization, that simultaneously grounded those products in history and sought to extract from the process of comparing past with present a set of universal techniques, lessons, or principles.

In sum, Holmes' interest in art and art history seems to have been precipitated less by aesthetic impulses than by a desire to "breath[e] ... different atmosphere[s]," to explore worlds outside Brahmin Boston. In that exploration he seems to have been proceeding with the same intuitive sense, expressed in the earlier observations of Henry Cabot Lodge and Henry Adams, that while his generation was habitually being exposed to messages from their elders—messages such as those communicated in Professor Bowen's classroom—those messages did not seem to make adequate sense of the world in which he was living. One of his responses to this feeling of intellectual dissonance with his elders was to escape to other realms and pursuits, such as collecting old prints and vicariously exploring the worlds from which those prints originated. Another was to search for alternative descriptions and explanations of his own experience.

In this search Holmes drew considerable inspiration from Ralph Waldo Emerson. While there has been some recent recognition of the influence of Emerson on Holmes, the closeness of Emerson's relationship to Holmes' household as Holmes was growing up has been exaggerated. Emerson and Holmes' father, while acquaintances, members of the Saturday Club, and active participants in the interlocking circles of Brahmin Boston, were not close friends, nor were their interests or temperaments similar. After Holmes Sr. completed a biography of Emerson for the American Men of Letters Series in 1884, a mutual friend wrote that he could not "conceive of two men more diametrically opposed in their natural traits."[151] There is no evidence to support the claim by two commentators that the younger Holmes referred to Emerson as "Uncle Waldo" as a child, and no support for the supposition that Emerson was a frequent visitor to the Holmes household.[152] Indeed Dr. Holmes had attacked one of Emerson's poems in an 1844 poem of his own, implying that Emerson and other Transcendentalists who posed questions such as "whence am I" and "wherefore did I come" were "deluded infants."[153]

Holmes Jr.'s connection with Emerson was, for the most part, intellectual. On Holmes' seventeenth birthday, which took place in the spring of freshman year at Harvard, his parents gave him five volumes of Emerson's works, and his old friend John Morse gave him another.[154] The impact of Emerson on Holmes in the next few months was obvious. In December 1858, Holmes published an anonymous essay in *The Harvard Magazine* that was a virtual echo of one of Emerson's essays, even bearing the same title.[155]

Emerson's essay had appeared in *The Atlantic Monthly* in January 1858 under the title "Books." The essay, also published anonymously,[156] advanced some generalizations about reading and its relationship to the advancement of knowledge. Emerson first noted that while there were a great many "extant printed books," the number of books actually worth an individual reader's attention were "few." He then gave "three practical rules" for reading, which consisted of "[n]ever read[ing] any book that is not a year old," "never read[ing] any but famed books," and "never read[ing] any but what you like." He believed that "famed" books were particularly important for two reasons: because they portrayed the experience about which they wrote in a fashion that made it accessible to others who had not shared it, and because their very "fame" suggested some qualities of universal appeal that would make them interesting to successive generations.[157]

The last argument was characteristic of Emerson's attitude toward history, which was that it was primarily useful as a way of confirming truths in which representatives of the present already believed, and that it was quite appropriately treated in that fashion. Thus Emerson saw no conflict between learning and reading only what one "liked," because he believed that the learning process was one in which the self shaped experience. He gave the example of the historian Herodotus, whose narrative contained "inestimable anecdotes," which had for some time "brought it with the learned into a sort of disesteem.'' But ''in these days,'' Emerson claimed, ''it is found that what is most memorable of history is a few anecdotes,'' since those had some universal appeal and the rest could and would be discarded by successive generations. Thus Herodotus' historical works were ''regaining credit.''[158]

Reading for Emerson, then, was a process by which the reader selected, out of the innumerable available published works, a few ''classics'' that simultaneously conveyed a sense of their own time and had particular appeal to the present. In the study of these classics one could find the ''seeds'' of ''recent civilization.'' In the writings of Plato, for example, Emerson found ''modern Europe in its causes and seed.''[159]

Most of Holmes' essay on ''Books,'' which alluded to Emerson, was simply a restatement of Emerson's arguments. In some portions of the essay, however, Holmes sought, both explicitly and implicitly, to apply Emersonian precepts to his immediate college experience. This dimension of his essay enhances its interest as a suggestive document.

Holmes began his essay by describing the perspective from which he was taking up the subject of books. It was that of one who believed that ''[t]he highest conversation is the statement of conclusions, or of such facts as enable us to arrive at conclusions, on the great questions of right and wrong, and on the relation of man to God.'' The author of ''Books'' was in search of ''higher food for thought'' and ''better things'' to talk about. He was interested in getting beyond ''the college gossip of the day''; he was among those ''who have somewhat higher aspirations than the mass of their companions.'' When such persons found ''none . . . in the ranks of boyish insipidity . . . who met or satisfy their desires,'' they ''must as an alternative take to books.''[160]

One of Holmes' biographers described the persona Holmes had assumed in his ''Books'' essay as ''that of an elderly gentleman of rather priggish enlightenment,''[161] and the characterization seems apt, at least based on the opening sentences of the essay. But the essay also conveys a sense of the particular intellectual urgency Holmes attributed to his generation, a generation that, for him, was in ''a peculiarly solemn position.''

> [W]e must at once in some shape understand the questions of the day . . .
> [A]lthough there always is a fight and crisis, yet are we not in a peculiarly
> solemn position? . . . A hundred years ago we burnt men's bodies for not
> agreeing with our religious tenets; we still burn their souls. And now some
> begin to say, why is this so? Is it true that such ideas as this came from God?
> Do men own other men by God's law? And when these questions are asked
> around us—when we, almost the first of young men who have been brought up
> in an atmosphere of investigation, instead of having every doubt answered—
> . . . when we begin to enter the fight, can we help feeling it is a tragedy? Can
> we help going to our rooms and crying that we might now think? And we
> whistle or beat on our piano, and some—God help 'em!—smoke or drink to
> drive it all away, and others find their resting-place in some creed which
> defines all their possibilities, and says, this far shall ye think, and no farther.
> No, no; it will not do to say, I am not of a melancholic temperament, and

mean to have my good time. It will not do for Ruskin to say, Read no books of an agitating tendency . . . We *must*, will we or no, have every train of thought brought before us while we are young, and may as well at once prepare for it.[162]

It is hard to read this passage without getting an immediate sense of the impact made on Holmes by the two major ideological forces of his experience at Harvard, orthodox religion and attitudes about slavery. The "peculiarly solemn position" in which Holmes finds himself and his contemporaries is immediately associated in the passage with "religious tenets" and the question of whether "men own other men by God's law." "Souls" are still "burnt" for "not agreeing with" religious orthodoxy; the ownership of humans by other humans is still affirmed as an idea that comes from God. And Holmes' generation, in his view, is "the first of young men who have been brought up in an atmosphere of investigation," rather than "having every doubt answered" by "some creed" which "says, this far shall ye think, and no further." The urgency conveyed in the passage is that of someone who has been encouraged to "investigate" large questions, rather than taking refuge in dogma, and has some big—and troubling—questions to ask.

Outside that passage, however, there was little distinctive or original in Holmes' "Books" essay. Indeed its structure so closely resembled Emerson's that one is not surprised that his father wrote an unnamed friend, about a year after "Books" appeared, that he was "not anxious" to have his son "appear in print, as he is forming opinions too fast to have much time to dress them up rhetorically."[163] Holmes echoed Emerson on the "almost innumerable" amount of books, and on the fact, as he put it, "that every grand book carries with it and implies ten thousand lesser ones."[164] He restated Emerson's maxim "that it best to read what we like."[165] And he gave a description of the qualities of a "great book" that applied Emersonian criteria. "[G]reat books," he said, "have, as it were, originated the very literature of that state and period from which they spring; . . . have drawn to their own mighty bulk the needs and strength of the time, and while everything around them has fallen to pieces, stand only in increased power and majesty."[166]

Holmes also followed Emerson in his view of history, to the point of using Herodotus as an example. "*History*," he argued, "should be the finest, the all-comprehending study." But "we do not find it so" because "facts and dates are mistakenly supposed to constitute its chief part." Instead, he suggested, "anecdotes . . . will often display the whole manners and customs of a period, when we should have laid down the statistics as ignorant as we took them up." He found the approach of "Herodotus . . . most pleasant" because "in a history of the great nations of the earth, he tells us such facts as that the mares that gained three races are buried by the side of their master in the road that runs through the hollows." It was these "details about each day" that best captured the spirit of an age; that insight could be illustrated by the proliferation of such details in "the daily newspapers." "[W]e must study the present," Holmes asserted, to "know the past."[167]

At the close of his "Books" essay Holmes made it plain where his approach to the subject originated. He mentioned Emerson, characterizing him as one who "probably takes about as large a view of men and events as any one we could point out now living in America.''[168] And he ended the "Books" essay with a metaphor appropriated from Emerson. Books were "little seeds ... seeming insignificant enough before the merest weed of real life," but they had the capacity to "be soaking in our minds, and when we least expect it [to] spring up, not weeds, but supporters that will be an aid in the sorest struggles of our life.''[169] The essay represented, in its whole, a mix of passion and pomposity, some genuine critical insight and some largely derivative posturing. Its chief significance was to demonstrate that by his sophomore year in college Holmes had internalized Emersonian interpretive criteria and was seeking to apply them to his immediate experience.

The "Books" essay is nonetheless useful in understanding Holmes' subsequent career as a scholar, for it exhibits, in a rudimentary form, some of the elements of his mature scholarly perspective. "Books" reveals, first of all, Holmes' sense that he and his contemporaries were placed in a "peculiarly solemn" cultural predicament, brought about by the collapse of orthodox religious dogma as an intellectual basis for making sense of experience, coupled with the appearance of some burning current issues—such as whether people could legitimately own other people—that seemed to require immediate explanation and understanding. However one might recoil from the pedantic or priggish tone Holmes adopted in defending reading and thinking, one grasps the urgency and seriousness with which he invested those tasks. The essay thereby underscores his participation in a generation with a distinctive perception of discontinuity with its immediate past, dramatized, in Holmes' view, by the simultaneous collapse of orthodox religion as a force for security and guidance, and the growing divisiveness of slavery in American culture.

In addition, the "Books" essay reveals that Holmes' perspective on the relationship between present and past was a historicist one. He followed Emerson in being conscious, on the one hand, of the distance between the past and the present, a distance most conspicuously revealed in "anecdotes" rather than in dates and statistics; and, on the other, of the "progressive" quality of change over time, so that the "greatness" of past books became successively distilled down through the ages, and ancients communicated to moderns at a universal, elemental level. Holmes, at this point in his career, also followed Emerson in seeing no contradiction between a belief that one, as a modern, was able to grasp "the whole manners and customs" of a period and a belief that history was a progressive process. The message of Emerson had been that the modern reader was capable of discerning "the great inspired books of all the great literatures" and extracting "the delicacy of the noblest and calmest books." That reader was capable, in short, of transcending time and contemporary experience. Great books were inspired and inspiring not because they were labeled as such by orthodox religion but because they revealed the capacities of the self as author and as reader. In adopting Emerson's assumption that the capacity to achieve or to recognize "greatness" in literature was innate in authors and readers, Holmes was implicitly adopting the perspective of what Emerson's followers called transcendentalism. Holmes may have been attracted to that perspective because it offered him an opportunity to "take a large view of men and events" without associating that view with the doctrines of established religion.

It may be surprising for those who have come to associate Holmes with the philosophical perspectives of skepticism, empiricism, or even resignation, to come to grips with the fact that in his initial effort at critical writing he was assuming the role of an Emersonian camp follower. Nonetheless it is understandable why Emerson, along with Ruskin, were the two commentators who set Holmes on fire in his youth. They were both, in their own fashion, seeking to enlist the past in a search for universals that could be reaffirmed as ideals for the present. They sought simultaneously to appreciate history and to be liberated from it.

In the remainder of Holmes' undergraduate essays, written on a variety of subjects, one can see continued reflections of the historicist and transcendentalist perspectives exhibited in "Books." In "Notes on Albert Durer," for example, an essay on the fifteenth- and sixteenth-century engraver Albrecht Durer written during the summer after his junior year, Holmes sought to formulate a "principle applicable in ranking the books and in settling the position of all artists."

[J]ust as the lowest form of good art is the mere portraiture of the single, unconnected fact, with no further view beyond . . . so art is great in proportion as it rises above this, and the presumption is always in favor of that picture being greatest in which the lowest truth of the individual is made subservient . . . to the profound truth of the idea. Knowledge of the stains of the earth, and of the decay that accompanies all earthly life, doubtless the painter needs, but higher than this is the sight which beholds the type disguised beneath the wasting form, and higher than anything connected with the individual is the conception of the harmonious whole of a great work, and this again is great, just as its idea partakes of what is eternal. And this striving to look on types and eternal ideas, is that highest gift of the artist, which is called the ideal tendency.[170]

Durer, for Holmes, was "a man who assumed in himself and represents in his works the great tendencies of his age and country." His "position as an artist" was set among "[t]he men of the fifteenth and sixteenth centuries." But Durer's impact was in his "combination of noble powers, coming at a thoughtful time."[171] His religious faith formed the impetus for his painting, but it was not the essence of that painting. The essence lay in Durer's ability to grasp "the type disguised beneath the wasting form," the "conception of the harmonious whole" that made his work "eternal" and thus "ideal." One could not understand Durer without appreciating the historical context of his "age and country," but one ultimately appreciated Durer for the extent to which he successfully transcended that context. The "principle" of art appreciation formulated in the passage quoted from "Notes on Albert Durer" can fairly be described as a "systematic elaboration of Emerson's ideas."[172]

Much of the rest of the Durer essay, which opened with a lengthy discussion of woodcut techniques and went on to emphasize the relationship of Durer's work to the religious faith of his time, was derivative of Ruskin's comments on Durer in *The Elements of Drawing*, a book which, as noted, was part of Holmes' collection of Ruskin's works.[173] As in the "Books" essay, Holmes had been motivated to write on a subject by the attention given to it by one of his intellectual mentors. He continued that pattern in another essay he wrote over the summer of 1860, "Plato,"[174] the other college essay mentioned in his autobiographical sketch. In his choice of subject Holmes was again tracking Emerson. In Dr. Holmes' biography of Emerson he listed the authorities Emerson had quoted or cited in his writings, and found that Plato had been referred to 81 times and Socrates 42 times. If references to Socrates are taken to be gleaned from Emerson's reading of Plato, the combined references represent the highest amount of citations to any of the authorities Emerson invoked in his work, surpassing Shakespeare, mentioned 112 times, and Napoleon, mentioned 84 times. "Emerson," Dr. Holmes concluded, "was an idealist in the Platonic sense of the word."[175] He noted that Emerson had also written appreciatively of Plato in his 1850 collection of essays, *Representative Men*, maintaining that "[o]ut of Plato came all things that are still written and debated among men of thought."[176]

Holmes later indicated that he had first read Plato "expecting to find the secrets of life revealed,"[177] and at the age of ninety he was still reading Plato's *Laws*, "Greek and translation opposite."[178] But while he concluded, in his "Plato" essay, that Plato was "a really great and humane spirit" who, along with Socrates, "fill me . . . [with] reverence and love," and in their dialogues represent "one of the grandest sights the world can boast,"[179] he did not find Plato a satisfactory philosophical model. His implicit criteria for evaluating Plato's contributions revealed that he was beginning to distance himself from Emerson.

Holmes treated Plato as a contributor to a progressive series of philosophical ideas that had become refined and "improved" with time, and emphasized Plato's limitations as much as his accomplishments. Whereas Emerson, and Holmes in his "Books" essay, had been more interested in extracting universal elements from the contributors of "great" historical figures, Holmes in "Plato," while retaining something of that emphasis, was equally interested in emphasizing the deficiencies of even the "greatest" of previous intellectual contributors, as seen from the perspective of what he called "science." With the addition of "science" as an evaluative criterion in his critical arsenal, Holmes began to complicate his relationship to the transcendentalist legacy he had borrowed from Emerson.

At one level the "Plato" essay was an exercise in what might be called "evolutionary" intellectual history: Plato's contributions were seen as a "stage" in the continual advancement of knowledge. Plato's primary deficiency as a theorist, and the chief advantage that Holmes felt that he and his contemporaries had gained in the passage of time since Plato's work had appeared, involved the role of "science" as a vehicle for understanding experience. "[W]hat should continually be taken into account in estimating [Plato's] views," Holmes asserted, was that "in these last days . . . an all-comprehending science has embraced the universe, showing unerring law prevailing in every department, generalizing and systematizing every phenomenon in physics, and every vagary of the human mind."[180] Plato's views, judged from a perspective resting on the insights of this "all-comprehending science," were "wrong," "loose and unscientific," "confused and doubtful," lacking "that exactness of science which [he] lived too early to attain," and "scientifically imperfect."[181]

Holmes' embrace in his "Plato" essay of a "scientific" perspective, and of the concept of "science" as an idealized intellectual standard, was to have significant ramifications for his subsequent career as a scholar, and was to create an inherent tension in his later scholarship between a professed goal of producing "scientific" work and the residue of historicist and transcendentalist perspectives he had previously internalized.

The use of the term "science" in the early nineteenth century did not convey the same associations it does to moderns, or even the associations it did to Holmes' contemporaries. "Science," as used to characterize works as diverse as treatises on moral philosophy and commentaries on legal subjects, referred to the organization of bodies of knowledge into systems. Techniques such as classifying and subclassifying subjects in accordance with some constructed hierarchy of significance were regarded as "scientific." On the whole, "science" was not equated with empirical observation or with "inductive" reasoning techniques, by which theories were "corrected" or qualified by the "facts" of experience. Nor was "scientific" methodology associated with the provisional formulation of hypotheses that were then "tested" experientially, but rather with the systemic organization of data in accordance with principles that were assumed to be valid.[182]

As such, the early nineteenth-century conception of "science" could easily coexist with religion. Religious principles, in fact, were just one of the various starting points for a "scientific" classification of bodies of knowledge. The radical feature of Darwinist evolutionary "science," as it came to be formulated in the years when Holmes was attending college,[183] was its methodology, in which generalizations about the course of human development were derived from the observation of changes in animal populations, even though the generalizations were eventually associated with religious conclusions about the origins of human existence. Had its conclusions been seen to follow from an organization of subject matter based on assumed principles, *The Origin of Species* could readily have been seen by contemporaries as a "scientific" work in the then conventional sense: another systemization and classification of a field of knowledge.

Holmes, however, took "science" as Darwin intended it to be taken: as a concept encompassing two discrete methodological aims, the conventional one of systematic classification and another one that more approximated the empiricist orientation that later generations would assume to be the central feature of "scientific" inquiry. Empiricism was, for one such as Holmes who was familiar with the historicist orientation of Ruskin and Emerson toward subjects located in a "distant" period in time, not a particularly dramatic methodological turn. By stressing the importance of anecdotes such as those narrated by Herodotus in capturing the customs and manners of a remote time, Holmes was in a sense endorsing an empiricist basis for historical generalization. In the "Plato" essay, however, he made a much more explicit association of "science" with empiricist methodology.

The following passage most clearly demonstrates the empiricist basis of Holmes' criticism of Plato for being "unscientific":

Dialectic, therefore, or logic, as concerned with . . . immutable ideas, which alone, as [Plato] holds, owing to their immutability, admit of definition, is exalted to this position, as science founded on observation, as concerned with mutable matters, must take a entirely secondary place. But logic is, in fact, merely an instrument which works with data previously obtained, whether from this very physical science or from intuition; and the unhappy fallacy in connection with this point . . . which runs all through Plato, is that he confounds this drawing of conclusions already contained in the premise, by logic, which can only develop a preexisting statement, with the finding of new data or statements, for which we must look to consciousness or to generalizations from experience.[184]

Holmes' point, of course, was that the very classification by Plato of "immutable ideas" as superior to and distinct from "mutable matters" presupposed that there was a basis for the classification in the first place. That basis either came from "intuition," which seemed perilously close to "drawing . . . conclusions already contained in the premise," or from "the finding of . . . data or statements," which seemed to be the equivalent of the "observation" of "mutable matters." Hence Plato was either an empiricist in spite of himself or one who was arguing that such ideas as "beauty" were "immutable" because he believed they were.

In the passage "science" was described as "founded on observation," and based on "data previously obtained." But in the paragraph immediately preceding that just quoted Holmes had said that in Plato's view "beauty . . . is the most sensible presentation of the good, which . . . embraces all the other permanent representative ideas." He then went on to say that

The good is the end of all philosophy, and as this is attained to by the study of the various ideas which represent it and which it comprehends, such study is philosophy, is science *par excellence*.[185]

Holmes' use of the term "science" in this excerpt more closely resembles the established early nineteenth-century conception of 'science' as systematic organization of knowledge, "the study of various ideas and [what these ideas] comprehend," organized around an "end," an overriding principle. In the excerpt "philosophy" and "science" are treated as comparable terms.

Holmes would continue to employ "science" in both its systemic and its empiricist guises in his mature scholarship. He would also seek to merge it with historicism, assuming that he could simultaneously treat legal subjects from the perspective of their historical development and from the perspective of the "philosopher/scientist" who ought to reorganize them in accordance with overriding principles or policies. These efforts, pursued over a ten year period of intense exposure to the history of common law subjects, would eventually culminate in his book *The Common Law*, which first appeared in 1881. The simultaneous attention he gave in his undergraduate essays to history and to "science," then, was to be replicated, in different form, in his most famous work of mature scholarship.

In carrying his historicist and "scientific" methodological orientations forward in his later career, Holmes did not trouble himself to explore the possibility that those two orientations might be mutually inconsistent or point in contradictory directions. He did, however, confront, as early as the "Plato" essay, the potential contradictions between a transcendentalist and an empiricist view of experience. Holmes was not fully prepared to press empiricism into certain realms, such as art, where he continued to believe, as the Durer essay revealed, in the capacity of the artistic rendering to transcend experience. In the Durer essay he characterized "the mere portraiture of the single unconnected fact" as "the lowest form of good art," and associated a "striving to look on types and eternal ideas" with the "highest gift of the artist" and "the ideal tendency" of art.[186] In "Plato" Holmes repeated those views. He then added a passage that echoed the Durer essay:

> How deeply would [Plato] have felt the difference of the plodder, who professing nature as his model, puts before him a flower, and copies every corrosion and chance stain upon its leaves . . . and the great artist who, seizing the type of the plant, paints that upon his canvas, and leaves the rest in the subordination in which it belongs. When [an] admirable artist . . . said that in every man and woman he tried to see their face and form as it would have been if it had descended from Adam . . . he was talking pure Platonism and true art.[187]

In at least two realms—"mathematical truth" and "true art"—Holmes was prepared to accept a nonempiricist approach to experience, an approach that closely resembled that of Emerson and his transcendentalist disciples. The implicit exception for those realms seems understandable for one who had made an investment in both Ruskin and Emerson as well as in "science." It also suggests that one should tread cautiously before concluding that Emersonian philosophy was simply an adolescent enthusiasm of Holmes'.

There is ample evidence, for example, that Holmes retained his interest in and attraction for Emerson well past his undergraduate years. He had given Emerson a copy of his "Plato" essay, precipitated by the advice Emerson had given him to "hold [Plato] at arm's length," and Emerson had allegedly responded by saying "I have read your piece. When you strike at a king, you must *kill* him."[188] In 1876 Holmes sent Emerson a copy of one of his legal history essays, "Primitive Notions in Modern Law," adding a note that described the piece as "a slight mark of the gratitude and respect I feel for you who more than anyone else first started the philosophical ferment in my mind."[189] In his ninetieth year he wrote his longtime friend Fredrick Pollock that "[t]he only firebrand of my youth that burns to me as brightly as ever is Emerson."[190] Holmes regularly appropriated phrases and lines from Emerson's poetry and essays in his own writing.[191] And Emerson, in 1870, published an essay, "Courage," in which he listed three qualities "as attracting the wonder and reverence of mankind": disinterestedness, practical power, and courage.[192] Those qualities were to find a place, in combination, at the very center of Holmes' mature belief structure.

Finally, one should not ignore the possibility of Emerson's belief in the power of the self to shape and even transcend experience surviving, in an inchoate fashion, in the mature Holmes. We will observe, in subsequent chapters, that alongside Holmes' growing sense of the cosmic helplessness of individuals before the vast forces of time, change, and majoritarian sentiment in the universe a kernel of romanticism, idealism, and exalted confidence in the self was retained. Because of Holmes' ability to convey vividly his sense of powerlessness or his skepticism about the capacity of individuals to make any difference in the course of events, and because of his unwillingness openly to celebrate himself, his achievements, or his potential to shape his experience, one might be tempted to view Holmes and Emerson as temperamental and philosophical opposites. To yield to that temptation is to miss one of the fundamental strains in Holmes' intellectual and emotional consciousness: his joy in life and in the potential power of the self.

Notwithstanding the uneven quality of Holmes' undergraduate essays,[193] they provide clear evidence that he devoted a good deal of his time in college to reading in, thinking about, and expressing himself on subjects that did not have a close connection with his classroom pursuits. Indeed if one were to recapitulate the principal foci of Holmes' years at Harvard—friendships with individuals of both sexes, engagement with social clubs, membership on the staff of *The Harvard Magazine*, the production of essays on art, philosophy, reading widely in those subjects, and participation in a circle of persons who increasingly came to believe that the institution of slavery in America should be abolished—it is not surprising that in Holmes' autobiographical sketch, after recounting his club memberships and literary activities, he wrote only one line about conventional academic pursuits, the fact that he had "tried for" and shared "the Greek . . . prize" for a composition he submitted in 1861.[194] The rest of his sketch described his activities as a volunteer in the Union army.

~

The last two months of Holmes' college career seemed to telescope most of the central themes of that experience. In his senior year he enrolled in Francis Bowen's course, "Political Economy," in which Bowen articulated a point of view squarely at odds with that Holmes advanced in the "Plato" and "Albert Durer" essays. Bowen believed that Darwin's *Origin of Species* was one of a number of "licentious and infidel speculations which are pouring in upon us from Europe like a flood,"[195] and that in the work of Emerson and other Transcendentalists "a glowing though vague conception of virtue takes the place of religion as a guild of life."[196] He set out to show in his course that the "sure and permanent support" for morality lay "in a recognition of its dictates as the commands of God."[197] He also believed that religion and laissez-faire economic principles went hand in hand: the idea that the economy regulated itself meant "that God regulates [it] by general laws, which always, in the long run, look to good."[198] He even suggested that population changes in the world were "indications of a beneficent arrangement of Providence, by which it is obtained that the barbarous race which now tenant the earth should work away and finally disappear, while civilized men are . . . to multiply."[199]

To say that Holmes, given his newfound enthusiasm for "science" and his obvious dissatisfaction with orthodox religion, reacted negatively to these tenets of Bowen would be to understate matters. When one recalls that in addition to being exposed to Bowen's views Holmes was participating in antislavery rallies and discussions in the winter and spring of 1861, and that Fort Sumter was attacked by Confederate forces on April 14, it is not surprising that a week after that attack the Harvard Faculty decided "that Hackett and Holmes, seniors," should be publicly admonished for "repeated and gross indecorum" in Bowen's class.[200] The "Hackett" in question was Frank Warren Hackett, Holmes' fellow staff member on the *Harvard Magazine*, a periodical that had already come to the attention of the President of Harvard for what he described to Dr. Holmes in a January 1861 letter as "printed

... acts of disrespect" to faculty members. That letter also referred to "oral acts of disrespect," a phrase that, since it was addressed to Holmes' father, may have been meant to apply to Holmes himself.[201]

By April 1861 Holmes may well have felt that a public admonition for outspokenness in Bowen's class amounted to a mite in his eye. He was in the process of leaving college to enlist in the Fourth Battalion, and he actually left Cambridge with the Battalion for guard duty at Fort Independence, in Boston Harbor, on April 25. We have seen that two days before his departure President Cornelius Felton again had to inform Dr. Holmes that his son had been publicly admonished for breaking windows and for continued disrespectful conduct toward Bowen.

The mysterious influence Felton described in that letter as affecting Holmes' conduct during the spring of his senior year at Harvard is not hard to discern. The progression of activities begun in the company of Penrose Hallowell in the winter of 1861 had culminated, after Fort Sumter, in a decision to fight on behalf of the antislavery principle. Later Holmes was to describe his conception of fighting against the South in the Civil War as "a crusade in the cause of the whole civilized world ... the Christian Crusade of the 19th century."[202] Enlistment was, as he said in that letter, an "example of chivalry." Alongside that gesture the petty rules and tiresome preachings of the Harvard faculty must have seemed hardly worth bothering about. It is clear that Holmes was inspired by the abolitionism of his friend Hallowell, with whom he enlisted; it is equally clear that he had no intention of returning to Harvard that spring. As he said in his autobiographical sketch, he expected to go south as a private after completing his training at Fort Independence.

Unfortunately Holmes and his fellow classmates found themselves in an awkward situation as the spring of 1861 waned. Although they had anticipated being sent southward into combat at the close of their training, the Fourth Battalion was not assigned to such duty; instead it was to remain in the Boston area and eventually be reduced to ceremonial duties. Finding this unsatisfactory, Holmes, Hallowell, and several others sought to enlist in one of the volunteer Massachusetts Regiments that were then being created. Securing a commission in those Regiments took time, however, and thus Holmes was confronted with the frustrating prospect of having no significant military duties to perform. On June 11, while Holmes was in limbo, President Felton again wrote Dr. Holmes about his son:

> The Faculty have been surprised that your son has not rejoined his class since he was relieved of military duty at the Fort; and I have been directed to give him notice that he will be expected to attend the examinations of his class, as a condition of being recommended to the Corporation for a degree.[203]

The Harvard Faculty's conclusion, signaled by Felton's letter, was that Holmes and Hallowell, whose extended absence had been discussed in a faculty meeting on June 10, could return, with the only penalty for their two months of absence from classes being accumulated deficiency points that would reduce their class ranks.

Holmes and Hallowell chose to return, took their examinations, and were deemed eligible to graduate. As a consequence Holmes was not listed in the top half of the students in his graduating class, and was not assigned a speaking part during Commencement exercises. It is not clear that he even attended those exercises, although

he did give the class poem on Class Day, June 21. His omission from those designated as being in the top half of the class nonetheless rankled his father, who complained to Felton:

> I have expressed the opinion incidentally to several friends that my son had not
> been treated by the Faculty as I should have expected. . . He left college
> suddenly, no doubt, but if he did not stop to kiss his Alma Mater, neither did
> many other volunteers stop to kiss their mothers and wives and sweethearts.
> He went with the expectation of going into active service, and has never
> ceased his military discipline and efforts to get into a post where he could
> serve his country. . .
>   For his promptitude in offering his services, at the very close of his college
> life he is not only deprived of the honors which I know you personally wished
> him to obtain, . . . but is consigned to the inglorious half of the Class, standing
> forever on the College records as one not worthy to be named along those who
> had achieved a decent mediocrity. . .
>   His case was entirely exceptional. Revolutions do not follow precedents nor
> furnish them. The enforcement of the scholastic rule in this instance seems to
> me harsh and unworthy of the occasion.[204]

Dr. Holmes had added in the letter he had "never heard a word of complaint"
from his son about the treatment and that he did not think Holmes had "bestowed
any thought upon the matter," and in his response Felton noted that "the faculty
took it for granted that in engaging in an employment so remote from College study,
for such a length of time, he had relinquished all expectation and desire of a commencement part, to secure what he considered of greater importance."[205] Felton's
instinct, though self-serving, seems sound. Holmes had, after all, not bothered to
return to college at all after his tour of duty at Fort Independence had expired. Indeed,
the incident may have confirmed for Holmes the irrelevance of Harvard and its rules
in a spring in which he, Hallowell, and others were embarking on a crusade to save
the civilized world.

    Thus it appears that, as in the case of Henry Adams and Henry Cabot Lodge,
Harvard College's most lasting contribution to Holmes' education was to afford him
stimulating companions and enough leisure time to pursue activities outside the
official curriculum. In a variety of unofficial activities he attempted to hone his
literary skills and pursue his interests in reading and in "high conversation." In
"conversations" with his clubmates and others he was exposed to the political and
social views of persons who were inclined, at that point in their lives, to devote a
fair amount of their energies to the romanticization of "honor," manliness, and the
martial virtues. When the Civil War broke upon Holmes and his contemporaries in
the spring of 1861, they were motivated to engage in it, having associated abolitionism and the destruction of corrupt Southern life with the chivalric crusades of
the middle ages. They were also inclined to recognize the vast contrast between the
world of soldiering and the world of student decorum and religious orthodoxy they
had encountered in official Harvard. By trivializing official student experience and
at the same time freeing its students to lead a richer and more stimulating unofficial

experience, Harvard had unwittingly prepared Holmes and his contemporaries to leave it, to go to war, without any regrets. Holmes' last entry in his autobiographical sketch declared that he was "too busy to say more" about his life up to July 1861. He was "too busy" trying to find a way to join the Union Army's crusade.

When one peruses Holmes' autobiographical sketch in search of a central theme, as distinguished from the details he chose to mention, a unifying tension seems to pervade the document. That tension emanates from a juxtaposition of the cumulative weight of Holmes' ancestral heritage against Holmes' selection of those features of his life that he regarded as essential. At least half of the sketch is concerned with Holmes' heritage, stretching from the opening sentences about his father to the sentence about his always having lived in Boston. The other half of the sketch discusses details that were, in July 1861, important for Holmes to emphasize about his current self: his clubs, his literary achievements, his participation in the war, the fact that Penrose Hallowell was his friend.

The arrangement of the sketch, with its implicit separation of heritage from current concerns, serves to underscore the fact that very few of the details Holmes mentioned in connection with his heritage were replicated in details he chose to mention about his present self. Holmes ignored any club memberships or social associations of his family members; he mentioned all those of his own. He devoted almost half of the "current" portion of his sketch to details of his efforts to volunteer in the Civil War; he mentioned only that "some of my ancestors have fought in the revolution," not giving their names. The detail that principally linked him to his heritage was his literary pursuits. In writing for the *Harvard Magazine* and the *University Quarterly* he was pursuing the "strong natural bent to literature" that was one of "[t]he tendencies of the family and of myself."[206]

The literary connection between heritage and current self, however, was dramatically qualified, even arguably obliterated, by the language that followed the phrase in which Holmes emphasized that connection. After mentioning the "natural bent to literature" that he shared with generations of Olivers, Wendells, and Holmeses, Holmes then wrote:

> at present I am trying for a commission in one of the Massachusetts regiments, however, and hope to go south before very long. If I survive the war I expect to study law as my profession or at least for a starting point.[207]

The use of the terms "at present" and "however" to frame Holmes' statement that he was "trying for a commission in one of the Massachusetts regiments" serves to create a dramatic break with the cumulative weight of his heritage. He and generations of ancestors may have a strong natural bent to literature, but "at present" he is not pursuing literature, but war, a pursuit that in the sketch he associated with his family only in a vague and oblique reference. His first goal on graduating from college, he indicated, would be to secure a military commission; his second to "survive the war"; his next "to study law as my profession."[208] While these goals did not represent a complete break with his heritage, as he has chosen to describe it, they did represent a break with the central connection between himself and his ancestors, an interest in literature. Moreover, the break appears to be a product of the urgency of circumstances: Holmes notes that he has written the sketch "in haste" and is "too busy" attempting to secure a military commission "to say more if I would."[209]

Seen in this fashion, the sketch appears as the statement of a person exceptionally mindful of the "pedigree" of his heritage, and equally mindful of the literary "tendencies" of his family and himself, who feels at the same time compelled, by events and his own inclinations, to pursue goals that on their face appear inconsistent with what it has meant, over time, to be an Oliver, a Wendell, a Holmes, or a Jackson. The tension one feels is that of a young man embarking on an unexpectedly different path from that toward which his "tendencies" and "natural bent" would have led him. It is also that of a young man taking a certain pride, and feeling a certain sense of independence, in his decision to venture into an unknown and dangerous future.

Holmes' July 1861 autobiographical sketch thus not only provides us with a vehicle for recapitulating the themes of his early life, but with an opportunity to encounter, at this early stage, one of the defining elements in that life as a whole. Literature, for Holmes, conveyed associations of ancestral accomplishment; it also signified a pursuit that seemed natural and inevitable for him, given who he was. At the same time literature was not to be his immediate concern on graduating from college; it was not even to be his choice of profession should he survive his wartime experience.

When Holmes had chosen to talk about himself, as distinguished from his ancestors, in the sketch, he had chosen to talk about his clubs, his wartime service, and his literary projects. In Holmes' later life social clubs and the attendant connections would play a comparatively small part, although his selection and pursuit of his social contacts would play a large role. War, primarily in the forms of a surrogate for immersion in the elemental forces of life and as a romanticized and yet disturbing memory, would also be a recurrent theme. Neither social connections nor war, however, were to occupy the central and ambivalent place in Holmes' life that was occupied by literature.

Holmes remained throughout his life a person for whom intimacy, of the kind he might have been seeking in his social affiliations at Harvard, was an attractive, if dangerous, pursuit. He also remained convinced that he and his contemporary volunteers—the generation he described as "touched with fire"[210]—had had their lives and sensibilities fundamentally altered by the experience of going to war. He explored the themes of social intimacy and war from many perspectives in the course of his life. But he did not explore, in an analytical fashion, the theme of "literature," especially the theme of having a "natural bent" for literature and yet adopting law as his profession. While he reflected on the difficulties, and eventual opportunities, of using law as a basis for philosophical inquiry, he did not reflect, at least openly, on what it meant to him to recognize his "natural bent to literature" and at the same time to define himself, professionally, as a lawyer, legal scholar, or judge. Alongside Holmes' acknowledgment in the sketch that the essential link between himself and his heritage was "literature," there was an additional, implicit acknowledgment— that in the "real world" of war and other "battles," and in the world of professional aspiration, literature was supposed to be subordinated to other themes. But this subordination, in Holmes' professional life, was never fully to take place.

CHAPTER TWO

The Civil War

~

IN AN address delivered approximately twenty years after he mustered out of
service with the Twentieth Regiment of Massachusetts Volunteers, Holmes said
that

> the generation that carried on the war has been set apart by its experience.
> Through our great good fortune, in our youth our hearts were touched with
> fire. It was given to us to learn at the outset that life is a profound and
> passionate thing. While we are permitted to scorn nothing but indifference, and
> do not pretend to undervalue the worldly rewards of ambition, we have seen
> with our own eyes, beyond and above the gold fields, the snowy heights of
> honor, and it is for us to bear the report to those who come after us.[1]

The passage is one of several in which Holmes, in his later career, sought to distill
the meaning of his experiences in the Civil War. That search was a persistent one.
An anthology of his writings includes five separate occasions, between 1864 and
1911, on which he made contributions devoted to the war,[2] and there were many
others in which he invoked martial themes, metaphors, or references. His tendency
to analogize life to war lasted, allegedly, at least until the day in 1932 when, shortly
after his inauguration, President Franklin Roosevelt called on Holmes and asked him
for advice on beginning his new job, and Holmes supposedly responded, "Form
your ranks and fight."[3] Moreover, Holmes' correspondence is filled with occasions
in which he remembered the war, his wounds, the deaths of his contemporaries, and
reflected on its meaning. Mark Howe was correct in observing that an analysis of
Holmes' experiences in the Civil War requires attention not only to "the war in
fact," but to "the war in retrospect."[4]

Holmes' Civil War experiences can be viewed from three interrelated perspectives. The first is a narrative chronology of Holmes' service, providing a framework
for Holmes' own reactions to the war, and underscoring the very large percentage
of time that Holmes spent being wounded or sick, recovering from injury or illness,
or witnessing the sufferings, woundings, or deaths of friends and acquaintances. A
narrative of Holmes' wartime service demonstrates that it was a notably stressful
experience.

The next perspective traces the evolution of Holmes' reaction to his wartime
experiences, based on his surviving Civil War letters and diaries. Those sources do
not, of course, constitute a complete, or unstructured, account of his reactions to the
war, since Holmes destroyed some of his letters, wrote some of his diary entries well

after the fact, and did not leave a record of the time he spent back home in Boston recovering from his wounds. The gaps in, and his efforts to varnish, his "eyewitness" account of his experiences are, in their own fashion, as interesting as his firsthand reactions, and some observations will be made about those "deficiencies" in Holmes' recording of his experiences. The effort is not to evaluate the accuracy of Holmes' perceptions, but rather to explore the sources of those perceptions: what they reveal about the posture from which Holmes observed and recorded his wartime service.

The last perspective recapitulates the "meaning" of the Civil War, as Holmes sought to convey that meaning in a series of retrospective addresses. An emphasis on the war in retrospect, as Holmes saw it, introduces a contrast between his experiences as a contemporary soldier and the memory of those experiences as a surviving veteran. While such a contrast is arguably present in any retrospective account of a wartime experience, it is of particular interest in Holmes' case. The suggestiveness of the contrast between the tone of Holmes' contemporary and retrospective accounts of his wartime experiences lies in its complexity. In both accounts Holmes was seeking, implicitly or explicitly, to draw meaning from the act of going to war. The meaning that he drew, in the two sets of accounts, appears to be radically different on the surface, but at the same time reveals an overriding similarity. Exploring the relationship of Holmes' contemporary and retrospective reactions to his Civil War experience helps locate the essential place of the Civil War in Holmes' life.

~

The ordinary details of Holmes' wartime experiences underscore the arbitrariness, drudgery, and myopia of war. In passage after passage from Holmes' letters and diaries his regiment is depicted as trudging over ground between battles, bivouacking in the cold and wet or wading through rivers and swamps in the heat, pausing only to confront the enemy and witness losses in its ranks. Bodies lie on the landscape; men with fearful wounds are transported behind the lines; officers in one moment rise to encourage their troops and in the next are slain. All the while there is no sense of where the regiment is headed or the overriding purpose of its maneuvering; encounters with the enemy seem random and devoid of any larger meaning. Most of the time Holmes and his comrades do not seem aware of why they are in a particular location or whether their aim is to attack the enemy or defend themselves. Sometimes they indiscriminately strike out at anyone in a different colored uniform; sometimes they avoid fighting altogether and exchange newspapers or canteens. Their war seems confined to the space around them; it seems to bear no relationship to anything else. Least of all does it appear like "a crusade in the cause of the whole civilized world," a description Holmes gave to it as late as April 1864.[5]

Such is the overall impression of Holmes' wartime environment. On the other hand his diaries and letters, together with secondary accounts, make it possible to give a chronological, if not an existential, order to his wartime service. That service had begun, we have seen, while Holmes was still at Harvard, when he joined the Fourth Battalion, and had only temporarily been interrupted during the months of June and July 1861, while he waited for a commission in what turned out to be the Twentieth Massachusetts Volunteer Infantry Regiment. His commission took a while to materialize, and there is evidence that his father intervened with the Governor of Massachusetts on his behalf.[6] By August the formalities of the enlistment process were complete, and Holmes had signed on for a three-year term as an officer.

Holmes' first assignment was to recruit additional men for the Regiment, and he was dispatched to Pittsfield, Massachusetts, in August to perform that task. It is not clear when he returned from Pittsfield to Camp Massasoit in Readville, Massachusetts, about eight miles from Boston, where the Regiment was encamped for training.[7] On September 4 the Regiment, now numbering about 750 men, was dispatched from Readville to Washington, D.C. The trip, made by steamer and train, took three days, with stops at Groton, Connecticut, New York, Philadelphia, and Baltimore. In New York most of the troops attended a dinner in barracks in Central Park, but Holmes and a few fellow officers stayed away, eating at Delmonico's restaurant. On arriving in Washington the Regiment disembarked at Camp Kalorama, located in Georgetown Heights, overlooking the northwest of the city. At that site they met other regiments of the Army of the Potomac, under the command of General George B. McClellan.[8]

From Camp Kalorama the Regiment proceeded to Camp Burnside on Meridian Hill closer to the center of Washington, and from there to Camp Benton at Poolesville, Maryland, following the Potomac River in a northwesterly direction from Washington. The Potomac marked the boundary line between northern and southern armies at the time, and Holmes' Regiment was assigned to picket duty at Edwards Ferry, two miles from Poolesville on the Maryland side of the river, where they could observe and communicate with Confederate soldiers on the Virginia side. They remained in the Poolesville area for the rest of September and a good portion of October, training and observing the enemy.[9] Holmes wrote his mother, on September 23, that "it seems so queer to see an encampment & twig men through a glass & think they are our enemies & hear of some of our pickets talking across & so on." "All these things," he added, "give reality to the life but I don't expect any fighting for the present."[10] He added that "all details like those I've written of our actual or probable movements are strictly private as we are strongly forbidden to write about such things."[11]

During the months of September and October the Twentieth Regiment was treated as part of General Charles P. Stone's Corps of Observation, which had been assigned by McClellan to monitor Confederate troop movements along the Potomac, from the Confederate stronghold in Leesburg, Virginia, forty miles up the river from Washington, to Washington itself. McClellan, relying on misleading intelligence reports, believed that the Confederates had amassed large numbers of troops along the Virginia side of the Potomac, and were preparing to attack Washington. As a result the Army of the Potomac remained inert during the months of September and early October 1861, despite considerable pressure from elements in Congress to launch an attack into Virginia.[12]

On October 19 McClellan, who was planning to make a foray across the Potomac, sent a telegram to Stone, suggesting that Stone make a "slight demonstration" of the presence of Union forces on the Maryland side of the Potomac so as to encourage the Confederate forces to vacate Leesburg. Stone assigned the responsibility for that demonstration to Colonel Edward Baker, a friend of President Lincoln's and former

United States Senator from Oregon who had very little military experience. Baker selected companies from several regiments, including the Twentieth Massachusetts Volunteers, and arranged for them to move across the river at Ball's Bluff, where supposedly there was a Confederate camp. On the night of October 20 and the morning of October 21 the Union troops moved across the Potomac, climbed a 150-foot bluff, and camped on a field at its top.

By afternoon the Confederate command post at Leesburg had learned that McClellan had abandoned his foray across the Potomac and that the Union forces encamped at Ball's Bluff were isolated in enemy territory, exposed in an open field, with a river at their back, inadequate boats to ferry the river, and no reinforcements. As a result Confederate forces moved forward, from the woods surrounding the field at the top of Ball's Bluff, and began firing on the Union forces. The fighting started at about 3:30 P.M. By 6 P.M. Union troops had been driven back to the bluff; by 8 P.M. the entire Union contingent had been forced back across the river to the Maryland side, and over half of the 1700 men originally assigned to the mission had been captured, killed, or wounded by Confederate soldiers. Among those captured was Colonel William R. Lee, in command of the Twentieth Regiment; among those killed was Colonel Baker; among those wounded was a twenty year old taking part in his first military battle, Oliver Wendell Holmes, Jr.[13]

Holmes had been shot in the chest,[14] the bullet entering on the left and lodging on the right side. One of the members of his company, First Sergeant Smith, dragged him to the rear, opened his shirt, squeezed out the bullet from a cavity it had made on the right side, and gave it to Holmes. He was subsequently taken down the bluff and transported, in a small boat, to a temporary hospital on Harrison's Island, a small island in the middle of the Potomac a few miles upstream from Edwards Ferry and in the vicinity of Ball's Bluff. He was examined by Dr. Nathan Hayward, the Surgeon of the Twentieth Regiment, who told him that he might recover, turned him over on his chest, and arranged to transport Holmes and other wounded men from Harrison's Island to the Maryland shore and then to Camp Benton. They eventually arrived there in the early morning hours of October 22, Holmes in a semiconscious state, having been given a dose of laudanum at Harrison's Island. By October 23, after being examined by a hospital steward, who plugged his wounds with lint, and Dr. Hayward, he was well enough to write a reassuring letter to his mother.[15] He had had a narrow escape from death, but the bullet had missed any vital organs and his wounds healed in an uncomplicated fashion.

By October 31 Holmes was well enough to be moved from Camp Benton to Philadelphia, where he was housed at the home of Penrose Hallowell's family and seen by a physician. Dr. Holmes journeyed to Philadelphia to retrieve his son, and they returned to Boston on November 9. From that time until March 26, 1862, he was not in active service, although in January and February he was sent to Pittsfield on recruiting duty.[16] By the time he returned to the Twentieth Regiment, it was stationed in Washington, having just arrived there from Camp Bolivar Heights, near Harper's Ferry, Maryland.[17] On March 27 the entire Army of the Potomac, including the Twentieth Regiment, sailed from Washington to Hampton, Virginia, where it disembarked at Fort Monroe. Just prior to his having returned to active duty Holmes had been promoted by Governor Andrew to Captain, but the official notice had not reached him and he assumed, to his delight, that he would serve as a lieutenant in Penrose Hallowell's Company. This assumption subsequently proved inaccurate, and Holmes and Hallowell ended up captaining different companies.[18]

The Army of the Potomac's task was to invade Richmond from the Tidewater, or eastern, side. Union forces had had some success in the late months of 1861 and the early months of 1862, and McClellan planned an advance on Richmond, led by his own army, in the hopes of securing a speedy end to the war. McClellan's strategy was to begin the advance in the spring, when he felt that the Tidewater roads would be sufficiently dry and the weather not yet hot, and reach Richmond before the summer set in. The Twentieth Regiment was to be part of that advance, which was to proceed from Fort Monroe to Yorktown, on the mouth of the York River, and then northwest in a direction parallelling the York and James Rivers toward Richmond.

The first anticipated action for the Regiment was to be a siege against Yorktown, which a relatively small Confederate force eventually evacuated on May 4. Between its landing at Hampton on March 31 and April 7 the Regiment moved slowly to Camp Winfield Scott, three miles south of Yorktown. McClellan was being cautious, preparing for a shelling of Yorktown prior to a direct attack on it, and as a consequence the Regiment stayed in the vicinity of Yorktown for the rest of the month. On April 23 Holmes wrote his parents that ''[t]he notion seems to be that McClellan is trying to out-general & catch 'em if poss[ible] without a big fight.''[19] During the interval between April 7 and May 4 the Regiment's activity consisted of marching and standing in mud, a product of heavy spring rains, and skirmishing with Confederates on picket lines. In the April 23 letter quoted above Holmes gave a description of the Regiment's situation that spring:

> We go to picket every third day and it would have made you smile to see Pen [Hallowell] and me yesterday morn'g sitting on a stump smoking our pipes & reading old letters after a night of raining like blazes, out in the woods with a constant popping of guns where the rebs and our men were exchanging compliments & every now & then *bang—boom*—as a shell was fired & exploded on the one side or t'other—we fire most—Now and then a bullet would whiz high over our heads from the other side. . . .[20]

After the Confederates, anticipating a major assault on Yorktown, withdrew in the direction of Richmond, the Regiment entered Yorktown and remained there until May 6, when it was dispatched up the York River to West Point, nearly due east of Richmond, to assist in an invasion of that city. The overall plan was for McClellan's Army of the Potomac to join forces with General Irvin McDowell's corps, which had been stationed near Fredericksburg, Virginia, to defend any Confederate forays in the direction of Washington. As McDowell prepared to advance south, however, Stonewall Jackson's Confederate forces created a significant diversion in the Shenandoah Valley, racing from Harrisonburg to New Market, Luray, Front Royal, Winchester, and just west of Harper's Ferry, winning skirmishes with Union troops and potentially threatening Washington from the west. McDowell's corps were ordered to chase after Jackson, preventing them from joining McClellan's advance. In the meantime General Joseph E. Johnston's forces retreated from Yorktown toward

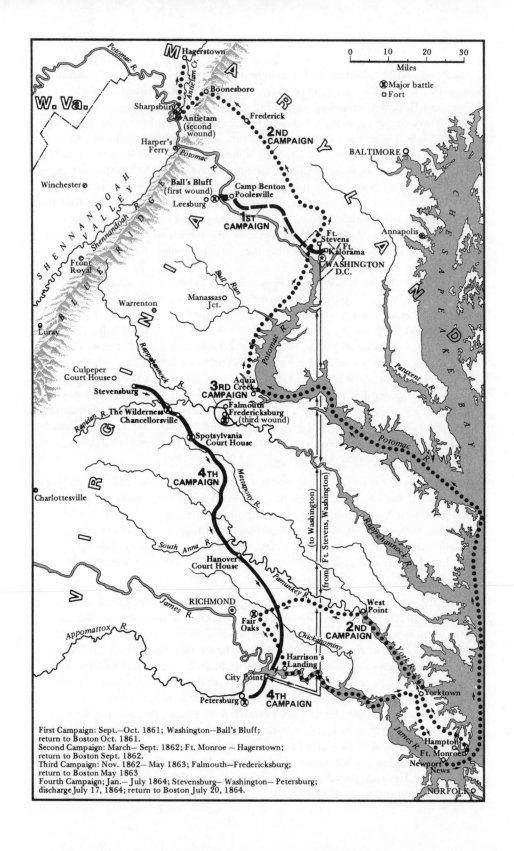

Hagerstown

Potomac R.

M

A

R

Boonesboro

W. Va.

Sharpsburg

Antietam
(second
wound)

Antietam Cr.

Frederick

2ND
CAMPAIGN

BALTIMORE

Harper's
Ferry

Potomac R.

Winchester

Ball's Bluff
(first wound)

Leesburg

Camp Benton
Poolesville

1ST
CAMPAIGN

Annapolis

Ft.
Stevens
Ft.
Kalorama

WASHINGTON
D.C.

SHENANDOAH VALLEY

Shenandoah R.

BLUE RIDGE

Front
Royal

Bull Run

Manassas
Jct.

Warrenton

Luray

Rappahannock R.

Culpeper
Court House

Stevensburg

Rapidan R.

The Wilderness
Chancellorsville

Aquia
Creek

3RD
CAMPAIGN

Falmouth
Fredericksburg
(third wound)

Spotsylvania
Court House

4TH
CAMPAIGN

Mattapony R.

Charlottesville

South Anna R.

Hanover
Court House

James R.

RICHMOND

Pamunkey R.

Appomattox R.

Fair
Oaks

Chickahominy R.

Harrison's
Landing

City Point

Petersburg

4TH
CAMPAIGN

West
Point

2ND
CAMPAIGN

York R.

Yorktown

James R.

Hampton

Ft. Monroe

Newport
News

NORFOLK

CHESAPEAKE BAY

Patuxent R.

Potomac R.

Rappahannock R.

(to Washington)

(from Ft. Stevens, Washington)

Potomac R.

0   10   20   30

Miles

⊗ Major battle
▫ Fort

First Campaign: Sept.—Oct. 1861; Washington—Ball's Bluff;
return to Boston Oct. 1861.
Second Campaign: March— Sept. 1862; Ft. Monroe — Hagerstown;
return to Boston Sept. 1862.
Third Campaign: Nov. 1862— May 1863; Falmouth—Fredericksburg;
return to Boston May 1863
Fourth Campaign; Jan.— July 1864; Stevensburg— Washington— Petersburg;
discharge July 17, 1864; return to Boston July 20, 1864.

Richmond and prepared to defend it. McClellan's army, including the Twentieth Regiment, slowly proceeded toward Richmond in May, a large force stopping on the north bank of the Chickahominy River, about six miles east of Richmond. The Regiment encamped on the north bank of the Chickahominy on May 28.[21]

At this point, after two months of comparative inactivity, Holmes and his regimental contemporaries again confronted war in earnest. On May 31 Johnston attempted to respond to the mounting pressure against Richmond by attacking the wing massing on the north bank of the Chickahominy. In the resulting battle, which lasted all that day and into the next, Johnston was wounded, and replaced by Robert E. Lee. Lee broke off fighting and the Army of the Potomac managed to cross to the southern bank of the Chickahominy. For the next three weeks Lee acted as if he was simply preparing to defend Richmond. Instead, relying on intelligence secured by a scouting run behind Union lines made by cavalry officer James E. (Jeb) Stuart, Lee prepared a counterattack on the Army of the Potomac, to be launched by Johnston's forces, aided by those of Stonewall Jackson, who had moved east from Charlottesville on June 17 to join Lee. On June 25 the counterattack was launched directly at Union forces that included the Twentieth Regiment. After seven days of nearly continuous, bloody fighting, the Regiment, along with the rest of the Army of the Potomac, retreated from the south side of the Chickahominy south to Harrison's Landing, about 8 miles from Richmond on the James River. Eventually the Regiment and the Army of the Potomac were to abandon the invasion altogether.[22]

Holmes wrote his parents of the heavy fighting in which he had been involved. In a June 2 letter, describing the Fair Oaks encounter, he wrote that "[i]t is singular with what indifference one gets to look on the dead bodies in gray clothes wh[ich] lie all around. . . . As you go through the woods you stumble constantly, and if after dark, as last night on picket, perhaps tread on the swollen bodies already fly blown and decaying, of men shot in the head back or bowels."[23] In a July 4 letter from Harrison's Landing he indicated that the Regiment had had "hard work for several days—marched all night—lain on our arms every morning and fought every afternoon—eaten nothing—suffered the most intense anxiety and everything else possible— . . . [Y]ou can't conceive the wear and tear."[24] And in a letter dated the next day he provided more details:

> June 29 we started from the trenches on our retreat—at Fair Oaks passed Rocket Guns & great quantities of stores wh[ich] had to be destroyed—. . . . Afternoon marched to Savage's Station where lots more stores were destroyed and a hospital stood where all the wounded had to be left to the enemy. Here the enemy shelled us—Several men hurt none of our Co.
>
> Marched all night rested at early dawn—marched and rested in woods noon—afternoon terribly thirsty (hardly any water to be had) came up double quick onto field of action (knapsacks on backs) . . . *Whang* goes a shell two men drop in Co. G. . . . [T]he Michigan 7th [Regiment] on our left breaks and runs *disgracefully* (private) . . . Not a waver in our Regt. . . . till Palfrey . . . gave the order to march double quick in retreat. We were flanked & nearly surrounded and that saved us. . . . The guns got so hot & dirty we couldn't load or fire more than ⅔ of them. That night June 30 we marched again (all

this time I only eating about 3 pieces of hard bread a day & not wanting more hardly sleeping at all & never washing). . . . The next morning a splendid line of battle (of the whole army) at Malverton where the Rebs shelled us (our brigade) hard. . . . At midnight started and marched through terrible rain & mud until we reached the James [River] the next day. The anxiety has been more terrible than almost any past experience.

I'm too tired that is too mentally inefficient to write well but I've sent 2 notes before including a leaf of my pocket book written some time to you in case I was ever killed.[25]

The note in his "pocket book" had been alluded to in another July 4 note: Holmes said that it had been written on June 13 "to show my feelings." Much later, when Holmes combed through his wartime correspondence, he destroyed that note, writing on the back of the envelope in which he sent that it was "rather pompous."[26] Regardless of the contents of that note, it was apparent from the letters recording the Regiment's activities in June and July 1862 that Holmes and his contemporaries had been exposed to some of the most difficult conditions of the entire war. In a September 17, 1862, letter to his parents Holmes noted that "[n]ever since the terrible exposures of Fair-Oaks have I been myself. . . . [O]ne damp night recalling those dreary times plays the deuce with me."[27]

From the perspective of those commanding the operations of the Union and Confederate forces, the battles of the "Seven Days" campaign marked a decisive point in the war. President Abraham Lincoln, realizing that the Army of the Potomac had been repulsed in its effort to invade Richmond and was now exposed to the hazards of hot weather in swampy conditions, where dysentery, typhoid, and malaria were known to flourish, resolved to evacuate the Army from Harrison's Landing and station it in the Washington area. At the same time Lincoln and his aides concluded that a swift, limited invasion of Richmond could not bring the war to a conclusion, and prepared to increase the Union military arsenal and engage in "total war." Moreover, a decision that Lincoln had been mulling over crystallized: he resolved to issue a proclamation freeing the slaves in the Confederate states, with the hope that this action would undermine the South ideologically as well as economically and militarily. Six days after Holmes wrote his parents recalling the hardships of the Seven Days battles Lincoln issued the Emancipation Proclamation.[28]

Meanwhile the Confederate commanders, buoyed by Lee's defense of Richmond, decided to continue their strategy of combining tactical retreats with aggressive forays into Union territory, with the eventual hope of invading Washington. In August, having reorganized his Army of Northern Virginia into two corps, one commanded by Jackson and the other by General James Longstreet, Lee ordered it to move north toward Washington. Jackson fanned west and successfully advanced to Manassas; Longstreet eventually joined him there, and together the Confederates forced a Union retreat from Manassas at the end of August 1862. At this point Lee resolved to continue to proceed north, crossing the Potomac into Maryland, with the goal of establishing a Confederate presence in a Union state and forcing the North to sue for peace.[29]

At this point the Union leadership resolved to mount a campaign against Lee's Army of Northern Virginia. They were apparently motivated by the deleterious effects on Northern morale of Confederate armies crossing into Union territory and threatening Washington, and by a belief that Lee's army had strayed too far from its support base in Richmond to be effective against increased northern forces. The Army of the Potomac, now numbering about 75,000 men, was delegated the task of attacking Longstreet's and Jackson's corps. Lee, becoming aware of the massing of Union troops, pulled his scattered army together at Antietam Creek, near Sharpsburg, Maryland, about a mile across the Maryland side of the Potomac River west of Washington. Both sides prepared for a major battle, which took place on September 17. At that battle's conclusion 6000 men had been killed and about 17,000 wounded.[30] With Antietam the course of the war decisively escalated: each side now sought the annihilation of the other.[31]

Among the Union units fighting at Antietam was the Twentieth Regiment. It had moved, with other units of the Army of the Potomac, from Harrison's Landing to Yorktown and Newport News in August 1862, embarking from Newport News for Washington on August 25 and arriving at Aquia Creek, on the Potomac south of Washington, on August 27. From there it marched north, eventually camping at Tennallytown, Maryland, on September 4. Between that date and September 17 it continued to advance in a northwesterly direction through Maryland, passing through Rockville, Hyattstown, and Frederick to Boonsborough and Keedysville, near Antietam Creek. Holmes' September 17 letter to his parents was written at 3 A.M. by candlelight; he noted that "we're in reserve & near to [the enemy] and may fight today.... All of us feel a deuced sight more like a fight than in that forlorn peninsula."[32]

The fight was to come within a few hours. On the morning of September 17 the Twentieth Regiment, designated as a reserve unit, was ordered up so far toward the front of Union lines that, as Holmes put it many years later, "we could have touched ... the front line ... with our bayonets." When the fighting began, "the enemy broke through on our left," and the Regiment, instead of being able to repel them, was "surrounded with the front," and an order to retreat was quickly given. Holmes remembered "chuckling to myself as I was leaving the field," since at Ball's Bluff *Harper's Weekly* had made much of the fact that he had been shot "in the breast, not in the back." This time he was "bolting as fast as I can ... not so good for the newspapers."[33] As he was retreating he was hit in the back of the neck, the ball "passing straight through the central seam of coat & waistcoat collar coming out toward the front on the left hand side."[34]

Holmes was taken to a farmhouse that was being used as a temporary hospital for Union troops, even though it was behind Confederate lines. Eventually the Confederates were driven from the area and the surgeon of the Fifteenth Massachusetts Regiment was able to examine Holmes. He "glanced hastily" at Holmes' wound and said "it wasn't fatal." Holmes was taken in an ambulance to Keedysville, Maryland, where he was attended to by Lieutenant Colonel William LeDuc, who was concerned about the nature of his wounds. LeDuc insisted that a Mrs. Kitzmuller put up Holmes in her house, plugged his wound with lint, and had him swallow an opium pill that a military surgeon, who claimed to have no time to attend to Holmes, had previously given him. LeDuc then telegraphed Holmes' parents that he had been "shot through the neck" but that the wound was "not thought mortal."[35]

By the morning of September 20 Holmes appeared well enough to be placed in a milk cart and taken to Hagerstown, Maryland, to take a train to Philadelphia and then eventually to Boston. As he walked through Hagerstown, however, he was approached by a young boy who offered him a place to spend the night. Holmes, "not feeling quite inclined to undertake the journey homeward immediately alone," accepted the invitation, and spent the next several days at the home of Mrs. Howard Kennedy. On September 22 he wrote his parents, with the aid of a young woman, that he was "not yet dead but on the contrary doing all that an unprincipled son could do to shock the prejudices of parents & of doctors." He had decided, he noted, "to remain [at the Kennedy's house] a few days, from which determination my having a good time here did not much detract." He advised the senior Holmeses that he did not "wish to meet any affectionate parent half way nor any shiny demonstrations when I reach the desired haven."[36]

Holmes' request not to be met was in vain. Not only had Dr. Holmes set out to find his son and accompany him back to Boston the day after receiving LeDuc's telegram, he was subsequently to publish an account of his journey in the December 1862 *Atlantic Monthly*. That account, entitled "My Hunt After 'The Captain,' " was additional proof for Holmes, if any was needed, that he was no ordinary Civil War enlistee. After being shot at Antietam he had written a note, "I am Capt. O. W. Holmes 20th Mass. Son of Oliver Wendell Holmes, M.D. Boston," as a precaution in case he "might faint & so be unable to tell who I was."[37] The note may have been intended to single himself out from other wounded, and LeDuc's account of his coming upon Holmes among other casualties at Keedysville suggests that it might have.[38] But if the enhanced attention produced by his being the son of Dr. Holmes had been helpful in that instance, Holmes did not always welcome it. The appearance of "My Hunt After 'The Captain' " made it plain that Dr. Holmes, for all the genuineness of his concern for his son's welfare, looked upon the incident of Holmes' wounding at Antietam as he regarded the rest of his immediate experience—material for stories that he could recount to the literary public. A sense of the mindset with which Dr. Holmes approached his journey to find his wounded son can be gleaned by his decision, on learning that he had missed his son in Keedysville and might expect to find him in Philadelphia, to take a detour before returning there to see "the great battle-field" near Antietam Creek, of which "it was impossible to go without seeing." Having done so, Dr. Holmes gave his *Atlantic Monthly* readers a full account of his efforts to retrace the course of the battle at which his son had been wounded. "The opposing tides of battle," he wrote about one spot, "must have blended their waves at this point, for portions of gray uniform were mingled with 'the garments rolled in blood' torn from our own dead and wounded soldiers."[39]

Dr. Holmes' account of his "Hunt After 'The Captain' " eventually came to the point when, after providing numerous descriptions of the countryside and several recordings of his conversations with other travelers he met along the way, the narrator arrived in Harrisburg, Pennsylvania, on September 24. The next morning he was hoping to meet the 7 A.M. train from Hagerstown, which his son was reportedly taking to Philadelphia. The train was due in at 11:15 A.M., but it was late, and Dr. Holmes fretted to his audience about railway accidents. Eventually it "came in so quietly that I was almost startled to see it on the track," and Dr. Holmes boarded and began a tour of the cars. "In the first car, on the fourth seat to the right, I saw my Captain . . . whom I had sought through many cities." In the account the Holmeses greeted each other, "How are you, Boy?" "How are you, Dad." Earlier Dr. Holmes had written that when he and his son would at last be reunited they would "observe the proprieties . . . no *hysterical passio* we do not like scenes. A calm salutation,—then swallow and hold hard. That is about the programme."[40]

When the account of Dr. Holmes' "hunt" appeared in print, Holmes was back in active service. His convalescence had been rapid and uneventful, lasting less than two months. By the middle of November he and his comrade Henry L. Abbott, who was also recovering from wounds in Boston, left that city for Washington in search of the Twentieth Regiment, which they eventually found at Falmouth, Virginia, between Warrenton and Fredericksburg. On November 7 Lincoln had replaced McClellan with Ambrose Burnside as commander of the Army of the Potomac. Holmes wrote his sister that "the Regiment is going to H_L as fast as ever it can," and that he had "pretty much made up my mind that the South have achieved their independence. . . . [B]elieve me, we never shall lick 'em."[41]

Burnside's plan was to cross the Rappahannock River at Falmouth, drive through Fredericksburg, and invade Richmond. After a successful start, the Twentieth Regiment and the other regiments in the Army of the Potomac were delayed for several days awaiting pontoon bridges, and Lee's Army of Northern Virginia was able to reinforce the defenses of Fredericksburg. When the Union attack eventually began on December 11, Burnside's troops were exposed to Confederate snipers, stationed on high ground overlooking Fredericksburg. Despite superior numbers, the Union forces were defeated, losing 13,000 men in a two-day battle, while Lee's forces lost only 5000. On December 15 Burnside withdrew, leaving Fredericksburg secure in Confederate hands. Another attack on Richmond had been repulsed.[42]

In the fighting around Fredericksburg the Twentieth Regiment had lost 165 men. Holmes had not participated at all. On December 12 he wrote his mother that he was in the hospital near Falmouth, "listless and miserable" from dysentery. For the next three days he gave an account of the Regiment's activities around Fredericksburg, punctuated by his frustrations about the state of his health and his inability to participate in the battles. He described his days as ones of "anxious waiting—of helpless hopelessness for myself, of weary unsatisfied questioning for the Regiment." On one occasion he "climbed a neighboring hill" near the hospital and "saw the battle—a terrible sight when your Regt is in it but you are safe." "Oh what self reproaches have I gone through," he added, "for what I could not help." The time he spent in the Falmouth Hospital, he said, was "one of the most anxious and forlornest weeks of my military experience."[43]

The Fredericksburg campaign seems to have been something of a turning point in Holmes' attitude toward his military service. In a letter to his father, written from Falmouth on December 20, he described the unsuccessful assault on Fredericksburg as "an infamous butchery in a ridiculous attempt" in which "I've no doubt our loss doubled or tripled that of the Rebs." He then added

I never I believe have shown, as you seemed to hint, any wavering in my
belief in the right of our cause—it is my disbelief in our success by arms in
which I differ from you. . . . I think in that matter I have better chances of
judging than you—and I believe I represent the conviction of the army—& not
the least of the most intelligent part of it—. . . . I see no farther progress—I
don't think . . . you realize the unity or the determination of the South.[44]

At about the time Holmes wrote this letter both the Army of the Potomac and the
Army of Northern Virginia resolved to stay in place over the winter and resume
fighting in the spring of 1863. Holmes took a brief sick leave in Philadelphia and
by late January was back at Falmouth.

At the same time, with morale in the Army of the Potomac at a distressingly low
state, Burnside was replaced in command by General Joseph Hooker, whose presence
seemed to have a salutary effect. Hooker prepared yet another invasion of Richmond
through Fredericksburg, and late in April Union forces pushed over the Rapahannock
in three separate forays, the largest group of troops securing a position at Chancellorsville, nine miles west of Fredericksburg. At that point Lee decided to attack the
Chancellorsville force, counting on the fact that the Confederates could advance
through the cover of woods. From May 1 through May 6 fighting raged, and eventually Hooker's forces withdrew across the Rappahannock. Thirteen thousand Confederate and 17,000 Union troops were killed or wounded. The battle was regarded
as a distinct success for the South, and played a part in Lee's subsequent decision
to invade Pennsylvania, which was to result in the early July 1863 battle of Gettysburg.[45]

The Twentieth Regiment, however, was not in the thick of the Chancellorsville
fighting. Its duties were to remain at Falmouth and then to secure Fredericksburg
and attack the Confederates from the rear, Chancellorsville being north of Fredericksburg. On May 3, while the Chancellorsville fighting was at its height, the Regiment marched through Fredericksburg, where a small rear guard of Confederate
forces remained on Marye's Heights, overlooking the city. Just outside Fredericksburg the Regiment encountered a canal and had to halt. As they did the Confederates,
observing their presence, brought in a cannon set up to fire spherical case shells
filled with shot. In a letter to his mother Holmes described the situation:

Pleasant to see a d'd gun brought up to an earthwork deliberately to bear on
you—to notice that your Co. is exactly in range—1st discharge puff—second
puff (as the shell burst) and my knapsack supporter is knocked to pieces . . .
2nd discharge man in front of me hit—3d whang the iron enters through garter
& shoe into my heel—[46]

Holmes was chloroformed and most of the shot extracted from his heel: he added a
line to his mother that he probably wouldn't lose his foot.

Ironically this particular wound, of the three Holmes was to suffer during his
Civil War service, was from its onset regarded as his least serious, yet required the
most prolonged recovery. Moreover, it was during an episode in which only he and
one other officer were injured, not an actual battle. Holmes had thus passed through
two of the most devastating battles of the war, had been shot in the chest and in the

neck, and had not only completely recovered but returned to action within a few months. In May 1863 he was struck by a random shot from a nuisance action by a rear guard in a situation where Union and Confederate troops were not even exchanging fire. He was to be on leave from the front for more than seven months.

While Holmes was on leave he began to consider the possibility of moving from the Twentieth Regiment to a less dangerous staff position. While he was encamped at Falmouth in the winter of 1862 he became acquainted with General John Sedgwick, commander of the Sixth Corps, who was also stationed that winter in the Army of the Potomac's headquarters at Falmouth. Sedgwick's aide-de-camp was Charles Whittier, an old friend of Holmes' from Harvard. Whittier had suggested the possibility of Holmes' joining Sedgwick's staff as an aide, and during his convalescence Holmes began to learn to ride, a prerequisite for a staff position in the Sixth Corps. Such positions, while not free from exposure to enemy fire, were less vulnerable than Holmes' current position as a captain of an infantry company.

Meanwhile events transpired to facilitate Holmes' departure from the Twentieth Regiment. While on leave the Governor of Massachusetts commissioned him a Lieutenant Colonel, but there were no vacancies at that position in the Regiment. When Holmes returned to the front at Stevensburg, Virginia, in January 1864[47] he found himself assuming the role of Captain in a unit in which his friend Henry Abbott was the Major and whose commander, George Macy, had been commissioned, but not mustered in, as Colonel. Since Macy technically held the position of Lieutenant Colonel, and there was no Major's position open, Holmes had no possibility of assuming a Lieutenant Colonelcy. While the situation prompted an angry letter from Dr. Holmes to Senator Charles Sumner,[48] it had the advantage, from Holmes' point of view, of enabling him to secure a temporary assignment to the staff of General Horatio Wright, division commander of the Sixth Corps. This took Holmes out of the direct line of fire.

Only six months more of service remained for Holmes, and those as a staff officer, but the experience was no less harrowing than what he had previously encountered. To be sure, he had missed the bloodbath of Gettysburg, where his first cousin Sumner Paine had been killed. But with the stalemate at Gettysburg having put an end to Lee's effort to end the war by a quick strike into Northern territory, the Union command, now unified under General Ulysses S. Grant, resolved to wear down the South in a dogged march through Virginia. The stage was thus set for the last year and a half of grim fighting that would conclude in April 1865 with Lee's surrender. Holmes himself was to witness his share of that fighting. In the spring of 1864 the Armies of Potomac and of Northern Virginia, having passed the winter a few miles from one another on the northern and southern sides of the Rapidan River near Wilderness, began to skirmish again, with Union forces moving south and Confederate forces seeking to counterattack them in the Wilderness forest. Fighting began in earnest on May 5, and continued through the rest of the month and into June. In one particular stretch of fighting, the infamous "bloody angle" at Spotsylvania Court House, about thirty miles north of Richmond, Union soldiers, investigating a battle site one morning, found 150 Confederate corpses piled in a trench that measured 200 square feet. Between May 5 and May 12 the Army of the Potomac had 32,000 men killed, wounded, or missing, and the Confederates 18,000. The

Union figure was greater than for all Union armies combined in any previous week in the war.

Holmes' letters and diary entries conveyed a clear enough sense of the horrors of the campaign. On May 6 he wrote that "[o]ur [headquarters] were exposed all day to pretty sharp artillery practice from 3 different directions."[49] On May 8 the Sixth Corps arrived at Chancellorsville, where Holmes "found woods afire & bodies of Rebs & our men just killed and scorching."[50] On May 10 he was "[u]p about 4 a.m." to witness "pickets firing tumultuously every little while" as the Battle of Spotsylvania began.[51] On May 11 he wrote his mother that "[t]oday is the 7th day we have fought . . . averaging a loss I guess of 3000 a day at least."[52] He described May 14, "with the night march before it, the long fasting, the much riding, the getting lost," as "one of the most fatiguing we have had."[53] A May 16 letter to his parents, written as the Spotsylvania campaign was ending, summarized the state of affairs. "Before you get this," he began, "you will know how immense the butchers bill has been—And the labor has been incessant—I have not been & am not likely to be in the mood for writing details. . . . Enough that these nearly two weeks have contained all of fatigue & horror that war can furnish."[54]

In that same letter Holmes announced, for the first time, that he had made up his mind to leave the army. "I have felt for sometime," he told his parents, "that I didn't any longer believe in this being a duty & so I mean to leave at the end of the campaign . . . if I'm not killed before." This letter was apparently misunderstood by his father, who thought that Holmes intended to leave after the spring battles ended. In a May 30, 1864, letter Holmes expressed pique at this interpretation, calling it "stupid" and adding, "I wish you'd take the trouble to read my letters before answering." He had meant that he would leave when "the campaign was over (i.e. next winter just near the end of my term of service)." He went to say that "I am convinced from my late experience that if I can stand the wear & tear (body & mind) of regimental duty that it is a greater strain on both than I am called on to endure— If I am satisfied I don't really see that anyone else has a call to be otherwise."[55]

As the spring campaign passed from May into June, Holmes' diary entries and letters continued to convey a cumulative impression of numbing horror and turmoil. He described "miserable days," "killing night marches," "the wear and tear of alternate march and fight," "infernal nasty time[s]," "nasty hot dusty day[s]," thunderstorms that made the roads "horrible," in short, a "most terrible campaign." A June 24 letter to his parents seemed to summarize his feelings. "These last few days have been very bad," he wrote. "I tell you many a man has gone crazy since this campaign begun from the terrible pressure on mind & body."[56]

All the while Holmes was conscious that in his new position as a staff officer "I am so much safer than any infantry officer." Eventually he was to waive promotion in the Twentieth Regiment in order to stay in a staff position: as he put it, "[t]he ostensible and sufficient reason [for waiving promotion] is my honest belief that I cannot now endure the labors & hardships of the line." When he eventually elected to muster out of the service rather than sign up for another term as an infantry officer, he noted that "I might, to be sure, stay long if I were one of the 3 aides allowed the Generals by law but as I'm not and am liable to go back to the Regiment if any change should take place, I leave." "I can do a disagreeable thing or face a great danger coolly enough when I *know* it is a duty,'' he wrote his mother in early June 1864, after the fighting around Spotsylvania had diminished, ''but a doubt demoralizes me as it does any nervous man—and now I honestly think the duty of fighting has ceased for me.''[57]

Given the conflicts and anxieties that accompanied Holmes' decision to leave the service rather than face the prospect of continued exposure as an infantryman, he was glad to report an episode of genuine danger, bravery, and triumph. It came on May 29, as the Sixth Corps advanced from the eastern side of the Pamunkey River in the direction of Hanover Court House, about 5 miles northeast of Richmond. Holmes was sufficiently pleased with his role in the incident that he recounted it on three separate occasions in his letters and diary: in a May 29 diary entry and in letters to his parents on May 30 and to his mother on June 7.[58]

The episode involved a request from General Horatio Wright for Holmes to carry a message to General David Russell ''and not to spare my horse.'' Holmes went off ''[a]bout an hour before sunset,'' and encountered a young boy who was a scout for Colonel Emory Upton of the Sixth Corps. The boy reported that he had been fired on by two Confederate cavalry soldiers and that Holmes should not go any further. Holmes concluded that he ''must go on,'' and rounded up three additional Union cavalrymen, who were foraging in the vicinity. When the group arrived at a bend in the road, near where the boy had been shot at, they encountered about twenty Confederates. Holmes then recounted in his diary that after he had

> trot[ted] to the place where boy was shot at—then [I] gallop[ed] to where the road bends to right—bang—whiz—''Halt'' ''Surrender'' from about 20 Rebs in line—I thought it was a mistake & they were friends & began to pull up but saw the gray jackets & clapped the spurs to my horse—much shooting— presently a fellow comes down the road—''Surrender''—he hadn't got his carbine quite unslung & I put my pistol to his breast & pulled trigger—missed fire—then he & others on right of road do shooting I lying along the side of my horse Comanche fashion—2 of my men got through with me—I soon struck pickets & [Colonel James] Duffy, General Russell's second-in-command], saw Russell & returned on other road with answer.[59]

Holmes noted that when he returned to General Wright's camp he ''[found] myself given over for lost,'' and that ''the staff to whom I spun my yarn intimated that they thought it rather a gallant thing . . . to get the order through & not knock under or turn back.'' In a June 7 letter to his mother he called the incident ''a jewel in the head of this campaign.''[60]

However pleased he may have been to recount the story of his ''narrowest escape'' from death during the war, Holmes continued to believe, as he wrote his parents on June 24, that any success that had been accomplished by the Union campaign through Wilderness and Spotsylvania toward Richmond had been ''at what a cost.'' By that date summer had arrived, and ''by & by,'' Holmes noted, ''the sickness will begin.'' He ''hope[d] to pull through but [didn't] know yet.''[61] As June ended, Grant's Army of the Potomac and Lee's Army of Northern Virginia seemed in a stalemate around Richmond.

At that time a group of Confederate troops from Lee's army, commanded by

General Jubal Early, had broken through Union lines northwest of Richmond, crossed through the Shenandoah Valley, and were threatening Washington. Grant ordered the Sixth Corps to leave the Richmond campaign, proceed to City Pant, Virginia, and take a steamer north to defend Washington. On July 6 Holmes and the other members of the Corps left their positions near Richmond and began their journey, eventually arriving at Fort Stevens, near Washington, on July 11 or, possibly on the 12th. Their presence deterred Early from attempting any attack on Washington, and his forces subsequently retreated south to rejoin the bulk of Lee's army.

It was during the abortive encounter between Early's troops and the Sixth Corps at Fort Stevens that perhaps the most celebrated incident of Holmes' wartime service allegedly occurred. President Lincoln had visited Fort Stevens on July 11 and again on the 12th, and on the latter day, according to subsequent accounts, was told roughly by a Union soldier to stand out of the line of fire. Over time the legend has sprung up that the soldier was Holmes.

The authenticity of the story is highly questionable. First, there are only two eyewitness accounts of Lincoln's presence at Fort Stevens, one by John Hay, Lincoln's private secretary, and one by General Wright, as related to George Thomas Stevens in the latter's 1870 history of the Sixth Corps. Hay's account has Lincoln visiting Fort Stevens on the afternoon of July 11, and also has General Wright and his staff arriving in Washington on that day. According to Hay's account, Lincoln told him, on returning from his visit, that he had stood on a parapet of the fort to observe Early's forces, and that "a soldier roughly ordered him to get down or he would have his head knocked off." According to Wright's account, Lincoln also visited Fort Stevens on the 12th, and again stood on the parapet, "until I told him I should have to remove him forcibly." Lincoln eventually was persuaded to sit "behind the parapet instead of standing upon it," but he persisted "in standing up from time to time, thus exposing nearly one-half of his tall form."

Both eyewitness accounts, then, have Lincoln present at Fort Stevens, standing on a parapet, and being told to remove himself. In Hay's version "a soldier" gave that order; in Wright's version, on a second day, the order was given by Wright himself. Neither account mentions Holmes; indeed there is no evidence that Holmes was at Fort Stevens on July 11 when Lincoln made his first visit. The accounts identifying Holmes as the soldier who ordered Lincoln to get down were written much later, by individuals who did not have firsthand information. The first was by Alexander Woolcott in a 1938 article in the *Atlantic Monthly,* relying on information supplied to him by Holmes' friend Harold Laski. The remaining two were oral comments made by Felix Frankfurter and Alger Hiss, based on conversations with Holmes himself.[62]

The difficulty with those accounts lies in the absence of confirmatory evidence in Holmes' own recollections of his service defending Fort Stevens. When Holmes took up residence in Washington as a Supreme Court Justice after 1902, Fort Stevens was a place he would often visit in the company of friends and law clerks. With the exception of Hiss, none of his law clerks ever recollected his identifying himself as having told Lincoln to get out of the line of fire. In discussing the story in his authorized biography of Holmes, Mark Howe, Holmes' legal secretary in the 1933 Term, indicated that "it remains surprising . . . that Holmes, who was generally not

reluctant to repeat to one friend a Civil War story that he had told to others, did not
. . . tell this story to more than a very few persons out of the many who accompanied
him to Fort Stevens."[63] Indeed Howe provided no evidence that Holmes had told
the story to anyone.

In addition, Holmes never mentioned the story in any of his written accounts of
his Civil War experience. On three separate occasions, in letters to Laski, he mentioned being at Fort Stevens on the occasion that Confederate forces came closest
to Washington, and seeing Lincoln there, but did not describe the alleged incident.[64]
Nor did he mention it in his numerous references to Lincoln in his correspondence
with Frederick Pollock or Lewis Einstein.[65] A typical description of his service at
Fort Stevens is that he gave to Einstein in March 1912, where he spoke of taking a
friend "in a motor car . . . round by the military road to Fort Stevens where in '64
I saw my General walking up and down the earthworks and President Lincoln standing within it and the big guns going and skirmish line over on the opposite slope
going up to the closest approach to the city that was made."[66]

It is likely, therefore, that while Holmes and Lincoln were together for a brief
moment at the very end of Holmes' military service, and while Lincoln was twice
ordered to refrain from exposing himself to enemy fire during his visits to Fort
Stevens, and while the skirmishes between the Sixth Corps and Early's forces at
Fort Stevens on July 11 and 12, 1864, were the closest encounter with Confederate
troops the Union capital was to have in the course of the war, those historic features
of Holmes' brief stay at Fort Stevens will have to suffice. The most memorable
aspect of Holmes' visit to Fort Stevens, in fact, was that it was five days before he
left military service. After Early's troops retreated in the presence of Union defenses,
the Sixth Corps returned to the Richmond area, and it was there, at Petersburg, 15
miles south of Richmond, that on July 17 Holmes was discharged. His friend Charles
Whittier wrote on the back of the document officially discharging him that "Citizen
Holmes will proceed at once to Boston and take drinks accordingly."[67] Two days
later Holmes arrived in Boston.

~

Such were the chronological outlines of Holmes' experiences in the Civil War; we
now turn to his contemporary accounts of the feelings those experiences engendered.
Holmes, as he put it in a June 1864 letter to his mother, had "started in this thing a
boy I am now a man."[68] He had enlisted in a burst of enthusiasm, had been three
times shot and three times returned to the front, had been hospitalized with dysentery,
and had reached a point in his service when "nearly every Regimental off[icer] I
knew or cared for is dead or wounded."[69] He had on one occasion hoped that he
might lose his foot so as not to have to return to service;[70] he had admitted to
demoralization; he had recognized, after the last awful campaign around Spotsylvania, that he could no longer "endure the labors & hardships of the line."[71] He
had undoubtedly left the war with a great sense of relief.

One can readily follow Holmes' changing attitude toward his wartime service in
his letters and diaries. He had been motivated to enlist, we have seen, by a conviction
of the corruption of Southern society, with its basis in slavery, by the example of
Pen Hallowell, who had joined him at Fort Independence and in the Twentieth

Regiment, and by a belief in the ideal of chivalry, whose devotees associated wartime service with the pursuit of honor and the advancement of civilization. It was in this frame of mind that he wrote his mother from his first station, Fort Independence, that "I'm in bully condition and have got to enjoying the life much," and composed a poem in which the poet, after "lost and long-wandering" in a "deep forest" with "hungry junipers," "dark rocks," and "lichen-ringed" shapes "of things that man outlaws," emerged to hear "a soft melodious rapture" and passed "upward [f]rom the dark valleys to sunlit hills."[72]

In Holmes' earliest Civil War letters this lightheartedness continued. He wrote of his diet ("milk, eggs, and lots of pies"), of hearing "cannonading" off in the distance, and of feeling "*very* well & in *very* good spirits."[73] But a month later came Ball's Bluff and his first exposure to combat. That experience introduced reality with a vengeance, and when Holmes returned to active service in March 1862 a different tone crept into his letters. It was "a campaign now & no mistake"; "there is real pluck shown now as there are real hardships to contend with"; while Holmes was "in good spirits," he "despise[d] the life in itself outside of special circumstances & principles."[74] And by June 2, in the midst of the Peninsula campaign, Holmes' account of his experience was drained of any romanticism:

We heard heavy firing . . . and soon our Div[ision] was under arms & marched 4 miles I should think—the last part through a stream above our knees and then double quick though mud a foot deep on to the field of battle. . . . Soon we filed round and formed under fire . . . and opened fire on the Reb. Line wh[ich] was visible—Our fire was stopped (by order) and we could see in the field. . . . Rebs. moving by twos & threes—apparently broken up—Then the order was given Forward in line—Double quick—At this point thinking there must be a battery nearer than I thought to be charged—I threw away my haversack wh[ich] impeded my motions containing all my food my dressing case my only change of stockings my pipe & tobacco. . . . Here we blazed away left oblique into the woods till we were ordered to cease firing & remained masters of the field. . . . We sat under arms waiting sleepless cold wet and hungry till morning for the renewal of the fight. . . . June 1st there was heavy firing from 7 am. till noon in the woods. . . . We stayed in line all day— formed sq[uare] to resist an expected attack of cavalry in the afternoon—OWH in the front rank of 1st front handling a sword & pistol—and were fired at several times during the day by sharp shooters—A bullet has a most villainous greasy slide through the air—

Today it is pleasant and hot—It is singular with what indifference one gets to look on the dead bodies in gray clothes wh[ich] lie around. . . . As you go through the woods you stumble constantly, and, if after dark, as last night on picket, perhaps tread on the swollen bodies already fly blown and decaying, of men shot in the head back or bowels—Many of the wounds are terrible to look at—Well we licked 'em and this time there was the maneuvering of a battle to be seen—splendid and awful to behold. . . . I doubt we fight more at present but we are in spirits though worn by fatigue and privation as well as mental anxiety—

If I am killed you will find a Mem. on the back of a picture I carry wh[ich] please attend to.[75]

After Fair Oaks Holmes' attitude toward the approach of military hostilities never again resembled the attitude with which he had begun the war. Thus in the September 17 candlelight letter from Antietam, while noting that "[a]ll of us feel a deuced sight more like a fight than in that forlorn peninsula," he added: "I don't talk seriously for you know all my last words if I come to grief. . . . Why should I say any more— It's rank folly pulling a long mug every time one may fight or may be killed—Very probably we shall in a few days and if we do why I shall go into it not trying to shirk the responsibility of my past life by a sort of death bed abjuration—.''[76]

Holmes' response to his situation during the Fair Oaks and Fredericksburg campaigns can be seen as part of a progression of disenchantment with war, which had begun for him as a buoyant crusade, quickly became a reminder of his own mortality with Ball's Bluff, evolved into a dispiriting quagmire with the Peninsula campaign, and became a source of sardonic humor after Antietam.[77] By Fredericksburg Holmes, who had, after all, applied for leave when his dysentery surfaced before the battle, was undoubtedly relieved not to be participating in it. At the same time the professional soldier ethos that he had come to internalize forbade shirking one's duty to fight and prohibited the disobedience of even suicidal orders, so Holmes' "self reproaches" were likely directed at his guilt for being secretly glad that he had missed the action. When Holmes described climbing the hill, from which he "saw the battle but . . . couldn't see the men," his most suggestive comment was "a terrible sight when your Regt is in it but you are safe.''[78] The Regiment, in which Holmes took increasing pride as his service continued, personified the ethos of the professional: at Fredericksburg the Regiment was in battle but Holmes was not, and Holmes was alternately relieved and troubled. This progression was to continue throughout the duration of Holmes' wartime service, in which he came to wish that he could suffer an injury so he could avoid going back to the front lines and finally came to resolve not to continue in service because "I cannot now endure the labors & hardships of the line.''[79]

The letter he wrote to his father after Fredericksburg in December 1862 reveals that Holmes had come to look at his wartime experience more fatalistically. His father had apparently, in an earlier letter, expressed concerns about Holmes' lack of support for the Union cause, and Holmes responded:

I think you are hopeful because (excuse me) you are ignorant. But if it is true that we represent civilization wh[ich] is in its nature, as well as slavery, diffuse & aggressive, and civilization & progress are the better things why they will conquer in the long run, we may be sure, and will stand a better chance in their proper province—peace—than in war. . . . At any rate dear Father don't, because I say these things imply or think that I am the meaner for saying them—I am, to be sure, heartily tired and half worn out body and mind by this life, but I believe I am as ready as ever to do my duty—[80]

In this letter Holmes juxtaposed "civilization" and "progress" against "war." It was as if he intended to emphasize that however lofty the ideals that made one go to war, the prosecution of war itself bore little relationship to those ideals and might actually not be their "proper province." It is hard to imagine, slightly more than eighteen months after his initial enlistment, that Holmes would have come to any other view of the relationship of ideals to war. What had his regiment, filled with aristocrats who saw their enlistments as part of a chivalrous crusade, done other than march, bivouac, crawl, and fight in harsh terrain, under taxing conditions, as part of a strategy that seemed elusive, directed against an enemy that alternated between being illusory and being deadly? How could anyone characterize the sojourns of the Twentieth Regiment as part of the march of progress?

Most of Holmes' enthusiasm, by this time, had been channeled into loyalty to the Regiment. In the letter quoted, after remarking on the unlikelihood that war was the appropriate province for fostering civilization and progress, he added that "the Regiment did behave gloriously in the late *rumpi*."[81] In a later letter he returned to the theme, noting that an officer from Pennsylvania had said, "your Regt is more like old times (meaning thereby the old Regular Army where Officers *were* Gentlemen) than anything I have seen in the Army, which in connection with other remarks about the perfection of their present condition and their behavior in the Field rather pleased me . . . I really very much doubt whether there is any Regiment which can compare with ours in the Army of the Potomac."[82]

In early 1863, around the time Holmes wrote the second of the two letters, he was given an offer to leave the Twentieth. Pen Hallowell wrote him in February with the news that he had accepted a Lieutenant Colonelcy in a newly formed black regiment, to be commanded by white officers. The regiment sought as officers "young men of military experience, of firm anti-slavery principles . . . superior to a vulgar contempt of color, and having faith in the capacity of colored men for military service."[83] Hallowell asked Holmes if he would consider becoming a Major in the new Regiment.[84] It is significant that Holmes turned this offer down. Hallowell had been his primary inspiration in enlisting in the war; chivalry and abolitionism his causes. By 1863, however, he had come to see his wartime service as linked to the Twentieth Regiment and its standards of gentlemanly professionalism.

Yet another stage in the progression of Holmes' responses to his wartime experiences began with his third wound at Chancellorsville, when for the first time he wished that he might be disabled so he could avoid any further military service. After Ball's Bluff, the Peninsula campaign, and Antietam he had submerged his fears and doubts in a posture of fatalism and professional stoicism; with the Chancellorsville wound came renewed feelings of terror and a desperation to leave the fight. His convalescence after the Chancellorsville wound was prolonged, and in the fall of 1863 word reached his companions that he was thinking of leaving the service.[85] By October Holmes had resolved to return, but did not do so until January 1864.[86] In the meantime, we have seen, he had learned to ride with the expectation of taking a staff position, which, while not a guarantee of safety, would keep him off the line. It was as a staff officer that he participated in the campaign to attack Richmond, in the spring of 1864, the campaign that prompted him to tell his mother that "these nearly two weeks have contained all of fatigue & horror that war can furnish . . . nearly every Regimental officer I knew or cared for is dead or wounded." In the midst of that campaign Holmes announced that "I have made up my mind to stay on the staff if possible till the end of the campaign & then if I am alive, I shall resign."[87]

Holmes' decision to resign allegedly marked a change from a posture he had taken, at least publicly, as late as April 1864. In a letter to Charles Eliot Norton at that time he had indicated that "[i]n all probability . . . I shall soon be mustered in for a new term of service" when his original enlistment expired in July 1864.[88] But his May 16, 1864, letter to his mother indicated that he had "felt for some time that I didn't any longer believe in this being a duty." Part of the reason for Holmes' decision was doubtless that the Twentieth Regiment was likely to be disbanded in July, since all of its members had initially enlisted for three years and absent any affirmative action on their parts would be discharged. In addition, virtually none of the officers with whom Holmes had enlisted were left, either having been transferred to other regiments, as in the case of Hallowell, or having been killed, as in the case of Henry Abbott, who fell in the battle of Wilderness. Holmes' transfer to General Wright's staff had been temporary, and had he reenlisted there was a distinct possibility that he might have been transferred back to the Twentieth as a line officer.

Nonetheless Holmes was apparently defensive about his decision. His parents took his May 16 letter as indicating that he intended to leave the service as soon as possible, and Dr. Holmes, we have seen, responded in a May 22 letter that must have expressed some misgivings about that judgment. In Holmes' May 30 letter, previously quoted, in which he attempted to correct the misunderstanding, he had written

> I must say I dislike such a misunderstanding, so discreditable to my feeling of soldierly honor, when I don't believe there was a necessity for it. . . . I am convinced from my late experience that if I can stand the wear & tear (body & mind) of regimental duty that it is a greater strain on both than I am called on to endure. . . . I am not the same man (may not have quite the same ideas) & certainly am not so elastic as I was and I *will not acknowledge the same claims upon me under those circumstances* that existed formerly.[89]

The letter is puzzling in one respect. Holmes' term of service was to expire in July, not "next winter," and so his comment about resigning at the "end of the campaign" would naturally have been taken to refer to the end of the present Virginia campaign. But it is clear that the "late experience" of the Virginia battles had pushed Holmes past the point of endurance. As he put it in a June 7 letter to his mother, "the campaign has been most terrible." He added that "I have been coming to the conclusion for the last six months that my duty has changed—I can do a disagreeable thing or face a great danger coolly enough when I *know* it is a duty—but a doubt demoralizes me as it does any nervous man."

Holmes picked up the theme of duty in the remainder of his letter. In 1861, when Holmes and his Harvard contemporaries were enlisting in volunteer regiments, one of them, William Everett, concluded that he would not enlist, but would spend the next years pursuing graduate study in England. Holmes had been critical of Everett's decision at the time, and now recalled it:

I honestly think the duty of fighting has ceased for me—ceased because I have laboriously and with much suffering of mind and body *earned* the right which I denied Willy Everett to decide for myself how I can best do my duty to the country and, if you choose, to God— . . . The ostensible and sufficient reason [for leaving the service] is my honest belief that I cannot now endure the labors & hardships of the line—Nothing further need be told abroad—[90]

Holmes' rationale was thus a combination of desperation at having endured so much carnage and conviction that he had earned the right to say "enough" by having exposed himself in so many battles. His concept of duty had thus progressed from an idea of fidelity to a cause to that of loyalty to a regiment and finally to that of loyalty to oneself.[91]

Holmes' progressive impressions of the experience of the Civil War, then, had evolved to the point where he saw war principally as a threat to one's being. In the end the central duty of wartime was the duty to do one's best to ensure the survival of the self. This, at any rate, was Holmes' unvarnished response to what he had seen at Ball's Bluff and on the Peninsula and at Antietam and at Fredericksburg and around Chancellorsville. But there were other, less naked responses. One was his professed attachment to the honor of the professional soldier and to the concept of duty to one's regiment and one's comrades in arms. Another was a residue of the ideals in whose pursuit he had first enlisted. One can see evidence of the survival of those ideals in the previously mentioned letter Holmes wrote to Charles Eliot Norton in April 1864 as he was awaiting the start of the Chancellorsville campaign. The letter had been prompted by an appreciation of the medieval crusades Norton had written in the *North American Review*'s April issue. Holmes wrote:

I have long wanted to know more of Joinville's Chronicle than I did, but the story seems to come up most opportunely now when we need all the examples of chivalry to help us bind our rebellious desires to steadfastness in the Christian Crusade of the 19th century. If one didn't believe that this war was such a crusade, in the cause of the whole civilized world, it would be hard indeed to keep the hand to the sword; and one who is rather compelled unwillingly to the work by abstract conviction than borne along on the flood of some passionate enthusiasm, must feel his ardor rekindled by stories like this. . . . In all probability from what I hear of the filling up of the Regt. I shall soon be mustered in for a new term of service as Lt. Col. of the 20th and so with double reason I am thankful to read of the great dead who have 'stood in the evil day.' No—it will not do to leave Palestine yet.[92]

The letter to Norton signifies the existence, by the spring of 1864, of a multilay-ered response on the part of Holmes to his Civil War service. He was abundantly clear, by this time, that he was one who was "compelled unwillingly" to the work of a soldier. The "passionate enthusiasm" that had accompanied him on enlistment had given way to a response in which the principal justifications for his continued participation in the war effort were a series of "abstract convictions," exemplified in the idea of duties: duty to one's comrades at arms, duty to the Regiment, duty to the ethic of professional soldiering. But what lay behind those duties? Was there a reason why the Regiment had been formed in the first place?

In his search for that reason Holmes returned to the idea of the war as a "Christian crusade." He and the other Union soldiers were fighting "in the cause of the whole civilized world." Their fighting was thus like the exploits of the early crusaders: in reading of those exploits in Norton's article Holmes was being exposed to "examples of chivalry." And it was those "examples," those reminders of the symbolic meaning of his participation in the war, that helped "us bind our rebellious desires to steadfastness." The "desires" he felt were desires to escape, to save oneself, to abandon the war effort. He needed a reminder that in choosing to be "steadfast" rather than "rebellious" he was acting in a chivalric fashion, reaffirming the ideals of his generation and his class. Specifically, he stood on the prospect of mustering in for another term of service in an infantry regiment, and "rebellious desires" were welling up in him. To read of the "great dead" who had followed the cause of chivalry in the past was to provide another reason to continue to endure the experience of war.

The letter thus signifies the transformation, in Holmes' mind, of the ethic of chivalry as a justification for participation in war. At the time of his enlistment the chivalry ideal was associated with the romantic exploits of knights, the pageantry of war preparations, the lightheartedness of youthful adventure. After Ball's Bluff and Antietam and Fair Oaks and Fredericksburg the ideal had assumed a different form. It now appeared as a restraint on the instinct to rebel: an "abstract conviction," not a "passionate enthusiasm." Chivalry had evolved to a version of a duty: duty to an abstract cause.

Holmes had, however, already fashioned a distinction, in letters to his family, between the rightness of the "cause" for which he was fighting and success in arms. However just the principle of fighting for "the whole civilized world," the Union armies might well never defeat their Confederate rivals. Continued fighting in the "cause" might well be an exercise in which one constantly exposed oneself to death in a conflict whose successful termination, from the point of view of the Union, was illusory. Chivalry thus became the ideal of fighting in a cause for its own sake, not a cause that one expected to prevail. It was a far more stoical ideal than it had been on Holmes' enlistment. It was also in direct conflict with the duty of self-preservation.

In the Norton letter one can see the seeds of a response to the wartime experience that would have a significant impact on Holmes' depictions of the Civil War in his later life. War was coming to be portrayed as a state of affairs from which one desperately wanted to escape, and yet to which one remained "steadfast." The motivating factors producing this "steadfastness" were not so much associated with a belief in the ultimate success of the war effort but with a belief in fighting for a cause that was just, or fighting because that was what a professional soldier did. War was coming to be seen as an experience that taught one about self-sacrifice. Honor and duty were coming to be associated with the suppression of one's "rebellious desires," particularly one's desire to want to survive.

And yet Holmes, about a month after writing this letter, was to announce that he had had enough of war; that he could no longer endure it. Having declared that he was planning to reenlist because he had been reminded about chivalry and past crusades, he reconsidered that decision and mustered out. In so doing he survived; in so doing he also chose to follow his desire to preserve himself rather than his desire to appear chivalric and honorable. As his feelings of immediate relief at his survival dissipated, and he considered the implications of his decision for the codes of his generation and class, he came to be troubled by his decision. The result was that when he came to talk of the war, and of participating in wars, he glorified those experiences with a vengeance. In the fullness of his rhetoric he hoped to conceal some of his guilt at not having "stood in the evil day" any longer.

~

The Civil War was to come to have as much significance for Holmes as memory as it had had as episode. While Holmes professed to have no interest in reading accounts of the war, he repeatedly called attention, in his correspondence, to the dates of the battles at which he had been wounded. He adopted martial themes and metaphors in his writings, and as he got further removed in time from the war he appeared to incorporate the ethos of the professional soldier as part of his general philosophy. The war as memory, however, did not take the same form for Holmes as the war in fact. We have seen that his response to his military service was a progressive realization that war in its essential state was an encounter with death, random, terrifying, and largely meaningless, that one sought to endure and ultimately to avoid. We have also seen that this acknowledgment of the essential nature of war was disquieting for Holmes, raising feelings of guilt and self-reproach, and that he adopted devices to blunt this disquiet, such as the endorsement of an ethic of professional soldiering or a belief in the code of chivalry and its attendant duties to causes greater than oneself.

As Holmes became more removed in time from his actual war experiences, his memory of the war came increasingly to emphasize the devices by which participation in a war experience was justified, as distinguished from the horrors of war itself. The result was that his retrospective accounts of the Civil War exhibited a tone quite at odds with his contemporary accounts. Whereas the earlier accounts had demonstrated, over time, a progressive recoil from his experience, later accounts illustrated a progressive romanticization of it. Holmes' romanticized memory of the Civil War, designed in part to give meaning to the war effort to survivors, also appears to contain elements of rationalization and self-justification. The exercise in recovering Holmes' "war in retrospect" becomes one in which the reader becomes increasingly aware of Holmes' capacity to use language as a device for concealing rather than revealing his feelings.

The first of Holmes' efforts to write about his wartime experiences was not intended for public consumption, but nonetheless represented an effort to distance himself from the immediacy of his surroundings. It was an account of his first wounding, the incident at Ball's Bluff, written either at the very end of his service or shortly after he had been mustered out.[93]

Holmes began by noting his sensations on being wounded ("I felt as if a horse had kicked me") and of being carried to the rear and observing other wounded men. "Then," he continued, "the thinking began." He first wondered whether he had been shot through the lungs, spit, and found blood in his mouth. He then remembered that in a book he had read as a child "the father of one of the heroines is shot through the lungs by a robber," and "died with terrible haemorrhages & great agony." He then remembered that he had brought "a little bottle of laudanum" in his coat pocket, and resolved to take it and commit suicide should the pain become unendurable.

His next thought, which occurred as he was being placed on the ferry boat for Harrison's Island, was that another man, groaning in the vicinity, should have gone before him. "Now wouldn't Sir Philip Sydney have that other feller put into the boat first?" he asked himself. In the reference to Sydney one sees the "ideals of conduct" for which Holmes had enlisted: Sydney was the archetypal apostle of chivalry. The question, Holmes felt, showed that even after being shot his mind was "still bent on a becoming and consistent carrying out of its ideals of conduct." But he did not defer to the other soldier: "I let myself be put aboard."

Bullets whizzed by as he was transported on the ferry, and he was carried, armchair style, to the small house on Harrison's Island that was serving as a makeshift hospital. Dr. Nathan Hayward examined him, and told him that he might recover, but "the chances are against you"; Holmes "felt for the laudanum and again determined to wait till pain or sinking strength warned me of the end being near." Hayward turned Holmes onto his stomach, and he began to feel sleepy. A doctor from a Pennsylvania regiment appeared, and Holmes "called him and gave him my address and told him . . . if I died to write home & tell 'em I'd done my duty—I was very anxious they should know that—and I then imparted to him my laudanum scheme—This he dissuaded and gave me a dose of some opiate . . . and when I slumbered I believe he prigged the bottle."

Thus far the theme of Holmes' recollections might be said to be the juxtaposition of the abstractions he associated with going to war against his survival instinct. While he thought of chivalry and duty, and was anxious that his parents know, if he died, that he had been faithful to those ideals, he also thought of whether he should live and the laudanum, his apparent respite from the agonies of death. It seems to have been no accident that he confided in the Pennsylvania doctor that he had the laudanum: what better way to ensure that he would not inadvertently take it? Thus while he may have initially gained some comfort from the laudanum he did not seem unhappy when it was "prigged" from him. Another means of death was gone.

At this point in his diary Holmes returned to his thoughts:

Of course when I thought I was dying the reflection that the majority vote of the civilized world declared that with my opinions I was en route for Hell came up with painful distinctness—Perhaps the first impulse was tremulous— but then I said—by Jove, I die like a soldier anyhow—I was shot in the breast doing my duty up to the hub—afraid? No, I am proud—then I thought I couldn't be guilty of a deathbed recantation—father and I had talked of that and were agreed that it generally meant nothing but a cowardly giving way to fear—Besides, thought I, can I recant if I want to, has the approach of death changed my beliefs much? & to this I answered—No—Then came in my Philosophy—I am to take a leap in the dark—but now as ever I believe that whatever shall happen is best—for it is accordance with a general law—and

good & *universal* (or *general law*) are synonymous terms in the universe. . . .
Would the complex forces which made a complex unit in *Me* resolve
themselves back into simpler forms or would my angel still be winging his
way onward when eternities had passed? I could not tell—But all was
doubtless well—and so with a "God forgive me if I'm wrong" I slept—

It is intriguing that in this passage Holmes made much of his decision not to
embrace religion as a "deathbed recantation": that was a coward's approach to
death. But what made "all . . . doubtless well" for him, on contemplation that he
might be dying but had no idea where he was going or in what form, was that
"whatever shall happen is best," a "philosophy" that he attributed to "a general
law . . . in the universe." The "general law" smacks of a kind of philosophic fatalism that comes very close to a form of religious belief. It is a close line between
saying "whatever shall happen is best" and saying "the Lord works in mysterious
ways." Both philosophies deny the power of humans fully to control events but
ascribe a benign purpose to that randomness. Moreover, Holmes attempted to square
himself should even this mild fatalism prove heretical. "God forgive me if I'm
wrong" hardly sounds like the thought of an unrepentant atheist.

In what he described as a "comatose" condition Holmes was ferried from the
hospital to the Maryland shore, "put in the hold of a canal boat," transported to
Edwards Ferry, and then taken in "one of the two wheeled ambulances" to the
hospital at Poolesville. The hospital steward, "a cockeyed Dutchman," looked at
his wound "and then left me uncomfortable but still exceedingly joyful, for he had
told me I should live." Two days after being shot Holmes was transported to Philadelphia.

In assessing the meaning of this diary account it is important to recall that it was
written much after the event occurred and very possibly at a time that Holmes
strongly suspected that he was not going to see any more combat. The account, in
short, was a survivor's account. In notes to the diary entry Holmes wrote that "[a]t
first I only intended to show the rapidity of thought & queer suggestions which occur
when one is hit, but as I always wanted to have a memorandum of this experience
. . . I have told the whole story." His obvious interest in having "a memorandum"
of the Ball's Bluff incident was that it was his first war wound, a serious one, and
he had survived. Moreover, the thoughts he presented were not "queer suggestions":
they were philosophical ruminations on the consequences of dying without an apparent belief in God. The emphasis in the account is on duty, bravery, fatalism in the
face of death, and a recognition that "whatever shall happen is best." "Tremulous"
sensations are suppressed. In a sense, Holmes' account of his wounding at Ball's
Bluff is the first of his descriptions of the war in retrospect.

The next occasion Holmes had to write of his wartime experiences came two
days after he had arrived home, discharged, in July 1864. On July 21 he attended a
dinner for the Harvard Class of 1861 and was asked, in his capacity as Class Poet,
to offer a poem for the occasion. He produced the following:

How fought our brothers, and how died, the story
You bid me tell, who shared with them the praise,

Who sought with them the martyr's crown of glory,
The bloody birthright of heroic days.

But, all untuned amid the din of battle,
Not to our lyres the inspiring strains belong;
The cannon's roar, the musket's deadly rattle
Have drowned the music, and have stilled the song.

Let others celebrate our high endeavor
When peace once more her starry flag shall fling
Wide o'er the land our arms made free forever;
We do in silence what the world shall sing.[94]

It is apparent, on reading this poem, that the professional soldier ethos is coloring Holmes' portrait of his wartime experiences. Others ask him to tell "the story" of how he and his companions fought and died, but his "lyre" has been drowned out by the din of battle. He is not inclined to "celebrate" what he concedes has been a "high endeavor"; that task he delegates to others once peace has been achieved. He and his fellow soldiers "do in silence what the world shall sing." Theirs is the tacit fellowship of the regular army.

After the issuance of this poem Holmes turned to other subjects, notably the law, and between the 1864 dinner and his next public discussion of his wartime experiences twenty years passed. Those were momentous years for Holmes. He graduated from law school, entered law practice in Boston, became an editor of the *American Law Review,* published an edition of Kent's Commentaries, wrote the Lowell Lectures, which became *The Common Law* and appeared in 1881, accepted a professorship at Harvard Law School, and resigned that position in 1882 to become Associate Justice of the Supreme Judicial Court of Massachusetts. At the same time, in that interval, the hostilities engendered by the war and the events and attitudes that preceded it had waned, and the Reconstruction era passed. The Civil War came to be seen less as a punitive strike against a corrupt South than as a vindictive eradication of traditional Southern culture by an aggressive North. In this context the celebration of Memorial Day was regarded as an effort to glorify the valor and courage of the soldiers on both sides of the conflict. Holmes, who was asked to give a Memorial Day address in Keene, New Hampshire, in 1884, expressed that conception of the holiday. As he put it, Memorial Day "embodies in the most impressive form our belief that to act with enthusiasm and faith is the condition of acting greatly. To fight out a war, you must believe something and want something with all your might."[95]

It was in this address that the first evidence that Holmes was seeking to distill something positive from his wartime experiences becomes apparent. In the early treatments his attitude had been stoic: fatalistically agnostic in the face of death, silent when asked to celebrate the glory and heroism of his contemporaries. With the passage of time, however, he searched for something to treasure from the war. What he found was the concept that to fight in war "you must be willing to commit yourself to a course, perhaps a long and hard one, without being able to foresee exactly where you will come out." War thus embodied "the feeling . . . that, as life is action and passion, it is required of a man that he should share the passion and action of his time at peril of being judged not to have lived."[96]

War thus taught that when one combined "passion" and "action" in life, one got more out of one's existence. Holmes' generation, the one "that carried on the war," was "set apart by its experience." It "was given to us to learn at the outset that life is a profound and passionate thing." The dead of the war "still live for us, and bid us think of life, not death—of life to which in their youth they lent the passion and glory of the spring."

But just what was it that set Holmes' generation apart? While there was a certain pleasure in remembering, from the perspective of safety and comfort, "the freezing winter bivouacs and . . . dreadful summer marches where every faculty of the soul seemed to depart one after another, leaving only a dumb animal power to set the teeth and to persist,"[97] Holmes seemed to be extolling more than simply the good fortune to have survived a war. There perhaps was something in war itself, and, more particularly, in the attitude that motivated soldiers to fight. "Passion" was as important as "action" in explaining the positive features of a wartime experience. And it was a peculiar kind of passion, one that so propelled those who possessed it that they committed themselves to a "course" without knowing where that course would take them. They felt so strongly about their beliefs that they were prepared to fight for them, even though they had no idea what form the fight would take or whether they would survive it.

What seemed to be ennobling about war for Holmes was that it was the end result of "passion," that it was a particularly satisfying release of passion—"action"—and that it was spontaneous, impulsive, and selfless action, action engaged in without any assurance that the actor would find his passion vindicated. But if this were the message of Holmes' 1884 address, it represented a curious contrast with the attitude he held for the bulk of his wartime service. After Ball's Bluff, we have seen, Holmes saw that there was no necessary relationship between ideals and military victory. While he claimed, at the end of his career, to continue to believe in the rightness of the Union cause and in chivalric ideals, he had long ago come to doubt that the Union army could defeat the South. He fought out of duty, not out of passion. When his sense that his numerous ordeals had earned him the right to reevaluate his duty he resolved to quit the service. So the translation of "passion" into "action" had taken him only as far as Ball's Bluff; from then on his motivation was quite different. It thus appears that in the 1884 address Holmes was seeking to substitute his earlier sense that not to enlist in the Union cause was "not to have lived" for the quite different sense of wartime that had emerged from his experience in service.

There was another dimension to Holmes' 1884 Memorial Day address. In a remarkable series of paragraphs, he summed up the memory of friends and companions from the Twentieth Regiment who had been killed in the war. His recollections were vivid and conveyed an aura of authenticity: they appeared as the war stories of a combat veteran. But one of the memories was inaccurate in an important respect, and that inaccuracy revealed one of the major ingredients of Holmes' portrait of the war in retrospect.

Holmes began his recapitulation of his dead comrades by announcing that "as surely as this day comes round we are in the presence of the dead." "I see them now," he said, "as once I saw them on this earth." The he began to particularize.

I see a fair-haired lad, a lieutenant, and a captain on whom life had begun somewhat to tell, but still young, sitting by the long mess-table in camp before the regiment left the State, and wondering how many of those who gathered in our tent could hope to see the end of what was then beginning. For neither of them was that destiny reserved. I remember, as I awoke from my first long stupor in the hospital after the battle of Ball's Bluff, I heard the doctor say, "He was a beautiful boy," and I knew that one of those two speakers was no more. The other, after passing harmless through all the previous battles, went into Fredericksburg with strange premonition of the end, and there met his fate.

I see another youthful lieutenant as I saw him in the Seven Days, when I looked down the line. . . . The officers were at the head of their companies. The advance was beginning. We caught each other's eye and saluted. When next I looked, he was gone. . . .

There is one who on this day is always present to my mind. He entered the army at nineteen, a second lieutenant. In the Wilderness, already at the head of his regiment, he fell, using the moment that was left him of life to give all his little fortune to his soldiers. I saw him in camp, on the march, in action. I crossed debatable land with him when we were rejoining the army together. I observed him in every kind of duty, and never in all the time that I knew him did I see him fail to choose that alternative of conduct which was most disagreeable to him. . . .

In action he was sublime. His few surviving companions will never forget the awful spectacle of his advance along with his company in the streets of Fredericksburg. In less than sixty seconds he would become the focus of a hidden and annihilating fire from a semicircle of houses. His first platoon had vanished under it in an instant, ten men falling dead by his side. He had quietly turned back to where the other half of his company was waiting, had given the order, "Second platoon, forward!" and was again, moving on, in obedience to superior command, to certain and useless death, when the order he was obeying was countermanded. The end was distant only a few seconds; but if you had seen him with his indifferent carriage, and sword swinging from his finger like a cane, you would never have suspected that he was doing more than conducting a company drill in the camp parade ground. He was little more than a boy, but the grizzled corps commanders knew and admired him; and for us, who not only admired, but loved, his death seemed to end a portion of our life also.[98]

Holmes was ultimately to refer, anonymously, to nine members of the Regiment who were casualties of the war. The list included Colonel Paul J. Revere and his brother, the surgeon Edward H. Revere, Charles Lowell, Holmes' cousin, and Brigadier General William Frances Bartlett, a class below Holmes at Harvard, who began the war as a Captain, lost a leg in the 1862 Peninsula campaign, returned to service only to be reinjured and taken prisoner in the 1864 union assault on Petersburg, and eventually died in 1876, his life shortened by his wartime privations.[99] Four of his comrades in the Regiment were discussed in the excerpted portion. The "fair-haired lad" who died at Ball's Bluff was William Lowell Putman, identified in Holmes' October 23, 1861, letter to his mother as having been killed[100] and in Holmes' diary of the battle as being described by the Regimental surgeon, Nathan Hayward, as having "a beautiful face or something of the sort."[101] The captain who "went into Fredericksburg with strange premonition of the end" was Charles F. Cabot, identified as having been killed at Fredericksburg in a December 12, 1862, letter from Holmes to his mother.[102] The lieutenant who exchanged glances and salutes with Holmes when he looked down the line was James Jackson Lowell, whom Holmes reported as "beyond doubt dead" in a July 5, 1862, letter to his mother from Harrison's Landing, Virginia.[103]

The fourth dead soldier remembered by Holmes in the excerpt was Henry L. Abbott. Holmes' extended treatment of Abbott in the address, coupled with the statement that Abbott was "always present to my mind" on Memorial Day, and that Holmes "admired" and "loved" him, testified to the significance of Abbott as an idealized figure in Holmes' reconstruction of his wartime experiences. Abbott invariably chose "that alternative of conduct that was most disagreeable to himself." He was "sublime" in action. He obeyed an order to march into "certain and useless death" with supreme indifference, swinging his sword "like a cane" as if he were "on the camp parade ground." In an omitted passage from the excerpt, Holmes said of Abbott that he was "a Puritan in all his virtues, without the Puritan austerity": a "master and leader" who, "when duty was at an end," could become "the chosen companion in every pleasure that a man might honestly enjoy." Abbott, in short, was the sort of man, like Pen Hallowell, that Holmes cherished as an intimate friend. Abbott's death, Holmes concluded, "seemed to end a portion of our life also."

But Holmes had not been one of the "few surviving companions" who had witnessed the "awful spectacle" of Abbott's advance at the head of his company in the streets of Fredericksburg. Holmes was not in the Fredericksburg streets at all, but in the hospital with dysentery. He had written his mother of watching the Regiment going to battle while he remained behind with tears in his eyes; after climbing a hill near the hospital he could see the battle but not the men.[104] To the extent he knew of Abbott's conduct during the battle, it was from second-hand accounts; he had not "seen [Abbott], with his indifferent carriage and sword swinging from his finger like a cane," marching to an expected death. His account, however, suggested that he had. Moreover, the account was part of a speech made not to fellow Regiment members, but to an audience in Keene, New Hampshire, that very likely included no one who had any idea of the identity of the anonymous comrades whose deaths Holmes chose to celebrate.

Several commentators have singled out Holmes' Civil War experiences as pivotal in the development of his mature philosophical beliefs. Only a handful, however, have noted the close connection between those beliefs and the psychological progression of Holmes' response to his wartime experiences.[105] The 1864 Memorial Day address, when placed alongside the contemporary observations of Holmes traced in this chapter, provides a particularly vivid illustration of that connection.

Holmes' stay in the hospital in Fredericksburg came at a time in his wartime service, we have seen, when he had abandoned his earlier lightheartedness, faced the prospect of his mortality, and sought to subsume his impulses for self-preservation in the ethos of the professional soldier. His journey south to rejoin the Regiment after his second wound, especially since it was made in the company of Abbott, was a gesture affirming his commitment to that ethos. Then, shortly after returning, he found the Regiment in the thick of fighting and himself an infirm spectator. His December 14, 1862, diary sentence, "a terrible sight when your Regt. is in it but you are safe," captured his feelings, and the next sentence, "Oh what self-reproaches I have gone through," revealed the conclusions he had drawn from the experience. Meanwhile, news filtered back to him that half his company had been wounded in the Fredericksburg battle; that Abbott's second lieutenant, William F. Perkins, had been killed;[106] and that Abbott had been saved from death only by an order being countermanded at the last moment.

Abbott and Holmes, two Harvard "gentlemen" brought together by their service in the Twentieth Regiment. Both wounded early in their service; both convalescents in Boston; both crossing "debatable land" in their effort to return to the campaign. Both, by now, united in a conviction that loyalty to the Regiment and duty to its command structure transcended any other reasons for fighting against the South. The one in Fredericksburg, obviously indifferent to his own survival, "sublime" in "action," treating a march into gunfire as if it were a parade ground drill. The other, in Fredericksburg, not in action, acutely conscious of his own safety.

Abbott and Holmes, two years later in the Wilderness campaign. The one, now briefly in command of the Twentieth Regiment,[107] still a line officer, struck down with a fatal wound, using his last moments to "give all his little fortune" to the men who served under him.[108] The other, now in a staff position, removed from the line, "all right," but, after realizing ten days after Abbott's death that "nearly every Regimental off[icer] I know or cared for is dead or wounded," determined to "resign . . . if I am alive."[109]

Abbott and Holmes, twenty years later nearly to the day, in Keene, New Hampshire, on May 30, 1884. The one among the ghosts whose graves were being decorated, who "come back and live" with Holmes and other survivors on Memorial Day. The other the author of *The Common Law,* Associate Justice of the Supreme Court of Massachusetts, in robust health at the age of forty-three. The one, Abbott, the very personification of soldierly duty and honor. The other, Holmes, a soldier who after being shot in the heel had hoped his foot might be amputated so that he could avoid returning to the war, who had chosen to leave service before Union victory was certain, who had admitted to his parents that he could no longer endure the blows and hardships of being a line officer, who had reproached himself for missing the battle that produced Abbott's legendary bravery.

In Holmes' 1884 Memorial Day address he was with Abbott at Fredericksburg. He was entitled to feel "touched with fire." He was a brave soldier, not a guilty survivor. He could claim the right to eulogize the ghosts of the Twentieth Regiment because he had fought along with them. He could claim the privilege of glorifying the soldier's ethos—that of subordinating one's life to the honor and duties of one's regiment, even if one is not confident about ultimate victory—because he had been with Abbott and the Regiment officers who had died. But he had not, in his mind, really been with Abbott and the others. That was why he chose to glorify them and their ethos, so that he might come to partake of it.

Another eleven years passed before Holmes was to speak again of his war experiences. Here again the context was a Memorial Day address, this time a ceremony at Harvard where he received an honorary degree. He was now fifty-four, and the United States had not been engaged in a war in thirty years. He expressed ironic pleasure at receiving the degree, suggesting in private that while it "comes too late for me to care much for it except negatively," it was "a mark that the President [Charles Eliot] has buried the hatchet and no longer bears me malice for giving up my professorship for a judgeship."[110] When his turn came to speak, he showed an awareness of the passage of time. "For although the generation born about 1840, and now governing the world, has fought at least two of the greatest wars in history,"[111] he began, "war is out of fashion, and the man who commands the attention of his fellows is the man of wealth." The "moralists and philosophers" of the 1890s "declare that war is wicked, foolish, and soon to disappear."[112]

In the face of a climate in which "[t]he aspirations of the world are those of commerce" Holmes sought to recapture the special experience of his generation and to glorify its encounter with war. "Most of my hearers would rather that their daughters or their sisters should marry a son of one of the great rich families than a regular army officer," he felt. "I have heard the question asked whether our war was worth fighting, after all." His answer was emphatically yes. "For my own part, I believe that the struggle for life is the order of the world, at which it is vain to repine." "[A]s long as man dwells upon the globe, his destiny is battle, and he has to take the chances of war." "The ideals of the past for men have been drawn from war. . . . For all our prophecies, I doubt if we are ready to give up our inheritance."[113]

But what were the "ideals . . . drawn from war"? They turned out to be the same ones that had driven Holmes to enlist in 1861: honor, chivalry, duty. And those ideals were particularly significant because they were deemed by the soldier to be more important than life. The name "gentleman" had been "built on . . . the soldier's choice of honor rather than life." To "be a soldier" meant "to be ready to give one's life rather than suffer disgrace." The ideals spawned by war were thus manifestations of "a splendid carelessness for life," a "senseless passion," a "faith . . . which leads a soldier to throw his life away in obedience to a blindly accepted duty, in a cause which he little understands, in a plan of campaign of which he has no notion, under tactics of which he does not see the use."

The references to campaigns and tactics reminded Holmes of his own anarchic wartime meanderings, and he observed that "most men who know battle know the cynic force with which the thoughts of common sense will assail them in times of stress." But those of his generation also knew "that in their greatest moments faith has trampled those thoughts under foot." Then came a recapitulation of his wartime experiences, this time through the filters of the war in retrospect:

> If you have been . . . ordered simply to wait and to do nothing, and have watched the enemy bring their guns upon you down a gentle slope . . ., have seen the puff of the firing, have felt the burst of the spherical case-shot as it came toward you, have heard and seen the shrieking fragments go tearing

through your company, and have known that the next ... shot carries your fate; if you have advanced in line and seen ahead of you the spot which you must pass where the rifle bullets are striking; if you have ridden by night at a walk toward the blue line of fire at the dead angle of Spotsylvania, where for twenty-four hours the soldiers were fighting on the two sides of an earthwork, and in the morning the dead and dying lay piled in a row six deep, and as you rode have heard the bullets splashing in the mud and earth about you; if you have been on the picket line at night in a black and unknown wood, have heard the spat of the bullets upon the trees, and as you moved have felt your foot slip upon a dead man's body; if you have had a blind fierce gallop against the enemy, with your blood up and a pace that left no time for fear—if, in short, ... you have known the vicissitudes of terror and of triumph in war, you know that there is such a thing as the faith I spoke of. ... You know that man has in him that unspeakable somewhat which makes him ... able to face annihilation for a blind belief.[114]

In this passage a number of Holmes' actual experiences are run together: the march into Fredericksburg, where his regiment was fired upon by Confederate soldiers stationed on a hill slope, while he lay ill with dysentery; the spherical caseshot that caught him in the heel at Chancellorsville; the gruesome battle of Spotsylvania; his grim picket-line duties in the Peninsula campaign; the wild ride to deliver the message where he dodged bullets by riding slung from saddle. All of this was recounted by one who knew the "triumph" of having survived as well as the "terror" of the memory; who had the luxury of claiming that for soldiers faith overrode cynicism. Holmes was not unaware, even in retrospect, that "[w]ar, when you are in it, is horrible and dull." But he insisted that "when time has passed ... you see that its message is divine."

So if his audience needed a further particularization, Holmes provided one:

In this snug, over-safe corner of the world we need [the message of war] that we may realize that our comfortable routine is no eternal necessity of things, but merely a little space of calm in the midst of the tempestuous untamed streaming of the world, and in order that we may be ready for danger. ... For high and dangerous action teaches us to believe as right beyond dispute things for which our doubting minds are slow to find words of proof. Out of heroism grows faith in the worth of heroism. ... Therefore I rejoice at every dangerous sport which I see pursued. ... If once in a while in our rough riding a neck is broken, I regard it, not as a waste, but as a price well paid for the breeding of a race fit for hardship and command.[115]

At this point Holmes' language seems to have run away from him. It is one thing to contrast the fatalistic acquiescence of soldiers with the complacent carping of civilians, and call the former heroism, but to equate polo playing with soldiering, to call a broken neck "a price well paid," and to speak of "dangerous sport" as "breeding ... a race fit for hardship and command" seems excessive. It is no wonder that Theodore Roosevelt, who was sent a copy of Holmes' 1895 commencement address after it appeared, was taken by it:[116] passages like that quoted above were

characteristic of the sophomoric and racist jingoism that Roosevelt and other advocates of the "strenuous life" propagated at the turn of the nineteenth century.

The loose language and excessive sentiment were unusual for Holmes, suggesting
that war in retrospect was a particularly emotional subject for him. We need not look
much further in "The Soldier's Faith" to find the basis of that emotion:

> As for us, our days of combat are over. Our swords are rust. Our guns will
> thunder no more. The vultures that once wheeled over our heads are buried
> with their prey. Whatever of glory yet remains for us to win must be won in
> the council or the closet, never again in the field. I do not repine. We have
> shared the incommunicable experience of war; we have felt, we still feel, the
> passion of life to its top.[117]

Again the experience of the Civil War is linked to a particular generation—that
"born about 1840, and now governing the world"—and to a special sort of "passion," the passion that comes from exposing oneself to mortal danger with the
attitude of "a splendid carelessness for life." And the sense that his generation had
been singled out to experience that passion—had been "touched with fire"—was
accentuated for Holmes by the fact that he could recreate his wartime experiences
as a survivor, knowing that "whatever of glory remains" for himself and his contemporaries, it would "never again [be won] in the field."

There is thus a good deal of the elemental Holmes in "The Soldier's Faith," as
there is in "Memorial Day": the familiar philosophic skepticism that marked his
mature perspective; the summoning up of ideals, such as duty, honor, and chivalry,
which he associated with gentlemanly codes and the professional ethic of the soldier;
his insistence that the Civil War had been both a pivotal and a distinctive experience
for his generation; his sense that unless one had experienced "high and dangerous
action" one had somehow not lived or fulfilled one's manhood. Above all, Holmes
intended in "The Soldier's Faith" to establish a juxtaposition that was central to his
thought, the juxtaposition between the anarchic reality of experience and the ennobling quality of ideals. Experience, most starkly personified by war, was random,
purposeless, "horrible and dull," but that fact did not lead to cynicism. For experience was given meaning by ideals, notwithstanding the imperfect correspondence
between ideals and reality. Thus the importance of the Civil War was "its message":
that exposing one's life in pursuit of ideals (including the ideal of soldierly duty,
personified in blind obedience) was a form of "passion" that constituted living life
"to its top."

Holmes the metaphysician is a familiar figure, with his frequently belittling references to the significance of the human race ("when one thinks coldly I see no
reason for attributing to man a significance different in kind from that which belongs
to a baboon or a grain of sand");[118] his mystical faith in "the cosmos" ("[t]he
ultimate, even humanly speaking is a mystery");[119] his historical relativism and
determinism ("[a]bsolute truth is a mirage";[120] "all great or general facts should be
looked at only as cosmical changes":[121] "property, friendship, and truth have a
common root in time");[122] his insistence on power, force, and the ability to kill one's
enemies as the predominant determinants of the universe ("[t]he world has produced
the rattlesnake as well as me; but I kill it if I get a chance";[123] "all society has rested

on the death of men'');[124] and, at the same time his exaltation of individual will, particularly toward some unknown goal (''the root of joy as of duty is to put out all one's powers toward some great end'');[125] (''Out of heroism grows faith in the worth of heroism.'')[126]

A good many of the metaphysical assumptions associated with this arguably paradoxical or arguably existential stance[127] could be traced to Holmes' Civil War experiences. The carnage of the war and the leveling character of wartime death may have served as a reminder that the social terms by which humans evaluated one another were ultimately meaningless. The randomness of death or survival may have been taken as ''proof'' of the mystery of ''the ultimate.'' The war itself, its course, and its conclusion, seemed determined by forces far larger than the troops who fought in it. There was a kind of historical inevitability to the process: why had slavery existed for so many years before humans resolved to kill one another over it? War was the quintessential environment to illustrate the central role of power, force, and death in the universe. And yet war was a particularly fertile breeding ground for heroism; it was an environment in which one could affirm what it meant to live all the more fully because one was continually facing death.

When one considers ''The Soldier's Faith'' in terms of Holmesian metaphysics, the address becomes more than a jingoistic tract. Holmes was not glorifying conquest and brutality and slaughter, but rather juxtaposing them against the ''heroism'' of stoic exposure to death in pursuit of ''gentlemanly'' ideals. Nonetheless, the tone and language of the address caused some contemporaries to take it as a glorification of war. When the speech appeared in the *Harvard Graduates Magazine* in December 1895 Wendell Garrison, a classmate of Holmes and the editor of *The Nation,* wrote a critique of it entitled ''Sentimental Jingoism,''[128] and E. L. Godkin, the editor of the New York *Evening Post,* followed with one entitled ''Force as a Moral Influence.''[129] Holmes complained to Frederick Pollock:

> Fancy my speech of last Memorial Day being treated as a jingo document! Greatly to my disgust it was put over in the *Harvard Magazine* and only came out a few days ago, . . . but now it seems to some of the godly as I were preaching a doctrine of blood! My classmate Wendell P. Garrison, Editor of *The Nation* . . . a most watery person but one who is, was, and ever will be flat, walked into me with a blunt knife . . . and I surmise that Godkin backed him in a No. 2 which was too clever for poor Wendell. I met the great Edward Atkinson [a Boston industrialist and pamphlet writer] this very morning and he shook his head & said, ''I don't like it. It's bad morals and bad politics.'' To which I civilly replied that I didn't care, but on reflection called his attention to my speech being on Memorial Day, not now.[130]

The ''bad politics'' of the speech came from its appearing at a time when relations between the United States and Great Britain were estranged as a result of conflicting colonialist aims in the Caribbean. While the Pollock letter displays Holmes' habitual prickliness at public criticism (he cannot resist describing Garrison as ''watery'' and ''flat''), the timing of the address' appearance was unfortunate in light of Holmes' purposes in describing the ''message'' of war. In a 1909 letter he pointed out that ''I tried in my speech The Soldier's Faith to bring home by example that men are eternally idealists—(a speech that fools took as advice to young men to wade in gore).''[131] On the other hand, Theodore Roosevelt's comparable misunderstanding of the speech may have been one of the factors that caused him to appoint Holmes to the Supreme Court. After the speech Roosevelt visited Boston, and a friend of Roosevelt's, William Sturgis Bigelow, who was also Holmes' fellow Porcellian, invited Holmes to dinner with Roosevelt, who, Bigelow told Holmes, ''wants to embrace you in connection with some recent Jingoid remarks attributed to you.''[132]

Holmes was to return to the theme of the war in retrospect on one more occasion. That was the fiftieth reunion of the Harvard Class of 1861, in June 1911. In a brief speech[133] Holmes returned to his characterization of his generation as having been peculiarly and importantly shaped by its wartime experience. ''It has been my fortune,'' he said, ''to belong to two bodies that seemed to me somewhat alike—the 20th Massachusetts Regiment and the class of '61. The 20th never wrote about itself to the newspapers, but for its killed and wounded in battle it stood in the first half-dozen of all the regiments of the north.'' Similarly ''this little class never talked much about itself, but . . . out of its eighty-one members it had fifty-one under arms.'' ''I learned in the regiment and the class,'' Holmes continued,

> the conclusion, at least, of what I think the best service that we can do for our country and for ourselves: To see so far as one may, and to feel, the great forces that are behind every detail . . . to hammer out as compact and solid a piece of work as one can, to try to make it first rate, and to leave it unadvertised.[134]

Here one sees the ethos of soldiering translated into an ethic of craftsmanship. The anonymous courage of the Regiment and his classmates in arms has become realized in ''hammering out'' compact and solid works and ''leaving [them] unadvertised.'' The ''training'' of a soldierly generation had emphasized ''discipline,'' ''stern experience,'' and ''duty.'' Holmes and his contemporaries had learned that ''pleasures do not make happiness and that the root of joy as of duty is to put out all one's powers toward some living end.''

In this address, written in his seventieth year, ten years into his tenure as a Supreme Court justice, one can see how the message of the war in retrospect remains ''passion,'' though transformed into unadvertised professional craftsmanship. Holmes was suggesting that ''feel[ing] the great forces'' and ''hammer[ing] out a . . . first rate . . . piece of work'' were part of the same passionate impulse generated by a splendid carelessness toward life, the impulse of the soldier, the impulse of his generation. Of course studying cases ''to the bottom'' or crafting memorable opinions was nothing like fighting a war in one basic sense, and Holmes knew that. One's life was not on the line in the former exercises. But Holmes wrote about producing work as if the producer's life *was* on the line, as if ''put[ting] out all one's powers toward some great end'' was the equivalent of fighting in battle.

Very early in his service, Holmes came to recognize that the war in fact bore little relationship to the ''war in theory,'' the ideals for which he had enlisted. Nevertheless, in his portrait of the war in retrospect he suppressed, or glided over, that dissonance, equating the ''message'' of the war with the pursuit of ideals. The memory of the war in fact, however, kept intruding upon him, but always from the perspective of one who had survived it. Thus the "passion" and "faith" and "duty" and "carelessness" of the war became a "joy" for Holmes, "splendid" and "divine" memories. And Holmes invariably conceptualized his later professional tasks as if they were versions of the task of fighting a war, enterprises in which one's whole being was directed but whose successful pursuit should remain "unadvertised." The fact that they were not—that a "splendid carelessness for life" never characterized Holmes' stance toward any of his postwar experiences—did not prevent Holmes from seeing them as if they were the equivalent of war; from seeing himself as the soldier rather than as the survivor.

So one has to conclude that however large the gap between Holmes' war in fact and his war in retrospect, and consequently how distorted the "message" that he drew from this wartime experiences, those experiences were central to his self-concept. When he spoke of being glad that he had left academic life for a judgeship because had he remained he felt he would have "declined the struggle offered me" and "taken the "less manly course,"[135] he was back at Ball's Bluff and Antietam and Fredericksburg and Chancellorsville and Spotsylvania, choosing "high and dangerous action" so that his passion for gentlemanly ideals could once again be demonstrated.

The war in retrospect became, in the end, an overarching, "official" memory that helped Holmes avoid recalling some more specific and more candid memories. There was the memory of his not declining to be placed on the boat in Ball's Bluff although the code of Sir Philip Sydney suggested that he defer to his enlisted men. There was the memory of his missing the ambush at Fredericksburg and feeling secretly glad and guilty at the same time. There was the memory of the cumulative terrors of the Wilderness campaign that resolved him to resign his commission rather than reenlist as an infantry officer. There was the memory of others in his class at Harvard and in his regiment who had died while he had survived. And there was the memory that relatively early on in the conflict he had lost faith in the Union Army's capacity to subjugate the South.

None of these memories was pleasant to recall from the perspective of a life now free from any further obligations to fight. Especially painful was the recollection that Holmes had mustered out before the end of the conflict; that he had given way to his recognition that "a doubt demoralizes me as it does any nervous man," and that he therefore could no longer "endure the labors and hardships of the line." In place of that particularly sensitive memory, and others that he preferred to dislodge from his consciousness, Holmes constructed his romanticized image of the war in retrospect.

The romanticization of his wartime experience took two forms. One was the familiar, and arguably plausible, equation of wartime service with fidelity to "the soldier's faith": duty to an often inexplicable cause. Holmes' generation had been "touched with fire" because they had had the opportunity to ascribe to that faith. For the remainder of his life Holmes and his contemporaries could take pride in their having being singled out to participate in a war and therefore to be "soldiers" in the extended meaning of that term.

The other was more imaginative, and consequently more revealing. It was that the experience of war communicated, in a vivid fashion, one of the elemental truths of life: that to feel passionately about a subject, and to act in carrying out that passion, was a prerequisite for living life to the fullest. One who had witnessed the archetypal example of passionate action—war—could replicate passionate action in other pursuits. And in so doing one could invest those pursuits with a cosmic importance reserved for elemental human tasks. Put prosaically, one could treat the creation of legal scholarship, or the adjudication of cases, as if they were activities capable of engendering ''high and dangerous action'' in the passionate pursuit of ideals.

It was on the one hand nonsensical for Holmes to equate legal scholarship or judging with fighting in a war. Legal scholarship and judging were activities associated with a ''safe, over-smug corner of the world.'' Holmes' life was not on the line in any direct fashion after 1864. On the other hand, it was important for Holmes to treat war and his subsequent pursuit of professional goals as if they were equivalently elemental exercises. By doing so he could reassure himself that he was still participating in the fight; that he had not escaped the war to survive; that he could continue to claim the privilege of having been touched with fire.

CHAPTER THREE

Friendships, Companions, and Attachments, 1864–1882

～

WHEN Holmes returned from the Civil War in the summer of 1864 he was confronted with the question of what to do with himself. For someone of his antecedents this was not an idle question. The Holmes family was not wealthy to the point where the life of an unemployed "gentleman," still a viable option for Holmes' upper-class Boston contemporaries, was financially possible, and nothing in Holmes' heritage suggested that he, unlike his father or his grandfathers, would be expected to lead a life of affluent leisure. He had signaled in his autobiographical sketch that the legal profession was to be his "starting point" for study if he survived the war, and so he prepared to enter Harvard Law School.

While Holmes had identified the law as his future profession, and while a number of his family members and friends, including his father, his uncle John, and a group of his father's literary contemporaries, such as James Russell Lowell, Henry Wadsworth Longfellow, and Emerson, had read law in their post-college years, Holmes had no familiar example, save his grandfather Jackson, of someone who had actually made the law the professional center of his life. If anything, the careers of those from his father's generation conveyed a different message. One may have read in the law, but one turned to medicine, literature, or even the ministry for one's profession. Moreover, there were disquieting messages about the prosaic character of legal study and the difficulty of finding intellectual inspiration in the subject of law itself. In an introduction to a book of essays that appeared in 1913 Holmes referred to those messages:

> When I began, the law presented itself as a ragbag of details. . . . The only philosophy within reach was Austin's *Jurisprudence*. It was not without anguish that one asked oneself whether the subject was worthy of the interest of an intelligent man. One saw people who one respected and admired leaving the study because they thought it narrowed the mind.[1]

In Holmes' correspondence from his first year as a law student there is evidence that he was struggling to find stimulation in his new field of study. In the spring of 1865 he wrote Henry Brownell, a poet whose writings on the Civil War Holmes had discovered with pleasure,[2] that he continued to be enthusiastic about poetry and philosophy[3] and that "Truth sifts so slowly from the dust of the law." There was a "danger" in law study, he confessed to Brownell: it was that one was so easily distracted from it. "It is so easy and so pleasant," he noted, "to go from day to day satisfying yourself for not having knocked off a hundred pages of Evidence or Contracts," but rather for having "turned over a few stones in some new mind . . . or [having] read some new poem or (worse) written one."[4]

Nonetheless Holmes indicated to Brownell that "my first year at law satisfies me,"[5] and noted in the fall of his second year that "it is interesting to understand how men come to prefer a professional to a general reputation—and for the sake of the former . . . will sacrifice every hope of the other."[6] By the time he had written this letter Holmes' course was clear: he would make the law his profession. The next seventeen years of his life, 1865–1882, were consumed with the implications of that decision.

There were two levels at which Holmes' decision to immerse himself in the profession of the law radiated through his life in that period, which ended with his becoming an Associate Justice of the Supreme Judicial Court of Massachusetts in December 1882. One level involved his personal relationships: his friendships, his marriage, his social pursuits. The effect of Holmes' immersion in the law on those relationships is the subject of this chapter. The other level, which is treated in the next chapter, involved his effort to define the particular aspects of being a lawyer that would provide him with the greatest amount of self-fulfillment. This effort led him, initially, to pursue more than one sort of legal activity at once: editorial writing, law practice, scholarship, law teaching. It eventually resulted in his conclusion that a judgeship best captured the professional niche in which he wanted to set his legal career.

Holmes' life from 1864 to 1882 can be seen as a study in professionalization. For Holmes, with his varied and deep intellectual interests, his lack of affinity for money-making for its own sake or for the world of business, and his abiding interest in developing a professional reputation, professionalization was an extended and sometimes painful and turbulent process. One of its most lasting effects was on the nature of Holmes' friendships. He began the professionalization process in his early twenties, a single man, living with his family, seeking to continue the pattern of close personal relationships, both with men and women, that he had established as an undergraduate at Harvard. His career choice played an important part in shaping and defining his friendships; eventually those friendships, and even his marriage, came to be structured around his overriding goal of making a mark in his chosen profession.

But the relationship between the personal dimensions of Holmes' life in his twenties and thirties and his pursuit of professional goals was not one-dimensional. Friendships, marriage, and social pursuits were not only shaped by Holmes' immersion in the law, they continued to serve as alternatives to the law, representations of the other enthusiasms of Holmes' life. Some of his friendships symbolized his continued interest in philosophy and literature; others his taste for flirtation and romance; others his continued desire periodically to partake of the atmosphere of places and societies far removed from Brahmin Boston. The very attraction Holmes found for the company of William and Henry James, or for the company of Fanny Dixwell and her young women contemporaries, or for traveling in England and on the Continent was that such experiences were alternatives to the intense professional regimen he had established for himself. But at the same time, as professional success became increasingly important to Holmes, those alternatives were redefined in terms of that pursuit. The years between 1864 and 1882 were ones in which the highly structured form of Holmes' mature life was first put in place.

~

One could argue that in terms of common human interest the years of Holmes' coming to maturity pale in comparison with other periods in his life. They lack the drama of his Civil War years or the visibility of his tenure as a Supreme Court justice; they even lack the romance of his middle years, when his private life took a surprising and eventful turn. Part of the reason for the comparatively prosaic quality of Holmes' life between 1864 and 1882 is readily supplied: there is not much information of a personal nature about those years. In those years Holmes was a young lawyer, attending law school, apprenticing himself to a lawyer's office, practicing with law firms, arguing cases in the Massachusetts courts. Young lawyers, however consumed by the demands of their profession, do not tend to perform highly visible tasks.

Nor was Holmes' private life conspicuously visible. He lived at home until his marriage in 1872, and then he and Fanny Dixwell continued to live with his parents. He socialized with a small circle of friends and recorded little of their comings and goings. His marriage was childless, his entertainments infrequent, and his sphere of contacts narrow. In many respects he lived the life of a conventionally ambitious lawyer, preoccupied by the demands of his profession and his own professional goals.

But the quality of Holmes' life from 1864 to 1882 is not fully explained by the social and professional circumstances in which he found himself. It was accentuated by the interaction of his professional role with his own temperament. Holmes was characteristic of the male members of his generation and class—Henry Adams, William and Henry James, John Chipman Gray—in delaying his professional commitments after the conclusion of the Civil War, in continuing to maintain an interest in speculative and literary pursuits, and in seeking to adjust himself to the business-driven world of the later nineteenth century.[7] But he was uncharacteristic in the intensity of his immersion in his profession once he had made a professional choice, and in his systematic concentration of his energies toward topics and pursuits that were connected to his professional ambitions. An 1876 comment by William James on Holmes seems to capture his intensity in the period. James called Holmes "a powerful battery, formed like a planing machine to gouge a deep self-beneficial groove through life."[8]

Two images—James' "planing machine" and another supplied by the mother of William and Henry James—seem to frame Holmes as he appeared to others in his early professional years. In 1873, while he was in the process of completing his edition of James Kent's *Commentaries,* Holmes dined at the Jameses. Mrs. James wrote her son Henry that Holmes'

whole life, soul and body, is utterly absorbed in his *last* work upon his Kent. He carries about his manuscript in his green bag and never loses sight of it for a moment. He started to go to Will's room and wash his hands, but came back for his bag, and when we went to dinner, Will said, "Don't you want to take your bag with you?" He said, "Yes, I always do so at home." His pallid face, and this fearful grip on his work, make him a melancholy sight.[9]

However Holmes' self-absorption was pictured, as self-centeredness by William James or, more charitably, as a form of anxiety by James' mother, the quality was evident to Holmes' contemporaries. The years between 1864 and 1882, for Holmes, were years of intense self-preoccupation, and the focus of that preoccupation was clearly professional recognition. In 1899 Nina Gray, the wife of John Chipman Gray and one of Holmes' oldest friends, wrote him a congratulatory note on his becoming Chief Justice of the Massachusetts Supreme Judicial Court. "I know," she said of Holmes' professional accomplishments, "you have had just a little the feeling that every man's hand was against you."[10] The letter suggests that Holmes had perceived his search for recognition as being undertaken in an environment that was at best indifferent to it—all the more reason for the intensity of his commitment.

Later in his life Holmes sought to capture, in graduation speeches, the atmosphere of his early professional years. In both instances he put it in terms of self-absorbed, lonely, hazardous journeys. "My way," he put it in an 1897 address,

has been by the ocean of the Law. . . . There were few of the charts and lights for which one longed when I began. One found oneself plunged in a thick fog of details—in a black and frozen night, in which were no flowers, no spring, no easy joys. Voices of authority warned that in the crush of that ice any craft might sink. . . . One saw that artists and poets shrank from it as from an alien world. One doubted oneself how it could be worthy of the interest of an intelligent mind.

This was "the first stage" of a professional journey, in which "one has companions." Eventually, after persistence, one "finds at last that there is a drift as was foretold"; one "has learned . . . that one is safe in trusting to courage and to time." But then comes the next stage:

So far his trials have been those of his companions. But if he is a man of high ambitions he must leave even his fellow adventurers and go forth into a deeper solitude and greater trials. He must start for the pole. In plain words he must face the loneliness of original work. No one can cut out new paths in company. He does that alone.[11]

Some years earlier Holmes had elaborated on the nature of original work:

Only when you have worked alone—when you have felt around you a black gulf of solitude more isolating than that which surrounds the dying man, and in hope and in despair you have trusted to your own unshaken will—then only will you have achieved. Thus only can you gain the secret isolated joy of the thinker.[12]

A good deal about Holmes' early professional years is revealed in these passages. There is first the anxiety he felt on entering into a profession that had repelled "artists and poets," who found it "an alien world." There is his own doubt as to whether the law could stimulate "the interest of an intelligent mind." There is the "thick fog of details," the lack of guiding "charts and lights" supplied to the beginning law student or the aspiring legal scholar. And there is, above all, the realization that while the first stage of entry is accompanied by "companions," themselves confronting an alien and unsettling experience, the conclusion of that stage—when one sees "a drift" after having been "frozen in . . . the ice"—is only the beginning of immersion in the legal profession for "a man of high ambition." The next stage is the lonely, isolated one of original scholarship.

In many respects the above passages provide a capsule summary of Holmes' early professional years. He began by entering Harvard Law School, in the fall of 1864, and encountering an intellectual atmosphere not unlike that which he had found at Harvard College. The Law School had three faculty members, Joel Parker, Theophilus Parsons, and Emory Washburn. All three had been practitioners; all three employed the lecture method of teaching. No examinations were given to the students; the only requirement for a degree was periodic attendance at lectures. The faculty recommended a list of reading materials, which Holmes conscientiously followed,[13] and moot courts were provided for the students, in which they argued cases before student and faculty judges. All in all it was a desultory, tedious experience. Five years later, in an unsigned notice in the *American Law Review,* which he was then editing, Holmes said that "for a long time the condition of the Harvard Law School has been almost a disgrace to the Commonwealth of Massachusetts." Its degrees represented "nothing except a residence for a certain period in Cambridge or Boston"; it had been "doing something every year to injure the profession throughout the country, and to discourage real students."[14]

Nonetheless after the close of his first year, we have seen, Holmes had pronounced himself "satisfied" with the law, and by the fall of his second year he had described it as "my enthusiastic pursuit," and noted how men, once exposed to a profession, tended to prefer a "professional to a general reputation," even though such reputations were necessarily limited.[15] While by this point Holmes had apparently resolved to forego other pursuits for the law, this did not mean that he equated legal study with attendance at law school classes. Two months after he wrote Brownell he stopped attending lectures at Harvard, attached himself to the Boston law office of his friend Robert M. Morse, and began "look[ing] up some cases."[16] Harvard nonetheless awarded him a degree in June 1866.

During his law school years Holmes lived with his parents on Charles Street in Boston. While he apparently did not feel the need to separate himself from his family in the same fashion that he had as a Harvard undergraduate, he nonetheless had a discernible circle of social companions his own age, whose members were female as well as male. This circle included Clover Hooper, later to be the wife of Henry Adams; Minnie Temple, the beautiful redhead from Connecticut who was to entrance all the men in Holmes' set and to die of tuberculosis on Holmes' twenty-ninth birthday, March 8, 1870, at the age of 25; John Gray, who graduated from Harvard three years earlier than Holmes, went on to Harvard Law School, and then spent the Civil War on the staff of the Judge Advocate General; Fanny Dixwell, who continued to live with her parents in Cambridge; Brooks Adams, the younger brother of Henry

Adams, who was in England; and the James brothers, Henry and William. Together the group went on outings to the seashore and the White Mountains, gave dinner parties, exchanged presents on Christmas, read poetry, and discussed literature. They also had some romantic interludes. Henry James subsequently wrote of a visit he made in the company of Holmes, Gray, and Minnie Temple to the White Mountains in the summer of 1865, how each man in the group was captivated by Minnie Temple, and how he felt inadequate in comparison to two Civil War veterans.[17] On one occasion the mother of Henry James reported that Minnie Temple, who had apparently admired Holmes, had become "quite disenchanted, and evidently looks at Holmes with very different eyes from what she did; that is she sees him as others do, talks of his thinness and pinchedness, as well as of his beautiful eyes, and seems to see his egotism."[18] Another time Clover Hooper wrote to a friend that she had attended "[a] pleasant little dinner at Brooks' with soup, fish, Sayles, & Gray—ditto at James' on New Years, with the variation which Boston affords of raw oysters, then soup, Gray & Holmes."[19]

Fanny Dixwell, Holmes' future wife, was also a regular companion of his during the years he attended law school and apprenticed himself to a law office,[20] and when Holmes wrote the woman who had housed him after his wounds at Antietam announcing his engagement to Fanny in 1872 he referred to Fanny as "for many years my most intimate friend."[21] That epithet, however, was possibly misleading. For at least the most intense, if not necessarily the most intimate, relationship of Holmes' early professional years was that with William James.

Holmes and William James had become acquainted after Holmes' return from the Civil War, and by 1866 James was referring to Holmes as "the only fellow here I care anything about."[22] Between 1867 and 1869, when James was abroad traveling and studying medicine, he and Holmes exchanged some long, animated letters. The principal subject of the letters was their mutual interest in philosophy: out of the letters came "The Metaphysical Club," a group of late nineteenth-century intellectuals who met periodically to discuss philosophical topics.[23]

One of the characteristics of James' and Holmes' friendship was the capacity of each to find the other intimidating. That conclusion is easily reached from a perusal of their correspondence in the 1860s. On December 15, 1867, Holmes began a letter to James:

> I shall begin with no apologies for my delay in writing except to tell you that since seeing you I have written three long letters to you at different intervals on *vis viva,* each of which I was compelled to destroy because on reflection it appeared either unsound or incomplete. . . . Writing is so unnatural to me that I have never before dared to try it to you unless in connection with a subject.[24]

The passage suggests that not only was Holmes concerned lest he render an unsatisfactory treatment of a philosophical topic to James, but that he was sufficiently self-conscious to claim that writing was "unnatural" to him even though he had written poetry and essays and kept a diary for several years.

Two other passages from the same letter are revealing. In one Holmes noted that "[m]y expressions of esteem are not hollow nor hyperbolical—nor put in to cover my neglect." He then continued:

In spite of my many friends I am almost alone in my thoughts and inner feelings. And whether I ever see you much or not, I think I can never fail to derive a secret comfort and companionship from the thought of you. I believe I shall always respect and love you whether we see much or little of each other.

The passage suggests the significance of James' friendship to Holmes at the time: it provided "comfort" and "companionship"; James was an object of "respect." At the same time Holmes alluded to being "almost alone in my thoughts and inner feelings": again one sees the images of solitude and self-preoccupation that were to characterize Holmes' early professional years.

In the second passage Holmes elaborated on his affection for James:

Oh! Bill, my beloved, how have I yearned after thee all this long time. [James had left Boston for Europe in April 1867.] How I have admired those brave, generous and magnanimous traits of which I will not shame thee by speaking. I am the better that I have seen thee and known thee—let that suffice.

Noteworthy in the passage is Holmes' ascription of selfless qualities to James and the claim that he was "the better" for having had James as a friend. When added to Holmes' portrait of himself as "almost alone in my thoughts and inner feelings," the passage gives a sense that Holmes valued his friendship with James in part because he regarded James' generous qualities as a contrast to his own.

Holmes had made a comparable if not identical impression on James. In March 1866, James wrote a friend, as noted, that "the only fellow [in Boston] I care anything about is Holmes, who is on the whole a first-rate article and improves by wear." James added that Holmes was "perhaps too exclusively intellectual, but sees things so easily and clearly and talks so admirably that it is a great treat to be with him."[25] During his time in Germany James reciprocated Holmes' enthusiasm for his company:

[H]ow I would prefer to have about twenty-four hours talk with you in that whitely lit-up room . . . I should like to have you opposite me in any mood, whether the facetiously excursive, the metaphysically discursive, the personally confidential, or the jadedly cursive and argumentative. . . . I feel as if a talk with you of any kind could not fail to set me on my legs again for three weeks at least.

In the same letter James, aware of Holmes' increasing immersion in legal matters, sought to encourage his friend to resist that trend:

I suppose you are sinking ever deeper into the sloughs of the law—yet I ween the Eternal Mystery still from time to time gives her goad another turn in the raw she once established between your ribs. Don't let it heal over yet.[26]

He then proposed the creation of what was to become "The Metaphysical Club."

Later that same year James wrote Holmes with comparable enthusiasm ("I have an esteem for you which is *tout particular,* and value intercourse with you"), but at the same time introduced a contrast between himself and Holmes:

> You have a far more logical and orderly mode of thinking than I . . . and when we have been together I have somehow been conscious of a reaction against the ascendancy of this over my ruder processes. I put myself involuntarily into a position of self-defense, as if you threatened to overrun my territory and injure my proprietorship. . . . *Some* of it may have been caused by the feeling of a too "cosmic-centric" consciousness in you.[27]

The passage suggests that James' view of the temperamental interaction in his friendship with Holmes was similar to that of Holmes himself: emotion, intuition, and generosity on one side, logic, order, and self-preoccupation on the other. A letter James wrote to his brother Henry a year later indicates that he was disturbed as well as threatened by the contrast:

> The more I live in the world the more the cold-blooded, conscious egotism and conceit of people afflict me. . . . All the noble qualities of Wendell Holmes, for example, are poisoned by them.[28]

James was, of course, the source of the "plane" image of Holmes, seeing his friend as gouging a "deep, self-beneficial groove through life." After 1870 the intensity of James' and Holmes' friendship waned, and while Holmes continued to note James' philosophical writings over the years, he regarded himself and James as very far apart in their views.[29]

In November 1866, Holmes noted in his diary that he had "debauched on Mill . . . by way of removing an old incubus before endeavouring to immerse myself in the law completely." This was nearly a year after he had resolved to abandon attendance at Harvard lectures and had attached himself to George Shattuck's law office. He added in the entry that immersion in the law was what "Shattuck says a man must [do] at some period in his career if he would be a first rate lawyer."[30] The contrast between the "debauched" pleasure philosophy provided for him and the "immersion" in his new profession was symptomatic of Holmes' early professional years. He was searching for the "conviction," which he finally noted to William James in April 1868, that "law as well as any other series of facts in this world may be approached in the interests of science and may be studied, yes and practised, with the preservation of one's ideals."[31] Also symptomatic was the allusion to Shattuck as the source of the principle of professional immersion. By the late 1860s Shattuck had replaced James as Holmes' most significant source of vocational inspiration.

Shattuck was twelve years older than Holmes, and had been in law practice since 1855. He was principally a trial lawyer, representing banks, merchants, and industrial enterprises. His practice was general, although he quite regularly litigated admiralty issues. In a tribute to Shattuck Holmes said that

> Mr. Shattuck in his prime was the ablest advocate I ever knew. . . . He was profound and far-reaching in plan. He was vehement in attack and stubborn in defense. He was fertile in resources and very quick in seeing all the bearing of a fact or a piece of testimony, a matter in which most men of weighty ability are slow.[32]

Unlike James Bradley Thayer, a partner of Shattuck's when Holmes joined his firm, or John Chipman Gray, Shattuck was not a scholar: he was what Holmes called a "man of action," a type to which Holmes was attracted.[33] He was also sufficiently unlike Holmes, sufficiently senior to him, and impressive enough in his intellectual powers to serve as a sort of role model for Holmes at a time when he was both seeking to move away from poetry and metaphysics and desirous of finding law an intellectually challenging experience. That a person of such obvious powers as Shattuck could find satisfaction in law and in the world of affairs was a confirmation of the value of the profession. That Shattuck also had helped usher Holmes into the profession by providing him with a place in his law firm accentuated Shattuck's importance in Holmes' life. "I owe to Mr. Shattuck more than I have ever owed to anyone else in the world, outside my immediate family," Holmes said in his tribute to Shattuck. He added:

> Young men . . . at the beginning of their professional life are very apt to encounter some able man a few years older than themselves who is so near to their questions and difficulties and yet so much in advance that he counts for a good deal in the shaping of their views or even of their lives. Mr. Shattuck played that part for me.[34]

If one were to generalize about the nature of Holmes' close male friendships in the period after his return from the Civil War, one would emphasize the close connection between those friendships and his search to find comfort in a vocation. William James and his brother Henry, with whom Holmes felt comfortable enough to accompany on summer vacations, represented Holmes' continued interest, notwithstanding his involvement with legal studies, in philosophy and letters. The James brothers and other acquaintances of Holmes, such as Chauncey Wright, John Fiske, and Charles Pierce, were late nineteenth-century intellectuals, concerned with erecting systems of philosophical belief in the face of what they regarded as the collapse of established religious and metaphysical efforts to explain the universe.[35] Holmes had been interested in that sort of pursuit since his undergraduate years at Harvard.

Other friends of Holmes, such as John Gray, Gray's law partner John C. Ropes, and Shattuck, were involved in the practice of law. It was not without significance that at the very time that Holmes' friendship with William James had begun to lose its intensity, and Holmes had come to believe that becoming a "first-rate lawyer" required total immersion in the law, John Ropes and John Gray offered Holmes the opportunity to contribute to the new law journal, *The American Law Review,* that they were editing. Holmes' contributions to *The American Law Review* were to lead him, eventually, to producing a twelfth edition of James Kent's *Commentaries on American Law;* to a series of essays on legal history; and in 1880 to the Lowell Lectures that were to become *The Common Law.* With this shift Holmes was not only to reorient his academic emphasis, he was to alter, subtly, the circle of persons he regarded as his professional peers.

~

Holmes' transformation from student philosophizer to lawyer was gradual and irregular. It was punctuated, in fact, by an interval of extended travel in Europe in which he did little academic study of any kind. His European trip nonetheless set a precedent for his later life. It was the first of what to become a periodic series of escapes from Boston to the society of London and its countryhouse environs, to a world that he found a decided, and stimulating, contrast to the one in which he was seeking professional recognition.

Travel in Europe in the years following college, as a kind of intellectual and cultural rite of passage, had been an established pattern of upper- and upper-middle-class Bostonians since Holmes' father's time. Moreover, Dr. Holmes' reputation and his contacts and those of his friends assured that his son would have an introduction to at least some social circles in London. Holmes had planned a journey to England and the Continent as early as the fall of 1865, and when he left Boston for London in April 1866 it was doubtless with expectations of having a stimulating as well as a memorable experience.[36] He was not disappointed, as his diary for 1866 reveals. Arriving in London on May 9, he recorded his first impressions:

> Began by going to Barings' [Bank] & to Mr. Adams' [the American embassy], then to Cook the tailor. Home to lunch. . . . After lunch purchases. . . . First impressions—common people like ours. Swells finer—2 types, saxon & dark, all dressed alike, lavender gloves & sailors ties. Evening, whores stop you everywhere.[37]

On his arrival Holmes used Henry Adams and his circle at the American legation as a point of social entry. His early notations in his diary are filled with accounts of lunches, dinners, walks, and conversations with Adams and his friends. On May 10 he wrote that "my mind made easier as to social differences." Holmes found "[f]ew of the gentlemen real ones," and felt that the "ladies [were] devilish frowsy in the hair," and "let their eyes wander while they talk to you, very freely." At a party at Lady Belper's on the next night he found "no one pretty there." On the 12th and 13th he visited the estate of "Mr. [Russell] Sturgis," a "regular country place," where the "turf is like moss in which the foot sinks deep," there were "lots of birds," and the "Thames [was] at the end of the lawn." The conversation, however, was "stiff and pedantic seeming," and another party he attended on the 17th was "signalized by bad dressing, bad looks, bad manners, and bad food."

Holmes engaged in a number of tourist activities, going to museums and churches, watching a horse race, visiting Oxford, taking river trips, and attending a cricket match. Through Adams he secured introductions to a number of prominent Englishmen. These included the Lord Chancellor, Lord Cranworth; Robert Browning; Motley's friends John Stuart Mill and Thomas Hughes (the author of *Tom Brown's School Days*), the latter of whom Holmes found particularly congenial;[38] James Fitzjames Stephen, with whom Holmes walked through London on the evening of June 1 and had "a good talk"; and Prime Minister Gladstone, who seemed to Holmes, later in life, as "the one man who was like an American," in "[coming] out to meet you and [having] gusto."[39] On May 26 Holmes, in the company of the Adamses, went to a reception at the Gladstones, where Gladstone "in consideration of my wounds made me sit and I was a great gun." He saw Gladstone again at a June 7 breakfast, where the Prime Minister "seated himself on my right." Henry Adams, who was also present at the breakfast, noted Gladstone's "extraordinary facility of conversation on almost any topic," and pointed to "a question proposed by Colonel Holmes respecting a group of figures in china," which prompted Gladstone to "launch . . . forth into a disquisition on that topic, which he delights in."[40] Adams told Holmes that the breakfast was "with hardly an exception . . . the pleasantest thing of the sort he had seen since he'd been in London."[41]

By early June Holmes' social life was crowded. On the 6th he noted in his diary that he had been asked to dine by the Lord Chancellor and John Stuart Mill but that "I was engaged to the Attorney General." On that day he had breakfast with "Col. Tighe" at the "A. & N. Club," then went to lunch at the Adamses, then "after lunch went with Mrs. Shaw to Regents' Park & I called on Lady Goldsmith and set forth my difficulty between her invitation & Lord Wensleydale's very frankly—and she kindly let me out of it—then left cards in succession on Duke of Argyll—Lady Waldgrave—Lady Belper—then to St. James Club [where Henry Adams had secured him a guest membership]. Accepted Lord W's invitation for the 9th. Dinner at the Attorney General's, delightful—Lady Laura bluff & pleasant. Took her down and sat on her left. Afterwards talked with her daughter about art."[42]

On the next day, June 7, Holmes renewed acquaintances with Leslie Stephen, whom he had first met in Boston in 1863, when he was recovering from his Chancellorsville wound.[43] The occasion of that reunion was a dinner given by Fitzjames Stephen, Leslie's older brother, whom Holmes had met on the 1st. At dinner the conversation turned to mountain climbing, about which Leslie Stephen was enthusiastic. Stephen was planning a climbing expedition to Switzerland that summer, and he invited Holmes to a meeting of the Alpine Club, of which Stephen was president, on June 12. Holmes attended the meeting, which consisted of dinner "at a pot house near Leicester Square," and then ate another dinner at the home of Countess Cowper, whose son, Henry, was to become one of Holmes' close English friends.

From mid-May through mid-June Holmes' diary entries suggest that his energies were almost exclusively directed toward social engagements. He ate breakfast, lunch, and dinner out nearly every day, regularly went dancing in the evening, and when he had spare moments went to the St. James Club or made calls on people. Characteristic of his attitude at the time was the contrast between his comments on art galleries (the French Gallery "disappointing" on May 10, the Kensington Portrait Gallery "had lots of poor stuff" on May 31) and those on private collections, such as that of the Cowpers. After going there for dinner on June 12 he wrote, "This is the way to see pictures. Van Dykes, etc., etc. around the dining and drawing rooms." The next sentence noted that he had "taken in the daughter of Countess Cowper to dinner."

Given the social whirl Holmes encountered on his first trip to London, it is not surprising that England came in his later life to symbolize a world in which he could release the gregariousness that was the other side of his solitary self-preoccupation. Two entries in the diary suggest the frame of mind with which he approached his London ventures. On June 11 he recorded that he had

dined at the Members [of Parliament] dining room with Mr. Mill with whom was Mr. [Andrew] Bain, psychologist. And we talked—I was struck with the

absence of imaginative impulse esp. in Mr. Bain—excellent for facts &
criticism but not open to the infinite possibilities—[44]

A day before Holmes had been invited to a dinner at the Cosmopolitan Club, where
he was "introduced to [Alexander] Kinglake, a military historian whose *History of
the Crimean War* Holmes had read in 1861 while convalescing from his Ball's Bluff
wound. Many years later Holmes described his encounter with Kinglake:

> I read Kinglake's *Crimean War* when I was in the army . . . I met Kinglake,
> who said he had a question to ask—I knew what it would be. Did our men
> fight in line? I grinned and said I remembered his speaking of that as an
> Anglo-Saxon prerogative, and asked if he really believed it, to which he—yes,
> he certainly did. I said of course our men fought in line, and that I believed
> you could make baboons do it if you had the right sort of officers.[45]

In these two entries one sees the increased self-confidence that Holmes had
acquired with his social successes in London. A month before he had needed reassurance from Henry Adams about "social differences"; now he was subjecting even
the more established British scholars to his wit and to his criteria for stimulation—
a sense of "the infinite possibilities." He was becoming aware that despite his lack
of social credentials, in the conventional British sense, and despite an occasional
fear that he had committed a faux pas (a June 5 entry noted that "[s]omehow though
I drunk little I felt the wine and was too talky and loud"), he was holding his own
in London society. Several years later he would comment on the criteria for accomplishment in that milieu:

> I always feel twice the man I was, after I visit London. Personality there is in
> higher relief than in my world here [Boston] with its limited experience and
> half culture. . . . You have to pay your way in London. No one takes you on
> faith—and I love it. You must be gay, tender, light-hearted when something
> misses fire, give your best, and all with lightness. London Society is hard to
> get into, not from any requirement of 16 quarterings, but because . . . there are
> too many interesting people in London. You must interest, and must interest
> people who, being in the center of the world, have seen all kinds of
> superlatives.[46]

Henry Cowper and Leslie Stephen, the two Englishmen with whom Holmes
developed friendships on his 1866 visit, met his criteria for what constituted an
"interesting" companion. In an 1867 letter to William James, precipitated by Cowper's visit to Boston, Holmes said that Cowper "made a decided impression on me.
He had the cosmos at heart . . . and we hammered at it into the night several times."[47]
As for Stephen, who shared Holmes' agnosticism, his taste for the novels of Sir
Walter Scott and chivalric ideals, and his interest in solitude, Holmes found him
"the best of fellows and companions all through."[48]

Sometime after their dinner with the Alpine Club members Stephen suggested a
climbing itinerary for Holmes in Switzerland, and on June 14, as the London social
season wound down, Holmes left for Paris, planning to spend two weeks there and
two weeks climbing. While he was in Paris he received a letter from Stephen, sug-

gesting that the two join forces for an Alpine climb on July 2.[49] He met Stephen at the Gare de Lyon station in Paris on that day, and they began a climbing excursion through Switzerland that continued until the 19th, when Stephen left to join a party of friends. Holmes continued to climb until the 24th, when he took a train to Geneva, stopped there for a day, then traveled on to Paris for two days and on July 27 took an overnight steamer to England.

Before leaving Paris for their climb, Holmes had spent two weeks as a conventional Bostonian tourist, passing time in the company of John Hay, a contemporary who was the American consul, and Charles Francis Adams, Henry's brother, as well as the Higginsons, the Crowninshields, and the Gardners, all Bostonians. He did not, if his diary can be believed, interact with French citizens to any great extent, although he did finally catch up with Dr. Pierre Louis, who had taught his father medicine in 1833 and 1834.[50] Despite his reactions to English art museums, he seems to have doggedly visited the Louvre, finally exclaiming, on his sixth visit,

> for perhaps the first time [I] really gloated—Van Eyck, Veronese—Valasquez—Rembrandt—. . . Delacroix—the little Van Eyck is absolutely perfect.[51]

Earlier he had seen the same paintings and noted that "the John Van Eyck opposite Paul Veronese's Marriage of Cana grows on me more and more—so does Veronese in a certain way."[52] In short, he had acted like a typical cultured Bostonian tourist, finding the food good, the theatre "stupid," and the night clubs "crowded and hot and fermenting."[53]

In contrast, the climbing expedition with Stephen was a memorable experience. Stephen had set a relentless pace, with Holmes "limping like the pilgrim who forgot to boil his peas, and swearing quietly . . . all the profane oaths you had ever heard in the war."[54] On one day they began climbing at 3:30 in the morning, reached the top of a peak at 10, descended, stopped to eat, then descended further down a glacier, arriving at the bottom at 5:30, and then walking back to Eggischorn, where they were staying, "burned, stiff, exhausted." Holmes likened the excursion to "an army march."[55] Still, the arduous climbing brought rewards. On July 6 Holmes climbed the Balme Horne peak, and "the finest sight I ever saw burst upon us beyond the precipice—vast rolling masses of cloud and, above and beyond that, a panorama of the greatest Alpine peaks. . . . Stephen said he never'd seen the like." On the 9th Holmes and Stephen "in the beautiful morning walked down to Grinderwald talking comfortably of metaphysics and regarding the lovely view." And on the next day the two "went at a rattling pace . . . down across the glacier and up the hillside, refreshing ourselves by milking a couple of goats . . . and at the cave [where they stopped] a first-class sunset was produced for our benefit." Holmes' feet hurt him continually on the trip, his face was badly sunburned, and he had to pass up a climb on the 17th because he was "too lame." But the trip was the combination of a physical ordeal and a solitary, sensory-laden experience that Holmes relished, especially in the company of a kindred spirit. Once Stephen left, Holmes did much less climbing: his diary entries refer to excursions in the company of "Miss Eugenia" and "Miss Bradlee," to champagne, and to walks and discussions in pine groves.

On his return to Paris on July 26, after leaving Switzerland, Holmes exhibited no enthusiasm for another round of tourist attractions and gatherings with Americans. He had written two English acquaintances, John Kennaway and the Duke of Argyll, and asked to visit them in their country estates in Devonshire and Inverary, outside Glasgow. When he arrived back in Paris he found their invitations waiting: he was to go to the Kennaways for a week, beginning on July 28, and to the Argylls on August 3 for an indefinite period. London was still empty in August, with its inhabitants scattered to their country retreats. Holmes described his journey to the Kennaways, after coming overnight from Paris:

> By 9:45 train to Salisbury where I had to wait nearly two hours . . . arrived at Ottery Road—found that [I] had been expected by earlier train—got a lift to the gate—as my graceful and athletic figure moved along the road, with umbrella in one hand & hat box in the other—in short—I met Miss K., then to the house—comfortable room & bath—dinner—Kennaways' ancestral acres— Devonshire cream—. . . . Pheasants—stable—gardens—beeches—Prayers— Bed—Dreams.[56]

The routine at the Kennaways consisted of rabbit shooting at dawn (on one day Holmes shot four rabbits, to his delight), then back to Escot Hall, the Kennaways estate, for breakfast and morning readings from the Bible. On Sunday the Kennaways went to church in the nearby village, where their family pew was "in the corner, fenced off from the rest" and the "country people . . . touched their hats" to Sir John and the rest of the Kennaway family. The next day Holmes accompanied Miss Kennaway on a drive and noticed the "common men touching their hats & the women dropping courtesies. . . . Everything smacking deliciously of feudalism." In the evenings he exchanged stories and drank grog. Near the end of the visit he drove to Stratford on Avon and saw Shakespeare's tomb and a bust. He found Shakespeare's "head rising toward [the] crown like Sir W[alter] Scott—mouth feminine and vinous—but this & a look about the cheek bones suggest a post mortem mask." The next day he took the train to Glasgow and the Argylls.[57]

It took Holmes three days to reach Inverary Castle, the Argyll family seat. On August 5 he stayed overnight in Arrochar, Scotland, and was "compelled by moral pressure to go to church," having "felt so solitary outside of it." In the afternoon and the evening, however, he "made up" for that burst of religiosity: "I made some good love to a maiden by name Campbell and then later walked largely into scotch whisky."[58] On the next day Holmes arrived at Inverary, where there was a celebration in honor of the twenty-first birthday of Lord Lorne, heir to the seat. "Guests began to pour in," and Holmes was "delighted to meet Miss Campbell of Stonefield again,"[59] whom he had met in London on June 2 and described as "[the] prettiest girl I've seen here." A "Mr. Howard" had prevented Holmes from talking to Miss Campbell on that occasion;[60] Holmes was to make up for his lost opportunity at the Argylls.

The attractions of Miss Campbell did not entirely preoccupy Holmes at Inverary. The next night he "was introduced to the pretty Jessie Robertson, daughter of the Duke's factor, to whom I would fain have made love," but Miss Robertson "threw me over for Sir John Orde."[61] And on the next night he "talked art and religion with Miss Orde, Sir John's daughter, and shocked her," and then got into some unpleasantness at a "county ball" which required the intervention of "Campbell of Islay (author of 'Frost and Fire', devilish good fellow"), who "stood my friend and no one was wiser."[62]

The routine at Inverary also consisted of shooting in the mornings, with grouse, deer, and rabbits the targets. Holmes was not particularly successful until Monday, August 13 ("[t]he great day of English sportsmen"), when he "killed four brace of grouse" and "a couple of wild ducks, . . . and wasn't I proud?"[63] Three days earlier he had shot a deer "smack through the head—it was better than [shooting] 10."[64] One day it rained, and Holmes "talked philosophy" with a Mr. Wood, went to church [and] saw Jessie Robertson at a distance," and read the sentimental Civil War poem, "Old Sergeant," to "the assembled family."[65] On Tuesday the 14th Holmes left the Argylls for a short visit with Sir John Orde, featuring more grouse shooting, after which he was expected at the Stonefield Campbells. On Thursday the 16th Holmes wrote the Campbells to say he was coming, but the next day he received word that Stonefield had taken ill, and so "invited myself to stay over Sunday" at the Ordes. The delay put Holmes "in such a funk that I fired quite wild" at the grouse.[66] On Sunday, however, Holmes ran into the elder Mr. Campbell at church, who told him that "Stonefield was much better" and that he could come the next day.[67]

Grouse shooting continued at the Campbells, but the social life picked up, as two more Campbell families arrived, both with daughters, one from Auchindarroch and the other from Skipness. After going grouse shooting on a "[b]eastly drizzling and blowy day," and staying out until 5:30 P.M., Holmes found himself "far from well on getting home." He had a rash on his legs and general aches and pains, and went to bed. At dinner, to his regret, he was seated near Miss Campbell of Stonefield but "couldn't talk much."[68] He felt better the next day, a Sunday, although "very stiff in every joint."[69] He was unable to go on an expedition to Edinburgh the next day, and finally sent for Miss Campbell of Auchindarroch to keep him company. She and her family left that afternoon; Holmes himself was scheduled to leave in two days.[70]

With his departure imminent, the young women began to pay more of an overt interest in him. On the morning of the 28th, a day before he left, Holmes went driving and amused his female companions by reciting extracts from poems; he reported Miss Campbell of Stonefield, whom he sat next to at dinner, "making eyes like a horned owl."[71] The next day he "spent the morning with the young ladies . . . as it was the last day," and received some grouse from Mr. Campbell to take with him on the ship back to America. He left Stonefield "feeling sad enough,"[72] took a boat and a train to Edinburgh, and prepared to go south to Liverpool, then to Chester and his trans-Atlantic crossing. He was overnight in Edinburgh, where he visited the castle overlooking town and the National Gallery ("where there are some interesting pictures").[73] In Chester he was "delight[ed]" to run into a Boston acquaintance, H. W. Jackson, who would also be sailing on the ship *China*.[74] The next day he sailed for Boston.

Holmes' 1866 journey to England furnishes a striking contrast to his experiences in Boston in the same period in his life, and throughout his life this contrast continued. In Boston, he led a relatively solitary, self-preoccupied existence, socializing with some close friends but hardly engaging in the perpetual round of lunches, teas, and dinners that he experienced in England. His close companions in Boston seemed to have been individuals of a comparably speculative and serious orientation; there is little mention of outdoor activities, parlor games, badinage. In Boston he was increasingly preoccupied with his legal studies and his career as a lawyer; there is no mention in his 1866 diary that he talked about law at all, save with older lawyers such as the Lord Chancellor. In Boston, in short, he functioned as an intense, driven, aspiring professional; in England he functioned as a young socialite. Moreover, while he had acted as a tourist in Paris, where he knew no natives, he had acted more as one of his English contemporaries might in London or in Devonshire or in Scotland. He had not merely observed English life; he had immersed himself in it.

From 1866 on England was to symbolize this immersion in social affairs for Holmes. As his patterns in Boston became increasingly solitary and reclusive, especially after his marriage in 1872 and his succession to a judgeship in 1882, he came to see England as an alternative to that existence. For a time he attempted to include Fanny on his English trips, but it was clear, after two attempts, that she did not take the same relish in the company of English socialites that he did. After 1882, with one brief exception, he traveled to England alone, visiting it in 1889, 1896, 1898, 1901, 1903, 1907, and 1913.[75] And he did not visit England as a tourist: he renewed old acquaintances, cultivated new ones, and went on the same sorts of rounds in London and at country places that he had frequented in 1866. With an occasional exception, his close friends in England were not lawyers; even after 1902, when he was on the Supreme Court, he did not go to England to seek out others in his profession or to be received by them. He went to immerse himself in the distinctively light but stimulating world of educated British society. That that society was strikingly different from its Boston counterpart was, in Holmes' view, to its credit.

A letter Holmes wrote in September 1898, after returning from his sixth visit to England, captures the role those excursions played in his life. Particularly revealing are Holmes' characterizations of the contrasts between his lives in Boston and in England, the effect English society had upon him, and the criteria for social success in London:

> The visit to your islands was a great success. It always is—I have almost more friends there whom I love, than I have here. Here I am a recluse. Most of my old friends are dead [an indication that the Civil War was still on his mind] and I do not make new ones, unless very rarely, as I do not give myself the chance. . . . I don't haunt lawyers especially—general society is the best thing—at least under my conditions . . . I always feel twice the man I was, after a visit to London. Personality there is in higher relief than in my world here with its limited experience and its half culture. . . . In the hotel [in England] you are a person not a number. On the other hand nothing is put up with but *real* personality. It must be the stiletto not a bogus masonic sword or stuffed club.[76]

~

After Holmes returned from Europe in 1866 he continued in the professional and personal routines he had established since his return from the Civil War. He affiliated himself with George Shattuck's firm, studied for the oral examinations that were then the only requirement for admission to the Massachusetts bar, and was admitted on March 4, 1867. For the next fourteen years he was to engage in one or another form of law practice in Boston. He began his contributions to the *American Law Review*, edited by his friends John Ropes and John Gray, and in 1870 was to succeed, along with Alexander Sedgwick, to the editorship of that periodical. Through his friendship with James Bradley Thayer, one of the partners of the Shattuck firm, he assumed the editorship of the sixth edition of Kent's *Commentaries*.[77] The experience of updating Kent caused him to engage in a close study of early American and English common law cases, an enterprise that stimulated him to pursue a series of scholarly articles on legal history that eventually led him to the subjects of his 1880 Lowell Lectures, which became *The Common Law*. Each of these pursuits confirmed his ''immersion'' in the law and his consequent abandonment of the two other scholastic passions of his early academic life, philosophy and literature. In 1870 Sedgwick said of Holmes, ''he knows more law than anyone in Boston of our time, and works harder at it than anyone.''[78]

Holmes' increased participation in matters directly related to his role as a lawyer also had, as we have seen, an effect on his friendships. After 1868 he saw less of William James; his diary recorded the daily events of his law practice and dropped references to reading poetry or taking outings to the countryside. Beginning in 1866 Holmes began a list of his readings,[79] and while titles from history, philosophy, and fiction continued to appear, they were outnumbered by legal titles. In the year 1871, for example, Holmes listed selections from Turgenev, Boswell's *Life of Samuel Johnson*, Montesquieu, Bret Harte's Condensed Novels, and a work on the ''Agricultural Community of the Middle Ages.'' Alongside these titles he listed eighteen works on law and jurisprudence.[80]

The general impression of Holmes' life from 1865 to the early 1880s is that of an existence increasingly being structured around the perceived obligations of his profession. While this structuring required some adjustment of Holmes' social as well as his professional relationships, there was one relationship that, on the surface, appeared to remain constant. In 1866 William James had written his brother that ''for eight years that villain Wendell Holmes has been keeping [Fanny Dixwell] all to himself over at Cambridge,''[81] and in 1872 Holmes married Fanny Dixwell, ''for many years my most intimate friend.'' To appearances, then, Fanny Dixwell may have seemed to represent a link to Holmes' earlier life, part of the social circle of his youth that had remained with him as he came to maturity. From another perspective, however, Fanny's continued presence in Holmes' life suggested that, unlike some of his other friends, she had implicitly acceded to his ''immersion'' in the law, and in marrying him was prepared to support, even reinforce, that immersion.

The marriage of Fanny Dixwell and Holmes was undoubtedly one of the significant events of his personal life, yet it remains difficult to reconstruct. One of the enigmas surrounding the marriage involves the circumstances by which it came into being. Holmes and Fanny Bowditch Dixwell had known one another at least since

1851, when Holmes had entered her father's Private Latin School. They were close friends from at least 1858 on,[82] and corresponded during Holmes' service in the Civil War.[83] In 1866 a letter from William James to Thomas Ward indicated that Fanny, with whom James was temporarily smitten, was identified with Holmes,[84] and on one occasion during his visit to Europe Holmes enclosed a letter to Fanny in one to his parents.[85]

During the years of Holmes' increased concentration on his profession, there is no indication that his intimacy with Fanny subsided, but there is also no indication that he felt any compulsion to marry her. His diaries suggest that he spent time in the company of other young women as well as Fanny, and in a letter to William James in 1868 he said that "[t]here are not infrequent times when a bottle of wine, a good dinner, a girl of some trivial sort can fill the hour for me."[86] By the early 1870s both Holmes' younger brother and younger sister had married. In *The Atlantic Monthly,* in a series of stories collected as *The Poet at the Breakfast Table,* Dr. Holmes had introduced two characters, "The Young Astronomer," previously mentioned, and "Scheherezade." Both characters were roomers at the boarding house that formed the setting of the stories, and in one episode the "Poet" analyzes the relationship between "The Young Astronomer" and "Scheherezade":

> If he would only fall in love with her, seize upon her wandering affections and fancies as the Romans seized the Sabine virgins, lift her out of herself and her listless and weary drudgeries . . . I am afraid all this may never be. I fear that he is too much given to lonely study, to self-companionship, to all sorts of questionings, to looking at life as at a solemn show where he is only a spectator.[87]

As an illustration "The Poet" recounts a scene where the Young Astronomer and Scheherezade observe a double star through his telescope. She says that "it must be so much pleasanter than to be alone in such a great empty space! . . . Does not a single star seem very lonely to you up there?" He responds, "Not more lonely than I am myself."[88] "The Poet" took this as an example of the Young Astronomer's disinclination to "warm his hands just for a little while in a human consciousness."[89]

On March 13, 1872, five days after his thirty-first birthday, Holmes finally put his father's fears to rest. Dr. Holmes wrote to his sister and to a friend on the 11th that his son's engagement to Fanny was "to come out" in two days. He referred to "[t]he attachment" between Fanny and Holmes as "a very long and faithful one— . . . both of them dating almost from childhood."[90] He indicated that the couple "did not see their way to marriage and consequently have not called themselves engaged until quite recently, though it was plain enough that they were entirely devoted to each other."[91] He suggested that "Wendell has found the reward of his fidelity to a young lady of most remarkable gifts and qualities."[92]

It is not clear what motivated Holmes to become engaged to Fanny in the spring of 1872, although the suggestion by Dr. Holmes that the couple "did not see their way to marriage" earlier may have been an allusion to finances. By 1872 Holmes had negotiated a $3000 contract to prepare an edition of James Kent's *Commentaries,* was lecturing on jurisprudence at Harvard Law School, and was practicing with his brother Ned; he may have felt that the combination had provided him with some short-term financial security.[93] At any event, it is apparent that Holmes did not see marriage as changing his life in any significant fashion. He and Fanny planned to live with Holmes' parents, where Holmes had been living; they had no honeymoon, and Holmes continued to plunge ahead in his work on Kent. His diary for 1872 noted on June 17 that he had married Fanny Bowditch Dixwell; the next sentence indicated that he had become the sole editor of the *American Law Review*. He continued to read legal and philosophical works during that month.[94] The comment by William James' mother about Holmes' "fearful grip on his work" and his obsession with his Kent manuscript, quoted earlier, was made after he and Fanny had been married.

It has been suggested that the marriage between Holmes and Fanny Dixwell was "arranged" by the families, and that there was no passion on either side.[95] It is clear, from a variety of sources, that Holmes and Fanny were close companions.[96] It is also clear that they were temperamental opposites, most particularly in their attitude toward social contacts. Holmes said of Fanny, after her death, that "I like solitude with intermissions, but she was almost a recluse. I have my work and a fair number of people whom I like to see. She shocked Gifford Pinchot once by saying 'I have no friends'; and it was true that there was no one except me with whom she was very intimate.'"[97] Several years earlier he had said that "[s]he is a very solitary bird, and if her notion of duty did not compel her to do otherwise, she would be an absolute recluse, I think. . . . She and I are a queer contrast in that way, as in many others.'"[98] There is evidence that Fanny was not close with any of the members of her family,[99] and she was not predisposed toward entertaining or traveling,[100] although she did accompany Holmes twice to Europe and gave regular teas when the Holmeses first arrived in Washington in 1902.

Part of the reason for Fanny's reclusiveness may have been the severe attack of rheumatic fever she suffered in July 1872, only a month after her marriage. Apparently a servant in the Holmes' household contracted the disease, and died of it, and Fanny also took sick.[101] In the late nineteenth century bacterial illnesses such as rheumatic fever were simply left to run their course. By October 1872 Fanny was still bedridden,[102] but she eventually recovered. Sometime in 1895 or 1896 the illness returned, this time apparently causing a loss of hair, which grew back in gray.[103] Several visitors to the Holmeses described Fanny, in later life, as conspicuously plain, taking no interest in her appearance. One said that "she really did look like a monkey with a long upper lip, darting black eyes and the restless manner of a small bird."[104] Another said that "[s]he had deep sunken eyes, and . . . had her hair skinned back. . . . [S]he never made any attempt to do anything with herself."[105] When the Holmeses arrived in Washington in 1902 Fanny was reported to have described herself as looking "like an abandoned farm in Maine."[106]

There is no direct evidence of a connection between Fanny's rheumatic fever and the Holmeses' childlessness, although rheumatic fever can damage heart valves and weakened heart valves can increase the risks of childbirth. The Holmeses' failure to have children has been the occasion of considerable speculation and some misleading commentary, by Holmes himself as well as others. Late in his life, on at least two occasions, Holmes intimated that he had chosen not to have children. In one instance he wrote Lewis Einstein that "I am so far abnormal that I am glad I have [no

children]. It might be said that to have them is part of the manifest destiny of man
. . . and that he should accept it as he accepts his destiny to strive; but the latter he
can't help and part of his destiny is to choose.''[107]

The other recorded occasion was a conversation Holmes had with Learned Hand,
sometime after Fanny died in 1929. On Hand's asking Holmes whether he had "ever
been sorry that you never had any children," Holmes, according to Hand, "waited
for a perceptible time and then said very quietly (still not looking at me): 'This is
not the kind of world I want to bring anyone else into.' ''[108] On the basis of these
comments, Mark Howe suggested that "[a]mong the avoidable burdens [of mar-
riage], there is some reason to believe that Holmes counted children," and that "[i]t
seems not unlikely that it was by his decision that no children were born of the
marriage.''[109]

Other biographers of Holmes have also speculated on the issue. Sheldon Novick,
who was aware, as Howe was not, of Fanny's early attack of rheumatic fever, stated
that "[t]he Holmeses' childlessness seems adequately accounted for by Fanny's age
[she was 32 when she married Holmes in 1872] and ill health," and that "Fanny
deeply regretted her childlessness.''[110] Liva Baker concluded that the Holmeses'
childlessness was "not surprising," alluding to "the risks of childbearing at [Fan-
ny's] advanced age in uncertain medical times," the possibility that Fanny may have
been infertile ("a common ailment among women who married later in life"), and
even to an unsubstantiated story that Holmes was sexually impotent.[111]

As a commonsensical proposition, it seems highly unlikely that the Holmeses
were childless by design. The issue of male fertility would have been a highly
sensitive one for Holmes, about which he quite conceivably might have been defensive, and thus his comments about choosing not to bring children into this world
and being glad he had no children strike one as rationalizations and evasions after
the fact. Had the Holmeses chosen not to have children, it is odd that Fanny would
have communicated her regret at not having them. Whatever tensions existed in the
Holmeses' marriage, it is hard to imagine a scenario where Holmes decreed that
there should be no offspring, and Fanny acquiesced in the situation while regretting
it. If other possibilities, including the risk to Fanny's health, are downgraded, the
most likely explanation for the Holmeses' childlessness appears to be that at least
one of the participants in the marriage was infertile, although there is no direct
evidence confirming that supposition. If infertility was the cause of the Holmeses'
childlessness, its implications may well have had a substantial effect on the Holmeses' marriage, raising issues of inadequacy or resentment in one or both partners.
Holmes' explanations for his childlessness, however, seem as contrived as the suggestion that the absence of offspring was a result of his alleged impotency.

Fanny's married life seems to have been preoccupied with domestic affairs,[112]
her embroideries, which she exhibited at the Boston Art Museum and the New York
Ladies Decorative Art Society in 1880 and 1881, and her pet birds. Her embroideries
drew rave reviews from critics after being exhibited,[113] but she never displayed them
again in public and destroyed all but a very few when the Holmeses moved from
Boston to Washington in 1902.[114] She did not share Holmes' interest in ideas, nor
was she involved in political or social affairs, with the exception of one short period
in her life. That was just after Holmes' appointment to the Supreme Court, when

the Holmeses encountered a custom of protocol in official Washington in which Cabinet members and Supreme Court Justices opened their homes for teas on designated afternoons. Fanny agreed to have an open house on Mondays, and for some years entertained callers, mainly wives and friends of persons in the Roosevelt administrations. Holmes wrote his friend Ellen Curtis that Fanny "has been a great success [as a hostess] although she won't believe it."[115] She also revealed herself to be a keen observer of the Washington landscape, stating to Holmes that she had seen "wives of men whom they had helped to arrive—and when they get here with their clothes they realize that now they are an encumbrance."[116]

The relationship between Holmes and Fanny seems to have been set in place by two compelling themes of their early marriage, his ambition and her illness, and to have remained largely constant over the years. It was not a distant nor an estranged relationship: Fanny read to Holmes in the evenings, played practical jokes on him,[117] teased him when he grew unduly solemn or pompous, and provided the emotional support that precipitated Holmes, on her death, to write Frederick Pollock that "for sixty years she made life poetry for me."[118] But it was a relationship in which two of the principal enthusiasms of Holmes' life—his work and his immersion in the social world of London—were not usually shared by Fanny.[119] In addition to those pursuits, it is fair to say that Holmes' other primary interests were his reading, which he shared only partly with Fanny, and his correspondence, which was obviously directed at others. The Holmeses' relationship was thus both close and limited: Holmes' life was divided into discernible spheres, and Fanny occupied only a portion of one of them. The relationship might be accurately described, in fact, as one in which Fanny implicitly permitted herself to be relegated to a distinctly bounded realm of Holmes' existence: a realm not less central for its bounded quality, but limited nonetheless.

Fanny's apparent tolerance of her "domestic" role in her husband's life, when seen in the context of altered expectations of men and women in marital relationships between the time frame of the Holmeses' marriage and the present, makes recreation of her motivation difficult. In a subsequent chapter it will appear that Fanny was well aware of, and tolerated, Holmes' tendencies to engage in flirtations with other women, and even encouraged him to travel unaccompanied by her to places where she knew he vigorously pursued female companionship. It is not clear how well informed Fanny was about the principal extramarital romance in Holmes' life, his attachment to Clare Castletown, the subject of that chapter. It appears that, on the one hand, Holmes took pains to conceal the existence of a longstanding, and intimate, correspondence that he engaged in with Clare Castletown, but that, on the other, Fanny was well aware of his friendship with Clare and her husband, Bernard Castletown, knew that on several trips to England and Ireland Holmes stayed with the Castletowns, and was conscious that Holmes kept a portrait of Clare in his study at home, along with portraits of other female friends.

In addition, Fanny tolerated, and even encouraged, the stark division in the Holmes household between professional and domestic spheres. Holmes paid no attention to household bills, the staffing of servants, the details of the twice-yearly moving of their household from Boston or Washington to their summer place at Beverly Farms, Massachusetts, or to the furnishing of the Holmeses' house at 1720

Eye Street in Washington, with the exception of the books Holmes placed in his study. As far as can be determined, Fanny paid no attention to Wendell's work as a judge or a scholar after she read the proof of his 1873 edition of James Kent's *Commentaries On American Law*.[120] A symptomatic ritual of the Holmeses' marriage was Fanny's reading aloud in the evenings, from "light" books selected by Wendell, while Wendell played solitaire. The ritual was designed to save Holmes' eyesight and enable him to reserve his solitary reading for selections that he felt improved his mind. It seemed to be of no consequence to either of the Holmeses that Fanny had had eye trouble as a young woman,[121] whereas there is no evidence that Wendell ever had any difficulties with his eyesight.

The central puzzle of the Holmeses' marriage centers on whether Fanny Dixwell tacitly recognized that her reclusiveness and disinclination to pursue social contacts served to frustrate a gregarious streak in Holmes, and accordingly allowed him a certain license to wander in search of female companionship as a kind of payment for sparing her the ordeals of socializing, or whether Holmes tacitly encouraged Fanny's reclusiveness when it served his own purposes, such as providing him the solitude to read, write, and engage in scholarship, and at the same time did not seek to include Fanny when he felt inclined to escape the confines of his professional life, because her presence was not consistent with his self-appointed role as a bon vivant. Perhaps an answer to the puzzle lies in a combination of its elements. Perhaps the structured professionalism of Holmes and the structured domesticity of Fanny complemented one another, with Holmes' occasional escapes into a social whirl and Fanny's tacit decisions not to accompany him in those escapades also serving analogous functions, in his case a release from professionalism and in hers a release from the social obligations of female domesticity.

~

One feature of Holmes' marriage in 1872 appears evident enough: it was hardly a respite from his consuming professional pursuits. His notebooks for that year reveal a steady progression of academic readings and work on the Kent edition, which he completed in November 1873. In March 1873, he went into practice with George Shattuck and William Munroe. From that year until 1881 he simultaneously practiced law, served as an editor of the *American Law Review,* and contributed a number of scholarly articles to that publication. The culmination of his scholarly efforts came in 1880, when he delivered the Lowell Lectures at Boston University, the text of which became *The Common Law,* which he published in March 1881. In October of that year President Charles Eliot of Harvard offered him a professorship on the Harvard Law faculty, and after a protracted series of negotiations he accepted the offer in February 1882. By December he had left Harvard to take a judgeship on the Supreme Judicial Court of Massachusetts, and a new phase in his professional life began.[122]

Holmes' law practice with the Shattuck firm brought its own attachments, even though it was neither remarkable nor unusual. He represented merchants, fire insurance companies, landowners, banks, and industrial enterprises, spending about half of his time counseling clients and the rest in court. Later in his life he revealed that he had been "the penman for an agreement on half a sheet of foolscap by which the

Atchison and the Denver and the Rio Grande [railroads] ended a private war and divided an empire.''[123] But on that occasion Holmes was simply the draftsman, the Atchison, Topeka, and Santa Fe Railroad being Shattuck's client, and for the most part his clients were individuals and enterprises on a more moderate scale. His principal area of expertise seems to have been admiralty, a useful specialty because so many mercantile or commercial transactions in Boston involved maritime commerce. Holmes typically represented shipowners or masters as distinguished from ordinary seamen.

An account of one such case has survived, *New Orleans Mutual Insurance Co. v. Joseph Nickerson,* in which Holmes represented a shipmaster whose ship had stranded while carrying cotton from New Orleans to Liverpool, resulting in the loss of ship and cargo. The account provides one example of Holmes' relations with his fellow members of the Boston bar. Richard Henry Dana, the author of *Two Years Before the Mast* and a prominent Boston admiralty lawyer, represented the Louisiana-based insurers of the vessel. Dana was assisted by his son, who kept a journal of the proceedings. The insurers claimed that because Captain Nickerson had known of the ship's unseaworthy condition before the voyage began, he was therefore liable to them for cargo claims they had paid. Holmes responded that an undetectable boiler leak had caused the loss of the ship, and that consequently the insurers could not recover against Nickerson.

Holmes prevailed in the federal District Court, and the insurers appealed to the federal Circuit Court, where, following then current practice, Justice Nathan Clifford of the United States Supreme Court, sitting on circuit in Portland, Maine, heard the arguments.

> After I was through, [the younger Dana wrote in his account of the arguments,] Mr. Holmes began. He made a decided attempt at oratory. He never spoke in a conversational tone. His sentences were well balanced and telling. He endorsed and made himself responsible for his clients, at which I was surprised, as he should have known better as a point of legal practice, and the well known slippery character of the Nickersons, especially old Joe, made it rather absurd, but probably had its favorable effect for him on the judge. The best example of rhetoric was calling our witnesses "wreckers" while the only testimony in which the word was used was that some wreckers had stolen some cotton lying on the beach [after the ship foundered]. The witnesses he referred to were, in fact, a retired Cunard captain, . . . the present Port Warden of Halifax [Nova Scotia, where the ship had foundered], the telegraph operator, [and] the [local] justice of the peace.[124]

Earlier in the case Richard Henry Dana the elder had intimated that at the trial court Holmes had harassed the insurers' witnesses and attempted to force them to establish trivial details, such as the fact that they were a corporation licensed to do business in Louisiana. Holmes then engaged in a colloquy with the elder Dana:

> MR. DANA: I would like Mr. Holmes to clarify the meaning of his remarks.
> MR. HOLMES: I am stating my case.
> MR. DANA: I want to get light.

MR. HOLMES: You must allow for some feebleness of intelligence on my part.
MR. DANA: I shall not do that.

Holmes then went on to say that "I sincerely trust that I may never forget, until my brother on the other side bids me forget it, that I owe to him some of the first kind advice that I ever had when I came to the bar; and so I shall trust that the comments of the counsel on the other side will end as they began." He then continued:

> I want it distinctly understood with regard to any suggestions of intimidation
> of witnesses . . . that the counsel for the respondents take the full responsibility
> for their acts, and we believe that there has been nothing done in this case,
> from beginning to end, . . . that has not been perfectly legitimate and proper.[125]

Holmes won the appeal, and the case was eventually settled after the Danas had filed an appeal to the Supreme Court of the United States.[126]

Holmes' expertise in admiralty matters became the basis of an opportunity for a federal judgeship that surfaced in 1878, an episode that yields some additional evidence of the way he was perceived by his professional colleagues. The death of the circuit judge on the First Circuit had created a vacancy, and it appeared very likely that the present district judge, John Lowell, would be promoted to the Circuit Court, thereby creating a vacancy on the District Court. In November 1878, Holmes' old friend John Gray wrote Charles Beaman, a Harvard College classmate of Holmes, urging that Beaman intervene with the U.S. Justice Department in support of Holmes for the judgeship. Gray pointed out that

> The business of the court . . . will be mainly in admiralty, and of admiralty law
> Holmes' knowledge is singularly exact and profound. His appointment would
> be a very popular one with the bar. . . [He] would be a worthy successor of
> Judges Sprague and Lowell. It is a rare chance to get a man of first rate calibre
> for the position.

"There is no time to be lost," Gray concluded, "as Congress meets next week. Holmes' wounds and sufferings in the war ought to help his chances."[127]

At the same time J. B. Richardson, a Boston practitioner, wrote a letter to Charles Devens, the Attorney General of the United States, endorsing Holmes' qualifications and enclosing a letter signed by seven other Boston lawyers, including Gray. Meanwhile Godfrey Morse, another practitioner, wrote to President Rutherford Hayes himself, who would make the appointment, referring to Holmes as "an able, learned, upright and good man and lawyer who would honor the bench."[128] Holmes himself wrote Pollock four days after Morse's letter:

> I am just now in a mild excitement. . . . Our local Circuit Judge having died
> last summer, there has been talk of promoting the District Judge Lowell, and a
> good many of the bar have mentioned my name as Lowell's successor if he
> goes up. The place is not desirable for the money, for the salary is only $4000.
> But it would enable me to work in the way I want to and so I should like it—
> although it would cost me a severe pang to leave my partners. . . . But the way
> the bar here have spoken about me has given me much pleasure, and I can't

help feeling nervous about the result until the thing is settled, although if I were appointed I should hardly know whether to be glad or sorry.[129]

One sentence in the letter is particularly revealing, that Holmes would have been attracted to a judgeship because "it would enable me to work in the way I want to." It suggests that he did not find law practice entirely congenial to his intellectual ambitions, and at the same time did not believe that a career as an editor and scholar would be sufficiently remunerative to engage in independent of practice. At thirty-seven he had already concluded that judging would offer an opportunity to do the sort of legal work that particularly suited him. But this judgeship was not to be, for reasons that remind one of the fortuitous nature of judicial appointments. A decision was made to promote Judge Lowell to the Circuit vacancy, and after one potential nominee turned down the position, Holmes' name came to President Hayes' attention. Hayes was attracted by Holmes' war record, and was inclined to nominate him. At that point Senator George Frisbie Hoar, no admirer of Holmes,[130] sought an audience with the President along with Charles Devens, the Attorney General. In his autobiography Hoar described the meeting:

[A] very strong recommendation of Mr. Oliver Wendell Holmes, Jr. . . . had been received by the President. He felt a good deal of interest in Holmes. I think they had both been wounded in the same battle. But, at any rate, they were comrades. The President then said: "I rather think Holmes is the man." I then gave him my opinion of Mr. Nelson [Thomas L. Nelson, a lawyer from Worcester, who had been an associate of Hoar's], and the President said to Devens: "Do you agree, Mr. Attorney General?" Devens said: "I do." And the President said: "Then Nelson be it."[131]

Thus not all of Holmes' professional attachments rebounded to his advantage. His judicial ambitions unfulfilled, he returned to law practice and scholarship, to write *The Common Law,* to accept an offer from Harvard Law School, and to leave that institution after less than a year for a judgeship. The years between the two judgeship possibilities for Holmes—the one in 1878 that never materialized and the one in 1882 that changed the course of his life—were assuredly the most productive and arguably the most significant in his scholarly career. In those years he increasingly withdrew from friends, companions, and attachments into what he would later call "the secret isolated joy of the thinker."[132]

CHAPTER FOUR

Coming to Maturity:
Early Legal Scholarship

~

IN 1876 Holmes wrote a letter to Emerson that captured his scholarly mission
between 1865 and the early 1880s. He said in the letter that "I have learned,
after a laborious and somewhat painful period of probation, that the law opens a
way to philosophy as well as anything else."[1] Just as the years between 1864 and
1882 were momentous in the personal and professional spheres of Holmes' life, they
were momentous in his development as a legal scholar. During that period Holmes,
after considerable effort and some false starts, developed an approach to scholarship
in which legal history, philosophy, and discussion of contemporary issues of policy
were integrated in an original and distinctive fashion, an integration that can be seen
to be the principal basis of *The Common Law*'s scholarly eminence. It was also
during that period that Holmes finally succeeded in applying to the field of law the
substantive and methodological concerns that had attracted him in his undergraduate
essays, and thereby demonstrated to himself as well as to others that the law was
capable of extended interpretive treatment.

The pursuit of scholarship was not simply a device through which Holmes, as
he came to maturity, sought to reassure himself that he had chosen the right profession. It was the professional center of his life during his late twenties and thirties.
After passing the Massachusetts bar in 1867 Holmes was busy with the daily practice
of law for the next fourteen years. But in that period the amount of time he spent
on legal scholarship rivaled and perhaps outdistanced the amount of time he devoted
to his law practice. His scholarly efforts included omnivorous reading in law, history,
and philosophy, preparing the twelfth edition of James Kent's *Commentaries on
American Law,* editing the *American Law Review,* and digesting English and American cases for that periodical. When Holmes was chosen to deliver the Lowell Lectures at Boston University in 1880, the result of which was *The Common Law,* that
opportunity was a stroke of good fortune that launched his career. But the opportunity
was hardly accidental. It was the culmination of a series of activities that all came
together in the creation of an original and comprehensive book.

With *The Common Law* in place, it is tempting to look back at the years that
preceded it and see echoes or hints of the distinctive perspective and arresting style
which marked that book. But the intellectual history of Holmes' early years is much
less neatly encapsulated. In the first place, his early efforts at scholarship involved
the sorts of methodological and philosophical fits and starts common to a scholarly

perspective in its early stages. Moreover, Holmes' early work was to an important extent derivative of the work of others, but the derivative aspects of his early scholarship are not readily discerned, because Holmes was loath to acknowledge influences on and antecedents of his work, and fiercely protective of contributions he regarded as original to him, even when their originality was perhaps cloudier than he claimed. Finally, the great interest Holmes' career as a judge has had for commentators has resulted in a tendency for persons coming into contact with his early work to see it as a prolegomenon to his later perspectives as a scholar and a judge, despite its being worthy of independent interest and at the same time not fully consistent with his later views.

The account of Holmes' early work offered in this chapter seeks to emphasize the degree to which his methodological and substantive orientation evolved over time. Holmes did not reveal, in his initial scholarly efforts, distinctively original views: he either adopted or reacted against existing commentary. In his search to make an original mark as a scholar he became attracted to certain intellectual approaches and concepts, such as the idea of formulating an analytical classification scheme for legal subjects based on the concept of a legal ''duty,'' that he subsequently abandoned. His development of an original and distinctive perspective came, essentially, by trial and error: through voracious reading, experimentation with various analytical schema, and an eventual fastening on what seemed to him to be elemental themes in the progression of legal subjects over time.

Implicitly, as he refined his scholarly perspective, Holmes adopted the epistemological priorities of his generation of late nineteenth-century intellectuals. He came to regard the study of history—or more particularly the study of history from an ''evolutionary'' perspective that emphasized the progressive changes in legal doctrine over time—as yielding the key to a ''scientific'' or ''philosophical'' investigation of legal subjects. He assumed, with his contemporaries, that history and ''science'' went hand in hand, and that a ''scientific'' classification of fields of law was desirable. He also assumed that ''scientific'' classifications of legal subjects had discernible policy implications, for such classifications revealed the policy grounds on which legal decisions had been made, and those grounds could be subjected to contemporary scrutiny. He saw no conflict in using history to derive contemporary policy. Even though he abandoned the idea of universal analytical criteria for structuring legal subjects, he did not abandon the belief that he could criticize legal doctrines from the perspective of their contemporary efficacy. In holding each of these assumptions he was representative of a generation of scholars who sought to derive secular organizing principles of knowledge through the association of ''empirical'' historical inquiry with ''scientific'' classification.

~

Markets and opportunities have a good deal to do with the production of scholarly work, and in Holmes' case his opportunity came with the launching of the *American Law Review* by John Ropes and John Gray in 1867. Ropes and Gray had both graduated from Harvard College, and John Ropes' brother Henry, as well as Gray, had served in the Civil War, Henry Ropes in the Twentieth Regiment. John Ropes and Gray had conceived the *American Law Review* as catering principally to practicing lawyers, but at the same time they had an ongoing interest in legal scholarship. The *Review*'s early volumes followed a prescribed format, consisting of several short scholarly articles; digests of English cases and of decisions of the Supreme Court of the United States, the federal district court for the district of Massachusetts, and selected state courts; short book reviews of legal treatises and other books on law, termed "notices"; and summaries of "events," compiled on a state-by-state basis, and sometimes including Congressional deliberations. The *Review* also published miscellanea, such as lists of federal and state judges and the dates of their appointments, deaths of prominent lawyers and judges, judicial salaries, anecdotes, and lists of new law books published in England and America. In following this format, the *Review* was not strikingly different from other law periodicals at the time, such as the *Law Digest* or the *American Law Register,* but it clearly was intended as a journal with a national audience and a somewhat more "highbrow" tone.[2]

Because of its extensive coverage of law books, the *Review* was interested in securing reviewers, and in the periodical's early years its compensation to reviewers for "notices" appeared to consist of a complimentary copy of the book under review. That at least was the arrangement made between the editors and Holmes in November 1866 when he was asked to review the sixth American edition of Henry Roscoe's *Digest of the Law of Evidence in Criminal Cases.*[3] He was also asked, at the same time, to review the sixth American edition of Alfred Swain Taylor's *Manual of Medical Jurisprudence,*[4] apparently under the same compensation arrangement. With those "notices" Holmes' career as a legal scholar was launched.

Neither of Holmes' reviews was particularly startling, and neither showed much evidence of original thought. In the Roscoe review he demonstrated his interest in the methodology of natural science, which had been an enthusiasm of his since college,[5] noting that "[t]he method of . . . arrangement" in Roscoe's treatise was to first state "general principles," and then proceed to a treatment of "the different species in detail," not unlike "that which is pursued in treatises on Natural History." He also contrasted the use of evidence in a criminal trial in the Anglo-American system with "the corresponding process before the courts of Continental Europe," pointing out that in the latter system "any evidence is admitted which will enable trained experts to furnish a theory" of guilt or innocence, whereas in the English and American courts "rules concerning the admission of evidence are determined, in the long run, by the average intelligence of juries."[6] This contrast, as Mark Howe has shown, was the same one that had been made by James Fitzjames Stephen in his *General View of the Criminal Law in England,*[7] which Holmes had consulted at the same time he was preparing the review of Roscoe.[8]

In the Taylor review Holmes complained about the effort to combine the subjects of two quite different professions in one volume. "We may express a doubt," he wrote, "whether doctors would regard a work on 'medical jurisprudence' as a sufficient hand-book of science; and we are very confident that few lawyers would feel strongly bound by its opinions on a point of law." A lawyer, in Holmes' view, "wants to know under what circumstances the courts have admitted [a medical] defense, [such as insanity,] in a criminal action." He could far better find that information, Holmes felt, in a note to an insanity case or a treatise on criminal law.[9]

While these comments were surely accurate as applied to the Taylor treatise, they were ones any legally trained reveiwer could have made.

Holmes reviewed one other book in the first volume of the *American Law Review*, Judge Isaac Redfield's ninth edition of Joseph Story's treatise, *Commentaries on Equity Jurisprudence*. Two features of the review are of interest. First, in the last paragraph of the review Holmes attempted to characterize the history of the subject of equity in the following fashion:

> The ecclesiastical conception of a right supplementary to the law, and at times transcending it, was an embryo of vague and doubtful figure. By an organic necessity, however, it has slowly developed into a stable body of principles. Centuries have firmly knit its tissues, and have shaped its exact contours. Many portions of its structure have even ossified so far as to have united with the rigid skeleton of legal doctrines. The rest may do so in time.[10]

The theory of doctrinal development advanced in this paragraph, complete with metaphors from natural history, strikingly resembles that advanced by Henry Maine in his book *Ancient Law*, which Holmes had read while at Harvard Law School.[11] Maine's evolutionary theory of legal change, in which doctrines came into being for contextual reasons, remained in place, and ultimately "ossified," producing "a stable body of principles," was one that Holmes was to adopt in modified form in *The Common Law*. But while Holmes reread Maine in 1868[12] and was described in 1875 by Henry Adams as "one of [Maine's] warmest admirers,"[13] he wrote Pollock in 1888 that "I do not think [Maine] will leave much mark on the actual structure of jurisprudence."[14] Holmes' public treatment of Maine was representative of his treatment of works of scholarship that influenced him in the early stages of his career. He tended to minimize the impact of those contributions, especially on his own work, and at the same time to emphasize the originality of his scholarly efforts.

Holmes continued to review books for the *American Law Review* after its initial volume, but he took on additional responsibilities for that periodical as well, and the emphasis of his reviews reflected that fact. Beginning with the April 1868 issue, Holmes prepared the *Review*'s digests of state reports for all issues through October 1869. In addition he prepared the Digest of English Law Reports for the October 1868 and October 1869 issues, and the Digest of the Decisions of the Supreme Court of the United States for the January 1869 issue.[15] These digests required him to read the contents of state court and English reporters, and he reviewed several such reports.[16] He also wrote a long, almost exclusively factual account of the impeachment proceedings against President Andrew Johnson in the April 1868 and July 1868 issues.[17] Given this attention to other features of the *Review*, his notices of treatises decreased, with only two appearing between January 1868 and October 1869. Of these one is of interest as giving evidence of a continued preoccupation with "scientific" schemes for classifying legal subjects that marked his early efforts at scholarship. In a review of Judah Benjamin's *Treatise on the Law of Sale of Personal Property* Holmes said that

> [I]t is worthy of notice that [an] earlier writer has considered almost all the law peculiar to the contract of sale. Were the law philosophically arranged, there

would be little to be added to what he has said. As it is, a book of reference on any subdivision of the law, in order to be satisfactory, must set forth at length, not only the principles constituting the specific difference of the subject-matter, but also those common to it and to many other classes of the same genus.[18]

By "philosophical" and "scientific" arrangements Holmes meant the same thing: classifications of legal subjects based on the methodology of natural science, with "general principles" serving as the equivalent of "genus" and the applications of those principles to specific legal issues serving as the equivalent of "classes" and "species." One of Holmes' first efforts, when he came to write his own scholarly articles, was to derive some "philosophical" arrangements of legal subjects.

In June 1870, Holmes was named co-editor of the *American Law Review* with Arthur Sedgwick, effective with the October 1870 issue, which began the *Review*'s fifth volume. The appointment ushered in a new stage in his scholarly career, that of author as distinguished from reviewer. The new role was one for which Holmes was well prepared. His extensive reading and other scholarly activities in the late 1860s and early 1870s fully justified the observations by contemporaries that he "knows more law than anyone in Boston of our time, and works harder at it than anyone,"[19] that his peers "had never known of anyone in the law who studied anything like as hard,"[20] and that Holmes had "a power of work."[21] His efforts for the *Review* had given him the opportunity to read English and state decisions with an assiduousness typically confined to those who are digesting sources for print. In addition, after November 1869 he edited the twelfth edition of Kent, which required him to read and annotate the text of Kent's four-volume treatise, bringing Kent's treatment in line with modern cases. When one adds to these labors Holmes' regular duties in law practice at the office of Chandler, Shattuck, and Thayer, his immersion in the law seems truly heroic.

It was also clear from the orientation of Holmes' work that he was not content to focus simply on the details of his practice. Knowledge of the contents of the Massachusetts Reports or English decisions might have been some use to him as a practitioner, but the same could hardly have been said for a perusal of the Wisconsin or Nevada or Michigan Reports. The digests Holmes prepared for the *Review* no doubt increased his mastery of his field, but it was not the kind of mastery a practitioner could put to ready use. Yet Holmes increased his commitments to the *Review* in his early years in practice, moving from notices to digests and finally to articles. At the same time he agreed to take on an edition of Kent when that labor, while it might increase his scholarly reputation, could not be expected to have much direct benefit to his skills as a practitioner.

In fact Holmes did not turn down any scholarly projects during his early years in practice, whether they involved working on Kent, taking over the editorship of the *Review,* or preparing articles. When conflict developed between those pursuits and his law practice, it was the latter that gave way. In 1870, after accepting the editorship of the *Review* and the twelfth edition of Kent, Holmes left Chandler, Shattuck, and Thayer to go into practice with his brother Ned, who had recently been admitted to the bar. This could hardly have been a move calculated to bring him more legal business or increase his prestige as a practitioner. It seems, on the contrary, one calculated to free him from office demands that might infringe on his scholarly pursuits.

~

The appearance of Holmes' first scholarship in 1870 can thus be seen as part of a progression of intellectual emphasis that had begun as early as college. Moreover, one can observe evidence, in Holmes' first scholarly efforts, that he regarded scholarship as an opportunity to address concerns that had surfaced in his reading in law school and the years immediately following. His first article, "Codes, and the Arrangement of the Law,"[22] illustrated his interest in achieving a "philosophical" classification scheme for law in light of the breakdown of the writ system of procedure that had served as the basis for doctrinal organization until the early nineteenth century.

Holmes' "Codes" essay drew on the contributions of two British jurists, Jeremy Bentham and John Austin.[23] Bentham had called for a reform of the English common law system and the creation of codes of legal subjects, and Austin had attempted to define the scope of "legal" relationships and to begin a classification of legal subjects. Both Bentham and Austin were interested in identifying the essential characteristics of a legal system and articulating its internal structure. Holmes, who had read Bentham and Austin as a law student and reread Austin's *The Province of Jurisprudence Determined* from 1868 through 1870,[24] shared those interests. He believed that the degeneration of the writ system of pleading into an arbitrary collection of pleadings,[25] the confusion created by an amalgamation of legal and moral issues,[26] and the promise of scientific methodologies as techniques for systematizing branches of knowledge had combined to create an opportunity for rearranging the subject of law.

In his "Codes" article Holmes had two goals. One was to emphasize his conviction that legal subjects should be classified philosophically, so as to achieve comprehensiveness and avoid the reiteration of overlapping subjects currently present in the treatise literature. He emphasized that a code, "being executed at the expense of government and not at the risk of the writer, and the whole work being under the control of one head . . . will make a philosophically arranged *corpus juris* possible."[27] He added that "if such a code were achieved, its component treatises would not have to be loaded with matter belonging elsewhere." Thus "a well-arranged body of the law would not only train the mind of the student to a sound legal habit of thought," it would, by eliminating the necessity of resorting to discrete treatises with overlapping content, "remove obstacles from [the] path" of persons seeking to learn legal subjects.[28]

Holmes was, however, skeptical that a code could deal adequately with the problem of "new cases . . . which will elude the most carefully constructed formula." Under the common law, new cases were dealt with by "a series of successive approximations— . . . a continual reconciliation," so that judges "decide . . . the case first and determine . . . the principle afterwards." The rigidity of a code posed problems for this accommodation process. "If the code is truly law," Holmes argued, "the court is confined to a verbal construction of the rule as expressed, and must decide the case wrong." On the other hand, if the court "may take into account that the code is only intended to declare the judicial rule, and has done so defectively, and may then go on and supply the defect,'' a code was "not law, but a mere text-book recommended by the government as containing all at present known on the subject.''[29]

Holmes thus stopped short of advocating codification. He was more interested in an "arrangement" of legal subjects that was "philosophical" in nature. The analytical key to such an arrangement, he believed, was a classification of legal subjects "based on *duties* and not on *rights*.''[30] In Holmes' view "[d]uties precede rights logically and chronologically'': even those laws that "in form create a right directly, in fact either tacitly impose a duty on the rest of the world, as, in the case of patents, to abstain from selling the patented article, or confer an immunity from a duty previously or generally imposed, like taxation.''[31] Thus Holmes sought to advance a classification of legal subjects based on different types of duties: "duties of sovereign powers to each other'' (international law); "duties without corresponding rights, or duties to the sovereign'' (taxation, criminal law); "duties from all the world to all the world'' (civil tort actions, such as "assault and battery, libel, slander, false imprisonment, and the like''); and "duties of all the world to persons in certain particular positions or relations'' (property ownership).[32]

In the last category of duties Holmes was inclined to place duties arising out of contract. He argued that since interference by third parties with contractual relations was generally actionable, parties to a contract could be said to be owed a duty by the rest of the world not to interfere with the contract's terms, and were thus like property owners. But Holmes conceded that "in contracts . . . the duty of the party obliged is all in all, and that of third persons is so rarely called in question, that it is hardly supposed to exist.'' He thus thought it "a fair question . . . whether contracts should not be kept for a fifth division,'' duties "of persons in particular relations.''[33]

While Holmes' classification system was ingenious, his general purpose in formulating it was not made clear in his "Codes" essay. Some clues interspersed throughout the essay, however, make possible a reconstruction of that purpose. Before setting forth his categories of duty Holmes had made an observation on the nature of law. Citing John Austin's definition of law as "a command . . . which obliges . . . to acts or forbearances of a class,''[34] he criticized the definition as insufficiently mindful of the enforcement dimension of commands. While the custom of wearing evening dress to dinner parties in London would technically not be a "law" under Austin's definition, it was enforced in the sense that violators were not "asked to similar entertainments.'' While "the only concern" of lawyers was "such rules as the courts enforce,'' and a court might well not enforce the evening dress custom, it was hard to say that in "common discourse" it did not amount to a "command.''[35]

Holmes' point was that attention to the enforcement dimension of legal rules focused one on their correlative character. Legal rules created duties only when their nonperformance resulted in official sanctions. Thus, in an action to determine possession, the law created a duty on the part of all the world to respect the rights of the possessor, but only because once possession had been determined the possessor could use "the officers of the law" to enforce his or her rights. As Holmes put it, "[a] duty, strictly so called, is only created by commands which may be broken at the expense of incurring a penalty."[36] This meant that certain customs that were unenforceable in the courts did not, strictly speaking, amount to duties. Holmes felt that it would be useful to distinguish between duties and the "sanctions . . . to which they are attached." This distinction would clarify the meaning of acts such as those when the law "seizes and sells the defendant's goods to satisfy [a] judgment" against him. Those acts were "quasi duties . . . sanctioned by liability to process for contempt."[37]

Holmes' first extended piece of legal scholarship was thus motivated by two concerns. One was to refine Austin's definition of law, and to narrow the scope of "the province of jurisprudence," by distinguishing between enforceable and unenforceable "commands." As he put it, "[r]ules not enforced by [the courts, with their attendant enforcement officials], although equally imperative, are the study of no profession" (the evening dress custom was an example). The other was to reach a clearer classification of types of legal relationships by restating those relationships in terms of duties and by distinguishing abstract "legal" duties from practical "enforcement" duties, or sanctions.

In a book notice in the *American Law Review* in 1872 Holmes restated his views in a more explicit fashion. The notice was of Frederick Pollock's article, "Law and Command," in the April 1872 issue of the *Law Magazine and Review*.[38] Always concerned to preserve the originality of his own views, Holmes was prompted by Pollock's essay to put into print "opinions which were expressed more at length in the beginning of a course of lectures on jurisprudence delivered at Harvard College while [Pollock's] article was going through the press."[39] The operative phrase in that comment was the last: Holmes wanted readers to know that he had formulated the ideas before reading them in Pollock. He had delivered the lectures in April and May of 1872, and had written them in the fall of 1871 and the early spring of 1872.[40] In the book notice Holmes said that Pollock's "results more or less coincide[d]" with his own.

Holmes first reiterated his criticism of Austin's failure to define law with sufficient precision, noting that to say that law was the command of the sovereign begged questions. He then stressed the enforcement dimensions of law, concluding that "it was doubted whether law . . . possessed any other common attribute than of being enforced by the procedure of the courts, and therefore of practical importance to lawyers."[41]

This was little more than a more pointed statement of views Holmes had expressed in his "Codes" essay. But then he offered a further refinement of his "enforcement" point:

It must be remembered . . . that in a civilized state it is not the will of the sovereign that makes lawyers' law, even when that is its source, but what a body of subjects, namely the judges, by whom it is enforced, *say* is his will. The judges have other motives for decision, outside their own arbitrary will, beside the commands of their sovereign. And whether those other motives are, or are not, equally compulsory, is immaterial, if they are sufficiently likely to prevail to afford a ground for prediction. The only question for the lawyer is, how will the judges act? Any motive for their action, be it constitution, statute, custom, or precedent, which can be relied upon as likely in the generality of cases to prevail, is worthy of consideration as one of the sources of law.[42]

In this passage the enforcement dimension of law seems to have obliterated any abstract sovereignty dimension, or perhaps sovereignty has been transferred to the enforcing powers, the judges. Moreover, "law" has been reduced to those sources that judges could expect to rely on in their decisions; that is, ones on which lawyers could predict how judges might act.[43] This comes close to suggesting, as Holmes later did, that "the prophecies of what the courts will do in fact, and nothing more pretentious, are what I mean by the law."[44]

The idea of law as predictions of how its enforcing officials would act marked a progression from Holmes' views in "Codes and Arrangements of the Law." In that essay he was content to accept Austin's definition of law as a working hypothesis, saying that "as a definition of what lawyers call law" it was "doubtless accurate enough." In the 1872 book notice he had shifted attention so fully to the enforcement dimension, and to the motives of judges, as to reduce Austin's definition to a meaningless abstraction. Moreover, Holmes disassociated himself in the book notice from Austin's view that a legal duty existed if there was a penalty for disobeying the sovereign's command. "A legal duty," Holmes argued, "cannot be said to exist if the law intends to allow the person supposed to be subject to it to an option at a certain price." "A protective tariff on iron," he pointed out, "does not create a duty to bring it into the country."[45] Shippers had the option of not bringing iron in.

The last example led Holmes to suggest that Austin had mistakenly believed that civil liability implied culpability. Austin "looked at the law too much as a criminal lawyer," Holmes thought: civil liability merely suggested that the defendant had chosen to pay rather than to desist from acting. The "object of the law," he maintained, was to give the defendant the option "to accomplish an external result." Wilfulness or negligence was made the basis of a civil action only in certain cases, when "the law . . . was secure of what it desires in the absence of wilfulness or negligence."[46] Holmes pointed out that in some instances civil liability was based on the principle that persons converting other persons' property or engaging in extrahazardous activities did so at their peril. Such persons were not "culpable" even though they were liable.

In the 1872 book notice we see germs of three jurisprudential propositions that were central to Holmes' mature scholarly views. The first was a positivistic conception of law as the decisions of bodies given power to enforce its rules, principally courts. That conception was not as uncompromisingly positivistic as it might first appear, for Holmes had excluded from the denomination of "laws" motives influencing those decisions that were based solely on the idiosyncratic reactions of the decisionmakers. In that sense Holmes was not fully equating law with judicial bias.

The second proposition was that many legal rules were not absolute commands, imposing duties, but were simply social judgments that certain activities ought to pay their own way in society. This suggested that not only was the definition of law as the command of a sovereign incomplete, the reach of law was narrower than one might suspect. Legal rules often gave an option of nonconformance on the payment of damages. This meant that the crucial step in the derivation of legal rules was some kind of public consensus as to which activities could be engaged in free of a "damage tax" and which could not. Here Holmes was anticipating his later expression of law being determined not by logic but by "the felt necessities of the times."

The last proposition was another central theme of Holmes' later scholarship, the distinction between internal and external standards of conduct, or, put another way, between subjective and objective theories of liability. At the time he wrote the 1872 book notice he had only recently arrived at the view that culpability was not a necessary prerequisite of liability, having written a year earlier that "a culpable state of mind is an element in most wrongs" and including negligence as well as wilfulness as examples of states of culpability. But by 1872 he had come to realize that the question in most cases, including criminal cases, was whether the defendant's conduct had subjected him or her to a penalty, not whether he or she held a "culpable state of mind." While culpability remained an apparent ingredient of those crimes, and also of civil actions in which the possession of an "intent" was part of the definition of the proscribed conduct, culpability was determined by a search for acts from which that intent could be inferred. It was thus arguable, Holmes came to believe, that the law was exclusively concerned with external and objective standards of liability. The development of this argument was one of his major purposes in *The Common Law*.

The 1872 book notice was thus an important, if attenuated, statement of themes that Holmes was to develop further in his mature scholarship. In two articles in the *American Law Review*, beginning in 1872, he sought to flesh out the details of the analytical classification of legal subjects based on "duties" that he had outlined in the "Codes" essay.[47]

It is interesting to speculate about the origins of Holmes' attraction to "duty" as an analytic concept. He gave no explanation for his initial belief in the centrality of "duty," and, when he subsequently abandoned the term, gave no explanation for his conclusion that it was now, as he put it, "open to objection."[48] Given this paucity of information, one can only advance some tentative suggestions. An initial suggestion might focus on the skepticism intellectuals of Holmes' generation held toward the concept of "rights." They found in that term two unfortunate associations: universal principles transcending time, which smacked of religion-based explanations for the universe; and power, within a society, being lodged somewhere other than with those charged with making that society's official decisions. To speak of persons having legal "rights" appeared to conjure up one or another of those associations. Holmes' contemporaries, notwithstanding their belief in extremely limited governmental involvement in the affairs of society, were firmly convinced that sovereign power, rather than natural rights or religious principles, dominated human affairs.

In this sense the idea of "duty," emphasizing social obligations imposed on individuals, may have appeared to be a more appealing concept to Holmes than the idea of "right." In addition, the term may have had a personal resonance. As early as his undergraduate years, and throughout his Civil War correspondence, Holmes had employed the term "duty" to describe his response to experience. He had thought it his duty to join the war effort; he had characterized his role as a soldier as that of living up to a prescribed code of duties; in his retrospective characterization of his wound at Ball's Bluff he had spoken of thinking about dying having done his duty "up to the hub"; when he resolved to resign rather than to reenlist for another three-year term he gave as one of his reasons that "I didn't believe any longer in this being a duty"; when he justified this decision in a subsequent letter to his mother he spoke of "the duty of fighting [having] ceased for me . . . because I have with much suffering of mind and body *earned* the right . . . to decide for myself how I can best do my duty."[49]

Duty, then, had been a concept that for Holmes seemed to capture the sorts of social obligations required of a scion of the Brahmin class, or a young man imbued with the ethic of chivalry, or a professional soldier. In contrast he had spoken of a "right," in his Civil War correspondence, as something one "earned" by doing one's duty. In that sense, in the worlds of Holmes' early manhood, duties logically preceded rights; he believed that in the world of jurisprudence, duties took similar precedence. Having enthusiastically formulated his conception of duty, and being prepared to develop it in his scholarship, Holmes was disconcerted to find that others had previously advanced it. For example, Shadworth Hodgson's *Theory of Practice*, which Holmes read sometime after he had finished the "Codes" article,[50] contained this passage:

> There is no more philosophical suggestion in Auguste Comte's writings than that in which he urges, that law should be approached and its object-matter arranged from the point of view of duties, and not from that of rights. . . .
> Names of rights are "second intentions"; the "first intentions" of which are the duties into which they are analyzable. To take rights and not the corresponding duties as the ultimate phenomena of law, is to stop short of a complete analysis.[51]

Nonetheless Holmes resolved to continue his investigation "as to how far what is commonly called law imposes what are properly called duties." He believed this effort was consistent with the goal of achieving a classification system that would "make the law *knowable*." The system that "best accomplishes that purpose," he suggested, was one "which proceeds from the most general conception to the most specific proposition or exception in the order of logical subordination." Since duties "logically preceded rights," they were a more "general conception," and Holmes assumed that a detailed investigation of types of duties might produce a useful system of classification.[52]

A sense of the framework of Holmes' approach can be gleaned by reproducing the "ground plan" for classification that he presented in his "Privity" article. That plan consisted of a table of the "primary divisions" in his organizational scheme, which featured duties, and the "subdivisions," which featured conventional legal subjects. Having made two general categories of duties, "duties of all the world," and "duties of persons in particular situations or relations," Holmes then subdivided each category into three types of duties, those "to the sovereign," those "to all the world," and those "to persons in particular situations or relations." He then included, within these subcategories, conventional legal subjects. Hence the law of prize and criminal law were included in duties owed by all the world to the sovereign; torts were included in duties owed by all the world to all the world; corporations, domestic relations, actions based on possession and ownership, and contracts were included in duties owed by all the world to persons in particular situations and relationships. In the other subcategory, duties owed by persons in particular situations or relations to the sovereign included eminent domain actions and property taxes; duties owed by those persons to all the world included nuisance actions; duties owed by those persons to other persons in particular situations included landlord and tenant actions, master and servant, and cases involving contracting parties.[53]

One effort of Holmes' early scholarship was thus to supply supplementary analytical principles that might help produce a clearer classification of legal subjects within the duty-based framework. An example was his article on privity, which sought to examine the problem created for duty-based classification systems by the practice of succession. Another example was his early work on torts, a subject Holmes had previously found inappropriate for legal scholarship because it represented an aggregate of analytically dissimilar subjects, such as trespass, libel and slander, and negligence.[54] In an 1873 essay in the *American Law Review* he said that "the worst objection to the title Torts is that it puts the cart before the horse, that legal liabilities are arranged with reference to the forms of action allowed by the common law for infringing them."[55] But on reflection, he concluded, "an enumeration of the actions which have been successful, and of those which have failed, defines the extent of the primary duties imposed by the law."[56]

By enumerating successful tort actions and analyzing them Holmes was able to arrive at a classifying principle: the culpability of the defendant. "[T]he legal liabilities defined by a book on torts," he argued, "are divisible into those in which culpability is an element and those in which it is not," and the "latter class may be subdivided into the cases where the facts which fix the liability are definitely ascertained, and those where the boundary line is in course of ascertainment, or from motives of policy is kept purposely indefinite."[57] In short, there appeared to be three types of torts cases, those in which culpability was an element of the action, those in which culpability was clearly not an element of the action (only factual proof of an injury and the tracing of that injury to the conduct of a defendant being required), and those in which culpability was not an element of the action, but actionability rested on a showing of particular facts or on policy grounds.

The tables Holmes added to his essays on privity and torts revealed that he intended them as extensions and refinements of the duty-based classification system he introduced in the "Codes" essay. But his method of investigating the topics of the essays ultimately proved incompatible with the duty-based system itself. In the "Privity" essay Holmes, confronting a legal doctrine inconsistent with the strict meaning of a duty-based system, found that the doctrine had not originated logically, but historically.

There were instances, for example, where "the law treats an individual as a party to a transaction in which he had no share in fact," such as the liability of masters for the torts of their servants or the "universal succession of the husband to the rights of the wife."[58] These examples could not be explained logically, as in the explanation that the master had somehow been careless in hiring the servant in the first place. Their explanation was supplied by the fact that in the Roman law, from which early English law drew many of its doctrines, servants and wives were treated as the slaves of masters and husbands, and thus inseparable from their persons. "When the notion had become familiar that one man could acquire rights, or be subjected to obligations by another who sustained his persona as part of the familia—the persona of the *paterfamilias* being the aggregate of the family rights and duties," Holmes argued, "it did not need a great stretch to extend the power of representation to a freeman."[59] Hence in the modern law the treatment of master and servant as identical entities was limited to the scope of the master-servant relation; outside it the parties were treated as separate persons. This treatment was purely a historical accident.

Similarly, in his essay on torts, by concluding that "an enumeration of the actions which have been successful, and of those which have failed, defines the extent of the primary duties imposed by the law," Holmes was conceding the difficulty of erecting a duty-based system on logical abstractions. Indeed he offered an account of the "growth of the law" that seemed to have little to do with logic:

> Two widely different cases suggest a general distinction, which is a clear one when stated broadly. But as new cases cluster around the opposite poles, and begin to approach each other, the distinction becomes more difficult to trace; the determinations are made one way or the other on a very slight preponderance of feeling, rather than articulate reason; and at last a mathematical line is arrived at by the contact of contrary decisions, which is so far arbitrary that it might have equally well have been drawn a little further to the one side or to the other. The distinction between the groups, however, is philosophical, and it is better to have a line drawn somewhere in the penumbra between darkness and light, than to remain in uncertainty.[60]

This passage shows the tension in Holmes' early essays between a desire for a "philosophical" arrangement of legal subjects and the recognition that doctrinal development in the law was a product of history and of the exigencies of cases. Holmes had begun his "Codes" essay by saying that "it is the merit of the common law that it decides the case first and determines the principle afterwards," and in the passage he was suggesting that principles and distinctions were a product of the fact situations in which they were announced. But at the same time the desire to avoid "uncertainty" in the law resulted in principles, in their application, hardening into rigid rules and arbitrary lines, which had ceased to provide adequate explanations of all the cases in which they were employed. The process suggested that logical classifications of legal subjects were not always responsive to the circumstances of cases, had their origins in other circumstances, and were sometimes purely arbitrary. This view of logical classifications was not calculated to inspire much confidence in them. But at the same time Holmes adhered to his view that even arbitrary classifications were valuable because they were "philosophical." He was subsequently to abandon that view.

～

Holmes contributed one additional piece of scholarship during this period of his career, his twelfth edition of Kent's *Commentaries*. The venture was in some respects an uncharacteristic project for Holmes to undertake, since his role was to be that of an editor, as distinguished from an original scholar, and since the purpose of the work was simply to update an established treatise by bringing it into accord with common law cases decided since its last edition, not to alter its structure or emphasis. Even on those occasions where the drift of current doctrine ran counter to propositions Kent had advanced in earlier editions, Holmes interpreted his role as that of one who was merely presenting the new cases rather than suggesting that Kent's conceptual organization had been unsound. The role caused a certain amount of strain for Holmes, who referred to himself as Kent's "valet" and said that as a consequence he had "to keep a civil tongue in my head" even though he had concluded that Kent had "no general ideas, except wrong ones."[61]

Holmes came to the Kent project in a fashion that suggests he would not have chosen to undertake it. In the late 1860s James Kent, Kent's grandson, resolved to prepare a twelfth edition of the *Commentaries,* and approached James Bradley Thayer, then a partner with George Shattuck's firm, about preparing the edition. Thayer agreed to take on the editorship, but made it clear to Kent that he could not do it alone, and suggested Holmes as someone to help with the preparation. In November 1869 Thayer asked Holmes to try a sample annotation and to inform him as to the problems that existed and his proposed solutions. Holmes responded by proposing an ambitious, and for the time a revolutionary, edition in which a new series of notes would be fashioned for many topics and the annotations of all previous editors, save Kent himself, would be dropped. "I cannot but think that if time allows," Holmes wrote to Thayer, "it is desirable that the notes should be somewhat full on points which are the present fighting grounds of the law."[62] That format was eventually adopted, and Holmes produced a number of extensive notes on such topics as the history of property in land, vicarious liability, easements, covenants running with the land, and warranty in the law of sales.[63]

In his letter to Thayer summarizing his views on the Kent project Holmes indicated that "[t]he plan which I have laid out is to do the work thoroughly at the first going over" and then to fill in recent cases from "the late Digests" of state decisions. He expressed concern that he could not do a thorough job in the time anticipated, which was two years. "You know," he reminded Thayer, "that I have devoted all my afternoons and a large part of my mornings to the work for the last three weeks or more—and I have hardly been able to attain the necessary pace."[64] On the basis of Holmes' investigations Thayer resolved to bring him into the project as an associate editor, and informed James Kent to that effect. In his letter to Kent, Thayer promised to serve as principal editor, and indicated that his name and that of Holmes would appear in the preface, but that Kent's name would appear on the title page, and Kent would have "the right of passing finally on the work which we shall furnish." He asked Kent for "some grace" about the two-year deadline, mentioning that Holmes had "already found that the work is going to require pretty close application." He also made it clear to Kent that Holmes "will have the laboring oar in getting together the material & getting it into shape."[65]

When the twelfth edition of Kent's *Commentaries* eventually appeared, in December 1873, it was apparent that the arrangement outlined by Thayer in his letter to James Kent had not been followed. Both the title page and the preface bore the name of Holmes as the editor. In the preface Holmes acknowledged Thayer's contribution as being the person "upon whom has rested the whole responsibility for my work to the owners of the copyright,'' and having ''read all that I have written, and . . . given it the great benefit of his scholarly and intelligent criticism.''[66] He did not mention James Kent at all. The arrangement prompted James Kent to write an angry letter to Thayer, saying he was ''much provoked'' by the appearance of the twelfth edition, having ''wanted [Thayer's] *name*'' on the volumes and believing that Thayer ''should have had the reward'' of public recognition for his participation in the project.[67] When Thayer apparently gave a diffident reply, perhaps indicating that Holmes had in fact done all of the actual editing and annotating of the volumes, Kent contrasted his pique to Thayer's diffidence by writing, ''You are a saint; I am an ordinary mortal.''[68] Later Thayer was to say of his experience with Holmes in the Kent project that it demonstrated that Holmes was ''wanting sadly in the noblest region of human character—selfish, vain, thoughtless of others.''[69]

It is not clear why the initial arrangement proposed by Thayer to Kent in December 1869 had been modified in the interval between that date and the eventual appearance of Holmes' edition of Kent's *Commentaries* four years later, so that Holmes was identified as the sole editor, Thayer relegated to a liaison and critic, and James Kent not even mentioned. Kent's, and to some extent Thayer's, reactions to the appearance of the preface and title page seem somewhat surprising, since Thayer was identified by Holmes as having read ''all that I have written.''

The incident, while arguably trivial, is nonetheless revealing of Holmes' attitude toward his personal relationships in the years under consideration in this chapter. He was obviously indebted to Thayer for his participation in the Kent project in the first place: James Kent had approached Thayer, not him. On the other hand Thayer had brought Holmes into the project because Thayer was unwilling, given the demands of his practice, to undertake it alone, and before the project had even started Thayer had informed Kent that Holmes would ''have the laboring oar'' in the preparation of the twelfth edition. In July 1872, Holmes gave Thayer a progress report on the edition that revealed that Holmes had done all of the work on it up to that point, and that Thayer had not read any of his annotations. In that letter to Thayer, Holmes spoke of having completed several of ''my notes'' to the volumes, of having taken ''the time necessary for thorough work,'' of the ''considerable pecuniary sacrifice'' he had undergone to work on the volumes, and of the fact that he expected ''to go to press very shortly.''[70] The letter suggests that neither Holmes nor Thayer contemplated that Thayer would have anything to do with the preparation of the twelfth edition until Holmes had completed all of his editing and annotating. If Holmes and Thayer were to remain as ''joint editors,'' Thayer would be taking considerable credit for his initial role in launching the project.

The identification of Holmes as the sole editor of the twelfth edition, and Thayer as a reader of Holmes' manuscript, was thus a fair representation of the division of labor that had actually occurred. Nonetheless, Holmes' claiming entire credit for the volume is revealing of his consciousness at the time. He was fiercely ambitious for scholarly recognition and jealous of his scholarly contributions. He was not inclined to allow even Thayer, a fellow member of his law firm and a close acquaintance, to take vicarious credit for his original work. For Holmes the fact that he owed his opportunity to prepare the edition of Kent to Thayer was irrelevant: he had done the work, and he wanted sole credit for it. If he considered that it might have been appropriate for a junior lawyer to bestow credit on a senior colleague who had provided him with a scholarly opportunity and read the finished product, that consideration paled beside his desire to be recognized for his "pecuniary sacrifice" and his hard work. Any personal loyalty he might have felt to Thayer was subordinated to his scholarly ambition.

Some of Holmes' contemporaries, in addition to Kent and Thayer, expressed concern about Holmes' behavior in the episode. In 1874 John Norton Pomeroy wrote an enthusiastic review of the edition for *The Nation,* and a draft of his review was seen by Arthur Sedgwick, Holmes' former co-editor on *The American Law Review,* who was at that time on *The Nation*'s editorial board. Sedgwick apparently wrote Pomeroy that in his judgment the review should include some mention of Thayer's role in the project. Pomeroy responded by stating that Holmes' preface had "very fully acknowledged" Thayer, and that in fact Holmes had been retained by Thayer to do the work on the edition. Any mention of Thayer, Pomeroy felt, would amount to "some general sort of puff." Nonetheless Sedgwick apparently insisted, because Pomeroy's eventual review mentioned Thayer's contribution.[71]

Sedgwick's reaction to Pomeroy's review is interesting because Sedgwick knew both Holmes and Thayer well. His reaction suggests that he may have found Holmes' relatively modest acknowledgment of Thayer consistent with a view he held of Holmes as self-preoccupied and ambitious. *The Nation*'s subsequent editing of Pomeroy's review to omit paragraphs in which Pomeroy praised Holmes' contributions could also be attributed to Sedgwick, whose previous tenure with *The American Law Review* might well have given him a reputation among *The Nation*'s editors as an expert on legal scholarship. The fact that the editing removed paragraphs praising Holmes suggests something amounting to animus on the part of the editor. There was no doubt that Holmes, however grudging his acknowledgment of Thayer, had prepared the edition himself. It was as if the anonymous editor of *The Nation* was seeking to respond to what he considered inappropriate behavior on the part of Holmes by depriving him of the opportunity to receive praise in print.

While Holmes was surely disappointed on learning from Pomeroy that the latter's praise of his efforts on the twelfth edition of Kent had been deleted from the printed version of his review, he could have taken some solace in the reviews of his edition that did appear. Russell Gray, John Gray's brother, reviewed the work in the *North American Review,* referring to Holmes as one of a group of scholars "who aspire to create or contribute to a consistent, rational, and universal system of jurisprudence, which shall be of general, or even universal, application." Holmes, to Gray, appeared as "a disciple of this new school" of jurisprudence or perhaps even a "prophet of one yet newer."[72] And the *Boston Daily Advertiser*'s anonymous reviewer described Holmes as "a *legal scholar*" with "a natural aptitude for study and research, for the patient collecting and sifting of abundant material." The reviewer speculated that "from the style of many of [Holmes'] notes . . . the writings of the metaphysicians had had no small share and influence in his mental training."[73]

~

In March 1873, as he was completing his work on Kent, Holmes made a decision that apparently signaled his abandonment of scholarship. In 1871 he had left Shattuck's firm to open his own law office, sharing office space with his brother Ned, who had returned to Boston after a tenure in Washington as secretary to Senator Charles Sumner from Massachusetts, a prominent architect of Reconstruction. Between 1871 and 1872 Holmes worked as co-editor of *The American Law Review,* and was the sole editor after July 1872. He continued to contribute essays and reviews to the *Review*'s pages, as well as preparing his edition of Kent and teaching courses in constitutional law and jurisprudence at Harvard College. His correspondence to Thayer suggests that his practice took a back seat to those commitments. We have seen that his leaving Shattuck's office, which was an active and growing concern, to open up his own office was a signal that he wanted to exercise more control over his time. In 1873, however, contemporaries regarded his formation of a partnership with Shattuck and William Adams Munroe, who had been affiliated together for the past three years, as a return to fulltime practice,[74] and Holmes gave up his editorship of *The American Law Review* and his lectureships at Harvard at the same time.

Holmes' decision to return to fulltime law practice amounted, however, to a shift in scholarly emphasis rather than an abandonment of scholarly concerns. Between 1873 and 1876 Holmes' scholarly readings actually increased in intensity. He brushed up on his German, which he had taken in college, so that he could read some sources in the original,[75] and he began to read widely in legal history, ancient and medieval history, and anthropology. By late 1874 he was reading studies of ancient legal systems, and by 1875 he was immersed in primary and secondary sources on legal history.[76] This reading and study would have a significant effect on Holmes' scholarship when he resumed it in 1876.

Given the changed direction of Holmes' scholarship after the three-year interval ushered in by his returning to fulltime law practice in 1873, it seems appropriate, before discussing the work he produced after that interval, to characterize the scholarly perspective that Holmes adopted in his early essays.

Holmes' first three essays had contained an unresolved tension between his search for a philosophical "arrangement" of the law, proceeding "from the most general conception to the most specific proposition in the order of logical subordination," and his conclusion, expressed in "The Theory of Torts" essay, that "an enumeration of the actions which have been successful, and of those which have failed, defines the extent of the primary duties imposed by the law."[77] Holmes had been initially enthusiastic about his duty-based classification system because he believed that the concept of duty came close to giving a fundamental account of legal relationships, and thus made possible a logical arrangement of legal subjects. But at the same time he had emphasized that the law's essence amounted to predictions about the decisions of courts; that lawyers were unconcerned about duties that were not enforced; and that therefore it made little sense to speak of a "duty" that was not recognized by judges.

The last set of observations had brought Holmes closer to the position that an enumeration of legal duties was nothing more than a description of the kinds of relationships that judges saw as creating rights or obligations that could be enforced in court. This made the classification of legal subjects an exercise in observation and prediction, designed to determine the sorts of relationships judges had enforced, and the sorts they could be expected to enforce in the future. "Law is not a science," Holmes had said in the "Codes" essay, "but it is essentially empirical."[78] But if legal rules were empirically based and if the derivation of legal duties was essentially a process in determining which sorts of actions had been successful and which sorts had failed, it seemed somewhat futile to attempt ambitious logical classifications of the kind Holmes had formulated in the "Codes" and "Privity" essays. In fact the historical orientation of the "Privity" essay had suggested that Holmes was undertaking empirical analysis even when purporting to be investigating a logically based classification system.

Holmes was eventually to settle on historical analysis as the methodology most conducive to deriving general observations about legal subjects, and to abandon both the concept of duty and his duty-based classification scheme. But we should not misunderstand the meaning of that change in his scholarly perspective. His shift from analytic to historical work did not mean that he had abandoned an effort to derive general organizing principles and propositions about law. It merely meant that he found the method of tracing legal doctrines over time a more convenient and arguably less vulnerable way of deriving such propositions. Holmes, we will see, made history serve the agenda of his theory.

Moreover, Holmes' shift in emphasis from logic to history did not mean that he had abandoned the idea of achieving some kind of philosophical classification of legal subjects. He simply had shifted the level of generalization at which that classification operated. Instead of emphasizing the types of duties into which legal subjects could be arranged, Holmes' later work focused on standards of liability in common law fields, with the goal of demonstrating an analogous progression in several fields toward a unifying standard. This was itself a classification, although of a more concrete and practical kind.

It is thus not accurate to see Holmes' early work as representing a sort of methodological dead end that he quickly abandoned. His early work had never represented pure logic-chopping, but had consistently relied on historical inquiry. His later work, while not employing analytical classifications and explicitly rejecting "logic" as a methodological tool suited to the law, was by no means contextually based history. He was an evolutionary historian, deriving fundamental principles from the change of legal doctrine over time. Those principles were more sophisticated versions of the logical abstractions of his earlier work.

In the passage of time between 1873 and 1876, when his next scholarly essay appeared in the *American Law Review,* Holmes, as noted, had begun to read much more extensively in works of legal history, particularly in German sources. Among the German works he read in the original during 1875 and 1876 were Goethe's *Faust,* Adolf von Scheurl's *Lehrbuch der Institutionen,* Rudolph Sohm's *Frankischen Reichs und Gerichts Verfassung,* and Heinrich Gengler's *Germanische Rechtsdenkmaler.*[79] To these titles he added a great many books, in French and English, on legal history. His reading list indicates that he read over fifty legal history books between 1873 and 1876, the largest number of titles on any one subject, and a particularly striking number in light of the comparatively few books on other aspects of the law that he read in the period. He seemed particularly interested in works on primitive legal societies, reading Henry Adams's edition of *Essays in*

Anglo-Saxon Law "twice—very carefully notes and references" in the fall of 1876.[80]

If the early goals of Holmes' legal scholarship and his eventual methodological orientation in *The Common Law* are both kept in mind, the interest he took in works on legal history, especially those by German scholars, is readily enough appreciated. The distinctive characteristic of German historical scholarship had been its extraction of philosophical principles from the materials of history. Whether the emphasis was on the universalistic nature of the principles (as in Immanuel Kant, Georg Puchta, and the Pandects [digests] of Justinian's *Corpus Juris*), or on the development of those principles through time (as in Frederick von Savigny, Georg Beseler, and Jacob Grimm), historical research confirmed for the German scholars the primacy of the autonomous concepts on which law was founded.[81]

German scholarship ultimately split into two camps, one enamored of preserving the basic principles of Roman law, which were taken to be timeless, another interested in exploring the origins and growth of German law from its sources in the practices of Teutonic tribes.[82] Of these Holmes was far more attracted to the latter school, but he recognized that it had less influence on continental jurisprudence. In a series of articles he set out to borrow from the techniques of German historical jurisprudence to discredit the philosophical claims of the Pandectist wing of German scholarship.

Before discussing those articles, it is worthwhile speculating on Holmes' motivation in returning to scholarship after what had appeared to be a conscious decision to leave it in 1873. One clue can be found in a letter Holmes wrote to James Bryce in August 1879 after he had resumed writing scholarly articles:

> There are so few men . . . who have any kind of idealism in their practice that
> I cling pretty closely to those who have. . . [T]he men who really care more
> for a fruitful thought than for a practical success are few everywhere . . . I wish
> that the necessity of making a living didn't preclude any choice on my part—
> for I hate business and dislike practice apart from arguing cases—though I
> have every reason to be thankful for the situation in which I am, given that the
> above necessity exists. As it is I console myself by studying toward a
> vanishing point which is the center of perspective in my landscape—but that
> has to be done at night for the most part and is wearing, and my articles
> though fragmentary in form and accidental in order are part of what lies in a
> whole in my mind—my scheme being to analyze what seem to me the
> fundamental notions and principles of our substantive law, putting them in an
> order which is a part of or results from the fundamental conceptions.[83]

It is apparent from this letter that Holmes had been motivated to join the firm of Shattuck, Holmes and Munroe for economic reasons. His compensation for the Kent project, $3000, was a considerable sum for the time, but the edition had taken him four years, and his only other income was from law practice with his brother. The editorship of the *American Law Review* was certainly not financially attractive, if it represented any compensation at all. In 1881, after he had been offered a professorship at Harvard, Holmes indicated that he was particularly concerned about his starting salary and any prospective raises "as I must live on my salary, [t]he property which I have saved being no more than a minimum fund to meet emergencies."[84]

Scholarship, then, was a financially inefficient endeavor for Holmes to pursue in his early thirties. But on the other hand the letter to Bryce indicates that Holmes did not like the ordinary routine of office practice, which consisted of advice to individuals engaged in "business," and that he distinguished between "a fruitful thought" and "practical success." Apparently he continued to be attracted, during the time he was concentrating on law practice, to the "vanishing point" of "putting . . . the fundamental notions and principles of our substantive law . . . in an order." It was with this goal in mind that he began to read intensively in legal history.

Two themes Holmes had been preoccupied with in his earlier articles had been the role of culpability in determining standards of liability and the relationship between rights, duties, and fact situations. In his 1872 lectures on jurisprudence, and again in his "Theory of Torts" article, he examined the former theme and suggested that Austin's insistence on culpability as a prerequisite for liability was misplaced. In his "Privity" article he had shown that in numerous instances persons who were treated as having succeeded to the rights of other persons did not occupy the same situations that gave rise to those rights; the succession was fictional, rationalized by the concept of privity. Now in 1876 and 1877 Holmes turned again to those themes, this time focusing on history.

The articles revealed the purposes of Holmes' reading in the years in which he had temporarily abandoned scholarship. Included in the sources he cited were Sohm on the procedures of salic law, Tylor on primitive cultures, the Black Book of the Admiralty, Henry Maine's *Early History of Institutions,* Savigny, Beseler, and the Icelandic sagas, as well as the more conventional sources of Roman and common law, Justinian, Ulpian, and Bracton. In the common pattern of historical scholarship, Holmes had juxtaposed original sources against secondary readings of them; his purpose was to criticize the interpretations offered in those secondary sources.

"Primitive Notions in Modern Law, No. I"[85] took up the culpability standard. In a footnote in the "Theory of Torts" article Holmes suggested that "[t]he peculiar liability for ferocious animals . . . seems to have been based upon the primitive notions that liability somehow attached upon the thing doing the harm."[86] In "Primitive Notions I" he sought to "explain that primitive notion more at length." First he gave some examples of liability that did not rest on culpability: the liability of persons for damage done by "extrahazardous things," such as animals "of known ferocious habits"; the liability of masters for the negligent acts of their servants; the surrender of objects that caused death in homicide cases.[87] To these Holmes added more examples: the surrender of children who had injured others; the sending of the lifeless bodies of persons who had committed suicide after having breached truces to the offended parties; even the destruction of trees whose limbs had fallen on victims.[88]

These examples were followed by a passage from Tylor's *Primitive Culture* emphasizing "the belief in the animation of all nature" that marked primitive societies.[89] Holmes suggested that "without clothing inanimate objects in personality, we cannot feel proper anger towards them," and that the "more undeveloped the institutions . . . the closer should we expect to find the liability to the immediate visible and tangible cause of the damage.''[90] He concluded that attaching liability to "the thing doing the damage" was a means of furthering the goal of legal proceedings in primitive societies, which was "vengeance, not compensation."[91] In Holmes' view this conclusion explained not only the surrender or destruction of offending objects or persons but the fact that once that surrender or destruction had taken place, limits on liability were imposed. In the case of a shipwreck, for example, if the ship was completely lost mariners had no action against her, but if any portion of the ship was saved, mariners retained a lien, since the animate object was still extant to be proceeded against.

At the time he wrote "Primitive Notions I" Holmes had not fully worked out the implications of his conclusion that early legal actions were rooted in a desire for vengeance. He observed that "practical conclusions can only be drawn with caution" from his findings.[92] But he suggested that the conventional explanation for the early actions, that "modern views of responsibility had not yet been attained,"[93] might be misplaced. That explanation presupposed that societies had progressed from a stage in which liability was simply based on a showing of injury to one in which liability was conditioned on intent or fault. But the goal of vengeance and the personification of inanimate objects suggested that some kind of responsibility was being attributed to the offending instrumentality, whether or not it was human. This indicated that primitive conceptions of liability were based on some attribution of responsibility. Holmes was to pursue this theme in *The Common Law*.

Holmes returned to the subject of "primitive notions" in modern law in the July 1877 issue of the *American Law Review*.[94] Here his focus was once again on the law of succession, which he had investigated in his "Privity" article. His purpose, he said, was "to prove the historical truth of a general result, arrived at analytically" in that article.[95] His "general result" had been that on many occasions in the law one who was said to have "succeeded" to the rights of another was not in fact in the same circumstances that gave rise to that other's rights, but was treated, through the concept of privity, as being in those circumstances. In "Primitive Notions II" Holmes sought to show that the historical origins of this version of succession— most prominent in rights to land—could be found in the law of inheritance. By analogy, Holmes demonstrated, persons taking possession of land from others were treated as if they had inherited the land from them, and thus held rights against outsiders. The transfer of rights to property was effectuated through an underlying, and fictitious, transfer of personal rights.

To say that Holmes' "proof" for this proposition was obscure would be to understate matters.[96] He ranged through commentators on Roman and German law, giving long quotations in Latin and treating those quotations as dispositive without further explanation, let alone translation. Most modern readers of "Primitive Notions II" are thus left disabled from assessing much of Holmes' argument, although those portions that are intelligible suggest that the language of inheritance certainly found its way into land succession cases. When Holmes concludes this portion of "Primitive Notions II" with the statement, "[s]o far as we have gone, we have found that wherever one party steps into the rights or obligations of another, without in turn filling the situation of fact of which those rights or obligations are the legal consequences, the explanation lies in a fictitious identification of the two individuals, which was in fact derived from the analogy of inheritance,"[97] one is tempted to take him at his word, especially since the point seems unexceptional.

The next part of "Primitive Notions II" is more interesting because of its relationship to jurisprudential beliefs Holmes developed in his subsequent work. In that part Holmes turned to an anomaly in the law of succession. The inheritance analogy only applied to "rightful" successions, that is, ones where the subsequent possessor of the land, while not inheriting it, had come into possession in a lawful manner. "If the change of hands was wrongful," as in the case of one who had forcibly ousted another from land, the successor could not claim the rights of the disseisee (the person who had originally owned the land).[98] But if the disseisee had acquired a right of way on the land, Holmes conjectured, and the disseisor then wrongfully ousted him, the disseisor nonetheless would have an action against any person "other than the rightful owner," should that person seek to obstruct the way.[99]

How was one to explain this anomaly? If the inheritance analogy was explained by a fiction that treated successors as heirs, that fiction presupposed lawful possession. The disseisor did not have lawful possession; why should she or he have greater rights than any other? The explanation, Holmes felt, was "to be found not in reasoning, but in a failure to reason."[100] As in the case of offending objects, primitive societies had personalized land, and land was thought of as having rights that were qualities of the land itself, and survived with it. Thus a right of way over land, even though it was itself an artificial creation of the law, was conceived of as attaching to the land itself. As in the case of offending objects, "a thing actually incapable of rights has been treated as if capable of them." Holmes concluded that the explanation for this phenomenon was "confusion of thought" or "grounds of policy."[101]

In that last phrase Holmes anticipated a major tenet of his later jurisprudential writing. He was to come to the view that doctrinal survivals whose origins could be traced not to "logic," but to history, were often perpetuated because they had beneficial policy consequences. Thus the rule that a disseisor would have an action for ejectment against all but the rightful owner, while based on a "confusion of thought" in which inanimate objects were personalized, could also be based on a policy ground that appealed to moderns, such as the security resulting from a quieting of land titles by recognizing the possessor's "succession" to all the rights of the former landowner. Through the recognition of the complex relationship between "confused reasoning" and "grounds of policy" in doctrinal anomalies, Holmes was to move to his famous organizing aphorism in *The Common Law* that "logic" and "experience" were both opposed and intertwined in legal reasoning.

At this point, after considering three of Holmes' exercises in historical scholarship—"Privity" and the two "Primitive Notions" essays—it seems worth commenting on the methodological orientation of that scholarship. I have suggested earlier that it is inaccurate to treat Holmes' work in legal history as antithetical to his analytical work; his historical explorations, as he admitted explicitly in "Primitive Notions II," were in the service of his earlier analytical formulations.[102] But in another sense his historical work was methodologically incompatible with his earlier analytic work, as his observations on the relationship between "confused reasoning" and "grounds of policy" revealed. Analytical jurisprudence presupposed that categories of legal analysis were universalistic in their nature: when Holmes said that duties logically preceded rights, he meant in any legal system at any point in time. But his historical explorations had revealed that some analytically based propositions, such as the idea that masters, even if they themselves had not been at fault, were vicariously liable for the negligence of their servants because they could be presumed to have been careless in hiring inept servants, were simply not true across time: they were later rationalizations of "confused thought" on "grounds of policy." The personalization of slaves or servants with masters had given rise to the doctrine of vicarious liability. Such "confused thought" could not be retained by moderns, so the fiction of carelessness in hiring was supplied in order to preserve a doctrine that had some functional utility.

Holmes, in short, had exhibited a historicist sensibility in his articles on legal history. He had recognized the inevitability of change with time, and the attendant inevitability that successive generations might find the intellectual assumptions of their predecessors "confused." In fact he had gone further, and presupposed a progression over time from less enlightened to more enlightened societies, hence his characterization of the tendency to personalize inanimate objects as "primitive." But historicism was incompatible with the universalistic assumptions of analytical jurisprudence. Since change over time was inevitable, categories erected in the present could never precisely apply to the past; starting assumptions and sensibilities were fundamentally different. Ultimately, Holmes' historical forays could not be reconciled with the intellectual assumptions that had produced his analytic work, and he would shortly come to recognize this fact.

~

Thus far, in the historical forays he had undertaken since his "Theory of Torts" article, Holmes had taken up the difficult questions of culpability and succession. His interest had been in explaining doctrinal fictions and anomalies that other jurists had sought to reconcile through appeal to modern ideological assumptions; Holmes' work suggested that the origins of those doctrines were in historical attitudes more consistent with "primitive societies." In 1878 he turned to two additional problems, the requirement of possession to bring an action to recover lost or stolen property, and the strict liability of common carriers at common law. Both problems had been suggested to Holmes in his reading of German sources. His approach to them was consciously directed toward undermining the impact of those sources.

"The only theory of possession with which common lawyers are acquainted," Holmes began his 1878 "Possession" article,[103] "is derived from a Roman source."[104] This state of affairs, he suggested, was a result of the fact that "the Germans have long had it all their way with the subject, and it has happened that those German philosophers who have written upon law have known no other system than the Roman."[105] Holmes argued that the impact of German jurists on theories of possession had had two unfortunate effects. First, the overall explanations advanced by the Germans about the law of possession were not consistent with common law decisions, and were thus simply wrong. Second, and of greater significance for Holmes, the explanations rested on an impoverished methodological emphasis in German legal scholarship, the emphasis on "logic," in which doctrines and theories were propounded that achieved logical symmetry and were philosophically satisfying, whether or not they were faithful to the actual cases.

Holmes chose the treatment of the rights of bailees as an example of the deficiency of German theories about possession. German jurists had, following Roman law, limited possessory remedies to those recognized as owners. "Paulus tells us," Holmes noted, "that depositaries and borrowers have not possession of the things intrusted to them; and it would shake the German theory of possession to its foundation to admit the possibility of such persons being possessors."[106] But at common law it was clear that bailees could recover from thieves, from persons who had damaged entrusted property, or from persons who had lost it; and these actions were permitted even though owners could recover as well. This demonstrated for Holmes that the "rights" of bailees were founded on possession. Those "rights" were simply the law's way of recognizing that facts consistent with possession were true with respect to certain persons. Holmes concluded that the "facts" of possession could be reduced to an intent to exercise dominion over specified property and the power to exclude others from it.

At this point in the analysis, Holmes concluded, the theories of German jurists proved "unsatisfactory."[107] By equating possession with ownership, the Germans insisted that "intent to deal with the thing as owner is in general necessary to turn a mere physical detention into juridical possession."[108] And this ascription of ownership to possessors was consistent with German legal philosophy. As Holmes put it,

[T]he German theories must exclude most bailees . . . from the list of possessors. In so doing, it singularly falls in with the Kantian philosophy of law. Kant . . . believed in the Rights of Man, and approached the law from that point. Possession for him was an extension of the ego, a setting of the will into somewhat external to it, and thus an appropriation of that somewhat, or as Hegel would have said, possession is an objective realization of free will; and the realized free will of the individual can only be restrained when in opposition to the freedom of all, to the universal will expressed by the State. The natural operation of this view on the minds of the German lawyers has been to lead them to consider the intent necessary to possession as primarily self-regarding. . . . The will of the possessor being conceived as self-regarding, the intent with which he must hold is thereupon treated in the same way: he must hold for his own benefit. . . . And thus philosophy confirms dogma, and dogma philosophy.[109]

Holmes sought to "begin afresh," with the consistent support of the common law for possessory remedies in bailees and with the principles of intent to exclude and the power to do so. He conceded that the analysis would not apply to servants, who were not deemed to be in possession of property entrusted to them by masters. The different treatment for servants, he suggested, was an anomaly that had surfaced for historical reasons, being one of "the many marks of the time when [servants were] slaves." Thus while the treatment of servants was one of the bases for the German jurists' attempt to confine possessory remedies to owners, Holmes' explanation was that "the grounds for denying possession and the possessory remedies to servants and agents holding as such ... are merely historical, and the general theory can only take account of it as an anomaly.''[110]

In short, the Germans had exhibited ''a characteristic yearning'' for ''internal juristic necessity drawn from the nature of possession itself,'' and had thus ''reject[ed] empirical reasons.'' But ''American and English readers'' would ''not have to be much argued with to [be] convince[d] ... that the grounds are empirical.'' Holmes pursued this last observation:

> Indeed, those who see in the history of law the formal expression of the development of society will be apt to think that the proximate ground of law must be empirical, even when that ground is the fact that a certain ideal or theory of government is generally entertained. Law, being a practical thing, must found itself on actual forces. It is quite enough, therefore, for the law, that man, by an instinct which he shares with the domestic dog, ... will not allow himself to be dispossessed ... of what he holds, without trying to get it back again. Philosophy may find a hundred reasons to justify the instinct, but ... [a]s long as the instinct remains, it will be more comfortable for the law to satisfy it in an orderly manner, than to leave people for themselves.[111]

On its face Holmes' ''empirical'' theory of possession appears to compare favorably with that of the German jurists, being more faithful to the cases, more flexible in taking account of exceptions and anomalies, and perhaps more sensitive to law's being ''a practical thing.'' But some difficulties remain. First, when pressed to justify the existence of possessory remedies Holmes pointed to ''an instinct'' in humans to resist others taking their property from them. It is hard to know how this ''instinct'' differs from the Germans' equation of possession with individual will or freedom, the philosophical basis of ownership. While Holmes' theory took account of possessory remedies not based on ownership, the same philosophical justification for those remedies could have been advanced by the Germans. ''Freedom of will'' seems only a more refined articulation of Holmes' ''instinct.''

Second, Holmes' ''empirical'' theory of possession comes close to saying that legal rules exist because they exist. Once one grants the presence of a possessory ''instinct'' and then posits that it is ''more comfortable'' for the law to respect that instinct than to ''leave people for themselves,'' one has an explanation for possessory remedies. But both the presence of the ''instinct'' and the tacit decision on the part of the law to respect it have been supplied by Holmes. Moreover, in those instances in which possessory remedies are not granted, as in the case of servants, one would still expect the retentive instinct to be present. There may be ''historical'' reasons for the different treatment, but their survival in an age when slave status has disappeared seems inconsistent with the acknowledgment of Holmes' ''instinct.'' So Holmes' ''empirical'' analysis seems to reduce itself to observations of existing rules and the claim that the law must be ''comfortable'' with such rules.

The positivistic cast of Holmes' empiricism seems particularly odd in light of an earlier passage in the ''Possession'' article:

> As has been said in several earlier articles, legal duties are logically antecedent to legal rights .... The business of the jurist is to make known the content of

the law; that is, to work upon it from within, or logically, arranging and distributing it in order from its *summum genus* to its *infima species*. Legal duties, then, logically come before legal rights. To put it more broadly and avoid the word duty, which is open to objection, the direct operation of the law is to limit freedom of action or choice on the part of a greater or less number of persons in certain specified ways; while the fact that the power of removing or enforcing this limitation is generally confined to certain other private persons is not a necessary or universal correlative.[112]

In this passage Holmes writes in a manner reminiscent of his earlier scholarship, even defining "the business of the jurist" as making logical arrangements of the law. He resurrects his "right/duty" distinction and restates it: the law restricts the freedom of action or choice of people ("duties") without necessarily giving others correlative powers to enforce those restrictions ("rights"). But what would Holmes' "empirical" analysis suggest about this right/duty distinction? It would seem to suggest that one cannot talk intelligibly of "rights" without an understanding of the "special facts" that give rise to them; and perhaps one cannot talk intelligibly of duties without a comparable analysis. Many people owe "duties" not to take the property of another, but just which duties could be enforced, and indeed whether they were owed at all, would seem to turn on "empirical" observation. So not only might the word duty be "open to objection," the entire right/duty distinction might be as well. The objection to the right/duty distinction would be the same as that to Germanic explanations of possession. It is an *a priori* rubric that tells one nothing in advance of the "facts."

~

The "Possession" article thus sees Holmes in a transitional stage in his scholarship, still clinging to a conception of "juristic" work as analytical and still seeking to find some value in his right/duty distinction, but having rejected all-encompassing "logical" explanations of doctrinal development and having loosed an "empirical" methodology that threatened to obliterate his earlier analytic work.[113] In his next article, "Common Carriers and the Common Law,"[114] which appeared in the *American Law Review* a year after his piece on "Possession," one sees Holmes more firmly in the "empirical" mode. The "Common Carriers" article, in fact, takes us nearly to the methodological frame of reference from which Holmes wrote *The Common Law*. In the article history, policy analysis, and philosophical rumination are fused in a manner distinctive of that work. It was as if Holmes had finally settled on a technique of analysis that could accommodate his historicist sensibility with his interest in remodeling common law doctrines to conform to the starting assumptions of a generation of Americans coming to maturity in the late nineteenth century.[115]

The question Holmes addressed in "Common Carriers and the Common Law" was why a steamship company that carried a mare on a voyage from London to Aberdeen, and lost the mare when she became frightened and severely injured herself during a course of rough weather, should be liable to the mare's owners even though the loss of the mare could not be attributed to any negligence on the part of the ship's employees. The basis for the liability was the principle that common carriers, such as steamships, hold themselves out as providing safe conduct for the passage of persons or goods that they transport, and are thus liable without fault if their cargo is damaged. In the case involving the lost mare two English judges commented on the origins of common carrier liability, one suggesting that it had been derived from the Roman law, the other that it had been carved out as a general exception to the principles of the law of bailments, which required a showing of fault on the part of the bailee.

Holmes' motivation in writing the "Common Carriers" article was threefold. First, he believed that both judges had been wrong in their statement of the origins of common carrier liability, and could be shown to be so. Second, he had come to be hostile toward any form of liability in tort that was not based on a showing of intentional harm or fault, and thus wanted an opportunity to expose the "peculiar" history of common carrier liability. Third, the process by which common carrier liability had come into being furnished Holmes with a fertile example of the relationship between history, social values, and legal doctrine, a relationship that he wanted to expound upon.

Holmes believe that he had already achieved the first goal in his "Possession" article, where he had argued that the early English law of bailment tracked patterns of self-help originating in the practices of Teutonic tribes. Those patterns emphasized that possession of a chattel conferred on the possessor a right to recover it if it had been stolen or to recover its value if it had been lost. "As a corollary to this," Holmes maintained, "the bailee was strictly answerable to his bailor; and in case the goods were lost, it was no excuse that they were stolen without his fault. The remedies were all in his hands, and therefore he was bound to hold the bailor harmless.[116]

Thus far Holmes had merely tracked his "Possession" article and added a corollary explaining the origins of strict liability for bailees. Under his explanation the origins were not Roman, but Teutonic, and the liability not exceptional, but common to all persons entrusted with goods who had possessory remedies. But there were some procedural complexities that had to be overcome before strict liability of carriers could be made out, Holmes suggested, such as the problem that the writ of detinue, typically used in possessory actions, would not allow damages to be recovered if the lost chattel could be returned, albeit in a damaged condition. To solve this problem the writ of trespass on the case was employed, with the complaining party alleging that the bailee had been engaged in a "common" calling, and that there was a general obligation on the part of persons exercising a public or common business to show skill in it. But these allegations had nothing to do with the law of bailments. As Holmes put it, "when the same form of action . . . came to be used alike for damage or destruction by the bailee's neglect, and for loss by a wrong-doer against whom the bailee had a remedy over, a source was opened for confusion with regard to the foundation and nature of the defendant's duty."[117]

Eventually, Holmes argued, "the defendant's common calling began to assume a[n] . . . importance," and "the liability of common carriers for loss of goods, whatever the cause of the loss might be," was placed on "a special principle peculiar to them, and not applicable to bailees in general." This marked the final stage in "[t]he confusion of independent duties" that had emerged with the substitution of writs in case for writs in detinue. Ultimately "the confusion became complete,[118] and all common carriers were made strictly liable for the loss of any goods they transported, except where they had not been paid for the transport. While many cases announcing common carrier liability spoke in terms of the "neglect" of the carrier, Holmes pointed out that this did not mean that the carrier was "negligent" in the sense of failing to meet a standard of ordinary care: negligence meant only "a failure de facto to keep safely."[119] The process had made common carriers insurers of the safety of goods in their possession.

Holmes was now prepared to summarize, and in his summary the methodology of his article became clear. As the original reasons for the emergence of common carrier liability—a "confusion" generated by the writ system and an inarticulate conviction that persons "who followed useful callings [should be held] up to the mark"[120]—became obscure, the liability came to be justified on contemporary notions of policy, such as "[t]o prevent litigation, collusion, and the necessity of going into circumstances impossible to be unraveled."[121] But those reasons might apply to some sorts of common carriers, such as railroads, "who may have a private individual at their mercy," but not to others, such as "a general ship or a public cab." The imposition of common carrier liability thus needed to be reexamined in cases where its policy basis did not seem justified.

Holmes' methodology in "Common Carriers" had several related purposes. One was to illustrate the jurisprudential claim that a "paradox of form and substance" lay within "the development of law." The "form" of the law's growth was allegedly logical, with "each new decision" deemed to have "follow[ed] syllogistically from existing precedents." But the discussion of common carrier liability had shown that "as precedents survive like the clavicle in the cat, long after the use they once served is at an end, and the reason for them has been forgotten, the result of following them must often be failure and confusion from the merely logical point of view." Common carrier liability did not follow logically from the possession-based liability of bailees, since it was much more broadly based; it could only be based on reasons that had nothing to do with logic. "[A]s the law is administered by able and experienced men," Holmes maintained, "who know too much to sacrifice good sense to a syllogism, it will be found that when ancient rules maintain themselves . . . new reasons more fitted to the time have been found for them." Legal doctrine was thus ultimately based on "the very considerations which the courts most rarely mention, and always with an apology . . . considerations of what is expedient for the community concerned." Every important principle that was developed in the common law, Holmes believed, "is in fact and at bottom the result of more or less definitely understood views of public policy."[122] The form of legal rules masked their substantive purposes; those purposes paradoxically reinforced doctrinal formalism.

This conclusion precipitated some additional observations. First, since doctrinal change occurred not only from an "attempt to follow precedents," but "to give a good reason for them," legal decisions were in significant part based on considerations of policy, which could be "consider[ed] . . . with a freedom that was not possible before" their importance had been appreciated. In the case of common carrier liability, for example, "if there is no common rule of policy, and common carriers remain a merely empirical exception from general doctrine, courts may well hesitate to extend the significance of those words.'' Exercises such as Holmes' had ''set at large . . . early precedent'' in the area, making possible ''argument on general principles.'' Pursuing such an argument, Holmes pointed out that ''notions of public policy which would not leave parties free to make their own bargains are somewhat discredited in most departments of the law.''[123] Common carrier liability was in that sense anomalous and open to reexamination.

A second observation was that the paradox of form and substance in the history of legal doctrine illustrated ''the failure of all theories which consider the law only from its formal side, whether they attempt to deduce the *corpus* from *a priori* postulates, or fall into the humbler error of supposing the science of law to reside in the *elegantia juris,* or logical cohesion of part with part.''[124] Logical consistency was unrealizable in the law so long as the growth of legal doctrine took place in the form supposed by Holmes. The law was ''forever adopting new principles from life at one end, and . . . always retain[ing] old ones from history at the other.''[125] In the process ''confusion of thought'' was inevitable, as doctrines serving a contemporary policy function were justified as logical extensions of precedent. One had to penetrate form for substance.

~

One additional essay remains to be considered in this discussion of Holmes' early scholarship, ''Trespass and Negligence,'' which appeared in the January 1880 issue of the *American Law Review.*[126] In this essay the crystallization of Holmes' methodological approach is again apparent, as he interweaves ''policy'' and a historical analysis of ''authority'' in his general argument. That argument was an attack on what Holmes took to be the two leading theories governing the liability for unintentional torts, one based on moral fault and the other on the assumption that a person acts at his or her peril when voluntarily undertaking duties. In the course of the attack Holmes sought to show that common law precedents were not consistent with either theory, that the theories reflected ''confusion of thought,'' and that an alternative theory, in which liability for unintentional torts was predicated on a violation of an externally based standard of reasonable care, was preferable.

Holmes began ''Trespass and Negligence'' by alluding to the two theories, attributing the moral fault theory to Austin, and putting that theory aside. He then took up the act-at-peril theory, which he found ''to be adopted by some of the greatest common-law authorities,'' and thus to require ''serious discussion before it can be set aside in favor of any third opinion which may be maintained.''[127] He summarized the arguments in favor of that theory. The first was ''consistency.'' In other areas of the law, such as when ''a man crosses his neighbor's boundary by however innocent a mistake, or if his cattle escape into his neighbor's field,'' liability was imposed without fault. Similarly if an auctioneer sold goods that had been sent to him for the purpose of being sold, but were actually owned by another, the auctioneer was liable to the rightful owner even though he could not have known the true ownership and even if he had ''paid over the proceeds and ha[d] no means of obtaining indemnity.''[128] Strict liability for unintentional tortious acts would be consistent with those examples.

The next argument in favor of act-at-peril liability was based on "policy." "Every man, it is said," Holmes noted, "has an absolute right to his person, and so forth, free from detriment at the hands of his neighbors." In cases where "the plaintiff has done nothing" and "the defendant . . . has chosen to act," the principle of autonomy would suggest that "the party whose voluntary conduct has caused the damage should suffer, rather than one who has had no share in producing it."[129] This principle would explain all of the cases previously mentioned as examples of act-at-peril liability. In each the defendant had done something, even though it was merely keeping an animal or walking on a neighbor's land, whereas the plaintiff had done nothing and had had his property lost or damaged.

Holmes next turned to "the argument from authority."[130] A number of cases, beginning with the "Case of the Thorns," decided in 1466, had affirmed that intent to injure another was not a prerequisite for liability in tort, although such intent was necessary in the criminal law. Thus when a landowner went on his neighbor's land to retrieve some thorns that had fallen there when he had cut a hedge, damaging the neighbor's land in the process, or when one accidentally shot another with a bow, or when in the course of building a house a landowner accidentally dislodged a timber, injuring his neighbor's house, or where one sought to defend himself with a stick, and accidentally struck a person behind him in lifting it, or even when a man entered onto a neighbor's land and took his horse under the threats of twelve armed men, liability would ensue despite the absence of any intent to injure or the existence of an excuse or justification for that intent.[131] The existence of such cases was so prevalent, in fact, that Holmes stated that "further citations are deemed unnecessary."[132]

Despite this evidence, Holmes proceeded to attack the act-at-peril theory. He not only argued that "such a rule is inconsistent with admitted doctrines and sound policy," he went further, claiming that "the common law has never known such a rule, unless in that period of dry precedent which is so often to be found midway between a creative epoch and a period of solvent philosophical reaction."[133] He suggested that consistency, authority, and policy all mitigated against the rule, notwithstanding the evidence he had already supplied.

Holmes' argument from consistency stressed that the act-at-peril principle swiftly led to unlimited liability. "The same reasoning," Holmes suggested, "would make [one] answerable . . . for the . . . damage similarly resulting from the act of his servant, in the course of the latter's employment." The same reasoning "would make a defendant responsible for all damage, however remote, of which his act could be called the cause." Thus if act-at-peril liability were made the touchstone of damages in tort, "any act would be sufficient, however remote, which set in motion or opened the door for a series of physical sequences ending in damage." Indeed "why need the defendant have acted at all, and why is it not enough that his existence has been at the expense of the plaintiff?"[134] For this reason Holmes believed that there had always been an implicit limitation of fault on actions in trespass. Either the defendant had intended to injure the plaintiff, in which case fault could easily be attributed, or the circumstances suggested that the defendant had fallen below a standard of reasonable care in being attentive to the plaintiff's interests.

This was a bold reading of the authorities that Holmes had previously cited, which had not employed any language conditioning tort liability on fault and had suggested that injury and causation alone were the tests of liability. But Holmes now claimed that the courts who had decided those cases could not have meant to endorse act-at-peril liability.[135] First, he maintained, "the general principle of our law is that loss from accident must lie where it falls, and this principle is not affected by the fact that a human being is the instrument of misfortune." Act-at-peril liability was inconsistent with that principle. Second, it was possible to read the act-at-peril cases as being based on an unarticulated notion of fault as a touchstone for liability. Thus in the thorns case "the falling of the thorns into the plaintiff's close, although a result not wished by the defendant, was in no other sense against his will."[136] Shooting and runaway horse cases, two other sources of the act-at-peril theory, turned out to contain language "put on the general ground of fault" except where shooting, "an extra hazardous act," took place in public places.[137] A leading unintentional injury case in Massachusetts had explicitly conditioned liability on intent or fault.[138] And the ancient examples of tort liability seemed to be confined to intentional wrongs.[139] The principle of act-at-peril liability had been erroneously engrafted from dissenting opinions and a misreading of the elements of the writ system.[140]

Holmes now turned to policy. He argued that the autonomy principle, applied so as to compensate anyone damaged by another's act, was inconsistent with the fact that "the public generally profits by individual activity." Since action "cannot be avoided, and tends to the public good," Holmes suggested, "there is obviously no policy in throwing the hazard of what is at once desirable and inevitable upon the actor."[141] He then continued:

> The state might conceivably make itself a mutual insurance company against accidents, and distribute the burden of its citizens' mishaps among all the members. There might be a pension for paralytics, and State aid for those who suffered in person or estate from tempest or wild beasts. As between individuals it might adopt the mutual insurance principle *pro tanto,* and divide damages when both were at fault, as in the *rusticum judicium* of the Admiralty, or it might throw all loss upon the actor irrespective of fault. The State does none of these things, however, and the prevailing view is that its cumbrous and expensive machinery ought not to be set in motion unless some clear benefit is to be derived from disturbing the *status quo.* State interference is an evil, where it cannot be shown to be a good. . . . Unless my act is of a nature to threaten others, unless under the circumstances a prudent man would have foreseen the possibility of harm, to make me indemnify my neighbor against the consequences is no more justifiable than to make me do the same thing if I had fallen upon him in a fit, or to compel me to insure him against lightning.[142]

The above paragraph, like Holmes' earlier statements about the "general principle of our law" being letting accident losses lie where they fell, seems different in tone from what we have previously encountered in his scholarship. It is an unreservedly contemporary statement, culled not from history nor authority, but rather from Holmes' own intellectual assumptions. No authorities are cited in support of "the general principle" of loss distribution and "the prevailing view" of state non-interference to redistribute losses; Holmes simply announces them as givens. Having done so, he proceeds to reexamine the conclusions drawn from innocent trespasses upon land, innocent conversions, and the escape of animals.

In the reexamination it turns out that "innocent" trespasses are not innocent because the trespasser "intends the very act or consequence complained of",[143] that "innocent" conversions were treated as giving rise to liability in order to preserve the security of titles or to encourage persons to ascertain the ownership of property[144]; and that the animal cases distinguished between animals whose nature it was to stray or to be fierce and those whose was not. In the latter cases liability did not ensue without fault, and in the former a reasonable owner should have known that certain animals strayed or were dangerous and taken precautions against it.[145] These cases were considered against the backdrop of a set of policy assumptions in which state interference to redistribute losses that "fell" in a certain place was deemed undesirable. A fault standard for such a redistribution was consistent with those assumptions.

Holmes was now prepared to formulate "the true theory of liability" for unintentional tort cases. He felt that his earlier analysis had demonstrated "that the general notion upon which liability to an action is founded is fault or blameworthiness in some sense." He thus turned to Austin's claim that fault in tort cases should be understood as the equivalent of "personal moral shortcoming."[146] That claim he found in need of qualification. "The standards of the law," he noted, "are standards of general application." The varieties of individual temperament, intelligence, and education were not taken into account in assessing the conduct of a defendant in a civil action. "If . . . a man is born hasty and awkward, is always having accidents and hurting himself and his neighbors," Holmes pointed out, "no doubt his congenital defects will be allowed for in the courts of Heaven, but his slips are no less troublesome to his neighbors than if they sprang from guilty neglect." Thus "his neighbors . . . require him, at his proper peril, to come up to their standard, and the courts which they establish decline to take his personal equation into account."[147]

In short, the law did "determine liability by blameworthiness," but it employed the concept of blameworthiness in a particular way. Blameworthiness was ascribed to a person who fell below the standard of care ascribed to "the average man, the man of ordinary intelligence and prudence." If a person did not possess the same characteristics as this hypothetical "average man," sometimes that fact was taken into account: blind persons, infants, and on some occasions insane persons were presumed not to be capable of meeting a standard of average care for themselves or others. But on the whole the law presumed that if "a man of ordinary intelligence and forethought . . . might and ought to have foreseen [a particular] danger," a person who did not "would [be] to blame" for not foreseeing it.[148]

In that sense blameworthiness was part of the law of unintentional torts. But it was a blameworthiness ascribed in general terms, to anyone who failed to meet a standard of ordinary care in a given case, and with reference to external standards of conduct as distinguished from judgments made about the particular qualities or characteristics of an individual. The moral element of unintentional torts, then, was in the ascription of "blameworthiness" to any conduct that fell below a standard of ordinary care. But the law was "wholly indifferent to the internal phenomena of conscience"; it was concerned with "external phenomena, the manifest acts and omissions." However much the law "may take moral considerations into account," what it "really forbids . . . is the act on the wrong side of the line [of ordinary prudent conduct], be that act blameworthy or otherwise."[149]

Holmes noted, in conclusion, that some analytical problems remained, such as how to achieve a degree of specificity in applying a standard of average prudence or reasonable conduct without delegating every case to the determination of a jury. He felt that "when standards of conduct are left to the jury, it is a temporary surrender of the judicial function, and may be resumed at any moment in any case when the court feels competent to do so." Otherwise, he maintained, "the almost universal acceptance of the . . . proposition . . . that the general foundation of liability in ordinary cases is conduct different from that of a prudent man" would have the result of leaving "all our rights and duties throughout a great part of the law to the necessarily more or less accidental feelings of a jury." This was not a situation he could "contemplate with pleasure."[150]

The important task of "Trespass and Negligence," Holmes believed, had nonetheless been accomplished. He had demonstrated that liability for unintentional torts was almost universally based on fault, but that fault was the equivalent of deviation from a standard of ordinary average prudent conduct, and hence not a moral concept in the conventional sense. The demonstration of the universality and moral neutrality of the fault standard harmonized admirably with Holmes' assumptions that damage caused by unintentional injury should ordinarily lie where it fell and that the state should not invoke its "cumbersome and expensive machinery" in the service of wealth redistribution. A fault standard placed the cost of damages from civil injury only on those whose conduct had fallen below the level of ordinary prudence. In so doing it created an incentive for individuals to achieve the redistribution of their own losses where they could trace them to another's "blameworthy" conduct, and also created an incentive for the state not to interfere in such situations, relying on civil lawsuits to effectuate the limited redistribution.

Indeed the "true theory" of unintentional tort liability proposed by Holmes in "Trespass and Negligence" was in such marked harmony with "the general principle" of no loss distribution and the "prevailing view" of no state redistributive influence that Holmes' analytical scheme appeared to be in service of those propositions. His claim that unintentional tort liability had always been based on fault appeared particularly suspect, given the decisions he cited, but it was certainly convenient.

~

With the "Trespass and Negligence" article Holmes concluded his early scholarship. In a footnote to the article he pointed out that his several essays on legal topics, "although written in an accidental order in the intervals of practice," were "parts of a connected scheme to analyze the fundamental conceptions of the law."[151] Shortly after "Trespass and Negligence" appeared Holmes was given an opportunity to develop that "connected scheme." He was asked to deliver "a course of Lectures" at Boston University's Lowell Institute in the fall of 1880, and resolved to base the lectures on his previous writings. The lectures, originally twelve, became the eleven chapters of *The Common Law,* which Holmes eventually published in March 1881. With the publication of *The Common Law* Holmes' emergence as a mature legal scholar was achieved.

Before turning to *The Common Law,* its relationship to Holmes' early scholarship, and its place in his career, it now seems appropriate to attempt a characterization of Holmes' early scholarship, with the labels others have assigned to it in mind.

Two characteristics of Holmes' scholarly efforts in the 1870s can comfortably be extracted from the recapitulation just given. First, it was not, methodologically, of a piece. There were three discernible methodological stages in the development of Holmes' early scholarship. First were the analytically oriented essays of the years before 1876, "Codes and Arrangements," "Privity," and "The Theory of Torts," in which Holmes' "right/duty" distinction figured prominently. Next came the historically oriented pieces, "Primitive Notions I," "Primitive Notions II," and "Possession," in which the distinction between rights and duties was placed to one side and ultimately abandoned, but historical exegesis was presented as reinforcing analytical work. Last were the remaining two essays, "Common Carriers and the Common Law" and "Trespass and Negligence," in which arguments from contemporary "policy" appeared much more prominently, and history was increasingly invoked in the service of jurisprudential generalizations and contemporary policy arguments.

By the last essays, in fact, Holmes had derived a surfacely coherent[152] and self-reinforcing methodological stance, one that both modified and incorporated his earlier work. He had abandoned "logic" in the form he had sought to employ in his first efforts to classify legal subjects. He presented the law as neither analytically coherent nor as a self-regarding set of philosophic universals. In abandoning logic as he had initially conceived of it, Holmes had implicitly abandoned his "right/duty" distinction, although he continued to speak of discrete areas of the law, such as torts or property, as yielding particular rights or duties. At the same time Holmes embraced history, but not in the antiquarian sense his forays into Teutonic and Roman law might have suggested. History provided him with the source of his "paradox of form and substance" that explained the growth of law. While the logical symmetry of doctrines, he argued, was retained on the surface over time to foster the impression of consistency and continuity, doctrines were under constant pressure to change, and this pressure came from contemporary notions of policy. Substantive change—produced by the "secret root" of considerations expedient to the community at any point in time—was masked by formal reasoning that emphasized the logical interconnectedness among common law principles, rules, and precedents. In fact rules and precedents did not survive merely because they had been in existence; they survived because they were recast in terms of contemporary policy considerations, on which principles were ultimately based.

History thus provided Holmes with the basis for exploring anomalies in the law, and the "confusion of thought" that in his view habitually marked the growth of legal doctrine. History also supplied him with the source of community pressures for doctrinal change. But by functioning as the source from which his overarching explanatory principle—the paradox of form and substance—was derived, history also became enlisted in the service of contemporary policy. For, as Holmes noted in his

"Common Carriers" article, "tracing the process" of history to illustrate the paradox of form and substance enabled one to be "at liberty to consider the question of policy with a freedom that was not possible before."[153] History thus set the policymaker free.

In the last stages of his early scholarship, Holmes offered a methodology in which the surface of legal doctrine—its purported logic—was viewed skeptically, in which historicist attitudes toward change predominated, and in which history was self-consciously employed in the service of contemporary assumptions about desirable social policies. It was a distinctive and enigmatic methodology, not easily labeled or located in time. Holmes' generation of intellectuals has been treated as having a conspicuous interest in deriving ordering and stabilizing principles of thought, allegedly in response to the awkward juxtaposition of mid-nineteenth-century romantic ideologies, of which abolitionism was one, and the chaos of the Civil War.[154] The same generation has been shown to have been particularly enthusiastic about the possibilities of "science"—by which they meant the mathematical and natural sciences—for providing theories and techniques for making sense of the universe.[155] Prominent among those theories was that of evolutionary "natural selection," which was endorsed not only in the natural sciences but in fields such as history, where the origins and growth of "civilized" societies from their "primitive" counterparts became a focal point of scholarship. Prominent among these techniques was the analogy to geometry, a science that offered a set of fundamental explanatory principles ("axioms"), and a technique for applying those principles to novel situations ("originals").[156] Finally, Holmes' generation has been characterized as the first in America fully to embrace historicist attitudes toward change, rejecting a conception of the growth of cultures in fixed stages, from birth through maturity to decay, for a conception of change as a permanent phenomenon that could be roughly equated with progress.[157]

All these generational tendencies appear in Holmes' work. One can observe a search for intellectual order and "geometric" reasoning in his early ventures in analytical jurisprudence; examples of evolutionary history in his work in the mid-1870s; and a historicist theory of doctrinal change in his "Common Carriers" and "Trespass and Negligence" essays. But the sources of those tendencies remain largely obscured. Doubtless Austin figured prominently in his early analytic formulations, although they were written in part to refute some of Austin's contentions.[158] Maine's historical scholarship, which was decisively in the historicist and evolutionary modes, was very probably a significant influence, perhaps all the more because Holmes declined to confirm that fact.[159] Henry Adams' and his associates' work on "primitive" societies was openly acknowledged by Holmes as a stimulus.[160] The German conceptualist jurists provided both a source of learning and a model to react against.[161] As we will see in our discussion of *The Common Law*, Christopher Columbus Langdell's distinctive methodological approach to legal subjects, caricatured by Holmes as "logic," may have served to crystallize a number of critical insights that Holmes had gained from his early work. There are even echoes, in Holmes' early lectures on jurisprudence and some of his analytic work, of the pragmatist outlook endorsed by some members of the "Metaphysical Club" to which he and William James had belonged in the early 1870s.[162] And the late essays in the period contain hints of a positivist theory of the source of legal rules and doctrines.[163]

But for all its familiar elements, Holmes' early work remains both distinctive and far from uniform. Its distinctiveness lies in the fact that while numerous nineteenth-century scholars had produced comprehensive treatises on legal subjects, while some had ventured into legal history, and while some had addressed policy concerns in their analyses, none had attempted to draw connections between history, policy, and doctrinal development to the extent that Holmes did. None save Maine had combined work in original historical sources with a historicist theory of cultural change; and Maine had not explicitly addressed the policy implications of his research. Others had emphasized an evolutionary approach to historical scholarship, but none of those treated the principle of evolution as freeing contemporary theorists from the burdens of past doctrines. Many others had attempted comprehensive philosophical and logical "arrangements" of the law, but none of those emphasized the paradoxical relationship between formal legal doctrine and substantive policy outcomes. Holmes, in short, fused the various intellectual enthusiasms of his contemporaries into a distinctive methodological approach.

That approach, we have seen, had been worked out in stages, and its emphasis shifted over time. Although Holmes claimed that his historical research in his "Primitive Notions" essays complemented his analytical work in his "Privity" article, it actually served to undermine it by suggesting that a comprehensive table of duties and rights only scratched the surface of doctrinal development. By the "Possession" article Holmes, while continuing to insist that "[l]egal duties... logically come before legal rights," had decided to "avoid the word duty, which is open to objection" in his formulations.[164] By 1880 he was prepared to concede that "[t]he form of continuity [in legal doctrine] has been kept up by reasonings purporting to reduce every thing to a logical sequence; but that form is nothing but the evening dress which the newcomer puts on to make itself presentable according to conventional requirements."[165]

In the same year that he delivered the lectures at the Lowell Institute Holmes gave a summary of the methodology he had worked out in the past decade:

> No one will ever have a truly philosophic mastery over the law who does not habitually consider the forces outside of it which have made it what it is. More than that, he must remember that as it embodies the story of a nation's development over centuries, the law finds its philosophy not in self-consistency, which it must always fail in so long as it continues to grow, but in history and the nature of human needs.[166]

This was the perspective from which Holmes was to write the lectures that were to change the course of his professional career.

CHAPTER FIVE

The Common Law

~

IN ONE of the notebooks in which Holmes listed the titles of books he was reading
and occasionally made comments about his scholarly projects, there is an 1880
entry stating that he was "[a]t work writing Lectures for Lowell Inst. which occupies
evenings, begun about Jan. 1."[1] The Lowell Institute, founded by the textile manufacturer John Lowell, Jr., in 1836 in order to offer public lectures that might demonstrate "the truth of those moral and religious precepts, by which alone . . . men
can be secure of happiness in this world and that to come,"[2] was offering a course
in Common Law in the fall of 1880, and Holmes, at the suggestion of John Lowell's
son A. Lawrence Lowell, later President of Harvard, was invited to give the lectures
that made up the course.[3] It is not known when the invitation came, but it must have
been in the calendar year of 1879, when Holmes' early scholarship had taken a
methodological turn.

The Lowell Institute course was an ambitious one, consisting of twelve lectures,
given on Tuesdays and Friday evenings in November and December. To be sure,
Holmes had written on many of the subjects he proposed to lecture on, such as early
forms of liability, trespass and negligence, bailment, successions, and the general
theories of tort law and possession. But the invitation meant that he would need to
explore additional subjects, such as criminal law and contracts, and that he would
be obliged to see if some overriding unity could be derived from his earlier scholarly
forays. In his "Trespass and Negligence" article he had spoken of having in mind
"a connected scheme to analyze the fundamental conceptions of the law"[4]; in letters
to friends in the 1870s he had uttered similar sentiments, writing to Arthur Sedgwick
of his ambition to construct "a new Jurisprudence or New First Book of the Law,"
and to James Bryce of a "scheme to analyse what seem to me the fundamental
norms and principles of our substantive law."[5]

When the final version of his lectures appeared as *The Common Law,* it was
apparent that Holmes had not only produced additional original work, he had considerably refined the work that he had previously done. He wrote to Frederick Pollock in June 1880 that his nights "have been largely devoted to preparing a course
of lectures for next winter,"[6] and in March 1881 that he had "failed in all correspondence and . . . abandoned pleasure as well as a good deal of sleep for a year"[7]
to produce the lectures. "I have worked hard," Holmes added, "for results that
seemed to me important."[8]

The significance of *The Common Law* for Holmes' personal and professional life
has been widely noted. Its publication on March 3, 1881, five days before Holmes'

fortieth birthday, demonstrated to him that he had in fact accomplished something significant before that date, which he felt to be the point beyond which professional accomplishments were not likely to come.[9] Despite the general lack of attention the book initially received, either its text or the lectures on which it was based[10] were regarded as possessing sufficient scholarly stature that in the same year of its publication Holmes was considered for a position on the Harvard Law School faculty. And despite the fact that the book is very rarely read in its entirety, and perhaps even less rarely understood, it has been regarded, at least since the 1920s, as one of the classic works in American legal scholarship.[11]

Holmes began *The Common Law* with one of the most celebrated passages in the history of American legal writing:

> The object of this book is to present a general view of the Common Law. To accomplish this task, other tools are needed besides logic. It is something to show that the consistency of a system requires a particular result, but it is not all. The life of the law has not been logic: it has been experience. The felt necessities of the time, the prevalent moral and political theories, intuitions of public policy, avowed or unconscious, even the prejudices which judges share with their fellow men, have had a good deal more to do than the syllogism in determining the rules by which men should be governed. The law embodies the story of a nation's development through centuries, and it cannot be dealt with as if it contained only the axioms and corollaries of a book of mathematics. In order to know what it is, we must know what it has been, and what it tends to become. We must alternately consult history and theories of legislation. But the most difficult labor will be to understand the combination of the two into new products at every stage. The substance of the law at any given time pretty nearly corresponds, so far as it goes, with what is then understood to be convenient; but its form and machinery, and the degree to which it is able to work out desired results, depend very much upon its past.[12]

While this passage, especially its fourth sentence, has been one of the most quoted in the history of American legal scholarship, it has not been one of the most easily understood. The modernist character of some of Holmes' sentences, referring to "experience," the unconscious, and the "prejudices" of judges, has made it so appealing to succeeding generations that its nineteenth-century referents have often been lost. But the passage was built on three such referents. One was the polemical use of "logic," which had an immediate contemporary reference, the work of Dean Christopher Columbus Langdell of Harvard. A second was the idea that the law was continually growing and changing, embodying changing "intuitions of public policy" as it developed. This idea was itself not original with Holmes, having come to him, very probably, from his reading of the work of Henry Maine and John Norton Pomeroy, the latter having perhaps been influenced in turn by Maine and the German jurist Karl von Savigny.[13] The idea of legal rules "evolving" over time was a resonant conception for nineteenth-century intellectuals, who were searching for a perspective that could reconcile a historicist attitude toward the past with an interest in deriving general organizing principles around which knowledge could be synthesized.[14]

In addition to the referents to "logic" and "evolutionary history" was a third which, while original with Holmes, can also be related to the intellectual context in which *The Common Law* appeared. It was Holmes' articulation of what he called the paradox of form and substance in the law, in which doctrinal development was simultaneously responsive to contemporary notions of policy and masked by formal adherence to precedent. The paradox of form and substance was an analytical device through which Holmes sought simultaneously to expose the fallacy of "logical" interpretations of common law and to demonstrate a connection between the historical development of legal rules and the policy goals those rules served.

In the paradox "form" played the role of concealing the underlying reasons for change in the law, which were, for Holmes' contemporaries, "historico-political."[15] Legal rules changed because their previous formulations had proven inexpedient: changes in legal rules thus confirmed the inevitable "evolution" of social phenomena in accordance with altered notions of social policy. But the form in which legal rules were articulated was designed to minimize or to conceal change, since the legal system had an investment in stability and continuity over time. This insight of Holmes explained, for his contemporaries, why the inevitabilities of change were not so apparent in the law. It made possible a reconciliation of the apparently static and precedent-driven character of the common law with their belief that history and contemporary politics were the principal explanations for cultural change.

A closer reading of the passage from *The Common Law* quoted above will reveal the role of each of these referents. Holmes' comments on the life of the law being experience rather than logic were repeated, verbatim, from a book notice he had written of Langdell's *Selection of Cases on the Law of Contracts*.[16] But other language in that notice was modified in telling ways in *The Common Law*. Here is the original passage from the book notice:

> The life of the law has not been logic: it has been experience. The seed of every new growth within its sphere has been a felt necessity. The form of continuity has been kept up by reasonings purporting to reduce every thing to a logical sequence; but that form is nothing but the evening dress which the newcomer puts on to make itself presentable according to conventional requirements. The important phenomenon is the man underneath it, not the coat; the justice and reasonableness of a decision, not its consistency with previously held views. No one will ever have a truly philosophic mastery over the law who does not habitually consider the forces outside of it which have made it what it is. More than that, he must remember that as it embodies the story of a nation's development through many centuries, the law finds its philosophy not in self-consistency, which it must always fail in so long as it continues to grow, but in history and the nature of human needs.[17]

In a comparison of the two passages it becomes clear that most of Holmes' modifications have the effect of making his observations more general and less pointed. In the Langdell review "the form of continuity" is juxtaposed rather severely against "felt necessity," "justice and reasonableness," and "human needs." The use of the words "kept up," "purporting," "presentable," and "conventional requirements," the references to "evening dress" and the distinction between "the coat" and "the man underneath" all convey the sense that doctrinal continuity is at best a convention and at worst a sham. In the *Common Law* version all of this language is dropped. Intuitions, prejudices, felt necessities, notions of convenience replace the more charged words, as if the author were looking at legal development from a more detached perspective.

Moreover, those who look at law as an exercise in logic are less pointedly castigated. In the Langdell book notice "no one [who emphasizes only logic] will ever have a truly philosophic mastery over the law"; in the *Common Law* version the law "cannot be dealt with as if it contained only the axioms and corollaries of a book of mathematics." The attack is shifted from a personal one ("Langdell can never be a 'master' of the law") to a methodological one (the analogy of legal science to the science of geometry is flawed). In the book notice one who seeks to understand the law must "habitually consider the forces outside of it which have made it as it is"; (as if Langdell's failure to do so discredits his work); in the *Common Law* version "in order to know what [the law] is, we must know what it has been, and what it tends to become. We must alternately consult history and theories of legislation" (as if Holmes and others are simply engaged in a common enterprise).

One might speculate that Holmes presented his *Common Law* version of the opposition between "logic" and "the forces outside" the law in order to avoid making too pointed an attack on Langdell, who may have been in the audience for the Lowell Lectures.[18] This is, of course, a possibility, but Langdell could hardly mistake the reference, assuming he was aware of the text of Holmes' book notice, which had already appeared when Holmes gave the first of his lectures, as well as the text of the lecture. It is more likely that the modification was made because the stark opposition between "logic" and extralegal forces, between form and substance, did not suit Holmes' general purposes in the lectures. In the Langdell review he had spoken of the "form of continuity," the consistency of a decision with "previously held views," as if they were unimportant in determining the growth of the law, and "the forces outside" as if they were all important. But in *The Common Law* he spoke of alternatively consulting "history" and "theories of legislation"; of comparing "[t]he substance of the law at any given time" with "its form and machinery." In sum, he signaled in the *Common Law* passage that his focus would not be exclusively on "the forces outside" the law; it would be, rather, on the relationship between formal doctrine and substantive policy over time.

Holmes' critique of logic was thus linked to the second late nineteenth-century referent in his opening paragraph in *The Common Law,* the idea that the course of law was similar to the course of evolution in natural science. "The law embodies the story of a nation's development through many centuries," Holmes announced, and therefore could not be dealt with as if it were a collection of mathematical axioms. While this comment was a criticism of "logical" jurisprudence that employed "geometric" reasoning, it was also an endorsement of what may be termed an "evolutionary" theory of doctrinal change. In the Langdell review this emphasis was more explicit. After suggesting that no one who emphasized only the logical connections among legal doctrines would ever have a "truly philosophic mastery" of the subject, Holmes had noted that the law found "its philosophy . . . in history and the nature of human needs." In the next sentence he called law "a branch of anthropology'' in which "the theory of legislation" was part of "a scientific study." The Langdell review thus suggested that the proper way to grasp the central meaning of legal development was to study "history" and contemporary "legislation," a word that in the late nineteenth century approximated our contemporary meaning of "policy," and was routinely contrasted with "law."[19]

The view that the law "is always approaching and never reaching consistency," that it "is forever adopting new principles from life at one end, and . . . retain[ing] old ones from history at the other which have not yet been absorbed or sloughed off," had, as we have seen, been expressed by Holmes in his "Common Carriers" essay before being repeated in the Langdell review. This "evolutionary" view of legal change has often been judged to be one of Holmes' most original contributions in *The Common Law,* especially in contrast to the "formalistic" jurisprudence of other late nineteenth-century writers. But Holmes' view was not particularly original,[20] nor was it unrepresentative of other scholars of his time.

Several reasons can be identified as contributing to the misunderstanding of Holmes' "evolutionary" conception of law, as presented in the *Common Law* lectures. First, the affinity between Langdell's extreme conceptualism and the formalistic methodology employed by many late nineteenth-century judges, when paired against the sharp reaction to conceptualist and formalist modes of legal analysis that surfaced in the early twentieth century, has led scholars to overestimate the reformist dimensions of Holmes' approach and to see him as in methodological kinship to the "antiformalists" of the Progressive era.[21] Second, Holmes' treatment of other jurisprudential writings in *The Common Law* gave the misleading impression that nearly every other nineteenth-century jurist, from Savigny through Langdell, had embraced the methodology of "logic," whereas Holmes stood virtually alone in emphasizing the importance of "felt necessities," "intuitions of public policy," and "forces outside the law" in shaping legal rules. Third, Holmes' inadequate citation of those writers who influenced his ideas, including not only those he characterized as opponents but those whom he simply ignored, has deprived scholars of the opportunity to locate Holmes' "evolutionary" approach in the writings of his contemporaries. Finally, Holmes' "evolutionary" theory of legal change remains obscure because he never actually applied it to substantive legal doctrines in the *Common Law* lectures. His efforts at legal history neither traced doctrine over time nor emphasized the "forces outside the law" that were purportedly shaping the content of doctrine.

Not all these reasons were fortuitous. Holmes, as we will see, had some clear ideological purposes in writing *The Common Law,* and it suited those purposes to lump several kinds of juristic writing together under the rubric of "logic." Moreover, Holmes, while markedly sensitive to the unacknowledged use of his scholarship by others, was himself loath to acknowledge obligations or influence. And despite the breadth and depth of the learning that Holmes brought to *The Common Law,* he was much more interested in using sources to reinforce polemical views he was advancing than to provide analytical or historical texture. He may have called for the replacement of "logic" with evolutionary history, but he was not particularly inclined to practice evolutionary history as a methodology.

The third referent, the paradox of form and substance, can be seen in the last sentences of the *Common Law* passage. "The most difficult labor," Holmes said, "will be to understand the combination of [history and theories of legislation] into new products at every stage. The substance of the law at any given time pretty nearly corresponds, so far as it goes, with what is then understood to be convenient; but its form and machinery, and the degree to which it is able to work out desired results, depend very much on its past.''[22] Here Holmes appeared to be signaling that much of his analytical work in the *Common Law* lectures would be focused on the paradox of form and substance. It was not enough simply to study the "forces outside" the law to understand the meaning of legal doctrine; it was necessary to compare the formal state of legal doctrine with its earlier formulations, in order to appreciate "the degree" to which formal constraints permitted those propounding doctrine "to work out desired results.''

Thus the celebrated passage with which Holmes began *The Common Law*, if its main components and their associations are dissected, yields clues about Holmes' methodological and polemical goals in the work. One was to expose the futility of all efforts to analyze legal doctrine solely in terms of "logic." Another was to juxtapose, against "logic," a grab-bag of other "forces" that shaped the law: "felt necessities of the time," "moral and political theories," "intuitions of public policy, avowed or unconscious," the "prejudices" of judges and other human actors. Still another was to highlight the paradox of form and substance in the law by simultaneously exploring "history," which confined doctrine to acceptable formal structures, and "theories of legislation," which provided the energy for doctrinal change.

If these goals are considered the animating forces of *The Common Law*, the work takes on a curious character at its very outset. The first goal would seem to be in direct opposition to Holmes' statement, three years earlier, that "the business of the jurist is to make known the content of the law; that is, to work upon it from within, or logically, arranging and distributing it in order from its *summum genus* to its *infima species*.''[23] It may be, as previously suggested, that Holmes' methodological orientation had changed since the "Possession" essay. And yet, as we will see, his analytical focus in the *Common Law* lectures was much more "from within," emphasizing the content of doctrine, than from without, on its context.

The second of the goals would appear to create a whole list of topics for further, more detailed attention: the ideological presuppositions of various generations ("felt necessities"); the substance of "moral and political theories" that have shaped the common law; an exploration of the "avowed" and "unconscious" dimensions of policy formulation; an inquiry into the role of "prejudices" and biases in judicial decisionmaking. But none of these topics was pursued in *The Common Law*. Its emphasis is almost wholly on the content of doctrine and the policy implications of that content.

When, however, we come to the third goal Holmes identified in the opening passage of *The Common Law*, we seem to have reached the methodological and polemical key to his narrative. Recall that the essay in which Holmes first identified the paradox of form and substance in the common law, his article on common carriers, had as its central purpose a reexamination of the doctrine that held common carriers strictly liable for damage to goods they transported. Holmes argued that such a reexamination was made possible because his tracing of the doctrine through history had revealed that it had been perpetuated for policy reasons that were now anachronistic. It would seem as if he were anticipating a similar analysis of the various subjects of his lectures, criminal law, torts, bailments, possession, contracts, and successions.

This supposition is reinforced by recalling that in his previous work on four of those subjects Holmes had suggested a doctrinal reorganization of each of them, and that that reorganization had been consistent with particularistic policy goals. It is further reinforced by Holmes' treatment of the subjects, criminal law and contracts, on which he had not previously written, which was oriented toward a comparable reorganization of those fields.

Thus one might expect that the analytical form of *The Common Law* would consist of a historical tracing of the roots of doctrine, a study of its formal content, an explication of the reasons advanced for its perpetuation, a critique of those reasons, and an alternative doctrinal orientation. The polemical form would then consist of policy arguments supporting that alternative. And, in a sense, this is what one finds, but in a highly attenuated form. Holmes presents the roots of doctrine, but in a conclusory fashion; the reader has to take Holmes' word as to the doctrine's content. He then has little to say about the changing content of doctrine, either with respect to its form or with respect to explanations for the change. At the most he notes that it has changed and gives illustrations. He is equally cryptic about the reasons for doctrinal continuity, occasionally offering a policy justification for it but more often merely noting the survival of an archaic formulation.

The bulk of *The Common Law* is devoted to a highly purposive reading of historical cases. Holmes begins with a theoretical formulation of the essence of a subject matter, such as the organization of a field around external standards of liability. He then reads history to demonstrate that this formulation has always been present in the field, although imperfectly recognized, or that the formulation follows from or constitutes a restatement of another cardinal principle of the field. One has to take Holmes at face value for evidence that historical research confirms his thesis. He cites no contrary evidence, and his readings of cases are principally paraphrases rather than renderings of the original language. Thus rather than creating an impression that the paradox of form and substance, demonstrated through history, "frees up" an area for reconsideration from a policy perspective, Holmes' analysis creates the impression that the reconsideration has already taken place and is now being confirmed by a reading of history. "I shall use the history of our law so far as it is necessary to explain a conception or interpret a rule, but no further," Holmes said in his introductory lecture in *The Common Law*. He proceeded to take that statement literally.

Holmes had three interconnected aspirations in writing *The Common Law:* to establish Teutonic rather than Roman practices and procedures as the principal historical sources of Anglo-American common law doctrines; to purge common law doctrines of their moral content by emphasizing that their standards of liability were objective and external rather than subjective; and to restrict the scope of liability for civil injuries as far as possible. There were some subsidiary projects that followed from these aspirations, such as critiquing the Austinian theory of civil liability, attacking the act-at-peril standard of liability in tort law, or reducing the influence of the "German" jurists' subjective theories of doctrinal application, but the essential thrust of Holmes' scheme was to rearrange common law fields so as to harmonize with his aspirations.

~

In his first chapter, on "Early Forms of Liability," Holmes began by saying that he would be discussing "the general theory of liability civil and criminal." This was itself a striking comment, suggesting that he was prepared to treat civil and criminal liability as based on equivalent standards. Having made the comment, he moved onto familiar ground, subjects he had tracked in "Primitive Notions I."

In the "Primitive Notions I" article, we will recall, Holmes had focused on Roman, Greek, Jewish, Salic, and maritime law to argue that the original purpose of legal actions was "vengeance, not compensation."[24] Part of his motivation in that effort was to show that, contrary to "analytical jurists," liability was not based on notions of culpability but on "the much more primitive notion, that liability attached directly to the thing doing the damage." The liability, Holmes suggested, "was not based on fault."[25] Now in the *Common Law* lectures he returned to those "primitive" legal systems, but his conclusions were strikingly different:

> It is commonly known that the early forms of legal procedure were grounded in vengeance. . . . Vengeance imports a feeling of blame, and an opinion, however distorted by passion, that a wrong has been done. It can hardly go very far beyond the case of a harm intentionally injured; even a dog distinguishes between being stumbled over and being kicked. Whether for this cause or another, the early English appeals for personal violence seem to have been confined to intentional wrongs. . . . It was only at a later day, and after argument, that trespass was extended to embrace harms which were foreseen, but which were not the intended consequences of the defendant's act. . . . Our system of private liability for the consequences of a man's own acts, that is, for his trespasses, started from the notion of actual intent and actual personal culpability.[26]

This was a striking reversal of Holmes' previous position, and his conclusion about the culpability-based character of early civil actions was based on no supporting evidence. He himself had been the source for his assertion that it was "commonly known" that early forms of legal actions were grounded in vengeance, and his claims that "vengeance imports a feeling of blame" were entirely unsupported. Indeed the thrust of his "Primitive Notions" articles had been to suggest that the early forms reflected a point of view in which intent to injure or fault were not considerations: the purpose of legal actions was to seek redress from an offending object, however that object had come to injure another. Astonishingly, however, Holmes presented precisely the same analysis of "primitive" and maritime law that he had presented in "Primitive Notions," but with different conclusions.

The first of those conclusions was simply a restatement of the paradox of form and substance he announced in his "Common Carriers" essay. It was initially unclear why this point necessitated repetition, despite its originality, until Holmes followed it with this paragraph:

[T]he process which I have described has involved the attempt to follow precedents, as well as to give a good reason for them. When we find that in large and important branches of the law the various grounds of policy on which the various rules have been justified are later inventions to account for what are in fact survivals from more primitive times, we have a right to reconsider the popular reasons, and, taking a broader view of the field, to decide anew whether those reasons are satisfactory. . . . [S]crutiny and revision are justified.[27]

Now it has become apparent that Holmes' forays into history will be undertaken to free up investigation of rules that amount to "survivals." Since those rules rested on grounds that are now outmoded, and continue to be justified on different grounds—"inventions"—they are peculiarly susceptible to revision.

Holmes had already made this point in the "Common Carriers" essay, and it was clear that he intended more than a simple classification of types of common law rules. He not only wanted to identify "survivals," he wanted to reconsider their validity. But he presented that goal in a somewhat cryptic and misleading form. The next paragraph of his "Early Forms of Liability" lecture read:

But none of the foregoing considerations, nor the purpose of showing the materials for anthropology contained in the history of the law, are the immediate object here. My aim and purpose have been to show that the various forms of liability known to modern law spring from the common ground of revenge. . . . [I]n the criminal law and the law of torts [that fact] is of the first importance. It shows that they have started from a moral basis, from the thought that someone was to blame.[28]

This passage is misleading in two important respects. First, Holmes' purpose in making his argument about the basis of early forms of liability had not been simply to demonstrate that those forms were rooted in a desire for vengeance. It had also been to attribute a concern for culpability to that "common ground" of the procedures. It was not so much that vengeance was the goal of the forms—it was that they sought to identify and to attribute blameworthiness. But even a reader who accepts Holmes' analysis as to the central purpose of the early forms of liability has only Holmes' assertions as a source for the connection between vengeance and blameworthiness. Indeed in "Primitive Notions," which represented Holmes' first use of his research on early procedures, he had come to the same conclusion about vengeance but specifically rejected the connections between vengeance and culpability.

The paragraph was thus misleading in its claims as to what Holmes' analysis had actually shown. It was also misleading about its "aim and purpose." Holmes wrote as if his only goal was to demonstrate the "common ground of revenge" from which the early procedures sprung. But in fact he had another, far more significant goal: to link that demonstration to the claim that the common law had "started with a moral basis." The purpose of his "Early Forms" chapter, from this perspective, was to prepare his audience for a subsequent argument, that the rules and standards of the common law were not only morally based but objectively determined and externally applied. This Holmes made abundantly clear in the last paragraph of his first chapter:

> It remains to be proved that, while the terminology of morals is still retained, and while the law does still and always, in a certain sense, measure legal liability by moral standards, it nevertheless, by the very necessity of its nature, is continually transmuting those moral standards into external or objective ones, from which the actual guilt of the party concerned is wholly eliminated.[29]

In concluding the analysis of the first *Common Law* chapter, it seems useful to summarize some tendencies that have been observed in Holmes' argument. First, he was not loath to use historical research he had earlier employed for one purpose— to suggest that "primitive" conceptions of liability did not demonstrate a conscious-ness of culpability—to show, antithetically, that in fact they demonstrated just that consciousness. Second, the general propositions that formed the core of his argu-ment, such as the connection between vengeance-based procedures and the attribu-tion of culpability, were not supported by any historical evidence. Third, the super-structure of Holmes' argument seemed of great importance to him, so much so that he was willing to risk commentary identifying him as having wholly changed his mind on the role of culpability in early procedural systems. He was prepared to ground the connections crucial to that superstructure—connections between ven-geance and culpability and between a moral basis for legal rules and the external and objective application of those rules—solely on the erudition of his prose.

~

In his second lecture, on criminal law, Holmes sought, as he had previously inti-mated, to link his assertions about the purpose of early forms of liability to his general argument that a unitary theory of liability, based on the objectification of conduct in the form of externally derived standards of reasonableness, characterized both the civil and criminal law. "The desire for vengeance," he began, "imports an opinion that its object is actually and personally to blame. It takes an internal standard, not an objective or external one, and condemns its victim by that."[30] This conclusion raised a question relevant to the criminal law: "whether such a standard is still accepted either in this primitive form, or in some more refined development."[31] Other writers on the criminal law had argued that its purpose was in fact "the gratification of revenge": under this theory criminal law stood "to the passion of revenge in much the same relation as marriage to the sexual appetite." If people sought revenge for wrongs committed against them, this argument ran, "the law has no choice but to satisfy the craving itself, and thus avoid the greater evil of private retribution."[32]

Nonetheless, Holmes argued, the central purpose of the criminal law was not to gratify vengeance, or, put in terms of theories of punishment, to effectuate retribu-tion. Its central purpose was rather "to deter the criminal and others from committing similar crimes."[33] He thus turned to a consideration of alternative theories of pun-ishment, fashioning an argument that deterrence was the basic goal of the criminal law. This argument was part of his more general effort to demonstrate the objectivity and externality of criminal law standards.

Holmes' entire discussion of theories of punishment—indeed all his argument in the lecture on criminal law—was conducted without any direct references to history.[34] While he eventually turned to the substantive elements of crimes as evidence of the validity of his claims, he did not engage in the kind of reading of historical sources he had undertaken in the first chapter. It is not clear why Holmes abandoned history in his discussion of criminal law. He had not written on the subject previously, and perhaps felt he did not have time to research it thoroughly; or he may have felt that the definitions of crimes that he used as illustrations were taken by his readers to be universalistic; or he may have felt that his audience would immediately perceive his discussion to be one of "policy," given that his subject was theories of punishment. At any rate Holmes spared his audience any conclusory assertions couched in the form of historical analysis in his second lecture. He immersed himself in policy arguments from the outset.

Of the three competing theories of punishment—rehabilitation, deterrence, and retribution—Holmes dismissed the first offhandedly. "Few would now maintain" that rehabilitation was the overriding purpose of the criminal law, he asserted. "If it were, every prisoner would be released as soon as it appears clear that he will never repeat his offence, and if he is incurable he should not be punished at all." Moreover, "it would be hard to reconcile the punishment of death with this doctrine."[35] He then turned to retribution. While a feeling that "the fitness of punishment following wrong-doing is axiomatic" was "instinctively recognized by unperverted minds," Holmes suggested that "the feeling of fitness [was] only vengeance in disguise." Otherwise one could not explain how persons who genuinely repented of their conduct and indemnified those they had injured would nonetheless be punished, or how defense of one's own life could exempt from punishment a person who had killed another.

In short, "[p]revention would . . . seem to be the chief and only universal purpose of punishment."[36] Acts were made crimes because society found them incompatible with its conceptions of civilized living, and the acts were punished in order to deter others from committing them. Society was indifferent to the variations of individual behavior that might surface in connection with such acts; it was solely interested in preventing the acts from occurring. "[T]he law," Holmes said, "does undoubtedly treat the individual as a means to an end, and uses him as a tool to increase the general welfare at his own expense." It "subordinates consideration of the individual to that of the public well-being."[37] Holmes was prepared to put this even more starkly:

No society has ever admitted that it could not sacrifice individual welfare to its own existence. If conscripts are necessary for its army, it seizes them, and marches them, with bayonets in their rear, to death. . . . [I]t seems to me clear that the *ultima ratio,* not only *regum,* but of private persons, is force, and that at the bottom of all private relations, however tempered by sympathy and all the social feelings, is a justifiable self-preference. If a man is on a plank in the deep sea which will only float one, and a stranger lays hold of it, he will thrust him off if he can. When the state finds itself in a similar position, it does the same thing.[38]

The law, then, was ultimately indifferent to the varieties of individual temperament and motivation in effectuating its goals, just as individuals were ultimately
indifferent to the welfare of their neighbors when their own preferences were at
stake. But Holmes was not primarily interested in advancing this Darwinist view of
the world in his criminal law lecture. His purpose in asserting that "public policy
sacrifices the individual to the general good," and "liability for punishment cannot
be finally and absolutely determined by considering the actual personal unworthiness
of the criminal alone," was to claim that "the purpose of the criminal law is only
to induce external conformity to rule."[39] Here one begins to see the structure of
Holmes' general argument. An attribution of culpability was at the root of early
forms of liability. But with respect to the most basic examples of culpability, acts
that the state defined as crimes, patterns of punishment suggested that the state was
indifferent to "the actual personal unworthiness" of the criminal. The culpability
was thus attached to the act; it was externally based.

This meant, for Holmes, that the roles of morality and subjectivity in the criminal
law needed to be understood in a different way. As he put it,

> It is not intended to deny that criminal liability . . . is founded on
> blameworthiness. Such a denial would shock the moral sense of any civilized
> community; or, to put it another way, a law which punished conduct which
> would not be blameworthy in the average member of the community would be
> too severe for that community to bear. It is only intended to point out that,
> when we are dealing with that part of the law which aims more directly than
> any other at establishing standards of conduct, we should expect there more
> than elsewhere to find the tests of liability are external, and independent of the
> degree of evil in the particular person's motives or intentions. The conclusion
> follows directly from the nature of the standards to which conformity is
> required. These are not only external . . . but they are of general application.
> They do not merely require that every man should get as near as he can to the
> best conduct possible for him. They require him at his own peril to come up to
> a certain height. They take no account of incapacities, unless the weakness is
> so marked as to fall into well-known exceptions, such as infancy or madness.
> They assume that every man is as able as every other to behave as they
> command. If they fall on any one class harder than the other, it is on the
> weakest. For it is precisely to those who are most likely to err by temperament,
> ignorance, or folly, that the threats of the law are the most dangerous.[40]

The morality of the criminal law was thus a morality directed at acts, not at persons;
and the standards of the criminal law reflected that orientation. They took no account
of subjective motives or intentions except insofar as they were reflected in acts. They
likewise gave no credit for extenuating circumstances save in those instances where
a person's condition was conclusive evidence that a "blameworthy" act was not in
fact blameworthy.

Holmes now sought to apply his conclusions to specific criminal law doctrines.
We need not follow the application in detail; suffice it to say that his argument was
that terms essential to the definition of crimes, such as "malice," "intent," and
"wilful," were for the most part terms of art that had an objective meaning. They

did not mean that the subjective state of mind of the defendant had been determined; they meant the actions of the defendant, under the circumstances, were consistent with the labels malicious, intentional, or wilful. The orientation of the criminal law was thus toward the facts surrounding an alleged crime, with a view of determining whether those facts were consistent with behavior signified by the labels. As Holmes put it, "the test . . . is the degree of danger . . . attending the act under the known circumstances of the case."[41] He then converted this test into a normative proposition: "[a]cts should be judged by their tendency under the known circumstances, not by the actual intent which accompanies them."[42]

The law of attempts was a particularly useful area for Holmes to illustrate his general analysis. That law generally attributed the intent associated with a crime even though the crime was unsuccessful, and punished the defendant accordingly. But it did so with reference to external facts rather than the defendant's state of mind. Holmes put two "attempt" cases as illustrations. If a man lit a match near a haystack, and then on discovering he was being watched blew it out, he was guilty of an attempt to burn the haystack. If, however, he started from Boston to Cambridge for the purpose of committing a murder when he arrived, but was prevented from crossing the Charles River because the drawbridge was not functioning, he was not guilty of attempted murder. The distinction turned exclusively on the degree of danger raised by the facts. "When a man buys matches to fire a haystack," Holmes maintained, "or starts on a journey meaning to murder at the end of it, there is still a considerable chance that he will change his mind before he comes to the point. But when he has struck the match, or cocked and aimed the pistol, there is very little chance that he will not persist to the end, and the danger becomes so great that the law steps in."[43]

The law of attempts thus demonstrated that an external standard of liability—the degree of danger raised by the facts of the alleged crime—was being employed. It also reinforced Holmes' view that the purpose of punishment was deterrence. If retribution or rehabilitation had been the goals of the criminal law, the man who blew out the match after lighting it near a haystack would not have been punished. He had stopped the dangerous act himself; there was no vengeance or rehabilitation to seek. But punishing him for an attempt sent a message to others who might be inclined to light matches near haystacks.

Holmes summarized his conclusions in the criminal law chapter as follows:

All acts are indifferent *per se*.

In the characteristic type of substantive crime acts are rendered criminal because they are done under circumstances in which they will probably cause some harm which the law seeks to prevent.

The test of criminality in such cases is the degree of danger shown by experience to attend that act under those circumstances.[44]

The chapter had, in some respects, been a remarkably effective performance. Not only had Holmes supplied a theory of the criminal law that explained a large proportion of its doctrines, he had linked that theory to his own views on the appropriate purposes of punishment. The theory had its analytical difficulties, of course, and appeared to be based both on a bleakly Hobbesian view of human nature and a bleakly positivistic conception of law. The substantive law of crimes is perhaps better described as a mix of subjective and objective criteria, suggesting that the law is not always indifferent either to acts or to the apparent motivation for them. Moreover, Holmes' assertions that since human actions are bottomed on self-interest, those of the state will be likewise, or that those instances in which criminal law standards appear to require more than the average foresight of the reasonable man can be explained by the simple fact that the state wanted that result, beg some questions. One might assume that "the moral sense of any civilized community" would be shocked by laws that merely imposed the arbitrary preferences of the state because force was the ultimate justification for law. But on the whole the lecture was a coherent and compelling statement of Holmes' views, suggesting that one of his goals in *The Common Law* was an overt reorganization of substantive fields around principles that he thought salient and policies that he thought sensible.

~

Holmes next devoted two chapters to torts. We have seen that in his previous writings on the subject he had employed both analytically and historically oriented methodologies, and that in his "Trespass and Negligence" essay he had first made the claim that early forms of action presupposed some fault or culpability in the offending party. His original intention in writing on torts had been to work out his right/duty distinction. He had felt that torts provided him with a particularly fertile field for the distinction because most tort cases involved persons in no preexisting relationships with one another, and thus illustrated the existence of duties owed by all the world to all the world. "[A]n enumeration of the actions which have been successful, and of those which have failed," he had argued in "The Theory of Torts," "defines the extent of the primary duties imposed by the law.... Torts ... contains in the first place duties of all the world to all the world."[45] But by "Trespass and Negligence," we have seen, he abandoned the right/duty distinction and introduced the claim that culpability was at the basis of all tort actions.

His *Common Law* chapters reiterated that claim and pursued some of its implications. As in "Trespass and Negligence," he rejected Austin's argument that tort law was based on "personal fault" (as distinguished from "blameworthiness" imposed by the community), rejected in most cases the act-at-peril theory of tort liability,[46] and asserted that the grounds of civil liability were essentially the same as those of the criminal law, that is, an externally based standard of reasonable care under the circumstances of the case. His arguments, as in "Trespass and Negligence," were based on policy considerations. He repeated his comments about the general assumption that losses should lie where they fell and the appropriateness of market distributions rather than state distributions of wealth; he reinterpreted old "act-at-peril" cases to suggest that given the practical difficulties of an act-at-peril standard they had in fact been based on fault.

Holmes next addressed what he took to be two of the major implications of his theory. One, previously mentioned, was that the standards of liability in criminal and civil law were the same: objective, externally determined, and emphasizing "blameworthiness," in the sense of acts that the community considered blame-worthy because of their dangerousness to others. This meant that across the spectrum of criminal and civil liability, from cases where "intent" was required to "act-at-peril" cases, the standard of liability was consistent and uniform. The presence or absence of an "intent" requirement was simply a response to the perceived dan-gerousness of conduct in given circumstances. Dropping a two-by-four off a high building onto a crowded street was so dangerous that one could presume intent to injure, even to kill; dropping the same object into a vacant lot was less dangerous and could not give rise to criminal liability. Keeping animals of known ferocious habits in zoos subjected the keepers to act-at-peril liability if the animals escaped and injured someone; keeping domestic dogs did not result in the same liability since dogs were not expected to be comparably dangerous.

The emphasis of the objective standard on the circumstances that gave rise to an injury suggested that jury determinations of the degree of danger in a given case would be crucial to the question of liability. This implication troubled Holmes, and he sought to narrow the ambit of jury power in tort cases. "If in the whole department of unintentional wrongs," he pointed out, "the courts arrived at no further utterance than the question of negligence, and left every case, without rudder or compass, to the jury, they would simply confess their inability to state a large part of the law."[47] But the tendency had been otherwise: "statutes and decisions have busied themselves . . . with substituting for the vague test of the care exercised by a prudent man, a precise one of specific acts or omissions."[48]

Holmes applauded this trend. He conceded that "the courts have been very slow to withdraw questions of negligence from the jury, without distinguishing nicely whether the doubt concerned the facts or the standard to be applied." But one should always recall that

> when standards of conduct are left to the jury, it is a temporary surrender of a
> judicial function which may be resumed at any moment in any case when the
> court feels competent to do so. Were this not so, the almost universal
> acceptance of the first proposition in this Lecture, that the general foundation
> of liability for unintentional wrongs is conduct different from that of a prudent
> man under the circumstances, would leave all our rights and duties throughout
> a great part of the law to the necessarily more or less accidental feelings of a
> jury. . . . [T]he tendency of the law must always be to narrow the field of
> uncertainty.[49]

In many areas of negligence, Holmes believed, "a state of facts" was "often repeated in practice."[50] In such instances "[a] judge who has long sat at *nisi prius* ought gradually to acquire a fund of experience which enables him to represent the common sense of the community in ordinary instances far better than the average jury." Furthermore, "the sphere in which [such a judge] is able to rule without taking [a jury's] opinion at all should be continually growing."[51]

Moreover, tendencies in the evolution of legal doctrine functioned to narrow the range of jury discretion. Here Holmes revived one of his earlier metamorphic gen-eralizations, originally presented in "The Theory of Torts":

The growth of the law is very apt to take place in this way. Two widely different cases suggest a general distinction, which is a clear one when stated broadly. But as new cases cluster around the opposite poles, and begin to approach each other, the distinction becomes more difficult to trace; the determinations are made one way or the other on a very slight perponderance of feeling, rather than of articulate reason; and at last a mathematical line is arrived at by the contact of contrary decisions, which is so far arbitrary that it might equally well have been drawn a little farther to the one side or to the other, but which must have been drawn somewhere in the neighborhood of where it falls.

In this way exact distinctions have been worked out upon questions in which the elements are few. . . . And although this attempt to work out an exact line requires much caution, it is entirely philosophical in spirit.[52]

With this exhortation to judges to trust in their experience, draw doctrinal lines, and limit jury discretion whenever they could, Holmes concluded his first chapter on torts. As had been characteristic of his earlier chapters, his boldest claims had been unaccompanied by extensive documentation. By the close of his first torts chapter he was prepared not only to assert that "the general foundation of liability for unintentional wrongs is conduct different from that of a prudent man under the circumstances," but to treat that proposition as having "almost universal acceptance."[53] The act-at-peril theory of tort liability had not only been read out of early cases, Holmes had taken his contemporaries to have concurred with him in this reading.[54]

Holmes began his second lecture on torts by emphasizing the same theme. His general proposition that both civil and criminal liability were based on standards of prudent conduct had two major difficulties, he conceded. "In the discussion of unintentional wrongs, the greatest difficulty to be overcome was found to be the doctrine that a man acts always at his peril." That difficulty being overcome, another surfaced. In crimes and in intentional torts "the difficulty will be to prove that actual wickedness of the kind described by the several words [used to define intentional torts, such as fraud, malice, and intent] is not an element in the civil wrongs to which those words are applied."[55]

At first blush it would appear that this difficulty was even more troublesome than the presence of an act-at-peril standard of liability. "Intent" and "malice," as elements of a tort, seemed quite far away from a standard of prudent care under the circumstances. But Holmes' criminal law chapter indicated that he was well prepared to address the problem. As he put it in the opening paragraph of his chapter discussing fraud, malice, and intent:

It has been shown, in dealing with the criminal law, that when we call an act malicious in common speech, we mean that harm to another person was intended to come of it, and that such harm was desired for its own sake as an end in itself. For the purposes of the criminal law, however, intent alone was found to be important, and to have the same consequences as intent with malevolence superadded. Pursuing the analysis, intent was found to be made up of foresight of the harm as a consequence, coupled with a desire to bring it about, the latter being conceived as the motive for the act in question. Of these, again, foresight only seemed material. As a last step, foresight was reduced to its lowest term, and it was concluded that, subject to exceptions which were explained, the general basis of criminal liability was knowledge, at the time of action, of facts from which common experience showed that certain harmful results were likely to follow.[56]

In his discussion of act-at-peril liability, Holmes had emphasized the policy dimensions of his argument, stressing the extensive liability that an act-at-peril standard would create, introducing complexities raised by causation, and noting the "general principle" of losses lying where they fell. Similarly in his discussion of the meaning of "intent" in intentional torts he emphasized policy considerations. A subjectivist definition of intent was impossible: intent needed to be inferred from acts. But acts depended on circumstances. Falsely stating "in the secrecy of the closet" that "a certain barrel contains No. 1 Mackerel" was different from making the same statement "to another man in the course of a bargain." Thus liability for the acts depended on "certain concomitant circumstances [being] shown." Holmes then took his analysis a step further:

> The principal question then is, whether this intent can be reduced to the same terms as it has been in other cases. There is no difficulty in the answer. It is perfectly clear that the intent that a false representation should be acted on would be conclusively established by proof that the defendant knew that the other party intended to act upon it. If the defendant foresaw the consequence of his acts, he is chargeable, whether his motive was a desire to induce the other party to act, or simply an unwillingness for private reasons to state the truth. If the defendant knew a present fact . . . which, according to common experience, made it likely that his act would have the harmful consequence, he is chargeable, whether he in fact foresaw the consequence or not.[57]

In short, "[t]he standard of what is called intent is thus really an external standard of conduct under the known circumstances, and the analysis of the criminal law holds good here.[58]

From that point Holmes quickly proceeded through the remaining intentional torts—misrepresentation, slander, malicious prosecution, conspiracy, and trover or conversion—employing the same analysis. He concluded that "the true explanation of the reference of [intentional tort] liability to a moral standard . . . is not that it is for the purpose of improving men's hearts, but that it is to give a fair chance to avoid doing the harm before he is held responsible for it. It is intended to reconcile the policy of letting accidents lie where they fall, and the reasonable freedom of others with the protection of the individual from injury."[59]

Holmes was now ready to summarize the entire field of tort law. There were instances in which the policy of letting losses lie where they fell and the autonomy principle allowed "certain harms to be inflicted irrespective of the moral condition of him who inflicts them." A person could establish himself in business even though the consequence might be "to diminish the custom of another shopkeeper, perhaps to ruin him." There were other situations in which "the law . . . may on grounds of policy throw the absolute risk of certain transactions on the person engaging in them, irrespective of blameworthiness in any sense.'' An example was engaging in especially hazardous activities, such as blasting or shooting. But ''most liabilities in tort [lay] between these two extremes, and [were] founded on the infliction of harm which the defendant had a reasonable opportunity to avoid.''[60] In those cases the defendant's liability ''will be determined by considering the degree of danger attending the act or conduct under the known circumstances.''[61] The test was whether an average person in the community would have forseen that danger to another would follow from the act, and therefore treated the act as ''blameworthy.''

Holmes regarded the first four *Common Law* lectures as of a piece, and it is worth recapitulating their connecting links. His discussion in those lectures, he said at the beginning of his fifth lecture, had been oriented toward ''the general principles of liability, and to the mode of ascertaining the point at which a man begins to act at his own peril.''[62] That discussion had been a progressive effort to show that the principles of criminal and civil liability were objectively determined and externally based, and that ''act-at-peril'' liability was, on close analysis, reserved for those situations in which a person had ''intentionally'' or carelessly ignored danger to others.

Holmes had argued that the tests of the criminal law, as well as the civil law, emphasized the degree of danger produced by conduct under given circumstances, and were thus objective rather than subjective. They were designed to ascertain whether a reasonable person in the position of the defendant knew or should have known of the dangers attendant on particular conduct.

When the tests of the criminal law were reconceived in this fashion, they demonstrated that its focus was on identifying dangerous conduct rather than stigmatizing behavior. That characterization harmonized with Holmes' argument for a theory of punishment whose purpose was to deter dangerous conduct rather than to rehabilitate or seek revenge upon criminals. In Holmes' analysis, society was as indifferent to the individual criminal as it was to acts *per se;* it was concerned only with dangerous conduct and its prevention. The question in criminal law was not why criminals had acted as they did; it was whether their acts were sufficiently dangerous to be labeled ''intentional'' or even ''malicious.''

A similar question was central to tort law. Since the standard of liability in torts was essentially the same as that in criminal law—''reasonable'' enough foreseeability of danger so as to cause the defendant's conduct to be labeled ''blameworthy''—the only difference between the two regimes was that in tort law the conduct in question was not, in most instances, sufficiently dangerous that in addition to giving rise to an action for damages it precipitated an interest on the part of the state in punishing the individual whose conduct had caused injury. A focus on acts, foreseeability, dangerousness, and ''reasonable'' versus ''blameworthy'' conduct characterized the law of torts as well as the law of crimes.

So summarized, Holmes' general principles of liability appeared neat, orderly, and consistent. His emphasis on reasonable conduct under circumstances raised problems of vagueness, but he urged experienced judges to respond to that problem by specifying negligent conduct as far as possible and thereby limiting the range of jury discretion. His system significantly underestimated the ambit of act-at-peril liability in torts, but that feature had the effect of throwing those instances where act-at-peril liability survived, such as common carrier liability and vicarious liability, into sharp relief, putting pressure on those doctrines. The system presupposed that inadvertent, non-negligent losses should remain on those who had the misfortune to encounter them, and thereby allowed a variety of dangerous activities to be conducted in society without those perpetrating the activities necessarily having to bear the costs of injuries they created. But it is arguable that in preferring order, certainty, and freedom to bargain in the marketplace to compensation and wealth redistribution, Holmes was simply mirroring the preferences of his late nineteenth-century contemporaries.[63]

~

The first four chapters of *The Common Law* had been demonstrably in the mode of the last stage of Holmes' early scholarship, which emphasized the fusion of history with contemporary policy. In the next chapters he appeared to resurrect earlier stages. He turned from "general" principles of liability to the "special relations out of which special rights and duties arise." These were possession and contract: by "special relations" Holmes meant that the duties owed to persons in possession of property or in contractual relations arose out of a particular status.

Chapters Five and Six, on bailment and possession, considered topics that Holmes had previously addressed in his "Possession" and "Common Carriers" articles. Unlike the chapters on contracts and torts, however, those on bailment and possession were historically oriented, with few explicit policy observations. It appeared as if Holmes were following his maxim, stated in the "Possession" essay, that "[t]he business of the jurist is to make known the content of the law; that is, to work upon it from within, or logically, arranging and distributing it, in order, from its *summum genus* to its *infima species,* so far as practicable."[64] But in fact Holmes had policy objectives in mind, ones that were consistent with those he had advanced in the earlier lectures. In summary, those objectives were to renew an attack on act-at-peril liability, this time in the form of the strict liability of common carriers for injuries to goods or persons they transported, and to convert questions of possession from abstract, philosophical inquiries to concrete, "empirical" ones, with the aim of reducing questions about the rights and responsibilities of those in possessory disputes to objective determinations of who in fact had physical possession of the goods in question.

The role of policy analysis in Holmes' "Bailment" and "Possession" chapters becomes apparent when one compares the text of those chapters to their original versions, his essays on "Possession" and "Common Carriers and the Common Law." The original purpose of the "Possession" essay, we have seen, had been to discredit "German" theories about the nature of possession and to demonstrate that "one who manifests physical control over a thing with the intent and power (judged by the manifested facts) to exclude others than the owner from it, acquires possession, whether he has or has not the intent to deal with it as owner."[65] The original purpose of the "Common Carriers" essay had been to attack a prominent example of act-at-peril liability.

In his *Common Law* chapters Holmes made two modifications in his use of the essays. He split the "Possession" essay in half, placing the first part in his "Bailment" chapter and reserving the second part for his chapter on "Possession." He then added much of the "Common Carriers" essay to his "Bailment" chapter, treating a common carrier as one prominent example of a bailee. At the same time he elaborated upon the remaining portions of his "Possession" article in his "Possession" chapter.

The analytical centerpiece of Holmes' reorganization of his earlier essays came in a passage at the beginning of his "Bailment" chapter:

> The test of the theory of possession which prevails in any system of law is to be found in its mode of dealing with persons who have a thing within their power, but who do not own it, or assert the position of an owner for themselves with regard to it—bailees, in a word. It is necessary, therefore, as a preliminary to understanding the common-law theory of possession, to study the common law with regard to bailees.[66]

One may wonder why Holmes was interested in maintaining that the treatment of bailees is "the test of [any] theory of possession." On reflection, it appears that bailees furnished him with a helpful example because the treatment of bailee liability necessarily raises the problem of "intent" in property law, a problem that had aroused Holmes' strong interest in criminal law and torts. Bailees do not have the "intent" to exercise dominion over property entrusted to them in the same sense that do owners of that property; they do not "intend" to exclude all the world from access to it. But at the same time bailees *can* exclude all but the owners of property entrusted to them; they act as if they are owners even though they lack the "intent" associated with ownership. For Holmes, then, bailees provided an illustration of the principle that one does not need "intent" to exclude others from possession; it is sufficient to have physical control and power to exclude all but owners.

In his "Possession" chapter Holmes put the case of a man who had bought a safe, and, having decided to sell it, sent it to another, and allowed him to keep his books in it until it was sold. When the keeper found money concealed in a crevice in the safe, the owner demanded it, and was refused. The keeper's refusal was upheld by a court; Holmes thought that decision wrong. If the keeper was a bailee, he reasoned, his possession of the safe gave him the power to exclude others from its contents, but not the owner. The owner may not have known about the hidden money in the safe, but he had the power to exclude the keeper from the contents of the safe, except insofar as he had permitted him to keep his books in it. The fact that he had no specific "intent" to exclude the keeper from the money, because he did not know about its existence, was irrelevant because he had the power to exclude the keeper from anything in the safe. As Holmes put it, "[t]he bailor has the power . . . to exclude the bailee from the goods, and therefore may be said to be in possession of them as against the bailee."[67]

It is now apparent that bailment was a convenient possessory relationship for Holmes because bailment furnished an example of possession without the "intent" to exercise dominion over the property in question. It followed for Holmes that just as the question of whether a bailee had responsibility to return property to the bailor turned on "empirical" facts, the liability of bailees to bailors ought to turn on equally objective and external criteria. In his analysis of common carrier liability he had argued that an initially objective standard of liability—whether the carrier had made a specific promise to be responsible for the loss or destruction of goods irrespective of fault—had degenerated into an act-at-peril standard, apparently based on the "common" or public status of the carrier. He had concluded that "[i]f . . . common carriers remain a merely empirical exception from general doctrine, courts may well hesitate to extend the significance of those words,"[68] resting liability on the circumstances of the loss rather than on the status of the carrier. He then generalized this conclusion at the close of his "Possession" chapter:

> Following the order of analysis which has been pursued with respect to possession, the first question must be, What are the facts to which the rights called ownership are attached as a legal consequence?[69]

The "Bailment" and "Possession" chapters, despite their historical focus, were thus of a piece with the earlier chapters. Their purpose was to organize common law doctrines around "empirical" investigation, external standards of liability, and objective application of doctrinal criteria. But Holmes' analysis contained an internal inconsistency. In discussing common carrier liability he had concluded that the act-at-peril standard reserved for them was "a merely empirical exception from general doctrine." But throughout the "Bailment" and "Possession" chapters he had argued that doctrinal standards *ought* to be derived empirically. In that argument empirical analysis functioned as a corrective to doctrine, an effort to clarify the dependence of legal "rights" on certain facts being present. But in his observations on common carrier liability "empirical," prefaced by "merely," was being used in a different sense, as an example of a historical quirk in the law that made no sense on policy grounds, existing only as a "survival."

In Holmes' former argument empirical analysis serves to conform doctrine to practice; in his latter argument it serves as an instrument of policy. If in disputes over property the rule is that owners prevail over possessors, empirical analysis reinforces that rule by helping to determine who "owns" a piece of property. But if with respect to common carriers the rule is act-at-peril, empirical analysis, by facilitating identification of "common carriers," should similarly undergird that rule. Since Holmes disapproved of the established rule for common carriers, however, he treated it as a "merely empirical exception." Empirical in that sense simply meant that it existed; its existence did not clarify anything.

This ambivalent use of "empirical" analysis is a fundamental characteristic of Holmes' methodology in *The Common Law*. At times Holmes acted as if the purpose of determining the factual underpinnings of doctrine was to permit doctrines to be tested against the circumstances in which they were applied, such as in torts (reasonable conduct), criminal law ("intent" as manifested in actions), and property ("ownership" or "possession"). While this approach stripped the element of subjectivity from doctrinal analysis, it had no effect on the substance of doctrines themselves, such as whether tort liability should turn on reasonable conduct or some stricter standard. Indeed the label "empirical" was in the service of substantive doctrine. When Holmes disapproved of substantive doctrine and found historical examples of it, he dismissed those as "merely empirical." It did not matter to

Holmes whether empirical analysis revealed a bailee to be a "common carrier," because the liability of common carriers was misconceived. In that example he was using "empirical" as a synonym for "existing as a historical fact."

Holmes' claim that "empirical" analysis would clarify doctrinal standards, and therefore that historical forays into the origins of doctrine would illuminate the policy reasons behind it, thus appears to be undermined by his own use of that analysis. If Holmes intended to show that existing doctrines were undermined in their application, so that the "law in action" was not the equivalent of the "law on the books," one could argue that he was using empirical analysis as a corrective or as a way of transcribing "reality." But where empirical analysis is simultaneously employed to undermine doctrine (as in Holmes' effort to show that tort cases had never adopted an act-at-peril standard) and dismissed as aberrational (as in Holmes' concession that the common carrier cases were "merely empirical"), one can have little confidence in it as an independent analytical tool. One suspects that it is in the service of policy formation.

These observations lead us back to the paradox of form and substance, originally formulated by Holmes in his "Common Carriers" essay, which he had affixed to his *Common Law* chapter on early forms of liability. One of the consequences of the paradox, for Holmes, was that since the formal justifications for legal doctrines never fully captured the basis of those doctrines, and yet, because of their formal nature, survived in place of hidden substantive justifications, one was free to use the artificial dimensions of formal reasoning as takeoff points for reexamination of doctrines on policy grounds. Holmes had explicitly said this in his "Common Carriers" essay.

One might have expected that the paradox of form and substance would have led Holmes toward an exploration of the substantive bases of surviving doctrinal rules. Such an analysis might have led to the conclusion that the bases were compatible with outmoded social assumptions and thus the rules could be reexamined. Instead, Holmes' analysis of bailment and early forms of liability had focused on the formal rules themselves, attempting to show that rules had been retained or modified out of "confusion of thought," meaning that phrase in a logical sense. The rules, being logically confused, were thus mere "survivals," not entitled to great weight, and the policy bases of the rules could accordingly be rethought.

Holmes' choice to approach "survivals" in this fashion implicitly relegated his historical analysis to a marginal status. He did not approach history from the point of view of a social or intellectual historian, seeking to explain the substantive bases of rules through an examination of their social context or the ideological presuppositions on which they were grounded. He simply recorded the formal transformation of doctrine, noting changes and "survivals," and demonstrated the "illogic" of many surviving doctrines by emphasizing their unfortunate contemporary consequences. Common carrier liability, for example, had survived because of the bailment analogy and because of an inarticulate notion that those who served the public owed its members some general obligation of care. Holmes did not reveal why the bailment analogy was regarded as compelling in relationships between railroads or ships and their passengers, or what lay behind the assumption that those who exercised a public calling bore a special responsibility. He merely noted that common carrier liability was "one of many signs that the laws were administered in the interest of the upper classes," that it ran counter to the principle that left "parties free to make their own bargains," and that "[a]n attempt to apply [the] doctrine generally at the present day would be thought monstrous."[70]

Holmes' use of history throughout *The Common Law* was thus not fully consistent with his opening observations about it. In his first chapter he suggested that while a "great many" legal rules "are quite sufficiently accounted for by their manifest good sense," some rules could "only be understood by reference to the infancy of procedure among the German tribes, or to the social condition of Rome under the Decemvirs." He proposed to "use the history of our law to explain a conception or interpret a rule." But his efforts at explanation or interpretation were confined to showing that the rule existed in older societies, occasionally speculating on why it might have come into being, and then labeling it a "survival." While this technique may have been intended to "free up" discussion of the rule by showing that it was founded on history and not on "manifest good sense," Holmes sometimes seemed to be using the "survivor" status of the rule as a justification for its continued existence, perhaps on the ground that it fostered certainty or consistency in the application of legal doctrines.[71]

The marginal status occupied by history—and, for that matter, "empirical" analysis of any sort—in Holmes' *Common Law* lectures might be perceived to be of only technical interest.[72] But the reputation that *The Common Law* has enjoyed makes that finding of somewhat greater significance. Principally on the basis of the celebrated passages from Holmes' introductory lecture, especially that contrasting "logic" with "experience" in the "life of the law," *The Common Law* has been seen as a pathbreaking work of legal philosophy, the first example of modernist jurisprudence. That image of the work is reinforced by the revelation that Holmes identified "logic" with the scholarly attitude of C. C. Langdell, which has led modern scholars to surmise that he meant his lectures to be understood as a reaction to Langdell's emphasis on the logical parsing and reconciliation of legal doctrine in appellate cases.

Holmes has thus been seen as a proto-Realist, focusing on the "prejudices" of judges and the "felt necessities" of generations as shaping forces in the law, as a legal anthropologist, ranging through the doctrines and practices of "primitive" societies, as a proto-economist, championing "empirical" analysis and market-based theories of liability, and above all as an arch-critic of formalist jurisprudence, the orthodox discourse of the late nineteenth-century elite legal profession, of whom Langdell was one of the high priests. But if one considers what Holmes actually engaged in in his *Common Law* lectures—apart from his riveting passages contrasting "prevalent moral and political theories" with "the syllogism"—one finds a methodology strikingly like that of Langdell.

Recall that in Holmes' unsigned 1880 review of Langdell's casebook on contracts, and in an 1881 letter to Sir Frederick Pollock, Holmes had fashioned a contrast between his jurisprudential approach and that of Langdell. He had claimed that in Langdell's contracts casebook "[d]ecisions are reconciled which those who gave them meant to be opposed, and drawn together by subtle lines which never were dreamed of before Mr. Langdell wrote.'' He had added the previous quoted sentences, ''[n]o one will ever have truly philosophic mastery over the law who does not habitually consider the forces outside of it which have made it what it is,'' and ''the law finds its philosophy not in self-consistency, but . . . in history and the nature of human needs.''[73] And in the letter to Pollock he had said that Langdell ''is all for logic and hates any reference to anything outside of it, and his explanations and reconciliations of the cases would have astonished the judges who decided them.''[74]

In this contrast Langdell's focus is on ''logic'': Holmes' on history and other ''forces outside the law.'' Moreover, Langdell's approach is presentist: his reconciliations of cases were ''never dreamed of'' before he wrote. But consider Holmes' treatment of early forms of liability, or of tort law, or of the law of criminal attempts, or of possession. His ''reconciliations'' were comparably breathtaking and comparably presentist. The kind of clear evidence suggesting that tort law had always been organized around a fault standard, or that subjectivity was not an element in criminal offenses, or that possession was grounded on exclusivity and power, was simply not present to the degree that Holmes' analysis suggested. He had introduced evidence congenial with his belief that external, objective standards should govern criminal law, torts, and property, his concern for promoting certainty and predictibility in common law subjects, and his interest in confining civil liability to injuries caused by deviations from a standard of reasonable conduct. His methodological focus had not precisely been that of Langdell—Holmes had been more open, if assertive and conclusory, in his use of policy arguments—but it was far closer to that of Langdell than that of a jurist interested in examining ''the forces outside'' the law.

One might ask why, if Holmes' approach in *The Common Law* was closer to that of the orthodox logicians he was criticizing than to those who would look past formal logic to the historical and social context of the law, commentators have repeatedly treated Holmes as a late nineteenth-century intellectual radical[75] and a precursor of modernist jurisprudential theories. The answer is both complex and straightforward, having to do with the glossing of *The Common Law* by early twentieth-century scholars and with the persistent failure on the part of students of Holmes' lectures to pay close attention to their details. The first dimension of the answer will be considered in more detail when Holmes' career on the Supreme Court of the United States is taken up: suffice it to say here that a generation of admirers who found a philosophic congeniality with some of Holmes' attitudes also found it convenient to ignore others.

The second dimension can be more succinctly explained at this stage. *The Common Law*'s detailed analysis is far less accessible or interesting than its generalizations, and perhaps mystifying to moderns in its ambivalent treatment of ''empirical'' data. Given the baffling features of Holmes' narrative and the memorable quality of some of his general observations, it is no surprise that readers have focused on the latter and ignored the former.[76] The consequence, of course, has been to make Holmes into a timeless figure and to deemphasize his affinity with contemporaries such as Langdell. This observation will be expanded upon in the concluding sections of this chapter.

The elements of Holmes' methodology in *The Common Law* are perhaps thrown into sharpest relief in his three chapters on contracts, where he considered, successively, the "history" and "elements" of contract law and the analysis of "void and voidable" contracts. Holmes, who had not previously written on the subject, produced his contracts lectures in the summer of 1880, doubtless stimulated by his reading of Langdell's contracts casebook. By that time the general scheme for Holmes' *Common Law* lectures was firmly in his mind, and the contracts lectures almost perfectly reproduced that scheme.

In recreating the history of contracts in his first contracts chapter, Holmes confronted the established explanation that English contract law reflected principles of Roman origin. Under this explanation, there were two such principles: that contracts containing certain formal requirements, such as a seal, would be sustained whether or not they were truly bargained-for exchanges, and that other contracts, not containing such requirements, would be sustained only for "cause"—a term signaling that courts would find that such contracts represented promises for which there was sufficient consideration. Contracts were thus examples of "a union of several wills to a single, whole and undivided will."[77]

Needless to say, this account of the history of common law contract doctrine was uncongenial to Holmes,[78] and he sought to trace the origins of each of the above principles to alternative sources. The first principle, originating in the action for debt, was "of pure German descent," having "the features of the primitive procedure which is found on the Continent."[79] To recover in "debt" a plaintiff needed to produce a written document stating the defendant's obligation, or a "transaction witness" that could swear as to the obligation's existence. The seal requirement for contracts, Holmes argued, evolved from the early Germanic procedure of having written documents whose seals identified the persons who owed obligations to others. The other requirement for contracts without seals—consideration—also evolved from Germanic procedure, in this instance the transaction witnesses. Over time the technical significance of these procedures diminished, but their apparent function was retained, that of verifying that a defendant who had promised something to a plaintiff had received something in return, making the plaintiff's allegation of a debt plausible.

Meanwhile, in Holmes' account, another action had surfaced, that of assumpsit, which originally was used in tort cases, being reserved for those cases where a defendant had promised to do something but had done it negligently. In this action consideration for the defendant's promise was not necessary. Eventually assumpsit came to be regarded as a form of action used in a special class of contracts, those in which the defendant received no benefit from his promise but the plaintiff was subjected to a detriment from the defendant's failure to perform. While courts sought to separate "assumpsit" actions from "debt" actions, which required consideration for the defendant's promise, assumpsit eventually expanded to cover transactions that had been reserved for debt. As Holmes put it,

> The illusion that assumpsit thus extended did not mean contract, could not be kept up. . . . A simple contract, to be recognized as binding by the courts of

Henry VI, must have been based upon a benefit to the debtor; now a promise
might be enforced in consideration of a detriment to the promisee. . . .
[Eventually assumpsit] supplanted debt, because the existence of the duty to
pay was sufficient consideration for a promise to pay. . . . [This] vastly
extended the number of actionable contracts.[80]

Holmes' analysis, with its characteristic emphasis on Teutonic procedures, common law writs, and "confusion of thought," closely paralleled the analysis he had
undertaken in his property and torts chapters. It had the advantage of marginalizing
the Roman roots of English contract law; it also had the advantage of suggesting
that in the period prior to the growth of assumpsit most contracts were not a "union
of several wills," but unilateral obligations assumed by someone who had no duty
to do so. Only in the latter stages of the history of contract, Holmes indicated, was
the assumption that contracts were founded on what he called "reciprocal conventional inducements"[81] in place.

Holmes elaborated on this last observation. "Nowadays it is sometimes thought
more philosophical," he noted, "to say that a covenant [an example of a contract
under seal] is a formal contract which survives alongside of the ordinary consensual
contract." But

[T]his is not a very instructive way of putting it either. In one sense,
everything is form which the law requires in order to make a promise binding
over and above the mere expression of the promisor's will. Consideration is a
form as much as a seal. The only difference is, that one form is of modern
introduction, and has a foundation in good sense, or at least falls in with our
common habits of thought, so that we do not notice it, whereas the other is a
survival from an older condition of the law, and is less manifestly sensible or
less familiar.[82]

In passages such as these one gets a glimpse of the occasional penetrating insight
contained in *The Common Law*. In one respect the passage represents a characteristic
treatment of "survivals" in Holmes' methodology. "Survivals" are examples of
doctrines that have lost the capacity to resonate with current notions of "good
sense," and are therefore more open to reexamination or relegation to an antiquated
status. But the passage also contains one of Holmes' illuminating observations about
the relationship between formal legal doctrine and substantive policy assumptions.
All doctrine is "formal," he suggests, and for a reason: it binds persons to legal
rules by stripping the rules of their subjective character. Contracts are followed not
because they are "mere expressions of the promisor's will," but because they com-
ply with the objective requirements for contract formation. But not all doctrine is
recognized as "formal," because that term, in its ordinary sense, suggests something
artificially technical rather than something naturally sensible. Consideration is the
latter sort of "form": reciprocally induced bargains are perceived as the "natural"
sorts of contracts. Contracts under seal, in contrast, appear "odd" and "technical,"
especially when unilaterally imposed. But both types of contracts are "formal" in
the sense that they meet the objective requirements for a binding legal relationship.
Both are evidence of the seriousness of purpose of the parties.

The passage thus reasserts Holmes' principle of the paradox of form and substance in the law in a way that was particularly helpful to his ultimate agenda for contract law. By elevating the doctrine of consideration to a "formal" status in the law of contracts, and at the same time suggesting that it "has a foundation in good sense" and helps "make a promise binding over and above the mere expression of the promisor's will," Holmes was suggesting that the substantive basis of the doctrine lay in its ability to replace subjective with objective standards in contract law. The seal represents a "form" in which the subjective intent of the promisor, coupled with a technical requirement, makes a promise binding. This is a "less manifestly sensible" form, and Holmes noted that the distinction between sealed and unsealed instruments was breaking down. The doctrine of consideration, however, especially if employed in its extended sense to include not just promises that benefit the promisor but those whose nonperformance works a detriment to the promisee, makes possible an analysis of contract formation on an objective basis.

The next logical step in Holmes' treatment of contract law would thus appear to have been an analysis of the elements of contract, with the same sort of emphasis on replacing subjective with objective standards that he employed in his chapters on criminal law and torts. And in fact Holmes did take that step. But he did so in an arresting fashion, interweaving his interest in reorienting common law subjects around objective standards with another of his interests, that of reducing the scope of common law liability.

After noting that the relationship between promises and consideration in contracts was one of "reciprocal conventional inducement," Holmes turned "to analyze the nature of a promise." He put a definition by the 1872 Indian Contract Act, which, because of its emphasis on the willingness of one party "to do or to abstain from doing anything, with a view to obtaining the assent of [another] to such act or abstinence," he read as confining a promise "to conduct on the part of the promisor."[83] This was not the way promises were treated under the common law of contracts. Holmes particularized:

> An assurance that it shall rain tomorrow, or that a third person shall paint a picture, may as well be a promise as one that the promisee shall receive from some source one hundred bales of cotton, or that the promisor will pay the promisee one hundred dollars. What is the difference in the cases? It is only in the degree of power possessed by the promisor over the event. . . . But the law does not inquire, as a general thing, how far the accomplishment of an assurance touching the future is within the power of the promisor. In the moral world it may be that the obligation of a promise is confined to what lies within reach of the will of the promisor. . . . But unless some consideration of public policy intervenes, I take it that a man may bind himself at law that any future event shall happen. He can therefore promise it in a legal sense.[84]

Holmes' distinction between the moral and legal definitions of a promise had "more important bearings," he felt, than "simply enlarg[ing]" that definition. The distinction went to the nub of the "theory of contract." As Holmes put it,

The consequences of a binding promise at common law are not affected by the degree of power which the promisor possesses over the promised event. If the promised event does not come to pass, the plaintiff's property is sold to satisfy the damages, within certain limits, which the promisee has suffered by the failure. The consequences are the same in kind whether the promise is that it shall rain, or that another man shall paint a picture, or that the promisor will deliver a bale of cotton.[85]

Thus promises that were accepted and made part of legally binding contracts had only one "universal consequence": "the law makes the promisor pay damages if the promised event does not come to pass." In other words, promisors do not promise that something will happen, only that if it does not happen, they will pay promisees. This was an arguably radical interpretation of contract theory in that it implied that there was no obligation on the part of contracting parties to perform their contracts, only to pay damages in the event of nonperformance. Traditional commentary on contract law had emphasized the obligations of persons who had bound themselves to legally enforceable agreements; Holmes asserted that "[i]n every case . . . a legally binding promise . . . leaves [the promisor] free from interference until the time for fulfilment has gone by, and therefore free to break his contract if he chooses.[86]

Since in most situations resulting in legally binding contracts both promisor and promisee desire the contract to be performed, why did Holmes choose to describe contract formation as if it were a process by which promisors exercised an option to perform or pay damages? He seems to have two goals in mind. One was to emphasize the limited scope of contract damages. "If a breach of contract were regarded in the same light as a tort," he noted, "it would seem that if, in the course of performance of the contract the promisor should be notified of any particular consequence which would result from its not being performed, he should be held liable for that consequence in the event of non-performance."[87] But contract damages were not so extensive. Special consequences of contract failure were not charged to the defaulting promisor unless they had been specifically incorporated in the contract. "The price paid in mercantile contracts," Holmes pointed out, "generally excludes the construction that exceptional risks were intended to be assumed."[88]

Suggestions that those breaching contracts should be liable for all the proximate causes of their breach were thus inappropriate: the measure of damages should be what reasonable persons in the position of the contracting parties took to be the ordinary consequences of a breach. This led Holmes to his second goal: reorienting contract law toward objective rather than subjective standards of liability. Stating "the common law meaning of promise and contract" as an option in the promisor to perform or to pay ordinarily expected damages "has the advantage," he felt, "of freeing the subject from the superfluous theory that contract is a qualified subjection of one will to another, a kind of limited slavery."[89] It also had the advantage, from his point of view, of distinguishing moral from legal obligations. A promisor might be unable to perform through no fault of his own; he was nonetheless liable for damages. A promisor might wilfully not perform for the most reprehensible of reasons; he was liable for the same sort of damages.

Limiting contract liability and continuing his reorientation of common law subjects from a subjective and internal to an objective and external set of standards were
thus at the bottom of Holmes' paradoxical definition of a legally binding promise.
Along the way he had placed emphasis on the importance of reciprocal inducements,
as exemplified by the principle of consideration, in contract formation.

In his final chapter on contract law, "Void and Voidable Contracts," Holmes
returned to the theme of objectifying contract doctrine.

He began his discussion by addressing some conventional excuses for nonperformance: mistake and fraud. These excuses were products of a theory of contract
formation that took for granted the failure of contracts in circumstances where mutual
assent was lacking, either because the assent had been erroneously based, secured
through deception, or secured under pressure. The theory assumed that the basis of
contracts was the conjoining of individual wills.

Holmes challenged this view. Mistake, misrepresentation, and fraud, he argued,
were "merely dramatic circumstances": the "true ground" of contract failure was
"the absence of one or more of the primary elements, which . . . are necessary to
the existence of contract."[90] He put three examples: cases in which "there is no
second party," cases in which "the two parties say different things," and cases in
which "essential terms seemingly consistent are really inconsistent as used."[91]

An example of the first line of cases was where "a man goes through the form
of making a contract with A through B as A's agent, and B is not in fact the agent
of A." In such a case, Holmes pointed out, "there is generally mistake on one side
and fraud on the other," but "no special doctrine need be resorted to." Because B
was not in fact A's agent, the promise offered to A had not been accepted by him,
and there had been no consideration issuing from him. The basic elements of a
contract, a reciprocal inducement between two parties, evidenced by mutual promises
and consideration on both sides, were not present. It did not matter what B's motivation in representing himself as the agent of A had been. He was not A's agent;
there were thus not two parties to the contract; the contract was void.

The second example was the case of the ship *Peerless,* on which a cargo of cotton
had been shipped from Bombay, and one person had agreed to buy and another to
sell the same.[92] The problem was that while the contract stipulated that the cargo in
question would "arrive ex Peerless from Bombay," there were two vessels bearing
the name *Peerless* that had sailed from Bombay, one in October and the other in
December. The seller meant the ship that had sailed in December; the buyer the one
that had sailed in October. Traditional analysis treated such contracts as void because
of "mutual mistake." Holmes argued that the contract should be void, but not
because of "the actual state of the parties' minds." The law, he argued, "must go
by externals, and judge parties by their conduct." It was not that "each party meant
a different thing from the other . . . but that each said a different thing." The seller
"said," according to Holmes, the "December ship *Peerless,*" the buyer "said" the
"October ship *Peerless,*" and thus the parties had not contracted to buy and sell
the same thing.[93] The seller had offered to sell cotton on the December ship, and the
buyer had agreed to buy cotton on the October ship. As in the first example, one of
the primary elements of the contract was lacking, and it was void.

In Holmes' third example A had agreed to buy, and B to sell, "these barrels of mackerel.'' The barrels in fact contained salt. Such a situation was traditionally treated as voiding the contract through mutual mistake, producing a ''difference between the actual subject-matter and that to which the intention of the parties was directed.'' Holmes analyzed it differently. It did not matter what the intention of the parties was; what mattered was that the ''essential terms'' of the contract were inconsistent as used. The contract was for the transfer of ''these barrels'' and of barrels of ''mackerel''; but the barrels designated contained salt. The parties could thus not transfer ''these barrels'' and transfer barrels of mackerel, nor could they transfer barrels ''of mackerel'' and transfer the barrels they had designated.

So far Holmes seemed on at least plausible ground in that each of the cases he chose for examples, if his somewhat artful reading of the ''Peerless'' case is accepted, could be seen as turning on what the parties did or said, not on their motivation. But Holmes conceded that there were numerous instances in which con- tracts containing a repugnancy in their terms were not treated as void (that is, non- existent), but voidable—that is, where the buyer had the option to rescind or to insist on performance. If in the barrels of mackerel example ''there had been fraud on the seller's part, or if he had known what the barrels really contained,'' Holmes noted, ''the buyer might have had a right to insist on delivery of the inferior article. Fraud would perhaps have made the contract valid at his option.''[94] Moreover, not all contracts in which terms were inconsistent as used were void on the grounds of repugnancy. If a ''piece of gold is sold as eighteen-carat gold, and is in fact not so pure,'' or if ''a cow is sold as yielding an average of twelve quarts of milk a day, and in fact she yields only six quarts,'' those bargains, Holmes admitted, ''would not be void. At the most, they would only be voidable.''[95]

Holmes turned those examples to the advantage of his argument. The existence of fraud resulted in a void contract being treated as a voidable one, as a way of punishing the fraudulent party, but fraud was nonetheless not an inquiry into motives: it was an objective concept. ''If a man makes a representation, knowing facts which by the average standard of the community are sufficient to give him warning that it is probably untrue, and it is untrue,'' Holmes pointed out, ''he is guilty of fraud in theory of law whether he believes his statement or not.'' Indeed in Massachusetts the courts ''seem to hold that any material statement made by a man as of his own knowledge, or in such a way as fairly to be understood as made of his own knowl- edge, is fraudulent if untrue, irrespective of the reasons he may have had for believing it and believing that he knew it.'' Thus a representation ''may be morally innocent, and yet fraudulent in theory of law.''[96] The emphasis was on facts, knowledge, average community standards, and a ''fair understanding'' of statements, not on individual beliefs and motives.

Nor was the different treatment accorded the mackerel/salt case and the gold or milk cases evidence that subjective elements had crept into the analysis. ''The dis- tinctions of the law,'' Holmes claimed, ''are founded on experience, not on logic.'' To void a contract ''the repugnant terms must . . . be very important—so important that the court thinks that if [they were] omitted, the contract would be different in substance from that which the words of the parties seemed to express.''[97] Salt was not mackerel, hence those terms were ''essential,'' and confusing them amounted to the creation of a repugnancy. Gold was still gold and milk still milk, even if the anticipated carats or output in quarts did not materialize. The principle of repugnancy was reserved for those contracts where essential terms were employed in a fundamentally inconsistent manner. That was to be determined by external evidence.

Fraud and mistake thus provided Holmes with good examples of contract doctrine that was derived by reference to external and objective standards, even though the words themselves appeared to focus on the subjective will of individuals. They were in that sense terms like "intent" in criminal law or torts and "fault" in tort law. As applied, their moral content was actually neutral. In the most arguably subjective sphere of the common law—private bilateral contracts created as a result of the subjective preferences of "free" individuals in a market setting—Holmes had insisted that objective and external standards predominated both with respect to doctrinal rules and theories of liability. Once again he had harmonized doctrine to his polemical purposes.

~

The last of Holmes' *Common Law* chapters, two on the law of successions, could be seen as anticlimactic. Holmes had originally been interested in successions when he was working out the analytical classifications on which his early scholarship centered. As we have previously seen, successions posed a puzzle to rights-based classification systems, because there were examples of persons who succeeded to a title in land even though, being mere possessors, they had no "rights" to it. Holmes had explained most successions, in his "Privity" essay, as resting on "a fictitious identification between the deceased [owner] and his successor," based on an analogy to the law of inheritance. He repeated that explanation in his first chapter on successions, and both his chapters on succession were firmly in his historical mode.

Two inconsistent doctrines of succession were each explained by history in the chapters. One doctrine treated successors as taking on the property rights of those from whom they acquired property, whether or not the succession was by inheritance or by purchase. The law regarded executors, even purchasers, as heirs. While based on fictions, this doctrine had the advantage of quieting titles and facilitating land transfers. The other doctrine, however, seems irreconcilable with the first. It permitted a possessor of land, even if his or her possession was unauthorized, to claim the benefit of easements or other conditions attached to the land. Holmes explained this doctrine as a holdover from the times when inanimate objects were attributed human qualities. Land was treated as capable of having rights; one piece of land was said to be capable of "enslaving" another through a restrictive convenant or easement. The consequence was, as in ordinary successions, that "a man is allowed to enjoy a special right [such as title to land or an easement over it] when the facts out of which the right arises are not true of him."[98] Holmes summarized:

The history of early law everywhere shows that the difficulty of transferring a mere right was greatly felt when the situation of fact from which it sprung could not also be transferred. Analysis shows that the difficulty is real. The fiction which made such a transfer conceivable has now been explained, and its history has been followed until it has been seen to become a general mode of thought. It is now a matter of course that the buyer [of land] stands in the shoes of the seller.[99]

The chapters on "Successions," while slightly to one side of the central purposes of *The Common Law*, should not be ignored. They represented early examples, for Holmes, of the paradox of form and substance in the law. One of the great contributions Holmes made in *The Common Law* was to show, through "technical" analysis of legal doctrines, that doctrinal continuity was, on the surface, "overvalued" by the common law system, being retained even when a particular doctrine was based on a fiction and thus "illogical." This was a significant qualification of the conclusion reached by a number of Holmes' nineteenth-century contemporaries that law "evolved" over time or "reflected" contemporary social attitudes. It raised the issue of the autonomy of the Anglo-American legal system: its investment in its own professional language, doctrine, and practice. The paradox of form and substance was Holmes' way of communicating the insight that law could both reflect and help shape its cultural context.

Of course the paradox led Holmes to go further, as he did in most of his *Common Law* chapters, using his discovery to "free up" discussion of a doctrine's substantive merits. That he did not take this step in the chapters on successions (perhaps because he had no quarrel with the substantive purposes of the "fictitious" doctrines he identified) should not detract from his general achievement. Holmes had shown, in *The Common Law*, that searching analysis of legal subjects required both an internal and an external perspective.

~

With the passage quoted above from his second chapter on successions Holmes concluded *The Common Law*.

In the original Lowell lectures Holmes had given a summary concluding lecture, which was omitted in the book version, although the analytical table of contents provided in the book version suggests that Holmes may have originally intended to end the book with a discussion of a central legal issue of his time, the alienability of property through trusts.[100] It now remains, with the foregoing analysis of the *Common Law* chapters in place, to assess their current interest and place them in historical context.

Modern readers who read the book through from beginning to end may well be befuddled by its apparent lack of thematic and methodological consistency. As we have seen, Chapters I (Early Forms of Liability, V (The Bailee at Common Law), VI (Possession and Ownership), and X and XI (Successions) adopted the historical orientation of Holmes' law journal scholarship after 1876. The other lectures, on criminal law, torts, and contracts, while containing historical material, used history in a very different fashion, less as a source of doctrinal anomalies that could then be subjected to reconsideration on policy grounds than as support for those policy arguments themselves.

It was as if in the course of writing the lectures Holmes had taken the final step in a methodological progression from analytic jurist to historian to contemporary political theorist. By "Common Carriers and the Common Law," we have seen, he had come not only to emphasize the paradox of form and substance in doctrinal development, but to urge that because of that paradox formal doctrine often persisted well after its original substantive basis had evaporated, and was thus ripe for reconsideration. The example he had chosen had been act-at-peril liability, a doctrine that offended both of the goals of his contemporary jurisprudential philosophy: objectively determined standards of liability (based on conduct, not on status) and a limited scope of liability in common law subjects.

In several *Common Law* chapters Holmes repeated and elaborated upon those policy goals. If such portions of *The Common Law* are emphasized, the work takes on the shape of a philosophically consistent, if polemical tract: a reformer's plea to reorient common law subjects around standards of liability that are objectively derived, externally based, and limited in their scope.

But the above passages, we have seen, represent only a fraction of *The Common Law*'s corpus. Most of the rest of the lectures are occupied with technical discussions of orthodox common law doctrines, tracings of the historical origins and development of subjects such as bailment or pleading or act-at-peril liability or the succession of land titles, and occasional criticism of other commentators, notably the "German" jurists. These portions were obviously intended by Holmes to complement and reinforce his polemical arguments. But Holmes rarely made explicit the relationship between the orthodox analytical and historical portions of his lectures. Where he did, as in the lectures on torts and to a less explicit degree in the lectures on contracts, polemical conclusions drove his historical and analytical expositions.

The methodological confusion that this creates has been noted by some specialist commentators.[101] But it has not been regarded as particularly interesting to many modern readers, especially in the face of the stylistically elegant, arguably profound, and apparently prescient jurisprudential passages scattered throughout *The Common Law*. To encounter a late nineteenth-century jurist who perceived and articulated the significance of social and intellectual "experience," as distinguished from technical "logic," in shaping the law, who openly recognized that judges are affected in their decisions by "prejudices," and who simultaneously affirmed the historical contingency and the outcome-driven character of legal doctrine has been overwhelmingly attractive to generations of twentieth-century readers. In the face of this deep juristic affinity, modern readers have not been inclined to dwell on the arcane details of a book whose subject matter content appears remote and alien.

The result is that *The Common Law*'s current status is a paradoxical one. As Morton Horwitz has recently observed, *The Common Law,* although Holmes' "masterpiece," a "great work," a "genuine classic," is nonetheless "obscure and inaccessible in addition to being very rarely read."[102] In emphasizing the book's contributions, Horwitz stresses its role as the seminal example of modernist American jurisprudence, but does not speculate on whether its juristic aphorisms continue to have the kind of appeal they did for earlier twentieth-century generations of readers.

In this regard, the methodological contradictions of the work are perhaps more fundamental than they might first appear. If one reduces the central juristic messages of *The Common Law* to four, and then speculates on their current intellectual appeal, an interesting phenomenon appears to be surfacing. In their reduced form, *The Common Law*'s messages are that "experience," not professional analytical "logic," controls the development of legal doctrine; that doctrine, while "formal" (comprehensive, continuous, and coherent) in appearance, is in reality based on inarticulate substantive premises and values; that given these first two messages, common law doctrine can only be based on objective and external standards, which themselves reflect current community premises and values; and that to preserve certainty and predictibility in legal rules, which govern the conduct of individuals in American society, common law doctrine *should* be based on objective and external standards, whether derived from history or from current policy assumptions.

Taken together, these messages apparently place a considerable premium, in the task of deriving enlightened common law doctrine, on a careful understanding by judges and scholars both of history and of current "theories of legislation," as manifested, in common law subjects, by the application of "objective" and "external" standards of conduct. In the juristic model proposed by *The Common Law*, judges search outside themselves for the standards around which common law subjects are to be organized. Their work is "empirical."

But we have seen that Holmes' own presentation of common law subjects in the lectures reveals the ambiguities in his conception of "empirical" work. His analyses of the respective subjects he treats are intended to replace "logic" and subjectivity with externally based and objectively applied concepts, such as the dangerousness and the carelessness of acts performed under given circumstances, or the existence or nonexistence of reciprocal inducements for mutual promises. Those concepts, however, are intimately tied to his own subjective policy goals, such as the promotion of certainty, the limiting of civil liability in tort and contract, and the deterrence of criminal behavior. Moreover, in those lectures where Holmes' analyses are primarily based on tracing historical doctrine, as distinguished from explaining doctrine in terms of contemporary policy goals, history, we have seen, is consistently in the service of contemporary policy. History provides evidence of the "confused" and thus vulnerable state of doctrine (as in common carrier liability) or of the source of doctrinal anomalies that can now be given a "true" explanation (as in bailment, possession, and successions), or, more generally, as evidence of the paradox of form and substance that makes possible continuous reconsideration of "formal" legal doctrine on grounds of current "convenience."

In sum, a contemporary student of the epistemological grounding of scholarly arguments might well recognize that despite Holmes' efforts to invoke history and other "empirical" phenomena as clarifying agents, an epistemological tension in *The Common Law* remains. That tension arises from the irreconcilability of Holmes' two central claims: that one needs to understand the common law not through contemporary intraprofessional notions of logical "correctness" but through the extraprofessional "experience" of history and community values, and that at the same time one needs to reorient common law subjects so that their doctrines and standards better conform to "correct" policy goals. "Correct" in each of those claims has to come from somewhere, and it seems in both claims to come from the same place, the juristic goals of the judge or the scholar. Thus "logic" can be seen to be not fully juxtaposed against "experience" in *The Common Law*. The two terms are simply different modes of implementing the goals of one who seeks to reform legal doctrine. Sometimes Holmes' version of logic is employed to show the absurdity of an archaic doctrine; sometimes the "prevailing view" of the contemporary community is summoned up to strengthen an argument for doctrinal change. In both instances a version of contemporary logic, presented in the form of a rhetorical argument, controls.

One of the striking features of commentary on *The Common Law* at the time it was first published, however, is that reviewers, while recognizing the simultaneous voices of Holmes as "evolutionary" historian and as contemporary "logician" and polemicist, did not find those voices discordant, or their simultaneous presence evidence of an abiding methodological tension within the work.

The Common Law was published on March 3, 1881,[103] and by May two reviews had appeared. Some of their nonsubstantive features, although apparently trivial, invite analysis. For example, both reviewers were familiar with Holmes' earlier essays, and noted that fact. Moreover, Roger Foster,[104] reviewing the lectures in the *Albany Law Journal,* pointed out that Holmes was "the son of the author of 'The Autocrat of the Breakfast Table.' " Finally, Foster alluded to "a certain obscurity of style which disfigured the [earlier] essays." That problem had "now been corrected," Foster felt, suggesting that "the necessities of addressing a somewhat popular audience from the platform" had contributed to the improved accessibility of Holmes' prose.[105]

John Warren's review in the May 1881 *American Law Review*[106] also began by noting that "[t]he habitual readers" of that journal "can need no introduction to Mr. Holmes," whose "essays on the historical development of the law . . . were parts of a scheme now accomplished" in *The Common Law*. And while Warren did not associate Holmes with his famous father, he likewise suggested that "the style could be made easier":

> The author has adopted the conciseness of the scholar, and has compressed to such a closeness that unpacking is made needlessly difficult. The reasoning in some cases is so very elliptical that it becomes almost obscure. He has sternly refused to let himself go where we feel sure he might go easily and pleasantly and to the great relief of his readers.[107]

These sets of remarks, while clearly intended as minor asides by the first two reviewers, nonetheless serve to identify some common characteristics of contemporary reviews of *The Common Law*. The reviewers were each specialists, familiar with Holmes' previous work. In several instances the reviewers identified Holmes as the son of a famous writer. And the reviewers alluded to Holmes' "obscure" style, sometimes paralleling the *American Law Review* in their comments.

The interrelationship of these common characteristics piques one's interest. One could argue that the "obscure" style that Holmes adopted in his scholarly essays and *The Common Law* represented a deliberate choice. He was, after all, an experienced writer with "a natural bent for literature"; he had been elected Poet of his undergraduate class; he had written ambitiously expressive letters to William James in the 1860s; he had created an embellished Civil War diary. His edition of Kent, in addition, was comprehensive and elaborate in its annotations, the opposite of "obscure." Nonetheless contemporary reviewers of *The Common Law* characterized its style as "terse," "epigrammatic," "elliptical," and "difficult."[108]

One is struck here by some comments Holmes made later in his life about his scholarly work and his father. He said that as a judge and a scholar he was writing for "one man in a thousand,"[109] and that he was "preparing small diamonds for people of limited intellectual means."[110] He also said that had Dr. Holmes not been "distracted into easy talk and occasional verse"[111] he "might have produced a great work."[112] Others have noted a progression in Holmes' early intellectual interests from literature (his "natural bent") through philosophy (where he "debauched," as he said to William James) to law, which he characterized as a work of "discipline."[113]

It is conceivable that Holmes' efforts to compress his thoughts, his rendering of ideas tersely and epigramatically, his constant references to arcane sources, and his delphic analogies in *The Common Law* were part of an effort to establish not just a professional, or a substantive, but a stylistic distance from his "famous" father. He may have seen the process of adopting the "obscure" and "difficult" style of the scholar as a way of moving from the larger "literary" world to the world of the erudite specialist, the person who had chosen not to be "popular."

Recall that in 1880, when Holmes' fortieth birthday was approaching and he was hurriedly bringing his "scheme" to reorient common law subjects into shape, Dr. Holmes was at the apex of his literary reputation. In 1879, when Holmes Senior had turned seventy, the publishers of the *Atlantic Monthly* gave him a commemorative breakfast, attended by Emerson, Julia Ward Howe, Harriet Beecher Stowe, and William Dean Howells. President Rutherford Hayes sent a congratulatory letter. The Boston *Daily Advertiser,* in reporting the occasion, called Dr. Holmes "[a] prophet . . . honored in his own land, a poet . . . revered by those whose praise is to him most precious, a wit [whose] . . . writings have the spring of the hickory, the smack of the cider, the tonic of the climate and the vigor of the type of men hardened by the struggle that has formed our national character."[114]

Holmes Jr. may have wanted to ensure that no one confused his scholarship with the "easy talk," the "occasional verse" and the sprightly, accessible prose of Dr. Holmes. In this vein, it is possible that the most distinctive feature of Holmes as a stylist, his epigrammatic terseness, was consciously or unconsciously adopted as a badge of identity. At any rate, the combination of a work clearly intended for a narrow, professional audience, yet "difficult" even for that audience, and the immediate association by reviewers of Holmes the son with Holmes the father is provocative. In this sense the casual comments of the early reviewers may take us closer to the central impulses from which Holmes wrote *The Common Law* than the tone of those comments might first suggest.

Just as the prefatory comments of contemporary reviewers may provide a clue as to *The Common Law*'s psychological origins, their substantive comments offer clues as to its contemporary intellectual messages. Here a modern reader, perhaps accustomed to thinking of Holmes as a prophet ahead of his time, may find some surprises. Consider this passage from Warren's review:

> Mr. Holmes recognizes fully that the course of the common law has been determined by the complications of life, and has always refused to grow in the shapes cut by logic. . . . [But] we are not sure . . . that Mr. Holmes does not go

even further than most lawyers would follow him in his belief in the constant
adaptation of law to the needs of the community. . . . The substance of the law
. . . is very little understood, but it is always treated as mysterious and
unintelligible to a degree which indicates a pretty wide separation between it
and the common affairs of life. . . . We think that most lawyers would hardly
say that the law can be trusted to meet the changing needs of society with
great promptness. . . .

One thing is probable, which is that the adaptibility of the law is decidedly
increasing. The legislative function of courts has hitherto been much disguised.
Judges trained in the peculiar conservatism of our system, venerating the old
law and professing only to discover and apply it, have gone out of their way
to conceal even from themselves their work in making new law. . . . Such
unconsciousness and such pretence are sure to weaken under the matter-
of-fact scrutiny of modern thought. The very book we are discussing
brings into unaccustomed clearness the legislative office of
the courts.[115]

In this excerpt the modern reader encounters some attitudes commonly associated
with the dominant American jurisprudence of the late nineteenth century: assertions
that the law is perceived as "mysterious and unintelligible," that judges "venerate
. . . the old law," that the system of common law adjudication exhibits a "peculiar
conservatism," and that judges conceive their function as discovering and applying
preexisting legal principles.[116] But each of the attitudes is treated as unselfconscious
or pretextual. Warren speaks of a "legislative function" of common law courts, or
the role of judges "in making new law," of deference to precedent as "fictitious"
or "unsubstantial," and, most tellingly, of the "weaken[ing]" of orthodox attitudes
"under the matter-of-fact scrutiny of modern thought." Moreover, the next sentence
unmistakably identifies Holmes as a "modern" in his recognition of the lawmaking
function of judges. In short, Holmes' voice in *The Common Law* is not treated as
alone in a jurisprudential wilderness but as a representative of "modern" attitudes
in the ascendancy.

Another suggestive passage occurs in the review by Foster:

[I]n the history of the evolution of jurisprudence and the progress of custom
and morality to positive law, . . . [American] authors have been, hitherto, far
behind those of the mother country. It is for this reason that the work on "The
Common Law," by the son of the author of "The Autocrat of the Breakfast
Table," will be welcomed by every student of the law. . . . The entire work is
written from the stand-point of the new philosophy, and those hackneyed terms
natural justice and *equity* are excluded from it. On the contrary we find . . . a
principle, which although familiar to most thinkers, we never saw so well
expressed:

"But it seems to me clear that the *ultima ratio,* not only *regum,* but of
private persons, is force, and that at the bottom of all private relations,
however tempered by sympathy and all the social feelings, is a justifiable
self-preference."[117]

This excerpt treats "positive law" as having displaced "natural justice" and "equity" in "the evolution of jurisprudence": Holmes is an advocate of the "new philosophy," positivism. Natural law, morality, custom, equity are earlier stages in the process; since those stages have passed, the terms are "hackneyed." Force and self-preference are "at the bottom of all private relations."

It is of course no surprise to find commentators treating Holmes as a modernist, an advocate of a "new" point of view, or a positivist. What is surprising is to find such commentators expressing those views at the very appearance of *The Common Law,* and treating positivist jurisprudence as "familiar" and the exposure of judicial lawmaking as "matter-of-fact." The comments suggest that the striking aphorisms of *The Common Law,* so habitually treated not only as vivid but as highly original for their time, were more representative of emerging late nineteenth-century modernist attitudes than commonly supposed.[118]

In short, the comments suggest that Holmes' thought in *The Common Law* had taken a significant turn since even his historical essays in the late 1870s. In the newer lectures, those on criminal law, contracts, and portions of those on torts, Holmes had been far more positivistic in his approach, emphasizing external standards and policy arguments and deemphasizing historical data. It is by no means clear that he had abandoned custom as an important source of legal doctrines; indeed the policy-oriented lectures can be read as elevating custom, as embodied in external standards that represented the "community's" perceptions of reasonable or prudent or dangerous conduct, to a position of great authority in the shaping of legal rules.[119] But it is also arguable that a progression from the historically oriented lectures to the policy oriented ones can be discerned, and that the progression roughly tracked that of substituting, as Roger Foster put it, "positive law" for "morality."

In this vein, the *American Law Review*'s comment that *The Common Law* represented "a manifestation of the tendency in modern ethics toward objective grounds, and away from intuitive and metaphysical theories of morals"[120] seems to have captured the attitude of many reviewers. The *Journal of Jurisprudence* noted that Holmes' effort was to "draw the province of jurisprudence clear of the quicksands of abstract morality,"[121] and characterized his argument in the torts lectures that "as the law has grown, even when its standards have contrived to model themselves upon those of morality, they have necessarily become external"[122] as a "brilliant analysis."[123]

Another review that quoted from Holmes' observations on morality and external standards in law was that by his friend Albert V. Dicey in the June 3, 1882, issue of *The Spectator.*[123] Dicey felt that "some important inferences" were suggested by "Mr. Holmes's view that what the law tends to make the test of liability is conformity or want of conformity to an external standard." Before discussing those portions of Dicey's review, which was the most lengthy and searching of the contemporary assessments of *The Common Law,* a brief note on the review's apparent origins seems appropriate.

Holmes had first met Dicey, who was a cousin of his old friend Leslie Stephen, in 1870, when Dicey came to visit Holmes in Boston.[125] In 1874 Holmes and Fanny encountered Dicey in London,[126] and Dicey was one of the individuals to whom Holmes sent his *American Law Review* articles as they appeared in the 1870s. In January 1880, Dicey wrote Holmes a long letter, prompted in part by the receipt of those articles. One paragraph of that letter began as follows:

> I am very much interested in your articles. What you say as to the very external nature of any legal standard, e.g. of negligence, strikes me as true, novel, & important.

Dicey then went on to make a more general comment on the articles, anticipating that they would someday be developed into a book:

> Having read your different articles at different times & missed some of them I am not quite in a position to judge of the whole work even as far as it has gone. I mention this since it probably in part explains a criticism which I venture to make because I am really anxious to call your attention to it before the work is finished. . . . A work on law may, it seems to me, be concerned with any or all of three questions, *first,* what is the law? (practical lawyer), *secondly,* what ought to be the law? (jurist or legislator), *thirdly,* what is the history of the law? (legal historian)
>
> I do not deny that these enquiries have a connection with each other but I think it greatly conduces to clearness to keep them distinct. Now as I read your work I feel as though I never [was] quite certain with which of the three questions we were dealing. I know that this does not arise from any real confusion on your part. The cause that I notice is, I think, . . . that you attach a speculative importance (which I do not attribute to them) to the dicta of the Judges. I care, to say the truth, much more to know what you think about negligence than to learn that say Coke used expressions which may be made consistent with a sound theory. . . . I certainly have occasionally thought that the question what is the nature of possession is mixed up rather unhappily with the enquiry how far can the text of Roman law be forced into consistency with a sound theory?[127]

Here we note the first recognition by a contemporary of *The Common Law*'s methodological ambivalence. The "dicta of the Judges," Dicey suggests, is being "forced into consistency with a sound theory" and at the same time treated as if it were of independent "empirical" significance. History, theory, and evidence are being intertwined in an ambiguous fashion: Holmes appears to be claiming that "sound theories" are derived from historical texts, when, in fact those texts are being "forced" into support for theories presumed to be "sound."

In his published review of *The Common Law* Dicey continued this critique, but in a much more muted and politic fashion. He began the review by calling *The Common Law* "the most original work of legal speculation which has appeared in English since the publication of Sir Henry Maine's *Ancient Law*," and referring to "Mr. Holmes' special qualifications for the task of legal speculation, and especially his combined interest in the historical and the logical aspects of law."[128] Such comments must have meant a great deal to Holmes, coming from a person of Dicey's stature, albeit a friend.[129] But then Dicey, after noting that the "special originality" of *The Common Law* was its "exhibiting in combination two different methods of treating legal problems," the "historical" and the "analytical," returned to the criticism he had made in the 1880 letter:

> [Holmes'] attempt to unite the historical with the analytical method of treating the problems before him, while it gives his work some very special and noteworthy merits, is, in our judgment, the cause of the only serious faults ... with which his treatise can fairly be charged. The chief of these defects is uncertainty of aim. Occasionally, the reader feels a doubt whether Mr. Holmes is contending that a given principle is in conformity with the decisions to be found in the year-books, or that it is in conformity with the dictates of right reason, or expediency.[130]

With the letter in mind, it is clear that in this passage Dicey was repeating his concerns that Holmes had not made it clear whether his simultaneous use of "historical" and "analytical" methodologies should be taken as attributing comparable importance to doctrine derived from history and doctrine derived from contemporary policy, two sources that Dicey did not find necessarily compatible. Holmes had said in the first page of *The Common Law* that "in order to know what the law is ... [w]e must alternately consult history and existing theories of legislation." Did this mean, Dicey wondered, that the two sources were to be given comparable weight as starting points for the derivation of "sound" doctrinal principles? Or, as Dicey suspected, was history sometimes to be deferred to, and sometimes ignored or criticized, in the service of contemporary policy arguments?

In short, Dicey had put his finger on the central methodological ambivalence of *The Common Law*. He captured that ambivalence succintly in the remainder of the paragraph previously quoted:

> Occasionally, the reader feels a doubt whether Mr. Holmes is contending that a given principle is in conformity with decisions to be found in the year-books, or that it is in conformity with the dictates of right reason, or expediency. The plain truth is that our author is too much of an apologist. He hardly distinguishes, in his own mind, between the doctrines of the common law and the dictates of common sense. ... Mr. Holmes, in short, deals with the texts of the common law in the same way in which speculative but orthodox theologians deal with texts of Scripture. They devote a great deal of ability to showing that certain doctrines are in themselves true, and at the same time labour, with equal assiduity, to prove that these doctrines may be deduced from, or are consistent with, a mass of texts which, to impartial readers, seem to have but a remote bearing on the matter in hand. The textualist, whether he be a jurist or theologian, is apt to make his readers feel that the force of a sound and sensible theory is weakened rather than strengthened by the mass of authorities quoted in its support.[131]

The critique offered in this passage so closely resembles current observations on the relationship between texts, interpretive structures, and historical evidence in works of scholarship that it is easily capable of being misunderstood. In his letter to Holmes, Dicey had not urged him to consider the problematic quality of arguments purportedly resting on evidence independent of the argumentative structure in which the arguments were embedded. He had simply asked him to consider whether he was writing as a "practical lawyer," a "jurist," or a legal historian. Dicey found all those methodologies defensible and capable of being separated; he simply wanted the separation made clear. In short, Dicey suspected that Holmes had interpreted texts to suit his theories, but did not conclude that that strategy was inappropriate, merely unnecessary. A "sound and sensible" theory, for Dicey, was not "strengthened," but "weakened," by a "mass of authorities quoted in its support." This was not because of any questionable relationship between evidence and interpretation, but simply because Holmes the jurist was far more illuminating to Dicey than the judges and jurists whose pronouncements Holmes enlisted in support of his arguments. Still, it must have galled Holmes to have Dicey compare him to a "theologian," the very term he had used to caricature Langdell.

Dicey's comments bring us to two reviews not previously discussed. One was that of Frederick Pollock in the *Saturday Review,* a London journal, for June 11, 1881.[132] Pollock began his review, which was unsigned but quickly recognized and appreciated by Holmes,[133] with these remarks:

> Before this we have called attention to the danger in which English lawyers stand of being outrun by their American brethren in the scientific and historical criticism of English institutions and ideas. The book now published by Mr. O.W. Holmes adds considerably to the advantage gained on the American side in this friendly contest. . . . [Holmes] gives us a searching historical and analytical criticism of several of the leading notions of English law; not an antiquarian discussion first and a theoretical discussion afterwards but a continuous study in the joint light of policy and history.[134]

What Pollock meant by "scientific and historical criticism" (the word "scientific" was used as the equivalent of "philosophical") is spelled out in a subsequent paragraph:

> [Holmes] shows us how dimly felt grounds of expediency, struggling with traditional rules of which the real grounds were mostly forgotten, have issued in the establishment of principles which are now capable of being expressed in a rational fashion for the most part, though many minute irregularities in their application, and here and there downright anomalies, preserve the memory of conflict and compromise.[135]

One will notice that in this excerpt and the preceding one Pollock thoroughly approved of Holmes' methodology. A "continuous study" of the common law "in the joint light of policy and history" was not only possible but desirable. "Traditional rules" whose "real grounds" had been forgotten but whose probable origin lay in "dimly felt grounds of expediency" could be restated in the reasoning of contemporary policy, because they were "now capable of being expressed in a rational fashion."

As an example, Pollock cited Holmes' discussion of negligence, which he called, along with that of criminal law, "the best part of the book." Pollock described Holmes' treatment of negligence in the following fashion:

Mr. Holmes goes on to show that the same principle of the external standard holds in the theory of civil wrongs, and particularly in that much confused subject, the law of negligence. What the law means by negligence, he strongly points out, is not, as assumed by some modern teachers, a state of the party's mind. . . . Negligence is the want of diligence. But diligence is not something in the party's mind; it is a matter of external conduct, the actual exercise of a certain measure of intelligence and caution. . . . The ground of policy on which the law rests is in that in order to carry on our affairs with freedom we must count on a certain amount of intelligence and good-will in a fellow-man apparently possessing normal faculties, and the law must hold him to make good that expectation.[136]

Why, for Pollock, is "now" the time that older common law doctrines can be recast in a "rational fashion"? Why has negligence been a "confused subject"? The answer to these questions is the same. Only recently has the "policy" of allowing individuals "to carry on our affairs with freedom" been recognized as of paramount importance. Objective and externally based standards of conduct for civil and criminal behavior are consistent with that policy, because, for Pollock, a presumption that one's neighbors possess normal intelligence, good-will, and caution allows one to go about one's business without worrying about interference from others. One can rely on the presumption, assume that the common law will enforce it except in "extraordinary circumstances," and thus carry on one's affairs with freedom.

The collective realization of his contemporaries that the objectification and externalization of conduct promotes that greatly valued principle, "freedom," is thus what renders Holmes' methodology acceptable to Pollock. One can fuse policy and history without raising epistemological dilemmas because of the great importance of this newly perceived insight. Recasting common law doctrine to make it conform to the policy of freedom to carry on one's affairs, for Pollock, constitutes a "scientific" approach to legal history. As Pollock put it in the concluding paragraph of his review, after discussing the negligence example:

We have no room to discuss at present Mr. Holmes's treatment of leading ideas in other doctrines of the law; but we must not forget to say that, even if his explanations be not wholly accepted, his research goes a notable way to dispel the obscurity that surrounds the English law . . . in its earlier stages. [In other lectures Holmes] . . . works historical materials into the fabric of a closely reasoned argument. . . . Altogether, Mr. Holmes's book will be a most valuable—we should say almost say an indispensable—companion to the scientific study of legal history.[137]

No wonder Holmes wrote Pollock, on seeing the review, that it was "worth a good deal of hard work" and "intimately pleasing to me."[138] But Pollock's was not the only contemporary review that found no potential contradictions in Holmes' fusion of history and contemporary policy and at the same time treated *The Common Law*'s exaltation of "freedom . . . to carry on affairs" as especially congenial. In a December 1882 notice the anonymous reviewer in the *Albany Law Journal* placed Holmes in a group of "several New England gentlemen who have lately made valuable contributions to the philosophical and the historical literatures of the common law."[139] While Holmes' investigations were "often made from the point of view of the historical jurist," the reviewer suggested, he was distinctive in "appl[ying] . . . profound theories of general application concerning the history of jural conceptions . . . to special cases, and [in] verif[ying] given theories by a special and laborious array of authority."[140] The reviewer particularized:

> We cannot gainsay that history and metaphysic serve Professor Holmes in good stead, for they have enabled him to produce a very good book—a book that well indicates the advance which the common law is now making toward a more scientific structure than it has ever before possessed. In early forms of liability, the author's account of the development of legal liability at common law is . . . mainly historical. . . . In the succeeding lectures on the Criminal Law and on Torts, the author's method is no longer that of the legal historian, but that of the analytic and philosophical jurist. We do not know in which character to prefer the author, both are excellent in their way.[141]

Notice that in this excerpt the reviewer finds Holmes' methodology congenial, or at least unremarkable, in two quite distinct respects. First, he treats "history and metaphysic" as if they were prologues to the "more scientific" intellectual structures of his contemporary world. The early forms of liability are illuminating, in part, because they show how "primitive" ancient conceptions of civil and criminal injury appear alongside modern conceptions. History thus reinforces the supremacy of contemporary assumptions about how the law should be organized; it underscores the "advance which the common law is now making." Second, the reviewer treats *The Common Law*'s employment of two discrete methodological orientations, "historical" and "analytic and philosophical," and Holmes' adoption of two discrete roles, that of the "legal historian" and that of the "jurist," as creating no epistemological tension. He not only assumes the orientations and roles are quite capable of being kept separate, he finds them "both excellent in their way." And while he parallels Dicey in dividing "jurist" from "legal historian," he does not recognize any complexities in that division of roles, or for that matter in their fusion. In sum, he assumes that history can reveal the analytic or philosophical essence of a legal doctrine, and that contemporary policy assumptions can be used to recast archaic or primitive doctrines.

At the same time the reviewer demonstrates his affinity for Holmes' principle of freedom to order one's affairs. Consider this passage:

> It is in the lectures on Contract . . . that Professor Holmes is at his best. Here he brings his extensive research to bear, with not a little originality, on important questions of history and of doctrine. Now in few other departments of law does history play a more important part than it does in that of contract. . . . History shows us that some former essentials to perfect contracts have since become non-essentials, and that a few nonessentials have become essentials. . . . For example, history teaches us that the development of a contract has been something like this: At first no promise is enforceable except

by caprice and by rude force; next, a ceremonial has become associated with the promise. . . . In the suceeding stage of development the promise is emancipated from the ceremonial and an obligation is attached to the mere promise—the promise has at last become all-important, the ceremonial unimportant. The highest stage of development is of course reached when it enables man to order his own affairs with the least possible interference from imperative law. This last stage is tolerably well exemplified in this country.[142]

A brief reconstruction of the logic of the paragraph will serve to demonstrate the kind of impact *The Common Law* made on its contemporaries. The reviewer begins by assuming that history "plays a[n] . . . important part" in contract doctrine. He then proceeds to give examples from that history, and the examples perfectly complement a theory of the common law of contracts as "developing" in stages, from a "primitive" state in which "caprice and rude force" serve as enforcement mechanisms, to a more "advanced" state in which the substance of promises is given greater weight than their form, to "the highest state of development" in which individuals are free to "order [their] own affairs with the least possible interference from imperative law."

The reviewer ends up, in his account, precisely where Pollock ended up. Just as the goal of negligence law is to promote freedom and autonomy in one's "own affairs," so is "the highest stage of development" in contract law. And just as Pollock ended his review by calling *The Common Law* "an indispensable companion to the scientific study of legal history," the *Albany* reviewer ended by describing the book as "an indispensable auxiliary . . . to every person who desires to be informed of the progress of the jurisprudence of the common law, and of what our scientific jurists are contributing to this progress." In both reviews "science," "philosophy," "history," an "analytic" orientation, and "progress" were mutually self-reinforcing concepts. Holmes could serve as a historian, a scientist, and a progressively oriented jurist at the same time.

～

It remains to explain the place of *The Common Law* within the culture of late nineteenth-century scholarship in which it first appeared, and to suggest some reasons for its continuing interest.

Commentators, particularly those struck by the importance of tacit ideological assumptions in shaping the methodological perspectives of scholars, have observed the several roles assumed by Holmes in *The Common Law* (historicist, analytic jurist, contemporary political theorist) and noted the discontinuity and discordance of those roles. I have made comparable observations in this chapter, although my vocabulary and perspective has differed from the other commentators.[143] But I have also emphasized that contemporary reviewers of *The Common Law*, while sometimes recognizing unresolved methodological tensions in the lectures, did not find *The Common Law*, as one modern commentator has put it, "a book at war with itself."[144] On the contrary, contemporary reviewers found *The Common Law* methodologically unproblematic and philosophically congenial.[145]

I have further suggested that the contemporary reviewers were attracted to the very methodological impulses in *The Common Law* that modern scholars have found discordant: its historicist impulse and what they called its impulse toward achieving a "scientific" organization of common law subjects. By "scientific" they meant, we have seen, a mode of analysis producing the orderly arrangement of evidence in a manner consistent with currently governing intellectual assumptions, particularly assumptions about the nature of "empirical" phenomena. They did not employ the term historicist, of course, because they equated the inevitability of historical change with the inevitability of progress from "primitive" to more enlightened cultures. But to the extent they perceived that the "historical" and "scientific" methodologies employed by Holmes in *The Common Law* were discrete, they treated them as self-reinforcing, expressing concern only that their discreteness be made clear.[146]

The reviews of *The Common Law* also demonstrate that the characteristic that made Holmes' historical and analytical chapters self-reinforcing for commentators was Holmes' assumption that both the course of history and the insights of contemporary policy and philosophy demonstrated the paramount importance of "freedom to conduct one's affairs." History revealed the gradual progression to a society (exemplified by late nineteenth-century America) in which this freedom was a core value. And since that value was held in such high esteem, a reorganization of legal subjects so as to emphasize doctrinal rules (such as external standards for civil and criminal liability, or objectivist legal concepts, such as reasonableness, reciprocal inducement, or dangerous conduct "under the circumstances") made philosophical and political sense and was thus "scientific."

In short, commentators were attracted to both the historicist and analytic modes of Holmes' methodological presentation in *The Common Law,* and took at face value his prefatory statement that "[i]n order to know what [the law] is, we must know what it has been, and what it tends to become." In characterizing *The Common Law* as a historical document, then, one may fairly call it a paean to "laissez-faire" or "liberalism," an example of Victorian scientific positivism, or an application of the theory of late nineteenth-century pragmatists that truth is an external phenomenon. Alternatively, one may fairly characterize *The Common Law* as a historicist attack on moral and religious fundamentalism, or a historicist critique of "theological" reasoning, or an affirmation of the determinism of history, the impermanency or even the contingency of "prevalent . . . intuitions of public policy," and the ultimate grounding of legal doctrine in current notions of common sense. There is material in the lectures to support any of those characterizations.

But the difficulty is that Holmes, while appearing unconcerned about the epistemological tensions between his two organizing methodological perspectives in *The Common Law,* nonetheless never treated them as uniformly self-reinforcing, as did the majority of his contemporary reviewers. He was careful, in his language, to convey subtleties, note exceptions to his generalizations, give attention to anomalies, and emphasize his paradox of form and substance in the "development" of the law. Reviewers noticed this circumspection. As one put it,

> Though beginning Mr. Holmes's book with some expectation of finding traces of an over-fine theorizing, we have read it with growing admiration of his

moderation. . . . He has suggested more than one theory about which we may feel doubts. . . . but we shall find that Mr. Holmes has himself suggested the most formidable difficulties and has softened nothing. However dextrous the argument and ingenious the interpretation of authorities, . . . we find ourselves in the hands of one whose sensitiveness to difficulties and objections is of the keenest, and who concludes only with caution.[147]

The result is that *The Common Law* evades any effort, even that of contemporary reviewers, to make it into a stereotyped or even a "representative" late nineteenth-century work of scholarship. Its historicist emphasis may ultimately be subversive of its "scientific" orientation, and its policy imperatives may overwhelm its treatment of historical evidence. But these are late twentieth-century judgments. The principal sense in which the *Common Law* chapters are manifestations of the intellectual climate of their time, their simultaneous historicism and "scientific" analytics, is difficult to capture with precision. Holmes appears at times to resemble a whig historian, deriving fundamental principles to guide the present from a study of the past, and at times to resemble a modernist historian, emphasizing the cultural gaps between past and present. His vivid, cryptic, but at the same time cautious and qualified language makes it extraordinarily difficult to locate the book in time. That language is no doubt the source of both the book's enduring interest and the inaccessibility of all but its "famous" passages, which are themselves by no means capable of unambiguous interpretation.

In another sense the evasive, cautious, and ambiguous language of *The Common Law* helps a reader locate the work within the course of Holmes' career as a scholar.

By the close of the 1870s Holmes, after considerable groping, was prepared to declare his scholarly independence and assert a comprehensive juristic perspective. In the course of that effort he sought to distinguish himself decisively from his influential juristic contemporaries. He separated himself from Langdell, beginning *The Common Law* with his famous logic/experience passage and offering in the contracts lectures a theory of contractual formation that implicitly and at times even explicitly rejected Langdell's doctrinal propositions. At the same time he separated himself from Austin and other subjectivists, and from Savigny and other German historical jurists. He even sought to distinguish himself, principally through erroneous citations or the absence of citation, from contemporaries whose insights he had adopted and extended, notably Maine, Pollock, and Pomeroy. In short, he did everything he could to convey his deep (but perhaps hesitant) belief that his book was one of conspicuous originality.

At the same time Holmes took pains to complicate the juristic perspective of his earlier scholarship and simultaneously soften the implications of that perspective. He reworked his earlier scholarship in *The Common Law*, eliminating signs that it was overtly argumentative (such as the outline of arguments in "Trespass and Negligence" and the separation of his form and substance paradox from its "Common Carriers" context) and stating propositions with greater caution, balance, and ambiguity, as reviewers noted. He retained his "elliptical" style but increased the number of elegantly cryptic generalized passages, the ones that have spanned time. And he treated his separate methodologies as self-reinforcing but also dialectical and complex in their interactions. The result was a book both internally inconsistent and marvelously complex, evocative, and penetrating.

The ultimate question about *The Common Law* is whether Holmes' alteration of his scholarly perspective at the time of its publication was a fully conscious one. Holmes never gave, as far as we know, a contemporary account of the process by which he reshaped his older work and added new lectures during the year in which he "put together some of the ideas which I deem most important in a regular order."[148] When he gave later accounts, they were varnished and, on balance, highly misleading. Consider this one to Harold Laski:

> You ask me what started my book. Of course I can't answer for unconscious elements. I don't think Maine had anything to do with it except to feed the philosophic passion. I think the movement came from within—from the passionate demand that what sounded so arbitrary in Blackstone, for instance, should give some reasonable meaning—that the law should be proved, if it could be, to be worthy of the interest of an intelligent man—(that was the form the question took then) . . . I don't think of any special book that put me on the track—though the works that I cited such as Lehuerou helped. I rooted round and made notes until the theory gradually emerged. I guess you have seen the MS book in which I collected texts and references on privity—the rights of a *res*—possession &c &c &c.[149]

On the surface, this explanation is remarkably evasive. Maine did far more than "feed the philosophic passion": Holmes adopted the same organizational structure of Maine's *Ancient Law*. Some works he cited "helped" much more than he let on; others that helped were not cited. Singling out Julien Marie Lehuerou as a particular "help" may have baffled Laski, since the only reference to Lehuerou in *The Common Law* came at the end of its preface, where Holmes advised "any one [who] should feel inclined to reproach me for want of greater detail" to recall "the words of Lehuerou, 'Nous faisons une theorie et non un spicilege.' "[150] The word "spicilege" has been read to refer to "the publication of historical trivia after the main outlines of a period have been known," but the word literally means gleaning the remnants of a field after harvest.[151] It is perhaps better translated, in Holmes' quotation, as "anthology," or "mere collection of data." But all the quotation then comes to is that Lehuerou helped Holmes by implicitly encouraging him to concentrate on theory rather than details. Of course Holmes concentrated on both in the *Common Law* lectures.

The passage is revealing, however, when read at another level. Holmes first signifies his awareness that "unconscious elements" may have affected his motivation in writing *The Common Law,* and then goes on to speak in terms of "passion" (using the word twice in two sentences), of the "movement" to write the book as coming "from within," of wanting to "prove" that the law was "worthy of the interest of an intelligent man," and of "rooting around" in "texts and references . . . until the theory gradually emerged." He also assumes that he and Laski know what "the theory" was. These sentences can be read as suggesting that Holmes' principal interest in writing *The Common Law* was to put forth an internally consistent and distinctive theory of common law doctrine, a theory original, comprehensive, and profound enough to "prove" that the law was an intellectually stimulating subject and, implicitly, that Wendell Holmes had chosen a "worthy" profession.

But the fascinating aspect of the passage is that its governing assumption—that "everybody" knew (and still knows) what *The Common Law*'s theory was—is not explored. The most striking feature of *The Common Law* is that its central theory is elusive and cryptically rendered.

So one needs to suspend judgment, at this point, both about Holmes' motivation in writing the Lowell Lectures and about their central meaning. What can be said with confidence is that *The Common Law* represented a decisive, but ambiguous, turn in Holmes' scholarly life. It revealed, beyond a doubt, the depth and complexity of his intellect and his singular control of language. Contemporaries noticed those strengths, and Holmes' career changed as a result. It also revealed how congenial the juristic perspective taken as being offered by Holmes in the lectures was to contemporaries. But that congeniality was a source of distortion: *The Common Law* was not quite what it seemed to contemporary readers, just as it has been not quite what it seems to many moderns. And the elusiveness of *The Common Law,* both as a work of scholarship and as a milestone in Holmes' career, cannot be dispelled simply by comparing the work to what Holmes had written (and done) before he wrote its lectures. One needs also to compare it to what he wrote and did in the remainder of his career.

Even then the enigmatic and paradoxical character of *The Common Law* may well remain. It was a book firmly grounded in the intellectual culture of its time, and yet a highly distinctive and individual work. It was a book with passages that have contained an enduring, arguably classic appeal, and yet it is a book whose scholarly apparatus remains obscure. It demonstrated its author to be a person whose control of language was masterly, and at the same time one capable of exercising his literary talents as much to conceal as to clarify. Its arguably greatest contribution—Holmes' recognition that the law is simultaneously influenced by internal professional and extralegal factors, and that legal doctrine is the product of a complex interaction between those sets of factors—was not emphasized by contemporary reviewers and has largely been ignored or oversimplified by subsequent commentators.

Much was to follow from the appearance of *The Common Law:* Holmes' professional life was not the same again. The book's appearance led him, in a roundabout fashion, to a career niche that he had coveted and that he found fulfilling, a judgeship. It also led him, in another fashion, away from original scholarship, as if he feared he could not again in that realm reach the level of performance he had achieved in his Lowell Lectures. In a sense *The Common Law* freed Holmes to become a "writer" again: to devote more of his time to the arts of speechwriting and correspondence, no longer obsessed with the necessity of building a professional reputation and confirming it with "professional" writing. Those corollaries of the 1881 appearance of *The Common Law* remain to be traced in detail. They will occupy us, along with other features of Holmes' life, in subsequent chapters.

CHAPTER SIX

"An All Round View of the Law,"
1882–1902

~

O N MARCH 3, 1881, Little, Brown and Company sent Holmes the first copy of
The Common Law. He inscribed the copy on the flyleaf and he and Fanny
opened a bottle of champagne; he saved the cork for the rest of his life.[1] As noted,
the book had appeared five days before his fortieth birthday, the point that indicated
whether "a man was to do anything."[2] Its publication must have signified a great
emotional release for Holmes. At last he had joined the company of his peers Pollock
and Dicey and Henry Adams and Leslie Stephen in publishing a book while still in
his thirties. But after the exultation of the moment when the first copy arrived,
anticlimax may well have set in. Holmes went back to his law practice, which continued as before. The book was greeted, as most books are, with a long silence. The
Lowell Lectures were over; the nights devoted to them and to their rewriting for the
book were suddenly empty. In the place of momentary euphoria came the more
familiar state of uncertainty. Would anyone review the book? Would Holmes' aims
in writing it be understood? Would his ambition to "take up the principal conceptions of our substantive law for the purpose of a new analysis"[3] be realized?

Two days after the first copy of *The Common Law* arrived Holmes was already
experiencing the anxiety of anticlimax. He sent Frederick Pollock a copy, noting
that he had "failed in all correspondence and . . . abandoned pleasure as well as a
good deal of sleep for a year" to produce the book, and added

> I should like it very much if my book was noticed in England but I suppose
> there are few anywhere who interest themselves in such things.[4]

A month later no reviews had yet appeared, and Holmes continued in the same vein
to Pollock. "I hope you will read my book," he wrote in an April 10, 1881, letter.
"It cost me many hours of sleep and the only reward which I have promised myself
is that a few men will say well done." He added that he had learned that copies had
been sent to the English journals *The Saturday Review* and *The Spectator,* but felt
"it is an accident whether it fall into the hands of people who will realize that the
work is at least a serious one."[5]

But although Holmes was unaware of it as he confronted the general silence with
which *The Common Law* was received, the publication of the book had changed his
professional life. Some indication of the book's reception was foreshadowed by a
letter James Bradley Thayer wrote to the Governor of Massachusetts in January 1881

shortly after Holmes' Lowell Lectures had been completed. The letter was in connection with a vacancy on the Supreme Judicial Court of Massachusetts: Thayer recommended Holmes for the position. He said to the Governor, John Davis Long, that Holmes' "recent course of lectures" had been "very remarkable and indicated the highest sort of legal capacity."[6] Long did not appoint Holmes, but Thayer's letter suggested that those in elite legal circles in the Boston community had come to recognize Holmes' intellectual talents.

It is not clear who was in the audience for Holmes' Lowell Lectures, but Thayer's comments to Long suggest that he may well have been. Thayer was at that time Professor of Law at Harvard Law School, which numbered four members on its faculty, Holmes' old friend John Chipman Gray, James Barr Ames, and the Dean, Christopher Columbus Langdell, whom, we have seen, Holmes had characterized as "the greatest living theologian" in American law.[7] At the time he was preparing the Lowell Lectures Holmes does not seem to have been close to Ames. He knew Thayer and Gray well, the former from his work on the 1873 edition of Kent. While there is no evidence that Holmes and Langdell were close, Holmes was keenly aware of Langdell's scholarship. In addition to his book review of Langdell's casebook on contracts, previously discussed, Holmes, we have seen, had written Pollock about his reaction to Langdell in April 1881:

> I have referred to Langdell several times in dealing with contracts because to my mind he represents the powers of darkness. He is all for logic and hates any reference to anything outside of it, and his explanations and reconciliations of the cases would have astonished the judges who decided them. But he is a noble old swell whose knowledge, ability, and idealist devotion to his work I revere and love.[8]

The previous June Holmes had made a reference to Langdell in a speech at the Harvard Commencement Dinner. In the course of suggesting that "[i]n every department of knowledge, . . . wonderful things have been done to solicit the interest and to stir the hopes of new inquirers," Holmes pointed to the "great contributions" made in law and stated that "not the least important of them have come from the great lawyer who presides over our own Law School, Professor Langdell."[9] While the setting of these remarks doubtless influenced their content, it is clear that Holmes had considerable respect for Langdell's intellect.

Other comments Holmes made at the 1880 Harvard Commencement also indicate that he had revised his earlier views about the quality of education offered at the Harvard Law School. In a previous chapter reference was made to an unsigned note that appeared in the *American Law Review* in 1870, one of the years Holmes was editing that periodical, in which Harvard Law School was described as "almost a disgrace to the commonwealth of Massachusetts."[10] The note went on to say that "[t]he object of a law department . . . is to furnish all students . . . the same facilities to investigate the science of human law, theoretically, historically, and thoroughly, as they have to investigate mathematics, natural sciences, or any other branch of thought."[11] This conception of legal education closely paralleled that of Langdell, whose use of casebooks and the socratic method in teaching followed from his assumption that "all the available materials of [legal] science are contained in printed books,'' and that ''the library is . . . to us all that the laboratories of the university are to the chemists and physicists.''[12]

There is thus evidence that by the 1880s Holmes was far more impressed with Harvard Law School as an educational institution than he had been a decade earlier. We have also seen evidence that he found legal scholarship a more satisfying enterprise than the general practice of law. In an 1879 letter to James Bryce, previously quoted, he complained that ''the men who care more for a fruitful thought than for a practical success'' were ''few everywhere,'' adding that ''I wish the necessity of making a living didn't preclude any choice on my part—for I hate business and dislike practice apart from arguing cases.''[13] After undergoing the experience of sustained scholarship that had resulted in a book, Holmes in the early 1880s may have been tempted to enter an environment in which such projects followed naturally from one's professional endeavors rather than being superimposed upon them. In short, he may have been tempted to consider abandoning law practice for a career in teaching and scholarship.

At the same time the Harvard Law School faculty began to take an interest in recruiting Holmes. At the opening of the 1881–82 academic year Harvard's enrollment had grown to 139 students, but it continued to be staffed only by four full-time professors, Langdell, Ames, Thayer, and Gray. Sometime in the fall of 1881 the President of Harvard University, Charles W. Eliot, contacted Holmes and inquired whether he would be interested in joining the Law School faculty, intimating that an endowment for a new professorship had been raised. Holmes, according to James Bradley Thayer, who was to play a considerable role in the process, ''deliberated for a considerable time'' after hearing Eliot's proposition, and then wrote him the following letter on November 1.

Dear Mr. Eliot:

Unless you take a different view I am not inclined to wait for contingencies the arising of which might not affect my determination. I am ready to accept a professorship in the Law School on the following terms if they are satisfactory as I believe from our conversations that they are.

1. I should prefer that the professorship should be entitled of Jurisprudence but the substance of the matter is not the title but the understanding thereby conveyed that I am expected to devote a reasonable proportion of my time to such investigations as are embodied in my book on the Common Law or other studies touching the history and philosophy of law.

2. The salary as I understand would be that of the other law professors, viz. $5000, and I suppose would be the result of a special endowment. As the taking of this place will invoke a pecuniary sacrifice which so far as I can foresee the future would probably in the long run be considerable I think I should ask that as soon as any law professor's salary is raised mine should be. I have to be particular on the money question as I must live on my salary.

3. If a judgeship should be offered me I should not wish to feel bound in honor not to consider it, although I do not know that I should take it and although my present acceptance will diminish the chance of such an offer and is for that reason against the advice of many of my friends.

4. If this letter meets your views the high respect I feel for the present faculty of the school including their presiding officer as well as the personal regard I entertain for them will make me look forward with eager anticipation to this new calling.

> With much respect
> Sincerely yours
> O. W. Homes, Jr.[14]

Three days after receiving Holmes' letter Eliot responded. He indicated that the title or substantive orientation of the professorship would be satisfactory and that "the salary of a full professor in the Law School would be raised if the resources of the School permitted." He then addressed the question of a judgeship. "In accepting a position here," he said,

> you do not pledge yourself to remain any definite time, & you remain free to accept a better position or more congenial environment elsewhere. On the other hand, your return to the practice of your profession simply within any period less than five years would be acceptable to the Corporation and Faculty only in the improbable case that you had not succeeded as a teacher of law.[15]

The thrust of Eliot's remarks on the judgeship question appeared to suggest that his principal concern, and that of Harvard as an institution, was that law professors not abandon teaching for practice without making a reasonable commitment to teaching, that is, five years. This concern may have been prompted by the higher salaries available to most law practitioners and perhaps by a feeling that Harvard was vulnerable to being used as a fulcrum to a more visible career in law practice. A judgeship, however, seemed to be a different category. Eliot referred to the prospect of "a better position" or a "more congenial employment" as an anticipated reason for leaving teaching. The exchange thus suggested that both parties had contemplated the possibility that Holmes might leave teaching for a judgeship and did not regard it as precluding an arrangement.

In his November 4 reply Eliot also said that he would "set about getting an endowment" for Holmes' professorship "at once, hoping to secure it in a few days." That proved a far more difficult matter than Eliot anticipated, and nearly resulted in Holmes' deciding not to join the Harvard faculty. Shortly after Eliot responded, according to James Bradley Thayer,

> Thereupon came the awkward difficulty that Eliot was mistaken; he had, I believe, given a wrong construction to something that John Lowell had said to him. Eliot, then, summoned in J[oseph] B. Warner and asked him to see if an endowment could be raised among the lawyers or by their means. He first had got Judge Lowell to promise $5000 if the fund could be raised and Holmes would come, and Mr. Sidney Bartlett promised as much more.[16]

Holmes, however, learned of Warner's efforts and the uncertain status of the endowment, and resolved to withdraw. On November 18 he wrote Eliot that "I have come to the conclusion that as the money to endow the professorship is not yet provided but will have to raised, I must withdraw my acceptance.'' Holmes felt that if ''a subscription should be raised on the understanding that I am pledged to fill the place,'' any contributors might regard their participation as ''a favor to me.'' Should the funds subsequently be raised, Holmes added, he might be inclined to accept the professorship, but he did not want to bind Harvard to securing it for him.

At this point Thayer decided to enter the negotiations. After hearing of Holmes' letter to Eliot, he spoke to Holmes, and on being reassured that Holmes was likely to come if an endowment could be raised without Holmes being designated as the prospective recipient of the professorship, told Holmes that he ''had great confidence that I could raise the money.'' He then offered his services to Eliot, and ''expressed the opinion that so young a man as Warner wasn't the best one for such a service.'' Eliot was noncommittal, not responding to Thayer's offer ''to give a part or the whole of the [Christmas] recess to the business if Eliot wished.'' At that point a vacancy developed on the Supreme Judicial Court of Massachusetts, and there was a possibility that Holmes might be named to it, so Eliot and Thayer agreed that they had better wait.[17]

The next time the matter was discussed was at the Law School Faculty meeting on January 10, 1882, which Eliot, Langdell, Ames, and Thayer attended. According to Thayer's recollection,

> Eliot put the question to those present, viz: Langdell, Ames & me, whether the faculty were prepared to make any effort to get an endowment. There was silence and then L[angdell] expressed the opinion that it was of no use to try; he didn't see how it could be done. Ames said the same. I then said I thought it could be done and should like to try but I should need a little time. There was no reply and no action was taken.[18]

Thayer then called on Eliot on January 11 and ''said to him that I did not wish to force my services on him but I should really like to take hold of this matter & if he approved I would give up some lectures during the next week and try.'' Eliot assented, and Thayer ''began to move about that day.''[19]

Thayer contacted Louis Brandeis, a graduate of Harvard Law School who had recently formed a partnership with Samuel Warren, previously an associate in Holmes' law firm. Brandeis ''named a number of young fellows as likely to help & perhaps as likely to give it all.'' Included in Brandeis' list was William F. Weld, Jr., whom Brandeis had tutored when Weld was a student at Harvard. Weld was ''lately heir to three millions by his grandfather's will.'' Thayer made repeated attempts to see Weld, who was reportedly going out of town, and finally managed to get Brandeis to ''break the matter'' to Weld and to set up a meeting between him and Thayer. The meeting was scheduled for three o'clock on Monday, January 16, at Brandeis' office, and Brandeis and Thayer agreed to get together an hour before the meeting.

At the conference with Brandeis, Thayer learned that Brandeis had mentioned the professorship to Weld, who expressed enthusiasm for endowing it and giving his name to it. Weld had also raised one possible difficulty. He had matriculated at Harvard but despite Brandeis' tutelage had not passed all his courses, including one he had taken with Thayer. He was considering returning to school and standing for a degree, but if he did, the fact of his endowing the professorship needed to be kept secret "because neither the college nor he would wish to have it supposed that he bid for a degree." Thayer assured him nothing would be said about it until "after the degree matter was over," and that the Law School would deal with him "with absolute impartiality." At the close of the meeting Weld agreed to give the money for the endowment, and Thayer "offered to prepare for him a paper" similar to that which Nathan Dane had employed when he created the Dane Professorship and designated Joseph Story as the appointee.[20] It was arranged that Weld would go to the office of Edward Hooper, the treasurer of Harvard University, the next morning to finalize the gift.

Thayer then decided to convey his remarkable news to all the interested parties. After meeting with Weld he stopped on his way out to Cambridge "and astonished Holmes at his office by saying that I thought it was all arranged & he had better make ready to come out." On arriving at Cambridge he "also called on Eliot & . . . told him that I thought it was all got from one man. He was entirely astonished & pleased." Thayer's final call was on Edward Hooper: he arranged with Hooper "to be at his office to meet an unknown gentleman at 10 and a half the next morning . . . he also was amazed." Eventually, on Thursday the 19th, Weld sent in a formal letter, which Thayer had prepared for him, giving about $90,000 to Harvard. Four days later the Harvard Corporation nominated Holmes as the Weld Professor. "Hooper told me afterwards," Thayer recalled, "that until I called W[eld] by name he didn't know who he was; but then he knew at once, he used to hold him on his knee."[21]

Thayer had written the account of his involvement in securing an endowment for Holmes in his memorandum book on January 29, 1881. Two weeks later he permitted himself the following summary of his accomplishments.

> On Saturday Feb. 11 the [Harvard] Overseers confirmed the appointment of Holmes as Professor; and at our faculty meeting on next Monday the 14th, instead of being where we were at the last one a month ago, with no money & no prospect of any for the new professorship, we shall have it all in hand & the new professor appointed and very likely actually present.[22]

Thayer might well have congratulated himself, and when one recalls his difficulties with Holmes over the credit for their work on the twelfth edition of Kent's *Commentaries,* his performance—indeed his consistent support of Holmes' efforts at career advancement in the 1870s and early 1880s—appears to have been an act of genuine selflessness.

Meanwhile Holmes, who had been informed of the Overseer's action by Eliot on February 11 and had accepted the professorship, made his plans to enter academic life. He was not to begin teaching duties until the fall, but he attended faculty meetings at the Law School in March and May 1882.[23] He was to offer several courses in the 1882–83 academic year: Torts for the full year, two hours a week; Agency and Carriers for the full year, one hour a week; Suretyship and Mortgage also once a week for the full year; Jurisprudence for an hour a week in the fall; Admiralty for an hour a week in the spring.[24] Of these all but the Torts course seem to have been lecture offerings. The Jurisprudence course mainly tracked the material of Holmes'

Lowell Lectures, with Holmes writing four additional lectures, two on the history of agency, including vicarious liability, and two on the early history of equity. He included the agency lectures in his Agency and Carriers course, and wrote additional lectures for that course and for Suretyship. While the structure of the lectures indicates that Holmes did not teach any of the classes except Torts socratically, he nonetheless assigned cases rather than selections from secondary sources for student reading.[25]

There is very little evidence about Holmes' reaction to his entry into law teaching. Later in his life he wrote that Fanny had thought that he "unconsciously began to grow sober with an inarticulate sense of limitation in the few months of my stay in Cambridge,"[26] but there is nothing in Holmes' notebooks or correspondence in the period between October and December 1882 that reflects that fact. He thought well enough of the scholarship he undertook after accepting the Harvard offer to publish it separately some years later.[27]

Both of the articles Holmes wrote after he joined the Harvard faculty were consistent with his jurisprudential orientation in *The Common Law*. The essay on equity argued that the early English Chancery courts essentially followed common law doctrines, rather than correcting them, except in two instances, one involving uses of land and the other breaches of covenants, where the equity courts simply sought to bring English law into harmony with earlier German doctrines. The essays on agency focused on the principle of vicarious liability, linking it to Roman conceptions of a slaveowner's responsibility for his slaves and suggesting that in modern society it was purely and simply a fiction. Indeed in Holmes' view "the whole outline of the law" of vicarious liability was "the resultant of a conflict between law and good sense."[28] While sometimes justified on policy grounds, vicarious liability was inconsistent with the principle that tort liability should be based on fault, and Holmes argued that the principle should be confined to "special cases upon special grounds."[29] In *The Common Law* Holmes had taken special pains to emphasize the influence of early Germanic doctrines on English law and to argue that liability in tort ought to be grounded on fault, so that both essays were in a sense derivative of the insights in that work.[30]

In December 1882, Holmes suddenly resigned from the Harvard Law faculty to accept a position of Associate Justice on the Supreme Judicial Court of Massachusetts. The offer of a judgeship to Holmes had come with unanticipated swiftness. In early December, Justice Otis Lord of the Supreme Judicial Court of Massachusetts announced his resignation. The timing of Lord's decision may have been prompted by the fact that the then Governor of Massachusetts, John Long, had not been a candidate for reelection that previous November and accordingly was in the last months of his term. The Governor-elect, Ben Butler, was a Democrat, and Lord and Holmes Republicans. Lord's decision thus gave Long, who had made two appointments to the Court in 1881, a third opportunity to appoint a judge before his term expired. Holmes knew of Lord's decision, and, on December 7, one W. C. Russell wrote Long recommending Holmes for the judgeship.[31]

On the next day, Friday, December 8, Holmes was having lunch with James Barr Ames in Cambridge when a carriage arrived with George Otis Shattuck, Holmes' law partner, and Fanny Dixwell Holmes in it. Shattuck informed Holmes that at noon on that day he had been summoned to Governor Long's office and told that Long meant to appoint Holmes to the vacant judgeship, but that Holmes' decision whether to accept the appointment was required before three o'clock that afternoon. The time constraints were caused by the fact that Long had only three weeks to serve in office, that judicial nominations were required to be considered by the Governor' Council for a week, and that the last apparent meeting of Long's Council was that afternoon. Shattuck, Fanny, and Holmes drove from Cambridge to the Governor's office and discussed the nomination; Holmes resolved to accept within the time limits. The next morning an article appeared in the Boston *Advertiser* announcing the nomination and giving details on Holmes' career.

The Harvard Law Faculty was thunderstruck. James Bradley Thayer, in a long memorandum to his diary written nine days after learning the news, described his initial reaction:

> On Saturday morning . . . , Dec. 9, I opened my Advertiser to read that
> [Holmes] was appointed to the bench of our Supreme Court and there was a
> long notice of him . . . It was surprising; the only explanation of it was that
> Long must have appointed him at a venture and trusted to his accepting; but
> that seemed unlikely. I called at the library on my way into Boston. Arnold our
> librarian said that Thorpe, a student in Shattuck's office (where Holmes still
> keeps up his connection), had called on Friday afternoon and mentioned that
> he had been appointed; it was utterly surprising to him. In the evening Gray
> (who is intimate with Holmes) happened to be [in the Harvard law library] and
> Arnold mentioned it to him; [Gray] also was surprised—entirely. He said that
> it must be a very sudden thing and put on his hat and went out quickly. [The
> next] morning Bolles, a student who writes for the paper, was in [the law
> library] and told Arnold that he had called on Friday evening on getting wind
> of this, upon Langdell and the President for information. Neither of them had
> heard a word of it. I at once said to Arnold, Very well, if that is so, I am
> relieved; I will bet $500 that the situation is this: he has told the Governor that
> he would consider the subject and the Governor has gone forward upon that.
> He never would accept without conferring with the President.[32]

But on investigating the matter further Thayer found to his astonishment that

> [Holmes] accepted the offer within the Governor's time and conferred with no
> one representing the college. He seems to have made no struggle for more
> time, not even to have conceived it *possible* that he could have more time or
> that it was any lowering of his own dignity or value to be pushed into a corner
> in this way, or that it should not have been *possible* for him to accept without
> a conference with Eliot. He had been on pay since Feb. 1, I think—March 1st
> at any rate; the year at the school had only begun; students were here who had
> been mainly induced to come by his being here, and all the students had
> rights—as the college had—which he was bound to consider carefully. But he
> accepted and it was blown abroad at once.[33]

Thayer then went on describe how in his judgment Holmes had compounded the difficulties:

Having done it, he did not post at once to see Eliot, he allowed him and all of us to learn it from the papers or any chance rumor. On Saturday morning . . . he called on Eliot and not finding him left his card (called twice it is said) and a verbal message that he might see him Monday morning. But not on Friday, or Saturday, or Sunday or Monday or Tuesday until Tuesday night at the Faculty meeting (coming to it late) did he have any communication whatever with Eliot or the authorities of the college. He made no effort other than the feeble one of Saturday morning after it was all published.[34]

At the Harvard faculty meeting on Tuesday evening, December 12, Holmes apparently attempted an explanation of his conduct. Thayer, who was not present and learned of the events from Eliot, reported that Holmes "made a long, excited and wholly ineffective attempt to account for his going . . . but no person said a word, *not one,* except E[liot] himself now and then, 'it did not seem kind,' he said, 'to leave him talking all alone,' '' After that meeting Holmes did not talk with Langdell or Thayer, and "seemed to have no sense of any impropriety in what he has done." Arnold, the librarian, subsequently reported that Holmes "wished it understood that this was all provided for in his letter of acceptance, that he had the documents, that 'the President did not blame him.' '' Thayer felt that this explanation of Holmes' was "about as bad a symptom as any in the whole business."[35]

It is clear that Thayer did not regard the correspondence with Eliot as a satisfactory explanation for Holmes' conduct. He conceded that "Holmes . . . is entitled to any excuse which this may furnish," and that "it cannot be denied that he was within the line of his legal right." But he then went on:

But what shall be said of his sense of what is morally admissible—of his sense of honor, of justice, of consideration for the rights of others and their sensibilities, when he could do what he did; of his personal self-respect, indeed.[36]

Thayer's complaint centered on the fact that there was no conceivable reason why Holmes could not have delayed his decision to consult Eliot and members of the Harvard Law faculty. "There were three weeks and more before Long's reign is over," Thayer pointed out. "If his council was not regularly to meet again for some days, yet could it not be called together in extra session?" Thayer wondered what Long "was going to do if H. *didn't* accept." He suggested that Holmes could "have intimated that he *probably* would accept and had the name go in and the news not published, and so have secured a chance to sleep over it and to confer with those who had a right to be consulted." But Holmes had accepted the offer at once, "and seems never to have thought and not to know now that it was an unhandsome, and indecent action."[37]

For Thayer, and apparently for others on the Harvard faculty, the fact that Holmes had acted "within the line of his legal right" was irrelevant. Some others at Harvard did not see Holmes' actions in quite the same light. The treasurer, Edward Hooper, wrote William Weld on hearing the news that while Holmes' departure was "a great blow to the Law School, as he expressly reserved the right to accept a judgeship, we cannot complain."[38] But those responsible for bringing Holmes to Harvard tended to agree with Thayer. In a 1924 letter to Holmes Eliot indicated that he "could not be reconciled" to Holmes' action at first, and reminded Holmes that "Langdell was never reconciled to that step on your part."[39] As for Thayer, he concluded his account of Holmes' departure with the following observations:

> He lost his head perhaps? But my experience in editing Kent, which I had been willing to forget, comes all back again and assures me that this conduct is characteristic—that he is, with all his attractive qualities and his solid merits, wanting sadly in the noblest region of human character—selfish, vain, thoughtless of others.[40]

Holmes gave few clues about his motivation in accepting the judgeship. In some correspondence, previously quoted, he identified one of the factors motivating him as what he called an "inarticulate sense of limitation" that he associated with his first months in law teaching. In December 1882, shortly after accepting the judgeship, he wrote James Bryce that "I had already realized at Cambridge that the field for generalization inside the body of the law was small and the day would soon come when one felt that the only remaining problems were ones of detail,"[41] suggesting that he was concerned about the future course of his scholarship. Several years later Holmes returned to this theme. In the letter to Bryce he had added that when one sensed that the field for generalization in law was small, and that much legal scholarship was filling in details, "as a philosopher" one would come to the realization that "he must go over into other fields—whether of ethics—theory of legislation—political economy or anthropology—history &c depending on the individual . . . he must extend his range."[42] In a 1920 letter to Harold Laski, prompted by the appearance of *Collected Legal Papers,* Holmes wrote that

> As to what you mention about going on to the Bench—the law *stricto sensu* is a limited subject—and the choice seemed to be between applying one's theories to practice and details or going into another field—and apart from natural fear and the need of making a living I reasoned (at 40) that it would take another ten years to master a new subject and that I couldn't bargain that my mind should remain suggestive at that age.[43]

Holmes' association of his concern for the future course of his scholarship with his decision to accept a judgeship does not quite ring true, especially given his decision to enter law teaching in the first place. He had decided to leave practice, in part, so that he could have more time and room to develop his scholarly pursuits, yet his letters to Bryce and Laski suggest that only a few months after having tried out some additional scholarship, in the Agency and Equity pieces, he had concluded that it would be merely sketching in the details of the jurisprudential outlines he had created in *The Common Law.* While it is possible that Holmes had not realized that he would "grow sober with an inarticulate sense of limitation" once he attempted to continue his scholarly efforts, there are some other themes in his letters about his decision to leave Harvard that appear more central to that decision.

In the Bryce letter Holmes had not listed his recognition that "the field for generalization inside the body of the law was small" as predominant among his motives for leaving Harvard. Paramount among those motives, he had written, was that I thought the chance to gain an all round experience with the law not to be neglected, and especially that I did not think one could without moral loss decline any share in the practical struggle of life which naturally offered itself and for which he believed himself fitted . . . I felt that if I declined the struggle offered me I should never be so happy again—I should feel that I had chosen the less manly course.[44]

And in a 1913 letter Holmes wrote to Felix Frankfurter a similar theme emerges:

[A]cademic life is but half life—it is withdrawal from the fight in order to utter smart things that cost you nothing except the thinking them from a cloister. . . . Business in the world is unhappy, often seems mean, and always challenges your power to idealize the brute fact—but it hardens the fibre and I think is more likely to make more of a man of one who turns it to success.[45]

In these letters the life of the academy is pitted against that of "business in the world." The former is "but half life," a "withdrawal from the fight"; the latter is a "struggle" that "hardens the fibre" of those who engage in it. Not to engage in "the practical struggle for life" is to choose "the less manly course"; to engage in the world of affairs with success is to become "more of a man." In moving from law teaching to a judgeship Holmes was, in his mind, moving from the cloister to the real world, reaffirming his masculinity.

One wonders why Holmes chose to conceptualize the choice in this fashion. He had, after all, practiced law for fourteen years before entering teaching; he had entered the world of practical affairs. Moreover, he had written Bryce earlier that he hated business and disliked practice except for arguing cases, the least "practical" and most "academic" of his professional tasks. If anything, the experience of practice had taught him that the profession of law could be a laborious, prosaic undertaking. Why did he think that judging would be significantly different? And why did he equate judging with "the practical struggle for life"? Did he believe that judges were the equivalent of businessmen, life on a state supreme court the equivalent of "business in the world"?

One recalls here the theme of survivor guilt that suffused Holmes' memory of his Civil War experiences. In his retrospective essays on the war the ordeal of fighting grew progressively more romantic as it grew more distant, until the soldiers who threw away their lives for a cause that they could not grasp became heroes, and the "horrible and dull" environment of wartime became transposed into a message that was "divine." In this view of the war even those who could barely endure it, those who had decided not to reenlist because they "could no longer endure the labors and hardships of the line" were more "manly" for the experience: they had had their fibre hardened. But in Holmes there remained the nagging doubt that in choosing not to reenlist he had chosen the less manly course; that he had opted to survive rather than kept the soldier's faith. To the extent that law teaching offered a comparable choice, a "withdrawl from the fight," Holmes was not going to make that choice again. His sense of self-esteem, even his belief in his own masculinity, were bound up in his decision to accept a judgeship.

In the 1924 letter to Holmes, Charles Eliot, after saying that initially he could not be reconciled to Holmes' action, which he thought precipitous and in bad taste, added that he had come to understand the decision, when Holmes had "explained to me your inheritance with regard to the function and status of judges." The reference was apparently to a conversation in which Holmes had told Eliot of his maternal grandfather Charles Jackson's service on the Massachusetts Supreme Judicial Court and of his desire to follow in his grandfather's footsteps. Left unsaid in that conversation, no doubt, was the fact that Holmes' father had not been and could not be a judge; that in following one family path Holmes was self-consciously rejecting another. Holmes Sr. was a Harvard professor in addition to being a literary figure; should Holmes Jr. have stayed on at Harvard and continued to do legal scholarship, he would have in a sense been mirroring vocational patterns in his father. To become a judge was not only to leave Harvard but to leave the world of letters. It was to choose Charles Jackson rather than Oliver Wendell Holmes, Sr., as a role model.

So it was unlikely that foremost in Holmes' mind, when he decided to leave Harvard for the Supreme Judicial Court of Massachusetts, was a perception that he had grown "sober with an inarticulate sense" of the limitations of a career whose magnum opus had been written at its beginning. Indeed the circumstances of Holmes' acceptance of the judgeship suggest that it was an impulsive decision, one made not through a careful balancing of future scholarly prospects but in the intuitive conviction that it was psychologically satisfying.

Three separable issues are run together in Thayer's account of Holmes' decision to leave Harvard. The first is whether the decision was inconsistent with the terms of Holmes' initial acceptance of the professorship. All parties to the incident appear to agree that it was not. Holmes insisted that the contingency had been provided for; Eliot did not dispute that; Hooper indicated that Harvard "[could not] complain" because Holmes had expressly reserved the right to accept a judgeship; even Thayer felt that Holmes was within his legal rights in leaving. Holmes' concern about the incident led him to retain Francis Parker, a Boston practitioner, to prepare for him a memorandum of law on the consequences of his and Eliot's arrangement, and Parker concluded that "the contract was expressly terminable upon Mr. Holmes' appointment as a judge," and "The College, therefore, took the risk of the time when it was so terminated, and this was an inducement for Mr. Holmes' accepting the place."[46] The judgeship offer, to be sure, had come at an awkwardly early time during Holmes' tenure at Harvard. But his correspondence with Eliot had said nothing about a time frame except for the understanding that Holmes would not return to law practice within a five-year period. A judgeship was not law practice.

The second issue was whether Holmes' conduct in accepting the judgeship and allowing the news to be made public without consulting anyone at Harvard was "selfish" and "thoughtless," as Thayer put it. The circumstances of Holmes' acceptance were certainly embarrassing to Harvard. He was leaving in the middle of the term, without any notice, and the news of his leaving was reported in the papers before anyone at Harvard had the slightest inkling that it was coming. Indeed Thayer was so sure that Holmes would not have accepted the position without consulting Eliot that he concluded that the newspaper account was mistaken. When the circumstances of Holmes' acceptance were made known, it was clear that he very probably could have delayed his acceptance, at least over the weekend, in order to consult

Eliot and others at Harvard. His not doing so gave the impression that in the face of the judgeship offered he cared very little about Harvard's sensibilities.

But Thayer's conclusion that Holmes' action was selfish and thoughtless assumes either that conversations between Holmes and Harvard acquaintances would have truly made a difference in his decision or were in any event necessary to save face and spare Harvard embarrassment. This leads to the third issue raised by the incident. Holmes might have concluded that Thayer's assumptions were incorrect: that is, he might have concluded that nothing would keep him from accepting the judgeship, so that conversations would have been futile, and that it was pointless, even awkward, to have such conversations when he had already made up his mind. The conversations would only reveal that Holmes cared relatively little for Harvard. Moreover, Holmes may have concluded that the risk that Long might not be able to persuade his council to meet again, or that he might choose another candidate who was willing to accept immediately, was not one that Holmes was prepared to take, and thus there was no reason for him to delay his acceptance. Given that conclusion, Holmes' conversations with persons at Harvard would quickly make it apparent that he was not even willing to delay overnight lest he jeopardize the judgeship.

By accepting Lord's offer, letting the announcement be made in the newspapers, and then not seeing anyone at Harvard for three more days, Holmes gave the distinct impression that the sensibilities of his Harvard colleagues were the farthest thing from his mind. This may have been imprudent and unnecessary, but it was very likely true. The offer of the judgeship had probably precipitated an emotional reaction in Holmes. Here at last was an office he coveted: one that dealt with the "business of the world" but was at the same time academic in nature; that paid a decent salary, higher than what he received at Harvard; that had been held by his grandfather Jackson; that carried with it the general prestige and stature of the judiciary and the special prestige and stature of the Supreme Judicial Court of Massachusetts, one of the more influential state courts in the nation at the time. Holmes had had the office of judge on his mind since 1878, when he had been mentioned in connection with a federal district judgeship. He had singled it out as continuing to be on his mind in his correspondence with Eliot.

Holmes' frame of mind on receiving the offer of the judgeship suggests that the prospect of a judgeship was so overwhelming to him, from an emotional standpoint, that when it came he literally did not think of anything or anyone else. Holmes was not a risk-taker where his professional prospects were concerned. After being nominated to the Supreme Court of the United States, for example, he delayed resigning from the Supreme Judicial Court of Massachusetts until his Senate confirmation was assured, even though that matter was purely routine. He was surely not going to take any risks with Lord's offer. Given those facts, not only did he not delay, he gave no thought to delaying. He simply blocked Harvard and his colleagues out of his mind. When Thayer, on being made aware of the sequence of events, grasped Holmes' thought processes, his resentment and infuriation surfaced. He understood that when Holmes was encountering decisions that touched a deep emotional chord within him, he thought only of himself.

Shortly after coming on to the Supreme Judicial Court Holmes announced that he "like[d] my work far more than I dreamed beforehand. The experience is most varied—very different from that one gets at the bar—and I am satisfied most valuable for an all round view of the law." He added that "one sees too a good deal of human nature, and I find that I am interested all the time."[47] While a year after beginning the judgeship he suggested that "for the present my [academic] investigations are at an end," he pointed out that he had retained the notes from his Harvard lectures and "may perhaps be able to shape certain portions into an article."[48] He envied Pollock's "learned explorations," which Holmes' absorption with "actualities and immediacies" prevented him from undertaking.[49] But he was not prevented from other sorts of writing, and soon he began to accept invitations to deliver extrajudicial addresses, the first of which was the 1884 commemoration of Memorial Day at Keene, New Hampshire, that produced his remarkable reminiscence of his Civil War companions.[50]

The emergence of Holmes as an extrajudicial speaker and writer signified that his work as a Massachusetts judge had neither completely satiated his capacity for work nor dulled the edge of his ambition. In 1887 he had reflected on the state of his professional life to Pollock:

My work is so hard that I don't dare attempt outside [scholarship]. When a few days leisure come I want to fall to and probably should, but my wife comes down on me with a picture of death as imminent if I do. So I fill such moments with talk about life, and reading poetry aloud, and French novels to myself. I wax impatient sometimes to think how much time it takes to do a little fragment of what one would like to do and dreams of. Life is like an artichoke: each day, week, month, year, gives you one little bit which you nibble off—but precious little compared with what you throw away. I enjoy it as keenly as most people however, I rather think. And I do despise making the most of one's time. Half the pleasure of life consists of the opportunities one has neglected. But already I have idled too long in making these few cosmical observations.[51]

Despite these observations, Holmes made time for his speeches. Between 1884 and the end of his tenure on the Massachusetts Supreme Judicial Court in 1902 he delivered a series of commemorative addresses, on the average of about two a year. His principal subjects were the profession of the law, including legal education; war; and the careers of distinguished lawyers. In these addresses he developed a distinctive style and introduced himself to the public as a literary artist. The addresses were also exercises in self-revelation, and are thus one of the best sources of Holmes' state of mind during the years he labored as a Massachusetts judge.

Of Holmes' extrajudicial addresses, the best known are those in which war was his central theme; these have previously been discussed. In his remarks on war Holmes took the opportunity to revisit his Civil War experiences from the perspective of the survivor, and to expiate some of the guilt he felt in that role by a determined glorification of soldierly duty. As early as 1880 he had ascribed to those of his classmates who had fallen in the war "a career of glory": they were "the most

brilliant of regimental commanders,'' the ''bluff, wise Christian captain,'' the ''gallant and gentle soldier.''[52] They were the source of ''stories . . . that add[ed] a glory
to the bare fact that the strongest legions prevailed.'' They were ''romantic figure[s],'' symbols of ''man's destiny and power for duty.'' They had ''toss[ed] life
and hope like a flower before the feet of their country and their cause.''[53] By honoring his contemporaries and romanticizing the war effort Holmes distanced himself
from the ordeal that he had endured and the guilt that he felt for having survived
and left the service before the war's end.

One theme of Holmes' years as a judge was thus working out a relationship
between himself and the memory of his Civil War experiences. He had emerged
from the war numbed and no doubt frightened by his recollections; his plunging into
legal scholarship could be seen as a form of blocking out wartime memories. When
he began again to talk of the war, in the 1880s, glorification of its meaning and of
its dead had begun to set in, so that by the 1890s, with ''The Soldier's Faith,'' he
had begun to sound like an arch militarist. But Holmes was more interested in the
self-abnegatory aspects of soldiering than in the jingoistic ones. He was well aware
of the ''swift and cunning thinking on which once hung life or freedom,''[54] of the
strength of the impulse toward self-preservation. He himself had swung to the side
of his horse when threatened with confederate fire, had transferred to an aide's
position to be able to escape the dangers of the infantry line, had mustered out of
service when it appeared that he could no longer remain an aide but needed to reenlist
as an infantry officer. When these memories of self-preservation surfaced, he spoke
instead of those who had willingly thrown their lives away. It was their faith that
was ''true and adorable.''[55]

In the 1870s the ''action and passion'' that Holmes regarded as so central to life
was pursued in the realm of scholarship. We have seen that he described himself as
one of the fortunate generation whose ''hearts were touched with fire''[56]: he could
take solace in having ''share[d] the passion and action of his time.''[57] But he recognized that ''we cannot live in associations with the past alone''; to be ''worthy
of the past'' his generation ''must find new fields for action . . . and make for
ourselves new careers.''[58] He thus set out to capture some of the glory he attributed
to those who had died in the war in his professional pursuits.

In order to equate his professional forays in the early years of his career with the
glorious episodes of his fallen Civil War compatriots, Holmes constructed two analogies. In the first of those the pursuit of intellectual knowledge through the legal
profession, especially through solitary scholarship, was likened to a physical adventure, a quest for glory. In the second the ideal of chivalry, with which Holmes had
associated service on behalf of the principle of antislavery, was also associated with
service in the legal profession. The solitary pursuit of scholarship was thus like the
soldierly pursuit of glory. Likewise the impulse that precipitated one toward the
legal profession was comparable, in its dedication to higher ideals, to the impulse
that had precipitated Holmes and his Harvard compatriots to participate in the Northern cause. In his extrajudicial addresses in the 1880s Holmes developed those analogies, and in the process of their development sought to equate his own career
pursuits with those of the Civil War comrades he honored.

In an 1885 address Holmes had foreshadowed his equation of law with physical adventure. He had asked what other profession "gives such scope to realize the spontaneous energy of one's soul," and "in what other does one plunge so deep in the stream of life—to share its passions, its battles, its despair, its triumphs . . . ?"[59] The next year he was asked to give a lecture to Harvard undergraduates on "The Profession of the Law." He concluded that lecture with a memorable passage:

> Of course the law is not the place for the artist or the poet. The law is the calling of thinkers. But to those who believe with me that not the least godlike of man's activities is the large survey of causes, that to know is not less than to feel, I say—and I say no longer with any doubt—that a man may live greatly in the law as well as elsewhere; that there as well as elsewhere his thought may find its unity in an infinite perspective; that there as well as elsewhere he may wreak himself upon life, may drink the bitter cup of heroism, may wear his heart out after the unattainable. . . .
>
> Perhaps I speak too much the language of intellectual ambition. I cannot but think that the scope for intellectual, as for physical adventure, is narrowing . . . I see already that surveys and railroads have set limits to our intellectual wildernesses—that the lion and the bison are disappearing from them, as from Africa and the no longer boundless West. But that undelightful day which I anticipate has not yet come. The human race has not changed, I imagine, so much between my generation and yours but that you still have the barbaric thirst for conquest, and there is still something left to conquer. . . . Your education begins when you . . . have begun yourselves to work upon the raw material for results which you do not see, cannot predict, and which may be long in coming. . . . No man has earned the right to intellectual ambition until he has learned to lay his course by a star which he has never seen—to dig by the divining rod for springs which he may never reach. In saying this, I point to that which will make your study heroic. For I say to you in all sadness of conviction, that to think great thoughts you must be heroes as well as idealists. Only when you have worked alone—when you have felt around you a black gulf of solitude more isolating than that which surrounds the dying man, and in hope and in despair have trusted to your own unshaken will—then only will you have achieved. Thus only can you gain the secret isolated joy of the thinker, who knows that, a hundred years after he is dead and forgotten, men who have never heard of him will be moving to the measure of his thought— the subtile rapture of a postponed power, which the world knows not because it has no external trappings, but which to his prophetic vision is more real than that which commands an army. And if this joy should not be yours, still it is only thus that you can know that you have done what it lay in you to do—can say that you have lived, and be ready for the end.[60]

In 1897 Holmes read Fridtjaf Nansen's *Farthest North,* a Norweigian explorer's account of his journeys in the Arctic, in search of the North Pole.[61] Holmes was taken with Nansen's account, and as early as May 1897 made an allusion, in one of his addresses, to "Nansen's power to digest blubber or to resist cold," which he thought an example of the "true resource of men." In the same address he claimed that "[t]he final test of this energy" was "battle in some form," such as "the crush of Arctic ice,'' or ''the fight for mastering in the market or the court.''[62] Then, in a commencement address at Brown University about two weeks later, he elaborated upon the theme of lawyer as solitary adventurer:

> My way has been by ocean of the Law. On that I have learned a part of the great lesson, the lesson not of law but of life. There were few of the charts and lights for which one longed when I began. One found oneself plunged in a thick fog of details—in a black and frozen night, in which there were no flowers, no spring, no easy joys. Voices of authority warned that in the crush of that ice any craft might sink. . . . And yet one said to oneself, Law is human—it is part of man, and of one world with all the rest. There must be a drift, if one will go prepared and have patience, which will bring one out to daylight and a worthy end. You all have read or heard the story of Nansen and see the parallel which I use. Most men of the college-bred type . . . have to go through that experience of sailing for the ice and letting themselves be frozen in. In the first state one has companions, cold and black though it be, and if he sticks to it, he finds at last there is a drift as was foretold. But he has not yet learned all. So far his trials have been those of his companions. But if he is a man of high ambitions he must leave even his fellow adventurers and go forth into a deeper solitude and greater trials. He must start for the pole. In plain words he must face the loneliness of original work.[63]

''Living greatly'' in the law was thus akin to a solitary adventure, to soldiering. And at the same time the legal profession was like a higher calling, whose practitioners were motivated by more than the motives of money or power. ''The world has its fling at lawyers sometimes,'' Holmes said in an 1885 address, but ''[i]t feels, what I believe to be the truth, that of all secular professions this has the highest standards.'' The legal profession was marked by a ''high and scrupulous honor.''[64] The ''torch of all high aspiration'' in the legal profession was that symbolized by fallen knights: law practice was a ''type of chivalry.''[65] On receiving an honorary degree from Yale in 1886 Holmes accepted it ''like the little blow upon the shoulder from the sword of a master of war which in ancient days adjudged that a soldier had won his spurs.'' He felt that ''[t]he power of honor to bind men's lives is not less now than it was in the Middle Ages.'' Honor was ''that which makes the man whose gift is the power to gain riches sacrifice health and even life to the pursuit.''[66]

One wonders why Holmes was determined to make the practice of law into a chivalric enterprise. He was well aware that much of law practice dealt with the world of business, which he would later describe as ''unhappy'' and ''mean.''[67] He was also aware of the late nineteenth century's fascination with wealth and with those who had achieved it: he began ''The Soldier's Faith'' address in 1895 by saying that ''the man who commands the attention of his fellows is the man of wealth.''[68] Yet he kept insisting that ''thoughts are mightier than things,'' and that ''ideals'' were ''more remote and vast than fortune.''[69] Why did he persist in likening the lawyer to the knight and in ascribing to the profession a spirit of honor?

A clue can be found in the letter, previously quoted, that Holmes wrote to Charles Eliot Norton in April 1864 when he was enduring one of his most discouraging stretches as a Civil War officer. We will recall that Norton had written an article in the *North American Review* likening the Northern war effort to a Christian crusade, and Holmes had responded by saying that "we need all the examples of chivalry to help us bind our rebellious desires to steadfastness in the Christian Crusade of the 19th century." "If one didn't believe that this war was such a crusade in the cause of the whole civilized world," he added, "it would be hard indeed to keep the hand to the sword."[70] The pursuit of ideals had driven Holmes to enlist; he was suggesting in the letter that those ideals had sustained him in the midst of discouragement. Comparable ideals, he intimated in his address, had motivated him to pursue his particular path in the law, a path that emphasized scholarship and service, not wealth. The chivalry example was thus a means of ennobling his profession and his professional choices.

The example was also a means of responding to the persistent sense of guilt and failure that nagged at Holmes when he recalled his war years. Despite professing fidelity to the ideal of chivalry, he resigned from service two months after writing the letter to Norton; he had chosen survival over ideals. Just as the characterization of his intellectual pursuits as lonely adventures was designed to recreate a place for him as the dogged soldier, the characterization of his profession as motivated by honorable ideals was designed to recreate a place for him as an idealist. While Holmes had pursued his solitary course through legal history principally because of a burning desire to produce original scholarship that would compete in stature with that of his peers and demonstrate his intellectual independence from his father, the version of that enterprise portrayed by his extrajudicial essays was that he had been one of those who had chosen "to think great thoughts" so as to be a "hero as well as [an] idealist."

Given this view of his professional activity, one might expect that in commemorative tributes to other lawyers Holmes would emphasize comparable qualities and comparable ideals in them. His tributory essays were in that vein. Sidney Bartlett was a lawyer who helped "establish, develop, or illuminate rules which are to govern the conduct of men for centuries"; as such "his is the most subtile, the most far-reaching power. His ambition is the vastest, as it is the most ideal."[71] Daniel Richardson was a "just, brave, tender, charitable, single-minded man" who "did a very great deal to lift up and maintain the character of the bar to which he belonged."[72] William Allen "would have preferred not to be celebrated . . . with all the pomp which properly is spent on those who have held power in their right hand." He appreciated that "such symbols do not express the vast and shadowy command which a thinker holds." He reminded one that "[o]ur prevailing ideals are somewhat coarse," and that "[c]omparatively few imaginations are educated to aspire beyond money and the immediate forms of power." His "ambition . . . look[ed] only to remote and mediated command," to "dreaming . . . the dream of spiritual reign."[73]

Even when Holmes was simply making off-the-cuff remarks, or introducing a speaker at a club dinner, his thoughts wandered to the same themes. On the occasion of his meeting the French essayist Paul Bourget he said that

> The sentimental optimism of New England thinks of war as all but over—if possibly commerce is not going to have everything its own way in the future, the types that are bred from war still have value for us. But if not—if, as,

externally, idealists usually are, the gentleman and the soldier is a survival, still it is a joy to some of us to see embodied . . . man's most peculiar power—the power to deny the actual and to perish.[74]

On a similar occasion, introducing a visiting English barrister, he spoke of an "old tradition which tells men that to be enduring and disciplined and brave is not less an end of life than to shine in the stock market and be rich."[75] In a series of remarks at the meeting of his Civil War regiment, he spoke of the "great trial in [our] youth that made [us] different . . . made us believe in something else besides doing the best for ourselves and getting all the loaves and fishes we could."[76] And in a banquet speech celebrating the victory of Admiral Dewey over the Spanish fleet in 1899 he distinguished between the "high heroic way of taking life" and the pursuit of "money and . . . personal advantage."[77]

In these extrajudicial essays Holmes sought to connect a number of propositions. The first was that the adventure of intellectual ambition was akin to that of the soldier engaging in battle or the knight embarking on a quest. A "man of high ambitions," he said in an 1897 commencement address, "must leave even his fellow-adventurers and go forth into a deeper solitude and greater trials."[78] The second followed from the first, that the pursuit of knowledge was an effort to achieve a disinterested ideal. The third was that there were opportunities to pursue knowledge in the law, and that those who did—the "thinkers"—rose above the mercenary and acquisitive ends sometimes attributed to their profession, and functioned like soldiers or knights. The last was that this dedication to the pursuit of the ideal of knowledge was a timeless source of inspiration that could be transferred down through the ages, just as the spirit of soldierly duty or chivalry could be transferred. In the 1886 address accepting an honorary degree from Yale University, previously quoted, he had combined those propositions in the following passage:

> I know of no mark of honor which this country has to offer that I should value so highly as this which you have conferred upon me. I accept it proudly as an accolade, like the little blow upon the shoulder from the sword of a master of war which in ancient days adjudged that a soldier had won his spurs and pledged his life to decline no combat in the future.
>
> The power of honor to bind men's lives is not less now than it was in the Middle Ages. Now as then it is the breath of our nostrils; it is that for which we live, for which, if need be, we are willing to die. . . . It is that which makes the scholar feel that he cannot afford to be rich.[79]

A striking feature of the propositions combined in this passage is that each, as Holmes was well aware, was a considerable overstatement. However lonely and frightening the pursuit of original scholarship, it could not be compared to "what it is to expect a bullet in [one's] bowels or to sail an iron clad over a mine."[80] The pursuit of knowledge had not been, in Holmes' own case, and was likely not in other cases, a disinterested exercise. On the contrary, Holmes had pursued scholarship because he wanted to advance his career and compete with those of his peers who were distinguishing themselves as academics. The comparisons Holmes had made in his 1897 commencement address between scholarship and Arctic exploration were apt. Arctic explorers did not primarily "start for the Pole" because they wanted to spread the gospel of Christianity or some other noble cause. Their central goal was to be the first to reach that remote spot and claim it for their own.

Nor had Holmes been entirely altruistic in first adopting and then rejecting a scholarly career. He had sought out scholarship in part because he "hated business and dislike[d] practice," and because he felt it was a vehicle through which he could gain some professional recognition. He had left academic life for a judgeship because he had an impression that academics was "half life" and because he was unclear how he could best put his talents to use after having written *The Common Law.* Finally, Holmes was abundantly aware that the legal profession was not the repository of selflessness and honor that his addresses suggested, and that those who sought to make their mark by helping fashion durable legal doctrine did not necessarily engage in that task for altruistic ends. Lawyers were paid to argue; judges to decide. Lawyers and judges took pleasure in the survival of their arguments or their decisions in part because of ego gratification.

In short, there was a dissonance between the propositions Holmes advanced in his extrajudicial addresses and his own experience as a lawyer, scholar, and judge. Yet Holmes clung to that dissonance and elaborated upon it as his collection of addresses grew during his years on the Massachusetts Supreme Judicial Court. It was as if in advancing the propositions he was seeking to convince himself that his career had been driven by goals other than those that motivated him to seek out success, recognition, and prominence. It was as if he recognized in himself the impulse toward self-advancement and power-seeking that he attributed to the commercialization of his age, and sought to make himself into a disinterested explorer, soldier, or knight instead. It was as if, nagged by the feeling that he might not have responded adequately to the ordeals of war, he sought to convince himself that by engaging in the loneliness of original work and aspiring to feel the "secret isolated joy of the thinker"[81] he was behaving like an honorable soldier after all. The thinker, the soldier, the idealist, the man who could disdain the apparent belief of Holmes' contemporaries that "[t]he aspirations of the world are those of commerce"[82] were to constitute Holmes' gallery of heroes.[83]

~

While Holmes' principal extrajudicial writing in his years as a Massachusetts judge took the form of ceremonial addresses, he did produce some scholarship. His initial scholarly efforts, as noted, were versions of lectures he drafted for his courses at Harvard, on the history of equity and agency, respectively, and represented work he had done in connection with *The Common Law.* But as he grew more comfortable with his judicial duties, and continued to yearn for recognition, he once again began to explore scholarly issues. In the 1890s, motivated by decisions in two labor cases in England, *Mogul Steamship Co. Ltd. v. McGregor* and *Temperton v. Russell,*[84] he reassessed the question of privilege where one competitor sought to undermine the economic position of another. The result was an 1894 article, "Privilege, Malice, and Intent," that demonstrated a significant shift in his views on the sources of common law rules from those he advanced in *The Common Law.*

In *The Common Law,* we have seen, Holmes had argued that even where the law spoke of rules or doctrines that appeared to be subjective, those rules, in application, evaluated conduct against an objective, external standard. Thus in his chapter on "Fraud, Malice, and Intent" he had maintained that "actual wickedness" was "not an element in the civil wrong" to which the word "fraud" was applied. "Malice" in the common law, he had suggested, did not mean "malevolence" in a lay sense or even "actual intent to cause the damage complained of." It was rather the equivalent of the "foresight or consequences" of a "reasonable man," based on external standards.[85]

In the cases that precipitated "Privilege, Malice, and Intent," however, the English courts did seem to be employing a subjective concept of malice, in which "doing harm to one's neighbor for the sole pleasure of doing harm" was treated as an unjustifiable and hence malicious motive. Otherwise, Holmes felt, there was no way to distinguish a case, such as *Mogul Steamship Company,* where merchants had provided shippers with incentives not to deal with a competitor, from a case, such as *Temperton v. Russell,* in which a union had ordered its members not to work for their employer if he sold goods to a buyer who did not hire union help. In the former case the merchants were simply attempting to improve their competitive position; in the latter the union was expressing its displeasure at an employer doing business with nonunion companies. "The ground of decision" in the two cases, Holmes suggested, "really comes down to a proposition of policy . . . concerning the merit of the particular benefit to themselves intended by the defendants, and suggests a doubt whether judges with different economic sympathies might not decide such a case differently."[86]

This treatment of labor cases suggested some difficulties for the jurisprudential theories Holmes had advanced in *The Common Law.* Recall that his posture in that work had been a combination of historicism and positivism. He had first argued that the law "evolved" in a series of decisions in which judges reconciled cases in accordance with the "felt necessities of the times," that is, current standards of conduct against which the community evaluated behavior. These standards, Holmes suggested at many points, were "objective" and could be ascertained empirically. At the same time, however, Holmes argued that objective standards in common law subjects were desirable because they demonstrated that rights-based jurisprudence was an insufficient theoretical formulation. In light of community pressures and expectations, rights were not absolute. Indeed to the extent that rights-based theories formed the basis for subjective standards of conduct, those standards were misguided and needed to be replaced by objective ones. Thus we have seen that in his *Common Law* chapters Holmes consistently argued, on policy grounds, for objective standards in common law subjects.

The divided jurisprudential basis of *The Common Law,* we have seen, created an internal methodological tension, one that Holmes appeared to have sought to resolve by adopting a positivist stance where it conflicted with a historicist one. In his discussion of vicarious liability, for example, he conceded that over the years courts had worked out a principle that masters were responsible for the negligent torts of their servants even though they could not be said to have been directly responsible for the servants' conduct. The principle was sustained by resort to the fiction that the masters had been careless in the selection of their employees. Holmes found this principle inconsistent with the general requirement that tort liability be based on fault and advocated its forthright abolition. The basis of his argument was that it made no sense to place the costs of injuries on persons who were unable to take steps to prevent them. His discussion presumed that judges could dismantle the doctrine of vicarious liability simply by recognizing that it was unsound in principle and in operation.

But such positivist arguments undermined the idea that legal doctrine evolved in response to community preferences. The "community" might prefer vicarious liability because it enabled injured plaintiffs to pursue additional, presumably wealthier defendants, even though those defendants could not have prevented the injuries from occurring. Holmes appeared to be inviting judges to ignore such community preferences when they were "unsound." In so doing he seemed to be suggesting that judges were not in fact bound by community norms.

In "Privilege, Malice, and Intent" Holmes pursued this last suggestion. If objective standards of liability were to be adopted in "unfair" competition cases, he reasoned, the successful invocation of a privilege to injure another by economic activity would turn on whether a reasonable person in the defendant's position could have foreseen that his conduct would injure the plaintiff. "Malice" would be subsumed in foreseeability. But this did not explain the results in the English cases. In both cases the defendants could have foreseen that their conduct would have injurious effects on the plaintiffs. Liability, however, was upheld only where "malice" had been shown, and malice was treated as a subjective concept. The judges had apparently reasoned that "malice" had been shown in the union boycott case because the union had no objection to management supplying goods to a particular buyer other than the fact that the buyer's work force was nonunion. The union was thus simply interested in directing its spite against the buyer rather than securing a competitive advantage against him.

Holmes suggested in "Privilege, Malice, and Intent" that the invocation of "malice" as an operative standard in unfair competition cases could be seen simply as a policy decision. In both cases an argument could be fashioned that the competitor, by offering below-cost rates as an incentive to keep customers from using a competitor's services or by boycotting sellers who proposed to do business with nonunion buyers, was seeking to improve its competitive position. That rationale was perhaps easier to discern in the former case, but in the latter it could be extracted: the union was seeking to improve its competitive position by making it more difficult for nonunion firms to survive in the market. The fact that judges had found "malice" in the union case but not in the other suggested that they disapproved of unions as market forces.

Once having recognized that "malice" was simply a basis for justifying decisions resting on grounds of policy, Holmes seemed unsure what to do with that insight. He conceded that the different judicial treatment of the two unfair competition cases signified that "[t]he time has gone by when law is only an unconscious embodiment of the common will." Law in such decisions, he argued, "has become a conscious reaction upon itself of organized society knowingly seeking to determine its own destinies."[87] But what followed from that argument? One conclusion that Holmes

came to was that the unfair competition decisions represented "very serious legislative considerations which have to be weighed," and that hereafter "the work
should be done with express recognition of its nature."[88] Another conclusion, however, was that "malice" ought to be retained as an intelligible legal standard, notwithstanding its subjective nature. "It is not enough," Holmes argued, "to say that
the defendant induced the public . . . not to deal with the plaintiff. We must know
how he induced them . . . If by advice, or combined action not otherwise unlawful,
motive may be a fact of the first importance." "It is entirely conceivable," Holmes
felt, "that motive . . . should be held to affect all, or nearly all, claims of privilege,"
even though "in all such cases the ground of decision is policy."[89] That is, he was
inviting judges to weigh, for themselves, the social advantages and disadvantages of
a competitor's action in determining whether it merited the label "malicious." He
had been a judge for 11 years since writing *The Common Law*.

The analysis advanced in "Privilege, Malice, and Intent" was not free from
contradictions. On the one hand, Holmes stopped short of abandoning "subjective"
criteria such as "malice," even though he had criticized them in *The Common Law*
and even though he now maintained that they were simply rubrics for decisions
arrived at on policy grounds. Although Holmes had admitted that the law was no
longer "only an unconscious embodiment of the common will," he seemed anxious
to retain the belief that "the advantages to the community, on the one side and the
other, are the only matters really entitled to be weighed."[90] In fact, he seemed to be
suggesting that judges be required explicitly to consider such factors in common law
cases, lest their decisions rest on "different economic sympathies." It was hard to
know, however, why judicial "balancing" of the sort Holmes anticipated would be
a reflection of community views, as distinguished from the views of the judges doing
the balancing.[91]

Three years later Holmes returned to the question of the sources for judicial
decisions in "The Path of the Law." Unlike the more modest scholarship he had
produced since leaving Harvard in 1882, "The Path of the Law" was reminiscent
of *The Common Law* in the breadth of its generalizations. The two works have often
been contrasted, and the current scholarly view appears to be that Holmes' jurisprudential views evolved considerably between the late 1870s and 1897.[92] But there are
some notable similarities between *The Common Law* and "The Path of the Law."
Language such as "the most important and pretty near the whole meaning of every
new effort of legal thought is to . . . generalize [doctrines] into a thoroughly connected system," or "the number of [such doctrines] when generalized and reduced
to a system is not unmanageably large"[93] could have been taken directly from *The
Common Law*. So could comments such as "[a] fallacy . . . is the notion that the
only force at work in the development of the law is logic," or "[t]he danger . . . is
. . . the notion that a given system, ours, for instance, can be worked out like mathematics from some general axioms of conduct."[94] Whatever his skepticism about
"general propositions," Holmes retained throughout his life the belief that pursuing
legal doctrines to their "bottom" required a degree of abstract synthesizing, and that
such efforts improved an understanding of the law. He also remained profoundly
suspicious of all attempts to equate law with geometric logic. Those judgments were
as firmly in place in "The Path of the Law" as they had been in *The Common Law*.

But there were some notable differences in outlook. One was suggested by Holmes' vivid metaphor of the "bad man" as a jurisprudential guide to the essence of legal decisionmaking. In *The Common Law* the process of his reasoning had begun with a critique of logic and then progressed through history to the derivation of external standards as doctrinal guidelines. While he conceded that the meaning of "reasonable conduct," or "malice," or "possession" would change with time, he treated those standards as intelligible entities. But the hypothetical "bad man" in "The Path of the Law" was not concerned with such abstractions. He wanted simply to know "the material consequences" of his conduct, that is, what the courts could be expected to let him get away with. The concepts that jurists dealt with—standards, "primary rights and duties,"—were simply "the scattered prophecies of the past upon the cases in which the axe will fall."[95] A legal duty was "nothing but a prediction that if a man does or omits certain things he will made to suffer . . . by judgment of the court."[96] By "the law," Holmes said, he meant "[t]he prophecies of what the courts will do in fact, and nothing more pretentious."[97]

These comments suggested that Holmes' view of legal decisionmaking had been significantly altered since his earlier scholarship.[98] He had originally been enthusiastic about the possibility of reorganizing jurisprudential classifications around the concept of a legal duty. While that idea, as an analytical device, had been muted in his work after 1876, his enthusiasm for intelligible legal standards remained. But his definitions in "The Path of the Law" indicated that he had reduced the process of common law decisionmaking to a consequentialist exercise. The question was not what doctrines or standards the judge formulated or applied, but whether a given court had prohibited or permitted a type of conduct. As he put it, pursuing the "bad man" conceit, "if we take the view of our friend the bad man we shall find that he does not care two straws for the axioms or deductions, but that he does want to know what the . . . courts are likely to do in fact."[99]

Holmes followed this theme through a variety of examples. There was no essential difference between "justified" and "unjustified" takings of property, such as eminent domain versus a wrongful conversion. In both cases the taking was permitted subject to the payment of damages: it did not matter whether one was called a tax and the other a penalty.[100] There was no "duty" to uphold a contract; there was only an option to uphold it or pay damages.[101] Liability for false statements "manifestly calculated to inflict temporal damage" did not rest on "any malevolent motive" in the speaker, but on the fact that the statement was of a kind reasonably certain to inflict harm.[102] The agreement of two parties to a contract did not rest on their meaning the same thing, but on their saying the same thing.[103] In short, the moral baggage of legal decisions was irrelevant to the decisionmaking process and hindered understanding of it.

But what was central to legal decisionmaking? The thrust of "The Path of the Law" suggested that techniques conventionally identified with the process—"analogy, discrimination, and deduction"—were not at its heart. Nor were moral beliefs. Holmes made it clear what he thought was at stake. "Behind the logical form," he argued, "lies a judgment as to the relative worth and importance of competing legislative grounds." The great majority of judicial decisions "[could] do no more than embody the preference of a given body in a given time and place."[104] Holmes argued that the training of lawyers should lead them "habitually to consider more definitely the social advantage on which the rule they lay down must be justified." Legal doctrines should no longer be "taken for granted without any deliberate, conscious, and systematic questioning of their grounds."[105] A body of law was "more rational and more civilized when every rule it contains is referred articulately and definitely to an end which it subserves."[106]

Holmes concluded "The Path of the Law" with a summary of the methodology he associated with a more realistic approach to legal decisionmaking. The first step in a "rational study," he argued, was "to a large extent the study of history." History provided "the precise scope of the rules which it is our business to know." But it was only the first step, because historical research revealed that most rules had persisted simply because they had once been established, without "being reshaped . . . with conscious articulate reference to the end in view."[107] This produced the paradox of form and substance that Holmes had identified in his earlier scholarship, in which the form of rules persisted even after their original substantive underpinnings had been discarded, and were reformulated only when their substantive implications were explicitly challenged. Holmes urged more attention to the process of reformulation, and especially more attention to the ends to which that process was being directed in a given case. "I look forward," he said, "to a time when the part played by history in the explanation of dogma shall be very small, and instead of ingenious research we shall spend our energy on a study of the ends sought to be attained and the reasons for desiring them."[108]

Holmes offered a final example of how his proposed methodology might work. He put a case where a landowner had granted a license to a person to use a right of way over his land on the erroneous supposition that that person was the agent of another whose use of the right of way the landowner approved. In fact the user was not the agent of the approved party, although the landowner took no steps to ascertain that fact. When after twenty years the landowner sought to deprive the user of access to the right of way, he would be met with the argument that open and adverse use over such a period of time would ripen into possession and title for the user. Should that argument be sustained where the user had not been granted initial access? Holmes argued that it should, not because of "the desirability of peace," or "the loss of evidence" that was presumed to occur when possession had taken place for twenty years, but because "a thing which you have enjoyed and used as your own for a long time . . . takes root in your being and cannot be torn away without your . . . trying to defend yourself, however you came by it." The landowner's neglect in ascertaining whether the user was the agent of the party he had given permission to use the right of way had "allowed the gradual dissociation between himself and what he claims, and the gradual association of it with another." The law should promote the value of autonomy furthered by such an association, especially where a complaining party's own conduct had served to disassociate himself from contested property.

The example served to illustrate the reformulation of established legal doctrines by a demonstration of the ends they served. It presented a clash between the doctrine by which the owner of land had a presumptive right to exclude all others from it, and the doctrine of adverse possession, which allowed those who used land openly and "adversely" for a given period to secure title to it. Holmes' argument in the illustrative case was that the adverse possession doctrine controlled in cases where the original owner had contributed to the adverse possession. He had rested that argument on the "end" of establishing an association between the use of land and its ownership. That end was desirable because it fostered the use and improvement of land and because it promoted personal autonomy.

But the case also served to illustrate that Holmes' methodology in "The Path of the Law" was at bottom a positivist methodology. The process he was urging was one in which judges, having used history to expose the ends that served as the justification for legal rules, then modified the rules if those ends were no longer socially desirable. In the process the judge was the arbiter of social opinion with respect to the desirability of a rule as well as the arbiter of legal doctrine. The case Holmes had put could have gone the other way: a court could have concluded that where a user of land had reason to know that he was using it under false pretenses, he had an obligation to reveal that fact to the owner. This decision would have promoted the social end of security of land titles and the inviolability of property rights. Judicial decisions to prefer one rather than another of competing legal doctrines, then, were ultimately decisions about who had the power to enforce a given preference. Since either of two irreconcilable preferences could be justified through appeal to the methodology described by Holmes in "The Path of the Law," the methodology only reinforced the fact that in common law decisionmaking judges were exercising what Holmes later called a "sovereign prerogative of choice."[109]

The last pages of "The Path of the Law" reaffirmed Holmes' belief that judicial extrapolations of the social ends served by legal rules represented the kind of professional ideal he had earlier associated with high-minded public service in the chivalric tradition. "To an imagination of any scope," he asserted, "the most far-reaching form is not money, it is the command of ideas." Those whose possessed "intellect great enough to win the prize" needed "other food besides success." For them happiness was not equated with "being counsel for great corporations and having an income of fifty thousand dollars," but with "becom[ing] a great master in your calling" by "connect[ing] your subject with the universe."[110]

The transition of Holmes' thought from his earliest scholarship to "The Path of the Law" can be illustrated by the relative importance he gave to systematic formulations of legal doctrine, as distinguished from the mere decision of cases. His earlier work, while recognizing the "practical" and "predictive" dimensions of legal decisionmaking, placed its emphasis on the derivation of standards or principles, either through use of the duty concept or through an analysis of cases over time that was designed to illustrate the progressive growth of standards such as externally based liability in tort or contract. Holmes' enthusiasm for historical methodologies in this period in his scholarly career was primarily because they made such demonstration of "growth" in the law possible.

With "Privilege, Malice, and Intent" and "The Path of the Law" Holmes had come to place far more emphasis on the element of judicial choice in legal decisionmaking. Whereas he had previously suggested, in discussing such phenomena as the paradox of form and substance, that the decay of older forms was simply part of the endless process of growth and change in the law, he now saw the paradox as revealing the discretionary nature of judicial decisions. Older forms were retained or abandoned because their substantive basis was either endorsed or rejected; judging was inevitably a matter of policy choices. The discretionary nature of judging and the fact that legal rules were inevitably reduced to policy choices prompted Holmes to emphasize the positivistic nature of law in his "bad man" metaphor. But he had another purpose as well in "The Path of the Law," to urge judges to be more self-conscious about the policy choices presented by cases and more explicit about articulating the policy basis of their decisions.

The latter feature of "The Path of the Law" made it less of a resigned capitulation to positivism than it might first appear. Holmes did not seem to be suggesting that all that one could say about judicial decisions was that they were choices by people holding power,[111] but rather that at the bottom of the decisions were competing policy alternatives, one of which had been embraced. By urging that judges become more explicit about the policies they were considering, embracing, and rejecting, he appeared to be calling for something like a policy science of judging. Should judges become more assiduous in stating the underlying policy reasons for their decisions, those reasons could be subject to the same sort of analysis and classification Holmes had attempted for common law rules in *The Common Law*. The purpose of such analysis would be reformist in the same sense that *The Common Law* was reformist: an effort to arrive at a more "scientific" basis for legal doctrines.

In his last major scholarly work, "Law in Science and Science in Law," Holmes pursued the idea of a policy science of judicial decisionmaking. He made it explicit that historical analysis was to be a prologue, a guide that "enables us to make up our minds dispassionately whether the survival which we are enforcing answers any new purpose when it has ceased to answer the old."[112] The use of history was "mainly negative and skeptical"; its "chief good [was] to burst inflated expectations." While history "sets us free" to make up our minds on contemporary policy issues, "[t]he true science of the law does not consist mainly in . . . a study of it as anthropological document from the outside." It was rather a study of the "establishment of [legal] postulates . . . upon accurately measured social desires."[113]

Holmes then proceeded to describe this "true science of the law" a little further. He first claimed stature for "[t]he man of science in the law." He was "not merely a bookworm"; he was "a great abstract thinker" directing his efforts toward "the successful study of problems . . . simply to feed the deepest hunger and to use the greatest gifts of his soul." But he was "in the fight," not one who had "give[n] up one-half of life that his protected talent may grow and flower in peace." He was concerned with "living questions" which "call[ed] upon your whole nature."

He then characterized the methodology of the "man of science":

We must think things not words, or at least we must constantly translate our words into the facts for which they stand, if we are to keep to the real and the true . . . [I]nasmuch as the real justification of a rule of law . . . is that it helps to bring about a social end which we desire, it is no less necessary that those who make and develop the law should have those ends articulately in their minds. . . . [W]hen a doubtful case arises, with certain analogies on one side and other analogies on the other . . . what really is before us is a conflict between two social desires. . . . The social question is which desire is stronger at the point of conflict. . . . Where there is doubt the simple tool of logic does not suffice, and even if it disguised and unconscious, the judges are called on to exercise the sovereign prerogative of choice.[114]

The "man of science" was thus supposed to function as a guide to the process of unearthing the competing "social desires" that lay beneath "doubtful" cases, of demonstrating that the judicial choice to apply one or another "analogy" was really a choice to embrace one rather than another of those desires, and of making that choice explicit. As an example, Holmes put the case of *Allen v. Flood,* another in the series of English interference with contract cases decided by the House of Lords. The case affirmed the principle that a mere intent to "better the defendant's union in a battle of the market" would not be sufficient evidence of "malice" for the purpose of interference with contract suits.

Holmes thought the case rightly decided, but noted that one of the grounds offered had been that "anything which a man has a right to do he has a right to do whatever his motives." He thought this reasoning "simply . . . a pontifical or imperial way of forbidding discussion." Even the "rights" to sell property or describe the character of others in employment situations could be confined: fraudulent sales or defamatory comments were actionable. In seeing "the vague generalization Right" invoked in support of an outcome, Holmes asked "whether it is definite enough to stand the strain." The fact was that interference with contract cases involved two competing "rights," that to pursue one's business interests freely and that to be free from malicious interference with one's business relationships (one could call those "rights," respectively, rights of "competition" and "property"). Whether an action was made out depended on a judicial resolution of those competing rights on policy grounds. The "man of science" could be helpful here because "it is finally for science to determine . . . the relative worth of our different social ends.[115] "For the rational study of the law," Holmes had said in "The Path of the Law," "the man of the future is the man of statistics and the master of economics."[116]

Holmes' conclusion that in "doubtful" cases judicial decisionmaking amounted to the exercise of the "sovereign prerogative of choice," the arbitrary selection of one competing "analogy" over another, thus did not thus mean that scholarly generalization about the law was impossible. Through the techniques of the "man of science," he suggested, the structure of judicial decisionmaking could be clarified and the competing social ends at the bottom of close cases revealed with greater particularity. "Prediction" might thus become less of a function of who held power than a function of which ends given judges were likely to embrace, and as those ends became better understood they might also be subjected to commentary and refinement. In the process law might more approximate a science of policy. "Very likely it may be that with all the help that statistics . . . can bring us," Holmes said, "there will never be a commonwealth in which science is everywhere supreme. But it is an ideal, and without ideals what is life worth?"[117]

Holmes' extrajudicial activities during his years as a judge on the Supreme Judicial Court of Massachusetts were, to an important extent, efforts to build a connection between his judicial and scholarly careers and his Civil War experience, and in so doing to convince himself that in a sense he continued to act as a soldier, explorer, or knight. While his essays and scholarly writings during his years as a Massachusetts judge may thus have been a source of personal satisfaction as well as professional recognition, frustrations remained. As Holmes' later scholarship suggested, judging could be reduced to a "trifling or transitory" experience or simply to a series of choices between competing social policies. On the one hand it had ceased to be an endless source of intellectual stimulation; on the other it had not been a basis for building a national reputation as a jurist. Holmes yearned for something more in his life. In particular, he yearned to pursue some "neglected opportunities": a dimension of life that he had once pursued and had carefully avoided while he sought to make a mark as a lawyer, scholar, and judge. That dimension of life had been the social whirl he had first encountered on his trip to England in 1866, the world of London dinner parties, country homes, flirtations, and "interesting" conversation. Beginning in the late 1880s Holmes would reenter that world. There, apparently for the first time in his life, he would find romance.

CHAPTER SEVEN

Travel and Romance

~

ROM the time he returned from Civil War service in the summer of 1864 until
his departure to Washington to serve on the Supreme Court of the United States
in December 1902 Holmes' life was overwhelmingly centered in Boston and overwhelmingly oriented toward his professional pursuits. He lived with his parents while
attending law school and during his first years in practice, and after his marriage in
1872 continued to live in his father's household for two years. In October 1873
Wendell and Fanny Holmes purchased a farm in Mattapoisett, Massachusetts, on
Buzzards Bay, where Holmes' partner George Shattuck was a summer resident, and
spent at least three weeks of every summer from 1873 to 1888, excluding 1882, in
Mattapoisett. They initially owned one-half of the house, with the caretaker living
in the other, and in 1883 purchased the whole. In the spring of 1888 the house
burned to the ground in a brushfire.[1]

Meanwhile Wendell and Fanny had found an apartment at 10 Beacon Street, not
far from the senior Holmeses, which they had moved into by the spring of 1875.[2]
In 1888 Wendell's mother died, and his younger sister Amelia went to live with Dr.
Holmes.[3] The next year Amelia, who had been afflicted with a weak heart, herself
died, and the junior Holmeses resolved to move into Dr. Holmes' house, with Fanny
assuming his care. That arrangement persisted until 1894, when Dr. Holmes died
and the junior Holmeses inherited his house. Amelia, who had married Turner Sargent in 1869 and been widowed from him in 1877, had on her husband's death
acquired property in Beverly Farms, Massachusetts, not far from Mattapoisett. The
senior Holmeses began spending portions of the summer there after Sargent's death,
and were continuing to do so when the farm in Mattapoisett burned. The successive
deaths of Holmes' mother and Amelia left the Beverly Farms property available to
the junior Holmeses, and they spent portions of the summers there, beginning in
1889.[4]

Before his appointment to the Harvard faculty Holmes was preoccupied with his
work, and he and Fanny had few social contacts. His assuming an academic position
made his summers free from responsibilities, and he wrote Frederick Pollock in April
1882 that he planned to spend the summer in England and the continent as "one of
the advantages of the professorship."[5] But the appointment to the Massachusetts
Supreme Judicial Court meant that Holmes' summers would be taken up, except for
intervals, with court business, further cementing the junior Holmeses' routine. Their
life, for most of Holmes' tenure as a Massachusetts judge, was centered around
Beacon Street and the courthouse, around Holmes' work and their role in the

extended Holmes family. Holmes traveled around the state on his circuit duties, occasionally attended meetings of the Saturday Club or the Tavern Club in Boston, and paid periodic social calls on female friends such as Nina Gray or Belle Gardner. There is no evidence that Fanny's world extended very far from Beacon Street.

There was, however, one exception to the prosaic routine of Holmes' extrajudicial life during the years he spent as a Massachusetts judge. This was his travels abroad, principally to England, and the social contacts and friendships he made during those travels. As the years in Boston passed, a pattern developed to the traveling: Holmes centered his visits on England, traveled alone, and threw himself into the whirl of the London social "season." It was clear by the late 1880s that these trips to England were an important part of Holmes' regimen: a form of release and rejuvenation. In the next decade it became clear that they were also a source of romance.

The first of Holmes' trips to England and the continent in 1866 has been previously described. The experience had made a marked impression on him, both as a source of intellectual stimulation and as an outlet for the social side of his personality. He had made friends with contemporaries in the British intelligentsia, men such as Pollock, Bryce, Dicey, and Leslie Stephen, and he had encountered John Stuart Mill, Alexander Bain, and William Gladstone.[6] He had also flirted with a number of young women, one of whom he characterized as "making eyes like a horned owl."[7] In short, he had felt appreciated both for his cerebral and his convivial talents, and he returned home resolved to make another European trip in the future.

An opportunity arose in the summer of 1874, when Holmes took a short break from the intense intellectual labors of the early 1870s, having seen his edition of Kent through to completion, resigned as editor of the *American Law Review,* and formed the firm of Shattuck, Holmes, and Munroe. By 1874 he had also completed two sets of course lectures to Harvard undergraduates and three law review articles; it appeared as if his new firm would mark a change in his orientation and a diminution of his scholarly intensity. By the summer of 1874 Fanny must also have been sufficiently recovered from her bout of rheumatic fever to travel. The Holmeses planned a three-month trip to England and the Continent, sailing in late May 1874.

The trip, at least in its English portions, was apparently designed to trace some of the steps that Holmes had taken alone in 1866, and so one of its features was the exposure of Fanny to her husband's intellectual and social companions. In that respect the trip was a mixed success. It started badly, as Fanny was seasick: she noted in a diary entry that she would "never, never, never put myself in such a fix again," and that her fellow women passengers were "beginning to get sick."[8] Once the Holmeses arrived at London, Holmes spent a fair amount of time in the company of his old friends and acquaintances, and Fanny was not included on some of those occasions. One evening when Holmes was dining out by himself, one of his friends, Sir John Kennaway, called on Fanny and suggested that the routine was "awfully lonely for you" and that had he not been engaged he would have insisted on taking her out to dinner.[9] Fanny noted in her diary that she liked Kennaway's attitude "better . . . than any of the others,"[10] which suggests that she might have felt somewhat ignored by her husband's intellectual friends.

With respect to the whirl of the London social season, Fanny was not unduly

impressed. She described one academic she encountered at a party as "very disagreeable in black stockings, long coat, black sash and ribbon round his head";[11]
she noted "[f]at old ladies with immense bosoms and larger stomachs";[12] and she
referred to her host on another occasion as a "twinkling hippopotamus."[13] She was
shocked at the size of the meals, listing an "*ordinary* breakfast" as including "omlet
Fish cutlets potted rabbit Mushrooms potato boiled eggs white and brown cold tarts
Toast hot bread three kinds of Jam—Honey—Fruit Tea [and] coffee."[14]

Fanny also remarked from time to time on Wendell's interest in other women.
At one party some Americans, whom Fanny had previously encountered on shipboard and did not like, "were . . . so delighted to see us in such good society," and
stopped to chat. The man said that a female friend of Holmes wanted to see him,
and that he could bring her over unless Fanny was jealous. When reassured that she
was not, the American said that "there has been cause for it in this case." "Scandal
in high life!," Fanny wrote in her diary. "Four pair of strange English eyes and one
eye-glass directed upon the group full of interest, and gossip in our case mingled
with a little sentiment and an instantaneous glance which seemed to say 'I too have
suffered.'" The friend of Holmes turned out to be a Miss Minton, whom Fanny felt
was "the last person under the last circumstances in the world" to whom her husband
would be attracted.[15]

There was also an episode with a Mrs. Willoughby, whom the Holmeses met at
the home of John Campbell, whom Holmes had visited on his 1866 trip. In her
description of that evening Fanny noted that "everybody [was] very cordial and
pretty," and that "I don't know when I have had such a pleasant time." Wendell
then added a line to the entry: "I sat next to Mrs. Willoughby whom I love."[16] Less
than a week later Mrs. Willoughby left a book for Wendell at the Holmeses' London
flat, and subsequently Fanny wrote that Holmes had departed one evening "to see
his charmer and return the book," but that he had "[b]rought the book back with
him."[17]

The Holmeses remained in London until July 11, when they left for Paris and
the Continent, traveling through France, Switzerland, and Italy before returning to
Paris and to London on August 2. They stayed in London until the 14th, when they
went to visit Kennaway in Scotland, sailing for Boston on the 26th. The trip, with
its emphasis on the London "season," a brief, tourist-oriented swing through
Europe, and visits to country houses after the London season ended, closely paralleled the structure of Holmes' 1866 visit. It was obvious that Fanny's tendency to
recoil from excesses in consumption or in conversation had made some features of
the trip stressful for her. One of Holmes' biographers advanced this characterization
of her about the time of the 1874 visit to Europe:

> While Mrs. Holmes could prick bubbles of pretention with a quick and
> scathing word . . . she evidently found none of the satisfaction and
> refreshment which her husband did in the virtuosity of talk. The shyness and
> reserve of New England made her an appreciative but slightly mistrustful
> observer of the world of social and intellectual fashion. . . . Doubtless the
> inclinations of an anchorite grew with the years, but it is not unlikely that her
> husband would have said of her in 1874 what he stated in 1912: "She is a

very solitary bird, and if her notion of duty did not compel her to do otherwise, she would be an absolute recluse, I think. . . . She and I are a queer contrast in that way, as in many others.''[18] It is probable . . . that one of the other ways in which Holmes saw himself and his wife as queerly contrasted was in their attitude towards intellectuality. No surviving records or memories of Mrs. Holmes indicate that she shared, or pretended to share, his exuberant interest in the world of ideas. In his later years he found a number of ladies who did the one or the other . . . I suspect that, not sharing his insatiable appetite for ideas, she saw herself as excluded from that segment of his life which was spent . . . in the pursuit of knowledge.[19]

The passage suggests that insofar as Holmes conceived trips to England as exercises in pursuit of ''the virtuosity of talk'' and ''the world of social and intellectual fashion,'' that conception was largely alien to his wife.

Nonetheless Fanny did accompany Holmes on another trip to Europe in the summer of 1882 that followed closely along the lines of the 1874 visit. Holmes renewed acquaintances with his English friends, who were now aware of his legal scholarship and *The Common Law*. Wendell and Fanny toured France and Switzerland as they had on the earlier trip, and added some time in Germany. They then returned to England and passed the balance of their stay in visits to friends in countryside locations.[20] Aside from an entry by Holmes that indicated Fanny was ''not well . . . for a short time''[21] during their stay in Paris, there is little evidence of their reactions to this visit, but the diary entries make clear that Holmes' familiar structure of intellectual and social pursuits was in place.

In the spring of 1889 the deaths of Holmes' mother and his sister resulted in the junior Holmeses resolving to leave their apartment and move into Dr. Holmes' house at 296 Beacon Street. Dr. Holmes wrote a friend in April 1889 that ''my household goes on smoothly, and not without a cheerful aspect'' because of the presence of ''[m]y daughter-in-law, a very helpful, hopeful, powerful, as well as brilliant woman.'' He added that ''[h]er husband the Judge will soon be established in the house,'' but that he would be ''a good deal away from home.''[22] At the same time Holmes wrote a friend that ''[i]t is settled now that we go to live with my father— the only practicable or possible thing,'' and added that ''Mrs. Holmes wants me to go abroad this summer prophesying that it will make the first summer easier for my father.''[23]

One of the reasons why Holmes might have been tempted to go abroad by himself in the summer of 1889 was his recent acquaintance with Ethel Grenfell, the niece of Henry Cowper, an aristocrat of intellectual and artistic tastes whom Holmes had first encountered on his 1866 visit to England and with whom he had renewed acquaintances on his 1874 and 1882 visits. Cowper, who had once referred to Holmes as his ''dearest friend,''[24] had died suddenly in 1887, and Holmes, who had not even known Cowper was ill, was shocked by the death. Ethel Grenfell, an orphan who had been raised by Cowper and his wife, had married the year of his death at the age of twenty, and the next year she traveled to Canada and America, stopping to visit the Holmeses in Boston in September. In May 1889, when she may have known that Holmes was thinking of coming to England, Ethel wrote him a letter, saying that "[y]ou were so *good* to me when we met & I have a great wish that we may always be friends. . . . I have since thought of so many things I should like some day to tell you."[25]

Holmes' connection with Ethel Grenfell opened up a new dimension to his English visits. She and her husband were part of a circle of young aristocrats, known as "the Souls,"[26] who were establishing themselves as significant figures on the London social scene. "The Souls," who had come into being in the late 1880s, were described by a London society journalist in 1889 as a "most aristocratic cult" that comprised "only the youngest, most beautiful and most exclusive of married women in London." He went on to say that "[c]ertain intellectual qualities are prominent among 'the Souls', and a limited acquaintance with Greek philosophy is a *sine qua non*."[27] The historian of "the Souls" has attempted a fuller characterization:

> They believed that they were moving society away from philistinism towards patronage of the arts; away from political divisions that meant neighbors barely spoke to one another, toward a greater tolerance on political matters; away from the belief that women were childish, pampered chattels, toward treating them as people with tastes and opinions worth cultivating. Above all, they believed they were restoring to the English upper classes . . . the art of intelligent conversation.[28]

As constituted, the group was an ideal circle for Holmes to frequent in London. Their numbers included people such as Arthur Balfour, later Prime Minister, and George Curzon, later Viceroy to India, who had a strong footing in contemporary politics. But their preoccupation was with stimulating conversation, engaged in by both men and women and regularly laden with sexual overtones. They were accomplished flirts as well as accomplished conversationalists; indeed the two skills were rarely distinguished.

～

There is evidence than in the late 1880s Holmes was not always interested in distinguishing conversation from flirtation. Prior to coming to England in the summer of 1889 he had written a number of friends and acquaintances, including Henry James, who was then living in London. Henry James' sister, Alice James, was also residing in England at the time, "taking a cure" for her chronic invalidism in Leavenworth Spa. On June 16, 1889, Alice made the following entry in her journal:

> H. writes that he has received an affectionate!!! letter from Wendell Holmes, a marvel explained by his near arrival in London. They say he has entirely broken loose and is flirting as desperately as ever. There is something so grim as to be out of nature in that poor woman's life and character. What is there but ugliness in any relation between two beings which doesn't work to soften their hearts and open their minds to their kind?[29]

The source of the comment that Holmes had "broken loose" and was "flirting as desperately as ever" was undoubtedly Henry and William James. William James had sailed with Holmes on *The Cephalonia* in May 1889 and wrote his brother that Holmes was "making himself delightful to all hands" on shipboard.[30] The observation suggests that Holmes' flirtations had been remarked upon before by members of the James family. It also suggests that Alice, at least, linked Holmes' behavior to "something so grim as to be out of nature" in Fanny.[31]

Holmes stayed in Mackellar's Hotel in London and wrote friends and acquaintances, informing them of his arrival. As in 1882, he took up with Frederick Pollock, Leslie Stephen, and other intellectuals, but he also contacted Ethel Grenfell. She invited him to Taplow Court, the Grenfells' estate outside London, where he encountered other members of "the Souls," including Arthur Balfour and Margot Tennant, the latter once described by a contemporary as possessing a "dangerous, graceless, disconcerting, invigorating, merciless, shameless, lovable candour."[32] Holmes struck up a friendship with Margot Tennant, who invited him to visit her at "The Glen," her father's country estate in Peeblesshire, Scotland, that August. On Holmes' return to America in September he initiated a correspondence with both Ethel Grenfell and Margot Tennant, the latter writing him that "your friendship . . . is not insincere or affected or 'modern' but [gives me] much happiness, much illumination, much encouragement, of the sort that comes from an assurance of the existence of what is true and strong."[33]

While Holmes was involved in the round of London dinner parties and country visits that constituted "the Souls" ' social activities, another upper-class circle was frequenting the London social "season." This was a group of Anglo-Irish landowners known as "the Ascendancy," whose estates comprised most of the choice acreage in Ireland. Their economic and political dominance stretched back to the sixteenth and seventeenth centuries, when British Protestant settlers had displaced the native Irish landowners. Their ties to England had been cemented when Ireland became part of the United Kingdom in 1800. They were Unionists, opposed to Home Rule, but at the same time Irish loyalists, interested in political representation for Ireland in Parliament. Their principal source of income came from their landholdings.[34]

Two of the prominent families in "the Ascendancy" circle were the FitzPatricks and the St. Legers.[35] The FitzPatricks were an ancient Catholic family who by the nineteenth century had become sufficiently connected to England to send Bernard FitzPatrick, who was born in 1849, to Eton and Oxford. Bernard was to occupy the expected roles of an "Ascendancy" landowner, serving in the Queen's Life Guards after Oxford and in 1880 being elected to Parliament for his district, and in 1883 suceeding at the death of his father to the title of Lord Castletown, whose name was taken from one of the ancient castles owned by the Fitzpatrick family. In 1874 Bernard married Emily Ursula Clare St. Leger, whose family dated back to the crossing into England of William the Conqueror. In the sixteenth century the St. Legers settled in Ireland, occupying an estate in County Cork. By the mid-nineteenth century the St. Legers occupied themselves with hunting and riding around their estate, Doneraile Court. The fourth Lord Doneraile, known as a "magnificent horseman and the best judge of hounds in the United Kingdom," met an untimely death in 1887 when he was bitten by a pet fox who turned out to be rabid. That Lord Doneraile was Clare St. Leger's father.[36]

Clare was born in 1855, educated at home, and married at nineteen. She and Bernard traveled extensively, and while in Ireland alternated residences between the

FitzPatrick estate, Granston Manor, in Upper Ossory, and the St. Leger estate in Cork.[37] In the summers Ascendancy families typically rented flats for the London season,[38] with Clare sometimes going by herself if Parliament was not in session. Bernard Castletown had been a classmate of Arthur Balfour at Eton and Oxford, so the Castletowns also had an entry to "the Souls" circle.[39] At one point, in the summer of 1889, Clare Castletown was introduced to Wendell Holmes at Wilton, the home of Lord and Lady Pembroke in Wiltshire, one "of the main Souls meeting places."[40] Holmes was sufficiently struck by the meeting to include Clare in a list of English acquaintances to whom he dispatched copies of the first printing of his extrajudicial addresses when it appeared in February 1891. She responded with a note that she was "so much pleased to receive your little book . . . & the letter which accompanied it & I feel quite flattered at your remembering my existence after all this time!" She added that if Holmes returned to England he should "let us know & come & stay with us."[41]

Holmes did not return to England until 1896, when he again traveled alone. On this occasion Fanny's absence was a product of her having suffered a second attack of rheumatic fever.[42] In the interval between 1889 and 1896 his father had died and he and Fanny had inherited his father's house at 296 Beacon Street; he continued his pattern of writing occasional scholarly articles and making speeches; he wrote friends that he was "a recluse."[43] We have previously seen that in this interval Fanny had again been seriously ill: she was bedridden for several months and lost a good deal of her hair, which grew back in a gray and ragged fashion.[44] Nonetheless, she encouraged Holmes to revisit England.

Ensconced again at Mackellar's Hotel, Holmes sent out his usual round of notes, including one to Clare Castletown, who had taken a flat on Green Street. She was out when he left his card, but responded with a note inviting him "to come to luncheon one of these days?"[45] Eventually, about a week after receiving that note, Holmes did go to lunch with Clare, and that visit began a pattern of frequent encounters, including lunches, dinners, and visits to exhibitions.[46] While that summer Holmes continued to see his friends in "the Souls," such as Ethel Grenfell and Margot Tennant Asquith, he did not make plans to stay with them after the "season" ended; instead he planned to go to Ireland.[47] Clare had invited him to visit at Granston Manor or Doneraile Court; the latter location seemed more convenient, as it was relatively close to his sailing destination, Queenstown.

On arriving at Doneraile Court, around August 14, Holmes found Bernard Castletown absent but three other guests, the Godfrey Levingers and Eustace Bechen, in residence. He nonetheless found some time alone with Clare, as the Levingers went sightseeing and Bechen hunted rabbits. In his diary entry for August 15 Holmes wrote the word "Jasmine," perhaps in reference to perfume Clare was wearing, perhaps recalling one of the scents in the conservatory, where they spent some time.[48] By the 22d, when he hurriedly left Doneraile Court for the hotel at Queenstown, Holmes had become smitten with Clare. He wrote her every day on ship, from Sunday the 23rd to through Friday the 28th, and mailed the letters in one bunch on Saturday the 29th, the day of his arrival in Boston. In that bunch of letters he proposed that they write each other on a regular basis, indicated that "no one sees your letters and they shall be destroyed if you prefer,"[49] and declared that "[n]othing has touched the freshness of the impressions under which I went off." "Oh what a lot of things I want to say," he added, "but hardly to write."[50]

The letters Holmes sent to Clare Castletown on his return to Boston from Europe initiated a correspondence that is unique among those of Holmes that have survived, and tantalizing in its obscurity.[51] The correspondence continued from 1896 until Clare's death in 1927, but a large fragment, covering the years from the middle of 1899 through 1913, has not survived. Moreover, only a handful of Clare's letters have survived, some of which are not dated. It was Holmes' intent to have both parties destroy letters they received, and he largely succeeded in doing that for her letters. She, however, did not destroy his letters, and in due course typescripts of them were made and found their way into the Holmes Papers.[52] The gap in the correspondence between 1899 and 1914 can only be explained as an inadvertent loss of the letters written in those years, since the parties continued to be in contact, and Holmes visited Clare at least three times during that period. Despite the breadth of the correspondence—over a hundred letters from Holmes to Clare have survived—its onesidedness makes the relationship between the parties difficult to reconstruct. It is clear, however, that Clare Castletown was not one of Holmes' casual English acquaintances.

In the first stages of the Holmes-Castletown relationship, judging from his end of the correspondence, both parties demonstrated a degree of infatuation. After sending his batch of shipboard letters Holmes finally heard from Clare, and the tone of her letter suited him:

> I have this moment received your most adorable letter. It is what I have been longing for and is water to my thirst. You say and do everything exactly as I should have dreamed. I shall keep it and when I am blue and you seem far away I shall take it out and read it and be happy again. Do I come back? I love your asking it. . . . Oh yes indeed I do and shall. I do not forget easily, believe me—and your letter was all that was wanting to assure me that we should abide together.[53]

Holmes then made an allusion to one of the moments he and Clare had spent together at Doneraile Court:

> I still carry in my pocket a handkerchief (one of my own) with a little infinitesimal dark smear upon it—with it I once rubbed away a ____ —Do you remember? Isn't that a fool thing for a serious Judge?[54]

He then became the "serious judge," and informed Clare that he was going to communicate with her in that role as well:

> By the by, I ordered the 2nd imprint of my speeches to be sent to you as soon as I arrived. Read them again and the 2nd memorial day one which you haven't seen, love them a little, for I put my heart into the accidental occasion—just enough that is to say to one who cares, you will understand, that there is high ambition and an ideal in this externally dull routine and much of the passion of life. The last sentence in the one on Wm. Allen is me.[55]

The last passage is particularly instructive. The tone of Clare's letter has encouraged Holmes to think that "we should abide together," and thus he ventures to involve her in matters into which he has "put my heart," his extrajudicial speeches sounding the themes of "high ambition and an ideal" that formed the justification for the "externally dull routine" of his professional life. The speech on William Allen had emphasized the fact that Allen's "ambition . . . look[ed] only to remote and mediated command"; that he had been interested in "wield[ing] . . . that most subtile and intoxicating authority which controls the future from within by shaping the thoughts and speech of a later time."[56] The last sentence had referred to "a few others" who "walk[ed] in meditative silence" and "dream[ed] the dream of spiritual reign."[57] Such was Holmes' ambition for himself. As he said to Clare, the last sentence speech on Allen was "me." "Abiding together" for Holmes thus included the opportunity to reveal to the other one's professional aspirations as well as the opportunity to engage in romantic byplay.

As Clare was entering into a correspondence with Holmes, she was occupied on other romantic fronts as well. During Holmes' visit to Doneraile she had received a letter from Percy La Touche, another member of the "Ascendancy" circle, who shared her interest in riding. The letter read in part:

> Don't work too hard and don't flirt with Mr. Holmes and don't let him flirt with you but remember that I love you with all my heart and soul, that I want you to be all and only mine, and that I would like to murder every man that dares to look at you or that you look at. Be good Dearest and remember.
>
> I don't feel at all inclined to laugh about your Bostonian and fairly hope he *will* go out shooting. How long is he going to stay? If he wasn't going to be at Doneraile on Friday I would come . . . and see you but I don't want to see *him* . . . I don't like his being there alone with you *at all* and I am sure you will find plenty to do with him and a great deal that I shouldn't like at all, and I don't know how much you will do or how far you will go and I am not happy but *jealous*.[58]

The content and timing of this letter throws some light on the posture from which Clare approached her relationship with Holmes. First, La Touche's tone suggests that he was considerably involved with Clare; subsequent evidence in the Castletown Papers confirms that a catalog description of him as being "a friend and clearly a lover" of Clare's is accurate. Second, the date of the letter reveals that Clare had not only told La Touche about Holmes' forthcoming visit, she had given him the impression that she might be inclined to "flirt" with Holmes, making La Touche unclear "how far [she] would go" in that flirtation. Third, notwithstanding Clare's evocation of jealousy in La Touche, she had treated her relationship with Holmes lightly, since La Touche took pains to dissuade her that he was "inclined to laugh about your Bostonian."

All of the above suggests that Clare had divined, before Holmes' visit, that a "flirtation" might well be in the offing, but that she had not taken it particularly seriously. But on August 31, nine days after Holmes had left and before she had received any shipboard correspondence from him, Clare received a letter from La Touche in response to two she had written him. One of the letters La Touche described as "sweet and gentle," but the other, he said, "hurt like anything." In the letter Clare had apparently confessed that she had been thinking about Holmes in the wake of his visit. "Do you recognize," La Touche responded, "how heart-

lessly cruel it was to undeceive me about those thoughts when I had deceived myself?
. . . That letter of yours—well it is burnt but its cruel words are burnt into my heart—
I do not ask you not to think but why why why must you tell me of your thoughts?''[59]

In the weeks following that letter, judging from Holmes' end of his correspondence with Clare, she continued to pour herself into their newly formed relationship.
In one letter she had apparently spoken of Holmes' ''uprooting'' her;[60] in another
he referred to three ''adorable'' letters from her, and to her apparent pique at his
writing ''as if I thought we were casual acquaintances.'' He took pleasure in pointing
out that she distracted him from his work (''you have done enough disturbance to
please even your imperious demands''). He even ventured a summary of the relationship at present:

> We both were very loud in our profession of familiarity with somewhat cynical
> views of life. But thank the Lord we neither of us are cynical at bottom and
> my guards are down long ago. I believe in you seriously and sincerely and it
> would be a deep grief to me to dream it possible that anything could interrupt
> our affection. My life is in my wife and my work—but as you see that does
> not prevent a romantic feeling which it would cut me to the heart to have you
> repudiate.[61]

During the period that Clare was writing Holmes ''adorable'' letters she had not
seen La Touche, and he began to exhibit considerable anxiety about his status with
her. On September 18 he wrote her that

> I can't help thinking it would make you happier (& me infinitely more happy)
> if you would acknowledge to yourself that you cared for me & that with my
> whole heart within your breast there was no more room, there never could be
> any room, for the heart of another man. I have oftened likened you to a snake
> . . . but I wish there was a little more of the deaf adder about you so that you
> would not unfold your lovely coils at the voice of a charmer (with an
> American accent) . . . I try & tell myself . . . that I am too strong to fear any
> foe however formidable & however insidious, that I *can* win you back & that I
> *will* do so. But I don't *know*—my heart aches with distrust. I have played for
> the highest stake for which ever man gambled & I almost dread seeing you for
> fear I may have lost it.[62]

In late September, Clare seemed to be more preoccupied with Holmes than with La
Touche. But then, perhaps because Holmes had reminded her that ''my life is in my
wife and my work,'' perhaps because of La Touche's geographic proximity, the
pendulum seemed to swing in La Touche's direction.

On October 17 Holmes wrote Clare a letter referring to a letter he had received
the day before from her in which he had felt ''a little cool breath of transitoriness.''
He added that ''I should like to know the name of the gentleman who knows mine
and who I fear flatters me by his malevolence,'' an indication that Clare had told
him about La Touche's reaction to his visit, without revealing La Touche's identity.
Clare had also apparently mentioned a tendency she had to follow her whims of the
moment, since Holmes asked, ''Do you not exaggerate a little the part which whim
plays in your life? It has an airy swaggering sound to say that one follows the fancies

of the moment, but somehow that does not fully answer my conception of you." He closed by saying that "I shall be . . . cheerful . . . when I get a letter from you with a little streak of tender feeling."[63]

That "little streak" was long in coming. On October 23 Holmes wrote Clare that he "long[ed] for a word from you like the first 3—no matter—you did write those."[64] On November 9, after a long silence, he finally heard from her and replied, "*[p]lease* don't let it be so long again."[65] And on November 21 his exasperation came to the surface:

> You do take a malicious satisfaction in hinting at transitory tragedies in your wanderings—and at a frame of mind not unlike some of those portrayed in Lettres de Femmes. . . . If we did not both of us appreciate that frame of mind we should not have become intimate so easily—but if we did not both feel something a good deal deeper than that we should not have been intimate at all. . . . For my part I hate the thought of anyone except me being admitted to know anything about your real feelings (some of your hints make me wonder almost if I know anything about you).[66]

In short, Holmes' stance toward Clare almost precisely mirrored that previously adopted by La Touche. Both men were particularly incensed that another should have access to Clare's feelings when they had that access. Neither seemed troubled by the fact that Clare was married to yet another man, had been for over twenty years, and would apparently continue to be: it was the presence of a rival for intimacy that especially piqued them.

Things continued rather badly for Holmes during the winter of 1896 and the spring of 1897. In a December 4 letter he noted, "how you delight . . . to put one on the outside and to hint at all manner of games to which he is not a party—at suggestions of expressed preference of the finite to the infinite." "Oh hang it," Holmes concluded, "I know very well as well as if you had told me that you are ready for adventures."[67] Two weeks later he began a letter addressed to "Dear Lady of Whims" by saying "I fear me that I suffer by not being on the spot."[68] On the 28th he supposed that "you perhaps are giving tea to some beggar who helps to relieve your moments off duty—may heaven confound him."[69] And on January 11 he wrote, in reference to a letter she had written him on New Year's day, that "as usual my head whirls with the hint of all manner of new men."[70]

As the spring of 1897 progressed, Holmes heard from Clare less frequently, but doggedly persisted in his letters to her. Finally in May he received "an adorable long letter," which prompted to him to exclaim:

> Time has only made our intimacy more settled, more certain. Is it not so? When I read between the lines I do not mistake do I? You have the gift of hints that may mean much or nothing. I take them to mean much. I think I shall keep your affection always.[71]

He then went on:

> I notice that for a long time I have heard no more of the substantial *other*—the same I suppose who wanted to kill me etc. Will you kindly advert to him. Is

he still in statu quo? Whatever that may have been? Has his importance grown? or how otherwise? or has he happily demised?[72]

Clare did not respond directly, but in a letter referred to by Holmes in his May 10 response, talked "of spring and of others saying pretty things."[73] He pressed her to "tell me when you turn the mystic phrase, that may mean much or little . . . am I to take [it] as meant all I can get out of it, or am I to appreciate it as giving far horizons and no more?"[74] She again declined to be specific, and he wrote, "You grieve me dear lady by the reserves implied in your not answering. There have been moments when your hints gave me very great delight and when I hoped it was only my infernal skeptical nature that pointed out to me that it depended on the reader whether they said much or little." "Each of your new enthusiasms," he added, "gives one a little stab . . . [I]f I were there I couldn't shoulder and compete with a lot of soupirants. If you did not prefer to see me and do your half I should sigh and walk away."[75]

The summer passed and Holmes wrote Clare about his reading, his bicycle trips with Brooks Adams, his nephew's marriage, and his occasional pique at "the new man who was to take you out on the river."[76] In an August 19 letter he observed that "you never speak of that other man—who was the dark horse earlier in our correspondence. Why? You will pass this question in silence & I shall remember & regret." And in a December 17 letter, by way of summarizing his frustrations with Clare throughout the year, he said that

> I wonder if I am to infer from a line that you have vouchsafed me at last . . .
> that you have been up to mischief and doing damage. Well I won't make
> myself miserable about it until you bid me to. . . . During the last year you
> have kept me pretty well at the point of your rapier. At times I could wish that
> you were not so constantly on guard—but I think that you are simpler in your
> feelings than you say or perhaps than you think—and I hope and quaveringly
> believe that your confidence in and regard for me haven't diminished with
> longer acquaintance. I think if you were not so constantly in the semi chaffing
> humor it would be easier to write one's feelings and interests to you from
> week to week but still I have talked pretty straight.

"I shall cut down to once a fortnight," Holmes wrote in conclusion, "if I don't hear from you once in six months—dear betrayer of my innocence."[77]

Meanwhile, Percy La Touche's correspondence with Clare suggested that Holmes' suspicions had been confirmed. In a May 11 letter La Touche reminisced about their liasions:

> I walked along the river to "our tree" & it was pretty to sit there & watch the
> dancing shadows . . . & to think of you. . . . Tomorrow I will go to Cork & I
> will see you all the way. First on the . . . bridge where we once picked violets
> together. Then at Moore Abbey where first I pressed my life upon your hand.
> Then . . . sweet recollections of one lovely night. . . . Then Doneraile & . . . all
> the moments of last autumn that I love to remember & none that I long to
> forget.[78]

And in an undated letter, probably written about the same time, he went into what to Clare might have been embarrassing detail:

> I do miss you so, my Beloved, not only in the silence of the night when I long to hear the soft murmur of your gentle voice, to see the love-light in your glorious eyes, the gleam of your white teeth, & all the exquisite beauty of your peerless form; to feel the perfume of your lovely arms, the beating of your heart within the fairest of all fair breasts, the maddening sweetness of your priceless kisses & all the indescribable rapture of "being loved by you"—Ah! it is sad indeed to miss you then, my love, when my heart is on fire with thoughts of such never-to-be-forgotten moments.[79]

Whatever her commitment to Percy La Touche, Clare began the year of 1898 by paying a little more attention to Holmes. She sent him a wallet for Christmas, and in the flush of his enthusiasm for it ("You can't tell how touched and delighted I was") he began to speak of coming over to visit her that summer. "If I put it off," he said, "there are always the horrible chances of time," but "on the other hand I can't bear to leave my wife until she seems better than she does now." Encouraged by her gift, he added that, "I deny that I talk law tediously and I scorn your threat to let another take my place in the conservatory." But he nonetheless wanted reassurance that "[w]hen I do come you will let me see a great deal of you."[80]

This letter ushered in a long period in which Holmes debated with himself about sailing to England. "For the last weeks," he wrote Clare in January 1898, "you have been adorable—and I keep saying to myself Oh if I *should* see her this summer—my wife rather eggs me on to go. It is pure generosity on her part because she thinks I will enjoy it."[81] Ten days later he told Clare he was planning to visit his doctor to "ask him whether it will be reasonably safe for me to come over this summer." He inquired where "the rooms are [in London] that you were good enough to think of for me," and asked whether "I should see a great deal of you if I come?"[82] At the end of January he was still concerned about time with Clare: "you have not yet answered whether I should see a lot of you if I come."[83]

By the middle of February Holmes appeared to have made a decision. He had checked with the Chief Justice of the Supreme Judicial Court of Massachusetts to see "whether if I decided to go to Europe he would put the last consultation forward from June 21 to a week earlier," and concluded that that request would be honored.[84] "I have very little doubt," he announced to Clare, "that I shall come over this summer unless something goes wrong unexpectedly." He added that his time in England would be comparatively short as he had "to report for duty on one of the first days of September," and he hoped that if Clare were planning to go abroad she would wait until he left. He then spelled out his expectations:

> You will do what you can to help me to see as much of you as possible won't you? I imagine all sorts of adorable romantic visits or excursions, such as England is full of . . . even a hansom [cab] in London is an enchanted solitude. . . . Would you dine with me some ev[ening]?[85]

The spring proceeded in this vein. In a March letter Holmes asked, "Do you think that if I come . . . I had better go to one of the places mentioned by you rather than to Mackellar's in Dover St?'' He noted that when he stayed at Mackellar's the last time ''I got a room and a little parlor on the ground floor which was rather handy. I have even known a lady to venture into it.''[86] Then, as his tantalizing negotiations with Clare with respect to their time together were progressing, his hopes of coming received a setback. Relations between the United States and Spain sharply deteriorated, and war appeared imminent. In a March 27 letter Holmes wrote that ''[m]y expectations as to England are clouded—partly . . . by the possibility of war. If war comes I rather should feel, or at least might possibly feel, that I ought to stand by and rearm—although my soldiering days are over.''[87] He added on April 1 that ''England this summer seems more doubtful and everything is shaken except my affection.''[88]

An additional element of uncertainty involved Clare's loss of a close male friend, who seems to have committed suicide. She first mentioned her concern for his welfare in February, and in March Holmes received the news of his death. ''I am truly grieved and shocked,'' he responded,

> and I sympathize with you with all my heart dear friend. You are pursued by sorrow. I wish that the knowledge that you also are accompanied by my eager anxious constant affection might be some little balm. As you say every detail which you mention makes the death more horrible. Poor chap—was it ennui— the feeling of being in a cul de sac—with no outlook that satisfied his longings?[89]

By early April Holmes had come to feel that this incident was an additional roadblock to his coming, as it seemed to have unsettled Clare. He wrote her that he had ''taken the refusal of a stateroom for June 25—but if war should come I should hesitate to leave the country as I have said—and generally the uncertainty remains.'' He added that ''it is intensified by the doubts you have thrown out,'' and asked again whether ''it would be possible for me to get an appreciable time with you or in your neighborhood.'' Earlier he had said that ''it looks so much as if war is upon us that although I never have felt as if it would come even my faith in the future is shaken.''[90]

But the Spanish-American war, once started, turned out to be a rout, ending in time for Holmes to sail. On April 29 he had written Clare that ''the view of England this summer grows dim,'' and ''I feel as if [the] wire between us has been cut,''[91] but four days later he said that ''Dewey's success gives me wild hopes,'' and ''[i]f the war is over I may come.'' By June the war seemed to have receded as a barrier, and Clare's spirits had improved. ''I simply love your letters latterly,'' Holmes wrote. ''They do not seem to keep one on the outside.'' He added, however, that he was still ''dreadfully shaky about going over this year.''[92]

As the war ceased to be a barrier to his sailing, and time drew closer to his projected departure date, Holmes brought up yet another potential obstacle. On June 7 he had written that ''it looks more as if I should come,'' but two days later he was once again uncertain. He tried to sum up his thinking to Clare:

> I had made up my mind that I ought to put it off and my wife now urges me to go and threatens horrid results to me if I do not. I fear I shall be a selfish pig if I do, and I don't know. If I do not come you will know that I do not give up

seeing you even for a time—i.e. put it off a year—without deep sorrow. Since I began to write I have almost decided not to come. I will not go into the reasons which really amount to a delicate balancing of what is the fair thing, etc. under existing circumstances—but I do entreat you neither to scold nor to turn away in vexation. . . . Life seems short and its chances few. One thing that tremendously urges me to go is the reflection that I am sur le retour and opportunities are not to be trifled with. . . . Oh my friend how will it be. Shall I get a cross answer or one of those in which you let out your adorable kindness?[93]

This letter seems to be a more accurate statement of Holmes' attitude toward returning to England to see Clare than his earlier statements of uncertainty. At the heart of his ambivalence appear to be feelings of guilt about leaving Fanny, apparently still recovering from rheumatic fever, and feelings of apprehension that Clare may not respond to his expectations of their relationship. He describes himself as "a selfish pig," and worries about doing "the fair thing . . . under existing circumstances," that is, responding honorably to his sense of duty to Fanny, especially given her condition and his obvious attraction for Clare. He also worries that his time in life—he was 57 and Clare 43 at the date of the letter—means that his opportunities for contact with Clare will not be extensive, and this "tremendously urges" him to seize this particular opportunity. But all the while he remains concerned about Clare's attitude. Will she be "cross" or "let out . . . kindness"; will she meet his accumulated hopes for romance or continue to keep him "at the point of [her] rapier"?

Nine days after dispatching the letter setting forth his ambivalence Holmes sent Clare a telegram to her London address. "Just settled sail Umbria June twenty five," the message ran. It was signed "Justice." A week later he was in London, staying again at Mackellar's.

Looking back on Holmes' correspondence in the first half of 1898, it furnishes a fair indication of the status of his relationship with Clare at that time. It was obvious that after the first burst of enthusiasm that followed upon his departure in August 1896, Clare retreated into a pose of coquetry from which she would only occasionally depart. Holmes' frequent inquiries about her attitude toward him should he come suggest that she declined to respond to his concerns. On the other hand, she seems to have dropped the practice of making allusions to her other male friendships, judging from the absence of comments about competitors in Holmes' 1898 letters. It appears that Clare became more open and "kind" in her letters once she sensed that she might see Holmes again in the near future.

Regardless of Holmes' professed constant affection for Clare and declarations of the fidelity of his commitment, his letters do not sound like those of one who has been physically intimate with his correspondent. The amount of time Holmes devoted in the 1898 letters to the question of whether he would have time alone with Clare suggests, to the contrary, that he could not even presume that she would want to be solely in his company. He may have fantasized about "adorable romantic excursions" with her, but he mentioned a ride in a hansom cab as an example of one of those. His stance of alternating excitement, guilt, and apprehension would seem consistent with that of one who recognizes his infatuation with another but is not at all clear about the other's attitude.

After the summer of 1898, however, one can note an altered tone in Holmes' correspondence that suggests that his relationship with Clare may have taken on a new dimension, or at least increased in intensity. Evidence of their meetings during that summer is scant. Holmes kept a diary of his trip, but his entries were cryptic. He had dinner with Bernard Castletown in London on July 11, meeting him for the first time; he stayed with the Castletowns at Granston Manor and again at Doneraile, on both occasions in the company of other guests. Bernard was present during his Granston Manor visit, but not during his stay at Doneraile. He spent a fair amount of time with other friends in London, but did not visit many of his English intellectual colleagues and was not an overnight guest at any of "the Souls" ' country places.[94] As far as can be determined, he wrote no letters during his 1898 visit to England that have survived in the Holmes Papers.[95]

Nonetheless, it is very likely that the time Holmes spent in the company of Clare Castletown during that visit intensified the nature of their relationship. That surmise rests on the tone of letters he wrote to her immediately after sailing for Boston on August 26.[96] On September 5, for example, he wrote her that he had returned "in the kind of collapse that comes after nervous tension." He had written her on shipboard, he said, and "I think you will see from it how I yearn and long for you." She had sent him a telegram on his arrival, "tendering" greetings; he wished "that I had found some expression as you did which I would entrust to the telegraph." He then summed up his feelings:

> And now do you think that you can meet time and distractions and still care for me as much? I believe you will. I firmly believe that time will make no difference to me. Oh my dear what joy it is to feel the inner chambers of one's soul open for the other to walk in and out at will. It was just beginning with you. Do not cut it off because of a little salt water. By the by permit me to suggest that you do not put my letters into the wastepaper basket which you trust so much. Fire or fragments and the water ways when you destroy if you do as I do. . . . It is rather odd to read letters of Sir W? Knollys to his sister, saying how much he would like to make many a mother if his existing incumbrances only might be gathered away, as he had a lawful lady.[97]

This comment is worth close analysis. While Holmes' statement that "time will make no difference to me" is of a piece with his earlier correspondence, in which he continually professed timeless devotion to Clare, the associated statement that she might be able to "meet time and distractions" and "still care for [him] as much" suggests, at a minimum, that he was confident of her attachment while he was at her side. The statement about feeling one's soul open for the other to walk in and out of at will indicates a degree of intimacy that Holmes had not previously claimed in the correspondence, and he attributes it to Clare ("it was just beginning with you") as well as to himself. The sentence about destroying letters intimates that the contents of letters may be compromising, and one should take particular care to ensure that they not come into public view. Finally, the allusion to Sir William Knollys' "incumbrances" and inclination to "make many a mother" seems to be an analogy to himself, who is "encumbered" with his "lawful lady" Fanny. On the whole, the tone of the letter is that of one who has become intimate with his correspondent, at least emotionally if not physically.

Another letter written three days later conveyed a similar impression of the relationship. Clare had written Holmes and expressed concern about his attack of shingles, which he had contracted in Granston Manor and kept with him for the rest of the time in Ireland and the voyage home.[98] "They merely meant somewhat less sleep," he reassured her, "an article which I would gladly exchange for the joy of being with you—and in the day while I was with you it didn't hurt." He went on:

Oh my dear I go with you to all the places where you remember me. Each has its own particular charm. Only it seems that if I might be with you in each once more I should be . . . much nicer than the last time and make sure that every memory was of unmixed charm. But mine are so now, and now that I am away you will be charitable and remember only what was sweet and dear to you. Do assure me that the pain of separation does not outweigh the joy of confidence and belief in the abiding.[99]

The tone of this letter sounds remarkably like that which Percy La Touche had written to Clare in the spring of 1897, complete with reminiscences about "all the places" they had been together. Holmes takes the liberty of assuming that Clare herself will feel pain in their separation. He also speaks of his "joy of confidence" in believing that their relationship will endure.

Holmes' feelings reached a crescendo in a letter written from Saturday the 10th to Monday the 12th of September, while he was at Beverly Farms. He began:

Separation from you is made bearable to me by the belief that we can now defy time and distance. . . . But I long to hear you repeat again and again that you do also—that it will not be different when you have become accustomed to separation and when all the distracting influences begin to work once more.

The last thought made him think of Clare's other suitors, and he recalled a luncheon he had spent in the company of one of them, possibly Percy La Touche himself:

I try vainly to recall the look of my vis a vis at luncheon on the day of your show, I think I looked at him with an inward inquiry and with appreciation, but I can't get back his face.

He then thought of his feelings for Clare, and how he wished she could be more closely connected to his professional life:

It is [those feelings], far more than the desire for appreciation for its own sake, that makes me wish so much that you entered into my scheme of life with full assent and understanding, and saw that it might be noble and great without the accessories of conspicuous position and immediate power . . . I should be in despair did I not have a timid confidence that I am worth it—but oh my dear despair is always so near at hand.[100]

Here Holmes has trotted out some familiar professional themes: his "scheme" to have his life regarded as "noble and great" even though he did not possess "the accessories of conspicuous position and immediate power''; his abiding sense that he was not adequately recognized, which made ''despair . . . always so near at hand''; his ''timid confidence'' that his contribution was nonetheless ''worth it.'' As in earlier letters, the moments when he feels the deepest intimacy with Clare are moments when he is moved to talk about his professional ambitions and doubts.[101]

He resumes the letter the next day, and returns to reaffirmations of their intimacy:

> Surely you will never again find it hard to talk from your heart. I feel as if we should begin where we left off, no matter what time had elapsed. Meanwhile let us talk straight in our letters as you do so adorably in the one which I received. . . . *Please* don't laugh at yourself, but be glad for a joy in life—for a dream which is true and never to be forgotten—for a shadow which has become substance—I put it on your heart.[102]

Again one is struck here of the similarity between Holmes' prose and that of La Touche, who also spoke of ''shadows,'' ''hearts,'' and ''never to be forgotten'' memories. One is also struck by the fact that Holmes now assumes that Clare has gone beyond coquetry in her stance toward him: they will now talk straight, talk from their hearts.

The last letter in this sequence was written on September 16. Holmes had begun to contemplate the possibility that Clare might drift apart from him again as other ''distractions'' surfaced. Referring to a note about a ''charming professor'' that Clare sent him, Holmes responded, ''I have conjectured that the groveller is no more— but hateful wonders push in whether there is one who does not grovel.'' But then he resolved to rest in his belief in Clare:

> Now I go partly on faith—need I tell you how deep the faith is? Whatever you say or don't say I believe in you and trust you and love you dearly. I long long long for you and think think think about you. You would be satisfied I think.[103]

The first part of the comment is in keeping with Holmes' new conception of the relationship as being beyond jealousy or coquetry. The last part, however, is unusual. Holmes loses control of his prose, writing clichéd sentences, and then seems to step aside from his emotions. ''You would be satisfied I think,'' he says to Clare, imply-ing that she might take satisfaction in reducing him to an adolescent level. The comment suggests that despite his strong feelings for Clare, he may have retained a perception of her as viewing the relationship as a sort of female conquest, in which he was finally reduced to the level of other ''soupirants.''

Thus ended the most intense phase of the surviving Holmes–Castletown corre-spondence, and very possibly the most intense phase of the relationship itself. Given Clare's temperament, the distance between the parties, and the infrequency of Holmes' visits to England, it was inevitable that she would not be able to sustain the level of intensity he may have assumed existed on his departure in August 1898. By May 1899 he was noting that ''it seems so long between each letter,'' and calling her attention to ''a little conversation we had the last moment we were [in the conservatory at Doneraile Court] and [memories of] many other places there and at

Granston." The next week, after receiving a letter from her saying "it is *impossible* to really keep in touch," he took the occasion to remind her that "I care for you just as much as when we were together. . . . You don't mean anything to the contrary of that I am sure. For you are a faithful wretch." But the last was wishful thinking: he had sensed a "suggestion of less nearness" that was characteristic of her stance when he was not likely to be in her company for some time.

As it turned out, their separation was longer, and perhaps more decisive, than either of them might have anticipated. Early in May 1899, while riding with Percy La Touche, Clare had a serious accident, which damaged the sight in one of her eyes and left her bedridden for some weeks. On not hearing from her Holmes eventually contacted Bernard Castletown directly and learned, in a June 16, 1899, letter, that Clare was "a little better but it is a very slow recovery." Holmes had sent her a letter, which Bernard had read to her; Bernard hoped "she will be able to read herself" by the time the next letter came. "My wife is charmed by your letters," he added, "and hopes soon to be able to write herself."[104] In the meantime the Boer War had broken out in South Africa, and Bernard resolved to join the campaign, with Clare to accompany him as soon as she was able to travel. The result was that the Castletowns were gone from England and Ireland for the next three years, arriving back, via Madagascar, Zanzibar, Aden, Malta, and Italy, in 1901.[105]

Some contact must have taken place between Holmes and Clare during her sojourn in South Africa, because Holmes made arrangements to visit the Castletowns again in the summer of 1901.[106] No correspondence has survived from the period, however, and Holmes' 1901 diary was as cryptic as that he kept for his 1898 trip. He managed to spend a good deal of time with Clare in London, seeing her on July 1, 2, 4, 5, 9, 12, 17, and August 5, and traveling to Doneraile Court for a visit beginning on August 13.[107] But he made no record of his reaction to those visits: the only evidence of his response to the trip can be found in two letters he wrote to his friend Nina Gray. In the first, dated July 15, 1901, from London, he said that "[t]his is the third week that I have been at it—hard," referring to "[l]uncheons and dinners every day." He added that he was planning "one or two flying visits" in the London area and then a stay in Ireland. "I have seen nearly all my old friends and they are properly effusive," he noted, "perhaps a trifle more gray hair in it than once—but the tremolo is not quite banished." He found English society the same: "[y]ou mark no points—and bid an eternal adieu by walking off in the middle of a casual sentence. . . . You must have something to contribute—but if you have you are passed round pretty quickly—and meet all sorts of people who can contribute." He liked "the eternally recurring problem of conversation with people you don't know and whose facts and gossip you don't care about." In such a setting "you have to feel round for the galvanic connection with general observations about life and the universe."[108]

In the second letter, written after he returned home, Holmes said he had had "the most complete time of all my times," but that he had "had enough of it so far as a time goes." "Nothing impressed me so much," he went on, "as a kind of resentment which I felt in the end at continuing the pursuits of pleasure." The visit had made him "gladder than ever before to be an American." He did not give details, promising to supply Nina Gray with "[p]articulars in small bills when we meet."[109]

Between 1901 and 1914, the next year from which correspondence between himself and Clare has survived, Holmes made three additional trips to England. He went over in 1907, and his diary indicates that he had dinner with Clare on the 20th of June, went to "Berkeley" with her on the 28th, called on her at her flat in Green Street on July 8, went to the Holland House flower show with her on the 9th, called on her again on the 16th, had lunch with her on the 20th, and visited her at Doneraile in August. During that trip he also had lunch with Bernard Castletown at least once, indicating that the latter had a friendly attitude toward him.[110]

Holmes and Fanny went again in 1909 in connection with his receiving an honorary degree from Oxford. They only stayed for three weeks in London and saw the Castletowns only briefly.[111] In 1913 Holmes traveled to Europe for the last time. Things had not gone well for the Castletowns in the interval. Canon Patrick Sheehan, the parish priest of Doneraile, reported to Holmes in 1910 that "Lady C. is only recovering from a serious operation on the eyes; and Lord C. is not so robust as usual,"[112] and a year later Holmes told Sheehan that "I know [the Castletowns] have had reverses and I gather he has collapsed, but I can't ask Lady Castletown questions, and I don't know exactly what it means."[113] Sheehan responded:

> The Castletown affair was very tragic. Lady C. has undergone a painful operation for the eyes in London; and was but partially relieved. They had returned here, and then the crash came. So unconscious was Lady C. that any danger impended, she had spent £400 in erecting a new Hall in the village. Her grief was pitiable; and so was Lord C.'s remorse. He had sold out all the *purchased* estates; and had speculated wildly (so it was said) in foreign investments, which proved useless. Receivers were at once sent down here to take charge of everything. Lord C. is at Granston; Lady C. in London. I understand they are allowed £2000 each per annum; and the latest news is, that the estate was not so involved as was at first supposed; and that possibly, they may be able to return at no very distant date. Meanwhile, Sir John Arnott, who has rented the place for the last few years during the hunting months, has now taken over [Doneraile] Court for 12 months. . . . The one agreeable feature was the universal sympathy awakened for Lord and Lady C. especially the latter. It was very touching.[114]

By 1913 things seemed to going better for the Castletowns. Sheehan reported that they had returned to Doneraile and called on him, with Clare "wondering whether you would pay the Green Isle a visit this year."[115] In April Holmes responded that he was considering "get[ting] abroad this year,"[116] and in June he informed Sheehan that "I am just replying to Lady Castletown that I shall come there after the [London] season has ended." "My doubt has been whether I ought to burden her," he added, "and I suggested going to Cork and motoring over—but she says come."[117] Sheehan responded that "I am distinctly of the opinion that your visit to the Castletowns would not only be a pleasure to them; but would raise Lord Castletown's spirits a good deal."[118]

Holmes arrived in London and immediately saw the Castletowns, having dinner with them on the 21st and 22nd of June. His diary indicates that he had dinner on two additional occasions with Clare, and that he saw Clare one last time for dinner

Dr. Oliver Wendell Holmes, Sr., in the study of his Beacon Street home, taken about 1888, when he was seventy-nine. *Courtesy of the Harvard Law School Art Collection.*

Holmes as an undergraduate at Harvard, about 1859. *Courtesy of the Harvard Law School Art Collection.*

Amelia Lee Jackson Holmes, taken in 1875, when she was fifty-seven. *Courtesy of the Harvard Law School Art Collection.*

Fanny Bowditch Dixwell, taken in 1860, when she was twenty. *Courtesy of the Harvard Law School Art Collection.*

Holmes in the first year of his Civil War Service, 1861. *Courtesy of the Harvard Law School Art Collection.*

Holmes in October 1872, three months after his marriage, when he was practicing law in Boston and finishing his edition of James Kent's *Commentaries on American Law. Courtesy of the Harvard Law School Art Collection.*

Holmes during the first year of his tenure on the Supreme Judicial Court of Massachusetts, taken in May 1883. Note that the Justices of the Supreme Judicial Court did not wear robes at the time. Holmes reinstituted the custom of wearing robes after becoming Chief Justice of the Supreme Judicial Court in 1899. *Courtesy of the Harvard Law School Art Collection.*

The "official" photograph of Clare Castletown, taken from a painting of unknown provenance. *Courtesy of the Harvard Law School Art Collection.*

An unsigned, unidentified photograph found in Holmes' papers. Clare Castletown had sent him a photograph of her in the fall of 1896, when she was forty-one. One might want to compare this with Clare's "official" photograph—the resemblance is striking. *Courtesy of the Harvard Law School Art Collection.*

Holmes in 1899, at fifty-eight, when he had become Chief Justice and his relationship with Clare Castletown was about to enter a new phase. *Courtesy of the Harvard Law School Art Collection.*

Holmes in 1909, on a visit to England to receive an honorary degree from Oxford. The photograph is one of several posed shots. *Courtesy of the Harvard Law School Art Collection.*

Holmes in his summer home at Beverly Farms, Mass., taken by his legal secretary Arthur Sutherland in September 1928, when Holmes was eighty-seven. *Courtesy of the Harvard Law School Art Collection.*

Holmes on his ninetieth birthday, March 8, 1931, taken in his study in 1726 Eye Street, Washington, D.C. *Courtesy of the Harvard Law School Art Collection.*

The last photograph of Holmes, taken by Clara Sipprell at 1726 Eye Street in December 1934, three months before Holmes' death. *Courtesy of the Harvard Law School Art Collection.*

on August 21, apparently in London.[119] A letter Holmes wrote to Frederick Pollock indicates that on this trip he reversed the usual order of his sojourns and went to Ireland in late July and early August. He told Pollock that "I have been a helpless spectator of misery after misery" on the trip, and that he had been at Doneraile. "Castletown," he noted, "has not yet fully recovered from his nervous collapse and sees things with a downward inflection," and his friend Canon Sheehan was dying.[120]

While Holmes and Clare were never to see each other again after that 1913 visit, they kept up a correspondence until her death in 1927. Only fragments have survived, making reconstruction of the relationship in those years difficult. It is abundantly clear, however, that the tone of intensity in Holmes' letters disappeared in those years; he treats Clare more like one of his numerous other correspondents, male and female. It is difficult to ascertain the cause or the timing of that loss of intensity, but Holmes' visit in 1903 may have marked a turning point. On that visit he wrote two letters to his friend Nina Gray. The first was from Granston Manor:

Here I intend to take a time of such quiet as I can get and rest . . . I realized that I am older. . . . It is time to be old—To take in sail—But London does much to make one forget which is a gain for a vacation at least—It is rather pleasant when everybody is making love all round, unless one is so out of it that he doesn't dare to speak to anyone for fear of interrupting a tragedy.[121]

The second was from Doneraile Court:

It is impossible to write a decent letter in the row of a household of people with a garden party in prospect—how I hate such disturbances of a quiet life! . . . [E]verything, pretty nearly, has gone according to one's wishes except the incursion of a lot of people when one longs for quiet. You would think it a boon and want 'em all—but I prefer the quiet corner out of the wind. They play bridge of an evening and I am left to some chance lady or a book . . . I cannot help a sort of amusement—I won't say that, it is too wicked—But the men I have known here turn up so far as they have not run off with their neighbors' wives or otherwise disposed of themselves . . . and it is not without a tragical side to come to places and think how more than possible it is that it is for the last time.[122]

At the time Holmes wrote the letter he had been appointed to the Supreme Court of the United States, had moved to Washington, and had written Nina Gray that "I don't see the women—I don't see the chance—I don't feel the inclination. . . . It is strange how small a part the society of women plays in my life here."[123] The letters from Ireland are consistent with that mood. Holmes is interested in "quiet," in "taking in sail"; he is "older"; he regards garden parties as "row[s]; he "prefer[s] the quiet corner out of the wind"; he even shuns bridge in the evenings. He also senses that he and Clare are on the downside of their relationship; he wonders whether this visit to Doneraile Court will be his last one. One might compare his characterization of London society in 1903, where he sees it as doing much "to make one forget" but being essentially a "vacation," with his characterization of

London in 1896 as "[a] wonderful romantic place," in which "an endless procession of possibilities streams before one's eyes."[124]

It may well have been that advancing age, the demands of his new position, and the passage of time had altered the intensity of Holmes' feelings about Clare. At any rate none of the passion of his earlier letters appears in his surviving correspondence with her after 1914. In its place are sentences such as "I am full of nothing but lovely recollections, dear thoughts and loving hopes,"[125] "I do hope things are as well with you as they can be in this time,"[126] or "I think affectionate thoughts of you."[127] In one letter, written in January 1915, Holmes wondered, "[w]hat has become of the other? I never keep his name in mind. I thought he had put my nose out of joint—and yet I am fond enough of you to really wish that you may have anything that makes life happier."[128] That was his last reference to the days in which he and Percy La Touche competed to be the only man privileged to know Clare's real feelings.

In 1916 the relationship changed perceptibly. That April Holmes had written Clare that "[y]our portrait still looks down upon me & I will not regale the censor with my thoughts but just send you my love—my hopes that you may endure to the end, that the end may be happy and that we may yet meet again. My age has not yet chilled me."[129] But then a long silence passed. He heard from her on June 19 (a letter that she had written a month earlier), and by July 30 had not heard from her again. Finally he heard from her on September 11, a letter she had sent him August 25. Mail to and from Ireland had been interrupted by the war and the Easter Rebellion, and was now being read by censors. And on December 20 Holmes received a distressing letter from a cousin of Clare's:

> My cousin Lady Castletown asks me to thank you for your kind wire & to send her greetings—I am sorry to say she had a slight stroke last week & for the time her speech & left side were affected—but I am thankful to say she is improving each day & both those symptoms are abating—In writing please make light of her illness as nervousness is to be avoided— . . . she will be allowed up on the sofa next week—she has a very good nurse & 2 doctors— her mind perfectly clear.[130]

Clare recovered from the stroke, and Holmes was able to tell her, in a May 1917 letter, that one of hers "gave me such satisfaction," and that he was "so filled up with memories and feelings."[131]

At that point in the correspondence another gap appears, and the only letters that have survived covering the years of the early 1920s are ones from Clare. Judging from their tone, the years after the end of World War I were not happy ones for her. The "Ascendancy" families continued to be beleaguered by the Irish Republican Army, which was active around both Doneraile Court and Granston Manor. Bernard Castletown wrote in his memoirs:

> We returned to Granston [in 1921], and things seemed likely to get quieter, but De Valera and his associates were bent on making this poor country impossible to live in. Chaos and disorders broke out everywhere; we had

attempts at cattle driving, nonpayment of rents, etc. . . . We had to insure our car against theft, as one attempt was made to take it away. . . .

During the year the civil war continued, and we had trouble with tenants and graziers. . . . In the south matters got very serious, and all communication with Cork was cut off, and for a month we heard nothing from that quarter. . . . The destruction of life and property has been very heavy, but so far we have escaped, and no houses in this county have been burned. I always count now from one week to another, as one never knows what may happen in any one week.[132]

Two letters from Clare to Holmes from about the same time period have survived. Neither is dated, but external evidence places them in the spring of 1922 and the summer of 1923. In the first Clare noted that the latest letter she had received from Holmes, sometime after the middle of March, had been dated January 29, "but nothing is surprising & I have quite ceased to expect anything to go right in this country—especially mail bags which are frequently used for bonfires on country roads." She added that she had been sick with influenza ("the variety they call *gastric* which is most poisonous") and that she was "half blind & deaf & lame & a few things of that sort." She wished him a happy eighty-first birthday.[133]

In the second letter Clare began by saying that "I am so glad you are all right & going to enjoy a lazy time at Beverley." The reference was very probably to Holmes' prostate operation the preceding summer, which had caused him to hospitalized for over a month and to convalesce slowly in the fall. He resumed his judicial duties but was still recovering the following summer, writing Pollock that "I don't know whether it is heart or what . . . but I don't find it wise to press exercise as much as I should like."[134] Clare then went on to describe her situation:

> I hope it will be nice & warm there & not like this where I am almost always shivering—& I *hate it so!* I am afraid you are right & I have not written for rather a long time but I always fancy I am ever so busy & can't stuff half my little jobs into the day—& they say that is always the way with idle people I am afraid—& besides I never have anything to say that is at all likely to interest you nowadays—vile murders being committed all over this wretched little country with apparent impunity & everybody more or less up in arms about everything—
>
> I rather wish we could go & settle for the rest of our days in California & never set foot in Ireland again—life has become so utterly futile & hopeless & generally disgusting here. . . . Fancy this being Ascot week! & Oh the merry days that we used to have there 100 years ago when all the world was young—& warmer & one didn't shiver in June—
>
> I think the longer one lives the less one likes living—[135]

One can see from this letter the quite different paths that Holmes' and Clare's lives had taken after the First World War. Clare never fully recovered from her 1899 riding accident, had a stroke, and was beleagured by the political turmoil in Ireland. She found herself shivering in June; she wished she could abandon Ireland; she had nothing of interest to report to Holmes; she felt that the "merry days" when she had been one of the belles of the London social season were "100 years ago." In short, she found life "utterly futile & hopeless & generally disgusting." Holmes, for his part, recovered from his prostate operation with few ill effects, plunged back into his work, and began to see himself recognized as one of the significant judges in American history. He wrote Pollock in 1922 that he had received "a puff in the *New Republic*" on the twentieth anniversary of his being on the Supreme Court and the fortieth year of his judicial career, and added that "I like it and want to produce as long as I can."[136] A little more than a year later he wrote Harold Laski that "I think my writing has kept up to the mark. Each of my last four cases has frightened me when it was assigned—but they all have satisfied me more than I expected."[137]

In 1926 Holmes did not hear from Clare for a very long time, and finally wrote her in August saying that he was "worried at your very long silence," and asking her "just to tell me how you are, if nothing else." Apparently he heard back from Bernard Castletown, for he wrote him on November 3:

> I feared but did not know she was ill. As I do not know the nature of the illness I can do nothing but hope it is not grave. Please give her my love and tell her I think about her a great deal and shall continue anxious until I hear more & I hope better news.[138]

By then Clare was bedridden. She had fallen on the stairs at Granston Manor in the spring of 1926, and had been moved to Doneraile, confined to the first floor with a day and night nurse to supervise. In October and November she was very ill, but rallied over the winter and died peacefully in her sleep on March 14, 1927.

Holmes learned the news from Ethel St. Leger, her cousin, who wrote him on April 11. Clare had played bridge the night she died, Ethel said, and at 10 had been fetched by the nurse and said goodnight to the company, their "never dreaming it was goodbye." "It was sudden at the end," Ethel added, "but most merciful as she never knew it was the end & had no pain or discomfort." She asked Holmes "not to mention I have written to you to Castletown." "There is an ethereal faint type of green on the trees," Ethel said in closing, "& the chestnut leaves have separated. The English spring is very beautiful & the dark trees show up the deciduous trees in contrast—I hope you will forgive my having written. . . . I thought I might take a liberty & do it on my own initiative."[139] Enclosed with the letter was an account of Clare's funeral in the *Cork Examiner,* which reported that "the passing of so outstanding a figure meant the removal of a personage who had in a host of ways merited and had bestowed upon her the highest esteem and regard of rich and poor alike. Her late ladyship had gained this endearment, not alone of a charming personality, but of the manner in which she had during her long connection with the district at all times taken so keen an interest in its progressive advancement."[140]

On April 22 Holmes heard from Bernard Castletown. He attributed Clare's death to her decision to go to Doneraile Court from Granston Manor. "As certain as I am writing this letter," he said, "this *accursed place* killed her. In my memory of it there have been 7 deaths in this house & in my own home in 73 years *not one* . . . there is a curse on it." He was "going every day to her resting place . . . & stay[ing] by her as long as I can bear." "I do not know what to do but to stick on here," he added. "My whole life was centered on her. I read to her & killed game for her &

lifted her & wheeled her about in her chair. I even sang to her which amused her. Now all is gone and I have no object in life."[141] "[F]ate is plucking the leaves from the old tree rather fast," Holmes wrote to Laski. "[Y]esterday [came] a letter giving me my first news of the death of Lady Castletown one of my oldest and most intimate friends. . . . [She] had had a stroke coming on top of other trouble so that death seemed probably a release, but it makes a great gap in my horizon."[142]

~

Thus ended Holmes' greatest romance, at least the greatest of which any evidence survives. Reconstruction of his relationship with Clare Castletown suffers from the sparse and scattered quality of the evidence and from difficulties in replicating, in the late twentieth century, the shades and nuances of Victorian social mores. But there are some clues on both sides, clues that permit a small amount of speculation.

On Clare's side the evidence of her relationship with Percy La Touche and her disclosure of Holmes' existence to La Touche suggests that extramarital liaisons were part of her life and that she took a certain degree of pleasure in playing off her suitors against one another. The concern La Touche exhibited in the fall of 1896 that he might be displaced by Holmes indicates that while Clare may have treated her friendship with Holmes as a lark in its initial stages, after his visit to Doneraile Court she developed a certain infatuation with him. But Holmes' letters to Clare in the late fall of 1896 and throughout the course of 1897 indicate that Clare had concluded that an investment in La Touche as a swain made more practical sense. The portrait of Clare implicitly sketched in Holmes' letters in that period is one of an adventurous woman seeking liaisons as a kind of amusement. It is also suggestive that when Clare realized that Holmes—who, after all, had told her that his life was in his wife and his work—might care enough to visit her again in the summer of 1898, the tone of her letters to him changed and she became less remote and flippant.

Speculation about the degree of physical intimacy between Holmes and Clare seems a fruitless exercise in light of the absence of evidence. We know, from the La Touche correspondence, that Claire was not loath to have affairs, and we also know that there were opportunities for her and Holmes to have become intimate during his visits to Doneraile Court in 1896 and 1898. If one judges only from Holmes' letters, however, physical intimacy seems a remote possibility. The letters indicate that he and Clare spent time alone together, but his descriptions of intimate moments involve settings, such as conversation in the conservatory, that do not seem conducive to physical intimacy. We also know from the letters and his travel diaries that he did not see Clare constantly while at Doneraile and that he saw her in London for lunches, dinners, flower shows, and other public occasions. Finally, Holmes' expectations of his visits, according to his letters, were not those of one who assumes that he and his correspondent will be physically intimate. Wondering whether he would spend any time alone with Clare does not seem to be the response of one who takes physical intimacy for granted.

But the relationship between Holmes and Clare is not principally interesting as a possible physical affair. It furnishes a significant example of Holmes' need for intimacy with a woman other than his wife, and of the nature of that intimacy. From Holmes' perspective, his relationship with Clare Castletown both perfectly captured the kind of intimacy he sought with women, and at the same time threatened to upset the structured nature of that intimacy.

Here one recalls the letter Holmes wrote to Lucy Hale during his freshman year at Harvard College. In the letter Holmes said that he "admire[d] and loved[d] ladies' society and like[d] to be on intimate terms with as many women as I can." He then spelled out what he meant by intimacy:

> So long as I write to you like a donkey I never can hope you'll have any real confidence in me but if I write in other terms than those of a silly flirtation I know that you at least could have a good influence on me—When you honestly speak to yourself don't you feel that these flatterers are not those that you would ever speak to about what you really deeply felt.[143]

Several hypotheses about the meaning of intimacy to Holmes were previously drawn from the Hale letter. First, Holmes' conception of intimacy with women, as articulated in the letter, was not one that required him to focus his attention on one person. On the contrary, he confessed that he would "like to be on intimate terms with as many women as I can." Second, intimacy to Holmes was not the equivalent of a "silly flirtation," in which a man wrote to a woman "like a donkey," flattering her. It was rather a relationship in which the man's attention gave the woman confidence to "speak . . . about what you really deeply felt." In the process the woman served as a "good influence" on the man. But while not a "silly flirtation," the relationship was not devoid of sexual overtones. After encouraging Lucy Hale to speak to him about what she "really deeply felt," Holmes continued, "[i]n the little [time that] I [have] seen you I tell you frankly that you seemed to me to have a good deal of capability as yet unaroused."[144]

On his 1866 trip to England Holmes appeared to be pursuing the sort of intimacy he outlined to Hale. We have seen that he sought out the company of several young women and enjoyed "making eyes" and "flirting" with them. This tendency was also characteristic of his life in Boston immediately after the Civil War, when he frequented a social circle that included other women in addition to Fanny Dixwell and when he wrote William James that he occasionally occupied his evenings in the company of "a girl of some trivial sort." But in the years after his marriage to Fanny any interest in intimacy with women seems to have been subordinated to his overriding desire to make a scholarly contribution. This was the period in which friends noted his reclusiveness and self-preoccupation, and in which he worked evenings as well as days.

Holmes' succession to a judgeship, and Fanny's illness and disinclination to socialize, seem to have set the terms of their life in Boston in the 1880s. As Holmes settled into the routine of his judicial duties, he found them less demanding, and began to read literature, write letters, and compose speeches and scholarly essays. He also began to socialize moderately in Boston, usually not in the company of Fanny. By his trip to England in 1889 others had noted a tendency to "break loose" and "flirt . . . desperately."

That England served as a liberating atmosphere for Holmes can be seen in three letters he wrote in the 1890s. In the earliest, written to the wife of Frederick Pollock, he recalled an incident in which two friends of mine walked by and with them a girl with a roving eye who seemed to take more notice than the usual tame bird. So the next day . . . I strolled up to my friend's house and soon was at it hammer and tongs with m'mselle. Of course she had been brought up in London. . . . You may say what you like about American women—and I won't be unpatriotic—but English women are brought up, it seems to be, to realize that it is an object to be charming, that man is a dangerous animal . . . and that a sexless *bonhomie* is not the ideal relation. . . . [I]f one knows his place and makes way for younger men when he isn't sure, it is better perhaps not quite to abandon interest in the sports of life.[145]

In this letter Holmes contrasts Englishwomen favorably with American women in recognizing that men are "dangerous animal[s]" and that sexual dimensions to relationships are worthwhile. He also admits that when a young girl looks him over he is inclined to follow up the encounter, and that even at his age he is not ready to give up flirting. In the 1920s Harold Laski wrote Holmes two letters in which he noted that Englishwomen had remembered Holmes in the 1890s as "the most perfect flirt in London,"[146] who had "a provocative gleam" in his eye.[147]

A second letter was to Lady Winifred Burghclere in 1898:

I always feel twice the man I was, after I visit London. Personality there is in higher relief than in my world here with its limited experience and half culture. . . . You have to pay your way in London. No one takes you on faith— and I love it. You must be gay, tender, hard-hearted when something misses fire, give your best, and all with lightness.[148]

That letter suggests that Holmes found London rejuvenating, a break from his "world [of] limited experience and half culture." In a previously quoted letter to Nina Gray, written in the midst of the first London season in which he had spent time in the company of Clare Castletown, he had particularized:

I have been whirling about in this place for 20 days. . . . A wonderful romantic place to an outsider momentarily let inside. . . . One is pretty sure that his neighbor at dinner will have a lot of psychologic small change at her command, enough to secure admission to the interior of the building. So an endless procession of possibilities streams before one's eyes which once in awhile realizes itself and you swear eternal friendship and forthwith vanish.[149]

But there was another dimension to Holmes' reaction to London. That letter to Gray continued:

I think one gets enough of the whole business in a month. After all one is not of it—. . . . It is play not what one wants to do for life. . . . One or two sketches of last time I am filling in with a little (water) color—but by growing more familiar everything becomes more nearly finite.[150]

In these sentences Holmes has stepped back from the "whirl" of the London season and recognized that its romance is "finite"; that "it is play not what one wants to do for life." He may have been referring to Clare in noting "[o]ne or two sketches of last time" that he was "filling in with a little (water) color," and if so, he was suggesting that even romantic attachments get "familiar" with time.

A last letter suggests that intimacy with women was part of a "chivalric" conception of gender relations that Holmes adopted during his visits to London in the 1890s, and that in a sense he was indifferent to the identity of his companions. In 1897, while in the midst of his romance with Clare, Holmes wrote Lady Pollock about another of his female friends, Lady Nina Campbell, "at whose feet" he had "somewhat vainly laid the devotion of an ever faithful heart" on his 1896 visit. This was the same trip on which Holmes had first spent time in Clare's company, and he recalled that he and Nina Campbell "had some charming moments together." But "my back once turned," he added, "she lapsed into silence," and thus the relationship did not evolve as did that with Clare.

All of this suggests that Holmes' search for intimacy, while actively pursued, was quite structured. He confined the search to environments outside Boston where he could "break loose"; he assumed the chivalric attitude of a "perfect flirt" with a deferential posture but a roving eye, not confined to any one woman; he was interested in including correspondence as part of the relationship. In one sense the heart of his relationship with Clare was in correspondence. There he could court her from a distance; there he could talk about his professional ambitions and his dreams of "spiritual reign"; there he could encourage her to talk about what she "really deeply felt." His greatest disappointment, during the time that her attention became distracted from him during the winter of 1896 and the course of 1897, was not that she had "vouchsafed him" by being "up to mischief and doing damage." It was rather that someone other than he might be "privileged to know [her] real feelings." He had tried not to write her "like a donkey": he had talked of philosophy and ambition and other "burning themes." In exchange he wanted the kind of closeness he had defined in his letter to Lucy Hale. But he also wanted to preserve a certain distance. His life was in his wife and his work, but that did not prevent a "romantic feeling" from surfacing which it would "cut [him] to the heart" to have Clare repudiate.

Control was thus one of the linchpins of Holmes' conception of intimacy. Control came from the fact that Clare and he were on separate continents, married to other people, of different worlds. Control also came from the fact that their principal contact was through letters. But even there the careful structure Holmes had erected broke down. He wrote Clare letters containing sentences such as "I long long long for you and think think think about you," the letters of "a donkey." In short, intimacy, as he defined it, gave way to romance. At some places his letters to Clare became indistinguishable from those of Percy La Touche. Just as London was "a wonderful romantic place" for Holmes, Clare Castletown was a wonderful object of romance. When he said that Clare's death "makes a great gap in my horizon" he was engaging in understatement. Clare had broken through Holmes' constructed version of intimacy: just as he could not fully control his prose, he could not fully control his feelings. Lack of control, especially of his emotions, was a state that made Holmes distinctly uncomfortable, and so it may have been with a sense of relief that he recognized, on the 1903 visit, that he and Clare had passed through the stormy period of their attachment, and it was time to take down the sails.

CHAPTER EIGHT

The Supreme Judicial Court
of Massachusetts

~

ON MARCH 7, 1900, on the eve of his sixtieth birthday, Holmes was given a
dinner by the Bar Association of Boston. He was at that time Chief Justice of
the Supreme Judicial Court of Massachusetts, having assumed that post in August
1899 on the death of Chief Justice Walbridge Field. In an after-dinner speech Holmes
reviewed his nearly twenty years on the bench. "I look into my book in which I
keep a docket of the decisions of the full court which fall to me to write," he said,

> and find about a thousand cases. A thousand cases, many of them on trifling or
> transitory matters, to represent nearly half a lifetime! A thousand cases, when
> one would have liked to study to the bottom and to say his say on every
> question which the law has ever presented, and then to go on and invent new
> problems which should be the test of doctrine, and then to generalize it all and
> write it in continuous, logical, philosophic exposition, setting forth the corpus
> with its roots in history and its justifications of experience real or supposed!
> Alas gentlemen, that is life. . . . We cannot live our dreams.[1]

In this excerpt the contrast between Holmes' expectations on becoming a judge and
his experience in that role was sharply etched. He would have liked to continue the
jurisprudential work he had begun with *The Common Law,* to "study to the bottom
and say his say on every question which the law has ever presented." He had looked
deeply into selected common law subjects and "said his say" in the lectures that
became *The Common Law,* reorienting the subjects of torts, contracts, criminal law,
and possession around the themes he found to be fundamental. He had "generalized" those subjects in a "continuous, logical, philosophic exposition." He had set
forth their roots in history and their policy justifications. He had wanted "to go on
and invent new problems" that "would be the test" of the doctrines he had laid
down in his treatise. Instead he had considered "a thousand cases, many of them
upon trifling or transitory matters." Judging had not been a continuation of the
"philosophical" search he had originated as a scholar. It had been a much more
mundane experience.

But the experience of judging changed Holmes' view of law. At the time he
became a judge he had thought of law as a philosophically continuous system, capable of being synthesized and generalized in a "scientific" fashion, encompassing
comprehensive principles. At the time he made the speech to the Boston Bar Asso-

ciation he had a much more limited view of law and a correspondingly limited view of the judge's function. Law was simply the aggregate of judicial decisions and the "prophecies" that could be made on the basis of those decisions; judging was simply the exercise of "the sovereign prerogative of choice."[2] Indeed Holmes in his 1900 speech gave a resigned, minimalist definition of judging and advanced a modest conception of its satisfactions:

> One begins with a search for a general point of view. After a time he finds one, and then for a while he is absorbed in testing it, in trying to satisfy himself whether it is true. But after many experiments or investigations all have come out one way, and his theory is confirmed and settled in his mind, he knows in advance that the next case will be but another verification, and the stimulus of anxious curiosity is gone. . . . [H]e sees it all as another case of the same old ennui, or the same sublime mystery—for it does not matter what epithets you apply to the whole of things, they are merely judgments of yourself. At this stage the pleasure is no less, perhaps, but it is the pure pleasure of doing the work, irrespective of future aims. . . . The joy of life is to put out one's power in some natural and useful or harmless way.[3]

William James, on seeing another version of the sentiments expressed in this paragraph, wrote to a friend that they represented Holmes' "set speech" celebrating "mere vital excitement," which for James was tedious and banal.[4] But for Holmes the idea that "doing the work" was "the joy of life" was both a great consolation and a source of continual motivation. At the very end of Holmes' judicial career, when he was still active at the age of ninety, Chief Justice Charles Evans Hughes marveled at the fact that Holmes "never seems to be bored at the unending and familiar task" of deciding cases. "For nearly fifty years" he had been hearing arguments and making decisions, Hughes noted, "but to each case he brings an undiminished and an unflagging zeal."[5] Even allowing for the exaggeration of a public tribute, Holmes' interest in "doing the work" for its own sake was evident. He had said in a national radio address, delivered at the same time as Hughes' tribute, that "the work never is done while the power to work remains. . . . For to live is to function. That is all there is in living."[6]

Although Holmes' commitment to "doing the work" of judging remained constant, his view of that work, we have already noted, had changed significantly during his years as a Massachusetts judge. He had ceased to see judging as an ambitious program of reorienting the common law in a continuous philosophic synthesis and had come to regard it as a minimalist task of doing one's job by deciding ordinary cases. At the same time his extrajudicial addresses revealed that he had come to equate idealism and respect in the legal profession with the modest and interstitial contributions of judges and lawyers to the corpus of legal doctrine. Moreover, his scholarship revealed the gradual erosion of his historicist theory of legal development, articulated in *The Common Law,* in which legal rules and principles gradually became more coherent and predictable as the policies undergirding them were better understood, and its replacement by the competing positivist theory, also present in *The Common Law,* that law was just the decisions of those having the power to decide.

The timing of Holmes' altered views about the nature of law and judging, combined with the contrast he made, in the 1900 speech, between a "study to the bottom" of legal questions which would produce a "continuous, logical, philosophic exposition" of "the whole corpus" of law and the decision of "a thousand cases, many of them on trifling or transitory matters," suggests that the basis for the change lay in his experience as a Massachusetts judge. In addition, one can see evidence of the contrast in letters he wrote about his work as a judge, ranging from an initial statement that "[t]he experience is . . . most valuable for an all round view of the law,"[7] something he had hoped for before going on the bench,[8] to a later comment that "[n]o very great or burning questions have been before me."[9]

Judging on the Supreme Judicial Court of Massachusetts (known locally as the SJC) was in fact very different from what Holmes had expected. It was in some respects a frustrating experience. Not only were Holmes' cases for the most part unimportant, the opportunities for him to reorient legal doctrine, at least in the cosmic fashion contemplated by the 1900 speech, were few and far between.[10] Then there was the problem of recognition: while one commentator in 1900 spoke of his "great reputation,"[11] for the most part his decisions were unknown to all but a handful of specialists. There were other frustrations as well: the provinciality and insularity of Boston, his continued overshadowing by his father, who remained alive until 1894, the illnesses and reclusiveness of his wife. Nonetheless, Holmes was being candid when he described the years he spent on the SJC as "the twenty happiest years of my life."[12] It was a time in which he was able to convince himself that although the vast scale of his initial professional ambitions might need to be tempered, he had learned the value of persistent, dedicated work and of postponed rewards. When in 1902 he serendipitously escaped the Massachusetts court for the more visible post of an Associate Justice of the Supreme Court of the United States, he could feel consummately prepared for that task. He may not have had the opportunity to study every legal question to the bottom, but he knew what judging was all about.

～

The court that Holmes joined in December 1882 was an institution whose procedures called attention to its colonial origins.[13] It was composed of seven members, who not only heard appeals in Boston but also traveled around the state, holding trial court sessions in county seats. For a portion of the year two of the seven justices traveled, sitting alone as trial court judges, while the other five remained in Boston, to make up an appeals court (the so-called Full Court). In the spring and fall all the justices traveled together to hear appeals in rural counties, with two then remaining on circuit as trial judges while the rest returned to Boston. The court's jurisdiction was technically very extensive, including original and exclusive jurisdiction of equity cases, divorce cases, and capital crimes, and also concurrent jurisdiction of all common law cases. As a matter of practice, however, the SJC justices, as a Full Court, tried comparatively few common law cases. While the justices could hear cases at the trial level *en banc*, they rarely did; instead a single justice from the SJC, sitting on circuit, would render an opinion, and the case would then be taken on appeal before the Full Court, including that justice if he were not on circuit at the time.

In Holmes' first full year on the Court, 1883, he began by sitting with the Full Court in Boston in January, remained in Boston through March, then went on circuit to hold equity trials in April and divorce trials in May, and returned to Boston for Full Court appellate sessions in June, where the justices reviewed the opinions that had been produced on circuit. The SJC then recessed in July, except for one of its members, who remained in Boston to hold equity court. It reconvened on circuit in September, holding appellate sessions in Berkshire, Hampshire, Hampden, Worcester, Plymouth, Bristol, and Essex Counties. In November the justices returned to Boston for another review of their fall cases; five then remained there for *en banc* sessions while the other two returned to circuit duties. In December the year concluded with Full Court appellate sessions in Boston.[14] The pace and routine of the work was exceptionally demanding, and Holmes, we have seen, initially concluded that he needed to curtail his other activities. He wrote Pollock in March 1883 that "I have pretty well given up dining out, as I can't do it and feel as well and fit for work the next day,"[15] and in August of that year he added that "[w]e are very hard worked and some of the older Judges affirm that no one can do all the work without breaking down."[16]

During the years of Holmes' tenure the Supreme Judicial Court's expansive jurisdiction was somewhat reduced: it ceased to have original jurisdiction over divorce, annulment, and child custody cases after 1887 and ceased to try capital crimes after 1891. But Holmes and his fellow justices continued to spend considerable time with their trial work. These trial court sessions, being scattered over the state and covering a great variety of legal disputes, were the backbreaking part of Holmes' duties. While there is evidence that Holmes was a skillful (and aggressive) trial judge,[17] only scattered archival records of his trial transcripts exist, and I have not included a discussion of his trial opinions in this evaluation of his work on the SJC. Suffice it to say, first, that Holmes' experience as a trial judge tended to confirm his confidence in his own intellectual powers and his lack of enthusiasm for jury decisions; and, second, that the materials exist for an extended scholarly treatment of Holmes as a trial judge.[18]

The kinds of cases that Holmes encountered on the SJC, while largely "trifling and transitory," provide exposure to the tapestry of late nineteenth-century New England life. A veteran sailor, injured while working on a tugboat, claimed that he was not responsible for his own injuries because the master of the tug had cursed at him, distracting his attention.[19] Liquor dealers were prosecuted under a Massachusetts statute for selling beer to minors or intoxicated persons, and defended on the ground that they had licenses from the state.[20] A person rode on the engine of a crowded train, disembarking at each stop and reboarding just before the train pulled away. At one stop he waited too long and was unable to reboard because others on the train were in his way. He jumped on the steps of one of the train's cars, fell off, and sued the railroad for his injuries, claiming he was a "passenger" owed a duty of safe conduct.[21] Charterers and owners of ships lost or damaged at sea sued marine insurance companies.[22]

Two men, in the course of driving a buggy on a dark night, were injured when the horse pulling the buggy stumbled into a caved-in portion of a city street. The horse was blind, and the city, conceding that it was responsible for keeping streets under repair, sought to defend on the ground that a blind horse was not a suitable horse to be driven on a public highway.[23] A married woman was promised a sum of money if she would return to her husband after the two had separated. When she returned, and subsequently sought to enforce the contract, she was met with the defense that there had been no consideration for her husband's promise because marital relationships could not be dissolved or resumed for money.[24] An action for fraud was brought in a case in which a stock prospectus was issued, and the stock turned out to be worthless.[25]

A pond owner, who used the pond to supply water to a manufacturing plant, sought an injunction against an adjoining landowner who, in the process of cultivating his hillside, brought manure and ashes onto the land, a portion of which were washed by rain into the pond.[26] Massachusetts statutes granted municipalities the power to take water for public purposes and provided compensation for landowners whose property was damaged by the operations of a municipality. Several landowners sued municipalities who sought to divert water from streams or brooks in order to build sewers. The municipalities claimed the protection of the statute; the landowners sought more extensive damages based on the common law of trespass or nuisance.[27] A man, in the process of using an outhouse on the right of way of a railroad, was killed when a train ran off the track and collided with the outhouse.[28] Massachusetts sought to prosecute two men who had sought to rob a store for breaking and entering. One defended on the ground that he did not actually proceed through the closed door of the store, but was let in by the other, who had come in under the pretense of wanting to purchase some goods.[29]

A Mr. Solomon ordered a mannequin for his store from a Mr. White. The arrangement called for Solomon to pay White a total of $35.00, with $10.00 down and the rest in monthly payments of $5.00. White shipped the mannequin to Solomon by a private express company; the mannequin arrived damaged and Solomon refused to accept it. White claimed he was owed the entire $35.00; Solomon responded that White's claim should be limited to the difference between a damaged mannequin and an undamaged one.[30] In a man's suit against a railroad for the loss of the company and affection of his wife because of injuries she had suffered from an accident in which the railroad had been negligent, the railroad sought to introduce evidence that the man had habitually kicked his wife with his boots on, and that the police had frequently intervened to break up domestic disputes involving the couple.[31]

A cigar makers' union sought to register its label under a Massachusetts statute authorizing the creation and registering of trademarks.[32] A man sued the owner of a horse for injuries when he was kicked. The owner had previously beaten the horse, and left him near a public sidewalk. He claimed that just as every dog was entitled to one bite, every horse was entitled to one kick.[33] Mrs. Bradley's lounge, made of a mahogany frame and upholstered with plush the color of old gold, was taken by one Hooker and converted to his own use. Hooker admitted taking and converting the lounge, and the parties disputed its value. At trial an expert testifying for Mrs. Bradley stated that the value of the lounge, if sold at auction, would be $15 to $20, but that an admirer of antique furniture would pay $50 for it. Hooker sought to exclude the expert's testimony about the $50 value.[34] Mr. Goddard, having slipped on a banana skin on the floor of North Station in Boston, sued the Boston & Maine railroad. The railroad introduced evidence that Mr. Goodard had not looked down before he slipped and thus could not determine how long the banana had lain on the floor.[35]

Two persons who were slaves in Virginia prior to the Civil War escaped, went to Massachusetts, and married in that state. The man had previously been married in Virginia, to another slave, and fathered three children from that marriage. After moving to Massachusetts, the man fathered two additional children with his second wife. Meanwhile his first wife, after not hearing from him for eleven years, remarried. After the Civil War the man's whereabouts became known to his children in Virginia, who visited him in Massachusetts. Eventually the man and his second wife, whose marriage had been certified in Massachusetts, died, and one of their two children, residents of Massachusetts, was named administrator of the man's estate. The man's first wife and surviving son from his Virginia marriage sued to share in the estate.[36] A passenger on a railroad train attempted to change cars while the train was stopped at a station. While walking down the train tracks in the dark, the passenger fell into a river over which the train had stopped, and sued the railroad's conductor for his injuries.[37]

A man named Newhall invested in a fraternal benefit organization, a common late-nineteenth-century type of insurance arrangement. Such organizations were not illegal in Massachusetts, but they had the reputation of taking advantage of the uneducated poor by issuing benefit certificates, payable on the death of the investor, that were not usually of equivalent value to the cumulative amount investors were assessed by the organization over time. In Newhall's case he had joined the American Legion of Honor in 1888 and taken out a certificate for $5000. The certificate provided on its face that it was subject to the bylaws of the American Legion of Honor, as currently existing "or hereafter adopted." In 1900 the organization amended its bylaws to reduce the highest amount it would pay on the death of a member to $2000. In 1901 Newhall died, and his wife sought to recover the value of his certificate, or $5000. The American Legion of Honor responded that compliance with their own bylaws required them to pay her only $2000.[38]

Such were some of the cases Holmes rendered opinions on during his years on the SJC.[39] While the facts of the cases give us a glimpse of a world frequented by horses and buggies, outhouses and railroads, the sons and daughters of slaves, thirty-five dollar mannequins and fifty-dollar plush-covered lounges, tugboats and fraternal benefit organizations, at the same time the cases appear "trifling and transitory."

In surveying Holmes' Massachusetts decisions I have started with his own guidelines: there were a great many cases and most were insignificant. I have chosen to approach his decisions from several perspectives. First, I have attempted to survey cases in areas of the law to which Holmes directed his special attention in *The Common Law*, with a view toward exploring whether, even in a modest fashion, he was able to conform his judicial decisions to the principles and policies he advocated in that work. Second, with an eye toward Holmes' later career on the Supreme Court, I have examined the small number of cases he decided that raised constitutional issues. Third, I have given some attention to the cases for which Holmes was best known as a state court judge, a handful of labor relations cases in which he allegedly identified himself as sympathetic to the emerging labor movement. Finally, I have sought to speculate about the effect of Holmes' career on the Supreme Judicial Court of Massachusetts on his intellectual and emotional perceptions of himself and his professional life.

~

In his chapter on criminal law in *The Common Law* Holmes had taken pains to emphasize that in that subject "the tests of liability are external, and independent of the degree of evil in the particular person's motives or intentions.[40] Although he had associated an external standard of liability in the criminal law with the idea that its primary purpose was one of deterrence, that association is something of a *non sequitur*,[41] and it has been pointed out that Holmes' principal purpose in championing an external standard of liability was to strip the criminal law, like other legal subjects, of the baggage of morals.[42] In particular, Holmes was interested in converting terms such as "malice" or "intent" from subjective to objective concepts, defined by reference to the actions of the defendant under the circumstances at issue. "Acts," he argued, "should be judged by their tendency under the known circumstances, not by the actual intent which accompanies them."[43]

In discussing the external standard of liability Holmes acknowledged that it fell more heavily on "the weakest" class in society. "For it is precisely to those who are most likely to err by temperament, ignorance, or folly," he pointed out, "that the threats of the law are the most dangerous."[44] In 1884 a case was decided in the Supreme Judicial Court of Massachusetts that, for Holmes, perfectly illustrated that dimension of the criminal law. Franklin Pierce, a Worcester physician, had administered a treatment to Mary Bemis, who had been taken sick with a bacterial or viral infection, which consisted of saturating a flannel shirt, drawers, and stockings with kerosene, and reapplying the garments every three hours. Pierce's theory was that the kerosene would act "like a poultice on a boil," drawing out the infection. It proved disastrous: Ms. Bemis' skin was burned and blistered by the kerosene flannels, eventually hastening her death.[45]

Commonwealth v. Pierce thus raised the question whether the existence in a physician of "an honest purpose and intent to cure" a patient precluded the physician's having the requisite intent to be convicted of manslaughter. As Holmes put it, the question in *Pierce* was "whether an actual good intent and the expectation of good results are an absolute justification of acts, however foolhardy they may be if judged by the external standard."[46] He concluded that an external standard should govern and the existence of a benevolent but foolhardy intent should not constitute a justification.

Holmes began his argument for criminal liability in *Pierce* by pointing out that the standard in civil cases was an external one, based on the evaluation of a defendant's conduct against that of "a man of ordinary prudence." He thought this standard sensible, since it had the effect of allowing "losses . . . to rest where they fall in the absence of a clear reason to the contrary" in civil suits, and argued that "there would seem to be at least equal reason for adopting it in the criminal law, which has for its immediate object and task to establish a general standard, or at least general negative limits, of conduct for the community, in the interest of the safety of all."[47]

Some early Massachusetts cases, however, following a dictum of an English decision, had held that a physician "who gives a person a potion, without any intent of doing him any bodily hurt, but with intent to cure" was not guilty of murder or manslaughter if the remedy, "contrary to the expectation of the physician," killed the patient. Holmes found that dictum inapposite in cases where the physician's actions could be shown to be reckless. He concluded that "the recklessness of the criminal no less than that of the civil law must be tested by what we have called an external standard," and that "the question whether [a physician's] act would be reckless in a man of ordinary prudence is evidently equivalent to an inquiry into the degree of danger which common experience shows to attend the act under the circumstances known to the actor."[48]

In *Pierce* the dangerousness of kerosene, when applied to substances coming into direct contact with a person's skin, was well known to common experience. The defendant could not escape liability "on the ground that he had less than the common experience." He knew that he was using kerosene, and the jury had found that its use under the circumstances was "the result of foolhardy presumption or gross negligence."[49] The defendant in *Pierce* was thus a member of the class of persons on which external standards of liability in the criminal law fell the hardest: those "most likely to err by temperament, ignorance, or folly."[50]

If one compares Holmes' language in *Pierce* with that of his criminal law chapter in *The Common Law,* it is clear that he saw the case as an ideal opportunity to put his theories into practice. In the chapter he had said that "the test" for criminal liability was "the degree of danger . . . attending the acts under the known circumstances of the case."[51] In *Pierce* he said that "the question whether [an] act would be reckless in a man of ordinary prudence is evidently equivalent to an inquiry into the degree of danger which common experience shows to attend the act under the circumstances known to the actor."[52] In *The Common Law* he had pointed out that "when we are dealing with that part of the law which aims more directly than any other at establishing standards of conduct, we should expect there more than elsewhere to find that the tests of liability are external, and independent of the degree of evil in the particular person's motives or intentions."[53] In *Pierce* he said that "the criminal law . . . has for its immediate object and task to establish a general standard . . . of conduct," and "we cannot recognize a privilege to do acts manifestly endangering human life, on the ground of good intentions alone."[54] In *The Common Law* he had argued that in the criminal law "[a]cts should be judged by their tendency under the known circumstances";[55] in *Pierce* he declared that "a man's liability for his acts is determined by their tendency under the circumstances known to him."[56]

Thus it was not surprising that Holmes wrote Frederick Pollock in early November 1884, when the *Pierce* case was being decided, that he had "written opinions in some very interesting cases," one of which was *Pierce.* "If my opinion goes through" in that case, he added, "it will do much to confirm some theories of my book."[57] "Confirmation" was an understatement: Holmes had extracted his language verbatim from *The Common Law* and applied it to *Pierce.* The consequence was an unfortunate result. A well-intentioned but foolish physician was convicted of a criminal offense when civil liability, based on medical malpractice, would have appeared a more appropriate outcome. But the result in *Pierce* would clearly cause doctors to think twice before applying home remedies to patients; it emphasized the criminal law's deterrent rather than its retributivist functions. That was also consistent with the views Holmes had expressed in *The Common Law*.

Had the bulk of the criminal law cases that came before Holmes been like *Pierce*, Holmes might have concluded that his work as a judge would give him regular opportunities to "confirm some theories of my book." But *Pierce* was the "interesting" exception to a mass of routine cases. In *Pierce* Holmes had encountered the combination of an unusual fact situation and a thorny technical problem: following Massachusetts precedent would have resulted in a subjective definition of justificatory motives in the criminal law. By being forced to confront precedent, in a case in which the defendant's acts, however well intentioned, were clearly foolhardy, Holmes was able to conduct his discussion at the level of policy, and thus offer the argument that it made sense for the criminal law to adopt external standards of liability. That he had already made that argument in *The Common Law* only heightened the opportunity *Pierce* presented to him. Such opportunities were few and far between.

If one surveys the criminal cases in which Holmes wrote opinions during his twenty-year tenure on the Supreme Judicial Court of Massachusetts, they reveal themselves to be a strikingly prosaic lot. Many involved reviews of rulings on evidence made at the trial court level, typically upheld by Holmes.[58] Several involved constructions of Massachusetts statutes prohibiting the unauthorized sale of intoxicating liquors,[59] the unlabeled distribution of oleomargarine,[60] the conduct of a lottery,[61] or the maintenance of "gaming" establishments.[62] Some involved technical definitions of specific crimes, such as robbery.[63] Holmes' majority opinions, for the most part, were brief, assertive, and devoid of copious citation. They were nearly all unanimous, in keeping with the Supreme Judicial Court's practice of not encouraging dissenting opinions.[64]

One exception to the routine character of Holmes' criminal law cases was presented by the facts of *Commonwealth v. Kennedy*.[65] The defendant in that case had been convicted of attempting to murder one Albert F. Learoyd by mingling rat poison with tea. He had bought an amount of poison known as "rough on rats" and placed a teaspoonful of the poison on the underside of the crossbar of a mustache cup, which was known to be the property of Learoyd's and used by him in drinking tea. Apparently Learoyd drank the tea, and subsequent evidence showed that it contained quantities of arsenic, which also showed up in Learoyd's urine. Learoyd became ill but survived. The question was whether Kennedy lacked the intent to murder Learoyd since his expectation that Learoyd would drink the tea from the mustache cup "may have been unfounded and unreasonable."

Holmes had discussed the law of attempts in his lecture on crimes in *The Common Law*, primarily to illustrate the purportedly external standard of criminal law liability. His example of a man being convicted for attempting to set fire to a haystack once he lit a match and held it near the haystack, but then blew it out when others arrived, was intended to suggest that it was the dangerous character of the acts perpetrated rather than the subjective "intent" of the perpetrator that determined whether an attempt had been made.[66] In *Kennedy* he returned to this theme. "We assume," he argued, "that an act may be done which is expected and intended to accomplish a crime, which is not near enough to the result to constitute an attempt to commit it."

He put the case of a person "shooting at a post supposed to be a man"; that act was not dangerous enough to qualify.[67] Traveling to Cambridge to commit a murder was not dangerous enough if the traveler was stopped on route by a drawbridge; if the traveler persisted to the point of actually cocking a gun at his victim, but did not fire, an attempt would have been made out. "The act done," Holmes concluded, "must come pretty near to accomplishing [a prohibited] result before the law will notice it."[68] This was because "the aim of the law is not to punish sins, but . . . to prevent certain external results."[69]

In the Kennedy case, Holmes argued, "the acts are alleged to have been done with intent that Learoyd should swallow the poison, and, by implication, with intent to kill him." The question was whether those acts were dangerous enough to make out an attempt when the defendant had no assurances that Learoyd would swallow the poison or that the dose swallowed would be mortal. Holmes thought they were. "Any unlawful application of poison," he reasoned, "is an evil which threatens death, according to common apprehension, and the gravity of the crime, the uncertainty of the result, and the seriousness of the apprehension, coupled with the great harm likely to result from poison even if not enough to kill would warrant holding . . . liability for an attempt." In the case of serious crimes even "impossibility of achievement" was not necessarily a defense.[70] Holmes' focus in *Kennedy* had been on the defendant's acts, not his state of mind. Kennedy may have been well founded or ill founded in his belief that putting a teaspoonful of rat poison in Learoyd's mustache cup would kill him; the gravamen of his crime had been in committing that dangerous act. "The danger becomes so great," Holmes had said in *The Common Law*, "that the law steps in."[71]

Holmes returned to the law of attempts in *Commonwealth v. Peaslee*,[72] a case decided after he had become Chief Justice of the Supreme Judicial Court of Massachusetts. The case so strikingly paralleled Holmes' illustrations in his discussion of attempts in *The Common Law* that one can imagine his satisfaction in encountering it. The defendant in *Peaslee* had "constructed and arranged combustibles" in a building "in such a way that they were ready to be lighted, and if lighted would have set fire to the building and its contents."[73] He then offered to pay a young man to go to the building and light the combustibles. As he and the young man were driving toward the building, the defendant changed his mind and drove away. "This is as near," Holmes said, "as he ever came to accomplishing what he had in contemplation."[74]

So described, the case seemed to come precisely between the two hypotheticals Holmes had put in his discussion of attempts in *The Common Law*. Were the defendant's actions in *Peaslee* like those of the person setting out from Boston to Cambridge to commit a murder who was prevented from crossing the Charles River because of a malfunctioning drawbridge? Or were they like those of the person who lit a match near a haystack but then blew it out? "The question on the evidence," Holmes said, "is whether the defendant's acts come near enough to the accomplishment of the substantive offence to be punishable."[75]

While *Peaslee* was like the two hypotheticals, there was a difference. In those examples the actor was acting alone; in *Peaslee* the actor was soliciting another to take steps to further develop the crime. Holmes noted that such cases were not commonly described as "attempts," but as "preparations." The distinction attempted to suggest that "an overt act, although coupled with an intent to commit the crime, commonly is not punishable if further acts are contemplated as needful." But the distinction was not clear-cut, Holmes maintained: "[i]t is a question of degree." Sometimes "preparations" were so far along that while more remained to be done, the intent had been clearly established. Thus in the haystack case the defendant did not actually apply a lighted match to a haystack, but only because he "discover[ed] he was being watched." Similarly "getting into a stall with a poisoned potato, intending to give it to a horse there," was an "attempt" even though the defendant was arrested before actually giving the potato to the horse. But "making up a false invoice at the place of exportation with intent to defraud the revenue" was not an "attempt" if the defendant did not attempt to use the invoice.[76]

On balance, a majority of the judges in *Peaslee* concluded that an attempt had not been made out because the defendant had only been indicated for preparing combustible materials with the intent that someone else should light them. He had not been formally indicted for soliciting the young man. "The necessity that the overt acts should be alleged has been taken for granted in our practice and decisions," Holmes wrote for the majority, "and is expressed in the forms and directions for charging attempts." Had "the indictment been properly drawn," he added, "we have no question that the defendant might have been convicted."[77]

The result contemplated by Holmes in *Peaslee,* should a proper indictment have been drawn, is difficult to square with the other cases he cited. In addition to the poisoned potato case, he cited a case holding that it was an attempt to pay a man to burn a barn, but also pointed out that a "mere collection and preparation of materials in a room for the purpose of setting fire to them" would not be an attempt "unaccompanied by any present intent to set the fire."[78] In *Peaslee* combustible materials had been collected and prepared, but the defendant, in turning away from the site of those materials, had not demonstrated any present intent to have those materials lit by the person whose aid he had solicited. It is hard to see how his "intent" differed from that of the person who made up a false invoice but then did not use it. Perhaps Holmes was suggesting that the collection of combustible materials was a more dangerous act than the preparation of a false invoice, since the materials might spontaneously burn, but he never made that suggestion explicit. The important feature of the case, for Holmes, seems to have been his demonstration that the distinction between preparations and attempts turned on "question[s] of degree." This was consistent with his general jurisprudential attitude toward distinctions in the law. In their starkest form distinctions clustered around two poles in a magnetic field; in application their component parts drew nearer and nearer and became "questions of degree," which ended up being separated by the arbitrary drawing of lines.

In twenty years of criminal law cases Holmes found only a handful that moved him to exercises of the kind he engaged in *Pierce, Kennedy,* and *Peaslee.* While in those cases he was able to "confirm" his views of legal doctrine or jurisprudence in the criminal law area, he could not have failed to notice the remarkably low number of such opportunities. The impression created by the cases is that while Holmes genuinely loved encountering the sort of intellectual puzzle presented by *Pierce* or *Peaslee,* in the bulk of his criminal law decisions he did little more than

ratify the Commonwealth of Massachusetts' concern with the distribution of intoxicating liquors or unlabeled oleomargarine.

~

Torts had been the central focus of Holmes' early scholarship, and arguably the area
in which he made his greatest intellectual contribution. Almost singlehandedly, he
had taken a field of law in its embryonic stages and suggested that it could be
systematized around the negligence principle. His argument for the primacy of negligence not only made possible a separate identity for torts, it had powerfully subversive effects on alternative principles of tort liability, such as strict enterprise
liability, that had surfaced in the nineteenth century and could have become significant features of American tort law in its formative stage.[79]

In Holmes' *Common Law* chapters on torts he had set forth several policy objectives for the field. One, previously mentioned, was the undermining of act-at-peril
liability as a doctrinal theory. A corollary to that objective was the enshrinement of
"fault"-based liability, personified by the negligence principle, as the touchstone of
tort law. Another goal of Holmes' was the objectification of the fault principle,
through the creation of a hypothetical standard of "reasonable" "blameworthy"
conduct against which the actions of defendants in tort suits were evaluated. Another
objective was the eradication of moral language from the negligence calculus, so
that "fault" was seen as strictly a legal concept, derived by the weighing of a
calculus of risk anticipation and risk prevention. Still another was the narrowing of
jury discretion in torts cases through the judicial derivation of precise definitions of
liability and clear doctrinal lines. A final goal was the injection into judicial analysis
of torts cases of the premise that losses caused by injuries "lay where they fell" in
the absence of a clear showing of fault. The image of tort law envisaged by these
objectives was that of a field of relatively limited liability with predictable rules and
comparatively little jury discretion.[80]

Holmes wrote the Court's opinion in tort cases more often than in any other field
of law during his tenure on the SJC. The plethora of cases and the well-developed
state of his theoretical views on tort law suggested that he might have abundant
opportunities to put those theories into practice. In fact his experience was similar
to that in the criminal law. The routine cases, in which he was constrained by the
issues or by other circumstances of the decisionmaking process, far outnumbered
the ones in which he was able to "confirm" his scholarly views. Several cases
involved the statutory duty of towns and cities to maintain public highways in a safe
condition, and the corresponding requirement that they be given adequate notice of
a defect.[81] There were a great many cases in which a plaintiff's assumption of the
risk of dangerous conditions precluded recovery even where the condition was the
result of the defendant's negligence.[82] There were a smattering of fraud cases,[83]
several cases involving the duties of landowners to persons coming on their premises,[84] and a handful of libel cases.[85] Most of the torts cases involved simple negligence actions, typically against railroads or streetcar companies, in which the issue
was whether the defendant had been negligent at all. In many of these cases a jury
had rendered a verdict for the plaintiff, and the defendant was appealing on the
grounds that it was not negligent as a matter of law. In a majority of the cases Holmes

agreed with the defendant. In general, with the exception of libel cases, his opinions had the effect of confining tort liability rather than extending it.

One of Holmes' simple negligence cases was doubtless interesting to him because it was a case of first impression, in which he was asked to construct legal doctrine from analogies and policy reasoning. The case was *Dietrich v. Northampton*,[86] decided in 1884. In *Dietrich* a pregnant woman slipped and fell on a defective highway, and successfully recovered damages against the town of Northampton under a Massachusetts statute making towns and cities responsible for maintaining streets and roadways in good condition. The fall also brought on a miscarriage, and a child was born prematurely, but was "too little advanced in fetal life to survive its premature birth." The administrator of the child brought an action against the town for the child's death. Holmes upheld a trial court finding that the child was not a "person" given an action against the town by the statute, even though "[t]here was testimony . . . based upon observing motion in its limbs, that it did live for ten or fifteen minutes."[87]

Holmes began his analysis by noting a dictum from Sir Edward Coke, "which seems to have been accepted as law in England," that "if a woman is quick with child, and takes a potion, or if a man beats her, and the child is born alive and dies of the potion or battery, this is murder." Could this analogy from the criminal law "be relied on," Holmes asked, "for determining the rule of civil liability?" He concluded that it could not. First, while "[s]ome ancient books seem to have allowed the mother an appeal for the loss of her child by a trespass upon her person," Holmes noted that "no case, so far as we know, has ever decided that, if the infant survived, it could maintain an action for injuries received by it while in its mother's womb."[88] He suggested that if a suit by the prematurely born child was the basis of the action, "the plaintiff . . . can hardly avoid contending that a pretty large field of litigation has been left unexplored until the present moment."[89]

But this was assuming that Coke's analogy was helpful to the plaintiff in *Dietrich* in that it laid down the principle that "an injury transmitted from the actor to a person through his own organic substance, or through his mother, before he became a person, stands on the same footing as an injury transmitted to an existing person through other intervening substances outside him." In fact, Holmes concluded, Coke's analogy was not helpful. Coke's rule "required that the woman be quick with child," and "quick," as defined by Massachusetts decisions, meant capable of having "some degree of quasi independent life at the moment of the act." A four- to five-month-old fetus was not "quick" within the meaning of those decisions.

Finally, Holmes maintained that even if Coke's analogy were accepted, and even if it were concluded that "a man might owe a civil duty . . . in tort to one not yet in being," there would then be the question whether "an infant dying before it was able to live separated from its mother could be said to have become a person recognized by the law" as having standing to bring an action in court. He noted, on this point, that the mother's cause of action against the town of Northampton had been statutory. He pointed out that while the Massachusetts statutes "punish unlawful attempts to procure miscarriage" (abortions), the statutes "greatly increase[d] the severity of the punishment if the woman dies in consequence of the attempt," but did not increase it at all if the child died, "even after leaving the womb."[90] This suggested that unborn fetuses were not considered "persons" within the meaning of the Massachusetts statute at issue in *Dietrich*.

Dietrich v. Northampton was a Holmes decision with an exceptionally long life. His statement that surviving infants could not recover for injuries suffered while in their mothers' wombs survived, as a general proposition, until 1949, and the *Dietrich* case itself was not limited until 1960. The decision was something of a prototype for Holmes' majority opinions in tort cases. He took an apparently sympathetic claim, suggested that its resolution in favor of the plaintiff would create a wide potential field of expanded tort liability, gave summary treatment to sources supporting his position, and reached a result that limited the potential scope of tort claims. After *Dietrich* prenatal injuries were eliminated from the class of compensable tort actions.

As Holmes' tort decisions progressed over time, the number of cases involving industrial accidents discernibly increased. In addition to cases stemming from railroad accidents, cases surfaced revealing that employment in late nineteenth-century industrial society was a hazardous enterprise. The hazards to workers, moreover, did not merely extend to the conditions of employment themselves. They also included legal doctrines that made recovery by injured employees against their employers a difficult enterprise. Chief among those doctrines were three: the "fellow servant rule," which precluded employees recovering against an employer when their injuries had been caused by another employee, and the doctrines of contributory negligence and assumption of risk, which completely barred recovery by injured employees who were found to have knowingly or carelessly exposed themselves to the risks of their employment.[91]

In 1887 the Massachusetts legislature attempted to address the problem of industrial injuries by passing a statute, the Employers' Liability Act, which was modeled on a comparable law in England. The statute, Holmes noted in *Ryalls v. Mechanics' Mills,* a case construing it, "was intended . . . to remove certain bars to [the right of employees] to sue for personal injuries based on their relation to their employer." In particular, the statute "purported . . . to do away with the defences that the workman impliedly took upon himself the ordinary manifest risks of his employment . . . or that the defect was due to the negligence of the person intrusted by the master with the supervision of the machinery, and that he was the plaintiff's fellow servant." The "main purpose of the statute," Holmes concluded, was "to extend the liability of employers in favor of employees."[92] Thus in the *Ryalls* case, in which an employee sued her employer for injuries caused by a defect in the machinery used in the mill in which she worked, Holmes concluded that the statute should be read as placing employees in no worse a position, and in sometimes a better position, than they had been at common law.

But the case of *Mellor v. Merchants Manufacturing Co.,*[93] decided the same term, qualified the meaning of that statement. In that case a very similar accident had occurred to that which had precipitated the litigation in *Ryalls*. A loom-fixer employed by a mill had noticed that a belt kept running off of a pulley on the shafting of one of the mill's looms. He called this to his superior's attention, and was informed that the belt would be fixed, but subsequently noticed it had not been. He then decided to repair it himself, and while he was waiting for the machinery to stop, as it automatically did at 6 P.M., the belt ran off again, catching his left hand and injuring it. He sued the mill for personal injuries, and was met by the defenses that in volunteering to repair the belt he had either assumed the risk of injuries from it or at least should have known of that risk.

Holmes concluded that the defenses abolished by the statute of 1887 were limited to those instances in which an employee "took the risk of the known dangers of the business . . . by reason of the parties not standing on an equal footing because of the [employee's] fear of losing a place." In *Mellor* the plaintiff had not, because of a vulnerable bargaining position, "assumed the risk" of all the dangers inherent in being a loom-fixer; he had voluntarily exposed himself to a risk that he had no obligation to encounter. He was not responsible for fixing the belt, and he had no reason "to put himself close to the source of danger when he knew that he could not work upon it until it was at rest . . . and when he knew also it would be at rest in a few minutes." The risk was thus not the result "of his contract of service," but "of his own free will."[94]

The *Mellor* case suggested that the doctrines of contributory negligence and assumption of risk were alive and well in Massachusetts despite the Employer's Liability Act. A pair of cases decided in the 1893 term tended to confirm that supposition. In the first of those, *Davis v. New York, New Haven, and Hartford Railroad Co.*,[95] a man repairing a track was run down by a train. He was facing north at the time, and bending over, and the trains came from the south, so that he had to rely on others to warn him of their approach. A foreman had been stationed near him, but had apparently given him no warning of the train's coming, and the train itself had apparently not whistled or otherwise signaled its approach. Despite the Employer's Liability Act, the railroad argued that the plaintiff had assumed the risk, and Holmes, in his opinion for a unanimous court, admitted that the risk of coming into contact with trains was one of the hazards of those who repaired train tracks. But in *Davis,* Holmes argued, the workman had not taken the risk "that a person entrusted by his employer with and exercising superintendence will be negligent in the exercise of his duty." If that were the case the 1887 statute "would be made of no avail," because an assumption of risk defense could be invoked against any employee injured by a train on the grounds that that was a risk inherent in the job.[96] In *Davis* that risk had been anticipated and provided against by the employer, and the fact that the person charged with warning persons repairing train tracks about the dangers of approaching trains had failed adequately to perform that function should not be a bar to recovery. If it were a bar, the effect would be not only to obviate the statute's effort to eliminate the assumption of risk defense when it rested on the inherent dangers of a job, but to resurrect the fellow-servant rule.

In the second of the cases, *Lynch v. Boston and Albany Railroad Co.*,[97] an employee of the railroad was engaged in cleaning under a switch bar in a railroad yard when he was struck and killed by a car that had been shunted off its proper track. As in *Davis,* the work was recognized as "of a kind which naturally withdrew attention from approaching trains," and the section foreman "generally looked out for the men the best way he could and warned them." But he was not required to keep a lookout, and testified that "even if the men were together they had to look out for themselves."[98] At the time of the accident, Holmes noted, "the deceased must be taken to have known that he was not relieved from the necessity of keeping watch for himself. If so, he was not free from negligence in failing to do so." Moreover, he could not expect a warning from a car should one "be shunted or kicked upon the track where he was working." In short, he "had no right to abandon the use of his own eyes" while repairing tracks.[99]

Davis and *Lynch* demonstrated that the effect of the 1887 Employer's Liability Act had not been to change radically the status of the common law doctrines of contributory negligence and assumption of risk. The occupations of track repairman or track custodian necessarily exposed those who held that employment to the risk of coming into contact with trains on the tracks where they were working. Unless the railroad affirmatively designated a supervisor to warn repairmen or custodians about oncoming trains, those risks fell on the jobholders. It is hard to imagine why the holders of such jobs were not within the class of persons whose inequality of bargaining position required them to engage in risky work. The statute had been designed to prevent such persons being barred from suits should they be injured by the very risks that made their job dangerous. And yet in *Davis* and *Lynch* Holmes allowed the former plaintiff to recover only because the railroad had provided a supervisor, who then failed to warn him, and barred the latter plaintiff from recovery even though it is hard to imagine how he could have cleaned under switch bars on tracks and watched out for trains at the same time.[100]

Among the consequences of industrialization and urbanization, in addition to the greater exposure on the part of the general population to dangerous machines, was a greater exposure to incidents calculated to place stress on the nervous system. Where such incidents resulted in emotional distress unaccompanied by physical injury, however, the common law treated them as not compensable. This treatment of emotional injury was based on the assumption that emotional distress was "speculative," not being capable of proof in the same manner as was physical injury, and that its ephemerality might encourage false claims. As the behavioral sciences developed in stature in the twentieth century, and the seriousness of emotional injury came to be more widely appreciated, suits for emotional distress alone came to be regarded as cognizable in the courts.[101] But during Holmes' tenure on the SJC that situation had not yet come to pass. Emotional injury unaccompanied by any physical injuries was not a basis for recovery in tort law.

This situation combined with another common law doctrine in the field of torts to create an anomaly that Holmes was forced to confront. Traditional common law tort damages for physical injury were assessed on the basis of an assumption that the defendant, if found liable, "took the plaintiff as he found him," so that a plaintiff whose susceptibility to a given injury was greater than that of the average person could recover the entire amount of his or her damages, even though they might be increased beyond the average by that susceptibility. Thus if a person was only slightly injured, but because of a susceptible temperament suffered emotional distress in addition to physical injuries, the person could include the emotional distress component in a damage claim. The following anomaly was thus created. If a carriage came up on the sidewalk and brushed a pedestrian, frightening him or her severely but causing inconsequential physical injury, the pedestrian could recover damages for the fright. But if the carriage missed hitting the pedestrian altogether, even though it frightened her or him to the same extent, no recovery at all was possible.[102]

Holmes dealt with this oddity of the law of emotional distress in several cases. In *Spade v. Lynn and Boston Railroad*[103] a drunken man was being removed from a railroad car when the conductor charged with removing him jostled another drunken man in the vicinity, throwing him upon Margaret Spade. "The fall upon her," Holmes noted, "seems to have been a trifling matter, taken by itself, but the fright caused by that and the rest of the occurrences in the car resulted in physical injury." Spade was thus a "slight impact" as distinguished from a "no impact" plaintiff under the law of emotional distress as it was then applied. She received a jury verdict for her injuries.[104]

Holmes, for a unanimous court, reversed and ordered a new trial. His opinion first concluded that the defendant railroad was not negligent. "So far as appears," he maintained, "the conductor was acting rightly in putting the drunken man off the car. As against the plaintiff, he was doing one of the things which she had to contemplate as liable to happen when she got into the car. . . . If the fall upon the plaintiff was the necessary consequence of a lawful and reasonable act, then it was one of the risks which she assumed when she took her passage."[105] Although the question of whether "a man is answerable for an injury inflicted upon an innocent stranger knowingly . . . if the injury is an unavoidable incident of lawful self-protection" was an interesting one that "deserves more discussion than it has received," Holmes noted that in *Spade* no negligence on the part of the conductor had been shown.

He then turned to two other points raised at the trial court, both of which had a bearing on the law of emotional distress. One was whether, if the plaintiff had been injured as a consequence of the defendant's negligence, she could have recovered "for such mental disturbance and injury as were caused by other acts of the conductor and the general disturbance in the car." This would have amounted to her being able to recover for some emotional distress that was unaccompanied by physical injury. Holmes held that she could not. Liability only extended to "consequences of the defendant's wrong to the plaintiff," not to "all consequences of the defendant's conduct." In the *Spade* case there was possibly a "difficulty in discriminating," he conceded, because "it seems quite possible . . . that the plaintiff's trouble was due in substance to the disturbance as a whole." But she could only recover if the jury concluded "that the impact on her person gave the detonating spark without which she would not have collapsed."[106]

That ruling meant that if two persons witnessed the presence of a drunken person in a railway car, and were upset by it, and in the process of attempting to remove the person a conductor carelessly waved a billy club in the air, brushing it against the clothing of one of the witnesses and narrowly missing the other, the one brushed could recover for subsequent emotional injury, even though much of the distress might have been precipitated by the presence of the drunk. This example points up what Holmes called "the difficulty in discriminating" between consequences directly related to the defendant's wrong to the plaintiff and other consequences of the event. It is hard to know why, in a case where someone had been brushed by a billy club, that person's emotional distress would be more genuine than if he or she had been narrowly missed by the same club. And in both cases the distress would seem to result from the experience as a whole, including the presence of an intoxicated person on a railway car and a subsequent altercation involving that person's removal.

Holmes then turned to the second point raised by *Spade:* whether, in emotional distress cases, defendants were required to take into account the peculiar emotional susceptibilities of the plaintiffs they injured. Here the objective standard of liability in tort law clashed with the principle that a tort defendant took victims as he or she found them. Counsel for the plaintiff in *Spade* argued that the conductor "had known the plaintiff for several years" and thus had increased obligations to her because "she was a particularly sensitive person." Holmes rejected that argument. "Ordinary street cars must be run with reference to ordinary susceptibilities, and the liability of their proprietors cannot be increased simply by a passenger's notifying the conductor that he has unstable nerves." The duty of a conductor thus only extended to the avoidance of conduct likely to harm an ordinary person. But if "the defendant's servant did commit an unjustifiable battery on the plaintiff's person," Holmes maintained, "the defendant must answer for the actual consequences of that wrong to her as she was, and cannot cut down her damages by showing that the effect would have been less upon a normal person."[107]

Holmes attempted to reconcile the different treatment of the two situations by saying that "[t]he measure of the defendant's duty in determining whether a wrong has been committed is one thing, the measure of liability when a wrong has been committed is another."[108] But his treatment appears confused. Defendants were not responsible for inflicting emotional injuries on others at all so long as the injury was entirely emotionally based. Thus the question of whether a given plaintiff was susceptible to emotional distress was irrelevant so long as he or she was not physically injured. There was, in short, no "duty" on the part of persons to avoid emotional injury to others at the time of the *Spade* case. The only sense in which emotional injury was recognized in tort law was as a component of damage once physical injury had occurred. And there were no "objective" limitations on that component. Holmes' discussion of "ordinary susceptibilities" thus had nothing to do either with the standard of liability or the measure of damages in emotional distress cases. The duty of a railway conductor in removing intoxicated persons from the train was to take reasonable precautions to avoid physical injury to passengers, not to avoid frightening them.

Some of the statements made in *Spade* were refined in two cases decided late in Holmes' tenure. In the first of those, *Homans v. Boston Elevated Railway Co.,*[109] a woman was thrown against the seat of a subway car when the car was negligently involved in a collision. She received a "slight blow" and "certain bruises," but subsequently suffered nervous shock and hysterical paralysis. The defendant in *Homans* argued that the *Spade* distinction between emotional injury directly related to physical injury and emotional injury arising from other causes should preclude recovery for emotional distress in *Homans,* since the plaintiff had not shown that her shock resulted from the blow that caused her bruises, as distinguished from the collision as a whole.

Holmes, for the court, concluded that since "the jar was due to the same cause as the blow, and both to the defendant's fault" it was unnecessary to make further refinements. The doctrine barring recovery for emotional distress alone was "an arbitrary exception, based upon a notion of what is practicable." Here "the reality" of the plaintiff's claim was "guaranteed by proof of a substantial battery to [her] person." There was thus no reason to deny recovery. In *Spade,* by contrast, "the defendant . . . was not responsible for the previous sources of fear" that had contributed to the plaintiff's distress. In *Homans* "the defendant was responsible for the trouble throughout."[110]

Similarly, in *Cameron v. New England Telephone and Telegraph Co.*[111] an accident produced physical and emotional distress in a manner that was difficult to separate. The company had set off a blast of dynamite, admittedly negligently, in the vicinity of a woman who was sitting on a rocking chair on her front porch. She suffered a fainting fit and subsequent miscarriage. It was not clear whether she had been thrown from her chair because of the explosion, or whether she had started to get up on hearing the explosion and then fallen. The defendant argued that she could not recover unless she had been thrown from her chair. The trial court instructed the jury that if the plaintiff fell and was hurt as a part of arising, or attempting to arise from her chair, she could recover. On appeal Holmes, for the court, found this instruction correct.

"The principle of the *Spade* case," Holmes declared in *Homans,* "is confined strictly to cases where the connection of the physical illness with the fright is wholly internal." Where "fright reasonably induces action which results in external injury, the defendant may be liable as well when the impact is brought about without the intervention of the plaintiff's consciousness." But in *Homans* it was possible that the plaintiff had not stumbled as a result of the explosion, but had simply gotten up from her chair, fainted, and fell. Her injury would then arguably have been emotionally derived. While conceding that "[s]uch a case would be different from those which heretofore have been before the court," Holmes thought that recovery would be likely, because "where the effect of the fright was to bring about an injury by impact, we should not distinguish between the different modes in which the injury was accomplished." In such a case "the reality of the cause is guaranteed sufficiently."[112] Holmes' comments indicate that he regarded the critical issue in emotional distress cases to be whether the circumstances of a case suggested that the plaintiff's claim was genuine. Had the plaintiff in *Cameron* simply heard the explosion, become frightened, stood up, and fainted, that would still have been a sufficient guarantee that her injuries, even if emotionally based, were genuine, because most persons would be frightened if exposed to an explosion of dynamite.[113]

The distinctions drawn in emotional distress cases reminded Holmes of what was at stake in many of the tort cases he decided. The reason for the "arbitrary" exclusion of emotional injury from the class of wrongs compensable in tort rested on a perception that every tort suit represented a clash between the social interest in compensating people for injuries suffered at the hands of their neighbors and the social interest in permitting people to conduct their affairs without fear of continually being subjected to lawsuits. In the case of emotional distress that clash had been resolved in favor of limiting compensable claims to those where the injury could be perceived as "genuine" and where the defendant could thus reasonably have perceived that his or her conduct could have expected to result in others being injured.

Emotional injuries were sometimes within the class of reasonably foreseeable harms, but often times were not, because they rested on the idiosyncratic reactions of one with heightened sensibilities.

This confrontation of competing social interests, Holmes noted, was common to torts cases. In *Patnoude v. New York, New Haven, and Hartford Ry.Co.*,[114] an otherwise unexceptional case, he illuminated the clash vividly. *Patnoude* involved a suit by the owner of a horse that had become frightened on observing an electric car covered with white canvas resting on a flat car on a railroad track near a highway. The car was in the process of being unloaded from the flat car and moved to a street railway car barn. As a consequence of the operation an eight-foot high fence screening the railroad tracks from the highway had been taken down. When the horse passed and saw the covered electric car because the fence was not there, it panicked and injured itself.

Holmes, writing for the court, denied recovery for the horse's injuries. The situation was a transitory one, he noted, and the process of unloading, the condition of the fence, and the existence of the canvas covering were all under the control of the street railway company rather than the railroad. But he did "not wish to be taken to intimate that if the plaintiff brings another action against the street railway company he can succeed." Even if "the car was an object likely to frighten horses," the question remained whether its existence on the railway company's land "was a legal wrong."[115] Holmes elaborated:

> As in many cases, perhaps it might be said in all, two principles of social desiderata present themselves, each of which it would be desirable to carry out but for the other, but which at this point come into conflict. It is desirable that as far as possible people should be able to drive in the streets without their horses being frightened. It is also desirable that the owners of land should be free to make profitable and otherwise innocent use of it. More specifically, it is desirable that a railroad company should be free to use its tracks in any otherwise lawful way for the carriage, incidental keeping and final delivery of any lawful freight. A line has to be drawn to separate the domains of the irreconcilable desires. Such a line cannot be drawn in general terms. . . .
> [S]ome uses of land might be imagined which would be held unlawful solely because of their tendency to frighten horses. . . . Others would be held lawful no matter how many horses they frightened.[116]

In *Patnoude*, Holmes felt, the line-drawing was easy. There was nothing unlawful about painting buildings or streetcars white. There was an obvious advantage in covering a streetcar with canvas when it was in the process of being transported, and there was an obvious advantage in temporarily taking down a fence so that a streetcar could be moved from one location to another. The fact that as a result a horse was exposed to a streetcar covered with secured white canvas was hardly a reason for the railroad company to be prevented from covering and transporting its cars on its own tracks. The case might have been more troublesome if the horse had kicked a passerby, who then sued the railroad: then it might have presented a truly contested conflict between the "domains of . . . irreconcilable desires" that Holmes' found competing in appellate cases.

In his *Common Law* chapters on property relationships Holmes had emphasized the status of a bailee as furnishing an analytical key to the concept of possession. Bailees lacked the intent to exercise dominion over the property they possessed; indeed they were interested in eventually transferring that property to someone else. While bailees had physical control over the property they held and the power to deny all access to it save the owner, they still did not have "possession" over it with respect to the owner. Bailment cases thus demonstrated that the question of possession was ultimately what Holmes called an "empirical" question. Did a relationship exist such that a person had the physical control of another's property under the permission of the owner? If so, that person's "intent" to exclude others from the property was irrelevant in determining whether he or she had possession of it. What was relevant were the facts that determined how the person came into physical custody of the property.

This "empirical" approach to bailment cases allowed Holmes to dispose of some issues readily. It also posed problems when applied to legal relationships in which one party appeared to act as agent for another in the delivery of goods. *Stiff v. Keith*[117] and *Andrews v. Keith*[118] provided examples of the former set of cases; *Hallengarten v. Oldham*[119] and *Smith v. Edwards*[120] the latter. In *Stiff* and *Andrews* Holmes, for the court, found that the role of third parties was only to facilitate bailments; once those bailments had come into existence, they had to be formally dissolved by the return of the property that formed the subject matter of the bailment. In *Hallengarten* and *Smith,* by contrast, third parties took on the status of bailees by being integral factors in the passage of property from one person to another in a distant locality.

In short, the few bailment cases that Holmes decided on the SJC tended to confirm his observation in *The Common Law* that bailment questions should be determined by a consideration of the specific facts surrounding the bailment. Where the facts suggested that a bailment had come into being, the bailor and bailee had particular obligations following from that fact. If the facts suggested that no bailment existed, no such obligations existed. And certain kinds of bailees, such as warehousemen *(Hallengarten)* or common carriers *(Smith),* had special obligations because the purpose of their possession of goods was often to facilitate the transfer of those goods from one party to another. None of these principles was counterintuitive, and none of the bailment cases memorable.

We have seen that Holmes came to his chapters on contracts in *The Common Law* at a later stage of intellectual development than the stages at which he encountered most of the other fields he wrote about. In torts, especially, in bailment and successions, and to an extent in criminal law, he modified his analytical approach and his substantive conclusions as he went along, arriving at the perspective that characterized his treatment of those subjects in *The Common Law* only briefly before writing the chapters. With respect to contracts, however, he had written nothing before the chapters, and thus they provided him with a good opportunity to employ his now characteristic methods to reach his now familiar conclusions.

Given Holmes' strong views on contract doctrine and the unorthodox orientation of his perspective, one might have expected that his contract decisions on the Supreme Judicial Court of Massachusetts would have been revisionist. To an important extent they were. In several decisions he attempted to strip the process of contract formation of its subjective elements and apply objective standards. One such case was *Hawkins v. Graham*,[121] an 1889 decision. In that case a millowner and an engineer entered into a contract for the installation of a heating system in a mill. The contract provided, among other things, that the temperature in any room in the mill could be raised to 70° Fahrenheit "in the coldest weather that may be experienced," and that if the equipment could not heat the rooms properly the engineer would remove it at his own expense. "In the event of the system proving satisfactory," the contract concluded, the millowner would pay $1575 to the engineer.[122]

When the equipment was installed the millowner complained that the temperature of the different stories of his mill varied, being higher by several degrees in the places where the hot air entered the rooms than in other portions of the room, and that this effect "did not prove satisfactory." He refused to pay the engineer, who sued him for the contract price. The question before the Supreme Judicial Court of Massachusetts was whether the "satisfaction" clause of the contract meant that the work had not been adequately performed.

"Such agreements usually are construed," Holmes began his opinion for the court, "not as making the defendant's declaration of dissatisfaction conclusive, in which case it would be difficult to say that they amounted to contracts . . . but as requiring an honest expression."[123] The phrase "it would be difficult to say that they amounted to contracts" is particularly telling. It suggests that Holmes was of the view that contract formation presupposed an objective rather than a subjective definition of "satisfaction," so that even if both parties knew that the specifications of an arrangement were tailored to one party's idiosyncratic taste, there were limits on what an idiosyncratic buyer could demand.

"In view of modern modes of business," Holmes conceded, "it is not surprising that in some cases eager sellers . . . should be found taking that degree of risk with unwilling purchasers, especially where taste is involved." But "when the consideration furnished is of such a nature that its value will be lost to the plaintiff . . . unless paid for," he added, "a just hesitation will be felt, and clear language required, before deciding that payment is left to the will, or even to idiosyncracies, of the interested party. In doubtful cases, courts have been inclined to construe agreements of this class as agreements to do the thing in such a way as reasonably ought to satisfy the defendant."[124]

This language is revealing of the way in which Holmes conceived contract formation. The problem with cases where the contract was tailored to one party's "satisfaction" was that an idiosyncratic buyer could resist payment simply by alleging that he or she was not "satisfied," thus delaying transactions and creating disincentives for sellers to provide specifications to taste. Holmes could have emphasized these practical consequences of the role of idiosyncratic taste and "satisfaction" in *Hawkins*. Instead he emphasized the role of consideration. When "the consideration furnished" was of the kind that "its value will be lost . . . unless paid for," he argued, idiosyncratic tastes could not fully control. This seems to be another way of saying that the nature of contract formation was incompatible with a subjective theory of contract. In almost all cases the value of "consideration furnished" would be lost unless the party furnishing goods or services was paid. The recital of consideration's playing an essential role thus seems to be principally a rhetorical device. To make his point apparent, Holmes added at the end of his *Hawkins* opinion that "the satisfactoriness of the system and the risk taken by the plaintiff were to be determined by the mind of a reasonable man . . . not by the private taste or liking of the defendant."[125] Put another way, a buyer can only expect reasonable, not perfect, satisfaction.

Hawkins v. Graham was thus an opportunity for Holmes to suggest that the subjective elements of contract formation were less dominant than perhaps supposed. In *Hobbs v. Massasoit Whip Co.*[126] he made a comparable suggestion with respect to offer and acceptance. A supplier of eelskins had on previous occasions furnished a manufacturer of whips with eelskins of varying lengths. On those occasions the price for eelskins over twenty-seven inches in length had been five cents a skin, and the price of eelskins between twenty-five and twenty-two inches in length two cents a skin. The manufacturer of whips had not requested skins less than twenty-two inches in length.

In February 1890, the eelskin supplier sent the whip manufacturer a shipment of 2350 skins. There was debate about the quality of this particular shipment. The supplier testified that 2050 skins were over twenty-seven inches in length and the remainder between twenty-two and twenty-seven inches. The manufacturer testified that he had not ordered the shipment of skins in question; that the skins that came in the February 1890 shipment were less than twenty-two inches in length and hence unfit for use; that he notified the supplier that the skins were unsatisfactory and would be held "subject to [his] order"; and that the supplier never responded to this notice, so that after several months the skins were destroyed.[127]

The trial judge instructed the jury that if they believed that the skins were received in the condition described by the whip manufacturer, and the manufacturer had notified the supplier, the supplier could recover nothing. But, the judge added, "if skins are sent to [the whip manufacturer] and [the manufacturer's people] see fit, whether they have agreed to take them or not, to lie back and say nothing, having reason to suppose that the man who has sent them believes that they are taking them, since they say nothing about it; then, if they fail to notify, you would be warranted in finding for the [supplier]."[128] The jury brought in a verdict for the supplier, apparently finding that the skins were suitable and that the whip manufacturer had not given notice of their alleged unsuitability. The manufacturer appealed on the ground that the instruction was erroneous.

"Standing alone and unexplained," Holmes wrote of the challenged instruction, "this proposition might seem to imply that one stranger may impose a duty upon another, and make him a purchaser, in spite of himself, by sending goods to him, unless he will take the trouble, and be at the expense, of notifying the sender that he will not buy." But this was not the case in *Hobbs,* he concluded. The parties were not strangers to one another, but persons who had dealt in eelskins "four or five times before," on which occasions the skins "had been accepted and paid for." The practice amounted to "a standing offer" on the part of the whip manufacturer for skins above twenty-two inches in length, "and even if the offer was not such that the contact was made as soon as skins corresponding to its terms were sent, sending them did impose on the [manufacturer] a duty to act about them.'' Thus "silence on [the whip manufacturer's] part, coupled with retention of the skins for an unreasonable time, might be found by the jury to warrant the [supplier] in assuming they were accepted, and thus to amount to an acceptance.''[129]

Hobbs thus might appear to stand for two familiar propositions of contract law. First, where ongoing business dealings exist between parties, terms established by custom and practice can amount to formalized agreements. Second, where a practice exists of regularized shipments to one party by another, with subsequent payment by the other party, silence on the part of the receiving party can, after a reasonable time, constitute acceptance on the terms established by the practice. But Holmes did not identify the *Hobbs* case as resting on either of those propositions. Instead he said that the decision "stands on the general principle that conduct which imports acceptance or assent is acceptance or assent in the view of the law, whatever may have been the actual state of mind of the party—a principle sometimes lost sight of in the cases.''[130]

The *Hobbs* case was another example, for Holmes, of the objective theory of contract formation. "The actual state of mind of the party" was not the central issue in the case. The question was not whether the whip manufacturer found the skins "suitable" or "satisfactory," but whether he had notified the supplier of his reaction. In other words, the arrangement between the parties did not contemplate that every time the whip manufacturer received a shipment of skins over twenty-two inches he would pay for them at the previously established rates; it contemplated only that if he did not notify the supplier that he did not want a particular load of skins he would be taken as having accepted them. The issue was thus not the "actual state of mind" of the whip manufacturer, but his conduct. Had he received a shipment of eelskins at the proper lengths, but rejected them and given proper notice, he would have been able to do so. The "principle sometimes lost sight of in the cases" was not in the *Hobbs* case at all. But it was a principle to which Holmes was committed in contract law.

Brauer v. Shaw,[131] an 1897 case, furnishes an even clearer example of the conduct/state of mind dichotomy. In that case a steamship company was negotiating with cattle shippers for space on the Warren line of steamships, sailing from Boston to Liverpool in May 1892. The company wrote a letter to the shippers stating that they "would probably accept fifty shillings" a head as the price for the space "if reply promptly," and adding that they should feel "duty bound to let [the space] to the first man making the best bid." The shippers responded by telegraphing a modified offer for the space. The company then telegraphed back, "Referring our letter yesterday first offer for number named has preference three parties considering. Wire quick if you want it." To this telegram the shippers responded, by telegram, "Have closed all your May spaces as per letter.''[132]

These exchanges were not, however, treated by the parties as concluding arrangements. Later in the same day on which the shippers had made their modified offer the company telegraphed them, "Subject prompt reply will let you May space fifty-two six." Twelve minutes after receiving this telegram the shippers responded accepting the offer. Their response, however, was not communicated until nearly an hour after they sent it, and in the meantime the company telegraphed them revoking the offer. By the time the shippers received this telegram, the company had already received their telegram accepting the offer. The question was whether a contract had been made between the parties for the shipment of cattle at fifty-two shillings, six-pence a head.

The case posed a classic puzzle in contract law. When difficulties in transmission result in an offer that has subsequently been revoked being accepted before notice of the revocation reaches the offeree, through no fault of the offeror, is there a contract? In *Brauer* the company clearly did not ''intend'' to let the space to the shippers at fifty-two shillings, sixpence a head; indeed they had informed the ship-pers that they had abandoned their previous inclination to do that. Through no fault of their own the shippers had not received that information. But, technically speak-ing, ''the offer was outstanding when it was accepted,'' since notice of revocation had not reached the shippers. Should the shippers be disabled from accepting the offer because the defendants had decided to revoke it?

Holmes, for the court, held no. There was a valid contract; the offer had been made and accepted before notice of its being revoked had reached the shippers. The relationship between the parties suggested that they were dealing with a fluctuating, competitive market for cattle space, and that the opportunity to secure that space at a favorable price turned on a shipper's prompt response to outstanding offers. Pre-vious dealings between the parties, in fact, suggested that the price had already fluctuated two shillings sixpence in one day. ''By their choice and act,'' Holmes maintained, the company ''brought about a relation between themselves and the [shippers] which the [shippers] could turn into a contract by an act on their part and authorized the plaintiffs to understand and to assume that that relation existed.'' Since the shippers ''had acted in good faith on the assumption,'' the company could not complain.

Here again the question of contract formation was analyzed by reference to exter-nal evidence and objective standards. Whatever the company's intent about the ask-ing price for cattle space on its May sailings, it had made an outstanding offer for space at fifty-two shillings sixpence. After having done so, it may have deeply regretted that act, and hastily revoked the offer. But so long as an offer was made before an acceptance, Holmes said, it did not matter whether it was made a longer or a shorter time before, so long as it was outstanding at the time of the accep-tance.[133]

''The whole doctrine of contract,'' Holmes had written in *The Common Law,* ''is formal and external.''[134] The point of *Brauer,* for him, was that whatever the parties' ''intent'' in leasing space for cattle on an Atlantic crossing, they had created mechanisms for a ''reciprocal conventional inducement''[135] to lease that space. Once those mechanisms were in place a contract existed to lease the space at a given price. It did not matter whether at the time the contract came into being neither party wanted to lease it at that price. The ''formal'' and ''external'' devices for contract formation had come into existence.

A final example of Holmes' commitment to the objectification of contract theory was the slightly bizarre case of *Martin v. Meles.*[136] There a group of leather manu-facturers agreed to contribute sums of $500 each to a committee appointed by the

Massachusetts Morocco Manufacturers Association. The sums were for "legal and other expenses . . . in defending and protecting our interests against any demands or suits growing out of Letters Patent for Chrome Tanning." The expectation was that "in case of suit against any of [the manufacturers] the committee shall take charge thereof and apply as much of the fund as may be needed to the expense of the same." The agreement also stipulated that "in no case shall the committee demand from any manufacturer . . . a total of subscriptions to exceed the sum of two thousand dollars."[137]

The committee was appointed and "undertook the defence of suits." Some months after the signing of the agreement in which the committee came into existence the Meles leather firm, which had not been a member of the Massachusetts Morocco Manufacturers Association but had signed the agreement, dissolved and two of its members "ceased tanning leather." They notified the committee of this act and refused to pay the remainder of their subscription to the committee. When sued for the balance of their subscription, they argued that no contract existed between them and the committee because there had been no consideration for their promise to pay the subscription.

This would seem to be a compelling argument for Holmes, given his view that consideration was not simply any benefit to a promisor or any detriment incurred by the promisee, but only those benefits and detriments that demonstrated evidence of "the relation of reciprocal conventional inducement . . . between consideration and promise."[138] The problem with the arrangement in *Martin* was that it was hard to imagine, at first blush, how the Meles firm was benefited by the committee's acceptance of the subscribers' money if the committee had not applied that money to the defense of any claim against the Meles firm. If one argued that the consideration for the Meles firm's promise was the committee's agreement to make use of that money should the need arise, it was still hard to imagine why the Meles firm would be benefited by subsequent acts of the committee when the firm had been dissolved and those of its members who were parties to the suit had left the leather tanning business. Finally, there was the problem that if the consideration for the Meles firm's promise to make subscription payments was the committee's reliance on those payments, it was unlikely that the committee would have done the acts it had promised to do whether the Meles firm had promised to subscribe or not, given that the Meles firm was not a member of the association that entered into the agreement with the committee.

Holmes nonetheless decided that there had been sufficient consideration for the Meles firm's promise. His opinion for the court first maintained that [the Meles firm] still had an interest [in the committee's defense of leather tanners] after going out of business, as they still were liable to be sued." The committee, moreover, had not simply promised to apply funds to legal defenses as they came in; it had promised to "undertak[e] . . . active and more or less arduous duties, . . . and mak[e] expenditures and incur liabilities" whether payments had come in or not. Further, although in consideration cases "[t]here must be some ground for saying that the acts done in reliance upon the promise were contemplated by the form of the transaction either impliedly or in terms as the conventional inducement, motive and equivalent for the promise," courts had "gone very great lengths in discovering the implication of such an equivalence."[139] Thus consideration could be found either in the promise or the subsequent acts of the committee.

At first glance Holmes' reasoning seems odd. To be sure, when the Meles firm first agreed to subscribe to the arrangement with the committee they had common interests with the other subscribers, even though they were not members of the Massachusetts Morocco Manufacturers Association. But after their firm dissolved, their only interest would seem to be in the defense of lawsuits growing from patent disputes involving them, which would surely have a finite duration. Moreover, it would seem that the committee would have behaved in the same fashion whether or not the Meles firm contributed payments. So a "reciprocal conventional inducement" between the Meles firm and the committee appeared lacking, especially with respect to acts performed by the committee after the Meles firm dissolved. And the only payments in dispute were those the committee sought to obtain from the Meles firm after its dissolution.

A passage from Holmes' opinion in *Martin* suggests what was at stake for him in the case. After acknowledging the argument that "the acts of the committee would have been done whether the defendants promised or not, and therefore lose their competence as consideration because they cannot be said to have been done in reliance upon the promise," Holmes responded:

> But that is a speculation upon which courts do not enter. When an act has been done, to the knowledge of another party, which purports expressly to invite certain conduct on his part, and that conduct on his part follows, it is only under exceptional and peculiar circumstances that it will be inquired how far the act in truth was the motive for the conduct, whether in case of consideration . . . or fraud.[140]

Here again the distinction between subjective (motive) and objective (conduct) elements is taken by Holmes to be at the root of a contracts decision. So long as the "formal" and "external" features of an arrangement are in place, such as acts that invite conduct and conduct that follows from the acts, courts should not speculate as to motives. Holmes seems to be saying that, as a practical matter, the arrangement between the committee and the subscribers was a kind of mutual insurance pact, in which the committee could expect payments from *all* the subscribers over the length of the agreement, and the subscribers could expect that the committee would defend any and all of them against lawsuits. Thus it didn't matter that the Meles firm subsequently went out of existence and ceased to have a common interest with the other subscribers: their situation was no different from an extant leather tanning firm that was not sued. What mattered was that a pledge had been made that invited the committee to act, and that the committee had promised to act and may have engaged in some activities in keeping with that promise. The formal shell of a "reciprocal conventional inducement" existed.

Seen in this light, *Martin v. Meles* was another in a series of cases in which Holmes followed the goal he had set forth for contract law in *The Common Law*, that of stripping contract doctrine of subjective elements where possible. The principal technique that Holmes employed to accomplish this goal, we have noted, was the formalization of contractual arrangements and the consequent diminution of their subjective or idiosyncratic dimensions. The backdrop against which such arrangements were evaluated was that of tort law, reasonable conduct under the circumstances. In making evaluations with that standard in mind Holmes repeatedly found arrangements to be in place that met the formal criteria for contract formation but were not what at least one of the "contracting" parties wanted. Neither the mill-owner in *Hawkins* nor the whip manufacturer in *Hobbs* nor the company in *Branch* nor the firm in *Meles* had desired that the arrangement that Holmes sanctioned come to pass. They had either sought to modify it or wanted to avoid it altogether. Holmes' decisions seemed to assume that their expectations were not controlling in light of what a reasonable person under the circumstances would have expected or in light of their conduct. In the main, Holmes was faithful in his Massachusetts contracts decisions to the principles of contract law he had affirmed in *The Common Law*.

～

When Holmes had settled into his second decade on the Supreme Court of the United States a group of early twentieth-century intellectuals began a process of canonizing his attitude toward constitutional adjudication. The story of that canonization process is reserved for a later chapter, but the attributes Holmes' supporters singled out for praise can be rendered simply enough at this stage. Holmes was regarded as an enlightened judge in the realm of constitutional law because he distinguished between judicial review of legislation affecting economic issues, where he advocated a deferential stance for judges, and judicial review of legislation affecting First Amendment rights, where he insisted on a more searching judicial scrutiny.

That characterization of Holmes was not without its difficulties, since it ignored both cases in which Holmes overturned economically based legislation on constitutional grounds[141] and cases in which he sustained legislative restrictions on speech.[142] But on the whole, especially during the 1920s, the characterization had some validity. In two cases decided during the 1931 Term, for example, Holmes joined a 5–4 majority invalidating a Minnesota statute allowing injunctions against newspapers that had printed allegedly defamatory material[143] and joined the same majority in sustaining a New Jersey statute regulating the fees paid to local agents by insurance companies against a Fourteenth Amendment due process challenge that claimed such arrangements violated a "liberty of contract."[144] The cases, taken together, suggested a double standard of review where speech interests and economic interests were concerned.

The opportunities Holmes had to construe provisions of the United States Constitution during his tenure on the SJC were limited. One reason was that the principal constitutional clause that had been read by early nineteenth-century courts as limiting the reach of state sovereignty—the Contracts Clause—had come to be read in a more restricted fashion by the years of Holmes' tenure, and another clause ostensibly placing limits on state regulation of private property, the Takings Clause of the Fifth Amendment, was treated as not applying against the states. Holmes decided a fair number of eminent domain cases and cases raising Contracts Clause issues during his time on the Massachusetts court, and in the overwhelming number of those cases sustained state insolvency legislation or eminent domain proceedings against constitutional challenges.[145] At the same time constitutional challenges to state legislation affecting First Amendment rights were few and far between, since the First Amendment had not been "incorporated" against the states under the Fourteenth Amendment's Due Process Clause, and state power to regulate expression was largely taken for granted.[146] There were thus comparatively few occasions when Holmes as a Massachusetts judge confronted the kinds of issues that were to play so important a part in the growth of his visibility as a Supreme Court Justice.

To the extent that he did consider constitutional issues during his Massachusetts tenure, however, Holmes gave no indication of treating economic and noneconomic issues differently. His position toward legislative power to restrict economic rights was consistently deferential. So was his position toward legislative power to restrict the right of free speech. A few selected cases will illustrate. In those cases Holmes was asked to interpret provisions of the Massachusetts constitution rather than the Constitution of the United States, so one cannot conclude that he would have necessarily adopted the same stance toward federal constitutional issues. His positions were nonetheless suggestive of tendencies in his later career.

Rideout v. Knox,[147] an 1889 decision, tested the effect of the Massachusetts constitution on a state statute declaring that fences or like structures "unnecessarily exceeding six feet in height, maliciously erected or maintained for the purpose of annoying the owners or occupants of adjoining property" were private nuisances. In November 1886 a landowner in Lynn, Massachusetts, erected an eleven-foot fence on his lot that blocked the view from some of his neighbor's windows. The neighbor asked the landowner to remove it, and he refused, saying that it had been erected as a trellis on which to trail vines. When the neighbor set forth the statute, the landowner responded by arguing that the statute was unconstitutional as applied to him, since it interfered with vested property rights and since he lacked the malicious purpose necessary to come within the statute. The trial judge held that the statute was constitutional and instructed the jury that it could be satisfied if the jury found that while a motive to annoy the neighbor was not the dominant purpose for erecting the fence, it was enough to bring the landowner within the statute if that was one of his purposes. The jury found for the neighbor, awarding him damages of one cent.

Holmes held that the "spite fence" statute was constitutional but that the trial judge's instructions to the jury on motive were incorrect. He conceded that "at common law a man has a right to build a fence on his own land as high as he pleases, however much it may obstruct his neighbor's light and air." He also conceded that "to a large extent the power to use one's property malevolently . . . is an incident of property which cannot be taken away even by legislation." Thus the Massachusetts Constitution prevented the legislature from prohibiting "putting up stores or houses with malicious intent." But a boundary fence built over six feet high was a different matter. "Some small limitations of previously existing rights incident to property may be imposed for the sake of preventing a manifest evil." The difference between a justifiable "small limitation" and an unjustifiable interference with property rights was "only one of degree," Holmes acknowledged. But "most differences are, when nicely analyzed," and "difference of degree [was] one of the distinctions by which the right of the Legislature to exercise the police power is determined."[148]

It followed from Holmes' analysis, however, that the statute required an actual malevolent motive, one that "without which the fence would not have been built or maintained.'' The legislature sought to "restrain . . . aggressive annoyance of one neighbor by another.'' If a fence over six feet high was "necessary" to the land-owner, the statute did not apply. And in *Rideout* such a motive had been shown. Holmes pointed out that the statute might even apply to fences or structures erected before it had been passed, as the one in *Rideout* had been, if a dominant malevolent motive could be shown. A neighbor merely had to complain about the structure, and if the landowner gave the neighbor leave to take it down or justified putting it up by stating a benign motive, the landowner could successfully defend against an action by the neighbor. Hence retroactive application of the statute was not a problem since the statute effectuated only an "insignificant curtailment of the rights of prop-erty.''[149]

The *Rideout* case, as Holmes conceived it, did not represent a very sweeping use of the police power, because the statute, as he construed it, only applied to a narrow range of cases. The case is interesting primarily not because of Holmes' view on the question of deference to the legislature but because of his recognition that the motives for acts could be a concern of the law as much as acts themselves. He had taken the position in *The Common Law,* we have seen, that terms such as "intent" and "mal-ice" were not to be given subjective definitions in fields such as criminal law and torts, but were to be inferred from objectively determined conduct. But the erection of a "spite fence" posed a more complex problem. If a statute that defined fences above a certain height as presumptively spite fences and proscribed them as nui-sances was a legitimate exercise of the police power, then it was not acts alone that the legislature was seeking to prevent, but certain motives that led to those acts. If the legislature had a legitimate interest in preventing the "aggressive annoyance" of one neighbor by another, it apparently had an interest in discerning "aggressive" motives. At the time Holmes wrote his opinion in *Rideout* he was rethinking the role of "malice" and "intent" in the law, and was eventually to conclude, as his "Priv-ilege, Malice, and Intent" article demonstrated, that subjective malice was some-times an important element of torts or crimes. Statutes such as the one in *Rideout* may have helped point him toward that conclusion.

The "intent" feature of *Rideout* was thus more central than the deference feature, although Holmes gave a clue to his attitude toward legislative regulation by arguing that all "vested rights" cases ultimately turned on questions of degree, and the legislature was in the business of making distinctions on the basis of degree under its police powers. In 1891, however, came two cases in which the attitude that Holmes exhibited as a Supreme Court Justice toward judicial review of legislation affecting economic interests was more clearly revealed. The first of those cases was *Commonwealth v. Perry,*[150] testing the constitutionality of a Massachusetts statute preventing employers in the weaving industry from imposing fines or withholding wages for imperfections that arose during weaving.

In *Perry* a weaver named Fielding had made a contract with his employer, Perry, that provided that Perry could deduct compensation from his wages once Perry had inspected Fielding's work and determined that it contained imperfections. After the passage of the statute Fielding sued Perry for the money deducted, claiming the deductions were illegal, and Perry defended on the ground that the statute was uncon-stitutional as a violation of "fundamental principles" and as an example of "class legislation."[151] In particular, the defendant claimed that the statute violated Article I of the Declaration of Rights of the Massachusetts Constitution, which defined among the "natural, inalienable rights of man" the right "of acquiring, possessing, and protecting property."[152]

A majority of the SJC agreed with the defendant, employing an analysis reminiscent of the "liberty of contract" doctrine Holmes subsequently was to find troublesome in such cases as *Lochner v. New York.*[153] "The right to acquire, possess and protect property," Justice Marcus Knowlton wrote for the *Perry* majority, "includes the right to make reasonable contracts, which shall be under the protection of the law." A statute "which forbids the making of such contracts, or attempts to nullify them, . . . violates fundamental principles or rights which are expressly recognized in our Constitution."[154]

Holmes dissented, and his language was strikingly like that which he was to employ in "liberty of contract" cases that came before the Supreme Court of the United States during his tenure as an Associate Justice. "The prohibition [of conduct given constitutional protection]," he said,

> must be found in the words of the Constitution, either as expressed or implied upon a fair and historical construction. What words of the United States or State Constitution are relied on? . . . So far as has been pointed out to me, I do not see that [the statute] interferes with the right of acquiring, possessing, and protecting property any more than the laws against usury or gaming. In truth, I do not think that that clause of the Bill of Rights has any application. It might be urged, perhaps, that the power to make reasonable laws impliedly prohibits the making of unreasonable ones, and that this law is unreasonable. If I assume that this construction of the Constitution is correct, and that speaking as a political economist, I should agree in condemning the law, still I should not be willing or think myself authorized to overturn legislation on that ground, unless I thought that an honest difference of opinion was impossible, or pretty nearly so.[155]

In this passage one can see the seeds of a perspective that was to become characteristic of Holmes as a Supreme Court justice. He made a sharp distinction between his own views as a "political economist" and his duties as a judge. He denied that he could overturn legislation simply because he thought it "unreasonable" unless he was clear that reasonable people could not differ on that point. In short, he declared himself prepared to tolerate legislative restraints on "property rights," whatever he thought of their efficacy, up to the point where they were clearly and indisputably unreasonable.

In the same year that he dissented in *Perry* Holmes wrote a separate statement in an advisory opinion the SJC justices issued on the constitutionality of the legislature's enacting a law conferring on cities or towns the power to purchase coal and wood for the use of fuel and sell it to their citizens at reduced rates. Five justices stated that they regarded the law as unconstitutional because it represented taxation "for purposes of private interest instead of a public use."[156] That distinction, which had been adopted by the Supreme Court of the United States,[157] was intended to restrict governmental functions to those historically conceived as "public." A majority of the justices maintained that buying and selling wood and coal for fuel was "a well known form of private business" whose pursuit did not "require the exercise of . . . powers derived from the Legislature."[158]

Holmes issued a brief separate statement in which he argued that "when money is taken to enable a public body to offer to the public without discrimination an article of general necessity, the purpose is no less public when that article is wood or coal than when it is water, or gas, or electricity, or education." The majority had distinguished public ownership of gas and electrical utilities on the ground that those entities regarded distribution of energy sources over a wide scale that would be impractical if left in private hands. Holmes thought that wood or coal were no less articles of general necessity than gas or electricity. He added one of his characteristic disclaimers: "The need or expediency of such legislation is not for us to consider." This would seem to suggest that he was not resting the power of the legislature to authorize cities or towns to go into the wood or coal business on any economic emergency. His position thus anticipated the emergence of governmental entities as economic actors in the twentieth century. The fact that Holmes expressed his position in a request for an advisory opinion adds to the significance of his views, since the SJC justices were expected to declare their views separately when they were asked for advisory opinions.

Not all Holmes' constitutional decisions involving legislative power to affect economic rights were solicitous of legislative prerogatives. In *Miller v. Horton*,[159] an 1891 decision, a Massachusetts statute had authorized the killing of horses "in all cases of farcy or glanders," contagious diseases. The statute provided for no compensation to the owner, and no hearing on the horse's condition. Another section of the statute authorized compensation for the burial expenses of the owner, but not for the value of the horse. A horse was condemned by the board of cattle commissioners of the town of Rehobeth, and two men were instructed to go to its owner's house and kill it. The owner resisted, and produced two veterinary surgeons, who examined the horse and concluded that it had no communicable disease. The commissioners refused to modify their order, and the horse was subsequently killed, whereupon the owner sued those who had killed it for its value, arguing that the statute that authorized the killing of an animal infected with a contagious disease was unconstitutional.

Holmes upheld the statute, but read it narrowly as authorizing the killing of horses only when they were in fact infected with farcy or glanders. The defendants in *Miller* had argued that this reading would undermine the process contemplated by the statute, because it would mean that in those instances where commissioners erroneously determined that a horse was infected, those instructed to kill the horse might be liable for its value, and thus "few people could be found to carry out orders on these terms."[160] Holmes rejected that argument because such a reading of the statute meant that an animal could be condemned without a hearing, and no recourse existed against those who subsequently killed the animal. Having no hearing in such cases raised the question "whether, if the owner of the horse denies that his horse falls within the class declared to be [nuisances], the Legislature can make the *ex parte* decision of a board . . . conclusive upon him."[161] That procedure, Holmes felt, would violate the provision in the Massachusetts Constitution that "no subject shall be deprived of his property but by the judgment of his peers." If a hearing could not be required before horses with contagious diseases were killed, Holmes maintained, it could be held afterward, with the owners entitled to compensation if the horses were found not to have been infected. As Holmes put it in summary:

> [T]here is a pretty important difference of degree . . . between regulating the precautions to be taken in keeping property, especially property sought to be brought into the state, and ordering its destruction. We cannot admit that the Legislature has an unlimited right to destroy property without compensation, on the ground that destruction is not an appropriation to public use within Article X of the Declaration of Rights. . . . And even if we assume that it could authorize some trifling amount of innocent property to be destroyed as a necessary means to the abatement of a nuisance, still if [the statute] had added in terms that such healthy animals as should be killed by mistake for diseased ones should not be paid for, we should deem it a serious question whether such a provision could be upheld.[162]

Miller suggests that although Holmes was more inclined than his colleagues to permit legislative regulation of economic activity, he was prepared to acknowledge that in some cases if the regulation was too intrusive, or unaccompanied by procedural safeguards, it amounted to a taking.

In another line of cases, those involving freedom of speech issues, Holmes suggested that government could restrict the noneconomic rights of its citizens as extensively as it could regulate their economic rights. In *McAuliffe v. New Bedford*,[163] for example, a policeman employed by the city of New Bedford had been removed by the mayor for violating a police regulation prohibiting the solicitation of money for political purposes and the membership of city employees in political committees. The policeman sued the city: among his arguments was the claim that his constitutional rights of speech and association under the Massachusetts constitution had been violated. Holmes responded:

> [T]here is nothing in the [Massachusetts] constitution . . . to prevent the city from attaching obedience to [the] rule [against political participation] as a condition to the office of policeman, and making it part of the good conduct required. The petitioner may have a constitutional right to talk politics, but he has no constitutional right to be a policeman. There are few employments for hire in which the servant does not agree to suspend his constitutional rights of free speech as well as of idleness by the implied terms of his contract. The servant cannot complain, as he takes the employment on the terms which are offered him. On the same principle that city may impose any reasonable condition upon holding offices within its control. This condition seems to us reasonable.[164]

One might notice that Holmes analogized public employment to private employment, treating the city of New Bedford as the equivalent of one who hires a servant. But if the policeman had "a constitutional right to talk politics," it would seem to be a right against the government rather than against private individuals, who could dismiss their employees if they objected to the employees' political views. *McAuliffe* raised the question whether there is a difference, in free speech cases, between the government as a lawmaking body and the government as a proprietor or employer. If the Massachusetts legislature passed a statute providing penalties for speaking on behalf of political candidates, Holmes seemed to think this would raise constitutional problems under the Constitution of Massachusetts;[165] why would it be different if the legislature dismissed one of its employees for stating his or her political views? The question is currently treated as a complicated one of First Amendment law, resting on a distinction between the government as proprietor and the government as regulator. Holmes' *McAuliffe* opinion seems to have assumed the existence of that distinction but did not explore its ramifications.

Holmes continued analogizing the powers of government to those of a private employer in *Commonwealth v. Davis*,[166] an 1895 case building on *McAuliffe*. William F. Davis, a lay preacher, was convicted for making a speech to his "congregation," the crowd peopling the Boston Common, without securing a permit from the city of Boston. He argued that the ordinance, since it conditioned speaking in a public place on securing a permit, was an unconstitutional restriction on free speech under the Massachusetts Constitution. Holmes conceded that an "ordinance . . . directed at free speech generally," such as one prohibiting public picnics or open-air dances, might be unconstitutional, but this ordinance was "directed toward the modes in which Boston Common may be used." He continued:

> For the Legislature absolutely or conditionally to forbid public speaking in a highway or public park is no more an infringement of the rights of a member of the public than for the owner of a private house to forbid it in his house. When no proprietary right interferes, the Legislature may end the right of the public to enter upon the public place by putting an end to the dedication to public uses. So it may take the lesser step of limiting the public use to certain purposes.[167]

"The argument [of unconstitutionality]," Holmes noted, "involves the same kind of fallacy that was dealt with in *McAuliffe v. New Bedford*."[168]

Davis provided another example of Holmes' analogizing the legislature to a private landowner, and treating the free speech issue as derivative of "proprietary rights." Since the government owned the land, it could prevent citizens from speaking on it. He added an argument that the greater power begets the lesser: since the legislature could eliminate public parks altogether, it could regulate their use. Both arguments seem specious as applied to the *Davis* case. Under the rationale of the first argument a city could prevent its citizens from speaking on the public streets because it owned them. Under the rationale of the second argument a city could create a public park and then restrict access to the park to citizens of a particular race. Holmes' position was in fact dependent on the same distinction between the government as proprietor and the government as regulator that he had implicitly made in *McAuliffe*. But he did not rest his arguments on that distinction. Instead he invoked a sweeping generality that implied that sovereign power could be made the basis for indiscriminate restrictions of constitutional rights. His approach begged a number of questions, and the Supreme Court of the United States eventually disapproved of Holmes' position in *Davis*.[169]

~

One set of cases from Holmes' tenure on the Supreme Judicial Court of Massachusetts remains to be considered, a set that includes his best known opinions as a state judge. The first was *Vegelahn v. Guntner*.[170] In that case a group of upholsterers who worked in a furniture factory in Boston had asked their employer for higher wages and shorter hours. The employer, Frederick Vegelahn, refused, and fired the workers' business agent, George Guntner. In response the workers went on strike and sought to persuade tradesmen not to deal with Vegelahn and insurance companies not to continue to insure his business. He advertised for new workers, and the strikers organized a patrol of pickets to discourage applicants for the positions and dramatize their grievances. After fights broke out, Vegelahn came before Holmes, sitting in the SJC's equity session, and asked for an injunction restraining the picketing and the "boycott" of Vegelahn's products.

Holmes found that in addition to the "persuasion" of persons not to deal with Vegelahn and the patrolling, there had been some "threats of personal injury or unlawful harm." He enjoined the workers from engaging in those threats in the future, but allowed the picketing, "so far as it confined itself to persuasion and giving notice of the strike," to continue.[171] Vegelahn appealed to the full Supreme Judicial Court, on this occasion made up of seven justices. In an opinion for five of the justices, Justice Charles Allen found that the picketing was "an unlawful interference with the rights both of employer and of employed." Employers had "a right to engage all persons who are willing to work for [them] at such prices as may be mutually agreed upon," Allen argued, and "persons employed or seeking employment have a corresponding right to enter into or remain in the employment of any person or corporation willing to employ them." He declared that "[t]hese rights are secured by the Constitution itself," citing *Commonwealth v. Perry*.[172] Allen enjoined the workers against persuasion and threats of any kind, as well as against picketing.[173]

Holmes dissented. He began his analysis by suggesting that *Vegelahn* was a classic case where the intentional infliction of temporal damage had occurred, and the question was whether that infliction of damage was justified. "[O]n the question of what shall amount to a justification," he felt, "judicial reasoning seems to me often to be inadequate." This was because "[t]he true grounds of decision [in such cases] are considerations of policy and social advantage, and it is vain to suppose that solutions can be attained merely by logic and the general propositions of law which nobody disputes." He noted that for some time the competition of one business with another had been regarded as justified even though the competitor "expects and intends to ruin [the established business] and succeeds in his intent." The competitor's actions were deemed justified because it was assumed "that free competition is worth more to society than it costs." So long as "force or threats or force" were not used, competition justified inflicting damage on one's competition.[174]

But in *Vegelahn*, Holmes noted, the majority had thought that competition "between employers and employed," or competition involving "a combination of persons," stood on a different footing. He thought this a mistaken idea. "[I]t is plain from the slightest consideration of practical affairs, or the most superficial reading of industrial history," he said, "that free competition means combination, and that the organization of the world, now going on so fast, means an ever increasing might

and scope of combination.'' He thought it ''futile to set our faces against this tendency,'' which was ''inevitable unless the fundamental axioms of society, and even
the fundamental conditions of life, are to be changed.''[175]

At this point Holmes had elevated *Vegelahn* from a case raising the narrow
question of whether a particular form of intentional infliction of temporal damage
was justified to a dissertation about industrial relations. He expanded on the latter
significance of the case:

> One of the eternal conflicts out of which life is made up is that between the
> effort of every man to get the most he can for his services, and that of society,
> disguised under the name of capital, to get his services for the least possible
> return. Combination on the one side is patent and powerful. Combination on
> the other is the necessary and desirable counterpart, if the battle is to be carried
> on in a fair and equal way. If it be true that workingmen may combine with a
> view, among other things, to getting as much as they can for their labor, just as
> capital may combine with a view toward getting the greatest possible return, it
> must be true that combined capital has to support their interests by argument,
> persuasion, and the bestowal or refusal of those advantages which they
> otherwise lawfully control. I can remember when many people thought that,
> apart from violence or breach of contract, strikes were wicked, as organized
> refusals to work. I suppose that intelligent economists have given up that
> notion today. I feel pretty confident that they equally will abandon the idea
> that an organized refusal by workmen of social intercourse with a man who
> shall enter their antagonist's employ is wrong, if it is dissociated from any
> threat of violence, and is made for the sole object of prevailing if possible in a
> contest with their employer about the rate of wages. The fact, that the
> immediate object of the act by which the benefit to themselves is to be gained
> is to injure their antagonist, does not necessarily make it unlawful, any more
> than when a great house lowers the price of certain goods for the purpose, and
> with the effect, of driving a small antagonist from the business.[176]

Holmes' dissent in *Vegelahn v. Guntner* was uncharacteristic of his Massachusetts opinions. He had prefaced it by saying that it had been his ''almost invariable
practice'' of deferring to his colleagues ''in silence . . . when I have been unable to
bring [them] to share my convictions,'' but he was departing from the practice in
Vegelahn because ''it will be of advantage to sound thinking to have the less popular
view of the law stated.''[177] But his statement of ''the law'' was in fact a statement
of economic theory in the arena of labor relations. By framing the case as a ''justification'' case and by noting that in such cases the true grounds of decision were
policy considerations, he had exposed the majority's reasoning as based on the policy
that combinations of labor were not justifiable even though combinations of capital
were. The only difference between a ''great house'' cutting its prices so as to drive
a smaller competitor out of business and a group of workers encouraging others to
boycott the products of an employer with whom they were having a wage dispute
was that one competitor was ''capital'' and the other ''labor.'' Just as labor-based
strikes had come to be an accepted feature of labor relations, so, Holmes predicted,

would peaceful picketing and boycotts. Freed from the confines of a majority opinion, he indulged his passion for theorizing.

Vegelahn v. Guntner became Holmes' best known state court opinion. He wrote Clare Castletown after his dissent came down that "[m]y dissent in the boycott case gets the adhesion of some who know what they are talking about and the abuse of a good many fools and incompetents including some newspapers,"[178] and that an acquaintance had told him that "he was at a dinner of men of weight in [Boston] and that majority opinion condemned me as a very dangerous man (i.e. in my judicial tendencies)." "I dare say I may have to pay for it, practically, before I die," he added.[179] At the same time he reportedly told a young friend that "I have just handed down an opinion that shuts me off forever from judicial promotion."[180] But the *Harvard Law Review* took a different view of Holmes' opinion in *Vegelahn*, indicating that while "[m]ost of the public . . . have a sufficient prejudice against anything that could be called 'picketing' to approve of the sweeping injunction issued by [the majority in *Vegelahn*], . . . the more carefully . . . the dissenting opinions, especially that of Mr. Justice Holmes, are studied, the more doubtful the question becomes." "It would seem," the *Review* continued, "that there is a serious discrepancy between the results reached in the cases of competition between rivals in the same trade, and the decisions in the cases where the struggle for economic advantage is between employers and employed." In *Vegelahn*, the *Review* suggested, the Massachusetts court had perhaps "gone too far in the dangerous direction of interfering with the struggle of economic forces."[181]

Most gratifying of all to Holmes may have been the *Review*'s notation that his "Privilege, Malice, and Intent" article had "cover[ed] the very ground of the *Vegelahn* case, and that "[n]othing could be more apposite to [*Vegelahn*]" than Holmes' comment in that article that "[t]he ground of decision really comes down to a proposition of policy . . . and suggests a doubt whether judges with different economic sympathies might not decide such a case differently."[182]

Four years after *Vegelahn* came *Plant v. Woods*,[183] another labor boycott case. In *Plant v. Woods* the boycott was engendered not by actions of an employer, but by competition between two labor unions of painters and decorators. One of the unions, in an effort to get members of the rival union to join its ranks, declared all such members "non union men," produced reinstatement certificates for those members and urged them to sign them, and then informed the members' employers of their identity and encouraged them to persuade recalcitrant employees to sign the reinstatement certificates. Although the union's interviews with the employers were peaceful, and it did not ask the employers to discharge the employees, a special master found that the union "intend[ed] that employers of [the recalcitrant employees] should fear trouble in their business if they continued to employ such men, and . . . [the trouble would be] in the nature of strikes or a boycott."[184]

A majority of the Supreme Judicial Court of Massachusetts enjoined the union from conspiring to compel the recalcitrant members to join them by threatening strikes or boycotts. While Justice John Hammond, writing for the majority, said that the case was a "justification" case, such as *Vegelahn v. Guntner*, and that Holmes' "Privilege, Malice, and Intent" article was relevant to it, he concluded that a "right to dispose of one's labor with full freedom" was implicated, and that "[t]he necessity that the plaintiffs should join this association is not so great, nor is its relation to the rights of the defendants, as compared with the right of the plaintiffs to be free from molestation, such as to bring the acts of the defendants under the shelter of the principles of trade competition.''[185] Hammond's analytical framework treated the inquiry into whether intentional interference with economic relationships was ''justified'' as requiring a balancing of the privilege of ''trade competition'' against the right ''to be free from molestation'' in pursuit of one's trade, and concluded that competition needed to yield. It ignored, as the majority opinion in *Vegelahn* had, the fact that enterprises routinely interfered with the economic relationships of their competitors by price structuring and other competitive devices.

Holmes again dissented, giving as a reason for departing from his typical practice of ''accept[ing] the law from the majority'' that Hammond's opinion had ''seen fit to adopt the mode of approaching the question which I believe to be the correct one, and to open an issue which otherwise I might have thought closed.''[186] By that he meant that the majority could simply have cited *Vegelahn* for the proposition that competition alone was not a sufficient justification for strikes or boycotts. Instead Hammond had adopted the analysis Holmes had set forth in *Vegelahn* and his ''Privilege, Malice, and Intent'' article balancing property rights against the goal of competition as part of a search for ''privilege'' and ''justification.'' Under that analysis, Holmes said, the issue in *Plant* was ''narrowed to the question whether, assuming that some purposes would be a justification, the purpose in this case of the threatened boycotts and strikes was such as to justify the threats.''[187]

Holmes found that the union's purpose in *Plant v. Woods* was ''to strengthen [it] as a preliminary means to enable it to make a better fight on questions of wages or other matters of clashing interests.'' The issue on which he differed from the other judges, he said, was whether the purpose of making unions more cohesive and stronger, so that they could better represent the interests of workers in their negotiations with management, was a legitimate one. On that issue, he concluded, ''unity of organization is necessary to make the contest of labor effectual.''[188]

Having not only suggested that union solidarity was a legitimate justification for interference with economic relationships, but that strikes and boycotts, if peaceably conducted, were also justified, Holmes then again indulged himself in a dissertation on economic theory. ''[A]lthough the law may not always reach ultimate economic conceptions,'' he declared, ''I think it well to add that I cherish no illusions as to the meaning and effect of strikes.'' He particularized:

> While I think the strike a lawful instrument in the universal struggle of life, I think it pure phantasy to suppose that there is a body of capital of which labor as a whole secures a larger share by that means. The annual product, subject to an infinitesimal deduction for the luxuries of the few, is directed to consumption by the multitude, and is consumed by the multitude, always. Organization and strikes may get a larger share for the members of the organization, but if they do, they get it at the expense of the less organized and less powerful portion of the laboring mass. They do not create something out of nothing. It is only by divesting our minds of questions of ownership and other machinery of distribution, and by looking solely at the question of

consumption—asking ourselves what is the annual product, who consumes it, and what changes would or could we make—that we can keep in the world of realities. But, subject to the qualifications which I have expressed, I think it lawful for a body of workmen to try by combination to get more than they now are getting, although they do it at the expense of their fellows, and to that end to strengthen their union by the boycott and the strike.[189]

In this paragraph one gets a glimpse of the distinctive combination of social Darwinism and Malthusianism that characterized Holmes as a political economist. While he assumed that life was a "universal struggle" and that strikes were simply a weapon in it, he thought that the allocation of resources in society was largely fixed, apparently by the class structure. There was allegedly a finite "annual product" that was available to be "consumed by the multitude," and if one portion of the "laboring mass" secured a larger share of that product for itself, it would only be at the expense of another portion. Holmes did not explain why an "infinitesimal deduction for the luxuries of the few" from this product would invariably take place, or why it would be "infinitesimal." Nor did he explain why "only by divesting our minds of questions of ownership and other machinery of distribution" and looking solely at consumption would economic theorists "keep in the world of realities." One could have seen cases such as *Plant v. Woods* as efforts on the part of unions to strengthen themselves, through pressure for solidarity, so that they could ultimately achieve greater control—through higher wages, fringe benefits, and better working conditions—of the means of producing goods in their industry. One might say that for Holmes to see those efforts as ultimately linked to "who consumes . . . the annual product" was to adopt a rather narrow view of late nineteenth-century economic life.

The point of Holmes' dissents in *Vegelahn* and *Plant v. Woods,* however, was that his judicial colleagues had simply regarded competition through the mechanism of strikes or boycotts as presumptively illegal. That was another way of saying that organized labor was an illegitimate form of competition. While Holmes' view of strikes and boycotts may have been colored by his belief that they were ultimately ineffectual, it was nonetheless in keeping with "the world of realities" in late nineteenth-century economic relations, in that workers had increasingly come to recognize that in many instances their interests were as "competitive" with those of their employers as were the interests of fellow producers. Holmes recognized that if the economic world was a "struggle," collective competition was inevitable as individual competition, and a strike or a boycott was no different than a price cut designed to affect the presence of a new producer in the market. That was why he thought legislative efforts to restrict the "combination" of enterprises in the name of "competition" incoherent. For him combination and competition went hand in hand.

The *Vegelahn–Plant v. Woods* sequence, because of the controversial nature of its subject matter, gave Holmes his greatest visibility as a state judge. When he was appointed to the Chief Justiceship of Massachusetts the *Albany Law Journal* reprinted a reaction in the Boston *Herald.* The *Herald* had suggested that "Judge Holmes may seem a radical, yet a practical one," and cited *Vegelahn* as an example. "The quality of a radical," the *Herald* noted, "is perhaps strikingly shown in his stand on industrial questions. . . . Strange as it may seem for a man of his environments, his legal opinions have leaned to the side of the laborer. . . . He thinks . . . that . . . workingmen may combine for getting the most they can for their labor, just as capital may combine with a view of getting the greatest possible return." And "if workingmen may combine for getting the most they can for their labor," the *Herald* continued, "just as capital may combine with a view to getting the greatest possible return, it must be true that when combined they have the same liberty that combined capital has to support their interests by argument, persuasion, and the bestowal or refusal of those advantages which they otherwise lawfully control."[190] The *Herald* did not treat these views as wrongheaded or heretical. It noted that "[a]s a magistrate [Holmes] has shown much learning and profound thinking."[191] In discussing Holmes' "stand in industrial questions" the *Herald* was ignoring Holmes' response to personal injuries suffered by industrial workers, which, we have seen, one could hardly characterize as "radical."

~

Despite *Vegelahn, Plant v. Woods,* and a few other memorable cases, Holmes was accurate in describing his Massachusetts cases as, on the whole, "trifling and transitory." The structure of the Supreme Judicial Court had contributed to that state of affairs, since the Full Court was required to hear appeals from many of the decisions that its members rendered singly during their assignments to equity or domestic relations or criminal sessions. This meant a large docket, requiring summary deliberations and encouraging short opinions. Moreover, no doubt in part because of the SJC's structure, separate opinions and dissents were discouraged. The typical Holmes opinion, then, was a case on appeal, usually one-sided in its issues, involving a comparatively trivial matter, in which Holmes was had been assigned to write for the majority. Under such circumstances, one might express surprise at the comparatively large number of opinions in which Holmes was able to persuade his colleagues to endorse views consistent with those which he had advanced in his scholarship.[192]

Far from being frustrated by the nature of his work as a state court judge, however, Holmes seemed to revel in it. In addition to characterizing his tenure as "the twenty happiest years of my life," he wrote Ellen Curtis in 1901 that "[w]e are smashing through the docket & everything is going with whiz," and that "I feel like Dr. Somebody who said that pure surgery was the highest pleasure of which the human mind was capable."[193] "The joy of life," he had said in his speech at the 1900 dinner honoring him, "is to put out one's power in some natural or useful or harmless way. . . . The rule of joy and the law of duty seem to me all one."[194]

One reason Holmes may have enjoyed being a justice on the Supreme Judicial Court of Massachusetts was the growing respect for his work demonstrated by specialist commentators. His dissent in *Commonwealth v. Perry,* for example, won praise from the *Harvard Law Review* as "the sounder and more liberal" view on the constitutionality of "wage fine" statutes. "Surely it is a permissible view," the *Review* argued, "that the Legislature, determining it to be for the public interest, should use its power for the protection of this large class." The view of the majority in *Perry,* the *Review* concluded, "would seem to be an extremely narrow one."[195]

In 1900 the *American Law Review* printed the entire text of Holmes' opinion for the Court in *Tyler v. Court of Registration,* sustaining the constitutionality of a Massachusetts land registration statute, taking pains to mention, as previously noted, "the . . . great reputation of the judge who wrote the majority opinion."[196] And in 1902, in recognition of his appointment to the Supreme Court of the United States, that review featured a commemorative piece on Holmes by one of its editors, the Boston lawyer and treatise writer Leonard A. Jones.[197]

Jones began his tribute by saying something that must have given Holmes mixed pleasure: "The famous and household name in literature of the father is supplemented by the son's famous and familiar name in jurisprudence."[198] He went on to survey Holmes' career, including a discussion of the Lowell Lectures that became *The Common Law.* "It was the privilege of the present writer," Jones said in connection with the lectures, "to hear these lectures which the lecturer delivered without referring to his manuscript, as if he were narrating offhand some interesting story, or telling of the happening of some event of absorbing interest. . . . The manner of delivery of these lectures seemed then, as it does now, a marvelous intellectual performance."[199] The publication of *The Common Law,* Jones suggested, "gave Mr. Holmes a great reputation at home and in Europe."[200]

Jones then turned to Holmes' judicial career. "Doubtless it has been [Holmes'] thought in rendering his judicial decisions," he suggested, "to make them harmonize so far as possible with ultimate scientific principles." Holmes did not, however, "think that it is the place of the judges to attempt to make a new system of law, or to reform it regardless of precedent and long established rules of practice." Jones quoted a passage from "Law in Science and Science in Law" in which Holmes said that "I do not expect or think it desirable that the judges should undertake to renovate the law. That is not their province . . . I am slow to consent to overruling a precedent, and think that our most important duty is to see that the judicial duel shall be fought out in the accustomed way." But then Holmes went on, Jones noted, to emphasize that a case represented "a conflict between two social desires," and that "[t]he social question is which desire is strongest at the point of conflict."[201]

Jones next emphasized Holmes' concern with theory in the law, quoting extensively from "The Path of the Law," his "high ideal of the law and the work of lawyers," quoting from an 1885 address to the Suffolk Bar Association and his 1886 address to Harvard undergraduates, and his advocacy of "a strenuous life," embodied in his "untiring work" on his profession.[202] He then turned to Holmes' decisions, typically emphasizing *Vegelahn* and *Plant v. Woods* as illustrations of Holmes' "independen[ce] in his views," and quoting from Holmes' comments on the efficacy of strikes in the latter case.[203] Jones concluded by predicting that Holmes' career on the Supreme Court of the United States "will be not less brilliant than it has been in every work in which he has been engaged and in every position he has been called upon to fill."[204]

Commentary of this sort may have led Holmes to feel that his efforts at extracting jurisprudential significance from trivial case had not entirely been overlooked. But it is likely that his greatest satisfaction in being a Massachusetts state judge came from another source. In the 1900 address he made a close connection between "joy" and "duty," and had suggested that the most vital pleasures of life came from the feeling that one was using one's intellectual powers to full advantage. Despite the backbreaking work of the court, Holmes could feel that he was consistently making decisions, doing his part to give some predictability to people's lives and to making interstitial contributions to the fabric of the law. His was a profession where one did not utter "smart things that cost you nothing"[205] from a cloister; it was continual exposure to the real world, whether it be industrial disputes or slip-and-fall cases or petty crimes or bailments or contracts among leather tanners. It was a profession that focused one's mind on action: one had, above all, to resolve disputes. It was a profession in which one could start every year with a crowded docket and watch the cases being swiftly disposed of, in which the results of one's work were tangible and immediate, not the ambiguous and muted results that followed from the publication of a work of scholarship.

It was, above all, a profession in which one's sense of "duty" could be easily grasped and readily pursued. As we have seen, Holmes had employed the concept of "duty" so regularly, in his scholarship as well as in his correspondence, that one would not be pressing very far into the realm of the psyche to suggest it had a special resonance for him. He had conceptualized a number of the episodes of his life as "duties": his enlistment and participation in the Civil War and his decision to leave military service; his work as a commentator on Kent's treatise. "Duty" had initially provided him with an organizing jurisprudential concept for his scholarly writing. The "duty" of a judge was easily discerned: it was to resolve controversies among antagonists who had turned to law rather than to violence or social disorder. By doing one's duty as a judge one was acting in the world. When that action gave one an opportunity to use one's intellectual powers, a feeling was created that one was participating in the "fight." For Holmes that was a feeling of joy. When he made his last speech before leaving the Supreme Judicial Court of Massachusetts to take up his position on the Supreme Court of the United States, he ended that speech with a characteristic description of the feeling:

> It is an adventure into the unknown. No man can go far who never sets down his foot until he knows that the sidewalk is under it. But, gentlemen, it is a great adventure, and that thought brings with it a mighty joy. To have the chance to do one's share in shaping the laws of the whole country spreads over one the hush that one used to feel when one was awaiting the beginning of a battle. . . . All is ready. Bugler, blow the charge.[206]

In likening his judicial duties to "an adventure into the unknown" and to "the beginning of a battle" Holmes was adopting the familiar metaphors by which he had sought to link his career as a scholar and a judge to his experience as a soldier. This tactic was by his sixtieth year habitual with him. But his judicial duties, if modest, had not only been fulfilling because they demonstrated to him that he had continued to be "in the fight" and that in leaving Harvard for a judgeship he had taken the "manly course." They had also been fulfilling in another, somewhat ironic respect.

In 1873, in his essay "The Theory of Torts," Holmes had made a generalization about the growth of the law, a portion of which has previously been quoted. He had said that

Two widely different cases suggest a general distinction, which is a clear one when stated broadly. But as new cases cluster around the opposite poles, and begin to approach each other, the distinction becomes more difficult to trace; the determinations are made one way or the other on a very slight predominance of feeling, rather than articulate reason; and at last a mathematical line is arrived at by the contact of contrary decisions, which is so far arbitrary that it might equally well have been drawn a little further to the one side or to the other.[207]

Holmes had formulated that generalization as a result of his historical studies. When he wrote it he had had comparatively little experience as a practitioner, none as a judge, and not a great deal as a scholar. His greatest amount of expertise had come from his work updating and analyzing Kent's treatise. Having studied the course of doctrine over time, he described it in terms of a metaphor drawn from science.

Twenty-six years later Holmes returned to the metaphor in the course of making a commentary on his work as a judge. "In our approach for exactness," he said of himself and his fellow judges,

we constantly tend to work out definite lines or equators to mark distinctions which we first notice as a difference of poles. . . . When [we] ha[ve] discovered that a difference is a difference of degree, that distinguished extremes have between them a penumbra into which one gradually shades into the other . . . [we realize that we have] to draw the line, and an advocate of more experience will show the arbitrariness of the line proposed by putting cases very near to it on one side or the other. But the theory of the law is that such lines exist. . . . We like to disguise the arbitrariness, we like to save ourselves the trouble of such nice and doubtful discriminations.[208]

Judging, then, had tended to confirm the insights Holmes had come to as a legal historian. He had initially observed the growth of legal doctrine taking place in an instinctive and arbitrary fashion; after having been a judge he knew that it took place that way. The excerpts and his *Patnoude* opinion were all of a piece: cases involved conflicts between "two principles of social desiderata" in which a "line ha[d] to be drawn to separate the domains of the irreconcilable desires." Such lines were arbitrary; judging involved "the sovereign prerogative of choice."

While the insight contained in these passages might first appear to be one calculated to reduce judging to a bureaucratic, relatively meaningless exercise, for Holmes it had a liberating effect. Because he had concluded that judging was not governed by formal doctrine but by choices between competing policies, he had come to realize that the most important thing that judges did was to decide cases. In his years on the SJC he had spent his energies on deciding cases. He had not belabored his explanations, although he had tried to "catch a glimpse of the universal in the particular" and to write up his results "with style."[209] A small number of cognoscenti had appreciated his achievement. If his dream of writing up the law in continuous philosophic series had dissipated over time, he had come to recognize what for him was the essence of judging.

Holmes' simultaneous realization that the "law of duty," as applied to judges, was to decide cases, and that by deciding cases one experienced the "joy" that came from the active use of one's mental powers was thus the primary source of his happiness in his years on the Supreme Judicial Court. But, as always with Holmes, there were ambiguities and complexities surrounding that state of happiness.

One set of ambiguities lay in Holmes' realization, very early in his judicial career, that his mind worked far more quickly and acutely than those of his judicial colleagues. In a letter to Nina Gray he spoke of being able to "twig in one minute what a man will take from 5 to 15 minutes to utter with due rherorical emphasis." While he couched that statement as a philosophical principle ("[t]hought is quick[er than speech]"), he was speaking of himself.[210] Holmes had a gift for penetrating to the core of an intellectual argument in a very brief time, and he knew it. That gift, coupled with his equally unusual capacity to express his thoughts rapidly and economically, resulted in his being able to do the work of an SJC justice in far less time than his colleagues. When one adds to the above gifts Holmes' "power of work," it is no surprise that he not only kept up easily with the burdensome tasks of his job, he sought to take on the primary responsibilities of his judicial colleagues. "I am tearing through cases writing decisions a deuced sight faster than I write you," he wrote Clare Castletown in 1897. "I should like to decide every case—and write every judgment of the court, but I'm afraid the boys wouldn't see it."[211]

The "joy" that Holmes found in simply doing the work of a judge—deciding cases and writing them up—was thus not just stoicism or, as Henry James felt, a celebration of mere vital excitement. It was a happiness based on the realization that one was supremely gifted at the essential tasks of one's profession. It was a confirmation of Holmes' exalted expectations for himself: a joy that came from the realization that he had the ability to be a great judge, a judge of discernibly higher intellectual stature than his peers. When Holmes talked, later in his life, of "jobbism," the idea that one simply did one's work as best as one could, that talk was taken by some of his admirers as a manifestation of his essential modesty, his self-abrogation, his "judicial humility." This was a misreading of Holmes' temperament. "Jobbism," for him, was the logical culmination of his own self-confidence in being a gifted professional. "I am such a damned egotist," he wrote Clare Castletown in February, 1897," so full of work, so eager to prove my power—that I get the fundamental vital happiness out of life in spite of everything."[212]

Invariably, however, with "joy" came "despair" for Holmes. His duties on the SJC barely scratched the surface of his energies and ambitions. He longed for recognition, for excitement and adventure, for, perhaps, a more prestigious and visible judgeship, one on the Supreme Court of the United States. In his letters to Clare during the period of their greatest emotional attachment, he spoke of feelings of despair that seemed so often to accompany his moments of joy. In the previously quoted letter to Clare, written after the reaction to his *Vegelahn* dissent, he concluded, after noting that he might have "to pay for it practically before I die," that "bitterness of heart is never far away."[213] In May 28, 1897, he spoke of "grind[ing his] teeth in secret rage at the public ignorance of the difference between the first rate and the second rate," an ignorance "I apply . . . to myself."[214] A year later he was more explicit, saying that "if I didn't go to England once in a while I should become almost a recluse, doing my work with a kind of bitter loneliness."[215] The statement about reclusiveness somewhat underestimated the extent to which Holmes was searching out and enjoying female companionship in Boston at the time. He could not resist telling Clare in an earlier letter that a "good looking" female friend of his, Clara Sherwood Rollins (later to become Clara Stevens), had published an 1897 novel, *Threads of Life,* that "show more or less traces of talks with me and I believe even introduces a personage more or less suggested by myself." But the statement about "bitter loneliness" perfectly captured one of the elements of his complex emotional stance in his years on the SJC.

When a series of fortuitous events in 1902 provided Holmes with a release from the SJC, and from Boston, he was confronted with another career choice that he knew he need not linger over. He wanted an appointment to the Supreme Court of the United States as badly as he had wanted a judgeship in the early years of his professional life. Even though he was not being insincere or self-deceiving in describing his years as a Massachusetts judge as the happiest in his life, his extraordinary ambition and his intense self-preoccupation, coupled with his residual bitterness, resulted in his regarding his professional life between 1882 and 1902 as somewhat unfulfilled. Here, in the Supreme Court appointment, was an opportunity for self-fulfillment. Holmes grasped it with relish. Yet, as we will see in the next chapter, his first reaction to the public announcement of his appointment was bitterness.

CHAPTER NINE

The Supreme Court, 1903–1916

~

IN FEBRUARY, 1901, Holmes was asked to make some remarks on "John Marshall Day," the 100th anniversary of the day on which Marshall took his seat as Chief Justice of the United States. Sixty-five years after his death Marshall had become a legend, and the legal journals and reports were filled with lush praise of his accomplishments. Holmes' comments were more reserved. At one point he said that "I should feel a . . . doubt whether, after Hamilton and the Constitution itself, Marshall's work proved more than a strong intellect, a good style, personal ascendancy in his court, courage, justice, and the convictions of his party." Then, perhaps with Marshall's example in mind, he continued:

> My keenest interest is excited, not by what are called great questions and great cases, but by little decisions which the common run of selectors would pass by because they did not deal with the Constitution or a telephone company, yet which have in them the germ of some wider theory, and therefore of some profound interstitial change in the very tissue of law. The men whom I should be tempted to commemorate would be the originators of transforming thought. They often are half obscure, because what the world pays for is judgment, not the original mind.[1]

As was usually the case with his speeches, Holmes' principal subject ended up being himself. One can see in this excerpt some of the lingering resentment he felt at implicitly being contrasted unfavorably with men of "judgment"—the silent, solid men of "reserved power"—because the world did not pay much for originality. He had made a great many "little" decisions during his tenure on the Supreme Judicial Court; he had tried to instill in them the germ of some wider theory. He had hoped that in so doing he was joining that group of persons, such as William Allen, "whose ambition . . . looks only to remote and mediated command," who wielded "that most subtle and intoxicating authority which controls the future from within by shaping the thoughts and speech of a later time," and who were to be honored "by a few others, lonely as themselves, walking apart in mediative silence, and dreaming in their turn the dream of spiritual reign."[2] He had come to see himself as one of "the originators of transforming thought." Such persons were often "half obscure."[3]

When Holmes delivered this address his expectation was very probably that his career would in no sense resemble that of Marshall. His subject had dealt with "great questions and great cases"; he was the "single figure" in which "American law [could] be represented.'' Holmes, by contrast, was an obscure Massachusetts judge. But a series of events was radically to alter that expectation. When the momentum of those events had culminated thirty years later with Holmes' ninetieth birthday radio address to the nation, he had become a rival to Marshall in the pantheon of eminent and visible judges, perhaps even more of a symbol than Marshall himself.

~

The first of the events was to be set in motion less than a year after Holmes made his remarks on Marshall, when Horace Gray, an Associate Justice of the Supreme Court from Massachusetts, fell ill, confirming earlier suppositions that he was likely soon to retire from the Court. The previous year Gray's failing health had prompted President William McKinley to inquire into possible successors for Gray, all of whom were expected to come from Massachusetts, in accordance with the then controlling criterion of geographic affiliation as a prerequisite for certain Supreme Court ''seats.''[4] McKinley sought the advice of John Davis Long, his Secretary of the Navy, who had appointed Holmes to the Supreme Judicial Court of Massachusetts. Despite that appointment, Long did not recommend Holmes for the position; instead he urged McKinley to nominate Long's former law partner, Alfred Hemenway. The offer of a nomination was actually communicated to Hemenway in the summer of 1901, and Hemenway indicated that he would accept the position.[5]

Matters then took another course. On September 6, 1901, in the course of greeting members of the public after a speech at the Pan-American Exposition in Buffalo, New York, McKinley was shot by a deranged assassin, and died eight days later. His successor, Vice President Theodore Roosevelt, did not feel bound to nominate Hemenway, and the matter was dropped, with Gray returning for another Term. In February 1902, however, Gray had a stroke, and it became apparent that his retirement was imminent. He formally retired in a July 9, 1902, letter to Roosevelt, but well before then political pressure was mounting to name a successor.

Holmes thus benefited from McKinley's assassination; had Hemenway been nominated it is unlikely that the Massachusetts ''seat'' would have come vacant at a time when Holmes, now over sixty, would have still been young enough to be given active consideration. Moreover, Holmes knew Roosevelt, who we have seen, had been so impressed by ''The Soldier's Faith'' speech that he sought a meeting with Holmes on a visit to Boston.[6] Most important, Roosevelt was an intimate of Henry Cabot Lodge, the junior Senator from Massachusetts, who as early as March 1902, had indicated that Holmes, whom Lodge had known since childhood, was his first choice for the Gray seat.[7] The Lodge-Holmes-Roosevelt relationship, a relationship involving Harvard graduates who were all Porcellians, would prove to be crucial in Holmes' securing the nomination, for opposition to Holmes surfaced, and the senior Senator from Massachusetts, George Frisbie Hoar, had been a longtime opponent of Holmes.

Lodge's pivotal role in the nomination was evident to interested parties, who began lobbying for their particular candidates. One such individual, the textile manufacturer Eben S. Draper, exchanged correspondence with Lodge in the spring of 1902 and declared that he was prepared to support a number of persons rather than Holmes. Holmes was, Draper suggested, ''erratic, and . . . not a safe man for such an important position."[8] When Lodge responded that Holmes was his first choice, Draper then endorsed Samuel Hoar, whom he had not supported previously, claiming that "the appointment of Mr. Hoar would give a great deal better satisfaction to all the business interests of the state than would the appointment of Judge Holmes."[9] But Lodge was not particularly concerned with such issues,[10] nor was he bothered by Holmes' apparent support of labor in *Vegelahn v. Guntner*[11] and *Plant v. Woods*.[12] On July 7 Lodge wrote Roosevelt that while some critics of Holmes based their reaction on "his one or two labor decisions," Lodge had "been talking quietly with lawyers [in Massachusetts] & there is no doubt that the great body of the bar would strongly approve" of Holmes. Lodge added that "[i]t would . . . be a sore disappointment to me if you should decide . . . to pass Wendell over . . . I am very fond of him & he is in line for the promotion."[13]

Roosevelt was also not deterred by Holmes' labor decisions. On the contrary, he wrote Lodge that

> The labor decisions which have been criticized by some of the big railroad men and other members of large corporations contribute to my mind a strong point in Judge Holmes' favor.
>
> The ablest lawyers and greatest judges are men whose past has naturally brought them into close relationship with the wealthiest and most powerful clients, and I am glad when I can find a judge who has been able to preserve his aloofness of mind so as to keep his broad humanity of feeling and his sympathy for the class from which he has not drawn his clients.[14]

Two features of Holmes' candidacy did give Roosevelt some pause, however. Roosevelt's enthusiasm for Holmes' "Soldier's Faith" address had been tempered by his reaction to Holmes' comments on John Marshall. He told Lodge that he thought the speech had displayed "a total incapacity to grasp what Marshall did," and had been "unworthy" of the occasion. Roosevelt regarded Holmes' comment that Marshall had "the convictions of his party" as disparaging, especially since Roosevelt thought such a quality necessary for one of his appointees. "[I]n the higher sense, in the proper sense," he wrote to Lodge, "[a judge of the Supreme Court] is not fitted for the position unless he is a party man." He "would like to know that Judge Holmes was in entire sympathy with our views, that is with your views and mine"; that he was "absolutely sane and sound on the great national policies for which we stand in public life."[15]

There was an issue that both Roosevelt and Lodge, being Republicans, regarded as a litmus test of Holmes' political ideology, the question of the constitutionality of tariffs on sugar and tobacco products produced in American possessions, such as Puerto Rico and the Philippines. That issue had significant political ramifications, since the status of colonial territories had been a major issue in the 1900 election. The Republican party's position had been that protectionist tariffs on American colonies were necessary to secure the position of domestic sugar and tobacco interests; the Democrats had argued that taxing the colonies without first allowing their residents to vote in American elections was unconstitutional and imperialistic. In the 1901 Term a bare majority of the Court had held the tariffs constitutional, but Horace Gray had been a member of that majority, and subsequent tests of the constitutionality of Congressional policies affecting the colonies would be affected by the position of Gray's successor. As Roosevelt put it to Lodge: "[A] minority so large as to lack just one vote of being a majority have stood for such reactionary folly as would have hampered well-nigh hopelessly this people in doing efficient and honorable work for the national welfare, and for the welfare of the islands themselves."[16]

Roosevelt proposed that he and Holmes meet secretly at Roosevelt's home in Sagamore Hill, New York, on July 25. Upon receiving Roosevelt's July 10 letter Lodge responded that he would talk with Holmes in advance of that meeting. "I can put [Roosevelt's concerns] to Holmes with absolute frankness," he said, "and shall, for I would not appoint my best beloved on that bench unless he held the position you describe."[17] In saying that, Lodge could be buoyed by his conviction that Holmes, with his positivist views on sovereignty, would have no difficulty sustaining the administration's position on the territorial cases.

Now that the opportunity of a Supreme Court appointment had become a realistic possibility, Holmes concentrated his powers on making sure that the offer would be forthcoming. Ideologically and socially, at least on the surface, he and Roosevelt appeared compatible. Holmes had been a nominal Republican all his life, had impressed Roosevelt with his patriotism and his apparent independence from malefactors of great wealth, and was someone with impeccable social connections, the same connections as Roosevelt himself. Roosevelt's concern about whether Holmes was a "party man" in the "high sense," while more telling than Roosevelt could have known, was easy enough to assuage, especially given Lodge's advance warning. Holmes could be abundantly charming and tactful when so inclined, and there were few occasions in his life in which he was more inclined than this forthcoming meeting.

In a subsequent letter to Nina Gray Holmes described his secret visit to Sagamore Hill:

> I dodged the reporters as the President was off for his day on his yacht and I suppose they were not on the lookout. When I got there the servant said [Roosevelt] would not be back to dinner but the children dined at 7.
>
> With some hesitation I titivated and came down at 7 to be received by a little Velazquez girl [Ethel Roosevelt] who curtsey'd and then proceeded to play the hostess with a delightful mixture of child and grown up. To us entered a little boy of about the same size and quality [Kermit Roosevelt]. They explained their regrets that their elder brother [Theodore Roosevelt, Jr.] could not appear as he was not feeling quite right having eaten an apple pie and a half. [Ethel was 11, Kermit 13, and Theodore Jr. 15 at the time of Holmes' 1902 visit.]
>
> Presently they discovered that I had been in the Civil War and asked me to tell my adventures. So I told them tales adapted to their years and gathered afterwards that I gave satisfaction.
>
> After dinner came a telegram that the Pres'dt. was stuck in a fog and would not get back till morning. I was to remain.
>
> Then as I sat smoking—a telephone from the secret service—I said that I

was a stranger. ''Judge Holmes?'' ''Yes.'' Then the speaker revealed his calling and wanted to know about putting men on duty—and so to bed.

In the morning between 9 and 10 the President and Mrs. [Edith Carow] Roosevelt came up very amiable. I had a little talk with him in which he said just the right things and impressed me far more than I had expected and then I bolted so as not to be seen by [George von L.] Meyer the Ambassador to Italy, who was the next to come.[18]

Holmes' account of his visit, especially given the timing and context of his letter to Nina Gray, is revealing. On August 12, 1902, Nina Gray had written Holmes:

Now that Horace [Gray] has himself announced that he is not going back to Washington, I am in suspen[s]e wondering what is to happen. Will Mr. Hoar put his finger in the pie, or will you have what you want (or at least what you wish to have offered to you)—this too? As you have had all else you cared to have in life, so far.[19]

Nina Gray and Holmes, we have seen, were intimate friends. She was one of the women to whom he would ''talk straight''—talk about his aspirations and disappointments as well as about his taste in literature or other women. She knew that he wanted Horace Gray's seat on the Supreme Court, or at the very least that he wanted the opportunity to sit in that seat. She also knew that Senator Hoar was a potential stumbling block to Holmes' chances, one who might ''put his finger in the pie.'' Finally, Nina Gray's letter shows that she regarded Holmes as something like a special favorite of the gods: someone who at the age of sixty-one had ''had all else you cared to have in life, so far.'' In short, Nina Gray was one of the women to whom Holmes had opened ''the interior'' of his being.

Yet Holmes chose to describe his visit to Sagamore Hill in terms similar to those he might have employed to a relative stranger. Other than Holmes' comments that he ''dodged the reporter,'' that he decided to ''titivate'' (a word no longer in common usage, the equivalent of the colloquialism ''spruce up'') with ''some hesitation,'' and that he ''bolted'' from Sagamore Hill after the interview, there is no impression in his letter of the intense excitement he felt at being secretly summoned for an interview about a position he coveted. On the contrary, there is another, misleading impression: the impression that Holmes was a detached observer, wryly recounting his adventures with children, the secret service, and even Roosevelt himself.

Holmes did not mention, for example, how the Roosevelt children ''discovered'' that he had been in the Civil War. They might have asked him, but the eldest of those present, Kermit, was born twenty-four years after that war ended, and Holmes was sixty-one at the time of the interview and hardly wearing his regimental uniform. It is probable that Holmes himself told the children he was a Civil War veteran and then launched into a recounting of his ''adventures,'' something that probably gave him great pleasure. Nor did Holmes mention what he said when Roosevelt and he ''had a little talk'' the morning after he arrived. Instead he said that Roosevelt ''said just the right things and impressed me far more than I had expected,'' as if he were interviewing Roosevelt for a position. Finally, while Nina Gray had made it clear that what was most on her mind was whether Holmes should be offered the Supreme Court nomination, he did not mention that result of the Sagamore Hill interview, even though he had noted, in his "black book" for 1902, "July 25. Presdt. offered me Judgeship."[20]

Doubtless part of Holmes' diffidence in his August 17 response to Nina Gray came from the fact that his nomination had just been publicly announced (when Nina Gray wrote Holmes on August 11, the day the announcement first appeared in the newspapers, she still did not know of it) and he had not been confirmed by the Senate. But it might seem odd, in light of the fact that Holmes' letter was written after his nomination had been made public, that his tone was consistent with that of someone being courted by the President of the United States. After all, when Gray received the letter she knew very well that the suitor's proposal had been accepted. And while Holmes may have wanted to make it abundantly clear that even though he had accepted the nomination, he had not been seeking it, Gray had already stated her conviction that Holmes "wanted" the nomination.

One thinks here of Holmes' response to the two other momentous professional decisions in his life. The first was his stance toward Charles Eliot in their negotiations surrounding Eliot's offer of a professorship at Harvard Law School. Holmes had first written Eliot that while he was determined to come, he wanted to reserve the right to consider a judgeship should one arise. He had then withdrawn his acceptance on hearing that the money for the professorship had not been raised. In short, the prospect of joining the Harvard faculty was not comparable, emotionally, to the prospect raised by his second significant professional decision, joining the Supreme Judicial Court of Massachusetts. When Holmes told Eliot he was not coming to Harvard because the money was not available, he was acting out of pride and out of the realization that Harvard might well raise the money in the future, but also out of a certain diffidence toward academic life itself. When, in contrast, Thayer pointed out that Holmes had undermined his dignity by accepting the SJC judgeship on such short notice, Thayer underestimated the extent of Holmes' emotional commitment. Holmes wanted a judgeship very badly, and therefore considerations of pride and dignity paled in the face of his fear that the opportunity might not come again.

The nomination to the Supreme Court was another instance, for Holmes, of an opportunity he wanted very badly surfacing for what seemed like a fleeting moment. Gray's seat was the only one for which Holmes, being from Massachusetts, was qualified. Even so, McKinley had not nominated Holmes, and Holmes assuredly knew of that fact. Roosevelt's presence as President, given that Roosevelt was close to Lodge and had previously been impressed with Holmes, made Holmes' nomination a serious possibility. Holmes knew through Lodge that Roosevelt was inclined to nominate him but had some doubts. If Holmes failed to impress Roosevelt, or if he delayed in his acceptance, a dream of his would likely be gone forever.

Thus Holmes sneaked off to Sagamore Hill because Roosevelt wanted secrecy. He charmed the Roosevelt children while waiting anxiously for Roosevelt's return. After dinner he waited some more, and then, when fog delayed Roosevelt, was required to wait overnight. He then was implicitly required to be charming and politically acceptable to Roosevelt the next morning, at the price of the nomination. Holmes was seventeen years older than Roosevelt. Holmes was the Chief Justice of the Supreme Judicial Court of Massachusetts, the author of *The Common Law,* recipient of honorary degrees from Harvard and Yale. Yet he was waiting on Roosevelt, entertaining children, focusing all his energies on not letting the nomination slip away. Dignity was a minor consideration, as it had been with the SJC appointment.

The realization that he had exposed his great desire for the Supreme Court nomination, to himself and perhaps to others, surfaced in Holmes' consciousness as he began to narrate his visit to Sagamore Hill in the letter to Gray. If he had perhaps been overly covetous, lacking in dignity, that was a thought he chose to keep to himself. He would certainly not compound any loss of dignity by openly confessing to Nina Gray that he had done everything in his power to secure himself the nomination. Instead he adopted a pose of diffidence, as if he had taken the position only because Roosevelt unexpectedly impressed him and "said just the right things." Diffidence was a posture in keeping with dignity. Thayer's comments, when Holmes left Harvard for the SJC, had been more revealing about Holmes than perhaps even Thayer intended.

After Roosevelt offered Holmes the nomination on July 25, and Holmes accepted, Roosevelt pledged Holmes to silence while he informed Senator Hoar, who had not been consulted at all on the matter. Holmes wrote Lodge thanking him for his "kind feeling" in the process, and indicating that Roosevelt had "said his mind was made up" although he was not making the nomination public.[21] For his part, Roosevelt wrote Lodge that he was "entirely satisfied" with Holmes' views.[22] Lodge responded that "he is our kind right through."[23]

Roosevelt and Lodge then turned to the unhappy task of placating Senator Hoar. On being informed of the news Hoar protested vigorously, but stopped short of publicly opposing the nomination. He wrote Lodge that Holmes' "accomplishments are literary and social . . . not judicial," and that "[i]n his opinions he runs to subtleties and refinements, and no decision of his makes a great landmark in jurisprudence."[24] He wrote Roosevelt that "[t]he old method" of making Supreme Court nominations had been departed from in Holmes' case. That method was "to let the public know of the vacancy, to allow a reasonable time for all persons interested, especially the members of the legal profession and the representatives of the States immediately concerned, to make known their opinions and desires."[25]

While Lodge and Roosevelt attempted to pacify Hoar, it became clear to them that their efforts would be fruitless. Lodge suggested to Hoar that he had not "do[ne] justice to Judge Holmes in his legal capacity" and that others, including Justice Horace Gray, thought Holmes able.[26] Roosevelt wrote that he had not consulted Hoar earlier because he had assumed that the Chief Justice of Massachusetts would be acceptable to anyone from that state, and he had only recently received Gray's letter of resignation.[27] Both responses were somewhat disingenuous, since neither Lodge nor Roosevelt had any intention of consulting Hoar, who had opposed Holmes for a federal district judgeship in 1878; they had also known for some time that Gray was planning to retire. At any rate, Hoar was not moved, writing Lodge that "I never heard anybody speak of Judge Holmes as an able judge," and that Holmes was regarded "as a man of pleasant personal address . . . but without strength, and without grasp of general principles."[28]

Despite Hoar's opposition to Holmes, there was little he could do to block the nomination. He was not personally close to Roosevelt and could not oppose Holmes publicly because of Holmes' standing as Chief Justice of Massachusetts and because Hoar's nephew, Samuel Hoar, had been mentioned in the newspapers earlier as a candidate for the position.[29] By August 11 Hoar had conceded, in a letter to Lodge, that Holmes' appointment "will be considered by the general public as entirely respectable," although adding that "those members of the profession whose opinion is of any value" would be disappointed, and would simply "have to make the best of it."[30] On receiving this letter Lodge wrote Roosevelt that "Mr. Hoar still growls mildly about Holmes not being a great lawyer but he is quieting and . . . all is well."[31] As we have seen, Roosevelt publicly announced the nomination that very day.

Hoar took one more step to publicize his doubts about Holmes. On November 5, 1902, before the Senate had acted on Holmes' nomination, Hoar wrote Chief Justice Melville Fuller about his new associate. After stating that Holmes' nomination "has been received with very great favor throughout the country," and that Holmes was "a gentleman, a man of integrity," who would "not be prejudiced or warped by his relations to any party, or desire to affect the political course of the government one way or the other," Hoar could not resist adding

> The best lawyers of Massachusetts, almost without exception, believe that while he has . . . excellent qualities, he is lacking in intellectual strength, and that his opinions carry with them no authority merely because they are his. We have contributed from New England some very tough oak timbers to the Bench, State and National. Our lawyers in general, especially those in the country, do not think that carved ivory is likely to be as strong or enduring, although it may seem more ornamental.[32]

Meanwhile Holmes, who had characterized his nomination to Lady Georgina Pollock as "a reward for much hard work,"[33] began to notice the public commentary on his nomination. It was overwhelmingly favorable, but it offended him nonetheless. On September 23, 1902, he wrote Frederick Pollock "a line of unreasoning—rage I was going to say—dissatisfaction is nearer." That "line" went as follows:

> There have been tacks of notices of me all over the country and the immense majority of them seem to me hopelessly devoid of personal discrimination or courage. They are so favorable that they make my nomination a popular success but they have the flabbiness of American ignorance. I had to get appreciation for my book in England before they dared say anything here except in one or two quarters. . . . And now as to my judicial career they don't know much more than that I took the labor side in *Vegelahn v. Guntner* and as that frightened some money interests, and such interests count for a good deal as soon as one gets out of the cloister, it is easy to suggest that the Judge has partial views, is brilliant but not very sound, has talent but is not great, etc., etc. It makes one sick when he has broken his heart in trying to make every word living and real to see a lot of duffers, generally I think not even lawyers, talking with the sanctity of print in a way that at once discloses to the knowing eye that literally they don't know anything about it. . . . [Y]ou can understand how in a moment of ostensible triumph I have been in a desert—when I hoped

to see that they understood what I meant, enough not to bully me with Shaw, Marshall, and the rest. If I haven't done my share in the way of putting in new and remodeling old thought for the last 20 years then I delude myself. Occassionally someone has a glimpse—but in the main damn the lot of them.[34]

The day after Holmes' nomination the *New York Evening Post* called him "more brilliant than sound,"[35] and the *Boston Evening Transcript* said that "[h]is striking originality will help . . . when it does not hinder."[36] These were comments that particularly vexed Holmes, as well as, perhaps, the *Evening Post*'s notation that Holmes was "more of a 'literary feller' than one often finds on the bench." They touched nerves that precipitated a kind of "rage" in Holmes. He may have wanted to call his reaction merely "dissatisfaction" to Pollock—after all how could one fairly "rage" at favorable comments about one's nomination to the Supreme Court of the United States—but "unreasoning rage," a loosing of pent-up bitterness, was closer to the mark.

Many of Holmes' longstanding frustrations surfaced in the letter. The reaction was, on the whole, "devoid of personal discrimination or courage," much like his now-regretted impulsive decision to muster out of Civil War service. The commentary had "the flabbiness of American ignorance," the same quality that had kept American reviewers from appreciating *The Common Law* until Pollock and Dicey had given it recognition. The newspapers hadn't studied his SJC decisions; they only knew that he "took the labor side" in *Vegelahn,* making him an unpredictable and eccentric judge in the eyes of "men of weight." It was such men, personified by Senator Hoar, who thought of him as "brilliant but not very sound," as talented but "not great." Their views had filtered down to the *Post* and the *Transcript*.

Even worse, his critics had attacked his judicial style, disparaging it as 'literary' and too 'original.' He had "broken his heart" in trying to make every word "living and real," but the commentators not only didn't "know anything about" what he was trying to say, they dismissed his efforts at originality of expression as "literary": "more brilliant than sound." He had hoped that they would have understood what he "meant": his goal of "putting in new and remodeling old thought," his dream of intellectual "reign." Instead they chose to "bully" him "with Shaw, Marshall, and the rest," judges who were "sound" presences, reliable, predictable, not "partial." The choice of Lemuel Shaw and John Marshall was particularly revealing: Shaw was the great "lawyer's judge" of Holmes' youth; Marshall the great "statesman" hero of Roosevelt. Holmes had doubts about whether he wanted to be, or could be, a "lawyer's judge" or a judicial "statesman." He saw himself as an original thinker, first and last. The idea that this talent was somehow incompatible with being a "great" judge was more than infuriating to him, it was devastating. He "damn[ed] the lot" of his apparent critics. Once again bitterness was never very far away from joy; in the midst of triumph he could feel, as he told Georgina Pollock, "very blue."[37]

Holmes was confirmed on December 4. In ascribing his appointment to "a reward for much hard work" he was somewhat misguided. The nomination had been the result of a series of somewhat improbable events: the assassination of McKinley; the close relationships among Roosevelt, Lodge, and Holmes; the fact that Roosevelt, much closer in age to Lodge than to Hoar, perceived the junior Senator from Massachusetts as a closer political ally than the senior Senator; the political criteria employed by Roosevelt in choosing a nominee, which included a combination of party affiliation and allegedly "progressive" leanings. The fact was that although Roosevelt's ties to Holmes had made Roosevelt inclined to nominate him, Roosevelt had no idea about Holmes' jurisprudence and did not particularly care, and he had a somewhat mistaken conception of Holmes' politics.

Roosevelt's lack of understanding of his nominee was illustrated in an episode that occurred during Holmes' second Term on the Court, when Holmes dissented in the *Northern Securities* case,[38] in which the Roosevelt administration sought to enjoin the merger of two previously competing railroads in a holding company, a consolidation that had the effect of preventing a third railroad from operating in the same territory. An antitrust action was brought against the holding company, based on the Sherman Act and on common law restraint-of-trade principles, and a 5–4 majority voted to dissolve the company. In dissent Holmes read the Sherman Act and the common law as permitting combination among firms in the same market so long as Congress had not expressly restricted the size of companies engaging in interstate commerce and so long as a monopoly, in the legal sense, had not been shown.[39] Roosevelt was reported as being incensed by the dissent: Henry Adams wrote his friend Elizabeth Cameron that "Theodore went wild about it."[40] Two years later Roosevelt wrote Lodge that

> [n]othing has been so strongly borne in on me concerning lawyers on the bench as that the *nominal* politics of the man has nothing to do with his actions on the bench. His *real* politics are all important. From his antecedents, Holmes should have been an ideal man on the bench. As a matter of fact he has been a bitter disappointment.[41]

While Roosevelt may have been disappointed with Holmes' judicial performance, it is unlikely that any other president would have nominated Holmes to the Court. Holmes had been a faithful Republican, but he was distinctly not one of the sort that captured Republican presidential nominations from Garfield on. He was a Brahmin Republican, like Lodge and Roosevelt: Harvard-educated, intellectual, imperialistic on foreign affairs questions, disdainful of patronage. He had not been the choice of McKinley and he would not have been the choice of Taft. His nomination was made possible by the death of a Republican president whose Vice-President had not been thought of as a serious presidential candidate that early in his life, and the fact that the first vacancy during Roosevelt's tenure came from Massachusetts. Whether or not Holmes had been a "bitter disappointment" to Roosevelt, he remained "our kind"—the social and intellectual compatriot of Lodge and Roosevelt—"right through."

~

Just at the time when Holmes had seemingly settled into a "half obscure" judicial life, he was transported to the national arena. The move to Washington was more than a change of locality for him: it was another stage in his professional and personal lives. He moved out of his father's house on Beacon Street and bought a house in

Washington, the first one he felt was truly his own. He "burn[ed] old papers which have cumbered and annoyed one for years," and as noted, Fanny burned most of her embroideries.[42] The Holmeses' private life was to change with their new surroundings and responsibilities. The wives of Cabinet officials and Supreme Court Justices were expected to hold weekly "at homes" to greet members of Washington political society, and the Holmeses were regularly invited to official dinners, including several at the White House. Holmes was also called on to occupy a new professional role. His work was different, consisting of many more public law cases and a higher percentage of cases of wide importance; he was the most junior member of a Court whose internal deliberations were affected by the seniority principle and who met all year en banc, with no single judge sittings. He was suddenly a national figure, if not yet one known to the public.

Holmes' move to Washington meant that his social patterns would also change. In Boston he and Fanny had essentially been recluses, he going out alone periodically to pay social calls on female friends; she going out very infrequently and rarely entertaining at home. In Washington, while the Holmes' immersion in social affairs would expand considerably, Holmes' social contacts were more formalized. In the place of conversations with people such as Nina Gray,[43] he began to expand his correspondence with friends, especially with women. It is in the correspondence from these friendships that his reactions to his new life can best be discerned.

The first theme that surfaces is Holmes' impression of the all-encompassing nature of his new work. He wrote Pollock of "[t]he variety and novelty of the questions, the remote spaces from which they come, [and] the amount of work they require."[44] At the same time he spoke of "the novelty, solemnity, and augustness of the work," which "has made my past labors seem a closed volume locked up in a distant safe."[45] His new colleagues were formidable as well: "[t]he men here may not be very strong on the philosophy or history of the law, but the abler ones administer it as statesmen governing an empire."[46] The Court was "a center of great forces," and "you must be powerful on a world scale to weigh [them]" in making decisions.[47] The job took "[a]ll my interest and energy" as he dealt with "this mighty panorama of cases from every part of our great empire involving great interests, raising questions I never have heard of, argued by the strongest men in the country."[48]

The demands of the work, Holmes felt, meant that he needed to reorder his priorities. "For the first time in my life," he confessed, "I have had flashes of a sense of responsibility." There was a "disappearance of personal thoughts in the absorption of great affairs."[49] "You don't hold time in the hollow of your hand as I got to feeling about the work of the Court in Boston," he noted, "and for the first time I feel too absorbed for curiosity." He said that "[f]or the present . . . I realize the frame of mind in which public affairs drown out private curiosities."[50]

By "curiosities" Holmes principally meant relationships with women. One of the central themes of his correspondence on arriving in Washington was how the atmosphere of the city and his new duties combined to reduce his opportunities for informal friendships with the opposite sex. "I have not looked upon a woman save in the way of kindness," he wrote Ellen Curtis[51] shortly after arriving. "I see no probability of new ventures."[52] Three weeks later he added that "I don't in the slightest degree wish to find an egeria here—and as my wife goes with me every-where I have all the companionship I need.''[53] In the middle of February he announced to Nina Gray that ''I don't see the women—I don't see the chance—I don't feel the inclination—not to speak of— . . . the Task takes all my time.''[54] ''For the first time in my life,'' he said to Curtis, ''I have found business to which I would postpone your sex.''[55]

His increased interest in his work was not the only reason Holmes appeared disinclined to pursue any ''new ventures'' in the realm of feminine company. The protocol of official Washington, with its emphasis on formal seniority in pairings at dinners and occasions, made casual acquaintanceships with the kind of attractive younger women to which Holmes tended to gravitate difficult. Moreover, Washing-ton was a small, provincial city, self-conscious and inclined to gossip. ''I dine out a good deal,'' Holmes wrote to Curtis, ''often being assigned a lady on principle of precedence not of selection. And I still meet others only for a flitting moment.''[56] Two months later he added that ''It remains true that I see no one intimately. One is in such a high light that eternal discretion is necessary.'' When he ''saw one woman the other evening who seemed aware of the differences of the sexes'' he thought that worth remarking upon.[57] ''[I]t is strange,'' he wrote to Nina Gray, ''how small a part the society of women plays in my life here. Apart from memory I hardly should know that they existed.'' Perhaps, he continued, that was ''just as well in this center of gossip.'' He had ''made one call of politeness of a Sunday afternoon and heard of it at once.''[58]

Another factor influencing Holmes' altered attitude toward socializing with women was the fact that Fanny played a much more active role in their social gatherings. When he first arrived he wrote Ellen Curtis that ''[t]he women here seem to have got up a good deal of formalism as to calling etc., but I don't think it will be unbearable to us.''[59] About a month later, noting that Fanny had begun to entertain at home on Mondays, he told Curtis that ''[s]he has been a great success although she won't believe it. Mrs. Lodge said she wrote to Boston the other day that my wife was It.'' Fanny still ''gets more pleasure from solitude than from society,'' Holmes added, ''and I think that some day when we have paid back some of our social debts . . . we shall drop out. . . . But at present we are on the top of the wave.''[60] Little as Fanny ''cares for society,'' he had written earlier, ''she takes it like a little man and you would think to see her that she liked it thoroughly.''[61]

Holmes' altered attitude toward woman was vividly captured in a vignette he described to Nina Gray in 1904:

> I somehow found myself talking to a very pretty girl whom I failed to get my wife to introduce me to the other evening and we gave each other notice of hostile intentions and that we were out for scalps & she told me I might play in her backyard if I didn't play with other girls. . . . But I fear the tragedy ends there, as I have don't have time to play in backyards. . . . I am hoping to read some philosophy or some law in the breathing spells—that does me more good than playing in backyards.[62]

The letter suggests what Holmes' ''flirtations'' were like at this stage in his life. The regularized rituals of official Washington entertainments meant that he was unlikely to run into "very pretty girl[s]" as a matter of course, since his dinner companions were apt to be the wives of those who were high on the Washington seniority ladder. His "somehow" testifies to the uncommon nature of his conversation with the young woman. What follows next is a typical description of Holmes' badinage with attractive women: conversations with a flirtatious element are described as competitions between the sexes, captured in the phrases "hostile intentions" and "out for scalps." Playing in a backyard appears to be a euphemism for paying court; "tragedy" was a favorite word of Holmes' to describe exchanges with a romantic dimension. But the point of the vignette is to inform Nina Gray that Holmes has rejected the offer to pay court. His work gives him limited time to indulge in outside activities, and in that time he has concluded that reading philosophy or law does him "more good" than indulging in flirtations. About a year before he had recorded the vignette Holmes had written another of his female friends to say that he planned "to close out that department," referring to flirtations with women, "and be a kindly cynic . . . and . . . a survivor."[63]

The move to Washington thus signified a new phase in Holmes' life. He and Fanny bought a house, at 1720 Eye Street, which Holmes described as having a "deep backyard with room for shrubs and small trees . . . and no danger the sunlight will be cut off by a big apartment house."[64] Holmes had written on coming to Washington that he "long[ed] for the day that I shall be in a house of my own," and when they finally moved in, in November 1903, he described the process with great pleasure:

> I have worked from 10 a.m. to 7 p.m. with half an hour out for luncheon, in arranging books. Oh the heavenly joy! It is always joy to see order where was confusion, and when the subject matter is books, and for the first time in one's life one can see what one has, it is *fecundissimus*.
>
> It is the devil of a job to transport all one's belongings . . . when one is over sixty, but is vitalizing; you get rid of dead matter, and the circulation is improved. . . . But the satisfaction is to have one's own surroundings about one instead of another feller's. . . . I really think you would say it was a pleasant place in a modest way, and the sun streams in at the back, and I feel that I am settled for good in a place which is mine. The Boston house never ceased to be my father's.[65]

A new house, a new set of rules for social life, a new position, a new role for Fanny, who had nonetheless performed her old, constant role of managing all the details of the move. The past seemed "a finished book—locked up far away, and a new and solemn volume opens."[66] The most important chapters in that new volume, from Holmes' point of view, would be those dealing with his work on the Supreme Court. He first found that work foreign and intimidating, but gradually came to take it in stride, and enjoyed it from the first moment. He was "more absorbed, interested and impressed than ever I had dreamed I might be,"[67] he wrote to Pollock, but at the same time noted that "this mighty panorama of cases" had raised "questions I never heard of, argued by the strongest men the country can show or submitted for peremptory action on big records which you have to get the point of in half an hour."[68] There were "some very powerful men amongst . . . the Judges," he noted, and "it is a pleasure to wrestle with them."[69]

Soon he wrote that he was "beginning to gain confidence." The other judges "seem to like what I have written so far," he noted, "and I feel as if I should count for more than merely one vote."[70] At about the same time he wrote Ellen Curtis that "[t]he feeling of mystery and awe about my work . . . has diminished," and while "[i]t ought to be done by demigods," he thought "I can hold up my end as things are." He was pleased that "I breathe in a larger air and enjoy the advantage of a position which makes what one says attended to simply because said from this place," instead "of having to creep into notice through textbooks when they happen to be intelligent enough to know a good thing when they see it."[71]

He expressed some concern about the comparatively short length of his opinions, which had been his style since becoming a judge. "I hope," he told Nina Gray, "my opinions will not be despised on account of their brevity, but thus far I have been pretty short as compared with the average."[72] A month later he continued to "shudder when I contrast my short little opinions with the voluminous discourses that are de regle," but also noted that he was finishing his assignments with sufficient dispatch that Chief Justice Melville Fuller could "unload a little of the work of some of the others on to me as I had some spare time."[73] Although he told Ellen Curtis that "I don't see that the cases need such a very long time to write them in, as is imposed," and that the other judges had been amused by the fact that "I have touched off mine pretty quick,"[74] he continued to "doubt whether my habit of writing short opinions will not make me seem less weighty at first with the general. They think that a great opinion indicates itself by padded breast and shoulders."[75] But on the whole Holmes was pleased and satisfied with his new position. "For the first time in my life," he wrote Curtis, "I am up against a greatness that comes from outside. Hitherto I have constructed from within what seemed like lines of the infinite. Now it is the simple grandiose—the external fact of feeling a vast world vibrate to one's determinations. . . . At bottom I am profoundly happy."[76]

~

The Court that Holmes joined in late 1902 was in several respects closer to that on which John Marshall had sat than to its current equivalent. Its courtroom was, as it had been since Marshall's day, in the Capitol, occupying the old Senate chamber. The justices had no offices of their own, working out of their houses. Their conference room was in the basement of the Capitol, along with a library that Justice Willis Van Devanter called "imperfect and dilapidated" on joining the Court in 1911.[77] They were provided with $2000 a year to hire a secretary, and were given a messenger. Most of the justices used that allocation to hire male stenographers, but Holmes, after his first Term, began to hire a graduate of Harvard as a "secretary" (really a research assistant, later called law clerk), relying on John Chipman Gray to select the person. Holmes was initially unusual in this practice, but other Justices came to adopt it and after 1919 Congress provided an appropriation for secretaries, who after that year became fixtures of the Court's staff.[78]

The Court's work was demanding, a function of its broad jurisdictional reach. The Judges' Act, limiting its appellate jurisdiction and creating the discretionary certiorari power, by which the Court can decline to hear the vast amount of cases petitioned to it, was not to be in place until 1925. In addition, *Erie Railroad v. Tompkins*[79] had not been decided, so the Court, like other federal courts, had no obligation to follow state law in most common law cases, and thus simple "diversity cases"—that is, cases involving contracts, accidents, or property disputes between citizens of different states—could find their rules of decision in "federal common law" as enunciated by the Supreme Court and the lower federal courts. In addition to these common law disputes, federal and state statutes had begun to proliferate in the early twentieth century, and constitutional issues had accordingly increased. On coming to the Court Holmes wrote Pollock about the kinds of cases he was encountering:

> I have written on the constitutionality of part of the Constitution of California, on the powers of the Railroad Commissioners of Arkansas, on the question whether a law of Wisconsin impairs the obligation of the plaintiff's contract. I have to consider a question between a grant of the U.S. in aid of a military road and an Indian reservation on the Pacific coast. I have heard conflicting mining claims in Arizona and whether a granite quarry is "Minerals" within an exception in a Railway land grant and fifty other things as remote from each other as these.[80]

In many respects the duties and practices of Supreme Court justices at the time of Holmes' joining the Court were ideally suited to his skills and temperament. The absence of a central building and offices meant that the collegial interchange of the Court was confined to its Saturday conferences. "Sembles," or "consultations," as the Supreme Judicial Court called conferences, were not a feature of his Massachusetts work that Holmes had relished. He liked the solitary, intellectual dimensions of judging: taking a case, thinking about it, arriving at a result, writing it up as best he could. He did not like conforming the language of his opinions to the demands of his colleagues, and he rarely consulted others on the analysis of a case. He enjoyed writing his assigned opinions with dispatch, and with the Court's docket overloaded, he felt he could contribute to the production of business through the swiftness with which he wrote.

Part of Holmes' productivity, of course, was achieved by the brief and summary character of his opinions. We have seen that he had written friends shortly after taking his seat that, as he put it to Nina Gray, "I don't believe in the long opinions which have been almost the rule here." He "tr[ied] every week to turn off my case, and to announce it the following Monday." He believed "that to state the case shortly and the ground of decision as concisely and delicately as you can is the real way. That is the English fashion and I think it civilized." He also felt that his swiftness "pleases the chief who as an Executive officer likes to get work done."[81] Others were less entranced by his terseness. Louis Brandeis once said that Holmes did not "sufficiently consider the need of others to understand,"[82] and even Holmes' fervid admirer Felix Frankfurter conceded, when he became a Supreme Court justice, that "Mr. Justice Holmes spoke for the Court, in most instances, tersely and often cryptically."[83] Holmes' old friend John Chipman Gray, in discussing the prospect of a clerkship with Holmes for Robert Taft in 1912, said that "[a]s you know, Judge

Holmes' opinions seem to lack lucidity,''[84] but argued that Holmes' illuminating talk on legal matters made up for that deficiency.

Robert Taft nonetheless turned down the offer of a secretaryship with Holmes, apparently agreeing with his father's view that it would not add significantly to the experience he had gained at Harvard Law School.[85] While Taft's decision may seem misguided in retrospect, it was an explicable response at the time. Holmes was still neither particularly well known to the general public nor deeply respected in elite legal circles by the close of his first decade on the Court. Moreover, his secretaryships were not designed to be heady professional experiences for the secretary.

Holmes played virtually no part in the initial selection of his clerks. Gray, or after Gray's death Frankfurter, screened candidates from Harvard Law School's third year class, selected one, and informed Holmes. Holmes then wrote the chosen candidate a formal letter of acceptance, invariably adding after the 1912 Term (when he had achieved sufficient age and seniority of service to be able to elect retirement at a full pension) that he reserved the right to retire or to die at any time. When the secretary arrived in Washington at the beginning of the Court's Term to take up his duties, he was often meeting Holmes for the first time. In the latter years of Holmes' tenure the secretary would stay with him throughout the summer.

Holmes had quite distinct criteria for the selection of a secretary. He wanted a socially presentable person, someone who could represent him in Washington society and thereby spare him the burden of having to socialize extensively. He wanted someone capable of participating in household affairs and, especially after Fanny Dixwell's death in 1929, capable of balancing his checkbook, paying his bills, and tending to his household accounts. He wanted a person of companionable temperament, someone with whom he could discourse about books and ideas. He wanted an unmarried man, one who could easily be on call and had no obligations of potentially comparable magnitude to his obligation to Justice Holmes. He assumed that Gray or Frankfurter would send him a talented law student, but he had very little interest in having his secretaries perform substantive research tasks. When Holmes was in the process of writing opinions in his study at 1720 Eye Street, he would ask his secretaries to find him citations, preferably to his previous opinions, but there is no evidence he ever asked a secretary to draft even the smallest part of an opinion for him. Secretaries, for Holmes, were primarily household staff members and intellectual and social companions. He called each of them ''sonny,'' and, despite being well aware of temperamental differences among them, treated them as interchangeable.[86]

Notwithstanding Holmes' expectations for the position, his legal secretaries were a distinguished group of people who, so far as is possible to discern, admired Holmes and enjoyed their time with him.[87] The internal canons of loyalty and confidentiality to which Supreme Court law clerks have typically if not universally subscribed prevent one from discerning the full, candid reaction of most of Holmes' secretaries to him, but the available evidence suggests that his secretaries found him stimulating, pleasant, sometimes inspiring, and invariably memorable. Nonetheless, generalizations about the impact of a year with Holmes on his secretaries are hazardous.

When Holmes arrived on the Court in late 1902 Melville Fuller was Chief Justice, and John Marshall Harlan, David J. Brewer, Henry B. Brown, Edward D. White,

George Shiras, Rufus W. Peckham, and Joseph P. McKenna were Associate Justices. By 1917 only White and McKenna remained on the Court, and by 1925 Holmes, who had been sixty-one years old on taking the oath of office, was the only remaining member of the 1903 Court still in service. In the course of his career Holmes was to sit with sixteen other judges, William R. Day, William H. Moody, Horace H. Lurton, Charles Evans Hughes, Willis Van Devanter, Joseph Lamar, Mahlon Pitney, James C. McReynolds, Louis D. Brandeis, John H. Clarke, William Howard Taft, George Sutherland, Pierce Butler, Edward T. Sanford, Harlan Fiske Stone, and Owen J. Roberts.

Despite the numerous associates Holmes had as a Supreme Court Justice, and the opportunities for close exchange presented by the collegial nature of Supreme Court decisionmaking, Holmes had few close friends among his colleagues and commented sparingly, and generally diplomatically, on the other men with whom he served on the Court.[88] He was close friends with White,[89] admired Hughes,[90] was mildly critical of Harlan,[91] and found McKenna an irritant.[92] Beyond that, with two exceptions, his judicial colleagues semed to have had remarkably little impact on his work as a judge or his life in general.

The role Holmes' Supreme Court colleagues apparently played in his life is captured by comments he made about them to Frederick Pollock, Harold Laski, and Felix Frankfurter. The first comment, made by Holmes in an 1918 letter to Pollock[93] and repeated in a 1920 letter to Laski,[94] was that the process by which Holmes presented his draft majority opinions to his colleagues occasionally resulted in "[t]he boys mak[ing] me emasculate one."[95] Holmes' correspondence to Pollock, Laski, and Frankfurter was filled with such comments, conveying an impression of bold, vivid, uncompromising Holmesian language being subdued or qualified by his more cautious fellow judges. Holmes' metaphor of emasculation suggests that he regarded vivid writing as a form of expressing his masculine self, and that he may have thought that the interest of his colleagues in qualifying his language reflected their lack of self-confidence.

The second comment was made to Felix Frankfurter in a 1922 letter. Holmes wrote Frankfurter in the midst of a brief recess from one of the Court's periodic conferences, in which the justices discussed and disposed of cases on which they had heard argument during a particular week. In concluding the letter to Frankfurter Holmes said, "I stepped out of a cloud of biting mosquitoes for a word of freedom with you. Now I go back to the swamp."[96] The connotations and imagery of Holmes' sentences are suggestive. In the Peninsula campaign of 1862 Holmes had marched through swamps and had doubtless been exposed to mosquitoes. The swamps inhibited his movements and the bites of the mosquitoes were an annoyance. But Holmes chose to render his temporary release from the "swamp" and the "cloud of mosquitoes" as a "word of freedom." A word, not a moment. The sentence suggests that Holmes may have found his colleagues on the Court inhibiting and annoying, but the principal effect of their presences was to inhibit and annoy his language. They made him long for the freedom to use his words as he saw fit, not as they thought prudent.

It is interesting that of the variety of ways in which Holmes might have chosen to express the impact of his Supreme Court colleagues upon him—as personalities, as sources of ideas, as friends or enemies—he chose to convey that impact in terms of the effect they had upon his language as a writer. They were "the boys" who "emasculate[d]" his opinions, as the "biting mosquitoes" who denied him "a word of freedom." It appears that despite the collegial nature of judging on the Supreme Court, in which the justices hear arguments in a body, confer to make collective decisions, and, from at least Holmes' time on, circulate draft opinions for the approval of others expected to join them, Holmes perceived his function as largely a solitary one in which he, the writer and jurist, was alone with his assigned case and his thoughts. His fellow justices were, to an important extent, hindrances in the performance of that function.

~

There were two exceptions to this general attitude of Holmes toward his colleagues in the Court. One was his relationship with Melville Fuller. That relationship, in retrospect, is intriguing. Willard King, Fuller's only biographer, said in 1950 that "the friendship of Fuller and Holmes [was] one of the most notable in the history of the Court."[97] King pointed out that while Holmes and Fuller, who grew up in Maine and attended Harvard Law School for the 1845–55 academic year, were both "descendants of . . . New England intellectuals" and had "similar . . . schooling," the two men differed sharply in their political affiliations, religious views, social attitudes, and "mental equipment." He concluded that the friendship was "unusual" and that Holmes "cultivated the Chief Justice . . . without the slightest suggestion of subservience."[98]

Holmes was sometimes attracted to men who were his temperamental opposites. He found Fuller an amiable, effective administrator as Chief Justice, writing in 1910 that Fuller "turned off the matters that daily called for action easily, swiftly, with the least possible friction, . . . and with a humor that relieved any tension with a laugh."[99] He may well have warmed to Fuller's modesty and been impressed by Fuller's combination of firmness and tact. He was shocked by the sudden death of Fuller's wife in 1904 from a heart attack, writing Fuller that "if it is any pleasure to you to hear that I think of you always with the same affection and faith I [would] like to tell it to you and hope that you know it beyond a doubt."[100] He undoubtedly took pleasure in the fact that Fuller, an uninspired writer, openly admired Holmes' literary style.[101]

But one of Holmes' implicit rules for personal relations—with men—was that he reserved his deepest friendships for persons whose intellects he regarded as "first rate." Fuller was clearly not in that category. However, Fuller was Chief Justice of the United States, and as such had the power to assign Court opinions when he was in the majority. We have seen that Holmes, as an Associate Justice on the SJC, had been voracious in his pursuit of opinions to write, being restrained from seeking to write most of the SJC's opinions only by the constraints of collegiality and judicial custom. One might have anticipated that as soon as Holmes felt comfortable in his new judicial position he would begin coveting opportunities to write majority opinions, and perhaps even wanting to write the lion's share of those opinions.

As a junior Supreme Court Justice Holmes had virtually no power to assign opinions himself, as he had had as Chief Justice of Massachusetts from 1899 through most of 1902. Seniority controlled the Court's assignment process, with the Chief Justice being treated as most senior. Thus Holmes' opportunities to write a disproportionately large number of majority opinions, or to write majority opinions in visible cases, were dependent, to an important extent, on the judgments of Melville Fuller. With this in mind, Willard King's statement that Holmes "cultivated" Fuller seems to have hit the mark.

On December 28, 1902, a little more than three weeks after he first sat on the Supreme Court, Holmes wrote a letter to Fuller. In it he said

> I enclose another opinion and have my third nearly ready. I have not heard from Harlan, Brewer, Shiras or Peckham JJ as to 41 Otis v. Parker. I suppose I am to do nothing until the next conference? Mr. J. Harlan to be sure said on the day he received it that he had read it and I understood him to agree—. . . . I cannot tell you how much I am impressed by and enjoy the work here.[102]

The reference to *Otis v. Parker*,[103] Holmes' first Supreme Court opinion, suggests that Holmes was unsure what the protocol was when Justices, some of whom had apparently voted with the majority, did not "sign on" to a circulated draft of the majority opinion. One could read the letter as reflecting a certain amount of impatience. Holmes would like to have his first opinion handed down as soon as possible; he is annoyed that some Justices, notably Harlan, who had told Holmes that he agreed with the opinion, had not formally endorsed it; he chafes at having to "do nothing" about the matter "until the next conference." One could also read the letter as a not very subtle reminder to Fuller that Holmes has no difficulty keeping up with the work on the Court. In about three weeks he has written and circulated one opinion, completed another, which he offers for circulation, and is "nearly ready" with a third. Finally, the letter could be seen as an effort to flatter Fuller. Holmes asks Fuller's advice, not only about internal Court protocol but, in a portion of the letter not included in the excerpt, about "what we are to do on New Year's day as to the president," referring to the then extant practice of the Supreme Court Justices paying a visit to the White House on New Year's Day.

Two months later Holmes was continuing to press Fuller for more work, and Fuller and the other justices were beginning to react to Holmes' attitude. In two letters, written a day apart in early February, Holmes informed Fuller that "I am on my last [assigned] case barring the one you told me not to write until further notice and the getting in of McKenna," that "[i]f you will give me some of your [assignments] I shall be grateful," that "I shall finish the last [of my assignments] tomorrow," that "[i]f there are 2 more weeks—I can write almost any old thing that anyone will give me," and that "a case doesn't generally take more than two days if it does that."[104] Fuller, himself interested in a prompt dispatch of the Court's business, wrote Justice Rufus W. Peckham four days after receiving the second of Holmes' letters. "Are you willing to part with No. 121 [Home Life Insurance Co. v. Fisher,][105] to Holmes, J?," Fuller asked Peckham. "I shall be glad to put it in his hopper."[106] The same day Peckham responded: "I will part with it in spite of __ __ as Brother Harlan would say!"[107]

The February 1903 exchanges among the Justices suggest that Holmes felt he need not flatter Fuller to get more assignments, but simply remind him of his eagerness to work, the speed with which he completed opinions (two days or less), and his ability to "write almost any old thing that anyone will give me." They also suggest that Fuller was inclined to encourage Holmes' zeal for work, since it could have the effect of improving the Court's collective productivity. However, when Fuller asked Peckham to relinquish an opinion in a minor case to Holmes,[108] Peckham, in the course of complying, took the occasion to add the ambiguous phrase" in spite of ___ as Brother Harlan would say!" The blanks in Peckham's phrase may have simply referred to a favorite curse of Justice Harlan's ("hell fire" or the like), in which case Peckham would have been signalling relief in giving up the assigned opinion. But they might also have referred to something like "damned Holmes," in which case Fuller would have been reminded that at least two of his colleagues did not care for Holmes' attitude.

A February 18 letter, written by Fuller to his wife, does little to clarify the ambiguous blanks in Peckham's note, but provides a good encapsulation of Fuller's early impressions of Holmes. Fuller pointed out that

> We shall dispose of more than fifty cases at our next meeting—more than ever before I believe—. The Nimble Holmes has got out his last—I delayed his progress for about a week but he deserved the obstacle & is free and clear & I suppose eager for more work.[109]

The letter makes it apparent that Fuller welcomed Holmes' participation in their mutual goal of disposing of cases. At the same time the letter reveals the existence of a distinction, in Fuller's mind, between the Court's collective efficiency and Holmes' individual desire to write as many opinions as possible. "The Nimble Holmes" was so quick to turn around opinions that "his progress" sometimes had to be "delayed" by a Chief Justice interested in preserving harmony among his colleagues. Holmes even "deserved" such delaying tactics, probably because Fuller believed that Holmes' combination of intellectual acuity, energy, and ambition could make him a source of resentment among the other justices.

A final incident casting light on the Holmes-Fuller relationship is Holmes' submission to Fuller, in the 1905 case of *Vicksburg v. Waterworks Co.,*[110] of an opinion deciding the case one way and a memorandum arguing for the opposite result. The case involved a construction of the Contracts Clause of the Constitution: the principal issue was whether a municipality could, by entering into binding contracts with private entrepreneurs, divest itself of its power to supply sufficient water to its residents. The city of Vicksburg, dissatisfied with the water service being provided by its original franchisor, decided to supply water itself, becoming a competitor of that franchisor. In an age in which utilities were not clearly defined as "private" or "public" entities, the city's action raised a vexing question of policy, but one that appeared to provide no difficulties for Holmes, given his views on sovereignty. If a state legislature could give a municipality power to supply water, it could also bind a municipality not to compete with private suppliers. But a subsequent legislature could change its mind and encourage competition. Supplying a necessity like water was one of the sovereign powers of the state.

There were two complexities in the *Vicksburg* case, however. First, the same case had come up to the Court only four years earlier, before Holmes' appointment,

and in a unanimous opinion, Justice George Shiras had intimated that once a municipality had entered into a binding contract with an "exclusive" franchisor, it could
not itself become a competitor of that franchisor during the time of the contract. To
do so, Shiras suggested, would violate the Contracts Clause of the Constitution unless
the contract did not make the franchise exclusive or was otherwise invalid.[111] While
Shiras was no longer a member of the Court, seven of the eight other justices that
had endorsed his 1901 opinion remained.

Second, the logic of Holmes' views on sovereignty vitiated all Contracts Clause
challenges to state legislation, at least where the state itself was a party to the prior
contract. If a state legislature could grant a private enterprise an exclusive franchise
for a designated period and then, within that period, change its mind and become a
competitor of the franchisor without running afoul of the Constitution, the categorical
language of the Contracts Clause ("no state shall impair the obligation of contracts")
was rendered meaningless. Holmes' views on sovereignty included an exception, to
his usual posture of deference to legislative power, for the "overwhelming constitutional mandate." Thus he might well have regarded *Vicksburg* as one of those
cases that could truly be decided either way, since it involved irreconcilable
principles (legislative versus constitutional supremacy) and thus amounted to an
exercise in "the sovereign preogative of choice." Accordingly, he wrote up justifications for deciding the case in favor of the franchisor, and also in favor of the city of
Vicksburg.

The incident reveals the degree to which Holmes could be simultaneously flippant and "jobbist" in his approach to the work of being a judge. In a letter accompanying the opinion and memorandum Holmes said that "I am about on the fence
as to the merits" of the case. That was not quite true: he believed that "on the
merits" the city of Vicksburg's position should prevail, but he was inclined to respect
a very recent precedent, even if he thought it wrongheaded. Being also inclined to
exercise his analytical and stylistic talents, he decided to write up an opinion reversing the first *Vicksburg* decision and, to complete the exercise, he wrote a memorandum arguing that the first decision should be followed. He informed Fuller that he
had sent both his memorandum and his draft opinion "to the printer—to be submitted
to the boys," and that "if the former *[Vicksburg]* opinion is sustained, I hope someone else will do it."[112] Eventually he joined an opinion by Justice William R. Day
that sustained the earlier *Vicksburg* opinion, thereby precluding the city of Vicksburg
from constructing its own water system.

The incident reveals that Holmes did not think it inconsistent with the integrity
of his office to produce rationales for both sides of a contested legal dispute and
then invite his fellow judges to pick whichever rationale they chose. Moreover, he
did not think that Fuller would disapprove of his actions. It was as if Holmes felt
comfortable, in the face of Fuller's restraining presence, to indulge a nihilistic streak
in himself, counting on Fuller to muffle or deflect any outrage Holmes' behavior
might produce among the other justices. It was as if Holmes enjoyed playing Sher-
lock to Fuller's Dr. Watson: the one brilliant, eccentric, whimsical, detached; the
other solid, conventional, prosaic, warm-hearted.

~

Holmes' second important relationship with a fellow justice was his friendship with Louis Brandeis. While a discussion of the Holmes-Brandeis relationship takes us past the chronological coverage of this chapter (Brandeis was appointed to the Court in 1916 and served beyond the time of Holmes' retirement in 1932), it seems justified at this stage to round out this discussion of Holmes' relations with his fellow justices.

William Howard Taft, in a 1928 letter to Henry Stimson, indicated that he regarded Brandeis as having exerted a marked influence on Holmes on the Court. "I am very fond of the old gentleman," Taft wrote, "but he is so completely under the control of Brother Brandeis that it gives to Brandeis two votes instead of one."[113] This comment was an embellishment on one Taft had made five years earlier, when he said that "I think perhaps [Holmes'] age makes him a little more subordinate or yielding to Brandeis, who is his constant companion, than he would have been in his prime."[114] Taft based his judgment not only on Holmes' age but on his perception of Brandeis, whom he once descrived as "belong[ing] to a class of people that have no loyalty to the Court . . . and wish to stir up dissatisfaction with the decision of the Court, if they don't happen to agree with it."[115]

Taft was not the only one with this perception of Brandeis' influence on Holmes. In a March 5, 1921, letter to Nina Gray, Holmes responded to her comment, "If only you stay thoroughly Anglo-Saxon." "I am tickled at your [remark]," he said.

> I take the innuendo to be that I am under the influence of the Heb's. I am comfortably confident that I am under no influence except that of thoughts and insights. Sometimes my brother B. seems to me to see deeper than some of the others—and we often agree. There is a case now on in which his printed argument convinced me contrary to my first impressions—I do not remember any other case in which the agreement was not independent. In two or three cases he has perhaps turned the scale on the question whether I should write— but in each of those I was and am more than glad that I did. . . . On the Cuba question I had written repeatedly before I ever knew or cared what he thought—and on free speech my best ebullition was independent though the Gov't prevented my opinion appearing by confessing error—I had turned that way long before he was on the bench. I don't suppose that I shall change your prepossession by what I say, but I am confident that you need not be uneasy on the score.[116]

Several reasons combined to make Brandeis a closer companion to Holmes than any of the other judges with whom he sat. First, Holmes, who liked to believe he was interested only in the views of the elite, placed Brandeis in that category. He had known of Brandeis' abilities since the 1870s; he had welcomed his appointment to the Court; he believed, as he wrote to Pollock in 1926, that Brandeis "has done great work and I believe with high motives."[117] There is no evidence that Holmes regarded any of the other judges with whom he sat as comparable to Brandeis in intellectual power and ability.[118] Brandeis' talents were particularly significant to Holmes in light of Holmes' self-image, that of one who dwelt in the realm of high intellect and was disinclined to devote his energies to extended companionship with lesser minds.

Second, Brandeis and Holmes, for quite different reasons, were united in opposition to the majority of the Court, especially during the 1920s, on major issues of
constitutional law. In a subsequent chapter we will see that after Holmes' opinions
in *Schenck v. United States* and the companion 1919 Espionage Act cases, a majority
of the Court regularly followed an orthodox "bad tendency" analysis of speech
issues, while Holmes, after his dissent in the case of *Abrams v. United States,* insisted
that his "clear and present danger" test for limiting speech, which he had first
formulated in *Schenck* and which he applied in an increasingly libertarian fashion
after *Abrams,* should control in the analysis of First Amendment questions.[119] Brandeis, who was supportive of free speech because of his commitment to education
and informed citizenship, also found the libertarian position congenial, and took the
opportunity to refine and expand Holmes' analysis. Thus on one of the most visible
issues of constitutional law in the 1920s, Holmes and Brandeis were in declared
opposition to the rest of the Court.

On the major area of constitutional disagreement in that decade, the use of the
Due Process Clauses to prevent regulatory social and economic legislation, Brandeis
and Holmes were likewise paired in opposition to a majority of the Court. After
some indications in the years immediately before and after World War I that the
Court was going to tolerate "social legislation" in the face of due process challenges,
a new postwar majority of the Court, composed in part of justices appointed by Taft
during his presidency and, after 1921, including Taft himself, closed ranks against
further "experimentation."[120] Of the justices who sat with Holmes and Brandeis in
the 1920s only Harlan Stone could have been said to be "tolerant" of the kind of
legislation on which "progressives" had placed such high hopes, and Stone did not
join the Court until 1925.

Holmes' and Brandeis' "tolerance" was based on different criteria. As his dissent
in *Hammer v. Dagenhart*[121] revealed, Holmes was offended by the doctrine of "liberty of contract," which a court majority employed to invalidate social legislation,
as a jurisprudential proposition and as a theory of constitutional interpretation. His
opposition did not imply any enthusiasm for the legislation it was being invoked to
challenge. Holmes repeatedly professed skepticism about the efficacy of hours and
wages legislation, child labor reform, and other policy goals of "progressives." The
only early twentieth-century "reform" he endorsed with enthusiasm was eugenics.[122]

Brandeis, on the other hand, believed in social experimentation at the state level.
He particularly felt that industrialization had its human costs, and that its victims
needed help, often from their own self-destructive tendencies. He was thus just as
enthusiastic about Prohibition as he was about minimum wage scales for women in
the District of Columbia. He also did not regard property rights as sacrosanct: in his
ideal polity government could and should regulate private property in the public
interest. In a conversation with Taft about appointments to the Court in 1923, Brandeis apparently told Taft that the crucial criterion for a nominee was not political
affiliation but "progressiveness, so-called—views as to property." Taft was reportedly not pleased by that comment, noting that "we can't go around looking for men
with certain creeds on property,"[123] but Brandeis intended the comment to mean
that in his judgment the most important thing the Court needed was justices who

were not indiscriminately wedded to the idea that property or contract "rights" were absolutes. Holmes shared this last sentiment, but for reasons unrelated to any enthusiasm for regulating property itself.[124]

A combination of circumstances, personal and contextual, thus meant that it was easy for Holmes and Brandeis to see themselves as allies within the Court in the 1920s, and easy for others to see them in that capacity as well. In addition to Taft's comments and those implied by Nina Gray, Charles Ross wrote in the *St. Louis Post Dispatch* in 1927 that Holmes and Brandeis "have achieved a spiritual kinship that marks them off as a separate liberal chamber of the Supreme Court. On the great issues that go down to the fundamental differences in the philosophy of government these two are nearly always together; often they are together against the rest of the court."[125]

But did Brandeis' and Holmes' association mean, as Taft suggested, that Holmes was under the influence of Brandeis? It is clear that the two justices, even on constitutional issues, did not invariably agree; when they did agree, in dissent, they sometimes expressed themselves separately.[126] And it is hard to imagine that on issues such as the proper interpretation of the Due Process Clauses or the appropriate doctrinal formulae for First Amendment cases Holmes would not have drawn upon his own experience rather than simply following Brandeis' lead. Indeed it is hard to imagine Holmes' following any other judge's lead on any matter that came to him. The essence of his judging was working out legal questions in a solitary fashion, "thinking [them] to the bottom." It was an important part of his self-concept that he did his work alone.

What, then, could Taft have meant? The answer seems to be that Taft, in a pique at not being able to marshal a unanimous front of justices on important constitutional issues,[127] had perceived that Brandeis had been "encouraging" Holmes to take public positions in cases where Holmes, although opposed to the majority view, might have remained silent.[128] While Taft rendered this as the equivalent of giving Brandeis "two votes," he may have been more concerned that Brandeis' "influence" on Holmes was resulting in two dissents, or at least a dissent joined by two of the illustrious names on the Court. In 1926, for example, Taft wrote one of his sons that Holmes "is not a great constitutional lawyer . . . but that is due to his training and point of view and influence which Brandeis has had on him."[129]

There is evidence that Taft's perception was accurate. It is clear, first of all, that Brandeis had highly developed views about the proper role of dissent in Supreme Court cases, especially constitutional cases, and that he was not loath to encourage Holmes to publicize his opposition when Brandeis shared that opposition. Brandeis believed that Holmes "has no realization of what moves men—he is as innocent as a girl of sixteen." He "ought to have more influence with the Court," but his constant tendency to "go off" on an abstract intellectual plane meant that he often did not sense the motivations of his colleagues.[130]

Brandeis perceived the inner workings of the Supreme Court during Taft's Chief Justiceship as dominated by majority justices, such as Willis Van Devanter, who lobbied successfully with their "conservative" colleagues to ensure larger majorities by suppressing dissents. Brandeis believed that there were "various reasons for withholding dissent," that it "all depends how frequent one's dissents have been

... or how important [the] case."[131] He thought that Holmes "is always in doubt as to whether to express dissent once he has 'had his say' on a given subject—and he has had his say on almost anything." The result was that a number of 5–4 decisions became rendered as 6–3 or even 7–2.[132] Dissent, Brandeis believed, had a "special function in constitutional cases." In "ordinary cases there is a good deal to be said for not having dissents—you want certainty and definiteness and it doesn't matter terribly how you decide so long as it is settled." But in constitutional cases, "since what is done is what you call statesmanship, nothing is ever settled."[133] In such cases Brandeis hoped to have "ample time to go over to Holmes and talk things over with him at length and modify his views."[134]

In Holmes' correspondence with Harold Laski, a young friend of his who was highly supportive of Brandeis, there are numerous references to Brandeis' being a catalytic factor in Holmes' decision to issue a dissenting opinion. The following are only some examples. On April 9, 1918, Holmes wrote Laski that "my labors are finished for the moment (unless I let Brandeis egg me on to writing a dissent in advance)." On May 25, 1918, he wrote that an opinion had come down "that stirred the innards of Brandeis and me and he spurred me to write a dissent."[135] On December 3 of that year he wrote that "when I get calm I am catspawed by Brandeis to do another dissent on burning themes."[136] On October 16, 1929, he wrote that "Brandeis ... reminded me of a case argued last term in which he said I should have to write a dissent."[137] and only two weeks before his retirement he wrote that "a dissent that the ever active Brandeis put upon my conscience waits untouched."[138]

Most significant of all, perhaps, was a letter Holmes wrote to Laski in February 1928. "I had but one case to deliver," he noted, "a majority opinion of no great interest—Brandeis dissenting." He then told Laski a story about the case. Justice McReynolds had held up the delivery of Holmes' opinion because he wanted to write a dissent; Holmes had "tried to put a shovel full of coals on [McReynolds'] head by handing him my prospective dissent [in another case] where we stand 5 to 4 unless he changes his mind." But he came back to Brandeis' position, saying that "Brandeis and I are so apt to agree that I was glad to have him dissent in my case, as it shows there is no preestablished harmony." The case was a minor one, involving a construction of the Anti-Narcotic Act as applied against packages of drugs shipped without revenue stamps, and would not have been likely to receive much notice. The fact that Holmes took pains to discuss the issue of "preestablished harmony" between himself and Brandeis, in a case in which their being on opposite sides would not likely have aroused much attention, is noteworthy. It suggests that here as elsewhere Holmes was extremely sensitive about his intellectual independence, and aware that Brandeis was in some sense an "influence" on him.

～

In one of his early letters after taking his seat on the Court Holmes had said that the jurisprudential universe of the Supreme Court of the United States was "much bigger than a state court." He had raised the same theme in an earlier letter to Pollock, describing his first set of cases, in which he stressed the "variety and novelty of the questions" he was being asked to consider. But his Supreme Court decisions were "bigger" in another sense. They involved "burning themes": public issues that contemporaries perceived as significant and controversial; decisions that would have widespread political impact. The best measure of the change from the Massachusetts court was the number of constitutional law cases Holmes encountered. One such case, *Otis v. Parker*,[139] the first opinion he delivered as a Supreme Court justice, foreshadowed his subsequent stance toward judicial review of the constitutionality of legislative acts.

In *Otis v. Parker* the constitutionality of a California statute prohibiting "all contracts for the sales of shares of the capital stock of any corporation . . . on margin" was challenged as a violation of the Fourteenth Amendment's Due Process Clause. The argument was a familiar one in late nineteenth-century constitutional jurisprudence, resting on the doctrine that the word "liberty" in that Clause included the right freely to enter into contracts. Holmes noted that "it is said that [the provision of the California statute] unduly limits the liberty of adult persons in making contracts which concern only themselves . . . thus depriving persons of liberty and property without due process of law."[140]

While conceding that "neither a state legislature nor a state constitution can interfere arbitrarily with private business transactions," Holmes maintained that "general propositions do not carry us far."[141] He then outlined, for the first time as a Supreme Court justice, his attitude toward judicial review of the constitutionality of legislative acts:

> While the courts must exercise a judgment of their own, it by no means is true that every law is void which may seem to the judges who pass upon it excessive, unsuited to its ostensible end, or based upon conceptions of morality with which they disagree. Considerable latitude must be allowed for differences of view as well as for possible peculiar conditions which this court can know but imperfectly, if at all. Otherwise a constitution, instead of embodying only relatively fundamental rules of right, as generally understood by all English-speaking communities, would become the partisan of a particular set of ethical or economical opinions.[142]

It is worth parsing this paragraph, since it contains a number of the assumptions that formed the starting place from which Holmes approached constitutional cases. He began by repeating the idea, which he had articulated in "The Path of the Law" and "Law in Science and Science in Law," that judges were often faced with cases in which principles of comparable importance were in collision, and simply had to exercise the "sovereign prerogative of choice." Here the principles were, respectively, legislative autonomy and the freedom of individuals to conduct private business. The latter principle did not shield all contracts, but on the other hand a legislature's power to make its own laws did not protect "arbitrary" legislative regulations.

Holmes' conception of judicial review identified the close potential connection between "arbitrariness" and perceived wrongheadedness, and sought to avoid equating the two in constitutional analysis. But he did not rule out the possibility that some legislation could be invalidated as being "arbitrary." The stance he assumed in *Otis v. Parker* thus appeared to assume that judges could fairly distinguish merely misguided legislation from legislation that trampled on "relatively fundamental rules of right, as generally understood by English-speaking communities."

"If the State thinks that an admitted evil cannot be prevented except by prohibiting a calling or transaction not in itself necessarily objectionable," Holmes said, "the courts cannot interfere, unless, in looking at the substance of the matter, they can see that it 'is a clear, unmistakable infringement of rights secured by the fundamental law.'"[143] The legislation in *Otis v. Parker* was a clear "infringement of rights," since it prohibited persons from entering into certain types of contracts. But Holmes obviously did not think those "rights"—allegedly subsumed in a "liberty" to contract—had been "secured by the fundamental law." Since the right to contract was not inviolate, the question was whether a particular restriction of it was reasonable as distinguished from arbitrary. He concluded that "[w]e cannot say that there might not be conditions of public delirium" in which the prohibition of sales on margins might make sense. He may have had in mind the fact that "short" sales of stock (sales on margin) are literally gambles on the part of buyers and sellers as to the future course of that stock, and when short sales are engaged in by large numbers of persons economic chaos can result. But the question was not whether such a prohibition made sense as an empirical matter, but whether "there might not be conditions in which it reasonably might be thought a salutary thing, even if we disagreed with the opinion."[144]

In the theory of judicial review applied in *Otis v. Parker,* the judge was largely a passive, "deferential" figure, notwithstanding his ultimate power as the sovereign interpreter of the Constitution. The theory introduced one of Holmes' familiar juxtapositions, that between his attitude toward the worth of a particular legislative provision and his responsibility as a judge evaluating that provision's constitutionality. With his Darwinist views on economic affairs, Holmes was not inclined to think that most legislation regulating the economy would have much effect. But he was inclined to believe that in most cases the legislature had the power to enact regulations that were ineffective. Given his conviction that consumption, not production, dictated the character of an economy, he had doubted if it made any difference whether the state or private individuals sold wood or coal to the citizens of Massachusetts. But he was willing to allow the state to go into the fuel business if it chose.[145] He was equally willing to allow California to regulate stock sales.

Otis v. Parker makes Holmes' celebrated dissent in *Lochner v. New York,*[146] decided two years later, appear to be one that could have been predicted by commentators. Over time, however, the *Lochner* dissent has come to be regarded as a major turning point in American constitutional jurisprudence, and the *Lochner* decision itself as one of the notorious moments in the history of the Court. It is not clear, at first blush, why *Lochner,* rather than *Otis v. Parker,* should have achieved celebrity status. On reflection, the great interest generated by *Lochner* seems to have been a function of two features of that case that were not present in *Otis v. Parker.* One was the contrast between Holmes' dissent, particularly its tone, and that of the other opinions, majority and dissenting, rendered by the justices in *Lochner.* The other was the *Lochner* majority's invocation of a liberty-of-contract argument to perpetuate the allegedly exploited status of a comparatively powerless group—nonunionized bakers—in the labor force. *Lochner,* in short, has been a case more commentators can relate to, and a case in which Holmes' position stands out more clearly, than *Otis v. Parker*. It was not a novel case for Holmes.

In the early twentieth century those who felt that the existing system of labor relations needed to be more responsive to the demands of an industrializing society often pointed to the deleterious impact of working conditions on the health of wage earners. In certain industries, critics charged, the situation was worsened by a practice of long working hours, which exposed workers in those industries to unhealthy conditions over an extended period of time. One such industry was the baking industry, which combined what one observer called "unreasonably long hours" with "[t]he constant inhaling of flour dust."[147] A report by the New York Bureau of Statistics of Labor found that the baking industry was among those "occupations involving exposure to conditions that interfere with nutrition," and recommended shorter hours of work in the industry. In response to those findings, New York passed a statute designed to improve conditions in "bakeries and confectionary establishments," which, in addition to mandating the ventilating and inspection of bakeries, limited the number of hours bakers could work to ten a day and sixty a week.[148]

The owner of a bakery in Utica, New York, was convicted of a misdemeanor under the statute for allowing one of his employees to work more than sixty hours in one week. He claimed that the statute was unconstitutional as an interference with the Fourteenth Amendment's "liberty of contract," and a majority of the Court eventually agreed with him. On the first vote the Court decided to sustain the statute, which was similar to a Utah statute requiring an eight-hour day for miners in 1898. But eventually one justice changed his vote, leaving a 5–4 majority for invalidation and turning Harlan's majority opinion into a dissent.[149]

Both Justice Rufus Peckham's opinion for the majority in *Lochner* and Harlan's dissent conceptualized the case as one in which the Fourteenth Amendment's "liberty of contract" was balanced against the state police power. "In every case that comes before this court," Peckham announced, "where [police power] legislation is concerned and where the protection of the Federal Constitution is sought, the question necessarily arises: Is this a fair, reasonable and appropriate exercise of the police power of the State, or is it an unreasonable, unnecessary and arbitrary interference with the right of the individual to . . . enter into those contracts in relation to labor which may seem to him appropriate or necessary for the support of himself and his family?"[150] Harlan put the inquiry in similar terms. "Granting . . . that there is a liberty of contract which cannot be violated even under the sanction of direct legislative enactment, but assuming . . . that such liberty of contract is subject to such regulations as the State may reasonably prescribe for the common good and the well being of society," he said, "what are the conditions under which the judiciary may declare such regulations to be in excess of legislative authority and void?" The answer was when the regulations were "plainly and palpably in excess of legislative power" because they bore "no real or substantial relation to [the] objects [of public safety, morals, or health] or constituted "a plain, palpable invasion of rights secured by the fundamental law."[151]

Both approaches assumed that "liberty of contract" was a viable constitutional doctrine and that the judiciary, in balancing Fourteenth Amendment "rights" against state police powers, could engage in a substantive reading of the Due Process Clause.

Language such as "fair," "reasonable," "arbitrary," "unnecessary," and "plainly and palpably in excess of legislative power" appeared to invite the judiciary to consider the wisdom of the legislation in question. Peckham's opinion concluded that the statute in *Lochner* was a "mere meddlesome interference with the right of the individual," whose "object and purpose were simply to regulate the hours of labor between the master and his employees . . . in a private business." "This interference on the part of the legislatures of the several States with the ordinary trades and occupations of the people," Peckham noted, "seems to be on the increase."[152] Harlan, in contrast, concluded that "[t]here are many reasons of a weighty, substantial character, based upon the experience of mankind, in support of the theory that, all things considered, more than ten hours' steady work each day, from week to week, in a bakery or confectionary establishment, may endanger the health and shorten the lives of the workmen."[153]

Placed against those two opinions, Holmes' dissent appeared to be a jurisprudential document of a different order. First, its tone, while characteristic of Holmes, provided a radical contrast to the other *Lochner* opinions, which by comparison appeared to have "padded breast and shoulders." Holmes' sentences were short and direct and his language less stilted and formal. Referring to the kinds of regulatory statutes that Peckham had called "mere meddlesome interferences with the rights of the individual," Holmes said that "[s]ome of these laws embody convictions or prejudices which judges are likely to share. Some may not," and then went on to suggest that the "particular economic theory" of a given statute was irrelevant in determining its constitutionality.[154]

Holmes' dissent in *Lochner,* in short, declined to accept "liberty of contract" as an established constitutional doctrine. He pointed out that "[i]t is settled by various decisions of this court that state constitutions and state laws may regulate life in many ways . . . which . . . interfere with the liberty to contract." He added that he thought that "the word liberty in the Fourteenth Amendment is perverted when it is held to prevent the natural outcome of a dominant opinion." He objected to judges making substantive readings of the Due Process Clause, maintaining that "[t]his case is decided upon an economic theory which a large part of the country does not entertain," and that "[t]he Fourteenth Amendment does not enact Mr. Herbert Spencer's Social Statics."[155] In summary, his position on "liberty of contract" and substantive due process was that

> a constitution is not intended to embody a particular economic theory, whether of paternalism and the organic relation of the citizen to the State or of *laissez faire*. It is made for people of fundamentally differing views, and the accident of [judges] finding certain opinions natural and familiar or novel and even shocking ought not to conclude our judgment upon the question whether statutes embodying them conflict with the Constitution of the United States.[156]

Despite this elegant language, and some other pithy phrases ("General propositions do not decide concrete cases. The decision will depend upon a judgment or intuition more subtle than any articulate major premise"),[157] Holmes' *Lochner* dissent was strikingly similar to his opinion for the majority in *Otis v. Parker*. In Otis he had pointed out that usury laws and Sunday closing laws had been sustained despite their interference with "liberty of contract." He had also mentioned that many states prohibited lotteries, even though those prohibitions directly interfered with freedom to contract. He repeated those examples in *Lochner*. His "general propositions" language in *Lochner* was similar to his statement in *Otis* that "general propositions do not carry us far." In *Otis* he had added that "[c]onsiderable latitude must be allowed for differences of view . . . [o]therwise a constitution . . . would be the partisan of a particular set of ethical or economical opinions." Finally, his standard of review was the same in both cases: whether "a rational and fair man necessarily would admit that the statute proposed would infringe fundamental principles as they have been understood by the traditions of our people and our law."[158] In *Otis v. Parker* he had said that the courts could not interfere with regulatory legislation "unless . . . they can see that it is a 'clear, unmistakable infringement of rights secured by the fundamental law.' "[159]

In light of the considerable similarities between the opinions, *Lochner*'s far greater notoriety among contemporaries seems to have come from its labor context. When Holmes said of the New York statute, at the close of his *Lochner* opinion, that "[a] reasonable man might think it a proper measure on the score of health," and that "[m]en whom I certainly could not pronounce unreasonable would uphold it as a first installment of a general regulation of the hours of work," he had identified the salient difference, for contemporaries, between *Lochner* and *Otis v. Parker. Otis* involved the kind of transactions—speculations in "wildcat" stocks of mining companies—that were generally perceived as risky and subject to manipulation. Where such transactions were concerned the general public arguably needed protection from its own gullibility. *Lochner,* by contrast, involved labor relationships, where employers and employees arguably knew their place in the market. The hours and wages of an occupation reflected that knowledge: for the state to regulate them struck of "meddlesome interference." *Lochner,* Holmes suggested, was merely the "first instalment of a general regulation of the hours of work." He went further, and maintained that a legitimate objective of state legislation was to equalize bargaining power between workers and employers. Thus Holmes highlighted what his contemporaries took to be the critical issue in *Lochner.* Would the Supreme Court sit by and allow states to effectuate this equalization, to enact "a general regulation of the hours of work?" The other justices in *Lochner* expressed concern about the effect of state efforts on freedom to buy and sell one's services in the marketplace. Holmes appeared to assume that such "freedom" was always at state suffrance. Holmes' views on "liberty of contract" and substantive due process notwithstanding, the truly alarming feature of his *Lochner* dissent to contemporaries was his apparent view on the states' role in labor relations.

Lochner thus appeared to identify Holmes as a "progressive" judge,[160] one sympathetic to legislative efforts to ameliorate the conditions of labor in industrializing America.[161] He had shown similar sympathies to labor interests in his *Vegelahn v. Guntner* dissent. But had more attention been given to the similarities between *Lochner* and *Otis v. Parker,* a different reading of Holmes' *Lochner* dissent might have surfaced. Holmes was suggesting in *Lochner* that the test for the constitutionality of regulatory legislation—whether a given statute was "reasonable" or whether it "infringe[d] fundamental principles as they have been understood by our people and our law''—was ultimately a test of majority opinion. If the public at large, through its legislative representatives, thought that the conditions of industrial labor should be regulated, the fact that judges thought the regulation ''meddlesome interference with the rights of the individual'' was irrelevant. If the public thought that such regulation—say one in which the state confiscated profits from companies and passed them on directly to workers—infringed ''fundamental principles,'' it would express its views by not enacting the legislation in the first place or voting those who had out of office. ''It does not need research'' to discern whether statutes such as that under scrutiny in *Lochner* were ''reasonable,'' Holmes felt.[162] One had only to look at public sentiment.

Holmes' response to *Lochner* was predictable in two other respects. His previous scholarship had demonstrated that he was deeply suspicious of words such as ''right,'' which Holmes had thought were ''nothing but prophecies'' of how courts might decide cases[163] or ''vague generalization[s]'' that amounted to ''pontifical or imperial way[s] of forbidding discussion.''[164] The invocation of the talismanic phrase ''liberty of contract'' could have been expected to generate a comparable response in Holmes. To say that such a ''liberty'' existed was for him simply another way of saying that courts would support all private bargains in labor contexts, however unequal the bargaining position of the parties. It was another pontifical way of forbidding discussion.

Moreover, Holmes' opinions in *Vegelahn* and *Plant v. Woods,* and his essay on ''Privilege, Malice, and Intent'' indicated that he saw capital and labor as similarly situated actors in the world of political economy. Just as there was nothing inappropriate in labor combining to seek an advantage in the marketplace, there was nothing inappropriate in a legislative majority, sympathetic to the ''plight'' of laborers, giving them special dispensations. The worth of that legislative policy need not concern Holmes, and his views on political economy suggested that he would be indifferent toward it, since he felt that capital and labor equally contributed to the flow of goods to the consuming masses, where the central issues of political economy played themselves out. In sum, nothing in Holmes' previous career and nothing about his established views on issues of jurisprudence and economic relations suggested he would find ''liberty of contract'' anything but a meaningless fiction.

Holmes also dissented from a case in which the majority employed a ''liberty of contract'' argument to strike down a regulatory statute in *Adair v. United States.*[165] In that case Congress had made it a criminal offense for a carrier engaged in interstate commerce to discharge an employee simply because of the employee's membership in a labor organization. The Congressional statute was invalidated on the ground that it interfered with the liberty of employers to discharge employees on the terms they chose. Holmes, in dissent, repeated his view that ''the right to make contracts at will that has been derived from the word liberty in the amendments has been stretched to its extreme,'' and noted that ''[w]here there is, or generally is believed to be, an important ground of public policy for restraint the Constitution does not forbid it, whether or not this court agrees or disagrees with the policy pursued.'' ''I quite agree,'' he concluded, ''that the question what and how much good labor unions do, is one on which intelligent people may differ ... but I could not pronounce it unwarranted if Congress should decide that to foster a strong union was for the best interest, not only of the men, but of the railroads and the country at large.''[166]

Similarly in *Coppage v. Kansas*,[167] Holmes dissented from an opinion invalidating a Kansas statute making it a misdemeanor for an employer to require his employees not to become members of any labor organization as a condition of their employment. The majority, citing *Adair,* found the statute violative of ''the right to make contracts for the acquisition of property.''[168] Holmes' entire dissent read:

> I think the judgment should be affirmed. In present conditions a workman not unnaturally may believe that only by belonging to a union can he secure a contract that shall be fair to him. If that belief, whether right or wrong, may be held by a reasonable man, it seems to me that it may be enforced by law in order to establish the equality of position between the parties in which liberty of contract begins. Whether in the long run it is wise for the workingmen to enact legislation of this sort is not my concern, but I am strongly of the opinion that there is nothing in the Constitution of the United States to prevent it, and that *Adair v. United States* and *Lochner v. New York* should be overruled. I have stated my grounds in those cases and think it unnecessary to add others that I think exist [citing *Vegelahn v. Guntner* and *Plant v. Woods.*] I still entertain the opinions expressed by me in Massachusetts.[169]

Another case along the same lines was *Noble State Bank v. Haskell*,[170] in which Holmes, for the Court, upheld the constitutionality of Oklahoma statute creating a fund to secure the repayment of bank deposits. The source of the fund was a one-percent assessment of the banks' daily deposits. The Noble State Bank challenged the fund as a violation of the Contracts Clause of Article 1, Section 10 of the Constitution and a taking of property without due process of law under the Fourteenth Amendment. Holmes dismissed the Contracts Clause claim out of hand, pointing out that the bank's charter was subject to alteration or repeal, and then turned to the due process claim.

His analysis was reminiscent of *Otis v. Parker, Lochner,* and *Adair:*

> In answering that question we must be cautious about pressing the broad words of the Fourteenth Amendment to a drily logical extreme. Many laws which it would be vain to ask the Court to overthrow could be shown, easily enough, to transgress a scholastic interpretation of one or another of the great guaranties in the Bill of Rights. They more or less limit the liberty of the individual or they diminish property to a certain extent. We have few scientifically certain criteria of legislation, and as it often is difficult to mark the line where what is called the police power of the States is limited by the Constitution of the United States, judges should be slow to read into the latter a [mandate to void] ... the legislative power. ...
>
> It may be said in a general way that the police power extends to all the great public needs. ... It may be put forth in aid of what is sanctioned by usage, or held by the prevailing morality or strong and preponderant opinion to

be greatly and immediately necessary to the public welfare. . . . With regard to the police power, as elsewhere in the law, lines are pricked out by the gradual approach and contact of decisions on the opposite sides.[171]

Notice that Holmes reasserted the *Otis* and *Lochner* arguments that the "liberty" of the citizen was infringed in a number of ways, repeated the general attitude on judicial review expressed in those decisions, defined police power as predicated on majoritarian sentiment, and offered yet another version of his "poles" metaphor for the growth of legal doctrine.

Holmes' "progressivism" in cases involving regulatory legislation, then, was a product of his fatalism about the power of majoritarian sentiment and his recognition of the sovereignty of the state to do what its citizens wanted. There were some instances, however, where he thought that the sovereign "power . . . to reconstruct society" needed to be expressly exercised in order to be legitimate, and one such instance, notorious in its day, illustrates how treacherous are characterizations of Holmes as a "progressive" judge.

One of the "great cases" of the early twentieth century was *Northern Securities Co. v. United States,*[172] a product of Roosevelt's efforts to use the Sherman Act to compel the dissolution of large industrial combinations—in this instance a holding company owning the stock of competitor railroads—whose presence tended to lessen competition. The Act outlawed "every contract, combination in the form of trust or otherwise, or conspiracy, in restraint of trade among the several States."[173] It provided criminal penalties for violations. Its application to the *Northern Securities* case raised three questions. Was the arrangement between the two railroads a "contract," "combination," or "conspiracy" in "restraint of trade"? Did the arrangement affect interstate commerce? If the first two questions were answered affirmatively, did the Act therefore prohibit any agreement that in some way affected interstate commerce? As Holmes put it, did it apply to "two small exporting grocers"?

A majority of the Court answered the first two questions affirmatively and finessed the third question. Four justices, in an opinion by Harlan, said that the arrangement met the definition of a "combination in restraint of trade" and that it had an effect on interstate commerce, but declined to pass on the question whether the Act could be made to apply to the activities of single individuals.[174] A fifth vote for dissolution was provided by Justice David Brewer, who indicated that the Act was not intended to apply to "those minor contracts in partial restraint of trade which the long course of decisions at common law had affirmed were reasonable and ought to be upheld." The particular arrangement in *Northern Securities,* however, was between corporations and had "the possibilities of combination, the control of the whole transportation system of the country." Brewer did not think such an arrangement "reasonable," and thus concurred in the result.[175]

Holmes dissented. He did not reach the commerce power question because he read the Sherman Anti-Trust Act literally, to include within its definitions of "contracts" and "combinations in restraint of trade" only those arrangements that were illegal at common law, and to apply to "every" person and to "any part" of interstate trade or commerce. The Act, in his reading, did not have as its purpose the complete eradication of any "contract," "combination," or "conspiracy" in restraint of interstate trade or commerce, but only those previously outlawed arrangements.

At common law, Holmes argued, contracts in restraint of trade were "contracts with a stranger to the contractor's business . . . which wholly or partially restrict the freedom of the contractor in carrying on the business as he ordinarily would." Their purpose was to protect the contracting party himself. Combinations or conspiracies in restraint of trade, by contrast, were "combinations to keep strangers to the agreement out of the business," and they were limited to monopolies or attempts to create monopolies, on the theory that such entities were against public policy.[176] Understood in this fashion, "contracts" and "combinations" in restraint of trade did not cover the arrangement that created the Northern Securities Company. It was not an arrangement that restricted the freedom of the two railroads that established the holding company, but one "which leaves the parties without external restriction."[177] Nor was it a monopoly in the legal sense of that term. It was not an attempt to exclude all interstate competition in railroads, even though it was clearly an effort to gain a greater footing in the interstate railroad market. The framers of the Act could not have meant to make all attempts to "monopolize" in the popular sense criminal under it, because then "Mr. [J. P.] Morgan could be sent to prison for buying as many shares as he liked of the Great Northern and the Northern Pacific" on the ground that he was seeking to "monopolize" control of those railroads.[178]

In short, Holmes believed that his reading of the Act was the only possible one because any other reading would mean that "a partnership between two stage drivers who had been competitors in driving across a state line . . . is a crime." Given the Act's language, "if the restraint on the freedom of the members of a combination caused by their entering into a partnership is a restraint of trade, every such combination, as well the small as the great, is within the act."[179] The Act, he felt, could not be construed "to mean the universal disintegration of society into single men, each at war with all the rest, or even the prevention of all further combinations for a common end."[180]

The difficulty in the *Northern Securities* case, Holmes concluded, was that the Sherman Anti-Trust Act was only clumsily applied to the situation the government was trying to prevent. "There is a natural feeling," he suggested, "that somehow or other the statute meant to strike at combinations great enough to cause just anxiety on the part of those who love their country more than money, while it viewed such little ones as I have supposed with just indifference." But while this notion "somehow breathes from the pores of the act," it was "contradicted in every way by the words in detail." While size seemed affiliated with "monopoly" in the popular mind, size in railroads was "an inevitable incident" of the railroad industry, and "even a small railroad will have the same tendency to exclude others from its narrow area that great ones have to exclude others from a greater area." The Sherman Act attacked small monopolies as well as large ones.

The events that precipitated the *Northern Securities* case, Holmes felt, were what had made it a "great" case. Such cases were "called great, not by reason of their real importance in shaping the law of the future, but because of some accident of immediate overwhelming interest which appeals to the feelings and distorts the judgment. These immediate interests exercise a kind of hydraulic pressure which makes what previously was clear seem doubtful, and before which even well settled principles of law will bend.''[181] The case had been a product of an inarticulate but deeply felt conviction among many early twentieth-century Americans that ''trusts''—combinations of companies designed to consolidate industrial power—had grown too large and were reducing competition by ''monopolizing'' markets. The Sherman Antitrust Act might have been passed out of a similar conviction. But the Act said nothing about preserving competition and nothing about a necessary connection between size and monopoly status. It used terms of art from common law and applied its prohibitions to every ''contract'' or ''combination'' in restraint of trade. As such it was an awkward instrument for ''trust-busting'' where the perceived difficulties of trusts lay in their size and their ''anti-competitive'' tendencies. Nonetheless, the Roosevelt administration, responding to popular anxiety about trusts, used it as the basis of an antitrust prosecution, and persuaded a majority of the Supreme Court that its application to the Northern Securities holding company was not too awkward. ''Great cases,'' said Holmes, ''make bad law.''[182]

Holmes, we have seen, infuriated Roosevelt with his dissent, and Roosevelt later complained that Holmes had been a ''bitter disappointment'' to him on the Court.[183] But Holmes was not consistently opposed to the use of the Sherman Act as a mechanism for dissolving combinations in restraint of trade. In *Swift and Company v. U.S.*[184] Holmes wrote the opinion, for a unanimous Court, applying the Sherman Act to a combination of shippers in fresh meat that had agreed not to bid against one another in setting prices for shipment of the meat to stockyards, to secure favorable rates for their shipments on railroads, and to establish uniform rules for giving credit to dealers in meat.

There were two issues in the *Swift* case. One was whether an ''intent'' to monopolize trade and commerce in fresh meat had been made out, given the fact that none of the acts were alone sufficient to produce a monopoly. Holmes dealt with that issue by resurrecting his Massachusetts opinion in the criminal attempt case *Commonwealth v. Peaslee*, which he had also cited in the *Northern Securities* case,[185] and arguing that ''[w]here acts are not sufficient in themselves to produce a result which the law seeks to prevent . . . but require further acts in addition to the mere forces of nature'' to bring the result about, intent could be made out by showing a connection among the acts and ''the consequent dangerous probability.'' ''It is,'' Holmes noted, as he had in *Peaslee,* ''a question of proximity and degree.'' He held that the ''unity of the plan'' in *Swift* had embraced ''all the parts.''[186]

The second issue was whether the ''combination'' in *Swift* affected interstate commerce. This issue was a delicate one for the Court even though the defendants' meat would eventually be sold across state lines, because earlier decisions had restricted the reach of the Sherman Act by making sharp distinctions between the manufacturing and distribution stages of commercial activity, and excluded from the Sherman Act's coverage manufacturing activities taking place within the borders of one state.[187] In *Swift,* however, Holmes argued, ''the subject matter is sales and the very point of the combination is to restrain and monopolize commerce among the States in respect to such sales.''[188] ''[C]ommerce among the States,'' he felt, ''is not a technical legal conception, but a practical one, drawn from the course of business.''[189] When cattle were sent for sale ''from a place in one State, with the expectation that they will end their transit, after purchase, in another . . . and when this is a typical, constantly recurring course, the current thus existing is a current of commerce among the States.''[190] Holmes' *Swift* opinion can be seen as one of the first recognitions by the Court that separating the process of commerce into artificial stages would produce unrealistic decisions.

～

After his retirement, for reasons that will subsequently be explored, Holmes came to be mythologized as a "liberal" judge. The characterization of Holmes as a liberal contained three discrete stands: support for organized labor, as evidenced by his decisions in *Vegelahn* and *Lochner;* deference toward "progressive" regulatory legislation, as in *Lochner, Adair,* and *Coppage;* and an alleged championing of civil liberties, as evidenced by his free speech opinions.

As we have seen, even those decisions in which Holmes supported the principle that labor could organize itself to compete with management in the market for services cannot fairly be taken as an indication that Holmes was sympathetic to labor interests. He simply felt that if a competitive advantage could be gained by combinations of capital or other anti-competitive practices, it could also be achieved by combinations of workers or collective labor tactics such as strikes or boycotts. He also believed that if the state wanted to prohibit industrial combinations or unions in the pursuit of some "reasonable" policy goal, the state could do so. He was thus "pro-union" only to the extent that his detachment contrasted with the decidedly anti-union views of his judicial colleagues. In addition to mischaracterizing Holmes' views, later twentieth-century "liberals" have occasionally assumed that since early twentieth-century reformers held "enlightened" views on economic issues such as labor relations (being pro-labor) and antitrust regulation (being in favor of such legislation), they held comparable views on the other identifying prong of liberalism, solicitude for civil rights. Such was very rarely the case. In the first thirteen years of Holmes' tenure on the Court the sorts of persons whose civil rights tend to be infringed by majorities—racial and ethnic minorities, political radicals, and aliens— fared comparatively poorly before the Supreme Court, and Holmes contributed to their relatively ineffectual showing.

A recent history of the Supreme Court during the tenure of Chief Justice Edward White has argued that notwithstanding the breadth and depth of racism in early twentieth-century American society, the Court was regularly solicitous toward the cause of black petitioners who sought relief against racial discrimination.[191] A review of the cases suggests that there may be some support for this argument when the Court is taken as a whole and the time period extended into the 1920s. But Holmes cannot easily be identified as a supporter of civil rights, for blacks or anyone else, in the years between 1903 and 1916. In fact, the Court's civil rights decisions during those years suggest that on more than one occasion Holmes' posture was sufficiently hostile to the claim of a petitioner to cause him to depart from his typical stance of deference toward the legislature in constitutional cases.

In *Giles v. Harris,*[192] however, Holmes was ultradeferential to the legislature. His approach, in fact, appeared to assume that the Court had no power to intervene in the entire race relations area because racial discrimination was a "political wrong."

The case involved an effort on the part of a black citizen of Alabama to compel the state registrars to register him and other blacks who sought to be registered prior to January 1, 1903, when more restrictive qualifications for Alabama voters went into effect. Giles' complaint, in the form of a bill for equitable relief, alleged that state officials had arbitrarily excluded blacks from being eligible to vote while allowing whites, and that the state Constitution, by prescribing restrictive qualifications for voters after the beginning of the 1903 year, had as its purpose the continued exclusion of blacks. Voters who qualified to vote prior to the 1903 requirements were eligible to vote for life, so that, according to the complaint, "[t]he white men are registered for good under the easy test and the black men are likely to be kept out in the future as in the past."[193]

Holmes concluded that equitable relief could not be granted. First, he declared that "the traditional limits of proceedings in equity have not embraced a remedy for political wrongs." While he did not rest his holding solely on that claim, it was an extraordinary one in the context of the case. The disenfranchisement of black voters was a "political" wrong only if blacks had no constitutional right not to be deprived of the franchise on grounds of race. After the Fifteenth Amendment they clearly had such a right. The fact that the motivation for excluding black voters from registration may have been "political" did not make the wrong any less legal, in the sense of a violation of existing constitutional rights. Holmes seemed to be suggesting that the whole range of practices in southern states in which blacks were deprived of legal rights on account of their race were merely "political" and thus beyond the reach of equity courts.

Holmes then passed on to two additional "difficulties which we cannot overcome." The first was that the plaintiff in *Giles* had claimed that the entire registration system in Alabama was invalid because it was fraudulently administered. If that were so, ordering the system to admit the plaintiff to the voting rolls would not cure its deficiencies. Admitting all qualified blacks would not solve the problem, because as a practical matter "there is no probability that any way now is open by which more than a few could be registered." And even if they all were, the plaintiff had maintained that the entire Alabama Constitution was defective because of its voting rights provisions, and to grant him relief would be to suggest that an original constitutional invalidity "could be cured by an administration which defeated [that Constitution's] intent."[194]

This argument amounted to saying that if a pervasive system of discrimination existed, no equitable relief could be granted because either the system could not as a practical matter be eradicated or no constitutional basis existed by which the system could be modified short of complete dissolution. That this was Holmes' intended meaning is buttressed by his second "difficulty" with granting equitable relief in *Giles,* that federal courts could not correct "political wrongs" created by states and the people of those states. Federal courts, he maintained, had "no constitutional power to control [the] action [of states] by any direct means." If "relief from a great political wrong" were desired, it "must be given by [the states] or by the legislative and political department of the government of the United States." This again suggested that "political" wrongs, which were in sharp distinction to "legal" wrongs, could only be corrected by "political" institutions. But such institutions regularly dealt with "legal" wrongs, as when state legislatures or Congress changed the definition of a crime or an offense under the tax or antitrust laws. Was Holmes suggesting that the federal courts had no power to enforce Congressional statutes? He appeared to be implying something else, that the federal courts ought not to intervene in the area of race relations.

Comparable deference to the "political" branches was shown by Holmes' opinion in *Moyer v. Peabody*,[195] a case where the petitioner's status was that of an ideological rather than a racial minority. The petitioner in *Moyer* was the president of the Western Federation of Miners, which was involved in labor unrest in Colorado. The Governor of Colorado declared one of its counties to be in a state of insurrection because of labor disputes, called out the State Guard to restore order, and arrested and detained Moyer. Moyer was imprisoned for about six weeks, with no effort being made to bring him before a court. He claimed that the Governor, as a state official, had violated his civil rights under Section 1979 (now 1983) of the United States Code, which provides for civil relief against deprivations of constitutional rights by state officials acting "under color of state law."[196]

Holmes held that the petitioner had stated no cause of action because he had not been deprived of a constitutional right. "[D]ue process of law," he announced, "depends on circumstances," and "varies with the subject matter and necessities of the situation." In *Moyer* a state of insurrection existed because the Governor had declared one, and the Governor's declaration was "conclusive of that fact."[197] Given the Governor's power to declare a state of emergency, he had comparable powers to call out troops and order precautionary arrests. "When it comes to a decision by the head of the State upon a matter involving its life," Holmes argued, "the ordinary rights of individuals must yield to what he deems the necessities of the moment. Public danger warrants the substitution of executive process for judicial process."[198]

The problem with Holmes' analysis is that it gave the Governor power summarily to detain persons by declaring a state emergency and then alleging that the safety of the state or the persons themselves warranted their detention. This seemed to give state officials a license to incarcerate people because of their political views. If a union threatened to strike, and the state's governor was unsympathetic, what prevented the governor, after *Moyer*, from declaring a state of insurrection and detaining the union's leaders so as to weaken the union's position in negotiations? The purpose of Section 1979 appeared to be to prevent state officials from using their powers to deprive their enemies of their constitutional rights, such as the right to a speedy trial once detained. Holmes acted as if in an "emergency" due process could be highly summary, even if the officials charged with due process violations had the power to create the emergency.

Moyer v. Peabody and *Giles v. Harris*, while certainly not responsive to civil rights claims, did not reveal Holmes as conspicuously indifferent to those claims among his colleagues on the Court, since in both cases his opinions were for a majority, although his *Giles* opinion produced three dissents. In two subsequent cases involving black claimants, however, Holmes wrote separately, and his position identified him as particularly unsympathetic to ideas of racial equality.

In *Bailey v. Alabama*[199] a black farm laborer named Alonzo Bailey contracted to work for a year at the rate of $12.00 a month, and received an advance of $15.00, which he was to repay by deductions of $1.25 from his monthly pay. Such contracts, coupled with state laws that made their breach criminal, in effect created a system of peonage, akin to involuntary servitude. Alabama had passed a statute in 1903 that provided that breach of a contract "shall be prima facie evidence of the intent to injure or defraud [one's] employer," and such intent was itself evidence of a criminal offense.

Bailey left his employment after a month without repaying the advance, and was arrested and tried for a criminal offense under the Alabama statute. After some initial confusion as to whether the Alabama statute created a mandatory presumption that a breach constituted fraud or simply a rebuttable one, the case was eventually sent back to an Alabama trial court, where a jury convicted Bailey. He then challenged the constitutionality of the statute in light of the Thirteenth Amendment, and the case was appealed to the Supreme Court of the United States. Counsel for Bailey and an amicus brief for the United States argued that the statute was designed to enslave blacks, since they were habitually required to accept advances in order to repay existing debts or to avoid incarceration for petty crimes. "It is common knowledge," the amicus brief pointed out, "that Alabama is chiefly an agricultural state and that the majority of laborers upon the farms and plantations are negroes."[200]

The 5–2 majority opinion[201] in *Bailey,* written by Justice Charles Evans Hughes, avoided the racial implications of the statute, declaring that "we may view the legislation in the same manner as if it had been enacted in New York or Idaho."[202] Hughes concluded that the statute made a breach of a labor contract *prima facie* evidence of fraud and permitted juries to convict on that evidence alone. This meant that the statute's "natural operation and effect" was to punish simple breaches of contract, and as such a person who terminated his employment without repaying an advance on a labor contract "stood stripped by the statute of the presumption of innocence, and exposed to conviction for fraud upon evidence only of breach of contract and failure to pay."[203] This was inconsistent with the Thirteenth Amendment, whose purpose was "to render impossible any state of bondage" and "to make labor free, by prohibiting that control by which the personal service of one man is disposed of or coerced for another's benefit."[204]

Holmes dissented in an opinion that was remarkable in its assumptions about the practice of farm labor contracts and the role of early twentieth-century juries in southern states where blacks were defendants. He had stated in *The Common Law* that contracts could not be regarded as a form of "limited slavery" because a party always had the option of breaching and paying damages. "If, when a man promised to labor for another," he had argued, "the law made him do it, his relation to his promisee might be called a servitude ad hoc with some truth. But this is what the law never does."[205] The presumption of criminal intent in the Alabama statute, however, plus the common inability of black laborers to repay their advances, had the effect of doing just that. Holmes conceded that "the liability to imprisonment may work as a motive when a fine without it would not, and that it may induce the laborer to keep on when he would like to leave." But he maintained that "if it is a perfectly fair and proper contract, I can see no reason why the State should not throw its weight on the side of performance."[206]

Holmes did not think his discussion of the purpose of the statute necessary, however, because he believed that the statute did not attach criminal liability for a mere breach of contract. He believed that it simply laid before the jury evidence that an employee had breached his contract, which, absent contrary evidence, created a presumption that the breach denoted fraudulent intent. He thought that presumption appropriate. "Is it not evidence," he asked, "that a man has a fraudulent intent if he receives an advance upon a contract over night and leaves in the morning?" Juries, he felt, through "their experience as men of the world," could draw inferences from the events of the breach. They might conclude, for example, "that in certain conditions it is so common for laborers to remain during a part of the season, receiving advances, and then to depart at the period of need in the hope of greater wages at a neighboring plantation, that when a laborer follows that course there is a fair inference of fact that he intended it from the beginning." Nor was it relevant to Holmes that Alabama also had a rule of evidence that barred persons charged with fraud from testifying as to their intent in breaching contracts. "If there is an excuse for breaking the contract," he said, "it will be found in external circumstances, and can be proved."[207]

In short, Holmes apparently believed that a white jury in Alabama, in a case in which a black laborer was accused of leaving a labor contract without repaying his advance, and where that laborer was not permitted to testify about his intent in breaching the contract, would weigh the "circumstances" and sometimes excuse the presumed fraud. Even though such juries were composed of "men of the world" who were aware of the transiency of laborers during the harvest season and who were exposed to stereotyped attitudes about the "reliability" of blacks, Holmes thought the Alabama statute compatible with the Thirteenth Amendment. Indeed he was perfectly comfortable with such statutes. "Imprisonment with hard labor," he noted, "is not stricken from the statute books. . . . [T]he power of the States to make breach of contract a crime is not done away with by the abolition of slavery."[208]

In the *Bailey* dissent Holmes had been uncharacteristically formalistic, emphasizing the formal distinction between conclusive and rebuttable presumptions. He had also been uncharacteristically solicitous of juries, suggesting that jurors carefully sifted evidence before presuming fraud from the fact of a contract's having been broken, a suggestion that did not square with his often expressed skepticism about the impartiality of juries.[209] In addition, he had pointed out that "[n]either public document nor evidence discloses a law which by its administration is made something different from what it appears on its face, and therefore the fact that in Alabama it mainly concerns the blacks does not matter."[210] This language suggested that he was acting as if the statute had been drafted to apply to all contracts and that the peculiar circumstances of black labor in Alabama played no part in its inception or its application.

In *United States v. Reynolds*,[211] however, Holmes took quite a different view of black labor in the post-Reconstruction South. The *Reynolds* case involved a practice that was the logical extension of the peonage practices invalidated in *Bailey*, the criminal-surety arrangement. Alabama and Georgia had statutes that permitted persons convicted of minor offenses, and ordered to pay fines, to enter into agreements with sureties by which the surety paid the fine and the convicted person agreed to work a given amount of time for the surety. If the convicted person failed to perform the work, he would be convicted and fined again, in an amount equivalent to the original damages paid by the surety. A recent study of the practice concluded that it was used almost exclusively in the case of blacks; that it resulted in large numbers of blacks being convicted of minor offenses; and that it meant that on some occasions serious crimes were scaled down to lesser ones so that a fine could be sufficient punishment.[212]

One person victimized by the criminal-surety system, Ed Rivers, presented an opportunity for the Justice Department to challenge its constitutionality. Rivers had pleaded guilty to petit larceny and was assessed $58.75 in fines and costs. He had no money to pay the fine and consequently entered into a criminal surety agreement with J. A. Reynolds, for whom he agreed to work for nine months and 24 days in exchange for his fine being paid. When Rivers subsequently quit Reynolds' employ, he was arrested and convicted of failing to honor the surety contract. He was fined again, and this time his fine was paid by another surety, who hired him for fourteen months at a rate of $6.00 per month. That story was enough for the Justice Department, who initiated, through a U.S. Attorney in the Southern District of Alabama, prosecutions against Reynolds and the other surety. They eventually worked their way up to the Supreme Court of the United States.

A unanimous Court held that the criminal surety statutes could not constitutionally be made the basis for indictments in cases such as that of Ed Rivers. Justice Day, for the Court, conceded that the criminal-surety arrangements were voluntarily entered into by the convicted persons and were alternatives to incarceration and service on the notorious forced-labor "chain gangs" present in Southern states. He also conceded that the terms of labor contracts between private individuals and their employees were, on the whole, not the state's business. The problem, for Day, was that the statutes instituted peonage, because once the surety paid the convicted person's fine any debt that person owed was to the surety, and the surety could enforce that debt through the state's criminal process. This meant that if the convicted person refused to work he could be punished again, as Ed Rivers had been, and be forced to enter into yet another surety contract. This meant, Day maintained, that "the convict is . . . kept chained to an ever-turning wheel of servitude."[213] It resulted in compulsory service based on debt, or peonage.

Holmes joined the majority in *Reynolds*. But he added a concurring paragraph spelling out his reasons:

> There seems to me nothing in the Thirteenth Amendment or the Revised Statutes that prevents a State from making a breach of contract, as well as a reasonable contract for labor as for other matters, a crime and punishing it as such. But impulsive people with little intelligence or foresight may be expected to lay hold of anything that affords a relief from present pain even though it will cause greater trouble by and by. The successive contracts, each for a longer term than the last, are the inevitable, and must have taken to have been the contemplated outcome of the Alabama laws. On this ground I am inclined to agree that the statutes in question disclose the attempt to maintain service that the Revised Statutes forbid.[214]

The contrast between Holmes' *Reynolds* concurrence and his dissent in *Bailey* is instructive. In *Bailey* he had emphasized the fact that the statutes making breach of a labor contract a crime were not race conscious, and that white juries in Alabama would carefully weigh evidence to determine whether black violators of labor contracts had an intent to defraud their employers. He had agreed with Hughes that the *Bailey* case was to be treated as if it had occurred in Idaho or New York, and the fact that the labor contract system mainly affected blacks was irrelevant. In *Reynolds,* however, he began his analysis by reaffirming the principle that a state could make breaches of contracts, including labor contracts, crimes. The problem with the criminal-surety practice in Alabama, then, was not that black laborers were fined for violating their contracts. It was that "impulsive people with little intelligence or foresight may be expected to lay hold of anything that affords a relief from present pain." It was, in short, that onerous surety arrangements would be "the inevitable . . . outcome" of the criminal surety statutes, since the "impulsive" black laborers involved would invariably choose immediate relief from their fines by entering into additional surety arrangements.

The motive of the Alabama legislature in passing such statutes, Holmes was suggesting, was thus "to maintain [compulsory] service," or peonage. The legislators knew that the laborers participating in surety contracts would overwhelmingly be black, and assumed that they would be "impulsive . . . with little intelligence." The legislation was thus race conscious. While Holmes thought that making breaches of contract crimes in the ordinary case (*Bailey*) was appropriate, since reasonable men knew the consequences of their actions, he thought that adding an "escape" from the ordinary consequences of the state's having criminalized breaches of labor contracts—incarceration and forced labor on a state chain gang—was inappropriate because black laborers would inevitably accept that escape, through the surety system, and bind themselves to perpetual service by entering into onerous surety arrangements. It was permissible, Holmes felt, for a state to criminalize breaches of labor contracts, even when black laborers were involved, but not permissible for states to take advantage of the "impulsive[ness]" of such laborers by allowing others to stand surety for them.

The *Bailey-Reynolds* sequence shows Holmes' positivism in tension with his interest in exposing the practical consequences of legal rules. His disinclination to recognize limitations on the sovereign capacity of the state had been behind his conclusion in *Bailey* that states could make breaches of contracts crimes, just as states could imprison persons for debt.[215] Given that view of sovereignty, he was not concerned with the circumstances under which white juries in Alabama would consider evidence rebutting a presumption that black laborers had intended not to honor their contracts. The Alabama legislature could have made breach a conclusive presumption of a fraudulent intent. In *Reynolds,* however, he could have rested on the same line of reasoning, but he did not. He could have argued that Alabama could criminalize breaches without giving breaching parties any option of escaping incarceration, so Alabama could surely provide such an escape. Instead he looked to the consequences of the criminal surety practice in a state in which the overwhelming number of affected laborers were black. He had ignored comparable consequences in *Bailey.*

Why did Holmes retreat to formalistic conceptions of sovereignty in one instance and not in the other? One possible explanation may lie in the fact that he wanted to facilitate transactions by reducing the opportunities of persons entering into them to do other than uphold their agreements or pay damages for breach. By making breach a crime, and providing for the option of fine or imprisonment for offenders, a state such as Alabama was deterring those who could not afford to pay damages for their breaches from entering into contracts in the first place. As Holmes had put it in his discussion of imprisonment for debt, the legislature could make "the purchase of the necessaries of life easier by giving special remedies against those who willfully try to avoid paying for them."[216] But by creating a third option in *Reynolds,* the state was allowing laborers to maintain the illusion that they could terminate their contracts and neither be fined nor imprisoned. They were too "impulsive" and ignorant to realize the consequences of entering into surety arrangements; hence they would continue to breach contracts in the future.

The *Reynolds* decision thus shows Holmes adopting an uncharacteristic pose of scrutinizing a legislature's motives and finding evidence of a race-conscious motive. The scrutiny, however, did not come from any assumption on Holmes' part that black laborers should be given an equal right to avoid peonage or incarceration for their contract breaches. On the contrary, it came from an assumption that black laborers were especially likely not to weigh the consequences of their acts and thus especially likely to end up in relationships that amounted to compulsory labor. It was a scrutiny based on notions of white supremacy.

Holmes participated in but did not write opinions in two other important civil rights cases in the first thirteen years of his tenure. In *Berea College v. Kentucky,*[217] the Court sustained a Kentucky statute preventing persons or corporations from operating educational institutions that accepted and did not separate blacks and whites. Berea College challenged the constitutionality of the statute, and a majority of the Court upheld it on the ground that states had plenary power to control the powers they conferred on corporations licensed within the state. All the Kentucky statute had done, the majority suggested, was bring Kentucky educational institutions in conformity with the principles of *Plessy v. Ferguson.*[218] Berea College could educate both blacks and whites if they were separated. Holmes concurred in the judgment of the Court but not in the majority's reasoning.

In the second case, *McCabe v. Atchison, Topeka & Santa Fe Railway,*[219] an Oklahoma "Jim Crow" statute affecting railroads was challenged under the Equal Protection Clause. The statute created an exception to the railroads' general obligation to provide "separate coaches or compartments . . . equal in all points of comfort and convenience . . . for the accommodation of the white and negro races."[220] Sleeping, dining, and parlor cars could be used "exclusively by either white or negro passengers, separately but not jointly."[221] The purpose of the exception was to permit railroads to decline to furnish certain accommodations to blacks if there was a limited demand. Luxury pullman cars were an example of such accommodations. Five black plaintiffs challenged the statute and, after their claim was dismissed by a federal district court and a 2–1 majority of the Eighth Circuit Court of Appeals, appealed to the Supreme Court.

In an opinion joined by four other justices, Justice Charles Evans Hughes denied relief on technical grounds but held that the exception in the Oklahoma statute was unconstitutional. An argument that separate accommodations need not be provided if the demand was insubstantial, he declared, "makes the constitutional right depend upon the number of persons who may be discriminated against, whereas the essence of the constitutional right is that it is a personal one." Once a railroad made a decision to provide accommodations to one race, Hughes said, it could not decline to provide comparable accommodations to another. "It is the individual," he concluded, "who is entitled to the equal protection of the laws."[222] Hughes held, however, that the black plaintiffs in *McCabe,* who had filed suit before the exception to the Oklahoma statute went into effect, had not actually been denied any accommodations by the railroad. They thus had no standing to sue, and judgment for the railroad was accordingly affirmed.

The split among the justices produced by Hughes' treatment of the statute suggests that four justices would have sustained its constitutionality. Holmes was one of these: the others—White, Joseph Lamar, and James McReynolds—were all Southerners. An exchange between Holmes and Hughes found among Holmes' papers suggests that Holmes thought Hughes' stance too abstract and removed from the world of "experience." Holmes had written a memorandum on the *McCabe* case, and on November 29, 1914, Hughes reponded. "I return herewith your memorandum in [the *McCabe* case]," Hughes began.

> I cannot construe the statute as requiring the carriers to give equal, though separate, accommodations so far as sleeping cars, dining cars, and chair cars are concerned. All agree—both parties and the Attorney General—that such cars may be provided exclusively for whites—that a black man must sit up all night just because he is black, unless there are enough blacks to make a "black sleeping car" pay.
>
> I don't see that it is a case calling for "logical exactness" in enforcing equal rights, but rather as it seems to me it is a bald, wholly unjustified, discrimination against a passenger solely on account of race.[223]

One can imagine that Hughes' use of the phrase "logical exactness" and his first sentence, were responses to Holmes' having urged him to give a reading of the Equal Protection Clause that took into account the economic and social realities of transportation involving the races in the South. Blacks and whites could not travel in the same cars and blacks could not, on the whole, afford luxury cars. Hence to make railroads furnish separate cars of a comparable type for all blacks and whites was to force them to put nearly empty luxury cars on a train. "Separate but equal," Holmes appeared to be suggesting, should not be interpreted with "logical exactness." Hughes replied to this argument that the proviso in the Oklahoma statute was not inserted to conform to railroad usage, but to force a black person "to sit up all night just because he is black." It was a "bald, wholly unjustified" discrimination against black passengers solely on account of their race. Hughes was intimating that the railroad would not have declined to furnish sleeping cars for white passengers, however small the demand.

We will recall that Holmes had left Harvard and enlisted in the Civil War because of his conviction that the cause of abolitionism was just. Later in his life he recalled that he was "deeply moved by the Abolition cause—so deeply that a Negro minstrel show shocked me.''[224] By the time he had come to be a Supreme Court justice that conviction had not resurfaced in a commitment to the civil rights of blacks. One extensive study of Holmes' opinions in cases in which civil rights claims were made by black petitioners has confirmed the tendency noted here: Holmes' "consistent reaction" was to "deny . . . the claimed right, sometimes in dissent against majority support of the right.''[225] That study analyzed twenty-five nonunanimous civil liberties cases, several of which involved black claimants, and concluded that Holmes supported the claim in only one case, and that did not involve a claim by a black.[226]

Why did Holmes' abolitionism not translate itself into a solicitude for the civil rights of blacks? That question may start from an erroneous premise, that support for the abolition of slavery necessarily engenders support for the equal rights of racial minorities. It is clear that Holmes was sympathetic to the abolitionists, at least through the early months of his Civil War service, but it is not clear that he was ever committed to equality for persons regardless of their race or skin color. Indeed two dimensions of Holmes' and his contemporaries' antislavery views would tend to negate that connection. First, several of his contemporaries, notably Henry L. Abbott, were enthusiasts for the principles of antislavery and soldierly duty, but were openly contemptuous of blacks, and there is no evidence that Holmes dissented from such views. When Holmes' great friend Penrose Hallowell approached Holmes about assuming the captaincy of a black regiment, Holmes declined.[227] Second, abolitionism was founded principally on opposition to the idea that men and women could make other men and women their property, not on opposition to the idea that one race was superior to another. Many abolitionists believed that the intermingling of the races was hazardous and that removal of blacks to Africa offered the best solution to the presence of large numbers of former slaves in America.

When Holmes discussed the ideals for which he went to war, he spoke of the effort of his contemporaries as a crusade on behalf of the "civilized world." Nowhere in his comments is there a suggestion that he equated civilization with the eradication of racial prejudice or with the goal of racial equality. Nothing in Holmes' world had prepared him to embrace that concept. He had had little contact with persons outside his class and had not shown any inclination to do so. As an upper-class Bostonian growing up in the mid-nineteenth century, his would have had few opportunities for associations with blacks. He was not an egalitarian nor a devotee of humanitarian causes; his affinity for the North's effort in the Civil War was as an aristocratic champion of honor and chivalry and duty. He had been exposed to the late nineteenth-century literature that stressed the survival of the fittest, the superiority of the white races, and the threat to "civilization" from excess proliferation of the "colored" peoples. While there is no evidence that he adopted racist anthropology and sociobiology in its crudest forms, there is no evidence that he avoided the racial stereotyping that was characteristic of his contemporaries.

Given Holmes' positivism, lack of humanitarian sympathies, exposure to racial stereotypes, limited contact with black persons, and age at the time he was deciding Supreme Court cases, there was no reason to suspect that he would be sympathetic to the legal position of blacks or inclined to treat the Equal Protection Clause as a mandate for substantive equality. Holmes did not believe that law could change the attitudes and practices of a culture. He believed the reverse, that law was a product of those attitudes and practices. If the political and economic dominance of whites in southern states combined with racial antagonisms to result in laws that were "bald discriminations" against blacks solely on account of their race, Holmes felt that was the way law worked. He was neither jurisprudentially nor personally inclined to do anything about the situation.

～

Holmes' lack of sympathy toward the civil rights of minorities may have been conspicuous in regard to race relations, but it was not confined to that area. We have seen that in *Moyer v. Peabody* Holmes had taken a summary view of the obligations of the executive to conform to constitutional guarantees. Not only did the determination of whether a state-wide "emergency" rest with the governor of that state, Holmes noted in *Moyer,* the judicial process deferred to executive processes once an emergency was declared. Thus if a state executive thought the presence of labor activity in a sector of the state economy sufficiently dangerous to justify an "emergency," that decision was discretionary with the executive, and if the executive further thought that the incarceration of labor leaders for an indefinite period would alleviate the tensions that had precipitated the emergency, *Moyer* suggested that decision was discretionary as well, even though it resulted in persons being incarcerated without any charges pending against them simply because a governor thought their ideas "dangerous."

Determinations by executive agencies of the status of aliens posed issues that Holmes viewed as comparable to those in *Moyer.* As in "emergency" cases, he deferred to the powers of the sovereign, in this instance embodied in an executive decision. Just as a state had the power to decide for itself when its very existence was threatened, a nation had the power to exclude undesirable persons from its borders. When those persons were aliens, present in the nation at suffrance, their opportunities to challenge exclusion were extremely limited. Such were the principles established by Holmes for the Court in a series of early twentieth-century cases, originally involving aliens of Chinese descent but extending to aliens as a class.

One can see Holmes' decisions in alien cases as a piece with the general attitude toward law, power, and society that he had exhibited in the civil rights cases. Since he did not believe that law had much independent meaning apart from majoritarian social attitudes, he did not think it operated as a restraint on those attitudes. The idea of there existing constitutional obligations that restrained members of society across time was thus foreign to him. Constitutional guarantees such as "equal protection" and "due process" were whatever majorities wanted them to be. The sovereign powers of the state, being an embodiment of majoritarian will, were thus nearly absolute. Holmes began with the premise that the state possessed a number of arbitrary authoritarian powers—terminating life, excluding persons from its borders, restricting access to its facilities or its employment—and that when it chose to exercise less restrictive versions of those powers its ultimate sovereignty always lay in the background. He was thus strikingly unresponsive to the claim that the state owed an obligation to conform the implementation of its powers to constitutional limits.

Alien cases presented a context in which the state's lack of constitutional obligations was particularly evident. Aliens had no rights of citizenship, and were subject to the most summary executive procedures. They were, for Holmes, the embodiment of a class of persons against whom the full powers of sovereignty could be exercised. As he put it in a 1913 case, he believed that "sovereign states have inherent power [over] aliens, and . . . Congress is not deprived of this power by the Constitution of the United States. . . . Furthermore, the very ground of the power in the necessities of public welfare shows that it may have to be exercised in a summary way through executive officers."[228]

United States v. Sing Tuck,[229] a case decided in Holmes' second Term on the Court, exemplified his view of alien "rights." In that case persons of Chinese descent had sought to enter the United States from Canada. They claimed they had been born in the United States, gave their names, and then declined to answer any further questions. An immigration inspector denied them admission, and they appealed on the ground that they were citizens of the United States and entitled to a judicial investigation of their status. An 1894 Congressional statute provided that "[i]n every case where an alien is excluded from admission into the United States . . . the decision of the appropriate immigration or customs officers, if adverse to the alien, shall be final, unless reversed on appeal to the Secretary of the Treasury."[230] The aliens argued that the statute could not apply to native-born citizens of the United States.

Holmes, for the Court, held that before a court could determine the question of citizenship the aliens had to exhaust their administrative remedies. This meant that they had to take an appeal to the Secretary of Commerce and Labor, which had replaced the Secretary of the Treasury as the appropriate official charged with hearing appeals in immigration exclusion cases. Under the existing procedures of the Secretary of Commerce and Labor, the examinations precipitated by appeals were not made public, the burden of proof of citizenship was on the complaining party, no persons except officials were permitted to communicate with the complaining party, no copies of the evidence were available to that party's counsel, and there were no opportunities to compel witnesses or take depositions.[231] Holmes concluded that this arrangement did not violate the Due Process Clause. "The whole scheme," he maintained, "is intended to give as fair a chance to prove a right to enter the country as the necessarily summary character of the proceedings will permit." He went further, and suggested that even after administrative remedies had been exhausted "[a] mere allegation of citizenship" would not be enough to precipitate judicial review; the petitioner needed to "make out a prima facie case."[232]

The problem with *Sing Tuck* was that the statute and its attendant procedures were concededly not designed to apply to American citizens, but the procedures themselves made proof of citizenship difficult to make out. There were at the time no universal registration cards that an American citizen could show to prove his or her status; the typical method of proof was to produce two witnesses who would attest that the applicant had been born in the United States. The summary character of the procedures in *Sing Tuck* virtually assured that applicants would not be able to produce those witnesses. Without such proof, Holmes suggested, a determination by an immigration officer that the entrant was not a citizen would not be reviewable by the courts unless the entrant had made out a *prima facie* case of his status as a citizen. But the very question at issue in proceedings such as that in *Sing Tuck* was whether the entrant could be subjected to a summary investigation of his eligibility to enter. He could only be thus subjected if he was an alien. So it would seem that a simple allegation of citizenship should have been sufficient to precipitate review by the courts on that issue. Holmes said that review, after a mere allegation, amounted to "an attempt to disregard and override the provisions of the statutes and the rules of the department and to swamp the courts."[233] But if the statutes and rules only applied to aliens, it would seem that a determination of alien status was necessary to their being triggered.

Sing Tuck had technically left the question open whether the entrants had shown enough to merit a judicial review of any administrative decision adverse to them on the question of citizenship. *United States v. Ju Toy*,[234] decided a year later, considered that question. A person of Chinese descent was detained by the master of a steamship after returning to the United States from abroad. He was denied permission to land on the ground that he had not been born in the United States. He appealed the decision of the immigration official to the Secretary of Commerce and Labor, who upheld it. He then filed a habeas corpus petition in federal district court. The court denied a motion to dismiss the petition on the ground that the administrative findings were conclusive, and decided, "seemingly on new evidence," that the petitioner was a native-born citizen of the United States.[236] An appeal of that decision was taken to the Court of Appeals for the Ninth Circuit and subsequently to the Supreme Court.

Holmes reaffirmed that *Sing Tuck* had established that a habeas corpus petition merely advocating citizenship was not enough to precipitate judicial review, and so the district court should not have entertained the case in the first place. "But as it was entertained, and the District Court found for the petitioner," he said, "it would be a severe measure to order the petition dismissed on that ground now." He had other grounds on which the petition could be dismissed. Foremost among them was his reading of the 1894 Exclusion Act, which, he claimed, "purports to make the decision of the Department final, whatever the ground on which the right to enter the country is claimed—as well when it is citizenship as when it is domicil." Since the statute was clearly valid insofar as it applied to aliens, it "must be valid to all that it embraces, or altogether void." Thus the statute's determination that an administrative official's finding of eligibility to enter the United States was conclusive *in every case*, even where citizenship had been alleged.

Holmes felt it necessary "to add a few words" to clarify the reach of his holding. When an entrant sought admission to the United States, he declared, "[t]he petitioner, although physically within our boundaries, is to be regarded as if he had been stopped at the limit of our jurisdiction and kept there while his right to enter was under debate." If one assumed that he was a citizen, and "the Fifth Amendment applies to him and to deny entrance to a citizen is to deprive him of liberty, we nevertheless are of opinion that with regard to him due process of law does not require a judicial trial." In other words, even where a citizen was seeking entrance into the United States, an administrative official could find that the entrant lacked citizenship status, deny him entry, and that finding would be conclusive. "That is the result of the [previous] cases [involving exclusion of aliens,]" Holmes argued, "and the almost necessary result of the power of Congress to pass exclusion laws."[236]

The breadth of Holmes' opinion in *Ju Toy* was extraordinary. It suggested that anyone returning to the country from abroad could be made subject to a conclusive administrative decision on the question of his or her citizenship. While this was not likely to take place in the case of a family returning from a Canadian vacation, it seemed to create an opportunity for immigration officials to make judgments about what kind of persons they wanted to let enter the United States. The *Ju Toy* result was particularly harsh since a district court had previously found the entrant to be a citizen. One commentator at the time felt that the decision was inexplicable unless it in fact applied only to Chinese entrants, whose immigration into the United States had long been a contentious political issue.[237]

A particularly instructive sentence in Holmes' argument in *Ju Toy* was that claiming that summary procedures in instances where persons sought to enter the United States were "the almost necessary result of the power of Congress to pass exclusion laws." Here Holmes was employing his familiar "the greater power includes the lesser" argument. Since Congress could exclude persons altogether from the country, it could condition the process of eligibility for inclusion. But no one suggested that Congress could arbitrarily exclude *citizens:* its sovereign powers to exclude rested on a necessary preference for its own subjects as opposed to those of foreign nations. It did not at all follow that because the power to establish summary criteria for excluding aliens could be subsumed in the greater power to exclude aliens altogether, comparable criteria for citizens raised no constitutional objections. Indeed the obvious consequence of summary procedures in cases such as *Ju Toy* was that some American citizens could summarily be deported from the country. Subsequent Supreme Court cases recognized that difficulty with Holmes' *Ju Toy* opinion and sought to limit it to "exclusion" as distinguished from "deportation" cases, reading "deportation" to include any instance in which a person was technically present in the United States.[238]

The *Sing Tuck–Ju Toy* sequence, while characteristic of Holmes in its broad assertions about sovereign powers and its unwillingness to put teeth into the Due Process Clause, could have been seen as contextually limited to the "Chinese immigration problem," an issue replete with stereotypes about the incapacity of Orientals to assimilate into American culture and the grave difficulties in distinguishing, in the "tightly knit" Chinese communities that had established themselves in certain American cities, American citizens of Chinese descent from resident aliens, illegal entrants, or visitors. But Holmes did not limit his invocation of sovereign power to discriminate against aliens to that context. In *Patsone v. Pennsylvania*,[239] for example, the petitioner was an alien of Italian descent, and Holmes' treatment of the claim was as summary as that in *Sing Tuck* or *Ju Toy*.

The *Patsone* case involved a statute passed against a backdrop of labor unrest in Pennsylvania. It had been enacted about a month after an agreement between coal mine operators and mine workers, many of whom were foreign-born, had expired. The statute made it unlawful for any unnaturalized foreign-born resident "to kill any wild bird or animal except in defence of person or property, and to that end" made it unlawful "for such foreign born person to own or be possessed of a shot gun or rifle."[240]

The statute was challenged on equal protection grounds as unjustifiably discriminating against aliens as a class. Holmes treated the statute as incorporating two causal sequences, one in which a connection was made between the use of rifles and shotguns and the killing of wildlife, and the other in which a connection was made between alien status and danger to wildlife. He thought the first casual sequence entirely unobjectionable. "The possession of rifles and shot guns," he maintained, "is not necessary for other purposes not within the statute. It is so peculiarly adopted to the forbidden use that if such a use may be denied to this class, the possession of the instruments desired chiefly for that end also may be."[241] That argument was curious. The very circumstances of the statute's passage suggested that the Pennsylvania legislature had an interest in keeping rifles and shotguns out of the hands of foreign-born miners. It is hard to imagine that the legislators believed that those rifles and shotguns would be used exclusively to shoot wildlife. Indeed if the preservation of wildlife were the paramount goal of the statute it would seem to have made sense to prohibit native-born as well as foreign-born persons from using them. But Holmes assumed that it was not necessary to have a rifle or a shotgun other than to shoot wildlife.

The singling out of aliens to be prohibited from using shotguns or rifles, the statute's second causal sequence, presented for Holmes "a more difficult question." One might have expected this reaction, since the statute presupposed that aliens were more likely to shoot wildlife than citizens, a supposition that might not seem obvious on its face. Holmes began his analysis of the question by noting "that a State may classify with reference to the evil to be prevented, and that if the class discriminated against is or reasonably might be considered to define those from whom the evil mainly is to be feared, it properly may be picked out." This was standard equal protection doctrine (not all discriminatory classifications violate the Equal Protection Clause), but it appeared to require that, at a minimum, Pennsylvania reasonably believe that the evil of danger to wildlife was mainly to be feared from resident unnaturalized aliens.

At this point Holmes adopted the stance of ultradeference. "The question," he said, "is a practical one dependent upon experience. . . . Obviously the question . . . . is one of local experience on which this court ought to be very slow to declare that the state legislature was wrong in its facts." He then continued:

> If we might trust popular speech in some States it was right—but it is enough that this court has no such knowledge of local conditions as to be able to say that it was manifestly wrong.[242]

In this passage Holmes appears to have transcended deference, even to the point of abdication of judicial responsibility. First, it is hard to see why the question of whether unnaturalized resident aliens posed a peculiar danger to wildlife in Pennsylvania was "obviously . . . one of local experience." The legislature did not seem in an advantaged position to determine that there was something about alien status that inclined an individual to kill wildlife, or that aliens lost that inclination on becoming citizens. Nor did it seem in a position of expertise on the question whether there was something about the conditions of life in Pennsylvania that made its resident aliens peculiarly dangerous to wild creatures.

Second, even if the relationship of alien status to dangerousness to wildlife was one requiring "local experience" to address, it is hard to understand the relevance of "popular speech in some States" to that question. If Holmes thought that persons in Pennsylvania were best suited to decide whether aliens in that state posed a danger to its wildlife, why should he take views expressed in other states into account? Since the question was "obviously . . . one of local experience," it would seem that such "popular speech" in other states was neither "local" in character nor based on experiences in Pennsylvania.

Third, why was it "enough" to satisfy the Equal Protection Clause that the Supreme Court had "no such knowledge of local conditions as to be able to say that [a state legislature] was manifestly wrong?" Under that standard it would seem that any state classification arguably based on "local conditions" would survive an equal protection challenge unless the Court was intimately acquainted with such conditions. But Holmes had already said that when "local conditions" were involved "this court ought to be very slow to declare that the state legislature was wrong on its facts." So when would the Court conceivably declare a state legislature "manifestly wrong"? If there ever was a case in which a state appeared "manifestly wrong," in fact, it was *Patsone* itself, since the premise of the legislature that unnaturalized resident aliens posed a special danger to wildlife seemed implausible on its face. Indeed the stated purpose of the Pennsylvania statute appeared to be pretextual, and the actual motive of the legislators to keep shotguns and rifles out of the hands of unnaturalized alien miners.[243]

Holmes' unarticulated reasoning in the *Patsone* case may have proceeded as follows. The state of Pennsylvania could, in the exercise of its sovereign powers, exclude all aliens from its borders. That being so, it could attach any conditions to the entry of aliens, including the condition that they not possess rifles and shotguns. Since the classification in *Patsone* had the same effect, it did not matter what reason the state gave for doing something it could already do. The reason may have been pretextual, but the result was permissible, so the Supreme Court ought not to look too closely into legislative motives. This line of reasoning would have been consistent with Holmes' general views on sovereignty and judicial review. It also would have revealed that he treated the Equal Protection Clause as having virtually no effect. Even if Pennsylvania could have barred aliens from possessing firearms, the classification it had made in *Patsone* between aliens and citizens, with respect to tendencies to be dangerous to wildlife, was based on the baldest of stereotypes. It discriminated against a class of persons solely on the basis of their alien status. Holmes was willing to justify that discrimination on the basis that "popular speech in some States" thought "it was right."

～

This review of Holmes' constitutional decisions has suggested that, even within the circle of his early twentieth-century contemporaries, he was no friend of civil liberties or of the rights of minorities in his first thirteen years on the Supreme Court. While in the *Lochner* and *Adair* cases he had earned the plaudits of "progressives" for deferring to state legislatures, he had also deferred to the legislatures that discriminated against blacks in *Giles v. Harris, McCabe,* and *Reynolds,* and against foreign-born miners in *Patsone,* and he had been perfectly comfortable with the executive decision that had incarcerated a "dangerous" union leader in *Moyer v. Peabody*. For every instance in which Holmes could arguably have been said to have been sensitive to the disfavored classes in early twentieth-century America, there were many more in which his indifference to those classes could have been documented.

But the case for Holmes as civil libertarian has not rested principally on his solicitude for the rights of racial, ethnic, or economic minorities. It has rested largely on his championing of free speech; on his image as a judge that was dedicated to "freedom," as he put it, "for the thought we hate."[244] Holmes' free speech opinions have been said to have encapsulated the heart of his stance as a judge, that of the dispassionate observer, concerned with creating a breathing space for intellectual exchange so that civilized and rational ideas would be able to compete with, and ultimately prevail over, their uncivilized and irrational counterparts. Holmes thus believed, it has been thought, that freedom to speak, like freedom to compete in the marketplace, was the basis of American society.[245]

While such has been Holmes' reputation, despite a number of more sophisticated assessments of his First Amendment decisions,[246] it would be hard to draw much evidence in support of that view from his First Amendment cases in the first thirteen years of his Supreme Court tenure. On the contrary, the two major First Amendment decisions Holmes authored in those years show a restrictive approach to free speech issues that reflected the jurisprudential orthodoxy of the early twentieth century. By 1915 Holmes' position on free speech questions did not seem to have deviated at all from his views as a Massachusetts judge. The right of free speech was as subject to the restrictions of the sovereign as any other constitutional right.

In light of the elaborate and extensive doctrinal apparatus that has been grafted on the First Amendment by modern courts and commentators, it may be startling to find that the orthodox view of the First Amendment prevailing at the time Holmes became a Supreme Court justice was that it was simply a codification of English common law. In the 1897 case of *Robertson v. Baldwin*,[247] the Court noted that the First Amendment, like other provisions of the Bill of Rights, did not institute "any novel principles of government," but merely codified "certain guaranties and immunities which we had inherited from our English ancestors, and which had from time immemorial been subject to certain well-recognized exceptions."[248] This meant that First Amendment protection did not extend to libelous, blasphemous, obscene, indecent, or "other publications injurious to public morals or private reputation."[249] Consistent with that view, the Court had allowed the conviction of a Mormon[250] and an anarchist[251] for belonging to groups whose views had a tendency to lead to socially injurious acts, such as polygamy or the overthrow of government, even though neither case presented a clear showing that the defendants had advocated performance of those acts.

Since, according to this view, the First Amendment merely codified the common law, it prevented only prior restraints on speech, such as government censorship of the press, not subsequent punishment for expressions that had a socially injurious tendency. This had been the view of William Blackstone in his *Commentaries,* purporting to summarize English common law. Blackstone had declared that "[t]he liberty of the press . . . consists in laying no *previous* restraints upon publications, and not in freedom from censure for criminal matter when published.''[252]

In his first free speech opinion as a Supreme Court justice, Holmes adopted this view, treating as irrelevant the fact that Blackstone's *Commentaries* did not take into account the text of the Constitution of the United States. The case was *Patterson v. Colorado*,[253] where an editor in Colorado had published articles and a cartoon allegedly "reflecting on the motives and conduct of the [judges of] the Supreme Court of Colorado in cases still pending.''[254] He was convicted of contempt, and appealed his conviction on the basis that "[t]o fine or imprison an accused person in contempt proceedings for publishing the truth about a judge or a court when the truth of the charge is pleaded in justification . . . is to deprive him of liberty or property without due process of law.''[255]

The precise constitutional basis of the editor's appeal in *Patterson* was unclear. He did not argue that the Fourteenth Amendment's Due Process Clause "incorporated" the First Amendment, but rather that the word "liberty" in the Fourteenth Amendment should be read as including freedom to speak and to write.[256] Nor did the state of Colorado address the incorporation issue, arguing only that if there was a liberty to publish true information it should give way to the state's interest in preserving the orderly administration of justice.[257] Justice John Harlan, however, dissenting in *Patterson,* argued that the Bill of Rights did apply against the States, relying on the privileges and immunities clause of the Fourteenth Amendment.[258] Holmes merely said that "it is easier to refer to the Constitution generally for the supposed right [claimed by Patterson] than to point to the clause from which it springs," but then left the incorporation issue open, since he concluded that "even if we were to assume that freedom of speech and freedom of the press were protected from abridgement on the part not only of the United States but also of the States, still we should be far from the conclusion that [Patterson] would have us reach.''[259]

The basis of Holmes' conclusion that no First Amendment right was involved in the *Patterson* case was that the First Amendment merely codified the law of criminal libel. "In the first place," he argued, citing decisions following Blackstone, "the main purpose of such constitutional provisions is 'to prevent all such *previous restraints* upon publications as had been practiced by other governments,' and they do not prevent the subsequent punishment of such as may deemed contrary to the public welfare." The question was then the routine one of whether a state could find "a publication concerning a matter of law before [a state court] as tending toward an interference . . . with [the] administration of the law." The "propriety and necessity of preventing interference with the course of justice by premature statement, argument, or intimidation," Holmes declared, "hardly can be denied.''[260] In the vocabulary of the time, *Patterson* was a simple "police power" case in which a "bad tendency" of a communication had been identified: the standard of judicial review was minimal.

But the editor in *Patterson* had not merely claimed a right to comment about public trials and the judges who decided them. He had also claimed that his statements about the corrupt and partisan motives of Colorado judges were true, and offered to prove their truth.[261] That fact did not matter to Holmes. At common law, he noted, "[t]he preliminary freedom extends as well to the false as to the true; the subsequent punishment may extend as well to the true as to the false. This was the law of criminal libel apart from statute in most cases, if not in all.''[262] In other words, the state of Colorado could decide that it did not promote the public welfare for persons even to make true statements about the conduct or motives of judges: it could treat those statements as criminal libels. If the statements had a tendency to interfere with the administration of the law, they could be suppressed without regard to their truth or falsity.

The combination of the "prior restraints" limitation on First Amendment claims and the "bad tendency" test announced as an evaluative standard for "police power" limitations on free speech made Holmes' *Patterson* opinion a very restrictive one. Under its reasoning a state could suppress even true speech if it concluded that the words had a tendency to promote socially injurious acts. If a newspaper said that a particular decision of the Governor of the state, or one of its courts, was reactionary and contrary to the public welfare, that comment could apparently, after *Patterson,* be made the basis for a contempt conviction simply because it might tend to undermine respect for elected officials or interfere with the administration of justice.

Eight years after *Patterson* Holmes again advanced a restrictive theory of freedom of speech in a Supreme Court case, once more sanctioning the use of "bad tendencies" as a justification for subsequent punishment of speech. The case was *Fox v. Washington,*[263] in which he spoke for a unanimous Court. The petitioner in *Fox* was an editor whose magazine had published an article, "The Nude and the Prudes," discussing the infiltration of the group whose members occasionally practiced nude bathing.[264] The group was infiltrated by "a few prudes," who "proceeded in the brutal, unneighborly way of the outside world to suppress the people's freedom," and ultimately had four members of the group arrested for indecent exposure.[265] The article called for a boycott of the "prudes' " businesses, declaring that "[t]he boycott will be pushed until these invaders will come to see the brutal mistake of their action and so inform the people."[266]

The state of Washington prosecuted the editor of the article under a state statute making it a gross misdemeanor to wilfully publish, edit or circulate any written matter "which shall tend to encourage or advocate disrespect for law or for any court or courts of justice."[267] A jury convicted the editor and, on appeal, the Washington Supreme Court held that his article was "not a criticism of the law, but was calculated to, and did, incite the violation of the law." It noted that the right of free speech did not mean "that persons may with impunity advocate disregard of law."[268] The editor attacked the statute primarily on the ground that its controlling standard, "disrespect for law," was too vague, since "who can say what language will produce that state of mind?"[269] The editor also claimed that the statute deprived him of his liberty under the Fourteenth Amendment and that the Court in *Patterson* had left open the question whether the First Amendment could be applied to the states.[270]

Holmes, in sustaining the conviction, said that "[w]e understand the state court by implication at least to have read the statute as confined to encouraging an actual breach of law," and "[i]t does not appear and is not likely that the statute will be construed to prevent publications merely because they tend to produce unfavorable opinions of a particular statute or of law in general." He asserted that in this case "the disrespect for law that was encouraged was disregard of it—an overt breach and technically criminal act."[271]

There was no evidence, however, that the Washington courts would construe the statute so as to limit its application to actual breaches. Indeed the facts of *Fox* suggested that the Washington courts would reach out to apply the statute to publications that "tend[ed] to produce unfavorable opinions." The article in *Fox* was such a publication. In sentences such as the one referring to "the privilege to bathe in evening dress, or with merely the clothes nature gave them,"[272] the article tended to communicate the "unfavorable" opinion that nudity in public was an appropriate activity. It appeared that the "disrespect for law" shown in the article was not the advocacy of a boycott, but rather the championing of public nudity.

Holmes further stated that "by indirection but unmistakably the article encourage[d] and incite[d] a persistence in what we must assume would be a breach of the state laws against indecent exposure."[273] He thus interpreted "disrespect" in the Washington statute as "manifested disrespect, as active disregard [for the] law.[274] As a result the statute fell into a class of laws that proscribed "encouragements that . . . if directed to a particular person's conduct, generally would make him who uttered them guilty of a misdemeanor" at common law. "Laws of this description," Holmes concluded, "are not unfamiliar."[275]

Fox thus illustrated another Supreme Court application of the "bad tendency" test to legislation restricting speech, a test that permitted states to suppress speech that had a "tendency" to incite or encourage socially undesirable acts. In *Fox* the Court applied the test quite broadly, since the speaker had not encouraged others to engage in public nudity but rather to boycott the businesses of those who had taken a "prudish" stance toward it. This suggested that any advocacy of an activity the state had forbidden—such as working on Sunday or dropping out of school at the age of twelve—had "bad tendencies" and could be made the basis of a criminal prosecution.

Taken together, *Patterson* and *Fox* apparently left very little room for the First Amendment to serve as a restraint on state legislation restricting efforts to criticize public officials or majoritarian views. The decisions were consistent with judicial orthodoxy in free speech cases prior to the United States' involvement in World War I. They were not consistent with a later characterization of Holmes as having "a solicitude for individual expression."[276]

~

When Holmes' first thirteen years on the Supreme Court are considered as a unit, there is not much evidence to base a prediction that by the close of his tenure he would be lionized by "progressives" and "liberals" as one of the greatest justices of all time. To be sure, he had staked out, in *Otis v. Parker, Lochner, Adair,* and *Noble State Bank,* a consistent and articulate position on judicial review of state legislation regulating economic affairs under the rubric of the police power. Commentators had begun to note his position, and those with a "progressive" orientation, such as Roscoe Pound and Felix Frankfurter, had described it favorably.[277] Moreover, Holmes' position ran against the grain of judicial orthodoxy in the early twentieth century. To a modernist critic of "mechanical" jurisprudence, disturbed by its insular attitude toward social and economic change and its naive or wilful theories of judicial interpretation of constitutional language, Holmes' posture appeared to be a breath of fresh air, although it was no different from the deferential stance he had taken toward legislative regulation as a Massachusetts judge. On the basis of the *Lochner* sequence, however, one could argue that Holmes had sewn the seeds of his later stature among those who came to describe him as a great "liberal" judge

But in all of the other constitutional areas considered in this chapter Holmes had not only affirmed the orthodoxy of his colleagues, he had been, for the most part, more indifferent to the constitutional claims of minorities than they. In the area of race relations he had been less sympathetic to the claims of black plaintiffs than Southerners such as White. In the area of alien rights he had been less inclined to support the claims of Chinese or Italian petitioners than Brewer or Peckham. In antitrust cases he had been less sympathetic to government efforts at regulation than Brown. In First Amendment cases one of his restrictive opinions had provoked a dissent from Brewer. In short, he had not only voted consistently against claimants alleging that their civil liberties had been violated, he had been less sympathetic to those claimants than justices typically identified as among the most "conservative" on the Court.

Thirteen years into his tenure, in his seventy-fifth year, greatness, in the eyes of the public, still awaited Holmes. A retrospective assessment of him at the time Edward White replaced Melville Fuller as Chief Justice in 1910, written by Alexander Bickel in the 1970s, is worth extended quotation. Bickel wrote:

> Nearly thirty years after the publication of *The Common Law* and his first judicial appointment, the public hardly knew him. . . . [I]n his seventieth year, even among his professional peers, the general acknowledgment of greatness was still to come for Holmes, and he himself felt its absence rather painfully. He was . . . often charged with obscurity and with a disinclination to take particular facts into account. . . . Holmes in 1910 . . . was almost all that he would be, lacking only the magnificence of very great age. But no one yet was writing that to know him was "to have had a revelation of the possibilities . . . of human personality."[278] No one was yet regarding him as "a significant figure in the history of civilization and not merely a commanding American figure."[279] And Benjamin Cardozo's later judgment of Holmes as "probably the greatest legal intellect in the history of the English-speaking judiciary"[280] had not yet been rendered.[281]

Despite his great enthusiasm for the new position he had assumed in 1903, by the time he had reached eligibility for retirement with full pay, on December 8, 1912, Holmes still felt that the kind of recognition he assumed would be commensurate with his abilities and contributions had eluded him. But that recognition, a new circle of friends, and a new phase in his life were close at hand.

CHAPTER TEN

Recognition

~

IN 1909, six years into his tenure as a Supreme Court justice, Holmes wrote two
letters about his work. In the first he said that "my friend and colleague White
. . . told me the other day that there was no man in the United States whose reputation
so little corresponded to what he had done."[1] In the second he said that "I have not
had as much recognition as I would like."[2] For Holmes, we have seen, the concept
of recognition had been a complex and central one in his professional life. He had
chosen to immerse himself in the law, and to forego literature and philosophy, in
part because he had not wanted to be recognized as the son of a father who had
combined professional and literary skills. He had shown a residual bitterness when
the fruits of his early ambition had not been adequately recognized, alluding to the
fact that *The Common Law* and his volume of speeches had largely been ignored
and that newspapers had referred to him as a "literary feller" in commenting on his
judicial career in Massachusetts.

He had regularly spoken of seeking to appeal only to a select audience of elite
professionals, and as late as 1911 he had said that his goal as a judge was "to hammer
out as compact and solid a piece of work as one can, to try to make it first rate, and
to leave it unadvertised."[3] But at the same time he had exhibited pique at the
glib characterizations of him in newspapers when he was appointed to the Court,
and newspaper comments continued to trouble him during the first decade of his
tenure. In 1904 he had complained that "when the newspapers begin to drivel . . .
they reduce one to confusion so far as to make him wonder whether everything he
ever did was in vain and whether some other kind of man is wanted."[4] In 1910 he
wrote Lewis Einstein that "when I read the newspapers the total absence of any
critical appreciation tends to make me gloomy. . . . One has a despairing sense that
popularity or popular appreciation is to be had only by the sacrifice of ideals."[5]

His appointment to the Supreme Court had not checked the voraciousness of his
ambition: he wrote Nina Gray in 1910, only partially in jest, that "I confine my
aspirations to being the greatest legal thinker in the world."[6] But as he approached
his tenth year on the Court and noted that he would be eligible to retire on a full
pension at the close of that year, he began to speak of retirement. In December 1911,
he had written Pollock that "[i]n my leisure moments . . . I speculate without conclusion whether I had better leave the bench when my ten years are up next year,"[7]
and in September 1912 he noted to Pollock that "I return to Washington . . . feeling
so free in the thought that by December I can leave whenever I want to."[8]

But in December 1912 Holmes reported to Pollock:

Last Sunday, December 8, was ten years, according to the Reports, from the day I took my seat. So now I am entitled to retire, and while I don't I am working for nothing, so to speak, as my pension would equal my salary. I don't intend to hop off while I feel all right and believe that I am as good as ever. When a man has made one outlet his only channel of experience for so many years, and when it is too late to expect to master a new subject and to produce results from it, it seems wise until one is ready for idleness to try to do as much as one can in one's chosen way. I am pretty sure they all want me to stay on.[9]

Holmes did not "hop off" the Court for another twenty years, and then reluctantly. In that twenty year interval the exalted recognition that he had sought since his decision to immerse himself in the field of law finally came to him. He had written, of John Marshall, that "[a] great man represents a great ganglion in the nerves of society . . . and part of his greatness consists of his being *there*."[10] With his sense of irony, he might have perceived that between 1912 and 1931 he was also "there" in the sense of finally having encountered a climate of intellectual opinion that was receptive to his ideas and appreciative of his style. But he also recognized that much of the "loneliness" he had equated with his lack of recognition had sprung from "egotism," as he put it to Canon Patrick Sheehan. His discontent in his first decade on the Court had come, he confessed to Sheehan, from "the feeling thrown back on oneself when one sees little attention given to what one thinks most important."[11] Now, suddenly, others thought Holmes and his attitudes very important indeed.

The story of Holmes' recognition in the last two decades of his judicial life is not, however, simply an episode in intellectual and cultural history. To be sure, the emergence of Holmes as a "great judge" was in part a function of his being "discovered" by a group of early twentieth-century intellectuals who found his jurisprudence congenial to the modernist, "progressive" world view they espoused. But another dimension of Holmes' emergence was personal, the product of an odd sociological interaction between an aging symbol of Brahmin Boston and a group of ambitious, upwardly mobile young professionals whose Jewish backgrounds had contributed to their sense of social marginality. Holmes was important, for this group of acolytes, not only because of what he was but because of who he was.

In one sense, then, the emergence of Holmes as a figure rivaling Marshall in significance was part of his being perceived as "a great ganglion" in the history of twentieth-century legal thought by a group of intellectuals who sought to redirect the emphasis of that body of thought. It was no accident that this group surfaced in the years prior to World War I; in terms of its composition or its ideas, it could not have surfaced twenty years earlier. Holmes came to be regarded as "great" in large measure because this group attributed qualities of "greatness" in a judge to him, and those qualities—philosophical skepticism, deference to the legislature in constitutional cases, a direct, "literary" style of opinion writing—would not have been identified with judicial distinction two decades before. Holmes had been primarily the same judge on the Massachusetts court in the 1890s, and no one had been his acolyte.

But if Holmes' "greatness" was culturally fortuitous in one sense, it was also the conscious product of a systematic campaign of publicity, a campaign in which Holmes participated. Holmes was fortunate to have as one of his principal boosters a person who was eminently suited to launch such a campaign and highly motivated to do so. The story of Holmes' rise to "greatness" is to an important extent the story of his friendship with Felix Frankfurter, whose own rise to prominence in the years between 1912 and 1931 bore a symbiotic relationship to the emergence of Holmes as an eminent judge.

Frankfurter's own emergence as one of the more visible and influential members of the academic legal profession was fortuitous in that it would not necessarily have happened twenty years earlier. While Frankfurter was by no means the first immigrant Jewish law school graduate to enter the legal profession, he was an unusual figure in the Harvard Law School class of 1906. He had come to America from Austria at the age of 12; his father was a furrier on the lower East Side of New York. He had attended City College of New York, and at Harvard he roomed with two other Jewish students, one of them Morris Raphael Cohen, later to become an eminent philosopher and a correspondent of Holmes. Although Frankfurter was a conspicuously successful law student, graduating first in his class, he encountered ethnic prejudice on attempting to secure employment in New York after graduation, recalling that he "was made to feel as though I was some worm going around begging for a job," and as if "the fact that I did very well at the Harvard Law School really didn't amount to much."[12]

Frankfurter's presence at Harvard was a product of a "meritocratic" philosophy of education identified with Charles Eliot, Harvard's president, who believed that so long as the numbers of talented Jews, blacks, and other minorities remained comparatively small, their presence would be a stimulating and diversifying presence for the Harvard community. The assumption behind this "meritocratic" approach was that such "outsiders" would be schooled in the mores and practices of the elite WASP community, not that they would embody cultural pluralism. One of the implicit corollaries of acceptance into bastions of WASP educational and professional culture was that aspiring Jews would become acculturated and thereby shed themselves of any negative characteristics associated with their heritage.[13]

The message that Frankfurter and his early twentieth-century Jewish contemporaries received from a "meritocratic" educational structure, then, was ambivalent. On the one hand their Jewishness was regarded as no bar to achievement, provided they had the intellectual firepower to excel at elite educational institutions; on the other hand their Jewishness was still a barrier to professional employment, especially if they had not taken on the patina of the WASP upper classes. In later life Frankfurter would see his Harvard environment as "democratic," indifferent to "wealth, family fortune, skin, creed," concerned only with "scholarship and character objectively ascertained."[14] But when he graduated from Harvard he deliberately accepted a job with a particular New York firm because "they had never taken a Jew and [allegedly] wouldn't take a Jew," and subsequently was asked by one of the partners of the firm to change his name.[15]

For much of Frankfurter's early professional life he continued to maintain a complex and ambivalent relationship with elite WASPs in the high strata of his profession. His mentors at Harvard were James Barr Ames, the Dean, who wrote him supporting letters to law firms, and Holmes' great friend John Chipman Gray, who asked him to be a research assistant after his first year in law school. The most important figure in his early years as a lawyer was Henry Stimson, who hired him at the U.S. Attorney's office in New York three months after he had accepted a job with the law firm and whom Frankfurter assisted, in a variety of capacities, from 1906 through 1912. Stimson personified the kind of elite WASP lawyer Frankfurter admired and respected, a person from an established social background who was involved in public service and "progressive" political reform. That was the sort of person Frankfurter aspired to be, and the sort of person he was at the same time quite conscious that he was not. When he fell in love, he chose as the object of his ardor Marion Denman, the daughter of a Congregationalist minister. His mother objected to the relationship, and the courtship was a rocky one, but eventually Marion Denman agreed to marry him.[16]

In 1911 Frankfurter, after having assisted Stimson in his unsuccessful 1910 campaign for Governor of New York, moved to Washington, at Stimson's urging, to take a job under Stimson in the Bureau of Insular Affairs in the War Department during the Taft administration. Frankfurter, who was single at the time, took up residence in a large house on 19th Street, dubbed "The House of Truth," which was owned by Taft's Commissioner of Indian Affairs, Robert Grovesnor Valentine. The "House of Truth" became a center of dissent within the Taft administration and a political and intellectual salon: Frankfurter later said that "it became a fashionable thing . . . almost everybody who was interesting in Washington sooner or later passed through the house."[17]

One of the visitors to the "House of Truth" was Holmes: indeed he may have begun the source of the place's name.[18] Frankfurter had come to Washington an admirer of Holmes, armed with a letter of introduction from John Gray.[19] Whether he first encountered Holmes at Valentine's residence, or whether he arranged a separate interview, Frankfurter soon made it plain that he was coveting a friendship with Holmes. He began, in characteristic fashion, to write Holmes flattering letters. One on February 10, 1912, said that "from the first time I came in contact with you, as a freshman in the Law School, through your *Common Law,* you had . . . 'the gift of imparting ferment.' " "That this bounty," Frankfurter continued, "should be enriched by the passion and persuasiveness of the living fire is a good fortune that makes my indebtedness everlastingly alive."[20]

That letter set the tone for Frankfurter's early correspondence with Holmes, the principal theme of those letters being Frankfurter's gratitude for being exposed to the freshness and inspiration of Holmes' ideas. In describing an episode in which he, Francis Hackett, and Walter Lippmann "in youngster fashion speculated on man and his destiny," Frankfurter said that "[n]aturally, in the course of talk, we turned to you and lingered there some time with the grateful realization that, in varying degrees, you have made the Green Young Things . . . see the job is the thing—with the added gift of formulating it in romantic terms."[21] And in thanking Holmes for a recent visit and conversation, Frankfurter wrote that "[t]he silent years alone can give proof of the gratitude for a shaping influence and a precious personality. But the internal man reverences the mortal day too deeply not to utter a syllable of rejoicing for the privilege that gives me a talk and a vision like Friday's."[22]

In the years before and during World War I Frankfurter flooded Holmes with letters like the above, asking his advice,[23] remembering his birthdays,[24] commenting on his opinions,[25] and generally expressing thanks for his presence.[26] One familiar with Frankfurter's career can easily recognize both the excessively flattering tone and the stilted language, common in his correspondence with persons he regarded as mentors or patrons.[27] And one familiar with Holmes' career could anticipate the pleasure he would take in the receipt of such flattery, notwithstanding the awkward way in which it was phrased.

Holmes' susceptibility to flattery, from both sexes, has previously been noted. But the depth of his reaction to Frankfurter's pursuit of a friendship with him may nonetheless be surprising. In the first year of the friendship he had written to Frankfurter:

> It will be many years before you have occasion to know the happiness and encouragement that comes to an old man from the sympathy of the young. That, perhaps more than anything else, makes one feel as if one had not lived in vain, and counteracts the eternal gravitation toward melancholy and doubt. I am quite sincere in saying that you have done a great deal for me in this way and I send you my thanks.[28]

The letter provides a clue to the attraction Holmes felt for Frankfurter. Written on Holmes' seventy-first birthday, the letter shows his consciousness of being "an old man" and his gratification at having secured "the sympathy of the young." While at one level Holmes surely did not feel "old," as his comments on his decision not to retire from the Court suggest, at another level he was afflicted with a "gravitation toward melancholy and doubt" that he characterized as "eternal" but which was highly personal. He remained anxious about recognition, perhaps even fearful that his time to secure the reputation he coveted was quickly passing. A representative of a younger generation, providing "sympathy and encouragement," raised the possibility that his reputation might endure, that his recognition might grow wider with time, even after his death.

There were other reasons why Holmes found Frankfurter's friendship an uplifting prospect. In addition to being young, Frankfurter was a graduate of Harvard, a participant in current political affairs, a person of intellectual tastes, and a friend or acquaintance of several prominent people. He was the sort of person Holmes coveted as an audience for his work: intelligent and discriminating enough to understand it and energetic and enthusiastic enough to prosyletize it. Holmes had spoken of writing for "the one man who did understand"[29]: Frankfurter was that sort of man. Moreover, as Holmes once put it, his friendship with Frankfurter "stepped in just when those of my youth have disappeared in death."[30] Between 1910 and 1921 a number of Holmes' closest old friends died, including Canon Sheehan, John Gray, William James, Henry Adams, his old Army first sergeant Gustave Magnitzky,[31] and Chief Justice Edward White. Frankfurter's presence, instead of reminding Holmes of his own mortality, provided him with a link to future generations.

In addition, Holmes' friendship with Frankfurter suggested an implicit shift in his priorities, especially in his definition of intimate relationships. Between 1889 and 1903 he had sought intimacy in friendships with women, culminating in his romance with Clare Castletown. After 1903, his move to Washington and his new judicial duties, the renaissance of his marriage, the aging of his English women friends, and the diminution of intensity in his relationship with Clare had resulted in his relying increasingly on correspondence to provide contact with women, minimizing his "flirtations" in Washington, and plunging into his work on the Court. Frankfurter was an ideal friend for this new phase of Holmes' life. He was nearly as interested about Holmes' work as was Holmes himself; he was a figure in the intellectual life of contemporary Washington; he was a man. The kind of intimacy Holmes secured with Frankfurter was the more measured intimacy of mentor and disciple, one that suited Holmes as he reached his seventies.

There was a final theme of the Holmes–Frankfurter relationship, that of the pairing of social opposites. With the exception of John Gray, Holmes had not remained close to the Brahmins of his youth. During his tenure on the Supreme Judicial Court of Massachusetts he had grown apart from the Jameses and Henry Adams, and he had never been close to the "solid" men for which Senator George Hoar had purported to speak at the time of Holmes' nomination to the Court. On the other hand he had not been loath to initiate friendships with persons outside his class, such as Canon Sheehan, the parish priest he had met at Doneraile in County Cork. He continued this tendency while on the Supreme Court, entering into extended correspondences with Harold Laski, the Chinese scholar John C. H. Wu, the journalist Franklin Ford, and on a smaller scale with the pacifist Rosika Schwimmer. While Holmes was conscious of ethnic differences, and continued to choose secretaries who were mostly WASPs, he did not share the anti-Semitic attitudes of many of his Brahmin contemporaries, such as Lawrence Lowell, President of Harvard during much of Frankfurter's tenure on the law faculty.[32] That Frankfurter and many of his "progressive" friends were Jewish seems not to have made any difference to Holmes.

It may well have made a difference to them, however. Frankfurter was conspicuous in searching out as mentors men who were discernibly upper-class WASPs. Holmes, Stimson, and Roosevelt were all examples, as was Robert Grovesnor Valentine, whom Frankfurter called "the closest friend of my own years" in a 1916 letter to Holmes.[33] Harold Laski, whose early letters to Holmes resemble those of Frankfurter in their flattering tone,[34] was described by Holmes, in a letter to Frederick Pollock, as "an astonishing young Jew whom Frankfurter brought over here the other day."[35] Holmes noted in a second letter that Laski was "unbelieving," that he was "one of the very most learned men I ever saw of any age," and was "an extraordinarily agreeable chap." He had allegedly "[b]eat the American champion at tennis" and was associated "with some of the younger men like Frankfurter and the *New Republic* lot, who make much of your venerable uncle and . . . bring . . . an atmosphere of intellectual freedom in which one can breathe."[36] Many, although not all, of the people who wrote for the *New Republic* on its founding were Jewish, and they saw in Holmes a particularly attractive figure, not the least because he seemed to be without class or ethnic antagonisms.[37] Walter Lippmann, writing in the *New Republic* in 1916, described Holmes as "[a] sage with the bearing of a cavalier," who "wears wisdom like a gorgeous plume."[38]

Above all, however, the link between Holmes and his young admirers was their conviction that they and the justice shared a modernist political sensibility. In this assessment they were not quite accurate. Frankfurter, Laski, and the "New Republic lot" believed that unregulated capitalism was passe; that experimental regulatory or redistributive legislation, with the goals of curbing the power of industrial enterprise and creating a more equitable and humane working environment, should be encouraged at the state level; that the "melting pot" was a viable social ideal; that the future was an improvement upon the past; and that a beneficent state should become more of a presence as a policymaking force.[39] Holmes did not fully hold any of those beliefs. He was an unreconstructed social Darwinist on economic issues, believing in competition but also in combination as the logical end of competition. He was not at all interested in the humanitarian dimensions of work in an industrialized society. He did not think that redistributive legislation had any meaningful effect, believing that consumption was the major pressure point of economic activity and that economic regulation only shifted the "bill" from one sector of the consuming public to another. He deferred to state legislation only because he did not think it appropriate for judges to pour substantive meaning into constitutional language absent an overwhelming textual mandate. He was not interested in social assimilation or the breaking down of class barriers, did not believe that the future was an improvement on the past, and did not favor the state as an omnipresent policymaking force. In short, Holmes "didn't believe that universal bliss would ensue if the world would only get a move on and obey when the *New Republic* says Hocus-Pocus-Presto-Chango."[40]

But Holmes' learning, antecedents, bearing, pithy informal style, and deferential attitude toward social and economic legislation were more than enough for his admirers. Beginning in the first decade of the twentieth century, a series of articles, notably by Roscoe Pound, began to appear in the law journals, decrying various features of jurisprudential orthodoxy, from syllogistic logic to substantive doctrines such as "liberty of contract," and calling for a greater attention on the part of judges to the social and economic conditions of contemporary American life.[41] Frankfurter did not contribute to this first wave of "progressive" scholarship, but he adopted its agenda.

In two letters to Holmes, written in connection with the prospect of his joining the Harvard faculty, Frankfurter made it plain that he was committed to the criticisms and suggestions of Pound and his fellow "sociological jurisprudes." "The job to be done," he wrote Holmes in the first letter,

> is to evolve this "sociological jurisprudence" Pound has been talking about. .
> . . If I have enough to meet the potentialities of the work my unscholarliness
> may be a help to save me and the students from Langdellian sterilization. . . .
> [I]t strikes me the school has to do a bigger job than high technique.[42]

In the second letter he was more explicit:

> [W]hat challenges me is to bring public life, the elements of reality, in touch
> with the University, and, conversely, to help harness the Law School to the
> needs of the fight outside. You know better than the rest of us how empirical,
> how inadequate the foundation of our legislative output, how un-thought out
> much of social reform legislation is, how meagre the data on which it is

based. . . . My years in the Government have taught me the utter inability of thoroughgoing thinking while in office and I feel the need of correlating this kind of analysis and research with the living economic and social facts of the day. . . . The economic clashes of the day are rich nourishment for me and it's with them that I want to deal but with more scientific geometry in a more tolerant temper and a deeper sense of limitations though no less of the passion that is faith which animates the social reformer of the day.[43]

Frankfurter, then, was intent on being a new sort of legal academic, one whose interests lay not in the "high technique" of parsing legal doctrine but in social reform. In his first four years on the Harvard law school faculty he produced four slight articles, all of them with a political spin. He was particularly concerned, in this period, with the Supreme Court's use of the due process clause to strike down legislation seeking to regulate relationships in the workplace and with the policy basis for such legislation, notably that affecting the wages and hours of laborers.[44] His scholarship not only reflected those interests, it revealed how his view of Holmes' jurisprudence had been integrated into his vision of social reform.

～

In 1916 Frankfurter organized a festschrift in the *Harvard Law Review* celebrating Holmes' seventy-fifth birthday. Such a tribute was unusual for a Supreme Court justice, and can be said to have marked the beginning of Holmes' rise to eminence in America.[45] Frankfurter's own contribution to the symposium was an article entitled "The Constitutional Opinions of Justice Holmes."[46] As an illuminating account of either constitutional law or Holmes' jurisprudence, the article was far from successful. Frankfurter said at one point that "[t]o discuss Mr. Justice Holmes' opinions is to string pearls,"[47] and the article primarily consisted of a number of long quotations from Holmes' opinions, interspersed with commentary that often bordered on the vapid. Nonetheless, the article is revealing as an example of the way in which Frankfurter and his "progressive" contemporaries converted Holmes to their own purposes and in the process began to make him into a figure of legend.

Frankfurter began the article by noting that the last thirty years had produced two major issues of constitutional law, "the scope of the power of Congress over Commerce, and the new limitations placed upon the states by the Fourteenth Amendment."[48] While that statement was accurate, it also reflected the regulatory agenda of "progressives": greater scope for the federal government's power to regulate industrial combinations through the commerce power and the Sherman Anti-Trust Act, and greater scope for the state governments to experiment with social and economic legislation, notwithstanding the Fourteenth Amendment's Due Process Clause. Frankfurter's formulation also reflected his emphasis on issues of federalism rather than issues of civil rights, a subject that had not fully penetrated the consciousness of early twentieth-century reformers.

Holmes' opinions, in Frankfurter's view, had formed "a coherent body of constitutional law" on the subjects of the commerce power and the Due Process Clause." Their "effect upon the development of the law" had been "the outstanding characteristic of constitutional history in the last decade."[49] This was an astonishing statement, since the *Northern Securities-Swift* sequence had suggested that Holmes did not view the commerce power broadly (at least in Sherman Act cases); and the *Lochner-Adair-Coppage* sequence demonstrated that his view of the Due Process Clause did not command a Court majority. Consequently, it is hard to know what "effect upon the development of the law" Holmes' opinions had had. But Frankfurter subsequently made clear what he meant. "Constant resort to the reviewing power of the Court" fostered by the new legislation raising commerce power and due process issues, he noted, "called again for a major premise as to the scope of the instrument which the Court must construe and the right attitude of the Court in its interpretive function." In a period of "legislative activity, in a period of especial unrest in the law, signifying an absorption of new facts and changing social conditions," Frankfurter claimed, citing Pound's "sociological jurisprudence" articles, "the starting point [for theories of judicial review] must be a conscious one, lest power and policy be unconsciously confused."[50]

It was clear that Frankfurter felt that Holmes had exhibited the "right" attitude in his opinions on the commerce power and the Due Process Clause. It was a little more difficult to show that Holmes' attitude was consistent with Frankfurter's agenda, but the showing was nonetheless made. After introducing a series of quotations from Holmes affirming his view that "[c]laim[s] or denial[s] of governmental power . . . reveal themselves not as logical antitheses, but as . . . matters of more or less, of questions of degree,"[51] Frankfurter concluded that nonetheless Holmes had "applied [the commerce] power with unimpaired depth and breadth," citing Holmes' majority opinion in *Swift* and his dissent in *Adair*. While he conceded that Holmes believed that "it is not enough to show that, in the working of a statute, there is some tendency, logically discernible, to interfere with commerce," and that "even nice distinctions" between federal and state police powers "are to be expected," Frankfurter insisted that Holmes was of the view that "the Federal power must be dominantly left unimpaired." A more accurate statement of Holmes' views, we have seen, would be that he regarded all federalism questions as "questions of degree," and balanced competing interests in a given case.

Frankfurter next turned to the due process cases. Here Holmes had been more consistently supportive of the view Frankfurter espoused, and Frankfurter's analysis showed less strain, although it ultimately converted Holmes' views to his own. Frankfurter began by noting the establishment of a substantive reading of the Due Process Clause in late nineteenth-century decisions of the Court, calling that reading an effort "to pour into the general words of the Due Process Clause the eighteenth-century 'law of nature' philosophy," and identifying the 1897 decision in *Allgeyer v. Louisiana*[52] as "the crest of the wave."[53] He then described Holmes' dissent in *Lochner* as the decision that precipitated "[t]he break" with substantive due process, and "the turning point" in a battle against "the unconscious identification of personal views with constitutional sanction." Quoting from the *Lochner* dissent ("It still needs to be quoted"), Frankfurter announced that "[e]nough is said if it is noted that the tide has turned."[54]

The *Lochner* dissent, for Frankfurter, was more than an enlightened exposure of substantive due process methodology. It reflected Holmes' "whole point of view towards constitutional interpretation." Frankfurter then summarized that view:

In all the variety of cases the opinions of Mr. Justice Holmes show the same realism, the same refusal to defeat life by formal logic, the same regard for local needs and local habits, the same deference to local knowledge. He recognizes that government necessarily means experimentation.[55]

None of these observations about Holmes' jurisprudence was supported by his *Lochner* dissent. It made no mention of "formal logic." It emphasized the scope of the police power to interfere with "the liberty of the citizen to do as he likes," but made no mention of local needs, habits, or expertise. Holmes' deference, as stated in the opinion, was to majoritarianism and to state sovereignty, not to "experimentation." In short, Holmes in *Lochner* neither opposed nor endorsed "progressive" legislation of the kind proposed for the baking industry by the New York legislature. He simply said that "my agreement or disagreement has nothing to do with the right of the majority to embody their opinions in law."[56]

On receiving his April issue of the *Harvard Law Review,* in which the symposium appeared, Holmes wrote Frankfurter. "I can't tell you how touched and charmed I am," he said. "Very few things in my life have given me so much pleasure." He added that "I well know that I owe it to your constant kindness that I receive such a crowning reward."[57] While Holmes may have winced at some of Frankfurter's conclusions in his symposium piece, such as that "from [Holmes'] opinions there emerges a conception of a Nation adequate to its great national duties and consisting of confederate States, in their turn possessed of dignity and power available for the diverse uses of civilized people,"[58] he recognized that Frankfurter's "constant kindness" to him would bear a close relation to any "crowning reward" he might receive in the future.

One of the reasons for the close causal relationship between Frankfurter's "discovery" of Holmes and the growth of Holmes' reputation was the ubiquity of Frankfurter's presence. In addition to being involved in a number of different professional ventures in the first two decades of his career, in which he made numerous contacts and acquaintances, Frankfurter's special talent, he believed, was "personalia," the ability to ingratiate himself with others and to bring them together.[59] Holmes described this quality in Frankfurter less charitably, saying that he had "an unimaginable gift of wiggling in wherever he wants to."[60] Frankfurter enjoyed talking to his friends about the accomplishments of his other friends, and there is ample evidence that he talked a good deal about Holmes. Moreover, as a Harvard law professor Frankfurter had additional opportunities to proselytize: Harold Laski reported to Holmes in 1916 that "Felix is teaching the growing youth . . . that cases like *Adair v. U.S.* and *Lochner* . . . have really got a philosophy within them."[61] It was Frankfurter who introduced Holmes to the group of young intellectuals who formed *The New Republic,* and their magazine to him; Frankfurter who first brought Laski to meet Holmes, thereby creating another publicist for Holmes' reputation; Frankfurter who organized the *Harvard Law Review* symposium.

Through an academic grapevine, including such persons as Roscoe Pound, Frankfurter, Laski, and Frankfurter's students, opinions such as the *Lochner* dissent penetrated the consciousness of elite "progressive" legal opinion. In 1916, for example, Laski confessed that law students needed to be taught that the dissent had "a philosophy'' within it; by 1919 he was writing Holmes that the dissent had ''become a classic.''[62] In 1920, in the course of searching for some superlatives to describe Holmes' dissent in the free speech case, *Abrams v. United States*,[63] Laski said that it ''will influence American thinking in a fashion to which only your work in *Lochner* and the *Adair* case have rivalry.''[64]

The emergence of Holmes' dissent in *Lochner* to ''classic'' status was not rapid. Comments on the *Lochner* case the year it was handed down did not distinguish between Holmes' dissent and that of Justice John Harlan, which had assumed that a substantive reading of the Due Process Clause was possible and balanced ''liberty of contract'' against the police power, coming down on the side of the latter. A comment by Ernest Freund, for example, said that ''the dissent is based on the ground that there was an issue of judgment, and the New York courts had approved of the judgment of the legislature.'' Freund believed the majority opinion in *Lochner* to have been ''wrongly decided'' because ''the choice between the comparative benefits of the public welfare and private liberty of action has, by the constitution, been committed to the legislature.''[65] Even Frederick Pollock, writing in the same year, referred to Harlan's argument that the Court was not competent to determine the working conditions in New York bakeries. Pollock also quoted extensively from Holmes' dissent, which he called ''plainly and boldly expressed,'' but indicated that the reason ''we are much inclined to agree with Mr. Justice Holmes'' was that ''English lawyers are perhaps naturally prejudiced in favor of the competence of legislatures.''[66]

It was not until 1909 that Holmes' *Lochner* dissent began to take on an identity of its own among commentators. Roscoe Pound, in that year, called Holmes' dissent ''the decisive objection to the position of the majority,'' and quoted the passage emphasizing that ''[a] constitution is not intended to embody a particular economic theory,'' but ''is made for people of fundamentally differing views.'' Those ''sentences,'' Pound said, ''deserve to become classical.''[67] Edwin Corwin, in the same year, also singled out Holmes' dissent, describing it as ''cutting ... through the momentary question of policy to the deeper, though inarticulate, major premise underlying all preference for or against the political will when it appears arrayed against private rights.''[68] And Louis Greeley, in an article on the attitude of the courts toward ''social legislation'' written in 1910, called the view expressed by Holmes' dissent in *Lochner* ''advanced'' and added that ''[i]f constitutional limitations were generally understood and applied in the way that Justice Holmes ... would apply them, there is surely nothing in them to prevent a very wide measure of social and industrial reform.''[69]

This growing tendency among legal commentators to isolate Holmes' *Lochner* dissent and to treat it as a fundamental critique of the Court's methodology in due process cases was echoed in popular journals.[70] As early as 1905 *The Outlook,* alone among lay periodicals, had isolated Holmes' dissent, saying that it had gone ''even more fundamentally into the question at issue'' than had that of Harlan.[71] In 1912 *The Outlook* ran an article by Theodore Roosevelt, a former *Outlook* editor who was campaigning for the presidency on the Progressive Party ticket, that cited Holmes' *Lochner* dissent as an example of appropriate judicial concern that the Court not restrict efforts at social legislation.[72] By 1915 *The New Republic* was employing the same language as Pound, writing in an editorial that "[w]e had supposed the *Lochner* opinion to have been discredited by the common consent of the legal profession," and that "the rational guidance to be derived from that case was to be found not in the . . . result but in the classic dissenting opinion of Justice Holmes."[73] The stage was thus set for Frankfurter, in 1916, to amass commentary critical of the *Lochner* majority[74] and to claim that with Holmes' dissent the "tide had turned" against judicial usurpation of legislative prerogatives.

Lochner was one element in the emerging image of Holmes as a "great judge," symbolizing the combination of his refusal to substitute his own judgments for those of legislatures in constitutional adjudication and his willingness to tolerate social and economic experimentation. By the 1920s two additional elements were in place. The first had been suggested by an observation made by *New Republic* columnist Philip Littell in a 1915 piece on Holmes, in which he had referred to Holmes as a "Puritan whom doubt had civilized." In that phrase Littell was seeking to revive the heritage of Puritanism while stripping it of its bigotry. "You do not resent the Puritan virtues when [Holmes] praises them," Littell maintained. "He tempts you to be tolerant of those men and women who always choose that alternative of conduct which is most disagreeable to themselves."[75] For Littell and his cosmopolitan contemporaries on *The New Republic,* Holmes was a "civilized" version of the old race of austere, self-abnegating Yankees. Eleven years later Elizabeth Sergeant, writing in the same journal, described Holmes as a descendant of "the natural Puritan aristocracy" who regarded life as "a rich but responsible adventure." He was a "gallant gentleman of old New England" who was "the most romantic of contemporary Americans."[76] Eventually this element was to reveal itself most vividly in a characterization of Holmes as one who transcended his class, "an aristocrat with a genuine interest in the welfare of the common man."[77] He was, in Sergeant's characterization, a "Yankee, strayed from Olympus."[78]

The second of the additional elements contributing to the image of Holmes as a "great judge" had been anticipated by Frankfurter's 1916 summary of Holmes' constitutional opinions, in which he had attributed to Holmes a "realism," an ability "to translate large words in terms of the realities of existence."[79] As "Realism" became a term of art in the 1920s and 1930s, designating a particular school of jurisprudential thought that criticized judicial decisions that were grounded on abstract concepts and urged that judges be responsive to current social and economic conditions, Holmes came to be claimed as an original Realist. In 1923 Frankfurter had said that Holmes' constitutional opinions were "but applications of his candid insight into the realities of lawmaking."[80] By 1930 one of the leading Realist spokesman was claiming that "Holmes' mind had travelled most of the road [toward Realism] two generations back,"[81] and another acknowledging that "whatever clear vision of legal realities we have attained in this country in the past twenty-five years is in large measure due to [Holmes]."[82]

The growth of Holmes' reputation can be seen in the comments on his volume of essays, *Collected Legal Papers,* which appeared in 1920. The publication of the essays was itself a testament to Holmes' stature, since all the essays had previously been published, many were quite dated, and several were on arcane topics. The genesis for the collection came from Harold Laski, who proposed the idea in the summer of 1919.[83] On October 16, 1919, Holmes wrote Laski that "[i]f the project of printing some of my things has not been given up as a bore" he was sending a list of possible speeches and articles for inclusion.[84] Laski responded the next day, indicating that the project was still going on, and eventually Holmes sent him two informally bound volumes of speeches and articles to facilitate the production process. While Laski expected that his receiving those volumes "would mean that I could [send] off the MS to the printer by November 19 and have the book out early in the New Year,"[85] it did not actually appear until November 1920.[86]

When *Collected Legal Papers* was published Holmes wrote Laski that "I don't see what anyone can say if any notice is taken of my book except that they are old chestnuts and the earlier of them dead on the author's avowed principles."[87] But on January 31, 1921, he wrote that he had seen "a generous review" by Morris Cohen in *The New Republic* and "an early puff in the [Boston] *Evening Transcript*."[88] A month later he wrote that he "was deeply pleased by another notice in *The Nation*— by Thomas Reed Powell—I think a professor at Columbia and esteemed there." He mentioned the Powell review again in a letter a week later, and on both instances added that "I am on the look-out for something that will take me down badly."[89]

But the critical reviews never materialized. Instead commentators demonstrated that, as Holmes had said in the preface to *Collected Legal Papers,* "[a] later generation has carried on the work that I began nearly half a century ago," and "the brilliant young soldiers still give [me] a place in their councils of war."[90] In particular, while commentators found in Holmes what suited them, they repeatedly stressed the degree to which his ideas, original and once remote from general discourse, had been absorbed into the fabric of contemporary scholarly thought. "His ideas," Roscoe Pound wrote in the *Harvard Law Review,* "have so thoroughly entered into the substance of our legal thought . . . that the epigoni could easily forget whose armor they were wearing and whose weapons they were wielding." Pound felt that a rereading of Holmes' essays, with attention to "the dates of their original publication" would demonstrate that "their author has done more than lead American juristic thought of the present generation. Above all others he has shaped the methods and ideas that are characteristic of the present as distinguished from the immediate past."[91]

Pound then exhibited another characteristic of the commentary on Holmes: he restated Holmes' views so that they more resembled those of the reviewer than those of the author. "Comparing twentieth-century science of law in America with the legal science of the last quarter of the nineteenth century," Pound announced,

> the most significant changes are, the definite break with the historical method; the study of methods of judicial thinking and understanding of the scope and nature of legal logic; recognition of the relation between the law-finding element in judicial decision and the policies that must govern lawmaking; conscious facing of the problem of harmonizing or compromising conflicting or overlapping interests . . . faith in the efficacy of effort to improve the law and make it more effective for its purposes; a functional point of view in contrast with the purely anatomical or morphological standpoint of the last century.[92]

Few of these characterizations were accurate descriptions of Holmes' jurisprudence. He had not made a "definite break with the historical method," either in *The Common Law* or elsewhere. He had not studied "methods of judicial thinking," including "legal logic": he had dismissed Langdellian logic as a subterfuge while continuing to employ his own version of logical analysis. His "conscious facing" of the problem of reconciling "conflicting or overlapping interests" consisted of the simple recognition that such reconciliation was what judges typically did in deciding cases. He had exhibited little "faith in the efficacy of effort to improve the law": he thought that "improvements" or other changes in the law were essentially predetermined by social forces and majoritarian prejudices. He had never endorsed a "functional point of view": that term belonged to Pound and his colleagues who believed in "sociological jurisprudence." In short, in describing Holmes' contributions Pound was describing those of Pound.

While Pound was sanguine in his conviction that Holmes' contributions had been absorbed into the thought of his contemporaries, Walter Wheeler Cook, reviewing *Collected Legal Papers* in the May 1921 *Yale Law Journal*,[93] was less so. Cook noted Pound's remarks, and responded that "[s]o far as a relatively small number of legal scholars are concerned this is perhaps true, but it is feared that the same statement will not hold for the vast majority of the leaders of our bench and bar, not to speak of the average lawyer."[94] Even law teachers, Cook felt, had not followed Holmes' methodology. Quoting a passage from "The Path of the Law," Cook described Holmes' methods as "follow[ing] the existing body of dogma into its highest generalizations by the help of jurisprudence," "discern[ing] from history how it has come to be what it is," and "consider[ing] the ends which the several rules seek to accomplish, the reason why those ends are desired, what is given up to gain them, and whether they are worth the price."[95] He felt that "much missionary work remains to be done before the methods of legal thinking exemplified in *[Collected Legal Papers]* become characteristic of . . . even the leaders of the legal profession."[96]

Cook's restatement of Holmes was far more accurate than Pound's: the passage he quoted can be taken as providing a summary of the very methodology Holmes had employed in *The Common Law.* He was also correct in suggesting that few legal theorists, whether of the orthodox "late nineteenth-century" variety that Pound had described or the "progressive" or "Realist" variety that had surfaced in Cook's time, had employed that methodology. "Progressives" such as Pound and Frankfurter were interested in criticizing doctrine, not in following the existing body of doctrine into its highest generalizations. Their concern was with particular decisions, such as *Lochner v. New York,* that exhibited an outmoded or wrongheaded judicial sensibility. They were not interested in "following" the evolution of the doctrine of liberty of contract. "Realists" such as Karl Llewellyn and Jerome Frank were not interested in the historical origins of doctrine—nor, for that matter, in doctrine itself. Their goal was to organize legal subjects in a way that reflected contemporary practices, customs, patterns of behavior, or economic or social conditions.[97] Of the three projects outlined by Holmes, Realists were only interested in the third, that of evaluating the "ends" that legal rules sought to accomplish, by way of making rules more "realistic." Cook, who was himself an exponent of Realism, was discerning enough to recognize that for Holmes the evaluation of social ends was part of a complex project in which legal doctrine was first taken seriously on its own terms and then seen as a historical and cultural phenomenon, preparatory to being evaluated critically. Few of the commentators who were enthusiastic about Holmes' essays had much interest in his project as a whole.

The unwillingness of commentators to pursue or even to accurately identify the methodological goals of Holmes did not diminish their enthusiasm for his ideas. He combined, for them, a modernist skepticism toward fixed or frozen legal dogma with a tolerance for social experimentation. One commentator, in an extended discussion of *Collected Legal Papers,* said that "Holmes has . . . firmly set himself against a block universe of legal conceptions and rigidly fixed social order," and "has sought to give man room to express his advancing needs in an orderly progressing society."[98] Another said that "[e]ven if we did not know that this writer was our greatest living judge, our most profound legal scholar, we would recognize in the pages of his Collected Papers a great personality, a seeker after truth."[99] A third, Albert Kocourek, writing in the *Illinois Law Review,* was the most effusive of all. In the course of his review Kocourek said of Holmes:

> He is already, it does not seem venturesome to say, as well established a figure in our law as Bracton or Coke, or Holt or Mansfield, or Marshall or Story. In range of learning no judge of the English common law can be thought of as a serious competitor. No other judge of this or any other generation has understood as profoundly what may be called the phylogeny of the English common law.
>
> If Holmes had not turned by some intellectual accident to the law, but had permitted his great native and acquired talents to fructify in the direction of those problems which lie deepest in his mind . . . he would, we are not reluctant to believe, have become one of the greatest metaphysicians of his time.[100]

The Harvard symposium and the response to *Collected Legal Papers* suggested that a number of forces were coalescing to secure Holmes the recognition he had so long coveted. By the appearance of *Collected Legal Papers,* however, he had not yet emerged as the "great liberal judge," a characterization that was to be at once the strangest and the most persistent of those that marked the last phase of his judicial career. In 1929 a comment in the *Oregon Law Review,* precipitated by Holmes' eighty-eighth birthday, demonstrated that the image of Holmes as "liberal" was firmly in place. "Justice Holmes," the comment noted,

> has been a great dissenter, but to his credit let it be said that this is perhaps due to the fact that he has been a great liberal. He has sturdily resisted the tendency of the Supreme Court of the United States to translate its own conceptions of social policy into the laws of the state. He expresses this in his own epigrammatic way in *Lochner v. New York.* . . . He has always resisted encroachment upon the states and has been favorable to the free play of states in working out their problems of taxation and of government. He has been wise and broad-minded and one who seems to understand the economic forces

in his treatment of the problems of big business, of industry and of labor. He has always been prone to sustain legislation wherever it was not clearly unconstitutional. Towards human interests and human liberties, no judge who has sat upon the bench has ever been more progressive in his attitude.[101]

Some of the elements attributed to "liberalism" by the comment had been associated with Holmes earlier, such as his deference to state legislatures and his reluctance to employ his office as a vehicle to "translate . . . conceptions of social policy." The reflexive citation to *Lochner* was in keeping with that association. But the characterizations of Holmes as a "great dissenter" and a "great liberal," and especially the depiction of him as "progressive . . . towards human interests and human liberties," were new elements in his image. To a noncontemporary, familiar with the pattern of Holmes' decisions from 1903 to 1916, those elements appear dissonant with the facts of Holmes' career. They were a product of a line of cases that began in 1919 and stretched through the reminder of Holmes' tenure, cases in which Holmes appeared as both a "liberal" and a "dissenter" on the issue of free speech. Treatment of those cases, and the metamorphosis of Holmes as a "liberal" judge, is reserved for the next chapter. Suffice it to say here that the inflation of Holmes' reputation in the years before and immediately after World War I was not a product of his purported role as a civil libertarian. It was a product of the attractiveness of Holmes as a philosophical and cultural figure to the generation of Frankfurter's contemporaries. In their effort to "shape . . . a jurisprudence to meet the social needs of the time"[102] they had made Holmes into one of their allies.

～

Of all the reactions to Holmes' recognition as a "great judge," the most interesting may well be that of Holmes himself. Some perspective on that reaction may be gained from a brief recollection of how swift and significant recognition for Holmes had been. As late as 1910 he had written to Pollock that "in spite of feeling as keen an interest in life as ever, the shadows begin to lengthen," and that "I reflect on the mistake that I have seen it to be in others to remain on the bench after seventy." "[A]s recognition gradually comes," he had added, "one should take it as a warning that the end is near."[103] The letter suggests that Holmes anticipated retiring from the Court when eligible to do so with a full pension, having completed a judicial career in which the kind of recognition he had sought had eluded him. But then, in a rush, had come his friendships with Frankfurter, Laski, and their contemporaries; the evolution of his *Lochner* dissent to a "classic"; the Harvard symposium on his seventy-fifth birthday; the publication of *Collected Legal Papers,* to widespread praise. To these accomplishments could be added the Roosevelt Medal for "distinguished service to the American people in the development of public law," which he received in 1924 and of which he said, in receiving it from President Calvin Coolidge, "for five minutes you make me believe that the dream of a lifetime has come true."[104]

Holmes' reaction to the elevation of his reputation, however, contained an undertone of what can best be described as anxiety. We have seen in his previous descriptions of his friendship with Frankfurter that the friendship was very important to him, and that he was apprehensive about some dimensions of it. In a 1915 letter he had spoken to Frankfurter of "my rather fearful hope that I may never fall from the place you have given me,"[105] and in a 1919 letter had said that a Frankfurter letter, written from the Paris Peace Conference, had "[brought] joy to my heart" because it was evidence that "your kindness for me has not been shaken by the sight you have had of some many impressive personalities in the old world."[106] The suggestion in those comments was that "the sympathy of the young" which helped counteract "the eternal gravitation toward melancholy and doubt"[107] that accompanied old age might be transient, especially as age brought weakness and increased isolation and irrelevance.

A similar attitude of apprehension accompanied Holmes' response to his growing recognition. One can observe this attitude in a succession of comments in his correspondence with Frankfurter during the 1920s, a decade in which his reputation continually grew in stature. In a February 17, 1920 letter, in reference to an attack on Laski in the Harvard *Lampoon,* Holmes said,

> Years ago I said to Arthur Sedgwick why is it that while we don't mind the attacks of fools their praise sets us up. . . . But later self observation has shown me that I mind the attacks more than the praise. And the reason is that we find so easy to think ill of ourselves than when anyone suggests it we say perhaps at least he's right.[108]

That letter suggests that beneath Holmes' self-confidence lay a degree of insecurity, and one might at first be inclined to accept that analysis at face value. Subsequent comments by Holmes about recognition, however, suggest a more complex attitude. Recognition for Holmes had consistently been seen as an entitlement, a "reward for hard work," as he described his nomination to the Supreme Court. He had, he felt, "worn himself out after the unattainable" in the pursuit of scholarship that led to *The Common Law;* "put his heart" into his extrajudicial addresses; attempted to see every one of his cases on the Massachusetts court "to the bottom." He believed that the "passion" with which he pursued his work as a scholar and a judge should be matched in a reputation of comparable dimension. Thus he would not have been surprised when recognition at last came; indeed he was frustrated that it had not come sooner.

Why did Holmes therefore receive the evidence of his recognition, as he had received the evidence of Frankfurter's devotion, with apprehension? I would suggest that his statements of fears were comparable to his statements of approaching old age or death, such as his continual, half-joking notation to his new secretaries that he reserved the right to die or resign during their tenure. In these statements Holmes was seeking to ward off his fears by declaring them openly, as in his metaphor of forcing the dragon out of its cave so that one could see its teeth and claws. He would talk of old age while admitting at the same time that he did not feel old; he would talk of retirement while noting that he had no plans to retire. Similarly, he talked to Frankfurter of his apprehensions that recognition and praise would ultimately usher in criticism and obscurity. "I have seen several notices [of *Collected Legal Papers*]," he wrote Frankfurter in August 1921. One was "superlative"; another "equally amiable." He had been "much surprised and a little worried by the outpouring."

This was because "[p]ride goeth before a fall—and whenever anything sets me up I expect very shortly to get taken down."[109]

When Frankfurter and others congratulated Holmes on the twentieth anniversary of his tenure on the Court, which came on December 8, 1922, Holmes responded by writing that "[i]t makes me tremble to have these kind expressions for fear I shall in some way fail to come up to them before I go up to the day of Judgment."[110] When he received a comparable notice of his anniversary in *The New Republic*,[111] he wrote at length:

> The very generous notice of my anniversary . . . renewed the terrors of which I have written you before but of course went to my heart. . . . Such a thing cannot but make one happy and feel as if the long day's task had not been in vain. . . . The terror is not only that one may fall down but that when people go to the top of the hill the next stop seems to be to come down again.[112]

Here one sees evidence of a theme that had surfaced earlier in Holmes' life but was to become more persistent as he grew older—the realization that his reputation and his destiny were ultimately tied to the judgments of others.[113] This was unsettling, not only because it revealed that even by hard work and talent one could not fully control one's future, but also because it dovetailed all too nicely with Holmes' belief in the "finitude" of ideas and the tendency of succeeding generations to ignore or repudiate what their predecessors had held dear. Sometimes Holmes reconciled himself to the evanescence of his contributions by adopting an attitude of philosophic fatalism or by asserting a belief in the durability of his disciples, as when he wrote Frankfurter in 1923 that while he was unsure how long he would stay on the Court "good men like you will carry on the work—and it does not bother me to think of it all being engulfed by the Cosmos."[114] But more commonly he reacted as he did in a 1927 letter. "[S]o long as one writes decisions," he said to Frankfurter, "he is concerned with the future and never can be sure that he won't find out that he really is a damn fool after all."[115]

Holmes' fatalism about his ultimate place in history should not be confused, however, with humility.[116] His statements that his reputation might "fall" or that criticism might follow praise, even his comment that "we find it so easy to think ill of ourselves," were not manifestations of an inner modesty, as some commentators have apparently believed.[117] Holmes may have thought that down deep he was not a completely admirable person—he refers more than once to his egotism and ultra-competitiveness—but he did not think that he was an ordinary intellect. A telling reminder of his self-esteem is his reaction to criticism. We have seen that as a young scholar Holmes was extraordinarily protective of his originality and extremely grudging in his praise of or even attribution of the work of others. He retained this quality throughout his life. Even in the period of his greatest recognition, the occasional criticism of his work drew his attention to a degree far exceeding praise.

Two examples from the years when he was gaining widespread recognition will illustrate. In 1915 and 1916 John M. Zane, a law professor at the University of Illinois, criticized two of Holmes' central jurisprudential propositions, that legislators were not bound by their own previous laws, since they embodied the arbitrary powers of the sovereign, and that judges "made" rather than "discovered" law.[118] On seeing Zane's articles Holmes immediately wrote to Pollock and Laski, making almost identical comments. That to Pollock went as follows:

> John M. Zane walks into me in the *Mich. Law Rev.* and later in the *Ill. Law Rev.* and thinks I am hopelessly precluded from the place that otherwise I should occupy by accepting the old notion of a sovereign being superior to the law that he or it makes and by believing that judges make law. I suspect he means a different thing from what I do by law and that the fight is more about words than he thinks. But there is a real difference expressed by him in a tone of dogmatism upon which I should not venture, although I think I could smash him if he would say what he thought and not only what he didn't believe.[119]

Laski responded indignantly, having read Zane's articles and concluding that "the man is . . . insolently ignorant." He suggested that both he and Roscoe Pound would respond with criticisms of Zane.[120] Holmes responded that

> if anyone takes the trouble to deal with [Zane] I think he should be handled lightly not wrathfully. A man who calls everybody a damn fool is like a man who damns the weather—he only shows that he is not adapted to his environment, not that the environment is wrong. . . . He seems to me to fall back on dogmatic dissatisfaction, and hardly to show his own hand if he has one. . . . Of course I have nothing to say if any one wants to talk back, but I should think that Pound, without giving dogmatism for dogmatism, ought to consider himself on a different plane and to retain that position. So in your own case. You are a scholar, while Zane . . . makes on me the impression of the son of a *nouveau riche* who is very fashionable in his carriage but shows by little things that the high way is not in his blood.[121]

Pound and Laski did not respond, but Holmes did not forget Zane over the years. In 1920, prompted by John Wigmore's attack on his dissent in *Abrams v. United States*,[122] Holmes wrote Pollock that while Wigmore had "grown rather dogmatic in tone, with success," he didn't "equal another Chicago man, Zane, who patronized and condemned me on other matters, and also with one sweep wiped all German jurists off the slate, and with another Hobbes, Bentham, Austin, etc., so that nothing seemed to remain but Zane, and what he stood for he didn't tell."[123] Six years later Holmes repeated to Laski that Zane "said that anyone who thought my *Kawanankoa* case was law might give up all hope of ever being a lawyer—which was rather hard on me."[124] Laski responded that he remembered Zane as "one who wrote boisterously but without learning," and that he "should not . . . take anything he said very seriously."[125] Holmes was not satisfied, however. He secured a copy of Sir Paul Vinogradoff's *Custom and Right,* which Zane had praised in a book review, in the hope that he would "think lightly of [it] for reasons of personal malevolence," since it had been "so very highly cracked up" by Zane.[126]

Then, a year later, Holmes brought up Zane again to Laski. He wrote that "[y]our old friend John W. Zane has written a book—*The Story of Law*—and James M. Beck [formerly the Solicitor General of the United States] writes a letter of introduction." Holmes then continued:

Zane has an irritating ability, at once undeniable and unsatisfactory. Evidently he has read a good deal, but he seems a *parvenu* in the world of intellect, from his arrogant dogmatism, and, unless I am wrong, his somewhat painstaking introduction of quotations or allusions that he thinks you will not expect. . . . [T]he conceit of the writer is amazing and I am sure that divine providence arranged that Beck should introduce him.[127]

Not waiting for a reply, Holmes wrote again six days later:

My judgment of Zane was not changed as I read on. There were some things that seemed to me disproportionate toward the end—and renewed surprise at the boorish dogmatism of one who pauses in a history to reflect on the advantages of being born a gentleman.[128]

Laski responded that he did "not know [the Zane book] even by name," but added that "I cannot . . . quite bear the thought that there is the hand of J. M. Beck upon it for the latter always seemed to me an intolerable pompous ass."[129] Holmes took the comment to mean that Laski did not know Zane himself, and with great pleasure repeated his earlier observations:

You did know of him and were savage—I forget exactly the occasion. You will be pleased to know that he said in an article that anyone who thought my *Kawanankoa v. Polyblank* decision right might give up all hope of being a lawyer. . . . He affects the tone of scholarship yet somehow seems to me a *parvenu* in the business. . . . I am not malevolent in my attitude to Zane, but it tickled all that is evil in me to have him introduced and recommended by Beck.[130]

The Zane sequence is interesting in several respects. First, Holmes was sufficiently moved by Zane's comments to write his close friends about them, and then to repeat the substance of Zane's criticism several years later, even though Pollock never responded to Holmes' first mention of Zane and Laski had difficulty remembering who Zane was. Holmes, on the other hand, remembered Zane well enough to read one of Zane's books that appeared ten years after the criticism, even though the book was an effort to make law explicable to lay audiences, the sort of work Holmes almost never read. Moreover, Zane's comment that anyone who agreed with the view of sovereignty Holmes expressed in *Kawanankoa v. Polyblank* ought to give up all hope of being a lawyer stung Holmes sufficiently that he repeated it four times in his correspondence with Laski, each time indicating that it was "rather hard on me." Finally, while Holmes claimed that "I am not malevolent in my attitude to Zane," he also admitted that he hoped he would not think well of Vinogradoff's work, since Zane had praised it, "for reasons of personal malevolence."

Particularly suggestive was Holmes' use of epithets from a class perspective to characterize Zane. While Holmes, when compared with his upper-class Brahmin contemporaries, was not overly inclined to characterize people on the basis of their social or cultural background, he was conscious of class differences and not disinclined to make class distinctions. His repeated references to Zane as "nouveau riche," "a parvenu," or "boorish," and his ridiculing of Zane's "reflect[ing] on the advantages of being born a gentleman'' may have been intended as comments on Zane's intellectual ability rather than his social antecedents. But the fact that Holmes, well aware that his own class was conspicuously that of "gentlemen," used the metaphors of class to characterize Zane suggests that Zane had surely gotten under his skin. It was unusual for Holmes to wrap himself in the mantle of privilege, and notable that he spent so much time making caustic comments about Zane.

A similar episode occurred when Judge Charles Merrill Hough of the U.S. Court of Appeals for the Second Circuit wrote an article in the *Harvard Law Review* on the Supreme Court's admiralty decisions that contained some criticism of Holmes.[131] The thrust of Hough's article was that the Court's admiralty decisions since 1906 "have not increased the certainty of maritime law, and . . . have impaired the tradition of enforceable customs of the sea." Hough noted that Holmes and Justice James McReynolds had written "almost one half of the opinions on maritime matters" between 1906 and 1924.

Along the way Hough took a number of gibes at Holmes. He said that Holmes' opinion in *The Blackheath*[132] had "started trouble" by undermining a contrary precedent without explicitly saying so.[133] He described Holmes in one case as "bagging an epigram as usual in his phrase hunting."[134] He found that a generalization advanced by Holmes in one case was "still somewhat obscure" in its application.[135] He described Holmes' statements in his dissent in *Southern Pacific v. Jensen*,[136] in which he had said that "the maritime law is not a *corpus juris*—it is a very limited body of customs and ordinances of the sea," and that "judges do and must legislate, but they can do so only interstitially,"[137] as "clever *mots*."[138]

Hough reserved his most stringent criticism, however, for Holmes' decision in *The Western Maid*.[139] The question in that case was whether the traditional maritime lien, which allowed affected persons to recover directly against a ship for collision damages, should attach when the collision had occurred while the ship was owned by the government (and therefore protected by sovereign immunity), even though the ship had passed into private hands at the time the lien was sought to be enforced. In *The Western Maid* Holmes, for the Court, held that since sovereign immunity prevented the government from being sued, the lien did not in effect exist, and could not be enforced against the ship even after she was no longer owned by the government. In the course of his opinion Holmes, in Hough's view, "announced one piece of law which goes far beyond the necessities of this admiralty question." Holmes' "singly controlling proposition," according to Hough, was that "the United States has not consented to be sued for torts, and therefore it cannot be said that in a legal sense the United States has been guilty of a tort."[140] This dictum was a characteristic statement of Holmes' ultrapositivist view of legal "rights" and "duties": if immunities or other barriers meant that the sovereign had granted suitors no remedy, those suitors had no legal rights and the persons who injured them no corresponding legal duty. Holmes went on to particularize this view in *The Western Maid*, stating that "[l]egal obligations that exist but cannot be enforced are ghosts that are seen in the law but that are elusive to the grasp," and that "there is no mystic over-law to which even the United States must bow."[141]

Hough responded that "[w]hen it comes to hurdling a legal difficulty Holmes J. is *hors concours*, but in this effort he has surpassed himself." He noted a "tone of mockery displayed in every reference to the doctrine of a lien attaching regardless of the shipowner's personal liability,''; pointed out that the doctrine that maritime liens ran with the ships even if they were unenforceable in certain instances had been adopted by two previous Supreme Court cases that Holmes ignored; and claimed that Holmes' dictum "disposes of an admiralty cause by refining on the meaning of a word [tort] unknown to the historic admiralty." "The Bumbles of the shipping world," Hough concluded, "will pass usual comment on [Holmes' dictum], which for 'interstitial' lawmaking takes the very highest rank."[142]

When Hough's article appeared, Holmes wrote Laski and Pollock about it. He mentioned to Laski Hough's remarks about "hurdling a difficulty" and "search[ing] for epigrams," and maintained that "I think I see deeper than he does in the matter he refers to . . . and I swear I don't hunt for epigrams."[143] In the letter to Pollock Holmes referred to Hough's article as "amusing" but "unconvincing." "The good Hough," he continued, "says that I refine on the meaning of a word unknown to the admiralty law—*tort*—that the admiralty only knows *collision,* that as I conclude that there was no tort I conclude that there was no collision." Hough's comment, he felt, suggested "several reflections too obvious to write out."[144]

Nonetheless Holmes did write down his "reflections" in a 1928 letter to Laski, in which he said,

> When the lamented Hough was alive and chaffing a decision of mine to the effect that a boat of the U.S. was not guilty of a tort in running into another vessel—he said we don't talk of torts in Admiralty but of collision, and would I say there had been no collision?—I wrote, alas just as he died, that if he preferred to talk Basque instead of French and to deny himself the benefit of the wider generalizations of a more developed system it was all right but that having but one word for two ideas he must distinguish. Collision in the sense of physical impact is not denied—but collision with legal responsibility—I certainly should deny. Collision might mean either—and I rather think Hough was the victim of his own ambiguity.[145]

As the above excerpt suggests, Holmes was not offended by Hough in the same fashion as he had been by Zane. In 1926 he wrote Pollock and Laski that Hough had come to visit him in Washington. He told the former that he "was very glad to see Hough," who had "chaffed me in the public prints." He added that Hough had "made criticisms that I think I easily could smash," the same language he had used in initially reacting to Zane, but that he "has said kind things also," and that he and Holmes "jabbered away like old acquaintances in two minutes."[146] To Laski, Holmes reported that Hough "has praised and criticized and chaffed me in articles in which, as in his opinions, he has a spicy tongue," and that "I liked him greatly."[147]

The episode of Hough's criticism is instructive because while Holmes distinguished between Hough's ideas and Hough's person, as he did not in the case of Zane, he nonetheless continued to bring up the criticism and eventually responded, both to Hough and to Laski. The points on which Holmes appeared most sensitive were his alleged tendency to search for epigrammatic phrases—a tendency that, notwithstanding his disclaimer, was sufficiently visible to others to have elicited numerous comments over the years—and his conclusory reasoning about sovereignty. As in the Zane episode, Holmes had decided to state his view of sovereign powers in a particularly categorical fashion, not choosing to make the distinctions he later made in response to criticism. He claimed he recognized that there was a difference between a physical collision and the right to sue for damages arising out of that collision, but in *The Western Maid* his language had blurred that distinction. Similarly his language, in *Kawanankoa v. Polyblank,* that "there can be no legal right as against the authority that makes the law on which the right depends" was too categorical: a legislature might decide to waive its sovereign immunity. Holmes believed that abstract talk of legal "rights" needed to confront the positivist origins of those rights, and he liked to put generalizations broadly and vividly, leaving others to worry about their application. His response to Hough's comments suggests that he may have recognized that his ultrapositivist position on sovereignty was vulnerable.

In the Zane and Hough episodes one can glimpse an underlying sense in Holmes that on some issues his jurisprudential positions required further refinement than he had been prepared to allot to them. But there is no corresponding sense of concern about the ultimate soundness of those positions. In both instances Holmes announces that he could "smash" his critics if he chose; indeed the exercise is not worth the effort. Holmes believed that in his early scholarship, and in the refinements on that scholarship which he had undertaken while on the SJC, he had thought through the question of the nature of law and the corresponding "interstitial" role of judges more fully and deeply than most of his contemporaries. The fact that he had chosen to state his conclusions in a bald and vivid fashion—exemplified in his "bad man" conceit in "The Path of the Law" and his aphorism that law was "nothing more pretentious" than "the prophecies of what the courts will do in fact"—did not mean that they were hastily or conclusorily reasoned. On the contrary, he felt, their elemental significance came from the insights of laborious research and hard thinking. When Holmes wrote Canon Patrick Sheehan and Nina Gray in 1910 that "my only ambition . . . is to do the best work that can be done,"[148] and that "I confine my aspirations to being the greatest legal thinker in the world,"[149] he may have meant those statements to be taken in jest, but he believed the goals were within his reach, despite the lack of recognition he had thus far received.

That is why the appearance of recognition, in the eighth decade of his life, must have been so profoundly gratifying to Holmes. In an important sense he had contributed to that recognition, by fostering, in his own way, the relationships with Frankfurter, Laski, and others that led directly to the publicization of his ideas and his opinions and the creation of his image as a "great judge." At one level Holmes believed that exalted recognition *must* come to him, as the Supreme Court nomination had, as a "reward" for his hard and accomplished work. But at another level he understood that just as he had been prepared to stay overnight at Sagamore Hill, waiting for Theodore Roosevelt to return so that Roosevelt could satisfy himself about Holmes' partisan soundness, he was prepared to ship copies of his scholarship to Laski to be assembled as *The Collected Legal Papers,* and to subscribe to *The New Republic* because that periodical thought him a "progressive" judge. If recognition was an entitlement, it was also a publicity campaign.

Recognition, for Holmes, came to symbolize others' investment in the person given homage, and his investment in them. In coming to understand the double-edged nature of recognition Holmes began, in his later life, to sense its evanescent nature and his inability to control its future course. The fact that by 1924, when he was awarded the Roosevelt Medal, he had reached "the top of hill" meant that inevitably he would start on the path down. This did not mean, he believed, that someone would expose him as an intellectual lightweight: that exposure could not take place because Holmes was a superior intellect. His path would inevitably be "down" because his time span, like all time spans, was finite. He was eighty-three years old when he told Coolidge that for five minutes his dreams had come true; in another five minutes he might be dead, and then who could tell what recognition he would secure? Recognition, like the other concepts that raised themes going to the core of Holmes' being, was double-edged.

CHAPTER ELEVEN

The Supreme Court, 1917–1931:
The "Progressive" Judge

~

WHEN the *Harvard Law Review* celebrated his seventy-fifth birthday with a symposium, Holmes may have inwardly rejoiced that he had not elected to retire on a full pension three years earlier, that at long last recognition was beginning to come. Had he been able to predict the future, however, he would have been astonished at what lay ahead. At an age at which most of his mid-career contemporaries were no longer alive, he would be able to live for nearly twenty more years, during all but the last three of which he would continue to sit on the Supreme Court. He would retain his physical and mental powers for almost all of those years, so that at ninety he would still be able to write a memorable birthday radio speech and to keep up with his work on the Court. As he aged and persisted the momentum of his recognition, swelled by his longevity, would grow to the point where his contemporaries applied to him epithets usually reserved for the dead. The years from 1917 to his retirement were, for the most part, a time of glory for Holmes, in which the vast reach of his ambition seemed closely approximated by the vastness of his reputation.

We have seen that an important ingredient in the emergence of Holmes as a "great" judge was the surfacing of a new audience for his work, the "progressive" intelligentsia of Frankfurter's generation. "Progressives," as noted, were particularly attracted to three features of Holmes: his "modern" and "realistic" conception of law and the judicial function; his tolerance toward what they termed "experiments" by the states in social and economic regulation; and, especially after World War I, his apparent solicitude toward constitutional claims based on the First Amendment's protection for speech. Although Holmes' admirers did not fasten on some of these virtues until he reached his eighties, they seemed to cement his image as the prototype of an enlightened judge.

In their haste to make Holmes into a figure of legend his enthusiasts, as suggested in Chapter Ten, showed an inclination to distort his views. This chapter considers in some detail two of the sets of opinions underlying Holmes' exalted reputation in his later years. The first set of opinions represented Holmes' paradoxical response to the problem of unconstrained judicial "lawmaking" in a democratic society, a response in which he freely fashioned common law rules that he conceded, as a jurisprudential matter, he lacked the power to make. The second set represented Holmes' persistent, but not universal, deference to a series of legislative "experiments" of an economic or sociological variety. In the first set, Holmes' admirers applauded his response at the level of theory and ignored it at the level of practice. In the second, they generally treated him as an enlightened "progressive" judge. Both views contained elements of wish-fulfillment. A third set of "progressive" opinions, dealing with free speech, will receive separate treatment in Chapter Twelve.

~

By the second decade of the twentieth century the jurisprudential message of Holmes' *Lochner* dissent had taken hold in a community of "progressive" legal intellectuals. Holmes' dissent had rested on the premise that judges should not substitute their judgment, in constitutional interpretation, for that of legislatures, except when facing an "overwhelming constitutional mandate." The exception, however, proved the rule, because where the Constitution placed explicit limits on a legislature, one sovereign (the supermajority that had ratified the Constitution) had imposed its power on another.

In short, everywhere in his exploration of jurisprudential issues Holmes saw the "fact" of sovereignty. Even where no legislative or constitutional mandate appeared to exist—the sphere of the common law—judges exercised a "sovereign prerogative of choice." Their choices were "sovereign" because the common law they created was itself the creature of the state. They derived their authority from the office that the state had conferred upon them, and the body of law they developed in their decisions could be legislatively changed. The great fallacy in jurisprudential thinking, Holmes believed, was the idea that judicial authority came from somewhere other than the sovereignty of the state. Common law was not the product of some independent system of reason ("logic") or the innate wisdom of judges.

Holmes' views paralleled those of two of his former colleagues on the Harvard faculty, James Bradley Thayer and John Chipman Gray, who in the late nineteenth and early twentieth centuries had published works on judicial review and sovereignty. In Thayer's 1893 paper, "The Origin and Scope of the American Doctrine of Constitutional Law,"[1] he argued for a limited scope of judicial review in constitutional cases. In the course of his argument Thayer sought to demonstrate that judicial review had developed in America only fortuitously, because of the experience of royal charters as a check on the powers of colonial legislatures; that there was no compelling reason for judges rather than legislators to be interpreters of the Constitution; that the "overwhelming constitutional mandate" standard for triggering judicial review was a well-established precedent; and that a modest judicial approach toward constitutional interpretation would encourage legislators to become more effective "statesmen." Holmes was less sanguine about the possibility of increased legislative statesmanship, but he agreed with Thayer that judges had no special insight into constitutional interpretation and no special mandate to substitute their interpretations of the Constitution for those of legislatures.

In 1909 Gray implicitly reinforced Thayer's views in the course of arguing that all jurisprudential theories that assumed the existence of an independent body of objective rules called "the law," and that assumed that judges merely "discovered" that body of "law" were fallacious. The law, Gray concluded, is made up of the rules for decision which the courts lay down; that all such rules are law; that rules for conduct which the courts do not apply are not law; that the fact that the courts apply rules is what makes them law; that there is no mysterious entity "the law" apart from these rules; and that the judges are rather the creators than the discoverers of law.[2]

It did not follow from these conclusions, Gray maintained, that there were no limits on the power of judges. "[T]he judges," he claimed, "are but organs of the state; they have only such power as the organization of the state gives them, and what that organization is, is determined by the wills of the real rulers of the state." "[O]n the most vital matters," Gray believed, "the rulers themselves determine what the organization of the body is and within what limits its organs shall work." Thus while judges were delegated power to lay down rules, the "rulers" could treat those rules as other than "law" if the rules were felt to be "inconsistent with the organization of the state . . . or . . . beyond the limits of the power of the court." In a democratic form of government, where the people were the titular "rulers," the test of whether a judicial declaration "was to be deemed law" was "the opinions of the community to that effect."[3]

Progressives such as Felix Frankfurter were inspired by Thayer's and Gray's work,[4] finding in it a theoretical justification for opposing judicial efforts to scrutinize early twentieth-century regulatory legislation on the basis of (judge-made) "dogma" such as the liberty of contract doctrine. For Frankfurter jurisprudential positions such as that articulated by Thayer and Gray were "progressive" in two respects. They were premised on the sanctity of democratic theory and thus harmonized with the general tendency of "progressives" to support a broadening and deepening of the popular base of American political institutions. They were also "modern" in their recognition that an older view of judges as the expositors of some disembodied entity called "the law," that existed independent of positivistic edicts by the sovereign, was outmoded. Such a view, in the minds of "progressives," was the last bastion of a conception of law as a universalistic, quasi-religious entity. "Moderns" had abandoned that conception, and consequently looked beneath the rhetoric of judicial decisions for evidence that judges were equating "the law" with their personal views.

Despite their difficulties with unconstrained judicial decisionmaking in the constitutional arena, early twentieth-century "progressives" did not express much concern about judicial decisionmaking in common law cases. Their failure to do so is instructive, because an apparent analogy to judicial usurpation of legislative prerogatives could be found in judicial practices in some common law subjects. In torts, for example, decisions of courts that took negligence cases away from juries in the interest of declaring uniform or predictable standards of law could have been seen as "countermajoritarian." Jurors were representatives of the community; many early twentieth-century judges, even at the state level, were unelected, unaccountable officials. In making a decision to fashion judge-made rules for negligence cases courts could be seen as resurrecting the outmoded conception of "law" as a disembodied collection of "principles," seemingly based on transcendent norms of reason or logic.

The practice of judges usurping jury prerogatives in negligence cases was arguably most "countermajoritarian" in cases in which the federal courts fashioned their own common law negligence doctrines, not necessarily relying on the negligence decisions made by the state courts in which they sat. Prior to the 1930s federal judges felt free, in a variety of common law cases, to derive rules from "principle" and "general authority," as distinguished from the law of the relevant state. This practice, which had been followed since the Chief Justiceship of John Marshall,[5] and expounded as a jurisprudential proposition by Justice Joseph Story in the 1842 case of *Swift v. Tyson*,[6] rested on the assumption that a "federal common law" existed independent of state-based decisions, and that federal courts could create their own common law in a number of cases, including negligence cases.

One of the most interesting features of Holmes' later years on the Supreme Court was that he simultaneously attacked the jurisprudential soundness of a body of "federal common law" and unabashedly contributed to developing it in negligence cases. Even though he claimed that the conception of an independent, transcendent body of federal common law was fallacious, since it ignored principles of sovereignty and resurrected the archaic image of law as "a brooding omnipresence in the sky,"[7] he continued to decide federal common law cases without recourse to the law of the state in which they arose, and in negligence cases substituted the judge-made rules of federal courts for the decisions of local juries. His "progressive" acolytes not only did not criticize this paradox, they did not even notice it.

Two of Holmes' negligence decisions in the 1920s are illustrative. In *United Zinc Co. v. Britt*[8] two boys, aged eight and eleven, were crossing land owned by the United Zinc Company, which had previously had a plant for the manufacture of sulphuric acid on the land. The land was on the outskirts of the town of Iola, Kansas, and in 1910 the company dismantled the plant's operations, tearing down a building but leaving a cavity where the building's basement had been. Water accumulated in the cavity and intermingled with sulphuric acid and zinc sulphate that remained on the plant site, creating a toxic pool, which was clear in appearance. The boys, noticing the pool, swam in it, were poisoned, and subsequently died. Their parents sued for negligence and won a jury verdict against the company, which ultimately appealed to the Supreme Court of the United States.

The United Zinc Company was responsible for maintaining the cavity on the land and allowing the toxic chemicals to mix with the water that filled the cavity. The boys, for their part, were trespassers on the land. The question in *Britt* was whether they should be treated as adult trespassers, who would under common law rules of landowner liability be owed no duty of care other than to warn against hidden traps on the land, or whether allowances should be made for their status as children and the fact that the clear, odorless pool constituted an attraction that could have lured them onto the land. If the boys were to be treated as adult trespassers, they were clearly contributorily negligent, and no jury could allow them to recover: the case would not even go to the jury. If, on the other hand, they were child trespassers, the case would turn on whether, under the circumstances, they had been attracted onto the land. That was a question for the jury to decide.

At the time of the *Britt* case state courts had split as to the treatment of child trespassers in so-called "attractive nuisance" cases.[9] One line of cases, influenced by the number of accidents to children caused by their coming into contact with unguarded railroad turntables, allowed such cases to go to juries on the ground that landowners should be expected to foresee that certain structures would be attractive but dangerous to children and that reasonable pains should be taken to guard them or otherwise make them inaccessible to child trespassers. The juries would then decide whether an "attractive nuisance" existed and whether the landowner had taken reasonable steps to protect children from it. Another line of cases, to which Holmes had contributed an opinion in Massachusetts,[10] treated trespassing children as the equivalent of trespassing adults and denied recovery on the ground that landowners owed no duty to protect trespassers from dangerous substances on their premises. The Supreme Court of the United States, in two turntable cases stretching over a twenty-year period, had associated itself with the former view.[11]

In *Britt*, Holmes held that the boys were "adult" trespassers and could not recover, adopting the doctrine of the Massachusetts cases. He acknowledged that although "children have no greater right to go upon other people's land than adults," it had been held that "knowingly to establish and expose, unfenced, to children of an age when they follow a bait as mechanically as a fish, something that is certain to attract them, has the legal effect of an invitation to them although not to an adult." He added, however, that "the principle if accepted must be very cautiously applied."[12] In the *Britt* case, he maintained, it was doubtful whether the water could have been "seen from any place where the children lawfully were and there is no evidence that it was what led them to enter the land." They had thus not even been "tempted," and surely not "invited" onto the land. There was no evidence that others had frequented the area near the poisoned water. In sum, Holmes concluded, "[t]here can be no general duty on the part of a landowner to keep his land safe for children, or even free from hidden dangers, if he has not directly or by implication invited . . . them to come there."[13]

Britt produced a dissent by Justice John Clarke, joined by Justice William Day and Chief Justice William Howard Taft, arguing that the Supreme Court of the United States had adopted the "trespassing children" classification in similar cases for the last fifty years; that the cavity filled with water had brick sides and "the appearance of an attractive swimming pool"; that there was no fence, sign, or other warning around the cavity; and that there were "several paths across the lot" owned by the United Zinc Company.[14] Clarke also noted that the question whether the pool was located such that the landowners should have anticipated that children might frequent its vicinity had been submitted to the jury, and by reversing the jury verdict the Court was saying that no reasonable jury could have found that the company should have foreseen children's being attracted to the pool.[15]

Holmes' opinion answered only one of these arguments. At the very end of his opinion he had written, "It is suggested that the roads across the place were invitations. A road is not an invitation to leave it elsewhere than at its end."[16] That pair of sentences was characteristic of Holmes' style of opinion writing. He did not respond to all the opposing arguments raised by the side whose cause he was not endorsing in his opinions, only those he found substantively or stylistically convenient. The presence of paths across the company's property was only one of a number of factors that suggested the company was maintaining an attractive nuisance.

Holmes' motivation for singling out that factor can be gleaned from his accompanying sentence. "A road is not an invitation to leave it elsewhere than at its end" was a memorable way to conclude an opinion, a pithily expressed generality.

The sentence was also highly erroneous, both as a general proposition and as applied to the *Britt* case. The "end" of a road is indeterminate in most instances. Indeed the purpose of roads is to link settlements in a continuous progression, not to "begin" or to "end" in a precise spot. To the extent roads have "an end," the great bulk of road users do not anticipate traversing them until the point where they become wilderness. On the contrary, they anticipate taking them to a point where it is convenient for them to get "off" the road, which continues. Roads are not like train tracks in that they do not have discernible points of origin and terminus. In short, roads do not "invite" those who use them only to take them to their "end."

Even if one were to claim that most roads were like train tracks and most persons took them to their termination point, the generalization hardly makes sense when applied to paths across the property of the United Zinc Company. Such paths had been tracked over the land by persons seeking short or convenient ways through undifferentiated territory. They were the prime example of roads that had no obvious "beginning" or "end," but merely designated traveled routes across terrain. It was quite likely, in fact, that one such path "ended" at the pool where the boys were poisoned in *Britt,* since the pool contained water that had collected in the foundations of an abandoned chemical plant. At one point many persons would have wanted access to that plant; a path might have been a vestige of that time. So if a path extended from the outer boundary of the company's property to the pool, it could well have been said, using Holmes' own dictum, to have been an invitation to visit the pool.

Shortly after the *Britt* decision had been handed down Holmes wrote friends about the case. In a letter to Pollock he suggested that his principal motivation in writing the opinion had been to reduce the impact of the doctrine the Court had previously endorsed in the turntable cases. "On Monday," Holmes wrote, "I fired off a decision cutting the turn table cases (children hurt on them) down to somewhat more precise limits. My brother Clarke uttered a larmoyant dissent that seemed to me more sentiment and rhetoric than reasoning, but the C. J. and Day agreed with him, I cannot but suspect, on reasoning of their own."[17] In a letter to Laski, written three days earlier, he said that he was about to deliver an opinion in a case involving "the liability (non-liability, I say) of a landowner for the drowning of children in a poisoned pool where it did not appear that the children had been in any way tempted to enter the land." The last sentence of the Laski letter was interesting because in his *Britt* opinion Holmes had said that "it is very plain that temptation is not invitation."[18] It is interesting that Holmes told Laski that the boys in *Britt* had drowned, as if they had fallen into an ordinary flooded basement cavity. In fact they had died from exposure to toxic chemicals, whose presence arguably should have made the company more inclined to fence off the site.

Britt was characteristic of Holmes' preference, in tort law, for rules that were sufficiently clear to take cases away from juries unless the liability of the defendant was patently evident. In *The Common Law,* we have seen, he had written that it was undesirable to "leave all our rights and duties throughout a great part of the law to the necessarily more or less accidental feelings of a jury," and had suggested in cases where "the elements are few and permanent," there had been "an inclination ... to lay down a definite rule," and although "this attempt to work out an exact line requires much caution, it is entirely philosophical in spirit." "[T]he tendency of the law," he felt, "must always be to narrow the field of uncertainty."[19] By "cutting" the doctrine of the turntable cases "down to precise limits," he was attempting to "narrow the field of uncertainty" for child trespasser cases in the federal courts.

Holmes' fondness for taking cases away from juries in negligence actions combined with the fact that he had never learned to drive an automobile[20] to produce one of his most notorious opinions. The case was *Baltimore and Ohio Railroad Co. v. Goodman*,[21] in which Nathan Goodman, a truck driver, had approached a railroad crossing that had an overhanging tool shed adjacent to it. As Goodman's lawyer put it in arguing before the Supreme Court,

> The Circuit Court of Appeals found that [Goodman] could not see north of the tool shed until the front of his truck was less than twenty feet from the west rail. The evidence was uncontradicted that the seat in which [Goodman] was sitting was six feet back from the front of the machine, and that the overhang of the railroad engine was two and one-half feet. Therefore, the front of his truck was within eleven and one-half feet from the danger point, before he could first see past the tool shed, behind which was the approaching train. . . . Hearing no signal, no bell, or other warning, he had been led into a trap.[22]

The Court of Appeals had sustained a jury verdict for Goodman on the ground that under the circumstances he had not been contributorily negligent and the railroad had been negligent in failing to warn of the approaching train. Holmes, for a unanimous Court, reversed and held Goodman contributorily negligent as a matter of law. "[N]othing," Holmes said, "is suggested by the evidence to relieve Goodman from responsibility for his own death. When a man goes upon a railroad track he knows that he goes to a place where he will be killed if a train comes upon him before he is clear of the track. He knows that he must stop for the train, not the train stop for him."[23] The fact that Goodman had "found himself in an emergency" and had "[done] all he could" was irrelevant: he needed to "reduce his speed earlier or come to a stop."[24]

Holmes then went on to lay down a "grade-crossing rule" for the federal courts for collisions between trains and motorists:

> [I]f a driver cannot be sure otherwise whether a train is dangerously near he must stop and get out of his vehicle, although obviously he will not often be required to do more than to stop and look. It seems to us that if he relies upon not hearing the train or any signal and takes no further precaution he does so at his own risk.[25]

Holmes conceded that in negligence cases "the question of due care very generally is left to the jury." But in cases such as *Goodman,* he argued, "we are dealing with a standard of conduct, and when the standard is clear it should be laid down once for all by the Courts.''[26] For Holmes *Goodman* was a case in which judges could eliminate the ''accidental feelings of a jury''[27] and lay down a rule ''once for all.''[28]

The problem with that approach was that Holmes' ''rule'' was absurd, and the idea of laying down a universal standard of conduct for grade crossing accidents equally absurd. Stopping at grade crossings and ''looking and listening'' for a train would not ensure that, in circumstances like Goodman's, the motorist would be able to avoid a speeding train that gave no warning of its approach. Getting out of cars might be more dangerous to motorists than not stopping, given two-way automobile traffic around grade crossings. In short, there was no easy way to determine in advance what conduct might be careless or prudent in a motorist when approaching an unguarded grade crossing. Cases such as *Goodman* were best left to juries. Holmes' opinion in *Goodman* was sharply criticized, both in the law journals and in the newspapers.[29] Although Pollock supported it, noting that ''[w]e have long ceased here to hold the verdict of juries in civil cases in any superstitious reverence,''[30] Holmes' formula for grade crossings was not widely followed by the lower federal courts, and seven years after the *Goodman* decision the Supreme Court eliminated Holmes' formula in *Pokora v. Wabash Railway,* a case with an almost identical fact situation to that in *Goodman.* Justice Benjamin Cardozo, who had succeeded to Holmes' seat in 1932, said of the *Goodman* formula:

> Standards of prudent conduct are declared at times by courts, but they are taken over from the facts of life. To get out of a vehicle is an uncommon precaution, as everyday experience informs us. Besides being uncommon, it is very likely to be futile, and sometimes even dangerous. If the driver leaves his vehicle when he nears a cut or curve, he will learn nothing by getting out about the perils that lurk beyond. By the time he regains his seat and sets his car in motion, the hidden train may be upon him. . . .
>
> Extraordinary situations may not wisely or fairly be subjected to tests or regulations that are fitting for the common-place or normal. In default of the guide of customary conduct, what is suitable for the traveler caught in a mesh where the ordinary safeguards fail him is for the judgment of a jury.[31]

Cardozo held that ''the opinion in Goodman's case has been a source of confusion in the federal courts to the extent that it imposes a standard for application by the judge,''[32] and that Holmes' formula would no longer be followed.

Holmes' opinions in the *Britt* and *Goodman* cases were predictable in the sense that since *The Common Law* he had been on record as advocating clear and predictable rules in common law subjects and as evidencing distrust in jury verdicts. At another level, however, the opinions were inconsistent with views that Holmes had persistently advanced about the nature and sources of law. *Britt* and *Goodman* had been products of a jurisprudence in which the federal courts, in common law cases, were deemed free to fashion their own substantive rules of law, not necessarily following the doctrines of the states in which they sat. This prerogative had made possible Holmes' strategy, in the *Britt* case, of refashioning the ''attractive nuisance'' doctrine in the federal courts to more resemble that promulgated in Massachusetts, even though the *Britt* case had originated in Kansas and the Kansas courts had adopted a more lenient standard of conduct for child trespassers. It had also made possible his effort in *Goodman* to articulate a uniform standard of conduct for grade-crossing cases in the federal courts.

The fact that Holmes was prepared to fashion federal common law on his own, however, did not mean that he believed that the practice was jurisprudentially sound. As early as 1910 he had dissented in a case in which the majority concluded that "the U.S. Courts were not bound to follow a State decision as [to] the effect of a deed of coal in the State."[33] He wrote Pollock about that decision:

> [The majority judges] follow an established though very fishy principle started by Story [in *Swift v. Tyson*], that in general commercial law the U.S. Courts would follow their own judgment, *non obstante* decisions of the State as to transactions within it. This has been extended to general law, while as to state statutes & constitutions the rule is the other way.

Holmes added that in defense of the principle the majority had declared that "we must use our independent judgment." "I reply," he told Pollock, "as to what? The state law. But the State judges and the State legislatures make the State law—we don't—and I refer to decisions and John Gray's recent book[34] to show that we have to recognize in other cases the law-making functions of the judges."[35]

Holmes felt that he had "punched a hole in [the] bottom" of those judges who sought to extend the "general law" practice,[36] but his views did not command a majority of the Court. In 1917, in the case of *Southern Pacific v. Jensen*,[37] the Court considered an accident to a seaman on the gangplank between a ship and its pier in New York harbor. New York had a workmen's compensation statute; the general maritime law offered no such remedy. The majority declined to apply New York law. Holmes, in dissent, described maritime law as "a very limited body of customs and ordinances of the sea," and said that in the absence of a Congressional statute governing maritime injuries "the natural inference is that . . . this court has believed the very limited law of the sea to be supplanted here as in England by the common law, and that here that means, by the common law of the state." His next sentence contained one of his most famous aphorisms, previously quoted. "The common law is not a brooding omnipresence in the sky," he said, "but the articulate voice of some sovereign or quasi-sovereign that can be identified," such as legislatures or courts.[38]

In the catchphrase "brooding omnipresence in the sky" Holmes was encompassing two of his favorite axioms, both of which John Zane had criticized, the axiom that judges as well as legislators made law and the accompanying axiom that law was nothing more than the enforcement of sovereign power. The axioms made it plain that to say that judges were merely applying the dictates of some "brooding omnipresence" when they fashioned "general law" doctrines, or to say that they could disregard the enforcement of the sovereign powers of the state by its courts, made no sense. In 1926 Holmes wrote Laski that

> There is a tendency to think of judges as if they were independent mouthpieces of the infinite, and not simply directors of a force that comes from the source that gives them their authority. I think our court has fallen into the error at times and it is that that I have aimed at when I have said that the Common

Law is not a brooding omnipresence in the sky and that the U.S. is not subject
to some mystic overlaw that it is bound to obey. When our U.S. Circuit Courts
are backed up by us in saying that suitors have a right to their independent
judgment as to the common law of a State, and so that the U.S. Courts may
disregard the decisions of the Supreme Court of the State, the fallacy is
illustrated. The Common Law in a State is the Common Law of that state
deriving all its authority from the State.[39]

The 1926 letter indicated that Holmes remained unrepentant on the unintelligi-
bility of "general common law." In a 1928 decision he was able to articulate his
position in a vivid dissent. The case, *Black and White Taxicab and Transfer Co. v.
Brown and Yellow Taxicab and Transfer Co.*,[40] involved an effort on the part of a
Tennessee taxicab company to secure exclusive taxi concessions at a Kentucky railroad station. A Kentucky statute prohibited such concessions, when held by Ken-
tucky-based corporations, as being against public policy. The Black and White cab
company, in order to circumvent the statute, dissolved itself in Kentucky, reincor-
porated itself in Tennessee, and secured a concession. When a rival taxicab company,
the Brown and Yellow company, attempted to maintain cabs at the Bowling Green,
Kentucky, station, the Black and White company sued to prevent it from doing so,
claiming an interference with its contractual relations with the railroad. A central
question in the case was therefore whether the Court would follow Kentucky decisions holding exclusive transportation contracts invalid. The Court majority concluded that "the decisions of the Kentucky Court of Appeals holding such arrangements invalid are contrary to the common law as generally understood and applied,"
and that "[f]or the discovery of common law principles applicable in any case,
investigation is not limited to the decisions of the courts of the State in which the
controversy arises." "The applicable rule sustained by many decisions of this
Court," Justice Pierce Butler wrote for the majority, "is that in determining questions of general law, the federal courts, while inclining to follow the decisions of
the courts of the State in which the controversy arises, are free to exercise their own
independent judgment."[41] Butler held that the contract was valid and that the Black
and White Taxicab Company could exclude competitors from the Bowling Green
station.

Holmes' dissent bears quoting at some length.

> The Circuit Court of Appeals had so considerable a tradition behind it in
> deciding as it did that if I did not regard the case as exceptional I should not
> feel warranted in presenting my own convictions again after having stated
> them in *Kuhn v. Fairmont Coal Company*. . . . But the question is important
> and in my opinion the prevailing doctrine has been accepted upon a subtle
> fallacy that never has been analyzed. If I am right the fallacy has resulted in an
> unconstitutional assumption of powers by the Courts of the United States
> which no lapse of time or respectable array of opinion should make us hesitate
> to correct.[42]

Holmes then went on to explain what in his judgment the "fallacy" was: "the often
repeated proposition . . . that the parties are entitled to an independent judgment on

matters of general law.'' By ''matters of general law,'' Holmes said, was meant ''the common law.''[43] He then continued:

> It is very hard to resist the impression that there is one august corpus [of the common law], to understand which clearly is the only task of any Court concerned. If there were such a transcendental body of law outside of any particular State but obligatory within it unless and until changed by statute, the Courts of the United States might be right in using their independent judgment as to what it was. But there is no such body of law. The fallacy and illusion that I think exist consist in supposing that there is this outside thing to be found. . . . [L]aw in the sense in which courts speak of it today does not exist without some definite authority behind it. The common law so far as it is enforced in a State . . . is not the common law generally but the law of that State existing by the authority of that State.[44]

Holmes then went on to note that the adoption of the ''common law'' by various state courts did not prevent them from ''refusing to follow . . . English decisions upon a matter where the local conditions are different'' and that Louisiana had not adopted the common law at all.[45] He also pointed out that state statutes were taken as superseding the common law, and indicated that he saw ''no reason why [state law] should have less effect when it speaks by its other voice,'' the voice of the state's courts.[46] He alluded to Story's decision in *Swift v. Tyson,* which he took to have been written ''evidently under the tacit domination of the fallacy to which I have referred,'' and indicated that he would ''not allow *[Swift v. Tyson]* to spread the assumed dominion into new fields.''[47] In short, he concluded, the *Taxicab* case raised ''a question of the authority by which certain particular acts, here the grant of exclusive privileges in a railroad station, are governed.'' In his view

> the authority and only authority is the State, and, if that be so, the voice adopted by the State as its own should utter the last word.[48]

Holmes' dissent in the *Taxicab* case was one of his most eloquent, and also one of his most predictable. His positivist theories of sovereignty, his longstanding conviction that judges ''made law,'' even if in some ''interstitial'' sense, his pride in having been a state judge, his disdain for jurisprudential theories based on metaphysics, and his concern that federal judges not usurp state prerogatives had united to produce a conviction that the line of ''general common law'' cases beginning with *Swift v. Tyson* was based on a fallacy that should be corrected. Two features of his dissent, however, invite some additional speculation.

One is that he did not apply the logic of his *Kuhn, Jensen,* and *Taxicab* dissents to his own ''federal'' common law opinions. He cheerfully went about ''cutting down the turntable cases'' in *Britt,* or announcing the ''stop, look, and listen'' formula in *Goodman* without so much as a nod to relevant state decisions that did not support his position. While vigorously refuting federal common law in *Taxicab* and the other dissents, he applied it unhesitatingly in *Britt* and *Goodman,* without reconciling, or even acknowledging, the flat contradiction.

The second interesting feature of Holmes' *Taxicab* dissent was his statement that the fallacy he had exposed was not only wrongheaded but had "resulted in an unconstitutional assumption of powers by the Courts of the United States." It is hard to know on what grounds Holmes thought unconstitutional the practice of federal courts declining to be bound by the substantive common law rules of states in which they sat. His dissents left no clue: the first mention of a constitutional objection had come in the *Taxicab* case itself. Nor had his early correspondence on the issue with Pollock and Laski shed any light, since in that correspondence Holmes had confined his attack to the "fallacy" on which Story had based *Swift v. Tyson*. In his 1926 letter to Laski, for example, he had added to the portion of his argument previously quoted the observation that Louisiana's complete rejection of the common law proved that "[t]he common law in a State is the Common Law of that State."

A 1928 letter to Pollock, prompted by the *Taxicab* case, gave only a hint at the basis of Holmes' constitutional objections. In the course of repeating much of what he had said in earlier correspondence, and referring to his "brooding omnipresence" aphorism, Holmes said that the "time-honored practice for the U.S. judges . . . to, if so minded, decline to follow the Supreme Court of the State . . . is a pure usurpation." Later in the letter he referred to the "arrogant assumption" of "some ex-circuit judges" that they could disregard state law if they chose.[49] It is possible that by those remarks Holmes was advancing an objection based on Article III, or perhaps the Ninth or Tenth Amendments, to federal courts usurping the reserved rule-making powers of the state courts. In his *Taxicab* dissent he cited an article by Charles Warren suggesting that the phrase "laws of the several states" in Section 34 of the Judiciary Act of 1789, which referred to the "rules of decision" in the federal courts, included state common law decisions as well as state statutes, contrary to Story's interpretation in *Swift v. Tyson*.[50]

Holmes then went on, however, to say that "this question is deeper than that," going to "the authority by which certain particular acts . . . are governed," and concluding that "[i]n my opinion the only authority is the State."[51] This would seem to be an argument from theories of sovereignty rather than from the Constitution. Nonetheless, the constitutional objection Holmes hinted at in his dissent became a basis for the overruling of *Swift v. Tyson* in *Erie Railroad Co. v. Tompkins*,[52] decided in 1938. In that case Justice Brandeis, who had joined Holmes' dissent in the *Taxicab* case, gave among his reasons for discarding the *Swift v. Tyson* principle that it represented "an unconstitutional assumption of powers by the Courts of the United States."[53]

The *Britt-Goodman* sequence and the *Kuhn-Taxicab* sequence, taken together, illustrate the idiosyncratic, antidoctrinal orientation of Holmes' jurisprudence. The latter sequence illustrates that Holmes felt strongly, as a philosophical matter, that the concept of a "federal common law" was misconceived, one of those metaphysical "fallacies" that beclouded the essence of judging. Federal judges had no "independence" from state common law rules, when deciding nonconstitutional cases originating in a particular state, because no corpus of "law" existed on which they could ground their decisions and thus affirm their independence. The professed "federal common law" was illusory. Federal judges lacked justification for ignoring the states' sovereign dictates and inventing their own rules, just as state court judges had no justification for ignoring state legislative enactments. *Swift* and its progeny had replaced the imperatives of sovereignty and federalism with gossamer metaphysics.

And yet the *Swift* line meant that in hundreds of ordinary common law cases federal courts were free to create their own rules of law. Among those cases were simple negligence cases like *Britt* and *Goodman,* which had come to the federal courts on diversity grounds. Metaphysically, *Britt* and *Goodman* were unsound. The Kansas courts had fashioned a "child trespasser" rule; the Supreme Court should have deferred to it. State courts had tended to treat questions of negligence and contributory negligence in grade-crossing cases as questions for the jury; Holmes' own formulation of the sovereignty issues in "federal common law" cases meant that he had no business laying down a grade-crossing rule for all the federal courts in *Goodman* or disregarding Kansas law in *Britt.* Not only did Holmes avoid the jurisprudential implications of his *Kuhn-Taxicab* analysis, he did so with relish. He disliked having juries decide negligence cases and he disliked a permissive rule for child trespassers. The *Swift* line gave him the power to infuse those views into federal common law doctrine; he did so.

Although commentators criticized *Goodman* and some of Holmes' colleagues refused to endorse *Britt,*[54] none of Holmes' acolytes, who waxed enthusiastic about the *Jensen-Taxicab* sequence,[55] were inclined to comment on the discrepancy between Holmes' critique of the jurisprudential basis of federal judges declaring an "independent" body of law in *Jensen* and *Taxicab* and his unabashed deviations from state common law rules in *Britt* and *Goodman.* The silence of Holmes' acolytes on this point is particularly striking because of their familiarity with, and approval of, the limited view of judicial lawmaking power endorsed by Thayer in his 1893 essay and the critique of law as an independent body of rules made by Gray in *The Nature and Sources of Law.* Because in *Britt* and *Goodman* Holmes arguably usurped state juries and state legislation, he raised the spectre of unrestrained judicial lawmaking. Holmes would no doubt have been aroused had the criticism he expressed in *Jensen* and *Taxicab* (which he had defended with a reference to Gray's book) been turned against him in *Britt* and *Goodman,* but it was not. His "progressive" admirers were more interested in finding consistency than in finding paradox.

～

Cases such as *Britt, Goodman,* and the *Jensen-Taxicab* sequence indicated that Holmes was still able, in his late years, to find large issues embedded within the routine and the mundane. On the whole, however, his cases during the last half of his tenure were relatively large in scope and increasingly visible to public attention. The conflict between the Court's Due Process Clause jurisprudence and "progressive" social legislation increased in intensity after World War I, as the Court majority persisted in affirming the "liberty of contract" doctrine, sometimes in contexts that precipitated public outcry. "Progressive" intellectuals began to rally around the proposition that the Due Process Clause ought to be legislated out of existence.[56] Meanwhile other constitutional clauses and doctrines were summoned to support legislative regulation, and the Court regularly resisted those on behalf of property rights. Here were cases sufficient to propel Holmes' positions into the public eye, and he made the most of them.

The context in which Holmes decided cases testing the constitutionality of social and economic legislation had changed significantly since Thayer's essay in 1893. The emergence of Progressivism and the increased presence of the federal government necessitated by World War I had made redistributive and paternalistic legislation more of a fact of American life. Frankfurter's generation of "progressives" welcomed this trend. They were, on the whole, not adherents of socialism; their vision of an ideal society was to an important degree restorative of an idealized small-town, middle-class, pre-industrial America. But at the same time they believed that economic interdependence was a reality of twentieth-century life, and that consequently government owed a responsibility to improve the conditions of those disadvantaged by industrialization and urbanization. In sum, they identified an "underprivileged class" of American workers, they felt members of that class were disadvantaged in an unregulated economy, and they therefore encouraged government to recognize the welfare of the worker as linked to the welfare of all society.

By World War I Holmes' views on political economy were firmly in place. They had arguably been so since 1873, when he had written a comment on "[t]he famous strike of the [London] gas stokers" in the *American Law Review*:[57]

[I]n the last resort a man rightly prefers his own interest to that of his neighbors. And this is as true in legislation as in any other form of corporate action. All that can be expected from modern improvements is that legislation should easily and quickly, yet not too quickly, modify itself in accordance with the will of the de facto supreme power in the community. . . . [W]hatever body may possess the supreme power for the moment is certain to have interests inconsistent with others which have competed unsuccessfully. . . . The fact is that legislation . . . is necessarily made a means by which a body, having the power, puts burdens which are disagreeable to them on the shoulder of somebody else.[58]

The statement was consistent with Holmes' belief that majoritarian power and force were the principal determinants of social policy, that such power and force were only temporarily held, and therefore that the "progression" of various policies in the history of a nation was simply one majority temporarily shifting its burdens to its neighbors. Such views were hardly consistent with enthusiasm for legislative policies in themselves, or even with enthusiasm for legislative "solutions" to perceived social problems, except as contrasted with the outright killing of the enemies of the majority.

Holmes' position derived from a combination of his early exposure to Herbert Spencer, his (remarkably late) exposure to Thomas Robert Malthus,[59] and his general lack of confidence in the capacities of what he called "the crowd." Spencer contributed the idea that legislation merely transferred obligations from one class to another; Malthus the argument that the tendency of humans (particularly those in the lower classes) to propagate would inevitably result in a dwindling food supply and perhaps the ultimate extinction of the species. Holmes added to those views the beliefs that the great percentage of economic resources was consumed by the lower classes ("the crowd"), and that the rich were principally vehicles for distributing products to the poor.[60]

Given Holmes' views on political economy, it was inconceivable that he could have been concerned about the economic inequalities that "progressives" thought industrialization produced, or sympathetic to those at the lower ends of the social and economic scale, or sanguine about the efficacy of legislative solutions to the perceived problems. His permissiveness toward regulatory and redistributive legislation derived wholly from his belief that in testing the constitutionality of legislation the judiciary should be extremely deferential. His one enthusiasm for a legislative policy was that for family planning as conceived by the eugenics movement; eugenics made sense to him because it attacked the problem of overbreeding among the lower classes. It was, in Holmes' view, a corollary to Malthusian axioms. Holmes had some hopes that through eugenics a "master race" could be bred, one that could withstand Malthusian inevitabilities. Beyond eugenics, legislation was just redistributing the burdens among interest groups.

Analytically, Holmes' notable constitutional opinions in cases involving social and economic regulation fall into two classes, those testing the constitutionality of regulations imposed by the federal government and those raising similar objections to regulations imposed by the states. In such classes of cases the text of the Constitution imposed a variant doctrinal framework. In cases involving federal regulation Congress had available the commerce power as an additional rationale; the state analog, much less precise, was the doctrine of the "police power" and the associated catchphrase "affected with a public interest." Due process attacks were possible against both sets of regulatory schemes, given the language of the Fifth and Fourteenth Amendments, but the Equal Protection Clause was, on its face, confined to state regulations. Finally, the doctrine of "liberty of contract" was pertinent to both sets of challenges. That shibboleth had been expanded from its original application (wages, hours, and working conditions) to include such arguably noneconomic subjects as the "liberty" to teach subjects in a classroom or to resist compulsory sterilization procedures.

The multiplicity of analytical paths gave Holmes an opportunity to expound his views on a number of established doctrinal formulas. But the central issue, for commentators on the cases, was the same, regardless of doctrinal overlays: could government employ its powers to improve the conditions of modern life in America? In some of the cases "progressive" commentators did not agree with a legislature's definition of "improvement," finding it parochial or repressive. Nonetheless the issue was essentially similar, whether the context was minimum wage legislation or prohibiting the teaching of foreign languages. Nearly always Holmes weighed in on behalf of government.

Chronologically, the first of Holmes' notable opinions on issues affecting social and economic legislation during the second half of his tenure on the Supreme Court was *Hammer v. Dagenhart*,[61] which considered the constitutionality of a Congressional statute. The Keating-Owen Act of 1916 sought to regulate the practice of child labor across the nation by prohibiting the interstate transportation of goods made in factories that employed children under the age of fourteen, or children between the ages of fourteen and sixteen, for more than eight hours a day. North Carolina had a state statute forbidding the employment of children under the age of twelve. The father of two boys who worked in a textile mill, one between twelve and fourteen

and the other between fourteen and sixteen, challenged the Act on the ground that
it was an invasion of the police powers of the states.

The nub of the challenge in *Hammer* was that the Congressional statute did not
aim at the products of enterprises that employed child laborers, but at the practice
of child labor itself. The statute was thus arguably not a regulation of "commerce,"
but one of "pre-commerce conditions of labor,"[62] the very distinction Holmes was
to employ four years later in the (now notorious) baseball antitrust case,[63] in which
he found, for a unanimous court, that major league baseball was not "commerce,"
even though teams crossed state lines to play one another, because the enterprise
consisted of "games" played locally. The majority in *Hammer* accepted this argument, reviving a bright-line separation, dating back to the Court's decision in *United
States v. E. C. Knight*,[64] between "production" and "commerce." As Justice William Day put it for the majority:

> The thing intended to be accomplished by this statute is the denial of the
> facilities of interstate commerce to those manufacturers in the States who
> employ children within the prohibited ages. The act in its effect does not
> regulate transportation among the States, but aims to standardize the ages at
> which children may be employed in mining and manufacturing within the
> States. The goods shipped are themselves harmless. . . . When offered for
> shipment, and before transportation begins, the labor of their production is
> over. . . . The making of goods and the mining of coal are not commerce.[65]

Given the state of Commerce Clause doctrine at the time of the *Hammer* decision,
Day's position was not startling. The Keating-Owen Act had not directed itself specifically at the shipping of products or at the quality of goods in interstate commerce,
but at the conditions under which goods were produced. Since the Court had accepted
distinctions between "manufacture" and "commerce" in construing the Commerce
Clause, it was not unreasonable to argue that the Act was an effort to stretch that
clause to impermissible limits by seeking to regulate activities that were not "commercial" in nature. Holmes, however, had said in *Swift v. United States* that commerce was "not a technical legal conception but a practical one, drawn from the
course of business,"[66] and he believed that where manufacturers received an economic
advantage from the conditions under which their products were made that advantage
was a "commercial" one, reflected in the costs of their products to interstate buyers.
Moreover, he believed that the Court's own precedents permitted, as he put it, "the
exercise of [a] constitutional power by Congress" even though that exercise had
incidental effects on the power of the states to control the methods of industrial
production within their borders.[67]

The bulk of Holmes' dissent in *Hammer v. Dagenhart* was thus a citation of
instances where the Court had permitted Congressional regulation of products even
though the effect of Congress' presence was to curtail state power. Congress had
levied a prohibitively high tax on colored oleomargarine. Congress had imposed a
tax on state banks. In the Sherman Act Congress had attempted to break up combinations in restraint of trade, even though its efforts interfered with the states'
control over production. Congress had regulated "innocent" but fraudulently
ordered food and drugs, interstate traffic in liquor, and white slavery.[68] In short,

Holmes concluded, Congress "may carry out its views of public policy whatever indirect effect they may have upon the activities of the States."[69] If there were no Constitution, he noted, the power of the states to send their products across state lines "would depend upon their neighbors." The Constitution had concluded that "such commerce belongs not to the states but to Congress to regulate."[70]

Holmes' *Hammer* dissent was thus unusual in that its categorical formulations— Congressional power to regulate interstate commerce not only implies a power to prohibit interstate commerce altogether but can be exercised whatever the indirect effects on the regulatory powers of the states—were less emphasized than the more orthodox authority of the Court's own prior decisions. "I flatter myself," Holmes wrote to Pollock, "that I showed a lot of precedent" in his *Hammer* dissent. In the same letter he noted that "as the law unquestionably regulated interstate commerce it was within the power of Congress no matter what its indirect effect on matters within the regulation of the states."[71] On this proposition the Supreme Court eventually agreed with him, overruling *Hammer v. Dagenhart* and declaring constitutional the Fair Labor Standards Act of 1938, which allowed the federal government to prohibit the shipment in interstate commerce of goods produced by "oppressive" child labor, thus establishing the broad reach of the commerce power.[72]

One of the bases on which federal "social legislation" rested, as the *Hammer* case indicated, was the Commerce Clause; a much rarer rationale analogized to state police powers. The Commerce Clause rationale was more straightforward and applicable in most cases, since most Congressional statutes involved the regulation of activities that crossed state lines. Occasionally, however, the Commerce Clause rationale proved inapplicable, and a version of the "police power" had to be invoked. An example was Congress' supervisory relationship with the District of Columbia. In 1918 Congress passed the District of Columbia Minimum Wage Act, establishing a Minimum Wage Board for the District of Columbia to fix minimum wage standards for adult women employed in any occupation within the District. The Act, relying on the "police power," allowed the Board to make recommendations "as to standards of minimum wages for women workers . . . to maintain them in health and to protect their morals."

A District of Columbia hospital employed "a large number of women in various capacities," some of whose wages "were less than the minimum wage fixed by an order of the board made in pursuance of the act."[73] It challenged the Act's minimum wage provisions on the basis of the Fifth Amendment's Due Process Clause. The Supreme Court, despite *Lochner*, had sustained two state efforts to regulate the hours of labor[74] and, in 1917 had (by a 4–4 decision) let stand an Oregon statute establishing a minimum wage for state workers.[75] The different results in successive cases suggested that wages and hours legislation was still regarded as pitting the "liberty" to bargain and sell one's services against the state's power to protect the health, safety, and morals of the public, and that the constitutionality of a given statute could not be taken for granted.

In the District of Columbia minimum wage case, *Adkins v. Children's Hospital*,[76] a majority of the Court found that the legislation violated the Fifth Amendment's Due Process Clause. The majority opinion, written by Justice George Sutherland, chose to elevate "liberty of contract" to a constitutional principle. "That the right to contract about one's affairs,'' he stated, ''is a part of the liberty protected by [the Due Process Clause] is settled by the decisions of this Court and is no longer open to question.'' Sutherland went on to say that ''[t]here is no such thing as absolute freedom of contract,'' but that ''freedom of contract is, nevertheless, the general rule and restraint the exception; and the exercise of legislative authority to abridge it can be justified only by the existence of exceptional circumstances.'' He cited no authority for those propositions, but nonetheless made them the basis of a general review of the Court's cases where statutes had been sustained against a ''liberty of contract'' challenge.

Not surprisingly, Sutherland found all of those cases distinguishable. In particular, he stressed that in no case had a statute limiting hours or wages been applied to all occupations within its coverage; that some cases had involved occupations ''affected with a public interest'' or had been temporary measures; that some had been ''for the protection of persons under legal disability or for the prevention of fraud''[77]; and that those ''especially relating to hours of labor for women'' had been predicated on a theory of gender relations that in Sutherland's view had been significantly modified since they had been handed down. He particularized:

> The decision[s] proceeded upon the theory that the difference between the sexes may justify a different rule respecting hours of labor in the case of women than in the case of men. It is pointed out that these consist in differences of physical structure, especially in respect of the maternal functions, and also in the fact that historically woman has always been dependent upon man, who has established his control by superior physical strength. . . . But the ancient inequality of the sexes, other than physical, . . . has continued with ''diminishing intensity.'' In view of the great—not to say revolutionary—changes which have taken place . . . in the contractual, political and civil status of women, culminating in the Nineteenth Amendment, it is not unreasonable to say that these differences have now come almost, if not quite, to the vanishing point. In this aspect of the matter . . . we cannot accept the doctrine that women of mature age . . . require or may be subjected to restrictions upon their liberty of contract which could not lawfully be imposed in the case of men under similar circumstances. To do so would be to ignore all the implications to be drawn from the present day trend of legislation, as well as that of common thought and usage, by which woman is accorded emancipation from the old doctrine that she must be given special protection or be subjected to special restraint in her contractual and civil relationships.[78]

In sum, Sutherland found that the statute singled out women for contractual protection without any showing that they needed it or that every business in the District of Columbia that hired women needed to give them special consideration. The statute, in Sutherland's view, bore no relationship to the value of the services rendered or to the extent of the benefits obtained from those services in the various occupations it governed. ''[A] statute which prescribes payment without regard to any of these things and solely with relation to circumstances apart from the contract of employment, the business affected by it and the work done under it,'' he concluded, "is so clearly the product of a naked, arbitrary exercise of power that it cannot be allowed to stand under the Constitution of the United States."[79]

Sutherland's opinion in *Adkins* elevated the stakes in the areas of substantive due process. After the majority's fulminations in *Lochner,* the Court had shown evidence of backing away from a categorical treatment of due process cases and of being tolerant of some "social legislation." No clear trend was evident, but the cases seemed to have reduced themselves to exercises in balancing, with the context of the legislation being decisive. Sutherland's opinion suggested that liberty of contract was "the rule" in due process cases; that any statutes governing a whole range of occupations were constitutionally suspect; that paternalistic rationales, at least as applied to women, were not to be given weight in the face of an adult individual's right to contract; and that legislation affecting wages was distinguishable from legislation affecting hours of work or the methods of wage payments or disabilities or fraud. His opinion meant that Frankfurter had been premature in identifying Holmes' dissent in *Lochner* as a "turning point" in the history of the Court's interpretation of the Due Process Clauses.

The breadth and scope of Sutherland's opinion may have provoked Holmes to respond in kind; at any rate he took the opportunity to summarize the attack on "liberty of contract" and other ideological glosses on constitutional language he had introduced with *Lochner*. He began by noting that "to remove conditions leading to ill health, immorality and the deterioration of the race" was an end that "no one would deny to be within the scope of constitutional legislation," and the means employed by the statute, the regulation of wages, had been thought "effective and worth the price" by "reasonable men." The only question therefore remaining, he concluded, was whether the statute in *Adkins* "might be invalidated by specific provisions of the Constitution." And the only "objection that can be urged" to the statute was "found within the vague contours of the Fifth Amendment, prohibiting the depriving of any person of liberty or property without due process of law."[80]

Holmes thus turned to the analysis of the Due Process Clauses. "The earlier decisions upon the same words in the Fourteenth Amendment," he argued, "went no farther than an unpretentious assertion of the liberty to follow the ordinary callings." But "[l]ater that innocuous generality" was "expanded into the dogma, Liberty of Contract." He then revived a familiar attack on that doctrine:

> Contract is not specially mentioned in the text that we have to construe. It is merely an example of doing what you want to do, embodied in the word liberty. But pretty much all law consists in forbidding men to do some things that they want to do, and contract is no more exempt from law than other acts.[81]

He then listed a series of laws "that seem to me to have interfered with liberty of contract quite as seriously and directly as the one before us."[82] These included a familiar group from his *Lochner* dissent and some others: usury laws, statutes of frauds, Sunday laws, statutes regulating insurance contracts, the methods for paying store employers or seamen, the size of loaves of bread, and women's hours of labor. He concluded that he would be hard pressed to say that women's wages were any different.

Turning to Sutherland's distinction between the power to fix maximum hours of work for women employees and the power to fix minimum wages for the same employees, "I fully assent," he said, "to the proposition that here as elsewhere the distinctions of the law are distinctions of degree, but I percieve no difference in the kind or degree of interference with liberty, the only matter with which we have any concern, between the one case and the other." Not only was there no difference between the kind or degree of infringement on "liberty" when wages and when hours were regulated, Sutherland's argument that a "revolution" had taken place in the status of women was specious. "It will need more than the Nineteenth Amendment," Holmes said, "to convince me that there are no differences between men and women."[83]

But the fundamental difficulty with the majority's position in *Adkins,* for Holmes, was that the statute did not "compel anybody to pay anything." It simply forbade employers in the District of Columbia to hire women "at rates below those fixed as the minimum requirement of health and right living." It was no different than the "hundreds of so-called police laws that have been upheld." The question was not whether "we believe the law to be for the public good." A number of reasonable people believed so, Holmes noted; he had his "doubts . . . whether the bill that has to be paid for every gain . . . was not greater than the gain was worth." But that was not a "matter . . . for me to decide."[84] The *Adkins* dissent, in sum, was a reprise of *Lochner,* strengthened and deepened by the proliferation of early twentieth-century "social" legislation and by Holmes' exposure of the dogmatic nature of the liberty of contract doctrine.

Adkins precipitated an outcry from legal and lay commentators,[85] incensed by the sweeping character of Sutherland's opinion, its dogmatic tone, and the uncertain prospect it created for minimum wage programs, which had been enacted in several states.[86] Frankfurter, who had argued the case for the losing side, and Laski made predictable comments about the unfortunate composition of the Court and its indifference to enlightened social experiments, and Frankfurter took to the pages of *The New Republic* to argue that after "fifty years of experiment with the Fourteenth Amendment" the Supreme Court could not "discharge with safety" its "centralizing authority over the domestic affairs of forty-eight widely different States."[87] Earlier, after *Adkins* came down, he had written Learned Hand that "[t]he whole thing we thought we had gained . . . is now thrown overboard and we are just where we were." In despair, he concluded that "the place to hit is the Amendments themselves."[88] Laski greeted the news of the *Adkins* decision by telling Holmes, "What an intolerable court you have just now."[89]

The *Adkins* decision was to remain intact until 1937, forestalling efforts to enact comprehensive minimum-wage legislation.[90] But in the meantime "social legislation" continued at the state level, and Holmes, for the most part, continued his posture of tolerance. There were, however, some exceptions to that posture, and some interesting ramifications, especially in terms of Holmes' reputation among "progressive" commentators.

In *Truax v. Corrigan*[91] the Court considered the constitutionality of an Arizona statute that, as interpreted by the Supreme Court of Arizona, provided that no injunctions could be issued by courts against peaceful picketing in labor disputes. Employees in a restaurant in Bisbee, Arizona, went out on strike and picketed the restaurant, and the owner sought an injunction against the picketers, claiming that the picketing had deprived him of business. The employees set up the statute as a defense, and the owner attacked it on two constitutional grounds, that it permitted injunctions in other disputes but not in labor disputes, thereby depriving other classes of persons of the equal protection of the laws, and that by preventing picketing from being enjoined it allowed striking employees to interfere with his business and thus deprived him of property without due process of law.

Chief Justice Taft, for the majority in *Truax,* held the statute unconstitutional. He argued that the picketing, whether "peaceful" or not, was an intentional interference with the contractual relations between the restaurant owner and customers, and was thus illegal. By prohibiting the enjoining of picketing in labor disputes, the statute legalized that activity, which Taft argued denied the restaurant owner due process of law. Finally, he concluded that since competitors of the restaurant could be enjoined from intentionally seeking to deprive the restaurant of business, the legislature's exemption for labor unions who sought to do the same thing violated the Equal Protection Clause. Holmes wrote Laski that he found Taft's opinion "rather spongy—copious citation of generalities become platitudes that don't bring you any nearer to the concrete case."[92]

Holmes' dissent was rather an offhand performance, although Laski called it "quite one of the most perfect little gems you have fired off in months," which "will have its place in the classic literature of the law."[93] His first paragraph attacked Taft's description of the goodwill in a business as "property" within the meaning of the Fourteenth Amendment, warning of "[t]he dangers of a delusive exactness in the application of the Fourteenth Amendment," and noting that "[a]n established business . . . is a course of conduct and like other conduct is subject to substantial modification according to time and circumstances." He then noted that some courts had authorized boycotts "in the aid of the employees' or the employer's interest," and saw no reason why the same could not be done by statute.[94] These comments seemed to be directed at Taft's due process argument, but Holmes did not elaborate.

He then turned to the equal protection argument, saying that "the selection of the class of employers and employees for special treatment . . . is beyond criticism on principles often asserted by this Court." He did not cite any authorities, but then noted that "the extraordinary relief by injunction may be denied to the class . . . without legalizing the conduct complained of." His point was that "many intelligent people believe" that there was more danger that injunctions would be abused in labor disputes, and the legislature could therefore prohibit their use in that context. He cited two Supreme Court cases upholding the prohibition of injunctions in support of that proposition.[95] This argument, like his comments on due process, appeared to be question-begging. Legislatures might believe that picketing in labor disputes was not the equivalent of intentional interference with contractual relations, or that courts were especially likely to grant injunctions in labor cases, but the question remained whether they could create exceptions for labor disputes in the face of the Due Process and Equal Protection Clauses.

Holmes' next argument, premised on federalism and sovereignty grounds, was that there was a "difficulty" in "requiring a State Court to issue an injunction that it never has been empowered to issue by the quasi-sovereign that created the

Court.''⁹⁶ This was likewise oddly cryptic. State courts had been ''empowered'' to issue injunctions, as an equitable remedy, in Arizona and all states that adopted the English common law system. The Arizona statute had taken away the power to grant injunctive relief in a designated set of cases. If its effort was unconstitutional, the statute was invalid, and the state courts' power to issue injunctions in all appropriate cases was revived.

In his last paragraph Holmes added a ''general consideration'' that was probably the basis for Laski's enthusiastic response to the *Truax* dissent. ''There is nothing that I more deprecate,'' Holmes said,

> than the use of the Fourteenth Amendment beyond the absolute compulsion of its words to prevent the making of social experiments that an important part of the community desires, in the insulated chambers afforded by the several States, even though the experiments may seem futile or even noxious to me and to those whose judgment I most respect.⁹⁷

This was language, with its emphasis on ''social experiments . . . in the insulated chambers afforded by the several States,'' right out of the Progressives' handbook for an enlightened polity. It suggests that Holmes, who had no particular enthusiasm for ''social experiments,'' may by 1921 have been exposed to the arguments of Brandeis, who believed deeply in social and economic reform at the local level, and may have adopted, consciously or unconsciously, some of Brandeis' vocabulary, which included the characterization of the states as ''laboratories'' for reform programs. Holmes added to this language his familiar caveat that the level of his enthusiasm for a given ''experiment'' should have nothing to do with its constitutionality. In *Truax* he was assuming the role of the ''wise'' judge who limits his own interpretive powers so that the states may experiment with social reform. Frankfurter, commenting on the case in an editorial in *The New Republic,* called the majority opinion ''fraught with more evil than any which [the Supreme Court] has rendered in a generation,'' and applauded Holmes' posture.⁹⁸

The pattern of Holmes' dissenting when the majority used the Fourteenth Amendment to invalidate state regulatory legislation continued in *Tyson & Brother v. Banton.*⁹⁹ A ticket broker challenged the constitutionality of a New York statute prohibiting the resale of theatre tickets at a price in excess of 50 cents more than the price printed on the face of the ticket. The statute declared that the price of admission to theatres and other places of public entertainment was a matter ''affected with a public interest,'' and thus within the state's police power. Sutherland, for a 5–4 majority, held the statute unconstitutional as a violation of the Due Process Clause, treating ''the right . . . to fix a price at which . . . property shall be sold'' as ''an inherent attribute of the property itself . . . and as such within the protection of the due process of law clauses.''¹⁰⁰

Having defined the right to set prices as an aspect of ''property,'' Sutherland proceeded to determine whether the business of selling tickets for theatres was one ''affected with the public interest'' such as to permit its regulation even though property rights were curtailed. After an elaborate discussion, he reached this conclusion:

A theatre is a private enterprise, which, in its relation to the public, differs obviously and widely, both in character and degree, from a grain elevator . . . or stock yards . . . or an insurance company. . . . Sales of theatre tickets bear no relation to the commerce of the country; and they are not interdependent transactions, but stand, both in form and effect, separate and apart from each other. . . . And, certainly, a place of entertainment is in no legal sense a public utility. . . . The interest of the public in theatres and other places of entertainment may be more nearly, and with better reason, assimilated to the like interest in provision stores and markets and in the rental of houses and apartments for residence purposes.[101]

Perhaps piqued by the categorical quality of Sutherland's argument, Holmes attacked the concept of "affected with a public interest" head on. In *Adkins* he had intimated that he thought the concept a fiction.[102] Now in *Tyson* he stated his view more starkly:

[P]olice power often is used in a wide sense to cover and . . . to apologize for the general power of the legislature to make a part of the community uncomfortable by change.

I do not believe in such apologies. I think the proper course is to recognize that a state legislature can do whatever it sees fit to do unless it is restrained by some express prohibition in the Constitution of the United States or of the State, and that Courts should be careful not to extend such prohibitions beyond their obvious meaning by reading into them conceptions of public policy that the particular Court may happen to entertain. Coming down to the case before us, I think, as I intimated in *[Adkins]*, that the notion that a business is clothed with a public interest and has been devoted to the public use is little more than a fiction intended to beautify what is disagreeable to the sufferers. The truth seems to me to be that, subject to compensation when compensation is due, the legislature may forbid or restrict any business when it has a sufficient force of public opinion behind it.[103]

Holmes then went through his familiar examples of restrictions, including on this occasion lotteries and "wine," whose consumption and distribution had been prohibited by the Eighteenth Amendment. "[W]hen public opinion chan ged [with respect to the value of wine], he noted, "it did not need the Eighteenth Amendment, notwithstanding the Fourteenth, to enable a state to say that the [liquor] business should end." He suggested that "[w]hat happened to lotteries and wine might happen to theatres in some moral storm of the future, not because theatres were devoted to a public use, but because people had come to think that way."

That argument settled the case for Holmes: constitutional adjudication was ultimately a matter of public opinion. On reading Holmes' dissent in *Tyson*, Frankfurter wrote him a congratulatory letter. "I am moved to rejoice over your new declaration of independence of all those sterile 'apologies' which 'police power' & 'affected with public interest' cover," he said. "You have never written a more illuminating opinion on Due Process—and I throw my hat into the air for it."[104]

The *Tyson* opinion was in fact one of Holmes' most illuminating, but not precisely in the way Frankfurter suggested. Holmes maintained in *Tyson* that there was nothing about economic activity that made it inherently immune from legislative regulation: whether or not it would be regulated was ultimately a question of the "force of public opinion." This assertion revealed, more clearly in *Tyson* than in many other instances in which Holmes expressed the same view, that Holmes was essentially fatalistic about the inviolability of legal "rights" against the state, and regarded the whole question of whether such "rights" could be restricted as one settled in the short run by contemporary political attitudes and determined in the long run by historical change. *Tyson* thus simultaneously demonstrates the strength of Holmes' positivism and his belief in historical determinism. In this context, Holmes' "tolerance" of legislative regulation was certainly not a result of his support for that legislation, nor even a result of his indifference to its consequences. It was more properly described as the product of a conviction that in the long run neither he nor any single individual could resist the force of public opinion.

Holmes' fatalism suggests that he would be as "tolerant" of benighted or repressive legislative activity as he was of the enlightened or "progressive" sort, and two cases will subsequently illustrate that observation. It also might suggest, however, that at bottom Holmes saw no limits on the power of legislatures to act, even in the face of constitutional provisions. That was not the case: occasionally he reached a limit, as in *Pennsylvania Coal Co. v. Mahon.*[105]

In the *Mahon* case a 1921 Pennsylvania statute sought to regulate the mining of anthracite coal by making unlawful the mining of coal under public buildings, thoroughfares, or private houses. It also authorized injunctions against violations. A homeowner sought an injunction against the Pennsylvania Coal Company from mining under its land in such a way as to "remove supports and cause a subsidence of the surface and of their house."[106] Title to the land had been conveyed by the Company in 1878, but the Company had retained subsurface rights, including the right to remove coal. Nonetheless, the homeowner argued that the 1921 statute abolished all preexisting subsurface rights in anthracite coal. The Company challenged the statute as unconstitutionally impairing contractual rights and taking property without compensation. The Supreme Court of Pennsylvania held that the Company did have preexisting contract and property rights, but that the statute had overridden those rights in a legitimate exercise of the police power.

Holmes, on appeal from that decision, held for a majority that the statute did violate the Contracts and Due Process Clauses. In this instance, he said, the diminution of property rights had been considerable, and there had been no compensation. He conceded that the question in such cases "depends on the particular facts," and that "[t]he greatest weight is given to the judgment of the legislature," but maintained that "the implied limitation" of the police power "must have its limits, or the contract and due process clauses are gone."[107] The destruction of property and contract rights had been extensive, Holmes claimed, because for practical purposes the right to own coal consisted of the right to mine it for profit. By forbidding the Company to mine, the statute was significantly reducing the value of its subsurface rights to the land.

"The general rule," Holmes said in summary, "is that while property may be regulated to a certain extent, if regulation goes too far it will be recognized as a taking." In the *Mahon* case, if the public had "been so short sighted to acquire only surface rights without the right of support" to the Company's land, "we see no more authority for supplying the latter without compensation than there was for taking the right away in the first place and refusing to pay for it because the public wanted it very much."[108] He then outlined the method of constitutional analysis that should prevail in such cases:

> The protection of private property in the Fifth Amendment presupposes that it is wanted for public use, but provides that it shall not be taken for such use without compensation. A similar assumption is made in the decisions upon the Fourteenth Amendment. . . . When this seemingly absolute protection is found to be qualified by the police power, the natural tendency of human nature is to extend the qualification more and more until at last private property disappears. But that cannot be accomplished in this way under the Constitution of the United States.[109]

The odd feature of this argument is that the methodology outlined above is almost exactly the reverse of that employed by Holmes in his due process dissents. Nowhere in those cases did he regard legislative regulations infringing on property rights, or "liberty of contract," as constitutionally impermissible. While in the excerpt quoted above he had stated that restrictions on private property could not be "accomplished in this way" even under the police power, in his due process dissents he had repeatedly said that the police power trumped private rights. At the close of the *Mahon* opinion he said that "[w]e are in danger of forgetting that a strong public desire to improve the public condition is not enough to warrant achieving the desire by a shorter cut than the constitutional way of paying for the change." But in *Tyson* he was to say that public opinion was the ultimate determination of constitutionality.

There is a way in which Holmes' opinion in *Mahon* can be reconciled with his due process dissents. He referred to it as a case involving the "Contracts" and "Due Process" clauses, which technically it was, because at the time *Mahon* was decided the Fifth Amendment's takings clause, requiring that property owners receive "just compensation" if their property was taken by the state under its eminent domain powers, was not regarded as applying against the states.[110] The Pennsylvania statute that invalidated the company's pre-existing subsurface rights was thus technically a deprivation of property without due process of law under the Fourteenth Amendment or an impairment of the obligation of contracts under Article I, section 10. But Holmes may well have regarded the statute as essentially a "taking": a use of the state's eminent domain power to appropriate the land of mining companies for uses more beneficial to the state. He spoke in his *Mahon* opinion of a legislative regulation amounting to "a taking," and cited "[t]he protection of private property in the Fifth Amendment."

Holmes thus may have regarded himself, despite technical problems, as essentially parsing the takings clause when he reviewed the legislative action in *Mahon*. If the case were a "takings clause" case rather than a conventional due process case, it was easier to see that the infringement on property rights was substantial and that the rights asserted were tangible, rather than being chimerical in the fashion of "liberties" of contract. A mining company did not want land for other than mining purposes. When it sold off its surface rights to land and retained its subsurface rights, it was retaining, from its perspective, the principal value of its land. When a legislature abolished those subsurface rights, which the company had contracted to retain, it was clearly infringing on substantial property rights, as well as arguably impairing the obligation of contracts. It was, in short, "taking" the company's property. Under takings clause analysis the company would be entitled to compensation. Since Pennsylvania had not compensated the company, its effort to "take" the company's subsurface rights was invalid.

Holmes' opinion in *Mahon,* which produced a dissent from Brandeis, was not popular with Holmes' constituency of "progressives." He sent it to Laski, who declined to comment on it, a noteworthy gesture in light of his almost constant praise of Holmes' opinions. Holmes noted to Laski that Frankfurter had also been silent: "[he] generally writes to me about any important opinions of mine and he has been silent as to the one I sent you in which Brandeis dissented; probably feeling an unnecessary delicacy about saying that he disagrees."[111] *The New Republic* issued an editorial comment, written by Brandeis' former clerk Dean Acheson, saying that "Justice Brandeis's view seems the superior statesmanship."[112] Holmes told Laski that he was "not going to reargue the matter now," but that he was "not greatly impressed" by Acheson's editorial, and that "statesmanlike" was "an effective word but needs caution in using it."[113]

To Pollock, who supported his position in the case,[114] Holmes was less defensive. While in the process of writing the *Mahon* opinion Holmes noted that "everybody seems to have misgivings about [his draft], which I believe to be a compact statement of the real facts of the law and as such sure to rouse opposition for want of the customary soft phrases." When he finished he sent it to Pollock, saying that "[m]y ground is that the public only got on to this land by paying for it and that if they saw fit to pay only for a surface right they can't enlarge it because they need it now any more than they could have taken the right of being there in the first place."[115]

Mahon was one of a series of opinions that Holmes' champions did not emphasize when offering evidence of his reputation as a "great judge." Not only did it reach the "wrong" result (Brandeis' dissent, which emphasized that property rights should yield to public safety, and which argued that the Court should defer to Pennsylvania's knowledge of its local conditions, was more "statesmanlike"), it adopted the "wrong" theory of judicial interpretation of constitutional restraints on legislative activity by indicating the existence of some restraints after all. Opposition to *Mahon* was thus not troublesome for Holmes' "progressive" supporters: they wrote it off as an aberration.

Holmes' position in two other due process cases decided during the second half of his tenure, however, created more of a dilemma for those who saw him as the archetype of a "progressive"judge. There he continued his familiar, and to his supporters honorable, pattern of deferring to the reasonable judgments of legislatures when a legislature had allegedly restricted due process rights. But neither case involved "rights" being asserted by the typical challengers to "social legislation" in the early twentieth century, corporations and other property holders. Instead the challengers in the cases were members of groups—school children, teachers, persons with disabilities—whose interests the ideological descendents of progressives would come to champion. In both cases Holmes was on the side of legislatures who sought to ignore the rights of those groups.

The first case, strictly speaking a pair of cases, considered the constitutionality of state statutes forbidding the teaching of modern foreign languages before the eighth grade.[116] One also considered the constitutionality of statutes in Iowa and Ohio flatly prohibiting teaching any languages except English before the eighth grade and German below the eighth grade.[117] In the foreign language cases a majority of the Court, in an opinion by Justice James McReynolds, conceptualized the cases as raising "liberty" issues under the Fourteenth Amendment's Due Process Clause. Because the "liberty" asserted to have been violated in the cases included what Holmes called the "liberty of teacher or scholar" to receive information, the cases can fairly be seen as embryonic First Amendment cases, although none of the justices who decided them treated them as such. They fit into the analysis of Holmes' evolving views on freedom of speech in the latter years of his career, and thus I will defer further discussion of them until Chapter Twelve.

In the foreign language cases, Holmes' deference to the legislature's decision to restrict access to foreign languages in public schools suggests that his celebrated respect for the "reasonableness" of state legislatures could cut both ways, in terms of early twentieth-century political ideology, and could sometimes produce a reflexive posture in him that was not consistent with his jurisprudential efforts in other areas. Modern commentators, wrestling with Holmes' reputation as a civil libertarian, have noted the foreign language cases as not conforming to that image.

The case that has most consistently troubled those who would describe Holmes as a champion of civil liberties, however, has been *Buck v. Bell*,[118] described by a recent biographer as "Holmes' most notorious opinion."[119] Virginia had sought to sterilize Carrie Buck, who had been committed to the State Colony for Epileptics and Feeble Minded, under a 1924 statute that provided for the sterilization of "mental defectives" who were confined to state institutions when, in the judgment of the superintendents of those institutions, "the best interests of the patients and of society" would be served by their being rendered incapable of producing offspring.[120] Counsel for Carrie Buck, in attacking a decision by the Virginia Supreme Court of Appeals ordering her sterilization, raised two constitutional objections to the statute: that it violated Buck's "constitutional right of bodily integrity"; and that in confining sterilization to "inmates of the state colony for epileptics and feeble minded" it denied her the equal protection of the laws, since other "defective" but unconfined persons were not singled out to be sterilized.[121]

In the United States Supreme Court a majority of the justices were inclined to sustain the statute, although some doubts existed. On April 23, 1927, Chief Justice Taft wrote Holmes a note indicating that he had assigned him the *Buck* case. "Some of the brethren," Taft noted, "are troubled about the case, especially Butler."

> May I suggest that you make a little full the care Virginia has taken in guarding against undue or hasty action, the proven absence of danger to the patient, and other circumstances tending to lessen the shock that many feel over such a remedy? The strength of the facts in three generations of course is

the strongest argument for the necessity for such state action and its reasonableness.[122]

Holmes followed Taft's suggestions. The first part of his opinion detailed the procedural safeguards afforded inmates who were candidates for sterilization. The superintendent of the facility in which the inmate was housed petitioned for steril-ization to the board of directors of his institution, with notice going to the inmate and his or her guardian, who was appointed by the local circuit court if none existed. In the case of minors notice was also given to the inmate's parents. The inmate was then accorded a hearing before the board, and invited to attend it if he or she desired. The findings at the hearing were reduced to writing, and the superintendent, the inmate, or the guardian could appeal them to the local circuit court. That court was permitted to consider, in addition to the evidence from the hearing, "such other admissible evidence as may be offered," and could affirm, reverse, or revise the board's order. Appeal could be taken from that decision to the Virginia Supreme Court of Appeals. "There can be no doubt," Holmes concluded, "that so far as procedure is concerned the rights of the patient are most carefully considered." He concluded that in the *Buck* case there was "no doubt that in this respect the [inmate] ... had due process of law."[123]

But counsel for Carrie Buck, Holmes noted, had contended "that in no circum-stances could such an order be justified." This brought him squarely to the question whether compulsory sterilization, based on a state interest in keeping "defective" persons from propagating themselves, was justified in light of a constitutional "lib-erty" to procreate. Holmes noted that the order in the *Buck* case had found that Carrie Buck "is the probable potential parent of socially inadequate offspring, like-wise afflicted, that she may be sexually sterilized without detriment to her general health and that her welfare and that of society will be promoted by her sterilization." In view of those findings, he concluded, "obviously we cannot say as a matter of law that the grounds [for sterilization] do not exist." He then set forth the rationale for compulsory sterilization of the mentally "defective":

> We have seen more than once that the public welfare may call upon the best citizens for their lives. It would be strange if it could not call upon those who already sap the strength of the State for these lesser sacrifices, often not felt to be such by those concerned, in order to prevent our being swamped with incompetence. It is better for all the world, if instead of waiting to execute degenerate offspring for crime, or to let them starve for their imbecility, society can prevent those who are manifestly unfit from continuing their kind. The principle that sustains compulsory vaccination is broad enough to cover cutting the Fallopian tubes .... Three generations of imbeciles are enough.[124]

This paragraph is a singular combination of familiar Holmesian arguments and non sequiturs. Holmes began with his common "the greater includes the lesser" argument, maintaining that if the state could send "the best citizens" to war, it could sterilize "those who already sap the strength of the State." Compulsory military service, of course, was not the equivalent of "call[ing] on the best citizens for their lives." Not all the "best citizens" were eligible for military service, and not all compelled to serve would lose their lives. Moreover, Holmes assumed that mentally disabled persons were clearly not among the "best citizens": indeed they sapped the strength of the state, apparently by being public charges. He also assumed that procreation by mentally disabled persons would necessarily result in "incompetent" offspring being produced, and that procreation by such persons would be at a high rate, so that sterilization was not only necessary to prevent the perpetuation of mental defectiveness but to keep the population from being "swamped" by defectives.

Holmes' next sentence assumed that the "degenerate offspring" of persons such as Carrie Buck would inevitably commit crimes, and crimes of sufficient seriousness that their execution would follow. He also assumed that in the alternative the "imbeciles" fostered by persons such as Buck would "starve for their imbecility," although the very system in which Carrie Buck was incarcerated would seem to suggest otherwise. He then laid down as a general proposition that "[i]t is better for all the world [that] . . . society can prevent those who are manifestly unfit from continuing their kind." This would suggest that compulsory sterilization for all "manifestly unfit" persons would not only be "better" for the rest of society, but better for them.

Finally, Holmes claimed that the same principle that sustained compulsory vaccinations was "broad enough" to sustain compulsory sterilization. It is hard to know how the "same principle" applied to the two situations. Compulsory vaccination had two purposes: to prevent disease in the individual and to prevent the spread of disease within the population. It had no substantial adverse effects on the person vaccinated save those instances in which vaccination offended that person's religious convictions. In such cases the strength of the social interest in preventing disease overrode the relative eccentricity of the conviction. Compulsory sterilization deprived a person of the opportunity to procreate. It had no beneficial effects on the person sterilized; its only purpose was to prevent that person from reproducing. The genetic unpredictability of mental disability and the difficulty in diagnosing mental illness—witnessed by Virginia's lumping together of the "feeble minded" and epileptics in the same state facilities—made it much less likely that sterilization of inmates would result in fewer criminals or "starving imbeciles" than vaccination would result in fewer cases of smallpox. In short, the "principle" of the vaccination cases seemed distorted when applied as a rationale to justify compulsory sterilization.

Holmes had one more argument to dispose of in *Buck v. Bell:* equal protection. The sterilization procedure was only applied to a narrow class of persons who happened to be wards of the state's "colonies" for the mentally disabled and epileptic. Numerous other "candidates" for sterilization were housed by the state, such as prisoners, and numerous other "feeble-minded" persons were not wards of the state. Holmes responded by assuming his most categorical posture. He said of the equal protection argument that "[i]t is the usual last resort of constitutional arguments." He then asserted that "the law does all that is needed when it does all that it can," as if that statement did not beg questions, such as what he meant by "can." What he meant, apparently, was that when the law "indicates a policy, applies it to all within the lines, and seeks to bring within the lines all similarly situated so far and so fast as its means allow," that was sufficient.

There was no indication, however, that Virginia was combing the environment for "feeble-minded" persons and seeking to incarcerate them as fast as it could. Incarceration in a facility such as that in which Carrie Buck was confined was not even instituted by the state, but by private persons, typically relatives, who felt they could not bear the burdens of caring for the "feeble-minded."

Holmes added that "so far as the [sterilization] operations enable those who otherwise must be kept confined to be returned to the world, and thus open the asylum to others, the equality aimed at will be more nearly reached." This was an odd argument to make in Carrie Buck's case, since one of the bases of Holmes' characterization of the case as involving "three generations of imbeciles" was that Carrie was "the daughter of a feeble minded mother in the same institution, and the mother of an illegitimate feeble minded child." It does not appear that her confinement had prevented her from reproducing her "defective" qualities, so it was not clear why she "must be kept confined" until she had been sterilized. In addition, the comment assumed that there were a limited number of spaces for the "feeble-minded" in asylums, and numerous "feeble-minded" persons outside the gates clamoring to enter and to be sterilized, so that "the equality" between the two groups would at some point "be more nearly reached." This did not seem to be a realistic prediction.[125] Indeed it suggested that Holmes thought the equal protection argument not serious enough to merit an intellectually coherent response.

Over the years the notoriety of *Buck v. Bell* has increased, as the Supreme Court has distinguished the case out of existence[126] and evidence has surfaced indicating that Carrie Buck was very probably not disabled, and that the Virginia sterilization procedures validated in the case were extraordinarily summary in their application.[127] Two features of the case appear to have been underemphasized in this development. One is that every member of the Taft Court, including Brandeis and Justice Harlan Fiske Stone, joined Holmes' opinion, with the exception of Butler, who did not offer any reasons for his dissent.[128] The idea of eugenic reform, to be effectuated through birth control, family planning, and voluntary or compulsory sterilization, was not thought to be a repressive one in the early twentieth century. On the contrary, it was associated with a paternalistic attitude toward the "lower classes," who were assumed to be ignorant of birth control methods and profligate in their relationships, thus producing children for whom they could not afford to care and perpetuating an underclass. The eradication of "feeble-minded" persons from the population, through sterilization procedures that were considered humane, was regarded as an enlightened effort to produce a better society.[129]

The second feature of *Buck v. Bell* is that it concerned a legislative "reform" about which Holmes did not have his customary skepticism. On the contrary, he was an enthusiast for population control devices, particularly those that promised to reduce "incompetence" in the population. He had no reason to doubt many of the assumptions of the eugenic reformers: that mental disabilities were inherited; that mental disability was linked to crime; that the very persons who were candidates for sterilization were the least likely to control their sexual impulses. He had written Pollock in 1920 that "I should be glad . . . if it could be arranged that death should precede life by provisions for a selected race," because "every society rests on the death of men,"[130] and that "[y]our remark that the men fit for military service on the whole are the better type . . . is precisely the reflection that makes me believe that it would be possible to breed a race."[131] He had written Laski in 1923 that "I do not regard the great multiplication of the species as a benefit."[132] and in 1925 that "I don't believe in millennia and still less in the possibility of attaining one ... while propagation is free and we do all we can to keep the products, however bad, alive."[133] He wrote Lewis Einstein in 1927, after the *Buck* decision, that "establishing the constitutionality of a law permitting the sterilization of imbeciles . . . gave me pleasure."[134] And he wrote Laski that when he wrote the opinion in the *Buck* case he "felt that I was getting near to the first principle of real reform."[135]

It therefore proves too much to associate Holmes' opinion in *Buck v. Bell* with a skeptical tolerance for "social legislation" of all sorts, which does not capture his attitude toward Virginia's sterilization statute. The notoriety of *Buck v. Bell* has increasingly cut into Holmes' image as a civil libertarian; it played an important part in the first major revision of that image by critics in the 1960s.[136] The question remains, however, how that image first surfaced, given Holmes' repeated skepticism about the efficacy of "progressive" legislation, indifference toward civil rights claims, disinclination to grant aliens any rights against the state, and ultrapositivist theories of sovereignty.

When progressives evaluated Holmes' general performance as a Supreme Court justice during the last fifteen years of his tenure they were undeniably pleased. To them the Holmesian mixture of deference toward legislative experimentation and "realism" about the nature of judicial decisionmaking was precisely the stance a "modern" judge ought to take. In the substantive due process cases Holmes had exposed "liberty of contract" for the interpretive overreaching that it was. In the *Jensen-Taxicab* sequence he had undermined anachronistic conceptions of law and lawmaking and given another rationale for limited judicial review of the decisions of more representative bodies of government. His admirers were willing to forgive him for the occasional case, such as *Mahon,* in which he seemed to have miscalculated the balance between property rights and legislative regulation. They ignored altogether the implications of his posture in *Britt* or *Goodman*. *Buck v. Bell* posed no particular problems for progressives: the eugenics movement, after all, was thought to be another of the social "experiments" responsive to a modernizing America.

On the progressives' balance sheet Holmes thus fared very well indeed. And when he began to consider free speech cases around the time of World War I, and after some reflection came down on the side of increased protection for dissident speech, his reputation as a great "liberal" judge was cemented: he even came to be portrayed as a friend of the common man. When one considers that the only "progressive" reform for which Holmes exhibited any enthusiasm was compulsory sterilization, that he repeatedly professed his skepticism toward the worth of wages and hours legislation or other efforts to redress inequalities in the marketplace, that he adopted an ultrapositivist view of governmental power to limit the rights of aliens, that he showed little solicitude for the civil rights of racial minorities, and that he ridiculed the positions of dissident speakers whose constitutional rights he supported, his image as a liberal appears to be a considerable distortion of his stance as a Supreme Court justice. The "discovery" of Holmes in the last two decades of his tenure on the Court testifies to the fortuitous process by which judicial reputations are created.

~

The exalted recognition Holmes achieved late in his career could never have occurred had he not left the Supreme Judicial Court of Massachusetts, with its principally local concerns, for a forum for which issues like those posed in *Lochner, Atkins,* and *Buck v. Bell* were regular fare. Had he not become a Supreme Court justice, he would surely not have been so important a figure for Felix Frankfurter; had he not been important to Frankfurter he might not have come to the notice of Frankfurter's "progressive" contemporaries, who played so important a part in the enhancement of Holmes' reputation and in his determination to forego retirement and serve as long as he could on the Court. Had Holmes not changed judicial jobs, in short, he would never have had the opportunity to outdistance his father's fame.

Holmes' tenure on the Supreme Court thus surely changed his life in the sense of creating opportunities that he would not have otherwise had. But had it changed the way he thought and acted as a judge? In one sense the question answers itself affirmatively, because by being on the Supreme Court of the United States Holmes was confronted with a spate of constitutional issues that he would not have encountered as a state judge. Before coming to the Court he had had no opportunity to interpret the Due Process Clauses, although he had been exposed to constitutional attacks on state police powers, and little chance to consider free speech issues. So many of the "great cases"—*Lochner, Adair, Hammer, Adkins, Northern Securities, Swift, Olmstead,* and the free speech decisions considered in the next chapter—in which Holmes' opinions received the attention of *The New Republic* and other organs of educated opinion would not have come to him at all as a state judge, and others would have come in a posture where his decisions would not be the ultimate word on constitutional issues. Being on the Court had given Holmes an opportunity to infuse his jurisprudential views into the discourse not merely of specialists but of an influential sector of the lay public.

Still, the question of judicial change is a more complicated one than that of opportunities for visibility. Holmes had undoubtedly taken advantage of those opportunities, but had he changed as a judge in the process? Here one's conclusions are more likely to be on the side of stasis rather than of movement. With the exception of free speech issues, subsequently to be discussed, there is very little evidence that Holmes' jurisprudential outlook differed from that in *The Common Law* or in his Massachusetts opinions. He was disinclined to defer to the verdicts of juries in common law subjects but inclined to tolerate the views of legislatures on constitutional questions. He was an advocate of external, "objective" standards in criminal law and torts and of determinate readings of documents in contracts. He tended to value certainty and predictability in common law rules more than humanitarian considerations. He regarded questions of law as ultimately questions of degree. He was disinclined to disturb the social judgments of legislatures whether he agreed with them or not; he was not averse to reforming common law doctrine if he thought it could be conformed to the intellectual standards he had formulated as a scholar.

He was a judge who, for the most part, worked alone, emphasizing his own thought and particularly his own expression. Colleagues were relatively unimportant in the process except as potential adversaries for his results and especially for his language. He was not inclined to quarrel with a colleague, nor to provoke or indulge in dissents: only late in his career did he dissent with any regularity, and only then did he enter into a close intellectual relationship with one of his colleagues, that with Brandeis. While he held no deep animosities toward any of the judges with whom he worked in Massachusetts or Washington, so far as can be determined, he did not achieve the intimacy with any of his colleagues, except Brandeis, that he did with, for example, Nina Gray, Frankfurter, Pollack, or Laski, friends he saw only occasionally.

As a judge, he was driven primarily by the "job" of making decisions and writing them up: by conclusions and language. This lent a coldness to his results and a cryptic quality to his explanations that offended some of his contemporaries and, periodically, later commentators. He was far more concerned with disposing of a case than with seeing that "justice," in a humanitarian sense, was done; he was far more concerned with stylistic elegance and pithiness than with technical legal analysis and exegesis. As a stylist he delighted in ambiguity and metaphoric expression; that those literary characteristics were not always virtues in a judicial opinion did not deter him from employing them. He came to the Supreme Court with a clear preference for the short, "civilized," elliptical opinion, and he retained that preference even in the face of opposition. Even when a case roused his deepest convictions, as *Adkins* or *Buck v. Bell* did, he never felt moved to write at length.

For his entire judicial career, he was remarkably detached, not only from those whose lives his decisions affected, but from the judges who joined him in the decisions, the lower courts who sought guidance from his opinions, the lawyers who argued the cases, and the public who reacted to the issues he resolved. Only when he received criticism of a sufficiently elevated sort, or when he received praise from persons whose admiration he coveted, did passion break through his detachment. Despite his disclaimers of indifference and fatalism, he adored recognition and thirsted after it, but still preferred it to come at a distance, as it were, in the form of written tributes. He was consistently piqued by criticism, defensive and aggressive in response to it, and mindful of it over the years. He was entirely convinced about the intellectual strengths of his mind and his qualities as a prose stylist, and when someone suggested that he evaded analytical difficulties or preferred epigrams to reasoning he bristled. At the same time he worried about not getting enough recognition or disappointing those who lionized him.

Apart from these instances, which give a glimpse in the mature judge of the intense self-preoccupation and intellectual competitiveness that had marked the younger scholar, Holmes went about his judicial life in comparative solitude, caring deeply about finishing his assignments and about the language he employed in his opinions, welcoming the opportunity to think about legal problems "to their bottom" or at least to revisit issues that he had already thought about, but being largely indifferent to much else in his professional life. Holmes as a judge, a scholar, a traveler, or an intimate friend was not indifferent to life itself. He recognized in himself a "passion" for activity as well as for achievement, a joie de vivre. When he wrote longtime correspondents or took drives around Washington or bicycle trips around Beverly Farms, when he conversed with a pretty girl at a party or held forth in the London social season, when he noticed the first signs of spring in the bloodroot and crocuses, when he took up his reading after a Term of Court, he did so with a freshness and an enthusiasm that could be described as joy. He said, on his ninetieth birthday, that "to live is to function—that is all there is in living," but he defined "function" to include gazing at flowers and writing letters as well as performing his judicial duties.

Holmes, in short, was not indifferent to the things that brought him pleasure; by contrast, he sought them with a passion. He did not, however, include among those things, in any large measure, a concern for the comings and goings of the people who filled his professional and personal lives. It is one of the ironies of Holmes' career that although he cared so much for recognition, and although so many persons, over the years, have made an investment in his ideas or his work or his life, he gave so little of himself to the persons around him, even those whom he loved.

CHAPTER TWELVE

The Supreme Court, 1917–1931:
Free Speech

~

Of all the opinions Holmes wrote during the fifty-odd years of his judicial career, by far the best known and most celebrated have been his free speech decisions. Unlike the great bulk of his cases, now simply historical documents, they are still quoted and anthologized. The lay public knows Holmes primarily as the judge who wrote memorable phrases about freedom of speech. Holmes' reputation as a "liberal" or civil libertarian rests to a large extent on his speech-protective interpretation of the First Amendment.

Several ironies tincture Holmes' association with free speech. First, for most of his tenure as a judge Holmes' consciousness of free speech claims was rudimentary and speech-restrictive. Second, when free speech issues came before him as a judge he tended to adopt orthodox views toward the role of the First Amendment, treating it as merely declaring common law protections for speech, which were confined to prior restraints on expression. Third, while Holmes was prominently associated with the emergence of modern First Amendment cases at the time of World War I, his opinions in the first group of those cases, testing the constitutionality of the Espionage Act of 1917, departed very little from jurisprudential orthodoxy and were restrictive rather than protective of speech. Fourth, when Holmes altered his position toward speech issues, beginning with his 1919 dissent in *Abrams v. United States,*[1] that alteration was to an important extent a response to suggestions implicitly and explicitly made to Holmes by others.

Finally, Holmes' free speech opinions, taken over time, lack analytic consistency. After treating speech for many years as simply "any other overt act we don't like,"[2] Holmes eventually came to believe that there was an important social interest in protecting speech as a means of informing public opinion in a democracy. Once he reached that belief, Holmes tended not only to protect speech claims but to conceptualize cases as raising speech issues where they arguably did not. On other occasions, however, Holmes deferred to legislative policies significantly restricting speech or did not see speech issues as being implicated in a particular decision. His solicitude for speech was also uneven and idiosyncratic; the memorable formulas he supplied in his analysis of free speech cases were not uniformly or consistently applied in his own decisions. Holmes' free speech opinions, from his point of view, seemed more about language and philosophy than about legal analysis.

The analysis of Holmes' free speech opinions set forth in this chapter has implications for what many commentators have seen as the central paradox of his judicial career. Observers of Holmes' opinions have noted the existence of what appears to be a significant contradiction between his generally deferential stance toward legislation in constitutional cases and his protective attitude toward speech.[3] In speech cases Holmes came to develop a framework that viewed legislative regulation of expression with suspicion and even hostility. Among the rationales he formulated to justify protection of "unpopular" speech was that of the "marketplace of ideas," in which novel opinions were given an opportunity to secure popularity and stature. The model of the "marketplace of ideas" has appeared radically inconsistent with Holmes' approach to cases involving economic regulation, where he was prepared to tolerate considerable legislative interference with existing market arrangements, whether he approved of the legislation or not.

In speech cases, in short, Holmes has appeared to commentators to have assumed a "countermajoritarian" stance, one shielding "unpopular" speech from efforts on the part of legislative majorities to suppress it. This chapter suggests that the assumption that Holmes' free speech decisions represent a dramatic departure from his habitual stance toward judicial review of the constitutionality of legislation is largely misplaced.

A survey of Holmes' free speech opinions over the course of his career on the Supreme Court reveals that his attitude toward free speech issues evolved in three discernible stages. In only one of these stages, the last, was his position ostensibly inconsistent with his general attitude of deference to majorities, and in that stage commentators have overemphasized Holmes' stirring rhetoric on behalf of the "principle of freedom of thought" and underemphasized the uneven and idiosyncratic pattern of his actual free speech decisions. In the first two stages Holmes' treatment of free speech cases was either not speech-protective at all or represented only a minor deviation from jurisprudential orthodoxy. Finally, there is evidence that Holmes' adoption, late in his career, of a more libertarian position on free speech cases was a reaction to arguments advanced by some of his "progressive" acolytes, and represented, rather then a considered reexamination of his general views on the proper stance of the judiciary in constitutional cases, something of a rhetorical spree. Indeed, the contradictions in Holmes' treatment of free speech cases reveal the idiosyncratic character of his jurisprudence, a jurisprudence that took delight in rhetorical ambiguity and overstatement.

~

Three years after Holmes' 1915 decision in *Fox v. Washington*,[4] he gave some inkling that he was beginning to reconsider his orthodox views on freedom of speech in *Toledo Newspaper Co. v. United States*,[5] which upheld a judge's contempt citation of a newspaper imposed for remarks criticizing the judge's conduct of a trial. The Ohio statute involved in *Toledo Newspaper* punished as contempt the "misbehavior of any person in [the] presence [of judges], or so near thereto as to obstruct the administration of justice."[6] The Court majority read "so near" as meaning "tending to," stating that the test of whether such a statute could restrict First Amendment rights was "the character of the act done and its direct tendency to prevent and obstruct,"[7] a restatement of the orthodox bad-tendency test. Holmes dissented, reading "so near as to obstruct" as "so near as actually to obstruct—and not merely near enough to threaten a possible obstruction."[8] That language, and his vote to overturn the conviction, appeared inconsistent with his endorsement of the bad-tendency test in *Fox*. Moreover, his assumption that the case raised a First Amendment issue did not seem to square with his view, previously expressed in *Patterson v. Colorado ex rel. Attorney General,* that subsequent punishment for objectionable speech did not violate the First Amendment at all, since the Amendment was confined to prior restraints against publication.

In addition, Holmes had written an unpublished dissent in the case of *Baltzer v. United States*,[9] which was ultimately reversed and remanded after the Justice Department decided to confess error and withdraw its prosecution. In *Baltzer* the defendant had been convicted for attempting to obstruct the draft by writing letters critical of the war effort to public officials. A majority of the Supreme Court voted to affirm the conviction, even though there was no evidence that the letters had been sent to anyone likely to participate in the draft. Holmes circulated a memorandum of his dissent to the other justices, the relevant portion of which read as follows:

> Real obstructions of the law, giving real aid and comfort to the enemy, I should have been glad to see punished more summarily and severely than they sometimes were. But I think that our intention to put out all our powers in aid of success in war should not hurry us into intolerance of opinions and speech that could not be imagined to do harm, although opposed to our own. It is better for those who have unquestioned and almost unlimited power in their hands to err on the side of freedom. We have enjoyed so much freedom for so long that perhaps we are in danger of forgetting that the bill of rights which cost so much blood to establish still is worth fighting for, and that no tittle of it should be abridged.[10]

Some impassioned sentences in Holmes' *Baltzer* memorandum might tempt a reader to see it as a manifestation that Holmes had suddenly developed a speech-protective consciousness. But the central distinction made in the memorandum was between "real obstructions of the law" that gave "real aid and comfort to the enemy" and dissenting opinions "that could not be imagined to do harm." This distinction was reminiscent of the one he had made in *Toledo Newspaper*, where he was prepared to tolerate critical comment on a judge's performance so long as the remarks had no probable likelihood of disrupting a trial. While *Baltzer* provides additional evidence that Holmes had moved beyond the view of the First Amendment he had expressed in *Patterson*, it is too much to say that in *Baltzer* Holmes "spoke as strongly for freedom of speech as he ever did"[11] in any of his free speech opinions.[12] Put another way, the unpublished *Baltzer* dissent was evidence that Holmes could wax eloquently about free speech ("no tittle of . . . the bill of rights which cost so much blood to establish . . . should be abridged") but it was hardly evidence that he had developed the kind of approach to free speech issues that he would exhibit in some of his subsequent opinions.[13]

While Holmes' departure from *Patterson* in *Toledo Newspaper* and *Baltzer* fore-shadowed his eventual abandonment of his orthodox views on free speech, his first postwar decisions in First Amendment cases were hardly speech protective. In 1919 the Supreme Court considered four cases under the Espionage Act of 1917, a statute that sought to prevent persons from causing insubordination in the armed forces or obstructing the recruitment or enlistment of soldiers.[14] In three of the cases, *Schenck v. United States*,[15] *Frohwerk v. United States*,[16] and *Debs v. United States*,[17] the Court concluded that the convictions did not violate the First Amendment.[18] Holmes wrote unanimous opinions for the Court in each of the three cases.

The three cases featured, for the first time in the twentieth-century history of free speech, extensive discussion of the First Amendment issues raised by prosecution under the Espionage Act. They demonstrated to commentators that previous scholarship on free speech, hitherto relegated to an incidental or marginal status, had suddenly become significant. As "modern" intellectuals became aware of the significance of free speech issues, they began to give more serious attention to this tradition of commentary.[19]

Alternative free speech jurisprudence had attracted commentators of sharply divergent ideological perspectives. Some were early twentieth-century political reformers who sought to expand the opportunities for critics of established governmental and societal practices to be heard.[20] A greater number of the commentators, however, were closer to Holmes in age. Some were late nineteenth-century bohemians and utopian reformers. Others can be identified with an established late-nineteenth century "liberal" ideology that emphasized the lack of legitimate power in the state to intrude into a private citizen's affairs.[21]

To understand the implications of alternative free speech jurisprudence for free speech cases in the period during and after World War I, it is necessary to understand the philosophical premises upon which the commentary was based. A premise central to the commentary, in its nineteenth-century versions, was that "liberty" subsumed a cluster of fundamental values, including individual autonomy in matters of taste and preference, freedom of exchange in the marketplace, and the fruits of property ownership. Liberty was thus a concept of great importance and potentially broad scope, whose promotion furnished one of the rationales for government itself. The assumed fundamental status of liberty in American culture was the base point from which arguments supporting the judicial doctrine of "liberty of contract" in late nineteenth- and early twentieth-century substantive due process cases were derived. Those same arguments were potentially applicable to cases raising Fourteenth Amendment objections to governmental restrictions on speech, and were advanced by several treatise writers and commentators in the late nineteenth century.[22] In summary, the arguments demanded that the same presumptions against governmental interference with individual liberty that had been invoked in cases involving governmental efforts to regulate economic relationships also be applied to governmental efforts to regulate speech.

While "liberty of contract" was a commonly invoked judicial concept in late nineteenth- and early twentieth-century case law, an analogous treatment of "liberty of speech" rarely appeared. There were two principal reasons for the hidden status of the "liberty of speech" argument. First, only a handful of federal and state statutes directly regulated speech during the time of the 1917 Espionage Act[23] and the 1918 Sedition Act,[24] and thus very few Supreme Court cases involved the issue of governmental power to restrict speech.[25]

Second, while "liberty of speech" was theoretically independent of other liberties, orthodox late nineteenth-century legal doctrine tended to subsume issues of "speech" in issues conceived as involving economic liberty. In two late nineteenth-century Supreme Court cases, for example, both sides treated the "free speech" issues as derivative of economic issues. In the first case, *In re Debs*,[26] a federal court order enjoining Eugene Debs and others from encouraging railroad workers to leave their jobs was regarded as an alleged infringement of a constitutional right to engage in the labor practice of a strike.[27] In the second case, *Davis v. Massachusetts*,[28] which affirmed Holmes' opinion in *Commonwealth v. Davis*,[29] the issue of a person's right to speak on the Boston Common was treated as derivative of the powers of municipal corporations to restrict activities on any kind of city property.[30]

The existence of a jurisprudential tradition grounding free speech protection on a broad interpretation of the concept of liberty was thus largely confined to scholarly literature prior to World War I. Moreover, that tradition differed from the orthodox view of free speech only in some respects. Those who conceptualized free speech as a liberty under the Fourteenth Amendment did not believe that the constitutional provisions on free speech merely codified the common law and therefore confined free speech protection to freedom from prior restraints.[31] It did not follow, however, that most of those individuals believed that free speech was to be given absolute or even extensive protection. On the contrary, most assumed that the liberty to speak could be balanced against the power of a government to defend itself in war or against attacks that threatened its own existence.[32]

It is not clear that the *Patterson* or *Fox* cases would have been decided differently had the late nineteenth-century view of speech as a liberty challenged Holmes' early orthodox view.[33] What is clear, however, is that when early twentieth-century political reformers began to devote greater attention to the question of expanding protections for political dissidents, an earlier tradition of commentary treating speech as a fundamental liberty was available to them. Along with that tradition, however, came part of its intellectual baggage: the identification of liberty with doctrines, such as liberty of contract, that by the early twentieth century had troublesome political implications for reformers.[34]

The potential use of liberty arguments as a source of protection for the controversial expressions of political dissidents, such as anarchists, labor organizers, and advocates of unconventional and arguably "obscene" sexual practices, caused a dilemma for early twentieth-century reformers inclined to challenge orthodox free speech jurisprudence. While they were prepared to resist judicial efforts to confine protection for speech to prior restraints, to permit suppression of expressions that had "bad tendencies," or to ignore free speech issues altogether, for them to do so on the basis of a broad-ranging conception of liberty would implicitly require acknowledging the primacy of that conception in the arena of economic affairs. In fine, the liberty premise of protection for free speech seemed to legitimate other protections—such as freedom of contract—to which early twentieth-century political reformers were distinctly unsympathetic.

Over the first two decades of the twentieth century political reformers who were supporters of free speech exhibited two different responses to the potential ramifications of the argument premised on liberty. One response was to disassociate freedom of contract from the general realm of protected liberties, either on the ground that liberty involved material possessions, which were necessarily secondary to the more fundamental right of human existence,[35] or on the ground that the liberty being protected was a fiction, given the unequal bargaining status of many contracting employers and employees.[36]

The other response had far greater significance for the development of modern First Amendment theory. It consisted of a reorientation of premises underlying a speech-protective interpretation of the constitutional provisions affecting freedom of expression. That reorientation took place in two discernible stages. In the first stage, a group of "progressive" political reformers confronted the implications of the liberty premise for numerous proposed legislative reforms and concluded that when the values associated with social progress conflicted with those associated with individual liberty, the latter set of values should give way to the former.[37] In the second stage, in part as a response to the implications of this conclusion, the liberty premise of free speech protection was reframed as a democracy premise. In that reformulation, the locus of philosophical energy animating solicitude for free speech was shifted from the individual as an autonomous being to the individual as a participant in a democratic society. The sources of protection for free speech became identified not with the interest of the individual whose liberty government existed to further, but with the social interest in furthering democratic principles by encouraging independent public discussion and debate.[38] Holmes was to emerge as one of the founders of modern First Amendment theory at the same moment in time when this second stage in the reorientation of the premises of free speech jurisprudence was taking place.

The Espionage Act cases of 1919 marked a transition phase in the modernization of free speech jurisprudence. As Holmes' opinion in *Toledo Newspaper* had suggested, the *Patterson* premise that the First Amendment only applied to prior restraints was coming to be abandoned, and in all the Espionage Act cases the government conceded that the First Amendment did not merely apply to prior restraints.[39] The government nonetheless maintained, in keeping with existing orthodoxy, that the test for finding a violation of the Espionage Act was whether the language complained of had a "bad tendency"—in these instances a tendency to prevent or obstruct the war effort. Holmes' opinion in *Schenck* provided the central basis for the Court's decisions in all the cases.

The defendants in *Schenck* had been Socialist Party officials who distributed leaflets to men who had been drafted to serve in World War I.[40] The leaflets intimated "that a conscript [was] little better than a convict," and "that conscription was despotism in its worst form and a monstrous wrong against humanity in the interest of Wall Street's chosen few."[41] The leaflet headings, addressed to the soldiers, read: "Do not submit to intimidation" and "Assert Your Rights."[42]

Holmes treated the facts of *Schenck* as an attempt to violate the Espionage Act, analogous to an attempt at criminal law. Under the criminal-attempt analogy, speech was just another act whose legality was to be judged by the intentions of the actor and the act's tendency to bring about a legislatively prohibited evil.[43] In his *Schenck* opinion, Holmes emphasized both those elements. "Of course," he concluded, "the document would not have been sent unless it had been intended to have some effect, and we do not see what effect it could be expected to have upon persons subject to the draft except to influence them to obstruct the carrying of it out."[44] Under orthodox analysis, then, "intent" and "bad tendency" both had been found.

Holmes then considered whether the fact that the circular distributed by the defendants was "protected by the First Amendment to the Constitution"[45] made any difference. He conceded that "the prohibition of laws abridging the freedom of speech is not confined to previous restraints, although to prevent them may have been the main purpose, as intimated in *Patterson v. Colorado*."[46] He also conceded that "in many places and in ordinary times the defendants in saying all that was said in the circular would have been within their constitutional rights."[47] He then continued:

> But the character of every act depends upon the circumstances in which it is done. The most stringent protection of free speech would not protect a man in falsely shouting fire in a theater and causing a panic. . . . The question in every case is whether the words used are used in such circumstances and are of such a nature as to create a clear and present danger that they will bring about the substantive evils that Congress has a right to prevent. It is a question of proximity and degree. . . . If the act (speaking, or circulating a paper), its tendency and the intent with which it is done are the same, we perceive no ground for saying that success alone warrants making the act a crime.[48]

This passage demonstrates how, as late as the Espionage Act cases, Holmes' view of First Amendment issues was still shaped by his common law experience, in particular his experience with the law of criminal attempts. As a Massachusetts judge, Holmes had implemented a view of criminal-attempt law that focused on notions of intent and tendency, emphasizing that the requisite intent to bring about an evil that the state had a right to prevent and the tendency to produce that evil were to be determined from the circumstances of the case.[49] We have seen that in two of his Massachusetts decisions, *Commonwealth v. Kennedy*[50] and *Commonwealth v. Peaslee*,[51] Holmes had addressed "intent" and "tendency" in terms of "proximity" and "degree."[52] In addition, he had also used the same terms in an earlier Supreme Court decision, the criminal conspiracy case of *Swift v. United States*,[53] in which he stated that the distinction between "mere preparation" and an attempt was one of "proximity and degree."[54]

These previous opinions suggest that Holmes' "clear and present danger" language in *Schenck* was merely another version of formulas involving "proximity and degree." That speech was involved added nothing to the analysis. Spoken words urging resistance to the war were treated the same as an unsuccessful effort to poison an acquaintance, as in *Kennedy*, or to burn down a building, as in *Peaslee*. Speech was, as Holmes told Harold Laski in July 1918, just another act the majority didn't like.[55] As in the case of prohibitions on overt acts in the common law of attempts, prohibitions on speech did not need to be closely tied to the imminence of success of the attempt.

Schenck then became the basis for the Court's decision to uphold the convictions in *Frohwerk* and *Debs*. Both cases were potentially distinguishable from *Schenck* on their facts. The defendant in *Schenck* had distributed leaflets directly to men who had been drafted.[56] The only question in that case was whether the language in those leaflets demonstrated a tendency to encourage draftees to resist their conscription. In *Frohwerk* and *Debs*, by contrast, the speakers had issued general criticisms of the war effort and had not made any real effort to direct them to draftees.[57] Moreover, in *Debs* the speaker had specifically restrained from urging draftees not to enlist.[58]

Holmes treated those facts as not making any difference. In *Frohwerk* he noted that "we have decided in [*Schenck*] that a person may be convicted of a conspiracy to obstruct recruiting by words of persuasion. . . . [S]o far as the language of the articles goes there is not much to choose between expressions to be found in them and those before us in *Schenck v. United States*."[59] He conceded that "[i]t does not appear that there was any special effort to reach men who were subject to the draft."[60] But on the record in *Frohwerk*, he concluded, "it is impossible to say that it might not have been found that the circulation of the paper was in quarters where a little breath would be enough to kindle a flame and that the fact was known and relied upon by those who sent the paper out."[61]

The *Frohwerk* opinion included some additional language suggesting that Holmes was treating "subversive" speech like an unsuccessful criminal attempt. He stated that "[w]e venture to believe that neither Hamilton nor Madison, nor any other competent person then or later, ever supposed that to make criminal the counselling of a murder within the jurisdiction of Congress would be an unconstitutional interference with free speech."[62] His comment seems unnecessary—no one at the time was suggesting that the First Amendment was an absolute—except to establish that an attempt to advise others to commit murder could be treated as an attempt to murder. Later in *Frohwerk* Holmes noted that "[w]e do not lose our right to condemn either measures or men because the Country is at war."[63] Again, the comment seems unnecessary unless Holmes was seeking to underscore the fact that the criminality of such condemnations should be treated as a question of proximity and degree, as embodied in formulas such as "clear and present danger." But Holmes did not repeat that formula in *Frohwerk*, and it is very difficult to see, despite Holmes' "kindle a flame" metaphor, how printing a circular intended for an audience of German-speaking socialists created a clear and present danger that the war effort would be obstructed.

The *Debs* case presented Holmes with another opportunity to apply his "attempts" analogy. This was the cause célèbre of the Espionage Act cases, in which Eugene Debs, the Socialist Party candidate for President in 1912, was convicted of obstructing the war effort on the basis of a speech he made at the Socialists' convention.[64] As Holmes conceded, Debs' "main theme" in the speech "was socialism, its growth, and a prophecy of its ultimate success."[65] Several particulars of Debs' speech, however, were made the basis of a criminal prosecution under the Espionage Act. Debs had alluded in the speech to a visit that he had made to three "loyal comrades" who were serving time in a workhouse for "aiding and abetting another in failing to register for the draft."[66] In discussing that visit, Holmes said in his opinion, Debs had "said that he had to be prudent and might not be able to say all that he thought, thus intimating to his hearers that they might infer that he meant more."[67] Holmes also noted that, in taking up the case of another Socialist who had been convicted of obstructing the enlistment service, Debs had "praised her for her loyalty to socialism . . . and said that she was convicted on false testimony, under a ruling that would seem incredible to him if he had not had some experience with a Federal Court.''[68] Finally, Holmes pointed out that Debs had said "I abhor war. I would oppose the war if I stood alone,''[69] and that the Socialist Party had adopted an " 'Anti-war Proclamation and Program' " at its convention, which Debs had said that he "approved of . . . in spirit and in substance.''[70]

The logic of Holmes' approach to criminal attempts applied easily to Debs' acts. Holmes maintained that the acts raised the possibility that "one purpose of the speech, whether incidental or not does not matter, was to oppose not only war in general but this war, and that the opposition was so expressed that its natural and intended effect would be to obstruct recruiting.''[71] He then concluded that "[i]f that was intended and if, in all the circumstances, that would be its probable effect, [Debs' speech] would not be protected by reason of its being part of a general program and expressions of a general and conscientious belief.''[72] According to Holmes, Debs' statement approving the Socialist Party's antiwar platform was telling in this regard. "Evidence that the defendant accepted this view and this declaration of his duties at the time that he made that speech," Holmes said, "is evidence that if in that speech he used words tending to obstruct the recruiting service he meant that they should have that effect.''[73]

Holmes' analysis of the issues in *Debs* is very difficult to square with his "clear and present danger" language in *Schenck*. Holmes argued that since Debs had accepted the antiwar platform of the Socialist Party and used "obstructionist" language in his speech, Debs intended to obstruct the recruiting service. There was no evidence, however, that Debs had used "words tending to obstruct the recruiting service" unless opposition to war itself had that tendency. The most that could be said of Debs' speech was that he had praised fellow socialists who had been convicted of obstructing the war effort and hinted that he would like to say more. Holmes' argument therefore makes no sense if Debs did not use any language that could fairly be labeled obstructionist. In Holmes' hands *Debs* thus established the principle that one could be convicted for opposing war generally.

Debs therefore was not a "clear and present danger" case unless Holmes was treating that formula as merely codifying the "tendency" element of criminal attempt law. While Debs' speech might have had a tendency to obstruct the war effort—assuming that some of his audience, sharing his antiwar sentiments and encouraged by his praise for convicted obstructionists, might have decided to encourage draftees to resist—it surely had not created a "clear and present danger" that the war effort would be obstructed. *Schenck, Frohwerk,* and *Debs,* taken together, suggest that Holmes' "clear and present danger" test was simply a restatement of "attempts" language found in his earlier opinions. If this conclusion is accurate, Holmes' Espionage Act decisions did not significantly modify his earlier free speech jurisprudence. The only clear modification in the cases was Holmes' abandonment of the "prior restraints" interpretation of constitutional provisions affecting speech.

～

After the three Espionage Act cases came down in the spring of 1919, a ground swell of criticism from "progressive" intellectuals surfaced. While the precise causes of that critical stance cannot be determined with certainty, there are several possible factors. With the end of World War I one of the most obvious and settled rationales for suppressing speech, fostering the national interest in wartime, diminished in significance. At the same time an awareness among Americans of the doctrines of radical collectivist European ideologies, such as socialism or syndicalism, had begun to emerge, sparked by the formation of the Communist Third International in March 1919. Radical collectivists were associated with a rash of bombings in the spring of 1919, one set of which affected Holmes personally.

On April 30 an employee of the New York City post office, reacting to the news of recent explosions of mail parcels containing bombs in Washington and Georgia, remembered noticing sixteen parcels, matching the description of the parcels that had exploded, in his own office. The parcels had been set aside for insufficient postage. When police investigated, the parcels were found to contain bombs timed to explode on May 1, the ceremonial holiday of the Bolshevik Revolution. J. P. Morgan, John D. Rockefeller, members of President Woodrow Wilson's cabinet, and Holmes were among the addressees of the parcels.[74] Holmes wrote Laski on May 1 that "I suppose it was the Debs incident that secured me the honor of being among those destined to receive an explosive machine."[75] When the October 1919 Term opened he was reminded of the incident, writing to Pollock that "[I]t is one of the ironies that I, who probably take the extremist view in favor of free speech . . . should have been selected for blowing up."[76]

The apparent emergence of radical collectivism as a moving force in American industrial life precipitated a "Red Scare," in which federal and state law enforcement authorities sought to expose the activities of radicals and curb their influence by restricting their opportunities to speak.[77] Those reacting to the Red Scare saw the suppression of radical doctrines as comparable to the suppression of "enemy" actions in wartime.[78]

The extension of repressive tactics toward controversial speech from the wartime to the Red Scare context alarmed a number of "progressive" intellectuals. During the year 1919, editorials in *The New Republic,* regarded by these individuals as their principal intellectual forum, increasingly described the tactics of those caught up in the Red Scare as excessive and hysterical, and called for a reaffirmation of the values of protecting free speech in a democratic society.[79]

Holmes had become aware of *The New Republic* shortly after its founding in 1914 and regularly discussed *The New Republic* articles and editorials in his correspondence with Felix Frankfurter and Herbert Laski.[80] In May 1919, an article by Ernst Freund appeared in *The New Republic* that was conspicuously critical of Holmes' opinion in the *Debs* case. Freund claimed Holmes had taken "the very essentials of the entire problem for granted"[81] by permitting the jury "to find a tendency and an intent to obstruct recruiting" when there was "nothing to show actual obstruction or an attempt to interfere with any of the [recruitment] processes."[82] "[T]o be permitted to agitate at your own peril, subject to a jury's guessing at motive, tendency and possible effect," Freund argued, "makes the right of free speech a precarious gift."[83] Freund thought Holmes' "fire in a crowded theater" analogy unsuited to "political offenses," and suggested that Holmes' view of free speech was an "unsafe doctrine" if "it has to be made plausible by a parallel so manifestly inappropriate."[84]

Holmes had already become aware of opposition to his *Debs* opinion before Freund's article had appeared and had responded to that opposition with a certain defensiveness. He wrote Frederick Pollock on April 5, 1919, that he was "beginning to get stupid letters of protest against a decision that Debs, a noted agitator, was rightly convicted of obstructing the recruiting service so far as the law was concerned."[85] He went on:

> I wondered that the Government should press the case to a hearing before us, as the inevitable result was that fools, knaves, and ignorant persons were bound to say he was convicted because he was a dangerous agitator and that obstructing the draft was a pretence. . . . There was a lot of jaw about free speech, which I dealt with somewhat summarily in an [earlier] case—*Schenck v. U.S.* . . . As it happens I should go farther probably than the majority in favor of it, and I daresay it was partly on that account that the C.J. assigned the case to me.[86]

With this letter Holmes began a pattern of correspondence with several commentators in which he expressed regret about the Espionage Act convictions and personal sympathy for Debs and the other defendants. At the same time, however, Holmes reaffirmed his view that the cases were rightly decided. Two weeks later, for example, he wrote Pollock that

> [o]f course there were people who pitched into the Court for sending Debs to prison under the espionage act, but there was no doubt that the Jury was warranted in finding him guilty or that the act was Constitutional. Now I hope the President will pardon him and some other poor devils with whom I have more sympathy.[87]

In the meantime Holmes sent Harold Laski his opinions in the Espionage Act cases. He felt compelled to add

> I greatly regretted having to write them—and *(between ourselves)* that the Government pressed them to a hearing. Of course I know that donkeys and knaves would represent us as concurring in the condemnation of Debs because he was a dangerous agitator. . . . But on the only questions before us I could not doubt about the law. The federal judges seem to me (again between ourselves) to have got hysterical about the war. I should think the President when he gets through with his present amusements might do some pardoning.[88]

Laski's response was a lukewarm endorsement of Holmes' opinions. He called Holmes' cry-of-fire-in-a-theater analogy "excellent" and conceded that "though I say it with deep regret [the decisions] are very convincing."[89] Laski added, however, that "I am not sure that I should not have liked the line to be drawn a little tighter about executive discretion."[90] Two weeks later, Holmes wrote again to Laski, informing him that the *New Republic* had written an editorial about *Debs*. The editorial stated that "[t]here is no doubt about the legality of his conviction. . . . [But] to let Debs serve his sentence would be both cruel and blind."[91] Holmes told Laski that he found the editorial "exactly right," but felt "it would not be proper . . . to say so publicly."[92]

On May 11, at the end of a letter discussing poetry, English literature, and a controversy brewing at Harvard Law School over some alumni's reaction to Felix Frankfurter, Laski wrote, "I am eager to hear if you read Freund in the *New Republic* of May 3rd and if you were at all influenced by his analysis."[93] The first part of that question was idle, for Holmes had already fired off a letter to Laski in which he had enclosed a letter he had prepared for Herbert Croly, editor of *The New Republic,* in response to the Freund article. Holmes wrote to Laski that he had "decided not to send" the letter to Croly "as some themes may become burning."[94] The letter was consistent with the defensive stance Holmes had adopted in his previous discussions of the Espionage Act cases. It read in part:

> As long ago as 1908 when I wrote *Harriman v. I.C.C.* it seemed to me that we so long had enjoyed the advantages protected by bills of rights that we had forgotten—it used sometimes to seem to me that the *New Republic* had forgotten—that they had had to be fought for and could not be kept unless we were willing to fight for them. . . . As I spoke of [that theme] to my secretary . . . he called my attention to the article on the *Debs* case which I had not seen. You had a short paragraph in an earlier number that struck me as exactly right. This article appeared to me less so if I understood its implications. The constitutionality of the act so far as the clauses concerning obstructing the recruiting service are involved was passed upon in *Schenck v. U.S.* and so all that was needed in the *Debs* case was to refer to that decision, and, given the finding of the jury, in my opinion it was impossible to have a rational doubt about the law. Freund's objection to a jury "guessing at motive, tendency, and possible effect" is an objection to pretty much the whole body of the law, which for thirty years I have made my brethren smile by insisting to be everywhere a matter of degree. . . . I hated to have to write the *Debs* case and still more those of the other poor devils before us the same day and the week before. I could not see the wisdom of pressing the cases, especially when the fighting was over and I think it quite possible that if I had been on the jury I should have been for acquittal but I cannot doubt that there was evidence warranting a conviction on the disputed issues of fact. Moreover I think the *clauses under consideration* not only were constitutional but were proper enough while the war was on. . . . But in the main I am for aeration of all effervescing convictions—there is no way so quick for letting them get flat.[95]

The Croly letter is interesting in several respects. First, even though Holmes had previously informed Laski that he thought it improper to tell *The New Republic* editors that their editorial on the *Debs* case was "exactly right," Holmes had been initially inclined to send Croly a letter with that very language in it. Sending the letter to Laski, who knew Croly well, made it quite possible that Croly would learn of Holmes' views. Second, Holmes' statement that *Debs* was foreclosed by *Schenck* was only persuasive if both *Schenck* and *Debs* were bad-tendency cases, because there was no evidence that Debs' speech had created a "clear and present danger" that the recruitment of troops would be obstructed. Holmes added that "it was impossible to have a rational doubt'' about the constitutionality of the statute because the jury had found against Debs. But the jury's finding might have been based on a mistaken impression that persons could be convicted under the Espionage Act for voicing a general opposition to war.

Holmes next repeated his view that all legal questions were questions of degree, a statement that was unresponsive to Freund's argument about juries' "guessing" in Espionage Act cases. Freund's point was not that the application of any test or standard directed toward determining whether speech could be suppressed in a given case involved guesswork. It was that the bad-tendency test unduly permitted juries to guess whether "bad" inferences could be made from very general statements, and thus permitted the Act to serve as a means of restricting speech that was merely unpopular.[96]

Along with emphasizing that his opinions in the Espionage Act cases were dictated by law, Holmes stressed that they were personally abhorrent. He confessed that he "hated" to "have to write" the *Debs* case; that he was sympathetic to Debs and even more so to the other defendants in Espionage Act cases; and that if he had been on the jury in *Debs* he would have been for acquittal.[97] He even intimated that some of the Espionage Act might be unconstitutional by underlining "clauses under consideration" in his remarks on constitutionality, and stated that now that the war was over it made no sense to prosecute "obstructionist" speakers under the Act.

The defensiveness Holmes exhibited in responding to criticism of *Debs,* as illustrated by his letters to Laski and Croly, could have been taken by his young friends as a gesture of reassurance. The letters might have conveyed a message to Holmes' "progressive" supporters that although his *Schenck* opinion had bound him in the subsequent Espionage Act cases, he was not unsympathetic to free speech arguments. The gesture could even have been taken as an invitation to continue talking to him about the subject.

At the time that Holmes was corresponding with Laski and Croly about free speech, he had already had discussions with yet another "progressive" intellectual, the federal district judge Learned Hand, on the same subject. In June 1918, Holmes had encountered Learned Hand on a train, and the two men had had a conversation about the First Amendment.[98] The discussion might have been prompted by the fact that Hand himself had previously issued an opinion in the case of *Masses Publishing Co. v. Patten,*[99] in which he advanced a libertarian interpretation of the First Amendment. In *Masses* the Postmaster General sought to exclude *The Masses* magazine from the mails under the Espionage Act on the grounds that it was willfully critical of the war effort.[100] Hand granted an injunction against the Postmaster General.[101] In the process, he articulated a test for evaluating the constitutionality of First Amendment challenges to legislation that focused on "direct incitement to violent resistance."[102] Under Hand's test the question in the Espionage Act cases would not have been whether "the indirect result of the language might be to arouse a seditious disposition," but whether "the language directly advocated resistance to the draft."[103]

Hand's direct incitement test was rejected, on appeal, by the U.S. Court of Appeals for the Second Circuit, and was implicitly not regarded as a plausible approach to First Amendment issues during Holmes' tenure.[104] Hand, however, continued to believe in it, and might have defended it in his train conversation with Holmes.

After the conversation the two men exchanged letters. Hand began by referring to a comment in the conversation in which he and Holmes had discussed the role of tolerance for the opinions of others in free speech theory. He argued that Holmes' view that there was a "sacred right to kill the other fellow when he disagrees," which had "silenced" Hand when Holmes said it,[105] needed to be limited. The right did not exist, Hand asserted, when "the victims insist upon saying things which look against Provisional Hypothesis Number Twenty-Six, the verification of which to date may be found in its proper place in the card catalogue," because if they are "spared, other cards may be added under that sub-title which will have, perhaps, an important modification."[106]

Holmes responded that "free speech stands no differently than freedom from vaccination."[107] He felt that if the legislature believed strongly enough in the evil of certain acts to enact legislation prohibiting them, the possibility that the belief might be wrong would be wholly irrelevant. While "[t]he occasions would be rarer when you cared enough to stop it," Holmes felt, "if for any reason you did care enough you wouldn't care a damn for the suggestion that you were acting on a provisional hypothesis and might be wrong. That is the condition of every act."[108] He was not inclined to think that the possibility that speech might lead those in power to alter their policies in the future was a sufficient justification for invariably permitting it in the present.

The correspondence then lapsed until February 1919, when Holmes wrote Hand that he had read Hand's *Masses* opinion and "will assume for present purposes that I should come to a different result."[109] He added, however, that "few judges . . . could have put their view with such force or in such admirable form."[110] The date of that letter suggests that Holmes might have been prompted to read *Masses* in connection with the Espionage Act cases, the first of which were handed down six days later. When the Espionage Act opinions were announced, Hand read them and wrote Holmes, prefacing his letter by saying that "this is positively my last appearance in the role of liberator."[111] While stating that Debs "was guilty under any rule conceivably applicable,"[112] Hand criticized Holmes' approach. He thought it dependent on an assumed causal relationship between words and their future impact. "In nature," he argued, "the causal sequence is perfect, but responsibility does not go pari passu."[113] Hand did "not understand that the rule of responsibility for speech" was that "the result is known as likely to follow."[114] In his view "[t]he responsibility only began when the words were directly an incitement."[115] He added that he thought "the test of motive" was a "dangerous test," since "[j]uries won't much regard the difference between the probable result of the words and the purposes of the utterer."[116] In short, Hand reiterated his *Masses* test as the touchstone for First Amendment cases.

Holmes responded in a letter that illustrates, in Gerald Gunther's words, "the primitiveness of Holmes's first amendment thinking at that time."[117] "I am afraid," Holmes began, "that I don't quite get your point."[118] He noted that he had "said nothing" in the *Debs* case "except to note that . . . the jury must be taken to have found that Debs's speech was intended to obstruct and tended to obstruct."[119] He then claimed that Hand's statement that "the responsibility only began when the words were directly an incitement" was the same as his "clear and present danger" formulation in *Schenck*. "I take it," he said, "that you agree that words may constitute an obstruction within the statute, even without proof that the obstruction was successful to the point of preventing recruiting. . . . So I don't know . . . how we differ so far as your letter goes."[120]

The point of Hand's letter, of course, was that any causal connections between a speaker's words and the evils that the Espionage Act sought to prevent had to be predicated on the speaker's directly advocating those evils. For Hand, whether the speaker "intended" the proscribed result or whether the speaker's language "tended" to accomplish that result was irrelevant if the speaker had not directly advocated illegal activity. Holmes' "clear and present danger" formulation was not responsive to that argument. Nor was Holmes' statement that since Hand agreed that a speaker could be convicted even if his speech had been unsuccessful in obstructing recruiting, he and Hand did not disagree in their basic approaches. Hand would prosecute only for direct incitements of illegal activity, regardless of whether they were successful. Holmes would allow prosecution for speech that could be taken as "tending" to incite illegal activity even though the speaker stopped short of doing so directly. The approaches were sufficiently different that Hand had written Ernst Freund, four days after Freund's critique of *Debs* had appeared, that "I was chagrined that Justice Holmes did not line up on our side."[121] Hand added to Freund that "I have so far been unable to make [Holmes] see that he and we have any real differences."[122]

The exchange with Hand demonstrated that while Holmes thought his "clear and present danger" test to be controlling in free speech cases (even though he had not referred to it in the *Frohwerk* and *Debs* cases), he treated it as merely declarative of the state of the law governing both criminal attempts and criminal appeals in speech cases. "Clear and present danger" articulated the focus in those cases: the speaker's (or actor's) words or acts. The test was designed to determine how closely those words or acts were connected to illegal activity. Based the closeness of that connection, could the speaker be presumed to have "intended" the illegal activity to take place? The test did not so much limit the scope of restrictions on free speech as provide a convenient litmus for analyzing "dangerous" speeches and other "attempts."

Thus it seems fair to say that as late as May 1919, when he wrote Croly defending his Espionage Act opinions, Holmes, however much he wanted to convey the impression that he was sympathetic to the position of the defendants in those cases, continued to treat unpopular speech as another "act you didn't like" and did not regard his "clear and present danger" formula as a test emphasizing the limits on governmental suppression of speech. By November 1919, however, Holmes had issued his dissent in *Abrams v. United States*,[123] and a month later, in a letter to Pollock discussing his dissent, Holmes said that "[a]s the *Debs* case and two others were assigned to me, in which the convictions were upheld, I thought it proper to state what I thought the limits of the doctrine."[124] From his *Abrams* dissent until the end of his career Holmes treated "clear and present danger" as a limiting test, an alternative to the bad-tendency test, and accordingly conceived of free speech problems as different from problems in the law of criminal attempts.

Abrams thus represented a major change in Holmes' attitude toward free speech, one that could not have been anticipated by his "progressive" friends on the basis of their correspondence with him in the few months after the Espionage Act trilogy. The correspondence with Laski and Hand, the editorials in *The New Republic,* and Ernst Freund's article had penetrated Holmes' consciousness, however, as his defensive response to criticism of the *Debs* case suggested. In addition, over the spring and summer of 1919 his young friends continued to encourage him to rethink free speech issues, he increased his reading on the subject,[125] and eventually he encountered a formulation of the rationale for increased protection for speech that touched a chord within him. This was the synthesis advanced by Zechariah Chafee, who combined an artful reconstruction of Holmes' treatment of speech in the Espionage Act cases with a recasting of the philosophical basis for protecting speech rights. Chafee's reformulation deemphasized the argument that speech was one of many liberties held against the state and emphasized the "social interest" in protecting speech as a means of furthering "the discovery and spread of truth on subjects of general concern"[126] in a democratic society.

In late July 1919, Laski invited Holmes, who was summering in Beverly Farms, to tea in Cambridge to meet Chafee, then an Assistant Professor at the Harvard Law School.[127] Prior to that meeting Laski had given Holmes a copy of Chafee's June 1919 article.[128] Laski heartily approved of the article, which included, in addition to its discussion of the Espionage Act cases, an argument that the Court's pre-Espionage Act treatment of free speech cases had been speech protective.[129] The article included a plea for enhanced recognition of the limits the First Amendment imposed on the power to suppress dissident speech,[130] and Laski wrote Chafee that "we must fight on it" with Holmes at the tea.[131] "I've read it twice," Laski said, "and I'll go to the stake for every word."[132]

Although Holmes' correspondence supplies no direct evidence that he had read Chafee's article, either before or after the tea, he had undoubtedly done so. The article was sent to him during a time, the early summer of 1919, when he had the leisure to read. It involved a subject about which Holmes was deeply interested and extensively discussed opinions he had written. Moreover, it had been critical of him and had been written by a person whose opinion he might presumptively have granted some weight, a young faculty member at Harvard Law School, scion of an aristocratic WASP family, who had contributed to *The New Republic*.

Several statements in Chafee's article might have attracted Holmes' attention. First, Chafee said that all the Espionage Act cases except *Debs* were "clear cases of incitement to resist the draft, so that no real question of free speech arose."[133] That statement was essentially inaccurate, but it conformed to Holmes' general view of the cases. Next, Chafee identified Holmes' "clear and present danger" formula as the "Supreme Court test"[134] for free speech cases. He then proceeded to construe it in a fashion that was remarkable, but sympathetic to Holmes. After arguing that earlier views of the First Amendment were incompatible with the bad-tendency test[135] and consistent with Hand's direct-incitement test,[136] Chafee claimed that Holmes' formula "substantially agree[d]" with the latter test and with "the history and political purpose of the First Amendment."[137] He said that Holmes, in his "clear and present danger" test, had "draw[n] the boundary line very close to the test of incitement at common law and clearly ma[de] the punishment of words for their bad tendency impossible."[138]

In light of *Frohwerk* and *Debs*, this last statement was surprising. Chafee attempted to reconcile it with those cases by suggesting that the defendant in *Frohwerk* had clearly incited others to resist the draft,[139] and that in *Debs* Holmes had unfortunately ignored the "clear and present danger" test.[140] Both suggestions provide clues to Chafee's purpose in writing the article.

The statement about *Frohwerk* was incorrect: the defendant had only made general statements critical of existing governmental policy. *Frohwerk* was a difficult case for Chafee's interpretation of Holmes' approach to the Espionage Act: Holmes had openly indicated the possible tendency in the defendant's circulars to impede the war effort and had not mentioned "clear and present danger."[141] Thus Chafee had nothing to gain from a detailed analysis of *Frohwerk*, which he did not undertake.

The statement about *Debs*, however, was very likely intended to touch a nerve in Holmes. *Debs* was the case for which Holmes had received the severest criticism, and the result in *Debs*, because of the defendant's deliberate effort to avoid making any explicit statement in support of resistance to the draft, was arguably the most vulnerable of the Espionage Act cases. Chafee devoted considerable attention to Holmes' opinion in *Debs*. If Holmes had applied the "clear and present danger" test in *Debs*, Chafee argued, it was "hard to see how [Debs] could have been held guilty."[142] Holmes had permitted the jury to convict Debs "merely because [it] thought his speech had a tendency to bring about resistance to the draft":[143] he had treated the verdict as "proof that actual interference with the war was intended and was the proximate effects of the words used."[144] For the "clear and present danger" test to "mean anything more than a passing observation," Chafee maintained, "it must be used to upset convictions for words when the trial judge did not insist that they must create 'a clear and present danger' of overt acts."[145] Only then would the test be functioning as it should: "to emphasize the social interest behind free speech, and show the need of balancing even in war time."[146] In *Debs*, Chafee concluded, Holmes "did nothing to emphasize the social interest behind free speech."[147] Holmes' "liberalism," Chafee concluded, seemed "held in abeyance" in the case.[148]

The option Chafee seemed to be implicitly presenting was that if Holmes wanted his clear and present danger formula to emerge as the Court's test for First Amendment cases, he needed to apply it with some degree of rigor. Chafee even provided a philosophical basis for "clear and present danger" limits on governmental suppression of speech: the assumption that "[o]ne of the most important purposes of society and government is the discovery and spread of truth."[149] Those familiar with Holmes' *Abrams* dissent will recognize that Holmes implicitly accepted Chafee's offer. He strengthened the "clear and present danger" test, separating First Amendment analysis from the common law of attempts, and reaching a result clearly incompatible with *Schenck*, even though purportedly based on the same analytical criteria.

It is worth noting, however, that at the tea where Holmes and Chafee met for the first time and "fought" about free speech doctrine, Chafee had no sense that he had brought Holmes over to his point of view. In September 1919, he wrote Judge Charles Amidon that while Holmes had indicated that as a juror he would have voted to acquit Debs, as a judge he was "inclined to allow a very wide latitude to Congressional discretion in the carrying on of the war," and that he "could not have gone behind the jury verdict" in *Debs*.[150] Chafee added that Holmes' "omission to state the principles" governing free speech cases was typical of federal judges at the time.[151]

Chafee's belief that Holmes remained unconvinced after their meeting should not be considered strong evidence that Chafee's analysis had not affected Holmes. Holmes was, as we have seen, defensive about criticism; in addition, he was disinclined to make public corrections and extremely sparing in his acknowledgment of the influence of others on his ideas. When confronted in a discussion with two younger men who were inclined to fight him on the *Debs* case, Holmes was not likely to confess error.

There is also reason to suspect that Holmes had incentives to accept Chafee's implicit invitation. Holmes had taken pains to communicate his personal belief that the Espionage Act prosecutions should not have been brought and his hope that the defendants would be pardoned. He also must have sensed, from the barrage of criticism that *Debs* had precipitated and from *The New Republic*'s adoption of a libertarian position on free speech issues, that free speech jurisprudence was at a crisis. Finally, he prided himself on not being "hysterical" with respect to unpopular speech in the same way that he was not "larmoyant" on issues that appealed to "sentiment."[152] His early and prominent involvement with the Espionage Act cases had given him an opportunity to fashion Court doctrine in an area that promised to be of widespread public interest. Chafee's reconstruction of "clear and present danger" and reformulation of the philosophical basis of free speech had provided him with opportunities to rethink that doctrine: *Abrams* would give him an early chance to express his thoughts. As the Court's October 1919 Term approached, Holmes wrote to Pollock after reading the latest of several works on free speech Laski had sent him over the spring and summer, E. S. P. Haynes' *The Decline of Liberty in England*. Although Holmes was not entranced with Haynes' book, he said that "I partly sympathized with his *animus*." He then added:

> The whole collectivist tendency seems to be toward underrating or forgetting the safeguards in bills of rights that had to be fought for in their day and are still worth fighting for. I have had to deal with cases that made my blood boil and yet seemed to create no feeling in the public or even in most of my brethren. We have been comfortable so long that we are apt to take it for granted that everything will be all right without our taking any trouble. All of which is but a paraphrase of eternal vigilance is the price of freedom— . . . [153]

My analysis of the *Schenck-Abrams* sequence rests on two assumptions. First, when Holmes employed the phrase "clear and present danger" in *Schenck,* he had not, despite his elegant language in the *Baltzer* memorandum, moved very far from his previous orthodox response to free speech cases. Second, it was the artful recharacterization of "clear and present danger" by Chafee, coming on the heels of other comments by young acquaintances of Holmes about free speech, that caused him to rethink that response. A letter Holmes wrote Chafee in 1922 provides indirect support for both these assumptions.

In it Holmes gave an account of the origins of "clear and present danger" which suggested that he never intended the formula to mean anything more than an encapsulation of the law of attempts. He told Chafee that the expression "clear and present danger"

> was not helped by any book that I know of. I think it came without doubt after the later cases (and probably you—I do not remember exactly) had taught me that in the earlier Pat[t]erson case, if that was the name of it, I had taken Blackstone and Parker of Mass. as unrefuted, wrongly. I simply was ignorant. But I did think hard on this matter of attempts in my *Common Law* and a Mass. case—later in the *Swift* case (U.S.)—and I thought it out unhelped.[154]

The passage is revealing in several respects. First, while "the later cases" (by which Holmes may have meant the *Toledo Newspaper* and *Baltzer* cases; he could not have meant *Fox v. Washington*) might have "taught" Holmes that the First Amendment was not confined to prior restraints, Chafee was surely not his teacher, since Holmes was not acquainted with Chafee or his work at the time he wrote *Schenck*.[155] Holmes remembered Chafee as having taught him something, however; possibly Chafee had taught him that "clear and present danger" had significant doctrinal possibilities and that the hypostasis for protecting free speech could be "democracy" and "search for truth" as well as "liberty."

Second, when Holmes discussed "clear and present danger" in the letter, his comments came exclusively from the law of attempts. He referred to *The Common Law*, which included an extensive discussion; to "a Mass. case" (probably *Peaslee*, possibly *Kennedy* as well); and to *Swift*. His restatement of the law of attempts in those cases, we have seen, was analogous to "clear and present danger," emphasizing "proximity and degree." The last sentence of the passage, referring to "it," brought the reader back to "this matter of attempts," as if Holmes still regarded the "clear and present danger" phrase in that context. In short, the letter suggests that Holmes' memory of the origins of the formula—which for him was firmly set in the law of attempts—was quite distinct from his memory of his subsequent education about First Amendment issues. With respect to that latter memory, he identified Chafee as one of his teachers.

The dialogue between Holmes and his younger contemporaries in the interval between *Schenck* and *Abrams* suggests that when Holmes considered *Abrams*, about a month after Chafee had described the results of their tea that July, he knew exactly what he was doing: he was seeking to reformulate the meaning of "clear and present danger." He used the facts of *Abrams* to aid him in that task.

In *Abrams* a group of Russian immigrants had published and distributed leaflets, both in English and Yiddish, criticizing President Woodrow Wilson's decision to send troops into Russia in support of persons fighting against the Bolshevik government.[156] The leaflets, apparently directed at factory workers in New York, also urged those workers to engage in a general strike, declaring that they were manufacturing weapons to use against their Russian comrades.[157] The leaflets were distributed when the United States was still at war against Germany.[158]

The case differed from the *Schenck* trilogy because the Espionage Act of 1917[159] had been amended by the Sedition Act of 1918.[160] The Sedition Act made it a crime, when the United States was at war, to "willfully . . . urge, incite, or advocate any curtailment of production . . . with intent . . . to cripple . . . the United States in the prosecution of the war."[161] Successful prosecution of the case required that the defendants had a specific intent to interfere with the war against Germany, as distinguished from the U.S. expedition to Russia.[162] Moreover, because the indictments rested on the broader language of the 1918 Amendment rather than the original language of the 1917 Act, the Court was required to confront seditious libel on the face of the Sedition Act. *Abrams* was undeniably a case in which the government sought to restrict speech itself.

The defendants in *Abrams* argued both that they lacked the requisite intent to be convicted under the Espionage Act as amended by the Sedition Act and that the entire Act was unconstitutional under the First Amendment.[163]

The majority in *Abrams,* in an opinion by Justice John Clarke, found the *Schenck* trilogy dispositive of the First Amendment claim. "Th[e] [defendant's] contention," Clarke asserted, "is sufficiently discussed and is definitely negatived in [*Schenck* and *Frohwerk*]."[164]

Clarke then turned to the question of statutory intent, resurrecting Holmes' language in *Debs.* A statement that was "part of a general program" of opposition to war, he mentioned, could be the basis for finding a specific intent to obstruct a particular war "if, in all the circumstances, that would be its probable effect."[165] "Men must be held to have intended, and to be accountable for," Clarke argued, "the effects which their acts were likely to produce."[166] The "obvious effect" of the leaflets was "defeat of the war program of the United States."[167] The defendants thus had the requisite intent for conviction.

The set of facts presented in *Abrams* made Holmes' dissent particularly interesting. Those facts arguably rendered the defendants' advocacy more of a "clear and present danger" to the war effort than any of the speeches delivered by previous Espionage Act violators. Schenck had delivered circulars to draftees, but the circulars had only spoken abstractly of the evils of conscription;[168] Frohwerk had not delivered circulars to anyone, and the pamphlets he printed were not directed specifically at draftees;[169] Debs had not said anything specific about draft resistance to World War I.[170] The defendants in *Abrams* had printed leaflets and thrown them out the window of a factory, knowing they might be received by munitions workers, whose factory was in the vicinity. The leaflets urged a general strike, which if undertaken would certainly have hindered the war effort.[171] Yet Holmes chose *Abrams* as an opportunity to argue that the First Amendment should be read as placing significant restrictions on the Espionage Act and comparable statutes.

A clue to Holmes' purposes in *Abrams* can be found in the way in which he described the leaflets. Clarke had quoted their language verbatim.[172] Despite this thorough treatment, Holmes chose to paraphrase the leaflets in a strikingly informal way. After including some vivid language in the leaflets, most of it without quotation,[173] Holmes said that one of the leaflets "goes on,"[174] and that another "winds up,"[175] and ends with "some usual tall talk."[176] Juxtaposing paraphrased sentences from the leaflets with these informal side comments considerably reduced the incendiary quality of the leaflets: they now appeared as caricatures of early twentieth-century radical prose. This was not accidental, for Holmes subsequently characterized the leaflets as "silly,"[177] as "poor and puny anonymities,"[178] and as products of a "creed of ignorance and immaturity."[179]

Holmes' distinctive recapitulation of the facts had a larger purpose: to imbue the phrase "clear and present danger," previously a formula akin to that of causation in the law of torts or crimes, with a substantive meaning, and to convert it to a standard of judicial review limiting governmental efforts to suppress speech. The act of throwing leaflets out the window to an audience of munitions workers had come far closer to the objective of bringing those leaflets into the consciousness of those engaged in the war effort than the act, in *Frohwerk,* of printing circulars. But "clear and present danger," under Holmes' reformulation, was no longer a mere matter of proximate cause. It also depended on the probability of the act's success. Holmes was suggesting in *Abrams* that the danger of proscribed conduct could be discounted by the "silly," "puny," and "immatur[e]" character of the leaflets' messages. Holmes' casting of the *Abrams* facts served his purpose of encouraging courts, in applying the "clear and present danger" formula, to consider the likely effectiveness of the speech sought to be suppressed.

Holmes' dissent also met other ends, including a suggestion that where First Amendment rights were implicated, the standard for finding the requisite intent for an offense differed from the common law standard. The majority had conceptualized *Abrams* as principally a case of statutory interpretation rather than constitutional law. Clarke had asserted that the First Amendment issue could be summarily disposed of; therefore the principal issue was whether the defendants had the requisite intent to come under the amended Espionage Act. In interpreting the Act, Holmes found the common law analogy, which had previously informed his discussion of First Amendment cases, now inapposite.

> I am aware . . . that the word intent as vaguely used in ordinary legal discussion means no more than knowledge at the time of the act that the consequences said to be intended will ensue. Even less than that will satisfy the general principle of civil and criminal liability. A man may have to pay damages, may be sent to prison, at common law might be hanged, if at the time of his act he knew facts from which common experience showed that the consequences would follow, whether he individually could foresee them or not.[180]

This treatment of intent, Holmes argued in his dissent, should not govern in *Abrams.* "It seems to me," he said, "that this statute must be taken to use its words in a strict and accurate sense."[181] Any other usage, in his view, "would be absurd."[182] Under a strict definition of intent "a deed is not done with intent to produce a consequence unless that consequence is the aim of the deed."[183] An actor "does not do the act with intent to produce [the consequence] unless the aim to produce it is the proximate motive of the specific act."[184] Holmes concluded that "[t]o say that [speech] might import a suggestion of conduct that would have interference with the war as an indirect and probably undesired effect seems to me by no means enough to show an attempt to produce that effect."[185]

Holmes gave no reasons for his abandonment of the analogy to causation in the common law of attempts, nor for his conclusion that intent in the statute "must be taken" strictly. He had, however, made a distinction between "act[s]" in the common law examples and "words" in his discussion of the construction of the statute. Because the First Amendment was implicated, Holmes seemed to be suggesting in this distinction, the statute needed to be interpreted strictly and the "indirect" test of causation abandoned.

The most significant purpose of Holmes' dissent in *Abrams,* however, was to advance a reconfiguration of First Amendment doctrine, purportedly based on his formula in *Schenck* and anticipated by Chafee. To do so he turned to what he considered "a more important aspect of the case," the First Amendment issue.[186] He first reasserted the primacy of the *Schenck* formula in evaluating First Amendment claims:

> I never have seen any reason to doubt that the questions of law that alone were before this Court in the cases of *Schenck, Frohwerk,* and *Debs* were rightly decided. I do not doubt for a moment that by the same reasoning that would justify punishing persuasion to murder, the United States constitutionally may punish speech that produces or is intended to produce a clear and imminent danger that it will bring about forthwith certain substantive evils that the United States constitutionally may seek to prevent. . . .
>
> But as against dangers peculiar to war, as against others, the principle of the right to free speech is always the same. It is only the present danger of immediate evil or an intent to bring it about that warrants Congress in setting a limit to the expression of opinion where private rights are not concerned. Congress certainly cannot forbid all effort to change the mind of the country.[187]

In this passage, some of Holmes' alterations of his *Schenck* dictum were bold; others were sufficiently subtle as virtually to escape notice. Holmes had invoked the *Schenck* trilogy and had referred to the murder example in an effort to maintain consistency and remind his audience that anyone must concede that free speech must have some limits. But he qualified the constitutional ability of the government to punish speech with the clear and present danger formula, which was also restated as "imminent danger." What had in *Schenck* been "substantive evils that Congress has a right to prevent"[188] became in the reformulation "certain substantive evils that the United States constitutionally may seek to prevent."[189]

These changes were not minor. Since Holmes had not referred to a "clear and present danger" in *Frohwerk* and *Debs,* and since he had employed the bad-tendency test in both those cases, the trilogy of 1919 cases could have been taken simply as attempt cases, with the "clear and present danger" phrase serving as one of Holmes' vivid aphorisms. In *Abrams,* however, "clear and present danger" moved to the center of First Amendment analysis. Only speech that "produces or is intended to produce a clear and imminent danger" could constitutionally be punished.

The position of the government in speech cases had also been altered. Instead of having "a right to prevent" substantive evils, the government was "seek[ing]" to prevent those evils, and only "certain" evils were appropriate—those that the government could "constitutionally prevent." Moreover, the government was now referred to as "the United States," not simply "Congress," so the limitations on restricting speech extended to executive and judicial as well as legislative acts.

Holmes then confirmed in his dissent the substantive nature of his reformulated test by saying that "the principle of the right to free speech [was] always the same," even in wartime, by restating the "clear and present danger" formula.[190] He also introduced a qualification that might easily go unnoticed. Once the "clear and present danger" test had been satisfied, Congress could "set a limit to the expression of opinion [in cases] where private rights are not concerned."[191] This intimated that First Amendment cases involving public matters were different; perhaps even that the "clear and present danger" test did not apply where the subject of the speech was private. It suggested that First Amendment protection might be closely linked to the public nature of the speaker's comments. In this observation Holmes was following Chafee, who had described the First Amendment as promoting "the public discussion of all public questions."[192]

Having reconfigured the appropriate test in First Amendment cases, Holmes applied it to the *Abrams* facts. "Now nobody can suppose," he maintained, "that the surreptitious publishing of a silly leaflet by an unknown man, without more, would present any immediate danger that its opinions would hinder the success of the government arms or have any appreciable tendency to do so."[193] Moreover, once the "strict" definition of intent was employed, Holmes "[could] not see how anyone can find the intent required by the statute in any of the defendants' words."[194] Further, "there is no hint at resistance to the United States as I construe the phrase."[195] In short, "the defendants are to be made to suffer not for what the indictment alleges but for the creed that they avow," a creed that "no one has a right even to consider in dealing with the charges before the Court."[196]

Holmes then addressed what he thought the *Abrams* case was all about: "[p]ersecution for the expression of opinions."[197] He had written Laski in 1918 that "if you are cocksure, and . . . you have no doubt of your power—you will do what you believe efficient to bring about what you want," but "[i]n most matters of belief we are not cocksure . . . we are not certain of our power."[198] In his *Abrams* dissent he repeated those sentiments:

> Persecution for the expression of opinions seems to me perfectly logical. If you have no doubt of your premises or your power and want a certain result with all your heart you naturally express your wishes in law and sweep away all opposition. To allow opposition by speech seems to indicate that you think the speech impotent, as when a man says that he has squared the circle, . . . or that you doubt either your power or your premises.[199]

While this passage seems at first blush to be articulating a rationale for suppressing speech, its actual purpose was to convey one of Holmes' central philosophical points in *Abrams:* that where matters of belief were concerned people rarely had "no doubt of [their] premises." He made that point in the following manner:

> But when men have realized that time has upset many fighting faiths, they may come to believe even more than they believe the very foundations of their own

conduct that the ultimate good desired is better reached by free trade in ideas—that the best test of truth is the power of the thought to get itself accepted in the competition of the market, and that truth is the only ground upon which their wishes safely can be carried out.[200]

In this paragraph one can see the interaction of Holmes' cultural determinism, which had led him in *The Common Law* to speak of experience overwhelming logic in the law, so that legal theories and legal doctrines inevitably came to reflect "the felt necessities" of the times, with Chafee's conception of "[t]he true meaning of free speech" as "the discovery and spread of truth on subjects of general concern."[201] One could value "free trade in ideas" even more than one valued "the very foundations of [one's] own conduct" because "fighting faiths" were ephemeral and subject to change. Equating "truth" with "the power of the thought to get itself accepted in the competition of the market" recognized the boundaries placed around ideas by current "felt necessities."

Holmes' conception of the "search for truth" was thus quite different from that of Chafee and the other early twentieth-century progressive theorists, who sought to shift the premises of free speech theory. For Chafee and those who emphasized the social interest in free speech, the search for truth was part of a process in which public opinion could become more informed and enlightened. For Holmes, "truth" was the equivalent of majoritarian prejudice at any point in time. He defined it to Laski as "the prevailing can't help of the majority,"[202] and to Learned Hand as "the majority vote of that nation that can lick all others."[203] The optimistic, democratic vision of Chafee and his "progressive" contemporaries had interacted with Holmes' skeptical resignation about the primacy of majoritarian sentiment. The "search for truth" metaphor, embodying both perspectives, had arrived in American free speech jurisprudence.

Holmes then emphasized the metaphor's constitutional significance. Immediately after associating "the ultimate good" with a "free trade in ideas" designed to search for truth, he announced:

> That at any rate is the theory of our Constitution. It is an experiment, as all life is an experiment. Every year if not every day we have to wager our salvation upon some prophecy based upon imperfect knowledge. While that experiment is part of our system I think that we should be eternally vigilant against attempts to check the expression of opinions that we loathe and believe to be fraught with death, unless they so imminently threaten immediate interference with the lawful and pressing purposes of the law that an immediate check is required to save the country. . . . Only the emergency that makes it immediately dangerous to leave the correction of evil counsels to time warrants making any exception to the sweeping command, "Congress shall make no law . . . abridging the freedom of speech."[204]

In this passage Holmes explicitly linked the "clear and present danger" test to the idea that thoughts gained or lost acceptance in "the market" of ideas and were "corrected" with time, producing "truth," an idea now characterized as "the theory of our Constitution." Somehow the "experimental" character of the constitutional scheme of government was linked to the "experimental" process by which ideas were tested and discarded in the marketplace. And since "the ultimate good" was reached by allowing this experimental process to go on, only those ideas that directly threatened the existence of the nation should be removed from the process by being suppressed. The First Amendment had become a "sweeping command" to test all ideas in the marketplace unless they immediately threatened the country.

Needless to say, after Holmes' reformulation in *Abrams,* his conception of the First Amendment generally, and of the "clear and present danger" test in particular, bore little resemblance to their counterparts in the 1919 Espionage Act cases. In Holmes' original treatment of the First Amendment issues in those cases, notwithstanding the clear-and-present-danger dictum, the presence of a First Amendment claim added nothing to an analysis that conceptualized the cases as common law attempts. Clarke's majority opinion in *Abrams,* in fact, had been faithful to the *Schenck* trilogy in its summary treatment of the defendants' First Amendment argument. It was Holmes who sought to change the rules.

Reaction to Holmes' dissent in *Abrams,* from the same sources who had initiated communication with him on First Amendment issues, was swift and, from Holmes' point of view, must have been eminently satisfactory. Laski wrote that "amongst the many opinions of yours I have read, none seems to me superior either in nobility or outlook, in dignity or phrasing, and in that quality the French call *justesse.*"[205] Felix Frankfurter wrote of "the gratitude and . . . the pride I have in your dissent," adding that "[y]ou speak there as you have always spoken," but "this time we need education in the obvious."[206] *The New Republic* wrote an editorial, *The Call to Toleration,* featuring Holmes' dissent,[207] and published an article highly critical of the majority opinion.[208] And Chafee devoted a law review article to the case, referring to "Justice Holmes's magnificent exposition of the philosophic basis" of the First Amendment,[209] and asserting that the effect of the majority decision "should be temporary in view of . . . the enduring qualities of the reasoning of Justice Holmes."[210] Chafee maintained that "[o]n the constitutional point, little can be added to the statement of Justice Holmes."[211] He believed that Holmes' dissent "must carry great weight as an interpretation of the First Amendment, because it is only an elaboration of the principle laid down by him with the backing of a unanimous court in *Schenck v. United States.*"[212] The "clear and present danger" test as reformulated, Chafee concluded, could now be taken as "marking the true limit of governmental interference with speech and writing under our constitution."[213] The first stage in the modernization of American free speech jurisprudence had been completed.

~

Abrams, the case in which Holmes decisively abandoned earlier orthodoxy and embraced a conception of the First Amendment that encompassed substantive limitations on governmental power, has rightly been identified as "the constitutional divide" in the evolution of his views on free speech.[214] In his post-*Abrams* free speech opinions Holmes regularly adopted speech-protective positions and thereby cemented his reputation among commentators as a libertarian on free speech issues.[215] Surprisingly little attention, however, has been paid to the language of those opinions, which is not easily reconcilable with Holmes' language in *Abrams*.

There is no question that Holmes' later speech decisions reflected his expanded consciousness of the First and Fourteenth Amendments, which treated them as constitutional provisions with significant substantive bite, rather than mere codifications of, or analogies to, the common law. The shape of Holmes' consciousness in the later free speech cases, however, was essentially idiosyncratic. While he continued to adhere, reflexively, to the "clear and present danger" test, he went well beyond it in some instances, apparently adopting an ultralibertarian perspective. Further, although Holmes now began to view some types of cases as raising free speech concerns, he nonetheless continued to resist any effort to treat speech as an essential liberty, akin to liberty of contract. Toward the end of his career, Holmes seemed far more concerned with exhibiting his enhanced sensitivity to the free speech implications of cases than with maintaining doctrinal consistency. In his attempts to exhibit a sensitivity to free speech issues Holmes provided some clues about his essential orientation as a First Amendment theorist and as a judge.

In his first post-*Abrams* free speech dissents, Holmes continued to exhibit his new sensitivity. In the 1920 Term he twice joined Brandeis in dissenting from opinions that applied the bad-tendency test and treated intent generally under the Espionage Act. Brandeis reiterated that the "clear and present danger" test should control judicial assessments of subversive speech[216] and that a specific intent to engage in prohibited activity should be required to sustain a conviction where speech rights were at stake.[217]

The next Term, Holmes dissented separately from Brandeis in *United States ex rel. Milwaukee Social Democratic Publishing Co. v. Burleson*.[218] There the Postmaster General had denied second-class mailing privileges to the *Milwaukee Leader* on the ground that the paper had printed articles critical of the war effort and was, therefore, a "non-mailable" publication within the meaning of the 1917 Espionage Act.[219] Although the Act did not address whether future issues of a "non-mailable" publication could be barred, the Postmaster General argued that because past violations had resulted in the newspaper's forfeiting its second-class mailing privileges, the government could decline to renew them.[220] The majority held that the articles clearly violated the Espionage Act and that the Postmaster General could presume that future publications would also violate the Act. Brandeis wrote an elaborate dissent, arguing that the Postmaster General had no discretionary authority to exclude publications from the mails based on a guess as to their future content.[221]

Holmes confessed that, until he had read Brandeis' dissent, he had been inclined to support the majority's position on the ground that "if a publisher should announce in terms that he proposed to print treason and should demand a second-class rate it must be that the Postmaster General would have authority to refuse it."[222] But Holmes had become convinced that "[t]he question of the rate has nothing to do with the question whether the matter is mailable," and that the Postmaster General could not determine nonmailability in advance.[223] The only thing the Postmaster General was empowered to do under the statute, Holmes felt, was to deny second-class mail privileges, and after the publications were mailed "to refrain from forwarding the papers . . . and to return them to the senders."[224] He was not empowered to decide, on the basis of a publication's content, that it could not be carried in the mails.[225]

Holmes argued that the Postmaster General lacked authority to deny access to the mails in the future, absent explicit statutory language conveying that authority.[226] So long as the United States maintained a Post Office, he suggested, "the use of the mails is almost as much a part of free speech as the right to use our tongues, and it would take very strong language to convince me that Congress ever intended to give such a practically despotic power to any one man."[227] Otherwise, the power claimed for the Postmaster General "could be used to interfere with very sacred rights."[228] According to Holmes, denial of second-class mailing privileges for the future was "a serious attack upon liberties."[229]

Holmes' response to the free speech implications of *Burleson* starkly contrasted with his earlier treatment of arguably similar cases. Conceding that "[t]he United States may give up the Post Office when it sees fit,"[230] he rejected the government's argument that "a citizen uses the mail at second-class rates not as of right—but by virtue of a privilege or permission, the granting of which rests in the discretion of the Postmaster General."[231] In fact, Holmes spoke in his opinion of "rights" and "liberties" in the use of the mails.[232] Yet in *McAuliffe v. Mayor, etc., of New Bedford,* the Massachusetts case involving a policeman who was fired for engaging in partisan political activity, he had summarily dismissed a First Amendment claim that the government could not condition access to its employment on conformity to its rules where those rules included a ban on the expression of political sentiments. *Burleson* embodied an analogous claim—that the government could condition access to its mailing privileges, which it could withdraw at any point, on a user's not engaging in seditious speech. And yet Holmes, who had announced that there was no constitutional right to be a policeman, suggested in *Burleson* that there was a constitutional right to use the mails. His shift of position was consonant with the enhanced sensitivity to free speech issues that his *Abrams* dissent had demonstrated.[233]

After *Burleson,* in the 1922 Term, Holmes wrote opinions in a cluster of cases that at first appear to bear no relationship to his free speech jurisprudence, but on closer analysis embroider his newfound solicitude for speech rights. The cases tested the constitutionality of efforts by three states to restrict the teaching of foreign languages in their public schools. The first case, *Meyer v. Nebraska,*[234] involved a Nebraska statute forbidding the teaching of any language other than English before the eighth grade. *Bartels v. Iowa,* [235] decided at the same time, consolidated four challenges to similar statutes in Iowa, Ohio, and Nebraska that prohibited the teaching of any languages except English before the eighth grade or prohibited the teaching of German before the eighth grade. A majority of the Court, believing that the cases raised liberty issues under the Fourteenth Amendment's Due Process Clause, invalidated all the statutes. Justice McReynolds, writing for the Court, gave a list of the sorts of activities encompassed within the term "liberty":

> Without doubt, it denotes not merely freedom from bodily restraint but also the right of the individual to contract, to engage in any of the common occupations of life, to acquire useful knowledge, to marry, establish a home and bring up

children, to worship God according to the dictates of his own conscience, and generally to enjoy those privileges long recognized at common law as essential to the orderly pursuit of happiness by free men.[236]

McReynolds thus echoed the arguments advanced by late nineteenth-century commentators, who had assumed that "liberty" in the Due Process Clause of the Fourteenth Amendment theoretically extended well beyond the familiar contract and property contexts. By the 1922 Term, however, no case had yet held that First Amendment protections were incorporated within that Clause and applied against the states. Even McReynolds' catalogue of liberties, although analogous to the First Amendment protections, did not presage incorporation. His list did suggest, however, that, like earlier commentators, he viewed the logic of the Court's substantive due process decisions as eventually leading to judicial inclusion of speech within the "liberty" protected by the Fourteenth Amendment.

Having thus characterized the foreign languages cases, McReynolds proceeded through the substantive due process analysis that had underlain the "liberty of contract" disputes. That analysis rested on the proposition that "liberty may not be interfered with, under the guise of protecting the public interest, by legislative action which is arbitrary or without reasonable relation to some purpose within the competency of the State to effect."[237] McReynolds concluded that the statutes restricting the teaching of foreign languages bore no reasonable relation to any end within the state's competency.[238] One stated goal of the legislation, he noted, was fostering civic pride and a homogeneity of ideals.[239] But given that ancient languages were exempt from the prohibition in Nebraska, and that the German language was singled out in Ohio, he concluded that the means adopted in furtherance of that end were too intrusive.[240] McReynolds intimated that "[u]nfortunate experiences during the late war and aversion toward every characteristic of truculent adversaries" may have precipitated the statutes.[241] He dismissed out of hand the claim that the legislation was intended to "protect the child's health by limiting his mental activities," pointing out that proficiency in a foreign language was associated with early exposure to it and that no evidence had suggested such exposure had deleterious health effects.[242]

Holmes dissented in all the cases except those in which the German language alone had been singled out for prohibition. His dissent was based on the proposition that "[w]e all agree . . . that it is desirable that all the citizens of the United States should speak a common tongue, and therefore that the end aimed at by the statute is a lawful and proper one."[243] The logic of that proposition is not easy to follow. One might assume that a state has an interest in promoting the common language of the nation and offering that language, whether or not it offers other languages, in its public schools. But would that interest bear a reasonable and fair relationship to state requirements precluding its citizens from speaking other languages? The statutes at issue in *Meyer* and *Bartels* did not merely establish English as the common language of public education, they also prohibited the teaching of language courses that had previously been offered. Moreover, they excluded only some languages, exempting ancient languages or, in Ohio, all other languages except German. The states thus appeared less concerned with promoting a common tongue than with preventing their citizens from access to certain undesirable tongues.

Holmes' dissent, however, assumed that if the purpose of the statute was arguably reasonable, the means by which that purpose was implemented were also reasonable, except where one foreign language was singled out for prohibition. He asserted that

> [y]outh is the time when familiarity with a language is established and if there are sections in the State where a child would hear only Polish or French or German spoken at home I am not prepared to say that it is unreasonable to provide that in his early years he shall hear and speak only English at school.[244]

And if a statute prohibiting the teaching of all foreign languages was reasonable, Holmes argued,

> it is not an undue restriction of the liberty either of teacher or scholar. No one would doubt that a teacher might be forbidden to teach many things, and the only criterion of his liberty under the Constitution that I can think of is "whether, considering the end in view, the statute passes the bounds of reason and assumes the character of a merely arbitrary fiat."[245]

These comments were striking, especially considering the time when Holmes wrote them. *Meyer* and *Bartels* were decided three terms after his *Abrams* dissent, but Holmes did not treat the claim that the statutes restricted "the liberty either of teacher or scholar" as precipitating an inquiry comparable to that which he urged in speech cases. Instead he treated the question as comparable to the "liberty of contract" dispute, where he asked only that legislation purportedly infringing on economic liberties be rational and not arbitrary. The language cases did not cause Holmes to scrutinize the legislation in an effort to detect "[p]ersecution for the expression of opinions."[246]

There are two possible explanations for Holmes' failure to subject the language cases to his new calculus on speech issues. First, he may not have seen them as primarily raising speech issues, just as late nineteenth-century commentators had subsumed the right to advocate the tactic of striking in labor disputes in the economic right to strike. Teaching a foreign language, in this vein, could have been regarded as an occupation rather than as a form of expression. This explanation ignores, however, Holmes' belief that the liberty purportedly being restricted by the statutes was that of a "teacher or scholar." By "scholars" Holmes must have meant students in the public schools who sought access to information about the languages of other nations, perhaps to improve their ability to participate in world affairs. This interest in access to information seems closely linked to the interest in access to diverse views which Holmes had identified as part of the "search for truth' in *Abrams*. It is unlikely, therefore, that he failed to recognize the free speech issues embedded in the language cases, especially in light of his increased sensitivity to those issues in other cases after *Abrams*.

A second, more likely, explanation is that the language cases made Holmes focus on protecting speech as a component of liberty, rather than focusing on a democracy's reliance upon speech in the search for truth. By interpreting the word "liberty" in the Fourteenth Amendment to include noneconomic as well as economic activities, McReynolds' opinion evoked the jurisprudence of liberty of contract.

Holmes responded as he invariably did when he believed a state's "experiment" was being subjected to an unjustifiable judicial attack based on a vague interpretation of "due process."[247] Although it would have been easy, and logical, to view the cases simply in terms of the teachers' rights to speak on subjects in which they were proficient, and the correlative rights of students to listen to that speech, Holmes chose to put the "liberty . . . of teacher or scholar"[248] into the "liberty of contract" context.

That Holmes, despite his language in *Abrams,* had not fully freed "speech" from the "liberty of contract" analysis is suggested by a comment he made to Laski in April 1923 before the *Meyer* and *Bartels* cases were decided.[249] Discussing his dissent in the case of *Adkins v. Children's Hospital,* where the majority had relied on "liberty of contract," Holmes added, "I am curious to see what the enthusiasts for liberty of contract will say with regard to liberty of speech under a State law punishing advocating the overthrow of government—by violence. The case was argued this week."[250] The case was *Gitlow v. New York,*[251] which was to be reargued and not decided until 1925; it was to produce one of Holmes' major free speech opinions.

Holmes plainly thought that "liberty of speech" would confound those who broadly applied "liberty of contract" since a comparable analysis might protect advocacy of subvesive activity. The comment to Laski presupposed that "liberty of speech" remained a gloss on the Fourteenth Amendment's Due Process Clause, although its incorporation of First Amendment rights was still unsettled in 1923. The *Gitlow* case was in fact to result in the First Amendment being incorporated in the Fourteenth; Holmes' response to the incorporation issue was particularly revealing.

Incorporation, however, was not the major issue that *Gitlow* raised for Holmes. By the time *Gitlow* was decided it had become apparent that he and other adherents of the "clear and present danger" principle faced a dilemma. That test had been designed to deal with situations in which a legislature had identified a proscribed end (e.g., obstructing the war effort), and the issue was whether a particular expresion related closely enough to that end. In *Gitlow,* however, the statute had criminalized the form of expression itself. A 1902 New York statute had provided criminal penalties for those who advocated "that organized government should be overthrown by force, or violence or any unlawful means."[252] The statute, originally passed in response to the emergence of anarchism, was applied against the publisher of *The Left Wing Manifesto,* a document that paraphrased *The Communist Manifesto,* calling for class struggle and "revolutionary mass action" toward the "annihilation of the parliamentary state."[253] The only specific action the *Manifesto* urged, however, was a series of mass political strikes.[254] The *Gitlow* majority, holding the statute constitutional, conceded that "[t]here was no evidence of any effect resulting from the publication and circulation of the Manifesto."[255] That lack of evidence, however, was arguably immaterial because the New York legislature, rather than proscribing action, had outlawed advocacy itself.

Writing for the Court, Justice Edward Sanford held that given the language of the statute, the "clear and present danger" test did not apply, and therefore the absence of any causal connection between the defendant's publication and any illegal activity did not matter.

It is clear that the question in such cases is entirely different from that involved in those cases where the statute merely prohibits certain acts involving the danger of substantive evil, without any reference to language itself . . . . [In the latter cases the "clear and present danger" test of *Schenck* governs]. . . . [That test] was manifestly intended . . . to apply only in [the latter] cases, and has no application to those like the present, where the legislative body itself has previously determined the danger of substantive evil arising from utterances of a specified character.[256]

Sanford's analysis assumed that the only question for the Court was whether *The Left Wing Manifesto* had advocated the doctrine "that organized government should be overthrown by force, or violence or any unlawful means." He concluded that it had, conceding that "[t]he statute does not penalize the utterance or publication of abstract 'doctrine' or academic discussion having no quality of incitement to any concrete action."[257] *The Left Wing Manifesto,* however, "advocates and urges in fervent language mass action which shall progressively foment industrial disturbances and through political mass strikes and revolutionary mass action overthrow and destroy organized parliamentary government."[258] It was immaterial to the majority that no effect had followed from the distribution of the *Manifesto* or that its authors had given no time frame for the "revolutionary mass overthrow" they urged.

Holmes, joined by Brandeis, dissented in *Gitlow.* The majority had summarily concluded that "[f]or present purposes we may and do assume that freedom of speech and of the press . . . are among the fundamental personal rights and 'liberties' protected by the Due Process Clause of the Fourteenth Amendment from impairment by the States."[259] Holmes, perhaps mindful that he had addressed and not resolved the incorporation issue in *Patterson v. Colorado,* agreed. "The general principle of free speech," he argued, "must be taken to be included in the Fourteenth Amendment, in view of the scope that has been given to the word 'liberty' as there used."[260] This echoed the comment he had made to Laski in the 1923 letter, when *Gitlow* was first argued, equating liberty of speech and liberty of contract. Holmes' point was that the Court's own extensions of the liberty language in the Fourteenth Amendment to protect rights in the economic arena would make it anomalous not to make the same extension where free speech was involved.

Holmes, however, had protested against the extensions of economic liberties and, in the foreign language cases, had resisted treating liberty of speech as bearing any more constitutional weight than liberty of contract. He thus added a cryptic sentence to the discussion of incorporation in his dissent. "[P]erhaps," he said, the application of the First Amendment against the states "may be accepted with a somewhat larger latitude of interpretation than is allowed to Congress by the sweeping language that governs or ought to govern the laws of the United States."[261]

Parsing that sentence and the one following it reveals the idiosyncratic frame of reference that Holmes had come to adopt in free speech cases. In the first sentence, he expressed a reluctance to endorse incorporation if it were premised on a substantive reading of liberty that might, in the guise of protection for speech, reinforce an expansive reading of economic liberties. Thus, according to Holmes, incorporation meant allowing "a somewhat larger latitude" to restrict speech rights in order to preserve a comparable latitude to restrict economic rights. On the other hand, he seemed eager to restate his new view of the First Amendment as "sweeping language" severely restricting Congress' powers, the view he had articulated in *Abrams* and, as his "ought to govern" language indicated, the court as a whole had nor endorsed.

The next sentence, however, muddied things considerably. Holmes said "[i]f I am right, then I think that the criterion sanctioned by the full Court in *Schenck* applies" and quoted the "clear and present danger" formula.[262] The relationship between the sentences is hard to fathom. "If I am right" would seem to refer to Holmes' discussion of the incorporation of the First Amendment against the states, the only issue he had thus far discussed in his *Gitlow* dissent. It could have conceivably referred, more particularly, to his view that free speech restrictions on the states ought perhaps to be less severe than those on the federal government. But in either case the application of "clear and present danger" to *Gitlow* seemed to come out of the blue. If the states had more latitude to restrict speech than the federal government, judicial tests developed in cases in which Congress had restricted speech might not necessarily be applicable. On the other hand, if *Schenck* controlled, and the "clear and present danger" test was a rule of causation, evaluating the closeness of the connection between advocacy and illegal acts, causation would seem to have been satisfied in those instances in which a legislature had outlawed advocacy itself. It was only if "clear and present danger" in its reformulated version—the version that Holmes insisted had been departed from in *Abrams* and *Schaefer*—was the correct test, that the legislative action in *Gitlow* deserved searching scrutiny. But if so, the same level of judicial scrutiny obtained in state and federal speech cases. Holmes' successive comments, then, appeared to contradict one another.

Nonetheless, Holmes proceeded as if the "clear and present danger" test applied, and concluded that "it is manifest that there was no present danger of an attempt to overthrow the government by force on the part of the admittedly small minority who shared the defendant's views."[263] If the publication of the *Manifesto* had been claimed to have been "an attempt to induce an uprising against government at once and not at some indefinite time in the future," Holmes argued, "it would have presented a different question."[264] That would have been a situation "with which the law might deal," he surmised, "subject to the doubt whether there was any danger that the publication could produce any result, or in other words, whether it was not futile and too remote from possible consequences."[265]

After *Abrams,* Holmes had come to see the "clear and present danger" test as a substantive evaluation of the seriousness of any threat posed by the speech at issue, even though he couched that inquiry in the "remoteness" language of causation. A speech, under this view, could pose no "clear and present danger," even if it was quite specific in its aims, if its own ineptitude or other circumstances suggested that it would not be taken seriously. A six year old's exhortation to other children of the same age to "take up arms against the President right now!" might under that analysis not qualify as a "clear and present danger." "Eloquence may set fire to reason," Holmes said, "[b]ut whatever may be thought of the redundant discourse before us it had no chance of starting a present conflagration."[266]

Intertwined with this familiar language, however, was some that, if taken seriously, suggested that Holmes was reaching yet another stage in his consideration of speech issues, one that might move him to adopt an ultralibertarian view of speech rights. The majority in *Gitlow,* after quoting passages from the *Manifesto,* had stated, "[t]his is not the expression of philosophical abstraction . . . it is the language of direct incitement."[267] Holmes responded:

> It is said that this manifesto was more than a theory, that it was an incitement. Every idea is an incitement. It offers itself for belief and if believed it is acted on unless some other belief outweighs it or some failure of energy stifles the movement at its birth. The only difference between the expression of an opinion and an incitement in the narrower sense is the speaker's enthusiasm for the result.[268]

Although this passage is often quoted, its implications for First Amendment analysis remain obscure. Given Holmes' stated position that normative ideas become "incitements" or "opinions" if presented with "enthusiasm," and that the "ultimate good" is best served by "free trade in ideas," "incitements" should be allowed to "offer [themselves] for belief" and, if accepted, for action. Statements urging others to overthrow the government at the conclusion of the speaker's remarks should receive their chance to come into the market. In breaking down distinctions between ideas, opinions, and incitements, Holmes appeared to adopt an ultralibertarian view of speech.

This interpretation is supported by another famous sentence in his dissent. "If in the long run," he wrote, "the beliefs expressed in proletarian dictatorship are destined to be accepted by the dominant forces of the community, the only meaning of free speech is that they should be given their chance and have their way."[269]

Although at first glance the sentence appears to be another version of Holmes' "free trade in ideas" approach, it contains some ambiguities. His language about "the dominant forces of the community" and his statement that "the only meaning of free speech" is that any stated belief should "be given [its] chance" suggest that he regarded any restrictions on free speech as ultimately fruitless. If the choices of the dominant forces of a community are the mechanism by which ideas become accepted, certain ideas will "have their way" regardless of their content. In choosing some of these ideas, however, the dominant forces are implicitly rejecting other ideas; indeed, those forces might even decide to bar some ideas from the marketplace altogether. Thus Holmes seems both to be advancing a view of speech in which the marketplace of ideas determines which speech is favored and which is not, and to be endorsing a positivist theory of the relationship between speech and the "dominant forces" of a community. It is not clear, from his language in *Gitlow,* whether the "only meaning of free speech" equates to the opportunity for all ideas to have a chance to "have their way" or means merely the prevailing attitudes of "the dominant forces of the community."

The dizzyingly contradictory implications of these several sentences suggest the risk inherent in assuming that Holmes' striking phrases express a developed ideology. Holmes the judge was often consumed by the sheer attraction of language itself. Phrases like "every idea is an incitement" and "the only meaning of free speech" exemplified his style. Although arresting and memorable, they often collapse as analytical guidelines.

Moreover, Holmes could not have expected that his unqualified language was establishing black-letter rules, because he believed all legal questions to be matters of degree. He was thus unlikely, despite having said that every idea is an incitement, to abandon the distinction between ideas that amounted to incitements and those that did not. Accordingly, Holmes was comfortable with his "clear and present danger" formula because such formulas, being tests of degree, invited him to distinguish between incitements and other types of speech. Indeed, the phrase "every idea is an incitement" might have been his way of making it clear to Learned Hand and his other young friends that he was not prepared to jettison the "clear and present danger" test for Hand's incitement test in *Masses Publishing Co. v. Pattern*.[270] In short, Holmes' *Gitlow* dissent is more an example of his distinctive literary style than an attempt to develop a new First Amendment jurisprudence.

Even if *Gitlow* did not signify a more libertarian trend in Holmes' views of speech, abundant evidence reveals his commitment, in the last years of his career, to a point of view irreconcilable with his Espionage Act opinions. The best example comes not from *Gitlow* but rather from Holmes' joining a series of cases, between 1925 and the end of his tenure, protecting free speech claims under a variety of theories, some more protectionist than "clear and present danger." These included Brandeis' concurrence in *Whitney v. California*,[271] which attacked the *Gitlow* approach by arguing that the First Amendment did not permit deference to legislatures on the evil of language itself, and by seeking to link prohibition of speech directly to incitements;[272] the decision in *Stomberg v. California*,[273] which declared a California statute comparable to the one sustained in *Gitlow* unconstitutional as applied to the display of a red flag at a political demonstration; and the decision in *Near v. Minnesota ex rel. Olson*,[274] which invalidated as a prior restraint a Minnesota statute that permitted the enjoining of "malicious, scandalous, or defamatory" publications. In only one free speech case after *Abrams* did Holmes fail to adopt a position in support of speech rights.[275] Replacing his thoughts about speech as simply "another act you don't like" were remarks like his 1925 aside (to Laski) that "I let out a page of slack on the right of an ass to drool about proletarian dictatorship. . . . Free speech means to most people, you may say anything that I don't think shocking."[276]

Perhaps the best evidence of Holmes' consciousness toward free speech issues in the last years of his tenure on the Court comes from his dissent in *United States v. Schwimmer*,[277] written two months after his eighty-eighth birthday. Rosika Schwimmer, a forty-nine-year-old Hungarian citizen, was a prominent pacifist who, in 1915, when she was still living in Hungary, persuaded Henry Ford to send a peace ship to Europe to, as she put it, "[bring] the boys out of the trenches by Christmas."[278] She had come to the United States in 1921 to visit and lecture, and had subsequently become a resident of Illinois.

In November 1921, she declared her intention to become a U.S. citizen and in September 1926 filed a petition for naturalization. As part of the naturalization process, she was given a "preliminary form" that required applicants to respond to various questions. Question 22 asked whether an applicant for citizenship was "willing to take up arms in defense of this country," and she answered in the negative.[279]

When Schwimmer subsequently filed a petition for naturalization in the District Court of the Northern District of Illinois, her petition was denied on the grounds that she was "unable . . . to take the prescribed oath of allegiance" and was, therefore, "not attached to the principles of the Constitution of the United States" nor "well disposed to the good order and happiness of the same."[280] The Court of Appeals for the Sixth Circuit reversed, finding that since Schwimmer was a woman and not eligible for military service, her refusal to bear arms was not any direct threat to the security of the nation.[281] The Supreme Court granted certiorari and heard the case in April 1929.[282]

A majority of the Court, through Justice Pierce Butler, reversed, concluding that "[w]hatever tends to lessen the willingness of citizens to discharge their duty to bear arms detracts from the strength and safety of the Government."[283] Therefore, "opinions and beliefs" as well as "behavior" were appropriate subjects of inquiry for the naturalization authorities.[284] Indeed, opinions and beliefs, in Butler's view, were "of vital importance, for if all or a large number of citizens oppose [the] defense [of the United States] the 'good order and happiness' of the United States can not long endure."[285]

Holmes dissented, joined by Brandeis, and converted the case from a routine naturalization case into a free speech case.[286] A portion of his opinion is worth quoting at some length:

> The views referred to are an extreme opinion in favor of pacifism and a statement that she would not bear arms to defend the Constitution. So far as the adequacy of her oath is concerned I hardly can see how it is affected by the statement, inasmuch as she is a woman over fifty years of age, and would not be allowed to bear arms if she wanted to. . . . Surely it cannot show lack of attachment to the principles of the Constitution that she thinks it can be improved. I suppose that most intelligent people think that it might be. . . . To touch a more burning question, only a judge mad with partisanship would exclude [an applicant for citizenship] because the applicant thought that the Eighteenth Amendment should be repealed.
>
> Of course the fear is that if a war came the applicant would exert activities such as were dealt with in *Schenck v. United States*. But that seems to me unfounded. Her position and motives are wholly different from those of Schenck. She is an optimist and states in strong and, I do not doubt, sincere words her belief that war will disappear and that the impending destiny of mankind is to unite in peaceful leagues. I do not share that optimism nor do I think that a philosophic view of the world would regard war as absurd. But most people who have known it regard it with horror, as a last resort, and . . . would welcome any practicable combination that would increase the power on the side of peace. . . . Some of her answers might excite popular prejudice, but if there is any principle of the Constitution that more imperatively calls for attachment than any other it is the principle of free thought—not free thought for those who agree with us but freedom for the thought that we hate. I think

that we should adhere to that principle with regard to admission into, as well as to life within this country.[287]

Before analyzing the free speech dimensions of Holmes' opinion, it is worth noting that the procedural posture of the *Schwimmer* case arguably mooted any First Amendment arguments. Schwimmer had been asked about her willingness to take up arms in defense of the country, and had given an answer that would have been grounds for a summary denial of citizenship except for the fact that as a forty-nine year-old woman she was ineligible for military service. The issue in *Schwimmer* was not whether Congress was infringing on First Amendment rights by asking the question and acting summarily if an applicant gave the "wrong" answer. No one seriously challenged Congress' power to condition American citizenship on the avowal of certain beliefs; aliens seeking to be naturalized did not possess First Amendment rights. Rather, the question was whether the United States could deny Schwimmer citizenship based solely on her disinclination to perform an act she would not likely ever be asked to perform.

Holmes, however, stating that "[i]t is agreed that [Schwimmer] is qualified for citizenship except so far as the views" she had set forth,[288] proceeded to analyze those views as in an ordinary First Amendment case. He found irrelevant Schwimmer's refusal to bear arms, because she was ineligible to do so anyway. He then trivialized her refusal to "defend the Constitution" as a mere belief that the Constitution can be improved—a belief that he suspected was shared by "most intelligent people."[289] Holmes further suggested that Schwimmer's views on the Constitution and war were akin to the belief that Prohibition should be repealed, and "only a judge mad with partisanship" would exclude an applicant who expressed the latter views.[290]

Holmes thus considered Schwimmer's views mild and inconsequential, like the leaflets he had described as "poor and puny anonymities" in *Abrams v. United States. Schwimmer,* he argued, might be thought similar to *Schenck* in that if war broke out Schwimmer might commit acts like those Holmes had found punishable in *Schenck*. He concluded, however, that Schwimmer was in a different "position" and had different "motives" than Schenck.[291] Schwimmer was a sincere pacifist; Schenck, by implication, a dangerous subversive. While Holmes himself did not share the optimism of pacifists,[292] nor did he think that the idea of war was philosophically absurd, he, like "most people who have known" war, regarded it with "horror, as a last resort . . . and would welcome any practical combination that would increase the power on the side of peace."[293]

After trivializing the dangerousness of Schwimmer's views, Holmes confronted the fact that some of her answers to questions about war and the obligations of citizenship "might excite popular prejudice."[294] It was this very sort of answer, Holmes suggested, that was protected by the First Amendment. The constitutional "principle of free thought" that "more imperatively calls for attachment than any other," was designed to ensure "freedom for the thought that we hate."[295] That principle should cover not only "life within this country" but proceedings where people sought citizenship.[296]

In light of Holmes' earlier decisions as a Supreme Court Justice, this language is rather extraordinary. First, it can be read to signify an abandonment of the "clear and present danger" test. While continuing to accept *Schenck* and seeking to distinguish it on the basis of the respective defendants' "position and motives," Holmes failed to use any "clear and present danger" language. Instead, he suggested that the "principle of free thought," including "freedom for the thought that we hate," was now a more significant constitutional principle than any other, which should apply to aliens—prospective citizens—who should not be punished for expressing their views even if those views were "hateful" to most Americans.

Second, this language suggests Holmes' abandonment, in free speech cases, of a positivist view of sovereignty. In the past, Holmes had been remarkably deferential to the power of the United States to treat aliens as lacking constitutional rights. Indeed, he had been the principal early-twentieth-century Supreme Court proponent of an ultrapositivist view of sovereignty and a starkly restrictionist view of the rights of those who sought to enter or to remain in the United States.[297] In contrast, Holmes' dissent not only suggested that a constitutional principle of free thought applied to naturalization proceedings, it stated flatly that the "principle of free thought" was of greater constitutional significance than "any other."

Holmes' personal correspondence about the *Schwimmer* case further illustrates the extent to which his view of free speech issues had become more libertarian. By the time of the *Schwimmer* decision, Holmes' life was centered around his work and his correspondence, and he was writing freely to intimates about his cases. In September 1928, he responded to a comment from Pollock criticizing "armchair pacifists"[298] with sentiments strikingly similar to those found in his *Schwimmer* dissent. "I agree with your condemnation of armchair pacifists," he wrote Pollock, "on the general ground that until the world has gotten farther along war not only is not absurd but is inevitable and rational." He added, however, that "I don't pass moral judgments."[299] And in June 1929, in response to a letter from Laski declaring the majority opinion in *Schwimmer* to be "an iniquitous injustice,"[300] Holmes said that he thought the opinion was affected by "a recollection of the anti-draft talk during the late war" and was "made easier by [Schwimmer's] somewhat flamboyant declaration that she was an atheist," which he had "alluded to . . . discreetly without mentioning" in his dissent.[301]

In January 1930, Holmes received a letter from Rosika Schwimmer. She expressed her "deep-felt gratitude" at his dissent, even "[a]t the risk of violating legal etiquette."[302] He responded, "You are too intelligent to need explanation of the saying that you must never thank a judge."[303] Holmes described a case as "simply a problem to be solved" and stated that if a judge's decision "was of a kind to deserve thanks, he would not be doing his duty."[304] Nonetheless he confessed that he was "gratified by [Schwimmer's] more than kind expression,"[305] and began a correspondence with Schwimmer that lasted until 1934, a year before his death.

It is not altogether surprising that Holmes, after admonishing Rosika Schwimmer for writing him, would then write her back and begin a correspondence friendship. She was thirty-six years younger than he, about the same age as Frankfurter, Laski, Chafee, and Learned Hand. Holmes had noted in his dissent that Schwimmer "seem[ed] to be . . . of superior character and intelligence."[306] Though he thought her pacifism was naive, he did not hold the same view of her atheism.[307] He could have seen her as part of the constituency of his old age: the progressive intelligentsia who had come to appreciate him and might pass on his contributions to posterity. In his correspondence friendships with this circle, Holmes grew comfortable expressing his instinctive affinity for the communicative arts, activities to which he had devoted his life. Just as he allocated an ever-increasing time in his later life to reading and writing letters, he devoted more time to taking seriously "the principle of freedom of thought." Holmes' correspondence with Schwimmer is further evidence both of the evolution in Holmes' thinking about speech issues and of his continued efforts to disseminate his ideas to a younger generation of intellectuals.

~

Holmes' opinions from *Schenck* through *Schwimmer* demonstrate that while the transformation of his ideas on free speech is readily discernible, the expression of that transformation in the form of consistent legal doctrine is not. Although on the surface Holmes appeared to continue to endorse the "clear and present danger" test as the best means for protecting speech rights, he made very little use of it in later opinions. He employed the formula as an analytical device only once in his later speech cases, the *Gitlow* dissent, which also appeared to endorse a variety of additional tests.

In other opinions written after *Abrams* Holmes inexplicably failed to apply the "clear and present danger" test at all. *Gilbert v. Minnesota*,[308] a 1920 case, involved a speaker convicted for suggesting that the practice of conscripting soldiers in wartime be put to a popular vote. It is hard to see how that comment could have resulted in a "clear and present danger" to the state under Holmes' *Abrams* reformulation.[309] Gilbert's conviction seemed harder to justify than Gitlow's, since Gitlow had explicitly called for class action having as its objective "the conquest by the proletariat of the power of the state."[310] Holmes nonetheless permitted Gilbert's conviction to stand, while insisting that the "clear and present danger" test called for a reversal of Gitlow's conviction.

Even when Holmes went to great lengths to argue for the protection of speech rights, as in the *Schwimmer* dissent, he did not apply the "clear and present danger" test. He merely stated that one ground for denying citizenship was "the fear . . . that if a war came the applicant would exert activities such as were dealt with in *Schenck v. United States*."[311] But if by mentioning *Schenck* he meant to suggest that *Schwimmer* was a "clear and present danger" case, and that Rosika Schwimmer's refusal to bear arms in the defense of the United States in some indefinite time in the future could hardly constitute a "clear and present danger," he did not make that suggestion clear. He only said that Schwimmer's "position" and "motives" were "wholly different" from those of the defendant in *Schenck* and then went on to discuss the "optimistic" and "sincere" quality of Schwimmer's pacifism.[312]

It would, of course, have been hazardous for Holmes to state openly that the "clear and present danger" standard actually governed *Schwimmer*, or even that the First Amendment was relevant to the case. Holmes did say, however, that the "principle of free thought" should pertain to "admission into, as well as to life within this country."[313] In that context his citation of *Schenck*, and his effort to distinguish the defendants in *Schwimmer* and in *Schenck*, seems doctrinally curious. It was not clear whether he was suggesting that in the future the "clear and present danger" test he had outlined in *Abrams* should be applied to naturalization proceedings, or simply that *Schenck, Abrams,* and *Schwimmer* were all cases in which the principle of "protection for the thought we hate" was implicated. In sum, all that one can conclude from a close analysis of Holmes' later free speech opinions is that he was regularly conscious of the free speech implications of cases and persistently solicitous of free speech claims. Even that conclusion needs to take into account *Gilbert* and the foreign language cases, in which he exhibited no solicitude for the free speech claim or no consciousness that there even was one. As for the "clear and present danger" test as a doctrinal formulation, Holmes might have wanted to give the impression that he continued to adhere to it, but he very rarely used it and in many instances did not even mention it.

~

This exercise in exploring Holmes' free speech opinions yields several conclusions. First, Holmes' 1929 sensitivity to the free speech issues had progressed logarithmically from *McAuliffe* and *Davis* in the 1890s, *Fox v. Washington* in 1915, and even from *Schenck* and the other Espionage Act cases in the spring of 1919. By the time of *Gitlow* and *Schwimmer,* Holmes had developed from a judge for whom speech issues seemed incidental or trivial or secondary to common law issues into one who accorded free speech central constitutional importance.

The evidence suggests that Holmes' shift resulted primarily from his personal experiences and relationships. Events in his personal life and his own unfulfilled career expectations made him more receptive to the ideas of Laski, Frankfurter, Hand, Chafee, and the circle of commentators who wrote in *The New Republic* during and immediately after World War I. The interest of those intellectuals in reframing free speech jurisprudence easily dovetailed with Holmes' interest in disassociating free speech from the jurisprudential underpinnings of "liberty of contract." When one undertakes a close comparison of Holmes' language in his *Schenck* and *Abrams* opinions, and places those opinions in the context of his intellectual friendships at the time, it is apparent that Holmes' exchange of views with younger intellectuals influenced him to abandon the analogy between the free speech cases and criminal-attempt cases and to reconfigure free speech as a broader principle. This reconfiguration led him to affirm the principle of "freedom for the thought we hate."

Holmes' change, however, was not philosophically or analytically consistent. He had attempted two general justifications for the protection of free speech: his statement in *Abrams* that the "theory of our Constitution" was that "the best test of truth is the power of the thought to get itself accepted in the competition of the market"[314] and his statement in *Schwimmer* that "if there is any principle of the Constitution that more imperatively calls for attachment than any other it is the principle of free thought—not free thought for those who agree with us but freedom for the thought that we hate."[315] These were inconsistent justifications. The first looked to majoritarian sovereignty in a democracy. Ideas that survived were ideas that exhibited power in "the marketplace of ideas," a marketplace driven by majoritarian tastes and sentiments. In protecting "truth" by relying on the "competition" of the marketplace, Holmes, as usual, was deferring to majorities.

The second justification, however, was openly countermajoritarian. The "freedom of thought" identified as worthy of protection in *Schwimmer* was freedom for unpopular thought, "the thought we hate." The speech receiving constitutional protection was speech that would *not* survive in the "marketplace of ideas" because it was deeply offensive to a majority. If offensive ideas were to be let into the market, so that they might have a chance to gain stature in the future, the judge, in the guise of interpretating the Constitution, would have to be regulating the market, or, in political terms, intervening against the wishes of a majority. Holmes never explained how the two philosophical justifications could be reconciled. He never related the marketplace theory, "the theory of our Constitution," to constitutional protection for the "thought we hate."

Moreover, although Holmes had said in *Schenck* that the "clear and present danger" test determined the limits of protection for speech "in every case," he failed to apply that test consistently after *Schenck*. In *Abrams* he reformulated the test, and in some later cases, such as *Schwimmer*, he went beyond the *Abrams* modification. In other cases, such as *Gilbert*, he failed to invoke the test or even to recognize the free speech issues at all. This failure is evidence that perhaps Holmes did not intend it as a doctrinal guideline at all. His recasting of the test in *Abrams* might simply have been an attempt to create an appearance of consistency between his dissent in *Abrams* and the earlier version of the test that he had formulated in *Schenck*.

One thus comes to see that Holmes' free speech opinions were not meant as conventional doctrinal formulations, providing guidance for the consistent interpretation of constitutional provisions. They were instead supposed to serve as vehicles for conveying Holmes' broader philosophical views to the world, vehicles by which Holmes implicitly sought to change the frame of reference within which free speech issues were viewed, to modernize First Amendment theory. They were also meant as literary exercises. Two letters Holmes wrote to contemporaries before World War I capture the essence of his sensibilities as a judge. In the first, written in 1911 to Lewis Einstein, Holmes said that

> The point that I have in view is continually to deepen and broaden the channels for the great forces that lie behind every detail. After a man has a working knowledge of his job it is less important to read the late decisions of other Courts, which generally are but the small change of thought than to let in as much knowledge as one can of what ultimately determines those decisions; philosophy, sociology, economics, and the like. I am not an expert in those matters; but I open as many windows on them as I can, and fondly hope that in some way the habit of trying to see the particular in the light of the universal will tell in one's writing.[316]

In the second, written to Canon Patrick Sheehan a year later, Holmes said,

> The thing I have wanted to do [as a judge] has been to put as many new ideas into the law as I can, to show how particular solutions involve general theory, and to do it with style.[317]

These excerpts reveal Holmes' implicit sense of priorities as he wrote opinions.

Philosophical inquiry, originality, and literary expression constituted the essence of judging. Conventional analytic consistency was comparatively unimportant.

Holmes expressed his sensitivity to free speech issues in a way consistent with the priorities he expressed to Einstein and Sheehan. When he first became attracted to the "new idea" that speech meant more than protection from prior restraints, he sought to express the limits of that protection in his *Schenck* dictum, placing the facts of *Schenck* in the universal language of "clear and present danger"—language that seemed at that time to capture for him the close connection between subversive speech and crime. As he rethought speech issues after *Schenck* in response to criticism he received from people whose opinions he valued, he sought to "open as many windows" as he could on the philosophical basis of protection for speech. One window that appeared promising was the reformulated basis of protection for speech as part of the "search for truth" in a democratic society that valued public discussion, and Holmes again sought to express that basis as a universal proposition embedded in the particular facts of *Abrams*.

The idea of the search for truth, however, did not fully justify the protection of speech rights. Though the search for truth was to take place in a competitive marketplace, that marketplace, in a democracy, was not completely free because it was controlled by majoritarian preferences. Thus, "getting accepted" meant, in some sense, "being popular"; if truth was to be equated with popularity a majority might choose to treat unpopular speech as untrue and suppress it. That was the problem in *Gitlow* and, in an abstract fashion, in *Schwimmer*. In both cases, representatives of a majority had deemed communism or pacifism unacceptable doctrines. Holmes responded by trying yet another universal formulation: the idea that the "only meaning of free speech" was that unacceptable doctrines be presumptively tolerated; that the Constitution embodied the principle of freedom for the thought that we hate. In both *Abrams* and *Schwimmer* his interest had been in the derivation of the formulation through philosophical inquiry, and the novel and original fashion in which the formulation was expressed. Others could wrestle with the analytical details.

Holmes' approach to free speech cases thus reveals, perhaps more clearly than any other subject matter area, his distinctive sensibility as a judge and his ambivalence about the professional role he occupied. Though Holmes had little interest in the orthodox dimensions of his own profession's work product—the "small change of thought" manifested by "the late decisions of other Courts"—he wanted to be recognized, and celebrated, as a judge. Holmes often treated judging as a kind of game, an exercise in which he tried to find "a form of words" to justify a result, as he would try to find fresh and arresting language to express a thought in a letter. At the same time, however, the game was a serious one for Holmes because he was also greatly interested in having his talents widely appreciated in the form of an exalted judicial reputation. In the sentence following his comment on doing his work with "style" in the 1912 letter to Sheehan, he had written, "I should like to be admitted to be the greatest jurist in the world."[318]

When one looks over the progression of Holmes' free speech jurisprudence, one cannot find a coherent theoretical pattern; one cannot fully square his stance with positivist premises or with conventional theories of judicial deference to the will of the majority. At times Holmes seemed to exhibit a minimalist view of speech, as "another act" majorities may not like; at other times he seemed to inflate protection for speech to the most important and imperative of constitutional principles. His philosophical conception of speech evolved through stages that initially seem to be the products of his intuitive responses and his personal and professional goals. His attitude toward First Amendment issues conflicts with some of his other jurisprudential positions. Liberty of contract, for example, was a dangerous illusion, an invitation to judicial overreaching; yet protection for the principle of "freedom for the thought that we hate" was at the core of the Constitution. When one examines Holmes' free speech opinions from the perspectives of doctrine and theory, one finds inconsistencies and contradictions at every turn.

Those opinions, however, were the products of a writer whose principal concern was to open "windows" on a philosophical issue, to see "the particular in the light of the universal." They thus appear less as doctrinal than as metaphorical statements. They aim not to achieve logical consistency but to offer "forms of words" that convey the universal dimensions of free speech theory. Whatever the limitations of "clear and present danger," "the search for truth," and "freedom for the thought that we hate" as analytical guides, they vividly encapsulate recurrent concerns and values, and they remind us that Holmes the writer has glimpsed the universal in the particular. In his free speech opinions Holmes did precisely what he told Canon Sheehan he wanted to do: to put new ideas into the law, to show how particular "solutions" to legal issues involved general theory, and to communicate with style.

Holmes the writer, however, was also Holmes the judge, who made decisions affecting lives, who tried to square his opinions with previous judicial utterances, and who operated within the confines of existing precedent. In his free speech opinions, as in his judicial work as a whole, the two personas conflicted regularly. Holmes felt the tension acutely, because while seeking to achieve the goals of a philosopher-jurist for whom writing was the means of communicating his insights, he also craved esteem as a judge. Since he assumed that doctrinal consistency and theoretical integrity were prerequisites for judicial eminence, he used "forms of words" to create an appearance of consistency and integrity. In the process his own instinct for glimpsing the universal in the particular betrayed him. Having invented a doctrinal formula in one free speech case, he saw its limitations in another and sought a principle even more universal.

Holmes thus became associated with the transformation of free speech theory in a fashion that served his goals as a jurist but collided with conventional expectations of the judge's role. Holmes' intellectual journey through free speech cases introduced four conceptions of speech in early twentieth-century American history: (1) speech as "another act we don't like," personified by the "criminal attempts" analogy; (2) speech as "the search for truth," personified by the reconfigured "clear and present danger" test; (3) speech as the vehicle by which "the dominant forces of the community" exercise their power; and (4) speech as "the principle of freedom for the thought that we hate." Each conception further complicated and refined the philosophical dilemma of protection for free speech in a modern constitutional democracy. Each conception carried with it a logically inadequate doctrinal formula for resolving speech issues. The cumulative inadequacy of the formulas served to demonstrate the complexity of the philosophical dilemma.

Holmes thus appears, in a history of his free speech opinions, as a lightning rod for cultural and ideological messages in the first thirty years of the twentieth century; as a jurist-philosopher, reflecting upon the intellectual conflicts of his time; and as a writer, communicating his reflections in vivid and memorable forms of words. His role appears less clearly, indeed almost incidentally, in his occupation as a judge. With Holmes' free speech opinions, as with his judicial work as a whole, what starts as a purported exercise in doctrinal analysis quickly disintegrates, revealing beneath the surface other language—language communicating the human, intellectual, and cultural dimensions of Holmes' opinions.

CHAPTER THIRTEEN

Aging

~

I N OCTOBER 1922, Holmes wrote Pollock from the Powhatan Hotel in Washington. He had had a prostate operation on July 12, and was slowly recovering. His weakness had resulted in his doctors recommending that an elevator be installed in his house to save him the labor of walking up a steep flight of stairs to his library and bedroom. The elevator had taken longer than expected, and the Holmeses were forced to stay at the Powhatan while awaiting its completion. Holmes' routine was upset, as he had to move his Court papers to the hotel and was not within easy reach of his books, and the opening of the Court's Term presented him with a series of new problems. "The total is," he told Pollock, "that I am distracted. It is the first moment of feeling like an old man."[1] Six months before Chief Justice William Howard Taft had written his brother that "Holmes . . . is suffering from asthma, and I suspect it is of a cardiac character. His breathing is stertorous at times, and he is evidently in great discomfort. . . . In my judgment, both Holmes and [Justice Joseph] McKenna ought to retire."[2]

These two letters were signals that Holmes, seemingly untouched by the passing of time, was mortal. He was to live thirteen more years, however, and the decline of his physical and mental capacities was astonishingly slight. In 1926, on the eve of Holmes' eighty-fifth birthday, Taft wrote his son Robert that Holmes was "full of good nature and comradeship, has the keenest sense of humor," and was "on the whole . . . an excellent member of the Court." Taft added that "[i]t is quite possible that [Holmes] may live to bury several of us," a prophecy that proved accurate in Taft's case.[3] Two days after Holmes was sent home from the hospital after his prostate operation he wrote Laski that "I am rather a feeble old man—who however is going in for 90 if he can get it,"[4] and not only did he reach ninety, he achieved that milestone still active as a Supreme Court Justice.

Aging, then, was a long, slow, and on the whole satisfactory process for Holmes. His last decade on the Court, we have seen, was arguably his most satisfying, certainly in terms of recognition and quite possibly for the significance and quality of his opinions. Several events described in this chapter, such as his health problems, Fanny Holmes' death, and his retirement from the Court, brought him sadness, and there were others, such as the death of Clare Castletown, that reminded him that as an octogenarian recluse he was no longer the dashing companion and bon vivant who had survived the Civil War and held forth in London society.

In growing old, however, as in many other aspects of life, Holmes seemed to have been favored in comparison to his fellow mortals. His last years were largely free from illness and discomfort, up to the very end of his life; he retained his capacity to perform intellectually challenging work almost to the close of his tenure on the Court; he had praise heaped upon him; he retained Fanny's companionship until his eighty-eighth year; his income and relative lack of familial responsibilities allowed him to live virtually as he chose. It is interesting, in the face of this largely benign older age, how fiercely Holmes battled to remain on the Court, to continue to meet his own high standards for self-performance, and, in the end, as his ninety-fourth birthday approached and his age made him incapable of writing letters, to stay alive. He had written, at least since 1886, of "be[ing] ready for the end."[5] At ninety he had said that death was plucking his ear and saying "live—I am coming."[6] But as death came upon him he fought it with all the passion in his competitive soul.

Health problems had not played a major part in Holmes' life since his Civil War wounds. In the 1890s he periodically wrote Clare Castletown of digestive problems, which were possibly a survival of the severe dysentary he had suffered in the war. In that correspondence he mentioned taking care about what he ate on shipboard or how much wine he drank, and he consulted a doctor before sailing to England in 1898. We have seen that he had an attack of shingles on returning from England that year, which was very likely brought about by stress, and there is no evidence the condition returned. He smoked an occasional cigar, limiting himself to one after dinner, and in general was considerably solicitous of his health, warning his younger correspondent friends, such as Laski, Frankfurter, and Lewis Einstein, not to "push [their] machine[s] too hard."[7] After moving to Washington he kept up a practice, initiated in Boston, of walking back and forth from his house to work, in this case a round trip of about three miles. There is no evidence he engaged in other forms of exercise save riding a bicycle in the 1890s, around his summer home at Beverly Farms.

Taft's reference to Holmes' asthma in the 1922 letter quoted earlier was evidence of a chronic complaint of Holmes', inherited from his father and also present in his brother Edward, which principally took the form of coughing fits in the evening, of which there were frequent mention in his correspondence.[8] While Holmes' asthma seems to have been relatively constant, especially as he grew older, there is no evidence it was debilitating. Taft reported in another place in the 1922 letter that Holmes "prides himself that he has never been away from court one meeting."[9] Holmes' prostate operation in the summer of 1922 was his first major health crisis in nearly sixty years.

The episode had been foreshadowed as the 1921 Term wound down. On May 3, 1922, he wrote Laski that he was "not feeling very well," still bothered by asthma and coughing at night, and that "if I went on long you would see that I am tired."[10] On May 12 he added that his health was "all right, bar a certain amount of coughing, which I expect has come to stay."[11] On May 21, as the end of the Term approached, he wrote Pollock that he was "pretty tired" after delivering his last opinions, and that he felt "a little languid."[12] On June 14, having arrived at Beverly Farms, he wrote Laski that "[w]e had a hard journey on to Boston—hot with the horrid Washington heat that gives you a fever—a jolting train—and [I] wish I could be quiet for a month."[13]

But Holmes had been invited to Amherst College on June 19 to receive an honorary degree. He had written Laski on May 12 that he had "provisionally accepted" that invitation, insisting on no speech, and on June 14 indicated that he was planning to "go . . . if I can," although "I dread it." On June 17, however, the date of his fiftieth wedding anniversary, "the lightning struck," as he told Pollock, and he was first bedridden and then hospitalized in the Corey Hill Hospital in Brookline, Massachusetts.[14] A letter he wrote to Lewis Einstein on June 19 spoke of his being "on my back, except the short instant of writing a letter or two," but attributed his condition only to "[t]he misfortunes of age—discomfort rather than pain and I hope and believe with no very serious threat for the future, but knocking me out now." "I suppose," he added, "I got too tired with my work and coming on [to Beverly Farms.]"[15] By June 23, however, it was clear that he required prostate surgery. He wrote Pollock from the hospital that "I am preparing—which will take from two to six weeks according to circumstances."[16] Two weeks later he told Laski that he had a "pipe from my bladder—glass of water every hour and operation when the doctor says."[17]

The operation was a success, and there is no evidence that Holmes had any recurrence of prostate trouble. By the 18th of July he was able to scrawl a note to Pollock[18] and on July 22 he wrote a brief one to Frankfurter, indicating that he was doing well but that recovery would be a long slow process.[19] Laski wrote on August 13 to say that Frankfurter had written him that "you plan to be at work in October,"[20] and Pollock wrote on August 23 that he was delighted that his earlier prophecy that the chances were 100 to 1 that Holmes would survive the operation had been justified.[21] Holmes responded that he had "a longish job to regain my strength," and on September 28, when he returned to Washington, was humiliated to report to Laski that he "was disgracefully wheeled in a chair from the [railroad] car to the taxi."[22] As late as December 14 he noted that while "I took something of a walk yesterday and was none the worse for it," the Holmeses did not "go about, dine out or give dinners," and he thought they would "drop out of society."[23]

By the spring of 1923 Holmes was clearly on the mend. That January he had written Nina Gray that "I am still rather shaky on my legs—and I get out of the carriage as if I were an old man, but we hope to cure these things with time."[24] He added to Pollock that "I certainly have improved since I have been here and have done my full share of work," but that "I still feel the shock of the operation."[25] A month later he said that "I think I grow stronger, though not yet *in statu quo ante*,"[26] and in March noted to Laski that "I stick to seclusion on the theory of letting my heart regain its strength."[27] and to Einstein that "I think I have slowly improved during the winter."[28] After that time references to his health largely disappeared from his letters. Meanwhile Taft reported that Holmes was "feebler physically, but I can not see that the acuteness of his mind has been affected at all,"[29] and that "his power of rapid work is still marvelous."[30]

From the spring of 1923 through that of 1931, when Holmes celebrated his ninetieth birthday, still an active Supreme Court justice, he seems to have had no significant health problems. But after turning ninety Holmes began to feel his age. In a June 1931 letter to Laski, who had visited him in Washington in May, he wrote that "[w]hen you left . . . I was feeling very feeble and finished—whichever way I look . . . there are only ghosts and memories."[31] By late July, after two months at Beverly Farms, he had recovered to some extent, noting that "I think I must have been tired on my arrival here. I meditated on death—but I do so no longer."[32] On August 10 he wrote Einstein that "I am going on with my routine," and that while "[t]ime every little while gives me a fresh notice of its advance," the "dilapidations are gradual and still consistent with life."[33] And on August 17 he wrote Nina Gray that "[a]ll is well here," that he was working on certiorari petitions in preparation for the Court's fall term, and that he was to receive a medal from the American Bar Association in September, which he planned to answer by radio.

Shortly after that time, however, came what he called to Lewis Einstein "a sort of cave in."[34] He was ill in the latter part of August and most of September, and had to cancel his radio address and plans he had made to visit Nina Gray in Boston before taking the train back to Washington. He wrote Gray, on September 22, that he had "given up writing almost altogether," that "[t]he vacation had been disappointing in my being ill most of the time," but that he planned to resume his work on the Court and "perhaps to utter similar croakings a year from now."[35] He did not write either Pollock or Laski throughout most of the fall, having his secretary inform Laski of his illness in September[36] and dictating a letter to Laski in October that said "I am not up to writing" and "I infer that I must be careful about my heart."[37]

In a 1980 interview with John Monagan, then preparing a book on the later years of Holmes' life, Chapman Rose, Holmes' secretary for the 1931 Term, said that Holmes had "had the heart attack that had led to the introduction of the elevators." Rose's "very clear recollection" was that an elevator had been introduced in the Beverly Farms house "about a year or two before I was there" (Rose was with Holmes during the summer of 1932).[38] Rose's statement is the only extant evidence that Holmes' illness in the summer of 1931 may have been heart trouble. In light of the absence of any other evidence to that effect, I am inclined to doubt Rose's conclusion. He was not Holmes' secretary at the time, and there is no evidence that an elevator was installed in the Beverly Farms house in the summer of 1931. In his October 9, 1931, letter to Laski Holmes said that "[m]y bed was moved downstairs at Beverly," which would have rendered an elevator unnecessary, and Rose may have confused the situation at Beverly with that at Holmes' house on Eye Street in Washington, which had an elevator.

It is possible that Holmes' illness, which as far as can be determined consisted primarily of excessive fatigue, may have been related to circulatory difficulties. In addition to his comment to Laski in the October letter that he inferred he needed to be careful with his heart, there is a statement in a November 12, 1931, letter that "I have been rather seedy since August," although "I don't feel tired all the time, as I did." The extreme fatigue that Holmes encountered during the late summer and early fall of 1931 is suggestive of some circulatory episode.

Also suggestive, along the same lines, is the fact that Holmes' 1931 illness apparently had an effect on his ability to write. He told Laski in late November 1931 that "[t]he physical act [of writing] comes hard. I don't know why or why I write smaller than I used to.''[39] This ushered in a condition that persisted throughout the rest of Holmes' life, to the point where his correspondence eventually dwindled to an occasional brief note. So it is possible that the ''cave in'' of late August 1931 was a mild stroke. In any event, while the episode undoubtedly accelerated Holmes' resignation from the Supreme Court in January 1932, it very probably did not shorten his life. He remained remarkable in his capacity to avoid serious illnesses, even at great age, and to recover from those he had.

~

Holmes' use of secretaries to assist him in his correspondence in 1931 and 1932, and the presence of secretaries at Beverly Farms in those years, testified to a major change in his life that occurred in April 1929 when Fanny Dixwell Holmes died. The circumstances of Fanny's death were of a piece with her life: obscure and unremarkable on the surface. From September 1928 through April 1929, she fell four times, the last time breaking her hip. In February 1929, Holmes wrote John Wigmore that ''[m]y wife had a tumble on Saturday, and aches, but no serious harm was done.''[40] On April 2, however, Holmes wrote Laski that while he was ''in good shape,'' Fanny was ''less so—however I think she is slowly improving from grippe and a succession of misfortunes.''[41] About three weeks later, however, apparently came the last of the falls. Chief Justice Taft, who because of his titular role and his friendship with Holmes was to be significantly involved in Fanny's last illness and death, described it:

> Mrs. Justice Holmes . . . had suffered three falls since September and then had one that broke her hip. It occurred at night when she was alone with the Justice, and he not having anybody within call had to lift her on to the bed and could not get a doctor until the next morning.[42]

When the doctor was summoned, he placed Fanny's hip in a plaster cast, but, as Taft reported, that technique, when applied to the aged, ''usually results fatally . . . because the suffering and exhaustion which attend the fixed position in which the patient has to be put usually produce a fatal result.''[43] On April 21 Louis Brandeis wrote Felix Frankfurter that ''Mrs. Holmes turned seriously ill Tuesday,'' and that Holmes ''seemed crushed, and fully twenty years older than he has been for months.''[44] On the 26th Holmes wrote Nina Gray

> Please do not mention it to anyone—although you may possibly hear it from others. Fanny is very ill and cannot write at present. You know how she hates to have people talk or know of her private affairs and therefore I say no more than is necessary. I try to keep occupied with work.[45]

On Sunday, the 28th, a relative of the Holmeses told Chief Justice Taft that Fanny was dying, ''but that the doctor . . . had not communicated to Justice Holmes what the impending result would be.'' The doctor, Taft said, ''was afraid that it might shock the Justice; that he would save him this. But Van Devanter and I sent for the doctor and told him that Holmes was a man who wanted to know the facts, and therefore he ought to tell him.''[46] That same day Brandeis wrote Frankfurter that ''OWH is making a grand fight. But it is a very hard one.''[47] On Tuesday evening, April 30, Fanny died.

Some mythology has sprung up about Fanny's funeral and subsequent burial in Arlington National Cemetery. Catherine Drinker Bowen, in her 1944 biography of Holmes and his family, stated that Holmes did not want a funeral at all, because Fanny ''hated all that kind of thing,'' and that Taft needed to convince Holmes that a funeral was necessary in the death of the wife of a Supreme Court Justice. Bowen also stated that Taft arranged for Fanny (and subsequently Holmes) to be buried in Arlington Cemetery because Holmes was reluctant to ask for a plot, even though as a Civil War veteran he was eligible for one.[48] Bowen's statements have been taken to be accurate by subsequent scholars.[49]

In fact Holmes did not resist a funeral for Fanny and had already secured the Arlington plot. Taft, along with Fanny's niece Mary Clark, did play a major role in the funeral arrangements, because of his role as Chief Justice and because, as he wrote one of his sons, ''Holmes can not attend to anything of that sort with comfort, and he seemed very grateful to me for relieving him.''[50] Taft told another of his sons that he ''really had to take charge of the funeral with Mrs. Clark.'' ''I went down to see her and met the Judge,'' he continued, ''and he did everything I suggested.''[51] The funeral was held at the Holmes' residence on May 3, 1929, at 11 A.M., officiated by Dr. Ulysses G. B. Pierce, minister of All Souls' Church in Washington.[52] Taft then described the burial site:

> It was a beautiful day, and we went out to Arlington where by virtue of his war record Justice Holmes is entitled to lie with his wife. He has the most beautiful site in Arlington. When Mr. Weeks was Secretary of War, Justice Holmes spoke to him about the matter of a lot, and he and Weeks went over to Arlington and selected the site. There is a great big beautiful tree on a large knoll, and I could not but feel envious that your mother and I did not have such a place.[53]

On May 15, after visiting Fanny's gravesite, Holmes wrote to Nina Gray that he had ordered a joint gravestone for himself and Fanny, since ''in a military place a woman has to be accounted for.'' He described the site as ''a beautiful little spot,''[54] and made it a practice, for the remainder of his life, to make regular visits to Fanny's grave. Chapman Rose described those visits during the time he spent with Holmes in 1931 and 1932:

> [H]e had a sort of pilgrimage that he would take, my recollection is once a month, out to the Arlington and a little ceremony that he went through. He'd walk up to the headstone and—a very characteristic gesture that I remember— run his fingers over the stone, the engraving on the stone, but without comment. Very stoical.[55]

For the engraving on the gravestone Holmes wrote:

Oliver Wendell Holmes
Brevet Colonel & Captain, 20th Mass. Volunteer Infantry
Justice Supreme Court of United States
March 1841

His Wife
Fanny B. Holmes
Dec. 1840   April 30, 1929[56]

Thus ended fifty-seven years of marriage for Holmes, and over sixty years in which Fanny was his closest friend and companion. The public reaction to her death tracked closely the role she had played in Holmes' life. The headlines to her obituaries did not list her by name, referring to her as "Justice Holmes' Wife," and gave very little information about her. The *Boston Globe* mentioned that she had presented a wood-carving of hers to the town of Gloucester, but neglected to mention her work with embroideries;[57] the *Washington Post* emphasized her being "a gracious hostess" who "before her health failed was at home every Monday." The *Post* described Fanny as "quiet and unassuming," but noted that her "conversation sparkled with bright and witty sayings."[58]

None of the obituaries captured Fanny's place in Holmes' life. Theirs had been a marriage of contrasts—her reclusiveness and his ambition and self-preoccupation—and also, very likely, a marriage in which the romantic intensity was stronger on her side than his. It was a marriage in which she soon resolved to, as he once said, "devote . . . all her powers to surrounding me with enchantments."[59] When, in her eighty-sixth year, she sensed that she was no longer in a position solely to manage the Holmes household, she secured the services of Mary Donellan as a housekeeper, and trained her to take care of Holmes and his surrounding domestic paraphernalia.[60] Despite her own lack of relish for social contacts, she first indulged Holmes in his and then, when he had passed from Anglophile to Washington personage, went through what must have been the ordeal of being a "gracious hostess." All the while she let Holmes know that she was not unduly impressed with his pontification or his charm. A symbolic ritual of their marriage was his playing solitaire in the evenings while she read to him. It was a event they shared, but it was her eyes that had been weak in their youth, and it was his that were rested to read professional documents and write opinions and letters.

Holmes' reaction to Fanny's death was characteristic. To close friends he acknowledged the vastness of his loss; at the same time he announced his determination not to let that loss divert him from his work and his goal of remaining on the Court as long as he could. He wrote Nina Gray that he was "reconciled to the situation by the fact that longer ills would have meant nothing but pain,"[61] and repeated similar sentiments to Pollock[62] and Laski.[63] He told both Pollock and Laski that "[f]or sixty years" Fanny had "made life poetry for me."[64] He noted that her death "seem[ed] like the beginning of my own."[65] But at the same time he told Frankfurter that his work seemed "to be done at a separate chamber of one's being—unaffected by any troubles."[66] He also told Taft, as Taft reported, that no one should anticipate that this loss would precipitate his retirement:

I was very much amused to have him say to me that he was going right on—
that he did not want any misunderstanding on that point. . . . He wrote an
opinion and sent it to me yesterday, the day she died.[67]

One of the first things he told me was that he did not propose to give up—that
the matter would go right on. I suppose that there are a good many who are
counting on his retirement. If so, they miss their guess. He proposes to remain
in the harness as long as the harness will hold him.[68]

Ten days before Fanny's death Brandeis had written Frankfurter of the necessity
for having Holmes' current secretary stay with him through the summer at Beverly
Farms. "He is needed," Brandeis said, "as no secretary ever has been."[69] The
secretary stayed, reading to Holmes in the evenings, and life, without Fanny, went
on.

~

Aging had also meant the piling up of honors and achievements. In 1922 had come
The New Republic's recognition of his twenty years on the Court and forty as a
judge, which had been especially uplifting after his long struggle to recover from
his prostate operation. In 1924 *Time* magazine put him on the cover of its March
15, 1926, issue, calling him "[a]s venerable as his father." That same year a custom of noting his birthdays on an annual basis began. Taft, in writing his sons in
celebration of Holmes' eighty-fifth birthday, said that Holmes was "in marvelously good form and greatly enjoys his old age," and that "[h]e is a remarkable
man." He could not forebear adding that Holmes was "a very poor constitutional
lawyer" who "lacks the experience of affairs in government that would keep him
straight on constitutional questions,"[70] a view that reflected Taft's frustrations on
noticing Holmes' increased inclination to join Brandeis in dissent on constitutional
issues.

The birthday celebrations reached a crescendo with Holmes' ninetieth in 1931,
where a nationwide radio broadcast was arranged, ostensibly by the editors of the
Harvard, Yale, and Columbia Law Reviews, but with the background guidance of
Felix Frankfurter. Preparations for the ceremony, which was to be held on Sunday,
March 8, began on Friday, when a number of newspaper photographers sought to
take Holmes' picture with Chief Justice Hughes, who had succeeded Taft on the
latter's death in 1930, as Holmes and Hughes left the Supreme Court for the noon
recess. Holmes declined, saying "I'm going to have my victuals first," but submitted
after lunch. A microphone was installed in his study so that he could respond to
tributes from Hughes, Dean Charles Clark of Yale Law School, and Charles Boston,
President of the American Bar Association. A hookup of the broadcast was set up
in Langdell Hall at Harvard Law School, and about five hundred people gathered to
hear it. The broadcast involved a coordination of Boston's and Clark's remarks,
which were made from a studio in New York, with the remarks of Hughes and
Holmes, which originated from Holmes' home in Washington. The Columbia Broad-
casting System broadcast the program.

Boston spoke first, quoting from Holmes' address on receiving an LL.D. from

Yale in 1886, which he had ended by saying that "I will try to maintain the honor you have bestowed," and adding, "[a]nd how marvelously he has done so through the nearly fifty years which have passed since then." Clark, whose function was described as that of introducing Chief Justice Hughes, nonetheless gave a brief outline of Holmes' career, concluding by describing "how [Holmes'] tolerance and sympathy have led him, often in dissent from his associates, to the expression of the loftiest of liberal opinions." "So often," Clark noted, "has [Holmes] been ahead of his generation in scholarship as well as in opinion that we may well hesitate to differ with him for fear he but expresses the views we will hold tomorrow."

Clark then introduced Hughes, who made an extended speech, giving highlights of Holmes' career and offering some tributes of his own. Some of those undoubtedly gave great pleasure to Holmes. On Holmes as a colleague, Hughes said that

> It is difficult for one who is in daily and intimate association with him to think of great age, as he is a constant contradiction of all that great age usually implies. He has abundantly the zest for life and his age crowns that eagerness and unflagging interest with the authority of experience and wisdom.
>
> In his important work, he is indefatigable. No one could be more scrupulous in meeting every obligation; no one more intense in devotion to his task. Every case that is presented to the Court arouses in him such immediate and earnest response that it is almost impossible to realize that in his service in the Supreme Court of the United States and in the Supreme Judicial Court of Massachusetts he has been listening to argument for almost fifty years.
>
> He has the dauntlessness and unquenchable fire of youth, ever ready, ever undismayed. His wit is as quick as ever, and his mental thrust as skillful and as vigorous. Above all, he is as lovable as ever, with the warm heart that resists the chill of years. While conserving his strength in a prudent and dignified withdrawal from the trivialities of conventional social intercourse, he is today, as ever, the best company in Washington, and I think that one could search the whole world in vain for any personality more electric and inspiring in its contacts.

On Holmes' life in general, Hughes said,

> The most beautiful and the rarest thing in the world is a complete human life, unmarred, unified by intelligent purpose and uninterrupted accomplishment, blessed by great talent employed in the worthiest activities, with a deserved fame never dimmed and always growing. Such a rarely beautiful life is that of Mr. Justice Holmes.[71]

Holmes had known about the radio program for some time, and had prepared his response well in advance. He had written Ellen Curtis in January 1931 that he was concerned about a "plunge into the unknown radio," a medium that was relatively new at the time, but that "what made me not positively refuse to take part in the radio talk was the thought of a line . . . with which I could wind up." That line, in its original form, was "Here's Death twitching my ear, 'Live,' says he, 'for I'm coming!' " Holmes rendered it to Curtis as "Death, plucking my ear, says, 'Live—I am coming.' "[72] In the response it was to take yet another form.

The source of the line was a book, *Medieval Latin Lyrics,* by Helen Waddell, which Alger Hiss, who had clerked for Holmes in the 1929–30 Term, had given him. During that Term Hiss and Holmes had read together Waddell's *The Wandering Scholars; Medieval Latin Lyrics* was a sequel. The poem from which the line was taken, "The Syrian Dancing Girl," had been attributed to Virgil. It was in praise of wine, gambling, and other hedonistic pleasures, but Holmes was to use it for different purposes.

Holmes wrote out his response in longhand, as was his custom. The final product bore only a few changes from the first draft, but some of those were interesting. When Holmes came to end with his quotation from "The Syrian Dancing Girl" he first wrote

> And so I then come to a line from a Latin poet of fifteen hundred years ago who said what I want to say, better, done in translation, than I can say it, "Death plucked my ear and said 'Live—I am coming.' "

In the final version that passage had become

> And so I end with a line from a Latin poet who uttered the message more than fifteen hundred years ago: "Death plucks my ear and says, 'Live—I am coming.' "[73]

The significance of the changes may be more apparent if Holmes' entire response is set forth. In the broadcast version of his remarks, he cleared his throat and said:

> In this symposium my part is only to sit in silence. To express one's feelings as the end draws near is too intimate a task. But I may mention one thought that occurs to me as a listener-in. The riders in the race do not stop short when they reach the goal. There is a little finishing canter before coming to a standstill. There is time to hear the kind voice of friends and to say to oneself: The work is done. But just as one says that, the answer comes: The race is over, but the work never is done while the power to work remains. The canter that brings you to a standstill need not be only coming to rest. It cannot be, while you still live. For to live is to function. That is all there is in living.[74]

Next came the closing reference to Virgil's poem.

Holmes' most revealing personal statements were arguably his public addresses: as he once told Clare Castletown, he put his heart into them. In this passage one particularly revealing thought is rendered in typically cryptic fashion, the idea that the combination of expressing one's feelings and contemplating the end of one's life is "too intimate" to bear. Holmes had regularly raised the theme of the dangers of fully letting his feelings run rampant: that response was "too intimate" for a person who preferred his structured version of intimacy. So one "sat in silence," at least with regard to the "passions" within.

He then turned to his "thought" about the "little finishing canter" that marked the end of a race. Holmes expressed that thought in a hopeful and at the same time fatalistic fashion. If life was a race, the riders did not stop when the race was over; there was that finishing canter, especially for those who had done well. But a cruel surprise lay ahead for the canterer hearing the "kind words" of wellwishers: when the canter stopped he either had to start another race or die. The work was never done while the power to work remained; the power to work, to "function," was all that life was about. "Function" was an ambiguous word, incorporating other things as well as working, and one could argue that "to live was to function." But the sentiment seemed more narrowly expressed. Once one no longer had "the power to work," one might as well cease living.

In this context Death's entry, plucking one's ear and saying "Live—I am coming," took on quite a different note from that of "The Syrian Dancer." In that poem Death's coming was an excuse for frivolity in life; in Holmes' version Death is saying something like "get back to work." When Holmes read the poem over the radio, he spoke the words "Live—I am coming" in a cadence, as if Death was mockingly suggesting that he would certainly arrive. The full "message" of the "Latin poet," then, in Holmes' version, was a teasing reminder from Death that mortality was, in case one had forgotten, inevitable, and in the meantime one had better "live," that is, "function," make use of one's "power to work." In the context of a distinguished person receiving tributes on his ninetieth birthday, the message seems something like, "Come on, Holmes, don't have your head turned by this recognition of your eminence and begin to think you are immortal. If you want to ward off death a little longer you had better get back in the race with the rest of the working riders."

It was an extraordinary performance, described by the *New York Times* as "perfect."[75] It affirmed the exalted status that Holmes had achieved at ninety, represented not only by the ceremony but by his being made an honorary Bencher of one of London's great professional and social centers, Lincoln's Inn (the first overseas individual to have been so honored); by the collection of essays edited by Frankfurter, *Mr. Justice Holmes,* which had been presented to him earlier on his birthday; and by a host of puff pieces and tributes in the press. Laski, who had been invited to Holmes' house for the event, wrote Holmes that "[t]hey were exquisite hours, among the very happiest that I have ever known."[76] The *Times,* in an editorial, called him "perhaps the greatest of living judges," who had experienced "[a] wonderful career, wonderfully maintained in the affection and reverence of his fellow citizens."[77] R. L. Duffus, in a "portrait of the great jurist" in the *Times,* said that "[h]is longevity has a connection with what must have been an early determination not to let life go until he had wrested from it the last secret that it had to offer."[78]

Some years later Laski told an unusual story about his visit. "Alone in [Holmes'] library at the house at Eye Street," Laski said, "we listened to the broadcast in his honor. . . . When the engineer had taken the radio apparatus away, he came and sat in the armchair on the other side of the fireplace from where I sat. As I looked at him, his eyes seemed far away, and the swift realization that I was watching the face of a very old man, very greatly moved, kept me silent. Then, after an interval, I saw a new light come into those blue-gray eyes, and then a gay smile that played over all his features. The words he spoke as that smile met the flash of those vivid eyes are as living today in my ears as they were almost seventeen years ago.

"When I came back from the Civil War," he said, "my father asked me what I was going to do and I told him I was going to the Harvard Law School. "Pooh!" said my father, "what's the use of going to the Harvard Law School? A lawyer cannot be a great man.'' Then there came into his voice an almost wistful tenderness. ''I wish,'' he continued, ''that my father could have listened tonight for only two or three minutes. Then I could have thumbed my nose at him.''[79] The Laski anecdote does not ring completely true. Sources have previously been quoted suggesting that Holmes Sr., as Holmes put it, ''kicked [his son] into the law,'' and ''put on the screws to have me go to the Law School'' when Holmes ''was full of thoughts about philosophy and in a vague way . . . thought about the medical school.''[80] It is clear that Holmes had doubts about whether a lawyer could ''be a great man,'' but there is no evidence that these doubts originated with his father. It is entirely possible that Holmes indicated to Laski that he wished his father could have heard some of the ceremony on Holmes' ninetieth birthday, and that he might have ''thumbed my nose at him,'' given the younger Holmes' competitiveness with his father. But the disparaging comment Laski reports Holmes Sr's having made about lawyers does not seem consistent with Holmes Sr.'s pressuring his son to enroll in Harvard Law School. In addition to several other comments along the same line, Holmes had written Laski himself, on May 18, 1919, that ''instead of philosophy I was shoved into the law.''[81]

Holmes wrote Charlotte Moncheur that his birthday ''went off wonderfully.'' ''Many things,'' he added, had ''moved me unexpectedly, for I am rather tough as against popular talk.'' He singled out the honorary Bencher tribute from Lincoln's Inn, a bust that the Columbia Law School had commissioned, letters ''from men that really count,'' the fact that many of his former secretaries had come to visit him on March 15, and ''even some letters from unknown people [which] had a note of feeling that touched me.''[82] He added to his old friend from Japan, Kentaro Kaneko, that he had been ''amazed and much moved by the kind expressions from many unknown to me,'' and had been impressed with Hughes's ''dear speech.''[83] ''Everything went off to my heart's content,'' he said to Nina Gray, ''and there came expressions that left me dumb. My work suffers this week, for I am overwhelmed.''[84] The last sentence was in keeping with his use of the ''Death plucks my ear'' quotation: after all the tributes one returned to the omnipresent stability of one's work. Taft had said on Holmes' eighty-fifth birthday that ''[h]e could not live without the Court.''[85]

~

When the October 1931 Term started it was beginning to be apparent that a combination of age and his recent illness had made Holmes less able to perform his duties. In his autobiography Hughes wrote that ''it appeared that [Holmes] was slipping. While he was still able to write clearly, it became evident in the conferences of the Justices that he could no longer do his full share in the mastery of the work of the Court.''[86] Chapman Rose, Holmes' secretary for the 1931 Term, remembered Holmes' eventual retirement as

> the culmination of a period of considerable worry because the way in which his age affected him was . . . an increasing fatigue. During the latter part of the day he would be very good and [it was] hard to imagine his ever having been better, during the hours when he was vigorous. But [a] pall would descend,

sometimes earlier, sometimes later . . . the attention span had gone without depriving him of the drive that he always had to finish any unfinished business. . . . So it was getting more difficult to prevent him from really exhausting himself and I remember, without having anyone to turn to about it, being considerably concerned about what if anything ought to be done.[87]

Eventually, after the Justices met on the matter and Hughes consulted with Brandeis,[88] Hughes made an appointment to visit Holmes at home on Sunday morning, January 12. Rose then picks up the story:

I was there as usual because I was observing a seven day a week schedule regularly and the Chief Justice went up to Justice Holmes' study in the room in the rear on the second floor and they conversed there for a time—I should think about 1/2 hour—and then sent for me and my assignment was to pull out from the shelves of the library the volume of the statutes that had to do with tenure and retirement and so forth which I did, and find the place that dealt with the subject and gave it to them and waited downstairs.[89]

After an interval Chief Justice Hughes came down the stairs from Holmes' study, "with tears streaming down his face." Rose thought it a "remarkable sight, with that impressive face [with a] beard." Hughes then left, and Rose "went upstairs to see the justice and Mary Donnellan [his housekeeper] was kneeling at his feet in tears. He was then and thereafter totally stoic about it. There was no expression of emotion one way or another."[90]

After Hughes left Brandeis arrived, "obviously by arrangement," Rose surmised,[91] and stayed with Holmes for about an hour. Mary Donnellan indicated that "even though [Holmes'] heart was breaking, he wouldn't let anyone know it." She indicated Holmes "thought it was the end," and "was lonesome." Donnellan added in an interview that Hughes "was hard" and "was very cold," but it was not clear that she was referring to his attitude on Holmes' retirement.[92] Hughes said in his autobiography that the visit to Holmes had been "a highly distasteful duty," and that his suggestion that Holmes retire had been "made as tactfully as possible."[93] In an interview with his authorized biographer late in his life, Hughes said that he had told Holmes "he was under too heavy a burden" and "should not strain himself by continuing to carry the load when his strength was no longer equal to it."[94] Holmes, Hughes said, "received my suggestion . . . without the slightest indication of . . . resentment or opposition."[95]

In his resignation letter Holmes said that "[t]he condition of my health makes it a duty to break off connections that I cannot leave without deep regret after the affectionate relations of many years and absorbing interests that have filled my life." He added that "the time has come and I bow to the inevitable."[96] Again the word "duty" figured prominently: Holmes was once again emphasizing the extent to which codes of appropriate behavior were imposing themselves on his will. He was not choosing to retire; he was bowing to the inevitable.

From January 1932 to Holmes' death in March 1935, two days before his ninety-fourth birthday, his world seemed telescoped. In a March 1932 letter to Laski he described his routine:

I find idleness lifegiving—I get up late—have a motor drive—this morning
to Mount Vernon and back in an hour and a quarter—easily brought down to
an hour. After luncheon my secretary reads to me and people call. I write
the few letters that I attempt. I find these come hard as I have told you
before.[97]

Holmes' comment on his difficulty in writing meant that his voluminous correspondences began to dry up in this period. His last letter to Pollock was written in May
1932; that to Laski in November of that year; his last to Lewis Einstein that Septem-
ber. He outlived Nina Gray, whom he last wrote in May 1932. He had outlived his
siblings Edward and Amelia, his old friends John Gray, Penrose Hallowell, Henry
Adams, William and Henry James, all the faculty members who served with him at
Harvard Law School, all the judges with whom he had served on the Supreme
Judicial Court of Massachusetts, and all of the justices of the Supreme Court of the
United States the year he joined it. He had outlived Clare Castletown and Fanny
Dixwell Holmes. Of the intimates of his life only his childhood friend John Morse,
Pollock, Laski, Frankfurter, and Ellen Curtis survived him. In December 1933, he
wrote the last letter of his that has been preserved to Ellen Curtis. "You know," he
began, "that I have been unable to write. . . . If we meet I still can talk a little and
keep a pretty long list of books. . . . But I am pretty well finished. This brings my
love and longing to say more."[98]

Most of the routine of Holmes' last years thus cannot be supplied from conventional sources. Recollections of two of his secretaries, Donald Hiss and James Rowe,
help fill in some details. Donald Hiss joined him in September 1932, beginning at
Beverly Farms and then journeying to Washington in mid-October. Hiss described
"our usual day" as follows:

I arrived at nine o'clock and worked a seven-day week. I took care of bills,
other matters of immediate concern, certain household affairs, and any letters
he received, particularly those from Sir Frederick Pollock or Harold Laski,
who were his most frequent correspondents during his retirement. I'd start the
day by asking if he wanted me to read to him, or whether he wanted to look at
some of his engravings or do other things on his own. Usually about 11:30 I
would read to him, and the selection was a joint effort. . . .

His tastes varied from Giorgio Vasari's *Lives of the Painters,* which we
read continuously with very few interruptions, to E. Phillips Oppenheim. In
between we read Bertrand Russell and Alfred North Whitehead. Occasionally
he would observe, "Sonny," as he called all of his secretaries, "at ninety-one,
one outlives duty. Let's read E. Phillips Oppenheim." He was very fond of
Oppenheim and the lighter things. But the reading and the discussion were
always varied.

At one o'clock we had lunch down in the dining room. His visitors ranged
from Owen Wister, Benjamin Cardozo, and Tom Corcoran, to Felix
Frankfurter, but most of the time we lunched alone. . . . After lunch he would
go upstairs and drop off for a very few minutes' nap, sometimes while I read
to him and other times without my reading to him. We always took a drive in
the afternoon. He referred to his chauffeur not as an employee but as a private

contractor. This probably was Holmes' way of limiting his liability in case of an accident. . . .

He always wore his swallowtail coat when he was driving. When he came in he had an old alpaca coat that he shifted to. After the drive we would read. At six o'clock I would leave and at seven o'clock he would have his supper, with Mary Donnellan in attendance. Except for a few instances when old friends . . . were in town, he dined alone. I would come back at 8:30 and read to him for an hour or so. This was the general routine, interspersed frequently with discussion of what we were reading or of almost any subject, because his interests were extremely wide. There was nothing that did not interest him except athletics.[99]

Brandeis, Cardozo, Stone, and McReynolds from the Court were frequent callers on Holmes during 1932 and 1933, Donald Hiss noted. Holmes would reminisce about the Civil War, his father, his honeymoon, and anecdotes of his early life. He read the *Atlantic Monthly* and the *New Republic,* but not the newspapers. Hiss, however, informed him about stories in the papers and read occasional articles to him, as Fanny had. He needed help up from his chair, where he would sit when reading or listening to the readings of others, and he expected to be helped on with his coat, but he was quite capable of dressing himself. Mary Donnellan shaved him, and he continued to take pains with his appearance.[100]

At the time he retired Holmes anticipated receiving an annual pension equal to his salary on retirement. That was the stipend provided for federal judges who were at least seventy years old and had served on the bench for at least ten years. Holmes, as we have seen, had been aware of his retirement annuity since at least 1910, when he began musing about retiring after he reached the age of seventy. In 1932, however, Congress passed a statute, designed to respond to the depressed economic conditions of the 1930s, that was interpreted as cutting in half the pensions of those federal judges who had "resigned," as distinguished from "retiring." The latter category of judges was still technically eligible to serve on the bench and thus could not have their salaries reduced "during their continuance in office" under Article I, section 1 of the Constitution. The statute had the effect of reducing Holmes's annual pension from $20,000 to $10,000 per year.[101]

Holmes was the most prominent judge affected by the statute, and in January 1933 the Attorney General asked Congress to eliminate the provision applying to federal judges, arguing that it had only saved $25,583 in the past year and would create incentives for federal judges to continue in office past the point of their effectiveness.[102] On February 6, 1933, the Senate adopted a measure restoring Holmes's salary to $20,000.[103]

On March 8, 1933, Holmes' ninety-second birthday, President Franklin Roosevelt, who had taken the oath of office for his first term only five days earlier, came to visit Holmes in the late afternoon, a visit arranged by Felix Frankfurter.[104] The day had included a lunch, attended by Frankfurter, Thomas Corcoran, and the Edward Holmeses, Holmes' niece and nephew, at which champagne, supposedly a gift from the British ambassador, was smuggled in, notwithstanding Prohibition. The afternoon drive was omitted, as Hiss wanted Holmes to remain fresh for the President's visit, and Holmes took a nap. Eventually Roosevelt's car drew up, with a crowd accompanying. On being informed that the President was coming to visit him, Holmes first said, "Don't be an idiot, boy. He wouldn't call on me," but then concluded that he had better put on his swallowtail coat.[105]

Roosevelt came up the elevator to Holmes' study, in his wheelchair, accompanied by Eleanor Roosevelt, James Roosevelt, one of the President's sons, and Frankfurter. As the guests sat down to chat in the study Hiss "hovered to see if I could be of any assistance." The conversation "was very animated," with President Roosevelt calling attention to a pair of swords over the fireplace that Holmes' grandfather Jackson had used in the French and Indian wars. At the end of the conversation there were two parting colloquies. Roosevelt asked Holmes whether there was anything he could do for him, and Holmes said that he would appreciate being able to get his money out of the bank—Roosevelt, responding to the economic crisis in existence at the time of his inauguration, had declared a "bank holiday" in the first days of his administration—so that he could pay his servants. Then Roosevelt asked Holmes if he had "any final advice to give me?" According to Hiss, Holmes said,

> No, Mr. President. The time I was in retreat, the Army was in retreat in disaster, the thing to do was to stop the retreat, blow your trumpet, have them give the order to charge. And's that exactly what you are doing. This is the admirable thing to do and the only thing you could have done.[106]

Donald Hiss' eyewitness account of Roosevelt's visit to Holmes on his ninety-second birthday is notable because two recent biographies of Holmes have stated that Holmes' response to Roosevelt's request for advice was "form your battalions and fight." If Holmes' advice had been expressed in those terms, rather than in the version given by Hiss, it is interesting that neither of the participants who recounted the meeting in print, Donald Hiss and Frankfurter, recorded Holmes as saying "form your battalions and fight."[107] Frankfurter made a contemporaneous record of the visit and discussed it subsequently in his memoirs, and Donald Hiss discussed it in his retrospective on clerking for Holmes. Had Holmes made the comment, it seems very likely that at least one of them would have remembered it and repeated it. Nonetheless the comment has joined the considerable amount of lore about Holmes that is eminently repeatable but not quite true.

In the 1934 Term, by which time James Rowe had succeeded Donald Hiss, and then Mark DeWolfe Howe, as Holmes' secretary, Holmes' routine remained virtually the same.[108] Rowe read a good deal to Holmes and accompanied him on drives every afternoon. He "kept his books . . . wrote his checks . . . did his income tax, that sort of thing." The job was seven days a week, as it had been for all the law clerks of Holmes' later life. Rowe would work during the day, go home for his dinner, and return in the evening to read to Holmes. Holmes had "five or six preferred places" to drive, including Fanny's grave at Arlington Cemetery, where they drove "about once a week." Another favorite spot was Fort Stevens, where Holmes had helped fight off a Confederate attack on Washington, and where in his old age he had come to believe that he had told Lincoln to get out of the line of fire.

Holmes "was quite an eater" even in the last year of his life, buying his food from Magruder's, an expensive grocer. He regularly received visits from Justices, especially Brandeis ("about three times a week"), Hughes, McReynolds, and Stone.

Laski, Pollock, and Frankfurter wrote regularly, and Rowe answered their letters. Holmes talked of the Civil War, how he "rather admired" the Confederates and disliked the abolitionists; how "he was rather huffy" that a fair number of his contemporaries avoided military service by buying substitutes; how "[h]e had felt it was his duty" to serve. He told Rowe the story of "Little" Abbott, jauntily marching to what seemed to be certain death at Chancellorsville. The last book Rowe read to Holmes before he died was Thornton Wilder's *Heaven's My Destination*.

~

On February 23, 1935, Holmes and James Rowe went for their daily drive. The next morning Holmes developed a cold, and it progressed into bronchial pneumonia.[109] Five days later newspapers began to report that Holmes was seriously ill. John Palfrey, Holmes' lawyer, and Felix Frankfurter came down from Boston to be with him, and his physician, Dr. Thomas Claytor, told the press that at Holmes' age all illnesses were serious. Oxygen tanks were brought to his house.[110] On March 2 the *Washington Post* reported that Holmes was holding his own, and quoted Frankfurter as saying that when he had been ushered into Holmes' company Holmes, in response to a jesting remark Frankfurter had made, had smiled and thumbed his nose.[111] Former secretaries Francis Biddle, Thomas Corcoran, Alger and Donald Hiss, and Mark Howe were reported as having visited the justice.[112] A "hurdy-gurdy man" inappropriately "set up his organ directly across the street" from Holmes' residence and "began grinding out the flippant strains of 'Let's All Sing Like the Birdies Sing.' " He was given a financial incentive to vacate the area.[113] Holmes' doctors were reported as encouraged because his condition had not worsened.[114]

The next day, however, Holmes weakened, and his doctors issued a statement saying that they found his condition "disturbing" in view "of his very advanced age. " Holmes was kept "almost constantly" under an oxygen tent, and not even Chief Justice Hughes was admitted to his bedroom.[115] On March 4 his condition was reported as grave, and his doctors declined to speculate on the outcome.[116] The *Washington Post* quoted a close friend as saying "It's just a matter of waiting."[117] On March 5 the doctors attempted glucose injections in his veins as an effort to maintain his strength, and friends were quoted privately as saying that they regarded any recovery as a "miracle."[118] At 2:15 on the morning of March 6 he died. Mark Howe announced his death to the press, and the *Washington Post* quoted Dr. Claytor as saying that Holmes died "more peacefully than anyone I've ever seen."[119]

A funeral service was held at All Souls' Unitarian Church on Friday the 8th. The justices of the Supreme Court served as honorary pallbearers. The Reverend Ulysses G. Pierce, who had presided at Fanny's funeral, gave a brief sermon, accompanied by organ music. The poem "Mysterious Night," by Joseph Blanco White, was read, as it had been read after Fanny died. Edward Holmes followed the coffin into the church.[120] Reverend Pierce, after quoting Holmes that "at the grave of a hero . . . we end, not with sorrow at the inevitable loss, but with the contagion of his courage; and with a kind of desperate joy we go back to the fight,"[121] added that Holmes "never turned his back, but marched straight forward." The service lasted thirty minutes.[122]

At the close of the service the coffin was placed in a hearse, which proceeded across the Memorial Bridge to the Fort Meyer gate of Arlington Cemetery. At that point the casket was transferred from the hearse to a cassion, and the Supreme Court justices, excluding Brandeis, who was reported as being too upset to attend the ceremony, and Willis Van Devanter, who was ill, accompanied the cassion to the grave, which was "situated on a knoll about half a mile northeast of the Lee Mansion." The United States Army Band played "Battle Hymn of the Republic." President Roosevelt, who had met the procession at the cemetery gate, accompanied it to the grave. A mixture of rain and sleet fell, but the President and other onlookers stood bareheaded. As the casket was lowered into the grave a three-volley salute was fired by soldiers and a bugler played "Taps." A reporter for the *Washington Post,* observing the proceedings, noted that a plane, attempting to land at National Airport in a low ceiling, flew dangerously low over the cemetery as President Roosevelt joined the procession, and that "[t]he melancholy 'whooo whooo' of a locomotive whistle across the river coincided with the bugler's first notes, producing a memorable effect." "Thus," the reporter concluded, "did the funeral of a hero close."[123] Mary Donnellan, standing next to James Rowe as the soldiers took the casket off the cassion to lower it into the grave, said "soldiers don't mind the rain."[124]

Holmes died a wealthy man for his times. His estate was valued at over $568,000: $500,000 in securities, cash, and other personal property; the Eye Street house ($53,752); and the Beverly Farms property ($15,000). John Monagan, one of Holmes' biographers, has speculated that $500,000 in 1935 dollars would currently be worth approximately $4.5 million, and has noted that until 1913 Holmes' income was tax free and that thereafter income tax rates ranged from 1 to 7 percent of gross annual income. Mary Donnellan, Holmes' housekeeper, received a salary of $840 a year plus room and board, and his other staff would have been paid less. In addition, Holmes had a yearly pension of $20,000 a year.[125] It is fair to say that he was one of the limited class of Americans on which the Great Depression of the 1930s had no appreciable impact.

Holmes' will bequeathed $100,000 to his nephew Edward Holmes, 25,000 to his cousin Dorothy Vaughan, for whom Holmes had assumed financial responsibility in the 1890s, and $10,000 to another cousin, Mary Clark, who had helped with Fanny's funeral arrangements. Edward Holmes also received all the editions of Holmes' works and those of Holmes Sr., as well as the desk on which Holmes had written his Supreme Court opinions. A gift of $25,000 was made to Harvard College, to be used preferably in the Law School, and a similar amount was given to the Boston Museum of Fine Arts.

Mary Donnellan, described in the will as a "parlor maid," was given $10,000, and Annie Gough, a servant who had lived with the Holmes since the time they had resided in Dr. Holmes' Beacon Street house, was given the same amount. Other household staff members received gifts ranging from $1000 to $5000. The remainder of the estate, about $290,000, was given to "the United States of America."[126]

Holmes' gift to the United States was placed in the Department of the Treasury's general fund, where it remained, without earning interest, for twenty years. In 1955, at the urging of then Supreme Court Justice Felix Frankfurter, Congress created a Permanent Committee for the Oliver Wendell Holmes Devise, with the Librarian of

Congress as chair, and authorized it to supervise the creation of a multivolumed history of the Supreme Court of the United States, to be called the Oliver Wendell Holmes Devise History. At the time that the series of volumes expected to constitute that history was identified, and various scholars commissioned to write the volumes, the anticipated date for the completion of the entire Holmes Devise History of the Supreme Court of the United States series was 1965. By that date none of the planned volumes had appeared. The first volume in the series appeared in 1971; at this writing nine of the eleven anticipated volumes are in print. John Monagan, in his discussion of Holmes' bequest to the United States, stated that "[t]he sorry history of the fund created by this bequest constitutes a disservice to [Holmes'] memory and a powerful argument against emulating his generous gesture."[127]

~

Holmes' death emphasizes the contrast between the public response to his last years and Holmes' own attitude toward that same period. The *New York Times,* in an editorial, called him "a great gentleman and scholar as well as a great judge," and said that "[s]peech dies in the throat when seeking words to fit the Master of Sentences who has gone."[128] This was typical of the public comments. In 1932, however, Felix Frankfurter wrote a memorandum of conversations he had had with Holmes that summer, after Holmes' retirement. On one occasion, Frankfurter noted, "[s]ome talk of affairs and events led H. to say, 'It's all very remote to me. I'm dead. I'm like a ghost on the battlefield with bullets flying through me.'" "Old men of achievement," Frankfurter concluded, "usually live on the juice of their achievements. Not O.W.H. His skepticism is so profound that he is skeptical—except for a flickering moment—of the importance of his own significance and so gets no warming and soothing comfort from dwelling on and in his past. . . . He feels the poignant edge of realization that his machinery is running down and that he is denied satisfaction of the range of his personality."[129]

In an addendum to that memorandum Marion Frankfurter, Felix's wife, summarized her impressions of Holmes that summer:

In all the visits this summer I have had an impression of a man in melancholy. Sustained interest or attention is gone. He brightens when something amuses him, laughs and chuckles as he always did, but these little moments never lead to anything. He constantly refers to being "dead." Twice when I have been alone with him he has seemed on the verge of unburdening himself. "Hasn't a man a right to be dead at 91?" he asked me rather fiercely. "I have a rendezvous with Death," he said another time. I referred to the change that must have come when he gave up his work. But to this he answered, "Well, I confess, that doesn't bother me at all." And another time he said that he liked being "dead" and not having to bother. But he falls to brooding again. "Oh dear dear," he will say half to himself, and his expression will be one of deep weariness, of loneliness, that I find poignant. There *isn't* anything one can say to prove his mood is false. . . . So when he turns to me and makes some flat statement of his dissolution, I agree with him. What he needs is playful affection and petting, but I have had awe of him for nearly twenty years and I find it hard to approach him now with anything more warming and human. I never before felt that he was a lonely man, but his isolation now could only be mitigated by children to play about him. We talked one day about "fame and honor." I said it was a confusion; what one wanted was simply to know within one's self that one had done his best. . . . But he went on to say that when anyone had reached his time of life, all that seemed to have little importance. "One can turn a trick here or there," he said, "but it all came to the same thing."[131]

In these excerpts Holmes' frequent references to himself as "dead" are serving contradictory purposes. At one level the remarks appear consistent with Holmes' method of warding off a fear by stating it openly. However much he said he was dead, he was not as long as he could say it. At times, in fact, calling himself "dead" appears to be an expression of relief: he was no longer burdened by the daily chores of being an active Supreme Court justice when those chores were getting ever more difficult to perform. But at another level, Holmes sees himself as no longer "on the battlefield," no longer doing work that counts. He feels anxiety and even a kind of guilt at not continuing to work while he is alive, hence the fierceness of his comment about one having "a right to be dead" at ninety-one. Although being "dead" was a way of escaping laborious "duties" yet still being alive, it was at the same time a recognition that Holmes, as he put it to Frankfurter in November 1932, had "dropped into the final obscurity," while Frankfurter, still active and working, was "a high light."

Nor did the "fame and honor" Holmes received seem to be a comfort. When Marion Frankfurter repeated what had been Holmes' traditional view of those subjects, that one only tried to do one's best for oneself and a handful of other cognoscenti, Holmes did not endorse her remarks. Instead he said "that when anyone had reached his time of life, all that seemed to have very little importance." An individual's contributions, in the long run, made very little difference: one could "turn a trick here or there but it all came to the same thing." Thus Holmes' skepticism appears to have led him not only to distrust praise, which he had once called to Pollock "a warning that the end is near," but ultimately to regard praise, and accomplishment itself, as making little difference in the flow of time. "What I want," his secretary for the 1932 Term reported his saying, "is that my days should pass as a rock in a bed of a river, with the water flowing over it."[131]

The Frankfurters' memoranda suggest that Holmes' own personality may have contributed to the melancholy they associated with his last years. He was, with his great intellect and his reserved, private style, a formidable personality, capable of inspiring awe in his younger contemporaries but not easily capable of facilitating intimacy. Marion Frankfurter felt that he needed "playful attention and petting" in his old age, but that any such behavior would jar the reverent awe his presence inspired. She wished that he had children to surround himself with; in fact he lived in a household with no relatives.[132]

There is a sense, in these accounts, that Holmes' early decision to concentrate his energies on his work, and to shape the rest of his life with that concentration in mind, may have been the source of his late melancholy, just as it had arguably been the source of his great achievements. From the moment he began legal scholarship he had staked everything on that project, working nights, avoiding former friends, becoming a recluse. After *The Common Law* appeared, and when he became a judge, he adopted the same approach to his judicial work. Without children, living with a wife who was only too happy to forego social contacts and apparently entirely prepared to ensure that he was freed from other responsibilities so that he could concentrate on his work, he had become singularly able to carve out his own routine of life.

The routine had been conspicuously successful in producing distinguished work for a very long span of time. A concentrated preoccupation with completing his opinions, ''improving'' his mind, keeping up his correspondence, and taking routinized breaks from work—solitaire, reading aloud, walks or drives, the occasional social call—was as characteristic of his life at eighty-seven as it had been more than forty years earlier. Yet almost no one else was intimately involved with the routine of his life. Fanny sustained it, as did his household staff, as did his secretaries. When Fanny died the routine persisted; when he retired from the Court its remnants remained; but there was suddenly no central purpose, nothing to conserve his energies for and to concentrate his powers on. At the end of his life the self-preoccupation that had vitalized him for so long became evidence that after more than ninety years he was essentially alone.

CHAPTER FOURTEEN

A Concluding Assessment

~

W HEN one seeks to sum up Holmes' central personal characteristics, the quality that first comes to mind is his vast and driving ambition. The theme of ambition emerges in many places and at many levels in Holmes' life—his intimidatingly prominent heritage and the burdens, as well as the advantages, that it created for him; the early idea, introduced perhaps by his father but internalized at least by his college years, that ''greatness'' was an expectation that he and others had for himself; his tacit decision, after finishing law school, that ''greatness'' required a concentration of his intellectual powers on one subject, the law, and a concentration of his emotional energies on his scholarly work. A concentration of intellectual and emotional energy, the suppression of ''distractions'' such as extensive social contacts, dabbling in philosophy or literature, even intimate relationships, and the achievement of ''greatness'' became linked in his mind.

Ambition also fostered Holmes' singular competitiveness, his extreme sensitivity to criticism, his thirst for recognition, even the perverse glumness with which he accepted praise and his insatiable desire for an even higher level of accomplishment. The particular form that Holmes' ambition took was that of the solitary scholarly quest, a mission that seemed to combine the appropriate measure of individual creativity, self-denial, and intellectual accomplishment that he desired. It was as if he had resolved not only to secure recognition comparable to that which his father had achieved, but to do so in an utterly different way, not by catering to popular taste or dramatizing the chatty conversation of his neighbors but by writing essays on obscure subjects for an audience of specialists.

Holmes' decision to take a judgeship was also a product of his ambition. From his earliest days in law practice the possibility had enticed him: it was a position that symbolized respect among his peers. By being a judge Holmes could decisively be something his father could not. Dr. Holmes had been a professional practitioner who taught on the Harvard faculty; Holmes had done the same. But Dr. Holmes, for all his prominence, could never be a person whose decisions about the law directly affected the lives of others. In becoming such a person Holmes was helping to distinguish himself from his father.

Ambition, then, led Holmes to become a judge, to continue to write speeches and academic essays while serving, to put himself in the way of a Supreme Court nomination, in part through his extrajudicial writings, and to uproot himself from Boston and his heritage at the age of sixty-one when that nomination came. Ambition underlay Holmes' discomfiture at the comments on his nomination, which too glibly identified him with his father and failed to appreciate the subtlety or power of his work, and of his vague but persistent dissatisfaction at not receiving adequate recognition his first ten years in Washington. In a roundabout way, ambition was an important motivating factor in Holmes' friendships with Felix Frankfurter and his contemporaries after 1912. In those friendships he may have discerned, correctly as it turned out, the possibility of recognition finally arriving on the scale he coveted.

Alongside ambition, among Holmes' central qualities, one would list what he called "passion." Despite the perceived docility of his temperament as a youth, it soon became clear to him, as well as to others, that he felt things intensely and periodically acted upon that feeling. One of the outlets for his intensity, during his college years, was writing: his undergraduate essays are deadly serious in purpose. Another was friendships: his wartime service arose out of those friendships. It is hard to imagine Holmes, nurtured in a community with little firsthand experience of the lives of blacks, northern or southern, and with little actual involvement, at least in his father's generation, with the fighting of a war, deciding to leave Harvard College to join a regiment of Massachusetts volunteers, unless he had made the cause of taking up arms one of comparable importance with the other causes of his undergraduate life. There seems little doubt that Holmes' conceptualization of military service as a "crusade" was not simply a product of his familiarity with the romances of Sir Walter Scott, but also an outgrowth of his friendship with Penrose Hallowell and others who associated chivalry with opposition to slavery.

Wartime service was for Holmes a release of passion. He fought; he suffered; he was wounded; he was violently ill. Despite the drudgery and terrors, despite his growing conviction that the actual details of war bore almost no relationship to the purported aims of the volunteers, he continued during most of his service to describe the war as a crusade. When the passions that had sustained him finally lost their force in the face of the carnage and the disheartening loss of friends and colleagues, he mustered out, but then he almost immediately began to romanticize war. In part, he glorified the stoic "message" of war, that a soldier's true honor came from performing his duty, even if he must throw away his life for a cause in which he no longer believed. But Holmes also expressed the romantic conviction that in going to war, in experiencing the constant presence of death, in willingly exposing himself to death, he was living life to the fullest, venting his passion.

Thus Holmes emerged from the Civil War with what became, in the course of his life, an anachronistic, tribalist perspective, glorifying war and its codes, such as duty, honor, chivalry, self-abnegation. He also emerged, of course, with considerable survivor guilt, which helped color his retrospective portraits of the wartime experience and may have been the explanation for his disinclination to read anything about the Civil War in his later life. War, he believed, was what had set his generation apart, touched it with fire. War had made his youth an appropriately passionate time, a time that had provided experiences which, reflected upon, proved that he had lived.

The theme of passion also surfaces in Holmes' image of his scholarly efforts after returning from the war: a lonely, physically trying adventure, like going on a quest or wrecking oneself on an ice floe. Nansen, the polar explorer, became a heroic figure for Holmes in middle life because Nansen had "started for the Pole," pursuing a goal whose achievement was uncertain for the sheer satisfaction of going alone where others had not gone. "Passion" also appears in the zest with which the young Holmes threw himself into social encounters in England in 1866 and later on his trips in 1874 and 1889. It appeared, in Holmes' middle life, in his tendency to engage in "flirtations" that were perceived as so unusual they troubled his contemporaries. It reached its greatest height in his relationship with Clare Castletown.

As Holmes' life progressed, the theme of passion became intertwined with control of passion. Holmes' intensity did not diminish, but others saw it as directed inward, toward subjects, like his edition of Kent or his historical essays, that involved only himself. His language, in his scholarship and his opinions as well as in his letters to Clare Castletown, became the language of controlled emotion. He seemed implicitly to emphasize the destructive side of passion and to devote some of his energy to suppressing or channeling his emotions. The result was a personality described by contemporaries as planing out a narrow, self-beneficial groove through life, or as having a fearful pallor, or as being two and a half people wrapped in one tight skin.

At the same time Holmes' passion reveals itself in an elemental fashion, as a zest for work and for life. Chief Justice Hughes marvels, when Holmes is ninety, at Holmes' boundless capacity to be enthused by the cases before him, at his fierce desire to complete his assignments. Chief Justice Taft speaks of Holmes' racing to complete his work, and asking for more; Justice Brandeis of his "firing off" opinions so quickly that others have no time to react. His secretaries testify to his great enjoyment in eating, his fondness for champagne, his love of good talk, his abiding interest in "improving his mind." His letters reveal that every spring in Washington he delights in the appearance of crocuses or bloodroot; that he never tires of taking drives to look at foliage in Virginia or the sites of Civil War battles; that in a hypothetical conversation with St. Peter, who tells him that his time has come, he asks for five more minutes. However internalized, the intensity of Holmes' passion remains one of his abiding characteristics.

Finally, Holmes displayed a complicated interaction between the Emersonian themes of the "self" and the "other," of an individual life being composed of the expression of one's will and the restraints placed on the self by external forces. In his complex life history one finds evidence of his early self-preoccupation, periodically rendered by contemporaries as selfishness; of his burying the news of his marriage among the run of entries in his "black book" of readings; of his tendency to believe that all his ideas were truly original and that others were borrowing from them without giving him proper credit; of his conviction that he was writing for, and communicating generally with, only the truly educated. His letters show constant awareness that his thoughts kept returning to himself. He grudgingly accepted honors, which came "too late" to really matter. He detached himself from close friends and the world at large when it suited his purposes. Most centrally, he took a dominant role in his marriage and his household, that of the figure around which everything revolved, who expected that others would devote their energies to making things "a path of beauty" for him.

At the same time one sees an awareness of the constant presence, and importance, of others. He participated in important friendships with such men as John Morse and

Penrose Hallowell.[1] He felt viscerally close to other Civil War veterans. He belonged to the "Metaphysical Club." He enjoyed a circle of young adult friends, including Clover Hooper, Minnie Temple, and Fanny Dixwell, and, in the years just after law school, an intimacy with William James. He was intimate, too, with John Gray during his first years of law practice. One could point to his regular invocation, throughout his life, of the concept of "duty," alternatively as an obligation to others or to an external code, such as the duty to serve in the Civil War or the duty constantly to improve one's mind, or as an intellectual construct, a jurisprudential substitute for "right" as the basis of a classification system. Holmes even began his retirement letter by saying that the condition of his health "made it a "duty" to break off connections with the Court. And, in his last years, he could report enjoying a mystery novel because, as he said, he had "outlived duty."

Pursuing these themes, one could note that Holmes' philosophy ultimately affirmed a fatalism in which the contingencies of time, change, and community attitudes overwhelmed the significance of individual contributions. But the themes of the "self" and the "other" did not manifest themselves in Holmes' temperament sequentially, with the commitment to self being pursued with great energy only to be ultimately overwhelmed by the forces of "experience." Instead the themes coexisted, as for instance, Holmes' almost excessive sentimentality, which could bring tears at the reading of a Civil War poem or joy from the appearance of the bloodroot for one more spring, and his sometimes chilling cerebral detachment. He genuinely doubted the universe had any reality independent of the individual's belief in it, and at the same time he pronounced the utter insignificance of the human species, fit only for eating and procreating.

In searching for a particularly central manifestation of the interplay between "self" and "other," the observer confronts Holmes' simultaneous concern with power and powerlessness. His intense pursuit of recognition, his insistence on completing his work, his self-proclaimed commitment to "jobbism" appear as efforts to impose one's will on one's appointed tasks—to manifest one's power by getting credit for the achievement. Yet the zest that Holmes found in work and in the praise that accompanied it was coupled with a constant insistence that the contributions of any individual would be dwarfed in the universe; that once he had retired as a Supreme Court justice he would become a "ghost."

The themes of self and other remained essentially unresolved. On the one hand Holmes' whole life, in its personal and intellectual dimensions, can be seen as a struggle to impose himself on his surroundings, whether as the "greatest jurist in the world" or as the oldest sitting judge in history, or as a dying man who allegedly thumbed his nose at his companions. On the other hand, as Holmes, pursuing self-improvement and recognition, deepened and refined his philosophical stance, he came more and more to recognize his own insignificance. His career thus simultaneously presents the example of one who carved out his own space in the universe as broadly and deeply as any, but who in the process came to sense that his efforts were very possibly useless. Holmes left the matter there. He could not truly tell whether he was in the universe or the universe in him; he had to guess.

When considering Holmes' intellectual qualities, one notices above all the juxta-position of his essentially "literary" and "speculative" orientation with the empha-sis on analytical marshaling of evidence that characterizes legal reasoning. When Holmes turned from literature and philosophy to law in the late 1860s, the turn was incomplete. He retained his interest, as a scholar and a judge, in placing data within the framework of generalizations and in finding a "form of words" to make those generalizations vivid and memorable. Thus he was far less interested in exhibiting the steps of his reasoning, or in amassing the details of his data. He combined, in *The Common Law,* arcane and attenuated allusions to ancient cases with breathtaking generalizations about the evolution of legal rules. His standard argument in oppo-sition to a legal principle, such as act-at-peril liability in tort, was that in "the prevailing view" it should not be followed, or that it was "uniformly disapproved." In short, he was arguably more interested in letting his language, as distinguished from his evidence or his logic, carry his arguments. In his opinions, and in his scholarship, he typically left out many of the steps in his reasoning. Brandeis once said that Holmes did not sufficiently consider the need of others to understand. Perhaps it is more accurate to say that he thought a well-turned "form of words" the equivalent of understanding.

Alongside Holmes' intellectual desire to plumb the depths of ideas, and to express them as freshly and vividly as possible, was a penchant for what could be called a "poetic" approach to his intellectual tasks. Holmes conceived of his role, whether judge or scholar, as a solitary, creative, original one. He did not, for the most part, consult others, and when he did, he denied any influence and gave no credit. He was not interested in "synthetic" presentations, whether in the form of narrative history or detailed statements of the facts of cases. Although he claimed in *The Common Law* that such extrajudicial factors as conditions of time and place were the ultimate determinants of legal rules, when analyzing contract, tort, or property cases he gave no attention to the historical context of the cases he discussed. When he stated facts, he did so only with his conclusions in mind. In *Buck v. Bell,* for example, he listed the procedural safeguards afforded persons eligible for sterilization at some length, but neglected to mention that Carrie Buck had never been shown to be an "imbe-cile."

Holmes' work was also self-consciously unconventional. In *The Common Law,* he undertook a fusion of historicist and policy methodologies that no Anglo-Amer-ican treatise writer had ever before attempted. As a judge he continued to write brief, cryptic opinions despite the custom, especially on the Supreme Court, of offering elaborate versions of syllogistic reasoning. He argued for a deterrence theory of punishment, objective standards in all of tort law, and an objective theory of contract formation, when none of those positions was generally accepted. He advanced a deferential theory of judicial review at the height of substantive judicial scrutiny of legislative acts. The ultrapositivism of his most mature jurisprudential essay, "The Path of the Law," cut against the prevalent view that law must track morality. His later radical skepticism starkly opposed his "progressive" supporters' faith in the perfectibility of social institutions. Holmes was a "poet," conceiving of his work as a process in which the individual thinker sought his own relationship to his material and expressed that relationship in an original, idiosyncratic manner.

Holmes was thus at bottom an individualist judge in a collegial profession. While he served all his career on courts that rendered decisions collectively, and while he allowed the norms of those courts to restrain too frequent dissents and too biting criticism of colleagues, he was essentially unconcerned with the views of others in his decisionmaking. "Others" included not only his fellow judges but those who had an interest in the outcome of his cases, whether because of their immediate impact on litigants or because of their larger social interest. Although Holmes obviously discussed cases in conference with other judges, and on occasion talked them over with intimates such as Brandeis, when it came to writing about them he was more interested in "firing off" and "finding a form of words" than in the process of collective decision. His interactions with his colleagues came primarily in the form of their removing too vivid or too sweeping passages in his draft opinions rather than any deliberation over the merits of the case.

In light of his individualistic interpretation of his role as a judge it is interesting that his judicial colleagues did not regard Holmes as a gadfly or a maverick, in the vein of Justices John Harlan the Elder or William O. Douglas. Some of Holmes' personal qualities seem to have militated against his being perceived in that fashion. As Taft's letters indicate, Holmes was universally polite and good-tempered to his contemporaries, suppressing anger in confrontations and apparently not indulging his wit or humor at the expense of others. Particularly striking in this regard is Holmes' lack of condescension for judges whom he regarded as his intellectual inferiors, of whom there were undoubtedly many. Holmes seems to have had a warm spot in his heart for successful men with strong personalities, whether or not they were intellectually inclined: he may have felt positively toward most of his colleagues even though he would not have wanted to engage them in intellectual discussion. Holmes was, of course, appreciated by most of his colleagues in his obvious dedication to his work. Although some did not welcome his voracious appetite for writing opinions, they could at least count on him not only to complete his own assignments but to take over theirs if they encountered difficulties.

Finally, although one gets a strong impression of Holmes as a philosophical skeptic, his skepticism was at war with other elements of his temperament and may have been, at some level, a pseudobelief or a defense. There is no sense, for example, that Holmes was skeptical about his own intellectual powers, or his capacity to write, or his ability to draw lines as a judge. There is no sense in his letters that he approached his work or his life with an attitude akin to "it doesn't matter in the end what I do"; on the contrary, the impression is that he approached everything, from opinions to walks or drives to letters and meals, with relish. I have alluded earlier to his "pseudohumility" on receiving honors or other forms of praise, as if by stating his fears about disappointing his acolytes or his disenchantment at receiving an award after it was past due he was getting them out in the open where they would dissipate.

One cannot fairly claim, however, that his skepticism was a pseudoskepticism. Every indication suggests it was a well-developed and refined philosophical position. But it seems just that: a belief that is affirmed as the sum of considered thought about the universe, but once affirmed ceases to be a guide to life. The only arena in which Holmes' skepticism actually functioned as a guide to his conduct is in its contribution to the melancholy state of his last years, when his ruminations on his own failing powers may have been reinforced by a conviction that in the end all that counted was the fullness of time, so that he was passing into insignificance. But his melancholy may have been simpler, only the result of a recognition that he could no longer function as he once did, and thus could no longer do the work that had so long diverted him from loneliness.

When Holmes' intellectual positions are placed alongside his unquestioned enthusiasm for nearly everything he chose to do in his life, one is reminded of a remark attributed to Fanny about her husband, "Wendell's latest plaything is Despair."[2] There is a sense that for all of Holmes' considered ruminations about the ultimate insignificance of man, the inevitable tyranny of the "crowd," and his own inability to prove that he was not dreaming or that the universe was not in him, rather than he in it, he either did not think that his fatalistic conclusions applied to his own life, or he resolved that whether they did or not he was going to live life to the fullest anyway.

Thus one has to consider the element of pose, as well as the element of warding off fears, in Holmes' "despairing" expositions. When Holmes said, in 1901, "[w]e are all very near despair," one is inclined to forget that in the preceding sentence he said that "[l]ife is an end in itself, and the only question as to whether it is worth living is whether you have enough of it."[3] He took pains to make sure that he had "enough" of the life that he wanted, and, however fatalistic he might have been about his ultimate destiny, he never doubted his ability to extract the juices of life.

～

In exploring the integration of Holmes' personal characteristics with his intellectual inclinations I have kept in mind the compartments into which he sought to divide his life: "two-thirds" or sometimes "half" in his work and the remainder in "his wife" or whatever remained outside work. He sought to effectuate something of a division between temperament, or certain features of it, and intellect. Put more precisely, he sought to suppress or channel some inclinations or features of his temperament lest they distract him from effective use of his intellect. When he sought diversions, he pursued them passionately, whether they were communications with Clare Castletown or the combination of solitaire and an absorbing book, but he tried to structure his life into "work" and "play" compartments.

Nonetheless, the connections between temperament and intellect come readily enough. His ambition lead him to a search to distinguish himself, from his father, from the "Brahmin" literary culture of his father's contemporaries, from their "softness" on philosophical questions. Distinction, for the son of so well known a personage, meant recognition, recognition in a different field, recognition in a medium that was intrinsically his own. Legal scholarship of a particularly demanding kind, expressed in a distinctive style, was a natural product of this process.

One can offer a comparable analysis of the emotional intensity that was characteristic of Holmes. His "passion," in its intellectual manifestations, led him to pursue issues "to their bottom," whether that involved coming to terms with Plato as an undergraduate or exploring "vis viva" with William James or investigating the origins of possession or determining the moving forces in the universe. The end result of these forays was, paradoxically, a philosophy that emphasized the mystical complexity of ultimates and fell back on the minimal "truths" of life, such as doing one's job, accepting that one "couldn't help" subscribing to certain faiths, recognizing the cosmic insignificance of man in the face of time and change. The fatalism of this philosophy did not, however, lead Holmes to nihilism or inertia; on the contrary, as noted, it encouraged him to plunge into the minimalist realms with gusto. Thus he cared deeply about finishing his assignments, thinking and writing as well as he could, improving his mind, mastering his profession. He cared, too, about his reputation, for, despite the insignificance of individuals in the long run, recognition was one of the minimalist features of life that gave satisfaction in the short space of time one was granted.

Of all the intriguing mysteries about life that Holmes discovered in his investigations, that of the inevitable coexistence of the "self" and the "other" seems to have intrigued him the most. He had grown up in a culture whose standards, whose styles of expression, whose social and intellectual tastes seemed firmly in place, a culture exalted and coveted by others. And yet that culture, as personified in the activities and inclinations of his father's generation, seemed stifling and unsatisfying. Beginning with his decision to leave Harvard to join a war effort for which his father's contemporaries initially had little enthusiasm, he struggled to distance himself from Brahmin culture. Yet in his own tastes and inclinations he remained deeply rooted in his heritage, very much his father's son.

Forty years after joining the Twentieth Regiment, years in which he had chosen his own profession, produced his own original scholarship, and assumed a position of power and influence in the world of affairs far outdistancing that of his father, he found himself still characterized as the son of Dr. Holmes, a "literary feller" whose brilliance and lack of "soundness" was unusual for a judge. At sixty-one, despite his frequent travels, despite his notable success in becoming a figure in London society, despite his romance with a member of "the Ascendancy," his life was overwhelmingly that of a Brahmin, circumscribed by a provincial social life and the reading and writing habits of a "man of letters." Even though he had "started for the Pole," and had felt the "secret joy of the thinker," he remained, for the most part, an obscure Massachusetts judge from the Brahmin class.

One of the canons of Brahmin Boston was civic and social responsibility, manifested, for Dr. Holmes' generation, less in political participation than in conscious efforts to establish and disseminate a distinctive American highbrow and middlebrow culture. The literary outpourings of Holmes Sr. and his contemporaries could be seen as part of the mission sketched in Emerson's "American Scholar," a mission to demonstrate to the educated world that American letters could rival its European counterparts in taste and intellect; that America, or at least Boston, deserved to be taken seriously as a cultural force. In Holmes this idea of civic responsibility was represented in the concept of "duty," which Holmes defined in terms quite different from those of his father's generation. Duty meant fidelity to chivalric codes, such as soldierly honor and loyalty to one's "cause." Duty meant pursuing one's profession with attention to "noble" ends, such as creating lasting scholarship or contributing to the fabric of the law's growth. Duty symbolized the continual presence of the "other" in one's life, rendered in the most palatable terms that Holmes, being of the generation "touched with fire," could imagine. It was the duty of the knight and the soldier, blind obedience to the noble cause.

Duty had its minimalist versions as well: never missing oral arguments or conferences, making decisions as swiftly and decisively as one could, completing one's assignments, reading the books an educated "gentleman" should have read before he died. But duty, and the heritage of Brahmin culture, had their stifling features. To be effective in his work, Holmes felt, he needed to structure the rest of his life, which meant usually foregoing social contacts for the company of his reclusive and eccentric wife. Over time this isolation chafed, producing the "bitterness" he wrote of to Clare Castletown and resulting in his making the world of upper-class London society a place to which he periodically escaped, released the spontaneous, convivial, and romantic elements in his nature, and "felt twice the man he was" before his arrival. The oppressive presence of the "other" in Holmes' Boston led him to seek a greater range of intimacy with others in London than he allowed himself at home, albeit a structured kind of intimacy, the intimacy of "play," not "what one does." London was a place where "a whole host of endless romantic possibilities" periodically surfaced, but a place that "one got tired of . . . in a month."

As his life progressed, Holmes' struggle to assert his individuality in the face of the "other" increasingly focused on his professional contributions, most intensely in his search for professional recognition. In the course of that search he encountered another culture, quite distant from Brahmin Boston, that of the early twentieth-century "progressive" intelligentsia. By involving himself with that culture Holmes furthered his quest for recognition, but, ironically, Felix Frankfurter and his contemporaries were in large part attracted by Holmes' Brahmin heritage. That a scion of privileged New England aristocrats should allegedly care about the "social experimentation" "progressives" felt necessitated by the increasingly heterogeneous and interdependent quality of modern American society made Holmes a rare catch for Frankfurter and his contemporaries. That an old-line Boston Yankee should enter into close friendships with young left-leaning Jews was part of Holmes' charm. It did not matter that Holmes cared nothing about "social experimentation," except from a jurisprudential point of view, and that he retained a keen consciousness of class and ethnicity. He was attractive to "progressives" in part because he had apparently disengaged himself from his Brahmin heritage while still embodying it.

Thus in some respects the lionization of Holmes in his last years, which could have been taken as a recognition of his unique accomplishments as an individual, was a lionization of a romantic figure from another time by a generation of "moderns." Holmes the old soldier, impeccably dressed in high collars, speaking with a trans-Atlantic accent, living in a house filled with Victorian and Georgian furniture, was as inspiring as Holmes the "great dissenter," the enlightened apostle of judicial self-restraint, the "progressive" or liberal judge. When the kind of recognition came to Holmes at the end of his life that he had sought so fiercely earlier, it was a recognition that expressed how powerfully the elements of his cultural heritage had superimposed themselves on his person, despite his efforts to detach himself from that heritage.

~

Holmes' lionization by a generation of "modern" intellectuals prevented discerning appraisals of his life and work for years. As late as the 1950s the only biographical treatments of him were a romantic, partially fictionalized portrait and a derivative journalistic account. His papers had been principally restricted to the use of his authorized biographer, a former secretary who had been selected by Felix Frankfurter. As late as 1967 that pattern of restricted access, and efforts to create an "authorized" portrait, were still in place. Meanwhile, Holmes had become an unexpectedly controversial figure in scholarly literature, being successively attacked for being soft on fascism and indifferent to civil liberties. Fewer and fewer generations of law students were being exposed to his opinions, as both his attitude toward constitutional adjudication and his substantive positions came to be considered obsolete.

Ironically, interest in Holmes was revived by the appearance of the first volumes of Mark Howe's "authorized" biography, which revealed the great complexity of Holmes as a person and as an intellect, and the large and interesting contributions that Holmes had made outside the realm of judging. By the end of Howe's second volume, Holmes had not yet decided a single case; nonetheless a reader could discern that Howe's subject was a compelling figure.

Just as it was ironic that Felix Frankfurter's "authorized" narrator of the legend of Holmes should have contributed to the collapse of that legend, at least in the form created by Frankfurter and his "progressive" contemporaries, it was ironic that Howe's untimely death, coupled with the abortive efforts on the part of Holmes' executors to commission another authorized biographer, should have resulted in the opening up to the public of another whole dimension of Holmes' life. With the abandonment of an "authorized" format, and the consequent collection and microfilming of Holmes' papers, the intricate and substantial world of Holmes' extrajudicial life, including his social life, came into public consciousness. An event symbolizing this new stage in Holmesian historiography was John Monagan's article publicizing the relationship between Holmes and Clare Castletown, as revealed in his letters to her. The existence of those letters, and of that relationship, had been known by Mark Howe and a handful of other "authorized" persons since World War II. The letters had been the property of Harvard Law School since 1967. When Monagan's article discussing them appeared in 1985, almost no one knew of their existence. Monagan first submitted the article to the *Boston Bar Journal;* its board of editors, made up of prominent Boston attorneys, turned the article down. Monagan then published the letters and his commentary in the *Boston Globe Magazine.*

The opening up of Holmes' papers precipitated considerable scholarly interest, and has made possible the appearance of two one-volume biographies that fill in details of Holmes' life and career that were largely unknown to all but a small circle of persons. But the appearance of these volumes has produced the next of a succession of ironies in Holmesian literature. In their apparent rush to convey "unknown" information about the latter part of Holmes' life, and to produce accessible, one-volume biographies of the best known judge in American history, the recent treatments have neglected to ask a question whose explanation has been made possible by the same circumstances that enabled full-length biographies of Holmes to appear after so many years. The recent biographies of Holmes rest on sources that permit a compilation of the narrative of his life as well as that of his work. Yet in the process of describing Holmes' life, the recent biographers only incidentally describe his work, and make little effort to explore the connections, and relationships, between life and work.

Such an exploration has been the effort of this volume. As a consequence, its emphasis has been internal, both in the sense of persistent attention to Holmes' mind and temperament and in the sense of regularly undertaking close analyses of Holmes' language, in its judicial and extrajudicial forms. While an overriding assumption of the volume has been that Holmes is a figure of great significance, whose life and career are amply deserving of focused examination, little time has been spent elaborating that assumption. It therefore seems worthwhile, at this juncture, to recapitulate the reasons for Holmes' historical importance and continuing interest.

Holmes has been unique, in the class of individuals who have been distinguished American judges, in being a figure of popular romance. Other judges have had significant extrajudicial careers in politics or public life: Brandeis, Frankfurter, Hughes, Hugo Black, Earl Warren come to mind. Other judges, ranging from John Marshall to William Brennan, have matched or surpassed Holmes in their impact upon American constitutional law. Other judges have had visible careers as scholars: Joseph Story, Frankfurter, Benjamin Cardozo. Several judges, ranging from Roger Taney to Douglas and Brennan, have approximated Holmes' longevity of judicial service. None, however, has presented the combination of culturally attractive features that Holmes presented: the son of the ''Aristocrat of the Breakfast Table''; the contemporary of William James, Henry James, and Henry Adams; a Civil War veteran; the author of the best known treatise on American law; the only judge to receive the Roosevelt Medal of Freedom; the only judge to have been given honorary degrees from Yale, Harvard, and Oxford; the only judge to have his birthday the occasion for a nationwide radio symposium.

Judges are, on the whole, not romantic figures, and it might be suggested that Holmes' distinction in that regard was largely fortuitous. He was favored both in his looks and in his antecedents; he was the right age to fight in the Civil War and lucky enough to survive it; despite being named to the Supreme Court at the age of sixty-one, he was fortunate enough to retain his physical and mental health into his nineties, allowing him to surpass his peers in longevity. One could argue that Holmes' eminence resulted in large part from genetic fortune.

Such an argument ignores the impressive uses to which Holmes put his advantages. Had he never been a judge, *The Common Law* would remain one of the great works of jurisprudence. In that book Holmes attempted something that no previous writer on jurisprudence had tried: a synthesis of common law subjects that was, at the same time, an argument for how the common law evolved and, implicitly, a statement of the policy goals it should be furthering in the future course of its evolution. Blackstone, Kent, and Story had produced earlier syntheses of common law fields, and Austin, Mill, Bentham, and Maine offered earlier statements of overriding jurisprudential principles or earlier efforts to explain how the common law changed. No previous writer had attempted the distinctive combination of history, analytics, and policy that Holmes forged in *The Common Law*.

Moreover, no late nineteenth-century writer on legal subjects, and especially no late nineteenth-century judicial writer, had critically examined the prevailing juris-prudential theory that judges merely declared a disembodied, self-centered entity called "law" as powerfully and as clearly as Holmes. He launched that critique as early as the 1870s, and continued it throughout his nineteenth-century scholarship. By the time he generalized the critique in his *Lochner* dissent, it had taken hold, and it would soon become commonplace wisdom. Few of the twentieth-century com-mentators who took for granted that judges "make" law and denied any meaningful separation between "the will of the law" and "the will of the judge" appreciated that Holmes had expressed those insights at a time when orthodox jurisprudence insisted that judging was a detached exercise in "finding" the law.

Holmes not only was a pioneer in articulating and disseminating the insight that the will of the law was inseparable from the will of the judge, he was a pioneer in developing the implications of that insight for judges in constitutional cases. In an age in which substantive judicial glossing of constitutional provisions was the norm, Holmes was the first prominent judge to question whether such glossing was per-missible in a majoritarian democracy, and to suggest that the proper stance for judges in a world where judicial "interpretation" and judicial "lawmaking" were often synonymous was deference to majorities. One could argue that Holmes was the first prominent expositor of the "countermajoritarian difficulty" and the accompanying posture of judicial "self-restraint" in constitutional cases that have dominated com-mentary on constitutional law issues for much of the twentieth century.

Having pioneered in the development of "deferential" judging in a majoritarian constitutional democracy, Holmes then pioneered the development of a counterde-ferential stance for judges in First Amendment cases. Despite the doctrinal incon-sistencies that abound in Holmes' free speech decisions, and the general difficulty in squaring his speech-protective approach with his deference to legislative or other constitutional cases, it is arguable that without his contributions the emergence of significant protection for dissident speech in American society would have been indefinitely delayed. His free speech decisions provided, in striking rhetoric, several of the modern rationales for protection of speech, including the rationale that a "marketplace of ideas," rather than governmental policy, should determine what constitutes "truth" in a democracy, and the rationale that the "principle of freedom for the thought we hate" was one of the fundamental principles of American society. If one, in short, were asked to single out three themes that have dominated American jurisprudence for much of the twentieth century, the list could quite plausibly com-prise deferential judicial review in constitutional cases, protection for free speech, and the belief that judges "make" rather than "find" law, which is itself the product of changing social conditions rather than innate "logic." Each of these themes was not only associated with Holmes, it may be said to have originated, in a considered jurisprudential form, in Holmes' work. While selecting these concepts for promi-nence obviously excludes others with which Holmes could not easily be associated— the growth of the principle of equality under law being the most conspicuous—one would be hard pressed to find any other judge in American history whose work was so closely associated with such seminal jurisprudence.

Finally, no judge in American history has left such a rich collection of correspondence, expressing so wide a variety of views on so many absorbing and important issues. Moreover, no judge in American history has written with such literary flair. Doubtless many students of the American judiciary would cite numerous other judges for having written more analytically satisfying, or intellectually honest, or doctrinally illuminating opinions than Holmes. But none equalled Holmes as a correspondent, as a kind of "man of letters." To the extent that "good writing" is an intelligible concept, Holmes was about as good a writer, judges and nonjudges included, as America has produced.

In sum, facets of Holmes appeal to a variety and diversity of people. If Holmes the judge seems to exhibit an impoverished sensibility, see Holmes the romantic, courting Clare Castletown. If Holmes' legal history essays seem overly pedantic or obscure, remember Holmes' Civil War battles. When tired of Holmes' views on Spinoza or Kent, consider his apercus on Jane Austen, John Galsworthy, or Marcel Proust. Balance surfeit with Holmes' celebration of living as an end in itself against Holmes the misanthrope and Holmes the apostle of despair. Holmes scholarship will never end, because his life and thought are nearly infinite in their variety.

~

When Holmes' safety deposit box was opened and the contents of his house inventoried after his death two findings were sufficiently interesting to be communicated to his authorized biographer. One was a "little paper parcel, the size of one finger, which, when opened, was found to contain two musket balls." On the paper was written, in Holmes' hand, "These were taken from my body in the Civil War." The other, from his bedroom closet, was a pair of "old Civil War uniforms," to which "was pinned a piece of paper, on which he had written 'These uniforms were worn by me in the Civil War and the stains upon them are my blood.' "[4] Thus Holmes preserved his great triumph, victory over death in the Civil War. He had, in his early days in that war, risked his life without knowing what war was about and without realizing the imperfect connection between military battles and the ends for which they were supposedly fought. Unlike his father and his father's generation, he had been touched with fire. And he had survived. The momentos, "taken from my body" and stained with "my blood," were testaments to that survival.

Holmes' capacity to survive dominates any consideration of his life. Capacity to survive in the face of physical danger and emotional turmoil; capacity not merely to survive, but to thrive, to live a very long time and to function, mentally and physically, at a very high level. The unreconstructed fatalism of Holmes' prose, his singular preoccupation with his somewhat narrow regimen, his periodic revelations of how little he cared for humankind in general and how mincing and structured was his affection, even for individual humans for which he cared, may tend to conceal the enthusiasm, the love, with which he approached life. Thus it is not just the pleasure one derives from being exposed to Holmes' thoughts and words that makes him a stimulating companion. It is the recognition, which closer acquaintance sharpens, of the pleasure he took in encountering life, in thinking about his encounters, and in writing up his thoughts with style.

Appendix

Holmes' Secretaries

~

1905–1906	Charles K. Poe
1906–1907	Augustin Derby
1907–1908	Howard Stockton
1908–1909	Erland F. Fish
1909–1910	Leland B. Duer
1910–1911	Irving S. Olds
1911–1912	Francis B. Biddle
1912–1913	Stanley Clarke
1913–1914	George L. Harrison
1914–1915	Harvey H. Bundy
1915–1916	Chauncey Belknap
1916–1917	Shelton Hale
1917–1918	Vaughn Miller
1918–1919	Lloyd H. Landau
1919–1920	Stanley Morrison
1920–1921	Day Kimball
1921–1922	Laurence Curtis
1922–1923	Robert M. Benjamin
1923–1924	James M. Nicely
1924–1925	W. Barton Leach
1925–1926	Charles Denby, Jr.
1926–1927	Thomas G. Corcoran
1927–1928	Arthur E. Sutherland
1928–1929	John E. Lockwood
1929–1930	Alger Hiss
1930–1931	Robert W. Wales
1931–1932	H. Chapman Rose
1932–1933	Donald Hiss
1933–1934	Mark DeWolfe Howe
1934–1935	James H. Rowe

Notes

~

Introduction

1. I have listed and commented upon many of those sources in the Bibliographical Essay, which follows.

CHAPTER ONE: *Heritage*

1. A recent biography of Holmes has placed the date of his graduation from Harvard as June 17. See Liva Baker, *The Justice from Beacon Hill* 100 (1991). Hereafter cited as Baker, *Justice from Beacon Hill*. The actual date of commencement was July 17. It is doubtful whether Holmes attended commencement, but he received his degree on that occasion. See Mark DeWolfe Howe, *Justice Oliver Wendell Holmes: The Shaping Years* 77 (1957). Hereafter cited as Howe, *Shaping Years*.

2. The official records in the Massachusetts State House give the date of Holmes' commission as July 10, but that date was obviously retroactive, since on July 12 a letter from John Lothrop Motley, a close friend of the Holmes family, indicated that Holmes' father, Dr. Oliver Wendell Holmes, Sr., was attempting to use influence to secure his son a commission. John Lothrop Motley to Mrs. John L. Motley, July 12, 1861, quoted in George W. Curtis, ed., *Correspondence of John Lothrop Motley* (3 vols., 1889), II, 12. For the commission see State House Archives, Boston, Mass.

3. Holmes added a footnote at this point and listed *The Autocrat of the Breakfast Table, The Professor at the Breakfast Table,* and Dr. Holmes' novel *Elsie Venner,* as well as his collection of poems and his medical lectures, *Currents and Counter Currents.*

4. The sketch appears in Harvard College, *Class of 1861 Album,* 329 Harvard Archives. It is quoted in full in Frederick C. Fiechter, Jr., "The Preparation of an American Aristocrat," 6 *New Eng. Q.* 3, 4–5 (1933).

5. The terms "plan" and "life plan" have been initially placed within quotation marks to emphasize that I am not claiming that Holmes Jr. self-consciously constructed every feature of the organization of his life. Indeed any "plan" attributed to Holmes Jr. can be seen as a set of intuitive as distinguished from self-conscious responses. Since those responses emphasize themes of control, however, the choice of the word "plan" seems justified.

6. See, e.g., Mark A. DeWolfe Howe, *Holmes of the Breakfast Table* 113–15 (1939). For a trenchant analysis of Dr. Holmes' cultural role in his *Autocrat* essays, see Peter

Gibian, "Opening and Closing the Conversation: Style and Stance from Holmes Senior to Holmes Junior, in Robert W. Gordon, ed. *the Legacy of Oliver Wendell Holmes Jr.* 186 (1992). Hereafter cited as Gordon, *Legacy.*

7. Oliver Wendell Holmes, Sr., to Phineas Barnes, March 28, 1828, in John T. Morse, *Life and Letters of Oliver Wendell Holmes* (2 vols., 1896), I, 55. Hereafter cited as Morse, *Life and Letters.*

8. Holmes Sr. to Barnes, September [no date given] 1829, id., I, 61.

9. Holmes Sr. to Barnes, January 13, 1830, id., I, 64.

10. Holmes Sr. to Barnes, March [no date given] 1831, id., I, 69. "Wistar's Anatomy" referred to the 5th edition of Caspar Wistar, *A System of Anatomy for the Use of Students of Medicine* (1830).

11. Holmes Sr. to Abiel and Sarah Holmes, August 13, 1833, Morse, *Life and Letters,* I, 107.

12. For a record of Holmes Sr.'s receiving the degree from Harvard Medical School, see Records of the College Faculty, 1836, Harvard University Archives, Widener Library, Harvard University, Cambridge, Mass. Hereafter cited as Harvard Archives. For evidence of his having joined the Massachusetts Medical Society, see Oliver Wendell Holmes Sr. Papers, Houghton Library, Harvard University. Hereafter cited as Holmes Sr. Papers. See also Eleanor M. Tilton, *Amiable Autocrat* 134 (1947). Hereafter cited as Tilton, *Autocrat.*

13. See Tilton, *Autocrat,* 203–08.

14. Id., 232.

15. Oliver Wendell Holmes, Jr., to Clara S. Stevens, July 26, 1914, Holmes Papers.

16. 4 *New England Q. J. Med.* 503 (1843).

17. See Tilton, *Autocrat,* 173–76. For an accessible version of the essay, see "Puerperal Fever as a Private Pestilence," reprinted in *The Writings of Oliver Wendell Holmes* (14 vols., 1891 ed.), IX, 106. Hereafter cited as *Writings of Holmes Sr.*, with volume and page numbers.

18. One might nonetheless concur with Gibian's assessment in Gordon, *Legacy*, at 215:

> Certainly we can understand the urgency and admire the courage of Holmes
> Junior's attempt to answer the deep questions left to him by his antebellum fathers.
> But we must admit that there is also an important honesty and humanity in the
> attempt to comprehend a tension of opposing voices—the "conversation of a
> culture"—rather than too suddenly to put on one's military mustache and march
> blindly into judgment.

19. Alice James, *The Diary of Alice James* 69 (Leon Edel, ed., 1964).

20. William James to Henry James, Sr., March 18, 1873, Harvard Archives, Houghton Library.

21. The most conspicuous example of this tendency is Catherine Drinker Bowen's biography of Holmes Jr. and his family, *Yankee from Olympus* (1944), in which Dr. Holmes and his son are portrayed as coexisting in a state of tension. See, e.g., 262–63, where Fanny Dixwell Holmes, recently married to Holmes Jr., is described as wanting to "ease this tension between father and son," and "make peace in [the] house." See also 122–23, 180–82.

The difficulty with Bowen's interpretation is that not only is it based on little actual evidence, it is presented in a narrative in which documented material is intermingled with material that is frankly imaginative. Bowen supplies thoughts for her characters, invents dialogue, and attributes attitudes without support. While she relied on confidential sources for many of her observations, none of those included persons who were present in the Holmes household during the time when Dr. Holmes and his son were reportedly at odds. Thus at a minimum such claims as "[f]or the past five years . . . Holmes had gone to absurd lengths . . . to avoid his father," Bowen at 323–24, need to be regarded as unsubstantiated. See also Francis Biddle, *Mr. Justice Holmes* 26–30 (1942), for a similar assessment, also undocumented.

Two other recent biographies have emphasized tensions between father and son. See Gary Aichele, *Oliver Wendell Holmes, Jr.* 2, 17, 23–24 (1989) (hereafter cited as Aichele, *Holmes, Jr.*); Sheldon Novick, *Honorable Justice* 10, 13–14, 20, 94, 140 (1988) (hereafter cited as Novick, *Honorable Justice*). I have found both those treatments one-sided. See G. Edward White, "Holmes' Life Plan," 65 *N.Y.U. L. Rev.* 1409, 1412–18 (1990).

22. Howe, *Shaping Years,* 11–28, and Baker, *Beacon Hill,* 60–64, are aware of the complexities in the father-son relationship, while their discussions differ in emphasis from mine.

23. Morse, *Life and Letters,* II, 33, 35.

24. Holmes to Felix Frankfurter, May 21, 1926, Holmes Papers.

25. Holmes to Baroness Charlotte Moncheur, October 7, 1928, Holmes Papers.

26. Holmes to Frankfurter, supra note 24.

27. Holmes to Nina Gray, April 30, 1905, Holmes Papers.

28. Felix Frankfurter, Memorandum, September 28, 1932, Holmes Papers. This account is not consistent with other autobiographical accounts that minimized the role of Holmes' father in Holmes' choice of profession. For an effort to make sense of this inconsistency, see Michael H. Hoffheimer, *Justice Holmes and the Natural Law* (1992).

29. Oliver Wendell Holmes, Sr., to Holmes, November 12, 1875, id.

30. Howe's reading of the same letter in *Shaping Years,* 27–28, is gentler than mine.

31. Holmes to Leslie Scott, August 22, 1908, id.

32. Oliver Wendell Holmes, Sr., "The Poet at the Breakfast Table," *Writings of Holmes Sr.* I, 147.

33. Dr. Holmes and his son, living together at 296 Beacon Street at the time, went out to watch the fire, and, as the Doctor put it in a letter, noticed that the burning buildings crumbled noiselessly, as if they were sinking into feather beds. Holmes Sr. to John L. Motley, November 16, 1872, in Morse, *Life and Letters,* I, 197.

34. The incident is described by Mark Howe, Holmes' law clerk for the 1933–34 Term, when Holmes was in his ninety-third year. Mark DeW. Howe, Diary of Clerkship Year with Justice Holmes, 1933–34, entry of Thursday, February 22, 1934, Mark DeWolfe Howe Papers, Harvard Law School Library.

35. The poem was written and published in September 1830. It appealed for the preservation of the frigate *The U.S.S. Constitution,* and was widely circulated in newspapers across the country. See Boston *Daily Advertiser,* September 15, 1830 (author described as "H."); Tilton, *Autocrat,* at 65. *The U.S.S. Constitution* was not dismantled, in part as a result of the poem.

36. See Tilton, *Autocrat,* 67–68, 142, 172, 176, 189.

37. Id., 161–62, 372.

38. See id., 373, 376.

39. See, e.g., O. W. Holmes, Sr., "The Autocrat of the Breakfast-Table," in *Writings of Holmes Sr.,* I, 230–33; O. W. Holmes, Sr., "The Poet at the Breakfast-Table," id., I, 147; O. W. Holmes, Sr., "The Professor at the Breakfast-Table," id., I, 94–95.

40. Letter from Oliver Wendell Holmes, Jr., to William James, April 19, 1868, in Holmes Papers, reprinted in Ralph Perry, *The Thought and Character of William James* (2 vols., 1935) I, 509.

41. See Mark DeWolfe Howe, *Justice Oliver Wendell Holmes: The Proving Years* 88 (1963) (hereafter cited as Howe, *Proving Years*), arguing that Holmes Sr. "could not bring himself, before the war, to condemn the slaveholders of the South"; Howe, *Shaping Years,* 24–25 (Holmes Sr. referred to himself as "an 'unconvinced' conservative or I might say as well a skeptical radical"); Tilton, *Autocrat,* 227 (describing Holmes Sr.'s ambivalence toward abolitionists).

42. See Holmes Sr., "The Inevitable Trial," in *Mechanism in Thought and Morals, Writings of Holmes Sr.,* VIII, 78, 90–91. For more discussion of Holmes Sr.'s views on the Union cause, see also Howe, *Shaping Years,* 145, and Tilton, *Autocrat,* 228.

43. John T. Morse, Jr., who knew both Holmes Sr. and Holmes Jr. intimately, quoted a contemporary, Edmund Gosse, as saying of Holmes Sr., "Perhaps no man . . . has given . . . a more extraordinary impression of wit in conversation." Morse, *Life and Letters,* I, 247.

44. Waldo Higginson to Henry Lee, Jr., September 15, 1842, quoted in Tilton, *Autocrat,* 161.

45. Catherine Cabot to Henry Lee, Jr., July 28, 1842, quoted in id., 162.

46. Mark DeW. Howe, Memorandum of conversation with Miss Loring, July 1942, Holmes Papers.

47. Amelia Jackson Holmes to Holmes, July 22, 1866, Holmes Papers.

48. Holmes to Amelia Jackson Holmes, September 11, 1861, in Mark DeWolfe Howe, ed., *Touched With Fire: Civil War Letters and Diary of Oliver Wendell Holmes, Jr. 1861–1864* 6 (1946). Hereafter cited as *Touched With Fire.*

49. Holmes to Amelia Jackson Holmes, September 23, 1861, quoted in id., 8.

50. Amelia Jackson Holmes to Lucy Hallowell, February 1, 1863, Holmes Papers.

51. A retrospective account of the formation of the Boston branch of the U.S. Sanitary Commission can be found in Thomas W. Higginson, *Massachusetts in the Army and Navy During the War of 1861–65* (2 vols., 1896), II, 588–89.

52. Remarkably, this unattributed comment about Amelia was made in an obituary of Dr. Holmes. See Boston *Post,* October 8, 1894.

53. Id.

54. Baker, *Justice from Beacon Hill,* 41.

55. Amelia Jackson Holmes to Henry Lee, Jr., September 21, 1838, quoted in Frances Rollins Morse, comp., *Henry and Mary Lee, Letters and Journals with Other Family Letters 1802–1860* 269–70 (1926).

56. Morse, *Life and Letters,* I, 70–71.

57. Holmes to Morris Cohen, February 5, 1919, quoted in Felix Cohen, "Holmes–Cohen Correspondence," 9 *J. Hist. Ideas* 3, 14–15 (1948).

58. Holmes allegedly made the comment to Alger Hiss during the time Hiss spent as Holmes' law clerk for the 1929 Term. Baker repeats the comment in *Justice from Beacon*

Hill, 42, citing an undated interview with Hiss. For a reference to Holmes' "perverse" reaction of feeling "very blue" after having been appointed to the Supreme Court of the United States, see Holmes to Lady [Georgina] Pollock, September 6, 1902, in 1 Mark DeWolfe Howe, ed., *Holmes–Pollock Letters* 105 (2 vols., 1961). Hereafter cited as *Holmes–Pollock Letters.* For a fuller discussion, see Chapter Ten.

59. Holmes to Amelia Jackson Holmes, July 8, 1864, in *Touched With Fire,* 151. Holmes had first notified his parents that he was contemplating leaving the Union army on May 16 of that year. See id., 122.

60. Amelia Jackson Holmes to Holmes, June 11, 1866, Holmes Papers.

61. Holmes made no mention of his sister, Amelia Jackson Holmes, or his brother, Edward Jackson Holmes, in the sketch. He does not seem to have been particularly close to either sibling, although he practiced law with Edward for a brief period between 1871 and 1873. Both Amelia and Edward died at comparatively young ages, Edward at thirty-eight in 1884 and Amelia at forty-six in 1889.

62. Howe, *Shaping Years,* 29.

63. A book published in 1852 estimated Jackson's wealth at $200,000. See Abner Forbes, *The Rich Men of Massachusetts* 37 (1852).

64. Charles Jackson, *A Treatise on the Pleadings and Practice in Real Actions* (1828). Jackson was to live until 1855. See Baker, *Beacon Hill,* 56, citing Jackson's will, probated in Suffolk County Probate Court Records.

65. *Baker v. Fales,* 16 Mass. 488 (1820). Jackson had also joined an earlier opinion sustaining a Massachusetts statute withdrawing tax relief for Calvinist clergy when such relief was unavoidable for other denominations. See *Adams v. Howe,* 14 Mass. 340 (1817).

66. Abiel Holmes, *Life of Ezra Stiles* (1798); *History of Cambridge, Massachusetts* (1801); *A Family Tablet* (1796).

67. The *Annals* went through two editions, one with the title *The American Annals* (1805) and the other *The Annals of America* (1829). My quotations are from the second edition.

68. Abiel Holmes, *The Annals of America* 432 (1829).

69. Id., 433.

70. Id., 489.

71. Id., 490.

72. Id., 520.

73. Holmes recollected the conversation in a discussion with Mark DeWolfe Howe, probably during the time in 1933 and 1934 when Howe was Holmes' law clerk. See Howe, *Shaping Years,* 14.

74. Dr. Holmes wrote to Harriet Beecher Stowe in 1871 that "to this day I do not read novels on Sunday, at least until 'after sundown'. And this not as a matter of duty or religion—for I hold the sabbatical view of the first day of the week as a pious fraud of the most transparent description, but as a tribute to the holy superstitions of more innocent years, before I began to ask my dear good father those *enfant terrible* questions which were so much harder to answer than anything he found in St. Cyprian and Tarretin and the other old books I knew the smell of so well, and can see now, standing in their old places." Oliver Wendell Holmes, Sr., to Harriet Beecher Stowe, September 25, 1871, quoted in Morse, *Life and Letters,* II, 230.

75. Holmes to Leslie Scott, May 21, 1923, Holmes Papers.

76. Speech, Tavern Club of Boston, November [no date given] 1902, Holmes Papers.

77. Holmes Sr. attended Phillips Academy in Andover, Massachusetts, at that time in its history a school with a heavily religious emphasis.

78. Abiel Holmes to Oliver Wendell Holmes, Sr., January 5, 1825, quoted in Morse, *Life and Letters,* I, 25.

79. Oliver Wendell Holmes, Sr., to Oliver Wendell Holmes, Jr., June 18, 1866, Holmes Papers.

80. Travel Diary, 1866, Holmes Papers.

81. Holmes to Baroness Moncheur, August 29, 1908, Holmes Papers.

82. Henry Cabot Lodge, *Early Memories* 15–18 (1913).

83. Henry Adams, *The Education of Henry Adams* 7–8 (1927 ed.).

84. Holmes to Baroness Moncheur, December 24, 1920, Holmes Papers.

85. A copy of the report card is in the Holmes Papers.

86. Holmes Papers.

87. Id.

88. Holmes to Harold Laski, May 5, 1918, in 1 Mark DeWolfe Howe, ed., *Holmes–Laski Letters* 154 (2 vols., 1953). Hereafter cited as *Holmes–Laski Letters.*

89. Edmund Wilson, *Patriotic Gore* 745 (1962).

90. Holmes to Frederick Pollock, May 26, 1919, *Holmes–Pollock Letters* II, 14.

91. "A Feast of Reason," January 9, 1850, O. W. Holmes, Jr., Copybook, Holmes Papers.

92. T. R. Sullivan to E. S. Dixwell, September 29, 1851, id.

93. Charles Francis Adams, *An Autobiography* 22–23 (1916).

94. Lodge, supra note 82, at 81–82.

95. Id., 82–83.

96. Henry Adams, supra note 83, at 39.

97. Lodge, supra note 82, at 83–84.

98. Epes Sargent Dixwell, *An Autobiographical Sketch* 43 (Mary C. D. Wigglesworth, ed., 1907).

99. E. S. Dixwell to Holmes, December 10, 1882, Holmes Papers. Holmes at that time had been married to Dixwell's daughter, Fanny Bowditch Dixwell, since 1872.

100. See M. Howe, *Shaping Years,* 11; Baker, *Justice from Beacon Hill,* 49–50. For a description of Holmes' library during his years as a Supreme Court justice, see Baker, 373–76.

101. Anonymous, quoted in Henry M. Rogers, *Memories of Ninety Years* 55–56 (1932).

102. Anonymous, quoted in Samuel Eliot Morison, *Three Centuries of Harvard* 307 (1936).

103. Henry Adams, supra note 83, at 55, 60.

104. Charles Francis Adams, supra note 93, at 35.

105. Morrison, supra note 102, at 260. The system had been established under the presidency of Josiah Quincy, who served from 1829 to 1845.

106. Orders and Regulations of the Faculty, 1857–61, Harvard University Archives. Hereafter cited as Orders and Regulations.

107. Id., quoted in Howe, *Shaping Years,* 38.

108. Orders and Regulations, 119.

109. See Baker, *Justice from Beacon Hill,* 82, citing Weekly Absences, 1857–61, Harvard Archives.

110. Orders and Regulations, 258.

111. Letter from C. C. Felton to O. W. Holmes, Sr., April 23, 1861, Harvard Archives.

112. See Holmes to Harold Laski, April 5, 1925, quoted in *Holmes–Laski Letters,* I, 727.

113. Both Howe, *Shaping Years,* 61–65, and Baker, *Justice from Beacon Hill,* 79–82, document Holmes' "repeated and gross indecorum" in Bowen's class and speculate on the apparent incompatibility between Bowen's religious-based explanations for social and economic phenomena and Holmes' increased skepticism about religious principles during his college years. For a fuller discussion, see below, pages 44–47.

114. Holmes' accumulated points are listed in Harvard University, Scale of Merit, 1849–62, Harvard Archives. His rank in class his junior and senior years appears in Harvard University, Monthly Returns, Examinations, and Term Aggregates, 1857–61, id.

115. Two contemporaries of Holmes subsequently gave accounts indicating that the Fourth Battalion was not sent south to fight, as Holmes had anticipated. See 1861 Diary of William F. Bartlett, Holmes Papers; Charles Francis Adams, *An Autobiography* 117 (1916). See also Boston *Post,* May 25, 1861.

116. See letter from C. C. Felton to Oliver Wendell Holmes, Sr., June 11, 1861, Harvard Archives.

117. Holmes to Lucy Hale, April 24, 1858, Holmes Papers.

118. See Hasty Pudding Club programs, Harvard Archives; Lloyd M. Garrison, *An Illustrated History of Hasty Pudding Club Theatricals* (1892).

119. Holmes, speech at Alpha Delta Phi (A.D. Club) dinner, September 27, 1912, in Mark DeWolfe Howe, comp., *The Occasional Speeches of Justice Oliver Wendell Holmes* 163 (1962). Hereafter cited as *Occasional Speeches.*

120. See Oscar M. Voorhees, *The History of Phi Beta Kappa* 54 (1945).

121. Quoted in Howe, *Shaping Years,* 46–47, citing Records of Christian Brethren and Christian Union, Harvard Archives.

122. See id., 47, citing Minutes of Christian Union, Harvard Archives.

123. Id., 293, citing an unpublished diary of William Francis Bartlett, a contemporary of Holmes at Harvard.

124. Quoted in id., 51, citing Porcellian Club records, Harvard University.

125. See Harvard University, *Annual Report of the President and Treasurer of Harvard University, 1859–60,* 4, Harvard Archives; Harvard College, *Class of 1861 Fiftieth Anniversary and Final Report* (1915).

126. Holmes, "The Race Is Over," Radio address to the nation, March 8, 1931, in *Occasional Speeches,* 178.

127. Quoted in 284 U.S. vi (1932).

128. Novick, *Honorable Justice,* 25, places the correspondence in Holmes' sophomore year at Harvard and surmises that Holmes met Lucy Hale the previous summer, that is, after his freshman year. The dates of the letters I am quoting clearly contradict that supposition. In the spring of 1858 Holmes was in his freshman year.

129. Holmes to Miss [Lucy] Hale, May 24, 1858, Holmes Papers.

130. The remark is quoted in Francis Biddle, *Mr. Justice Holmes* 148–49 (1946). The context in which Biddle presents the remark suggests that Holmes made it in late March 1919, when he was seventy-eight, but Biddle was clerk to him in the 1911–12 Term. Biddle drew frequently on the anecdotes of other clerks and friends of Holmes in writing *Mr. Justice Holmes,* which was undocumented.

131. Holmes to Lewis Einstein, April 17, 1914, in James B. Peabody, ed., *Holmes–Einstein Letters* 89 (1964). Hereafter cited as *Holmes–Einstein Letters.*

132. This information comes from a conversation between Emily Hallowell, a daughter of Penrose Hallowell, and Mark Howe, May 24, 1942, Holmes Papers, and from a letter from Amelia Holmes to Lucy Hallowell, the mother of Penrose Hallowell, supra note 50.

133. Holmes to Arthur Garfield Hays, April 20, 1928, Holmes Papers.

134. Holmes to Harold Laski, November 5, 1926, *Holmes–Laski Letters* II, 893.

135. Holmes to Einstein, supra note 131.

136. For the details of the meeting, see Howe, *Shaping Years,* 66–68.

137. See *Richard P. Hallowell: "A Solider in the Army of the Lord"* (undated pamphlet), quoted in id., 294. Penrose Hallowell's participation as a bodyguard is inferred from the fact that his brother was organizing the protection for the speakers at the January 24 meeting.

138. R. P. Hallowell to Holmes, January 23, 1861, Holmes Papers.

139. See Howe, *Shaping Years,* 67–68, citing contemporary accounts.

140. Harvard University, 16 *Orders and Regulations of the Faculty* 81 (1861), Harvard Archives. In his autobiographical sketch Holmes described the Greek prize as "[t]he only college prize I have tried for." A translation of Holmes' Greek essay appears in Hoffheimer, *Justice Holmes and the Natural Law,* 129.

141. Holmes's childhood reading emphasized adventure stories and romances, such as the works of Sir Walter Scott and Sylvania Cobb, Jr. See Howe, *Shaping Years,* 11, and Baker, *Justice from Beacon Hill,* 49–50, citing Holmes' library, Rare Books Room, Library of Congress.

142. See Holmes to Lewis Einstein, January 1, 1916, *Holmes–Einstein Letters,* 121.

143. Baker, *Justice from Beacon Hill,* 91, citing Holmes's library, Library of Congress.

144. Holmes's library records his having acquired Ruskin's *Elements of Drawing* (1857), *Pre-Raphaelitism* (1851), *The Stories of Venice* (1853) and *The Political Economy of Art* (1858), the last two gifts from his family. See Baker, *Justice from Beacon Hill,* 91.

145. During Holmes' freshman year at Harvard the Holmes family withdrew three additional books on art history from the Boston Athaneum Library. See Howe, *Shaping Years,* 42, citing Boston Athaneum Library records, 1857–61.

146. Holmes to Einstein, January 1, 1916, supra note 142.

147. Holmes to Baroness [Charlotte] Moncheur, August 28, 1911, Holmes Papers.

148. Holmes to Morris Cohen, February 5, 1919, Holmes Papers.

149. See R. Stein, *John Ruskin and Aesthetic Thought in America 1840–1900* (1967).

150. See Dorothy Ross, "Historical Consciousness in Nineteenth Century America,"

89 *Am. Hist. Rev.* 909 (1984); G. Edward White, *The Marshall Court and Cultural Change, 1815–1835* 5–10, 964–75 (1988).

151. Henry Bowditch, "Did Mr. Emerson Sympathize with the Abolitionists," November 19, 1885, quoted in *Autocrat,* 344. Holmes Sr.'s biography was entitled *Ralph Waldo Emerson* (1884). Hereafter cited as Holmes Sr., *Emerson.*

152. The "Uncle Waldo" claim was originally made by Fiechter, supra note 4, at 11, and repeated by Aichele, *Holmes, Jr.,* 17, and by Novick, *Honorable Justice,* 16. None of the claims is documented, and neither Howe, *Shaping Years,* nor Baker, *Justice from Beacon Hill,* advance the same claim. Novick's assertion that Emerson "came often from Concord" to visit the Holmeses and "made a center around which the room seemed to revolve" is also undocumented. Novick, *Honorable Justice,* 16–17. Aichele goes even further, asserting that Holmes "felt closer to Emerson . . . than to his own father." Aichele, *Holmes, Jr.,* 17.

153. Oliver Wendell Holmes, Sr., "Terpsichore," 24 *Graham's Magazine* 10 (1844), quoted in Tilton, *Autocrat,* 177–78.

154. See Baker, *Justice from Beacon Hill,* 85, citing Holmes's library, Library of Congress.

155. All of Holmes' contributions in *The Harvard Magazine* were anonymous. In 1914 a classmate of Holmes', Frank Warren Hackett, supplied an index identifying the authorship of unsigned articles and book reviews in *The Harvard Magazine.* The index is in the Harvard Archives. Holmes was elected a senior editor of *The Harvard Magazine* in the fall of 1860. See Howe, *Shaping Years,* 58.

156. Ralph Waldo Emerson, "Books," 1 *Atlantic Monthly* 343 (January 1858). The identities of "anonymous" contributors were well known to regular readers of nineteenth-century journals and periodicals, and Holmes would surely have known Emerson to be the author of "Books," because Holmes' father was a founder of *The Atlantic Monthly.*

On the relationship of Holmes to Emerson, see the remarkably prescient analysis in Sanford V. Levinson, *Skepticism, Democracy, and Judicial Restraint: An Essay On the Thought Of Oliver Wendell Holmes and Felix Frankfurter* 15–32 (PhD. dissertation, Harvard University, 1969). Levinson's analysis anticipates the other important treatment of the Holmes-Emerson relationship, Hoffheimer, *Justice Holmes and the Natural Law,* by over twenty years.

157. Id., 345–47.

158. Id., 346.

159. Id., 346, 349.

160. Holmes, "Books," 4 *Harvard Magazine* 408 (December 1858), reprinted in Michael H. Hoffheimer, ed., "The Early Critical and Philosophical Writings of Justice Holmes," 30 *B.C. L. Rev.* 1221, 1250 (1989). After this book was in production Hoffheimer's *Justice Holmes and the Natural Law,* appeared. That volume also reprints the "Books" essay, along with Holmes' other early writings, at 95–134. It will no doubt supplant Hoffheimer's *Boston College Law Review* collection as the most accessible source of Holmes' early writings. My text for this chapter is Hoffheimer's *Boston College Law Review* collection, which contains a valuable introduction.

161. Howe, *Shaping Years,* 43.

162. Holmes, "Books," Hoffheimer, supra note 160, at 1251–52.

163. Holmes Sr. to Joseph Cook, December 12, 1859, Flavius Josephus Cook Papers, Duke University Library, quoted in Jay B. Hubbell, "Oliver Wendell Holmes, Rev. Joseph Cook, and the *University Quarterly*," 31 *New Eng. Q.* 401, 409 (1958).

164. "Books," in Hoffheimer, supra note 160, at 1250–51.

165. Id., 1251.

166. Id.

167. Id., 1252–53.

168. Id., 1253.

169. Id.

170. Holmes, "Notes on Albert Durer," 7 *The Harvard Magazine* 41 (October 1860), reprinted in Hoffheimer, supra note 160, at 1253. The language quoted appears at 1258, 1259. Holmes was sufficiently proud of this essay to list it in his autobiographical sketch.

171. Id., 1259.

172. Hoffheimer, Introduction, id., 1244.

173. See Michael Hoffheimer's comparison of "Notes on Albert Durer" with Ruskin's analysis of Durer in *The Elements of Drawing* in Hoffheimer, supra note 160, at 1241–44.

174. Holmes, "Plato," 2 *University Quarterly* 205 (1860) reprinted in Hoffheimer, supra note 160, at 1260.

175. A table of Emerson's "authorities" is found in Holmes Sr., *Emerson,* 382. The comparison of Emerson to Plato appears in id., 391. See also Hoffheimer, id., 1233.

176. Holmes Sr., *Emerson,* 198.

177. Holmes to Learned Hand, May 6, 1924, Holmes Papers.

178. Holmes to Lewis Einstein, July 7, 1931, *Holmes–Einstein Letters,* 326.

179. Holmes, "Plato," in Hoffheimer, supra note 160, at 1272–73.

180. Id., 1272.

181. Id., 1265, 1268, 1269, 1272.

182. For examples of this conception of science in early nineteenth-century writings in law, see St. George Tucker's 1803 edition of *Blackstone's Commentaries,* Peter Du Ponceau's *A Dissertation on the Nature and Extent of the Jurisdiction of the Courts of the United States* (1824), and Joseph Story, "Progress of Jurisprudence" (1821), reprinted in William W. Story, ed., *Miscellaneous Writings of Joseph Story* 198 (1852). See the discussion in White, *The Marshall Court and Cultural Change, 1815–1835,* supra note 150, at 81–85, 144–55.

183. Charles Darwin's *The Origin of Species* first appeared in 1859, and in January 1860, Francis Bowen, no friend of Darwin's theories, described the book as "making a great sensation." Bowen, unpublished letter of January 27, 1860, quoted in Howe, *Shaping Years,* 35. Despite the presence of a marked copy of an 1860 edition of *The Origin of Species* in Holmes' library, he claimed not to have read the book until 1907. See Holmes to Clara S. Stevens, April 28, 1907, Holmes Papers, quoted in Howe, *Shaping Years,* 156.

184. Holmes, "Plato," in Hoffheimer, supra note 160, at 1266.

185. Id.

186. Holmes, "Notes on Albert Durer," in id., 1259.

187. Holmes, "Plato," in id., 1269–70.

188. Holmes recounted these conversations with Emerson in a December 7, 1926, letter to Elizabeth S. Sergeant, Holmes Papers. The conversations are quoted in Howe, *Shaping Years*, 54.

189. Holmes to Emerson, April 16, 1876, Harvard Archives, quoted in Howe, *Shaping Years*, 203.

190. Holmes to Frederick Pollock, May 30, 1930, *Holmes–Pollock Letters* II, 264.

191. For some examples, see Baker, *Justice from Beacon Hill*, 85–86. Compare also the first line of Emerson's poem "Terminus," first read in 1866 ("It is time to be old, to take in sail") in Holmes Sr., *Emerson*, at 247, with Holmes to Nina Gray, August 14, 1903, Holmes Papers, "I realize I am older . . . It's time to be old—to take in sail."

192. See Holmes Sr., *Emerson*, at 259. The "Courage" essay was in Emerson's 1870 collection, *Society and Solitude*.

193. In addition to the essays previously considered, Holmes contributed two groups of comments entitled "Editor's Table," three book notes, and an essay on the pre-Raphaelites, all in *The Harvard Magazine*. These pieces are printed in Hoffheimer, supra note 160. A complete list of Holmes' undergraduate writings would also include his poem "Alma Mater," read at the "Sophomore Supper" of his class, in the spring of 1859. The poem is reproduced in id., 1259–60, and in Howe, *Shaping Years*, 50. Suffice it to say that the subsequent election of Holmes as Class Poet by his contemporaries, if based on an exposure to "Alma Mater," suggests that there were very few aspiring poets in the class of 1861.

194. See 7 *Harvard Magazine* 362 (July 1861) for a statement that Holmes' submission won the annual prize for Greek composition.

195. Francis Bowen, *Principles of Metaphysical and Ethical Science Applied to the Evidences of Religion* vii (1855).

196. Id., 47.

197. Id.

198. Francis Bowen, *The Principles of Political Economy* 23 (2nd ed., 1859).

199. Id., 141.

200. Minutes, Harvard Faculty, 1861, Harvard Archives.

201. Cornelius Felton to Oliver Wendell Holmes, Sr., January 17, 1861, id.

202. Holmes to Charles Eliot Norton, April 17, 1864, Harvard Archives, quoted in *Touched with Fire*, 122.

203. Cornelius Felton to Oliver Wendell Holmes, Sr., June 11, 1861, Harvard Archives.

204. Oliver Wendell Holmes, Sr., to Cornelius Felton, July 24, 1861, id.

205. Cornelius Felton to Oliver Wendell Holmes, Sr., July 26, 1861, Harvard Archives, quoted in Howe, *Shaping Years*, 77.

206. Holmes, supra note 4.

207. Id.

208. Id.

209. Id.

210. Holmes, Address, May 30, 1884, in *Occasional Speeches*, 15.

CHAPTER TWO: *The Civil War*

1. O. W. Holmes, "Memorial Day," address delivered May 30, 1884, Keene, New Hampshire, *Occasional Speeches,* 4.

2. Max Lerner, *The Mind and Faith of Justice Holmes* 5–27 (1943). Hereafter Lerner, *Mind and Faith.*

3. The story of Holmes' advice to Roosevelt has been told numerous times: for an eyewitness account, see Donald Hiss, Interview, in Katie Louchheim, *The Meaning of the New Deal: The Insiders Speak* 36–38 (1983). For a fuller discussion of the authenticity of Hiss' report, see Chapter Thirteen.

4. *Touched With Fire,* vii.

5. Holmes to Charles Eliot Norton, April 17, 1864, Holmes Papers. It is suggestive that a month after sending that letter Holmes wrote his parents that he had resolved to leave the service at the end of his regiment's present campaign, giving as a reason that "I have felt for some time that I didn't any longer believe in this as a duty." Holmes to Oliver Wendell Holmes, Sr., and Amelia Jackson Holmes, May 16, 1864, *Touched With Fire,* 122.

6. Apparently the Twentieth Regiment was attempting to recruit former members of the Fourth Battalion, but Holmes was not among the early recruits. Colonel William R. Lee, a native of the Boston area, had been charged with organizing the Twentieth Regiment, in connection with Lieutenant Colonel Francis W. Palfrey, a graduate of Harvard who had been in the Fourth Battalion. Palfrey recommended several Harvard graduates from the Fourth Battalion for captaincies and lieutenancies in the Twentieth Regiment, but Holmes was initially not among those. It was not until July 22, when two companies of men from the Twentieth were transferred to the Nineteenth Regiment, already in active service in Virginia, that additional vacancies occurred in the Twentieth, and Holmes was given a Lieutenant's commission. Prior to that date Dr. Holmes had apparently written Governor John Andrew and visited Colonel Lee on his son's behalf, and John Lothrop Motley had indicated, in a letter to his wife, that the younger Holmes could expect a commission. But apparently it was not until after July 22, when it became obvious that the Twentieth Regiment was going to require more officers, that Holmes' commission was secured. See Tilton, *Autocrat,* 265, citing letter from A. J. Browne to Col. William R. Lee, John Andrew Papers, Massachusetts Historical Society; John Lothrop Motley to Mrs. J. L. Motley, July 12, 1861, in Curtis, ed., *Motley Correspondence,* II, 11; George A. Bruce, *The Twentieth Regiment of Massachusetts Volunteer Infantry, 1861–65* 5–6 (1906). Hereafter cited as Bruce, *Twentieth Regiment.*

7. It is not clear how long Holmes stayed in Pittsfield or when he returned. In a letter to Felix Frankfurter, written in 1916, Holmes said only that "I . . . went off to Pittsfield recruiting, and thereafter into camp and to the war." Holmes to Frankfurter, November 2, 1916, Holmes Papers. There is a recollection of Holmes' visit to Pittsfield by Carolyn Kellogg Cushing, who was nine years old when Holmes arrived, in "The Gallant Captain and the Little Girl," 155 *Atlantic Monthly* 545 (May 1935), but some of the chronology in Cushing's account is inconsistent with Holmes' returning to the Regiment before it left the Boston area for Washington on September 4, 1861. Holmes was a lieutenant, not a captain, when he visited Pittsfield.

8. Details of the Regiment's trip can be found in Bruce, *Twentieth Regiment,* 12. See

also Holmes to Amelia Jackson Holmes, September 8, 1861, *Touched With Fire,* 4–5, for a discussion of the New York to Washington portions of the trip, including his dinner at Delmonico's.

9. See Bruce, *Twentieth Regiment,* 14–15.

10. Holmes to Amelia Jackson Holmes, September 23, 1861, *Touched With Fire,* 8, 12.

11. Id., 12.

12. See James McPherson, *Battle Cry of Freedom* 361–63 (1988); Joseph D. Patch, *The Battle of Ball's Bluff* 12–15 (1958); Bruce Catton, *Mr. Lincoln's Army* 75–80 (1951).

13. See McPherson, *Battle Cry of Freedom,* 362; Patch, supra note 12, at 10–25.

14. Holmes was actually shot twice, the first shot being a spent bullet that struck him in the solar plexus, knocking him down. When he ascertained that he was not seriously hurt, he rose and advanced in the direction of the Confederate forces, only to be shot through the chest. See Holmes to Amelia Jackson Holmes, October 23, 1861, *Touched With Fire,* 13.

15. The details of Holmes' wounding at Ball's Bluff are taken from his October 23, 1861, letter to his mother, id., and a diary entry, probably written near the close of his military service in 1864, reprinted in id., 23–33.

16. During the initial period of his convalescence in Boston, Holmes had so many visitors that his mother kept a list of "Visitors to the Wounded Lieutenant" for the month of November 1861. The list numbered 133, and he also received four bouquets of flowers from unknown persons. Among the visitors were President Cornelius Felton of Harvard, Senator Charles Sumner of Massachusetts, and his future wife, Fanny Bowditch Dixwell. Dr. Holmes wrote to his friend John Lothrop Motley on November 29 that "Wendell is a great pet in the character of young hero with wounds in the heart." Holmes to Motley, November 29, 1861, Morse, *Life and Letters,* II, 158. For Amelia Jackson Holmes' list of visitors, see "Visitors to the Wounded Lieutenant," Holmes Papers.

17. On Holmes' journey from Poolesville to Philadelphia and then to Boston see Howe, *Shaping Years,* 101, citing a telegram from Anna Hallowell to Oliver Wendell Holmes, Sr., November 1, 1861, a letter from William Hunt to Oliver Wendell Holmes, Sr., November 3, 1861, and a letter from Oliver Wendell Holmes, Sr., to Amelia Jackson Holmes, all in Holmes Papers. On Holmes Jr.'s recovery and recruiting duty during the months of November and December 1861, and January and February 1862, see Oliver Wendell Holmes, Sr., to John L. Motley, November 29, 1861, quoted in Morse, *Life and Letters,* II, 157, Holmes to Motley, February 3, 1862, id., 163; Mrs. James T. Fields, quoted in Howe, *Shaping Years,* at 112, describing a breakfast visit from Holmes and Dr. Holmes on December 7, 1861. On the movements of the Twentieth Regiment between the battle of Ball's Bluff and March 25, 1862, see Bruce, *Twentieth Regiment,* 80; Holmes to Dr. and Mrs. Oliver Wendell Holmes, Sr., March 25, 1862, *Touched With Fire,* 37. On Holmes' return to active service on March 26, see id.

18. See Holmes to Dr. and Mrs. Oliver Wendell Holmes, Sr., April 7, 1862, *Touched With Fire,* 42; Holmes to Dr. and Mrs. Oliver Wendell Holmes, Sr., April 23, 1862, id., 45. Holmes initially resolved not to accept the Captaincy, since his regimental commander, Francis Palfrey, had not been consulted, but relented or was ordered to do so.

Compare Holmes to Dr. and Mrs. Holmes, Sr., April 23, 1862, where he wrote "I shan't accept the Captaincy" with Holmes to Dr. and Mrs. Holmes, Sr., June 2, 1862, id., 47, where he indicated that he was the captain in command of Company G.

19. Holmes to Dr. and Mrs. Oliver Wendell Holmes, Sr., April 23, 1862, *Touched With Fire*, 44. For general details of the Army of the Potomac's advance on Richmond in the spring of 1862, see McPherson, *Battle Cry of Freedom*, 423–27.

20. Holmes to Dr. and Mrs. Oliver Wendell Holmes, Sr., April 23, 1862, supra note 19.

21. For the details of Jackson's Shenandoah campaign and its effect on the 1862 invasion of Richmond, see McPherson, *Battle Cry of Freedom*, 454–60. Details of the Twentieth Regiment's activities from May 6 to May 28 can be found in *Touched With Fire*, 47–48.

22. For details of the May 31–June 1 battle at Seven Pines and Fair Oaks, east of Richmond, and the "Seven Days' Battles" east and south of Richmond from June 25 through July 2, see McPherson, *Battle Cry of Freedom*, 461–71.

23. Holmes to Dr. and Mrs. Oliver Wendell Holmes, Sr., June 2, 1862, *Touched With Fire*, 51.

24. Holmes to Mrs. Oliver Wendell Holmes, Sr., July 4, 1862, id., 56.

25. Holmes to Dr. and Mrs. Oliver Wendell Holmes, Sr., July 5, 1862, id., 58–60.

26. See id., 57 n. 2.

27. Holmes to Dr. and Mrs. Oliver Wendell Holmes, Sr., September 17, 1862, id., 62–63.

28. For a discussion of the political and military consequences of the Army of the Potomac's unsuccessful invasion of Richmond in May–July 1862, see McPherson, *Battle Cry of Freedom*, 489–510.

29. For details of the Confederate forces' invasion of northern Virginia and Maryland in August and September 1862, see id., 510–38.

30. The magnitude of those figures can be seen in some comparisons with other wars in which American troops have participated. The total killed at Antietam/Sharpsburg represented more than twice the number of U.S. forces killed in the War of 1812, the Mexican War, and the Spanish-American war combined. The total number of casualties represented four times the number of Americans killed on the first day of the invasion of Normandy in June 1944.

31. See McPherson, *Battle Cry of Freedom*, 538–46.

32. Holmes to Dr. and Mrs. Oliver Wendell Holmes, Sr., September 17, 1862, *Touched With Fire*, 63–64. For an account of the Twentieth Regiment's movements between the time it disembarked from Newport News on August 25 and its arrival near Antietam Creek on September 15 or thereabouts, see id., 61–62; Bruce, *Twentieth Regiment*, 148–58.

33. Holmes to Frederick Pollock, June 28, 1930, *Holmes–Pollock Letters* II, 270. The reference to *Harper's Weekly* was an editorial, "New England Never Runs," that had appeared in the November 9, 1861, issue, in which the writer, in discussing the battle of Ball's Bluff, had noted that "Lieutenant Holmes, said the first brief dispatch [of the battle], 'wounded in the breast'; not in the back; no, not in the back. In the breast is Massachusetts wounded, if she is struck. Forward she falls, if she falls dead."

34. Holmes to Dr. and Mrs. Oliver Wendell Holmes, Sr., September 18, 1862, *Touched With Fire,* 64.

35. An account of LeDuc's intervention on Holmes' behalf can be found in Alice Sumner LeDuc, ''The Man Who Rescued 'The Captain','' 180 *Atlantic Monthly* 80 (August, 1947). See also *Touched With Fire,* 65–66.

36. Holmes to Dr. and Mrs. Holmes, Sr., September 22, 1862, *Touched With Fire,* 67. The letter was written for Holmes by Ellen Jones of Philadelphia, a young woman who was staying with the Kennedys. For an account of Holmes' stay in Hagerstown, see Anna Howell Kennedy Findlay, ''Where the Captain Was Found,'' 33 *Maryland Historical Magazine* 109 (June, 1938). Ms. Findlay was the daughter of Mrs. Howard Kennedy.

37. Undated note, Civil War Scrapbook, Holmes Papers, quoted in Howe, *Shaping Years,* 128.

38. See Alice Sumner LeDuc, ''The Man Who Rescued 'The Captain','' supra note 35.

39. Oliver Wendell Holmes, Sr., ''My Hunt after 'The Captain','' 10 *Atlantic Monthly,* 738, 749 (December, 1862).

40. Id., 759, 760, 747.

41. Holmes to Amelia Holmes, November 16–20. 1862, *Touched With Fire,* 72–73.

42. For details of the attack on Fredericksburg, see McPherson, *Battle Cry of Freedom,* 569–75.

43. Holmes to Amelia Jackson Holmes, December 12–15, 1862, *Touched With Fire,* 74, 76, 77.

44. Holmes to Dr. Oliver Wendell Holmes, Sr., December 20, 1862, *Touched With Fire,* 79–80.

45. For an account of the Chancellorsville and Wilderness campaign, see McPherson, *Battle Cry of Freedom,* 639–46.

46. Holmes to Amelia Jackson Holmes, May 3, 1863, *Touched With Fire,* 92.

47. See *Touched With Fire,* 94.

48. Oliver Wendell Holmes, Sr., to Charles Sumner, November 3, 1861, Holmes Papers, quoted in Howe, *Shaping Years,* 160.

49. *Touched With Fire,* 106.

50. Id., 109.

51. Id., 110.

52. Id., 114.

53. Id., 118–19.

54. Holmes to Dr. and Mrs. Oliver Wendell Holmes, Sr., May 16, 1864, id., 121–22.

55. Holmes to Dr. and Mrs. Oliver Wendell Holmes, Sr., May 30, 1864, id., 135.

56. Holmes to Dr. and Mrs. Oliver Wendell Holmes, Sr., June 24, 1864, id., 149–50.

57. Holmes to Amelia Jackson Holmes, June 7, 1864, *Touched With Fire,* 142, 143; Holmes to Amelia Jackson Holmes, July 8, 1864, id., 152.

58. See id., 133–34, 136–37, 142.

59. Diary entry, May 29, 1864, id., 134. For a similar account, see Holmes to Dr. and Mrs. Oliver Wendell Holmes, Sr., May 30, 1864, id., 136–37.

60. Holmes to Amelia Jackson Holmes, June 7, 1864, id., 142.

61. Holmes to Dr. and Mrs. Oliver Wendell Holmes, Sr., June 24, 1864, id., 150.

62. The Woollcott article, "Get Down, You Fool," 161 *Atlantic Monthly* 169 (February, 1938), was reprinted in Alexander Woollcott, *Long, Long Ago* 15 (1943). Frankfurter's account is in a letter to John H. Cramer, May 19, 1943, Felix Frankfurter Papers, Library of Congress, quoted in John Cramer, *Lincoln under Enemy Fire* 123 (1948). The Hiss comment was made in an interview Alger Hiss gave to Liva Baker, quoted in Baker, *Justice from Beacon Hill,* 152.

63. Howe, *Shaping Years,* 169. The elliptical fashion in which Howe made his observations about the authenticity of the story may have been a result of the fact that he knew that Felix Frankfurter, who had strongly supported Howe's effort to write on Holmes, claimed to have heard the story from Holmes himself.

64. See Holmes to Laski, May 27, 1921; Holmes to Laski, March 11, 1922; Holmes to Laski, March 26, 1922, *Holmes–Laski Letters,* I, 339, 410, 414. In each letter Holmes spoke of "my private show of Fort Stevens—where I saw Lincoln and the enemy nearer in to Washington than they ever were again." Id., 410.

65. See, e.g., *Holmes–Pollock Letters* I, 152, 243; II, 10, 44, 243, 271.

66. Holmes to Einstein, March 27, 1912, *Holmes–Einstein Letters,* 67.

67. Civil War Scrapbook, Holmes Papers.

68. Holmes to Amelia Jackson Holmes, June 7, 1864, *Touched With Fire,* 142.

69. Holmes to Dr. and Mrs. O. W. Holmes, Sr., May 16, 1864, id., 122.

70. See Charles A. Whittier to Holmes, May 15, 1863, Holmes Papers, quoting Dr. Nathan Hayward, the Twentieth Regiment's surgeon, as having said that Holmes was at first sorry that he would not lose his foot after having been wounded in the heel near Fredericksburg. Holmes confirmed those feelings in a conversation with Mark Howe, January 30, 1934, quoted in Howe, *Shaping Years,* 155.

71. Holmes to Amelia Jackson Holmes, June 7, 1864, id., 142.

72. The letter was dated May 1, 1861, and the poem was attached to another letter written September 8, 1861. See *Touched With Fire,* 3, 6.

73. Holmes to Amelia Jackson Holmes, September 11, 1861, id., 8.

74. Holmes to Dr. and Mrs. Oliver Wendell Holmes, Sr., Tuesday, April 7, 1862, id., 38, 39, 42.

75. Holmes to Dr. and Mrs. Oliver Wendell Holmes, Sr., June 2, 1862, quoted in id., 48–52.

76. Holmes to Dr. and Mrs. Oliver Wendell Holmes, Sr., September 17, 1862, quoted in id., 62.

77. See Charles Walton to Dr. Oliver Wendell Holmes, Sr., October 1, 1862, Holmes Papers, in which Walton mentioned Holmes' comments about the "moving accidents" of the Antietam campaign.

78. Holmes to Amelia Jackson Holmes, supra note 43.

79. Holmes to Amelia Jackson Holmes, June 7, 1864, *Touched With Fire,* 141.

80. Holmes to Oliver Wendell Holmes, Sr., December 20, 1862, id., 79.

81. Id.

82. Holmes to Oliver Wendell Holmes, Sr., March 29, 1863, id., 90–91.

83. Letter from Governor John Andrew to Robert Shaw, January 30, 1863, id., 153.

84. Hallowell to Holmes, February 7, [1863], Holmes Papers.

85. See Henry L. Abbott to Holmes, September 22, 1863, Holmes Papers. In that

letter Abbott said that "we can't afford to lose you," and "[i]f any impudent stay-at-home wide-awake asks you when you are coming back, punch his head."

86. See Oliver Wendell Holmes, Sr., to Charles Sumner, January 4, 1864, Charles Sumner Papers, Houghton Library, Harvard University, *Touched With Fire*, 160.

87. Holmes to Dr. and Mrs. Oliver Wendell Holmes, Sr., May 16, 1864, id., 121.

88. Holmes to Charles Eliot Norton, supra note 5.

89. Holmes to Dr. and Mrs. Oliver Wendell Holmes, Sr., May 30, 1864, *Touched With Fire*, 135 (emphasis in original).

90. Holmes to Amelia Jackson Holmes, June 7, 1864, quoted in id., 141.

91. Later in his life Holmes seems to have had some concerns about whether he had acted appropriately in leaving the service. In a letter to Felix Frankfurter in 1917 he said "now I should allow less than I did . . . 50 years ago to the consideration of the special faculties that one may attribute to oneself as a ground for not taking the chances of war." Holmes to Frankfurter, March 5, 1917, Holmes Papers. By "special faculties" Holmes was probably alluding to the cumulative physical and mental stress that he was suffering from in the late spring of 1864. He had written a young friend on June 21 that "[o]ur medical director (6th C[orps]) told me the other day that I was not keeping up by the strength of my constitution but by the stimulus of this constant pressure to which we have been subjected." Holmes to Agnes Pomeroy, June 21, 1864, *Touched With Fire*, 143. Apparently over time Holmes had come to feel that this "battle fatigue" was not unique to him, and thus furnished less of a compelling reason to quit the service.

92. Holmes to Charles Eliot Norton, supra note 5.

93. Mark Howe, in going through Holmes' papers in connection with the preparation of his biography, discovered some loose sheets enclosed in a diary that Holmes had kept of his wartime experiences. The sheets, which contained an account of Holmes' wounding at Ball's Bluff, "were evidently torn from another memorandum book which has not survived." Howe, *Shaping Years*, 299. Passages in the account, such as "I always wanted to have a memorandum of this experience—so novel at that time to all & especially so to me from the novelty of the service and my youth" suggest that the account was written well after the wounding. The tone of the account is also suggestive of one writing when he knows that the immediate danger of death has passed.

94. The poem was delivered at a dinner at Young's Hotel in Boston, June 21, 1864. It is reprinted in Lerner, *Mind and Faith*, 8.

95. Holmes, "Memorial Day," supra note 1.

96. The address is also reprinted in Lerner, *Mind and Faith*, at 9; I am using that as my text. The passage quoted appears in *Mind and Faith*, 10.

97. Id., 15.

98. Id., 11–13.

99. For a discussion of the men referred to in Holmes' 1884 Memorial Day address, see Hiller B. Zobel, "The Three Civil Wars of Oliver Wendell Holmes: Notes for an Odyssey," 27 *Boston Bar Journal* 18, 19–21 (February 1983).

100. *Touched With Fire*, 18.

101. Id., 31.

102. Id., 74–75.

103. Id., 60.

104. Id., 74–76.

105. Notable are Edmund Wilson's chapter on Holmes in *Patriotic Gore* (1962); Saul Touster "In Search of Holmes from Within," 18 *Vand. L. Rev.* 437 (1965); and Hiller Zobel's essays, one of which is cited supra, note 99.

106. *Touched With Fire,* 76.

107. Colonel George N. Macy, the Regiment's commander, was wounded in fighting around Wilderness on May 6, 1864. Abbott, second in command, assumed Macy's position, only to be fatally wounded on the same day. Id., 105.

108. Holmes to Dr. and Mrs. Oliver Wendell Holmes, Sr., May 6, 1864, id., 105.

109. Holmes to Dr. and Mrs. Oliver Wendell Holmes, Sr., May 16, 1864, id., 122.

110. Holmes to Lady Pollock, July 2, 1895, *Holmes–Pollock Letters* I, 57.

111. Holmes was referring to the Franco-Prussian war of 1870 as well as to the Civil War.

112. Holmes, "The Soldier's Faith," address delivered on May 30, 1895, reprinted in Lerner, *Mind and Faith,* 18. Subsequent citations are to *Mind and Faith.*

113. Id. at 20.

114. Id. at 20–21.

115. Id. at 23.

116. See the discussion in Chapter Nine.

117. Lerner, *Mind and Faith,* 24.

118. Holmes to Pollock, August 30, 1929, *Holmes–Pollock Letters* II, 252.

119. Holmes to Laski, January 11, 1929, *Holmes–Laski Letters* II, 1125.

120. Id.

121. Holmes to Alice Stopford Green, October, 1901, Holmes Papers.

122. Holmes to Laski, April 13, 1929, *Holmes–Laski Letters* II, 1146.

123. Holmes to Lewis Einstein, May 21, 1914, *Holmes–Einstein Letters,* 93.

124. Holmes to Laski, December 9, 1921, *Holmes–Laski Letters* I, 385.

125. "The Class of '61," June 28, 1911, *Occasional Speeches.*

126. "The Soldier's Faith," supra note 112, at 23.

127. If one were inclined to emphasize paradox, one could consider why humans should strive to be "heroes," or whether heroism is even possible, if humankind is so cosmically insignificant. Alternatively, one could argue that Holmes is urging humans, in a world whose meaning cannot be traced to extrinsic sources (the ultimate is a mystery; absolute truth a mirage) to create their own meaning through "heroic" acts that affirm their vitality.

128. [Garrison], "Sentimental Jingoism," New York *Evening Post,* December 16, 1895, reprinted in 61 *The Nation* 440 (December 19, 1895).

129. New York *Evening Post,* December 17, 1895.

130. Holmes to Pollock, December 27, 1895, *Holmes–Pollock Letters,* I, 66.

131. Holmes to Clara Stevens, September 3, 1909, Holmes Papers.

132. Bigelow to Holmes, undated, Holmes Papers. Roosevelt added a handwritten note to the letter which read "Can't I have a chance just to shake hands with you?"

133. Holmes, "Parts of the Unimaginable Whole," address delivered June 28, 1911, reprinted in Lerner, *Mind and Faith,* 25.

134. Id., 26.

135. Holmes to James Bryce, December 31, 1882, Holmes Papers.

CHAPTER THREE: *Friendships, Companions,*
and Attachments, 1864–1882

1. Holmes, "Introduction to the General Survey by European Authors in the Continental Legal Historical Series," 1913, in Oliver Wendell Holmes, *Collected Legal Papers*
298, 301–02 (1920). Hereafter cited as *Collected Legal Papers*.

2. See Holmes to Henry H. Brownell, May 9, 1865, Holmes Papers; see also Oliver
Wendell Holmes, Sr., to Brownell, May 9, 1865, quoted in Tipton, *Autocrat*, 280.

3. On April 21, 1865, the poet Forceythe Willson, who had also written about the
Civil War, wrote Holmes a letter, in response to one he had received from Holmes, in
which he described Holmes as "stand[ing] before two of God's own mighty gates—
Poetry and Philosophy!" and speculated that "[t]he more of an 'idealist' you may happen
to be the finer your promise as a poet." Willson to Holmes, Holmes Papers, quoted in
Howe, *Shaping Years*, 196.

4. Holmes to Brownell, supra note 2.

5. Id.

6. Holmes to Brownell, October 31, 1865, Holmes Papers.

7. See George Frederickson, *The Inner Civil War* 183–235 (1965).

8. William James to Henry James, July 5, 1876, quoted in Ralph Barton Perry, *The
Thought and Character of William James* (2 vols., 1935), I, 371.

9. Mary James to Henry James, Jr., February 28, 1873, quoted in Perry, supra note
8, I, 58.

10. Mrs. John C. Gray to Holmes, July 28, 1899, Holmes Papers.

11. Holmes, "Commencement Address—Brown University, June 17, 1897," *Occasional Speeches*, 97–98.

12. Holmes, "The Profession of the Law," id., 30–31.

13. See Eleanor Little, "The Early Reading of Justice Oliver Wendell Holmes," 8
Harvard Library Bulletin 163 (1954). Hereafter cited as "Early Reading."

14. [Holmes], "Harvard Law School," 5 *Am. L. Rev.* 177 (1870). The notice was
prompted by the Law School's decision that year to require all degree candidates to take
written examinations as a prerequisite to graduating.

15. Holmes to Henry Brownell, supra note 6.

16. Holmes, diary entry, September 27, 1866, Holmes Papers. Among the cases
Holmes "looked up" were ones on fraud, interpretation of wills, the rule of interest on
an overdue note, and the dissolution of a partnership, the standard materials of general
law practice.

17. James' recollection of the visit was set forth in Henry James, *Notes of a Son and
Brother* 450–60 (1914).

18. Mary James to Alice James, January, [1867], quoted in Jean Strouse, *Alice James*
99 (1980).

19. Marian Hooper to Eleanor Shattuck, January 10, 1870, George Shattuck Papers,
Massachusetts Historical Society, Boston. George Shattuck, who practiced law with
Holmes in the 1870s, was one of Holmes' early professional mentors.

20. See, e.g., diary entry for December 12, 1866, Holmes Papers, indicating that
Holmes had visited Fanny on her birthday; diary entry for December 31, 1866, id.,

indicating that Holmes and Fanny had met and exchanged pictures. The entries are quoted in Howe, *Shaping Years,* 252–53.

21. Holmes to Mrs. Howard Kennedy, March 11, 1872, quoted in Anna Howell Kennedy Findlay, "Where the Captain Was Found," 33 *Maryland Historical Magazine* 109, 121 (1938).

22. William James to Thomas W. Ward, March 27, 1866, in Henry James, ed., *Letters of William James* (2 vols., 1920), I, 73.

23. See James to Holmes, January 3, 1868, Holmes Papers, quoted in Ralph Barton Perry, *The Thought and Character of William James* 91 (1964): "When I get home let's establish a philosophical society to have regular meetings and discuss none but the very tallest and broadest questions—to be composed of none but the very topmost cream of Boston manhood." This society, "The Metaphysical Club," has been attributed considerable significance in the formation of Holmes' mature philosophical views, but its significance has probably been exaggerated. See, e.g., Philip Weiner, *Evolution and the Founders of Pragmatism* (1949). See the discussion in Chapter Four.

24. Holmes to William James, December 15, 1867, Holmes Papers.

25. William James to Tom Ward, March 27, 1866, in Henry James, ed., *The Letters of William James* (2 vols., 1920), I, 75.

26. James to Holmes, January 3, 1868, quoted in Perry, supra note 8, II, 507.

27. James to Holmes, May 15, 1868, quoted in id., 512.

28. William James to Henry James, October 2, 1869, quoted in id., I, 307.

29. See, e.g., Holmes to James, October 13, 1907, Holmes Papers: "I have read the work and my general feeling about it you probably know already. I heartily agree with much—but I am more sceptical than you are. You would say that I am too hard or tough minded."

30. Holmes, diary entry, November 24, 1866, Holmes Papers.

31. Holmes to James, April 19, 1868, Holmes Papers.

32. Holmes, "George Otis Shattuck," 14 *Proceedings of the Massachusetts Historical Society* 361, 367 (2d. series, 1900).

33. See Holmes to Harold Laski, October 9, 1921, *Holmes–Laski Letters* I, 373. In that letter, after speaking of his "reverence for men of action," Holmes said that "not being a man of affairs and affairs being at least half of life I look up to those who have profound insights and foresights and successfully act on them."

34. Holmes, "George Otis Shattuck," supra note 32, at 367.

35. Wright, Fiske, and Pierce were members of "The Metaphysical Club" along with William James.

36. See Oliver Wendell Holmes, Sr., to John Lothrop Motley, October 10, 1865, in Morse, *Life and Letters,* II, 177. In that letter Dr. Holmes told Motley that his son was anticipating going to Europe and would like Motley's introductions to John Stuart Mill and Thomas Hughes.

37. Holmes, diary entry, May 9, 1866, Holmes Papers.

38. Holmes was invited to Hughes' home for dinner on May 27, and apparently flirted with Hughes' twelve-year-old daughter, a fact Hughes initially joked about but then apparently began to take seriously when Holmes repeatedly inquired about her in correspondence. Eventually Hughes expressed his concern and Holmes reassured him that he had no serious designs on the young woman. See Thomas Hughes to Holmes, Decem-

ber 31, 1866, Holmes Papers; Hughes to Holmes, February 26, 1868; id. Both letters are quoted in Howe, *Shaping Years,* 231.

39. Holmes to Harold Laski, February 4, 1927, *Holmes–Laski Letters,* II, 918.

40. Henry Adams' comments were quoted in Charles F. Adams, Jr., *Charles Francis Adams* 370 (1900).

41. Holmes, diary entry, June 7, 1866, Holmes Papers.

42. Holmes, diary entry, June 6, 1866, Holmes Papers.

43. See John Pollock, Introduction, *Holmes–Pollock Letters,* xxv.

44. Holmes, diary entry, June 11, 1866, Holmes Papers.

45. Holmes to Frederick Pollock, June 9, 1930, *Holmes–Pollock Letters,* II, 267. Pollock, whose sense of humor was not his most outstanding characteristic, responded by saying, "Could you have taught baboons the required steadiness and confidence, not to speak of shooting? I doubt it." Pollock to Holmes, June 19, 1930, id., 269.

46. Holmes to Lady Burghclere, September 17, 1898, Holmes Papers.

47. Holmes to James, December 15, 1867, id.

48. Diary entry, July 14, 1866, id.

49. Stephen to Holmes, June 28, 1866, id.

50. For a discussion of Dr. Holmes' study in France, see Tilton, *Autocrat,* 96–131. Mark Howe reported in his first volume on Holmes that "Holmes made a number of unsuccessful efforts to meet with . . . Louis," Howe, *Shaping Years,* 235, but a diary entry of June 26 reads, "Drove up to Neuilly . . . and saw Louis." Two days earlier Holmes had written, "[T]ried for Louis again, who called today—didn't find him."

51. Diary entry, July 1, 1866, Holmes Papers.

52. Diary entry, June 29, 1866, id.

53. Diary entries for June 26, 28, id.

54. This was an account of the journey as told by Stephen to Tom Hughes and repeated to Holmes in Hughes' letter of December 31, 1866, Holmes Papers.

55. Diary entry for July 11, 1866, id.

56. Diary entry, July 28, 1866, id.

57. Diary entry, August 2, 1866, id.

58. Diary entry, August 5, 1866, id.

59. Diary entry, August 6, 1866, id.

60. Diary entry, June 2, 1866, id.

61. Diary entry, August 7, 1866, id.

62. Diary entry, August 8, 1866, id.

63. Diary entry, August 13, 1866, id.

64. Diary entry, August 10, 1866, id.

65. Diary entry, August 12, 1866, id.

66. Diary entry, August 18, 1866, id.

67. Diary entry, August 19, 1866, id.

68. Diary entry, August 25, 1866, id.

69. Diary entry, August 26, 1866, id.

70. Diary entry, August 27, 1866, id.

71. Diary entry, August 28, 1866, id.

72. Diary entry, August 29, 1866, id.

73. Diary entry, August 30, 1866, id. Holmes left Stonefield on the 29th, spending the night in Edinburgh, toured the next day, then took a 9 P.M. overnight train to Liverpool. From there he caught a train for Chester, where he stayed the night at the Washington Hotel, sailing for America on September 1.

74. Diary entry, August 31, 1866, id.

75. In 1909 Holmes received an honorary degree from Oxford, and Fanny accompanied him to the ceremony. The visit was a comparatively brief one. See Novick, *Honorable Justice*, 293–94, citing a letter from Holmes to John Wigmore, August 18, 1909, Holmes Papers.

76. Holmes to Lady Burghclere, September 17, 1898, Holmes Papers.

77. The circumstances under which Holmes assumed the editorship of the twelfth edition of Kent's *Commentaries* are discussed in Chapter Four.

78. Arthur Sedgwick to Henry James, Jr., January 30, 1870, James Family Papers, Harvard Archives, quoted in Howe, *Shaping Years*, 273.

79. The preservation of Holmes' reading lists in his papers deserves some comment. The reading lists are contained in three notebooks. The first notebook is Holmes' diary for 1866, which contains primarily notes of his trip to Europe that year (quoted from extensively in this chapter), and also contains a list of books Holmes read between 1865 and his May 1866 trip to Europe and during the remainder of 1866. The second notebook, covering the years 1867 through 1880, consists of a diary of his activities during the year 1867 and a list of books he read between that year and 1880. The listings in the first two notebooks, excluding the diary entries, are included in the Little article, "Early Reading." The third notebook, colloquially referred to as "The Black Book" by Holmes' secretaries and other close acquaintances, is a volume of 159 pages that includes a list of all the books he read from 1881 to 1935, the year of his death, and also includes some notes on his reading, beginning with books he read in 1876. For a fuller description of the contents of the notebooks, see "Early Reading," 163.

80. Holmes, Notebooks, Holmes Papers, reprinted in "Early Reading," 182–84.

81. William James to G. W. James, March 21, 1866, James Papers, Houghton Library, Harvard University, quoted in Baker, *Justice from Beacon Hill*, 173.

82. See William James to G. W. James, supra note 81.

83. Holmes' Civil War letters and diary indicate at least three occasions (April 25, 1862, May 2, 1864, and May 18, 1864) when he received letters from Fanny and one occasion (May 20, 1864) when he wrote her. See *Touched With Fire*, 47, 101, 126, 128.

84. See James to Thomas W. Ward. March 27, 1866, in Henry James, ed., *The Letters of William James*, (3 vols., 1920), I, 76.

85. See Amelia Jackson Holmes to Holmes, July 16, 1866, Holmes Papers.

86. Holmes to James, April 19, 1868, Holmes Papers.

87. Oliver Wendell Holmes, Sr., *The Works of Oliver Wendell Holmes* (13 vols., 1892), III, 58–59 Hereafter cited as Holmes, Sr., *Works,* with volume and page numbers.

88. Holmes, Sr., *Works,* III, 59.

89. Id.

90. Dr. Oliver Wendell Holmes, Sr., to Ann Holmes Upham, March 11, 1872, Holmes Papers.

91. Dr. Oliver Wendell Holmes, Sr., to Charles [last name not given], March 11, 1872, id.

92. Dr. Holmes to Upham, supra note 90.

93. Holmes' decision to go into practice with his brother might seem surprising since there is no evidence the two were close and Ned was just beginning his career. It is likely that by 1872 Holmes felt less compulsion to make money in practice, having negotiated the Kent contract, and wanted the luxury of his own practice. Ned had married into the affluent Wigglesworth family in 1871, see Baker, *Justice from Beacon Hill*, 205, and may likewise have not been unduly concerned with the financial rewards of his practice.

94. See "Early Reading," 184.

95. Mrs. Faneuil Adams to author, October 10, 1989.

96. See the sources cited in John Monagan, *The Grand Panjandrum: The Mellow Years of Justice Holmes* 49–61 (1988). Hereafter cited as Monagan, *The Grand Panjandrum.*

97. Holmes to Lewis Einstein, June [no date given] 1929, *Holmes–Einstein Letters,* 297.

98. Holmes to Ethel Scott, January 6, 1912, Holmes Papers.

99. Mark Howe, Holmes' authorized biographer, quoted Thomas Barbour, "an intimate friend of Holmes," whose wife was a cousin of Fanny's, as saying that Fanny "had no close friends and 'hated' most of her sisters." Quoted in Howe, *Shaping Years,* 200.

100. On her 1874 trip to Europe Fanny kept a diary, which included this entry, on May 30:

Will never, never, never put myself in such a fix again. 14 days more of it perhaps.

101. See letter from Dr. Oliver Wendell Holmes, Sr., to Thornton Hunt, July 16, 1872, which indicates that "my daughter-in-law is down with rheumatic fever," and letter from Holmes Sr. to Hunt, October 4, 1872, which states that "[m]y daughter-in-law has not yet got downstairs," and speaks of "the severe and long-continued illness of my daughter-in-law." Dr. Holmes has two daughters-in-law at the time, but Ned Holmes and his wife, Henrietta Wigglesworth, were in Europe in the summer and fall of 1872, so Fanny was clearly the subject of Dr. Holmes' remarks. The letters are in the Thornton Hunt Papers, Keats House, London, England.

102. See Holmes Sr. to Hunt, October 4, 1872, Thornton Hunt Papers.

103. Just when Fanny developed rheumatic fever for a second time is uncertain. Holmes traveled to England in the summer of 1896, and it is unlikely he would have made that journey if Fanny had been seriously ill. In a July 20, 1897 letter to Lady Georgina Pollock, the wife of his longtime friend Sir Frederick Pollock, Holmes wrote that "my wife . . . hasn't by any means got back to where she was before her rheumatic fever," but added that Fanny "seemed to awaken to a life and joy which she had not known for a good while" on a trip they had taken to New Hampshire. Holmes to Lady Pollock, July 20, 1897, *Holmes–Pollock Letters,* I, 75. Given the recovery period of rheumatic fever, this would suggest that Fanny might have taken sick while Holmes was in Europe in the summer of 1896, or possibly the summer before, 1895. Sheldon Novick, in his biography of Holmes, places the onset of Fanny's illness in the fall of 1894, but Novick cites no evidence for that dating, and it is hard to imagine that nearly three years after the illness Fanny would still have been suffering from its effects, as Novick asserts. See Novick, *Honorable Justice,* 201, 381.

104. Mrs. James B. Ayer, interview with Mark Howe, undated, Holmes Papers.

105. Isabella Wigglesworth (the wife of Fanny's nephew Frank Wigglesworth), interview with John Monagan, quoted in Monagan, *The Grand Panjandrum,* 54.

106. Quoted in id.

107. Holmes to Einstein, August 31, 1928, *Holmes–Einstein Letters,* 289.

108. Learned Hand to Mark Howe, April 29, 1959, Holmes Papers, quoted in Howe, *Proving Years,* 8.

109. Id.

110. Novick, *Honorable Justice,* 433, citing Mark Howe interview notes, Holmes Papers. See also Howe, *Shaping Years,* 200, quoting Mrs. Edward Jackson Holmes, the wife of Holmes' nephew, to the effect that Fanny "on more than one occasion spoke with profound sorrow of the fact she had no children."

111. The inclusion of that story in Baker's biography of Holmes is in contrast to her generally careful and prudent treatment of sources. The story is based on a memorandum dated April 5, 1961, apparently written by Mark Howe, in the Holmes Papers. In the memorandum Howe noted that he had lunched with Samuel Eliot Morison, a historian on the Harvard faculty, and Lewis Einstein, a longtime friend of Holmes, and that Morison had reported that John T. Morse, Jr., Holmes' contemporary, had many years before told him that Holmes was sexually impotent. Howe added that "[n]either Morison nor Einstein seemed to take any stock in Morse's announcement." See Baker, *Justice from Beacon Hill,* 225.

The episode would hardly seem a sufficient basis for any claim about Holmes' sexual potency. Baker nonetheless spends the next several paragraphs of her biography speculating that "[f]or Holmes, a diagnosis of impotence is not impossible." Among her grounds for speculation are the fact that the bullet that lodged in Holmes' neck in Antietam might have "damaged a nerve connected to his lower anatomy"; that "[p]hysicians today recognize connections between back ailments and sexual impotence" (Holmes never had any known back ailment); and that "[Holmes] and Fanny's fears of the results of sexual intimacy, singly or in combination, may well have contributed to a state of sexual helplessness in Wendell and also perhaps to Fanny's ability to respond, inhibiting the free expression of sexual feelings in both." Id., 228–29.

112. The Holmes Papers indicate that Fanny made all the household purchases, and Holmes' correspondence indicates that she took charge of decorating, refurbishing, and other matters pertaining to the Holmes household. She also bought the train tickets for the Holmeses' journeys from Boston or Washington to Beverly Farms, hired the domestic help, arranged the meals, and generally took charge of their living arrangements.

113. See, e.g., The Boston *Daily Advertiser,* April 19, 1880, which called Fanny's embroideries "the most remarkable needlework ever done," and *The Nation,* April 21, 1881, which said that "Mrs. Holmes . . . is an American artist of noticeable qualities."

114. Mrs. James B. Ayer to Mark Howe, quoted in Howe, *Shaping Years,* 255.

115. Holmes to Ellen Curtis, February 7, 1903, Holmes Papers.

116. Id.

117. A commonly described one originated with Francis Biddle, who was Holmes' secretary in 1911. Holmes was in the habit, after breakfast, of going down to the cellar in his house to find some worms to feed Fanny's birds. On April 1, 1912, as Biddle told the story,

He should have been warned on that particular April morning by something in Fanny's eye, as she looked across at him at breakfast from behind the kidneys she was stewing for him. . . . And the secretary had turned up early when he was still at breakfast, which was a suspicious circumstance in itself, knowing the secretary. Somehow they inveigled him into making a tour of the house. . . . [O]n that particular morning they all three went to the cellar, and Fanny was mumbling and muttering something about "cockroaches."

Suddenly the secretary cried: "Come over here, Mr. Justice, I think I see one."

He moved toward the flour barrel. "Nonsense, my lad, no cockroaches would live in a house with Mrs. Holmes."

"But Mr. Justice, look." Sure enough, large as life, there it was, sitting on the flour in the half-empty barrel.

They all craned.

"Brr," said Mrs. Holmes, and shivered. "Nasty thing." He looked at her suspiciously. She didn't often shiver. "You grab it," she said to the secretary.

But that young man hesitated.

The Judge pulled back his coat sleeve. "One, two, three!" And he plunged his arm deep in the flour, and brought forth a cockroach, made of wire.

"April fool, old man," said Mrs. Holmes.

He eyed the two conspirators with a deep, long chuckle of enjoyment. And then, to his wife: "You she devil!"

Francis Biddle, *Mr. Justice Holmes* 140–41 (1946).

118. Holmes to Pollock, May 24, 1929, *Holmes–Pollock Letters*, II, 243.

119. Fanny did participate in the editing of Holmes' volume of *Kent's Commentaries* and regularly discussed public affairs with him, since he declined to read newspapers. See Howe, *Proving Years*, 23.

120. Diary entry, March 3, 1873, Holmes Papers.

121. See Holmes to William James, December 15, 1867, Holmes Papers; Holmes to William James, April 19, 1868, id.

122. The details of Holmes' acceptance of an offer from Harvard Law School and subsequent resignation of his professorship are set forth in Chapter Six.

123. Holmes to Lewis Einstein, April 26, 1918, *Holmes–Einstein Letters*, 164.

124. Richard Henry Dana III, manuscript journal, quoted in Bliss Perry, *Richard Henry Dana 1851–1931* 104 (1933).

125. Opening Argument for Defendants, *New Orleans v. Joseph Nickerson*, 4, 8 (1878), Library of Congress.

126. See *New Orleans v. Nickerson*, Case #778, 779, 780, Circuit Court for the District of Massachusetts, 1877, Federal Records Center, Dorchester, Mass.

127. John Chipman Gray to Charles C. Beaman, November 29, 1878, Records of the Department of Justice, National Archives, Washington, D.C. The letter is quoted in Howe, *Shaping Years*, 131.

128. Morse to Hayes, December 5, 1878, National Archives, quoted in id., 131.

129. Holmes to Pollock, December 9, 1878, *Holmes–Pollock Letters*, I, 10.

130. In 1902 Hoar attempted to block the nomination of Holmes to the Supreme Court of the United States. See the discussion in Chapter Nine.

131. George F. Hoar, *Autobiography of Seventy Years* (2 vols., 1903), I, 416–19.

132. Holmes, "The Profession of the Law," February 17, 1886, *Occasional Speeches,* 31.

CHAPTER FOUR: *Coming to Maturity:*
Early Legal Scholarship

1. Holmes to Ralph Waldo Emerson, April 16, 1876, Harvard Archives, quoted in Howe, *Shaping Years,* 203.

2. The *Review's* format was nearly identical to that of the *American Jurist,* an earlier Boston-based journal that ceased publication after the Civil War.

3. George Sharswood, ed., *Roscoe's Digest of the Law of Evidence in Criminal Cases* (6th ed. 1866). Mark Howe, basing his conclusion on an entry by Holmes in his diary for 1866, wrote that Ropes and Gray had given Holmes Sharswood's edition of Roscoe as "plunder" in exchange for his noticing the book in the January 1867 *American Law Review.* Howe, *Shaping Years,* 265. Holmes' reading list for 1866 indicates that he was reading Sharswood's *Roscoe* as late as December 15, 1866. See "Early Reading," 173.

4. Alfred Swain Taylor, *A Manual of Medical Jurisprudence* (Clement Penrose ed. 1866). Holmes was also reading Taylor as late as December 15, 1866. See "Early Reading," 173.

5. Recall Holmes' comment in his essay on Plato, discussed in Chapter One: "[I]t is only in these last days that anything like an all-comprehending science has embraced the universe, showing unerring law prevailing in every department, generalizing and systematizing . . . every vagary of the human mind." Holmes, "Plato," 2 *University Quarterly* 205, 216 (1860).

6. Holmes, Book Notice, 1 *Am. L. Rev.* 375, 376 (1867).

7. See Howe, *Shaping Years,* 267–68. In his *General View,* Stephen had written that in the English system rules of evidence were judged "by considering whether they are well fitted to . . .provide a security that no one shall be punished till his guilt is proved by plain solid reasons, such as experienced men act upon in important affairs of their own." In Holmes' review he wrote that "[i]n the English and American courts the object [of rules of evidence] is to enable ordinary men . . . to come to a conclusion such as they would feel justified in acting on in a business matter of their own." James Fitzjames Stephen, *A General View of the Criminal Law of England* 264 (1863); Holmes, supra note 6, at 376.

8. See "Early Reading," 172.

9. Holmes, Book Notice, 1 *Am. L. Rev.* 377 (1866).

10. Holmes, Book Notice, 1 *Am. L. Rev.* 554, 555 (1867).

11. See "Early Reading," 169.

12. Id., 178.

13. See Henry Adams to Henry Maine, February 22, 1875, quoted in Harold Dean Cater, *Henry Adams and His Friends* 64 (1947).

14. Holmes to Frederick Pollock, March 4, 1888, *Holmes–Pollock Letters* I, 31.

15. The articles, digests, and notices in the *American Law Review* were anonymously authored. The identity of authors for the first four volumes was supplied by John Gray's copy of those volumes, currently in the Oliver Wendell Holmes Papers, Harvard Law School.

16. See notices of Michigan Reports, 3 *Am. L. Rev.* 141 (1868); Wisconsin Reports,

id., 147; Nevada Reports, id., 148; Ellis & Ellis, Queen's Bench Reports, id., 150; Iowa Reports, id., 357; Illinois Reports, id., 556; Michigan Reports, id., 757.

17. 2 *Am. L. Rev.* 547, 747 (1868).

18. Holmes, Book Notice, 3 *Am. L. Rev.* 541 (1869).

19. Arthur Sedgwick to Henry James, January 30, 1870, James Papers, Harvard University Archives.

20. William James to Henry Bowditch (quoting John Ropes), May 22, 1869, in Ralph Barton Perry, *The Thought and Character of William James* (2 vols., 1935), I, 297.

21. Mrs. Henry James, Sr., to Henry James, Jr., August 8, 1869, James Papers.

22. 5 *Am. L. Rev.* 1 (1870). My text for Holmes' early articles, except where otherwise noted, is Frederic Rogers Kellogg, *The Formative Essays of Justice Holmes* (1984) (hereafter Kellogg, *Formative Essays*), which has the advantage of accessibility, in addition to being a photographic reproduction of the original essays. Holmes' "Codes" article begins at page 77 of Kellogg.

23. In addition to being aware of the writings of Bentham and Austin, Holmes had read large portions of the work of John Stuart Mill and met Mill on his trip to England in 1866. "Early Reading," 169, 171, 173, 174, indicates that Holmes read Mill and criticism of Mill from 1865 through 1867.

The relationship of Holmes to the mid-nineteenth-century British utilitarian jurists is the subject of H. L. Pohlman, *Justice Oliver Wendell Holmes and Utilitarian Jurisprudence* (1984).

24. See "Early Reading," 169, 177, 181.

25. Holmes spelled out this concern in a book notice in the January 1871 issue of the *American Law Review,* the next to appear after his "Codes" article had been published. "If those forms [the common-law writs] had been based upon a comprehensive survey of the field of rights and duties, so that they embodied in a practical shape a classification of the law, with a form of action to correspond to every substantial duty," he argued, "the question would be other than it is. But they are in fact so arbitrary in character, and owe their origin to such purely historical causes, that nothing keeps them but our respect for the sources of our jurisprudence." Holmes, Book Notice, 5 *Am. L. Rev.* 359 (1871).

26. In his book notice of Redfield's edition of Story's *Commentaries on Equity Jurisprudence,* Holmes had decried Redfield's "habit of moralizing, which is notably out of place among the rules and precedents of courts." "When the learned editor calls in the authority of religion to make weight against the authority of the Master of the Rolls," Holmes dryly commented, "by doing so he only renders the want of legal authority more conspicuous." Holmes, Book Notice, supra note 10, at 554.

27. Kellogg, *Formative Essays,* 78.

28. Id., 78–79.

29. Id., 77–78.

30. Id., 79. Emphasis in original.

31. Id., 79.

32. Id., 82.

33. Id., 84–85.

34. Id., 80.

35. Id., 80–81.

36. Id., 88.

37. Id., 88–89.

38. Pollock, "Law and Command," 1 *Law Magazine and Review* 189 (1872).

39. 6 *Am. L. Rev.* 723 (1872). The notice is reprinted in Kellogg, *Formative Essays*, 91.

40. See "Early Reading," 183, 184.

41. Kellogg, *Formative Essays*, 91.

42. Id., 92.

43. Holmes excluded "singular motives" based on idiosyncratic human reactions, such as "the blandishments of the emperor's wife," as "not a ground of prediction." He thus stopped short of equating law with "what the judge ate for breakfast." Predictions were based on the availability to the judge of sources commonly regarded as authoritative.

44. Holmes, *Collected Legal Papers*, 173. This statement first appeared in "The Path of the Law," 10 *Harv. L. Rev.* 467 (1897).

45. Kellogg, *Formative Essays*, 92.

46. Id., 93.

47. The articles were "The Arrangement of the Law. Privity," 7 *Am. L. Rev.* 46 (1872), in Kellogg, *Formative Essays*, 95, and "The Theory of Torts," 7 *Am. L. Rev.* 652 (1873), id., 117. For reasons that will be subsequently explored, Holmes then abandoned analytically oriented essays and turned to legal history.

48. Holmes, "Possession," 9 *Am. L. Rev.* 688 (1878), in Kellogg, *Formative Essays*, 167, 181.

49. Holmes to Dr. and Mrs. Oliver Wendell Holmes, Sr., May 16, 1864; Holmes to Amelia Jackson Holmes, June 7, 1864, *Touched With Fire*, 122, 143.

50. The precise time that Holmes read Hodgson and noted the passage quoted below is not clear. Holmes' reading list did not include Hodgson among its titles. In Holmes' manuscript of the "Codes" essay, in the Holmes Papers at Harvard Law School, there is a notation in the margins, near his formulation of the rights/duties distinction, that he had not seen Hodgson until the "Codes" essay had appeared in print. But in Holmes' bound copy of Volume Five of the *American Law Review*, in the Library of Congress, Holmes wrote the following:

> My coincidence [with Hodgson and Comte] is so striking that it is proper to say
> that [Hodgson's] book was received at the Athenaeum (where I first saw it) August
> 24/70 at which time this [the "Codes" essay] was in print. I had noted the idea in
> the flyleaf of Austin long before, and never saw the passage in Comte.

This comment is odd in light of the fact that Holmes' reading list indicates that he finished writing the "Codes" essay on August 27, 1870. See "Early Reading," 181.

Holmes had not claimed in the "Codes" article that his rights/duties distinction was original, but he obviously regarded it as such, and believed that it was significant enough to build additional scholarship on. The fact that he began his next article using the distinction by quoting the passage from Hodgson and saying that in suggesting that classification of the law be grounded on duties rather than rights "we believed ourselves at the time to be original" indicates that he was anxious that others not believe he had passed off Comte's insight as his own. The Hodgson book, he said, was "believed not to have reached this country until after the ["Codes"] article was in print." Holmes,

"The Arrangement of the Law. Privity," 7 *Am. L. Rev.* 46 (1872), reprinted in Kellogg, *Formative Essays,* 95.

51. Shadworth Hodgson, *Theory of Practice* (2 vols., 1870), II, 169–70, quoted in Holmes, supra note 48 at 46; Kellogg, *Formative Essays,* 95.

52. Holmes, "The Arrangement of the Law. Privity," in Kellogg, *Formative Essays,* 95.

53. For the entire table, see id., 97.

54. Holmes, Book Notice, 5 *Am. L. Rev.* 340 (1871).

55. Holmes, "The Theory of Torts," 7 *Am. L. Rev.* 652 (1873), in Kellogg, *Formative Essays,* 117.

56. Id., 124–25.

57. Id., 124.

58. Id., 111.

59. Id., 111–12.

60. Id., 119.

61. Holmes to John Norton Pomeroy, May 22, 1872, Holmes Papers, quoted in Howe, *Proving Years,* 16.

62. Holmes to Thayer, December 10, 1869, Holmes Papers, quoted in Howe, *Proving Years,* 12.

63. See Oliver Wendell Holmes, ed., James Kent, *Commentaries on American Law* (4 vols., 12th ed., 1873), IV, 441, II, 260, III, 419, IV, 480, II, 479. Hereafter cited as Holmes, *Kent's Commentaries,* with volume and page numbers.

64. Holmes to Thayer, December 10, 1869, supra note 62.

65. James Bradley Thayer to James Kent, December [no date given], 1869, James Bradley Thayer Papers, Harvard Law School Library, quoted in Howe, *Proving Years,* 12–13.

66. Holmes, *Kent's Commentaries,* I, viii.

67. James Kent to James Bradley Thayer, December 16, 1873, Thayer Papers, Harvard Law School Library, quoted in Howe, *Proving Years,* 14. Emphasis in original.

68. James Kent to James Bradley Thayer, December 17, 1873, Thayer Papers, Harvard Law School Library, quoted in id., 14.

69. Thayer, diary entry, December 18, 1882, Memorandum Book D, 144, Thayer Papers, Harvard Law School Library. A complete account of the entry is set forth in Howe, *Proving Years,* 265–68. See also Chapter Six.

70. Holmes to Thayer, July 15, 1872, Thayer Papers, Harvard Law School Library, quoted in Howe, *Proving Years,* 15.

71. Sedgwick's reaction to the draft of Pomeroy's review is set forth in a letter Pomeroy wrote to Holmes, February 9, 1874, Holmes Papers, quoted in Howe, *Proving Years,* 14. In a subsequent letter to Holmes, Pomeroy expressed annoyance that while he had agreed to acknowledge Thayer's contribution, he had not expected that his review would be edited such that his praise of Holmes' efforts would be omitted. See Pomeroy to Holmes, February 14, 1874, Holmes Papers. The review appeared in 18 *The Nation* 110 (February 12, 1874).

72. [Gray,] Book Notice, 118 *North American Review* 387–88 (April, 1874).

73. Boston *Daily Advertiser,* January 2, 1874. Emphasis in original.

74. Jeremiah Smith, an associate of Holmes' who was to have a distinguished career

as a practitioner, judge, and professor at Harvard Law School, wrote Holmes in the spring of 1873 that his affiliation with Shattuck and Monroe amounted to a "return to active practice." Smith to Holmes, April 18, 1873, Holmes Papers, quoted in Howe, *Proving Years*, 24.

75. See Holmes to James Bryce, May 17, 1871, Holmes Papers, quoted in Howe, *Proving Years*, 24, indicating that Holmes could not read German well enough to understand scholarly sources. By December 1874, Holmes' reading list listed Rudolph Sohm's *Der Procesz der Lex Salica*, a German source.

76. See "Early Reading," 187–91. It was in this period that Holmes first read Henry Sumner Maine's scholarship on the early history of legal institutions. See id., 189, 193.

77. Holmes in Kellogg, *Formative Essays*, 124–25.

78. Holmes, "Codes, and the Arrangement of the Law," in Kellogg, *Formative Essays*, 80.

79. "Early Reading," 190, 192, 194.

80. Id., 194.

81. For examples of the various approaches of the German scholars whose works Holmes read, see Immanuel Kant, *Metaphysische Anfangsgruende der Rechtslere* (1797); Friedrich Karl Savigny, *Das Recht des Besitzes* (1803); Georg Frederick Puchta, *Cursus der Institutionen* (1841–46); Bernhard Windscheid, *Lehrbuch des Pandektenrechts* (1862–70). For a detailed treatment of Holmes' relationship to late nineteenth-century German scholarship, see Mathias Reimann, "Holmes' *Common Law* and German Legal Science," in Gordon, *Legacy*, 72–114.

82. For an extended discussion, see Reimann in Gordon, *Legacy*, 81–85.

83. Holmes to James Bryce, August 17, 1879, Holmes Papers.

84. Holmes to Charles Eliot, November 1, 1881, Holmes Papers. The letter was first written by Holmes on October 24, and a revised version was sent to Eliot on November 1.

85. 10 *Am. L. Rev.* 422 (1876); Kellogg, *Formative Essays*, 129.

86. Id., 117.

87. Id., 130–31.

88. Id., 133–35.

89. Id., 135.

90. Id., 137.

91. Id.

92. Id., 144.

93. Id.

94. "Primitive Notions in Modern Law, No. II," 11 *Am. L. Rev.* 641 (1877); Kellogg, *Formative Essays*, 147. This article and "Primitive Notions I" were signed, the first time that Holmes had authored signed scholarly articles.

95. Id., 147.

96. In *The Common Law*, where one of Holmes' chapters was based on a lecture on "successions" modeled on "Primitive Notions II," he characterized the theory of *inter vivos* succession to property as the "most difficult and obscure part of the subject." Holmes, *The Common Law* 353 (1881).

97. Kellogg, *Formative Essays*, 159.

98. Id., 159–60.

99. Id., 160.

100. Id.

101. Id., 166.

102. Reimann makes a similar observation in "Holmes's *The Common Law* and German Legal Science," in Gordon, *Legacy,* 79.

103. "Possession," 12 *Am. L. Rev.* 688 (1878); Kellogg, *Formative Essays,* 167.

104. Id.

105. Id.

106. Id., 177.

107. Id., 179.

108. Id., 180.

109. Id., 180–81. As Reimann has shown, this reading of German possession theory was superficial and inaccurate in several ways. The question for German theory was not whether possession, as a practical matter, yielded a "right" in the possessor to exclude others—which German jurists accepted—but whether possession could be formally termed a "right" within the meaning of a civil law system, which contains "a great number of general rules concerning rights as such." Reimann, in Gordon, *Legacy,* 89.

110. Holmes, "Possession," in Kellogg, *Formative Essays,* 181, 186, 191.

111. Id., 198–99.

112. Id., 181.

113. By *The Common Law,* Reimann has argued, Holmes had come to recognize the inconsistency between formal analytical jurisprudence and his "empirical" approach, and had launched a potential attack on "formalism" in both its German and American versions. See Reimann in Gordon, *Legacy,* 91–95. Compare the discussion in Chapter Five.

114. Holmes, "Common Carriers and the Common Law," 13 *Am. L. Rev.* 909 (1879), in Kellogg, *Formative Essays,* 201.

115. See generally Dorothy Ross, *The Origins of American Social Science* (1991). Hereafter Ross, *Origins.* Ross argues that the Civil War provoked a "crisis" in intellectual authority in America, as religious-based explanations for the universe lost their authoritative status and the emergence of massive industrialization and class conflict made it abundantly clear to American intellectuals that cultural change might well be a permanent, inevitable phenomenon. A search thus emerged for intellectual devices through which the ability of the exceptional American republic to resist time and change could be reaffirmed: "science" was regarded as one of those devices. Id., 53–59.

Ross identifies Holmes as one of a post-Civil War generation of intellectuals who sought to formulate "positivist laws of historical progress" through the use of "scientific" methodology. Holmes was unusual, Ross believes, in being overtly positivist in his orientation: his contemporaries more commonly used "science" to derive universal, timeless principles. See id., 66–67.

If Ross' terminology is adopted, Holmes' early analytical work on "duties" more closely resembles the "orthodox" orientation of his contemporaries, in which "science" (in Holmes' case logic) is used to flatten out history; and his later historical work gives evidence of the acceptance of inevitable change over time. If one considers Holmes' undergraduate work, however, there is evidence that he possessed a nascent historicist sensibility even before the beginning of his scholarly career. Thus Holmes' belief in the analytical promise of the concept of "duty" would appear to be something of a distraction, explained, perhaps, by Holmes' and his contemporaries' eagerness to invest "science" (by which Holmes originally meant analytical philosophy) with the capacity to substitute for religion as an "all-comprehending" discipline capable of systematizing experience.

116. Holmes, "Common Carriers and the Common Law," in Kellogg, *Formative Essays,* 203.

117. Id., 207.

118. Id., 215.

119. Id., 219.

120. Id., 221.

121. Id.

122. Id., 223.

123. Id., 222–23.

124. Id., 223. This language anticipated Holmes' unsigned book review of Christopher Columbus Langdell's *Selection of Cases on the Law of Contracts,* in which he said that "Mr. Langdell's ideal in the law . . . is the elegantia juris, or logical integrity of the system as a system." Holmes, Book Notice, 14 *Am. L. Rev.* 233 (1880). See the discussion in Chapter Five.

125. Kellogg, *Formative Essays,* 223.

126. Holmes, "Trespass and Negligence," 14 *Am. L. Rev.* 1 (1880); Kellogg, *Formative Essays,* 225.

127. Id., 225–26.

128. Id., 226–27.

129. Id., 227.

130. Id., 228.

131. Id., 229–30 and cases there cited.

132. Id., 231.

133. Id.

134. Id., 232–33, 235.

135. His arguments were repeated, almost verbatim, in *The Common Law.* See the discussion in Chapter Five.

136. Holmes, "Trespass and Negligence," Kellogg, *Formative Essays,* 243.

137. Id., 242–43.

138. Id., 244, referring to *Brown v. Kendall,* 6 Cush. 292 (1850).

139. Id., 240–42.

140. Id., 241–43.

141. Id., 236.

142. Id.

143. Id., 237.

144. Id., 237–38.

145. Id., 252–54.

146. Id., 245.

147. Id., 245–46.

148. Id., 246–47.

149. Id., 247.

150. Id., 259.

151. Id., 225.

152. I am postponing questions about the epistemological coherence of Holmes' methodology until Chapter Five, where the methodological premises of *The Common Law* are discussed.

153. Holmes, "Trespass and Negligence," in Kellogg, *Formative Essays*, 223.

154. See E. Wilson, *Patriotic Gore* 743–96 (1962); George Frederickson, *The Inner Civil War* 79–112 (1968); Ross, *Origins*.

155. Frederickson, supra note 154, at 199–216; Gordon, "Holmes's *Common Law* as Legal and Social Science," 10 *Hofstra L. Rev.* 746 (1982); Ross, *Origins*, 56–71, Thomas C. Grey, "Langdell's Orthodoxy," 45 *U. Pitt. L. Rev.* 1, 16–20 (1983).

156. See Ross, *Origins*, 59–62; Grey, supra note 155, at 16–20; Michael H. Hoeflich, "Law and Geometry," 30 *Am. J. Legal Hist.* 95 (1986).

157. See Ross, "Historical Consciousness in Nineteenth Century America," 89 *Am. Hist. Rev.* 909 (1984); Ross, *Origins*, 58–67.

158. See Howe, *Proving Years*, 66–78.

159. See Holmes to Harold Laski, June 1, 1922, *Holmes-Laski Letters*, I, 429. "You ask me what started my book," Holmes wrote. "I don't think Maine had anything to do with it except to feed the philosophic passion. . . . I don't think of any special book that put me on the track."

For a discussion of the originality of *The Common Law*, and Holmes' general attitude toward acknowledging the contributions of other scholars toward his work, see Chapter Five.

160. See Holmes, Book Notice, 11 *Am. L. Rev.* 327 (1877). In that notice Holmes reviewed Adams' edition of *Essays in Anglo-Saxon Law*, which he said "prepare the ground for a truly philosophic history of the law."

161. For more on Holmes' debt to the Germans Savigny and Jhering, which he underplayed, see Chapter Five. See also Reimann in Gordon, *Legacy*, 96–104.

162. The relationship of Holmes to pragmatism has been the subject of several studies. See Max T. Fisch, "Justice Holmes, the Prediction Theory of Law, and Pragmatism," 39 *Journal of Philosophy* 85 (1942); Philip Weiner, *Evolution and the Founders of Pragmatism* (1949); Thomas C. Grey, "Holmes and Legal Pragmatism," 41 *Stan. L. Rev.* 787 (1989).

163. For a discussion of Holmes as a positivist, see Chapters Five, Six, Nine, and Twelve.

164. Holmes, "Possession," in Kellogg, *Formative Essays*, 181.

165. Holmes, Book Notice, supra note 124, at 233.

166. Id.

CHAPTER FIVE: The Common Law

1. See "Early Reading," 202, for the 1880 entry.

2. The quotation is from John Lowell Jr.'s will creating the Institute, cited in Robert Dalzell, *The Associates* 145–46 (1988). For more detail on the Lowell Institute, see Harriette Smith, *The History of the Lowell Institute* (1898); Edward Weeks, *The Lowells and Their Institute* (1966).

3. No doubt by 1880 instruction in "moral and religious precepts" was not a prerequisite of Lowell Institute lectures, otherwise it is hard to imagine Holmes as coming to mind as a lecturer. In a letter written to Mark De Wolfe Howe on May 19, 1942, A. Lawrence Lowell indicated that John Lowell had invited Holmes to give the 1880 lectures on Lawrence Lowell's recommendation. See Howe, *Proving Years,* 136.

4. Holmes, "Trespass and Negligence," in Kellogg, *Formative Essays,* 225.

5. Holmes to Arthur G. Sedgwick, July 12, 1879; Holmes to James Bryce, August 17, 1879, Holmes Papers.

6. Holmes to Pollock, June 17, 1880, *Holmes-Pollock Letters,* I, 14.

7. Holmes to Pollock, March 5, 1881, I, 16.

8. Id.

9. Holmes to Mrs. Charles S. Hamlin, October 12, 1930 ("if a man was to do anything he must do it before 40").

10. The Boston *Daily Advertiser* published a summary of the lectures in its January 1, 1881, issue. The reviewer noted that "[n]o other course in the [Lowell] institute has been attended by so large a proportion of young men—an evidence both of the interest they have in the law and the power of Mr. Holmes to interest them." The summary suggested that Holmes may have retained in the skeleton of his lectures some of the analytical classifications he had made early in his career. At one point the summary had Holmes saying that "some rights and liabilities require special facts to be true of plaintiff, defendant, or both, before they can exist. The chief of these groups of special facts are possession and contract." In his table of duties, affixed to his "Privity" article, Holmes listed possession and contract among duties "owed to persons in particular situations or relations." See Kellogg, *Formative Essays,* at 97. The reviewer concluded by noting that "[h]aving sketched his course, Mr. Holmes gave a few minutes at the close of the lecture to a picture of the scope, beauties, pleasures and horrors of the law."

11. One indication of *The Common Law*'s status is that it has never been out of print since its initial publication.

12. Holmes, *The Common Law* 1–2 (1881).

13. On page 1 of *The Common Law* Holmes said that "[t]he law embodies the story of a nation's development through many centuries." On page 168 of his treatise, *An Introduction to Municipal Law,* (1864 ed.) John Norton Pomeroy had written, "[A] nation's law is most intimately connected with their civilization, and is some sort of an exponent of the people's attainment in general culture."

Holmes had read Pomeroy's *Municipal Law* in the spring of 1871. See "Early Reading," 183. Pomeroy had cited Maine's *Ancient Law* and Savigny's *Traduit de l'Allemand* in his preface. *Municipal Law,* ix. Holmes had also read Maine in 1871 and again in 1875, and had read Savigny in 1870, 1876, and 1877. "Early Reading," 181, 184, 189, 193, 194. See also Joseph Story's 1829 essay, "The Value and Importance of Legal Studies," in William W. Story, ed., *Miscellaneous Writings of Joseph Story* 526 (1852), for a similar view of the "developing" character of law.

14. See Ross, *Origins,* 58–61; William LaPiana, "Victorian from Beacon Hill: Oliver Wendell Holmes' Early Legal Scholarship," 90 *Colum. L. Rev.* 809, 811–13 (1990).

15. See Ross, *Origins,* 66–69, for a discussion of efforts on the part of late nineteenth-century intellectuals to develop the field of "historico-politics." By that term Ross means an approach to history designed to confirm, through an exploration of the evolution of

institutions and ideas over time, the primacy of certain principles of political government. As Ross puts it, the approach assumed that a "scientific" study of "the facts" of history "would yield those underlying principles that guided political progress." Id., 71.

16. Holmes, Book Notice, 14 *Am. L. Rev.* 233 (1880).

17. Id.

18. Howe, *Proving Years,* 157, surmised that "[i]t is not unlikely that Langdell, Thayer, Ames, and Gray—the entire Faculty of the Harvard Law School—were in the audience" for Holmes' opening Lowell Lecture, and speculates that Holmes "would hardly have pointed a finger of scorn" at Langdell as the principal architect of a "logical" approach to the law. But see Reimann, "Holmes' *Common Law* and German Legal Science," in Gordon, *Legacy,* 95–105, arguing that in attacking "Germans" in *The Common Law* Holmes was surreptitiously attacking Langdell.

19. For an example, as late as 1906, of a contrast made between "legislation" and "law," see C. C. Langdell, "Dominant Opinions in England During the Nineteenth Century . . ." 19 *Harv. L. Rev.* 151 (1906).

20. Compare, for example, Holmes' statement that the law was "always approaching and never reaching consistency" with Joseph Story's 1829 comment that the law "moves onward in the path toward perfection; but never arrives at the ultimate point." Story, "The Value and Importance of Legal Studies," supra note 13, at 526.

21. The most influential interpretation has been that of Morton White in *Social Thought in America: The Revolt Against Formalism* (1948). A number of recent scholars have begun to emphasize the connections between Holmes' and Langdell's approaches, despite their obvious differences. For a discussion of several of those efforts, see H. L. Pohlman, *Justice Oliver Wendell Holmes and Utilitarian Jurisprudence* 144–61 (1984). See also LaPiana, supra note 14, at 826–30; Reimann in Gordon, *Legacy,* 109–111.

22. Holmes, *The Common Law,* 2.

23. Holmes, "Possession"; Kellogg, *Formative Essays,* 181.

24. Holmes "Primitive Notions I"; Kellogg, *Formative Essays,* 137.

25. Id., 132, 138.

26. Holmes, *The Common Law,* 4.

27. Id., 37.

28. Id.

29. Id., 38.

30. Id., 40.

31. Id.

32. Id., 41–42. The comparison of the criminal law to marriage and "the sexual appetite" had been made by Holmes' friend James Fitzjames Stephen in his *General View of the Criminal Law of England* 99 (1863).

33. Holmes, *The Common Law,* 42.

34. Holmes began the discussion by referring the reader back to his first chapter, but only by way of contrasting the "internal standard" of liability he associated with "[t]he desire for vengeance" with the "objective or external one" of contemporary criminal law. Id., 40.

35. Id.

36. Id., 46.

37. Id., 46–47.

38. Id., 43–44.

39. Id., 48–49.

40. Id., 50–51.

41. Id., 57.

42. Id., 66.

43. Id., 68–69.

44. Id., 75.

45. Holmes, "The Theory of Torts"; Kellogg, *Formative Essays,* 117, 124–25.

46. It is fair to say, in fact, that Holmes entirely rejected the act-at-peril theory of tort liability as a theory. He permitted liability based on other than a violation of reasonable care in a limited class of circumstances, but explicitly on the ground that social policy required this "exceptional" treatment. Act-at-peril liability for accidents caused by dangerous animals or substems was an example. See Holmes, *The Common Law,* 154–55.

47. Holmes, *The Common Law,* 111–12.

48. Id. at 112. Holmes was apparently less troubled by jury determinations of "intent" in criminal law cases because of the requirement that crimes be particularized and their elements precisely determined.

49. Id., 126–27.

50. Id., 123.

51. Id., 124.

52. Id., 127–28.

53. Id., 126.

54. David Rosenberg has argued that in rejecting an "act-at-peril" standard Holmes was not rejecting what Rosenberg calls "foresight-based," as distinguished from "cause-based," strict liability. "Fault" for Holmes, Rosenberg believes, encompassed failure to prevent forseeable consequences of acts whose occurrence was very costly to prevent, such as water escaping from land whose soil was porous to an extent that could not have been known to the landowner. Rosenberg's analysis thus makes Holmes into a supporter of strict liability in cases where injuries could be foreseen, even where the chance of injury was remote.

Rosenberg's analysis reveals a dilemma for Holmes' general theory of liability in tort, but it does not necessarily suggest that Holmes recognized and resolved the dilemma. If foreseeability is to be the test of liability, one could argue—as Holmes did—that a decision to build a reservoir on one's land amounted to a "choice" to take the risk that water from it might escape. But under that analysis any act that could be factually linked to a subsequent injury to another would be a "choice." Holmes had specifically rejected liability in that situation in *The Common Law*. See id., 95. So for Holmes to allow recovery in the case of water escaping from a reservoir built on porous land—as distinguished from the case of water escaping from a reservoir in a very heavy rain—he would have to conclude that the former circumstances were "foreseeable" and the latter not. This stretches foreseeability to the breaking point.

It is far more likely that Holmes, by "foreseeability," meant "reasonable" foreseeability, as defined by the community, than any "foreseeable" relationship, however remote. Rosenberg's distinction between "cause-based" and "foresight-based" liability was never explicitly made by Holmes in *The Common Law*. Morever, Holmes may have allowed recovery in the case of a reservoir on porous land because he knew that in such a case, *Rylands v. Fletcher,* 3 H. L. 330 (1866), the House of Lords had found liability, and Holmes wanted to fit *Rylands* into his general theory. He therefore turned *Rylands* into a "foreseeability" case. See id., 116.

Rosenberg's analysis is in David Rosenberg, *Oliver Wendell Holmes and Strict Tort Liability* (unpublished manuscript, June 1992 draft).

55. Holmes, *The Common Law,* 130.

56. Id., 130.

57. Id., 133.

58. Id., 134.

59. Id., 144.

60. Id., 145.

61. Id., 162.

62. Id., 164.

63. He stated elsewhere in *The Common Law* that "norms of public policy which would not leave parties free to make their own bargains are somewhat discredited in most departments of the law." Id., 205. The phrase "are somewhat discredited" was a typical example of Holmes' appealing to what he took to be the preferences of many of his contemporaries. In this instance he may have been accurate in his reading of those preferences.

64. Holmes, "Possession"; Kellogg, *Formative Essays,* 181.

65. Id., 199.

66. Holmes, *The Common Law,* 164–65.

67. Id., 224–25.

68. Id., 205.

69. Id., 246.

70. Id., 203, 205.

71. An example would be "the fictitious identification between the deceased and his successor" for the purposes of transferring property ownership, which has the advantage of quieting title to land. Id., 342.

72. I am not the first to note Holmes' marginalization of history in his scholarship. See Howe, *Proving Years,* 140: "[Holmes] followed the historian's path . . . not for the purpose of increasing understanding of the past but to the end of comprehending the character of legal institutions."

73. Holmes, Book Notice, 14 *Am. L. Rev.* 233 (1880).

74. Holmes to Pollock, April 10, 1881, *Holmes–Pollock Letters* I, 17.

75. See G. Edward White, "The Rise and Fall of Justice Holmes," 39 *U. Chi. L. Rev.* 51, 77 (1971).

76. One astute reader of *The Common Law* noted in 1977:
The lectures have long since become unreadable unless the reader is prepared to put forward an almost superhuman effort of will to keep his attention from flagging and his interest from wandering. . . . [T]he historical underpinning [of Holmes' lectures] was patently absurd, even when it had not been deliberately distorted . . . [Holmes] was making a highly original, essentially philosophical statement about the nature of law. For reasons which he never explained, he chose to dress his statement in the misleading disguise of pseudo-history.
Grant Gilmore, *The Ages of American Law* 52 (1977).

77. See Thomas Holland, *Elements of Jurisprudence* 173–74 (1880), quoting Karl von Savigny.

78. In addition to his opposition to the principles themselves, the use of Roman sources was tainted for Holmes because those jurists, principally the German Pandectists, who had emphasized the primacy of Roman law doctrines in the common law, had at the same time stressed the fact that those doctrines embodied universal principles, such as possession and free will. Since Holmes was hostile to the methodology of the German jurists, he was also hostile to the purported dominance of their Roman sources.

79. Holmes, *The Common Law,* 252.

80. Id., 237–38.

81. Id., 293–94.

82. Id., 273.

83. Id., 198.

84. Id., 298–99.

85. Id., 299.

86. Id., 301.

87. Id.

88. Id., 303.

89. Id., 300.

90. Id., 308.

91. Id., 315.

92. The case was decided under the name *Raffles v. Wichelhaus,* 2 H & C. 906 (1864).

93. Holmes, *The Common Law,* 309. Holmes' interpretation of the word "said" in his analysis was a liberal one. The contract actually provided that the plaintiff would sell and the defendant would buy a cargo of cotton "to arrive ex Peerless from Bombay." Neither party "said" the "December ship Peerless" or the "October ship Peerless"; Holmes read them as "saying" those words.

In fact the case is much more straightforwardly characterized as one in which the "mutual mistake" was about what the parties "meant" when they both "said" "ex Peerless from Bombay." But since Holmes was interested in using the case as an example of how objective evidence rather than subjective intent governed the law of contract formation, he was not interested in characterizing the case in that fashion.

94. Id., 311.

95. Id., 311–12.

96. Id., 312.

97. Id.

98. Id., 407.

99. Id., 409.

100. Compare id., x, with id., 409.

101. See, e.g., Saul Touster, "Holmes a Hundred Years Ago: *The Common Law* and Legal Theory," 10 *Hofstra L. Rev.* 673 (1982); Robert Gordon, "Holmes' *Common Law* as Legal and Social Science," id., 719. See particularly the discussions by Touster, 685–88, and Gordon, 719–21.

Mark Howe's detailed treatment of *The Common Law* in Howe, *Proving Years,* 135–248, shows ample evidence of an awareness that Holmes was simultaneously employing what Howe calls "analytical" (or "philosophical") and "historical" methodologies.

But Howe was much less interested in exploring the apparent contradictions in Holmes' thought than in establishing connections between the historical portions of *The Common Law* and its juristic messages.

102. Morton J. Horwitz, "The Place of Justice Holmes in American Legal Thought," in Gordon, *Legacy,* 31, 32.

103. Holmes to Mrs. Charles S. Hamlin, October 12, 1930, Holmes Papers.

104. Foster signed his review with his initials. Given the conventions of authorship in legal journals in the 1870s and 1880s, when anonymous articles and book reviews were beginning to give way to initialed and authored ones, it is likely that Foster was one of the editors of the Albany Law Journal. His identity was determined from a consultation of one of the inside leaves of Holmes' own, autographed copy of *The Common Law,* which is available in the Special Collections Room at the Harvard Law Library. On that leaf Holmes listed the journals and other academic sources that had "noticed" the book, including the identity of some reviewers, none of whom had signed their names to their reviews. The list is impressionistic: in some instances Holmes did not list the names of reviewers whose identity he knew, and he gave no indication as to how he had discovered the identity of those reviewers whose names he listed.

105. [Roger Foster], "Holmes on the Common Law," 23 *Albany L. J.* 380 (1881).

106. Warren's review was also unsigned. Holmes listed his identity on the leaf of his edition of *The Common Law.*

107. [John Warren], "Holmes's Common Law," 15 *Am. L. Rev.* 331, 338 (1881). Note Warren's use of the currently fashionable term "unpacking" to describe the analysis of a text.

108. See, e.g., 23 *Albany L. J.,* supra note 105; 15 *American Law Review,* supra note 107; 25 *Journal of Jurisprudence* 646, 647 (1881).

109. Quoted in Silas Bent, *Justice Oliver Wendell Holmes* 306 (1932).

110. Holmes to Pollock, December 1, 1925, *Holmes–Pollock Letters,* II, 173.

111. Holmes to Felix Frankfurter, June 26, 1928, Holmes Papers.

112. Holmes to Clara Stevens, July 26, 1914, id.

113. See., e.g., Touster, supra note 101, at 682.

114. Boston *Daily Advertiser,* December 4, 1879.

115. 15 *Am. L. Rev.,* supra note 107, at 334.

116. Cf. G. Edward White, *The American Judicial Tradition* (2d. ed., 1988), 147–49. The fact that these jurisprudential attitudes were widely held at the time of the publication of *The Common Law* does not, of course, suggest that they were consistently treated as unproblematic. See id. 145, 149.

117. 23 *Albany L. J.,* supra note 105, at 380.

118. Ross, *Origins,* describes Holmes as part of a "brief effort in the 1870s to establish a somewhat different historical-political science," and as one of "a few Americans, influenced by positivist scientific ideals, [who] hoped for the discovery of laws of historical development." She suggests that this "overt positivism . . . did not sink academic roots in the 1870s and 1880s," but it was nonetheless in the air. Id., 64, 66.

119. See Horwitz in Gordon, *Legacy,* 43–55.

120. 15 *Am. L. Rev.,* supra note 107, at 336.

121. 25 *Journal of Jurisprudence* 646, 647 (1881).

122. Holmes, *The Common Law,* 162.

123. 25 *Journal of Jurisprudence,* supra note 108, at 647.

124. [Albert V. Dicey], "Holmes's Common Law," 55 *The Spectator* (Literary Supplement, June 3, 1882), reprinted in Touster, supra note 101, at 712. For convenience I have cited from the reprinted version. The review was unsigned: Dicey's authorship was discovered by Touster and Professor Robert Tener. See Touster, supra note 101, at 696.

125. See Howe, *Proving Years,* 31.

126. Id., 102.

127. Albert V. Dicey to Holmes, January 19, 1880, Holmes Papers.

128. 10 *Hofstra L. Rev.* 673, 712 (1982).

129. Dicey was named Vinerian Professor of Law at Oxford the same year he wrote the review, being selected over Frederick Pollock. See Holmes to Pollock, March 25, 1883, *Holmes–Pollock Letters,* I, 20.

130. 10 *Hofstra L. Rev.,* supra note 128, at 714.

131. Id.

132. 51 *Saturday Review* 758 (1881).

133. See Holmes to Pollock, July 5, 1881, *Holmes–Pollock Letters,* I, 18: "The notice in the *Saturday Review* (which I had already attributed to you on internal evidence before receiving the copy with your initials) was worth a good deal of hard work. . . ."

134. 51 *Saturday Review,* supra note 132, at 758.

135. Id.

136. 51 *Saturday Review,* supra note 132, at 759.

137. Id.

138. Note that Holmes again chose the word "intimate" to describe his response to a highly meaningful event in his life.

139. 26 *Albany L. J.* 484 (1882). The review also singled out Henry Adams' *Essays in Anglo-Saxon Law* (1876); and Melville Bigelow's *Placita Anglo-Normanica: Law Cases from William I to Richard I* (1879) and *History of Procedure in England from the Norman Conquest.* Holmes had, we have seen, reviewed the first of those books and read the second in manuscript. See also Howe, *Proving Years,* 139–48.

140. 26 *Albany L. J.,* supra note 139, at 484.

141. Id., 484–85.

142. Id., 485.

143. See, e.g., Touster, supra note 101, at 684–704; Gordon, supra note 101, at 722–43; Horwitz, in Gordon, *Legacy,* 36. Horwitz differs from the first two commentators in finding "contradictions in the thought of . . . Holmes" only "seemingly irreconcilable," and seeks to explain Holmes' methodology through strategies similar to those I have employed in this chapter, although he reaches quite different conclusions.

144. Gordon, supra note 101, at 720–21.

145. Holmes, in a letter to Frederick Pollock in 1902, indicated that *The Common Law* was not widely noticed or appreciated in America when it first appeared. As he put it, "I had to get appreciation for my book in England before they dared say anything here except in one or two quarters." Holmes to Pollock, September 23, 1902, *Holmes–Pollock Letters,* I, 106. Since Holmes noted the early reviews of *The Common Law* on the back of his own copy, it is clear that he was aware of the Pollock and Dicey reviews, and may have had those in mind in his comment. See Howe, *Proving Years,* 249.

As a result of this statement and the fact that no subsequent American edition of the work appeared until 1909, while two additional English editions appeared in 1882 and 1887, commentators have been inclined to accept Holmes' view that the book was initially better received in England than in America. But in a recent essay, Jordan D. Luttrell of Meyer Boswell Books has suggested that all subsequent editions of *The Common Law* that appeared between 1881 and 1909 were printed from the same electroplates, and has discovered three different sets of printers' marks on titles bearing 1881 as a copyright date. These printers' marks suggest that three separate American presses, two in Cambridge, Mass., and one in Boston, printed editions of *The Common Law* between 1881 and 1909, and that one of the English editions bears American printers' marks. Moreover, Luttrell has discovered five variant bindings of early editions of *The Common Law,* four of which are American in origin. Luttrell's findings suggest that there may have been more of a demand for *The Common Law* in America, during its early history, than Holmes' letter to Pollock suggested. The Luttrell essay appears in Catalogue Fourteen of *Rare and Unusual Law Books,* Meyer Boswell Books, Inc. 1–3 (Winter 1991).

146. Dorothy Ross' comment about Holmes' contemporaries in the decades after the Civil War seems appropriate to the first generation of reviewers of *The Common Law:*

> Through empirical method social scientists hoped to discover fundamental laws at work alike in nature and history. . . . [T]heir dawning awareness of historical change, their sense of living in a natural and historical world that must generate its own principles of order, made them . . . more dependent than before on the force of scientific law.

Ross, *Origins,* 60.

147. 15 *Am. L. Rev.,* supra note 107, at 333.

148. Holmes to Pollock, June 17, 1880, *Holmes–Pollock Letters,* I, 15.

149. Holmes to Laski, June 1, 1922, *Holmes–Laski Letters,* I, 429–30.

150. Holmes, *The Common Law,* iv.

151. See Gilmore, *The Ages of American Law,* supra note 76, at 128.

CHAPTER SIX: *"An All Round View of the Law"* 1882–1902

1. See Holmes to Mrs. Charles S. Hamlin, October 12, 1930, Holmes Papers, indicating that the cork was in the right-hand drawer of his desk as he wrote her.

2. Id.

3. Holmes to Frederick Pollock, July 16, 1879, *Holmes–Pollock Letters* I, 12.

4. Holmes to Pollock, March 5, 1881, id., 16.

5. Holmes to Pollock, April 10, 1881, id., 17.

6. James Bradley Thayer to John D. Long, January 13, 1881, Massachusetts Archives, Executive Department Letters, quoted in Howe, *Proving Years,* 259.

7. [Holmes,] Book Review, 14 *Am. L. Rev.* 233 (1880).

8. Holmes to Pollock, April 10, 1881, *Holmes–Pollock Letters,* I, 17.

9. Holmes, "Remarks at the Harvard Commencement Dinner," in *Occasional Speeches,* 2.

10. Note, 5 *Am. L. Rev.* 177 (1870). The note prompted a response by Joel Parker, who had been a professor at Harvard Law School during the time of Holmes's residence

as a student, that characterized Holmes and his co-editor Arthur G. Sedgwick as "two young men . . . who about four years since, consented to receive the honors of the school in the shape of a degree of Bachelor of Laws, without insisting on a preliminary examination to show that they deserved them." Parker added that he was hardpressed to say "which is more prominent in [the note], the conceit which dictated it, or the entire lack of courtesy manifested by it." Joel Parker, *The Law School of Harvard College* 5 (1871).

11. 5 *Am. L. Rev.* at 177.

12. C. C. Langdell, *Cases on Contracts* ii (1871). In 1886 Holmes recalled that in the brief time he taught at Harvard Law School he had employed the socratic method in a course in Torts. "With some misgivings," he noted, "I plunged a class of beginners straight into Mr. Ames's collection of [Torts] cases, and we began to discuss them together in Mr. Langdell's method. The result was better than I even hoped it would be." Holmes, "The Use of Law Schools," in *Occasional Speeches*, 43–44.

13. Holmes to James Bryce, August 17, 1879, Holmes Papers.

14. Holmes to Charles W. Eliot, November 1, 1881, quoted in Howe, *Proving Years*, 260. A copy of the letter, with the date "October 14, 1881," is in the Holmes Papers. Apparently Holmes originally wrote Eliot a draft of the letter on October 24, corrected that draft and mailed a clean copy of the corrected version between that date and November 1, and at the same time retained the corrected October 24 draft for himself.

15. Charles W. Eliot to Holmes, November 4, 1881, Holmes Papers, quoted in Howe, *Proving Years*, 261–62.

16. James Bradley Thayer, Memorandum, January 29, 1882, in James Bradley Thayer Papers, Book D, 103, Harvard Law School Library. This memorandum, written after Holmes had joined the Harvard faculty, should not be confused with a subsequent memorandum of Thayer's, dated December 18, 1882. See note 32 below.

17. Id., 104.

18. Id.

19. Id.

20. Id., 105–06.

21. Id., 107.

22. Id., 108 (entry of February 12).

23. See Howe, *Proving Years*, 272, quoting Minutes of Law School Faculty, Harvard Archives.

24. Harvard Law School Catalogue, 1882–83, quoted in Howe, *Proving Years*, 272.

25. See Howe, *Proving Years*, 279, citing student notebooks for Holmes' classes in Jurisprudence and Agency. Holmes' 1886 description of "plung[ing] a class of beginners straight into Mr. Ames' collection of [torts] cases," quoted supra note 12, provides evidence of his socratic orientation in Torts.

26. Holmes to Felix Frankfurter, July 15, 1913, Holmes Papers, quoted in Howe, *Proving Years*, 282.

27. Holmes' lectures on the early history of contracts and uses in equity were published as "Early English Equity," 1 *L. Q. Rev.* 162 (1885), and his lectures on agency as "Agency," 4 *Harv. L. Rev.* 345 (1891) and 5 *Harv. L. Rev.* 1 (1891). These articles were reprinted in *Collected Legal Papers*, 49, 81.

28. Holmes, "Agency," *Collected Legal Papers*, 101.

29. Id., 115.

30. Holmes had anticipated some of his views on agency in his notes to the twelfth edition of Kent's *Commentaries*. See, e.g., II, 260–61, where Holmes criticized the vicarious liability of masters for the negligent acts of their servants and suggested that the master–servant relationship was analogous to that of principal and agent.

31. W. C. Russell to John D. Long, December 7, 1882, Holmes Papers.

32. James Bradley Thayer, Memorandum, December 18, 1882, Thayer Papers, Book D, 140. Reprinted in Howe, *Proving Years*, 265.

33. Id., 141–42; Howe, *Proving Years*, 266–67.

34. Id., 143; Howe, *Proving Years*, 267.

35. Id., 143–44; Howe, *Proving Years*, 267. The silence of James Barr Ames at the faculty meeting is particularly intriguing, since it was Ames that had lunch with Holmes the day that he first learned of the news of his appointment. There is no evidence that Ames learned anything about the situation from Shattuck's and Fanny's arrival. If he did, it is curious that he did not mention Holmes' appointment to John Gray, whom Thayer reported as being "surprised—entirely" by the news.

One wonders why Ames did not ask Holmes, his lunch partner, why Holmes had not seen fit to inform Ames the reason he was so precipitously departing from their lunch. Or, if Holmes had informed him, why he chose not to bring that fact up at any time.

36. Id., 144; Howe, *Proving Years*, 268.

37. Id.

38. Edward W. Hooper to William F. Weld, date illegible, Harvard University Archives, Houghton Library, Harvard University, quoted in Howe, *Proving Years*, 269–70.

39. Charles Eliot to Holmes, March 28, 1924, Holmes Papers, quoted in Howe, *Proving Years*, 269.

40. Thayer Memorandum, December 18, 1882, supra note 32, at 144; Howe, *Proving Years*, 268.

41. Holmes to James Bryce, December 31, 1882, Holmes Papers, quoted in Howe, *Proving Years*, 280.

42. Id.

43. Holmes to Harold Laski, November 17, 1920, *Holmes–Laski Letters* I, 291.

44. Holmes to James Bryce, supra note 41.

45. Holmes to Frankfurter, July 15, 1913, Holmes Papers.

46. Francis Parker, Memorandum of Law and Morals, December 23, 1882, Holmes Papers, quoted in Howe, *Proving Years*, 271.

47. Holmes to Frederick Pollock, March 25, 1883, *Holmes–Pollock Letters*, I, 21.

48. Holmes to Pollock, March 9, 1884, id., I, 25.

49. Holmes to Pollock, January 17, 1891, id. I, 34.

50. The address is reprinted in *Occasional Speeches*, as well as in Lerner, *Mind and Faith*. Holmes's interest in giving extrajudicial addresses may also have been stimulated by the fact that his father had a considerable reputation as a Lyceum lecturer. See Chapter One.

51. Holmes to Pollock, January 17, 1887, *Holmes–Pollock Letters*, I, 29.

52. Holmes, "Remarks at the Harvard Commencement Dinner, June 22, 1880," *Occasional Speeches*, 1–2.

53. Holmes, "Harvard College in the War, June 25, 1884," id., 18, 19.
54. Holmes, "Memorial Day," May 30, 1884, id., 8.
55. Holmes, "The Soldier's Faith," May 30, 1895, id., 76.
56. Holmes, "Memorial Day," id., 15.
57. Id., 6–7.
58. Id., 14–15.
59. Holmes, "The Law," February 5, 1885, id., 21.
60. Holmes, "The Profession of the Law," February 17, 1886, id., 28–30.
61. See Howe, *Proving Years,* 2.
62. "George Otis Shattuck," May 29, 1897, *Occasional Speeches,* 95.
63. "Commencement Address," June 17, 1897, id., 97–98.
64. Holmes, "The Law," February 5, 1885, id., 20.
65. Holmes, "The Puritan," February 12, 1886, id., 24.
66. Holmes, "On Receiving the Degree of Doctor of Laws," June 30, 1886, id., 32.
67. Holmes to Frankfurter, supra note 45.
68. Holmes, "The Soldier's Faith," May 30, 1895, *Occasional Speeches,* 73.
69. Holmes, "The Use of Colleges," February 3, 1891, id., 64.
70. Holmes to Charles Eliot Norton, April 17, 1864, *Touched With Fire,* 122.
71. Holmes, "Sidney Bartlett," March 23, 1889, *Occasional Speeches,* 54.
72. Holmes, "Daniel Richardson," April 15, 1890, id., 56–57.
73. Holmes, "William Allen," September 15, 1891, id., 67–68.
74. Holmes, "Paul Bourget," December 4, 1893, id., 70.
75. Holmes, "Rudolph C. Lehmann," November 24, 1896, id., 91.
76. Holmes, "The Fraternity of Arms," December 11, 1897, id., 101.
77. Holmes, "Admiral Dewey," October 14, 1899, id., 110.
78. Holmes, "Commencement Address," June 17, 1897, id., 98.
79. Holmes, "On Receiving the Degree of Doctor of Laws," June 30, 1886, id., 32.
80. Holmes, "Admiral Dewey," October 14, 1899, id., 110.
81. Holmes, "The Profession of the Law," February 17, 1886, id., 31.
82. Holmes, "The Soldier's Faith," May 30, 1895, id., 73.
83. In elevating soldiers, intellectuals, and anti-commercial "idealists" to cultural heroes Holmes was, of course, mirroring the attitudes of late nineteenth-century "mugwump" reformers. See John Sproat, *The Best Men* (1968).
84. In *Mogul Steamship Co., Ltd. v. McGregor,* 23 Q.B. 598 (1892), the court allowed merchants to combine to offer unprofitably low rates to shippers in order to prevent a prospective competitor from entering the market. In *Temperton v. Russell,* 1 Q.B. 715 (1893), a union was prevented from striking its employer in response to the employer's having supplied goods to a non-union buyer. Holmes treated those cases in "Privilege, Malice, and Intent," 8 *Harv. L. Rev.* 1 (1894), reprinted in *Collected Legal Papers* 117, 127.
85. Holmes, *The Common Law* 45, 104 (1881).
86. *Collected Legal Papers,* 128.
87. Id., 129–30.
88. Id., 129.
89. Id., 130.
90. Id., 129, 130.

91. Morton Horwitz has suggested that Holmes' treatment of "malice" in "Privilege, Malice, and Intent" represented "the first time . . . that a fully articulated balancing test . . . entered American legal theory," and for that reason "perhaps . . . the moment we should identify as the beginning of modernism in American legal thought." Morton Horwitz, "The Place of Justice Holmes in American Legal Thought," in Gordon, *Legacy*, 56–57.

92. See, e.g., Horwitz's discussion in Gordon, *Legacy*, 67–70.

93. Holmes, "The Path of the Law," address delivered at Boston University School of Law, January 8, 1897, *Collected Legal Papers*, 167, 168, 169.

94. Id., 180.

95. Id., 168.

96. Id., 169.

97. Id., 173.

98. We have seen that there were hints of Holmes' "prediction" metaphor in his earliest scholarship. In his 1872 comments on Austin in the American Law Review, for example, he said that "it was doubted whether law . . . possessed any other common attribute than of being enforced by the procedure of the courts, and therefore of practical importance to lawyers," and added that "[t]he only question for the lawyer, is how will the judges act?" Holmes, Book Notice, 6 *Am. L. Rev.* 723, 724 (1872); Kellogg, *Formative Essays*, 91–92.

Care should be taken in associating these remarks with a full-blown positivist theory of legal decisionmaking. In the same review from which the above comments were taken, and in which appeared others, such as "the rule is inserted in the law books for the empirical reason . . . that it is applied by the courts and must therefore be known by professional men," Holmes indicated that he was interested in probing "[t]he notion of duty," and the fact that "the object of the law is to accomplish an external result." His early scholarship attempted to develop, as he put it, "a sound classification of the law . . . on the basis of the ultimate conception *duty*." Holmes, "The Arrangement of the Law: Privity," 7 *Am. L. Rev.* 46 (1872); Kellogg, *Formative Essays*, 95 (italics in original). It is hard to imagine that Holmes would have treated "duty" as an "ultimate conception," or have been interested in classifying legal doctrines around the notion of duty, had he believed that "the law" was simply the aggregate of what was applied in the courts. Indeed his interest in deriving a classification system from the duty concept suggests that he was seeking to reformulate decisions that had hitherto been intelligible only as results.

99. *Collected Legal Papers*, 173.

100. Id., 188–89.

101. Id., 175.

102. Id., 176–77.

103. Id., 178. This proposition, of course, tracked Holmes' discussion of the "Peerless" case in *The Common Law*. See Chapter Five.

104. Id., 181.

105. Id., 185.

106. Id., 186.

107. Id., 187.

108. Id., 195.

109. Holmes, "Law in Science and Science in Law," January 17, 1899; 12 *Harv. L. Rev.* 443 (1899); *Collected Legal Papers*, 210, 239.

110. Holmes, "The Path of the Law," id., 201–02.

111. Horwitz, in Gordon, *Legacy*, 68–69, reads "The Path of the Law" in that fashion.

112. Holmes, "Law in Science and Science in Law," *Collected Legal Papers*, 225.

113. Id., 225–26.

114. Id., 238–39.

115. Id., 242.

116. Id., 187.

117. Id., 242. In this respect Holmes can be said to have retained, as late as the opening of the twentieth century, the enthusiasm of his post Civil War contemporaries for "science" as a methodology that could help bring a kind of order to a post-religious universe.

CHAPTER SEVEN: *Travel and Romance*

1. The details of Holmes' purchase of the Mattapoisett property and its eventual destruction are set forth in a letter Holmes wrote to Mrs. Charles S. Hamlin. See Holmes to Mrs. Hamlin, October 12, 1930, Holmes Papers. See also Howe, *Proving Years*, 23; Novick, *Honorable Justice*, 142, 183. Holmes admitted in the letter to Mrs. Hamlin that his memory of the timing of the house's destruction might not be precise.

2. See Howe, *Proving Years*, 106.

3. In 1886 Amelia Jackson Holmes' health had begun to fail. She suffered a "breakdown" in July, and Dr. Holmes hired a companion for her. Her mental state continued to deteriorate, and in February 1888 she died. See Holmes to Pollock, December 21, 1886, *Holmes–Pollock Letters* I, 28; Holmes to Pollock, March 4, 1888, id., I, 30; Oliver Wendell Holmes, Sr., to Amelia Jackson Holmes, July 11, 1884, Holmes Papers; Baker, *Justice from Beacon Hill*, 291–93.

4. See Novick, *Honorable Justice*, 186, 200.

5. Holmes to Pollock, April 8, 1882, *Holmes–Pollock Letters* I, 19.

6. See Chapter Three. See also Howe, *Shaping Years*, 228–230.

7. Diary entry, August 27, 1866, Holmes Papers. See also Howe, *Shaping Years*, 243.

8. Fanny Holmes, diary entry, May 30, 1874, Holmes Papers. See also Howe, *Proving Years*, 96–97.

9. Fanny Holmes, diary entry [no date], 1874, Holmes Papers. See also Howe, *Proving Years*, 102.

10. Id.

11. Fanny Holmes, diary entry [no date], 1874, Holmes Papers. See also Howe, *Proving Years*, 97.

12. Fanny Holmes, diary entry [no date], 1874, Holmes Papers.

13. Fanny Holmes, diary entry [no date], 1874, Holmes Papers. See also Howe, *Proving Years*, 97.

14. Fanny Holmes, diary entry [no date], 1874, Holmes Papers. See also Novick, *Honorable Justice*, 143.

15. Fanny Holmes, diary entry [no date], 1874, Holmes Papers. See also Howe, *Proving Years*, 98.

16. Fanny Holmes, diary entry, June 28, 1874, Holmes Papers. See also Howe, *Proving Years*, 99.

17. Fanny Holmes, diary entry, July 9, 1874, Holmes Papers. See also Howe, *Proving Years*, 99.

18. Holmes to Lady Ethel Scott, January 6, 1912, Holmes Papers, quoted in Howe, *Proving Years*, 103.

19. Howe, *Proving Years*, 103.

20. The trip was recorded by Holmes in his 1882 diary, Holmes Papers.

21. Holmes, diary entry [no date], 1882, Holmes Papers, quoted in Howe, *Proving Years*, 273.

22. Oliver Wendell Holmes, Sr., to Elizabeth S. Ward, April 13, 1889, in Morse, *Life and Letters* II, 263–64.

23. Holmes to Owen Wister, April 14, 1889, Holmes Papers.

24. See Howe, *Proving Years*, 104.

25. Ethel Grenfell to Holmes, May 4, 1889, Holmes Papers. Ethel had married William Grenfell in 1887. Grenfell was named Lord Desborough in 1905. Angela Lambert, *Unquiet Souls* xvii (1984) (hereafter Lambert, *Unquiet Souls*). Consequently Ethel Grenfell is called Lady Desborough in the Holmes Papers.

26. The origins of the name ''Souls'' is said to have come from the members of the group's sense that ''in order to become one of the coterie, it was necessary to possess a soul above the ordinary.'' See Lambert, *Unquiet Souls*, 32, for a social history of ''The Souls.''

27. *The World*, July 16, 1889, quoted in Lambert, *Unquiet Souls*, 10.

28. Lambert, *Unquiet Souls*, 32.

29. Alice James, diary entry, June 16, 1889, quoted in Anna Robeson Burr, ed., *Alice James—Her Brothers—Her Journal* 93 (1934).

30. William James to Henry James, July 1, 1889, quoted in Ralph Barton Perry, *The Thought and Character of William James* 174 (1964 ed.). Perry also indicates that William James was a passenger on *The Cephalonia*'s May 1889 sailing.

31. Id.

32. Desmond MacCarthy, quoted in Lambert, *Unquiet Souls*, 15.

33. Margot Tennant to Holmes, January 8, 1890, Holmes Papers. Margot Tennant married Henry Asquith in 1894, who was named Lord Asquith in 1925. See Lambert, *Unquiet Souls*, xv, 184. She is consequently referred to as Lady Asquith in the Holmes Papers.

34. See Mark Bence-Jones, *The Twilight of the Ascendancy* 13–16 (1987). Hereafter cited as Bence-Jones, *Ascendancy*. The name for the set signified that for most of the nineteenth century they were the ''lords and . . . landowners of Ireland,'' dominating its politics as well as its economy. Id., xv.

35. The details of the St. Leger and FitzPatrick families in this and succeeding paragraphs are from Bernard Castletown's memoirs. See Lord Castletown, *Ego* 46–59 (1923) (hereafter Castletown, *Ego*).

36. See Bence-Jones, *Ascendancy*, 68.

37. There is a picture of Doneraile Court in Bence-Jones, *Ascendancy*, 284. An extensive description of Granston Manor is given in an article in *The World*, April 12, 1899, 633. Included in the article was a description of Clare's "boudoir, a fascinating little room."

38. Bence-Jones, *Ascendancy*, 63–64.

39. Castletown, *Ego*, 8.

40. Lambert, *Unquiet Souls*, 68. In Novick, *Honorable Justice*, 188, the statement is made that Holmes met Clare Castletown "[a]t a picture gallery." There is no evidence given in support of this statement, and it is possible that Novick may have been confused by a letter Holmes wrote to Clare on August 6, 1897, in which he said that "it was in the middle of July that we went to the Exhibition and I noticed you had a quick eye for pictures." In that same letter Holmes noted that "[b]efore this time last year I had found you," referring to 1896, when he and Clare first became friends. Holmes to Clare Castletown, August 6, 1897, Holmes Papers.

The meeting of Holmes and Clare at "Wilton" is confirmed by a letter Clare wrote to Holmes on February 19, 1892, in which she thanked him for the gift of a volume of his speeches. She said, "I suppose you have been back in England again since that time at Wilton but I have been laid up almost ever since (with a spine that I damaged out hunting) so we haven't had a chance of meeting." Clare Castletown to Holmes, February 19, 1892, Holmes Papers.

41. Clare Castletown to Holmes, February, 19, 1892, Holmes Papers.

42. The timing of Fanny's second attack cannot be precisely established. Novick, *Honorable Justice*, 201, speculates that it came in the autumn of 1894, perhaps as a response to nursing Dr. Holmes in the last stages of his life. On June 16, 1896, Holmes wrote his friend Nina Gray that "my wife has had the rheumatic fever and although much better still seems weak," Holmes to Nina Gray, Holmes Papers, and in July, 1897 wrote Frederick Pollock that "my wife . . . hasn't by any means got back to where she was before her rheumatic fever," Holmes to Pollock, July 20, 1897, *Holmes–Pollock Letters* I, 75. These letters would seem to place the date of Fanny's illness in late 1895 or early 1896. If it had been closer to the spring of 1896, it is unlikely Holmes would have traveled to England, and since he wrote Lady Pollock in September 1895 that he was planning to come to England in the summer of 1896, it is unlikely the attack had come before that September. See Holmes to Lady Pollock, September 13, 1895, in *Holmes–Pollock Letters* I, 62.

43. See, e.g., Holmes to Frederick Pollock, April 2, 1894, in *Holmes–Pollock Letters* I, 51; Holmes to Lady Pollock, August 11, 1895, in id., I, 59; Holmes to James Bryce, November 5, 1894, Holmes Papers.

44. See Howe, *Shaping Years*, 200, citing an interview with Mrs. Arthur D. Hill, a contemporary of Fanny's.

45. Clare Castletown to Holmes, "Saturday" [July 4], 1896, Holmes Papers.

46. Notations of the visits can be found in a diary Holmes kept for the 1896 trip, Holmes Papers.

47. See Novick, *Honorable Justice*, 209, citing Holmes' diary, 1896, Holmes Papers.

48. Holmes, diary entry, August 15, 1896, Holmes Papers.

49. Holmes to Clare Castletown, August 27, 1896, Holmes Papers.

50. Holmes to Clare Castletown, August 28, 1896, Holmes Papers.

51. The correspondence, long in the possession of Mark Howe, was discovered in the Holmes Papers by John Monagan after those papers were made available to the general public, and portions were discussed in Monagan's article, "The Love Letters of Justice Holmes," *Boston Globe Magazine,* March 24, 1985, 15. For some reason Novick, *Honorable Justice,* quotes extensively from Holmes' letters to Clare Castletown, but makes no mention of Monagan's article or his role in publicizing the letters. Baker, *Justice from Beacon Hill,* 314–17, cities Monagan's article in her bibliography, but does not discuss it.

52. After Bernard Castletown's death in 1939 Doneraile Court came into the possession of the St. Leger family. The seventh Lord Doneraile died in 1956, and his wife, originally a resident of New Zealand, continued to live in the house. Mark Howe became aware of the relationship between Holmes and Clare Castletown in the course of writing his authorized biography of Holmes, and through intermediaries discovered that Doneraile Court contained a number of letters from Holmes to Clare. Howe acquired typescript copies of the letters in the 1940s, and on his death in 1967 an arrangement was made by which Lady Doneraile presented those typescripts to the Harvard Law School Library. My thanks to Mrs. Mary Manning Adams for her help in filling in details of the appearance of the Castletown letters. See also Bence-Jones, *Ascendancy,* 283–84; Monagan, *The Grand Panjandrum,* 90–91.

53. Holmes to Clare Castletown, September 5, 1896, Holmes Papers.

54. Id.

55. Id.

56. Holmes, "William Allen," September 15, 1891, *Occasional Speeches,* 67–68.

57. Id.

58. Percy La Touche to Clare Castletown, August 17, 1896, Castletown Papers, Bisbrooke Hall, Uppingham, Rutland, England. Emphasis in original.

The existence of letters from Percy La Touche to Clare Castletown in the Bisbrooke Hall Collection was very probably not contemplated by either of the parties. One of Clare's closest friends in the "Ascendancy" set was Doty Bandon, the wife of the Earl of Bandon, who lived on an estate, Castle Bernard, near Doneraile Court in Cork County. During "the time of troubles," ushered in by the Easter Rebellion of 1916 and revived by the creation of the Irish Free State in 1920, the Irish Republican Army placed several of the large estates in Cork County, including Doneraile Court, under siege, and in 1921 burned Castle Bernard. Shortly after the burning the Bandons left Ireland permanently for England, and after Lord Bandon's death Doty, whose family, the Cadburys, had connections in Rutland County, settled there, using her widow's annuity to buy property. On Doty Bandon's death she left her Rutland County property, 'Laxton,' to her companion Mary Gaussen, who died in 1968, leaving the property in trust for Rupert Boyle, a descendant of the Cadbury family.

When Doty Bandon left Ireland she carried with her a number of Clare Castletown's personal papers. After the Boyle family succeeded to the 'Laxton' property, the papers were moved to another Boyle family estate, Bisbrooke Hall, presently occupied by Robert Boyle, Esq.

Why Clare retained her correspondence with Percy La Touche and entrusted it (along with other routine correspondence about household matters) to Doty Bandon is one of those secrets of family history that will probably remain forever unexplained. See Bence-

Jones, *Ascendancy*, 54, 99, 109, 193, 234 for descriptions of Percy La Touche, including a picture; see also 209–14 for a description of the Bandon family under siege. My thanks to Robert Boyle for filling in the details of the travel history of the Castletown Papers.

59. La Touche to Clare Castletown, August 31, 1896, Castletown Papers.

60. Holmes to Clare Castletown, September 17, 1896, Holmes Papers.

61. Holmes to Clare Castletown, October 7, 1896, id.

62. La Touche to Clare Castletown, September 18, 1896, Castletown Papers. Emphasis in original.

63. Holmes to Clare Castletown, October 17, 1896, Holmes Papers.

64. Holmes to Clare Castletown, October 23, 1896, id.

65. Holmes to Clare Castletown, November 9, 1896, id.

66. Holmes to Clare Castletown, November 21, 1896, id.

67. Holmes to Clare Castletown, December 4, 1896, id.

68. Holmes to Clare Castletown, December 18, 1896, id.

69. Holmes to Clare Castletown, December 28, 1896, id.

70. Holmes to Clare Castletown, January 11, 1897, id.

71. Holmes to Clare Castletown, May 7, 1897, id.

72. Id.

73. Holmes to Clare Castletown, May 10, 1897, id.

74. Holmes to Clare Castletown, May 20, 1897, id.

75. Holmes to Clare Castletown, June 10, 1897, id.

76. Holmes to Clare Castletown, August 9, 1897, id.

77. Holmes to Clare Castletown, August 9, 1897; December 17, 1897, id.

78. La Touche to Clare Castletown, May 11, 1897, Castletown Papers.

79. La Touche to Clare Castletown, undated, Castletown Papers. This letter was found inside the envelope in which the May 11, 1897, letter was contained.

80. Holmes to Clare Castletown, December 31, 1897, Holmes Papers.

81. Holmes to Clare Castletown, January 10, 1898, id.

82. Holmes to Clare Castletown, January 18–21, 1898, id.

83. Holmes to Clare Castletown, January 28, 1898, id.

84. Holmes to Clare Castletown, February 17, 1898, id.

85. Holmes to Clare Castletown, id.

86. Holmes to Clare Castletown, March 3, 1898, id.

87. Holmes to Clare Castletown, March 27, 1898, id.

88. Holmes to Clare Castletown, April 1, 1898, id.

89. Holmes to Clare Castletown, March 27, 1898, id.

90. Holmes to Clare Castletown, April 8, 1898, id.

91. Holmes to Clare Castletown, April 29, 1898, id.

92. Holmes to Clare Castletown, June 6, 1898, id.

93. Holmes to Clare Castletown, June 9, 1898, id.

94. Holmes, diary, 1898, Holmes Papers.

95. There are very few letters from Holmes to Fanny Dixwell Holmes, or from her to him, in the Holmes Papers. Since Holmes made a number of trips to England alone, and the parties would obviously have corresponded, it seems clear that only a few letters have survived.

96. There is also a letter Holmes wrote to Judge A. Inglis Clark, an Australian judge

and scholar, on September 4, 1898, soon after returning from Ireland. In the letter Holmes said that he had "just been in the midst of friends in England and Ireland who though made in later years love me I think and whom I love I know." Holmes to Clark, September 4, 1898, A. Inglis Clark Papers, University of Tasmania Library. One cannot make too much of the word "love" in such context, but the letter does seem to capture Holmes' sense of the distinction between his committment to Clare ("I know") and hers to him ("I think"). My thanks to James A. Thomson of the Crown Law Department in Perth, Australia, for making copies of the Holmes–Clark correspondence available to me.

97. Holmes to Clare Castletown, September 5, 1898, Holmes Papers.

98. Entries in Holmes' diary for 1898 indicate days in which he was affected by the disorder.

99. Holmes to Clare Castletown, September 8, 1898, Holmes Papers.

100. Holmes to Clare Castletown, September 10–12, 1898, id.

101. See, for example, the letter of September 5, 1896, quoted supra note 53.

102. Holmes to Clare Castletown, September 10–12, 1898, supra note 100.

103. Holmes to Clare Castletown, September 16, 1898, Holmes Papers.

104. Bernard Castletown to Holmes, June 16, 1899, id. The accident probably took place on May 10. A letter from Annette La Touche, Percy's wife, to Bernard Castletown on May 11 indicates that Clare and Percy had both fallen from horses but that Percy was not seriously injured. Annette La Touche to Bernard Castletown, May 11, 1899, Castletown Papers. Clare's accident was reported in the Cork *Herald* on May 15, 1899 (Castletown Papers). Holmes somehow heard the news of Clare's accident and sent Bernard Castletown a telegram expressing "Anxious Sympathy" on May 31 (id.) The June 16 letter from Bernard Castletown to Holmes may have been in response to that telegram.

Clare was still not able to write in August. Bernard wrote Holmes an August 5 letter, congratulating him on being named Chief Justice of the SJC, in which he said that "[m]y wife is certainly better. . . . She wishes me to say she is quite able to read letters now as she has one quite good eye and the other improving." Bernard Castletown to Holmes, August 5, 1899, id.

105. See Castletown, *Ego,* 209–212.

106. In March 1901 Holmes wrote Judge Inglis Clark that "I have been pretty hard at work since Sept. 1 [and] propose to turn my weary steps . . . for a short vacation . . . to [that] pleasing centre of Evil doing . . . England." Holmes to Clark, March [no date], 1901, Clark Papers.

107. Holmes, diary, 1901, Holmes Papers.

108. Holmes to Mrs. John Chipman (Nina) Gray, July 15–17, 1901, id.

109. Holmes to Nina Gray, September 15, 1901, id.

110. Holmes, diary, 1907, id. In the June 16, 1899, letter in which Bernard Castletown gave Holmes details of Clare's accident, he began the letter, "I quite reciprocate your view of our friendship," and urged Holmes to "let us hear if there is any chance of your visiting these shores." In his autobiography Bernard mentioned Holmes as "the greatest and most interesting" of the "succession of pleasant visitors" he and Clare entertained. Castletown, *Ego,* 41.

111. On August 23, 1909, after he had returned from England, Holmes received a letter from Canon Patrick Sheehan, the parish priest at Doneraile, with whom he had

struck up a friendship after first being introduced to him by Bernard Castletown in 1903. See David Burton, ed., *Holmes–Sheehan Correspondence* 3 (1976). Hereafter cited as *Holmes–Sheehan Correspondence*. In the letter Sheehan said that "Lady Castletown mentioned that you had been over; but I think they regretted they had not seen you, or you were unable to visit. Lord and Lady Castletown were much pleased with the Oxford affair." Sheehan to Holmes, August 31, 1909, *Holmes–Sheehan Correspondence*, 29.

Holmes responded to this letter on September 13, 1909, by saying that he "saw the Castletowns as I flitted through London." Holmes to Sheehan, id., 30.

112. Sheehan to Holmes, August 26, 1910, id., 36.

113. Holmes to Sheehan, March 1, 1911, id., 37.

114. Sheehan to Holmes, March 25, 1911, id., 39.

115. Sheehan to Holmes, February 25, 1913, id., 61. Clare's comment to Sheehan suggests that she and Holmes were not in close contact.

116. Holmes to Sheehan, April 16, 1913, id., 64.

117. Holmes to Sheehan, June 20, 1913, id., 64.

118. Sheehan to Holmes, June 21, 1913, id., 65.

119. Holmes, diary, 1913, Holmes Papers.

120. Holmes to Pollock, August 13, 1913, *Holmes–Pollock Letters* I, 207. The letter was written from Lincolnshire in England, where Holmes was staying at the time.

121. Holmes to Nina Gray, August 14, 1903, Holmes Papers.

122. Holmes to Nina Gray, September 2, 1903, id.

123. Holmes to Nina Gray, February 1, 1903, id.

124. Holmes to Nina Gray, July 17, 1896, id.

125. Holmes to Clare Castletown, April 16, 1914, id.

126. Holmes to Clare Castletown, October 30, 1914, id.

127. Holmes to Clare Castletown, November 22, 1914, id.

128. Holmes to Clare Castletown, January 10, 1915, id. In the very same year Percy La Touche wrote Clare a letter in which he described his life as a series of failures, including being prevented from standing for Parliament by his parents, missing out on the Klondike gold rush, and wasting a profitable financial opportunity in Dublin because he had "spent the little money I had." The one "success" in his life, Percy concluded, had been his great love for Clare. Percy La Touche to Clare Castletown, December 6, 1915, Castletown Papers.

129. Holmes to Clare Castletown, April 20, 1916, Holmes Papers.

130. Mary Aldsworth to Holmes, December 20, 1916, id.

131. Holmes to Clare Castletown, May 10, 1917, id.

132. Castletown, *Ego*, 233–34.

133. Clare Castletown to Holmes, undated, Holmes Papers. The reference to Holmes' eighty-first birthday places the letter in the spring of 1922.

134. Holmes to Pollock, August 2, 1923, *Holmes–Pollock Letters* II, 120.

135. Clare Castletown to Holmes, June 14 [1923], Holmes Papers.

136. Holmes to Pollock, December 31, 1922, *Holmes–Pollock Letters* II, 109.

137. Holmes to Laski, February 1, 1924, *Holmes–Laski Letters* I, 587.

138. Holmes to Bernard Castletown, November 3, 1926, Holmes Papers.

139. Ethel St. Leger to Holmes, April 11, 1927, id.

140. "Late Lady Castletown," *Cork Examiner,* March 15, 1927, id.

141. Bernard Castletown to Holmes, April 22, 1927, id.

142. Holmes to Laski, April 29, 1927, *Holmes–Laski Letters* II, 938.

143. Holmes to Miss [Lucy] Hale, May 21, 1858, Holmes Papers.

144. Id.

145. Holmes to Lady Pollock, August 11, 1895, *Holmes–Pollock Letters* I, 59.

146. Laski to Holmes, July 29, 1924, *Holmes–Laski Letters* I, 640.

147. Laski to Holmes, May 7, 1927, *Holmes–Laski Letters* II, 941.

148. Holmes to Lady Winifred Burghclere, September 17, 1898, Holmes Papers.

149. Holmes to Nina Gray, July 17, 1896, id.

150. Id.

CHAPTER EIGHT: *The Supreme Judicial Court of Massachusetts*

1. Holmes, address, March 7, 1900, *Occasional Speeches,* 123–24.

2. As discussed in Chapter Six, this was the position adopted by Holmes in his essays, "The Path of the Law," written in 1897, and "Law and Science and Science in Law," written in 1900.

3. Holmes, address, March 7, 1900, *Occasional Speeches,* 124–25.

4. See William James to Frances R. Morse [1901], quoted in Perry, *The Thought and Character of William James* (1935 ed.), II, 251.

5. Hughes, "Mr. Justice Holmes," 44 *Harv. L. Rev.* 677, 678 (1931).

6. Holmes, "The Race Is Over," March 8, 1931, *Occasional Speeches,* 178. Mark Howe, who edited the 1962 edition of Holmes' speeches, gave this address the title, "The Race Is Over," but the speech is referred to as "Death Plucks My Ear" in the Holmes Papers.

7. Holmes to Frederick Pollock, August 27, 1883, *Holmes–Pollock Letters,* I, 22.

8. See Holmes to James Bryce, December 31, 1882, Holmes Papers, describing his decision to leave law teaching for a judgeship: "I thought the chance to gain an all round experience of the law not to be neglected."

9. Holmes to Frederick Pollock, April 1, 1892, *Holmes–Pollock Letters,* I, 42.

10. For an elaboration of this point, based on the "institutional constraints" Holmes faced on the Supreme Judicial Court of Massachusetts, see Patrick J. Kelley, "Holmes on the Supreme Judicial Court: The Theorist As Judge," in Russell Osgood, ed., *The History of the Law in Massachusetts: The Supreme Judicial Court 1692–1992* 275 (1992).

11. "Notes of Recent Decisions," 34 *Am. L. Rev.* 109 (1900).

12. Holmes, "Twenty Years in Retrospect," speech, December 3, 1902, in *Occasional Speeches,* 154.

13. The best source on the history of the Supreme Judicial Court of Massachusetts is Osgood, ed., *supra* note 10.

14. See William Caleb Loring, "Ought the Full Bench To Be Required To Go Circuit," 5 *Mass. L.Q.* 65 (1919) for a review of the SJC's docket.

15. Holmes to Frederick Pollock, March 25, 1883, *Holmes–Pollock Letters* I, 21.

16. Holmes to Pollock, August 27, 1883, id., 22.

17. See Holmes to Clare Castletown, June 3, 1897, Holmes Papers: "[T]he younger men—or I dare say the bar generally, think I talk too much and don't give 'em chance enough to develop their ideas."

18. Hiller B. Zobel's "Oliver Wendell Holmes, Jr., Trial Judge," *Boston Bar Journal*

(March/April 1992), 25, and Zobel's "What a Medley of a Man!" catalogue to a March 8–June 6, 1991 exhibition at the Harvard Law School, have brief but incisive discussions of Holmes as a trial judge. Justice Zobel plans a full treatment of the subject.

19. *Williams v. Churchill,* 137 Mass. 243 (1884) (Holmes found for the master).

20. *Commonwealth v. Tabor,* 138 Mass. 496 (1885); *Commonwealth v. Patterson,* 138 Mass. 498 (1885); *Commonwealth v. Murray,* 138 Mass. 508 (1885) (Holmes limited the statute's reach to cases where the jury was given proof of one or two illegal sales of alcohol and could thereby infer an ongoing practice of such sales).

21. *Merrill v. Eastern Railroad Co.,* 139 Mass. 238 (1885) (Holmes found for the train company on the ground that the claimant never had the status of a passenger, and therefore the train owed no duty to him).

22. *Lincoln v. Boston Marine Ins. Co.,* 159 Mass. 337 (1893); *Boardman v. Boston Marine Ins. Co.,* 146 Mass. 442 (1888).

23. *Breckenridge v. Fitchburg,* 145 Mass. 160 (1887) (Holmes concluded that a jury might have found that the horse's blindness was insignificant to the case, as the darkness was such that even a sighted horse could not have seen the road).

24. *Merrill v. Peaslee,* 146 Mass. 460 (1888) (Holmes, dissenting, thought that the wife's relinquishing of her legal right to sue for divorce was sufficient consideration, making the contract valid).

25. *Reeve v. Dennett,* 145 Mass. 23 (1887).

26. *Middlesex Company v. Lowell,* 149 Mass. 509 (1889) (Holmes held that no injunction was warranted unless the drainoff became particularly offensive).

27. *Bates v. Westborough,* 151 Mass. 174 (1890); *Collins v. Waltham,* 151 Mass. 196 (1890).

28. *Dillon v. Connecticut River Railroad Co.,* 154 Mass. 478 (1891) (Holmes found that the man's heirs could not recover against the railroad because the man was a trespasser on the railroad's right of way).

29. *Commonwealth v. Lowrey,* 158 Mass. 18 (1893) (Holmes held there was a breaking and entering because the defendant gained entrance with the help of an accomplice).

30. *White v. Soloman,* 164 Mass. 516 (1895) (Holmes ruled in favor of White, concluding that White's side of the bargain was complete when White delivered the mannequin to the express company).

31. *Sullivan v. Lowell & Dacut Railway,* 162 Mass. 536 (1895) (Holmes limited the evidence to the issue of damages).

32. *Tracy v. Banker,* 170 Mass. 266 (1898) (Holmes held that the union label was a trademark).

33. *Hardiman v. Wholley,* 172 Mass. 411 (1899) (Holmes concluded that a jury could find that the owner was negligent in leaving a nervous horse near a sidewalk).

34. *Bradley v. Hooker,* 175 Mass. 142 (1900) (Holmes ruled that the jury might hear the expert's testimony).

35. *Goddard v. Boston & Maine Railroad,* 179 Mass. 52 (1901) (Holmes held that the railroad was not liable, as Mr. Goddard had not shown that it had adequate notice of the banana's presence on the floor).

36. *Irving v. Ford,* 179 Mass. 216 (1901) (Holmes held that the Virginia marriage was not valid, but did not decide the question whether the first wife and surviving son could share in the estate).

37. *Kellogg v. Smith,* 179 Mass. 595 (1901) (Holmes held that the railroad incurred no liability since the passenger did not act as a reasonably prudent person in his position would have).

38. *Newhall v. American Legion of Honor,* 181 Mass. 111 (1902) (Holmes ruled for Newhall's wife, stating that submitting to a fraternal benefit organization's bylaws could not mean submitting to the risk that the bylaws would be amended to make the face value of the benefit certificate insecure).

39. An early comprehensive survey of Holmes' SJC opinions can be found in Perlie P. Fallon, "The Judicial World of Mr. Justice Holmes," 14 *Notre Dame Lawyer* 52, 163 (1939). Fallon's articles are marvelously evocative, if eccentric.

40. Holmes, *The Common Law,* 50.

41. In a 1963 book review of Mark Howe's *Proving Years,* H. L. A. Hart pointed out that "[Holmes'] proof [of the connection between external standards in the criminal law and a deterrence theory of punishment] is that since the law only requires outward conformity in its prescriptions and does not care, so long as the law is obeyed, what were the intentions or motives of those who obeyed or whether they could have done otherwise, so it should equally disregard these subjective matters in dealing with the offender when the law has been broken." Hart argued that "even if the general justification of punishment is the utilitarian aim of preventing harm . . . it is still perfectly intelligible that we should defer to principles of justice or fairness to individuals and not punish those who lack the capacity or fair opportunity to obey." Hart, Book Review, *The New York Review of Books,* October 17, 1963, p. 16.

42. Yosal Rogat, "The Judge as Spectator," 31 *U. Chi. L. Rev.* 213, 224 (1964).

43. Holmes, *The Common Law,* 66.

44. Id.

45. *Commonwealth v. Pierce,* 138 Mass. 165, 168–69 (1884).

46. Id. at 176.

47. Id.

48. Id. at 177–78.

49. Id. at 180.

50. Holmes, *The Common Law,* 51.

51. Id., 57.

52. 138 Mass. at 178. One could argue that the phrase "circumstances known to the actor" in this standard makes the standard a mix of subjective and objective elements. Holmes did not emphasize that argument.

53. Holmes, *The Common Law,* 50.

54. 138 Mass. at 176, 179.

55. Holmes, *The Common Law,* 66.

56. 138 Mass. at 179.

57. Holmes to Pollock, November 2, 1884, *Holmes–Pollock Letters* I, 26.

58. E.g., *Commonwealth v. Doherty,* 137 Mass. 245 (1884) (inferences permissible from direct testimony); *Commonwealth v. Moinehan,* 140 Mass. 463 (1886) (cross-examination of defendant); *Commonwealth v. Hyland,* 155 Mass. 7 (1891) (credibility of defendant's testimony).

59. E.g., *Commonwealth v. Tabor,* 138 Mass. 496 (1885); *Commonwealth v. Patter-*

son, 138 Mass. 498 (1885); *Commonwealth v. Gavin, 148 Mass.* 449 (1888); *Commonwealth v. Lyons, 160 Mass.* 174 (1893).

60. *Commonwealth v. Bean,* 148 Mass. 172 (1889); *Commonwealth v. Russell,* 162 Mass. 520 (1895); *Commonwealth v. Ryberg,* 177 Mass. 67 (1900).

61. *Commonwealth v. Wright,* 137 Mass. 250 (1884); *Commonwealth v. Sullivan, 146 Mass.* 142 (1888).

62. *Commonwealth v. Healey,* 157 Mass. 455 (1892); *Commonwealth v. Emerson,* 165 Mass. 146 (1896).

63. E.g., *Commonwealth v. Ryan,* 154 Mass. 422 (1891).

64. Holmes issued only twelve dissenting opinions, and voted in dissent a total of twenty-three times, in his twenty-year tenure, in which he decided over a thousand cases. See Harry Shriver, *Judicial Opinions of Oliver Wendell Holmes* 325 (1940). For a discussion of the tradition of unanimity on the Supreme Judicial Court of Massachusetts, see Kelley, supra note 10, at 277–79.

65. 170 Mass. 18 (1897).

66. Holmes, *The Common Law,* 67.

67. 179 Mass. at 20. Holmes had previously discussed this case, *M'Pherson's case,* in *The Common Law,* 69.

68. 170 Mass. at 20.

69. Id.

70. Id. at 21–22.

71. Holmes, *The Common Law,* 69.

72. 177 Mass. 267 (1901).

73. Id. at 271.

74. Id.

75. Id.

76. Id. at 272.

77. Id. at 274.

78. Id. at 272.

79. On Holmes' early contributions to American tort law see G. Edward White, *Tort Law in America: An Intellectual History* 6–44 (1980). Hereafter White, *Tort Law in America.* On his efforts to subvert strict enterprise liability, reflected in decisions such as *Rylands v. Fletcher,* see Clare Dalton, *Losing History: The Case of Rylands v. Fletcher,* unpublished manuscript. David Rosenberg's unpublished work, *Oliver Wendell Holmes and Strict Tort Liability,* disagrees with Dalton. I am inclined to agree with Dalton, although I think Rosenberg's analysis raises the possibility that Holmes was more interested in achieving predictable rules than in endorsing any particular liability standard. See the discussion of Rosenberg in Chapter Five.

80. See the discussion in Chapter Five; see also White, *Tort Law in America,* 12–19, 56–62.

81. E.g., *McCabe v. Cambridge,* 134 Mass. 484 (1883); *Dietrich v. Northampton,* 138 Mass. 14 (1884); *Fortin v. Easthampton,* 142 Mass. 486 (1886); *Powers v. Boston,* 154 Mass. 60 (1891); *Bourget v. Cambridge,* 156 Mass. 391 (1892); *Dobbins v. West End St. Ry.,* 168 Mass. 556 (1897); *Spillane v. Fitchburg,* 177 Mass. 87 (1900); *McNeil v. Boston,* 178 Mass. 326 (1901); *Brummett v. Boston,* 179 Mass. 26 (1901).

82. E.g. *Russell v. Tillotson,* 140 Mass. 201 (1885); *Coullard v. Tecumseh Mills,* 151

Mass. 85 (1890); *Sullivan v. Fitchburg Ry. Co.*, 161 Mass. 125 (1894); *Whittaker v. Bent*, 167 Mass. 588 (1897); *Ellsbury v. New York, New Haven, & Hartford Ry. Co.*, 172 Mass. 130 (1898); *Quinn v. New York, New Haven, & Hartford Ry. Co.*, 175 Mass. 150 (1900); *Lamson v. American Axe & Tool Co.* 177 Mass. 144 (1900); *Goddard v. Boston & Me. R.R.*, 179 Mass. 52 (1901).

83. E.g., *Deming v. Darling*, 148 Mass. 504 (1889); *Windram v. French*, 151 Mass. 547 (1890); *Latham v. Aldrich*, 166 Mass. 156 (1896); *Whiting v. Price*, 169 Mass. 576 (1897); *Emmons v. Alford*, 177 Mass. 466 (1901).

84. E.g., *Cutter v. Hamlen*, 147 Mass. 471 (1888); *June v. Boston & Albany R.R.*, 153 Mass 79 (1891); *Chenery v. Fitchburg Ry. Co.*, 160 Mass. 211 (1893); *Oxford v. Leathe*, 165 Mass. 254 (1896); *Palmer v. Gordon*, 173 Mass. 410 (1899); *Riley v. Harris*, 177 Mass. 163 (1900).

85. E.g., *Hurley v. Fall River Daily Herald Pub. Co.*, 138 Mass. 334 (1885); *Hanson v. Globe Newspaper Co.*, 159 Mass. 293 (1893).

86. 138 Mass. 14 (1884).

87. Id. at 15.

88. Id.

89. Id. at 16.

90. Id. at 17.

91. See White, *Tort Law in America*, 41–55.

92. *Ryalls v. Mechanics' Mills*, 150 Mass. 190, 193 (1889).

93. 150 Mass. 362 (1889).

94. Id. at 363–64.

95. 159 Mass. 532 (1893).

96. Id. at 535–36.

97. 159 Mass. 536 (1893).

98. Id. at 537.

99. Id. at 538.

100. Kelley, supra note 10, at 75–77, explains Holmes' posture on assumption of risk cases by emphasizing Holmes' insistence on an external standard of tort liability that was based on the concept of reasonably foreseeable danger. Since in assumption of risk cases the dangers were as foreseeable to plaintiffs as to defendants, both parties were "blameworthy," or negligent, and since any negligence on the part of plaintiffs barred them from recovery against negligent defendants, Holmes denied recovery. In cases such as *Lynch*, however, the plaintiff's job seemed incompatible with adequate protection against risks.

See also *Robinska v. Lyman Mills*, 174 Mass. 432 (1899), where Holmes, for a unanimous court, allowed the assumption of risk and contributory negligence doctrines to bar the claim of a young immigrant woman who was injured by a factory machine whose warning sign she was unable to read.

101. See White, *Tort Law in America*, 102–06.

102. Id., 102–03.

103. 172 Mass. 488 (1899).

104. Id.

105. Id. at 488–89

106. Id. at 490–91.

107. Id. at 491.

108. Id.

109. 180 Mass. 456 (1902).

110. Id. at 47–48.

111. 182 Mass. 310 (1902).

112. Id. at 312.

113. Modern emotional distress cases have focused on the same question, whether the circumstances of the plaintiff's injury establish a ''guarantee of genuineness'' with respect to his or her claim. See, e.g., *Molien v. Kaiser Foundation Hospitals*, 27 Cal. 3d. 916 (1980).

114. 180 Mass. 119 (1901).

115. Id. at 121.

116. Id. at 121–22.

117. 143 Mass. 224 (1887).

118. 168 Mass. 558 (1897).

119. 135 Mass. 1 (1883).

120. 156 Mass. 221 (1892).

121. 149 Mass. 284 (1889).

122. Id. at 285–86.

123. Id. at 287.

124. Id. at 287–88.

125. Id. at 289.

126. 158 Mass. 194 (1893).

127. Id. at 195–96.

128. Id. at 196.

129. Id. at 197.

130. Id.

131. 168 Mass. 198 (1897).

132. Id. at 199.

133. Id. at 200.

134. Holmes wrote this comment in the margin of his own copy of *The Common Law* at page 230. See Mark Howe's edition of Holmes' copy, which Harold Laski gave to Harvard Law School after initially receiving it from Holmes. Mark DeW. Howe, ed., *The Common Law* (1968).

135. Holmes, *The Common Law*, 230.

136. 179 Mass. 114 (1901).

137. Id. at 115.

138. Holmes, *The Common Law*, 230.

139. 179 Mass. at 116–17.

140. Id. at 117.

141. See, e.g, *Pennsylvania Coal Co. v. Mahon*, 260 U.S. 393 (1922).

142. See, e.g., *Schenck v. United States*, 249 U.S. 47 (1919).

143. *Near v. Minnesota*, 283 U.S. 697 (1931).

144. *O'Gorman v. Hartford Ins. Co.*, 282 U.S. 251 (1931).

145. For two representative decisions see *Taft v. Commonwealth*, 158 Mass. 526 (1893); *Murphy v. Manning*, 134 Mass. 488 (1883).

146. See David M. Rabban, "The First Amendment in its Forgotten Years," 90 *Yale L. J.* 514 (1981). See also Chapter Eleven.

147. 148 Mass. 368 (1889).

148. Id. at 372.

149. Id. at 373.

150. 155 Mass. 117 (1891).

151. Id. at 119.

152. Id. at 121.

153. 198 U.S. 45 (1905).

154. 155 Mass. at 121.

155. Id. at 124.

156. Opinion of the Justices, 155 Mass. 598 (1892).

157. *Loan Association v. Topeka,* 20 Wall. 655 (1880).

158. 155 Mass. at 606.

159. 152 Mass. 540 (1891).

160. Id. at 541.

161. Id. at 543.

162. Id. at 547–548.

163. 155 Mass. 216 (1892).

164. Id. at 220.

165. The Massachusetts Constitution has a free speech clause.

166. 162 Mass. 510 (1895).

167. Id. at 511.

168. Id.

169. The *Davis* case was appealed to the Supreme Court of the United States, which unanimously sustained Holmes' position in *Davis v. Massachusetts,* 167 U.S. 43 (1897). In a series of cases in the 1930s and 1940s the Court changed its mind and repudiated *Davis.* See *Hague v. CIO,* 307 U.S. 496 (1939); *Schneider v. State,* 308 U.S. 147 (1939); *Jamison v. Texas,* 318 U.S. 413 (1943).

170. 167 Mass. 92 (1896).

171. Id. at 95–96.

172. Id. at 97.

173. Id.

174. Id. at 106.

175. Id. at 108.

176. Id. at 108–09.

177. Id. at 104.

178. Holmes to Clare Castletown, November 13, 1896, Holmes Papers.

179. Holmes to Clare Castletown, November 21, 1896, id.

180. Catherine Drinker Bowen, relying on a conversation she had with Arthur Hill, a neighbor of Holmes', reported this comment in her biography of Holmes, *Yankee from Olympus,* 305 (1943).

181. Note, 10 *Harv. L. Rev.* 301 (1896).

182. Id.

183. 176 Mass. 492 (1900).

184. Id. at 494–95.

185. Id. at 502.

186. Id. at 504.

187. Id. at 504–05.

188. Id. at 505.

189. Id.

190. "Judge Holmes' Opinions," 60 *Albany L. J.* 118, 119 (1899).

191. Id., 118.

192. Kelley, supra note 10, argues persuasively that Holmes persistently attempted to inject his theoretical views into the common law of Massachusetts, despite the limited number of cases in which he had such opportunities.

193. Holmes to Ellen Curtis, December 4, 1901, Holmes Papers.

194. Speech at Bar Dinner, March 7, 1900, *Occasional Speeches,* 125.

195. Note, 5 *Harv. L. Rev.* 287, 288 (1891).

196. "Notes of Recent Decisions," 34 *Am. L. Rev.* 109 (1900).

197. Leonard A. Jones, "Oliver Wendell Holmes, The Jurist," 36 *Am. L. Rev.* 710 (1902).

198. Id.

199. Id., 713.

200. Id., 714.

201. Id., 715–16.

202. Id., 717–20.

203. Id., 721.

204. Id., 722.

205. Holmes to Felix Frankfurter, July 15, 1913, Holmes Papers.

206. Holmes, "Twenty Years in Retrospect," December 3, 1902, *Occasional Speeches,* 157.

207. Holmes, "The Theory of Torts," 7 *Am. L. Rev.,* 652, 654 (1873).

208. Holmes, "Law and Science and Science in Law," 12 *Harv. L. Rev.* 443 (1899), reprinted in *Collected Legal Papers,* 210, 232–33.

209. Holmes to Canon Patrick A. Sheehan, December 15, 1912, *Holmes–Sheehan Correspondence,* 56.

210. Holmes to Nina Gray, October 2, 1896, Holmes Papers, quoted in Zobel, supra note 18.

211. Holmes to Clare Castletown, February 11, 1897, Holmes Papers.

212. Holmes to Clare Castletown, February 2, 1897, id.

213. Holmes to Clare Castletown, November 21, 1896, id.

214. Holmes to Clare Castletown, May 28, 1897, id.

215. Holmes to Clare Castletown, June 2, 1898, id.

CHAPTER NINE: *The Supreme Court, 1903–1916*

1. Holmes, "John Marshall," February 4, 1901. *Occasional Speeches,* 134.

2. Holmes, "William Allen," id., 67–68.

3. Holmes, "John Marshall," id., 134.

4. Even though numerous states had joined the Union by that time, certain regions invariably had representatives on the Court. New England was one of them. Holmes was appointed to a seat previously held by Justices William Cushing (Massachusetts), Joseph

Story (Massachusetts), Levi Woodbury (New Hampshire), Benjamin Curtis (Massachusetts), Nathan Clifford (Maine), and Horace Gray. The presumption of a New England "seat" ended on Holmes' retirement in 1932; his replacement, Judge Benjamin Cardozo, was from New York. See generally Henry J. Abraham, *Justices and Presidents* (1992 ed.).

5. For details of Holmes' appointment to the Supreme Court of the United States, see John Garraty, "Holmes' Appointment to the U.S. Supreme Court," 22 *New Eng. Q.* 291 (1949); Richard E. Welch, Jr., "Opponents and Colleagues: George Frisbee Hoar and Henry Cabot Lodge," 39 *New Eng. Q.* 182 (1966); Novick, *Honorable Justice,* 234–36; Baker, *Justice from Beacon Hill,* 339–51.

6. On June 5, 1895, as we have seen, Roosevelt wrote Henry Cabot Lodge, "By Jove, that speech of Holmes's was fine." Henry C. Lodge, ed., *Selections from the Correspondence of Theodore Roosevelt and Henry Cabot Lodge* (2 vols., 1925), I, 146. Hereafter cited as Lodge, ed., *Selections.* Around the same time Roosevelt prevailed on William Sturgis Bigelow to invite him and Holmes to dinner so that Roosevelt could shake hands with Holmes. See Chapter Two.

7. Henry Cabot Lodge to Eben S. Draper, March 3, 1902, Henry Cabot Lodge Papers, Massachusetts Historical Society, quoted in Garraty, supra note 5, at 293. Further citations to the Lodge Papers are from Garraty unless otherwise indicated.

8. Draper to Lodge, May 7, 1902, Lodge Papers, quoted in Garraty, supra note 5, at 293.

9. Draper to Lodge, June 13, 1902, Lodge Papers, quoted in Garraty, 294.

10. Lodge had written Roosevelt, before receiving the second Draper letter, that "I am absolutely for Holmes." Lodge to Roosevelt, June 5, 1902, Lodge Papers, id.

11. 167 Mass. 92, 104 (1896).

12. 176 Mass. 492 (1900).

13. Lodge to Roosevelt, July 7, 1902, Lodge Papers, quoted in Garraty, 295.

14. Roosevelt to Lodge, July 10, 1902, in Lodge, ed., *Selections,* I, 517–18.

15. Id.

16. Id.

17. Lodge to Roosevelt, July 19, 1902, quoted in Garraty, 296.

18. Holmes to Nina Gray, August 17, 1902, Holmes Papers.

19. Nina Gray to Holmes, August 12, 1902, id.

20. Holmes entry, 1902, "Black Book" List of Readings, 1881–1935, Holmes Papers.

21. Holmes to Lodge, July 25, 1902, Lodge Papers, quoted in Garraty, 297.

22. Roosevelt to Lodge, July 25, 1902, Theodore Roosevelt Papers, Library of Congress, quoted in id.

23. Lodge to Roosevelt, July 26, 1902, Lodge Papers, id.

24. Hoar to Lodge, July 29, 1902, Lodge Papers, id., 298.

25. Hoar to Roosevelt, July 28, 1902, Roosevelt Papers, id.

26. Lodge to Hoar, August 8, 1902, Lodge Papers, id., 297.

27. Roosevelt to Hoar, July 30, 1902, Roosevelt Papers, id.

28. Hoar to Lodge, August 11, 1902, Lodge Papers, id.

29. See Boston *Globe,* May 18, 1902, quoted in id., 294.

30. Hoar to Lodge, August 11, 1907, Lodge Papers, id., 299.

31. Lodge to Roosevelt, August 17, 1902, Lodge Papers, id., 300.

32. Hoar to Fuller, November 5, 1902, quoted in Willard King, *Melville Weston Fuller* 285 (1950). Hereafter cited as King, *Fuller.*

33. Holmes to Lady Pollock, September 6, 1902, *Holmes–Pollock Letters* I, 105.

34. Holmes to Pollock, September 23, 1902, id., 106.

35. Editorial, New York *Evening Post,* August 12, 1902, p. 4.

36. Boston *Evening Transcript,* August 12, 1902, p. 6.

37. Holmes to Lady Pollock, supra note 33.

38. *Northern Securities Co. v. United States,* 193 U.S. 197 (1904).

39. The case is discussed in more detail below, text at notes 173–182.

40. Henry Adams to Elizabeth Cameron, March 20, 1904, in Worthington Chauncy Ford, ed., *Letters of Henry Adams* (2 vols., 1938), II, 429.

41. Roosevelt to Lodge, September 4, 1906, Lodge Papers, quoted in Garraty, 301.

42. Holmes mentioned burning his papers in a November 14, 1902, speech to the Tavern Club, *Occasional Speeches,* 150. Fanny's destruction of her embroideries was reported to Mark Howe by Mrs. James B. Ayer: see Howe, *Proving Years,* 255.

43. Anita Lyman (Nina) Gray had married Holmes' old friend John Chipman Gray in 1873, and beginning in the 1880s Holmes made it a practice to call on Nina Gray about once a week. His surviving correspondence with her dates from 1887 to 1932.

44. Holmes to Frederick Pollock, December 28, 1902, *Holmes–Pollock Letters* I, 109.

45. Holmes to John G. Palfrey, December 27, 1902, Holmes Papers.

46. Holmes to Clara Stevens, January 10, 1903, id.

47. Holmes to Nina Gray, January 4, 1903, id.

48. Holmes to Ellen Curtis, December 21, 1902, id.

49. Id.

50. Holmes to Nina Gray, supra note 47.

51. Ellen Curtis was a neighbor of the Holmeses in their summer residence, Beverly Farms, Massachusetts. She and Holmes, in addition to regular visits during the summer months, had an extensive correspondence. Holmes' last dated letter of those that have survived, December 19, 1933, is to Ellen Curtis. Holmes Papers.

52. Holmes to Curtis, December 21, 1902, Holmes Papers.

53. Holmes to Curtis, January 12, 1903, id.

54. Holmes to Nina Gray, February 15, 1903, id.

55. Holmes to Curtis, March 3, 1903, id.

56. Holmes to Curtis, January 12, 1903, id.

57. Holmes to Curtis, April 1, 1903, id.

58. Holmes to Nina Gray, February 15, 1903, id.

59. Holmes to Curtis, December 21, 1902, id.

60. Holmes to Curtis, February 7, 1903, id.

61. Holmes to Curtis, January 12, 1903, id.

62. Holmes to Nina Gray, February 8, 1904, id.

63. Holmes to Anna Codman, February 15, 1903, id.

64. Holmes to Curtis, February 24, 1903, id.

65. Holmes to Lewis Einstein, November 23, 1903, *Holmes–Einstein Letters,* 6–7.

66. Holmes to Pollock, December 28, 1902, *Holmes–Pollock Letters* I, 109.

67. Id.

68. Holmes to Curtis, December 21, 1902, Holmes Papers.

69. Holmes to Curtis, January 12, 1903, id.

70. Holmes to Nina Gray, January 4, 1903, id.

71. Holmes to Curtis, February 24, 1903, id.

72. Holmes to Nina Gray, January 16, 1903, id.

73. Holmes to Nina Gray, February 15, 1903, id.

74. Holmes to Curtis, February 23, 1903, id.

75. Holmes to Nina Gray, May 3, 1903, id.

76. Holmes to Curtis, March 21, 1903, id.

77. Willis Van Devanter to W. Riner, January 16, 1911, Willis Van Devanter Papers, Library of Congress, quoted in Alexander Bickel and Benno Schmidt, *The Judiciary and Responsible Government, 1910–21* (1984). Hereafter cited as Bickel and Schmidt, *Judiciary.*

78. Holmes' ''secretaries'' (never referred to as law clerks during his lifetime) were research assistants only in a limited sense. They are better described as intellectual companions. See the reminiscences of Holmes' ''clerks'' in Katie Louchheim, *The Making of the New Deal: The Insiders Speak* (1983). Hereafter cited as Louchheim, *The Making of the New Deal.*

79. 304 U.S. 64 (1938).

80. Holmes to Pollock, December 28, 1902, *Holmes–Pollock Letters* I, 109.

81. Holmes to Nina Gray, March 2, 1903, Holmes Papers.

82. Quoted in Alexander Bickel, *The Unpublished Opinions of Mr. Justice Brandeis* 227 (1957).

83. *Federal Maritime Bd. v. Isbrandtsen Co.*, 356 U.S. 481, 523 (1958) (Frankfurter, J., dissenting.)

84. John Chipman Gray to William Howard Taft, November 9, 1912, William Howard Taft Papers, Microfilm Edition, Alderman Library, University of Virginia. Hereafter cited as Taft Papers. See also Bickel and Schmidt, *Judiciary,* 70.

85. See William Howard Taft to Robert A. Taft, November 19, 1912, Taft papers. See also Bickel and Schmidt, *Judiciary,* 70.

86. For support for the statements made in this paragraph, see the reminiscences of Holmes' secretaries, supra note 78; the memoirs of Arthur E. Sutherland, Jr. (secretary for 1927–28) and Mark DeWolfe Howe (secretary for 1933–34) in Arthur E. Sutherland, Jr., Papers and Mark DeWolfe Howe Papers, Harvard Law School Library; and Augustin Derby, ''Recollections of Mr. Justice Holmes,'' 35 *N.Y.U. L. Rev.* 345 (1935).

87. For a list of Holmes' secretaries, see the Appendix.

88. See G. Edward White, ''Holmes as Correspondent,'' 43 *Vand. L. Rev.* 1707, 1750–55 (1991).

89. See Holmes to Nina Gray, January 16, 1903, Holmes Papers; Holmes to Pollock, September 24, 1910, *Holmes–Pollock Letters* I, 170; Holmes to Charlotte Moncheur, May 16, 1912, Holmes Papers.

90. See Holmes to Laski, May 27, 1921, *Holmes–Laski Letters,* I, 339; Holmes to Alice S. Green, April 26, 1910, Holmes Papers.

91. Holmes wrote Pollock on April 5, 1919: ''As to Harlan's qualified concurrence in Kawananakoa v. Polyblank, that sage, although a man of real power, did not shine

either in analysis or generalization and I never troubled myself much when he shied. I used to say that he had a powerful vise the jaws of which couldn't be got nearer than two inches to each other.'' *Holmes–Pollock Letters* II, 7–8.

92. See Bickel and Schmidt, *Judiciary,* 238–41, describing ''[a]n odd and in most ways pointless little rivalry'' (238) between Holmes and McKenna, which tended to manifest itself in competition as to who could complete his assigned opinions faster. Bickel and Schmidt also assert that Holmes ''did not hold McKenna in high regard,'' citing a letter from Felix Frankfuter to Alexander Bickel, January 6, 1956, quoted in id., 239.

93. Holmes to Pollock, January 24, 1918, *Holmes–Pollock Letters* I, 258.

94. Holmes to Laski, November 17, 1920, *Holmes–Laski Letters* I, 291.

95. Holmes to Laski, supra note 90.

96. Holmes to Frankfurter, March 28, 1922, Holmes Papers.

97. King, *Fuller,* 313.

98. Id.

99. Holmes to William L. Putnam, July 12, 1910, William L. Putnam Papers, quoted in id., 334.

100. Holmes to Melville W. Fuller, August 18, 1904, quoted in id., 299.

101. See King, *Fuller,* 296, quoting interview with Colley Bell, a former secretary of Fuller's, August 1946.

102. Holmes to Melville W. Fuller, February 28, 1902, Mrs. Rivers Genet Papers, quoted in King, *Fuller,* 289–90. The papers of Mrs. Rivers Genet, Fuller's granddaughter, were made available to Willard King in connection with his biography of Fuller. See King, *Fuller,* vii. Hereafter cited as Genet Papers.

103. 187 U.S. 606 (1902).

104. Holmes to Melville W. Fuller, February 5–6, 1902, Genet Papers, quoted in King, *Fuller,* 291.

105. 187 U.S. 726 (1903).

106. Fuller to Rufus W. Peckham, February 10, 1903, Genet Papers, quoted in King, *Fuller,* 291.

107. Rufus W. Peckham to Melville W. Fuller, February 10, 1903, Genet Papers, quoted in id.

108. *Home Life Insurance Co. v. Fisher* involved the construction of a life insurance policy.

109. Fuller to Mary Coolbaugh Fuller, February 18, 1903, Genet Papers, quoted in King, *Fuller,* 291.

110. 202 U.S. 453 (1906).

111. 185 U.S. 65, 81–83 (1902).

112. Holmes to Fuller, May 18, 1906, Genet Papers, quoted in King, *Fuller,* 319.

113. Taft to Stimson, May 18, 1928, Taft Papers.

114. Taft to Helen Taft Manning, June 11, 1923, id.

115. Taft to Horace Taft, November 28, 1925, id.

116. Holmes to Nina Gray, March 5, 1921, Holmes Papers.

117. Holmes to Pollock, October 31, 1926, *Holmes–Pollock Letters* II, 191. In his reference to ''high motives'' Holmes may have been thinking of his reaction to Brandeis in the Richard A. Ballinger-Gifford Pinchot hearings on corruption in the Taft admin-

istration's policies on natural resources. Brandeis, representing *Collier's* magazine, which first raised the issue of corruption, publicly embarrassed then President Taft by demonstrating, before a number of reporters, that Taft had approved Ballinger's policies as Secretary of the Interior without having information about what Ballinger was doing. In a May 13, 1916, letter to Clara Stevens (Holmes Papers) Holmes said, "I didn't like [Brandeis'] mode of conducting the Ballinger case." On the Ballinger-Pinchot controversy, see James L. Penick, *Progressive Politics and Conservation: The Ballinger-Pinchot Affair* (1968).

118. Brandeis, for his part, had a high opinion of Holmes, dating back to the time when he had helped raise money for Holmes' chair at Harvard Law School, described in Chapter Six. When Brandeis was nominated for the Supreme Court in 1916 he wrote a contemporary that "[m]y views in regard to the constitution are as you know very much those of Mr. Justice Holmes." Brandeis to Thomas Watt Gregory, April 14, 1916, in Melvin Urofsky and David Levy, eds., *Letters of Louis D. Brandeis* (5 vols., 1975), IV, 165.

119. For a detailed discussion, see Chapter Twelve.

120. For a detailed discussion, see Chapter Eleven.

121. See the discussion in Chapter Eleven.

122. See Chapter Twelve.

123. Brandeis reported the conversation with Taft to Felix Frankfurter, quoted in Bickel and Schmidt, *Judiciary*, 6.

124. In a July 19, 1923 conversation with Frankfurter, Brandeis said that Holmes' opinion in *Pennsylvania Coal Co. v. Mahon*, discussed in Chapter Eleven, was the result of "class bias." Holmes' solicitude for property, Brandeis suggested, reflected "views not of his manhood but childhood." Quoted in Melvin I. Urofsky, ed., "The Brandeis—Frankfurter Conversations," 1985 Sup. Ct. Rev. 299, 321. Hereafter cited as Brandeis–Frankfurter Conversations.

125. Ross, St. Louis *Post Dispatch*, June 19, 1927.

126. See the cases discussed in Chapter Eleven and Twelve.

127. In 1929 Taft wrote his brother that "I must stay on the Court in order to prevent the Bolsheviki from getting control." Taft to Horace Taft, November 14, 1929, Taft Papers.

128. Taft was increasingly irritated with Holmes and any other dissenters in his later years as Chief Justice. In 1928 he wrote that Holmes' dissent in the care of *Myers v. United States* was "only one of a great number of opinions that he is writing now to indicate that he really does not believe in the constitution at all, as he really does not, when it imposes any limitation upon legislative authority." Taft also wrote his brother that "[i]f Holmes' dissents in constitutional cases had been followed, we should have had no constitution." Taft to Stimson, supra note 113; Taft to Horace Taft, June 8, 1928, Taft Papers.

129. Taft to Robert A. Taft, March 7, 1926, Taft Papers.

130. Brandeis to Frankfurter, July 1, 1922, Brandeis–Frankfurter Conversations, 307.

131. Brandeis–Frankfurter Conversations, July 2, 1924, 328.

132. Brandeis–Frankfurter Conversations, July 6, 1924, 330.

133. Brandeis–Frankfurter Conversations, July 1, 1923, 314.

134. Brandeis–Frankfurter Conversations, September 1, 1923, 327.

135. Holmes to Laski, May 25, 1918, *Holmes–Laski Letters* I, 157. The case may well have been *Hammer v. Dagenhart,* which was formally issued on June 3, 1918.

136. Holmes to Laski, December 3, 1918, id., I, 176.

137. Holmes to Laski, October 16, 1929, id., II, 1192.

138. Holmes to Laski, December 26, 1931, id., II, 1347.

139. Supra note 103.

140. Id. at 608.

141. About a year later he wrote Pollock, "My intellectual furniture consists of an assortment of general propositions which grow fewer and more general as I grow older. I always say that the chief end of man is to frame them and no general proposition is worth a damn." Holmes to Pollock, September 24, 1904, *Holmes–Pollock Letters* I, 118.

142. 187 U.S. at 608–09.

143. Id. at 609.

144. Id.

145. Opinion of the Justices, 155 Mass. 598 (1892).

146. 198 U.S. 45, 75 (1905).

147. Id. at 70, citing Hirt, "Disease of the Workers."

148. Id. at 46.

149. King, *Fuller,* 372, argues that "the Justice who switched [in *Lochner*] must have been either Brown or McKenna, or both." He bases this claim on the fact that Brewer, Peckham, and Fuller had dissented in a previous case, *Atkin v. Kansas,* 191 U.S. 207 (1903), in which a law restricting state employment to 8 hours a day had been upheld.

150. 198 U.S. at 56.

151. Id. at 68.

152. Id. at 61, 63, 64.

153. Id. at 72.

154. Id. at 75.

155. Id.

156. Id. at 75–76.

157. Id. at 76.

158. Id.

159. 187 U.S. at 609.

160. The term "progressive" is placed in quotes to signify that it was a label that certain early twentieth-century political reformers attached to themselves. Many of those individuals were identified with the progressive movement in American policies, which emerged as an influential political force in the early years of the twentieth century. See G. Edward White, *Patterns of American Legal Thought* 103–04 (1978). Hereafter White, *Patterns.*

161. This was the identification many early twentieth-century commentators made. But that identification was slow to develop. Initial reaction to *Lochner* did not give prominent mention to Holmes' dissent; the first set of comments in that vein did not appear until 1908. It was not until the First World War that Holmes' *Lochner* dissent was treated as a major jurisprudential statement. For a detailed discussion of early reactions to *Lochner,* see Chapter Ten.

162. 195 U.S. at 76.

163. Holmes, "The Path of the Law," *Collected Legal Papers,* 169.

164. Holmes, "Law and Science and Science in Law," id., 241.

165. 208 U.S. 161 (1908).

166. Id. at 191–92.

167. 236 U.S. 1 (1913).

168. Id. at 14.

169. Id. at 26–27.

170. 219 U.S. 105 (1911).

171. Id. at 110, 112.

172. 193 U.S. 197 (1904).

173. The text of the Act is quoted in 193 U.S. at 318–20.

174. Id. at 333.

175. Id. at 361, 363.

176. Id. at 404.

177. Id. at 406.

178. Id. at 409.

179. Id. at 410–11.

180. Id. at 407.

181. Id. at 400–01.

182. Id. at 400. See also Holmes's dissent in *Dr. Miles Medical Co. v. Park & Sons Co.,* 220 U.S. 373 (1911), where the majority applied the Sherman Act to invalidate agreements between a manufacturer of proprietary medicines and druggists and their representatives in which the prices of patent medicines were fixed. In his dissent Holmes said that "I think that, at least, it is safe to say that the most enlightened judicial policy is to let people manage their business in their own way, unless the ground for interference is very clear," and that "it seems to me that the point of most profitable returns marks the equilibrium of social desires and determines the fair price in the only sense in which I can find meaning in those words." Id. at 411, 412.

183. Roosevelt was not so estranged from Holmes, however, as to forego the opportunity to quote from Holmes' opinions when it suited him. For example, Roosevelt's opening address to the 1908 National Conservation conference quoted extensively from Holmes' opinion in *Hudson Water Co. v. McCarter,* 209 U.S. 349 (1908). Holmes and Roosevelt shared an interest in the conservation of natural resources, an interest Holmes retained for his entire Supreme Court career. See, e.g., *New York v. New Jersey,* 283 U.S. 336, 342 (1931), where he wrote that "a river is not an amenity, it is a treasure."

184. 196 U.S. 375 (1904).

185. 193 U.S. at 409.

186. 196 U.S. at 396.

187. E.g., *United States v. E. C. Knight Co.,* 156 U.S. 1 (1895).

188. 196 U.S. at 397.

189. Id. at 398.

190. Id. at 398–99.

191. Bickel and Schmidt, *Judiciary,* 726–27.

192. 189 U.S. 475 (1903).

193. Id. at 482.

194. Id. at 487.

195. 212 U.S. 78 (1909).

196. Id. at 83.

197. Id.

198. Id. at 85.

199. 219 U.S. 219 (1911).

200. Brief for United States as Amicus Curiae, 10, quoted in Bickel and Schmidt, *Judiciary,* 862.

201. At the time *Bailey* was argued, October 20 and 21, 1910, two vacancies existed on the Court: Chief Justice Fuller died on July 1 and Justice Moody, suffering from arthritis, retired on October 3. Bickel and Schmidt, *Judiciary,* 31, 861.

202. 219 U.S. at 231.

203. Id., 235, 236.

204. 219 U.S. at 241.

205. Holmes, *The Common Law,* 235–36.

206. 219 U.S. at 247.

207. Id. at 248–49.

208. Id. at 247.

209. Holmes said in *Bailey* that: "I take it that a fair jury would acquit if the only evidence were a departure after 11 months' work and if it received no color from some special well-known course of events." Id. at 242. In 1897 he had written Georgina Pollock that "I think there is a growing disbelief in the jury as an instrument for truth, the use of it is to let a little popular prejudice into the administration of law (in violation of their oath)." Holmes to Lady Pollock, April 11, 1897, *Holmes–Pollock Letters,* I, 74.

210. 219 U.S. 245–46.

211. 235 U.S. 133 (1914).

212. See Ray Stannard Baker, *Following the Color Line* 96–98. (1964 ed.) Baker's book first appeared in 1906. See Bickel and Schmidt, *Judiciary,* 749.

213. 235 U.S. at 146–47.

214. Id. at 150.

215. In *Brown's Case,* 173 Mass. 498, 500 (1899), Holmes had indicated that in his view legislatures could enact "unconditional imprisonment in case of failure to pay."

216. 235 U.S. at 150.

217. 211 U.S. 45 (1908).

218. 163 U.S. 537 (1896), affirming that "separate but equal" interstate transportation facilities for blacks and whites did not violate the Equal Protection Clause of the Fourteenth Amendment.

219. 235 U.S. 151 (1914).

220. Oklahoma Comp. Laws, Section 860 (1910).

221. Id.

222. 235 U.S. at 161–62.

223. Hughes to Holmes, November 29, 1914, Holmes Papers.

224. Holmes to Arthur Garfield Hays, April 20, 1928, id.

225. Yosal Rogat, "Mr. Justice Holmes: A Dissenting Opinion," 15 *Stan. L. Rev.* 254, 255 (1963).

226. Id. at 307–08.

227. Abbott wrote Holmes, learning that he had turned down Hallowell's offer, "I believe you have done ... what is thoroughly right and proper, instead of absurdly

wasting yourself before the shrine of the great nigger.'' Abbott to Holmes, October 8, 1863, quoted in Howe, *Shaping Years*, 159.

228. *Tiaco v. Forbes*, 228 U.S. 549, 556–57 (1913).

229. 194 U.S. 161 (1904).

230. Id. at 163.

231. Id. at 167.

232. Id. at 170.

233. Id. at 168.

234. 198 U.S. 253 (1905).

235. Id. at 259.

236. Id. at 263.

237. See Thomas Reed Powell, ''Judicial Review of Administrative Action in Immigration Proceedings,'' 22 *Harv. L. Rev.* 360, 361 (1909).

238. See, e.g., *Ng Fung Ho v. White*, 259 U.S. 276 (1922).

239. 232 U.S. 138 (1914).

240. Id.

241. Id.

242. Id. at 144.

243. It is possible that the state purpose in *Patsone* was to conserve scarce natural wildlife resources for its own citizens. If that were so—and such a purpose was not stated in the *Patsone* case itself—it would seem that the state could more efficiently implement it by preventing aliens from acquiring hunting licenses than from denying them access to firearms altogether.

244. *United States v. Schwimmer*, 279 U.S. 644 (1929).

245. See, e.g., Lerner, *Mind and Faith*, xliv, xlvi.

246. See the sources discussed in Chapter Twelve.

247. 165 U.S. 275 (1897).

248. Id. at 281.

249. Id.

250. *Davis v. Beason*, 133 U.S. 333 (1890).

251. *Turner v. Williams*, 194 U.S. 279 (1904).

252. William Blackstone, *Commentaries on the Laws of England* (4 vols., 1769), IV, 151–52.

253. 205 U.S. 454 (1907).

254. Id. at 459.

255. Id. at 456. Patterson did not specifically rely on the First Amendment, assuming in his argument that it was incorporated into the Fourteenth Amendment's Due Process Clause. Holmes addressed this issue briefly in his opinion in *Patterson v. Colorado*.

256. Id.

257. See id. at 458.

258. Id. at 464 (Harlan, J., dissenting). It was not until eighteen years later that a majority of the Court was to hold, without discussion, that the Fourteenth Amendment did incorporate the First Amendment. *Gitlow v. New York*, 268 U.S. 652 (1925). For a discussion of Holmes' opinion in the *Gitlow* case, see Chapter Twelve.

259. Id. at 461–62.

260. Id. at 463.

261. Id. at 461.

262. Id. at 462.

263. 236 U.S. 273 (1915).

264. Id. at 276.

265. Id.

266. Id. at 276–77.

267. Id. at 275 (quoting Wash. *Remington & Ballinger's Code,* section 2564).

268. *State v. Fox,* 127 P. 1111, 1112 (Wash. 1912).

269. Brief for Plaintiff-in-Error, 15, *Fox v. Washington,* 236 U.S. at 273.

270. 236 U.S. at 273.

271. Id. at 277.

272. Id. at 276.

273. Id. at 277.

274. Id.

275. Id. at 277–78.

276. Lerner, *Mind and Faith,* 289.

277. The reception of Holmes' position by "progressive" commentators is described in the next two chapters.

278. Morris Cohen, 82 *The New Republic* 206 (April 3, 1935).

279. Felix Frankfurter, *Mr. Justice Holmes and the Supreme Court* 3 (1961 ed.).

280. Quoted in id., 29.

281. Bickel and Schmidt, *Judiciary,* 70–71.

CHAPTER TEN: *Recognition*

1. Holmes to Clara Stevens, January 6, 1909, Holmes Papers.

2. Holmes to Clara Stevens, March 6, 1909, id.

3. Holmes, address to Harvard University graduation, June 28, 1911, *Occasional Speeches,* 160–61.

4. Holmes to John G. Palfrey, April 1, 1904, Holmes Papers.

5. Holmes to Einstein, December 19, 1910, *Holmes–Einstein Letters,* 57–58.

6. Holmes to Nina Gray, December 2, 1910, Holmes Papers.

7. Holmes to Pollock, December 31, 1911, *Holmes–Pollock Letters* I, 188.

8. Holmes to Pollock, September 15, 1912, id., 202.

9. Holmes to Pollock, December 15, 1912, id., 205.

10. Holmes, "John Marshall," February 4, 1901, *Occasional Speeches,* 132.

11. Holmes to Sheehan, September 3, 1910, *Holmes–Sheehan Correspondence,* 36–37.

12. Felix Frankfurter in Harlan Phillips, ed., *Felix Frankfurter Reminisces* 35–36 (1962). For accounts of Frankfurter's early life, see Michael Parrish, *Felix Frankfurter and His Times: The Reform Years* (1982) and H. N. Hirsch, *The Enigma of Felix Frankfurter* (1981).

13. See Hugh Hawkins, *Between Harvard and America* 133–35, 180–90 (1972); Seymour Martin Lipset and David Riesman, *Education and Politics at Harvard* 99–102 (1975).

14. Felix Frankfurter to Roscoe Pound, August 28, 1921, Roscoe Pound Papers, Har-

vard Law School, quoted in Parrish, *Felix Frankfurter and His Times,* supra note 12, at 156.

15. Frankfurter in Phillips, supra note 12, at 37–38.

16. See Hirsch, supra note 12, at 58–61, for more details.

17. Frankfurter in Phillips, supra note 12, at 106–07.

18. Michael Parrish, in his biography of Frankfurter, reports an incident at "The House of Truth" in which Holmes and Fanny observed the sculptor Gutzon Borglum draw a sketch of his proposed "Black Hills" monument. Parrish, supra note 12, at 52. Felix Frankfurter also reported the incident in Phillips, *Felix Frankfurter Reminisces,* supra note 12, at 137.

Max Freedman, in his undocumented history of the friendship of Franklin Roosevelt and Felix Frankfurter, stated that "Mr. Justice Holmes, with facetious intent, referred to [Valentine's residence] as the House of Truth." Max Freedman, *Roosevelt and Frankfurter: Their Correspondence 1928–1945* 308 (1967). Freedman cited no source for that statement, and a more thorough investigation of the origins of the name "House of Truth" has expressed doubt about whether Holmes coined the phrase. See Jeffrey O'Connell and Nancy Dart, "The House of Truth: Home of the Young Frankfurter and Laski," 35 *Cath. U. L. Rev.* 79 (1985).

19. Hirsch, *The Enigma of Felix Frankfurter,* supra note 12, at 21.

20. Frankfurter to Holmes, February 10, 1912, Holmes Papers.

21. Frankfurter to Holmes, February 19, 1912, id.

22. Frankfurter to Holmes, December 16, 1912, id.

23. E.g., Frankfurter to Holmes, July 4, 1913, id., concerning Frankfurter's decision whether to accept a position on the Harvard Law School faculty.

24. E.g., letters of March 7, 1912, March 8, 1915, March 6, 1917, id.

25. E.g., Frankfurter to Holmes, March 28, 1914, id., referring to Holmes' opinion in *LeRoy Fibre Co. v. Chicago, Milwaukee & St. Paul Railroad,* 232 U.S. 340 (1914); Frankfurter to Holmes, January 27, 1915, id., referring to Holmes' dissent in *Coppage v. Kansas,* 236 U.S. 1 (1915).

26. E.g., Frankfurter to Holmes, March 6, 1917, Holmes Papers. "Behind the forces of faith . . . I feel your dominant presence, unflinching in the face of all that makes one hesitate, passionate against every compromise with the unknown, in your very self you give one's faith validity and give the gay impetus to new faith."

27. For examples, see Frankfurter's correspondence with Henry Stimson, selections of which are quoted in Hirsch, *The Enigma of Felix Frankfurter,* supra note 12, and with Franklin D. Roosevelt, quoted in Freedman, *Roosevelt and Frankfurter,* supra note 18.

28. Holmes to Frankfurter, March 8, 1912, Holmes Papers.

29. Quoted in Francis Biddle, *Justice Holmes, Natural Law, and the Supreme Court* 38 (1961). Biddle added that while Holmes liked to write for the one man who did understand, "sometimes Holmes missed him."

30. Holmes to Frankfurter, March 8, 1916, Holmes Papers.

31. Magnitzsky has been rumored to have saved Holmes' life in the battle of Ball's Bluff, and as a result to have been made office manager of the Shattuck, Holmes and Munroe law firm. Holmes, according to the rumor, suppressed the information that Magnitzsky saved his life by, in effect, buying Magnitzsky's silence. Magnitzsky managed trust accounts of the Holmes family in addition to his duties at Shattuck, Holmes and

Munroe. For Holmes' reaction to Magnitzsky's death, see Holmes to Lewis Einstein, September 20, 1910, *Holmes–Einstein Letters,* 55. For a discussion of the rumor, see Monagan, *The Grand Panjandrum,* xi.

32. On Lowell's anti-Semitism see Hirsch, supra note 12, at 68.

33. Frankfurter to Holmes, December [no date] 1916, Holmes Papers.

34. Laski first met Holmes in July 1912 when Frankfurter brought him to Beverly Farms. On July 11 Laski wrote a thank you note, saying that "I do not say 'thank you'— not merely because it is inadequate but because from one's master one learns that it is simply duty to receive. You teach our generation how we may hope to live." *Holmes–Laski Letters,* I, 3.

35. Holmes to Pollock, July 12, 1916, *Holmes–Pollock Letters,* I, 238.

36. Holmes to Pollock, February 18, 1917, id., 243–44.

37. For more on this theme, see David A. Hollinger, "The 'Tough-Minded' Justice Holmes, Jewish Intellectuals, and the Making of an American Icon," in Gordon, *Legacy,* 223–28.

38. Lippmann, "To Justice Holmes," 6 *The New Republic* 156 (1916).

39. On *The New Republic* as a "progressive" institution, see Charles Forcey, *The Crossroads of Liberalism* (1961); Christopher Lasch, *The New Radicalism in America* 181–224 (1965).

40. Holmes to Laski, September 7, 1916, *Holmes–Laski Letters,* I, 17.

41. Notable among those writings were those of Roscoe Pound. See, e.g., Pound, "Do We Need a Philosophy of Law?" 5 *Colum. L. Rev.* 339 (1905); Pound, "The Need of a Sociological Jurisprudence," 19 *Green Bag* 607 (1907); Pound, "Mechanical Jurisprudence," 8 *Colum. L. Rev.* 605 (1908); Pound, "Liberty of Contract," 18 *Yale L. J.* 454 (1909). See also Joseph Bingham, "What Is the Law," 11 *Mich. L. Rev.* 1, 109 (1912), and Bingham, "The Nature of Legal Rights and Duties," 12 *Mich. L. Rev.* 1 (1913).

42. Frankfurter to Holmes, July 4, 1913, Holmes Papers.

43. Frankfurter to Holmes, September 6, 1913, id.

44. See Frankfurter's articles, "The Present Approach to Constitutional Decisions on the Bill of Rights," 28 *Harv. L. Rev.* 790 (1915); "The Law and the Law Schools," 1 *A.B.A.J.* 532 (1915); "Hours of Labor and Realism in Constitutional Law," 29 *Harv. L. Rev.* 353 (1916).

45. One could argue that Holmes had been regarded as eminent in England earlier. Oxford gave him an honorary degree in 1909 for his work in legal history, and the 11th edition of the *Encyclopedia Britannica,* in an appendix to the article on Oliver Wendell Holmes, Sr., described him as "one of the greatest jurists." Holmes may not have been pleased that he was still being treated as an "appendix" to his father, but he was delighted to be grouped in the same sentence with Sir Edmund Coke and Lord Mansfield by English author Henry Mitchell Webster in his 1916 novel, *The Real Adventure.* He commented to Pollock, "Is it not fame for a judge to be referred to by the lay gents in that way?" Holmes to Pollock, March 24, 1916, *Holmes–Pollock Letters,* I, 235.

46. 29 *Harv. L. Rev.* 683 (1916).

47. Id., 693.

48. Id., 684.

49. Id.

50. Id., 685.

51. Id., 686–87.

52. 165 U.S. 578 (1897).

53. Frankfurter, "The Constitutional Opinions of Justice Holmes," supra note 46, at 690.

54. Id., 691.

55. Id.

56. *Lochner v. New York,* 198 U.S. 45, 75 (1905).

57. Holmes to Frankfurter, April 13, 1916, Holmes Papers.

58. Frankfurter, "The Constitutional Opinions of Justice Holmes," supra note 46, at 698.

59. See Frankfurter to Marion Denman, March [no date] 1919, Felix Frankfurter Papers, Library of Congress, quoted in Hirsch, supra note 12, at 12, where Frankfurter describes his job, a representative of the American Zionist Organization at the Paris Peace Conference of 1919, as "personalia . . . nursing and mediation."

60. Holmes to Laski, July 30, 1920, *Holmes–Laski Letters* I, 272.

61. Laski to Holmes, July 22, 1916, id., 7.

62. Laski to Holmes, November 27, 1919, id., 223.

63. 250 U.S. 616, 624 (1919).

64. Laski to Holmes, April 2, 1920, *Holmes–Laski Letters* I, 257.

65. Ernest Freund, "Limitation of Hours of Labor and the Federal Supreme Court," 17 *Green Bag* 411, 416 (1905).

66. Frederick Pollock, "The New York Labor Law and the Fourteenth Amendment," 21 *L. Q. Rev.* 211, 212 (1905).

67. Roscoe Pound, "Liberty of Contract," 18 *Yale L. J.* 454, 464 (1909).

68. Edwin Corwin, "The Supreme Court and the Fourteenth Amendment," 7 *Mich. L. Rev.* 643, 669 (1909).

69. Louis Greeley, "The Changing Attitude of the Courts Toward Social Legislation," 5 *Ill. L. Rev.* 222, 227–28 (1910).

70. Not all commentary on the *Lochner* majority opinion was unfavorable. George Wickersham, in an article in the *Harvard Law Review* in 1914, said that "[i]f the views suggested by Mr. Justice Holmes . . . should prevail . . . written constitutions had better be avowedly and formally abolished, as bills of rights would then become mere mockeries." George Wickersham, "The Police Power, A Product of the Rule of Reason," 27 *Harv. L. Rev.* 297, 308 (1914). And *The Nation,* commenting on the decision when it was handed down, described the majority's position as "old fashioned but salutary" in its opposition to the monopolistic tendencies of labor unions. "This Week," 80 *The Nation* 301 (April 20, 1905).

71. 79 *The Outlook* 1017, 1018 (Saturday, April 29, 1905).

72. Theodore Roosevelt, "Judges and Progress," 100 *The Outlook* 40 (January 6, 1912).

73. Editorial, 5 *The New Republic* 132 (December 11, 1915).

74. See Felix Frankfurter, "Hours of Labor and Realism in Constitutional Law," supra note 44, at 370–71.

75. Philip Littell, "Books and Things," 3 *The New Republic* 100 (May 29, 1915).

76. Elizabeth Sergeant, "Oliver Wendell Holmes," 49 *The New Republic* 59, 60, 63–64 (December 8, 1926).

77. James Pollard, "Justice Holmes, Champion of the Common Man," *New York Times,* December 1, 1929, section 4, p. 4.

78. Sergeant, supra note 76, at 59.

79. Felix Frankfurter, "The Constitutional Opinions of Justice Holmes, supra note 46, at 691, 693.

80. Felix Frankfurter, "Twenty Years of Mr. Justice Holmes' Constitutional Opinions," 36 *Harv. L. Rev.* 909, 929 (1923).

81. Karl Llewellyn, "A Realistic Jurisprudence—The Next Step," 30 *Colum. L. Rev.* 431, 454, (1930).

82. Jerome Frank, *Law and the Modern Mind* 253 (1930). Frank also characterized Holmes as "[s]keptical about the inevitable validity of existing rules merely because they exist," and having "an unquenchable zeal for an honest facing of the facts." These two traits were important for the Realists' self-definition of their movement, but not necessarily apt descriptions of Holmes' tendencies as a judge. For more examples of commentators' tendency to see in Holmes intellectual qualities they sought in themselves, see G. Edward White, "The Rise and Fall of Justice Holmes," 39 *U. Chi. L. Rev.* 51 (1971).

83. Holmes to Laski, September 1, 1919, Holmes Papers. The letters from Laski to Holmes between May 30 and October 8, 1919, were unaccountably lost, and thus are not in the Holmes Papers or in the *Holmes–Laski Letters.* The September 1 letter is the earliest recorded evidence of the project, but it indicates that the project had been the subject of discussion by Holmes and Laski over the summer.

84. Holmes to Laski, October 16, 1919, *Holmes–Laski Letters* I, 215.

85. Laski to Holmes, October 17, 1919, id., 216.

86. Holmes to Laski, November 17, 1920, id., 291: "And this week my book is out!" It is not clear what caused the delay. On November 5, 1919, Laski wrote Holmes that "[t]he typing of the book goes merrily forward." Id., 220. On February 19, 1920, Holmes wrote Laski that he had "a letter this p.m. [from the publisher], Harcourt Brace, with specimens. I stick to the original form and think it will be handsome." Id., 244. At the end of March Laski wrote Holmes that he had "corrected half the galley proof of your *Essays,*" and that he had told the publisher that Holmes should see the page proofs. Laski to Holmes, March 31, 1920, id., 257. By May 11 Holmes had seen the proofs, and made corrections; he then sent them to Laski, who acknowledged receipt on May 15. Holmes to Laski, May 11, 1920, id., 261–62; Laski to Holmes, id., 262. There was a slight problem with one of the essays, for which reprint permission had not been secured: Holmes noted it in a May 20 letter and wrote the publisher directly, enclosing a stamp so that they could write Laski. Holmes to Laski, May 20, 1919, id., 264.

On June 4 Holmes wondered whether "the book of my essays &c [is] finished—or has anyone charge of it, if not?" Holmes to Laski, June 4, 1920, id., 266. Laski, who had accepted a position at the London School of Economics and was about to leave America for England, wrote back on June 8 that "[y]our book proceeds rapidly," and that he had "told the publisher that after the 16th [of June, shortly before Laski was sailing for England], he is to send page-proof to you." He also asked Holmes if he wanted "to write a little preface by way of postscript." Laski to Holmes, June 8, 1920, id., 267. Then nothing happened for several months. On September 17 Holmes wrote Laski that the book was "hoped for in October subject to trouble with printers &c." Id., 281. But on October 19 he wrote that "I have heard nothing of my little [book] since the publisher wrote that they hoped to bring it out early in October." Id., 288. Finally, on November 17, 1920, Holmes received the book. Id., 291.

The lesson of the story might appear to be that it is unwise to attempt to produce books through the use of intermediaries, especially when they leave the country. But Laski seems to have been assiduous in forwarding materials to the publisher, and by early June he had nothing further to do with the project. Holmes needed to write a preface, but Holmes was invariably prompt about assignments, and the preface was only two paragraphs. See Holmes, *Collected Legal Papers* iv (1920).

The inexplicable delays seemed to have occurred between June and October 1920 when the page proof was in the publisher's hands and only a preface remained to be supplied, since no index was planned. Holmes seems not to have paid any attention to the book over the summer, since he and Laski corresponded several times without mentioning it. Laski was preoccupied with his return to England and at any rate would have had no further responsibilities in the production process. It is quite possible that in this period the manuscript was left neglected at the publisher's. It would not be the first time in publishing history that such an occurrence had transpired.

87. Holmes to Laski, November 17, 1920, *Holmes–Laski Letters* I, 291.

88. Holmes to Laski, January 31, 1921, id., 307.

89. Holmes to Laski, February 25, 1921, id., 315.

90. *Collected Legal Papers*, iv.

91. Roscoe Pound, "Judge Holmes' Contributions to the Science of Law," 34 *Harv. L. Rev.* 449 (1921).

92. Id., 450.

93. Walter Cook, Book Review, 30 *Yale L. J.* 775 (1921).

94. Id., 775–76.

95. Id., 775.

96. Id., 776.

97. See Laura Kalman, *Legal Realism at Yale, 1927–1960* 1–44 (1986).

98. James H. Tufts, "The Legal and Social Philosophy of Mr. Justice Holmes," 7 *A.B.A.J.* 359 (1921).

99. O. K. McMurray, Book Review, 10 *Calif. L. Rev.* 266, 267 (1921).

100. Albert Kocourek, Book Review, 16 *Ill. L. Rev.* 156 (1921). In reading the review Holmes might have noted that the same issue in which Kocourek lavished such praise on him contained a notice by John Wigmore of the death of Melville Bigelow, one of Holmes' contemporaries in the days in which he, Henry Adams, and others were pursuing work in legal history. See Editorial Note, "Melville Madison Bigelow," 16 *Ill. L. Rev.* at 120.

101. Charles E. Carpenter, "Oliver Wendell Holmes, Jurist," 8 *Ore. L. Rev.* 269, 270 (1929).

102. Frankfurter used this statement in a memorandum he wrote on July 5, 1913, summarizing the pros and cons of accepting an offer to teach at Harvard Law School. The memorandum is set forth in Phillips, supra note 12, at 80–84; the quoted sentence appears at 81.

103. Holmes to Pollock, September 1, 1910, *Holmes–Pollock Letters* I, 167.

104. Holmes quoted these remarks of his in a December 20, 1924, letter to Frankfurter, Holmes Papers. There is also an undated memorandum, in Nina Gray's hand, of a comment Holmes made to her, probably in the summer of 1924, when he returned from Washington to Boston and Beverly Farms. The comment was, "Mr. President: For five minutes you make the dream of a lifetime seem true. But one who is on the firing line cannot dream long. I hope that the short time that is left will not dim the honor of today." Being closer to the event, this version may be a more accurate statement of what Holmes said, but one has to rely on Nina Gray's transcription. See Zobel, "What a Medley of a Man!" catalogue, 29.

105. Holmes to Frankfurter, March 9, 1915, Holmes Papers.

106. Holmes to Frankfurter, September 25, 1919, id.

107. Holmes to Frankfurter, March 8, 1912, id.

108. Holmes to Frankfurter, February 17, 1920, id.

109. Holmes to Frankfurter, August 30, 1921, id.

110. Holmes to Frankfurter, December 8, 1922, id.

111. The notice, which was unsigned, described Holmes as "the symbol at once of the promise and the fulfillment of the American judiciary," and called his dissenting opinions "dissents that shape history and record prophecy." "Mr. Justice Holmes," 33 *The New Republic* 84 (December 20, 1922).

112. Holmes to Frankfurter, December 22, 1922, Holmes Papers.

113. For earlier evidence of this theme, see "Twenty Years in Retrospect," Holmes' December 3, 1902, address to the Middlesex Bar Association, in *Occasional Speeches,* 154. "At the moment," Holmes said in the speech, "the work of twenty years comes up for judgment, and that . . . is not without its sadness. You are the judges. . . . " Id., 155.

114. Holmes to Frankfurter, September 20, 1923, Holmes Papers.

115. Holmes to Frankfurter, December 20, 1927, id.

116. In its 1922 editorial *The New Republic* had described Holmes as "compounded of humility and humor." "Mr. Justice Holmes," supra note 111, at 84. The phrase suggests that the author of the editorial may have been Felix Frankfurter.

117. Yosal Rogat, a discerning critic of Holmes, noted this distinction in an essay on Holmes in 1964. In commenting on another Frankfurter encomium to Holmes, in which Frankfurter described Holmes as exhibiting "tolerance and humility in passing judgment on the experience and beliefs expressed by those entrusted with a duty of legislating," Rogat suggested that "if humility were actually a 'decisive factor in constitutional adjudication,' Holmes would tie for last with General DeGaulle." Yosal Rogat, "Mr. Justice Holmes—The Judge as Spectator," 31 *U. Chi. L. Rev.* 213, 253 (1964), quoting Frankfurter's essay on Holmes in the *Dictionary of American Biography* 423 (1st Supp., 1944).

118. John M. Zane, "German Legal Philosophy," 16 *Mich. L. Rev.* 287 (1918); John M. Zane, "A Legal Heresy," 13 *Ill. L. Rev.* 431 (1919). The first of the articles dealt with Holmes' view of judicial decisionmaking, the second with Holmes' view of sovereignty. In the second article Zane said that Holmes had a "bad philosophy of law," exemplified by his decision in *Kawanankoa v. Polyblank,* 205 U.S. 349 (1906), where Holmes had said that "[a] sovereign is exempt from suit, not because of any formal conception or obsolete theory, but on the logical and practical ground that there can be

no legal right as against the authority that makes the law on which the right depends,''
id. at 353. Zane, 13 *Ill. L. Rev.* 441. Holmes translated Zane's comment to mean that
anyone who subscribed to his view of sovereignty ''couldn't hope to be a lawyer.''
Holmes to Laski, January 3, 1926, *Holmes–Laski Letters* II, 817.

119. Holmes to Pollock, January 24, 1919, *Holmes–Pollock Letters* II, 3.

120. Laski to Holmes, January 29, 1919, *Holmes–Laski Letters* I, 181.

121. Holmes to Laski, February 1, 1919, id., 183.

122. John Wigmore, ''*Abrams v. United States:* Freedom of Speech and Freedom of
Thuggery in War-time and Peace-time,'' 14 *Ill. L. Rev.* 539 (1920).

123. Holmes to Pollock, April 25, 1920, *Holmes–Pollock Letters* II, 42.

124. Holmes to Laski, October 13, 1926, *Holmes–Laski Letters* II, 886.

125. Laski to Holmes, October 23, 1926, id., 888.

126. Holmes to Laski, November 1, 1926, id., 892.

127. Holmes to Laski, November 23, 1927, id., 998–99.

128. Holmes to Laski, November 29, 1927, id., 999.

129. Laski to Holmes, December 3, 1927, id., 1002.

130. Holmes to Laski, December 14, 1927, id., 1003.

131. Charles Hough, ''Admiralty Jurisdiction—Of Late Years,'' 37 *Harv. L. Rev.*
529 (1924).

132. 195 U.S. 361 (1904)

133. Hough, supra note 131, at 533.

134. Id., 535–36.

135. Id., 537.

136. 244 U.S. 205, 220–21 (1917).

137. Id. at 221.

138. Hough, supra note 131, at 538.

139. 257 U.S. 419 (1922).

140. Hough, supra note 131, at 542–43, quoting Holmes, 257 U.S. at 433.

141. 257 U.S. at 433, 432.

142. Hough, supra note 131 at 543, 544.

143. Holmes to Laski, March 16, 1924, *Holmes–Laski Letters* I, 601.

144. Holmes to Pollock, May 5, 1924, *Holmes–Pollock Letters* II, 135.

145. Holmes to Laski, April 17, 1928, *Holmes–Laski Letters* II, 1046.

146. Holmes to Pollock, October 1, 1926, *Holmes–Pollock Letters* II, 189.

147. Holmes to Laski, October 3, 1926, *Holmes–Laski Letters* II, 878.

148. Holmes to Sheehan, August 14, 1910, *Holmes–Sheehan Correspondence,* 32.

149. Holmes to Nina Gray, December 2, 1910, Holmes Papers.

CHAPTER ELEVEN: *The Supreme Court, 1917–1931:*
The ''Progressive'' Judge

1. *Harv. L. Rev.* 17 (1893). For a contemporary discussion of Thayer's essay, see
Symposium, 88 *Nw. U. L. Rev.* (Fall, 1993).

2. John Chipman Gray, *The Nature and Sources of Law* 116 (1909).

3. Id., 116–117.

4. See Frankfurter in Phillips, *Felix Frankfurter Reminisces,* 347, describing Thayer's
essay as ''the great guide for judges.''

5. See G. Edward White, *The Marshall Court and Cultural Change* 111–122 (1988).

6. 16 Pet. 1 (1842).

7. *Southern Pacific v. Jensen,* 244 U.S. 205, 222 (1917).

8. 258 U.S. 268 (1922).

9. See Peter Karsten, "Explaining the Fight Over the Attractive Nuisance Doctrine," 10 *Law and Hist. Rev.* 45 (1992).

10. *Chenery v. Fitchburg R. R. Co.,* 160 Mass. 211 (1893), following *Daniels v. Railroad Co.,* 154 Mass. 349 (1891), a decision in which Holmes participated.

11. *Railroad Co. v. Stout,* 17 Wall. 657 (1873); *Union Pacific Ry. Co. v. McDonald,* 152 U.S. 262 (1893).

12. 258 U.S. 268, 275 (1922).

13. Id. at 275, 276.

14. Id. at 278.

15. Id. at 279.

16. Id. at 276.

17. Holmes to Pollock, March 29, 1922, *Holmes–Pollock Letters* II, 92.

18. 258 U.S. at 275.

19. Holmes, *The Common Law,* 126, 127, 128.

20. Holmes was in his late sixties when automobiles first became available as a mode of transportation, and the Holmeses did not acquire an automobile until 1925, when Holmes was eighty-four. See Monagan, *The Grand Panjandrum,* 39, indicating that the first accounts by secretaries of Holmes' taking car rides occurred in 1926.

21. 275 U.S. 66 (1927).

22. Id. at 67–68.

23. Id. at 69–70.

24. Id. at 70.

25. Id.

26. Id.

27. Holmes, *The Common Law,* 126.

28. 275 U.S. at 70.

29. See, e.g., Note, 43 *Harv. L. Rev.* 126 (1930); *New York Times,* November 1, 1927; February 25, 1928.

30. Pollock to Holmes, January 12, 1928, *Holmes–Pollock Letters* II, 211.

31. 292 U.S. 98, 106 (1934).

32. Id.

33. Holmes to Pollock, January 7, 1910, *Holmes–Pollock Letters* I, 157, describing *Kuhn v. Fairmont Coal Co.,* 215 U.S. 349 (1910), where Holmes dissented, id. at 370.

34. Holmes had read *The Nature and Sources of Law* shortly after it appeared in 1909. See Holmes' "Blackbook" (list of readings), 1909, Holmes Papers.

35. Holmes to Pollock, supra note 33.

36. Id., 158.

37. 244 U.S. 205 (1917).

38. Id. at 222.

39. Holmes to Laski, January 29, 1926, *Holmes–Laski Letters* II, 822–23.

40. 276 U.S. 518 (1928).

41. Id. at 528, 529–30.

42. Id. at 532–33.

43. Id. at 533.

44. Id.

45. Id. at 534.

46. Id.

47. Id. at 535.

48. Id.

49. Holmes to Pollock, February 17, 1928, *Holmes–Pollock Letters* II, 215.

50. 276 U.S. at 535. Holmes called the article "an examination of the original document by a most competent hand."

51. Id.

52. 304 U.S. 64 (1938).

53. Id. at 79. Brandeis quoted from Holmes' dissent in *Taxicab.*

54. It is also noteworthy that all the other justices on the Court in 1927, including Brandeis and Stone, endorsed Holmes' opinion for the Court in *Goodman.* No doubt some of that group relished the idea of having very few grade crossing cases come up to the Supreme Court in the future, as would be the case after Holmes' "stop, look, and listen" formula became the standard for grade crossing accidents in the federal courts.

55. See, e.g., Laski to Holmes, October 5, 1920, *Holmes–Laski Letters* I, 286 *(Jensen);* Laski to Holmes, April 29, 1928, id., II, 1050 *(Taxicab).*

56. In 1924 Frankfurter wrote an anonymous editorial in the *New Republic* arguing that the Due Process Clauses of the Fifth and Fourteenth Amendments, given their invocation by a majority of the Court as a barrier against "progressive" legislation, "ought to go." [Felix Frankfurter], "The Red Terror of Judicial Reform," *The New Republic,* October 1, 1924, in Philip H. Kurland, ed., *Felix Frankfurter on the Supreme Court: Extrajudicial Essays on the Court and the Constitution* 167 (1970). Hereafter cited as Kurland, *Frankfurter on the Supreme Court.*

57. [Holmes], "The Gas Stokers Strike," 7 *Am. L. Rev.* 582 (1873).

58. Id., 583–84.

59. None of Malthus' works are listed in Holmes' early readings. In an August 30, 1914 letter to Pollock he spoke of reading Malthus, and in an October 16, 1916 letter to Pollock he described that experience as "epoch-making." *Holmes–Pollock Letters* I, 219, 238. A September 2, 1914, letter to Lewis Einstein conveys a similar impression that Holmes was reading Malthus for the first time. *Holmes–Einstein Letters,* 99.

60. It is not clear where Holmes derived his views on the importance and extent of lower-class consumption. Similar views were held by some other nineteenth-century "mugwumps." In a 1911 letter to the economist Frank Taussig, Holmes stated that "the crowd" consumed over 98 percent of what society produced. Holmes to Taussig, July 18, 1911, Holmes Papers. On the views of Holmes' contemporaries, see John W. Cawelti, *Apostles of the Self Made Man* (1965). For a good general discussion of Holmes' views on political economy, see Stephen Diamond, "Citizenship, Civilization, and Coercion," in Gordon, *Legacy,* 115.

61. 247 U.S. 251 (1918).

62. Id. at 261.

63. *Federal Baseball Club of Baltimore, Inc. v. National League of Professional Baseball Clubs,* 259 U.S. 200 (1922).

64. 156 U.S. 1 (1895).
65. 247 U.S. at 272.
66. 196 U.S. at 398.
67. 247 U.S. at 278.
68. Id. at 279–80.
69. Id. at 281.
70. Id.
71. Holmes to Pollock, June 14, 1918, *Holmes–Pollock Letters* I, 267.
72. *United States v. Darby,* 312 U.S. 100 (1941), where the Court declared that "[t]he power of Congress over interstate commerce is not confined to the regulation of commerce among the states. It extends to those activities intrastate which so affect interstate commerce or the exercise of the power of Congress over it as to make regulation of them appropriate means to the attainment of a legitimate end." Id., 118.
73. *Adkins v. Children's Hospital,* 261 U.S. 525, 541 (1923).
74. *Muller v. Oregon,* 208 U.S. 412 (1908); *Bunting v. Oregon,* 243 U.S. 246 (1917).
75. *Stettler v. O'Hara,* 243 U.S. 269 (1917).
76. 261 U.S. at 525 (1923).
77. 261 U.S. at 554.
78. Id. at 553.
79. Id. at 559.
80. Id. at 567–68.
81. Id. at 568.
82. Id.
83. Id. at 569–70.
84. Id. at 570–71.
85. For a summary of critical articles by both legal and lay commentators, see National Consumers' League, *The Supreme Court and Minimum Wage Legislation* (1925).
86. Two years after *Adkins* the Court summarily affirmed a lower federal court's decision that a minimum wage statute enacted by the Arizona legislature was unconstitutional. Holmes concurred on the ground that *Adkins* was controlling *Murphy v. Sardell,* 269 U.S. 530 (1925).
87. [Frankfurter], "The Red Terror of Judicial Reform," supra note 56.
88. Frankfurter to Learned Hand, April 11, 1923, Felix Frankfurter Papers, Library of Congress, quoted in Parrish, *Felix Frankfurter and His Times,* 165.
89. Laski to Holmes, April 13, 1923, *Holmes–Laski Letters* I, 493. Holmes wrote Laski back, indicating that he had sent him copies of the opinions, and said that "I think that what I said was plain common sense. It was intended . . . to dethrone Liberty of Contract from its ascendancy in the Liberty business." Holmes to Laski, April 14, 1923, id., 495.
90. In *Morehead v. Tipaldo,* 298 U.S. 587 (1936), a 5–4 majority of the Court declared a New York minimum wage statute unconstitutional, following *Adkins,* but the next year, in *West Coast Hotel v. Parrish,* 300 U.S. 379 (1937), the Court sustained an almost identical minimum wage law from Washington and expressly overruled *Adkins.*
91. 257 U.S. 312 (1921).
92. Holmes to Laski, January 15, 1922, *Holmes–Laski Letters* I, 398.

93. Laski to Holmes, January 22, 1922, id., 401.

94. 257 U.S. at 342–43.

95. Id. at 343.

96. Id. at 344.

97. Id.

98. [Frankfurter], "The Same Mr. Taft," *The New Republic,* January 18, 1922, in Kurland, *Frankfurter on the Supreme Court,* 55–56.

99. 273 U.S. 418 (1927).

100. Id. at 429.

101. Id. at 439–40.

102. 261 U.S. at 569.

103. 273 U.S. at 446.

104. Frankfurter to Holmes, March 19, 1927, Holmes Papers.

105. 260 U.S. 293 (1922).

106. Id. at 412.

107. Id. at 413.

108. Id. at 415.

109. Id.

110. The Marshall Court had held the Fifth Amendment inapplicable to the states in *Barron v. Mayor of Baltimore,* 7 Pet. 243 (1833), and no decisions had yet "incorporated" provisions of the Bill of Rights against the states in the Fourteenth Amendment's Due Process Clause. See the discussion in Chapter Twelve.

111. Holmes to Laski, January 13, 1923, *Holmes–Laski Letters* I, 473.

112. 33 *The New Republic* 136 (January 3, 1923). Holmes identified Acheson as the author, spelling his name wrong, in the January 13, 1923, letter to Laski, supra note 111. Acheson had been secretary to Brandeis for the 1919–20 Term.

113. Holmes to Laski, supra note 111.

114. See Pollock to Holmes, February 5, 1923, *Holmes–Pollock Letters* II, 111.

115. Holmes to Pollock, December 31, 1922, *Holmes–Pollock Letters* II, 109.

116. *Meyer v. Nebraska,* 262 U.S. 390 (1923).

117. *Bartels v. Iowa, Bohning v. Ohio, Pohl v. Ohio,* 262 U.S. 404 (1923).

118. 274 U.S. 200 (1927).

119. Novick, *Honorable Justice,* 477.

120. 274 U.S. at 206.

121. Id. at 201–2.

122. Taft to Holmes, April 23, 1927, Holmes Papers.

123. 274 U.S. at 206–7.

124. Id. at 207.

125. Yosal Rogat, in his analysis of Holmes' treatment of the equal protection issue in *Buck v. Bell,* suggested the following:

Holmes began with the idea that mental deficiency and antisocial traits were inherited with a directness close to that producing the color of sweet peas. All those who were "inadequate" must therefore be prevented from "continuing their kind." At this point in his thinking he was already committed to the belief that they should all be either confined or sterilized. However, he seemed to believe that there were so many within these categories that they could not, practically

speaking, all be locked up. . . . He therefore envisioned a sequence of incarceration, sterilization, release, and creation of new asylum vacancies.
Yosal Rogat, "Mr. Justice Holmes; A Dissenting Opinion," 15 Stan. L. Rev. 3, 254, 290 (1963).

126. *Skinner v. Oklahoma,* 316 U.S. 535 (1942), invalidated on equal protection grounds an Oklahoma statute providing for compulsory sterilization of felons. The statute failed to distinguish between persons convicted of felonies, which included successive petty misdemeanors, and other crimes, and as such was highly vulnerable to an equal protection attack. Moreover, the statute assumed that "criminal tendencies" were inheritable, a proposition that had not been substantiated empirically, whereas there was some scientific evidence that certain kinds of mental disorders were genetic in origin.

127. There is also evidence that *Buck v. Bell* was a test case, arranged to legitimate the sterilization statute passed by the Virginia legislature, which was seen as a model for other states. See Paul Lombardo, "Three Generations: No Imbeciles: New Light on *Buck v. Bell,*" 60 *N.Y.U. L. Rev.* 30 (1985).

128. Butler, the only Catholic on the Court at the time, may have objected to compulsory sterilization on religious grounds.

129. See Lombardo, supra note 127, at 32–33; Mary Dudziak, "Oliver Wendell Holmes as a Eugenic Reformer," 71 *Iowa L. Rev.* 833, 843–48 (1986).

130. Holmes to Pollock, February 1, 1920, *Holmes–Pollock Letters* II, 36.

131. Holmes to Pollock, April 25, 1920, id., 41.

132. Holmes to Laski, August 12, 1923, *Holmes–Laski Letters* I, 523.

133. Holmes to Laski, July 17, 1925, id., 761.

134. Holmes to Einstein, May 19, 1927, *Holmes–Einstein Letters,* 267.

135. Holmes to Laski, May 12, 1927, *Holmes–Laski Letters* II, 942. In his 1915 article, "Ideals and Doubts," 10 *Ill. L. Rev.* 1 (1915), reprinted in *Collected Legal Papers,* 303, Holmes had said that "I believe that the wholesale social regeneration which so many now seem to expect . . . cannot be affected appreciably by tinkering with the institution of property, but only by taking in hand life and trying to build a race. That would be my starting point for an ideal in law." Id., 306. And in 1923, in his last scholarly contribution, an introduction to John Wigmore's *The Rational Basis of Legal Institutions,* Holmes said that "I can understand . . . legislation that aims . . . to improve the quality rather than increase the quantity of the population. I can understand saying, whatever the cost, so far as may be, we will keep certain strains out of our blood." Quoted in Lerner, *The Mind and Faith of Justice Holmes,* 400–01.

136. The most representative revisionist essay on Holmes' image as a civil libertarian is that of Rogat, supra note 125. Rogat has a lengthy and impassioned analysis of *Buck v. Bell.* Id., 282–90. On changes in Holmes' reputation over time see White, "The Rise and Fall of Justice Holmes."

CHAPTER TWELVE: *The Supreme Court, 1917–1931: Free Speech*

1. 250 U.S. 616, 624 (1919).

2. Holmes to Harold Laski, July 7, 1918, *Holmes–Laski Letters* I, 161.

3. For a particularly clear statement of this apparent contradiction, see H. L. Pohlman, *Justice Oliver Wendell Holmes: Free Speech and the Living Constitution* (1991).

4. 236 U.S. 273 (1915). See the discussion in Chapter Nine.

5. 247 U.S. 402 (1918).

6. Id. at 418.

7. Id. at 419.

8. Id. at 423.

9. 248 U.S. 593 (1918).

10. Memorandum, December 3, 1918, Holmes Papers.

11. See Sheldon Novick, "Justice Holmes and the Art of Biography," 33 *Wm. & Mary L. Rev.* 1219, 1230 (1992).

12. Novick, supra note 11, may have been misled by a March 1921 letter Holmes wrote to Nina Gray in which, in the course of discussing the question of Brandeis' influence on him, he said that "on free speech my best ebullition was independent, though the Gov't prevented my opinion appearing by confessing error." He added that "I had turned that way long before [Brandeis] was on the bench." Novick may have (correctly) taken the letter to refer to *Baltzer,* but Holmes' credibility is impaired by his comment about "turning" on free speech issues long before Brandeis joined the Court. Brandeis became a Supreme Court Justice in 1916, one year after *Fox v. Washington* and two years before *Toledo Newspaper* and the *Baltzer* memorandum.

13. Novick, supra note 11, finds the *Baltzer* memorandum to be additional support for his previous claim that Holmes did not change his position on speech issues from 1918 on. Novick first expressed that view in *Honorable Justice,* 473–74. This chapter suggests Novick's analysis has some considerable difficulties. See also G. Edward White, "Justice Holmes and the Modernization of Free Speech Jurisprudence: The Human Dimension," 80 *Calif. L. Rev.* 391 (1992).

14. Espionage Act of 1917, ch. 30, 40 Stat. 217 (1917). The overwhelming number of prosecutions under the Espionage Act were brought under title I, section 3 of that Act, which provided that

> Whoever, when the United States is at war, shall willfully make or convey false reports or false statements with intent to interfere with the operation or success of the military or naval forces of the United States or to promote the success of its enemies and whoever, when the United States is at war, shall willfully cause or attempt to cause insubordination, disloyalty, mutiny, or refusal of duty, in the military or naval forces of the United States, or shall willfully obstruct the recruiting or enlistment service of the United States, to the injury of the service of the United States, shall be punished by a fine of not more than $10,000 or imprisonment for not more than twenty years, or both.

Id. ch. 30, tit. 1, § 3, 40 Stat. at 217.

15. 249 U.S. 47 (1919).

16. 249 U.S. 204 (1919).

17. 249 U.S. 211 (1919).

18. The Court dismissed *Sugarman v. United States,* 249 U.S. 182 (1919), for want of jurisdiction. In a unanimous opinion by Brandeis, the Court held that there had been no "substantial" constitutional issue properly raised in the case. Id. at 185. *Sugarman* dealt with a Socialist party member who had been convicted for describing World War I as a capitalist conspiracy in which workers should not participate. Id. at 183. The only basis for a constitutional issue in the case was purportedly erroneous instructions on the

First Amendment. See id. at 185. On review, however, the Court found that the instructions were adequate.

19. For discussions of this alternative strand of free speech commentary, see Mark A. Graber, *Transforming Free Speech: The Ambiguous Legacy of Civil Libertarianism* 17–65 (1991), hereafter Graber, *Transforming Free Speech;* David M. Rabban, "The First Amendment in its Forgotten Years," 90 *Yale L. J.* 514, 559–79 (1981), hereafter Rabban, "First Amendment"; David M. Rabban, "The Free Speech League, The ACLU and Changing Conceptions of Free Speech in American History," 45 *Stan. L. Rev.* 47 (1992), hereafter "Free Speech League."

20. Examples were Ernst Freund, Henry Schofield, and Gilbert Roe. See Graber, *Transforming Free Speech,* 54–65; Rabban, "First Amendment," 560–75; Rabban, "Free Speech League," 78–80.

21. Some of the commentators were Ezra Haywood, P.M. Bennett, Edward Bond Foote, Moses Harman, Edwin Cox Walker, and Theodore Schroeder. See Graber, *Transforming Free Speech,* 17–44; Rabban, "First Amendment," 560, 563–64; Rabban, "Free Speech League," 59–77.

22. See, e.g., John W. Burgess, *Political Science and Comparative Constitutional Law* (1890); Thomas M. Cooley, *A Treatise on the Constitutional Limitations Which Rest Upon the Legislative Power of the States of the American Union* (1868); Christopher G. Tiedeman, *A Treatise on the Limitations of Police Power in the United States* (1886).

23. Espionage Act of 1917, 40 Stat. 217 (1919), supra note 14.

24. Sedition Act of 1918, 40 Stat. 553 (1919).

25. See Paul L. Murphy, *The Meaning of Freedom of Speech* 16–17 (1972); Paul L. Murphy, *World War I and the Origin of Civil Liberties in the United States* 51 (1979).

26. 158 U.S. 564 (1895).

27. Id. at 574–75.

28. 167 U.S. 43 (1897).

29. See the discussion of *Commonwealth v. Davis* in Chapter Eight.

30. 167 U.S. at 46–48.

31. Cooley and Tiedeman directly challenged that view. See Cooley, *Constitutional Limitations,* supra note 22, at 421; Tiedeman, *Police Power,* supra note 22, at 191–92.

32. See Cooley, *Constitutional Limitations,* supra note 22, at 428; Tiedeman, *Police Power,* supra note 22, at 192. See also Thomas M. Cooley, *The General Principles of Constitutional Law in the United States of America* 277–78 (1880), arguing that government could intervene to suppress speech threatening "the abolition of republican institutions."

33. The defendants in *Patterson* and *Fox* arguably threatened the existence of "republican institutions" by encouraging disrespect for the law or its officials. See the discussion in Chapter Nine.

34. The "liberty of contract" doctrine was criticized during the first decade of the twentieth century for being unresponsive to changing social and economic conditions. See, e.g., Roscoe Pound, "Liberty of Contract," 18 *Yale L.J.* 454, 464 (1909). See also White, *Patterns,* 99, 102–07.

35. See Theodore Schroeder, *Free Speech for Radicals* 13, 94 (enlarged ed., 1916).

36. See, e.g., Ernst Freund, *The Police Power: Public Policy and Constitutional Rights* 539 (1904).

37. See Graber, *Transforming Free Speech,* 75–86, discussing the belief of many progressives that "preserving social community under modern conditions required an individual conformity inconsistent with broad rights of political dissent." Id., 76.

38. See, e.g., Roscoe Pound, "Interests of Personality," 28 *Harv. L. Rev.* 445, 453 (1915); Henry Schofield, "Freedom of the Press in the United States," 9 *Am. Soc. Soc'y: Papers & Proc.* 67 (1914).

39. See David M. Rabban, "The Emergence of Modern First Amendment Doctrine" 40 *U. Chi. L. Rev.* 1205, 1255–56 (1983). Hereafter Rabban, "Emergence."

40. *Schenck,* 249 U.S. at 49–50.

41. Id. at 50–51.

42. Id. at 51.

43. Id. at 52.

44. Id.

45. Id.

46. Id. at 51–52.

47. Id. at 52.

48. Id.

49. This view had, of course, been first promulgated by Holmes in *The Common Law.* See Holmes, *The Common Law* 65–66. See also the discussion in Chapters Five and Eight.

50. 170 Mass. 18 (1897).

51. 177 Mass. 267 (1901).

52. See *Peaslee,* 177 Mass. at 268; *Kennedy,* 170 Mass. at 19–20. See the discussion in Chapter Eight.

53. 196 U.S. 375 (1905).

54. Id. at 402. See the discussion in Chapter Nine.

55. Letter from Holmes to Laski, July 7, 1918, *Holmes–Laski Letters* I, 161.

56. *Schenck,* 249 U.S. at 50.

57. See *Debs,* 249 U.S. at 214–15; *Frohwerk,* 249 U.S. at 208.

58. See *Debs,* 249 U.S. at 213.

59. *Frohwerk,* 249 U.S. at 206–07.

60. Id. at 208.

61. Id. at 209.

62. Id. at 206.

63. Id. at 208.

64. *Debs,* 249 U.S. at 212.

65. Id.

66. Id. at 213.

67. Id.

68. Id.

69. Id. at 214.

70. Id. at 215.

71. Id. at 214–15.

72. Id. at 215.

73. Id. at 216.

74. *New York Times,* May 1, 1919; see the discussion in Richard Polenberg, *Fighting*

Faiths: The Abrams Case, the Supreme Court, and Free Speech 162–63 (1987). Hereafter Polenberg, *Fighting Faiths*.

75. Holmes to Laski, May 1, 1919, *Holmes–Laski Letters* I, 199.

76. Holmes to Pollock, October 26, 1919, *Holmes–Pollock Letters* II, 29.

77. See William E. Leuchtenberg, *The Perils of Prosperity 1914–32* 69, 73–76 (1958); Robert K. Murray, *Red Scare: A Study in National History, 1919–1920* 92–94, 121–22 (1955). Hereinafter cited as Murray, *Red Scare*.

78. See Murray, *Red Scare,* 122–65.

79. See David W. Noble, "The New Republic and the Idea of Progress, 1914–1920," 38 *Miss. Valley Hist. Rev.* 387, 397, 400 (1951). On the role of *The New Republic* as an organ of progressive intellectuals, see Charles Forcey, *The Crossroads of Liberalism* (1961) and Christopher Lasch, *The New Radicalism in America* 181–224 (1965).

80. See, e.g., Laski to Holmes, July 19, 1916, *Holmes–Laski Letters* I, 5 ("Please don't fail to read Phil Littell in this week's *New Republic,"); Holmes to Frankfurter, Jan. 28, 1916, Holmes Papers ("The New Republic is on my table but I am [behind and] hav[e] been frightfully busy. I note your recommendations.").

81. Ernst Freund, "The *Debs* Case and Freedom of Speech," *The New Republic,* May 3, 1919, 13, 14.

82. Id., 13.

83. Id., 14. It is interesting that Holmes' posture on jury findings in free speech cases ran directly counter to what he had endorsed in *The Common Law* and in the *Goodman* case. See the discussions in Chapters Five and Eleven.

84. Id.

85. Holmes to Pollock, April 5, 1919, *Holmes–Pollock Letters* II, 7.

86. Id.

87. Holmes to Pollock, April 27, 1919, id., 11.

88. Holmes to Laski, March 16, 1919, *Holmes–Laski Letters* I, 190.

89. Laski to Holmes, March 18, 1919, id., 191.

90. Id.

91. Editorial Note, *New Republic,* April 19, 1919, 362.

92. Holmes to Laski, April 20, 1919, *Holmes–Laski Letters* I, 197.

93. Laski to Holmes, May 11, 1919, id., 201–02.

94. Holmes to Laski, May 13, 1919, id., 202.

95. Holmes to Herbert Croly, May 12, 1919, id., 203–04. Emphasis in original.

96. See Freund, supra note 81, at 15.

97. This view was not entirely consistent with what he expressed to Pollock, supra note 87, and to Wigmore. He told Wigmore that the jury's finding in *Debs* was correct. See Holmes to John P. Wigmore, June 7, 1919, Holmes Papers.

98. See Gerald Gunther, "Learned Hand and the Origin of Modern First Amendment Doctrine, Some Fragments of History," 27 *Stan. L. Rev.* 719, 732 (1975). Hereafter Gunther, "Learned Hand." Learned Hand became a judge on the U.S. Court of Appeals for the Second Circuit in 1923, and remained there until 1961.

99. 244 F. 535 (S.D.N.Y. 1917).

100. Id. at 538–39.

101. Id. at 543.

102. Id. at 540.

103. Id. at 542.

104. See *Masses Publishing Co. v. Patten,* 246 F. 24 (2d Cir. 1917). Hand himself intimated in correspondence to Holmes that no other court had endorsed his approach. Hand to Holmes, March 7, 1919, Holmes Papers, quoted in Gunther, "Learned Hand," 758.

105. Hand to Holmes, June 22, 1918, Holmes Papers. Quotations from this and subsequent letters from Learned Hand to Holmes are reproduced by permission of Gerald Gunther and Jonathan Hand Churchill.

106. Id.

107. Holmes to Hand, June 24, 1918, Holmes Papers.

108. Id.

109. Holmes to Hand, February 25, 1919, Holmes Papers.

110. Id.

111. Hand to Holmes, March 7, 1919, Holmes Papers.

112. Id.

113. Id.

114. Id.

115. Id.

116. Id. Hand might also have pointed out that an inquiry into "motive" as part of the "bad-tendency" or "clear and present danger" tests was inconsistent with Holmes' general disdain for subjective tests or standards in the law.

117. Gunther, "Learned Hand," 741.

118. Holmes to Hand, April 3, 1919, Holmes Papers.

119. Id.

120. Id.

121. Gunther, "Learned Hand," 736, quoting letter from Learned Hand to Ernst Freund, May 7, 1919.

122. Id.

123. 250 U.S. 616, 624–31.

124. Holmes to Pollock, December 14, 1919, *Holmes–Pollock Letters* II, 32. Holmes wrote similar letters to Nina Gray and Albert Beveridge at the same time. See Holmes to Nina Gray, December 10, 1919, Holmes Papers; Holmes to Albert Beveridge, December 8, 1919, Holmes Papers.

125. Holmes' "Blackbook" for 1919 (p. 124) lists a number of titles that were relevant to an exploration of free speech issues. As Richard Polenberg and Anthony Lewis have pointed out, Holmes' reading for the spring, summer and early fall of 1919 can fairly be seen as evidence "that Holmes spent much of that [time] thinking the problem of free speech through again." Anthony Lewis, *Make No Law: The Sullivan Case and the First Amendment* 81 (1991); see also Polenberg, *Fighting Faiths,* 224–27. Included in Holmes' readings for 1919 were eight books that bore directly or indirectly on the history or philosophy of free speech: John Stewart Mill's *On Liberty;* James Ford Rhodes' *History of the Civil War* (1917), which denounced Lincoln's "arbitrary interference with the freedom of the press in [some Southern] States" (p. 68); Laski's *Authority in the Modern State* (1919), which asserted that "no mind is in truth free, once a penalty is attached to thought" (p. 55); Walter Lippman's *The Political Scene,* representing the current *"New Republic"* view on contested social issues; Charles H. Mc-

Ilwain's *Introduction to the Political Works of James I* (1918), sent to him by Laski [see *Holmes–Laski Letters* I, 199]; Graham Wallas' *The Life of Francis Place* (1918), a biography of an early nineteenth-century English reformer who opposed government taxation of newspapers; Locke's *Essays on Government,* which Holmes had not previously read (see *Holmes–Pollock Letters* II, 22); and E. S. P. Haynes' *The Decline of Liberty in England.* The last book, which seemed to Holmes "to succeed in being obscure in matters that had no obscurity in them," Holmes to Pollock, September 19, 1919, *Holmes–Pollock Letters* II, 25, nonetheless precipitated an interesting reaction from him. See text at note 153.

126. Chafee made this argument, in identical language, in two articles. See Zechariah Chafee, "Freedom of Speech in War Time," 32 *Harv. L. Rev.* 932, 956–57 (1919); Chafee, "Freedom of Speech," *The New Republic,* November 16, 1918, 66–67. Hereafter, respectively, Chafee, "Speech in War Time,"; Chafee, "Freedom of Speech."

127. See Fred D. Ragan, "Justice Oliver Wendell Holmes, Jr., Zechariah Chafee, Jr., and the Clear and Present Danger Test for Free Speech: The First Year, 1919, 58 *J. Am. Hist.* 24, 43 (1971), citing letter from Laski to Chafee, July 23, 1919, Zechariah Chafee, Jr., Papers, Harvard Law School Library. Hereafter cited as Ragan, "Holmes and Chafee."

128. Ragan, "Holmes and Chafee," 43. The article Laski gave to Holmes was Chafee, "Speech in War Time," supra note 126.

129. Chafee, "Speech in War Time," 955–59.

130. Id., 934, 957, 973.

131. See Ragan, "Holmes and Chafee," 43, quoting Laski to Chafee, July 23, 1919, Zechariah Chafee, Jr., Papers.

132. Id., quoting Laski to Chafee, July 23, 1919, Chafee Papers.

133. Chafee, "Speech in War Time," 967.

134. Id., 968.

135. Id., 949–53.

136. Id., 960–64.

137. Id., 967.

138. Id.

139. See id., 967 and n. 122.

140. See id., 968.

141. See *Frohwerk v. United States,* 249 U.S. 204, 209 (1919).

142. Chafee, "Speech in War Time," 967–68.

143. Id., 968.

144. Id.

145. Id.

146. Id.

147. Id.

148. Id., 969.

149. Id., 956.

150. Rabban, "Emergence," 1315, quoting Chafee to Judge Charles Amidon, September 30, 1919, Chafee Papers.

151. Id.

152. The reference is to Holmes' opinion in *United Zinc & Chemical Co. v. Britt,*

258 U.S. 268 (1922), discussed in Chapter Eleven. A dissent by Justice John Clarke criticized Holmes' position for the majority in *Britt* as "harsh." Id. at 280. As noted, Holmes called Clarke's dissent "larmoyant" and based on "sentiment." Holmes to Pollock, March 29, 1922, *Holmes–Pollock Letters* II, 92.

153. Holmes to Pollock, supra note 125.

154. Rabban, "Emergence," 1265–66, quoting letter from Holmes to Chafee, June 12, 1922, in Chafee Papers. Ragan's reading of the letter as saying "Patriotic" rather than "Pat[t]erson" is clearly incorrect. See Ragan, "Holmes and Chafee," 26 n. 12.

155. There is no indication in Holmes' correspondence that he had been exposed to Chafee's 1918 article on free speech in *The New Republic*, and in any event that article did not discuss the issue of whether the First Amendment was confined to prior restraints.

156. 250 U.S. at 619–20.

157. Id. at 621.

158. Id. at 617.

159. Espionage Act of 1917, ch. 30, 40 Stat. 217 (1919), supra note 14.

160. Sedition Act of 1918, ch. 75, 40 Stat. 553 (1919), supra note 24.

161. Id., ch. 75, § 3, 40 Stat. at 553.

162. *Abrams,* 250 U.S. at 621.

163. Id. at 618–19, 621.

164. Id. at 619.

165. *Debs v. United States,* 249 U.S. 211, 215 (1919).

166. *Abrams,* 250 U.S. at 621.

167. Id.

168. See *Schenck v. United States,* 249 U.S. at 49–51.

169. See *Frohwerk v. United States,* 249 U.S. at 205.

170. See *Debs,* 249 U.S. at 213–14.

171. For a thorough account of the facts of *Abrams,* see Polenberg, *Fighting Faiths,* supra note 125, at 224–27. See also Zechariah Chafee, Jr., "A Contemporary State Trial—The United States Versus Jacob Abrams et al.," 33 *Harv. L. Rev.* 747, 747–48 (1920). Chafee indicated that the circulars were thrown out of the window in the early morning when a crowd was loitering at a street corner directly below the window. Chafee, id., 747. Many of the crowd were waiting to begin work in a nearby manufacturing building. Id. Hereafter Chafee, "A Contemporary State Trial."

172. 250 U.S. at 619–23.

173. See id. at 625–26.

174. Id. at 625.

175. Id. at 626.

176. Id.

177. Id. at 628.

178. Id. at 629.

179. Id.

180. Id. at 626–27.

181. Id. at 627.

182. Id.

183. Id.

184. Id.

185. Id. at 629.

186. Id. at 627.

187. Id. at 627–28.

188. *Schenck v. United States,* 249 U.S. at 52.

189. *Abrams,* 250 U.S. at 627.

190. Id. at 628.

191. Id.

192. Chafee, "Speech in Wartime," 934.

193. 250 U.S. at 628.

194. Id.

195. Id. at 629.

196. Id. at 629–30.

197. Id. at 630.

198. Holmes to Laski, July 7, 1918, *Holmes–Laski Letters* I, 160–61.

199. 250 U.S. at 630.

200. Id.

201. Chafee, "Speech in Wartime," 956.

202. Holmes to Laski, January 11, 1929, *Holmes–Laski Letters* II, 1124.

203. Holmes to Learned Hand, June 24, 1918, Holmes Papers.

204. 250 U.S. at 630–31.

205. 2Laski to Holmes, November 12, 1919, *Holmes–Laski Letters* I, 220.

206. Frankfurter to Holmes, November 12, 1919, Holmes Papers.

207. "The Call to Toleration," *The New Republic,* November 26, 1919, 360.

208. See Gerard C. Henderson, "What is Left of Free Speech," *The New Republic,* December 10, 1919, 50.

209. Chafee, "A Contemporary State Trial," 769.

210. Id., 771.

211. Id., 769.

212. Id.

213. Id., 771. Of those who had participated in the conversations with Holmes about free speech only Learned Hand continued to express reservations, although Chafee privately concurred in some of Hand's concerns. Hand felt that the "clear and present danger" test gave too much leeway to juries to define the limits of protection for speech in an impressionistic fashion. See Gunther, "Learned Hand," quoting letter from Hand to Chafee, January 2, 1921, Chafee Papers, Harvard Law Library.

214. Rabban, "Emergence," 1317.

215. In 1941, Zechariah Chafee wrote of the *Schenck-Abrams* sequence: "Looking backward . . . we see that Justice Holmes was biding his time until the Court should have before it a conviction so clearly wrong as to let him speak out his deepest thoughts about the First Amendment." Zechariah Chafee, Jr., *Free Speech in the United States,* 86 (1941 ed.).

216. *Schaefer v. United States,* 251 U.S. 466, 482–83 (1920) (Brandeis, J., dissenting).

217. *Pierce v. United States,* 252 U.S. 239, 271–72 (1920) (Brandeis, J., dissenting).

218. 255 U.S. 407, 436 (1921) (Holmes, J., dissenting).

219. Id. at 410–12.

220. Id. at 412.

221. Id. at 417.

222. Id. at 436–37.

223. Id.at 437.

224. Id.

225. Id.

226. See id.

227. Id.

228. Id. at 438.

229. Id.

230. Id. at 437.

231. Id. at 427.

232. See id. at 437–38.

233. For another case demonstrating Holmes' enhanced sensitivity to free speech issues, see *Leach v. Carlile*, 258 U.S. 138, 140 (1922) (Holmes, J., dissenting). In *Leach* Holmes found a First Amendment violation in the Postmaster General's refusal to deliver mail to a company that had advertised "Organo Tablets," which it manufactured as a general cure for illness, an advertisement that the Postmaster considered fraudulent. Id. at 139. "If the execution of this law does not abridge freedom of speech," Holmes wrote, "I do not quite see what could be said to do so." Id. at 141.

234. 262 U.S. 390 (1923).

235. 262 U.S. 404 (1923).

236. *Meyer,* 262 U.S. at 399.

237. Id. at 399–400.

238. Id. at 402.

239. Id.

240. Id.

241. Id.

242. Id. at 403.

243. *Bartels,* 262 U.S. at 412.

244. Id.

245. Id.

246. *Abrams,* 250 U.S. at 630.

247. Because promoting "a common tongue" by prohibiting language instruction up to a certain age in the public schools was a matter "upon which men reasonably might differ," Holmes concluded he was "unable to say that the Constitution of the United States prevents the experiment [from] being tried." *Bartels,* 262 U.S. at 412.

248. Id.

249. See Holmes to Laski, April 14, 1923, *Holmes–Laski Letters,* I, 495.

250. Holmes to Laski, April 14, 1923, *Holmes–Laski Letters,* I, 495.

251. 268 U.S. 652 (1925).

252. Id. at 654–55, quoting New York Penal Law § 161 (Matthew Bender, 1909).

253. Id. at 658–59, quoting *The Left Wing Manifesto.*

254. Id. at 659.

255. Id. at 656.

256. Id. at 670–71.

257. Id. at 664.

258. Id. at 665.

259. Id. at 666.

260. *Gitlow,* 268 U.S. at 672.

261. Id.

262. Id.

263. Id. at 673.

264. Id.

265. Id.

266. Id.

267. Id. at 665.

268. Id. at 673.

269. Id.

270. 244 F. 535 (S.D.N.Y.), *rev'd,* 246 F. 24 (2d Cir. 1917). In *Masses,* Hand wrote that, "[i]f one stops short of urging upon others that it is their duty or their interest to resist the law, it seems to me one should not be held to have attempted to cause its violation." Id. at 540.

271. 274 U.S. 357, 372–80 (1927).

272. Id. at 373, 374, 376.

273. 283 U.S. 359 (1931).

274. 283 U.S. 697 (1931).

275. In *Gilbert v. Minnesota,* 254 U.S. 325 (1920), Holmes concurred in sustaining the conviction of an official of the Non-partisan League for giving a speech urging that the policy of conscripting soldiers in wartime be put to a popular vote. Id. at 333–34. Although Holmes gave no reasons for his concurrence, it is possible that he thought doing so would require the same substantive reading of liberty that he had resisted in the foreign language cases.

276. Holmes to Laski, June 14, 1925, *Holmes–Laski Letters* I, 752.

277. 279 U.S. 644 (1929).

278. See "Rosika Schwimmer Dead at Age of 70," *New York Times,* August 4, 1948, 21.

279. 279 U.S. at 647.

280. Id. at 646.

281. *Schwimmer v. United States,* 27 F.2d 742 (7th Cir. 1928), *rev'd,* 279 U.S. 644 (1929).

282. *United States v. Schwimmer,* 279 U.S. 644, 645 (1929).

283. Id. at 650–51.

284. Id. at 651.

285. Id.

286. Id. at 653. Technically *Schwimmer* was not a First Amendment case. Neither the majority nor Holmes mentioned the First Amendment. The majority pointed out that "aliens . . . have no natural right to become citizens, but only that which is by statute conferred upon them" and that the burden was on applicants "to show by satisfactory evidence that [they have] the specified qualifications" for citizenship. Id. at 649.

The question in *Schwimmer* was therefore whether she had met the burden of establishing "the requisite facts" to make out a case for admission. The majority held that she had not met the burden because of her testimony that she would not bear arms and that she was ''an uncompromising pacifist with no sense of nationalism but only a cosmic sense of belonging to the human family.'' Id. at 651–52. ''[O]pinions and beliefs as well as . . . behavior,'' Butler pointed out, ''are subjects of inquiry under the statutory provisions governing naturalization.'' Id. at 651. The process thus contemplated that First Amendment issues would not be raised if the government denied an applicant citizenship solely on the ground of his or her beliefs. Even though the Naturalization Act of 1906, ch. 3592, 34 Stat. 596, which established the naturalization procedures used in *Schwimmer,* would in effect be an example of ''Congress . . . abridg[ing] the freedom of speech,'' the First Amendment did not apply to aliens.

Holmes, in his dissent, spoke of the ''principle of free thought'' and called that a ''principle of the Constitution.'' Id. at 654–55. He also cited the *Schenck* case, as if *Schwimmer* was doctrinally comparable. Id. at 654. But he avoided mentioning the First Amendment.

287. Id. at 653–54.

288. Id. at 653.

289. Id. at 653–54.

290. Id. at 654.

291. Id.

292. Indeed Holmes had written Laski on April 13, 1929, before the *Schwimmer* case had been decided, that ''[a]ll 'isms [including pacifism] seem to me silly—but this hyper-aethereal respect for human life seems perhaps the silliest of all.'' Holmes to Laski, April 13, 1929, *Holmes–Laski Letters* II, 1146.

293. *Schwimmer,* 279 U.S. at 654.

294. Id.

295. Id. at 654–55.

296. Id. at 655.

297. See generally Yogal Rogat, ''Mr. Justice Holmes: A Dissenting Opinion,'' 15 *Stan. L. Rev.* 3, 254 (1962), discussing Holmes' restrictive views on alien rights.

298. Pollock to Holmes, September 9, 1928, *Holmes–Pollock Letters* II, 229.

299. Holmes to Sir Frederick and Lady Pollock, September 20, 1928, *Holmes–Pollock Letters* II, 230.

300. Laski to Holmes, June 4, 1929, *Holmes–Laski Letters* II, 1155.

301. Holmes to Laski, June 15, 1929, id., 1158. Schwimmer's atheism may have been what Holmes was ''allud[ing] to'' when he said that ''[s]ome of her answers might excite popular prejudice.'' *Schwimmer,* 279 U.S. at 654.

302. Schwimmer to Holmes, January 28, 1930, Holmes Papers.

303. Holmes to Schwimmer, January 30, 1930, Holmes Papers.

304. Id.

305. Id.

306. *Schwimmer,* 279 U.S. at 653.

307. Holmes had exhibited a skepticism about the existence of God by the age of twenty. See Howe, *Shaping Years,* 109–10; *Touched With Fire,* 27–28.

308. 254 U.S. 325 (1920). For the facts of *Gilbert* see supra note 275.

309. The defendant in *Gilbert* also said that ''[i]f they conscripted wealth like they have conscripted men, this war would not last over forty-eight hours.'' 254 U.S. at 327.

310. *Gitlow v. New York,* 268 U.S. 652, 658 n. 2 (1925). It is possible that Holmes declined to protect the speech in *Gilbert* because of the necessity of relying on a "liberty of speech" argument. But on its facts the *Gilbert* case hardly represented a "clear and present danger" as Holmes had come to apply that test after *Abrams.*

311. *Schwimmer,* 279 U.S. at 654.

312. Id.

313. Id.

314. 250 U.S. at 630.

315. 279 U.S. at 654.

316. Holmes to Lewis Einstein, June 24, 1911, *Holmes–Einstein Letters,* 59.

317. Holmes to Patrick Sheehan, December 15, 1912, *Holmes–Sheehan Correspondence,* 56.

318. Id.

CHAPTER THIRTEEN: *Aging*

1. Holmes to Pollock, October 15, 1922, *Holmes–Pollock Letters* II, 103.
2. William Howard Taft to Horace Taft, April 17, 1922, Taft Papers.
3. William Howard Taft to Robert A. Taft, March 7, 1926, id.
4. Holmes to Laski, August 19, 1922, *Holmes–Laski Letters* I, 439–40.
5. "The Profession of the Law," *Occasional Speeches,* 31.
6. "The Race Is Over," id., 178.
7. See, e.g., Holmes to Laski, November 25, 1916, *Holmes–Laski Letters,* I, 38.
8. See, e.g., Holmes to Laski, February 25, 1921 ("The Doctor . . . inspected me as I have puffed and panted more than I used to and said I was all right in heart and lungs."); Holmes to Laski, April 22, 1922 ("Personally I have been much bothered by coughing, etc., and really was relieved when the Doctor told me that I had a smart attack of asthma.") *Holmes–Laski Letters,* I, 315, 418.
9. Taft to Horace Taft, supra note 2.
10. Holmes to Laski, May 3, 1922, *Holmes–Laski Latters* I, 422.
11. Holmes to Laski, May 12, 1922, id., 426.
12. Holmes to Pollock, May 21, 1922, *Holmes–Pollock Letters* II, 95.
13. Holmes to Laski, June 14, 1922, *Holmes–Laski Letters* I, 431.
14. Holmes to Pollock, June 23, 1922, *Holmes–Pollock Letters* II, 99.
15. Holmes to Einstein, June 19, 1922, *Holmes–Einstein Letters,* 207.
16. Holmes to Pollock, supra note 14.
17. Holmes to Laski, July 7, 1922, *Holmes–Laski Letters* I, 434.
18. *Holmes–Pollock Letters* II, 100.
19. Holmes to Frankfurter, July 22, 1922, Holmes Papers.
20. Laski to Holmes, August 13, 1922, *Holmes–Laski Letters* I, 440.
21. Pollock to Holmes, August 23, 1922, *Holmes–Pollock Letters* II, 100.
22. Holmes to Laski, September 28, 1922, *Holmes–Laski Letters* I, 453.
23. Holmes to Laski, December 14, 1922, id., 463.
24. Holmes to Nina Gray, January 1, 1923, Holmes Papers.
25. Holmes to Pollock, January 25, 1923, *Holmes–Pollock Letters* II, 110.
26. Holmes to Pollock, February 24, 1923, id., 114.
27. Holmes to Laski, March 1, 1923, *Holmes–Laski Letters* I, 485–86.

28. Holmes to Einstein, March 24, 1923, *Holmes–Einstein Letters* 213.

29. Taft to Learned Hand, March 3, 1923, Taft Papers.

30. Taft to Helen Taft Manning, June 11, 1923, id.

31. Holmes to Laski, June 20, 1931, *Holmes–Laski Letters* II, 1319.

32. Holmes to Laski, July 25, 1931, id., 1320.

33. Holmes to Einstein, August 10, 1931, *Holmes–Einstein Letters,* 329.

34. Holmes to Einstein, October 9, 1931, id., 330.

35. Holmes to Nina Gray, September 22, 1931, Holmes Papers.

36. See Laski to Holmes, September 17, 1931, *Holmes–Laski Letters* II, 1329, indicating that Robert Wales, Holmes' secretary for the 1930 Term, had written him about Holmes' illness. It was Holmes' practice, after Fanny's death in 1929, to bring his secretaries with him to Beverly Farms, where they would remain until a new secretary joined him in Washington in October.

37. Holmes to Laski, October 9, 1931, id., 1334.

38. H. Chapman Rose, interview with John Monagan, September 17, 1980. My thanks to John Monagan for supplying me with a transcript of his taped interview with Rose.

39. Holmes to Laski, November 21, 1931, *Holmes–Laski Letters* II, 1340.

40. Holmes to John Wigmore, February 27, 1929, Holmes Papers.

41. Holmes to Laski, April 2, 1929, *Holmes–Laski Letters* II, 1144.

42. William Howard Taft to Charles P. Taft, May 5, 1929, Taft Papers.

43. Id.

44. Louis D. Brandeis to Felix Frankfurter, April 21, 1929, in M. Urofsky and D. Levy, eds., *"Half Brother, Half Son": The Letters of Louis D. Brandeis to Felix Frankfurter* 370 (1991).

45. Holmes to Gray, April 26, 1929, Holmes Papers.

46. Taft to Charles P. Taft, supra note 42.

47. Brandeis to Frankfurter, in *"Half Brother, Half Son,"* supra note 44, at 371.

48. Catherine Drinker Bowen, *Yankee from Olympus,* 419.

49. See Monagan, *The Grand Panjandrum,* 61; Novick, *Honorable Justice,* 368.

50. Taft to Robert A. Taft, May 5, 1929, Taft Papers.

51. Taft to Charles P. Taft, supra note 42.

52. Memorandum of Chief Justice Taft's engagements for May, 1929, Taft Papers; Taft to Charles P. Taft, supra note 42.

53. Taft to Charles P. Taft, supra note 42.

54. Holmes to Nina Gray, May 15, 1929, Holmes Papers.

55. Chapman Rose, interview with John Monagan, September 17, 1980, supra note 38.

56. Holmes to Nina Gray, May 15, 1929, supra note 54.

57. *Boston Globe,* May 1, 1929, p. 21, col. 6.

58. *Washington Post,* May 1, 1929, p. 1, col. 4. See also *New York Times,* May 1, 1929, p. 31, col. 4.

59. Holmes to Canon Patrick Sheehan, April 1, 1911, *Holmes–Sheehan Correspondence,* 41.

60. See John Monagan, "The Triumph of Annie Mary Donnellan Coakley," *Washington Post,* June 19, 1985.

61. Holmes to Nina Gray, May 15, 1929, supra note 54.

62. "I am reconciled by the certainty that a continuance of life would have meant only a continuance of pain and suffering of which my wife had had too much before the final accident." Holmes to Pollock, May 24, 1929, *Holmes–Pollock Letters* II, 243.

63. "I am reconciled to my wife's death as the alternative seemed inevitably a life of nothing but pain." Holmes to Laski, May 23, 1929, *Holmes–Laski Letters* II, 1152.

64. Holmes to Pollock, supra note 62; Holmes to Laski, supra note 63.

65. Holmes to Laski, May 30, 1929, *Holmes–Laski Letters* II, 1152.

66. Holmes to Frankfurter, May 31, 1929, Holmes Papers.

67. Taft to Horace Taft, May 1, 1929, Taft Papers.

68. Taft to Robert A. Taft, May 5, 1929, id.

69. Brandeis to Frankfurter, April 21, 1929, supra note 44.

70. Taft to Charles P. Taft, March 7, 1926, Taft Papers.

71. The quotations from Boston, Clark, and Hughes are taken from *The New York Times,* March 9, 1931, p. 18, cols. 1–3.

72. Holmes to Curtis, January 13, 1931, Holmes Papers.

73. The original of the first draft is in the Holmes Papers. A copy is reproduced in *Occasional Speeches,* 178, along with the final version.

74. *Occasional Speeches,* 178.

75. *New York Times,* March 11, 1931, p. 24, col. 5. In the same article the *Times* identified the source of Holmes' "Death plucks my ear" quotation and noted that "the last of these hedonistic verses, lingering in the memory of Mr. Justice Holmes, gains a nobler, a Stoic sound."

76. Laski to Holmes, March 16, 1931. *Holmes–Laski Letters* II, 1308. Apparently Laski had been invited to the birthday ceremony some time earlier: he wrote Holmes from England on January 10 that "you note that I can now definitely accept an invitation to be in Washington on your birthday." Laski to Holmes, January 10, 1931, id., 1304.

77. Editorial, *New York Times,* March 8, 1931, section 3, col. 2.

78. Duffus, "At Ninety, Justice Holmes Marches On," *New York Times,* March 8, 1931, Section 5, p. 3.

79. Laski, "Ever Sincerely Yours, O. W. Holmes," *New York Times Magazine,* February 15, 1948, p. 56.

80. See, e.g., Memorandum of Felix Frankfurter, September 28, 1932, Felix Frankfurter Papers, Library of Congress, quoting a conversation he and Judge Billie Hitz had with Holmes at Beverly Farms.

81. Holmes to Laski, May 18, 1919, *Holmes–Laski Letters* I, 205.

82. Holmes to Moncheur, April 5, 1931, Holmes Papers.

83. Holmes to Kaneko, April 26, 1931, id.

84. Holmes to Nina Gray, March 11, 1931, id.

85. Taft to Robert A. Taft, March 7, 1926, Taft Papers.

86. David J. Danelski and Joseph S. Tulchin, eds., *The Autobiographical Notes of Charles Evans Hughes* 299 (1973). The notes were dictated by Hughes in 1945, for the use of his children and grandchildren. A microfilm copy was deposited in the Library of Congress. Danelski and Tulchin published an annotated version, with an introduction.

87. Rose, interview with Monagan, supra note 38.

88. Hughes, supra note 86, at 299.

89. In Charles Evans Hughes' recollection of the visit to Holmes on January 12, 1931, he stated that "at [Holmes'] request I got out from his bookshelves the applicable statute." Hughes, supra note 86, at 299. Of the two accounts Rose's seems more plausible. It would have been unlikely that Hughes would have interrupted a delicate interview with Holmes to search for a volume among Holmes' bookshelves, and Rose, who was on the scene, would have been presumed to be in a good position to find the volume, being familiar with Holmes' library.

90. Rose, interview with Monagan, supra note 38.

91. Id.

92. Annie M. Donnellan Coakley, interview with John Monagan, November 28, 1979, in John Monagan Papers, Harvard Law School. My thanks to John Monagan for directing me toward this interview.

93. Hughes, supra note 86, at 299.

94. Charles Evans Hughes, interview with Merlo Pusey, January 7, 1946, quoted in Merlo Pusey, *Charles Evans Hughes* (2 vols., 1951), II, 681.

95. Hughes, supra note 86, at 299.

96. Holmes to President Hoover, quoted in 284 U.S. at vii. (1932).

97. Holmes to Laski, March 18, 1932, *Holmes–Laski Letters* II, 1370.

98. Holmes to Curtis, December 19, 1933, Holmes Papers.

99. Donald Hiss in Louchheim, *The Making of the New Deal*, 32–34.

100. Id., 33–36.

101. See *New York Times*, August 14, 1932, p. 19, col. 5.

102. *New York Times*, January 21, 1933, p. 3, col. 3.

103. *New York Times*, February 7, 1933, p. 21, col. 3.

104. See Felix Frankfurter, *Felix Frankfurter Reminisces* (Harlan Phillips, ed., 1962), 241–42.

105. Donald Hiss in Louchheim, supra note 99, at 37.

106. Id., 38.

107. Baker, *Justice from Beacon Hill*, 641; Novick, *Horable Justice*, 396. Baker cites a memorandum from Felix Frankfurter, dated March 15, 1933, in the Frankfurter Papers in the Library of Congress, and Novick cites Alger Hiss' *Recollections of a Life* 33 (1988), quoting his brother Donald. The Frankfurter memorandum does not use the phrase "form your battalions and fight," and Alger Hiss' recollection of his brother's account was over fifty years after the event.

108. James Rowe in Louchheim, supra note 99, at 42–46. Subsequent quotations in the next two paragraphs are from James Rowe's interview.

109. Monagan, *The Grand Panjandrum*, 144.

110. *New York Times*, March 1, 1935, p. 1, col. 2; *Washington Post*, March 1, 1935, p. 1, col. 4.

111. *Washington Post*, March 2, 1935, p. 1, col. 6.

112. Id.

113. *New York Times*, March 2, 1935, p. 3, col. 3.

114. Id.

115. *New York Times*, March 3, 1935, p. 3, col. 3.

116. *New York Times*, March 4, 1935, p. 8, col. 3.

117. *Washington Post*, March 4, 1935, p. 1, col. 4.

118. *New York Times*, March 5, 1935, p. 15, col. 2. The *Washington Post*, on the same day, reported that Mark Howe had announced, at 1 A.M., that Holmes was still alive, although under an oxygen tent. Howe's statement was made in response to a New York radio station's anno2uncement that Holmes had died. *Washington Post*, March 5, 1935, p. 1, col. 1.

119. *Washington Post*, March 6, 1935, p. 1, col. 6.

120. *Washington Post*, March 8, 1935, p. 4, col. 1; *New York Times*, March 7, 1935, p. 16, col. 5.

121. Holmes had made these comments at courtroom ceremonies honoring Chief Justice Walbridge Field, November 25, 1899, *Occasional Speeches*, 118.

122. *Washington Post*, March 9, 1935, p. 1, col. 4; p. 4, col. 4.

123. Id., p. 4, col. 4.

124. James Rowe to Felix Frankfurter, March 22, 1935, Frankfurter Papers, Manuscript Division, Library of Congress. My thanks to John Monagan for calling my attention to this letter.

125. See Monagan, *The Grand Panjandrum* 33, citing *Historical Statistics of the United States*, Bureau of the Census, 1985.

126. *New York Times*, March 10, 1935, p. 1, col. 6.

127. Monagan, *The Grand Panjandrum*, 45. For more on the remarkable history of the Holmes Devise History of the Supreme Court of the United States, see Alfred S. Konefsky, "The Marshall Court and the Writing of Law and History," 66 *Virginia Q. Rev.* 160 (1990). In the interest of full disclosure, I should add that I am one of the Holmes Devise authors, although not one of the group originally commissioned by the Permanent Committee of the Devise in the 1950s. See the preface to White, *The Marshall Court and Cultural Change*, now volumes III–IV in the Devise History.

128. *New York Times*, March 7, 1935, p. 22, col. 2.

129. Frankfurter, memorandum, August 10, 1932, Holmes Papers.

130. Marion Frankfurter ("M.D.F."), addendum to Felix Frankfurter memorandum, supra note 129.

131. H. Chapman Rose to Liva Baker, quoted in Baker, *Justice from Beacon Hill*, 639.

132. It is hard to imagine Holmes, in his nineties, being surrounded by his "children," who would have been at least in their sixties. Nonetheless Holmes' childlessness, together with his aloofness, surely contributed to the solitary quality of his last years.

CHAPTER FOURTEEN: *A Concluding Assessment*

1. It is not without interest that even though Morse was still alive at Holmes' death and Hallowell lived until 1914, when Holmes was seventy-three, Holmes had comparatively little contact with either of them after he entered the legal profession in 1865, although he corresponded with Morse over the years. Nonetheless, he regarded Morse and Hallowell as intimate friends because they had, for a short space of time, been so closely connected to the central themes of his life in secondary school and college. Holmes wrote Lewis Einstein in 1914 that although he and Hallowell had "ceased to

have much intercourse,'' Hallowell's death had left ''a great space bare'' for him. Holmes to Einstein, April 17, 1914, *Holmes–Einstein Letters,* 90.

2. See Mark Howe, Memorandum, August 10, 1964, Holmes Papers, quoted in Baker, *Justice from Beacon Hill,* 430–31.

3. ''John Marshall,'' February 4, 1901, *Occasional Speeches,* 126.

4. John Flannery to Mark D. Howe, May 13, 1942, Holmes Papers.

Bibliographical Essay

~

HOLMES leads all American judges, and most American historical personages, in the amount of scholarly and popular literature he has engendered. This essay comments on only a small amount of that literature, but seeks to single out those sources that a reader desiring more information or insight about Holmes' life and career should first consult. The sources are divided into two types, primary source materials and secondary writings, and the latter category is keyed to the topics taken up in the respective chapters of this work.

PRIMARY SOURCES

When Holmes died in 1935 his papers were placed in the hands of John Gorham Palfrey, his executor. Shortly after Holmes' death Palfrey made the papers available to Felix Frankfurter, who was Holmes' original choice to write the authorized biography of his life. When Frankfurter was appointed to the Supreme Court of the United States in 1939 it became apparent to him that he would not have the time to write the biography, and he eventually selected Mark DeWolfe Howe, who had been Holmes' secretary in 1933–34 and who was then on the law faculty of Buffalo University (now the State University of New York at Buffalo) to produce the authorized account of Holmes' life. Howe left Buffalo to join the Harvard Law faculty after the Second World War, and began work on the biography, using Holmes' papers and acquiring some additional materials. Howe edited three of the important early printed sources on Holmes: his Civil War letters and diaries, and his letters to Frederick Pollock and Harold Laski. Eventually two volumes of Howe's biography were published, one in 1957 and the second in 1963. Howe also edited a volume of Holmes' speeches in 1962 and an edition of *The Common Law* in 1963.

In 1967 Mark Howe died, and after some consultation Paul Freund of the Harvard Law Faculty, who had succeeded Palfrey as Holmes' literary executor, appointed Grant Gilmore, then on the faculty of Yale Law School, to continue the authorized biography to its conclusion. The Holmes Papers were transferred from Harvard to Gilmore, who retained possession of them until his death in 1982. Although Gilmore published two books during the time he held exclusive access to the Holmes Papers, he did not accomplish any further work on the biography. In 1985 Harvard Law School decided not to seek any further authorized treatment of Holmes' life and to release the papers to the general public. This was done in the form of an arrangement between Harvard University and University Microfilms, Inc., in which a microfilmed edition of the Holmes Papers, complete with an annotated guide, was produced and sold to depositories. The result is that a virtually complete version of Holmes' papers is now readily available, with the Harvard Law School Library retaining the original papers in its Special Collections.

Access to the Holmes Papers is thus a relatively routine matter for scholars and other interested persons. The papers primarily consist of Holmes' voluminous correspondence, cataloged chronologically by individual correspondent. In addition, the papers contain a variety of miscellaneous printed and other matter, ranging from travel diaries to household accounts to press clippings. Holmes' copies of his judicial opinions during his tenure as a Supreme Court Justice are included, as is a docket of cases, some containing notations, from his tenure as Associate Justice of the Supreme Judicial Court of Massachusetts. The papers include some important unpublished correspondences, such as those between Holmes and Felix Frankfurter, Holmes and Nina (Mrs. John Chipman) Gray, and Holmes and Clare Castletown.

Because of the Holmes Papers' relative accessibility and volume, students of his career should consider consulting them in pursuing any project about Holmes. At this juncture in their history, however, the papers do not contain a great many surprises. Many of Holmes' extensive correspondences have been published, and those that remain unpublished do not offer startlingly new information. Holmes tended to repeat himself in his letters, and while his correspondence, taken as a whole, is a fascinating collection, it does not reveal many "secrets" that commentators have not already unearthed. Nonetheless, the Holmes Papers provide an excellent opportunity for the serious student of Holmes' career to come to grips with him.

As previously noted, some portions of the Holmes Papers have been published. The largest collection of Holmes letters currently in print is Mark DeWolfe Howe's 1953 edition of the correspondence between Holmes and Harold Laski, *Holmes–Laski Letters, 1916–1935* (2 vols., 1953). Howe also issued an edition of Holmes' correspondence with Sir Frederick Pollock, *Holmes–Pollock Letters, 1874–1932,* in two volumes in 1941, and published a one-volume edition in 1961. Both editions contain helpful annotations by Howe and extensive indexes. Howe also issued *Touched With Fire: Civil War Letters and Diary of Oliver Wendell Holmes, Jr., 1861–1864* (1946), an annotated account of Holmes' letters to his parents and a diary he kept during his Civil War service.

In 1964, James B. Peabody published an edition of Holmes' correspondence with the British diplomat Lewis Einstein, *The Holmes–Einstein Letters,* that covers correspondence between 1903 and 1935. David M. Burton has edited two additional volumes of Holmes' correspondence, *Holmes–Sheehan Correspondence: The Letters of Justice Oliver Wendell Holmes and Canon Patrick Augustine Sheehan* (1976), and *Progressive Masks: Letters of Oliver Wendell Holmes Jr., and Franklin Ford* (1982). Sheehan was an Irish parish priest Holmes met on a visit to Doneraile, Ireland, in 1907; Ford an American journalist and man of letters who corresponded with Holmes between 1907 and Ford's death in 1917. Additional published sources of Holmes' correspondence are Felix Cohen, ed., "The Holmes–Cohen Correspondence," 9 *J. Hist. Ideas* 3 (1948), containing selections from letters exchanged by Holmes and the philosopher Morris Cohen, and John Wu, ed., *Justice Holmes and*

Dr. Wu: An Intimate Correspondence (1947), selections from the correspondence of Holmes and John C. H. Wu, a Chinese scholar and acolyte of Holmes.

Perhaps the best introduction to Holmes as a correspondent, however, is Richard Posner's *The Essential Holmes* (1992), a collection of Holmes' essays, letters, speeches, and judicial opinions, commented upon with acumen. Included among the selections are letters from Holmes to Laski, Pollock, Einstein, Ford, Cohen, and the Irish historian Alice Stopford Green. Posner also provides a provocative overview of Holmes and a good list of relevant secondary works.

Holmes' other extrajudicial writings are also widely available in print. In addition to Mark DeWolfe Howe's edition of Holmes' speeches and addresses, *The Occasional Speeches of Justice Oliver Wendell Holmes* (1962), three collections of Holmes' extrajudicial scholarship are available, his *Collected Legal Papers* (1920), which includes his major scholarly writings, Frederic Rogers Kellogg's edition of his early unsigned articles and book reviews, *The Formative Essays of Justice Holmes* (1984), and Harry C. Shriver's collection of miscellany, *Justice Oliver Wendell Holmes, His Book Notices and Uncollected Letters* (1936), which includes some pieces not included in the other two collections. Michael H. Hoffheimer has reprinted Holmes' undergraduate essays in "The Early Critical and Philosophical Writings of Justice Holmes," 30 *B.C. L. Rev.* 1221 (1989). The Hoffheimer edition contains some particularly valuable and incisive commentary on Holmes' early writings. For an updated and expanded version of Hoffheimer's *Boston College Law Review* essay, as well as a complete edition of Holmes' early writings, see Michael H. Hoffheimer, *Justice Holmes and the Natural Law* (1992). Finally, for a comprehensive bibliography of Holmes' published correspondence, see James A. Thomson, "Playing with a Mirage: Oliver Wendell Holmes Jr. and American Law," 22 *Rutgers L. J.* 123, 168–71 (1990).

The Common Law, Holmes' best known work of scholarship, has gone through a series of editions since its first publication in 1881, and continues to fascinate. Mark Howe's 1962 edition remains the best annotated treatment. Holmes' judicial opinions are also widely available in edited form. Harry C. Shriver's edition of *The Judicial Opinions of Oliver Wendell Holmes: Constitutional Opinions, Selected Excerpts and Epigrams as Given in the Supreme Judicial Court of Massachusetts* (1940) contains a number of Holmes' opinions as a Massachusetts judge. In 1929 Alfred Lief edited a volume of Holmes' opinions in the Supreme Court of the United States, *The Dissenting Opinions of Mr. Justice Holmes*, that signified Holmes' emergence in the decade of the 1920s as a "great dissenter." In 1931 Lief issued another volume, *Representative Opinions of Mr. Justice Holmes*, which remains a good introduction to Holmes' work on the Supreme Court of the United States. But the best single-volume collection of Holmes' opinions and extrajudicial addresses remains Max Lerner's *The Mind and Faith of Justice Holmes* (1943), a marvelous distillation by one of this century's most perceptive commentators on Holmes. If one were limited to two introductory samples of Holmes' work as judge, jurist, and correspondent, the Lerner and Posner volumes would be the ones to choose. At this writing the University of Chicago Press has in production a four-volume collection of Holmes' extrajudicial writings, including *The Common Law*, edited by Sheldon Novick, one of Holmes' recent biographers.

SECONDARY SOURCES

As noted, the discussion of sources in this portion of the bibliographical essay is keyed to the coverage of individual chapters in this work, but at the outset some attention should be given to other works that have sought to cover Holmes' entire life and career. The first of those efforts was Silas Bent's *Justice Oliver Wendell Holmes* (1932), which appeared while Holmes was still alive, and which Holmes appropriately characterized as "harmless." Bent had no access to Holmes' papers, and the book is most revealing for what it says about public perceptions of Holmes on his retirement.

In 1944 the most widely read of all books on Holmes, Catherine Drinker Bowen's *Yankee from Olympus,* appeared. While the Bowen book, which described itself as a history of "Justice Holmes and His Family," created consternation in scholarly circles, it remains an accomplished literary performance. Unfortunately Bowen, who interviewed a number of sources for the book, including Holmes' niece Dorothy Upham and Holmes' former law clerk Francis Biddle, was more interested in dramatic narrative than in balance or accuracy, and much of her account better deserves the label fiction than history. She was particularly captivated by the relationship between Holmes and his father, Dr. Oliver Wendell Holmes, Sr., and took many opportunities to suggest that there was continuous and abundant tension between father and son. In other respects Bowen's feel for human interest concerns overrode the authenticity of her data but, as a kind of historical novel, *Yankee from Olympus* is still good reading.

The decision on the part of Holmes' executors to commission an authorized biography and the consequent restriction of Holmes' papers meant that scholarship on Holmes, of which there was considerable, was confined to the journal and periodical literature until 1957, when the first volume of Mark Howe's biography, *Justice Oliver Wendell Holmes: The Shaping Years,* appeared. That volume was followed six years later by *Justice Oliver Wendell Holmes: The Proving Years,* which carried Holmes' life forward through December 1881 when he resigned from a professorship at Harvard Law School to become an Associate Justice of the Supreme Judicial Court of Massachusetts. While Howe's coverage of the first forty years of Holmes' life was scrupulous and thorough, his untimely death in 1967 meant that Holmes' entire judicial career remained to be covered.

Nonetheless Howe's two volumes represent a remarkable achievement. A loyal former secretary and diffident biographer, Howe nonetheless managed to expose some tensions and shortcomings in his subject, as well as to illuminate the emotional and intellectual sources of Holmes the mature scholar and judge. Intellectual and social history was Howe's forte, and his analyses of the Brahmin subculture in which Holmes grew up, and the growth of Holmes' scholarly perspective during his twenties and thirties, remain starting points for understanding Holmes. On occasion Howe may seem overly kind to his subject, but if one reads carefully one will notice the occasional critical insight nestled in melliflous prose. Above all Howe recognized Holmes as the solitary, self-preoccupied intellectual that he was, and since those themes were ones that engaged Howe, the result was an effective meeting of biographer and subject. Thirty years after the appearance of Howe's second volume his effort retains its importance.

The combination of Howe's death, the transfer of the Holmes Papers to Gilmore, and Gilmore's death stifled biographical attention to Holmes for over twenty years. With Harvard's decision to disseminate the Holmes Papers in 1985, however, came a rush of scholarly attention. The first book to take advantage of the availability of the Holmes Papers was John S. Monagan's *The Grand Panjandrum: The Mellow Years of Justice Holmes* (1988), which focused on the latter portion of Holmes' life and was exclusively directed toward Holmes the person. Monagan, who in the course of his research had come upon Holmes' "love letters" to Clare Castletown, was particularly interested in the domestic circles of Holmes' life. The result is a charming, and deceptively probing, account of the many-sided features of Holmes' character. While not claiming scholarly erudition or expertise about Holmes' scholarship or judicial career, the Monagan volume is nonetheless an insightful portrait.

The principal gap created by the deaths of Howe and Gilmore was a dearth of information about the last fifty years of Holmes' life. In the late 1980s scholars moved to fill that gap, and three biographies appeared. The first of those, Gary J. Aichele's *Oliver Wendell Holmes Jr., Soldier, Scholar, Judge* (1989), in the Twayne Biography series, closely resembled in coverage and analysis the 1980 Twayne volume, David H. Burton's *Oliver Wendell Holmes, Jr.* While a fair amount of scholarship on Holmes had appeared between the dates of the Burton and the Aichele volumes, and Aichele discussed the availability of the Holmes Papers, his accounts and conclusions were not strikingly different from those of Burton. Both books relied heavily on secondary sources and did little to dislodge conventional scholarly wisdom about Holmes. Both were more concerned with brevity and conciseness than with detailed coverage or analysis.

Also in 1989 the first modern trade biography of Holmes, Sheldon Novick's *Honorable Justice,* appeared, followed two years later by Liva Baker's *The Justice from Beacon Hill.* Both the Novick and Baker volumes sought to fill in the details of Holmes' life and career resulting from the attenuated coverage of Howe's biography, and both made extensive use of the Holmes Papers. Since the appearance of Monagan's book, Holmes' relationship with Clare Castletown had become part of Holmesian lore, and both volumes quoted extensively from Holmes' letters to Castletown. Both books were also similar in occasionally not resisting the temptation to sensationalize, as in Novick's description of Holmes in his preface as "a violent, combative womanizing aristocrat . . . who in personal letters seemed to espouse a kind of fascist ideology,"[1] and Baker's veiled claim that Holmes was sexually impotent.[2] Finally, the Novick and Baker books are similar in their determined inattentiveness to Holmes' work as a scholar and a judge, a task that Novick described as "daunting" and conceded "remains to be done."[3]

Despite those similarities, the Novick and Baker books can be readily distinguished. The Baker volume, notwithstanding its limitations as a scholarly account of Holmes' career, is a competent trade biography, culling information from a variety of accessible and inaccessible sources into a readable and largely accurate narrative. Along the way Baker provides some deft sketches of members of Holmes' family and consistently places Holmes in the context of his times. As a general introduction to Holmes' life, the Baker book is a good place to start. The Novick volume seems uncertain as to its emphasis. Despite his disclaimers about attempting a treatment of

Holmes' ideas, Novick at times engages in extensive analysis of Holmes' scholarship or judicial decisions, typically in lengthy footnotes. At other times he declines to engage in analysis altogether, as in his chapter on Holmes' relationship with Clare Castletown, where after an initial narrative he simply quotes from Holmes' letters to Clare without any comments at all. The Novick volume, unlike that of Baker, is also uneven in its use of source material, citing letters in the Holmes Papers extensively but not always accurately, and exhibiting, from time to time, a misplaced reliance on secondary sources.

Two other very recent works on Holmes should be mentioned. In 1992 Stanford University Press published a collection of essays on Holmes, *The Legacy of Oliver Wendell Holmes, Jr.,* edited with an introduction by Robert W. Gordon. The essays, which were originally papers delivered at a symposium at Stanford Law School, contain some important recent work on Holmes, some of which has not appeared elsewhere. Particularly notable are Gordon's introduction and the essays by Morton Horwitz, "The Place of Justice Holmes in American Legal Thought," Mathias Reimann, "Holmes' *Common Law* and German Legal Science," Robert A. Ferguson, "Holmes and the Judicial Figure," and David A. Hollinger, "The 'Tough-Minded' Justice Holmes, Jewish Intellectuals, and the Making of an American Icon." In addition, Michael H. Hoffheimer's *Justice Holmes and the Natural Law* (1992), which first became available from Garland Press early in 1993, deserves serious attention from anyone interested in Holmes' "intellectual biography." The Hoffheimer volume is one of the more searching treatments of Holmes in the Holmes literature.

~

There is a good deal of material on Holmes' familial and educational heritage, but a surprising dearth of modern studies. There is no biography of Abiel Holmes, but Mark A. DeWolfe Howe, the father of Mark DeWolfe Howe, and Eleanor Tilton produced biographies of Oliver Wendell Holmes, Sr., *Holmes of the Breakfast Table* (1939) and *Amiable Autocrat* (1947). Howe's is the more analytical of the two volumes, but unfortunately contains no documentation. The Tilton account is thorough, being based on Holmes Sr.'s papers, but bland. In many respects the most revealing source on Holmes Sr. is John T. Morse's authorized biography, *Life and Letters of Oliver Wendell Holmes* (2 vols., 1896). Morse was a cousin and family friend who knew the Holmes family intimately, and many of his observations represent the fullest available effort by a contemporary to reflect on the complexities of Dr. Holmes' personality.

The relationship between Holmes Sr. and Jr. has been addressed by a number of scholars, beginning with Bowen's *Yankee from Olympus* and continuing in Francis Biddle's *Mr. Justice Holmes,* which appeared in 1946, two years after Bowen's biography. Since Biddle was an important source for Bowen, and since the Bowen and Biddle analyses of the father-son relationship parallel one another, one may surmise that much of the tension attributed to the relationship came from interpretations Biddle placed on events described to Biddle by Holmes when Biddle was Holmes' law clerk during the 1911 Term. Bowen colored and romanticized the father-son relationship, making it one of her principal themes in *Yankee From Olym-*

pus, and the stereotype of father-son tension has persisted. Some subsequent biographers, notably Aichele in *Oliver Wendell Holmes Jr.* and Novick in *Honorable Justice,* have perpetuated the stereotype, but others, such as Howe in *Shaping Years* and Baker in *Justice from Beacon Hill,* have portrayed the relationship between Holmes Sr. and Holmes Jr. in a more complex fashion. Saul Touster's essay, "Fathers and Sons: The Self-Analysis of Dr. Holmes," in the Gordon volume of essays, represents an extended effort to apply psychological techniques to the father-son relationship. My chapter agrees with numerous others as to the importance of Holmes Jr.'s relationship with his father in shaping the themes and concerns of his own life and emphasizes the continuity in the two men's lives as well as their conflicts. Liva Baker's biography represents the most extended treatment of Amelia Jackson Holmes, Holmes' mother, a figure of greater significance in his life than previous scholarship has suggested.

The Holmes Papers and the Howe volumes contain a good deal of information about Holmes' childhood and early education, and the writings of Holmes' contemporaries, such as Henry Cabot Lodge and Henry Adams, cited in Chapter One, are helpful in recreating the social and intellectual atmosphere of the Boston in which Holmes grew up. While Howe discusses Holmes' undergraduate writings, the best source on those essays in Michael H. Hoffheimer's introduction to "The Early Critical and Philosophical Writings of Justice Holmes," which makes a sustained effort to place Holmes' early scholarship in the context of other works he was reading at the time, notably those by Ralph Waldo Emerson and John Ruskin. See also Sanford v. Levinson, *Skepticism, Democracy and Judicial Restraint: An Essay on the Thought of Oliver Wendell Holmes and Felix Frankfurter* 15–32 (Ph.D. dissertation, Harvard University, 1969) which in the course of an extended comparison of the ideas of Holmes and Frankfurter, offers an insightful and sophisticated analysis of the relationship between Holmes and Emerson.

Mark Howe's edition of Holmes' Civil War letters and diary, *Touched With Fire,* is the starting place for an understanding of Holmes' wartime experience. The sources in *Touched With Fire* need to be used with care, since Holmes destroyed some of his Civil War letters and wrote the extended account of his first wound at Ball's Bluff (which is presented as if it were a contemporary description) near the very end of his service. My chapter seeks to contrast the actual events of Holmes' wartime service with his successive memory of those events throughout the remainder of his life. James M. McPherson's *Battle Cry of Freedom* (1988) and Howe's annotations to *Touched With Fire* are helpful in recreating the chronology of Holmes' active service in the war, and Novick's chapters on Holmes' Civil War experiences are among the most successful portions of *Honorable Justice.* Howe made use of his scholarly research for *Touched With Fire* in his chapters on the Civil War in *Shaping Years,* and also consulted contemporary accounts by fellow soldiers of Holmes. The result is that it is possible to reconstruct the details of Holmes' Civil War years with some precision.

Scholars have regularly emphasized the importance of the Civil War in shaping Holmes' latter beliefs. Their analyses have taken two forms, those emphasizing the impact of the war on Holmes' generation of intellectuals, who emerged from it with an enhanced skepticism, a distrust of religion and other "metaphysical" belief systems, and varying degrees of enthusiasm for Darwinist explanations of the universe, and those emphasizing the psychological dimensions of Holmes' "survivor guilt," which manifested itself first in his early mustering out of service and subsequently in his romanticization of war. The first category of studies includes Edmund Wilson's essay on Holmes in *Patriotic Gore: Studies in the Literature of the American Civil War* (1962), an analysis that goes well beyond the wartime context to create a complex portrait of Holmes' mindset. George Frederickson, *The Inner Civil War: Northern Intellectuals and the Crisis of the Union* (1965), includes Holmes in a group of late nineteenth-century intellectuals whose enthusiasm for order and science he associates with the loss of faith in established governmental institutions precipitated by their wartime experience.

The second category of Civil War scholarship on Holmes, personified by Saul Touster's "In Search of Holmes from Within," 18 *Vand. L. Rev.* 437 (1965) and Hiller B. Zobel's "The Three Civil Wars of Oliver Wendell Holmes: Notes for an Odyssey," 26 *Boston Bar Journal,* (December 1982) 13; 27 id. (January 1983), 18; 27 id. (February 1983), 18, emphasize the impact upon Holmes of being severely wounded, missing important battles, and surviving where many of his contemporaries died. Both the Touster and Zobel articles are among the finest work on Holmes. My chapter seeks to build on the theme of "survivor guilt" first identified by Zobel, and relate it to Holmes' progressive romanticization, in his extrajudicial speeches, of his wartime experience and of war itself. The major sources for my analysis are essays available in *Occasional Speeches* and letters in the Holmes Papers.

~

Much of the material on which Chapter Three is based comes from the Holmes Papers, particularly Holmes' correspondence with William James, Holmes' travel diary for 1866 and Fanny Dixwell Holmes' travel diary for 1874, and other letters of Holmes. While all of Holmes' biographers have been interested in his "courtship" of Fanny Dixwell, there is little material on that courtship in his papers or elsewhere, and the details of my account do not differ significantly from those in Howe or Novick or Baker. Howe comments on the growing isolation of Holmes in this period, and his consequent withdrawal from previous close friendships; my chapter makes that isolation a more central theme. The chapter also gives a relatively full account of Holmes' 1866 trip to England and the Continent in order to emphasize the degree to which Holmes found self-fulfillment in the roles of young upper-class "gentleman" and flirt. One of the major themes of this study is thus first introduced in this chapter: Holmes' implicit division of life into "work" and "play" segments, and his association of "play" (by which he meant throwing oneself into a round of social engagements) with an environment other than Boston.

~

In the course of approaching *The Common Law,* scholars, from Mark Howe on, have recognized the significance of Holmes' unsigned essays and book reviews in the *American Law Review* during the 1870s. Frederic Rogers Kellogg has collected and published those works in *The Formative Essays of Justice Holmes,* and has argued that Holmes' early essays reveal the development of an ultimately coherent political philosophy, which Kellogg labels pragmatism. Howe's analysis of the essays in *Proving Years,* on the other hand, emphasizes their connections with the "evolutionary" history being produced by late nineteenth-century American scholars such as Henry Adams. My approach treats the essays as representing different stages in the emergence of Holmes' mature scholarly perspective, the first stage analytical in orientation and influenced by the work of British scholars such as Austin and Pollock; a subsequent stage, beginning with Holmes' essays in 1876, overtly historical, in the mode of Adams' work; and a final stage, signified by works that appeared while Holmes was writing the lectures that became *The Common Law,* representing Holmes' effort to combine history with policy arguments, and implicitly to argue that those arguments could be derived from historical exegesis. This last stage set the tone of *The Common Law.* I have also sought to include the role of Holmes' 1873 edition of Chancellor Kent's *Commentaries on American Law* in the process of his scholarly development. In the course of discussing the Kent volume, I have reviewed the steps through which Holmes came to take sole credit for the 1873 edition, an episode James Bradley Thayer thought relevant to Holmes' later decision to leave the Harvard law faculty to accept a judgeship.

My analysis of Holmes' early work suggests that a line of scholarship emphasizing the philosophical orientation of the early essays, and seeking to identify the sources of Holmes' philosophical perspective, may have underemphasized Holmes' interest in the methodologies of "evolutionary" history and comparative anthropology, and may have read too considered a philosophical approach into Holmes' early work. My account thus deemphasizes the significance of the "Metaphysical Club" of young Cambridge intellectuals, which William James first conceived in an 1868 letter to Holmes, in Holmes' early scholarship, and assumes that Holmes' early scholarship can best be characterized as a search for a distinctive, indigenous methodology, rather than as a response to British utilitarian jurisprudence. For alternative views, see Philip P. Wiener, *Evolution and the Founders of Pragmatism* (1949); H. L. Pohlman, *Justice Oliver Wendell Holmes and Utilitarian Jurisprudence* (1984). William P. LaPiana's "Victorian From Beacon Hill: Oliver Wendell Holmes' Early Legal Scholarship," 90 *Colum. L. Rev.* 809 (1990) is one of the few sustained, and successful, efforts, to place Holmes' early work in a historical context.

～

The ubiquitous fascination of *The Common Law,* still in print after more than a century, remains one of the phenomena of American intellectual history, especially because of the difficulty a modern reader has in understanding the work. The great interest of *The Common Law* has resulted in its being the subject of some very accomplished treatments, beginning with Mark Howe's *Proving Years.* Howe's chapters consist of a fascinating extended recreation of Holmes' reading and reflections as *The Common Law* took shape, and they remain a good starting place for students of the work. The centennial of *The Common Law*'s publication resulted in a series of important essays, three of which were grouped in a book, *Holmes and The Common Law: A Century Later* (1983), published by Harvard Law School in its Occasional Pamphlet series. The essays are Benjamin Kaplan, "Encounters with O. W. Holmes, Jr.," Patrick Atiyah, "The Legacy of Holmes Through English Eyes," and Jan Vetter, "The Evolution of Holmes: Holmes and Evolution." Two other essays appearing at the same time are Saul Touster, "Holmes a Hundred Years Ago," 10 *Hofstra L. Rev.* 673 (1982) and Robert Gordon, "Holmes' *Common Law* as Legal and Social Science," id., 719. A second essay by Touster, "Holmes: The Years of *The Common Law,*" 64 *Colum. L. Rev.* 230 (1964), also deserves attention. Morton Horwitz seeks to place *The Common Law* in the progression of Holmes' scholarship in his essay in Gordon's *The Legacy of Oliver Wendell Holmes, Jr.* Mathias Reimann's essay in the Gordon volume is a helpful analysis of the role German scholarship played in preparing Holmes to write *The Common Law.*

Of the above sources, my approach parallels most closely those of Gordon and Horwitz in seeing *The Common Law* as a unique, epistemologically confused, and time-bound work. I have tried to demonstrate that Holmes attempted to create an indigenous fusion of historicist and presentist methodologies that would establish the "validity" of certain legal principles Holmes found congenial. Holmes' contemporaries regarded the work as simultaneously one of "history" and one of "policy," and welcomed that emphasis as fresh and relevant. Neither he nor they regarded a historicist approach to past sources as being epistemologically incompatible with the use of history to vindicate contemporary policy judgements.

～

The interval, from the fall of 1881 until the winter of 1882, in which Holmes successively decided to leave law practice to join the Harvard law faculty, and then to leave Harvard to accept an appointment as Associate Justice of the Supreme Judicial Court of Massachusetts, was arguably the most momentous sequence of events in his career. Yet we continue to know relatively little about Holmes' motivation in those decisions. Howe's *Proving Years* discusses the decisions, and quotes extensively from the most detailed source available, James Bradley Thayer's memorandum describing the events of Holmes' leaving Harvard. I have sought to expand on Howe's treatment, but to some extent Holmes' thought processes in the two decisions remain a mystery. My approach emphasizes how significant a judgeship was to Holmes psychologically, so that when the opportunity came he reacted spontaneously and perhaps impulsively, and surely did not give serious attention to the feelings of others who might be affected by the decision.

Holmes' extrajudicial scholarship is an important source of the continued development of his jurisprudential views for the balance of the nineteenth century. Some secondary works have assumed that Holmes' perspective remained constant from *The Common Law* through "Privilege, Malice, and Intent," "The Path of the Law," and "Law in Science and Science in Law." The issue had not received extended treatment by biographers, since Howe's coverage did not take him past *The Common Law* and the more recent biographers have either ignored Holmes' scholarly writings or given them only cursory treatment. Some of the essays in *The Legacy of Oliver Wendell Holmes, Jr.,* however, address the issue. Morton Horwitz concludes that there was considerable movement of Holmes' views from *The Common Law* to "Law in Science and Science in Law," and that the later Holmes is more of an uncompromising positivist than the earlier, whose writings share his late nineteenth-century contemporaries' enthusiasm for custom as a principle limiting legal rules. I agree with Horwitz that by the end of his judicial service on the Supreme Judicial Court of Massachusetts Holmes was an uncompromising positivist. This did not prevent him, however, from developing an attachment to legal principles, such as free speech, that served to limit the effect of a majority's positivistic edicts. In his attachment to free speech, I suggest in Chapter Twelve, Holmes was less interested in philosophic consistency than in articulating his convictions as vividly and memorably as he could. Dorothy Ross' *The Origins of American Social Science* (1991) is useful in placing Holmes in the company of other late nineteenth-century American intellectuals.

The focus of Chapter Seven is Holmes' relationship with Clare Castletown, a relationship I find central to an understanding of Holmes' mature conception of intimate relationships. While the relationship was known to previous biographers, including Mark Howe, who chose to suppress its existence until he reached the point where it was chronologically relevant, I did not find previous treatments complete enough or otherwise satisfactory, and so I set out to recapituate the context of the relationship in as full a fashion as I could. This meant investigating the social milieu in which Holmes and Clare Castletown first met, a milieu frequented by two inter-locking upper-class sets, the "Souls" and the Anglo-Irish "Ascendancy." By understanding the mores of those groups, I felt, one might gain a greater understanding of the nature of Holmes' and Castletown's relationship.

Some secondary sources were helpful in that effort. John Monagan, who had first publicized the existence of the Holmes-Castletown letters, had in the course of his research for *The Grand Panjandrum* investigated collections of private papers in England that housed letters written by Clare Castletown. The catalogue description of one such collection, Bisbrooke Hall in Leicestershire, England, suggested that Clare had had an extramarital affair with one Percy La Touche, a resident of Cork County, Ireland. With the help of John Monagan, Dr. A. P. W. Malcolmson of the British Public Records Office, and George Boyle, the owner of Bisbrooke Hall, I secured access to letters between Clare Castletown and La Touche. The timing and content of the letters made it clear that during the late summer and fall of 1896, when Clare's relationship with Holmes was first taking on a romantic dimension, she was also involved in an intimate relationship with La Touche, who was aware of Holmes' existence and extremely jealous.

In the course of seeking to reconstruct the kind of social world Clare Castletown frequented I was aided by two histories of the "Souls" and "Ascendancy" circles, Angela Lambert's *Unquiet Souls* (1984) and Mark Bence-Jones' *Twilight of the Ascendancy* (1987). On the basis of these sources and information in the Holmes Papers, I was able to trace the first meeting of Holmes and Clare Castletown in the summer of 1889, their subsequent meeting in London in the summer of 1896, and most of the rest of their contacts. The Lambert and Bence-Jones volumes were particularly helpful in depicting the attitudes of Bernard and Clare Castletown's contemporaries toward male-female friendships, extramarital liaisons, marriage, and divorce. The La Touche-Castletown letters provided me with an example of a married member of Clare's circle who was involved in an extramarital affair with a woman married to someone else, and that member's reaction to the appearance of a "competitor."

On the basis of the information I secured, I was able to clarify some of the puzzles of the Holmes-Castletown relationship. One puzzle was the existence of a gap in the correspondence between 1899 and 1914, which had tempted some scholars to conclude that the relationship may have dissipated over time. My evidence suggested simply that the correspondence, which Holmes had sought to destroy and had assumed that Clare Castletown was not preserving, had somehow been lost for that period, because there was abundant evidence that Holmes and Clare saw one another in England or Ireland in 1901, 1903, 1907, 1909, and 1913.

A more significant puzzle was the precise nature of the relationship between Holmes and Clare Castletown. The La Touche letters and the histories of the "Souls" and "Ascendancy" circles established that Clare was not loath to have extramarital affairs, that her relationship with Percy La Touche was known among the "Ascendancy" families, and that La Touche, at any rate, regarded Holmes as a potential lover of Clare's. The very ease with which extramarital liaisons were tolerated among Clare's contemporaries, and Holmes' social companions in London, suggests that if Holmes and Clare had been inclined to have had a physical relationship few barriers would have existed. Nonetheless, as Baker pointed out in *Justice from Beacon Hill,* Holmes' "love" letters to Clare do not read like those of a person who has been physically intimate with his correspondent. On the contrary, they read like those of a person within whom a large amount of unrequited emotion has welled up. La Touche's letters, on the other hand, read like those of a person who cherishes the physical intimacy he has experienced and is fearful that another may be in a position also to experience it. As Chapter Seven suggests, Holmes and La Touche were in a sense fearful of the same thing, that Clare would let another man "close" to her, but Holmes described the closeness exclusively in intellectual terms.

The waxing and waning of Holmes' relationship with Clare Castletown thus sheds a great deal of light on Holmes' friendships with others, both male and female; on Holmes' attitudes toward women; on Holmes' marriage to Fanny Dixwell; on the role England and English social life played in Holmes' life; and on the changes Holmes' life went through after his appointment to the Supreme Court of the United States in 1903. The relationship also demonstrated Holmes' inherent tendency to romanticize and intellectualize his experiences. Chapter Seven is thus intended to take the reader into the very center of Holmes' personality structure.

～

Unlike much else about Holmes, his Massachusetts decisions have elicited a comparatively sparse amount of commentary. The explanation for that state of affairs largely has to do with the course of Holmes' authorized biography. In the plan of Howe's biography, Holmes' Massachusetts cases were next to be considered, and Howe's research notes indicate that he had begun the process of collecting and summarizing cases and had commissioned bibliographical studies of periodical and newspaper commentary on the decisions. Gilmore, who had long been a teacher of private law subjects, planned to make Holmes' Massachusetts cases one of the centerpieces of his volume. A collection of Gilmore Papers at the Harvard Law School Library reveals that Gilmore had not only begun preparing summaries of Holmes' Massachusetts decisions, he had begun research in the historical decisions that Holmes had cited as a commentator and a judge. From scattered remarks in the two books Gilmore published while he was working on the Holmes biography [*The Death of Contract* (1974) and *The Ages of American Law* (1977)], one can infer that Gilmore was highly skeptical of Holmes' use of historical materials, although not necessarily critical of Holmes' skills as an historian.[4] But Gilmore died before he completed any systematic survey of Holmes' Massachusetts opinions.

There matters have largely remained, since none of the recent Holmes biographers have had the inclination to examine Holmes' Massachusetts cases in detail. That decision may not completely be the result of inertia or diffidence in the biographers. On the whole, Holmes' Massachusetts opinions are brief, cursory, and not very significant. They primarily deal with common law questions centered in the rules and precedents of Massachusetts, sometimes reflecting the eccentricity or parochialism of Massachusetts doctrines. The court on which Holmes sat was one that valued collegiality and unanimity in its opinions and gave considerable weight to precedent in its jurisprudence, so not only were dissenting opinions unusual during Holmes' tenure, any evidence of collegial discord was rare. The result is that only a few of Holmes' opinions from Massachusetts have been included in his anthologized corpus of writings, and those—Holmes' dissent in *Vegelahn v. Guntner*[5] being an example—tend to give a misleading impression of Holmes as an outspoken, "liberal" state judge.

A few specialized studies of Holmes as a state judge exist. The most comprehensive is Perlie P. Fallon, "The Judicial World of Mr. Justice Holmes," 14 *Notre Dame Lawyer* 52, 163 (1939). The Fallon articles, which are more expository than analytical, are rarely cited in the Holmes literature. They were helpful to me in providing a sense of the kind of cases Holmes routinely heard on the SJC. Mark Tushnet, "The Logic of Experience: Oliver Wendell Holmes on the Supreme Judicial Court," 63 *Va. L. Rev.* 975 (1977), is a relatively complete modern analysis, covering most of Holmes' important cases. In "The Integrity of Holmes' Jurisprudence," 10 *Hofstra L. Rev.* 633 (1982), I surveyed torts opinions of Holmes in five-year intervals in the course of an argument that the principal insight Holmes gleaned from being a state judge was that most cases were relatively tedious or trivial, with few opportunities to plumb the depths of philosophical analysis or to remake the corpus of the law. Chapter Eight, which takes up the subjects Holmes had lectured on in *The Common Law,* does not significantly depart from that argument, although it seeks to demonstrate that in several respects Holmes self-consciously, and with some success, sought to reorient common law doctrine consistent with the policy views he had expressed in *The Common Law.* Patrick J. Kelley's essay, "Holmes on the Supreme Judicial Court: The Theorist as Judge," in Russell Osgood, ed., *The History of the Law in Massachusetts: The Supreme Judicial Court 1692–1992* 275 (1992), makes that same argument in considerably more detail. Kelley and Hiller B. Zobel have work in progress that will enrich our understanding of Holmes' years on the SJC.

One of the surprises for me, in following Holmes through the course of his professional life, was how very late in his career he gained the reputation of an eminent
jurist. Holmes was so central a figure to the generation of lawyers and law professors
which preceded mine that I and my contemporaries received repeated attention to
him in our law school years. While his reputation was arguably less exalted by the
1960s and 1970s than it had been in the 1940s and 1950s, he was nonetheless
acknowledged to be—and still is—one of the central figures, perhaps the central
figure, in the history of American law. (For a commentary on the significance of
Holmes to a lawyer coming to maturity in the 1930s, see Kaplan, "Encounters With
O. W. Holmes, Jr.," previously cited.)

As late as the years just preceding the First World War, however, Holmes was
still an obscure figure. In Chapter Nine I sought to probe some of the sources of that
obscurity, beginning with Holmes' nomination to the Supreme Court. The history
of that nomination, which is the subject of John A. Garraty, "Holmes' Appointment
to the United States Supreme Court," 22 *New Eng. Q.* 2291 (1949), reveals that
Holmes' nomination was not entirely "a reward for hard work," as he described it.
Theodore Roosevelt, the nominating President, had very likely never read any of
Holmes' scholarship and was unfamiliar with the great bulk of Holmes' Massachusetts opinions; Holmes' greatest attraction for Roosevelt was as the author of "The
Soldier's Faith." Holmes would surely not have received the nomination had President William McKinley not been assassinated; indeed McKinley had already nominated another candidate from Massachusetts whose confirmation would very likely
have resulted in Holmes' never sitting on the Court. Holmes' nomination, in short,
was fortuitous; and, as the public reaction to the nomination suggested, Holmes was
best known as a scholar, a speechmaker, a "literary feller," the son of the Autocrat
of the Breakfast Table. It is important, in light of Holmes' subsequent great eminence, to appreciate his relative obscurity at the age of sixty-one.

With Holmes' obscurity and subsequent eminence in mind, Chapter Nine
explores his decisions in the first fourteen-odd years of his Court career in search of
a potential explanation for his later prominence. That explanation is not readily
forthcoming. While Holmes wrote one of his most celebrated opinions, his dissent
in *Lochner v. New York,* in the period, his very first opinion, *Otis v. Parker,* was
strikingly similar to *Lochner* in its attitude toward judicial review, and attracted little
attention. Nor at first did *Lochner* itself attract much attention. Only when its apparent solicitude for state legislative "experimentation" came to be regarded as "progressive" did it begin to achieve the status of a "classic." Nor were any other
opinions harbingers of Holmes' subsequent status as a "liberal" and a "great dissenter." He dissented only rarely in the period, and was conspicuously indifferent
to the claims of blacks, aliens, and other minorities. He exhibited no solicitude for
free speech claims, adopting Blackstone's view that confined protection to prohibiting prior restraints. Of the forty-nine opinions anthologized in Max Lerner's *The
Mind and Faith of Justice Holmes,* only ten came from his first thirteen years on the
Court.

Given the cast of Holmes' early years as a Supreme Court justice, it is no surprise
that few commentators have focused on that portion of his career. One exception is

the treatment of Holmes in Alexander Bickel and Benno Schmidt's Holmes Devise History, *The Judiciary and Responsible Government, 1910–1921,* covering the years of Chief Justice Edward White's tenure. But that volume portrays Holmes as relatively obscure. The circumstances surrounding its authorship doubtless contributed to this treatment. Bickel had planned to write the entire volume, but died after completing only a portion of the manuscript. Schmidt then took up the project, and decided to focus exclusively on cases involving racial discrimination. Thus Holmes' first modern free speech opinions, *Schenck v. United States* and *Abrams v. United States,* were omitted from a volume whose chronological coverage suggested their inclusion. Nonetheless, the Bickel–Schmidt volume examined cases testing the constitutionality of social legislation in detail. Although Holmes wrote as many opinions as his colleagues in those cases, he was not singled out for prominent treatment. Robert Post's forthcoming Holmes Devise volume, covering the Taft Court, is expected to pay Holmes far greater attention.

To the extent that recent scholars have focused on Holmes' early years on the Court, they have questioned his image as a champion of civil liberties. In a series of influential articles first undertaken in 1963 and completed, posthumously, in 1984, Yosal Rogat attacked Holmes' reputation as a civil libertarian. As Chapter Nine suggests, Holmes' decisions in pre-World War I cases affecting the rights of minorities provided Rogat with ample documentation for his thesis. See Yosal Rogat, "Mr. Justice Holmes: A Dissenting Opinion," 15 *Stan. L. Rev.* 3, 254 (1963), and Rogat and James M. O'Fallon, "Mr. Justice Holmes: A Dissenting Opinion—The Speech Cases," 36 *Stan. L. Rev.* 1349 (1984). See also Rogat's trenchant overview of Holmes, "The Judge as Spectator," 31 *U. Chi. L. Rev.* 213 (1964). Benno Schmidt's chapters on race relations in *The Judiciary and Responsible Government* also identify Holmes as something other than a civil libertarian, on a Court that Schmidt argues protected the civil rights of blacks to a surprising degree. David Rabban's article, "The First Amendment in its Forgotten Years," 90 *Yale L. J.* 514 (1981) analyzes the Holmes opinions I discuss in Chapter Nine and is an excellent source of jurisprudential commentary on free speech issues prior to World War I.

～

The period from 1903 to 1917, however, produced major changes in Holmes' life, although those changes had not yet resulted in an altered public reputation. In Chapter Ten I seek to summarize those changes and describe how they eventually brought Holmes recognition on a scale commensurate with his exalted ambition. Most of the changes involved Holmes' private life, although they were arguably related to his new career as a Supreme Court Justice. He gradually began to reduce the degree of his "flirtations" with women, which had been a habitual, if confined, part of his routine in Boston and had preoccupied him on his visits to England in the 1890s. As he became more conscious of his position as a member of official Washington society, and he and his wife began to entertain, he gradually dropped his custom of seeking out new friendships with women, relying on maintaining, through an increased correspondence, those he had previously established. At the same time his relationship with Clare Castletown apparently diminished in intensity after 1899, when the Castletowns left England for two years and Clare was affected by injuries suffered in a riding accident. While the gap in the Holmes-Castletown correspondence precludes any confident characterization of the relationship after 1899, it seems safe to say that the level of romantic intensity waned after that year. By 1903 Holmes, in letters to England, was talking about how his lady friends and he were growing older.

The absence of close female friends, a growing sense that his work remained unrecognized, and the contemplation of approaching retirement seems to have instilled an attitude of loneliness in Holmes in the early years of the twentieth century: at any rate the term "lonely" appears frequently in his correspondence, which increased dramatically in the period. It thus seems fair to say that the changes brought about by his new life in Washington and the approach of his eighth decade created something of a void in Holmes' life, and into that void stepped Felix Frankfurter and his circle of young intellectuals, with their "progressive" visions of the future twentieth century. If Holmes inspired Frankfurter and the rest, they in turn were meaningful figures for Holmes: buffers against age, links to posterity.

Despite the widespread acknowledgment of the significance Frankfurter, Harold Laski, and their "progressive" contemporaries played in the transformation of Holmes' reputation and arguably his rejuvenation on the Supreme Court, very little has been written on the relationships between Holmes and his younger friends. This is surprising, because Howe's edition of the *Holmes–Laski Letters* has been available since 1953, and the importance of Progressivism as a political movement in American history and of the *New Republic* as a "progressive" organ has long been recognized. Nonetheless, Chapter Ten, to the best of my knowledge, represents the first sustained attempt to explore the relationships between Holmes and his "progressive" friends and to trace the impact of that relationship on his reputation. David Hollinger's essay, "The 'Tough-Minded' Justice Holmes, Jewish Intellectuals, and the Making of an American Icon," in Gordon, *Legacy,* 216, which came too late for me to take advantage of its insights, makes a start in that direction. A subsidiary puzzle is why the Holmes–Frankfurter letters, a correspondence rivaling those between Holmes and Pollock and Holmes and Laski in breadth and variety, have nor yet been published, especially since the younger of the two correspondents has been dead since 1965.

~

The diversity and significance of Holmes' Supreme Court opinions between 1917 and 1932 required two chapters, and the great importance of Holmes' free speech decisions, coupled with the large amount of secondary literature on those decisions, suggested that they should be treated separately. This left a patchwork quilt of decisions in other areas, most but not all involving constitutional cases, which I treated in Chapter Eleven. Here the secondary literature is more extensive, although still surprisingly scanty in comparison with the writing on Holmes as a scholar. Bickel and Schmidt discuss a few of the cases in *The Judiciary and Responsible Government*. David P. Currie's *The Constitution in the Supreme Court: The Second Century, 1888–1986* (1990) gives trenchant, if brief, attention to all the constitutional cases. *Buck v. Bell* has spanned a substantial literature, the most important recent contributions being Paul A. Lombardo, "Three Generations, No Imbeciles: New Light on

Buck v. Bell,'' 60 *N.Y.U. L. Rev.* 30 (1985), and Mary L. Dudziak, "Oliver Wendell Holmes as an Eugenic Reformer: Rhetoric in the Writing of Constitutional Law," 71 *Iowa L. Rev.* 833 (1986). E. F. Roberts, "Mining with Justice Holmes," 39 *Vand. L. Rev.* 287 (1986) discusses the *Mahon* case.

~

H. L. Pohlman's *Justice Oliver Wendell Holmes: Free Speech and the Living Constitution* (1991) is the place to start for a one-volume discussion of Holmes' free speech decisions and relevant commentary. Pohlman's views are provocative, and I disagree with most of them in Chapter Twelve. Nonetheless, the Pohlman volume is the most accessible compilation of almost all the relevant literature on Holmes and free speech, of which there is a considerable amount. I have cited most of the commentary in my notes to Chapter Twelve: the following is a listing of the most important sources. One should preface that listing by noting that in light of the great deal of material on Holmes and free speech, as distinguished from other legal issues Holmes considered during his career, the treatment of Holmes' free speech cases in all the recent biographies is disappointing, being a mere rehash of existing literature, not even adding any new biographical information.

As noted in Chapter Twelve, a debate exists among scholars as to the origins of Holmes' "modern" approach to free speech cases and the precise evolution of that approach. Pohlman, *Justice Oliver Wendell Holmes,* and David S. Bogen, "The Free Speech Metamorphosis of Mr. Justice Holmes," 11 *Hofstra L. Rev.* 97 (1982), maintain that Holmes' position from *Schenck v. United States* through *Abrams v. United States* is consistent and originates in Holmes' view of the law of criminal attempts. Gerald Gunther, "Learned Hand and the Origins of Modern First Amendment Doctrine: Some Fragments of History," 27 *Stan. L. Rev.* 719 (1975), and David M. Rabban, "The Emergence of Modern First Amendment Doctrine," 50 *U. Chi. L. Rev.* 1205 (1983), argue that Holmes' positions in *Schenck* and *Abrams* cannot easily be reconciled and that the latter opinion represents a more speech-protective formulation. Neither Gunther nor Rabban are interested in integrating Holmes' free speech cases after *Abrams* into their analysis; Chapter Twelve argues that a consideration of those cases further complicates the matter.

My investigation of Holmes' free speech jurisprudence considers the role of his "progressive" friends, such as Frankfurter, Laski, Learned Hand, and Zehariah Chafee, in reshaping his attitude toward speech cases. Holmes' conversations with that group during the summer and fall of 1919 are also discussed in Gunther, "Learned Hand," Rabban, "Emergence," and Fred D. Ragan, "Justice Oliver Wendell Holmes, Jr., Zechariah Chafee, Jr., and the Clear and Present Danger Test for Free Speech: The First Year, 1919," 58 *J. Am. Hist.* 24 (1975). My analysis of the role of "progressive" intellectuals in the formation of Holmes' views on speech supports the conclusions of those sources. I go on to argue in Chapter Twelve, however, that the transformation from *Schenck* to *Abrams* represents only one stage in the progression of Holmes' free speech jurisprudence, which I conclude ultimately defies doctrinal characterization. Other relevant sources on Holmes and free speech are Harry Kalven, "Professor Ernst Freund and *Debs v. United States,*" 40 *U. Chi. L. Rev.* 238 (1973); Rogat and O'Fallon, "Mr. Justice Holmes: A Dissenting Opinion—

The Speech Cases,''; Douglas Ginsburg, "Afterword," 40 *U. Chi. L. Rev.* 244 (1973); and Edward J. Bloustein, "Holmes: His First Amendment Theory and His Pragmatist Bent," 40 *Rutgers L. Rev.* 283 (1988). Richard Polenberg, *Fighting Faiths: The Abrams Case, The Supreme Court, and Free Speech* (1987) is a thorough account of *Abrams*. Mark Graber, *Transforming Free Speech: The Ambiguous Legacy of Civil Libertarianism* (1991) and Rabban, "The First Amendment in its Forgotten Years," and David M. Rabban, "The Free Speech League, the ACLU, and Changing Conceptions of Free Speech in American History," 45 *Stan. L. Rev.* 47 (1982) are the best sources for an understanding of late nineteenth- and early twentieth-century free speech jurisprudence.

～

On Holmes' last years the best source is Monagan, *The Grand Panjandrum,* which relied in part on interviews with some persons, such as Holmes' housekeeper Mary Donnellan, who had an intimate acquaintance with Holmes during the last period of his life. Also useful are the interviews with Holmes' secretaries during the latter part of his tenure, such as Thomas Corcoran, Alger and Donald Hiss, and James Rowe. Those interviews are collected in Katie Louchheim, *The Making of the New Deal: The Insiders Speak* (1984). Two of Holmes' secretaries, Mark Howe and Arthur Sutherland, left diaries of their years with Holmes in their collections of papers in the Harvard Law School Library. I have relied on those sources and on contemporary newspaper accounts, as well as correspondence in the Holmes Papers, for information about the final illnesses and deaths of Fanny Dixwell and Holmes. A recording of Holmes' radio address on his ninetieth birthday is in the Harvard Law School collection, and there are contemporary accounts of the event in the *Washington Post* and *New York Times*.

～

Finally, the following sources, written for a variety of purposes, contain important observations on Holmes: Walton Hamilton, "On Dating Justice Holmes," 9 *U. Chi. L. Rev.* 1 (1941); Daniel Boorstin, "The Elusiveness of Mr. Justice Holmes," 14 *New Eng. Q.* 478 (1941); the debate between Henry Hart and Mark Howe about Holmes' "positivism" in Howe, "The Positivism of Mr. Justice Holmes," 64 *Harv. L. Rev.* 529 (1951) and Hart, "Holmes' Positivism—An Addendum," id., 929; H. L. Mencken, "The Great Holmes Mystery," 26 *American Mercury* 123 (1932), revealing Mencken's less than adulatory view of Holmes; Elizabeth S. Sergeant, "Oliver Wendell Holmes," 49 *The New Republic* 59 (1926), a striking piece of Holmesian hagiography; Augustin Darby, "Recollections of Mr. Justice Holmes," 12 *N.Y.U. L. Rev.* 345 (1935), which should be compared with the recollections of other secretaries; Ben W. Palmer, "Holmes, Hobbes, and Hitler," 31 *A.B.A.J.* 261 (1945), characteristic of the anti-Holmes reaction in the years around World War II; and Morton White's effort to include Holmes among a group of early twentieth-century "antiformalists" in *Social Thought in America: The Revolt Against Formalism* (1948). On the whole, Holmes' general good fortune has persisted in the quality of his scholarly assessments.

Notes

1. Sheldon Novick, *Honorable Justice,* xvii.
2. Liva Baker, *The Justice from Beacon Hill,* 228–30 (1991).
3. Novick, *Honorable Justice,* xviii.
4. "A startling aspect of [Holmes'] lectures," Gilmore said of *The Common Law,* "is the repeated insistence that the principles of liability appropriate to the late nineteenth-century United States had been laid down in the English yearbooks of the fourteenth and fifteenth century." *Ages of American Law,* 54. At another place Gilmore said that Holmes' "historical underpinning was patently absurd, event when it had not been deliberately distorted." He added that "I do not meant to suggest that Holmes was a poor historian or that he did not know what he was doing. He was an excellent historian and knew more about what he was doing than most of us do. He was making a highly original, essentially philosophical statement about the nature of law. For reasons which he never explained, he chose to dress his statement in the misleading disguise of pseudo-history." Id., 52.
5. 167 Mass. 92, 104 (1896).

Index

~

Abbott, Henry L., 59, 61, 69, 78, 79, 342, 471
Abolitionism (antislavery movement)
 and Holmes Sr., 13
 and Hallowell, 31, 32, 45
 OWH's support for, 32
 and Civil War service, 46
 as romantic ideology, 146
 and OWH's civil-rights record, 341–42
 vs. racial egalitarianism, 342
 and OWH old-age recollections, 471
Abrams v. United States, 412, 430–34, 579n.171
 and "clear and present danger" test, 320, 426–27, 428, 432–34, 436, 443, 451
 Laski on, 364
 Wigmore attack on dissent in, 372
 and *Schwimmer*, 447
 and "search for truth," 452
Academic life, OWH on, 206
Acheson, Dean, 403
Act-at-peril liability theory, 140–42
 and critique of Austin, 120
 and *The Common Law*, 154, 161, 163, 164, 165–66, 264
 and paradox of form and substance, 180
 and foreseeability, 526n.54
Adair v. United States, 328–29, 333, 348, 352, 362, 363
Adams, Brooks, 91–92, 236
Adams, Charles Francis, 23–24, 25, 99
Adams, Henry, 89
 on Boston education, 21, 24, 34
 and Harvard College, 25, 46
 and OWH in England, 96–97
 and OWH's admiration of Maine, 115
 and study of primitive societies, 130, 146
 on TR and *Northern Securities*, 307
 death of, 358
 OWH distanced from, 359
 OWH outlives, 468
 as OWH contemporary, 486

Adkins v. Children's Hospital, 394–97, 400, 410, 441
Admiralty or maritime law, 155, 374–76, 386
 OWH argues case in, 109
 Black Book of the Admiralty, 131
Adverse possession, doctrine of, 220–21
Albany Law Journal, review of *The Common Law* in, 189–91
Alien cases, and OWH on Supreme Court, 343–48, 445–48, 449–50
Allen, Charles, 287
Allen, William, 213, 232–33, 298
Allen v. Flood, 223
Allgeyer v. Louisiana, 362
American Law Review, 113–14
 OWH as editor of, 91, 105, 108, 112, 116, 128, 130, 226
 OWH as contributor to, 95, 103, 114–16, 119, 121, 123, 129, 132, 391
 and Thayer, 127
 The Common Law reviewed in, 182, 185
 OWH opinion printed in, 293
Ames, James Barr, 197, 198, 200, 202, 356–57
Amherst College, OWH honorary degree from, 457
Amidon, Charles, 429
Ancient Law (Maine), 115, 186, 194. *See also* Maine, Sir Henry
Andrews v. Keith, 273
Anti-Semitism
 against Frankfurter, 356
 OWH vs. Brahmins on, 359
Antislavery movement. *See* Abolitionism
Antitrust cases
 Northern Securities case, 307
 OWH Supreme Court decisions in, 330–33
Arbitrariness in law, OWH on, 124, 295. *See also* Sovereign prerogative of choice
Argyll, Duke of, 100
Arnott, Sir John, 244